ROY JENKINS

John Campbell is the author of many biographies including one of Edward Heath, for which he won the 1994 NCR award, *The Iron Lady: Margaret Thatcher, from Grocer's Daughter to Iron Lady* and, most recently, *Pistols at Dawn: Two Hundred Years of Political Rivalry from Pitt and Fox to Blair and Brown*. He is married and lives in Kent.

JOHN CAMPBELL

Roy Jenkins

A Well-Rounded Life

VINTAGE BOOKS
London

First published in Great Britain in 2014 by
Jonathan Cape

Vintage
20 Vauxhall Bridge Road,
London SW1V 2SA

www.vintage-books.co.uk

A Penguin Random House Company

Penguin
Random House
UK

global.penguinrandomhouse.com

A CIP catalogue record for this book
is available from the British Library

ISBN 9780099532620

Penguin Random House is committed to a
sustainable future for our business our readers
and our planet. This book is made from
Forest Stewardship Council® certified paper.

Typeset by Palimpsest Book Production Limited,
Falkirk, Stirlingshire
Printed and bound in Great Britain by
Clays Ltd, St Ives plc

For Kirsty again, in love and gratitude,
and also for the next generation –
Barnaby, Willow and Angus,
Rosie and Isabel

Contents

List of Illustrations

John Harris (© UPP/TopFoto)

Jenkins, as Home Secretary, inspecting the London Fire Brigade, 1966 (The Bodleian Library, University of Oxford. Jenkins Paper Box 3, 6942/B/London Metropolitan Archives)

Visiting the scene where three policemen were shot, 1966 (Getty Images)

The Chancellor of the Exchequer arriving at the Treasury, 1968 (Photograph by Neil Libbert)

Jenkins leaving 11 Downing Street to present his first budget, 1968 (Getty Images)

Roy Jenkins and Harold Wilson, 1970 (© The Economist Newspaper Limited, London (1970))

The Opposition Front Bench, 1970 (Getty Images)

Tennis at East Hendred, 1969 (Getty Images)

Tennis at East Hendred, 1976 (Getty Images)

Speaking at the Labour Party special conference on the Common Market, 1975 (Getty Images)

Jenkins with Jeremy Thorpe and Edward Heath during the European Referendum Campaign, 1975 (Getty Images)

The television debate between Jenkins and Tony Benn, 1975 (Getty Images)

Struck by a flour bomb, 1975 (© PA Photos/TopFoto)

Jenkins in his study at East Hendred (*The Times*/Newssyndication.com)

Receiving an award to mark twenty-five years as MP for Stechford (Mirrorpix)

Plate Section III

Jenkins on an official visit to Timbuctoo (The Bodleian Library, University of Oxford. Jenkins Paper Box 2, 469)

President Jenkins in session in the Berlaymont building, Brussels, 1977 (© European Union, 2013)

With President Giscard D'Estaing (Getty Images)

With Chancellor Helmut Schmidt (Bundesregierung/Detlef Gräfingholt)

With British Foreign Secretary David Owen (Getty Images)

With President Carter and Margaret Thatcher (Archivio Cameraphoto Epoche/Getty Images)

Delivering the Dimbleby Lecture, 1979 (© Neil Libbert, first published in the *Observer*)

The Gang of Four after the Limehouse Declaration, 1981 (Getty Images)

Jenkins announcing his intention to fight the Warrington by-election for the SDP, 1981 (Getty Images)

Canvassing in Warrington (left) (*The Times*)

Canvassing in Warrington (right) (© PA Photos/TopFoto)

Laughing in the rain, Warrington, 1981 (© PA Photos/TopFoto)

Jenkins returning to the House of Commons, 1982 (Popperfoto/Getty Images)

The Leaders of the Alliance: Jenkins and David Steel, 1983 (The Bodleian Library, University of Oxford. Jenkins Paper Box 5, 472)

Jennifer and Roy, Great Yarmouth, 1982 (Photograph by Neil Libbert)

Writing in Tuscany, 1993 (By permission of Lord Rodgers of Quarry Bank)

In procession as Chancellor of Oxford University (© Copyright Billett Potter, Oxford)

Winning the Whitbread Biography Award, 1995 (UPP/TopFoto)

Roy and Jennifer in 1999 (donfeatures.com)

Acknowledgements

M Y greatest debt is to Dame Jennifer Jenkins for inviting me to write her husband's biography and allowing me the exclusive use of his papers, then still held at East Hendred, in order to do so. It was an enormous privilege to be able to stay in the house while working on them. I am grateful for her generous hospitality over several extended visits, and for many wide-ranging and candid conversations about her life with Roy. I am also grateful to Charles and Ivana Jenkins, Cynthia Jenkins and Edward and Sally Jenkins for their help, hospitality and input, setting me right on a number of points. It cannot be easy having a biographer probing your family life but, as the children of a biographer themselves, they were understanding and very tolerant.

I am also indebted to Patricia Williams for her help and valuable advice at various stages of the work; and to Andrew Adonis for sharing with me some of the work he had done towards the biography before he had to give it up, notably his notes of an interview with John Harris.

I am grateful to Rosie Alison for making available to me Roy Jenkins' letters to her aunt, Barley Alison; Leslie Bonham Carter for lending me her collection of press cuttings and allowing me to quote her letters; Craig Brown for Jenkins' last postcard enjoying his parody of *Twelve Cities*; Sir David Butler for allowing me to quote from his invaluable collection of contemporary interviews with all the leading politicians over many decades; Ruth O'Neill and Graham C. Greene for permission to quote Tony Crosland's letters; David Gilmour for allowing me to quote his mother's letters; Patricia Grigg for letting me see her husband John's letter written after visiting Brussels in 1978; and Bill Rodgers for letting me see extracts of his diary and correspondence with Roy Jenkins.

I am grateful to Random House for permission to quote from the diaries of Richard Crossman and Tony Benn; to David Higham Associates for permission to quote from the published and unpublished diaries of Barbara Castle; to Peters Fraser & Dunlop for permission to quote from the diary of Paddy Ashdown; and to Bernard Donoughue and Giles Radice for allowing me to quote from their published diaries.

I am grateful to the following for permission to reproduce cartoons in the text: the Telegraph Media Group and Nicholas Garland himself for Garland cartoons; Express Newspapers for Cummings; Solo Syndication for Illingworth; Susannah Gibbard for Gibbard; Claire Calman for Calman; Janet Slee for David Austin; and the British Cartoon Archive at the University of Kent for Richard Willson. Every effort has been made to trace other copyright holders; if one or two have slipped through the net I can only ask them to be forgiving.

I am additionally grateful to an enormous number of old friends and former colleagues and associates of Roy Jenkins for interviews and in many cases generous hospitality, sharing with me their memories and judgements: The Marquess and Marchioness of Anglesey; Lord Armstrong of Ilminster; Lord Ashdown of Norton-sub-Hamdon; Michael and Anne Barnes; Mme Marie-Alice de Beaumarchais; Tony Benn; Mrs Alannah Brennan; Dr Michael and Mrs Eleanor Brock; Sir David Butler; Nicholas Byam Shaw; Professor David Cannadine; Sir John Chilcot; Mrs Celia Cotton; the late Susan Crosland; Jan Dalley; Tam Dalyell; Richard Davenport-Hines; Sir Geoffrey de Deney; David Gilmour; Oliver Gilmour; Lord and Lady Goodhart of Youlbury; Dr Andrew Graham; Mrs Patricia Grigg; Lady Harlech; Robert Harris; Sir Max Hastings; Lord Hattersley of Sparkbrook; Lord Healey of Riddlesden; the late Sir Nicholas Henderson; the late Anthony Howard; Sir Michael and Maxine Jenkins; Dr John Jones; Sir Anthony Kenny; Lord Lester of Herne Hill; Lord Liddle of Carlisle; Sir Colin Lucas; Donald and Elsa Macfarlane; Sir Ronald McIntosh; Lord Maclennan of Rogart; Lord Mandelson of Foy; Professor David Marquand; Dr Christopher Mason; Bob Morris; Mrs Sara Morrison; Lord Oakeshott of Seagrove Bay; Brian Oakley; Lord Owen of Plymouth; Sir Hayden and Laura Phillips; Tom Phillips; Lady Antonia Pinter; Lord Radice of Chester-le-Street; Lord Rodgers of Quarry Bank; Tom Rosenthal; Professor Jean Seaton; Lord Steel of Aikwood; Lord Taverne of Pimlico; Lord Thomas of Swynnerton; Sir Crispin Tickell; Lord Tugendhat of Widdington; Sir Stephen Wall; Sara Wheeler; Baroness Williams of Crosby; Mrs Barbara Wren; and Philip Ziegler.

I am conscious that there are many more people who knew and

worked with Roy Jenkins whom I could and perhaps should have spoken to. To them I apologise that I did not get to see them; I can only plead that I would never have finished the book if I had spoken to everyone. I do regret, however, that Tony Blair was unable to find the time to talk to me.

I must also thank Helen Langley, Head of Modern Political Papers, and her colleagues at the Bodleian Library, Oxford for her help and understanding while the Jenkins papers were still at East Hendred and since their removal to the Bodleian; Alan Mumford for advice about cartoons; and M. Nicolas de la Grandville, chef du protocol at the European Commission for giving me an invaluable tour of the Berlaymont building in Brussels.

As always I am grateful to my agent of many years, Bruce Hunter of David Higham Associates, for helping set up the project in the beginning; to my current agent, Andrew Gordon, for seeing it through to completion; and to my editor at Jonathan Cape, Dan Franklin, for his patience, enthusiasm and support throughout. I am also grateful to Mandy Greenfield for her editing, Alison Rae for her eagle-eyed proof-reading, Clare Bullock for checking the final text for remaining inconsistencies and Caroline Wood for her tireless picture research.

Finally, once again, my deepest gratitude is to my wife Kirsty, whose love, encouragement and practical support, from research assistance to proofreading, has sustained me through the period of writing the book. I could not have done it without her and the book is dedicated to her.

John Campbell
December 2013

Introduction

R OY Jenkins enjoyed an exceptionally long career at or near the top of British politics. He was first elected to Parliament at the age of twenty-seven in 1948. He sat in the House of Commons for the next twenty-eight years, rising in that time to be Home Secretary twice, Chancellor of the Exchequer and deputy leader of the Labour party, and appeared well placed to succeed Harold Wilson as Prime Minister until he wrecked his position in the party by his determined support for British membership of the European Common Market. After four years out to serve as the first (and so far only) British President of the European Commission, he returned to the Commons for a further five years as one of the founders of the Social Democratic Party, which, after initial heady success, narrowly failed to break the stranglehold of the Conservative and Labour parties on British politics; he then moved to the House of Lords, where he continued to play an influential role for another fifteen years until his death in 2003. This active parliamentary span of almost fifty-five years is surpassed only by Gladstone in the nineteenth century and Churchill in the twentieth – the titanic subjects of two of Jenkins' bestselling biographies – and matched by very few others.

Moreover, though he failed in his ambition to become Prime Minister – and indeed only held office for just over eight years – Jenkins left a greater mark on British life and politics than many who did success-fully climb Disraeli's greasy pole. In three distinct areas – his Home Office reforms of the 1960s, Britain's membership of the European Union and the reshaping of the centre left of British politics – his legacy is enduring.

First, as Home Secretary for the first time in 1966–7, he saw onto the Statute Book a shopping list of overdue reforms which between them transformed the ethos of British life: legalising homosexuality between consenting adults, allowing easier abortion (ending the scandal of thousands of women dying every year from illegal operations), abolishing stage censorship by the Lord Chamberlain, ending corporal punishment in prisons (capital punishment had already been suspended, after a campaign in which he played a leading part, just before he took office) and taking the first steps to outlaw racial discrimination and (in his second spell at the Home Office in the 1970s) sex discrimination, as well as radically restructuring the police service and reforming key parts of the criminal justice system. When subsequently demonised by conservatives as the godfather of the 'permissive society' and all its attendant ills, Jenkins was always able to point out that no subsequent government – not even Margaret Thatcher with her three-figure majorities – ever tried to reverse any of these measures, which in combination helped to make Britain a freer and more equal society. No doubt they would all have come about sooner or later, but it took extraordinary determination, courage, clarity of purpose and skill on Jenkins' part to drive them through in a very short space of time when he had the opportunity.

Second, he played a role second only to Edward Heath in taking Britain belatedly into the European Community, campaigning consistently for British membership from the late 1950s onwards, leading a large rebellion of Labour MPs against the party whip to carry the decisive vote in favour of entry in 1971, and then taking a leading part in the cross-party referendum campaign that confirmed British membership in 1975. At the time, and for thirty years afterwards, this seemed an historic and irreversible decision. Today that certainty is called into question. Not only has Britain consistently baulked at committing to the further evolution of what is now the European Union, from the Social Chapter and the Schengen Agreement to the single currency, but there is now for the first time a serious possibility of Britain leaving the EU altogether. Though in his later years Jenkins was frustrated by the Blair government's failure to join the euro, he was convinced that it was only a matter of time; withdrawal from Europe entirely was unimaginable at the time of his death. Since then the rising tide of Euroscepticism, driven by a relentlessly hostile press and apparently vindicated by the near-collapse of the euro in 2012, inevitably tarnishes this part of his once unquestionable legacy. Nevertheless the argument is not over. In or out, Britain's relationship with Europe will remain a critical subject for debate and decision for years to come; and the pro-Europeans are beginning cautiously to find their voice again. Arguments about markets and sovereignty apart, from the moment he took up the cause the central thrust of Jenkins' case for membership was the belief that Britain must shake off the hangover of empire and learn to live with her continental neighbours as one medium-sized European power among others. In the decade since his death the experience of Afghanistan, Iraq, Libya and other ill-advised attempts to play the world's policeman alongside the United States has shown that this lesson has still to be learned.

Third, though Jenkins' bold attempt to recast the ossified structure of British politics ended in the short run with the failure of the SDP to break the mould in 1983, the shock of the SDP defection helped to drag the Labour party back from the clutches of the far left and led within barely more than a decade to the creation by Tony Blair, Gordon Brown and Peter Mandelson of 'New Labour' – a post-socialist makeover that made Labour electable again by adopting practically everything the SDP had stood for, from continued membership of NATO and the EU to the abandonment of nationalisation and the ending of old Labour's institutional subservience to the trade unions. The merger of the SDP with the Liberals to form the Liberal Democrats in 1988 created a much stronger and more disciplined third force than the old Liberal Party. Then, in the 1990s, Jenkins hoped to heal the historic breach between the Labour and Liberal parties, which had allowed the Tories to dominate the twentieth century, by persuading Tony Blair to form a Labour–Lib Dem coalition and cement it by introducing some form of proportional representation. Blair's landslide majority in 1997 and the refusal of his senior colleagues to give up a system that had rewarded Labour so handsomely put paid to that: Jenkins' recommendations were kicked into the long grass in 1998 and electoral reform was decisively rejected again by the referendum of 2012. Here again, however, the debate is not over. The devolved parliaments of Scotland, Wales and Northern Ireland, the Mayor of London and British members of the European Parliament are all elected by more or less proportional systems: first-past-the-post for Westminster is increasingly an anomaly, and pressure for reform will continue as elections with a low turnout and a multiplicity of parties continue to produce increasingly bizarre and unpredictable results. Jenkins' 1998 proposals will continue to be the starting point for discussion of a practical and principled alternative.

Thus while Jenkins' social reforms of the 1960s remain unchallenged and irreversible, the other two great causes of his later years appear to have suffered serious setbacks since his death. Britain's membership of Europe could yet turn out to be an historic cul-de-sac; the reformers may never succeed in overcoming the vested interest of the two dominant parties in maintaining the existing voting system. But in the long run the overwhelming likelihood is that in both cases Jenkins' vision will eventually be realised. Britain cannot for ever evade the geographic facts of life that make it ineluctably a part of Europe, single currency and all; and Westminster must one day accede to the justice of a properly representative electoral system. In all three areas, I believe, Jenkins will ultimately be seen as having been on the side of history.

But Jenkins was much more than just an unusually thoughtful politician. He was also a prolific writer, author over his lifetime of twenty-one books, including four full-length political biographies, four shorter biographies, two biographical collections, his own autobiography and several volumes of assorted essays, speeches, book reviews and other journalism. His writing was done mainly on holiday, in parliamentary recesses and at weekends; but it was much more than a hobby. It was a second career, which he sustained alongside his primary dedication to politics – while somehow managing to earn a reputation for being lazy! Except for the relatively few years when he was in government Jenkins, like Churchill, earned far more by writing than he did from politics and supported his family and an expensive lifestyle largely by his pen. And at least three or four of his books will continue to be read for years to come.

Above all, Jenkins was for at least the last thirty years of his life the embodiment of Britain's liberal establishment – that calmly (or complacently) superior elite of overwhelmingly Oxbridge-educated politicians, dons, mandarins, judges, broadcasters and commentators loathed equally by the old Labour left and the Thatcherite new right. From an early age Jenkins made it his business to know everyone in this cosy world, anatomised in 1990 by his friend Noel Annan in his book *Our Age*. He belonged to all the most exclusive clubs and dining clubs in London and lunched with some member of 'the great and the good' almost every day of his adult life. He collected honours and awards of every sort, from the chancellorship of Oxford University and the presidency of the Royal Society of Literature to the Order of Merit. He was the Grand Panjandrum or Pooh-Bah of British public life – an extraordinary apotheosis for a miner's son from Abersychan. This is why I have thought it important to try to narrate his political career in the context of this wider social, literary and quasi-academic life: more than any other individual, Jenkins' immense network of friendships

4

illuminates the assumptions and values of the British governing elite of the second half of the last century. It is also why I have not shied away from revealing his unconventional private life which reflects so much of the hidden world of that class in that era. I have tried to present the whole man in the round, and not just the politician.

I also believe, however, that Jenkins' long career throws a particularly clear light on the transformation in the conduct of politics over this half-century. When he was first elected to the House of Commons in 1948 the life of politics had not changed essentially since the days of his hero Asquith forty years earlier. Reputations were made and lost by speeches in the Commons chamber, while communication with the public was by speeches at packed and sometimes rowdy meetings up and down the country, fully reported in the newspapers. Television was in its infancy and even radio was largely barred from discussing current affairs. Politics was completely dominated by two class-based, ideologically opposed and well-supported parties: one predominantly middle- and upper-class and capitalist, the other largely working-class and avowedly socialist – though of course there was some overlap at the edges and generally cordial relations of mutual respect between the two. Both equally assumed that the future would be increasingly collectivist and egalitarian: Labour welcomed and sought to advance this process, while most Conservatives – before Margaret Thatcher – merely hoped to slow it. Up until the mid-1980s politics was genuinely a contest of ideas, between parties and within them: party conferences – particularly the annual Labour conference – were occasions for real argument and real power struggles, passionately conducted in public – and in due course televised – even if the vote was decided in advance by union block votes in smoke-filled rooms.

This was the world in which Jenkins rose to become deputy leader of the Labour Party. He did it largely by being the most effective debater in the Commons when the floor of the House was still the cockpit of political conflict. By the time he left for Brussels in 1976 this was already beginning to change, as more and more political debate took place in radio and television studios, in interviews and soundbites rather than in set-piece speeches. When he returned to the Commons in 1982 Jenkins no longer fitted in. The Asquithian style that had dominated the House in the 1960s now seemed ponderous and old-fashioned; the satirical sketch-writers who had largely replaced the straight reporting of Parliament mocked his pomposity, and he was embarrassingly uncomfortable on television. Briefly in its early days the SDP managed to resurrect the crowded public meetings of an earlier age; but it did not last. Under Mrs Thatcher and Tony Blair and the insatiable demands of twenty-four-hour news, politics became the affair of strictly controlled media manipulation, trivial point-scoring and damage limitation that we suffer today. If I have devoted considerable coverage to the controversies and arguments of Jenkins' era, it is because they seem to come from a different age when politics was a serious pursuit, taken seriously by serious people and seriously reported – yet at the same time more fun and more rewarding because real issues were felt to be at stake. Above all, it was still an age of optimism and rising expectations, unlike the present dismal era of cutbacks, economies, narrowing options and widening inequality. Coming out of the war, Jenkins' generation (Labour and Conservative alike) had perfect confidence in a future of ever-increasing national wealth, expanding public services and personal leisure – a confidence which mounting economic difficulties, the unpredicted rise of Thatcherism, climate change and global terrorism have sadly dented. They may not have felt much like it at the time, but from the perspective of the early twenty-first century the 1950s and 1960s now seem almost a golden age. Of course the over-confident illusions of Jenkins' generation contributed to the failures that Thatcherism set out to remedy; but the cure has been in its own way as bad as the disease. Over the whole seventy-year span from 1945 to the present no single career illustrates the heyday and retreat of social democracy in Britain more painfully than Jenkins'.

For all these reasons this is a long book: I could not have done justice to all the facets of Jenkins' career in a shorter one. It is based on a wide range of unpublished sources. First, since being appointed official biographer I have had full access to Roy Jenkins' own papers, stored until recently at his home in East Hendred, now transferred to the Bodleian Library, Oxford. I am immensely grateful to Dame Jennifer Jenkins for giving me the free run of this collection, including the wonderful wartime correspondence between herself and Roy of which I have made extensive use in Chapters Three and Four. This archive naturally provides the core of the book, though frustratingly for the biographer there are a lot more incoming than outgoing letters: as a professional writer Jenkins did not like to put pen to paper more than necessary unless paid to do so, and always preferred to respond to correspondents over lunch or on the phone. Nevertheless his papers testify to the extraordinary range of his friendships as well as preserving the drafts of all his books, the text of hundreds of speeches and articles, his contemporary notes towards his memoirs, the full typescript of his Brussels diary, his bank statements, tax returns and wine merchants' bills and – most valuable of all – his meticulously kept engagement diaries, which make it possible to trace his movements and whom he lunched with almost every day for more than fifty years.

In addition to this private goldmine I have used the official records of the 1964–70 and 1974–6 Labour governments, housed in the National Archives at Kew; the Labour Party archive now in the People's History Museum in Manchester; the SDP archive at the University of Essex in Colchester; and other collections of private papers held at the Bodleian (Harold Wilson, Barbara Castle, James Callaghan), the London School of Economics (Tony Crosland, Peter Shore and one or two others), University College London (Hugh Gaitskell) and Churchill College, Cambridge (Enoch Powell, Lord Hailsham, Neil Kinnock and others). I have been lent valuable private material by individuals, including particularly Rosie Alison, Lord Hattersley, Lord Rodgers of Quarry Bank, Robert Harris and Patricia Grigg; and I have conducted more than fifty interviews with surviving friends, colleagues and contemporaries, as well as with members of the Jenkins family, who have given me every help and encouragement. Finally I have of course drawn extensively on the immense published literature about the Labour Party, the Wilson governments and the SDP: the diaries of Hugh Dalton, Richard Crossman, Barbara Castle, Tony Benn, Paddy Ashdown and others; the memoirs of Harold Wilson, Jim Callaghan, Denis Healey, David Owen and a dozen more; biographies by Ben Pimlott, Philip Ziegler, Susan Crosland and Giles Radice, to name just a few; countless studies of the period by journalists and historians; as well as Hansard, *The Times* and other newspapers and journals. No period of political history can have been so thoroughly documented as the second half of the last century.

Finally I must declare my bias. Roy Jenkins was the first public figure I was aware of and always the one I most admired. I grew up as a near-neighbour of the Jenkins family in Ladbroke Square. I remember vividly his vigorously eccentric style on the tennis court in the communal garden and the policeman outside his front door when he was Home Secretary; I even remember when someone scrawled 'ASQUITH' on one of the pillars. I was a Liberal at university – an endangered species in the late 1960s – and in the 1970s I was one of those consciously waiting for Jenkins and the Labour moderates to break out of the Labour Party, certain that they would have to do so sooner or later. When they did I was an enthusiastic foot soldier in the SDP, voted for Jenkins as leader and even wrote a short biography of him – my third book – published just before the 1983 election, in the course of writing which I helped at the Hillhead by-election in 1982. I was naturally a strong supporter of merger with the Liberals and took a dim view of David Owen. I met Jenkins several times when he was President of the local SDP branch in Kensington, where I then still lived, and continued to admire him almost without reservation, though to my regret I never came to know him well. I was disappointed when I heard that he had appointed Andrew Adonis to be his official biographer, and correspondingly delighted when the opportunity eventually fell to me after all. All this, I realise, makes me less than wholly objective as a biographer. In previous books, despite having lived through their premierships, I have written of Edward Heath and Margaret Thatcher from a judicious distance. I can only hope that in this one my admiration and affection for my subject have not rendered me entirely uncritical.

John Campbell
September 2013

1 His Father's Son

DURING his lifetime a typically British controversy surrounded Roy Jenkins' origins. To his critics in the Labour party – themselves often guiltily middle-class and privately educated – it was almost inconceivable that this grand figure, with his drawling accent and air of lordly entitlement, should have been born and raised in the very heart of the labour movement. The son and grandson of miners, raised in the South Wales coalfield between the wars, his father actually imprisoned during the General Strike: romantic class warriors like Michael Foot and Tony Benn would have given their eye-teeth for such an impeccable socialist pedigree. Long before he abandoned Labour to found a rival party in 1982, Jenkins' enemies accused him of having rejected his roots and betrayed his class, practically from the moment he went to Oxford. Some alleged a purely political betrayal, asserting with Denis Healey that he was 'never really Labour at all'.[1] Others – most prominently Leo Abse, Labour MP for Pontypool and mischievous amateur Freudian – diagnosed a deeper apostasy: the authentic Welsh working-class identity which Jenkins derived from his father was undermined, Abse claimed, by the influence of his anglicised and socially ambitious mother, leaving the young Roy rootless, pretentious and déclassé.[2]

But most of this is nonsense. Roy Jenkins was indeed born into the heart of the South Wales Labour movement; but he was born into a Labour elite that saw itself confidently on the way to becoming the new governing class. His father had been a miner, certainly, but there was never any question of Roy following him down the pit. By the time Roy was born, on 11 November 1920, Arthur Jenkins was already a full-time union official, chairman of the Pontypool Labour party and a Monmouthshire county councillor.* He later became an alderman, Justice of the Peace, Vice-President of the South Wales Miners' Federation (SWMF), a member of the National Executive of the Labour Party and in 1935 – when Roy was fourteen – MP for Pontypool. He then quickly became Parliamentary Private Secretary (PPS) to the party leader, Clement Attlee, and held that position throughout the war when Attlee was deputy Prime Minister. He was briefly a minister in the 1945 government before his early death. In short, Arthur Jenkins was not just a pillar of the local establishment in South Wales – where Labour already *was* the establishment – but also, when Roy was growing to political awareness, at the very heart of government and national politics. More than all this, however, he was also gentle, bookish, internationalist and resolutely unmilitant: all characteristics that he passed on to his son.

Arthur exemplified, in Alan Watkins' words, 'the great (now largely lost) tradition of Welsh self-improvement'.[3] He was born in 1882 at Varteg, a bleak moorland mining community five miles up from Pontypool in the easternmost valley of the Welsh coalfield, and educated up to the age of twelve at the Varteg Board School, when he left, like most of his contemporaries, to follow his father down the pit. After a dozen years at the coalface, however, educating himself through evening classes and discussion groups, he won a miners' scholarship (worth £30 a year) to Ruskin College, Oxford – the enlightened institution founded in 1899 to offer the opportunity of higher education to working men who would otherwise have had no chance of it. The fact that Ruskin was not strictly part of the university did not stop Arthur regarding himself ever afterwards as an Oxford man. From there he gained another scholarship to study in Paris for ten months, where with his friend Frank Hodges (later general secretary of the Miners' Federation) he forged lasting contacts with leading French socialists while learning to speak and read French better than his son ever did. 'The classics of Russian fiction in his considerable library,' Roy wrote years later, 'were in French translations, which was unusual in the house of a South Wales miners' agent.'[4] Jenkins' love of France in particular, and Europe in general, was directly inculcated by his Francophile father.

Returning to Pontypool in 1910 after this two years' mind-expanding absence, however, Arthur had little choice but to go back down the

---

* It may not be unimportant that Roy was born on the second anniversary of the Armistice, which meant that throughout his childhood his birthday was marked by solemn ceremonies, brass bands and processions. 11 November was a very special date in the calendar in the 1920s.

pit. Working in a reserved occupation, he was spared the still greater horrors of the trenches which culled so many of his generation; but he spent less and less time underground as he made his career in the union. In 1911 he became secretary of the Pontypool Trades Council; in 1918 he was appointed deputy miners' agent for the Monmouthshire Eastern Valleys, and in 1921 he succeeded as agent. By this time he was also a county councillor and a governor of several local schools. Arthur was a good speaker and evidently not without ambition; yet he was an unusually unassuming politician – not at all a firebrand in the florid Welsh style associated with Nye Bevan, for example, raised in the next valley a decade and a half later. When Arthur died in 1946, aged only sixty-three, the obituaries all emphasised his scholarly manner. 'This gentle and sensitive son of Wales seemed, at a first meeting, to be more the poet or the student than the man of action,' wrote the *Daily Herald*.[5] The *South Wales Argus* mourned 'a man of outstanding personality and vision – an idealist and an internationalist, a self-taught man who started at the bottom of the ladder and, by perseverance and brilliant attainments, gained nationwide distinction without seeking it'.[6] Other tributes praised his integrity and selflessness. Attlee called him one of the three most unselfish men he had met in politics.[7]

Meanwhile Arthur had married, in 1911, Harriet (always known as Hattie) Harris, daughter of the foreman of the Bessemer steelworks at Blaenavon, three miles further up the valley. In the social hierarchy of the Welsh valleys her background was several notches above his. But her mother died when she was four and her father when she was seventeen; so when Arthur met her she had come down in the world, living in lodgings in Pontypool and working as an assistant in a music shop. By marrying the already up-and-coming Arthur it was Hattie who was bettering herself, though doubtless she was keen to regain the social position to which she had been brought up. After three years in a miners' cottage at Talywain, Arthur and Hattie moved to a small but respectable terraced house set rather grandly above the main road through Abersychan – then a distinct village a couple of miles up the valley from Pontypool, with its own shops, police station, Working Men's Institute and no fewer than six chapels – Baptist, Methodist and Congregational – as well as an Anglican church and a Catholic chapel.[8] They named it Greenlands after the house where Hattie grew up. In 1915 she bore a stillborn son, and it was another five years before she conceived again, by which time she was thirty-four and Arthur thirty-eight. As the only child of mature parents, it is not surprising that Roy was cosseted and somewhat spoiled. Curiously, however, Arthur's diary for the days around his birth barely mentions the event. He merely noted that 'H. is going along very nicely indeed' and went into Newport as usual on 11 November for a council meeting.[9] Fathers did not get involved in childbirth in those days.

Before Roy was three the family moved again, 300 yards down the Snatchwood Road to a slightly larger house – also called Greenlands – less elevated but boasting a bathroom and a sizeable back garden running down to a railway track (and a monkey-puzzle tree in the tiny front garden). Arthur was now earning an unquestionably middle-class salary of £300 a year. Their neighbours were the headmaster of the local primary school on one side and the builder who had developed the terrace on the other. They had a live-in maid, and the union soon gave him the use of a motor car. The front room of the house was Arthur's office, where a constant stream of people came to see him about their problems or union business. A cousin, interviewed in 1972, remembered 'a very cosy house . . . there were always bright fires during the winter and vases of fresh flowers in the summer. And books! Why, there were books everywhere.'[10]

This cousin denied that Roy was spoiled, 'but his parents thought he was absolutely IT, there was no doubt about that'.[11] Another agreed that Hattie 'was very ambitious for him, from the earliest age, and made a tremendous fuss of him'.[12] When, years later, the press began to look into his background, neighbours were happy to furnish memories of a rather pampered little boy. For instance, Derek Powell – the son of the next-door builder and one of Roy's two best boyhood friends – remembered:

Hattie literally smothered Roy with love. She would hardly let him walk down the street alone. He was always a shy boy. I sometimes wonder if that was because his mother swamped him . . . His mother . . . tried to shelter him from everything. For example when he was at primary school she religiously saw him across the village road every day. He could have become stand-offish as a result of this, and of being an only child. But with me and our little gang he was not given the chance.[13]

The daughter of the other neighbours agreed:

His mother was loth to let him out of her sight. When he had an ordinary appendix operation in hospital Hattie stayed with him for three days and nights refusing to go home. Even when Roy went down the road to Pontypool railway station to collect train numbers, along would go Hattie to sit and knit on the platform with him.[14]

That may be a bit unfair. The appendix operation, when Roy was seven, was serious enough to involve three weeks in hospital and six months off school; and Hattie certainly did not follow him around all the time, as Derek Powell's memory of their 'little gang' makes clear. In most respects Roy was a quite normally active, if privileged, boy:

> We were pretty lucky kids. Other boys in the valley . . . played on slag heaps. They had little else to do. But Roy and I had bicycles and splendid model railways and plenty of good things at Christmas.[15]

He also loved cricket, rugby and swimming. Moreover he was not entirely an only child, since for much of his childhood two elder cousins, Sybil and Connie Peppin, the daughters of Hattie's widowed sister, stayed with the Jenkinses much of the time, particularly in the school holidays: Sybil and Connie played with Roy in the sandpit, and later cricket in the garden – not cowboys and Indians, as Hattie did not allow guns; and in the summer the two families would go together to Swansea, Porthcawl or Weston-super-Mare. Later, when their mother died, Connie came to live with the Jenkinses. She was five years older than Roy, but he used to treat her, with a boy's assumed authority, as though she were the younger: 'He treated me like a sister. He'd give me worms to hold.'[16]

At the same time he was always a studious boy; and unusually – indeed, obsessively – numerate. 'The main thing about Roy as a boy was his addiction to numbers,' Connie remembered. 'He was always silent and counting or working out some sum. He was like that ever after!'[17] He loved collecting facts, and once he had learned them he never forgot them, as he characteristically demonstrated in an essay on Glasgow written in the last year of his life:

> An excellent encyclopaedia (Harmsworth's) published in the early 1920s, to the study of which I devoted many childhood hours, gave with complete confidence the exact population of every major city down to the last digit. Glasgow then scored 1,111,428 compared with Edinburgh's 320,318.[18]

Likewise he relished cricket not so much for the game itself as for the statistics that it generated. As a boy, he wrote nostalgically in 1996, 'my life was dominated by cricketers, their scores and their enshrinement in the temporary pantheon of Players' cigarette cards'.[19] All his life he loved making lists and grading things – cities, wines or Prime Ministers – in rank order.

Like many boys in those days, his love of numbers found an outlet in trainspotting. Not only did the Eastern Valley line from Newport up to Ebbw Vale run past the bottom of his garden; but Pontypool Road, just three miles away, was then a major railway junction where the GWR (Great Western Railway) expresses from Bristol and Plymouth up to Manchester and Glasgow crossed – 'sometimes exchanging coaches' – with those from Cardiff to Birmingham.* 'The train for Glasgow, I remember vividly, had two engines, which made me feel that it must be both a distant and an important destination.'[20] Trains and distant destinations captivated him. 'He used to plan train journeys,' another schoolfriend recalled, '– complete with times and interchanges – to Jerusalem and Constantinople, and he could recite all the stations on the Paris metro at a very young age.'[21] Though not a mathematician, this numerological precision stayed with him all his life.

They were a very close family. Among themselves they all had animal nicknames. Arthur was 'Jumbo', Hattie was 'Pony' and Roy was 'Bunny'. Even when Roy was grown-up and away in the army, Arthur still signed his letters to him 'Jumbo' and gave him the news of 'Pony'. The maid, Kathleen Tuttle, remembered that Roy wanted her to have a nickname too: 'He started calling me "Kathlet", but his mother put a stop to that. I think she felt I might think it cheeky but I really rather liked it.'[22] Kathleen did not think Roy was spoiled, rather that he was quite strictly brought up, always made to do his homework and piano practice (which he hated). Arthur could be stern if Roy disappointed his expectations, whereas Hattie more easily forgave him. But Kathleen never once heard Arthur raise his voice. If Roy was naughty, which was not often, his punishment was not to be allowed to join Arthur on his evening walk on Penyrhoel, the nearby hill. 'That would really hurt Roy. He worshipped his father, and because Arthur had to give so much of his time to dealing with the problems of other people, Roy used to clutch at the moments he could spend with him.'[23]

---

* Looking at the map today, this seems surprising. But until Dr Beeching slashed the railway network in the 1960s, trains from the South-West went through the Severn tunnel to Newport before proceeding north via Pontypool, Shrewsbury and Carlisle to Glasgow.

Arthur, for his part, took Roy around with him to political meetings and union conferences all over South Wales and beyond. His earliest memory was of being taken to the Empire Exhibition at Wembley in 1924, when he was three. On Sundays they would drive to Abergavenny, Raglan or other places of interest around Monmouthshire. They went quite frequently to Cardiff – twenty-two miles away, but 'very much the local metropolis' – for shopping, theatre visits, rugby internationals or 'semi-celebratory meals' in the best hotels;[24] and occasionally to London. In 1929, when Roy was eight, Arthur took him (with Hattie) abroad for the first time, to Brussels where he was attending a Socialist International meeting. Two years later they went to Paris for six days, visiting all the usual sights but also the house that Arthur had stayed in twenty years before. To a ten-year-old from Pontypool, Paris in those days was 'a very attractive but slightly shabby city . . . interesting but strange, and potentially hostile'.[25]

In 1993 another boyhood friend whose memories had been awakened by reading Jenkins' memoirs wrote him an almost idyllic recollection of these days:

> Snatchwood Road, games in 'the wood' . . . cricket in back gardens (those 'Test Matches'), the swimming pool, or rather baths, at Pontrenewydd with Derek Powell pounding out length after length much to the astonishment of us all, your kindly, caring mother and father, trips to the country in your father's car (if memory serves me right, an early Jowett), brown blazers and brown caps, listening to rugger internationals on the radio . . . What a happy and carefree, but cosseted childhood we had.[26]

The most famous episode in Roy's childhood, however, was one he was unaware of at the time. Roy was not yet six when Arthur was involved in a violent incident at the Quarry Level colliery in Pontypool in August 1926, one of many such skirmishes during the bitter miners' lockout which continued for seven months after the collapse of the General Strike in May. Pickets at the pithead were attempting to stop around forty 'scabs' from going to work, while the police tried to escort them. Stones were thrown and the police baton-charged the pickets – the sort of scenes that were to be familiar again half a century later in 1972 and 1984. As agent, Arthur had undoubtedly helped organise the picketing; but he was almost certainly trying to prevent violence, not foment it: anything else would have been utterly out of character. The *Times* report the next day supported this interpretation:

15

Mr Arthur Jenkins, the miners' agent, scrambled to the top of a coal truck and called a truce. He then addressed the crowd, saying: 'I have seen all that has happened here. The attack was a most ferocious one on the part of the police without the slightest cause.' Members of the crowd shouted: 'Let's give it to them.' Mr Jenkins replied: 'No, we don't want that. I shall say what I have to say elsewhere.' The police ordered the demonstrators to leave the premises, and they dispersed.[27]

Nevertheless Arthur was arrested with several others for riotous assembly, and additionally charged with inciting his co-defendants to commit riot and damage. When the case was heard at the Pontypool police court three weeks later the police gave evidence that he had told the crowd, 'I can do no more. They have . . . decided to work. I now leave them to you', as a result of which the crowd turned hostile and started throwing stones.[28] The case was passed up to the Monmouthshire Assizes in November, where it lasted for five days. Several impeccable witnesses testified to Arthur's good character; but the police, in his view, 'lied terribly',[29] and Mr Justice Swift chose to believe the police. 'I am satisfied,' he declared, 'that from the early morning of August 30 . . . you were laying plans to intimidate these workers and to thwart the police.'

> Your position was deplorable. You were a man of high position, not only in the Miners' Federation, but in the county, and it was above all things your duty as a public man, as a member of the County Council and as one of the Standing Joint Committee, to have assisted the police in maintaining order.

His co-defendants got three months; but Arthur was sentenced to nine months in prison.[30]

The sentence was widely seen as a travesty of justice and a campaign was launched, supported not only by local and national newspapers but by the chairman of the South Wales coal owners, to have it reversed. Far from considering Arthur disgraced, his fellow county councillors placed flowers on his seat to mark his absence. Ramsay MacDonald, Labour Leader of the Opposition, raised the case in the House of Commons,[31] and a petition of 40,000 signatures was presented to the Home Secretary, Sir William Joynson-Hicks. Perhaps fortunately for Arthur, the notoriously hardline 'Jix' was ill; deputising for him, Lord Birkenhead (the former F.E. Smith, now Secretary of State for India) ordered his release after only three months. He returned home to a hero's welcome, with miners and their wives cheering his car as it passed through every village in the valley.

Roy remembered the emotional homecoming, but not until years later did he learn where Arthur had been. At the time he was merely told that his father was visiting coalmines in Germany – the sort of thing he did quite regularly – while Hattie took Roy away from Abersychan (he had not yet started school) to stay with friends in Newport. Leo Abse alleged that Hattie kept the truth from Roy 'not out of protectiveness but from sham respectability';[32] in her defence Alan Watkins wrote that 'most Welsh mothers would have behaved in the same way. In any case, she had been instructed to act as she did by Arthur, who did not wish his son to grow up with hatreds or prejudices.'[33] Even so, Connie Peppin remembered that 'Aunt Hattie took it all very badly. Absolutely knocked out. She needed a lot of support at that time, otherwise she would have stayed in her own house. But she couldn't, and could never bear to talk about it.'[34] Nor could Arthur. 'To the end of his life,' Roy recalled, 'my father hated the memory of that jail sentence.'[35] Even three months must have been a painful ordeal for a man of his tastes and temperament, and Hattie believed it did lasting damage to his health. But he had no wish to pose as a martyr or make political capital out of his imprisonment; nor did he want his son to do so, and Roy never did. The one lasting effect it had on him was to instil a healthy scepticism about police evidence.

Roy did not go to school till he was seven (and then he had six months off following his appendix operation – possibly an example of Hattie's over-protectiveness). For the next three years, however, he attended the local primary school at Pentwyn, which was dramatically sited between a bare mountainside and a large coal-tip: his memories of sliding down the latter on his way home contradict the idea that Hattie accompanied him everywhere. From Pentwyn he easily won a place at one of the two local grammar schools. West Monmouth, a semi-boarding school partly owned by the Haberdashers' Company, was universally recognised as the top school in the area. Arthur was a governor and would have had no difficulty in sending Roy there. Instead he chose to send him to Abersychan County School, slightly closer, but much less highly regarded. The choice was strange since Arthur was already determined that Roy should follow him to Oxford. There survives in Roy's papers a fragment of a letter or diary entry dated 21 May 1929 – when he was just eight and a half – typed but childishly spelled:

This year for Witsun we decided to go to Oxford so that I could deside whitch college I wanted to go to . . . When we arrived at Oxford Daddy drove up to Russgin Colleg to see the . . .[36]

Ivor Bulmer-Thomas, a family friend, believed that Arthur was torn – like many a Labour parent since – between his ambition for his son and his political need to support the local school. He was a governor of Abersychan too, and thought highly of the headmaster; so on this occasion he made the political choice. But Bulmer-Thomas believed it set Roy back academically.[37]*

One or two more childish letters have survived. From one, dating from April 1930, typed on SWMF paper – 'Agent: Alderman Arthur Jenkins' – it seems that Roy was being allowed to have a dog:

> Dear Jum,
>   I think I have decided to have one of Peter's brothers or sisters . . . one that rolles over on her or his back, and wags his wager . . . who has a nice dispsishon and is very playful . . . I am in diviculty bying a he or a she i want to by a she but mammer wants me to buy a he. you do not mind me having it? do you!
>   xxxxxxxxxxxxxxxxxx
>   LOVE FROM
>   Bun[38]

Another, six months later, handwritten in pencil, shows a marked improvement in spelling. Arthur and Hattie were evidently in London:

> Dear Mammy & Daddy,
>   I got your letter this morning. I thought you would enjoy the journey up . . . Walter Daniel has got a scooter and I can't half go on it . . . I read Oliver Twist in three hours this morning . . . Mrs Thomas told me two tell you that I have been a good boy . . .
>   Love from Bun xxxxxxxx[39]

---

* Ivor Bulmer-Thomas had a remarkable career. Born plain Ivor Thomas in 1905, the son of a brickyard worker, he progressed from West Monmouth – where Arthur first took an interest in him – to a brilliant academic career at Oxford and then, via journalism, into Labour politics, before crossing the floor to join the Tories in 1949, marrying into the Bulmer cider family and devoting the rest of his life to saving 'friendless' churches. He remained a friend of Roy's up to his death in 1993.

Roy started at Abersychan in September 1931, two months before his eleventh birthday, and left at sixteen. Being so young, and the son of a local bigwig, he was given a rough initiation. Another new boy named Norman Edwards recalled, sixty-five years later, how he had got into a fight trying to protect Roy and been given a hundred lines for his pains:

> What struck me . . . was that you were unwilling to defend yourself or me, and that the fashionable dogma of Ghandi [*sic*] of passive resistance . . . held sway. My view was that a miner's son fought for every crust of bread and principle.

The charge of reluctance to fight would frequently be levelled at Jenkins in years to come. Looking back, however, Edwards saw things differently:

> You were hard on yourself when you say that you lacked steel. You must not forget that you were 1 year younger than the rest of us, and that makes a vast difference in academic attainment, physical prowess and sheer guts. You lived with that for six years.[40]

Roy was already a budding journalist with a high sense of his own importance. At the age of ten he produced two editions of a newspaper called the *Greenlands News*, filled with items about pets, illnesses and cricket scores, all broken up into paragraphs with a crossword and weather forecast. The first edition contained the following report:

> Important Member of Greenlands Ill
> From our special correspondent Middle Bedroom Wednesday.
>   It is reported that Roy H. Jenkins who is suffering from Broncitis is improving rather rapidly. But I regret to state that he is unable to run in his School sports at Talywan on Friday July the 3rd where he would undoutbably have won![41]

Two years later he relaunched the newspaper on a larger scale, reporting TERRIBLE SNOW STORMS and DOG'S TERRIBLE FRIGHT, but also:

> The following agreement has been written out and drawn up by Sir R.H. Jenkins K.C.
>   'It is hereby agreed, sealed and signed that Arthur Jenkins shall

pay Roy Harris Jenkins the sum of 6d (six pence) every Saturday morning without fail.

Should R.H. Jenkins get into Class B, then the amount will become 1/- (one shilling) and should R.H. Jenkins get into Class A then the amount will become 2/6 (two shillings and sixpence).

Should Arthur Jenkins fail to pay on Saturday morning, then he must pay the amount plus 3d as soon as possible.

It now remains for the signatures to be added.'

There was also 'OUR GRAND COMPETITION . . . S'EASY. Send in your efforts with two penny stamps to Roy Jenkins, Snatchwood Road Abersychan Mon not later than Sunday March 5th'; and a useful fact: 'ON THIS DAY 1882 – Electric tramcars were first intriduced into the world'.[42] The twelve-year-old editor was already an avid newspaper reader.

Despite some initial bullying, Jenkins claimed in his memoirs to have been 'thoroughly happy' at Abersychan, though academically he did not shine.[43] 'It wasn't an intensely competitive school,' another boyhood friend, Hugh Brace, recalled, with no tradition of sending boys to university beyond Wales. The quality of the teaching was variable: the French mistress was 'particularly bad', the history teacher 'all right, but no more'.[44]* But Roy, oddly, did no history for two years before the sixth form – which he later blamed for gaps in his knowledge. For his School Certificate in 1935 he took six subjects (English, geography, French, maths, physics and chemistry), to which he added Latin – 'absolutely necessary for Oxford' – the following year. (He and Hugh were taught Latin together by the head.) Then, after a misguided flirtation with chemistry, he switched course and took history, geography and English for his Higher Certificate. His reports recognised his intelligence, but thought he lacked concentration. 'I am convinced that if Roy would concentrate more resolutely in class he would improve his position very considerably,' his form master wrote at the end of his first year: significantly he did better in exams than course work. In his final year his English master described the budding writer pretty well:

Thinks for himself and is interested in life & books . . . Work expresses mental alertness and keen interest in ideas and literature.

* Near the end of his life Jenkins recalled it more candidly in an unguarded interview in the *Spectator*. 'I got into Balliol 62 years ago from a most awful school – no, I mustn't say that, but . . . it was a very, very minor school, with very little good teaching.'[45]

Essays are clear and logical and vocabulary expressive. Roy has read outside the limits of his books and has acquired general ideas. He would be wise to confine himself to set books for the next few weeks . . . If he does himself justice he should do very well.[46]

It is clear from this that he was already reading widely. Asked by a newspaper in 1995 to nominate his favourite Penguin, he chose Aldous Huxley's *Crome Yellow* (first published in 1921):

In the summer of 1937 when I was driven by my parents around Devon and Cornwall they (although far from being anti-books) complained that there was little point in showing me the splendours of the coasts and moors of South-West England if I spent the whole time sitting in the back of the car engrossed in Huxley. His aura of sophistication was alluring for a sixteen-year-old.[47]

This was just after he left school. But asked on another occasion for a favourite poem, he picked 'Prospice' – a meditation on death by Robert Browning, which he said he had studied for his Higher Certificate and still found 'powerful' in his seventies.[48] Outside the classroom Roy was 'more enthusiastic than skilled' at games, though he played in the scrum at rugby, was not a bad slow bowler and won prizes for swimming. He was popular enough to become a prefect, though the girls – it was a co-ed school – thought him 'a bit uppish and detached'.[49] Hugh Brace remembered him 'going around with the girls a bit in the sixth form, one in particular', who must have been his first girlfriend.[50]

By this time Arthur had become MP for Pontypool when the previous Member retired in 1935. From now on he normally stayed in London during the week when the House was sitting, lodging with other Labour Members in a hotel in Bloomsbury, and came home only at weekends. But that year the family moved to a much larger house reflecting his new status.* This third Greenlands – rented from the GWR – was two miles further down the valley on the edge of Pontypool, near the railway station, a square white-stuccoed house standing in a substantial garden, with an open aspect to the south-east towards England. It was not a 'big house' in the full sense of the word,

---

* MPs' pay was raised in 1937 to £600 p.a. This was a solid professional salary, but it was supplemented by no additional expenses beyond the train fare to their constituencies, hence the need for cheap accommodation in London during the week.

but in the context of Pontypool it was a substantial residence. Here Arthur and Hattie frequently entertained parliamentary colleagues for the weekend: the Attlees and Arthur Greenwood, Herbert Morrison and Hugh Dalton, among others. The teenaged Roy thus grew up knowing all these leading figures of the 1945 government as family friends – though the guest who most impressed him was his own future Cabinet colleague, Dick Crossman, then a thirty-year-old Oxford don who stood as Labour candidate at a Birmingham by-election in 1937. 'His blend of verve and paradox I found very exciting at sixteen.'[51]*

If Roy was not already hooked on politics, he certainly became so now:

> As a schoolboy, I was an assiduous gallery-sitter in the House, whenever I could persuade my parents to take me up to London, which was not too infrequently . . . I remember on one occasion, during I think the long drawn-out debates on the 1936 Unemployment Assistance Bill, being very indignant when, at 4.00 a.m., my father insisted on sending me home to his hotel in a taxi and refused to allow me to see the night through from the Gallery.[53]

As well as politics, the young Roy was habituated very early to taxis, hotels and restaurants.

In February 1935 he wrote a detailed account of a trip to London with his mother and a friend, which included breakfast on the train. Food was something he already took very seriously:

> This was very sound – the usual G.W.R. breakfast. Porridge, Corn Flakes or Grape Nuts with a peculiar kind of extremely rich and good cream. Some kind of fish, generally kipper, plaice or haddock (the former two of which I like, the latter one I eat), any variety of eggs, bacon, sausage, cold ham etc., and finally toast, some very good butter (frozen or half-frozen), and marmalade, all washed down with two, or even three large cups of good coffee. The coffee on the G.W.R. is always very good. There is never the least suspicion of skin about it. I dislike intensely coffee on which skin is prone to form.

---

* Arthur took Roy with him when he went to speak for Crossman at this by-election – Roy's first visit to the city he was to represent for twenty-seven years. His principal memory was of Birmingham's impenetrable one-way traffic system.[52]

They stayed at the Strand Palace Hotel which, he noted, was 'in many ways, an amazing hotel. It is very large and, despite the fact that the charges are quite reasonable, extremely luxurious.' They went up the dome of St Paul's, met Arthur for lunch at the Strand Corner House and went to Selfridges, before going to see *Love on the Dole* – a very suitable choice for a Labour MP – at the Garrick Theatre. 'It was a very good play,' Roy wrote, 'but was not particularly marked by its cheeriness.' The next day they went to the Science Museum, the zoo and Madame Tussaud's. ('I had never been there before, and I cannot say that it impressed me very much'), before catching the 5.55 back from Paddington and having a good dinner on the train.[54]

A few months later he did it again, this time on his own. At Newport station, doubtless feeling very grown-up, he bought the *Daily Mirror*, the *News Chronicle* (a Liberal paper) and the *Humorist* magazine. Breakfast was up to standard, 'the kipper being one of the best that I have ever tasted'. But lunch at the Strand Palace was disappointing. 'The lunch is not nearly so good as the dinner is, although I have no doubt that they bear a very distinct relation to one another.' The dinner he confidently judged 'one of the most amazing in London', comprising six or seven courses for three shillings and sixpence.[55] But he was not interested only in food. After one of these London trips he compiled an exhaustive description, in nine chapters, of the unfolding view from the train window. 'The journey from Newport to Paddington,' it began, 'must be, for its length, one of the most beautiful in the country.' The scenery was 'varied and interesting', and he counted it a recommendation that 'the line passes no areas that are disfigured by basic industries'.[56] Artlessly these teenage journals foreshadow the man he would become.

In the summer of 1937 he left school, but his Higher Certificate results were 'indifferent' and he was not yet ready to try for Oxford. So he went for a year to University College, Cardiff – an interlude he omitted from his entry in *Who's Who*. Hugh Brace thought it was 'a kind of crammer . . . because he was so young'.[57] It was really more like a sixth-form college, intended to bring him up to the level needed to achieve his father's ambition. Soon after he had started there, Arthur – away in London as usual – wrote him a characteristic letter on his seventeenth birthday:

My dear Roy,
    This is your 17th birthday and I am writing this note to wish you many happy returns.
    You are now starting on your university career. In school you

have done splendidly. With good health and perseverance you will no doubt be equally successful in the next five or six years. I wish you well.

A good rule in life is never to do to anyone what you would not like done to you. I once heard Sir Harry Lauder say he had never said or done anything in his profession he would be ashamed for his mother to hear or know. That, I thought, was a proud record. May you be able to achieve that high standard!

Pony and I are very proud of you. I know you will do everything possible to preserve that pleasure for us.

I enclose a small token of our love.

Yours affectionately,

Jumbo[58]

Looking back in a piece written for the college centenary in 1982, Roy claimed to have enjoyed his seven months at Cardiff. He lived at home and travelled in each day by bus, an hour and a quarter each way, so he did not experience much of university life, partly because he was so young, but also because his focus was so firmly fixed on Oxford. But he remembered that the food was 'rather good, better certainly than that which I subsequently had to accustom myself to at Balliol', and claimed to have made two lasting friends with whom he made frequent expeditions to the Kardomah Café to drink Russian tea 'in glasses with straw holders, which we thought a rather daring drink'.[59] He was supposed to be brushing up his history and French and starting some economics. He was presumably taught by Hilary Marquand, soon to be a minister in the 1945 government but at this time Professor of Industrial Relations at Cardiff, since he named Marquand, along with his headmaster, as a referee in his application to Oxford; but he mainly remembered writing nineteenth-century history essays for Dorothy Marshall, later a distinguished historian of the eight-eenth century, whom he credited with teaching him to write in the approved Oxford style.* At any rate, this year at Cardiff did the trick. In March 1938 he sat the history scholarship for a group of six colleges, including Balliol – then the only Oxford college operating admission solely by competitive examination. Sending his application to the Balliol admissions tutor, he wrote naively that he had 'obtained past papers

---

* More than half a century later Jenkins was able to invite Dorothy Marshall, now aged ninety-two, to lunch at East Hendred. She greatly appreciated his reference to her in his memoirs and was 'as excited as a schoolgirl' at seeing him again.[60]

from an Oxford publishing firm, but they gave no indication of the scope of the work required', and asked for some advice.[61]* The tutor replied reassuringly that the extent of his reading was less important than the power of using the material he possessed: the point was whether he had the sort of mind that would enable him to gain a First, not whether he had the knowledge now that would be expected at the end of three years.[62] He failed to win a scholarship; but the college evidently did detect first-class potential and he was offered a place to read PPE (philosophy, politics and economics, otherwise known as Modern Greats), already the course of choice for aspiring politicians.

That goal achieved, Arthur took him again to Paris where Roy stayed on for a month on his own, staying in a *pension* near Montparnasse and exploring the city on foot and by metro. This was when he acquired 'almost a taxi-driver's knowledge of Paris' – but not yet a taste for wine. 'It was rather nasty wine they served us,' he recalled years later, 'a *vin ordinaire* which most people diluted with water. But I didn't like it, diluted or undiluted.'[63] As the war clouds gathered over Czechoslovakia, however, he hurried back to England ten days before Munich bought a temporary reprieve, then went up to Oxford at the beginning of October 1938, still a month short of his eighteenth birthday.

---

* He signed this letter 'R. Harris Jenkins'. It is not clear whether he then saw Harris as his preferred Christian name or as part of a double-barrelled surname. At any rate he dropped it very quickly as soon as he got to Oxford.

2 David and Jonathan

OXFORD has been the nursery of aspiring politicians ever since the young William Gladstone was President of the Union in 1830. Whatever the competing academic claims of Cambridge, it is overwhelmingly from Oxford that the governing elite has reproduced itself, generation after generation. The rise of the Labour Party interrupted the tradition only briefly. The pioneers naturally did not go to university at all. But by the time Labour came to maturity as a governing party after 1945 – under the Oxford-educated Attlee – its younger leaders were overwhelmingly Oxford graduates and very often dons, like Hugh Gaitskell, Douglas Jay, Patrick Gordon Walker, Dick Crossman and Harold Wilson. Almost half of the twenty-three members of Wilson's first Cabinet in 1964 had been to Oxford, and five of the six contenders for the succession in 1976 – though on this occasion it was the exception, Jim Callaghan, who took the prize. On the Conservative side the picture has been similar: in the thirty-five years between Churchill's retirement and the accession of John Major (roughly the span of Roy Jenkins' political career) all five Tory leaders had been to Oxford. More recently Tony Blair, David Cameron, George Osborne, William Hague and the Miliband brothers have maintained the pattern.*

But if the dominance of Oxford has been remarkable, the pre-eminence of a single college is almost equally so. Balliol is one of the oldest of the Oxford foundations but architecturally one of the least distinguished and academically has never been outstanding. 'I am not

---

* The only substantial breach in Oxford's near-monopoly was made by the post-Thatcher generation of younger Tories, almost all of whom – Kenneth Clarke, Michael Howard, Norman Lamont, Leon Brittan, John Gummer, Michael Portillo, Peter Lilley and David Mellor – went to Cambridge.

sure,' Jenkins wrote in 1988, 'that Balliol has been responsible for any major foray beyond the established perimeter of knowledge since Adam Smith'; while in his own time 'I do not think it had a single don of towering intellectual stature'.[1] It boasted a remarkable tally of eminent literary alumni, from Matthew Arnold and Algernon Swinburne in the nineteenth century to Aldous Huxley and Graham Greene in the twentieth. But Balliol's distinctive ethos, combining an unusually meritocratic admissions policy with a commitment to public service, was first established under the mastership of Benjamin Jowett in the 1870s. The archetypal Balliol man of Jowett's time was H.H. Asquith, the brilliant son of a Yorkshire wool merchant who coined and in himself epitomised the phrase 'effortless superiority', becoming a young Home Secretary in 1892 before rising with smooth inevitability to the premiership in 1908. From 1924 the Jowett tradition was carried on by another outstanding Master, A.D. ('Sandy') Lindsay – a Labour-voting Scot and champion of adult education who was briefly Professor of Philosophy at Glasgow before going back to Balliol at the age of forty-five. Amid the upper-class frivolity that still largely characterised Oxford between the wars, Lindsay's Balliol was a serious college which mixed scholarship boys from state schools with the best of the public schools and a substantial element from overseas and self-consciously trained them up to be the next generation of Cabinet ministers, ambassadors, Permanent Secretaries and bishops.

This mix of egalitarianism with high-minded ambition suited the young Jenkins admirably – as it did the serious young organ scholar, three years ahead of him, 'Teddy' Heath, the son of a Broadstairs builder, and the brilliant, bullish yet solitary son of a Bradford technical college head, Denis Healey, two years ahead. 'Life,' it was once said, 'is one Balliol man after another'; and in the post-war decades the famous joke was scarcely an exaggeration. Within his own college Jenkins was able to get to know several of those who would be his colleagues and rivals in the House of Commons over the next half-century: not only fellow grammar-school products like Heath and Healey, but also well-connected scions of political families like Julian Amery, Maurice Macmillan, Hugh Fraser and Mark Bonham Carter (Asquith's grandson). Though very different, all these men perceptibly carried the Balliol impress: that air of innate self-confidence and an inability to suffer fools. From the moment he arrived in Oxford Jenkins slipped smoothly into the same mould.

He was always shy. Yet Balliol, with its unusual mix of privileged Etonians and clever scholarship boys, Scots, Jews, American Rhodes

Scholars and princely Indians, was 'an intrinsically friendly place'[2] and his provincial background was no serious bar to fitting in. Two lifelong friends he made within the college were Madron Seligman (also a close and faithful friend of Ted Heath, much later a Member of the European Parliament); and Ronald McIntosh (later an industrialist who headed the National Economic Development Council (NEDC) in the 1970s). A third was Neil Bruce, who became a BBC foreign correspondent but died relatively young. Their memories of Jenkins differed slightly. Seligman remembered him as quiet, diffident and bookish, whereas McIntosh recalled him as 'good company, with a well-developed sense of fun and a lively, though not scholarly, mind . . . A naturally gregarious character, he was always at ease with himself socially and had no hang-ups about being a Welsh miner's son.'[3] Jenkins himself admitted that he might not have felt so comfortable in most other colleges at the time; he remembered feeling 'fairly uneasy' when invited by Gavin Faringdon to his family seat at Buscot Park towards the end of his first year.[4] But when David Ginsburg – another grammar-school boy who came up to Balliol the next year – first heard him speak in the Union, he took him for a peer's son.[5] If he did not already have it when he went up – and he always maintained that his father spoke little differently from himself – he very quickly acquired the distinctive drawl, with no trace of a Welsh accent, that was to be the delight of impressionists in years to come. It was doubtless his inability to pronounce his 'R's that led someone to describe him as 'one of Nature's Old Etonians'. It was unlucky that his own name began with 'R'; but perhaps for this reason he never shied away from words beginning with the difficult letter.

Somehow Arthur contrived that Roy was not short of money. He lived in college in his first year – Staircase 15, Room 17 – and thirty years later his 'scout' (college servant) remembered him as 'one of the best tippers' he ever knew. Scouts reckoned anything over £5 as generous. 'Mr Jenkins always gave me between £5 and £10 and when he left college to go into digs he gave me the tea service he had been using.'[6] He had always liked his food, but now he quickly discovered a taste for wine. His school friend Derek Powell, who had preceded him to Oxford, recalled that Roy used sometimes to dine with him at Merton. 'We had a little clique of bon viveurs – and our college food was better than Balliol's . . . Our wines were better too, and Roy appreciated them. He loved a good claret then as he does now and his taste for living became Balkan Sobranie all the way once he got to Oxford.'[7] Ginsburg too, who also became a lifelong friend – a Labour and then an SDP MP – remembered Jenkins, as an undergraduate, introducing him to Château Margaux.[8]

Michaelmas term 1938 was a tense but politically exciting time to go to Oxford. For a brief moment Neville Chamberlain's expedient deal with Hitler at Munich seemed to have bought a reprieve; but the shadow of war still loomed, and no freshman going up that year could feel confident that he would be able to finish his degree. By chance Oxford – and Balliol in particular – was immediately at the heart of the national crisis of conscience about Munich. In a famous by-election that autumn the adopted Labour candidate, the future Foreign Secretary Patrick Gordon Walker, was persuaded to stand down in favour of 'Sandy' Lindsay, who stood as an Independent anti-government candidate to unite all those opposed to appeasement: an unprecedented action for the head of an Oxford college. The government was defended by the thirty-one-year-old Quintin Hogg, while Lindsay's supporters, including some dissident Tory MPs, campaigned on the slogan that 'A Vote for Hogg is a Vote for Hitler'. Jenkins, along with most of Balliol, was swept up in Lindsay's campaign – an intoxicating introduction to Oxford politics. 'I remember canvassing up sodden and leafy half-drives in North Oxford, when I was shocked to discover that Conservative loyalty to Chamberlain and Hogg was rather stronger than academic solidarity with Lindsay.'[9] Hogg won, saving Chamberlain's face, but his majority was halved. A few weeks earlier, in the first Union debate of the term, Teddy Heath – hitherto a model young Conservative – had courageously teamed up with the Labour ex-president Christopher Mayhew to denounce Munich. In the most crowded house for years they carried the vote by 320:266. Then, following another debate in which he memorably accused the Prime Minister of turning 'all four cheeks' to the enemy, Heath was elected president by a margin of 280:155. Jenkins 'almost certainly' voted for him,[10] though it was Mayhew's speech that he most vividly remembered.*

With his family background and his own political ambition, it was inevitable that Jenkins' life for the next three years centred on the Union and the Labour Club. In retrospect, he regretted that he wasted so much of his energy on the Union, neglecting the range of other opportunities that Oxford offered. But at the time politics consumed his whole existence. His friends were almost exclusively political, while

---

* Reviewing Heath's memoirs in 1998, Jenkins recalled the first time he ever saw 'Teddy', '60 years ago, leaning against the club fender of the Balliol Junior Common Room after breakfast and reading *The Times* with great seriousness'.[11]

Roy Jenkins

Balliol provided five consecutive presidents in his first five terms, including Heath, Seligman and Hugh Fraser: his most ardent ambition was to continue that succession. The Oxford Union in those days took itself very seriously as a miniature House of Commons where national and international issues were debated along party lines; arguments, mannerisms and even jokes were honed which would soon be heard at Westminster; rivalries formed that would later be played out on the national stage. It is easy to mock these privileged young pretenders in tailcoats playing at politics; yet in 1938–41, debating questions of war and peace, socialism, communism or fascism, they were debating matters of life and death to their generation, and their arguments vividly illuminate the controversies of the time.* The Labour Club was dominated by Communists, boldly proclaiming an allegiance most of them would subsequently outgrow. Healey, for instance, was a Communist party member while at Oxford: decades later Jenkins could still see him 'walking purposefully through the Balliol quad in a belted mackintosh, full of ideological certainty'.[13] John Biggs-Davison was another 'straight-down-the-line fellow traveller' who later swung right across the political spectrum to land on the far right of the Tory party.[14] Jenkins, by contrast, was always firmly in the moderate Labour mainstream. A socialist by inheritance and upbringing, not rebellion, he had no need of adolescent posturing to establish his credentials. So long as the Communists were part of the broad left alliance against Nazism, however, and the Chamberlain government was still half-heartedly exploring possible cooperation with Stalin to contain Hitler, the latent division within the Labour Club did not come to a head.

In his first term Jenkins attended Union debates assiduously, but did not speak. He made his maiden speech at the beginning of his second term in January 1939 on a Labour motion condemning the domestic policy of the National Government. Isis, the student newspaper, judged this first effort – carefully prepared and rehearsed – 'very fluent' and 'quite good'.[15] The political colour of Oxford at the time was reflected in a comfortable victory (129:84) for the anti-government side. Two weeks later Jenkins again took the loyalist Labour line against a motion that 'This House welcomes the breaking down of the traditional party lines': 'Mr G.C. Grey (Hertford), summing up for the Ayes, thought a Popular Front could sweep the country, but Mr R.H. Jenkins (Balliol),

* Some, like Healey, had no time for all the dressing up: but Jenkins loved that side of it. He bought his Union tailcoat in Cardiff, and congratulated himself that he was still wearing it for state banquets sixty years later – 'an evening coat having the advantage over a morning one that it does not have to be done up in the middle'.[12]

30

summing up for the Noes, thought this most unlikely.'[16] This time, in a much smaller House, he was on the losing side by 82:46. He spoke a third time in March to deplore Britain's recognition of General Franco, recently victorious in the Spanish Civil War. At the end of this term he stood for the Library committee and did pretty well to get sixty-five votes. In the summer term, however, he spoke only once, again following the orthodox Labour line – despite the imminence of war – *against* immediate conscription; and again failed to be elected. *Isis* did not yet see him as a 'Union prospect'.[17]

Altogether he did not make much impact in his first year. Outside the Union he remembered playing college hockey, going to the cinema a lot and eating walnut cake in Fuller's Tea Rooms. Meanwhile he made heavy weather of his preliminary exams ('Pass Mods'), which he managed to spread over three terms instead of the usual two: doubtless the result of spending too much time on politics. As a result he looked back on his first year with much less affection than the next two. That last summer of peace he took part in the Balliol Players' annual tour, taking a production of Aristophanes' *The Birds* (in English) to various picturesque locations around southern England ('Roy was an enthusiastic member of the chorus').[18] In July he made his first recorded public speech, appearing on a platform with his father and the eighty-year-old George Lansbury in support of the Labour candidate at a by-election in Monmouth.[19] Then he went to France for five weeks, where he got a job escorting British visitors across Paris – and was annoyed to run into Denis Healey offering to show him around – but also travelled as far as the Spanish border with Ronnie McIntosh, staying in a villa owned by a girlfriend of Biggs-Davison. When the bombshell of the Nazi–Soviet Pact scuppered the last hopes of peace, they all hurried back from Toulon just before the declaration of war. But there was no immediate call-up of young men under twenty – indeed no British involvement in hostilities at all for seven months; so after a gloomy few weeks at home in Pontypool he went back to Oxford in October.

His horizons expanded considerably in his second year. First, to accommodate the evacuation of Chatham House from London, much of Balliol was moved next door to Trinity, where Jenkins shared a staircase with Madron Seligman: two large rooms each instead of the 'bed-sitter' he had occupied in Balliol, with log fires and better food. 'For long afterwards,' he wrote in his memoirs, 'whenever anyone asked whether wartime Oxford had not been a sad decline from the splendours of peacetime, I said that, on the contrary, it had put my standard of living up by about half.'[20] Second, since all four of the elected officers of the Union immediately left to join the forces, unelected replacements had to be co-opted in their place: in this way Nicholas ('Nicko') Henderson of Hertford, later to be one of Jenkins' closest friends but at this point no more than an 'amical acquaintance',[21] became president and Seligman treasurer. Jenkins got his foot on the ladder by joining the Standing Committee and the next term, when Seligman became president, moved up to secretary. Third, he made a number of important new friends: David Ginsburg; two Old Etonians, Anthony Elliott and Michael Ashcroft, who joined the Foreign Office and the Treasury respectively after the war; Isaiah ('Shy') Halevy, with whom he shared digs in his third year (but who was killed in 1944); and above all Tony Crosland – 'the most exciting friend of my life' – with whom his career would be intimately entangled for the next thirty-eight years.[22]

Crosland was fifteen months older than Jenkins and a year ahead of him, having gone up to Trinity in 1937 as a classical scholar after a turbulent career at Highgate School. His father was a senior civil servant, his mother an academic; but, most importantly, Joseph and Jessie Crosland were Plymouth Brethren: members of a strict Christian sect that rejected any form of priesthood. This conflicted background – professional upper-middle class, materially comfortable yet at the same time fiercely puritanical – set up all sorts of complicated tensions in their son which were exacerbated by Joseph's death in 1935. Partly in emulation of his parents, partly in reaction against them, young Tony embraced a form of socialism that was at once cerebral and romantic, egalitarian and elitist, and a personal lifestyle that was simultaneously hard-working and hedonistic. At Oxford he cut a striking figure, as Jenkins recalled in an obituary tribute written in 1977:

> I first saw Tony Crosland in 1938 or early 1939. He was 20, and I was 18. The gap seemed bigger. He was a very impressive undergraduate, showing every sign of intellectual and social self-assurance. He was immensely good-looking, and even in those days rather elegant. He wore a long camel-hair overcoat, and drove a powerful low MG known as the Red Menace. I, like many of his near-contemporaries, admired him from afar, and was rather intimidated.
>
> Then, one winter's evening a few months after the outbreak of the war, he came to my rooms, probably on some minor point of Labour Club business, and having settled it, remained uncertainly on the threshold, talking but neither sitting down nor departing for nearly two hours. His character was more ambivalent than I had thought, but also more engaging.

Thereafter, I saw him nearly every day for the next six months until he left Oxford.[23]

In the early days of their relationship Jenkins was clearly the junior partner. Crosland was not only older but intellectually more confident. He introduced his younger friend to Marxism, and taught him the importance of socialist theory and the class struggle – in which Roy, deriving his political allegiance unquestioningly from his father, had hitherto felt little interest. At the same time Tony deeply envied Roy's roots in the Labour movement, which he, as a middle-class intellectual, could never match. As their friendship developed, Roy took Tony back to Pontypool to meet his parents, as he did most of his Oxford friends.* But Arthur and Hattie took particularly to Tony, so much so that he became almost an adopted son. Hattie mothered him in a way that his own mother never had, and Arthur – the first of several surrogate father-figures in Tony's life – played a major part in weaning him from his initially over-theoretical understanding of socialism. Thus Roy and Tony formed a very close and complementary relationship: personal as much as political. Tony at this time was openly gay – it was part of his slightly dangerous glamour – and part of Roy's attraction for him was probably sexual. There is certainly a strong homoerotic undercurrent in his letters; and years later Roy confessed that Tony had successfully seduced him at least once.[25] Jenkins was not by nature gay – far from it; but it is clear that he fell for a time so wholly under Crosland's spell that he might have tried anything.

The teasing balance of their relationship (both personal and political) is well conveyed in the first surviving letter that Tony wrote Roy at the end of 1939, when Roy was back in Pontypool for Christmas and Tony was staying with his mother in Sussex:

My dear Roy,
    Your kind uncle is sending you Christmas card, letter, & fabulously expensive present all at once. But your uncle is also very annoyed with you for not sending back that 'Labour & the War' very soon, as you promised to do; I wanted it rather badly

---

* Seligman, McIntosh, Elliott, Ashcroft and Bruce all enjoyed Arthur and Hattie's hospitality in Pontypool. 'In the much less travelling world of the 1930s,' Roy wrote with some exaggeration, 'it was almost like being taken to visit a Druse stronghold in the Lebanon.' The 'sense of local power . . . was intriguing [to] conventionally-educated upper-middle-class boys from London or the Home Counties'.[24] This is a very rare example of Jenkins playing up his roots to impress his friends.

at Oxford, but it doesn't matter now at all, so you are magnanimously forgiven.

How have you been getting on with your 'beautiful' boy friend? Personally I think that however gold his heart may be (& I rather doubt even that) his exterior is bordering on the repulsive. However, one who wears political blinkers is likely to be aesthetically blind as well – it's all one can expect of a Social Democrat.

'Social Democrat' was of course intended as a friendly insult. Tony was critical of Labour from a far-left perspective. 'I still cling rather pathetically to my hopes in the Party,' he wrote, but he thought it insufficiently socialist, and suspected Roy of the same weakness. 'Fundamentally it's your nice liberal outlook again – the "we're-all-decent-chaps-at-heart-so-why-can't-we-all-pull-together-after-all-remember-what-Nelson-said" sort of outlook – one which is diametrically opposed to Marxism.' He concluded teasingly:

Well, Roy, write to me soon and tell me your ideas about Liverpool [the upcoming Universities Labour Federation (ULF) conference]. And don't forget – drink, women and sleep are all things to be taken in small quantities! What a thrill the Pontypool girls must get each vac. when their handsome (& pansy) Beau Geste comes back to them again! God, what an awful thought!

Yrs etc. Tony[26]

But if Tony was clearly the dominant partner, Roy did not follow him uncritically. The Oxford Labour Club was deeply divided over whether or not to support the war. Since the Nazi–Soviet Pact the majority had followed the Communist line that it was an imperialist war, like 1914, which the working class should not support. Tony and Roy took the minority view that Labour should support the war but not Chamberlain, in the belief that it could be turned to socialist ends. Tony, however, as a good Marxist, was still prepared to justify the Nazi–Soviet Pact, and Soviet threats to Finland, on grounds of self-defence. Roy, following Attlee and the Labour leadership, was not. On 22 November he proposed a motion at the Union that 'Recent Soviet policy has not been in accordance with socialist principles':

Mr R.H. Jenkins (Balliol), who opened the debate, stated that he was a socialist, but that he thought a country's policy should not necessarily be guided by what Marx would have thought or Lenin would have done. He was not prepared to accept the dictates of Moscow as infallible reason.[27] . . . Stalin's policy was inconsistent with the war aims propounded by Mr Attlee, and Russia's withdrawal from the Peace Front had betrayed Socialism by precipitating bloodshed, war and disorder.[28]

In the *Oxford Magazine* Nicko Henderson commented that 'Mr Jenkins made, as usual, a very sound and sensible speech; but he should try and get his arguments home by using more emphasis and thrust at the right moments'. In reply, Tony made what Henderson considered 'the best speech Mr Crosland has made in the Union'. But the House was against him – 'His *sang-froid* was useful against interruptions' – and Roy won the debate by 93:40.[29]

A week later Soviet troops invaded Finland. The Labour Club's cyclostyled *Bulletin* carried three distinct reactions. Leo Pliatzky – another undergraduate Communist who finished up as Permanent Secretary in the Department of Trade in the 1970s – defended the invasion. Jenkins condemned it as wanton aggression and a violation of self-determination. Crosland, with characteristic ambivalence, still excused it on military grounds but condemned it as a diplomatic blunder on Stalin's part which would only fuel anti-Soviet outrage in the West – as it did.[30]

After Christmas Tony (with Pliatzky) paid his first visit to Pontypool, where they doubtless carried on the argument and Arthur took them down a coalmine. (Tony had been down a mine before, whereas Roy – to judge from the way he describes the experience in his memoirs – surprisingly had not.) From there they all drove in Tony's car to the ULF conference in Liverpool, beginning on 2 January 1940, where they found themselves in an even smaller minority against the Communist domination of student Labour politics.* The Oxford Labour Club was divided; but most other university Labour clubs were virtually monolithic. Crosland, supported by Jenkins and another Oxford delegate, moved a counter-resolution in support of the war; but it was defeated

---

* 'As we moved up through the Welsh marches on that short January day,' Jenkins remembered at Pliatzy's memorial service sixty years later, 'Pliatzky and Crosland kept up their spirits by singing left-wing songs. I was not able to join in, not out of ideological disapproval, but because of an inability, despite my Welsh origin, ever to sing a note. But the recital left its mark on me, and nearly fifty years later I caused mild surprise by choosing the Soviet Airmen's Song . . . as one of my choices for *Desert Island Discs*. It was really in memory of that day.'[31]

by 49:9 and the invasion of Finland supported by 46:6.[32] As a result of these votes the ULF was disaffiliated from the Labour party.

Back in Oxford, Seligman as president invited the Finnish ambassador to the Union, where he pleaded for 'all possible help' to be given to his beleaguered country. Jenkins spoke in his support; Crosland did not speak, but staged a pro-Soviet demonstration, lowering a banner from the gallery demanding 'Hands Off Russia'. In a crowded House the motion was carried by 295:141; but Seligman and the ambassador had to fight their way out of the building through a crowd of left-wing bullies. This was Crosland's last pro-Soviet flourish. In all the other debates that term, as the war in the West still hung fire – the so-called 'Phoney War' – he and Roy were on the same side. On 1 February they both condemned the Chamberlain government's policy on the home front. On 15 February Roy spoke 'on the paper' and Tony from the floor against Labour joining an immediate coalition. The next week Roy used his father's influence to secure Arthur Greenwood (Labour's deputy leader) as guest speaker to advocate a socialist Britain, supported by Tony and Henderson, but did not speak himself. On 29 February he argued against banning the Communist Party. He was now winning some plaudits as a speaker. 'He has a fine control of language,' the *Oxford Magazine* allowed, 'and is a convincing debater.'[33] But on 7 March he drew the short straw in another high-profile debate when the exiled President of Czechoslovakia Eduard Beneš was the star guest, supported by Ted Heath, returning as an ex-president to the scene of his former triumphs. Jenkins proposed – surely against his own belief – the motion that 'This House has no faith in liberal Western democracy as a basis of government'. Against the usual leftist trend, but doubtless in guilty expiation of Britain's betrayal of Czechoslovakia at Munich, it was rejected by acclamation. Despite this, Jenkins was elected librarian for the summer term. Crosland stood for the presidency, but lost to a Tory, Robin Edmonds from Brasenose (later a diplomat). He was probably punished for toeing the Moscow line too long.

Despite their political differences, it was in this term and the next that Roy and Tony were at their closest. During the first seven months of 1940, Tony later wrote to Hattie, he and Roy enjoyed 'an exceedingly close & intense friendship of a kind that neither of us are ever likely to experience again':

> We used to spend practically the whole day together, we automatically did the same things, had the same friends, in fact practically shared our two lives, in complete mutual absorption and (as

I then thought) complete mutual loyalty. The proof of our friendship was that during the whole period neither of us had any
relations at all with members of the other sex – we were each
too wrapped up in our own two interwoven lives.[34]

As well as their own hopes, ambitions and emotions, they argued
about life, politics and socialism. They started from utterly opposed
directions. Though outwardly fiercely rational, Crosland once confessed
to his friend Philip Williams that his socialism derived from 'the emotional
need for a God, a religion, a Heaven, for something to believe in that
transcends the individual'.[35] This quasi-spiritual need was quite unlike
Jenkins' wholly secular, humanist approach. In an obituary appreciation
– written with the benefit of thirty more years' acquaintance, but surely
based on these early conversations – Roy contrasted Tony's rigorous
intellectualism with his own more pragmatic sense of history:

He had a mind of high perspective, yet cared little in a personal,
as opposed to an aesthetic sense, about the past. He had practically
no sense of nostalgia. He believed in applying highly rational
standards to decision-making (he always thought me hopelessly
intuitive) but he was full of strong emotions.[36]

During the Easter vacation Tony went again to Pontypool; but only
after a prickly exchange of letters, of which only one, from Roy, survives.
Its length and complexity vividly suggest the tortuous sensitivities of
their relationship:

My dear Tony,
I will begin by countering the charges you directed against my
letter. The statements that you made were quite correct, but the
conclusions that you drew were all wrong. You said that it was
hardly worth reading and that the only thing that it accomplished
was that it made you change, or rechange, your mind about coming
to P'pool. But that was the sole purpose of the letter. I had nothing
of particular interest to tell you and I should not have thought of
writing at that stage had I not been continually terrified by the
thought that the great but temperamental Tony, the complex
character, the difficult boy, would suddenly erect a façade of
sulkiness and for some obscure but significant reason refuse to
communicate with me for the rest of the vac., thereby infusing
his whole being with a feeling of intense satisfaction . . .

I did think at the end of last term that you really wanted to come to Pontypool, but the general effect of your letter that came this morning was to completely contradict this . . . I should hate you to feel that you were under any obligation to come down here. I should in fact be bitterly dissappointed [*sic*] if you did not arrive next week, but you need not feel that you have to carry out the task of amusing me for ten days or so.* Finally, I hope that you will not be so foolish as to misunderstand this paragraph. I want you to come v. much indeed.

The rest of the letter was concerned with politics and suggested that Roy was still very much under Tony's influence. He hoped that Tony would introduce him to 'some of your more eminent political acquaintances' in London – it is not clear whom he meant – 'or would a stooge make things difficult?' Despite his speech criticising Soviet policy, he was still worried by Labour's hostility towards Russia since the Nazi–Soviet Pact, and by the expulsion of the fellow traveller D.N. Pritt from the Labour Party for defending the invasion of Finland. 'In all political matters,' he admitted, 'I am feeling very desperately the need for your guidance.' He ended by asking Tony to telephone Pontypool to confirm when he was coming; and signed off 'Love, Roy'.[37]

But the influence was not all one-way, since it was in the course of their conversations at Pontypool that the two friends determined to break away from the Communist-dominated Labour Club and form a rival Democratic Socialist Club committed explicitly to the Labour party. Clearly they were swayed by 'energetic' discussions with Arthur, who warned them – Tony in particular – that the only road to socialism in Britain was through Labour. When they had returned to Oxford, Arthur wrote Tony an avuncular letter from the standpoint of a practical politician. Doubtless he had often spoken in similar terms to Roy.

My dear Tony . . .
I think I can understand the struggle you are having with yourself, and the reason for it. I have a feeling that you have been living alongside, a sort of neighbour of, the real Labour movement. You are, I am certain, in deadly earnest to do the right thing. That is the quality that will put you right in the end. What you have lacked, and do not misunderstand when I say it, is experience of the average

* Jenkins at this period could never spell 'disappointed', but regularly spelled it and similar words with a double 's'.

working man and woman . . . Oxford is a first-rate place for a Socialist if it can be joined to experience of the South Wales coalfield, or a similar industrial district. Perhaps a pure Oxford socialist is like pure gold, too soft to stand the wear and tear of usage! But you are blessed with a faith in the future of Labour that will urge you to gather experience of the real world, and when you have got that you will have one political god, and not several . . .

Yours very sincerely,

A.J.[38]

Tony wrote to Philip Williams that 'Papa' (as he called Arthur) was 'practically neurotic on the subject of the Left, with a very marked anti-middle-class intellectual bias'.[39] Nevertheless he took his advice. In years to come, when Crosland had become Labour's leading intellectual, he never forgot the importance of staying close to the Labour movement and the unions, investing his Grimsby constituents with a simple wisdom that Roy and others thought sentimental, if not positively phoney. In this respect Arthur could be said to have had, in the long run, more lasting influence on Tony than he had on Roy.

The split in the Oxford University Labour Club (OULC) was precipitated by the National Executive's decision to disaffiliate the ULF. At first, when some moderates began to talk of a breakaway, Roy and Tony were against it. Roy wrote a piece in the *Bulletin* arguing that a splinter club would not attract enough support to be viable (it had been tried at Cambridge): the moderates, he urged, must just work harder to counter the Communist influence. 'It is by attempting to get more control of the existing organisation and not by wrecking everything that has been built up, that we can best hope to propagate the Labour Party line'[40] – exactly the argument, ironically, used by Labour loyalists against the SDP in 1981. In February the OULC again debated Finland. Pliatzky again defended the Soviet action; Crosland – 'with his customary suavity and self-assurance' – now condemned it; but Denis Healey scornfully dismissed his apostasy, proposing a new version of Marx's slogan: 'Workers of the World unite! You have nothing to lose but your Liberals, and possibly your Social Democrats!'[41] One wonders if he remembered this in 1981.

Over Easter, Labour finally voted to disaffiliate the ULF ('So the blow has fallen,' Crosland and Jenkins wrote jointly in the *Bulletin*).[42] At a packed meeting in the first week of the summer term they and a trade union-funded mature student called Ian Durham moved a proposal to sever the club's connection with the ULF and reaffiliate with Labour. It was rejected by 182 votes to 108. But the rebels – or loyalists – were ready. 'The following day,' the *Oxford Magazine* reported, 'leaflets were in circulation announcing that a new body had been formed under the logical, if ill-omened, title of the Democratic Socialist Club, and had already been recognised by the Labour Party.'[43] Crosland was the first chairman, Durham was secretary and Jenkins treasurer; David Ginsburg and Anthony Elliott were also on the committee. G.D.H. Cole had agreed to be president and Patrick Gordon Walker senior treasurer, and they already had two messages of support, one from Attlee and another from ten leading dons including Sandy Lindsay, Dick Crossman, Frank Pakenham and A.L. Rowse (later joined by A.J.P. Taylor). An impressive programme of speakers was announced, including Herbert Morrison, Hugh Dalton, Cole and Crossman. It was an extremely well-organised coup. The printed membership card stated the formal objects of the new club:

> The Club stands for a policy of Democratic Socialism. It associates itself with the struggle of the Labour Party and the Trade Union movement to win Socialism by democratic methods, and it asserts its solidarity with the forces of Democratic Socialism throughout the world.[44]

The leaflet gave a more colloquial version of its *raison d'être*:

> *Who and What We Are*
> Following the disaffiliation by the Labour Party of the old University Labour Federation . . . on the grounds that it was a Communist organisation whose whole policy was contrary to that of the Labour Party, we, the supporters of the Labour Party in Oxford have set up a NEW and BETTER Socialist Society.

> *Under Entirely New Management*
> We don't like Hitler and we're rather coy with Stalin. So we have NOTHING in common with the Stalinist anti-war policy of the old 'Labour' Club.

Labour supported the war, the leaflet affirmed, but 'WE ARE NOT CHAMBERLAIN'S STOOGES!' Chamberlain must be replaced if the victory was to be for democracy. 'THE DECKS ARE CLEARED FOR THE WAR ON TWO FRONTS! NAZISM MUST BE DESTROYED! CHAMBERLAIN MUST GO!' The leaflet included an application form. 'We welcome as members all those interested in democratic socialism.'[45]

The new club quickly attracted 400 members, not just defecting members of the OULC, but others previously alienated by its hard-left line. It was an uncanny anticipation, on a miniature scale, of the SDP breakaway from Labour in 1981 in which Jenkins again played a leading part – though more successful, since the OUDSC did succeed in trouncing the old Labour Club. Eventually the two were reunited, but the breakaway was to be repeated at regular intervals by future generations, with more premonitions of the SDP: by Bill Rodgers, Shirley Williams and Dick Taverne in 1950, and by Alec McGivan and Matthew Oakeshott – with Jenkins' support – in 1967. The fault line between the far left and centre left remained astonishingly persistent over forty years. Among those who stuck with the pro-Soviet OULC in 1940 were Healey ('more from inertia and indifference than from conviction,' he claimed in his memoirs),[46] Edmund Dell (another member of the Callaghan Cabinet in the 1970s who would join the SDP in the 1980s) and Leo Pliatzky. Another unrepentant Stalinist was Iris Murdoch, treasurer of the OULC. As her opposite number in the OUDSC, Jenkins had to wrangle with her over the division of assets and liabilities. 'Both our different ideological positions and the arm's length nature of our negotiations,' he recalled, 'were indicated by our respective salutations. "Dear Comrade Jenkins," she began. "Dear Miss Murdoch," I replied.'[47] Forty-two years later the now-celebrated novelist made amends by joining the SDP.

No sooner had the OUDSC been launched than the 'Phoney War' ended with the German invasion of the Low Countries on 10 May, Chamberlain's replacement by Churchill, the British evacuation from Dunkirk and the collapse of France. During these critical weeks, to his subsequent shame, Jenkins was more exercised by his campaign for the presidency of the Union than by the cataclysmic events across the Channel. In his anxiety he spoke almost every week. On 25 April – the day after the Labour Club vote – he had the support of two prominent MPs, Beverley Baxter (Conservative) and Harold Nicolson (National Labour) in moving 'That . . . German aggression has left no place for neutrality'. His opening speech was 'at once a direct attack on neutrals and a sidelong attack on the Government'. But in a packed House he only just prevailed by 237:221.[48] On 2 May – a week before the House of Commons debate that toppled Chamberlain – he supported a motion 'That HMG is incapable of winning the peace', which was carried by 81:48. ('The Librarian' – as Roy now was – 'advocated a Socialist peace effectively'.)[49] On 9 May Jenkins and Crosland both successfully opposed the motion 'That this House dislikes Signor Mussolini less than it does

M. Stalin'. ('The Librarian desired at least a pact of non–aggression with Russia'.)[50] But on 16 May, in a poorly attended debate after Labour had joined the government, they differed again. Roy loyally supported the motion 'That this House has confidence in Mr Churchill's coalition'. But Tony declined to do so, on the ground that several of the discredited appeasers remained in office.[51]*

Two weeks later came the presidential debate, on the motion 'That without a great growth of Socialism, this war will have been fought in vain'. Jenkins had hoped to secure Attlee – now deputy Prime Minister – as his guest speaker, but had to make do with the editor of the *New Statesman*, Kingsley Martin, and the Labour MP (and leading internationalist) Philip Noel-Baker. His opponent was James Comyn, an Irishman from New College, later a judge, who was supported by a Liberal barrister, A.S. Comyns-Carr, KC. Jenkins' speech, the *Oxford Magazine* reported, was 'fluent and well-prepared'. 'Nazism,' he argued, 'was a religion.'

> We too must fight inspired by belief in a new world order. The League of Nations had failed because of Capitalism's inherent tendency towards war . . . A Socialist Germany was vital for European peace. The power of the international financier must be destroyed if social justice was to be won.[53]

Comyn made the case for liberalism against socialism. Jenkins comfortably won the debate by 104 votes to 68; but he lost the presidency the next day by five votes, 117:112.

He was bitterly disappointed by his failure. His friends had urged him to make more of his working-class background, but he refused. 'The poor are poor,' he told them. 'You don't want any sob-stuff on that.' David Ginsburg thought that this fastidiousness cost him the presidency. 'The grand effete manner of Roy Jenkins,' he told the *Sunday Express* in 1972, 'is nothing new.'[54] In fact he probably failed because he was not quite enough of a personality. He was still seen as worthy, shy, diligent, but a bit dull: Tony Crosland's sidekick, his speeches highly competent, but not brilliant. Alternatively the members may simply have had enough of Balliol treating the presidency as its exclusive preserve.

Crosland still had a year of his four-year 'Greats' degree to go. He

---

* The rump Labour Club unrepentantly denounced Labour for joining the government: 'The Labour Party leaders now accept office under Churchill in order to bring even greater misery and destruction to the peoples of Europe.'[52]

could have stayed on to finish it, but he was nearly twenty-two and, in the crisis of 1940, fighting Hitler seemed more urgent than Greek philosophy, so he decided to volunteer at once. While awaiting the call he stayed again with Roy at Pontypool – a period that he was soon recalling as an idyllic interlude, his normal cynical insouciance dented by the harsh prospect suddenly before him:

> The summons came as a bit of a shock, as I was not expecting it so soon, & at odd intervals during the day I felt rather like bursting into tears, particularly at moments when my thoughts turned to some of our happy moments together at Pontypool.[55]

He was posted to the Royal Welch Fusiliers – 'whoever they might be' – based at Northwich in Cheshire. The day before leaving (from London) he wrote to Roy that he had been to see the film *Black Velvet* again. 'But I didn't enjoy it a tenth as much as when we saw it together & I thought of you all the time.' He mentioned that he had booked Roy a place at a Fabian Society conference at Dartington in the first week of August, and signed off 'Love from a very dismal Tony'.[56] His journey north was a further shock, the Oxford Marxist suddenly finding himself thrown in with a lot of working-class cockneys with whom he felt nothing in common. 'I spoke to nobody and was quite literally on the verge of tears the whole time.' He hoped to be sent to officer training in about two months, 'For which thank God. One day's democracy is quite enough for me. I've never been so miserable & sick for f . . . [friends?] in my whole life.'[57]*

A week or two later Tony wrote again, thanking Roy for his letters, which unfortunately do not survive. He was settling down now, gradually discovering the more educated men in his company and even getting on better with the cockneys, who regarded him as a complete 'cissie' because he swore only moderately and did not perpetually make crude jokes:

> The lack of political consciousness is almost incredible . . . Seen from this close proximity to a cross-section of the young British working class an awful lot of the N.S. [*New Statesman*] & Tribune appears even bigger balls than it did before . . . The only political issue in which these people are at all interested is the question of duty-free cigarettes for the troops.

---

* The corner of this letter, including the ending, is torn off.

Meanwhile he had managed to spend an afternoon's leave in Northwich, having 'a beautiful long bath & a glorious tea' in an expensive hotel. 'It was exactly the sort of afternoon which we used to spend so blissfully together.' He signed off with an extraordinarily fond endearment, which leaves little doubt of his feelings for Roy: 'Well, my angel, I envy you your Dartington holiday sincerely. Love, Tony.'[58]

Tony also wrote twice to Arthur and Hattie, letters which reflect his close relationship with the family. The first, to Hattie alone, thanked her for sending him socks: 'It was very kind of you to remember the lost (and black?) sheep of the family!'

I'm afraid the Army is having the effect of increasing violently all those bad characteristics of mine to which you used to draw attention, particularly the intolerance & the bitterness.

As to the general morale & feelings of the men, their attitude to the army & the wider question of the war, it seems to me a political question of vital & urgent importance. But I won't say anything about it, because if I did I'm quite certain Mr Jenkins would disbelieve it, & put it down to my Leftist deviations & general political unreliability . . .

He was not sure he could get through the period till his OCTU (officer training) 'without running mad and murdering an officer or two'. Meanwhile, he concluded, 'I only wish I could have got leave from here to come down to Pontypool, as the wise, peaceful & philosophic atmosphere of Greenlands is just what I need at the moment. Please give my respects to Mr Jenkins. Yrs affectionately, Tony.'[59]

The second, addressed to both Arthur and Hattie, was a serious account of how much he had learned from mixing with the ranks, and the urgent need for political education to make them understand what the war was about. Labour, he urged Arthur, needed to take more interest in the army, which was still dominated by regular army attitudes inappropriate to a conscript force. Nevertheless, he added, 'I can assure you that the last few weeks have greatly strengthened my attachment to the L.P. [Labour Party] & I have moved even further away from "Left" intellectualism.'[60]

Meanwhile Roy was doing his bit in the form of a two-week forestry course in Shropshire with David Ginsburg and Anthony Elliott, at the end of which he contrived to meet Tony for dinner in Crewe. Finding himself in that part of the world again three years later, he dined in the same hotel and found it 'pregnant with memories of Tony . . . It was there,' he recalled cryptically, 'that he gave me the orange tie – a very symbolic gift.'[61] Symbolic of what? We can only guess. In the interval, Roy's life had been transformed, because that August at Dartington he met Jennifer Morris.

3 The Gate at Dartington

JENNIFER was the daughter of Parker Morris, Town Clerk of Westminster, a somewhat austere public servant who had enjoyed a meteoric career in local government, rising from deputy Town Clerk of Salford to Town Clerk of Chesterfield and thence, aged only thirty-eight, to the pinnacle of his profession in 1929. He was knighted in 1941 for his civil defence work in London, but is best remembered today for chairing a committee for the Macmillan government which recommended minimum standards for floor space, ceiling height and so on. 'Parker Morris standards' were made compulsory for new homes in 1969 and are still the benchmark in debates about housing to this day. Jennifer – born in Buxton in January 1921 and thus just two months younger than Roy – fully inherited both her father's ability and his devotion to public service, plus a strong feminist commitment from her mother, who had been one of the first women journalists on the *Manchester Guardian* during the First World War. She was tall, slim, elegant and serious-minded, something of a bluestocking. After boarding school at St Mary's, Calne, she went on to read history at Girton College, Cambridge, where by the end of her first year she was already chairman of the Labour Club. In this capacity she attended the Fabian summer school at Dartington (in south Devon) in August 1940 with her friend Jane, daughter of G.D.H. and Margaret Cole, then the leading Fabian couple. These summer schools were a combination of serious political discussion with rather self-consciously hearty relaxation. Roy wrote that it was a mixed cricket match on the fifth day that incongruously threw him and Jennifer together. 'Inspired by some exhilaration of attraction, I captained one side, performed unusually well and lost some inhibitions in the flush of victory.'[1] In that moment

– sanctified in their private memory as 'The Gate at Dartington' – their lives were changed for ever. As Jennifer wrote in 1942:

> Before it we were just interested in each other and might easily have said goodbye without ever seeing each other again and without thinking much of each other – at least after a week or two had passed. And then the Gate came – almost like a miracle. After that, even tho' we still didn't know each other v. well everything was completely changed. After that we always expected each other to want to see one and to spend all possible time with one.[2]

When the summer school ended the next day they left together – she to a fruit-picking camp near Evesham, he back to Pontypool – travelling together as far as Bristol. From Evesham, Jennifer wrote Roy the first letter in what was to become an immense (and immensely revealing) correspondence over the next five years. This letter, Roy confessed in 1942, he knew almost by heart, 'because I read it so often in vain searches for any signs of special affection. I was much too stupid, or perhaps merely too unconfident, to realise that its having been written on the Saturday evening was a much more important sign than anything I could hope to find inside.'[3] He was so besotted that when he went to London a few days later – while Jennifer was still in Evesham – he went up to Hampstead to gaze at the house where she grew up.[4] Over the following weeks they met again several times in London, where Roy had got a temporary job with the Fabian Society, and were caught up in one of the first air-raids. (Arthur wrote to Tony that Roy was 'caught in a cinema during an air-raid warning' – he did not yet know about Jennifer – 'and was there till 4 a.m.')[5] Roy was also invited one weekend to Henley, where Parker Morris had evacuated his family for the duration of the war.

Jennifer visited Roy in Oxford at least once during the following term and they both declared their love after spending some more time together in early December, before returning to their families for Christmas. 'My darling Roy,' Jennifer wrote, 'You know I think I've loved you ever since that gate at Dartington – it was quite surprising how much I missed you at Evesham.' She had been reading a Chinese philosopher called Lin Yutang who taught that detachment was a protection against being hurt, but believed that 'it must also prevent you from feeling so intensely happy as we've been the last week'. She thought that instinct and emotion were more important than intellect. 'I don't know that you agree, I know I go too far the other way, and am very bad at analysing and thinking clearly . . . You think of things and analyse things I have never thought of.' 'Darling I do love you,' she concluded. 'Very very much love, Jennifer.'[6]

Roy wrote to her the same day. 'We were so close together during the last week and you almost seemed to have become so much a part of me that I just can't realise that we won't see each other again for nearly four weeks.'[7] But it took her letter – 'by far the most exciting letter that I have ever received' – to impel him to a similar, but characteristically qualified, declaration: 'I'm glad that you think you loved me ever since the gate at Dartington; I'm practically certain that I've loved you ever since then.' He thought 'the philosophy of your Mr Lin Yutang . . . a little muddled'; but ended with the assurance that 'I love you too'.[8]

This was to be the character of their letters over the next four years: Roy always trying to analyse, quantify and date their love, his every expression of happiness at being together or misery at being apart carefully weighed against previous occasions that were happier or less happy, more or less miserable, expressing his mania for precise calibration even in matters of love; Jennifer by comparison more spontaneous and occasionally irritated by his qualifications. But from now on neither of them had any serious doubt that their lives were totally bound up in one another.

Roy returned to Oxford in October with 'a singularly well-timed injection of confidence and optimism'.[9] He did not live in college this year, but took over Crosland's former digs at 2 St John Street, sharing them with 'Shy' Halevy and another man. He was elected president of the Balliol Junior Common Room – a post previously held by both Ted Heath and Denis Healey – a measure of his growing confidence and popularity: another freshman who came up that year remembered 'a slim young man with no signs of greatness but bursting with Welsh charm'.[10] But he still devoted most of his energy to the OUDSC and the Union. The OUDSC continued to thrive, with an impressive programme of speakers for the autumn term including Harold Laski, Ellen Wilkinson and the publisher of the Left Book Club, Victor Gollancz. Jenkins continued as treasurer for this term, before succeeding Durham as the third chairman in January. Unusually, he also made a second bid for the presidency of the Union. He spoke twice in October – against Labour remaining in coalition with the Conservatives after the war, then in favour of abolishing the House of Lords – before his second presidential debate on 21 November on the motion 'That this House does not wish to hear of the Conservatives again'. The guest speakers were Aneurin Bevan, then the most prominent Labour left-winger, on Jenkins' side, and a little-known Tory MP called Samuel Hammersley on the other.* Jenkins mounted a sweeping attack on the Tories, inviting the House to vote 'on the past deeds of the Conservative Party' rather than on his Tory rival's aspirations:

> The past deeds conclusively showed that twenty years of virtual power had only succeeded in destroying post-war hopes of better things to come. Conservative power began with victorious Britain and ended, he hoped never to be resurrected, with a Britain discredited and distrusted in the world. At home their idea of justice was the Means Test; abroad, the strengthening of their potential enemies. Mr Jenkins was, as usual, sincere and impressive, and he concluded by addressing what was almost a personal appeal to the Treasurer [Roger Gray, later a QC] to jettison the vanquished Conservatives and take his true place with the victorious progressives.[11]

Arthur came up to Oxford to hear the debate and was delighted by Roy's performance, as he wrote proudly two days later:

> Your speech pleased me more than I could tell you. It gave me one of the best thrills I ever had . . . You opened so well that I felt you could not keep it up, but you did, in voice, manner and deportment, if that is the correct word. It was first-rate, the star of the debate.[12]

Jenkins and Bevan duly won the debate, by 118 votes to 80; but Jenkins had directed his fire at the wrong target. In the presidential vote Gray, the Tory, was eliminated on the first ballot; but most of his redistributed votes went – perhaps on imperial grounds – to Bahadoor Singh, an Indian from St Catherine's (later an Indian diplomat) who comfortably beat Jenkins on the second ballot by 123:96. Roy took this second defeat more philosophically than the first. The Union remained the centre of his life for the rest of his time in Oxford. He continued to attend and occasionally speak in debates 'in what I juvenilely imagined was an elder-statesman sort of way';[13] he lunched, read

---

* A group photograph taken before the debate shows Jenkins and Bevan together in the front row. Sadly, however, nothing came of this previous meeting when Roy joined Nye in the House of Commons eight years later.

the papers and did much of his work for his finals (known as 'Schools') there. But the double failure to win the presidency never ceased to niggle him.

Meanwhile Roy's new love for Jennifer was causing acute jealousy to Tony, who sensed the difference in his friend almost immediately. As early as 8 October he was complaining like a jilted lover that 'after a very long interval' he had received just 'a brief type-written note' and suggesting bitterly that 'the problem of our correspondence will soon solve itself as you will soon be able to get everything you have to say on the back of a postage-stamp'. Roy had evidently told Tony something about Jennifer, since he sent her his love.[14] A fortnight later Roy had obviously confessed rather more, since Tony now turned sarcastic. 'I was particularly interested to hear some details of your amour – I had not quite realised how far Jennie was leading you on; weekends at Henley must have been tremendously thrilling. It makes me very happy to think that despite my absence our friendship has remained so close & our mutual confidence so great.' This letter was coolly addressed to 'Dear Roy' and signed 'Yrs, Tony'.[15]

Tony got his commission in November and was posted to Barmouth on the mid-Welsh coast for his OCTU. His billet was quite comfortable, he told Roy, but he was having to share a double bed with another young officer ('I can assure you he is quite safe as yet').[16] In two further letters from Barmouth he addressed the question of their relationship. Of one, only the last paragraph survives:

> You may have thought the whole thing out more carefully than I & decided that it's not worth trying. But if you haven't, I suggest you might come & spend a night (or even a weekend when the Menace is available) at Highgate some time after Christmas. Then, without indulging in any unnecessary recrimination or undesirable introspection, we could see how we got along together, and decide accordingly whether to let the thing slide completely into oblivion, or whether to try to recapture at least a fraction of our former intimacy. It would at any rate be convenient, to put it no higher, to know where we stood. What do you think?
> My regards to Jennifer, please.
> Yrs, Tony[17]

Unfortunately we do not have Roy's side of this correspondence – this was exactly the moment when he was declaring his love for Jennifer; but he evidently invited Tony to Pontypool a few days after

Christmas. Tony's cautious (but fractionally warmer) acceptance was postmarked 23 December:

> My dear Roy . . .
> I'm getting increasingly sceptical about how much there is left to be salvaged from the wreck of our strange bizarre relationship, attacked as it is so violently on all sides, but at least I should like to see you before we make up our minds; anyway, I still think there's a chance I may be wrong, tho' all the evidence points in the other direction.
> At all events, I'm very much looking forward to seeing you!
> Much love, Tony[18]

This Christmas visit evidently reassured Tony that he had not lost Roy entirely. In January 1941 he wrote again, approving in an elder-brotherly way of Roy's decision to join the Royal Artillery when he was called up ('You will certainly have a very much easier and more comfortable time, physically and psychologically, than if you had gone into the Infantry') and ending confidently: 'Very much love, my pet, Tony. N.B. I agree with you entirely about the 3 days at Pontypool – I have no fears at all for the future.'[19]

His next surviving letter, dated 26 January, was mainly about OUDSC affairs, advising Roy again with an elders authority about meetings and speakers and how to handle the committee:

> I got the impression on my last leave that you were tending to exaggerate the degree of domination . . . which you had achieved last term . . . I didn't say anything because I think it's frightfully important that you should acquire this self-confidence; *but* beware of getting it prematurely – it's the worst position of all. I have complete faith in your being able, during the course of this term, to establish yourself completely; but you may find it a more uphill task than perhaps you realised. So don't be put out if people seem a bit over-critical at first; I know that you'll be able to deal with them quite satisfactorily.

But he ended in the language of a lover: 'I am very lonely for you, & longing to be with you again, darling. Very much love, Tony.'[20]

In a considerable coup, obviously arranged by Arthur, Roy had managed to book Attlee to address the first OUDSC meeting of the new term. A few days later he reported to Tony at length about how it had gone. His typed letter conveys a vivid flavour of their political discussions and shows Roy still clinging to some startlingly left-wing attitudes:

> In some way the Attlee meeting was a big success. We managed to get it quite well publicised in the City and the Union was very full (probably about 1000). A crisis arose about an hour before the meeting when he suddenly announced that he couldn't possibly be expected to answer questions at a public meeting! Only herculean efforts and a good deal of subtle flattery from my father . . . succeeded in making him change his mind to the extent of agreeing to answer four. This wasn't very satisfactory . . . but at least it was something.
>
> From a purely oratorical point of view (if one can apply that criterion to Attlee) his speech was a good deal better than I had expected. It was very well received throughout and he got the most colossal applause when he sat down. It wasn't particularly right-wing . . . but it left me feeling vaguely unhappy and for the last week I have been more politically depressed than for a long time past . . . You may remember how, a little over a year ago, you completely changed my political outlook by making me accept the class struggle as the fundamental tenet. In the period immediately after this I think that we both suffered (if you don't mind being coupled with me) from a too rigid adherence to this doctrine . . . Since then our move to the right has, I'm sure, been mainly the result of an increasing distrust of the a priori, although aided and caused by external circumstances, of course. But even now our (insert 'my' instead, if you like) political outlook starts off from a fundamental belief in class antagonism . . . Attlee, on the other hand, starts from exactly the opposite direction. His a priori proposition is that most men, particularly if they happen to be members of the British House of Commons, are fundamentally good and right-hearted . . . I don't suppose that this is of great practical importance, but it makes me feel that I could never feel any real spiritual unity with him; and this depresses me. Also the complete lack of interest . . . that he showed in the affairs of the Club didn't have the most inspiring effect on the Standing Committee.*

---

* Arthur, by contrast, wrote to Tony that Attlee's speech was 'pretty sound'. He added that 'Roy did very well in the chair.'[21]

The rest of this long letter was mainly about, first, the government's suppression of the Communist *Daily Worker* (of which, on balance, Roy approved); and, second, John Strachey's new line (expounded at another OUDSC meeting the following week) that a third way between socialism and fascism would become possible after the war, namely a sort of modified capitalism on the lines of Roosevelt's New Deal. In influential books like *The Coming Struggle for Power* Strachey had been a leading Marxist theoretician before the war; but he was now moderating his views – he finished up as a middle-of-the-road minister in the Attlee government. Jenkins very soon followed the same evolution. At this stage, however, he felt that Strachey's 'chief fallacy lay in the fact his examples are nearly all taken from the US, which is still in a rather different stage of development to any European country'. But he wanted to know Tony's view.

Finally Roy described his army medical. 'Despite the fact that I could read nothing with my one eye and was feeling absolutely at death's door, they put me a Grade One with a certain gay abandon . . . I think that I'm probably safely in the Artillery . . . though I don't know definitely,' before ending by assuring Tony that he was 'looking forward immensely' to seeing him on 1 March. 'Saturday afternoons in this term make me want you and the Red Menace v. badly. We must get a car from somewhere and have one drive and one Trust House tea together during your leave . . . Very much love, Roy.'[22]

Tony replied from Rhyl, where he was on weekend leave. Having previously persuaded Roy that class was fundamental, he had now – after six months' experience of the army – realised that Marx was wrong: the working class, he had discovered, was not primarily moved by class feeling, but by patriotism, religion, liberalism and 'strong conservatism'. Moreover Strachey was right about Roosevelt's New Deal: 'modified State capitalism, given efficient leadership, should be quite able to ameliorate w-c standards of living to an enormous extent'. Having led Roy up the Marxist path, Tony was now leading him down it again. He too was looking forward to the next weekend, and hoped that Roy would be able to get hold of a car. 'I'd awfully love to spend the first night at 2 St John St, so that we could chatter on as long as we liked, but I suppose Mrs P. could only offer me that sleep-destroying sofa. Write soon. Very much love, Tony.'[23]

Evidently Roy did not need to find a car, since Tony brought the Red Menace to Oxford. Jennifer was there too, to attend a conference, and so met Tony for the first time: the three of them had a 'wildly dangerous drive to Woodstock'.[24] They continued to make an awkward triangle for the next two years until Tony was posted abroad in 1943. At the same time as beginning to work hard for his Schools that spring, Roy saw both Jennifer and Tony as often as he could. Jennifer clearly resented the fact that Roy still felt obliged to see Tony whenever he got leave, sometimes ahead of her. Roy and Jennifer were still writing passionate letters assuring one another of their love, but they were not yet sure that it would last, obsessively anticipating what they called 'the BB' – presumably the 'Big Break'. After they had spent what Jennifer called 'an absolutely lovely week' together in March – 'I do love you absolutely, utterly and exclusively and you must believe it otherwise it will worry both of us'[25] – Roy wrote: 'I still think that the BB is a good deal further away than I thought it to be at Xmas & I still hold that it's conceivable that it may never come. But I don't awfully like your solution – that our love should achieve permanence by reducing itself several stages. My romanticism is so incorrigible that I would almost prefer to remember you when we loved each other completely than to have you when we loved each other partially or, at least, rather unexcitingly.'[26]

A fortnight they spent together in Pontypool and Oxford over Easter was marred by arguments over Jennifer's insistence on her need for 'independence'. Having returned to Pontypool to see Tony, Roy wrote to Jennifer that he was 'horribly worried about our future relationship':

> I have an unpleasant fear that it means that we shall probably have a summer of increasingly frequent disagreements & minor 'scenes'. This doesn't necessarily mean the end, unless, as is v. likely, you begin to think that the whole thing is hardly worth while.

Noting that she seemed to think the BB was inevitable and was 'even tactfully working up to it', he went on:

> I don't imagine that you will come to any different conclusion about the 'virginity' issue. It's probably not really v. important, thinking about it since, I have decided that it was merely another facet of the independence difficulty that came up at Pontypool and, as such, is pretty disturbing.[27]

Jennifer, back in Cambridge, replied that, on the contrary, their last row had made the BB less likely. 'It made us realise that we couldn't do without each other and know how acutely miserable we could make each other . . . . I no longer think I am or ever will be dominated by you Darling, we shall just become part of each other and the influence will be mutual and of course the restaurant argument illustrating who's on top is v. important from my point of view!'[28] But two days later she had backtracked slightly from this flash of feminism: 'I am completely happy about our present relationship . . . I didn't mean all that silly stuff about dominating and independence . . . All I want is that we should be a complete unity.'[29]

A couple of weeks later again Roy had clearly been discussing the question of 'emotional independence' with Tony, since Jennifer now wrote that 'I'm sure one can't love anyone as much as we do and still retain it and anyhow I think Tony's completely wrong to have had that as an object. I'd far, far rather have times of such perfect happiness as we have had, even if they entail such intense misery afterwards, than just go on being moderately happy.'[30]

Tony was now training as a signals officer in Wrexham. (He was rather annoyed at this posting, but recognised that it might reduce his chance of getting killed.) In the summer term he wrote three further letters, which showed that he had not yet given up on Roy. In one, dated 11 May, he apologised for not writing earlier:

> Another reason for delay was that I was toying with the idea of writing a long introspective letter about our friendship, discussing the effects on it of various factors such as June [presumably a girlfriend], Jennie, your decisions about the Army, our enforced separation, David Graves [a fellow officer, son of the poet Robert Graves] and other persons & factors. I had actually started this letter, but then decided it would perhaps be wiser to drop it, for fear of your misinterpreting certain things I was going to say . . . Don't let's have another fortnight's delay before I get your next letter. I love you still very much, Tony.[31]

In the second, of 3 June, he recalled happy times the previous summer – before Roy met Jennifer – in terms irresistibly reminiscent of Charles Ryder and Sebastian Flyte in *Brideshead Revisited*. It was now, as then, swelteringly hot – 'just like some of those days last summer when we used to go out in the Red Menace together':

> Do you remember a day in Pangbourne when we had tea almost alone in a rather palatial hotel, and laughed cynically together at the photographs in the 'Tatler'? Or a drive back from, I think,

Henley? Or lying in the grass by a ruined Abbey just near Burford? One of the great joys of those expeditions was that even on the way home we always had a flick [film] in the evening to look forward to.

I'm glad I came back for that brief 48 hrs. We at last had the introspective discussion that otherwise would have been much less satisfactorily carried out through the post, and we have once again settled a problem that seemed at first sight all but insoluble. Perhaps we have even been taught, once again, the folly of being so absurdly introspective about our friendship! . . .

Well, no more news. Work hard, and don't let down the old-established and well-known firm of Crosland and Jenkins, which for all its turbulent history is still united by bonds as strong and close as ever. Very much love, Tony.[32]

Two weeks later (18 June) came a rather briefer letter:

My dear Roy,

I'm a little disappointed not to have had any reply from you to my last letter; but I'm very tired of all this mutual suspicion and recrimination that have so often marked our friendship, so I will put it down to School's [*sic*] & say no more about it.

He planned to spend the first day or two of his next leave in Pontypool, then London and Oxford, if that suited Roy. 'All the best in Schools, Tony.'[33]

At Easter Roy had belatedly decided that he had better start doing some work for his Schools. Since his first year he had, by his own account, entirely stopped going to lectures; and most of his reading had been directed to Union speeches and OUDSC affairs. Fortunately at least two-thirds of PPE overlapped with his political interests, so he had read and absorbed the prophets of modern British socialism: Cole, Laski, Hugh Dalton and Evan Durbin. Within Balliol he was taught philosophy by 'Sandy' Lindsay, politics by John Fulton (many years later the author of an influential report on the reform of the civil service) and economics by a young Hungarian, newly arrived in Oxford, Thomas Balogh. Balogh was eccentric but in Jenkins' recollection 'by far the best teacher I had'.[34] He used to provoke Roy by attacking Attlee so that Roy would have to defend him.[35] Roy also wrote history essays for a senior Fellow called A.B. Rodger, some of which survive: to a modern eye they are very old-fashioned diplomatic history on subjects

like 'The Near Eastern Crisis from 1875 to 1878' or 'The Problem of
Franco-German Security up to Locarno', and very dull. Nevertheless
Rodger, while sometimes doubting the depth of his knowledge,
praised his writing style, which pleased Jenkins so much that he quoted
the compliment in his memoirs fifty years later. Because so many of
the Balliol Fellows were away at the war, he was also taught by dons
from other colleges, including G.D.H. Cole. Looking back, he thought
that his heroes were already Keynes and Roosevelt, 'balanced by an
interest in and affection for all things French . . . I was infused by
liberal optimism, tempered but not hobbled by a tendency to make
mildly mocking jokes about the people and institutions I most admired.
That was essentially the cast of mind which Oxford, working on my
natural proclivity, gave me.'[36]

But then Balogh warned him that he (and Ginsburg, with whom
he shared tutorials) must do some work, or both would fail and he
would lose his job. So, encouraged also by his flatmate Halevy, Jenkins
set himself a schedule of eight hours a day, seven days a week for eighty
days – that is, from late March to mid-June 1941 – reworking his old
essays and Crosland's (on philosophy, presumably), which Tony had lent
him, filling in the gaps with intensive reading. This was the first exercise
of a hitherto unrevealed capacity for concentrated work over a short
period, which later served him well in politics. At the time, however,
his mood veered between 'a considerable degree of optimism and
absolute despair'.[37] At one point, still in Pontypool, he was convinced
that he was 'absolutely set for a 3rd, if not a 4th'.[38] Back in Oxford,
he fretted that 'my state is getting progressively worse':

> I'm completely failing to work on anything approaching a plan.
> I am only managing to do an average of about 6 hours . . . Most
> of the time I just sit, doing absolutely nothing at all. This getting
> up at 6.0 A.M. started off v. well, but has now developed into the
> most ghastly vice . . . It merely means that I am losing 2 hours
> of very necessary sleep.[39]

In Cambridge Jennifer also had exams, part one of her history tripos,
and her nerves too were getting frayed. 'It's a good thing you're not
here perhaps Darling,' she reflected, 'as it might bring the BB considerably nearer. Also if we were together I very much doubt if either of
us would do eight hours a day.'[40]

They still found time to exchange political views, with Jennifer
tending to be the more radical. She was involved in the same sort of

battles with the Communists that Roy and Tony had been fighting in Oxford; but she was also worried by the formation of a middle-of-the-road 'New Britain Club', which 'the wretched [J.B.] Priestley' was coming to address (having turned down the Labour Club):

> I very much hope, darling, that you agree in thinking that these 'non-party progressive' movements are peculiarly insidious. They are in fact the greatest danger that the L.P. will have to face in the next few years. They have such a very obvious appeal to middle class socialists who have come to the L.P., but who have no sound theoretical (Marxist, if you like) background. Fortunately the danger of working-class penetration is not so great, since these new movements tend to be strongly anti-TU.[41]

She might have been a Labour loyalist warning about the SDP in 1981! Unfortunately Roy's reply has not survived. But a few weeks later – soon after Tony had made his U-turn on the class struggle – he told her somewhat pompously that she was 'in increasingly grave danger of falling into all the faults of the "left-wing intellectual" attitude to politics . . . I must try to put you right again when you come to Oxford.'[42] It seems he had only temporary success, since a couple of weeks later she was unrepentant:

> You probably succeeded in removing my left-wing deviation fairly effectively but after the summer when I've had time to read a lot and have enough data to base a proper opinion on you won't . . . I shall convert you from your reactionary tendencies.[43]

On the other hand, Jennifer was prepared to consider 'a modified form of proportional representation – say four or five member constituencies', as proposed by the Liberal historian Ramsay Muir;[44] while Roy – ironically, in the light of his position half a century later – dismissed Muir's idea as 'complete nonsense', merely 'an attempt to give the poor Liberals a new place in the state'. Just like the critics of his own scheme in 1998, he argued first that PR would mean that 'Govts are chosen, not by the electorate, but by the manoeuvres of various groups in the House. A British electorate [unlike the French] gets what it thinks it wants'; and, second, that 'Coalition or minority govt. must inevitably be weak', except in the special conditions of wartime. 'The gt. virtues of the 2-party system are, as you are no doubt aware, that it gives some measure of continuity & . . . responsibility.'[45]

Over Easter Roy somehow found time to write an article on the future of the Labour Party. He sent it to Jennifer for approval; but her praise was qualified:

I think your chef d'oeuvre's rather good . . . As you say, it's quite impossible to put the case for socialism in a few words, but you seem to have selected the principal problems and shown how they could be solved fairly effectively, tho' I don't know that it's all quite enough thought out.

She still took a hard line on the question of class war:

I don't quite see the point of the paragraph on taking the class war out of politics. It's obviously v. desirable and it obviously would come, in any socialist state, but just as obviously (I should have thought) it will [illegible] as long as the L.P. is trying to effect far-reaching changes in the distribution of power and wealth and the present possessing-classes are trying to keep what they've got. I'm afraid this sounds like the criticism of an essay but I assure you Darling I was very interested and most impressed! I hope it arrived in time to be included in the book.[46]

On 1 May Roy spoke in a Union debate against the continuation of the coalition after the end of the war. According to the *Oxford Magazine*, he was 'more merciful than usual to the Conservatives, but still demanded a completely Labour Government carrying through a completely socialist programme'.[47] His speech, he told Jennifer, was nevertheless 'regarded as disgustingly right-wing & was therefore badly received by lunatics like Anthony [Elliott] and Michael [Ashcroft]. I think if I had more time I should develop a new political line: we must work on it during the vac; although you almost certainly won't agree.'[48] Jennifer responded firmly:

I v. much deplore your right-wing speech in the Union – and fear there must be something very reactionary if Michael, Anthony and David were all up in arms against it. This time Darling I expect it will have to be me who will have to put you on the right lines again![49]

A few days later it seemed that Roy's line had weakened further: 'The more I think about it,' Jennifer now told him, 'the more I think your idea of a short opportune Conservative–Labour Coalition at the end of the war would be disastrous' – first, because it would be impossible to keep the Labour party together; second, because 'after the war any government which doesn't put through a very sweeping programme . . . will become v. unpopular and there will be a great revulsion of feeling against it for not fulfilling everybody's wartime ideals. If the L.P. can't use the critical moment for its own policy it should do its best not to share the general opprobrium any government will get'; and, third, because 'Any democratic socialist party must as soon as it gets a clear majority put thro' a programme to change the economic structure of the country – a policy of social reform is not much good and can easily be revoked.'[50] These letters display both shrewd political judgement and a remarkable confidence that Labour could win a postwar election on its own – not at the time a widely shared view.

Roy's hard work paid off. He surprised both himself and his tutors by narrowly achieving a First. Balogh claimed to have needed a stiff drink to recover from the shock. Lindsay was disappointed by his low mark in philosophy – allegedly the lowest by a Balliol man since PPE was established in 1924 – but told Roy that he had gained straight alphas in 'descriptive history'.[51] At least one family friend claimed not to have been surprised. The deputy Prime Minister sent his typically laconic congratulations: 'My dear Roy . . . I had a bet with Arthur that you would pull it off all right . . . C.R. Attlee.'[52]

To celebrate, Roy took Jennifer out to dinner at one of his favourite restaurants, Boulestin in the Strand, before going home to Pontypool, where Jennifer wrote to him the next day:

> Yesterday was lovely Darling and it was v. sweet of you to let me share your First . . . As I said before a First is an achievement anyhow but it's a great achievement when you've managed to do so much else as well and haven't had to retire to a metaphoric cell and live a solitary devoted life. I feel most honoured to be allowed to say to myself that you've got a First and that you actually love me (unless of course you are already beginning to experience a reaction!). I can't think of anything else to say except that as you know I'm as glad as if I'd got a First myself and I love you like hell.[53]

Roy had been afraid that he might be called up immediately; but he was not, and they were able to spend most of the rest of the summer together, mainly in Oxford, Henley and London. Although not uninterrupted – Roy spent at least two weekends with Tony – this was the longest period they would spend together before they were married; 'just the most marvellous and most perfect and most exciting time I've ever had,' Jennifer called it:[54] a golden four months to which they both looked back longingly during the separations and hardships of the next three years. They still analysed their love endlessly, as is clear from a letter Jennifer wrote one weekend in July when Roy was at Pontypool with Tony. She was sorry if her honesty had hurt him:

> But it may help you not to idealise me and therefore prevent equal or more severe shocks in the future. For one thing in spite of your remarks about self-sacrifice I am definitely extremely selfish – probably more so than you. I love you more than I can ever say for saying all you did – you gave me more in that short time than any vague idea of virginity you think you have caused me to lose. I don't suppose I can ever give you half as much.[55]

Among other things, they made a return pilgrimage to Dartington in August, as Jennifer recalled in another letter in September. (For some time Roy had been calling her his 'darling giraffe'; she called him her 'jaguar'.)

> That was an awful moment leaving Dartington wasn't it? I felt quite sentimental about it. It will always be very, very much bound up with you my Darling and very, very sacred. If we were really middle class and settled down in a nice little villa I'm sure we should call it 'Dartington' or if that were impossible we'd call our unfortunate eldest giraffe it instead . . . Whenever I think of giraffes I think of you saying 'You look bloody giraffe-like' and I think God how I love you. There is now an added longing to get the war over in addition to all its beastliness and it is the chief longing of all – to finish it so that we can be together for ages and ages. We must love each other like hell if we've been together all this summer and thought it was a long time, but in fact it's gone so quickly . . . After all this time I think there's a damn good chance that we'll go on loving each other so much that we'll want to live together – as long as we can avoid too many scenes – tho' in a way they prove how very, very much we love each other.[56]

In the autumn Jennifer went back to Girton, while Roy got what he called 'an easy-going job' at the American Embassy in London (the

Ambassador, John Winant, was a friend of his father), going back to Oxford twice a week for some very light military training[57] and spending most weekends in Cambridge, as he characteristically recalled a year later:

> The weekends in Cambridge during that autumn really were frightfully good. Coming down from L'pool St for the first one was frightfully exciting. I still hardly knew Cambridge at all and, to me, it was still a place where the pre-Dartington Jennifer, which still intrigued me, had spent a lot of time . . . Also, to one so used to the G.W. [Great Western] line from Paddington it was a rather mysterious journey through very odd country in a train with ridiculously steamed up windows . . . Do you remember Ely the next afternoon?[58]

She did. 'I too remember last autumn incredibly well – Ely, St Edmundbury [Bury St Edmunds] and the journeys in the train there and back. The Lion [where Roy stayed] and Girton and the Arts [where they saw *The Cherry Orchard*]. And your reading nothing but Trollope.'[59]

Yet all the time they were still agonising – Roy particularly – about whether their relationship might be cooling down. 'We once talked about the possibility of us coming to love each other rather differently,' he wrote in November, 'I'm horribly sure that that would be quite impossible. If one once began to suspect that there was a tendency for things to fall off, one should become so acutely miserable that it would be quite impossible to go on. I'm rather frightened that quite soon, I may begin to feel that . . . I really am quite worried about this, although I am sure that you think it all very foolish, my darling.'[60]

The same day Jennifer was writing cheerfully about what pictures they might have in their future house together – something Dutch in the Queen Anne dining room in Cowley Street, or Douanier Rousseau in their first flat 'in a modern block on Highgate Hill' – though she felt it necessary to explain who Rousseau was, 'your knowledge of modern French art being rather slight'.[61] More seriously, a few days later on the train back to Cambridge after a miserable parting on Oxford station, Jennifer wrote an important letter warning of possible conflict between Roy's political ambitions and her desire for a career of her own. She would subordinate herself, but only to a certain extent:

> Oh my Darling I do hope terribly that we go on loving each other as intensely as we do now and have done since the

beginning. I think that it's essential that we should for the next few years even if our love changes and becomes calmer later on. I do hope you won't find this waiting period and the army so dull that you will need a new and ipso facto more absorbing emotional experience. I do hope that the combination of Labour Club and work won't erect a barrier between us by pulling me in the opposite direction or making me v. tired, but if it does I will give up the Labour Club. You do, and always have, come first. You always must come first and I therefore agree that an independent career is a danger, because I'm not and never will be one of those people who will be satisfied with looking after the house and later on the small giraffes. People who are satisfied with that kind of life, or even before the small giraffes appear, with a job that is quite uninteresting and unimportant, can put their husbands etc. first easily. I'm not and there's no doubt it makes things more difficult.

Comparing their relationship with those of a number of her girl-friends, she was sure that their love was fiercer and more absorbing than any of her friends'. 'Therefore we must reach more perfect peaks than they do, but at the same time it makes our love more delicate than theirs and it makes us more likely to have petty scenes.' But that only made it more imperative that they should stick together:

We've got such a lot of things to do together and life seems quite pointless without you. I think I'd have to go v. religious or something if we did have the BB. Although the independent career is a danger it is less so in our case than it would be in most because we work together at the same things. One thing I'm certain of – I think my Darling that we'll have at least to be officially engaged at your first election or the Conservatives will make up some slander . . . It will be as much fun fighting our first election as going on our Grand Tour.[62]

In December they had a typical lovers' spat. 'We had been having a quarrel (I cannot remember what about),' Roy wrote much later, 'and I spent nearly 3 hours trying to phone you at Girton from the call-box in the corner [at the Oxford Union]. I had some idea of coming over to Cambridge that evening but it became too late for that and so instead, we met in London the next morning and had a wonderful reconciliation scene behind a telephone box at Liverpool St. We then had coffee at F. & M. [Fortnum & Mason] & went back to Oxford for the weekend.'[63]

Before Christmas Jennifer stayed at Pontypool again, where they seem to have played some form of hockey in the garden ('They were bloody good those games weren't they?') and she came away with a memorable mental picture of Roy 'in that white sweater and with your socks over your trousers and a cigarette hanging out of your mouth – looking lean and lithe and tough'.[64] In January 1942 they managed a couple more weekends in Cambridge – he went up for her birthday on the 18th, when they tried to be economical by having dinner in a Lyons Corner House – but Roy spent most of the month kicking his heels in Pontypool while waiting for his call-up, unable to find a job in London and unable to afford to live there without one, wallowing in the misery of being apart:

> Oh my darling, darling Jennifer I love you much more than I have ever done before & it's a terrible shock not to have my giraffe bobbing up & down at my side – which means more to me than anything else in the world. The only comfort is that this time I have no doubts & no fears about you – I can remember your tears so vividly that they are impossible.
> I can't think of an ending that wouldn't be pure bathos.
> I just love you.
> Roy[65]

But all the time Tony was still on the scene. He had now been posted to Dorset, from where he was still able to meet up with Roy quite regularly, either in London or for weekends in Pontypool. Their relations were still difficult. 'Has Tony recovered from his idea that you played him false?' Jennifer asked.[66] And on another occasion: 'I hope you will have a good weekend with Tony and find a modus vivendi.'[67] In November Roy reported to Jennifer that he had spent a day with Tony in London – just drifting around, having tea and dinner and seeing *Citizen Kane* – before going back to Hampstead where Roy was staying, where they talked until three in the morning.[68] Then in January 1942 Tony wrote what Roy called 'a wildly introspective letter' to Hattie, 'giving all his reactions to you & explaining the change in his attitude towards me – all rather frightening, but it seems to have passed all right, thank God'.[69] Part of this letter, describing their relationship before Jennifer came between them, has already been quoted. But the rest is worth quoting in full:

Dear Mrs Jenkins,

I am writing at once to clear up once & for all this business of my 'new relations with the Jenkins family'. I'm very sorry to have made it sound more significant than it is: because in actual fact it has not made the slightest difference to my desire to come down to Pontypool as soon as possible.

Your guess as to the cause of the change was perfectly right up to 4 months ago, but since then this particular cause has been replaced by another one.

[Here followed Tony's account of his 'exceedingly close & intense friendship' with Roy between January and July 1940.]

Well, I went off into the Army, and, as was both natural and inevitable, Roy came under the spell of the first nice girl he met – who, fortunately, will make him an admirable partner: that I genuinely believe. This, of course, was a revolutionary break in our friendship, as Roy obviously realised, since he omitted to mention the matter at all to me, although we were corresponding regularly. As a result I only learned of it quite accidentally from an outside source, and this I was not easily able either to forget or forgive.

[In fact Tony knew about Jennifer by early October, so Roy did not keep her existence secret very long.]

It so happened that the exigencies of Army life and my misogynistic principles precluded me from finding a similar solution to the problem. So there followed several months during which the whole balance of our friendship was very unevenly weighted. I was both jealous and bitter, and despite two or three visits to Pontypool during my leaves we were never able to re-introduce any genuine harmony into our relationship. So much for Conflict no. 1, which you diagnosed in your letter.

Then, to make matters worse, during last August and September, I underwent two or three experiences which have lasted up to the moment of writing. I can't very well describe them in a letter: suffice it to say that they had the good effect of ridding me of all my bitterness and jealousy, the bad effect of making me very largely forget all about Roy. Almost of a sudden, the whole complicated affair seemed unimportant and irrelevant: and, as a result, on my last leave, Conflict no. 1 was replaced by the fresh difficulty, and the unequal balance toppled right over in the other direction.

However, I see no reason why the picture should remain so gloomy and melancholy. All that has happened is that from travelling along very fast in top gear we have had to change down to bottom gear: and the gears crashed rather badly on the way. From being David and Jonathan we shall, when the gearing down is completed, become two normal people on conventionally friendly terms. Many of the high hopes are gone, many bold gay plans for the future are dead: and somewhere a spark has been put out. But it may well be that the new state of affairs is more healthy than the old: and, to repeat, nothing has altered my desire to remain an adopted member of the Greenlands household – if they will still have me!

I have betrayed no confidences in this letter, as I have previously told Roy all that I have written here. I have no objection to his knowing I wrote this letter, and, if you should wish, reading it.

Always in hopes of moving nearer P'pool.

Yours affectionately,

Tony[70]

What Hattie made of this we cannot know; but she evidently did show the letter to Roy. Nor do we know what the two or three mysterious 'experiences' were that caused Tony to forget about Roy. A girl? Another man? Or something entirely different? Neither of Crosland's biographers – his second wife, Susan (unsurprisingly), nor Kevin Jefferys – knows much about this crucial period of his life. All we know is that Roy and Tony did eventually settle down to a more normal pattern of friendship (though it could never be entirely easy, given how close they had been) and Tony remained on quasi-filial terms with Arthur and Hattie.

Very soon after this, Roy was finally called up and his life entered a new stage.

4 Captain Jenkins

Roy did his officer training, incongruously, at Alton Towers, in Staffordshire. It was not then the garish theme park it has since become, but a rather genteel pleasure garden, full of 'elegant little footbridges' and 'tearooms disguised as Swiss chalets', which served poached eggs and cucumber sandwiches'.[1] Nevertheless the shock of army life on a hitherto somewhat pampered young man was considerable. His memoirs naturally recall his years of military service with a distanced colouring of wry amusement, even 'some nostalgia'.[2] By then he had read Evelyn Waugh's *Sword of Honour* trilogy and the three wartime volumes of Anthony Powell's *A Dance to the Music of Time* – two of his favourite authors – and could refract his own experience through their satirical depiction of the tedium and absurdity of army life. His letters to Jennifer at the time, however, paint a rather less happy picture:

> I'm still feeling completely dazed and find it quite outside my comprehension to spend six god-forsaken months in this place . . . The great snag is that one seems to have so little time to spare from cleaning, polishing etc. I have spent most of this morning trying to shine a mess tin which has to be presented for an inspection by the Major tomorrow . . . I am quite hungry enough to eat most things that I am given, but a few days ago, eating lunch at Isola for instance, I would never have believed that I could eat liver & messy potatoes ladled out of a bucket affair . . . I now have to go & sew name tabs onto blankets & so I suppose I must finish.[3]

Jennifer's reply to this *cri de coeur* was sympathetic, but just a touch ironic: 'I can't imagine you polishing and sewing Darling . . . but it should make you a v. useful and helpful, practical husband jaguar!'[4] (If she really hoped for that, she would be disappointed.) In further letters over the next few weeks Roy described the uncongenial rigours of gun drill, marching and strenuous map-reading exercises: 'racing up & down huge hills in the blazing sun [it was now May] pursued by the wretched Colonel with his hunting horn', which left him in 'a quite exceptional state of physical exhaustion'.[5] The Colonel, he reported, 'also likes one to beagle! I may be forced to take it up, as the only alternative appears to be rugger.'[6] Actually beagling turned out to be more enjoyable than expected; and 'the Colonel fell in a ditch, which was something'.[7] But there was also compulsory boxing, which he did not enjoy. 'I have discovered that I am incapable of boxing . . . I'm afraid that is very immasculine, darling, and I hope you won't decide that you have made an awful mistake.'[8]

In compensation, he still got leave two weekends out of three, and delighted in working out complicated train timetables by which they could spend the maximum amount of time together, variously in Alton or Cambridge, London or Pontypool. Yet his letters were still full of tortuous self-analysis about their relationship. Roy called Tony introspective, but he was just as bad. For instance, after a day together in London in April:

> Yesterday was an awful parting, but it is ridiculous for you to make yourself feel worse by any doubts as to whether I love you. Yesterday had the one beneficial result that it made me far more certain and, in a sense, a lot happier about our relationship than I have been for quite a long time. The real cause of my doubts at Alton was that I had never quite recovered all the consciousness (sensibility, if one likes to be vain) that I lost during the first few days in the army. The most surprising thing was that I quite lost the ability to be sentimental about you, or about anything else for that matter . . . and I never properly recovered it until last night . . . I accepted the partings a great deal too philosophically for my frame of mind about us . . . Yesterday completely changed all that . . . Last night I felt horribly but reassuringly sentimental.[9]

The whole correspondence over the next three years is full of lengthy passages like this in which they both – but particularly Roy – reassured one another that they still loved each other as much as, or even more than, ever. Once, feeling 'rather statistical & mathematical today', Roy drew 'a little graph showing the intensity of our respective curves over 18 months'.[10] His lifelong compulsion to measure and compare was applied even to the emotions.

Jenkins did not mix easily with his fellow trainees and kept himself largely to himself. One with whom he did become friendly, Gordon Scotney (later a headmaster), remembered that Roy found the gunnery training 'intellectually satisfying':

> But I soon became aware that he was a bit different from the rest of us. A copy of *Hansard* arrived every week, and he would go off to his billet to read it alone. He never mentioned it, and I never asked him about it.[11]

Roy soon learned that trying to talk politics in the mess was not productive. Years later he recalled thinking that the death in office of the Chancellor of the Exchequer, Sir Kingsley Wood, in September 1943 would make a promising topic of conversation with a hitherto unknown group of fellow officers – he had just been transferred to a new unit – only to find that 'none of them seemed to have heard of him'.[12] Politics, then as now, was a minority interest.

It was while doing gunnery training at Alton that Jenkins had an experience which never ceased to haunt him. He described it lightly to Jennifer at the time:

> I performed a most prodigious feat yesterday & fired the gun that sent a round 1½ miles off the range! Actually it was entirely the fault of No. 1 (I was No. 3) who loaded charge 3, instead of ch. 1, with the result that it went about 6000 yards instead of 2500. It was a miracle that it didn't land on the railway station . . . For all I know it may still have killed off a few innocent people.[13]

In fact someone *was* killed – the Colonel's driver, no less; and Roy was not sure that it was not his fault. Five decades later he confessed the episode to a colleague: it evidently still worried him.[14] Ironically this was the nearest he came to firing a shot in anger during the war.

Meanwhile Jennifer was working hard for her tripos, suffering the same mixture of panic and apathy that Roy had experienced a year earlier. 'The one thing that comforts me,' she wrote selflessly on 17 May, 'is that you got a First and I'd rather I got the Third than you, if one of us had to'.[15] In fact she got a good Second, but she allowed herself no time to celebrate. She got a job almost immediately as a supervisor in a Hoover factory in Tottenham that had been adapted to making propellers. This was quite a test of her mettle: a twenty-one-year-old girl straight down from Cambridge thrust into disputes over working hours and absenteeism with recalcitrant, often Communist, shop stewards. Wartime industrial relations were not always characterised by patriotic cooperation. Often she had to work nights, which made it harder to get time off to coincide with Roy's leaves and meant that she was frequently exhausted when they did get together. She found digs with a Mrs Stutchbury in Muswell Hill. 'The big advantage is the 'phone,' Roy wrote – not that telephoning during the war was either easy or private.* And it was not certain that he could stay. 'Is the woman horribly moral,' he wondered, 'or would she allow us to use the room?'[17]

Contraception was still a problem for unmarried couples in the 1940s. 'It might be easier than we thought,' Jennifer had written while still at Cambridge. 'I think I'll see if old Havelock [the American sexologist Havelock Ellis] is in the Girton library after the exams.'[18] By September she was trying to make an appointment with a doctor who was only available in working hours. But clearly a frontier had been reached:

I definitely want to culminate Darling if you can bring yourself to forget the extreme English miss-ish-ness of the Dartington me† and if you think it won't make me even more of a split personality when you think of me. Seriously though, I think we have reached a stage where not doing so creates a barrier and even tends to drive us apart slightly. We both want to so much, and we both presumably find our present stage increasingly unsatisfactory, so that that in itself unconsciously makes things just slightly difficult. Also we have gone along very naturally up to now, enjoyed each new stage very much, and it becomes definitely unnatural to stop now. Also psychologically at the moment we are both a bit on the defensive about it. I quite agree that we need a night together for the first time and that there's no need to hurry unduly, particularly as the 2nd Front now looks as tho' it's off for a bit.[19]

---

* 'We are awfully distant on the phone, aren't we Darling?' Jennifer wrote in 1941. 'Especially when one is limited to three minutes we don't really talk about anything in case the pips go . . . I think of all the things we do, telephone calls are the only things that are disappointing.'[16]
† *The English Miss*, by R.H. Mottram, was a book they had both read and mocked the previous year.

The Second Front was a constant worry. Soon after Jennifer had started at Hoover, Roy got his commission and was posted to the 55th West Somerset Yeomanry, stationed at West Lavington on the edge of Salisbury Plain, with the expectation that they might be sent abroad quite soon. They lived under canvas and did gunnery exercises in pouring rain. 'The bloody, god-forsaken regiment is part of an armoured Guards division,' Roy wrote, 'containing among other things the 2nd Coldstreams. It all sounds horribly, horribly shock troop & I wasn't at all prepared for supporting tanks.'[20] The abortive raid on Dieppe in the middle of August 1942 seemed to presage further landings. Roy wondered if he should start learning Danish or Dutch. These weeks, he recalled, were 'the peak of my strictly military career'.[21] When nothing happened, however, army life became merely uncomfortable and tedious, with nothing to do in the evenings except drink and smoke around sixty cigarettes a day.* He tried to keep up his political interests by reading Hansard and running classes for the Army Bureau of Current Affairs (ABCA); he also represented one of his men who was up on a driving charge. (Later in the war he acted for another before a court martial.) But he was disappointed not to be appointed an Intelligence officer; and he was soon angling to be transferred to a civilian job. Arthur used his contacts to try to find him another opening at the American embassy, but soon gave it up as hopeless. In December Roy had hopes of landing a staff job in London, a prospect that briefly excited Jennifer:

It would be absolutely wonderful if you came to live in London . . . We might even think about getting married sooner than we had thought. If you get a captaincy and staff pay you should be able to afford a ring with a little assistance from me![25]

In fact none of these possible escape routes came to anything.

Instead his unit moved just after Christmas 1942 to more comfortable quarters near Bristol, where they had very little to do beyond

* Jennifer was always trying to get Roy to smoke less – she thought even six to eight a day 'quite a lot'[22] – and so did his parents, though his letters are studded with requests for cigarettes. In June 1944 he suddenly announced that he had given up. 'I started 2½ days ago . . . and since then no nicotine has besmirched my lips. I think that I do feel slightly better as a result and I am quite intoxicated by the financial saving that will be involved. I think that I will endeavour to smoke nothing for a month and then to revert to as many cigars as I can get without paying for them.'[23] But he evidently did not keep it up, since later in the year Jennifer was again promising him 'a very good prize if you don't smoke until Friday week'.[24]

some rather desultory drilling. A typical letter in January 1943 described what he called 'an energetic week':

> We had a 5-mile run on Monday afternoon and another today, in boots, denims and tin hats this time. On Wednesday I played a bastard but extremely suicidal form of rugger & then went to Bristol to see my mother. She stayed until 7.45 and I then went back and had a long & solitary dinner at the Grand and then caught the 9.45.[26]

Never one to stint on his food, Roy always made sure of a good dinner whenever he could and made a point of telling Jennifer where, and often what, he had eaten and what wine he had drunk. 'You know Darling,' she told him once, 'you must be fundamentally more extravagant than I am as it's what one does alone that's the test: I would never go to Isola by myself – it somehow wouldn't seem right.'[27] But her mild protests never stopped him. He still did not socialise much with his fellow officers, but preferred to go out on his own, or else stay on his bed, reading voraciously. 'I was remarkably ill-read when I got my Oxford degree,' he wrote years later, 'but much less so when I emerged from the army.'[28] Among other things he got through Proust for the first time and most of Trollope.

That spring he had much more leave: they congratulated themselves on six consecutive weekends, as well as longer spells together in both Ponytpool and Henley. Yet this seems to have been an exceptionally tense period, partly because Tony, having joined the Parachute Regiment, was about to be sent to North Africa ('He is rather depressed about the prospect, not unnaturally,' Roy reported to Jennifer)[29] and insisted on seeing Roy in Oxford before he went; and partly due to an extraordinary storm in a teacup occasioned by Roy's former tutor, Thomas Balogh, a notorious womaniser, then unmarried, who made a play for Jennifer. The two strains came together in a letter Jennifer wrote in March:

> I don't know why I felt so depressed this evening but I did. It was partly I suppose because Tony was on embarkation leave, partly because he, you and I are an awkward trio, partly because we had such a short time together and that not completely in harmony . . .
> I suppose that the reason why you were slightly peeved about the Tommy incident was my lack of courage in making it clear

that you were the only person who matters. And of course you were right – I was rather cowardly tho' I don't know why . . . I'm not perfect and a dislike of disagreeing with people does sometimes make me appear rather faithless. It's not a sign that I love you any less – and if you just tell me it will be OK.[30]

But Roy was more than slightly peeved, and some days later, after a couple of unsatisfactory phone calls, sent her an astonishingly dispro-portionate démarche:

My darling Jennifer . . .
    The obvious way to start the main part of this letter would be to tell you my reactions now but, as you appear to treat them with such indifference, I don't very much want to entrust you with further statements of emotional weakness. When I told you that I had answered Tommy by saying that I was going to marry you it made my eyelids burn with tears, for some odd reason, and I looked at you and you gave me exactly the right sort of look and I felt that we were closer together than we had been all day. You changed your attitude and more or less said that you had every intention of making the wildest professions of loyalty for me.

But then he had somehow convinced himself that she did not really mean it, but was merely being polite:

I can't for one moment claim that, as a result of all this, I don't love you or that I consider a final break (the BB, do you remember?). Were it peace-time I should probably make no attempt to see you at all soon, but time is today much too pressed for that and I need you far too badly to be without you for long. Nevertheless I now believe:

(i) That you are psychologically extremely selfish.
(ii) That you are very far from being proud of your love for me.
(iii) That you have very little moral courage and moral honesty.
(iv) That you are very much less sensitive than I believed . . .
(v) That our mutual frankness is at least half a myth . . . I can honestly say that, at the moment, I do not know whether or not he tried to or did kiss you . . . If so, how beautifully you would develop the argument that it was the best way to get rid of him.

73

But after all this he concluded that 'if you don't see Balogh again, my relationship with him is made impossible'!

If this was not bewildering enough, he finished by sending utterly conflicting messages:

> If you love me, after reading this, there is only one answer, a very simple one, to this & the week-end problem, but I am so tired of watching you fail to find the right answer to these problems that I shall probably phone you tomorrow or Friday night & make the arrangements myself. I want you so much that I have not the strength of will to waste even a possible twelve hours.
>
> This letter is probably a much nastier one than the silly note that I wrote from Oxford, but it is a much more serious one and I am quite sure that, in a year's time I, at least, will not laugh over it. I have just read it through & I still believe every word of it & also a lot more that I have not said.
>
> It is now 1.15 a.m. & you are probably asleep long ago.
>
> Roy[31]

We cannot know how rows of this sort were resolved; but it evidently ended happily, since a few days later Jennifer was talking of buying an engagement ring. She continued to see Balogh, which was apparently what Roy wished. But in April she wrote that Balogh had been so persistent that she had finally told him that she was going to marry Roy: she hoped Roy would not be cross, but she had no choice![32] Many years later Roy recalled the incident philosophically to Balogh's biographer:

> Thomas was keen on Jennifer . . . he was rather an old satyr . . . She was only twenty and Thomas was forty-five or something but I think she, though not swept off her feet, was mildly flattered and retains an affection for him.[33]

In fact Balogh was only thirty-eight in 1943, while Jennifer was twenty-two. But they did all remain friends through the 1950s and 1960s, despite adhering to different wings of the Labour Party, and Roy was godfather to one of Balogh's children in 1957.

A week later Jennifer told Roy that while visiting her brother in Cambridge she had indeed bought a ring – an unusual inversion of convention:

I wish you had been there to see it and approve, but I hope you will like it. It is small and square – three small diamonds – cost £12-12-0d. It was a little over our price, but I thought it was worth it as I couldn't see anything else I particularly liked.[34]*

Soon after this they spent a week together in Pontypool, when they presumably told his family. 'It was a lovely week,' Jennifer wrote, 'and we were very, very happy together, loved each other very, very much. It is so good to be together for a few days after having had only odd days and parts of days for so long . . . The day at Monmouth was very good . . . and then in the field at Chepstow, and the castle at Abergavenny, and above all – just the house and garden.'[36]

Roy's parents warmly approved of Jennifer: Arthur used to take her for lunch or dinner in London, though Hattie was sometimes upset if Roy devoted all his leaves to seeing her instead of coming home. When Roy failed to write or telephone they would ring Jennifer to make sure he was all right. Her parents were more difficult. Sir Parker Morris (he was knighted in 1941) thought that Roy was distracting Jennifer from her work and wrote to tell him so. Jennifer was furious. 'I feel so angry that I can hardly hold my pen firmly. It really sounds a most hypocritical letter. The stuff about taking my mind off my work is of course stuff and nonsense . . . What is very much more likely to take my mind off my work is not seeing you and therefore feeling miserable and trying to work out wild schemes of meeting.'[37] Her relations with her parents were never as easy as Roy's with his.

About this time, however, she managed to secure a much less stressful job as a temporary civil servant in the Ministry of Labour, where she started at the beginning of May. It was good timing, she told Roy, as it avoided a lot of congratulations from her workmates. 'It would be a little difficult to explain that we had really been engaged for nearly three years.'[38] The new job was all about training ex-servicemen for new careers after the war. 'We are quite high up and are treated politely, which is more than I ever was at Hoovers! . . . It seems so funny after being treated as the lowest of the low at Hoovers.'[39] The work itself

---

* To friends they had been describing themselves as engaged for some time. Gordon Scotney remembered meeting up with Roy at Waterloo on the way to join their unit in Salisbury in August 1942. Roy turned up with 'a radiant looking young girl on his arm' whom he introduced as his fiancée. 'They were obviously very much in love. Jennifer was astonishingly beautiful and vivacious – a real catch.' Characteristically they all went off to tea at Fortnum & Mason.[35]

varied between periods of boredom with too little to do and others when she had too much to cope with. Once, in June 1944, she wrote that she was trying to sort out which professions and which training course for each profession should be covered by different schemes. 'It is taking a long time, but I rather enjoy getting muddles straight – and this is an awful muddle.'[40] But the Ministry gave her much more time for social life and her letters in 1943–4 are full of reports of lunches, theatre-going and tennis. Later that year she left her digs in Muswell Hill and moved to Chelsea to share a flat with two girlfriends in Markham Street just off the King's Road.

Meanwhile Roy too moved again, to Sussex – another cushy posting with the Leicestershire Yeomanry billeted in a mock-Elizabethan housing estate at Angmering-on-Sea. Here he saw a much more classy side of the army than he had encountered hitherto. 'Several of the officers occasionally turned up in top boots and breeches and there was more wine in the mess';[41] while the battery commander, Robin Wilson, was a man of some social position, whose pretensions in retrospect amused him. But at the time, as an impatient young socialist, Roy found him hard to take:

Meals are intolerable. He never seems to turn up till about half an hour late and you hang about waiting for him. Then you aren't allowed to leave the table till he finishes an extremely leisurely meal. It may be alright for other members of the Battery, but I think that I have something better to do than sit sheepishly around a table while a rather 2nd class Leicestershire country gentleman finishes his coffee.

Moreover he thought his new men inferior to the West Somersets. 'My sergeants were really quite well educated – the best specimens of the L.M.C. [lower-middle class], those here are just typical army toughs, with a really bad spirit.'[42]

Sussex did have the advantage that it was easier to get to London to see Jennifer, or for her to come to Brighton, most weekends. In May they both managed to attend some of the Labour Party conference, which during the war was held in the Central Hall, Westminster. Then in August Roy got a temporary staff job for six weeks as ADC to General Walter Clutterbuck, based in Haywards Heath. It was 'quite a compliment', Jennifer wrote, and 'would seem to be an opportunity for getting something else better . . . I expect you are living in very comfortable quarters now and eating well. I hope you are not drinking too much? . . . If you ever do get any time off, Haywards Heath is extremely near – 45 minutes from London.'[43]

Roy did go to London at least once in his staff capacity. He had no time off to see Jennifer, but dined at Bentley's, the famous fish restaurant off Piccadilly. 'The fact that I had never heard of it is just another example of the enormous gulf between the military and us,' he reflected. 'Living in a Mess with senior regular officers really is extraordinarily revealing & in some ways they are far worse than I ever believed possible.'[44] But by the end of September he was back with his battery and finding it 'very bleak':

I always knew that it would be slightly grim, but I never quite realised how quickly all the petty little duties would crowd back upon one. I should think that the chances of getting a weekend off are quite remote, so many ridiculous little things does Robin find for one to waste time over. It really is incredible that the General managed to spend about half as much time running a division, not incompetently, as Robin does running a battery, and plagued his subordinates a great deal less too. This afternoon I had to do a barrack damage statement, which meant walking round all the billets with a little book in my hand writing down how many windows were broken etc. It seemed a symbolic first duty!

More than anything Jenkins hated wasting time; he was impatient to get on with his career and was beginning to think that the whole army experience was a pointless cul-de-sac:

In some ways this interlude at div. [Divisional HQ] was rather like my two months at the American Embassy. They were both slightly unusual, almost distinguished jobs. But neither of them built anything up or led to anything or lasted long enough to give me any really useful experience of anything . . . It is extraordinarily depressing to think how purposeless life has been since June 1941. Instead of being a fairly continuous stream as it had been before, it has been nothing but a series of unconnected interludes, some pleasant, some unpleasant but none of them of any long-term use . . . From a literary point of view I am slightly more well read than I was two years ago; but from every other aspect I know infinitely less and, politically, I believe that I have become less mature and much more inclined to be influenced by passing feelings.[45]

Jennifer's reply was a model of wifely wisdom:

To answer your letter – I think that political balance and maturity are only achieved when one is thinking about the political situation constantly and to some purpose, and when one is trying to formulate and carry out a definite day to day policy. In the army you never think out the political implications of any particular situation – e.g. Italy – for any definite purpose such as a speech or article, nor are you thinking constantly and steadily about either the long term policy or the day to day tactics. In addition one is inevitably more subject to passing impressions and feelings when one's living a life that one doesn't like and is therefore slightly bitter and depressed . . . If you have in fact lost political maturity, I think it's only a temporary loss, not due to any softening of the brain, but to the circumstances of the life you are living. I don't really think that you will find the time since leaving Oxford a dead loss. You have always been most conscious of the defects of armchair politics and Army life will make it less likely that you will become a victim to these defects in the future. After all you aren't a person who is likely to 'mix' v. freely and easily and probably this enforced 'misery' will be quite useful later on.[46]

Here one gets a little taste of the quality of the political support that Jennifer gave Roy for the rest of their lives together.

Roy was still pulling every string available to him to try to get a transfer to some more rewarding posting. Apart from anything else, there was an increasing likelihood of his being sent abroad as – in Jennifer's words – 'the shadow of the 2nd Front becomes more menacing'.[47] At first he still hoped that his father might manage to get him a permanent job in the American Embassy; then he applied unsuccessfully for a desk job in the War Office. Finally he set about trying to get into Intelligence, to which end he started furiously trying to learn German. In his memoirs he implies that his eventual posting to Bletchley Park at the end of 1943 came out of the blue, thanks to the unprompted influence of 'Sandy' Lindsay exerting 'the traditional role of Masters of Balliol . . . of placing Balliol men in what they regarded as appropriate jobs'.[48] Lindsay was indeed instrumental, but he was not unprompted. Arthur had been pressing Roy's cause on him for several months, initially through Frank Pakenham (the future Lord Longford), then a don at Christ Church. In June he had an hour's talk with Lindsay in Oxford and told Roy that 'The Master . . . wants to get you fixed in

Maurice Allen's show. That's Intelligence par excellence . . . The Master is a very good friend of yours. He thinks you are a fine lad.'⁴⁹* Roy wrote optimistically to Jennifer that 'Lindsay, I gather, went so far as to say "Maurice Allen will get whom he asks for and he will ask for whom I recommend". I hope he is right.'⁵⁰ But a couple of weeks later he was not so confident. 'I rang up my father last [night] & asked him to make yet another try at the I. Corps or something. I hope to God he can do something.'⁵¹ But for some time nothing happened. Jennifer warned against placing too much hope in Lindsay and thought Roy should make use of his temporary staff posting:

> I must say I don't think you can count on the I.C. – Lindsay's scheme sounds very vague and rather back door. I should be careful of turning things down. The best plan is obviously to ask the General – you are probably in the best position you will ever be for getting a good job, so it's worth using it.⁵²

Writing to his parents, Roy wondered if 'the Lindsay thing' would ever materialise. There might be an Intelligence job in the brigade coming up. 'Trying to decide what to do has made me thoroughly miserable for the last few days.' Perhaps he should ask the General.⁵³ But then in October Arthur's efforts suddenly bore fruit. 'I hope you are concentrating on German,' Jennifer exulted. 'It really is incredibly good to have heard from Intelligence in nine days. Lindsay certainly does keep his word!'⁵⁴ Thus it came as no surprise, but a huge relief, that Roy was finally translated to Bletchley for the last year of the war.

Now that they were engaged, Jennifer at least began to look forward to the time when they might be married. She had taken a fancy to Chelsea – 'It is a very nice part of London and one we might well live in . . . There are quite a lot of small old houses that have been renovated and would suit us beautifully'⁵⁵ – and even started choosing pictures: 'I should also like a Cézanne [presumably she meant a repro- duction] – preferably one of the views of Estac – the sea and the hill – and some of those Chinese drawings of animals – do you know them?'⁵⁶ But she still made it clear that she had no interest in domes- ticity. Visiting a cousin who was about to have a baby, she wrote: 'I only hope that if ever I produce any small giraffes or jaguars I shan't

---

* Maurice Allen was a Balliol economics don who had an unspecified role in Intelligence during the war. After the war he became an adviser to the Bank of England and a director of the Bank when Jenkins was Chancellor, where he still enjoyed a somewhat mysterious reputation.

be as bored as I am when being shown round the equipment of other people's children.'[57] Though the child when it arrived was sweeter than she expected ('I usually hate babies'), she was still appalled by the amount of work involved in feeding and changing it. 'One thing I am certain of is that one must have enough money to have lots of cooks, nurses etc. when one starts having children – then one leaves everything to them.'[58] She was no keener on cooking and once, after staying with Jane Cole, told Roy bluntly: 'You ought to marry her if you want to marry a good cook Darling.'[59] Jennifer looked forward to a marriage of equals, like that of the great Fabians, Sidney and Beatrice Webb:

> One does feel that with the Webbs it was vital that they should have met and had a life together, whereas with most people one feels that if they hadn't married one person, they would have married another and got on quite as well. It is rather presumptuous to think of us after the Webbs, but I am absolutely certain that we were made for each other and that we could neither of us lead a happy or fruitful life without the other – and that really neither of us could ever find a substitute for the other.[60]

While still in Sussex that autumn Roy caught 'the worst flu I have ever had',[61] which turned into jaundice. After a miserable week being looked after by his batman, he was allowed to go home to Pontypool to the care of his mother. He was there for nearly four weeks, during which time Jennifer came down at least twice. But he complained when she did not write:

> You don't seem to be quite as dutiful about writing this week . . . Perhaps you think that I am better and that it is not therefore so important. At any rate it must be the first time for about a year that I have written to you without having first had a letter from you!

He spent his time feeling sorry for himself, doing five hours of German a day ('or even a bit more'), reading Proust ('but not much') and dreading going back to his battery after such a long absence.[62] Far away in Italy, Tony, now on active service but still getting letters from Arthur and Hattie, heard about Roy's illness and wrote sarcastically to his friend Philip Williams that Roy thought 'this should entitle him not only to a wound stripe, but also to the 1939–43 Star, and I believe he is making representations to this effect in the highest quarter'.[63]

Roy's relatively comfortable war would always leave him vulnerable to gibes from those like Crosland and Healey who had been tested under fire.

Nevertheless Roy's contribution to winning the war was as important in its way as theirs. After three months' training at a cipher school in Bedford, playing 'intellectual parlour games' with an incongruous assortment of academics and other unmilitary oddballs plucked from the universities,[64] he was assigned in April 1944 to Bletchley Park in Buckinghamshire, the headquarters of the now famous but then top-secret Intelligence operation by which the British successfully cracked the supposedly unbreakable German ciphers, allowing them to read signals sent to the German commanders in the field. This brilliant achievement – made possible by the mathematical genius of Alan Turing and others less celebrated but no less important – may not have decided the outcome of the war but is usually reckoned to have shortened it by two or three years. Reading the German 'Enigma' codes in 1941–3 – particularly the naval codes – enabled the Allies first to sink a lot of shipping in the Mediterranean, starving Rommel of supplies that might have enabled him to take Egypt; then to halt the devastating toll of German U-boats on Allied shipping in the North Atlantic; and finally to accomplish the landings in Italy with the fewest possible casualties. Then, in a second stage from 1943, they began to be able to read German army signals sent by a non-Morse system known at Bletchley as 'Fish'. By means of a machine called Colossus, built out of Post Office spare parts, which was the precursor of the modern computer, they gained access first to German plans on the Russian and Balkan fronts, and then to German dispositions to counter the D-Day landings in Normandy in June 1944.

Colossus began operating in December 1943. Jenkins was one of a second wave of cryptanalysts, both civilian and military, recruited to decipher the material produced by this amazing breakthrough. They worked in two sections, both housed in Block F, one of several low brick buildings hurriedly built to replace the original wooden huts in which Turing and the other pioneers had worked in the early days of the war. The first section, under Professor Max Newman (and therefore known as 'the Newmanry'), worked mathematically to reduce the astronomical probabilities to less mind-boggling proportions; the second, under Major Ralph Tester ('the Testery'), then attempted to decode the signals by sheer intellectual ingenuity and patience. Jenkins was assigned to 'the Testery', where a twenty-year-old classicist recruited straight from Balliol named Donald Michie (later Professor of Machine Intelligence at Edinburgh) was given the task of teaching the 'uniformed and exquisitely charming' new boy the Baudot code.[65] Once trained, the breakers worked day and night, in eight-hour shifts. The night shifts were the worst. Since the secrecy surrounding Bletchley was lifted in the 1970s many of those who worked there have described the brain-hurting work, the long hours of tedious frustration relieved by the occasional exhilarating success, trying to work out the possible patterns of letters that might make German words. Roy did not speak German; but he had taught himself enough over the previous few months, by reading the German émigré newspaper *Die Zeitung* and carefully making lists of words, to recognise words and likely combinations of them that might come up. Problem-solving of this sort suited his cast of mind; but it was grinding work, as he told one historian in 1998:

> We had to work on a semi-intuitive basis and sometimes your intuition worked and sometimes it didn't. It was a curious life. It could be very wearing, particularly if it didn't succeed. You could spend nights in which you got nowhere at all. You didn't get a single break, you just tried, played around through this bleak long night with total frustration and your brain was literally raw. I remember one night when I made thirteen breaks. But there were an awful lot of nights when I was lucky if I made one. So it was exhausting.[66]

'We tried extremely hard,' he wrote in his memoirs, 'feeling that it was the least that we could do as we sat there in safety while the assault on the European mainland was launched and V-1s and V-2s descended on London. And trying hard meant straining to get the last ounce of convoluted ingenuity out of one's brain, rather like a gymnast who tries to bend his bones into positions more unnatural than he had ever achieved before.'[67] Once, after a run of poor results, he was taken off breaking and demoted to less demanding work. This ironically coincided with his promotion to Captain (underlining that military rank counted for little or nothing at Bletchley). But after a few weeks he was relieved to be restored to the elite.

Jenkins joined Bletchley too late to contribute to the early successes of Enigma. He did not decode any of the signals that helped save the lives of Crosland and Healey in the Italian campaign. But he was part of the team that enabled the Allied commanders to read the movements of the German forces in France before D-Day. Thanks to the 'Fish' decrypts, the Allies knew the whereabouts of fifty-eight out of sixty German divisions: the damage the other two were able to inflict showed that accurate intelligence was critical to the success of the invasion. In the later stages of the war, as the Germans were pushed slowly back towards Berlin, Jenkins and his colleagues broke several more 'Fish' links, which helped to hasten the final victory. At the time, however, and for many years afterwards they had no idea what they were achieving.

By the end of the war there were around 9,000 people working at Bletchley – three-quarters of them young women, mainly ATS and Wrens – all sworn to absolute secrecy about what their work entailed. None of them lived on site; Roy was billeted in a nearby military camp, others in surrounding villages. But there was a thriving social life, with concerts and dances organised for the (mainly male) code-breakers and their (mainly female) assistants to maintain morale. Roy took little part in any of this: as before, he kept himself largely to himself. He was reunited with at least two Oxford contemporaries, in just the way that the same characters keep recurring in Anthony Powell's novels: Michael Ashcroft, who had been at Bletchley since 1941 and transferred to the Newmanry in 1944; and another Balliol Old Etonian, Peter Benenson, later the founder of Amnesty International, who worked alongside Roy in the Testery. He also made one important new friend, the historian Asa Briggs, who had been deciphering Enigma (as a civilian) since 1942: he and Jenkins talked history, politics and economics and discussed the pros and cons of an academic or a political career after the war. Jenkins also proofread Briggs' first book. But Briggs thought Roy unusual in that, faithful to Jennifer, he had no eyes for any of the highly intelligent and usually well-connected girls who comprised most of the workforce at Bletchley.[68]*

The secrecy of the work meant that he could write very little about it in his letters to Jennifer, except to complain of exhaustion. But at least he could now hope that he was doing something useful. Another drawback was that he got less time off. 'The weekend seems very boring and barren without you,' Jennifer wrote in March 1944. 'It is quite a long time since we haven't been able to see each other on Saturday or Sunday, even if only for a short time.'[69] Their letters were still full of complicated arrangements for contriving the maximum possible time

---

* There survives in his papers, however, an invitation from the Wrens of 'C' Watch requesting the pleasure of the company of Captain R. Jenkins at their dance on Thursday 9 November at Woburn Town Hall. The fact that he kept it suggests that he went.

together, and miserable partings on station platforms. At first they managed about one weekend a month in either Oxford or London, until at the end of May Roy gave 'the very dismal news that we have been placed under a travel ban':

> We are not allowed to go more than 25 miles or be away for longer than 24 hours. That means of course that London or Henley is out of the question, but I think that, as it specifically says a radius not a distance, Oxford may be alright.* As, however, it will obviously make it v. difficult for us to see each other, I wonder whether you might change your plans to the extent of coming to Woburn for a certain amount of your leave.[70]

There was still a neurotic edge to many of Roy's letters. He was always assuring his 'darling, darling giraffe' that he loved her more than ever, as if he had never been quite certain before, or telling her that 'last week was extraordinarily reassuring, darling'.[71] After a frustrating day in London when they could not shake off Jennifer's brother David, he wrote:

> I thought you were wonderfully beautiful yesterday, darling & I have never wanted so badly to kiss you, as you probably saw. I do love you fantastically much and I am sorry if my doubts of your love for me are irritants to you. I think that the desire for a more complete possession than one can ever attain is a necessary accompaniment to loving anyone as much as I love you. Or perhaps it is just the result of too much Proust.[72]

That summer London came under attack, for the first time in three years, from flying bombs – Hitler's last throw. Roy, safe at Bletchley, worried about Jennifer; but his anxiety only irritated her, as she explained with admirable sangfroid after one evidently fraught weekend together:

> Darling, I am sorry about being irritated, but I honestly can't bear the continual conversation about buzz bombs . . . I do and will take care . . . but if one is to live in London one must take them casually and one must continue to work and eat. They don't worry me nearly as much when I am actually in London, where everyone

---

* This was typically ingenious, but incorrect. Even as the crow flies, Oxford is twenty-eight miles from Bletchley.

else takes them calmly, as they do when I am with, or have just been with, you. I know you are worried, darling, and it is of course natural and very reassuring to me that you should be, but please try not to repeat warnings at short notice throughout the weekend and try not to restrict the conversation to this one subject. I don't of course mind telling you what happened during the week or day, but I find it a great strain (far greater than the buzz bombs) to talk about it the whole time. I hope you don't mind this Darling, but I just must say it.[73]

Jennifer was now sharing a flat, which made it easier for them to sleep together when Roy could get to London. But contraception was still a problem and Jennifer made a point of telling Roy about a friend who had got pregnant: 'an unfortunate accident, which seems to emphasise the need for care!'[74] More often she went to Bletchley, fitting in with his shifts, and stayed nearby at Woburn Sands. But she was becoming increasingly anxious that 'as soon as there's a chance of being able to live together we should get married. It would be so good to have somewhere of our own.'[75] In July they finally came to 'an important decision . . . which we have put off for so long';[76] but telling their parents was evidently still tricky. In August they managed a week's holiday together, walking and cycling around Buckingham and Brackley, but it seems to have caused Jennifer some difficulty with her parents when she got home to Henley:

> I have had a fairly cool evening with the family not saying much and they're not asking me about the holiday much! I feel that it is for my mother to take the initiative in effecting any reconciliation.[77]

Arthur and Hattie were more amenable. Somehow Roy and Jennifer contrived another ten days' leave in September, most of which they spent in Pontypool, before Jennifer went off to an agricultural camp helping to harvest oats and barley – curiously enough at Alton. 'It was very mis saying goodbye at Newport, Darling,' she wrote from the train:

> Still we ought not have to go on having these partings for too much longer. It was a very, very good leave, Darling, and I loved you so much. There were lots of good moments – playing tennis against the house, playing cricket, in the train to Newport and the [illegible] on the Sugar Loaf, on the river at Oxford.[78]

Roy stayed another day and braved speaking to Hattie.

> I talked to my mother about the details of our wedding for a short time last night. You will be glad to know that she thinks you wd. be foolish to be married in white! . . . . I think that she is now reconciled to our being married more or less any time in the next 6 months, whether the war is over or not. I think that I have really been v. courageous & efficient. I hope that you will be equally so, darling.
> I certainly love you more than ever.[79]

'I certainly think you have been v. courageous and efficient viz a viz your parents,' she replied. 'I too hope that I shall be equally so viz a viz mine.'[80] Roy also told her that he had been persuaded – presumably by his mother – to choose a china service, which they had meant to do together. He chose a tea and breakfast set that was said to be eighteenth-century.[81] Jennifer thought he was 'very brave to choose the china – is it hideous? Even if it is it will no doubt be v. useful as long as we don't have to keep it in a glass cupboard.' She was not sure that he should not have chosen the larger service. 'Nevertheless if the other was more attractive you were quite right to choose it.'[82]

Two weeks later she was able to tell Roy that her mother had greeted the news that they wanted to get married soon 'with equanimity . . . Her main request was that we should give them due warning.' She thought her mother would have liked a white wedding and considered a registry office – which she presumed the Jenkinses wanted – 'rather dull'. But she also thought they should not wait too long: 'that not many people fell in love at the age of 19 and then got married 4½ years later [and] neither of us showed much initiative in finding other people! I assume that she will tell my father.'[83]

With the end of the war in sight, Roy was now looking seriously for a parliamentary seat to fight at the General Election, whenever it came. In uniform, but not abroad, he was better placed than many would-be candidates to pursue possible vacancies. Better placed certainly than Tony, who was stuck in the Mediterranean – moving between Italy, France and Egypt – and feared, as he wrote to Hattie in February 1944, that he might be in the Far East by the time of the election. ('I wish . . . I was back in Pontypool,' he added, 'ruining the garden by playing cricket every day.')[84] He briefly had hopes of Henley or Luton; but soon recognised that he had no chance as long as he was overseas. Writing to Roy in September, he reflected that it would do him no harm to wait five years, but in the meantime he would have to earn his living. 'Oxford and the Army give me no qualifications for anything at all: and while that is an undoubted advantage in politics, it is apt to be a drawback in other forms of life.' But he thought Roy's prospects were good.[85] Roy's first target was one of the Cardiff seats, where his father might be expected to have some influence. On the basis of what he told her, Jennifer was optimistic:

> South Cardiff sounds most hopeful and your meetings with all the ex-Lord Mayors very encouraging. If they choose Marquand or Thomas this time they will hardly be able to resist the glamour of a service candidate for East Cardiff.[86]

But a few days later Roy was gloomy:

> My father says that the wretched Granville West, a most inferior man, seems to be making the most progress and is likely to beat Marquand. I shall be rather annoyed if he gets it. I had an illegible but, as far as I could tell, pleasant but non-committal letter from Jim Griffiths.[87]*

In fact Hilary Marquand, Professor of Industrial Relations at Cardiff University, got East Cardiff and George Thomas from Tonypandy (the future Speaker) got Cardiff Central, while South Cardiff chose a thirty-three-year-old Inland Revenue official, James Callaghan, who had served in the navy, but had no Welsh connections at all. All three were duly elected in 1945. Granville West, a Pontypool solicitor, got nothing for the moment but would cross Roy's path again very soon. Jenkins was briefly excited to get a letter from Sowerby (in Yorkshire) inviting him to apply there, until he discovered that Asa Briggs had received the same letter and realised that they had circulated everyone on the Transport House list! He replied that he was very interested, but that travelling restrictions would made it difficult to get there – an odd argument since Yorkshire was not much further from Bletchley than South Wales.[88]

His best opportunity came at Aston, in Birmingham. Jennifer was not keen, telling Arthur on the phone that 'other chances equally good, if not better, are sure to come'. He thought she was probably right.[89]

---

* Jim Griffiths was the MP for Llanelli, soon to be Minister of National Insurance in Attlee's Cabinet and much later the first Secretary of State for Wales in 1964.

Jennifer advised Roy to stick to Welsh seats. 'Aston certainly seems to raise difficult problems. If you had a chance for either Monmouthshire or Newport it would be better to hang on, but neither of the latter seems to be very sure.'[90] In fact Roy decided to go for Aston, was interviewed there in early October and made a good enough impression to be shortlisted. He gave Jennifer a graphic account of the interview. His first impression of Birmingham – 'enormous and gloomy' – was not favourable. But he felt he spoke reasonably well for twenty minutes ('not exceptionally well, I thought, but quite moderately so') before facing an hour of questions. 'They were not difficult – much less so than I had expected – but as I had to talk and think at the same time almost continuously I was quite exhausted at the end.' The first question, oddly, was about a united Ireland ('It was comparatively easy to waffle on that'). Others sought his views on finance, trade unions, state control of industry and whether, if he lost Aston he would stay and nurse it ('My reply to the last was a masterpiece of equivocation').

On the whole I should say that my chances were much better at the end than at the beginning. Unless finance weighs very heavily against me, or the two people today (young but unknown to me) are exceptionally good, I think that I can get it. There is going to be a final selection conference 5 weeks today and I think that we might both go to B'ham then. I am not sure that I wd not like it. It ought really to be winnable and might suit me better than Monmouth.[91]

But one of his rivals was Woodrow Wyatt; and it was Wyatt who won the nomination and went on to win the seat. He subsequently attributed his success to the fact that he had stayed with the local party secretary 'in a back-to-back house without indoor sanitation', while Roy preferred to stay in a hotel. 'It was the only time I ever did anything politically better than Roy.'[92] If so, Roy retorted, 'it was a considerable feat to lose to Woodrow Wyatt on the ground of being too sybaritic'.[93] In fact Roy too had stayed with the secretary on his first visit to Aston (though he did confess to Jennifer that 'a hotel would have pleased me better') and claimed that he only stayed in a hotel the second time – 'the old LMS [London, Midland and Scottish] Queen's Hotel, famous for the gleam of its chandeliers'[94] – because Jennifer came with him. (The hotel apparently had no problem with this, even though they were not yet married.) At the time Roy felt that he lost out to Wyatt's superior rank – at least that was how he rationalised his defeat, somewhat bitterly, to Tony:

> I was beaten by a candidate who was very much of my own type. He was a staff major called Wyatt, aged twenty-six, who was at Oxford . . . for the three years up to the beginning of the war. As far as I know his political conversion does not date back very far and I do not think that he was even a member of the Labour Club . . . [He] seemed to be quite intelligent, not very well-informed politically and possessed of a surprisingly affected manner . . . My final verdict . . . is that Wyatt won largely through being a major at 26 (they were very impressed by that) and having a better war record than I had. God knows, though, it was modest enough compared with yours!

Roy believed that Tony would have won the nomination easily, had he been able to go for it. He himself still hoped that his father's standing with Attlee might yet secure him a winnable seat. When Labour's deputy national agent, Dick Windle, encouraged him to settle for Monmouth he was disappointed. 'Monmouth is certainly as good as I deserve for a first fight, but I was a little unsettled by having seen Clem only a few hours before, who had suggested far more ambitious things.' Windle also told him that Attlee was keen to find Crosland a seat.[95]

By this time Tony knew that Roy and Jennifer were planning to marry. His response was tolerant and amusing:

> I am very glad to know that you and Jennifer are going to get married this winter. I must confess that if I were (a) the marrying type, (b) engaged, (c) in love, (d) moneyed, (e) faithful, (f) at home: and if I had (a) any means of earning a living, (b) a tolerable home, (c) equanimity, (d) a set of green budgerigars, and (e) some idea of how to go through the wedding ceremony – I should do exactly the same in your position. And I do quite seriously think it is a very wise thing to do.

He wished he could get home for the wedding, but there was no chance. After a lot of questions about the political situation (was it certain that Attlee would lead Labour into the election? Would the party consider pacts with the Liberals, Common Wealth or the Communists?) he ended:

Tell Jennifer from me I am very glad she is getting married: and
that I naturally think her lucky to marry the best friend I ever had.
Wasn't that nicely said?
Write soon.
Love, Tony[96]

The wedding was set for 20 January 1945. It took place, rather grandly,
in the Savoy Chapel with the reception afterwards in the Savoy Hotel.
This was arranged by Sir Parker Morris, drawing on his contacts in
Westminster – though he did consult Arthur Jenkins about whether
such a smart venue might be used against Roy politically. He also
produced, Jennifer told Roy, 'an enormous list of guests, many of whom
I don't know. He may, however, decide not to ask all of them if your
family want to ask a lot.'[97] On the contrary, Roy's mother thought that
'very few people from P'pool would come to Henley or London' – it
was, after all, still wartime.[98] In fact Jennifer's recollection is that far
more of his side attended than hers. But it is clear from an unusually
bitter letter that Hattie wrote Roy in October that she felt that Jennifer's
family was taking over:

> So the Parker Morris' really got down to business did they –
> what was it you said. 'They were more businesslike than we
> were.' What was it we lacked in sonny? You know that is one
> of the things with a son that perhaps hurts a bit, that one is only
> a looker on. Never mind that does not matter a scrap if we are
> only lookers on, if it is on your happiness we are looking, which
> I have no doubt it will be.[99]

In Tony's absence, Roy asked Ronnie McIntosh to be his best man;
but he too was unavailable as he was in the merchant navy and his
ship was sailing. (Hattie thought it should be delayed for her son's
wedding!)[100] His third choice was Michael Ashcroft, with Asa Briggs,
David Ginsburg and Ivor Bulmer-Thomas acting as ushers. Roy's
political pedigree was underlined by the presence of Attlee, who made
the principal speech. V-2 rockets were still landing on London: one fell
a mile away while the newly-weds were signing the register, and another
uncomfortably close when Roy went back to Jennifer's flat in the
evening to collect some clothes. They spent their first night in the Savoy
and the second in Cambridge, before going on to Edinburgh for a
week's honeymoon before Roy had to return to Bletchley and Jennifer
to the Ministry of Labour.

On 6 February – just seventeen days after the wedding – Jennifer wrote her new husband a devastating letter:

My darling Roy,
  I'm afraid that our married life is not starting as well as it might. Ever since the day we were married you have been full of grievances against me. On January 20th you were thinking that I ought to give up the M/L and come to live at Bletchley; on January 29th you were thinking the same thing, with the additional grievance that if I couldn't or wouldn't give up the M/L now I should at least give it up as soon as possible after the war; on February 4th you were angry because I didn't come to meet you, on February 5th you were angry because I didn't come to Euston with you and wasn't in when you phoned. Behind all these grievances is the feeling that I don't love you as much as you love me – if I did I would show it by coming to Bletchley and finding a part-time job. It makes it all the more sad as I do love you with all my love. If my love is inadequate you shouldn't have married me. You have known what it is since August 1940 and in the last year you have begun to complain that it is insufficient. I'm afraid that one's love is like one's nose – it is there and there is nothing one can do about it if one doesn't like it. But if you don't like it you shouldn't have married me.
  The other thing is the M/Labour. You know well that I'm not the kind of person who would be satisfied with housekeeping and cooking. You should also know that it is very difficult for a woman (merely because she is a woman) to get an interesting job except teaching. I shan't remain in the M/L after the war because of the marriage bar, but during the war, while I am obliged to have a job, even though I am married, I should like to remain. You also knew that before we were married, and if you didn't like it you should have said so.
  It should be unnecessary for me to have to defend my love. I have loved you since August 1940, and since then I have never looked at anyone else, never kept anything secret from you and I have devoted as much time as was humanly possible to being with you. This winter I have had the misfortune to be ill, which irritates you because I can't be with you and devote as much energy to you as I otherwise should.* Instead of thinking of this

---

* Jennifer had been ill at home in Henley for ten days in October, during which time Roy visited her at least once.

as outside my control you attribute it – consciously or unconsciously
– to my fault I think and say that it means I don't love you as
much.

You may feel miserable when you accuse me of not loving you
enough, but it makes me feel equally miserable when you so
accuse me.

I don't know whether you will get this before you leave
tomorrow, but I hope so.

With all my love
Jennifer[101]

How had it come to this? Had they really not talked before the
wedding about what they would do afterwards? Even in the surviving
letters Jennifer made it very clear that she was not going to be a
conventional domestic wife. How could Roy have imagined that she
would give up her job to look after him? Anyway it is clear that he
was already coming to London the next day, a Wednesday. They had a
sleepless night – not surprisingly – presumably talking the problem
through, since the next day she was very tired at work; but then she
had a better night (alone) and got into work late on Friday morning,
from where she wrote to him again:

My Darling
I am keeping my second promise and writing to you this
morning. After our somewhat disturbed night, I felt too tired
yesterday evening to do anything but lie in a chair and read, I
can't think how you managed to work – if you did . . .

Darling, I love you more than ever and hope you haven't started
feeling aggrieved again. I too would love us to live together, and
want to do so more and more. Last night, I felt very lonely without
you – more than ever.

All my love Darling
Jennifer[102]

One must assume that an accommodation was reached, and that
Roy gained a better understanding of the calibre of woman he had
married. Jennifer did give up her full-time job at the end of the
war; but she never became just a housewife. She subordinated herself
loyally to his career; but even when she had young children she
always maintained a career of her own – eventually a very distinguished one. These letters, which recall her worries about her

'independence' at the very beginning of their relationship, are the only surviving evidence of a tension that remained at the heart of what was nevertheless an extraordinarily successful fifty-six-year marriage.

5 False Starts

As the war ended, Jenkins had only one ambition: to make up for lost time and join his father in the House of Commons as soon as possible. With the first General Election for ten years likely to be held as soon as practicable after Germany surrendered, an unusually large number of veterans retiring and many ambitious young hopefuls like Tony Crosland still abroad, he should have had a good chance of finding a winnable seat. He was not only the obviously able son of a respected father, with a First Class degree and a good record in university politics, but he had excellent contacts in the party leadership. One drawback may have been that, since he could not mention Bletchley Park, he could not boast a particularly impressive service record: Captain Jenkins had already lost out to Major Wyatt at Aston. Yet others – Harold Wilson, for one – managed to secure safe seats without having been in uniform at all. Whatever the reason, Jenkins failed to secure a constituency that gave him a real chance. He came closest in another Birmingham seat, Sparkbrook, at the time a Tory-held marginal, where he lost by a single vote to a popular local councillor who went on to win the seat and held it until his death in 1959.* Had he won that extra vote, Jenkins' career might well have taken off rather earlier than it did, since Attlee would surely have given him office sometime before 1951.

But it was better to win his spurs by fighting a hopeless seat than to have no constituency to fight at all; so he was relieved finally to be

* Sparkbrook fell to the Tories at the 1959 General Election, so it was not completely safe. But Roy Hattersley won it back for Labour in 1964 and held it until 1997; so the likelihood is that, as the sitting Member, Jenkins could have held on in 1959.

selected – again by a single vote – for Solihull, an overwhelmingly middle-class suburb of Birmingham where the Tory majority in 1935 was 31,000. He was selected at the end of April 1945, a couple of weeks before VE Day. Two weeks after that Labour withdrew from the coalition government and Churchill called the election for 7 July. As prospective candidate for Solihull, Jenkins attended the Labour party conference at Blackpool in May, where he would have heard, among other blood-curdling speeches, Major Denis Healey, the candidate for Pudsey and Otley, deliver a fierce denunciation of the international capitalist class – 'selfish, depraved, dissolute and decadent' – which must now be overthrown.[1] Jenkins did not get to speak; but he and Healey were photographed together, both in uniform, as promising representatives of Labour's new generation. Then, like other serving officer-candidates, he was given five weeks' leave from Bletchley to fight the election. He launched his campaign jointly with the candidates for two adjoining seats at the Fox and Goose pub in Washwood Heath on 17 June. Attlee spoke at Birmingham Town Hall on 19 June and came to Solihull the next day – clearly a personal favour, since it was scarcely a marginal seat. Over the next two weeks Captain Jenkins, as he was billed, held meetings nearly every day, mainly in schools, but sometimes outside pubs at closing time. With Jennifer at his side when she could get the time off work, he had what he recalled as 'an educative few weeks', learning to speak to audiences 'less self-consciously precious than the Oxford Union'.[2] He eschewed class-war rhetoric, but hammered home Labour's message that the same sort of planning that had won the war was equally necessary to win the peace. The response was so positive that he and Jennifer actually dared to believe that he could win – as he claimed confidently at his eve-of-poll meeting: 'Capt. Roy Jenkins . . . said he had fought and, he believed, won, the election largely on the question of jobs for all. Col. Lindsay appeared to have fought largely on what Mr Lansbury said in 1932.'*

Here in Solihull the issue is clear. It is the future against the past. I am fighting for new factories, new houses, new schools, new hospitals. I want equal opportunity for children, freedom from drudgery for housewives, security of employment and hope of promotion for men, and a decent living with dignity for the aged.

* The Tory candidate, Lt-Col. Martin Lindsay, DSO, was a regular army officer who had achieved fame as an Arctic explorer before the war. He sat for Solihull from 1945 to 1964 without achieving office, before receiving one of the last baronetcies awarded by Macmillan in 1962.

The alternative for Solihull is to vote [for] old promises, catch-words, nightmares and the eternal Tory line.[3]

In order to allow time to collect the forces' ballots, the count was delayed for three weeks until 26 July. In the interval Roy and Jennifer enjoyed a lazy holiday in Cornwall and made a sentimental return to Dartington. Then Roy went back to Solihull, via Pontypool, to await the result, while Jennifer returned to London. From Pontypool he wrote her his first letter for six weeks:

The holiday was certainly wonderful, darling and I am beginning to feel horribly nostalgic for Fowey . . . I do hope that you enjoyed Dartington & Totnes and that, on reflection, you do not think it to have been a mistake going there. It was bound to make one feel rather sad but, for me, it produced at least one moment of extreme happiness, and had re-awakened some incredibly good memories. I am sure that our first seaside holiday tog[ether] was a great success and that we will not disagree too violently about what we want to do.[4]

The same day, she wrote him a letter to await him in Solihull:

You won't get this till Wednesday afternoon or evening, by which time I expect that you will be feeling pretty apprehensive. It will be rather an unpleasant ordeal and I wish I could be there to console you. It will be absolutely wonderful if all goes well and you win. It will be a great achievement to win a place like Solihull and so young. We will have some terrific celebrations.

She too thought their holiday a success. 'We will be able to have some jolly good holidays in the next few years.' Now back at work – attending a conference on the training of blind people under the Disabled Persons Act – she felt 'very depressed all day and longed to be in Fowey – bathing, sailing and lying in the sun together'. She ended: 'All my love my Darling – and I'll be waiting for you to ring on Thursday – except between 1.10 and 1.40. I shan't be able to think of anything else till then. Jennifer.'[5]

Roy wrote again on the train from Pontypool to Birmingham. At Greenlands he had found his father 'a good deal less well', which had helped take his mind off the election result. He too wished they were back in Cornwall. But 'I am now reconciled to the fact that there can be no further peace or rest or holiday until it is over and so I wish no longer to postpone it.' Then he reverted to Dartington with a Proustian sense of *temps perdu*:

> I do not think our visit to Dartington in any way pricked the bubble. In many ways it has made my feeling for the place even stronger and has certainly heightened the dangerous desire to go back and stay in the school for a week. There is a real danger, of course, that as time goes on we will remember, not the actual 'gate' scene, but its many reconstructions.
>
> I hope that you will not feel that I was in any way peeved or hurt by your sadness on Saturday evening. I felt much too nearly the same way myself for that. Our love is now obviously far deeper and our dependence on each other far greater than it was in 1940. But, for all that, one can never quite recapture the delirious feeling of that August and it is an infinitely sad thing. At the time, of course, there was no sadness and yet there was real reason for it; for we had used up something quite irrevocably. In some ways there was far more reason for regret than there is on becoming 30, or coming down from university or passing any of the other stages that normally cause people to mourn their youth!

The count was now expected to be quicker than anticipated, 'so you may expect the fateful telephone call rather earlier. If it does not come by midday,' he added, 'I think you may assume that we are enduring the agony of a recount.'[6]

That was wildly optimistic. In fact Jenkins did exceptionally well, but not nearly well enough, achieving a swing of 20 per cent (against the national average of 11.8 per cent) and cutting his opponent's majority to just over 5,000:

Lt-Col. Martin Lindsay (Conservative)	26,696
Capt. Roy Jenkins (Labour)	21,647
Conservative majority	5,049[7]

But he was bitterly disappointed, since so many of his contemporaries had been elected. With 393 members against just 213 Tories and twelve Liberals, Labour had achieved an historic and – it seemed at the time – possibly permanent revolution. Amid the exhilaration of Labour's sweeping triumph, Jenkins feared that he had missed the bus. He was despondent not to be one of the avalanche of new Members ushering in the socialist millennium.

Not yet demobilised, he had no choice but to go back to Bletchley. Though married, he and Jennifer could not yet live together: she was still working for the Ministry of Labour and living in Chelsea. It was a frustrating and demoralising time, especially since the work at Bletchley had become simultaneously less urgent and more difficult. The Russians had captured the German 'Fish' machines, changed the settings and were using them to communicate with their armies 'liberating' eastern Europe. Transferred to the 'Newmanry', Jenkins found himself out of his mathematical depth. Eventually, however, with less and less to do, he found a useful way to occupy his time. Finding a quiet room where he was not disturbed, he settled down to read, one after another, the 'tombstone' biographies (most of them multi-volume) of all the major figures of late-Victorian and Edwardian politics: Gladstone, Joseph Chamberlain, Lord Randolph Churchill, Salisbury, Asquith and half a dozen more. This concentrated crash course laid the foundation of what was to become his major intellectual hobby for the rest of his life and the basis of his secondary career.

Meanwhile he had to decide what to do when he was finally released, since politics was for the moment closed to him. Had the war not intervened, he would 'almost certainly' have read for the Bar on coming down from Oxford in 1941;[8] and Arthur still thought this was what he should do, as he wrote slightly testily to Roy and Jennifer in July. (He clearly did not expect Roy to win Solihull.)

> When do you propose to start reading for the Bar? A decision will soon have to be taken on that. If Jennifer will join 'Pony' & me in that I think we might soon force a decision.
>   Yours ever, 'Jumbo'[9]

By 1945, however, Roy had had enough of exams.

The other possibility was academia. Back in 1943, when Sandy Lindsay was pulling strings to get him into Intelligence, there was talk of Roy getting a scholarship to America, then coming back to Balliol to take a doctorate before concentrating on politics, 'because that is your natural bent'.[10] 'The Master,' Arthur told Roy, 'does not think you should go to Harvard but to a university in the Middle West.'[11] Roy would certainly rather have gone to Harvard. Failing that, he applied – with 167 others – for the job of International Secretary of the Labour Party: a consolation prize secured by Denis Healey, who had narrowly failed to win Pudsey and Otley.[12] In the end, however, Roy found a job through another of his father's useful contacts. William Piercy was one of those shadowy but powerful figures who flitted between business and public service between the wars. During the Great War he had worked in Lloyd George's Ministry of Munitions and helped set up the Ministry of Food; between the wars he helped establish the first unit trusts; during the Second World War he returned to Whitehall to work for Attlee. Then in early 1945 he was chosen to head a new organisation, the Industrial and Commercial Finance Corporation (ICFC), established by the Bank of England to raise investment for small and medium-sized business. Needing to recruit from scratch, Piercy offered a job to Arthur's economist son.

The attraction for Roy was that it carried with it early release from the army. He was demobilised on 1 January 1946 and started work three weeks later as an assistant economist on a salary of £500 a year for a five-and-a-half-day week. The downside was that he was not in the least interested in banking. On paper it should have been useful experience for an aspiring politician whose knowledge of economics had so far been entirely academic. If not exactly socialism, the ICFC – privately funded and independent of the government – was the acceptable face of capitalism: a perfect expression of Keynesianism in action, harnessing City finance to fuel the economic growth that Labour badly needed. But Jenkins was quickly bored by the work and got on badly with his first two bosses, who found him irritatingly superior. Years later one of them recalled feeling 'slightly resentful' at Roy's powerful connections. 'I remember the day I said to him, "You must not be under the impression that dining at Number 10 on Wednesday night absolves you from doing the filing on Thursday morning." But I don't think he agreed with me.'[13] Eventually Roy found a manager with whom he did get on: the senior controller, John Kinross, who became a lifelong friend. In his memoirs Kinross wrote that Jenkins 'did first-rate work' and claimed to have seen him even then as a future Chancellor.[14] In turn, Jenkins recalled in his memorial address for Kinross in 1989 that 'Working for John Kinross not only engaged my loyalty and affection but also seized my imagination and fully engaged my mind.'[15]* His most memorable achievement working with Kinross was lending Charles Forte the money – £168,000 – to expand his catering business from milk bars to hotels.

---

* He also noted a fundamental difference between them. Kinross had an instinctive feel for making money, but no desire to spend it. By contrast, 'I had practically no feel at all for making it, but quite a considerable desire to spend it.'[16]

Meanwhile Jennifer had left the Ministry of Labour and got a job with Political and Economic Planning (PEP) – an early think tank – working on manpower needs on a salary of £400 a year. Their combined incomes enabled them, a year after they were married, to settle down at last to life together, first in a bedsit in Kensington but soon moving to a modest flat above a snack bar, surrounded by bomb sites, in Marsham Street, five minutes from the House of Commons. By the standards of the time they were by no means badly off. They went to the cinema and the theatre and ate out quite regularly: Roy's pocket diaries for these early post-war years contain the phone numbers of several of their favourite London restaurants, including the White Tower (MUS 2181), Martinez (REG 5066) and Boulestin (TEM 7061). Despite severe restrictions on taking money out of the country they also managed several foreign holidays: to Ascona on Lake Maggiore in 1946, with a quick trip down to Milan; to Paris in June 1947, and to Venice and Lake Garda in September, the beginning of a lifelong love of Italy. Nearer home they spent weekends with Jennifer's parents, even after the Parker Morrises had moved back from Henley to Hampstead Garden Suburb: in the great freeze of 1947 they enjoyed 'four or five successive Saturdays and Sundays of intensive tobogganing on Hampstead Heath'.[17]

Trying to get away from banking, Roy still saw possibilities in academia and applied for two university jobs. The first, for which he was recommended by Lindsay despite his poor mark in philosophy in his Schools, was a philosophy lectureship at Manchester: this he described in his memoirs as 'a lucky escape'.[18] The second was still more ill-advised. Like many others whose university careers had been interrupted by the war, Tony Crosland had taken up the option to return to Oxford at the mature age of twenty-seven. He switched to PPE and took his degree – a First, naturally – in a single year, at the same time resuming the chairmanship of the OUDSC and becoming a somewhat elderly president of the Union. On graduating he became an economics lecturer at Trinity, but was quickly elected a Fellow, leaving his lectureship vacant. Tony suggested that Roy should take it over. Roy duly applied, and by his own account wanted very much to get it. Fortunately the college chose someone else – Fred Atkinson, later chief economic adviser to the Treasury. As Roy later realised, 'it would have been a great mistake for me to have worked directly under Crosland, close and on the whole happy though our relationship was in those days'.[19] But it is striking that he was still so influenced by Tony. Indeed, he showed little independent initiative of any sort at this period. Everything he did was at someone else's prompting: his father, Lindsay or Crosland. The same was true also of his next lucky escape.

After seven years' loyal service to the deputy Prime Minister, Arthur had been appointed Under-Secretary in the Ministry of Town and Country Planning in the last days of the coalition government in March 1945 – though Attlee had to insist in order to get Churchill to agree.[20] But his health was already failing, and he only got through the election 'with considerable difficulty'.[21] Attlee nevertheless promoted him to Parliamentary Secretary at Education under Ellen Wilkinson; but almost immediately Arthur was ill again. Prostate trouble that would be easily treated today was neglected and spread to his kidneys. He only narrowly survived what was then a major operation in September and resigned from the government in late October. He battled on, and as late as March 1946 was the main speaker at a conference in Pontypool presciently aimed at bringing new industries to the eastern valley. But very soon afterwards he underwent a second operation which he did not survive. He died at St Thomas' hospital, just across the river from the House of Commons, on 25 April, aged sixty-three.

In a touching gesture, Violet Attlee came to the hospital and took Hattie and Roy back with her to stay the night in Downing Street – the only time in his life that Roy slept in Number Ten. The next day they returned to Pontypool by train. The funeral was three days later in St James' Anglican church, with an address by the Archdeacon of Newport, and Arthur was buried in Trevithin churchyard, even though he (unlike Hattie) was not a believer.* There were 800 mourners in the church and crowds lined the streets outside to pay their respects. Under the headline 'Romantic Career of a Man of the People', the *Monmouthshire Free Press* commemorated 'A Man Who Had No Enemies'.[23] Attlee was unable to attend, but was represented by a junior minister, Lord Henderson.

Roy was not the only one to be devastated by his father's death. The clearest evidence of how close Tony had grown to both Arthur and Hattie is contained in a remarkable letter that he wrote to Hattie from Oxford on the evening of the funeral. It is a long letter, but worth quoting in full for what it says about all three of them:

---

* 'He was not hostile to religion or clergymen,' Roy wrote, 'but quietly agnostic', which was precisely his own position all his life. Hattie, by contrast, was a devout chapel-goer until Arthur's death, after which she never attended again. 'I never asked her why, but I think she must have thought that God had let her down.'[22]

Dear Mrs Jenkins,

I didn't really have a proper opportunity for a talk with you in Pontypool today, so I feel I must write to you and tell you one or two things that are in my mind. This is *not* just a polite letter of sympathy, but a very special one since as you know I've always looked on you as almost a second mother.

Surely you must have been comforted and fortified by the enormous turnout of people at the funeral. It was the most impressive tribute to a man that I have ever seen in my life or ever expect to see. And I couldn't help noticing that the people in the streets didn't behave as though they were there out of curiosity – they behaved as though they had lost a real & beloved friend, as indeed they had.

Yet, thinking it over, there is nothing surprising in this spontaneous tribute. Your husband had the most astonishing power of inspiring love and affection, especially in young people – there was something so genuine and generous and sincere about him. I don't know what his religious convictions were, but the only way I can describe it is by saying that he was a 'very perfect Christian gentleman', in the highest sense of the term.

As far as I am concerned, his was one of the dominating influences in my life. I shall never forget as long as I live the profound effect which he had during the first year of the war on my whole attitude to life. I think he liked me, and had confidence in me: I only hope I shall prove worthy of that trust.

When I saw you first this morning, you said how unreasonable such a tragedy seems to be, how cruelly unnecessary: and that is bound to be one's instinctive feeling. Yet (and I hope you will forgive me for saying this) I wonder whether death may not prove to have been a kind release for him. He had such vitality and joy in life that I am sure he could never have endured living on as a partial invalid or restricted in his activities. If that was the alternative perhaps this was the most merciful way.

But I particularly want to say this. Whether you realise it or not, a large part of his influence with people was due to you. Even if I had not met Mr Jenkins, I should still have got enormous pleasure and benefit from visiting Greenlands and talking to you; and I'm sure this is true of many others as well. You mustn't mind my saying this: but I'm terribly anxious that you should gradually take up your old life again – meeting people, being active in Pontypool, and helping and encouraging people (as you helped me) by your wisdom and kindness.

I have at least an inkling of how you must feel through having seen my mother go through the same agony when my father died. I know she felt that the whole bottom had dropped out of her life. But bit by bit she took up her old teaching activities again, and I really think has done a lot of good. I know it's what my father would have wished her to do.

I can't tell you how much I appreciated you asking me to go with you and your family at the funeral. It moved me very deeply and I shall never forget the honour you paid me by doing it.

I do hope I have said nothing in this letter which may irritate you. If I have, please forgive it, because it was said from a full heart.

Please don't reply to this letter. I shall be thinking of you often, and I know that you'll face the next few weeks with the same courage you showed during the ordeal this afternoon.

With very, very much love,

Tony[24]

The most remarkable thing about this letter is that it makes no mention of Roy whatever.

In her grief, Hattie decided that the best tribute to Arthur's memory would be for Roy to take over his seat in Parliament. On paper the idea was not unreasonable. He had already fought a seat at the General Election and done well. He was looking for another to contest and was just the sort of bright young man the Labour Party wanted in the Commons. What could be more natural than that he should stand for his home town? The proposal found some support. 'What better memorial,' a former chairman of Pontypool council wrote to the local paper, '. . . than to send his son to the House of Commons to carry the torch that his father lit nearly fifty years ago on Varteg Hill?'[25] But other voices were raised against. Ernest H. Parker of Pontnewydd denied that Arthur would have wanted Roy to follow him:

I know it would not be Alderman Jenkins' wish that we should, out of sympathy, resuscitate the old practice of hereditary representation. We who knew Alderman Jenkins for many years knew his very decided opinions on that question . . . If Mr Roy Jenkins is to be Member for Pontypool, it must not be because he is the son of an illustrious father.[26]

Again Roy let himself be led, this time by his mother. 'At one level of consciousness', he admitted in his memoirs, he knew quite well that it would be folly for him to try to replace his father.[27] For all his cosmopolitanism, Arthur was above all a miners' MP. As his *Times* obituary noted, 'The welfare of miners was always his chief interest';[28] and Hansard bears that out. Roy Jenkins could never have been credible as a miners' MP. His interests already lay far from Pontypool and he would always have been a poor surrogate for his father. Moreover he would have had his mother, a prominent and controversial local personality in her own right – magistrate, school governor, stalwart supporter of the local hospital, the Red Cross, youth clubs and pensioners' organisations – forever standing over him: he could never have been his own man. Hattie's unpopularity in the town has probably been exaggerated. But one local councillor who claimed in 1972 that Arthur wished Roy to succeed him certainly thought her a liability to his cause:

> I remember her so well, walking about the town always elegantly dressed, usually in black – a cape and hat, that sort of thing. She wasn't just Hattie Jenkins. She was Mrs Arthur Jenkins, wife of the MP. She was a good sincere woman, but Arthur's long years of public service seemed to have left her with a conviction that only a Jenkins could serve the valley.
>
> With all respect to her, I still feel she was a stumbling block to her own ambitions for her son. I still feel that if he had been able to persuade her to go away for a fortnight's holiday during that fight for the nomination we might have pulled it off for Roy. But with her taking him from door to door I'm afraid his chances were very much reduced.[29]

Roy went hard for the nomination. He addressed meetings and canvassed influential individuals. Pontypool was a rock-solid Labour seat, so there was a lot of competition. Eventually twelve hopefuls were invited to a selection conference on 29 June, attended by 220 local members. Roy got down to the last two, but in the final ballot he was comfortably beaten (134:76) by Granville West, the local solicitor who had missed out on the Cardiff Central selection in 1944. West duly won the by-election, but subsequently made little impact in the Commons or (when surprisingly ennobled by Gaitskell) in the Lords. For Jenkins it was another fortunate escape. Leo Abse, who followed West in 1959, claimed that he was deeply scarred by his rejection and was ever afterwards 'almost phobic where Wales was concerned'.[30] But this is rubbish. After his parents died he had little reason to go back to Wales, except occasionally to speak as he did in every other part of Britain. He always thought it false to make too much of his Welsh identity; but he had no particular hang-up about it and in fact became more attached to it as he got older. He actually continued to bank with Barclays in Pontypool to the end of his life – scarcely the act of a man who was 'phobic' about his origins. It was Hattie who felt his rejection most keenly. She continued with her public activities, as Tony had advised, becoming a county councillor in 1949 and chairman of the bench in 1953, and lived long enough to see Roy safely elected for another seat; but she never forgave the local party and was never really happy again. She died in 1953, aged only sixty-seven. All in all she had far less influence on Roy's career than Arthur did.

His next venture proved more fruitful than his previous efforts. But once again he owed it entirely to Attlee's patronage. As he himself put it: 'By acts of almost inexplicable generosity not obviously stemming from his detached character the Prime Minister launched me on a writing career.'[31] First Attlee invited his late friend's son to edit a volume of his speeches between May 1945 and November 1946. Jenkins selected them – twenty-nine speeches or extracts from speeches, grouped not chronologically but under eight headings – and wrote an entirely factual three-and-a-half-page introduction, for which he was paid (by Attlee personally) £50. The book was published by Heinemann in 1947 under the typically vapid title for such collections, *Purpose and Policy*. Then Attlee gave Roy free access to his papers to write his biography. Despite having been Labour leader since 1935 Attlee was still so little known that there was a gap to be filled, and Heinemann paid Jenkins a very decent advance of £200, with an option on his next two books (which suggests that they saw him as a writer with a future). In fact he found nothing of a personal nature in the papers and wrote an almost entirely public record of the Prime Minister's career up to May 1945, which added little to public knowledge. He wrote it in the evenings and weekends over twelve months between November 1946 and November 1947. It is unmistakably a young man's book – earnest and dutiful, in the manner of all those Victorian tombstones he had consumed at Bletchley, but mercifully shorter – with no word of criticism and very few flashes of his mature style, though admittedly Attlee remains to this day a difficult subject for any pen to bring to life, and the tyro author was scarcely in a position to be critical, even had he wished to be. Attlee made a few corrections, but was generally happy with the result.[32] Looking back, however, Jenkins thought it a mistake to have tried to write about someone towards whom he was so clearly in 'a client relationship'; and he never again wrote about a living subject.[33]* Nevertheless *Mr Attlee: An Interim Biography* was 'not a bad book', and he still thought it read 'unembarrassingly' forty-five years later.[38] The reviewers – including George Orwell in *Tribune* – were generally kind. It sold around 3,500 copies. Above all, it gave him his start as a political biographer.

But his primary ambition was still to get into Parliament as soon as possible; and in 1948 – just before *Mr Attlee* came out – another opening arose when the Member for Central Southwark suddenly resigned. It was not a prospect which attracted much interest, since the seat was due to disappear at the next election. Comprising a narrow wedge of working-class housing stretching from the Elephant and Castle towards Camberwell, the constituency had been heavily bombed during the war – 'whole streets were wiped off the canvassers' lists'[39] – and much of its population evacuated. Even on paper the electorate was now only 27,000, and fewer than half that number had voted in 1945, when Labour won by 9,336 votes to 3,654. Thus Central Southwark offered no more than a temporary toehold in Parliament, especially since the Member for North Southwark, the Minister of Labour George Isaacs, had already been promised the new enlarged constituency. Nevertheless Jenkins judged that two years would give him enough time to make a name that would help him to something more secure. Just as he was in very different circumstances thirty-four years later, he was so impatient to find a seat that he was willing to take on anything that came along. He applied for the nomination and was selected (beating a local councillor by twenty votes to eight) on 23 March.

The speech with which he won the backing of the local committee combined a becoming modesty with socialist conviction and a display of economic expertise. It offers the fullest statement, at the moment of his entry into grown-up politics, of how Jenkins presented himself and what he believed, in 1948, the Labour party stood for. After an elegant expression of regret at the passing of the constituency and

---

* Such insights as there are derived mainly from his own very limited experience. Thus he wrote that Attlee's eight hours' work a day for his Schools was 'about the maximum';[34] that 'the organisers of political meetings are notoriously flattering in their letters to possible speakers';[35] and that Attlee avoided the mistake 'often committed by younger intellectuals of attempting to judge his military superiors by standards more applicable to . . . a university don or a writer in a Left-wing periodical'.[36] Already he compared Attlee with Asquith and revealed an early prejudice against Lloyd George. But almost the only flourish that might have come from one of his mature biographies is a remark (apropos Oswald Mosley) that 'Only the politically illiterate regarded Moscow and Mussolini's Rome as the same place, but one could start for either by taking the boat train to Dover.'[37]

a tribute to the retiring Member, he began with four personal points. First, he was careful to point out that, 'although I have been lucky enough to receive a first-class university education', he was not brought up 'in an atmosphere detached from the harsher facts of life'. In South Wales he had seen dole queues longer than they had known in South London. Second, 'I was brought up in a family that had its whole being in Labour politics . . . I know how important a part of an MP's job lies not in Westminster, but in Pontypool or in Central Southwark or wherever his constituency may be.' Third, though not strictly a local candidate, he lived only a mile from the Elephant and Castle, 'and it is a mile which it would be my intention to cover very frequently'; and his wife, 'who shares to the full my interest in politics', would be 'equally willing to play her part'. Fourth, he had already fought one campaign in a difficult area.

These points made, he went on to praise the achievement of the Labour government with characteristic historical perspective. 'If one compares the legislative record of this Government with that of almost any previous administration one realizes how big is the step towards social equality and a decent ordering of the nation's resources which we have taken since 1945.' The social security system, the National Health Service, 'the rehabilitation of the coal industry', 'the reorganisation of the country's transport' – each one of these measures would in normal times be sufficient to ensure a government's claim to reforming fame. Moreover, all this had been achieved at a time of desperate economic stringency. The problem was that the country was living above its income and must now take steps to 'balance our account'. But that only enhanced the need for a Labour government, not a return to bad old Tory remedies:

> If times are difficult and many goods are scarce, it is more than ever essential that the Labour policy of fair shares for all should be supported. If we face a period of possible economic crisis, then let us ensure that it is the socialist solution of increased production and a planned allocation of resources which is applied, and not the old Tory solution. For don't let us forget that the Tories have a solution of a sort to our present economic difficulties. By creating a certain amount of unemployment, by allowing a slashing of wage rates to follow from this, by applying all the old deflationary methods, by ending scarcity by the illusory method of taking purchasing power from the pockets of the people, they might cut down the volume of our imports, not because people

didn't need them but because people couldn't pay for them. But we don't want that. I am pretty sure that the people of Central Southwark don't want that. I am pretty sure that the people of the country as a whole don't want it.

If selected, he thought he could fight a successful campaign 'which would give us a great victory at the polls and which would also make a contribution to the task of educating the people to the facts of our economic situation, and thus strike a blow in the vital battle for production, with which is bound up the whole future of our movement and of our Government'.[40] This might have been the Chancellor of 1968 speaking.

A by-election so close to Westminster drew a good deal of coverage in the national press, so once the campaign started his performance came under some scrutiny.'Mr Jenkins,' the *Manchester Guardian* reported, 'is a tall young man with a rather shy manner. But he warms up on the platform and has a Welsh flair for oratory.'[41] More perceptively, the *Observer* suggested that soaring oratory was not really his style:

A Labour meeting here is apt to be quiet. The audience appears to listen with polite inattention . . . In these uninspiring circumstances Mr Jenkins deals soberly with the larger issues, as becomes Mr Attlee's man. Patiently struggling against a training which inclines him to speak above the local heads, he stands as counsel for the defence of a Government which might be accused of failure and calls for an impressive acquittal.[42]

He held meetings nearly every evening in the ten days before polling on 29 April. Again the constituency's proximity to Westminster meant that he was supported by an impressive line-up of Cabinet ministers (Hugh Dalton and James Griffiths), junior ministers (Edith Summerskill and Douglas Jay) and MPs (including Bessie Braddock and the young Member for next-door Bermondsey, Bob Mellish), as well as friends of his own, including his boss at the ICFC, John Kinross. His Tory opponent was a man named James Greenwood who had left school at fourteen and made much of being the local candidate – legitimately, in that he ran an advertising agency based in the constituency and had long been active in local politics; but Jenkins pointed out that he actually lived in Hampstead, six times further away than he himself did! Greenwood tried hard to bring the campaign down to street level, shouting against the trams and asserting that the threatened closure of a local market mattered more to the people of Southwark than the United Nations. Jenkins, by contrast, at his 'orderly and rather stuffy meetings',[43] kept firmly to the bigger picture, maintaining that the eyes of the country – indeed, the world – were on Southwark, looking for a big vote of confidence in the Labour government. Full employment was his trump card, illustrated in leaflets showing a long queue outside the labour exchange in Walworth Road before the war, contrasted with a recent picture of the same building now with no queue. Other photographs showed the dapper young candidate talking with building workers and pensioners; the back page of his election address featured Jennifer asserting that 'the housewives and mothers of Southwark stand solidly behind Labour's policy of fair shares for all'. Repeatedly Jenkins damned the Tories as the party of unemployment who would cut the living standards of the workers: 'The leopard does not change his spots.' And in his eve-of-poll speech he ridiculed a Tory poster that showed a tug-of-war – the Labour Party plus Communists plus Fascists against the Conservative party plus the people:

Poor Tories! They still believe that they are the people and those who vote against them are just the riff-raff. But what is the truth? It is that the Labour Government is the greatest bulwark against totalitarianism of any sort, both in this country and in Europe as a whole. It offers freedom with social justice, it offers an end to industrial unrest and to the long dole queues, which are the most dangerous breeding grounds of totalitarianism.

That is why its success is so important to other countries. That is why people all over the world are watching it, almost with bated breath.[44]

Jenkins held the seat quite easily – Labour did not drop a single by-election between 1945 and 1951 – but his share of the vote was down:

Roy Jenkins (Labour)	8,744
James Greenwood (Conservative)	4,623
Labour majority	4,121[45]

Greenwood claimed that a similar swing across the country at the next election would give the Tories a working majority; but Jenkins was well pleased. 'The result shows that, despite the present national difficulties, the majority of people do appreciate the way the Labour

Government is trying to solve our problems.'[46] He had fought a good campaign, served the government well and achieved his own first ambition at the same time. However precariously, he was – at twenty-seven – the youngest Member of the House of Commons. He had got his toe on the bottom rung of the ladder.

6 Baby of the House

JENKINS arrived at Westminster not, like most new Members, with a sense of excitement and novelty at the strangeness of the place, but rather with a slightly blasé sense of relief that – young though he was – he had come into his entitlement at last. He already knew the House pretty well, not only from watching debates from the gallery since he was a boy, but from meeting his father in the bars and corridors of the building. During the war he had more than once waited for Arthur in the deputy Prime Minister's room.* He knew most of the senior members of the Labour government, from Attlee downwards, who had been his father's friends; and this exalted connection was reinforced by Attlee insisting on acting as one of his sponsors when he was formally introduced on 3 May 1948. (The London area whip was, more conventionally, the other.) To Attlee this was a natural favour to his old friend's son who had just written his biography; but it inevitably cast Jenkins in the eyes of his new colleagues as a sort of teacher's pet. This was not the best start to a parliamentary career.

He nearly compounded it by immediately becoming PPS to Hugh Dalton. The former Chancellor, who had been obliged to resign after an unwitting budget leak six months earlier, was about to return to the Cabinet as Chancellor of the Duchy of Lancaster. Before Jenkins was even elected Dalton had floated the possibility of taking him on, and found Attlee warm to the idea.[1] Either Dalton thought better of it or Jenkins had the sense to refuse. But Dalton was an assiduous

---

* In 1948 the Commons were still sitting in the House of Lords, as they had been since their own House was bombed in 1940. They did not move back into the rebuilt Commons chamber until 1950.

III

patron of young talent, and Jenkins quickly joined the circle of his young protégés. At the party conference at Scarborough in mid-May Dalton recorded having Roy and Jennifer at his table as well as his particular favourite, for whom he nursed a homoerotic attraction, Tony Crosland. Two weeks later Jenkins wrote to congratulate Dalton on his return to the Cabinet. 'I don't know whether I am entitled to address you as "Dear Hugh", but you once told me that you liked impertinent young men.'[2] But Roy could never be as impertinent as Tony.

Jenkins described his first impressions of the House in a speech to the Newport Model Parliament.* With a candour that no new MP would risk these days, he admitted that the first weeks after his election were 'a period of relief, of relaxation, almost of anti-climax, after the rigours of a by-election campaign'.[3] In his memoirs, too, he recalled his time as Member for Central Southwark as 'an easy life'. Labour's still enormous majority meant that whipping was light; and Southwark itself was 'undemanding':

> I went there often – it was only a ten-minute and one-penny tramcar-ride away – and tried to find non- or quasi-political organisations to address. But no-one seemed to expect this. Neither of the other members did it, nor had my predecessor. Constituency correspondence was negligible. Advice bureaux were more popular, but not much. It was one of the last of the pocket boroughs.[4]

What he most enjoyed, after the constraints of a nine-to-five job at the ICFC and before that the army, was the freedom to allocate his own time. It was not that he did not work hard: he did, all his life, belying his image as a lazy hedonist. But he liked to set his own time-table and hated being answerable to others. The relative autonomy of an MP's life in the late 1940s and 1950s suited him down to the ground.

The absence of constituency obligations allowed him to concentrate on making his name in the House. He waited only a month before making his maiden speech. It was a polished and typically loyal effort. Stafford Cripps had presented his first budget in April, and the Finance Bill was still going through the House. One of its provisions was a one-off capital levy – euphemistically called a 'Special Contribution' – on investment income over £250 p.a. The Tories denounced it

---

* Model Parliaments were an admirable Victorian exercise in civic participation which still survived in some places, where local people met to debate current issues in a sort of mock House of Commons, like a less privileged Oxford Union.

furiously as 'a bad tax . . . economically bad and morally bad';[5] but Jenkins saw the chance to make his debut in its defence. Reminding the House that he represented some of the lowest-paid people in the country, he called the contribution 'an indispensable weapon' against inflation – not so much because of its direct deflationary impact as for its 'psychological effect' in assuring the poor that the rich were sharing the burden of austerity:

> I know that hon. Members opposite pretend to be rather shocked by the thought that the Government are influenced by consider-ations of this sort. They regard it as playing politics, but I and the majority of members on this side of the Committee do not regard it as playing politics. It is not a question of that, but a question of righting the balance and putting rather more on the shoulders of the rich, who were looked after so well by successive Conservative Governments, and putting less on the shoulders of the poor, who were not so well looked after by the same Conservative Governments. If the Labour Government abandoned this policy in its financial plans it would not only be politically foolish but morally wrong and socially unjust. Therefore, I submit, it would have been virtually impossible for the Chancellor to carry out the general design of his Budget without some additional impost on the rich.[6]

Maiden speeches have an uncanny way of anticipating the speaker's subsequent career. Jenkins wrote later that the austere, teetotal Cripps 'exercised a considerable fascination over me at this time'.[7] Certainly Cripps' 'special contribution' made a lasting impression on him. Though no two men could have been more different, when Jenkins found himself as Chancellor twenty years later facing the same urgent need to squeeze consumption in order to boost exports, he remembered Cripps' precedent and imposed a similar levy himself. Back in 1948 he saw that Cripps faced the same sort of political/economic judge-ment that he would have to make in 1970. 'It was better to have a somewhat harsh Budget that would cure inflation rather than a generous popular Budget which would merely undermine the purchasing power of the pound.'[8] He spoke for only fifteen minutes, having learned his text carefully by heart, but he already sounded like an embryonic Chancellor. All maiden speakers are congratulated by those who follow them, but Sir Arthur Salter, the Tory member for Oxford University, was more than conventionally complimentary: 'I can say with complete sincerity that I have hardly ever heard an hon. Member speaking for the first time in this House, and without notes, who has spoken so charmingly and with such clarity as the hon. Member for Central Southwark.' Another Tory envied his 'apparent self-confidence . . . fluency and logicality'.[9] Despite his support of the government, he won noticeably more compliments from the other side of the House than from his own.

He spoke once more before the end of the session, balancing gratitude for Marshall Aid – the enlightened American project for rebuilding war-shattered Europe – with a recognition that it would not by itself solve Britain's problems. 'I believe that it would be churlish not to stress the first point, and that it would be unbelievably foolish not to stress the second.' He conceded that the Truman administration's motivation might not be wholly disinterested, but thought 'far-sighted self-interest . . . a great deal more rare and more welcome than short-sighted self-interest'.[10] The Tory who followed him mocked his naivety:

I hate to shatter the delightful oasis of self-deception and unreality in the matter of what America thinks of the present Government in which he lives. I suggest that the first use of the dollars that the Chancellor will get might be to pay for a trip for the hon. Member to go to America and learn the real naked truth of what the American people, and a good deal of American labour, think of the hon. Gentleman's Government.[11]

Jenkins would not pay his first visit to the United States for another five years; but he never qualified his rose-tinted view of the Americans' essential benevolence.

In September the Commons was recalled for an extraordinary session to carry for a second time the Parliament Bill – reducing the delaying power of the House of Lords from two years to one – which the Lords had rejected in June. This was an issue that Jenkins had already identified as the subject of his next book, and he did not miss the chance to intervene briefly in support of the government's measure: 'a modest step, but a step which is well in keeping with the needs of the times'.[12] Then in November he made his longest speech so far in support of nationalising the steel industry. Characteristically he made the case for nationalisation on grounds that were determinedly non-doctrinaire: the simple fact was, he argued, that the money to finance the industry could no longer be raised privately:

With the steel industry we have reached the point when nationalisation is the natural next step. It is an industry in which I believe the money must come from public or semi-public sources. It is an industry in which free competition is dead. It is an industry in which even the party opposite admits there must be a good deal of State control. Now, when that position is arrived at – public money, State control, no competition – who are the doctrinaires? Those who want to take the natural and logical step and put the thing under public ownership as well as under public control, or those who despite all these things insist in saying that it must still remain under private ownership?[13]

That autumn Jenkins also started writing regularly in *Tribune*, the left-wing weekly founded in 1937, financed largely by Cripps and now edited by Michael Foot. Soon it would be transformed into the main organ of Bevanite opposition to the Labour leadership; but for the moment – so long as Nye Bevan was in the government – it was thoroughly loyal. Jenkins' first piece for the paper, headlined 'When Lloyd George called the Lords "Mr Balfour's Poodle"', was on House of Lords reform, which was probably his way in;[14] but thereafter he used the platform to display his credentials as an economist. On 5 November – ten days before his Commons speech on the subject – he rehearsed his argument that the City could no longer finance the steel industry. 'Sooner or later the state will have to provide the bulk of the money for steel. It would be ludicrous to do this while leaving the control of the industry in private hands.'[15] This drew another withering response from an anonymous writer in the *Financial Times*, who insisted that the City had already raised £50 million for the South Wales tinplate industry, castigated 'the iron curtain of ignorance and prejudice which surrounds Mr Jenkins', and concluded that 'If the opponents of nationalisation are to have no more serious arguments than this to contend with, they should have no difficulty in persuading even Mr Jenkins that the case for nationalisation is as weak as a new-born kitten.'[16] Steel was the most contentious of Labour's nationalisations after 1945; it was eventually carried in 1949, but the Tories committed themselves to reversing it, and did so in 1953. It then remained the front line of the dispute between public and private ownership for the next four decades, renationalised by Labour in 1967, then privatised again by Mrs Thatcher in 1988, while Jenkins' enthusiasm for nationalisation steadily diminished.

In January 1949 he enjoyed a nice little perk when he managed to get himself included in a parliamentary delegation to newly democratic

Italy, led by the Speaker and including among its number 'Rab' Butler, John Boyd-Carpenter and Ivor Bulmer-Thomas. For a francophile railway enthusiast and budding gourmand, it was heaven.

> We went to Paris by Golden Arrow, dined at the Embassy, and proceeded by the Simplon express from the Gare de Lyon . . . At Milan we transferred to two saloons of the royal train of the House of Savoy which had been taken over by the Republic, and so proceeded to Rome.[17]

There they were magnificently wined and dined – in striking contrast to still-rationed Britain – at a series of lunches and dinners with the President, the Prime Minister (Alcide de Gasperi) and other Italian parliamentarians. At one dinner Jenkins sat next to the former Prime Minister, Vittorio Orlando (who had been one of the 'Big Four' with Lloyd George, Clemenceau and Woodrow Wilson at the Paris Peace Conference in 1919), which pleased his sense of history. They also met the Pope (Pius XII) and visited Naples, where Jenkins and Bulmer-Thomas slipped away to visit the elderly philosopher Benedetto Croce. On this jaunt Jenkins also took the opportunity to draw out the wonderfully indiscreet Butler, who treated the young Labour Member to some typically barbed 'Rabbisms' about his Tory colleagues ('The trouble with Anthony [Eden] is that he has no intellectual interests') and even hinted at some sort of centre party as Jenkins recorded:

> I doubt if there is anything substantial, except steel, in our home policy with which he disagrees . . . At times it seemed . . . as though Butler were expecting a position in 10 years or so in which the C.P. [Communist Party] would be strong and the bulk of the L.P. [Labour Party] might form a centre party with him & some other Tories. He thinks it is only Ramsay MacDonald who prevents a coalition today.[18]

This was fantasy, but it is a reminder that MacDonald's 'great betrayal', when he abandoned the Labour party to form a National Government with the Tories in 1931, continued to haunt Labour throughout the post-war period. The allegation of 'MacDonaldism' would still be spat at Jenkins himself as late as the 1980s.

The next month he got a second chance to get his foot on the bottom rung of the ministerial ladder when he was invited to become PPS to the Commonwealth Relations Secretary, Philip Noel-Baker;

and this time he took it. ('Mr Attlee is a fellow who looks after his apples,' 'Crossbencher' commented in the *Sunday Express*.)[19] Jenkins had no interest in the Commonwealth and little regard for Noel-Baker ('He was unco-ordinated, lacked critical judgement and was a weak minister'); but the appointment did not stop him speaking on the subjects that did interest him and it gave him his only experience of the inside of a government department before he became a minister himself in 1964. He did the job for a year – enjoying 'the frequent Government hospitality meals over which Noel-Baker presided with grace';[20] but he declined the same position with another minister after the 1950 election.

In this year, too, he and Jennifer started a family. At the end of 1948, when Jennifer was already six months pregnant, they moved from their poky flat in Marsham Street to a much larger flat occupying the top two floors of a tall Victorian house in Cornwall Gardens, South Kensington.* Though still only four stops along the Circle Line, this was not only less convenient for the House of Commons, but far from ideal for bringing up young children. In March 1949, however, Jennifer gave birth to their first 'giraffe' – a son whom they christened Charles. The ceremony took place, inevitably, in the crypt of the Palace of Westminster, with Attlee and Crosland as a contrasting pair of godparents. Roy and Jennifer stayed in Cornwall Gardens for five years, during which time their second child, Cynthia, was born (in June 1951); so that Jennifer soon found herself carrying two children and a large 1950s pram, as well as coal and shopping, up and down seventy-nine steps several times a day. By the time they moved again she was expecting their third.

During 1949 Jenkins continued to work hard at being a diligent young MP. With no future in Southwark he needed to make a mark quickly in order to find a safer berth before the next election. To that end he intervened early and often in the debates on Cripps' second budget, defending it particularly against the criticism of the Communist Phil Piratin, and praising rather too fulsomely the unflinching way in which Labour's 'Iron Chancellor' was discharging his 'difficult and thankless task'. He even ended one speech by quoting Robert Louis Stevenson's *Weir of Hermiston*: 'Uncheered and undismayed, he marches up the broad, bare staircase of his duty.'[22] 'I was a tremendous loyalist during my first years in the House,' he wrote slightly apologetically in

---

* The rent was £240 p.a. – nearly half Roy's MP's salary of £600 p.a. – but, with a friend of Jennifer's lodging with them, their housing costs were 'almost negligible'.[21]

his memoirs. 'I waited to see what the Government was going to do and then devoted my speeches to defending decisions made rather than attempting to influence those which were still to be taken.'[23] In this spirit he vigorously backed the government's Profits Tax Bill (which clawed back some of the increased profits made by dollar exporters as a consequence of devaluation) as a small blow for greater equality, by contrast with the Tories' 'intolerable policy . . . of narrow selfishness'.[24] Schooled in the Oxford Union, he was already a polished performer with an elegant turn of phrase and a veteran's ease with the courtesies of parliamentary speech – 'It is within the knowledge of the hon. Member'; 'I am glad to see the right Hon. Member in his place'; but at the same time he could be waspish and aggressively partisan. Years later he admitted to being influenced by Dick Crossman's way of holding attention by logical acrobatics. 'I was sufficiently impressed as a young MP that he was the only parliamentarian I ever consciously tried to emulate.'[25]*

He also contributed articles to *Tribune* and other Labour journals like the *New Statesman* and *Socialist Commentary* – earnest pieces on such subjects as wage stabilisation (his first engagement with the question of incomes policy), the need for a capital gains tax and the nationalisation of cement; attended Fabian conferences; and wrote long letters to *The Times*.[27]† At the same time – as a safety net in case he failed to secure another seat – he was beginning to do some more popular journalism. In July he had a big article in *Picture Post*, spread over seven pages, illustrated with grim photographs of dole queues and hunger marchers, under the headline 'If US Depression Spreads CAN WE ESCAPE THE BLOW?', in which he warned against repeating the policy mistakes of the 1930s.[29] In addition he began a lifelong ability to turn his travels to profit by writing about the problems of the Italian socialist parties for the *New Statesman*.[30] Already he was developing a useful second income to supplement his MP's salary.

In June – the last time it was held in the summer – he managed to speak at the party conference at Blackpool. He spoke in the economic debate, once again defending Cripps against a resolution supported by practically every previous speaker pleading for some relaxation of wage

---

* A letter to Dalton in October 1950, however, suggests that he was beginning to find Crossman's compulsive love of paradox merely tiresome. 'One ought at least to pretend to believe in the ideas one puts forward.'[26]
† He was also willing, slightly surprisingly, to put his name to Cold War propaganda prepared by the Foreign Office for dissemination in non-aligned countries like Norway, articles with titles such as 'Soviet Sharp Practices Exposed: How Yugoslavia was Exploited'.[28]

control. As sternly as his master, Jenkins warned that inflation always hit the wage-earner hardest. But he balanced that unwelcome message by asking Cripps to make the 'special contribution' of his 1948 budget permanent. 'I hope . . . that a general capital levy is still possible.'[31] Cripps, however, made no concessions to Jenkins or anyone else, but in an 'unrelenting' reply, which, *The Times* reported, 'left his audience intellectually helpless though probably emotionally unconvinced', simply reiterated his stark message of continued austerity until the country had balanced its trade gap.[32] For the moment party discipline was still such that conference swallowed its medicine without a vote.

That summer Jenkins suffered from what he called in his memoirs 'a prolonged bout of the imprecise, lowering, although never disabling psychosomatic pains which have occasionally afflicted me throughout my adult life'.[33] The likelihood must be that he was getting anxious about finding another seat and worried that his political career might be about to end before it had properly begun. He went to see a psychiatrist who depressed him further by telling him that he might hope to live a normal span so long as he avoided any undue strain. In later life Jenkins liked to recall this diagnosis with some amusement; but at the time it was not so funny. Seats were becoming vacant, but boundaries had been redrawn, making it hard to assess the winnability of the new constituencies. He turned down the opportunity to contest Hammersmith North, for instance, where the Labour candidate in 1945 – up against the Independent, effectively Communist, D.N. Pritt – had lost his deposit. In fact the new Labour candidate, Frank Tomney, easily defeated Pritt in 1950 and held the seat till his retirement in 1979; so Jenkins passed up the chance of a safe London seat. He did apply for two more promising constituencies: Eton and Slough, which preferred the veteran peace campaigner Fenner Brockway; and Ogmore – another Welsh valley seat some thirty miles west of Pontypool – which chose the president of USDAW (the shop workers' union). He found the experience of hawking himself around the country 'at once nerve-racking and mildly humiliating', and was becoming 'dismayed and a little desperate' by the time the Member for Birmingham Yardley decided to stand down.[34]

Jenkins had actually had his eye on Birmingham all along, where a new constituency had been created on the eastern side of the city, formed in roughly equal proportions from the old Yardley and Erdington divisions and the more working-class parts of Solihull, where he had fought in 1945. It seemed certain to be a cast-iron Labour seat, and one where he already had some credit in the bank. One of his strongest supporters in Solihull had been Joseph Balmer, a Birmingham city councillor, later to be Lord Mayor; now, as chairman of the new constituency party, Balmer backed Jenkins equally strongly for Stechford. At the selection meeting on 16 October 1949 Jenkins had to deny that he was being foisted on the constituency as Attlee's favourite son; he emphasised, as in Southwark, his 'solid working-class stock on both sides of my family', his training as an economist and the fact that his wife was 'as keenly interested in socialist politics as I am' and would play a full part in his campaign – an important selling point in a seat where the Tory candidate was a woman.[35] In a three-way contest he narrowly squeezed through on the second ballot between the local party chairman (who led on the first ballot) and Fred Mulley (then a Cambridge academic, later to be a ministerial colleague in the Wilson governments), who came third. It was a huge relief. After six years of trying he finally had a secure base for a long parliamentary career.

Stechford was as different from Southwark as another urban seat could be. Central Southwark was a doomed but still lively community, its ageing electorate crowded together in crumbling Victorian tenements ripe for redevelopment. Stechford, by contrast, was an anonymous stretch of new housing estates mainly inhabited by skilled manual workers employed in the booming Birmingham motor industry and allied trades. If Southwark was a traditional Labour seat in which any of the early pioneers would have felt at home, Stechford epitomised the new world of Labour, in which some of the activists were still left-wing but the voters were less interested in socialism than in the size of the weekly pay packet and increasingly, as the 1950s went on, in the washing machine, the family car and the package holiday in Spain. When old socialists like Nye Bevan deplored the growing materialism of the working class, it was of places like Stechford that they were thinking.

Jenkins represented Stechford for twenty-six years, and its character, or lack of it, inevitably affected the development of his ideas over the next two and a half decades. He was a conscientious Member in the days when there was no expectation that MPs should live in their constituencies or visit more than once or twice a month. Local problems were dealt with by local councillors, who resented an MP who interfered. After some early tensions he enjoyed excellent relations with his local party, particularly with Joe Balmer, his agent S.G. Cooke and a couple called Austin and Dora (Dink) Hitchman, with whom he stayed during elections. He had some historical feeling for the city which Joe Chamberlain had made his personal fiefdom in the previous century, though Chamberlain was far from being one of his heroes. Yet in a quarter of a century as a Birmingham MP he acquired little affection for the place. As early as 1952 he was playing his favourite game of drawing comparisons between cities in an article for the weekly illustrated magazine *The Sphere*. He did his best to present Birmingham as a 'great and proud city', with 'a certain civic dignity . . . good theatres and good shops'. But 'compared with European cities of roughly equal size – Marseilles or Milan or Munich – it lacks pulsation at the centre. It is essentially a place where people live and people work, rather than where people congregate.'[36]* In his last completed book, published the year before he died, he wrote that in the 1950s and 1960s 'the city's restaurant resources were minimal'. He never identified with Stechford as he did later with Glasgow, Hillhead, or romanticised it as Tony Crosland did Grimsby. Yet he was always grateful that it sustained his political career for twenty-six years 'with steady and undemanding generosity'.[37]

He only had to nurse Stechford for four months while still representing Central Southwark. In that time, however, he was caught out by the taxman claiming for expenses to which he was not entitled. In those days MPs only received travelling expenses to and from their constituency, plus telephone calls within London and postage to government departments. (The need for second homes had not yet arisen.) But in July 1950 Jenkins' claim for £40 for travel to Birmingham in the months before the election was rejected on the ground that he did not yet represent the constituency.[38]

Attlee called the election in February 1950. The government and all its senior ministers were palpably exhausted; while the Tories, still led by the seventy-five-year-old but rejuvenated Churchill, burning to reverse his defeat in 1945, were able to exploit public weariness with the years of rationing and socialist controls. Jenkins fought Stechford against this returning Tory tide. He had told his selection conference in October that the election would be 'one of the most bitterly fought in our whole political history', and that Labour would have to fight 'the greatest defensive battle in the history of the labour movement'.[39] In this spirit, his election address was a serious and notably well-written 1,000-word statement of Labour's achievements – full employment, increased production, social security and the National Health Service – in the face of enormous economic difficulties. Above all, he contrasted

---

* He had recently been to Milan, but it is not clear that in 1952 Jenkins had yet visited either Marseilles or Munich.

Labour's policy of fair shares for all with the Tories' hankering to turn the clock back:

> The alternative would be a return to power of the Conservative Party, with its policy dressed up a little for electoral purposes, but with its basic ideas the same as in pre-war days. The results would be much worse than in pre-war days, for the war has destroyed many of the advantages which we used to enjoy in our trading relations with other countries. Tory ideas of a fair distribution of wealth, which brought enough misery in the easy days, would now be intolerable; and Tory neglect of our productive resources . . . which was dangerous enough fifteen years ago, would now mean national disaster.

'Since 1945,' he concluded, 'we have had, for the first time, a Parliament which has . . . worked for the whole community, and not just for a selected few. I ask you to elect another such Parliament on February 23rd.'[40]

With thirteen Birmingham constituencies to cover and Stechford assumed to be safe, the local press did not pay him much attention. His opponent, Edith Pitt – an industrial welfare officer and local councillor who campaigned mainly on what were called 'women's issues', specifically the cost of living – got rather more coverage. Reporting one of his meetings, the *Birmingham Gazette* commented that Jenkins 'looks like a young Conservative – one of the more serious type', describing his emphatic gestures with his right hand while his left stayed mainly in his jacket pocket – 'so much more graceful than the trousers' pocket'; but conceded that 'this new arrival in Birmingham is one of the city's most impressive Labour candidates'.[41] The *Birmingham Post* reported that Jennifer came up 'from the South' as often as she could to help him, both speaking at meetings and canvassing (as she had done in Solihull and Southwark); she also featured prominently on his election leaflets, contributing her own 'Message to the Women Electors of Stechford', mainly about prices and family allowances. Hattie too came up from Wales.[42] But very little was reported of what any of them said.

The national result left Labour still the largest party, but its huge majority melted away and the government was left with a bare overall majority of just five. Attlee was able to stagger on for another twenty fractious months; but the socialist millennium, so confidently hailed in 1945, had run into the sand. In Stechford, however, Jenkins was comfortably returned to a House of Commons where he could now feel he properly belonged:

Roy Jenkins (Labour)	33,077
Miss E. Pitt (Conservative)	20,699
S.W. Haslam (Liberal)	2,789
Labour majority	12,378[43]

The *Birmingham Gazette* reported, slightly satirically, that the newly elected Member 'wasted no time in seeking relaxation. He went to the pantomime at the Theatre Royal, Birmingham, last night, with 200 Labour Party members, settled down in his seat and forgot the huge task ahead of him. Today he is going to London with his wife for a brief rest.'[44] The pantomime, suitably enough, was *Jack and the Beanstalk*. He was now ready to start climbing.

7 Fair Shares for the Rich

THE new Member for Stechford was a serious young socialist. He had fought the election on the Labour government's record since 1945. But at his selection meeting the previous autumn, facing an exclusively party audience, he had set out where he believed the Labour movement should be aiming in the years ahead. It was widely agreed that the government had run out of reforming steam since its initial burst of energy in 1945–8. Jenkins listed three steps – more radical than anything in the 1950 manifesto – which he suggested the next Labour government should take towards creating 'a more genuinely equal and democratic society': first, 'a large-scale capital levy', to spread the ownership of wealth more widely; second, the destruction (or at least the absorption into the state system) of the public schools, which was 'essential' to creating greater equality of opportunity; and, third, moves towards industrial democracy, starting in the nationalised industries. These were all mechanistic matters of social engineering. But he concluded with a statement of the broader purposes of socialism, as he understood them, of which much more would be heard over the next decade:

> I am by training an economist. Day to day politics . . . are becoming more and more an affair of economics. But do not let us for that reason begin to think that socialism is something solely concerned with economics. It is nothing of the sort. Economic policies, measures of nationalisation, these are only the means to an end. The end is the creation of a society in which everybody can live full, contented and worthwhile lives, working in a decent atmosphere and living in good houses and pleasant surroundings. This

is the end, and we must never lose sight of it. I think that so far we have made fairly good progress in the right direction, but that we still have a long way to go. It is our task in the Labour movement to see that we get there.[1]

For the moment, however, he still projected himself very specifically as an economist. He was at once loyal to the government and distinctly left-wing; aware of the country's severe economic difficulties, yet determined that the transformation of society should not be halted by them. Speaking on the budget in April 1950, he repeated his call for a capital levy to reduce 'the gross inequality of property . . . which . . . I believe to be totally incompatible with a truly democratic society'. He thought Cripps had been 'a little over-cautious' this year, but pompously conceded that his record was so good that he was entitled to the benefit of the doubt! This speech also gave him the opportunity to congratulate Tony Crosland, who had been elected for South Gloucestershire, on his 'striking maiden speech', which took much the same line.[2] No doubt they had discussed it together. Over the spring and summer he made several more short speeches and interventions in the debates on the Finance Bill. 'On two occasions,' the Birmingham Labour paper, the *Town Crier*, noted with approval on 24 April, 'he entered the debate, and with great skill exposed the arguments of the Tories for the sham they were.'[3] In June he asked his first oral question, of the President of the Board of Trade, Harold Wilson, about exports to the United States; and in the new session, beginning in November, he made several more fairly technical speeches about raw materials and the cost of living.

At this stage the tribal rift that was soon to split the Labour party had not yet opened up; but in so far as its outline was already visible, Jenkins identified as much with the left as with the right. His two heroes in the government were Cripps, whose roots lay on the left despite his post-war reincarnation as the prophet of austerity, and Nye Bevan, still Minister of Health, but about to be moved to the Ministry of Labour. Jenkins was never personally close to Bevan (something he later regretted), but he admired him at this time 'to the verge of extravagance' and was briefly one of the 'large circle of intimates and would-be intimates' who gathered around him in the smoking room as the Welsh magician cast his spell over his disciples;[4] he was also on good terms with several of the future Bevanites, including Michael Foot (for whom he was still writing regularly in *Tribune*), John Freeman and Tom Driberg. With Freeman and Driberg, indeed, Jenkins, Crosland

and Woodrow Wyatt formed an illicit canasta school during late-night sittings of the House. (Canasta was then a fashionable card game.) In these early years he came under some left-wing pressure from his constituency party, as is clear from a letter he wrote Hugh Dalton in October 1950. He thought Dalton underestimated what he called the 'Russia complex' in the party, possibly because he sat for 'good solid Durham'. 'If you sat for a Birmingham seat,' Jenkins told him, 'I think you would be shocked to discover how many prominent people in the party are still emotionally violently pro-Russian and violently anti-American.'[5] This was one issue on which Jenkins was always robustly right-wing. He probably thought it prudent to play up to Stechford's expectations in some other respects.

In the spring of 1951 he published a *Tribune* pamphlet which he later described as 'the apogee of my excursion to the left'.[6] In later years, when Jenkins was seen as a plutocratic fat cat, its ironic title, *Fair Shares for the Rich* – actually supplied by Foot – was twisted to suggest that it was an appeal for clemency to the rich. On the contrary, it was an 'almost Robespierrean' demand not merely for the reduction but for the *abolition* of large private fortunes, by taxing them on a scale rising from 50 per cent between £20,000 and £30,000 up to 95 per cent over £100,000. To minimise the shock, the government might pay back to the former owner, for his lifetime, the income he would have got from his capital. But the essence of Jenkins' carefully detailed scheme was a swift, sharp act of confiscation; death duties and capital gains tax he dismissed as ineffective because too slow.* Anticipating Conservative howls of protest, he argued that *all* taxation was confiscation; and – reflecting his growing historical interest in the pre-1914 Liberal government – compared his proposals with Lloyd George's 'People's Budget' of 1909, which precipitated the House of Lords crisis of 1911. For the Tories to suggest that the redistribution of wealth by democratic means was unacceptable, he asserted, was a far more outrageous challenge to democracy than any tax, in 1950 as it was in 1910. Thus even at this most left-wing point of his career, when advocating a measure that he would soon come to regard as embarrassingly extreme, Jenkins explicitly placed his proposals in the Asquithian tradition of liberal reform.

At the same time *Fair Shares for the Rich* concluded with a passage

---

* A typical review in the right-wing weekly *Time and Tide* condemned his punitive attack on wealth: 'The sole purpose is to prevent anyone living at a standard of life, on his own money and after paying his taxes, of which Mr Jenkins disapproves. This is the Socialism of the dead-level and the dead-end.'[7]

on nationalisation which anticipates much of the 'revisionist' Labour position of the later 1950s. With the abolition of great private fortunes, Jenkins argued, it would no longer be possible for 80 per cent of industry to remain in private hands. 'There will simply not be enough rich people to own it.'

> A large capital levy therefore implies an extension of nationalisation. But it will be nationalisation for a different object, and therefore of a different pattern, from that which we have seen in the past five years.
>
> The coal industry, the railways, gas and electricity, were all brought under public control because it was thought necessary to take the particular industry, to reorganise it, to impose a certain structure upon it, and to run it as a unified whole. These nationalisation measures were essentially planning measures. They called for the control of whole industries, and they called for the control of particular industries. It would have defeated the whole object to have taken merely one of the four main-line railway companies, or to have substituted catering for coal.
>
> After steel the position will be different. Future nationalisations will be more concerned with equality than with planning, and this means that we can leave the monolithic public corporation behind us and look for more intimate forms of ownership and control. It will not matter if a large number of public bodies – municipalities, co-operatives and the like – and not merely the central Government, participate in the ownership. It will not matter if only sections of industries are publicly owned, so that they have to meet competition from the sections remaining in private hands. It will not matter if only a part of the shares of a particular company, and not necessarily the controlling part, are in the hands of a public body. It will indeed be positively desirable that all these things should occur, for the widest possible diffusion of control and responsibility is an essential aim of democratic socialism.[8]

In this respect *Fair Shares for the Rich* reflected the thinking of the 'new right' that began to emerge in the last year of the Labour government, as the confident consensus of 1945 fragmented in recrimination and uncertainty about what to do next. The scope and form of future nationalisation was the central, symbolic issue. Nye Bevan's 'controlling heights of the economy' – coal, gas, electricity, the railways, the Bank of England and finally steel – had all been nationalised between 1945 and 1950. Labour fought the 1950 election committed, rather unconvincingly, to adding cement and sugar to the public sector; but the rift was already opening up between the pragmatists, who recognised that further nationalisation, unless clearly justified on practical grounds, was not an election winner, and the fundamentalists who would countenance no dilution of the aim of a fully socialised economy. Under the dominating influence of Herbert Morrison, Labour went into the 1951 election with no more specific commitments to nationalisation, merely a list of criteria by which future candidates might be assessed. Morrison represented the old right of the party, which wanted only to consolidate the gains made since 1945. The younger right, headed by Hugh Gaitskell (who succeeded Cripps as Chancellor in October 1950), sought a more flexible way forward on lines first explored in the writings of Evan Durbin, Hugh Dalton and Douglas Jay before the war and fully developed by Tony Crosland in *The Future of Socialism* in 1956. Jenkins' 1951 pamphlet was a minor contribution to this gathering consensus on the right of the party that envisaged no further large-scale nationalisation on the Morrisonian model, but rather the piecemeal extension of public ownership, within the framework of a mixed economy, in the name of a non-doctrinaire socialism that placed its highest priority on equality.

Jenkins covered similar ground again in an essay on 'Equality' that he contributed to a collection entitled *New Fabian Essays* edited by Dick Crossman. These emerged from a series of Fabian conferences from 1949, but the book did not appear until May 1952 – after the Bevanite split. The other contributors included both Tony Crosland (on 'The Transition from Capitalism') and Denis Healey (on foreign policy) from the right, and Ian Mikardo (on trade unions) and Crossman himself from the left, with a balancing preface by Attlee. Crosland's was the most theoretical piece – anticipating *The Future of Socialism* – which deservedly attracted more attention than Jenkins' more superficial offering; but they were both singing from the same hymn sheet.* Without the emotional intensity of their Oxford days, Roy and Tony had largely restored their old friendship; but Tony was still unquestionably the leader, as Woodrow Wyatt later recalled:

---

* *New Fabian Essays* was noticed, among other reviewers, by two American writers whom Jenkins would later count among his closest friends. The historian Arthur Schlesinger criticised both Jenkins and Crosland for their misguided emphasis on equality of outcome, not merely of opportunity; while J.K. Galbraith shrewdly sensed that Jenkins was 'clearly troubled by his topic. Of the end he is not in doubt: he is distinctly and candidly worried about the means.'[9]

Roy was oddly respectful of Tony, letting him overwhelm him in arguments. He thought Tony was the most brilliant man he knew, much above himself intellectually. I had to say, 'Don't be silly, Roy. He's just more bullying, bombastic and abusive than you are. You're much cleverer than he is', which was true.[10]

It would be some years before Jenkins realised that, if not necessarily cleverer, he was certainly the better politician.

Even at the height of his flirtation with the left, therefore, several countervailing pressures were already pulling Jenkins to the right. First was his ingrained loyalty to Attlee and thence to the Labour government as a whole – including, when it came to the crunch, the new Chancellor, Gaitskell, whom as yet he barely knew. The second was the former Chancellor, Hugh Dalton – a fierce opponent of the left since pre-war days and now Gaitskell's principal mentor and champion. A big, bald, booming Old Etonian, Dalton was a much more approachable figure than the austere and private Cripps. Many years later Jenkins wrote an affectionate portrait of him in his book *The Chancellors*, comparing him to one of his favourite fictional characters, Anthony Powell's Kenneth Widmerpool: unlike Widmerpool, however, Dalton, though a full generation older than Roy, was 'teasable . . . capable of laughing at himself and highly enjoyable to be with'.[11] He was also compulsively indiscreet and an excellent source of malicious gossip. In the 1950 Parliament his three special protégés were Jenkins, Crosland and Wyatt, for whose advancement he pulled every string he could. That autumn, for instance, he congratulated himself that he had helped both Roy and Tony gain some attention by speaking at conference.[12] Jenkins seized the opportunity to rehearse again his argument for capital taxation. But Dalton always put Crosland first. In May 1952, when Labour was back in opposition, he urged Gaitskell to choose one of them to sit on an economic policy committee. 'I said they were both very good young men. I thought Tony had the better brain & would be more use to the committee . . . I hope, & believe, that you will choose Tony . . . I said Roy was good, but not so good.'[13]

A third factor was the Korean war which broke out in June, when the Americans intervened (under the aegis of the United Nations) to prevent Communist North Korea annexing the South. The Labour government – Bevan initially included – not only supported the American action but sent British troops to help and undertook an ambitious programme of rearmament, despite the country's parlous economic state. Jenkins' later view was that Attlee should have told the

Americans that Britain could not afford such a burden.[14] But at the time he was as hawkish as anyone. Such was their enthusiasm, indeed, that Jenkins, Crosland and Wyatt conceived the mad idea of waiving their parliamentary exemption from military call-up and volunteering for some weeks' training in the reserves, to encourage others to join up. Wisely the War Office declined their offer.

More important, the cost of rearmament put Gaitskell's 1951 budget under additional strain. He responded by deciding to impose charges for National Health Service false teeth and spectacles (hitherto free), which in turn provoked Bevan's resignation from the government. Bevan had been restless for some time, under-employed since the completion of the Health Service in 1948, but denied the promotion he felt he deserved. The last straw was Attlee's choice of Morrison as Foreign Secretary when Ernie Bevin had to retire in March; but Bevan's greater grievance was the earlier appointment of Gaitskell as Chancellor: a forty-four-year-old Wykehamist who symbolised for Bevan the take-over of the party by public-school intellectuals with no roots in the labour movement. Though he had initially supported the war and swallowed (when proposed by Cripps) the principle of charging within the NHS, he took Gaitskell's determination to introduce charges into what he thought of as *his* Health Service as a personal affront delib-erately designed to provoke his resignation; and after a couple of weeks' blustering he duly obliged on 21 April, joined by one other Cabinet minister (Wilson) and one junior minister (Freeman). This was the defining moment which split the Labour party for the next ten, if not twenty, years.

Jenkins and Crosland – in common with the great majority of Labour MPs – supported Gaitskell's budget. They did not question the need to spend an additional £1,100 million on rearmament for Korea, but approved the way Gaitskell achieved it mainly by raising taxes on the better-off. Pensions were protected and overall spending on the NHS actually increased; the charges on teeth and spectacles were minimal (£23 million in a full year) and widely felt to be inevitable, if not positively desirable. 'I think that most people,' Jenkins declared on the second day of the budget debate, 'have been surprised that the weight of the burden of rearmament on the nation's economy has been as small as it has been, and . . . are greatly impressed by the ingenuity with which the Chancellor has managed to spread it.'[15] In short, they believed there was nothing for anyone to resign over. They were shocked by Bevan's self-indulgent tantrum. From Dalton they heard how he had tried to hold his colleagues to ransom – 'Aren't I worth twenty-three millions?' – and personalised the issue into a choice between himself and Gaitskell.[16] Michael Foot in *Tribune* raised the stakes by likening Gaitskell to the turncoat Philip Snowden, Labour's first Chancellor who had followed Ramsay MacDonald into the National Government in 1931; and when Bevan finally resigned he immediately widened the issue to attack the whole rearmament programme which he had previously supported with an appalling display of boorishness and megalomania at the party meeting. Gaitskell, by contrast, conducted himself with modest reasonableness.

Dalton's three musketeers had no hesitation in agreeing that Bevan was in the wrong. The next weekend they went public in their constituencies. The *Birmingham Gazette* reported that Jenkins and Wyatt – both known as writers in *Tribune* – had made 'slashing attacks' on Bevan: Wyatt in the *Town Crier*, Jenkins at 'a public forum organised by Ten Acres and Stirchley Co-operative Society', where he declared that Bevan had 'tried to hold a pistol at the head of the Cabinet'.[17] Yet Jenkins at least was anxious not to widen the rift in the party and quickly denied that he had made 'a slashing attack':

> This I did not do and I have no intention of doing so in the future. There have already been too many bitter attacks delivered on leading figures in the Labour movement. What I did do was to point out that I could not agree with Mr Bevan either in his reason for resignation or in the manner in which he made it, but Mr Bevan could do service to the country by using his freedom to help hammer out an original and forceful Labour programme for the next election.[18]

This was an admission that the party singularly lacked such a programme at present and indicated a concern to keep Bevan's undoubted charisma and creativity within the fold. The worry was that – egged on by Foot and other flattering acolytes – he might kick over the traces entirely and condemn Labour to the wilderness of opposition. At the height of the resignation crisis, the political columnist of the *Yorkshire Post* wrote a flattering piece naming Jenkins and Crosland as two of the party's up-and-coming intellectuals. Jenkins he described as 'a likeable young man who has not yet allowed early success to go to his head', clearly destined for office 'if the Socialists ever return to power in his lifetime. But the way they are going, it doesn't look as if his chances of ever sitting on the Front Bench are very good'.[19] That was just what Labour's young hopefuls were afraid of.

In the reshuffle following the three resignations it was rumoured that Jenkins might get a job. In fact it was Wyatt who got the nod and became – briefly – Parliamentary Secretary at the War Office. At least in hindsight Jenkins claimed not to have been disappointed, thinking he had probably received enough patronage from Attlee and had plenty of time. But it meant that when Labour finally returned to office under Harold Wilson in 1964 he was not among the handful of MPs with previous experience of office.

In his diary Dalton described Jenkins' dismay at the division in the party, and his attempt to avoid taking sides:

Roy has hated recent atmosphere in the House of Commons so much that he has only gone there to vote. Jennifer is expecting a second baby in a week or so . . . Roy – and many others – have been deeply shocked by Nye and his 'sub-human' performance at Party Meeting.

But already, with Dalton's not-so-subtle encouragement, Jenkins was clear that Gaitskell should be the next leader, bypassing Morrison:

Roy hopes Clem will go on long enough to be able to hand over direct to Hugh. Under Herbert, it would not be a happy Party . . . We agreed that Hugh had, as yet, no Public Face in the Labour Movement in the country, though he had it in Parliament and in public opinion generally. But this would come.[20]

The government struggled on with its tiny majority over the summer until Attlee threw in the towel and called an election on 25 October. Labour pulled itself together sufficiently to fight a good rearguard action, but the political momentum was now with the Tories, exploiting public weariness with socialist austerity under the slogan 'Set the People Free'. In Stechford Jenkins strenuously denied that socialism had 'failed'. On the contrary, he claimed, the Tories were desperate to get Labour out because they had been 'too successful':

Too successful in bringing the poor up and the rich down. Too successful in giving millions of people a new status. Too successful in ending the unemployment queue. Too successful in transforming a Tory Britain into a Labour Britain. That is why they want us to go. Not because we have failed, but because we have succeeded.

Somewhat contradictorily he argued that the Tories had promised not to undo Labour's achievements, while simultaneously accusing them of wanting to turn the clock back to the 1930s. Labour still had much to do, he insisted, which was why the government needed an increased majority.[21] In a newspaper article he clutched a straw of hope from Tory over-confidence and President Truman's unexpected re-election against the odds in 1948.[22]

This was the only election in his life that Roy had to fight without Jennifer beside him. Now with two young children – prominently featured in his election literature – she had her hands full. Hattie came from Pontypool to support him instead. But there was no real need, since Stechford was perfectly safe. One of the local papers described the thirty-year-old Jenkins' confident performance at a crowded meeting at Audley Road school:

Last night one felt that the secret of his success lay in his platform manner. Never once did he talk down to his audience; whether discussing the international situation or home affairs he was always with them and of them, speaking for some 40 minutes without a voice being raised against him.[23]

There was no Liberal candidate this time, so he had a straight fight against the same Tory opponent, Edith Pitt. As a result his majority was slightly cut, though his vote actually went up:

Roy Jenkins (Labour)	34,355
Miss E. Pitt (Conservative)	23,384
Labour majority	10,971[24*]

This closely mirrored the national result. On a slightly reduced (but still 82 per cent) turnout, Labour recorded its highest-ever vote, nearly fourteen million – 200,0000 more than the Conservatives; but by the vagaries of the electoral system the Tories won twenty-six more seats. By this ambiguous verdict the seventy-seven-year-old Churchill was returned to Downing Street, flanked by the much younger Anthony Eden and Rab Butler and several of his wartime cronies. Despite Labour's divisions, few imagined that the party would be out of office for thirteen years.

* Edith Pitt went on to become MP for Edgbaston from 1955 to 1962. She held several junior offices under Eden and Macmillan, became a Dame in 1962 and died in 1966.

On the contrary, such was the left's faith in the inevitable march of progress that they took it for granted that Labour would be back very soon. *Tribune* thought it 'a tragedy that Labour's period of government has been interrupted' by what it called Churchill's 'stopgap administration'; while Attlee expected to be Prime Minister again within two years.[25] The civil war that convulsed the party for the next four years was so bitter precisely because both sides – Bevanites and Gaitskellites – believed they were fighting to set the agenda of the next Labour government. Though Attlee and Morrison remained as leader and deputy leader, much of the burden both of opposing the government and of preparing for Labour's anticipated return to office fell upon Gaitskell, who was almost the only senior figure to emerge from the party's defeat with his reputation enhanced and his energy undimmed. Though only forty-four, he had enjoyed a rapid rise to the second position in the government as the old warhorses – Bevin, Cripps and Dalton – had died or retired. Hitherto a prim and somewhat donnish figure, he had displayed in his showdown with Bevan a new assertiveness which led the powerful right-wing union bosses – pre-eminently Arthur Deakin, Sir Tom Williamson and Will Lawther, leaders respectively of the Transport & General Workers, the Boilermakers and the Miners – to embrace him as the champion they had been looking for. He now had an extraordinary opportunity to shape the party's future, and in his quiet way he was determined to seize it.

Jenkins had been impressed by Gaitskell's cool handling of his dispute with Bevan and became a Gaitskellite almost overnight, though it took a little longer before he was drawn into his inner circle. During the last months of the Labour government he made a number of strongly supportive speeches in economic debates which earned Gaitskell's gratitude; then when the party went into opposition he took a hard line in favour of withdrawing the whip from fifty-seven left-wingers who voted against the Tory government's defence estimates, and quickly emerged as a reliable voice against the Bevanites in party meetings. 'Chris [Mayhew], Woodrow, Tony and Roy have all done well,' Gaitskell noted in March 1952, 'and thus set an example to others.'[26] As an economic specialist, Jenkins was thus an obvious pick for the small team (also including Crosland) that Gaitskell assembled to fight Butler's first budget. His particular contribution was to lead the attack on what he later called 'a complicated piece of window dressing' known as the Excess Profits Levy, which was supposed to claw back some of the easy profits generated by the rearmament programme. Though Labour might have been expected to applaud such a measure, Jenkins persuaded his colleagues that it was at best a marginal sop in the context of a broadly regressive budget, and devoted the whole of April and May to fighting it – gathering support, briefing interested parties, drafting and moving amendments, and conducting guerrilla warfare through eight long nights on the floor of the House. This, he recalled, involved 'more detailed parliamentary drudgery . . . than I had ever done before or was ever to do again . . . When this part of the Finance Bill came to be debated I think I understood it more completely than did the then Chancellor and more completely than I was ever to understand any complicated part of a Finance Bill which I was to introduce myself nearly two decades later.'[27] So it was a good apprenticeship. A warm cross-party camaraderie develops over the course of such campaigns, and one night there was some bantering disagreement between Jenkins and Crosland about the meaning of a particular clause, to the amusement of the Tories, before Gaitskell intervened to explain that they were both right.[28] Another time the future Tory Chancellor Reginald Maudling gracefully complimented the 'joint eloquence' of the Members for Stechford and South Gloucestershire, 'to which this Committee have now become fairly well accustomed. Their eloquence and persuasiveness is well known.'[29] Not for the first or last time, they made an effective double-act: Crosland the more brilliant, Jenkins more painstaking. They did not of course defeat the bill. But they made a thorough nuisance of themselves, helped to raise Labour morale and confirmed their own growing reputations. 'Tony and Roy have been magnificent,' Dalton wrote after one all-night sitting, 'and quite established themselves.'[30]

It was while working together on the 1952 Finance Bill that Jenkins got to know Gaitskell well. 'Private relations were very close amongst the group,' he later wrote, 'and Gaitskell could be treated with as much mocking but friendly disrespect as anyone else.'[31] He had already been impressed politically by Gaitskell's seriousness and integrity; now he was still more captivated by his private gaiety and his determination to enjoy a social life beyond politics, which matched Jenkins' own widening sense of priorities. Their friendship, he wrote on Gaitskell's death, 'although it arose out of politics, was not primarily a political one'.[32] Around this time he became a member of XYZ, the economic dining club founded by Dalton and others before the war, which now brought together people like Douglas Jay and Patrick Gordon Walker of Gaitskell's own generation, a number of academic economists and Labour-supporting bankers, and some younger MPs among whom Jenkins and Crosland were the most prominent. From now on Roy and Tony were invariably spoken of together as Gaitskell's brightest young lieutenants, though Crosland was always Gaitskell's favourite, as he was Dalton's: though he had outgrown his youthful homosexuality (he married his first wife in 1952), there was still about him a trace of that sulphurous homoeroticism that had dazzled Roy at Oxford. Wyatt wrote opaquely that between Gaitskell and Crosland there was a bond 'which Socrates would have understood';[33] and Jenkins wrote in his memoirs that 'In my retrospective view, with both of them long dead, Gaitskell was more excited by the idea of Crosland than he was by the idea of me, but found me rather easier to deal with. As a result he saw about an equal amount of one as of the other, but mostly though not always separately.' At the same time he and Tony 'saw at least as much of each other as either did of Gaitskell, and when one of us disagreed with him we were mostly united.'[34]

Labour's 1952 conference, held that year for the first and only time at Morecambe, was the most poisonous ever. Several Bevanite motions – reaffirming the principle of a free Health Service and the nationalisation of 'key and major industries' – were carried against the platform; and others more extreme (including one advocating strikes to bring down the government) won significant support. Speakers from the right were jeered and booed; while in the voting for the constituency section of the National Executive the Bevanites swept six of the seven places, with Morrison and Dalton kicked off, to be replaced by Wilson and Crossman. (Gaitskell got barely half the vote of Crossman, the lowest elected Bevanite.) The atmosphere, in Michael Foot's words, was 'rowdy, convulsive, vulgar, splenetic'.[35] To the left, this was simply the grass roots asserting themselves against a complacent and out-of-touch leadership corrupted by the compromises of office. To the right it was an irresponsible eruption which threatened the very survival of Labour as a party of government. Two days later, in a speech at Stalybridge on his way home, Gaitskell hit back, alleging that 'about one-sixth of the Constituency party delegates appeared to be Communists or Communist-inspired' and declaring that it was 'time to end the attempt at mob rule by a group of frustrated journalists' – he mainly meant *Tribune* – 'and restore the authority and leadership of the solid sound sensible majority of the movement'.[36] If there was a moment when Gaitskell cast off his previously donnish image and declared himself a future leader, this was it.

Jenkins was enthusiastically behind him. The day the conference ended he asked Gaitskell to attend a meeting he was trying to organise 'from our point of view' in Birmingham, to counter a successful Brains Trust which the Bevanites had held earlier in the year, assuring him that the local leaders, 'who were rather wobbly beforehand, have been so shocked by Morecambe as to be driven very hard our way – I don't want them to be discouraged'.[37] Like Gaitskell, he had great faith in the fundamental good sense of ordinary members of the party, if firmly led. He also had, already, an unusual sense of the need to appeal beyond Labour's traditional base. Since the beginning of the year he had been working on a little book entitled *Pursuit of Progress*, designed as a counter to Bevanism. His theme was that Labour, having achieved its historic breakthrough in 1945, must not now, as the Bevanites appeared to want, regress to it origins as a purely class party, but must face up to the problems and responsibility of remaining a party of government, representing the whole left-leaning half of the electorate. He had been developing this idea in articles and speeches to various audiences since 1950, even including a talk on Finnish radio. Labour's problem was that between 1945 and 1951 it had achieved its first tranche of objectives: nationalisation of key industries, full employment, the National Health Service, social security and a good start in reducing poverty and inequality. The question was what to do next: how to win the voters' continued support for progressive policies when the worst injustices of unemployment and the Means Test had been removed and most people were so much better off than before the war. In a letter to Dalton, Jenkins used a slightly bizarre analogy which some of their colleagues might have considered frivolous. 'Most people,' he wrote, 'will go to more trouble to get rid of a shoe that pinches than save up for a trip to Naples.' (Why Naples, one of the poorest cities in Europe, except that he had recently been there and evidently saw it as an epitome of a post-war *dolce vita*?) 'We have helped people to get rid of their pinching shoes, but it is at least possible that they will not allow us to conduct them to Naples.'[38] Socialism, on this analogy, was a sort of mass charabanc trip to the continent!

In fact the domestic agenda set out in *Pursuit of Progress* was still pretty radical. There was some retreat from his earlier proposal to confiscate private fortunes at a stroke: redistribution, he now conceded, might have to spread over a generation, but the objective was unchanged. Likewise, Jenkins no longer wrote of abolishing the public schools, only of making the state system so good that it would be able to absorb them. But while he took a swipe at 'those who regard nailing one's colours to the mast of nationalisation, without much regard to what it is designed to accomplish, as an infallible proof of robust radicalism', he remained committed to greatly increased public ownership as a means of promoting equality:

It is quite impossible to advocate both the abolition of great inequalities of wealth and the acceptance of a one-quarter public sector and three-quarters private sector arrangement. A mixed economy there will undoubtedly be, certainly for many decades and perhaps permanently, but it will need to be mixed in very different proportions from this.

Whether it would require 'a thirty per cent, fifty per cent or seventy per cent public sector' it was impossible to say. 'The answer will become clearer as the goal is approached.' This was a very characteristic formulation: whether in the advancement of socialism, the unity of Europe or the evolution of the SDP–Liberal Alliance Jenkins always believed the direction of advance was more important than spelling out a precise goal. But in 1953 he still insisted that 'the whole concept obviously demands a much more vigorous and far-reaching nationalisation policy' than the vague list of criteria on which Labour had fought the 1951 election. While tolerating 'the indefinite continuance of some form of private enterprise', he took for granted the government's responsibility to plan the economy as a whole.[39]

It was rather in foreign policy that Jenkins directly confronted the Bevanites – in particular their continuing sentimentality towards the Soviet Union, their ambivalence towards the United States, and their hankering for a 'socialist' foreign policy that would seek a neutral posture between the two. For Jenkins, as for Gaitskell, one of the Attlee government's greatest achievements was Ernest Bevin's unswerving alignment of Britain with the United States in NATO, repudiating, in the face of the Soviets' brutal crushing of democracy in central Europe, the wishful 'left can talk to left' naivety with which the party had come to power. Critical as he was of American capitalism, he recognised that the US was at least a democracy, and therefore capable of evolving towards socialism, whereas the USSR was a thoroughly unsocialist tyranny. He was as realistic about Russia as he was optimistic about America:

> If it is thought that the most difficult task of modern socialists is not so much the undermining of capitalism (which is happening in any event) as the prevention of its development into a horrid managerialism, of which the hallmarks will be the centralisation of power and the existence of grossly privileged groups, the Soviet system has little to its credit beyond that of being somewhat ahead in the race to beastliness.[40]

Capitalism, he implied, was doomed anyway: the battle of the future was between democratic socialism and 'horrid managerialism'.

Meanwhile neutralism was not an option for a progressive party:

> Neutrality is essentially a conservative policy, a policy of defeat, of announcing to the world that we have nothing to say to which the world will listen . . . Neutrality could never be acceptable to anyone who believes that he has a universal faith to preach. And those countries which have successfully adopted it in the past have paid the price of becoming little islands full of frustrated hedonists. Switzerland and Sweden are as ideologically sterile as they are physically undevastated.[41]

Here, for the first time in Jenkins' writings, is a hint of the theme that would define his career over the next half-century. The idea of a 'socialist' foreign policy was a delusion based on an outdated view of Britain's place in the world: 'a subconscious faith in the omnicompetence of British policy . . . the essential foundation of utopianism'.[42] In 1953 the idea of the European Common Market was only just beginning to take shape; and for some years yet Jenkins adhered to the conventional view that Britain could not think of joining it. But this passage shows him already seeking the appropriate vehicle for Britain's engagement with the modern world.

Having rejected neutralism, he continued, Labour must also reject its lingering pacifism and accept the need for defence expenditure commensurate with Britain's reduced but still significant weight as a middle-ranking power. The spectacle of the Minister of Defence, Emanuel Shinwell, being voted off the National Executive in 1951 to salve the left's guilt about armaments exemplified the party's confusion. It was an honourable part of the Labour tradition to be suspicious of the use of force; but it was unrealistic to pretend that the ability to exert any influence in the world did not require a military capacity. If Labour was to be a governing party again, and not a permanent opposition, the leadership must be ready to take on the neutralists and pacifists. It was better to face a temporarily damaging split in the short term than risk 'the destruction, by schism, perhaps for a generation, of the whole progressive movement in the country'.[43]

'The whole progressive movement in the country': this was what Jenkins thought Labour now was and must take care to remain. After a messy period of transition between the wars, he believed that Attlee's Labour party had taken over from the Asquithian Liberal party as the embodiment of the non-Conservative half of the electorate. In the penultimate chapter of *Pursuit of Progress,* entitled 'The Swinging Pendulum', Jenkins argued that defeat in 1951 should not be seen as a setback for Labour. The voters would always tire of any government, but the Tories habitually prospered by adopting their opponents' policies. Socialism would advance not smoothly but by fits and starts, punctuated by periods of Tory government which would not reverse Labour's achievements, but merely give Labour time to prepare the next advance. Labour did not have to be in power all the time, but should accept this pattern of advance. 'The confident heyday of capitalism will recede still further as time goes on,' he blithely predicted, but the Tory party was resilient. 'It may well survive the transition to a classless society and a largely non-capitalist pattern of production with little more difficulty than it survived the nineteenth century shift in the social balance.' Accordingly Labour should have confidence in its own ideas and 'devote more time to leadership and less to the anxious study of the Gallup polls'. It should show 'a philosophical acceptance of the fickleness of the electorate combined with a determination to use periods of power, when they occur, to the greatest possible advantage'.[44]

'The first duty of a party of the left,' he concluded, 'is to be radical in the context of the moment, to offer the prospect of continuing advance, and to preserve the loyalty of those whose optimistic humanism makes them its natural supporters.'[45] 'Optimistic humanism' was another characteristic formulation which described his political mindset for the rest of his life. In 1953 he still called it 'socialism', but increasingly it was 'radicalism', 'progress' or simply 'reform'. The essential divide, on this view, was temperamental rather than doctrinal, between the selfish-defensive pessimism of Toryism on one side and liberal-socialist-progressive optimism, under whatever label, on the other: a belief, not in the perfectibility of man (the preserve of utopian revolutionaries), but in the possibility of society being improved by rational action in gradual steps. It was a simple philosophy, arguably a woolly one, certainly not intellectual, but essentially pragmatic. Thirty years later, as leader of the SDP, Jenkins was still offering the country the same hazy combination of 'hope and realism' or – in an echo of Gladstone – 'conscience and reform'. The specific content of his policies evolved over the intervening years as the march of socialism was halted and capitalism made an unexpected comeback. He admitted in 1981 that he had not used the word 'socialism' for years. He generally called himself a liberal, and ended as a Liberal Democrat. But his essential yardstick – 'to be radical in the context of the moment' – was perfectly consistent.

As was normal in those more serious days, *Pursuit of Progress* was widely reviewed in both the national and local press, with an equally wide diversity of judgement on both the style and the content, ranging from the Aberdeen *Press and Journal* ('fresh and interesting') to the Glasgow *Evening News* ('prosy and excessively dull') and the *National and English Review* ('rather sententiously written'). The *Manchester Guardian* somewhat surprisingly thought that 'Some of Mr Jenkins' arguments may seem strong meat for candidates with tender constituencies'; but the Communist *Daily Worker* predictably judged its value 'zero'. In the *New Statesman* Dick Crossman found it 'a little anaemic'; but Jenkins' old tutor Thomas Balogh, in *Tribune,* while not uncritical, welcomed 'a provocative historical analysis of permanent value'. Most balanced was *The Economist,* whose anonymous reviewer judged that, as a miner's son who was also an intellectual, 'Mr Jenkins can look at politics with a detachment rare among members of parliament on either side.' His book, it concluded sagely, was 'an important contribution to contemporary political thinking; that it raises far more questions than it answers is merely symptomatic of contemporary thinking'.[46]

Sixty years on, the unquestioning assumption of a socialist future seems both misguided and painfully naive. But in 1953 – when the Tories too had embraced Keynesian planning – several reviewers questioned what was distinctively socialist about Jenkins' prescription. One, his father's old protégé Ivor Bulmer-Thomas (recently defected to the Tories and writing in the *Daily Telegraph*) wondered if Roy too was in the wrong party, but concluded shrewdly that he did belong with Labour on account of his belief in 'progress': 'The great thing is apparently to keep advancing: it does not seem to matter so much where we get.'[47] Another – the left-wing novelist-MP Maurice Edelman, writing anonymously in the *Times Literary Supplement* – perceptively suggested that Jenkins and the Gaitskellites in general were excessively complacent about the steadily improving future and the ability of the liberal revisionists to keep control of the party if things turned out less comfortably:

For if there is peace [in Korea], accompanied by an American slump with two million unemployed in Britain, will not the Utopians and the nationalisers and the Russia-lovers and all the rest of them once again seek a more radical transfer of power than Mr Jenkins proposes? And even in a less extreme hypothesis, are not Mr Jenkins and the Oxford economists of the Labour movement unduly self-content in a dangerous world?[48]

Time would eventually prove Edelman right; but not just yet.

8 Expanding Horizons

As Labour settled into what turned out to be an eternity of opposition, Jenkins' life expanded enormously. Living was becoming more comfortable as the war receded and the austerity of the immediate post-war years gave way to the growing affluence of the 1950s. As a young MP with the security of a safe seat but no early prospect of office, he could afford to relax and enjoy himself – and he did. His new, more expansive life comprised three distinct strands, which all overlapped and informed one another. He was still first and foremost a conscientious politician whose daily life was centred in Parliament; but he was also developing a successful secondary career as a prolific writer, both of books and journalism, while at the same time beginning to cultivate an extensive social life. Though the balance between them fluctuated, these three elements remained the components of his existence for the rest of his life.

He later claimed to have attended the House 'virtually every sitting day' in these early years.[1] At least up to 1955 the Conservative government's majority was small, and unless paired he was required to be there every day to vote. Like most Members in those days he had no office, but had to dictate his correspondence wherever he could find space in a corridor. But he spent no more time than he could help in the Chamber listening to debates, nor did he serve on any Standing Committees. He was usually to be found in the library researching or writing his articles and books. He spoke in debates about four or five times a year, contributing carefully crafted and well-delivered speeches, almost exclusively on economic and financial matters, and asked questions, usually on technical points about sterling or the Bank Rate. He always spoke in the budget debate, and for a few weeks in the early summer would put aside his writing to focus on the Finance Bill ('For that period I try to be a full-time legislator').[2] He was also careful to raise questions of concern to Birmingham. In May 1952, for instance, he initiated a Friday afternoon debate on lay-offs in the motor industry; and in March 1953 he opened an adjournment debate (at two o'clock in the morning) on unemployment in Birmingham.[3]* Altogether Hansard shows that he spoke a good deal more than Tony Crosland between 1951 and 1955, but much less frequently than Woodrow Wyatt. He was invariably complimented by the next speaker, but his style was already distinctly mannered. One Tory remarked in 1951 that Jenkins combined 'the impetuosity of youth' with 'the gestures of the elder statesman';[4] and in April 1954 Sir Waldron Smithers – an archetypal knight of the shires – offered the usual felicitations with more than usual emphasis: 'I do congratulate the hon. Member on his fluency. I think the way he spoke was wonderful, though I do not agree with him.'[5]

He enjoyed his first distinct parliamentary success in February 1954 when he was chosen to introduce a Labour motion calling for an inquiry into a spate of predatory takeover bids – most prominently Sir Charles Clore's bid for the Savoy Hotel – which, he alleged, were not genuine business developments at all, but 'financial manipulations . . . dealing almost exclusively with quick money returns', which 'put large untaxed capital profits into the hands of certain individuals and undermined the policy of dividend restraint'. The Tory who followed him condemned his 'spiteful and vicious party political propaganda', exemplifying Labour's 'pathological hatred of profit'.[6] But the respected Labour Member for Leeds North-West, Charles Pannell, noted in his local paper that Jenkins spoke with few notes and 'with remarkable authority for a young man. There was wit and polish and a buoyancy about it all.' According to Pannell, he scored a particular hit with a neat riposte to Rab Butler, who had sought to defuse the issue by saying that they should remain 'cool, calm and collected'. 'It seems to me,' Jenkins mocked, 'that Mr Clore and Mr Samuel remained pretty cool, pretty calm and they certainly collected.'[7] Unfortunately this crack does not appear in Hansard; maybe he only made it privately, or on another occasion. Winding up the short debate, Gaitskell repeated Labour's call for an inquiry, but Butler batted it away, and the motion was comfortably defeated.

---

* In what is usually considered a period of full employment, unemployment in Birmingham was just 1.4 per cent compared with a national figure of 2.2 per cent. But this disguised a lot of part-time working.

Jenkins' constituency obligations were not onerous, but he was perfectly assiduous by the standards of the time, when MPs were not expected to spend much time in their constituencies, still less live there. (In his autobiography Roy Hattersley remembered a newly elected Member for Sheffield in 1950 promising to visit the constituency every three months – and this being taken as a very handsome commitment.)[8] Jenkins normally went to Stechford one weekend and one other evening every month to do a 'surgery' with his new agent, Harold Nash, and attend church bazaars, school prize-givings and the like; but there was no demand for political meetings, so he rarely had to make a serious speech. Each September he would pay a longer visit of seven to ten days – more from habit than because it was very useful. Members for rural seats, he wrote in a newspaper article at the time, used to tour the outlying villages of their constituencies:

But my constituency has no villages. It is a suburban chunk of a very big city, and, apart from elections, three public meetings a year, at selected points, cover it quite adequately. I therefore spent my time, not in addressing the public, but in holding policy discussions with the active members of my local party and in talking over administrative problems – housing, education and the like, with the members and officials of the vast Birmingham municipality.

This year (1952), however, 'lacking . . . the nervous stimulus of an election atmosphere', he confessed to finding 'ten days a long time'.[9] No doubt that feeling grew over the next decade. Visiting Washington for the first time in 1953 and finding most of the Congressmen and Senators out of town, he commented unfavourably on the 'excessively close attention to their constituencies which the American system demands', clearly grateful that the same was not expected of British MPs.[10]

In twenty-six years Roy and Jennifer never bought a home in the constituency and no one ever suggested that they should. He – and more rarely she – used to stay with Austin and Dora (Dink) Hitchman and their two daughters, all of whom became good friends. Austin Hitchman was a skilled craftsman – he serviced bakery ovens, not in Birmingham alone, but all round the country; they were Labour members, but not very politically engaged, so they kept Jenkins relatively insulated from local rivalries, which was as he liked it. He enjoyed businesslike relations with the city councillors – in those days major local dignitaries who jealously guarded their independence of central government. 'The town clerk and the other major officers were figures of great, rather frosty authority,' he recalled, who did not expect their MPs to interfere in local matters.[11] He gave advice when asked, and always came up for the local elections, but that was all. In return, the local party largely respected his freedom of conscience on national issues. His only moment of real difficulty came over German rearmament in 1954. Since 1950 the Labour leadership, in government and then in opposition, had reluctantly accepted the need for rearming West Germany under NATO; but the left – supported by some violently anti-German right-wingers like Dalton – was strongly opposed, and the issue provoked several backbench rebellions. The Stechford party was unanimously Bevanite on this as on other matters, and in March 1954 Jenkins faced a showdown with his activists, with the real possibility that he might be disowned. But he took the argument boldly to them, persuaded them to respect his right to differ and won by thirty-two votes to two. This meeting, he confessed in his memoirs, was 'a watershed. Before it, I had been rather nervous of the Stechford party; after it I was not.'[12] He had no more trouble with his constituency until the 1970s when the character of the Stechford constituency party, like others, began to change.

After only five years as a Birmingham MP, following the 1955 election, Jenkins was elected chairman of the Birmingham group of Labour Members, succeeding Victor Yates, the Member for Ladywood, one of seven Bevanites suspended the previous year for voting against German rearmament.* Woodrow Wyatt in one of his many memoirs claimed that Jenkins virtually asked his permission to stand. 'You're playing for the big stakes aren't you? Do you mind if I stand . . . ? I think it is more important to me than to you.'[13] If true, this would suggest a surprising diffidence on Jenkins' part. But the story is nonsense, since Wyatt had lost his Aston seat through redistribution earlier that year, so was not eligible to stand. The *Birmingham Gazette* saw Jenkins' election as 'a tribute to the esteem in which he is held, since he does not live in Birmingham'; whereas Yates was a habitual rebel, Jenkins was 'known as an unswerving supporter of the official leadership and policy of the Labour Party'.[14] But some already recognised him as more than

* Labour held eight of the thirteen Birmingham seats in 1955, but the MPs were an undistinguished lot. Jenkins apart, the only one of any note was Denis Howell (Small Heath), a former football referee who achieved brief fame as minister for the weather in the 1970s. Their calibre increased in the 1960s with the election of Brian Walden (All Saints) and Roy Hattersley (Sparkbrook).

that. The political correspondent of the *Birmingham Mail* hoped to see Jenkins and the young Tory Member for Handsworth, Sir Edward Boyle, rising together to the leadership of their two parties. 'The fancy is tickled by the prospect of these two Birmingham members, each with a political lifetime stretching ahead, forming a kind of Gladstone–Disraeli rivalry throughout the decades of the mid-twentieth century in the Commons.'[15] Boyle indeed rose rapidly to the Cabinet, but sadly for this prediction chose to leave politics in 1969, just as Jenkins was reaching the top.

Years later Jenkins had to write to the press to deny a persistent story that he disliked Birmingham and breathed a sigh of relief each time he left it: on the contrary, he insisted, what he missed on leaving Parliament in 1976 was not the House of Commons, but his constituency – by which he meant some of the people in it, the Hitchmans, the Balmers and some others.[16] In truth there was little to love in Stechford itself, or in Birmingham, which at the end of his life he described coolly – and slightly egotistically – as 'a very worthwhile place to represent'.[17] He liked to play with the idea that Birmingham was a 'border town', equidistant between the North, the South and Wales (which suited his own ambivalence), and all Brummies therefore immigrants: Welsh, Scots, Irish and, increasingly by the 1960s, Caribbean and Asian. But he felt for Birmingham none of the real affection he later felt for Glasgow, Hillhead. Nevertheless he was 'deeply grateful' to the city and the constituency not only for sustaining his career for a quarter of a century but for allowing him to be – as he put it in 2002 – 'a latter-day example of that now distinctly endangered species the part-time MP'.[18]

The other half of his working life was writing. Once he had secured his future in politics, Jenkins was keen to have another string to his bow, partly to supplement his income, but also to stave off boredom and give himself another interest – though since almost all his writing was about politics, it was more of a busman's hobby than a complete contrast. But he was already determined not to be confined by politics. In 1951 he admired the effortless way Dalton seemed to manage his departmental work ('He thought I was exceptional among ministers', Dalton recorded, 'in wanting to read books, meet people and go to places unconnected with my Department').[19] This was a model Jenkins would try to emulate when he held office himself. Throughout the 1950s and 1960s he made a point of reading widely – not only history and politics, but contemporary fiction: he kept up with the latest works of all the leading novelists of the day, Evelyn Waugh and Anthony

Powell being his particular favourites, as well as continuously revisiting Proust. He also discovered that he was a compulsive writer, and once he had got the habit he was, for the rest of his life, almost never without a book on the go, except for the relatively few years when he was in office, producing eventually some twenty-three titles as well as a continuous outpouring of journalism. No other front-rank politician besides Churchill has ever written so much – or so well.

His first historical book, following his worthy but dull Attlee biography, was an elegant short account of the House of Lords crisis of 1911 which came out in February 1954. He had been working on it for some time, but put it aside in 1952 to write *Pursuit of Progress*. Like most of Jenkins' books, *Mr Balfour's Poodle* was based entirely on secondary sources – the biographies of the leading personalities, supplemented by Hansard and the *Annual Register*. Nevertheless in the period just before the explosion of academic history that followed the expansion of the universities and the opening of official papers in the late 1960s, it was quite an original venture and enjoyed considerable success. It was historical, but described events of only forty years before with unmistakable contemporary resonance. It indulged Jenkins' identification with the Edwardian period, but at the same time underlined his view of Attlee's Labour party as the natural inheritor of Asquithian Liberalism, while the Tories of 1950 were implicitly the lineal descendants of the ermined reactionaries of 1910. This continuity was explicitly spelled out in an appendix comparing the seats won by the Liberals in 1906 with those won by Labour in 1945. The title – derived from Lloyd George's famous gibe that the House of Lords, far from being 'the watchdog of the constitution', had been reduced to the Leader of the Opposition's 'poodle' – was criticised by some reviewers as too flippant, and some bookshops allegedly shelved it under 'pets'. But it was generously praised by A.J.P. Taylor, Harold Nicolson and Leonard Woolf, among others, and also by Asquith's daughter, the redoubtable Lady Violet Bonham Carter, who reviewed it in the *Observer* and wrote to her son Raymond: 'It is by a young Labour MP called Roy Jenkins & is extremely good reading, very amusing & very pro-Father.'[20] *Mr Balfour's Poodle* established Jenkins' reputation as a serious popular historian overnight. It did not sell particularly well – it earned him just £247 at the time – but it was republished at regular intervals and remains in print to this day.

Its success led immediately to his next project. He was actually already in negotiation with Heinemann to write the official biography of Ernest Bevin, who had died in 1951. He had been approached by

Arthur Deakin, Bevin's successor as boss of the TGWU, and was initially 'flattered and excited' by the idea, which was for a major project in several volumes, to be financed by the union.[21] But the negotiations stalled over Deakin's insistence on retaining an unacceptable degree of editorial control. Jenkins soon came to realise that Bevin was not really his sort of subject – in fact a less suitable subject can hardly be imagined, trade union affairs not being among his interests – while Deakin began to wish he had commissioned Alan Bullock (as he eventually did) instead. So Jenkins was already looking for a way out when he was offered, out of the blue, a much more attractive alternative.

Following the launch of *Mr Balfour's Poodle* he and Jennifer were dining at the House of Commons with Tony and Caroline Wedgwood Benn when Mark Bonham Carter, who was dining at another table with his brother-in-law Jo Grimond, approached him to suggest that he should write a biography of the Victorian radical Sir Charles Dilke. This was a turning point in Jenkins' life. Bonham Carter was Asquith's grandson; he was also a director of the publisher William Collins. He and Jenkins had overlapped at Balliol, but Bonham Carter was two years younger and they had not been friends. Now, however, when Jenkins jumped at the Dilke commission, Bonham Carter became not only his publisher for the next thirty years, but one of his closest friends, as well as a useful link to the Liberal Party, which was still dominated by the Asquith connection.*

Dilke was a wonderful subject, not primarily because he was an important figure in late-Victorian politics, a Cabinet minister under Gladstone and an ally and rival of Joseph Chamberlain, but because his career was wrecked by a sensational divorce scandal. Jenkins quickly read up on the case and accepted Bonham Carter's invitation to jump ship. His contract, signed in June 1954, required him to deliver the book in eighteen months for an advance of £500. Collins were to have his next book too, unless it was a biography of the French socialist Leon Blum for Weidenfeld – another idea he had evidently been considering.[22] In fact it took him twice that time. This time he did use unpublished sources – Dilke's private papers, which were left by his executrix to the British Museum and only opened, under the terms of her will, in 1955. He thus had the biographer's dream: a cache of previously unseen material, as well as all the ingredients of a sexual

---

* The Liberals then had just six MPs and the party was very close to extinction; more than anyone else, Jo Grimond, who became leader in 1956, kept the flame alive and laid the foundation of its steady revival over the next half-century. He was married to Mark Bonham Carter's sister, Laura.

whodunnit to spice up the politics. Dilke was in many ways an admirable and interesting figure, but his biography would not have been a commercial prospect were it not for the scandal that brought him down.

He had been well placed as a possible successor to Gladstone when he was accused, in July 1885, of having had an affair lasting some two and a half years with the young wife of a Liberal lawyer named Donald Crawford, who sued for divorce, naming Dilke as co-respondent. There was no substantial evidence against Dilke except Mrs Crawford's uncorroborated word; but her story was highly circumstantial and included the titillating detail that their intercourse had sometimes included a third party – a servant girl named Fanny – 'all three in a bed together'.[23] Dilke strongly denied the allegation. But his counsel decided not to put him in the witness box, since he *had* enjoyed other affairs (including one with Mrs Crawford's mother) which might have been revealed in cross-examination. In law his failure to give evidence did not count against him. The judge ruled that Dilke had no case to answer and dismissed the case against him; but at the same time he granted Crawford his divorce. This ambiguous result might have satisfied a private individual, but to a prominent politician whose name had been already dragged through the newspapers it was worse than useless. 'The verdict,' as Jenkins wrote, 'appeared to be that Mrs Crawford had committed adultery with Dilke, but that he had not done so with her.'[24] Public opinion, fanned by the pioneering investigative journalist W.T. Stead, assumed him to be guilty.

Dilke had the case reopened, without success, and spent the remainder of his life collecting evidence to discredit Mrs Crawford's story. He did actually succeed in resuming his political career; but he never held office again and was effectively ruined. There was in truth ample evidence that Mrs Crawford was a malicious fantasist who had relations with numerous other men but chose to accuse Dilke – for reasons unexplained – in order to secure a divorce from her husband. By his other irregular liaisons, however, Dilke had laid himself open to an accusation that he could not disprove. It was an extraordinary story, with wider political ramifications. It was whispered that either Lord Rosebery or Joe Chamberlain (supposedly Dilke's closest ally) was behind the conspiracy to destroy his rival: both had curious dealings with Mrs Crawford. In his biography Jenkins was forced to conclude that the truth will never be known; but not before he had spent 150 pages – two-fifths of his book – scrupulously examining and testing the various allegations and hypotheses. No detail was spared, yet he contrived to treat the subject with perfect taste, for which the *Times'* anonymous reviewer was profoundly grateful:

> Everyone who was aware of the extraordinary facts of Dilke's life knew that once the papers could be got at there would be a sensational biography. It might well have been a pornographic one . . . One shudders to think what treatment this Life might have been given had it got into the hands of a brash biographer. Happily Mr Jenkins has treated it in just the right way.[25]

The book, published in October 1958, reads quite dully today, but at the time it attracted enormous interest. Of all the generous reviews, perhaps the most gratifying was A.J.P. Taylor's in the *Observer*:

> Mr Jenkins is an admirable writer who gets better with every volume that he produces. No Member of Parliament spends his time more rewardingly. Instead of gossiping in the smoking room, he works in the library; and puts every reader increasingly in his debt . . . If all Members of Parliament were as gifted as Mr Jenkins, professional writers would have reason to worry.[26]

In addition, Jenkins received dozens of letters – from friends, from the great and good and from members of the public – congratulating him and offering new theories or titbits of evidence. He replied to them all. The Irish historian, diplomat and politician Conor Cruise O'Brien wrote that he believed Chamberlain was behind the conspiracy to ruin Dilke. Jenkins replied: 'I agree entirely with what you say in this respect, but I could not tie up the details in a way to make me feel at all convinced that he was behind the whole matter.' But he did not exclude it.[27] Forty years later, when he contributed the Dilke entry to the new *Dictionary of National Biography*, Jenkins still acknowledged 'considerable circumstantial evidence' against Chamberlain, 'but an absence of a convincing motive'.[28] Ultimately, therefore, the story was frustratingly inconclusive. Meanwhile the mystery was made into both a television drama and, in 1964, a successful stage play, which ran for a year in the West End (under the title *Right Honourable Gentleman*) starring Anthony Quayle and Anna Massey. Jenkins received no money from this, though the play was clearly based on his book, but decided not to sue.

The second strand of his writing was journalism. During his first three years in Parliament he had written about once a month for

Tribune and occasionally elsewhere, mainly on economic subjects; but between 1951 and 1956 he enjoyed a wonderful opportunity to learn the harder discipline of writing a weekly column for an Indian paper called *The Current*, published in Bombay by a wealthy anti-Nehru MP, D.F. Karaka, who had been president of the Oxford Union in 1934 and married Roy's cousin, Connie Peppin (now known as Pita). It was a bizarrely Anglophile publication, which billed itself (despite copious glamorous pin-ups of Western film stars) as 'The Paper That's Read in *Clean* Indian Homes' and claimed a circulation of 'under 1,000,000'. Puffed as 'one of the most brilliant young members of the British House of Commons', Jenkins was paid £5 per column: more important was the chance to hone his journalistic craft, week in, week out, with little likelihood of anyone in Britain reading what he wrote. His audience was assumed to be closely interested in the minutiae of British politics, so much of what he wrote was a commentary on the week's events at Westminster, which he described with a freedom and a satirical edge that he would not have risked in a British publication. A second theme was international affairs: he expatiated with seeming authority about the emergence of Communist China, the French defeat at Dien Bien Phu, the prospects of German reunification, and a good deal about European politics – French, Italian, Yugoslav, all in a rigidly Cold War context – at a time when he never spoke on foreign affairs in the Commons. Finally he gave his readers a commentary on the British social scene, describing phenomena of such burning interest to the Bombay middle class as the Boat Race, 'Teddy Boy' fashion and Princess Margaret's romance with Peter Townsend. These more trivial columns are in fact the ones of most enduring interest. He described the smog in London, the appalling traffic and Britain's terrible roads; the thrilling draw in the Lord's Test of 1953, which brought the House of Commons to a halt; declining standards of crowd behaviour at Wimbledon, with – already – few British players to support; and Billy Graham's latest missionary crusade, which he thought unlikely to succeed, as 'The English do not much like being evangelised'.[29] Whether he actually went to Wembley to witness this event for himself before writing about it, however, must be doubtful. He filed an equally colourful report of the Coronation, describing peers and peeresses in their robes and coronets queuing at High Street Kensington tube station for a special train to take them to the Abbey – although he was actually in Pontypool, convalescing from glandular fever!

This piece contained some interesting thoughts about the new Elizabethan age, however. He anticipated a long reign – he was right there at least – but also major changes to the monarchy that would render the 'semi-feudal splendour' of the Coronation still more incongruous, so that it might be the last ceremony of its kind.[30] In the same vein he used his column to try out his progressive views about controversial social questions which he would shortly make his own: the campaign for equal pay (March 1954); homosexuality (April 1954); the prosecution of leading publishers for obscenity (November 1954); the first Commons vote to abolish hanging (February 1955); and the execution of Ruth Ellis (July 1956). Most characteristically, perhaps, he constantly described the weather – always an obsessive preoccupation. His very first column, in September 1951, set the tone: 'It has been a dismal week, with the worst weather of the summer adding itself to the more serious disappointments of the breakdown of the Korean armistice talks and the failure of the Stokes mission to Persia.'[31] Another, in 1955, began: 'The Christmas weather has been calm and mild; but into the Foreign Offices of the Western World the French National Assembly has injected an atmosphere of storm.'[32] In August 1954 he devoted a whole article to the miserably wet summer and speculated whether it was due to hydrogen bombs, jet aircraft or simply a bad year with seventeenth-century parallels in Pepys' diary. The whole five-year span of these columns adds up to an extraordinarily vivid chronicle of the political and social scene in the early 1950s; it also turned Jenkins into a thoroughly accomplished journalist.

A third genre that he began to develop in these years was travel-writing. The first year he appeared in *Who's Who* (1949) he listed his recreation as 'foreign travel'; and for the rest of his life he was addicted to it, making a point of recording how many times he had visited each country, where he had stayed and dined and what he ate. The apotheosis of this habit was his penultimate book, *Twelve Cities*, published in 2002, in which he stated, among other similar statistics, that he had visited Paris twenty times between 1947 and 1959 and New York nearly 200 times over five decades. Some of these trips were purely recreational, accompanied by Jennifer; but mostly they had some political or journalistic pretext, and he became very good at combining the two. Wherever he went he usually managed to get an article out of it, initially for *The Current*, then later and more lucratively for various British papers. In September 1951 he visited Yugoslavia and opened his report from Ljubljana with a strikingly evocative sentence: 'The season for the starting of European wars is drawing to a close, and the Yugoslavs, more than most peoples, heave a sigh of relief for every week that passes without a Russian move.'[33] In 1953 he went to America for the first time and not only described his general impressions over several weeks in *The Current*, but also wrote a long piece for *The Sphere* about the American iron and steel industry. And later in the decade, in 1958, he visited the Middle East and wrote four partly political, partly descriptive articles for the *Birmingham Mail* – from Kuwait, where he saw the new oil wealth beginning to change the traditional society ('Cadillacs instead of camels');Teheran, which he thought 'a dull city . . . the streets have a nondescript air which I associate with the less attractive parts of Washington'); Beirut, where the leader of the Muslim insurgents received him with 'three tommy guns hanging rather ostentatiously on the wall'; Baghdad ('a hot, sticky, ugly town') and Amman, which 'reminded me more of Ebbw Vale than of a capital city'.[34] His pieces on Jordan and Iraq were reprinted in the *Spectator*.[35] Here, as in some of his more serious columns for *The Current*, one can see Jenkins beginning to fancy himself as a future Foreign Secretary.

His 1953 visit to America opened an important new dimension to his life. He travelled – by sea, arriving in New York on the *Queen Mary*, no less – as part of a US government scheme to bring 'young leaders' to America; and in his case it was money well invested. Hitherto he had been, as he later wrote, 'a young backbencher with few American contacts',[36] a staunch supporter of the Atlantic Alliance, grateful for Marshall Aid but critical of American capitalism. The two months he spent in the autumn of 1953, however, mainly on the East Coast in Washington, New York and Boston, but including a quick swing around the West Coast, the Midwest and the Deep South, 'transformed my thinking and my emotions about the United States'. Since then, he wrote in his memoirs, 'I have believed (probably falsely) that I understood America, and have felt very engaged with it'[37] – an engagement that was not at all diminished by his later commitment to Britain's role in Europe. His understanding was in truth very partial, since the contacts he made were almost entirely with the East Coast Democratic elite. He met the leading liberal Senator of the day, Hubert Humphrey, in Minnesota, and had an hour's interview in Kansas City with ex-President Truman, whom he revered as a great president, but was naively disappointed to find showed 'no evidence of genius, either hidden or overt'.[38] But above all at Harvard he met the historian Arthur Schlesinger and the economist J.K. Galbraith, intellectual pillars of the Democratic establishment who became two of his closest friends: more than anyone else, their friendship enabled him henceforth to feel equally at home in liberal circles on both sides of the Atlantic.

Quite early in his tour, however, he received news of his mother's death – from a stroke at the age of sixty-seven. He had to fly home (from Detroit) for the funeral, but returned the next day to resume his interrupted schedule. As a result he missed out Chicago: an omission he compared to visiting Athens without seeing the Parthenon.[39] He then continued on his way, reporting to *The Current* from Washington (on the ongoing McCarthy hearings and fears of an American slump), from San Francisco (on the West Coast's preoccupation with China rather than Europe) and from Atlanta (on marginally improved conditions for African Americans – by which he meant fewer lynchings, though he was optimistic that 'the discrimination which still exists has only a fairly short life ahead of it'), while never failing to describe the weather: the energy-sapping heat in Washington or the fog in San Francisco.[40] He missed the Labour Party conference, but returned in time for the beginning of the new session of Parliament in November.

Hattie's death made possible a huge change in Roy and Jennifer's family and social life. By the end of 1953 their third child, Edward, was on the way, joining Charles (born 1949) and Cynthia (born 1951). The flat in Cornwall Gardens was not exactly too small for this growing family – it was a big flat, on two floors – but it was increasingly inconvenient. No one wishes their parents' death, but his mother's passing fortuitously enabled Roy to sell Greenlands and look to buy somewhere more commensurate with his expanding lifestyle. They eventually found a tall early-Victorian house in North Kensington, just off Notting Hill Gate. Notting Hill, so expensive today, was then a run-down and still bomb-damaged area – the communal gardens fenced with chicken wire and the houses mainly divided into bedsits. As late as 1967 the *New York Times* described Ladbroke Square, not inaccurately, as 'a comfortable island in the somewhat seedy Notting Hill area of London'.[41] But 33 Ladbroke Square was a fine house and an excellent investment, as more middle-class professional families started to move into the area in the late 1950s and 1960s. Roy and Jennifer bought it for £5,250, but had to spend another £1,750 doing it up. To pay for this Roy negotiated an overdraft of £1,200 with Barclays in Pontypool; Tony Crosland stood guarantor for half of this loan.[42]

They moved in the summer of 1954, shortly before Edward was born. With three young children as well as a large house to run, Jennifer was now primarily a housewife and mother – not at all the life she had imagined during the war. But she was far too energetic and public-spirited to be confined to the home. She had been obliged to give up her job with PEP in 1948, but she had not surrendered her independence: she did some extramural lecturing in the early 1950s and was soon laying the foundation for a remarkable career with a succession of admirable organisations. She was involved with the Consumers' Association from its foundation (by the sociologist Michael Young, a former director of PEP) in 1957, joined the board and in 1965 succeeded Young as chairman. She quickly proved to be a consummate committee woman, and further appointments followed as she had more time: with the Design Council, the British Standards Institution and the Ancient Monuments Society – of which she was secretary (initially from Cynthia's bedroom) in 1972–5 and ultimately president. She also served as a juvenile magistrate (standing aside when Roy was Home Secretary) and much later as chairman of the Historic Buildings Council (now English Heritage) and the National Trust, as well as a director of Sainsbury's and the Abbey National. From the beginning of their marriage, or certainly from the moment Roy got into Parliament, they lived very independent lives: when Roy was not at the House of Commons until all hours he would often be away, in Birmingham or somewhere else around the country or abroad, for politics or pleasure, or the two combined. Yet it remained an exceptionally strong marriage, despite the strains that Roy imposed on it. Jennifer took an active interest in his career, yet allowed him freedom to pursue his own amusements; he relied heavily on her political judgement at every major turning point, while leaving domestic matters – even questions relating to the children – entirely to her. 'It is not a matter of principle to me that the mother should make decisions about the children rather than the father,' he told the *Observer* in 1967, 'but equally it isn't a matter of principle the other way. One thing is right in one family, and another is right in another family. This solution is right in my family, and I am perfectly happy that it should be so.'[43]

It clearly suited Roy; but it also suited Jennifer. Apart from the fact that he was hopelessly impractical – he could not hang a picture, let alone boil an egg – she would not have consulted him on the choice of curtains and he had little interest in looking at alternative schools. This was not unusual: fathers in that generation did not generally change nappies, nor did husbands do the shopping. The demarcation was quite clear: not having to ask him about every domestic decision left Jennifer more time for her own career. Roy confessed some slight guilt at the imbalance. 'I think I get more out of it than my wife does. She helps with my problems more than I help with hers'; but this, he explained, was 'because I respect her judgment so much'.[44] Jennifer always insisted that she was happy with the separation of functions. When asked if she did not have political ambitions of her own, she replied that one politician in the family was enough. But she was never a very hands-on mother. When the children were young they had a succession of au pairs to get them off to school in the mornings: two of the favourite ones with whom the family stayed in touch were German. Jennifer always tried to be home in the afternoons to give them their tea; but then she and Roy went out so much in the evenings that Cynthia once asked her why they had children at all. The strain of combining a young family, an exacting husband and her own career left Jennifer in those years often exhausted.

As the children grew up, Roy was a fairly distant father. In his very last book he wrote that Franklin Roosevelt, 'partly by nature, partly by geography, remained aloof from most of the adolescent problems of his children';[45] he might have been describing himself. Like other ambitious politicians, he was simply not there much of the time; when he was, he was often preoccupied, or just not interested in the concerns of children. When he did give them his full attention, however, he could be great fun. He would take them, individually or with a friend, on outings – to Battersea funfair, Hampton Court maze or the viewing terrace at Heathrow to watch the planes – and embellish their adventures outrageously to Jennifer when they got home. In many ways, Cynthia reflected, he was more like a favourite uncle than a father. As they got older he would treat them as adults and listen seriously to their views, so that the conversation at meals – as Charles recalled at his funeral – was more likely to be about capital punishment or divorce than football or pop music. For family holidays they usually took a large house not too far from London – Sussex or Kent – and invited friends with children the same age to come and stay; they hit on the clever idea of renting a prep school with excellent facilities that they could use: a swimming pool, tennis courts and cricket nets. Roy enjoyed playing games with his children, but he gave no quarter; he was always intensely competitive.* On the other hand, even on holiday he always worked for a good part of the day: he usually had a book in hand – he thought 'a holiday without any work is as barren as a working day without a conversational meal'[47] – and all his life treated holidays as a time to get on with his writing. He would emerge for lunch and

---

* In his memoirs he recalled an epic set of tennis with Charles, then aged thirteen, which Charles won 18–16. 'He had never beaten me before. I never beat him again.'[46] In later years Edward was one of the few people who could beat Roy at croquet.

perhaps play games for a couple of hours, but then go back to work. He never really relaxed for very long.

The three children grew up very different: Charles shy, quiet and intense; Cynthia prickly, with an often embattled relationship with her father; Edward more easy-going than the other two. Charles suffered the most from having a famous father: at thirteen he was sent to Winchester and found it an ordeal. As a reward for surviving his first term Roy took him to Berlin, rather as Arthur had taken him to Paris at a similar age. It was just after the building of the Wall, and the sight of goose-stepping communist soldiers at Checkpoint Charlie inoculated Charles for life against the appeal of the far left. 'That in itself,' Roy wrote years later, 'made the journey well worth while.'[48] He was doubtless comparing Charles with Cynthia, who as an Oxford student at the height of campus radicalism in the early 1970s reacted angrily against his establishment politics, marched against the Vietnam War and threw herself into community activism and the women's movement. Most of the time Roy was quite tolerant of this youthful rebellion and enjoyed winding her up; but it was often difficult for Jennifer, caught in the middle. Charles meanwhile had left Winchester – for purely personal reasons, unconnected with criticism of Labour ministers sending their children to private schools – to go instead to Holland Park comprehensive in Kensington (one of the flagship comprehensives in the country), where he was much happier and met his future wife. It is fair to say, however, that both the elder children found growing up in their father's shadow hard.*

Meanwhile the move to Ladbroke Square enabled Roy and Jennifer to live in the style he thought appropriate to a rising young Member of Parliament. Anthony Wedgwood Benn, as he was then known – who already lived just around the corner in an equally large house in Holland Park Avenue – described Jenkins in 1957 as 'a caricature of an up-and-coming young politician in a Victorian novel';[49] and there is no doubt that Roy was almost consciously playing the part. Another future colleague who had the same impression was Bill Rodgers. Oxford-educated, but still close to his Liverpool roots, Rodgers was rather shocked by his first experience of lunch at Ladbroke Square on Christmas Eve 1956:

---

* Despite Jenkins' earlier disapproval of private education, all three children attended private schools: Cynthia St Paul's Girls' School, and Edward the City of London School. After Oxford, Charles joined the *Economist* Intelligence Unit, where he stayed for his entire career, becoming European editor. Cynthia qualified as a solicitor, worked for some years in community law centres and later for the London Assembly. Edward went to Cambridge and became a barrister, taking silk in 2000.

I like Roy, who improves on acquaintance: and also Jeniffer [*sic*], who seems very English, in the nicest way . . . Roy is working on Edwardian England . . . I think he fancies himself living with some of the elegance of those days. His children have turn-of-the-century names – Charles, Cynthia, Edward: his house is roughly that period (interior – it is rather older in structure): he has slightly studied personal manners – and a furry coat which goes well with a cigar: there was sherry before lunch, wine with and brandy after. All this is perhaps summarised by good living and liberal ideas – in the best sense; both worth a lot . . . But it is *so* different from the envirement [*sic*] of most Labour supporters (as also 99% of the population).[50]

Jenkins had developed a taste for wine while still at Oxford, but he could not afford to drink it regularly until after the war. Ladbroke Square, however, boasted a wine cellar under the pavement, next to the coal cellar, 'so damp and dirty that bringing out a bottle was rather like fetching a sack of damp potatoes'. In a magazine interview in the 1990s he pinpointed a key moment in his life:

Sometime between 1950 and 1955, wine changed from a drink you were pleased to find at a meal, but didn't expect, to something you almost began to expect. And, at that time, I changed from buying it at the local off-licence on the day of the dinner party, to buying wine in advance.[51]

From the beginning he concentrated on claret, calculating that by restricting himself to one region he could build up a serious expertise in a way that he could not if he tried to cover the whole field. Of course the field was relatively limited in the 1950s, before New World or even Spanish wines began to be widely sold in Britain, and the choice of good wine lay pretty much between Bordeaux and Burgundy.

Lunch and dinner parties played a central part in his mock-Edwardian lifestyle. Roy and Jennifer made a point of entertaining a wide circle of political, literary and diplomatic acquaintances: a shrewd mix of old university friends, political colleagues like the Gaitskells and the Jays, and interesting people they wanted to know better, many of whom quickly became friends. One of the latter was Nicholas ('Nicko') Henderson, who was surprised the first time he was invited, since he had known Jenkins only slightly at Oxford, but rapidly became one of his best friends. Another was a dashing young French diplomat, Jacques de Beaumarchais (a descendant of the creator of Figaro), then serving in London, who with his elegant wife Marie-Alice also became lifelong friends. The ground floor dining room could seat ten or twelve, and they held about a dozen dinner parties a year: so even allowing for repeat invitations they must have entertained over a hundred guests a year. Jennifer had help in the kitchen, but even so the food was unpretentious; the wine, the company and the conversation – by no means confined to politics – made up for it. In his memoirs Roy listed those present on what he claimed were two typical evenings in 1955. The first, on 8 February, comprised Jacques and Marie-Alice de Beaumarchais; the zoologist and government scientific adviser Solly Zuckerman with his wife Joan; Thomas Balogh; Woodrow Wyatt; Thea Elliott (wife of Roy's Oxford friend, now in the Foreign Office, Anthony Elliott); and Barley Alison, an unmarried young publisher then with Weidenfeld & Nicolson. The second on 5 October threw together J.K. Galbraith, visiting from the States; the Labour MP Kenneth Younger and the editor of the London *Evening Standard*, Charles Wintour, with their wives; and (on her own) Caroline Wedgwood Benn.[52] Of course such invitations were often reciprocated, so it was an excellent way for a young MP to widen his circle of contacts. Roy also made a point of lunching with someone interesting nearly every day.

One friend whom Roy and Jennifer did not invite to dinner was Tony Crosland. 'Famous for his flounces and his unconcealed disapproval of those he might be asked to meet, he was too hazardous a guest for dinner parties.'[53] 'He used to go on about it,' Jennifer told Nicko Henderson, 'as if he had some mission in life to stop us seeing our friends. In the end I told him not to come any more.'[54] Tony was going through a bad time in the mid-1950s. Probably in an effort to shake off his youthful homosexuality, he had married in 1952 Hilary Sarson, a pretty girl nowhere near his intellectual level. The marriage did not work out and they were divorced in 1957. He also lost his seat in 1955, which at least allowed him time to finish *The Future of Socialism*; but he then fell into a wild period – described by his biographer as 'his Dukes' Daughters period'[55] – when he drank too much while going through a string of glamorous girlfriends. (Woodrow Wyatt wrote that Crosland was successful with girls because he made them laugh; he went to bed with them 'to convince himself that he had triumphed over his homosexual side, which had been in the ascendant at Oxford'.)[56] Wedgwood Benn (whom he had taught at Oxford) attended his divorce party and tutted disapprovingly about the people he met there: 'a sort of rootless crowd of nondescript men and rather sulky women';[57] and the historian A.J.P. Taylor, then married to Crosland's sister, wrote him a well-meant but pompous letter (which Crosland furiously resented) warning him that he was in danger of wasting his great ability.[58] Throughout this period Tony's relationship with Roy was strained, but never broken. In the end he pulled himself together, helped by winning a new seat (Grimsby) at the 1959 election and marrying in 1964 a new wife, the American journalist Susan Barnes, who gave him a stability and (with her two young daughters) a family life that he had never previously enjoyed.

Ladbroke Square was the largest communal garden in London, whose assets included a somewhat soggy grass tennis court; so Sunday afternoon tennis parties, followed by tea, became another feature of Roy and Jennifer's entertaining. Nicko Henderson, in his wry memoir *Old Friends and Modern Instances*, painted a graphic picture of these occasions, when he and Roy used often to play together against Crosland and Douglas Jay. Crosland could evidently be invited more safely to tennis than to dinner; but Jay had his own method of scoring:

> Playing against these two, Roy and I came to realise that many points had to be won twice over. This was so especially following those strokes we thought our best. First we had to get the ball over the net and then, if it was a deep shot to the far baseline, we had to shout 'in' before there was any chance of Douglas giving his contrary verdict upon it. Tony feigned not to mind whether it was in or out. Roy liked this aspect of the struggle. He also relished the chance for backchat and quips that tennis provided . . .
>
> Apart from his interest in the game itself and the complicated task of winning, Roy was, I believe, sensitive, as always to his surroundings. On those late afternoons, he liked the sunset flickering through the trees and the row of houses in the square seen intermittently through the branches. Architecture is one of his realms of acute observation.

Though competitive, Jenkins was a vigorous rather than a stylish tennis player (Jennifer, well coached as a schoolgirl at St Mary's, Calne, was a good deal better):

> If one part of his game could be singled out as even less good than the rest it was his serve. It was an elaborate performance which started with him walking back to the rear enclosure of the

court, then turning round and advancing fast and purposefully to the service line where he would stop abruptly, swing his left arm fiercely, and, with an audible intake of breath, give the ball an almighty blow – the result of which, whether in pace or direction, rarely did justice to the careful preparation and windmill activity that had gone into it.[59]

Woodrow Wyatt was another often invited to play tennis; he had a rather different memory of playing with Crosland and 'one of his ever-changing string of girlfriends, in front of whom he disliked being beaten'.[60] In due course, in the early 1960s, Jennifer raised the money to build a hard court in the Square – almost directly opposite no. 33 – where the tennis parties continued for a time even after Labour came to power in 1964.* But soon after this Roy and Jennifer bought their house in the country, with its own court where the Home Secretary could play without the attentions of photographers. So they never played in Ladbroke Square again.

Jenkins made a point of cultivating a wide acquaintance beyond the narrow world of politics; and it was noted early on – with amusement by his friends, more critically by many in the Labour party – that he had a weakness for aristocracy, which led to accusations that he was a social climber, or a snob. There was undoubtedly some truth in this: he did take visible pleasure in moving in socially exalted circles a long way from his upbringing in Pontypool. But he had no respect for aristocrats as such: he was quickly bored by people he thought stupid, or merely privileged, while politically he was still committed to promoting greater equality.† He liked the company of clever people of any class; but he especially enjoyed the social ease and sophistication that the well-born and well-connected tended to possess. In addition he enjoyed their society because it connected him to the late-Victorian/ Edwardian political world he wrote about in his books and which he liked to imagine himself inhabiting, a world in which great magnates like the Salisburys and Derbys still held enormous sway but the bearers of old names could still be Liberal as easily as Conservative. For the same reason he was irresistibly drawn to the Asquith/Bonham Carter

---

* The author vividly remembers, about 1965, seeing the Minister of Aviation and the Education Secretary (Crosland) with their wives playing together on the new court in Ladbroke Square. Jenkins' idiosyncratic service action was exactly as Henderson described it.
† Reminded many years later that he was always 'very fond of ducal drawing rooms', Jenkins replied: 'Yes, but I was always very choosy about which dukes.'[61]

dynasty. Though not strictly aristocrats, Asquith's descendants were political royalty, and by mixing with them he could feel close to his political model. As early as 1951 Hugh Dalton noted him taking 'an Asquith' to dinner after his speech on Gaitskell's budget.[62]

As a historian Jenkins was fascinated by class, and the subtlety of class gradations. As he grew grander himself, this fascination could become faintly ridiculous. In his 1998 book *The Chancellors*, for instance, he wrote of Sir John Anderson, a man of middle-class background who was much invited to grand houses in the 1930s: 'The Abercorns, the Athlones, the Willingdons were typical hosts, although there was also a leavening of Lady Cunard and Lady Colefax.'[63] Not one in a thousand of his readers would have appreciated the difference; but Jenkins loved these fine distinctions. He was equally precise in calibrating middle-class distinctions too, describing Hugh Dalton and Harold Macmillan, for example, as 'fellow-inhabitant[s] of the no-man's land between the upper and the upper-middle class';[64] and for one who had so recently sought to abolish the public schools, he was curiously fascinated by the supposedly different character of Etonians and Wykehamists, or the pecking order of Old Carthusians and Old Haileyburians. As the son of a sometime miner who had raised himself into the middle class by the time he was born, Jenkins was both acutely aware of class origins and determined to transcend them. He was an observer as well as a participant, like Charles Ryder in Waugh's *Brideshead Revisited*, or Nicholas Jenkins in Anthony Powell's twelve-volume sequence *A Dance to the Music of Time*, which he lapped up as they came out between 1951 and 1975. It was coincidence that Powell's hero was called Nicholas Jenkins, but there is no doubt that Roy Jenkins closely identified with his namesake's journey through mid-century English society.

His enjoyment of contemporary fiction was genuine; but he also relished the sense of straddling the worlds of politics and literature. By 1958 *Mr Balfour's Poodle* and *Dilke* had gained him unimpeachable credentials in an age when history was a more literary genre than it is today. In 1960 he was delighted to be elected a member of the Literary Society, a select dining club founded by Wordsworth and others in 1807 which still met monthly at the Garrick: its membership comprised precisely that social-literary pantheon to which he aspired, from T.S. Eliot and John Betjeman to Harold Nicolson and Kenneth Clark. The last three members elected before him were Anthony Powell, Osbert Lancaster and the Duke of Devonshire; and over the following years most of the leading (male) novelists and playwrights, historians and philosophers, critics and publishers of the day were elected – Kingsley

Roy Jenkins

Amis and V.S. Pritchett, Isaiah Berlin and Robert Blake, Raymond Mortimer and Michael Holroyd – but very few politicians, and those distinctly well-connected: Harold Macmillan, Jo Grimond and (not an obviously literary figure) Alec Home.[65] Jenkins felt as much at home in this company as he did among politicians, and rather more so than he did in the Labour party. Nicholas Davenport, a rare Labour-supporting banker and leading member of the Gaitskellite dining club XYZ, used to entertain weekend guests at his house near Oxford in the mid-1950s:

> Roy and Jennifer Jenkins were among our favourite political guests because they were free from the compulsion to talk politics and really enjoyed talking about art and literature. When politics came up, Roy would always have interesting historical analogies to bring into the argument, for his scholarship was profound and in consequence his political ideas never partisan.[66]

This lack of partisanship should not be exaggerated – Jenkins was still by day a fully engaged Labour politician – but his historical perspective enabled him to make friends easily across the political divide. 'As is so often the case in politics,' he wrote years later of Labour's first Chancellor, Philip Snowden, 'he found it easier to get on with his opponents, while reserving his contempt and even enmity for his honourable friends.'[67] Jenkins did not feel enmity or contempt for many people in his world, but he undisguisedly preferred the company of those who shared and – through their possession of agreeable country houses – helped to feed his increasingly expensive tastes. One such was John Jacob ('Jakie') Astor, the fourth son of Waldorf and Nancy Astor, who was Tory MP for Plymouth, Sutton, and Jenkins' House of Commons 'pair' – that is, they cancelled each other out when both were absent from the House – until he stood down in 1959. Through Jakie, Jenkins got to know the rest of the Astor dynasty: his brothers Bill (the third Viscount, later caught up in the Profumo scandal); David (the editor-proprietor of the Observer); and Michael (also briefly an MP in the late 1940s). Jakie owned a big house at Hatley in Bedfordshire, and from 1961 let the dower house to Roy and Jennifer for holidays and weekends, with use of its large park, including tennis court and swimming pool, where Roy could play at being a country gentleman.

Another important connection was Ann Fleming. Born Ann Charteris, granddaughter of the ninth Earl of Wemyss, married successively to the third Baron O'Neill (who was killed in the war), the second Viscount

164

Rothermere (the owner of the *Daily Mail*) and now (not very happily) Ian Fleming, the creator of James Bond, she was one of those dazzling, witty, but essentially shallow aristocratic women who found her métier as a hostess, entertaining a lively salon of writers, artists and academics, as well as the more interesting politicians, first at her London house in Victoria Square and later at her country house at Sevenhampton in Wiltshire. Though a thoroughgoing Tory and a crashing snob, she enjoyed catching Labour politicians in her net, most prominently Hugh Gaitskell, with whom she conducted a discreet affair from 1956 until his death, but also the rising stars of the party, including both Jenkins and Crosland.* According to one friend, the publisher George Weidenfeld, she liked Roy 'for his urbane conversation and slightly deferential affection', and Tony for his 'acerbic intellect and sheer good looks. She also liked their wives, which was rare.'[69] Crosland lent Gaitskell his Chelsea flat for his assignations with Ann; she allegedly confessed that when in bed with Gaitskell she liked to imagine herself in the arms of the more dashing Crosland.[70] Ann's guilt-free adultery was typical of the smart world in which she lived – an Edwardian world, part aristocratic, part Bloomsbury, to which Jenkins was powerfully attracted and whose relaxed sexual mores he enthusiastically embraced.

From quite early in his marriage he was an unfaithful husband. After the first intensity of their wartime romance the physical side of the Jenkins' marriage was never satisfactory. Like many driven men, Roy was highly sexed. Jennifer was not. She bore him three children between 1949 and 1954, but he was already seeking variety elsewhere, and Jennifer soon accepted – probably with relief – that he should do so, so long as there was no scandal, which there never was because he was not in the normal sense of the word a womaniser. He did not pursue his secretaries. All his extramarital relationships were first and foremost friendships – *amitiés amoureuses*, in which the *amitié* came first and the *amour* was secondary, like the cigar after a good dinner. They were all enduring relationships with mature, sophisticated and intelligent women, and well known to Jennifer. There was no scandal because he was careful to conduct all his affairs within strong marriages which they never threatened to break up; the two most important girlfriends of his middle and later years were the wives of two of his best friends. In the upper-class society of the 1950s and 1960s this was not unusual;

---

* 'Those whom she chose to like adored her,' the biographer Frances Donaldson wrote in her memoirs, 'everyone else disliked her very much because she made no attempt to disguise not wanting to know them. Everyone she did not wish to know was designated "a bore".'[68]

and those who moved in those circles embraced the same freedom from middle-class morality. Gaitskell's affair with Ann Fleming did not endanger his marriage to his wife Dora, nor did it weaken her devotion to his memory after his death. It was pretty well accepted that men had mistresses, and that wives too – once they had borne two or three children – had lovers. Roy and Jennifer were genuinely devoted to one another; but Jennifer accepted that Roy was 'gregarious' and had (like many charismatic politicians, from David Lloyd George to John F. Kennedy and Bill Clinton) exceptional sexual energy. She was actually grateful – 'within limits' – to those who took the burden off her, so long as she liked them, which she generally did, and trusted them not to steal Roy from his primary loyalty to her. It was not perhaps what she had imagined when she married; but it was 'not intolerable'. He in turn said that he 'could not imagine loving anyone who was not very fond of Jennifer'. She put up with it because, with all his faults, she loved Roy, was devoted to his career and enjoyed his company and conversation more than anyone else's; meanwhile he allowed her the independence, as the children grew up, to live her own life and pursue her own career.[71]

His infidelities probably started around 1950 or 1951 – that is, a year or so after Jennifer gave birth to their first child – when he became infatuated with Barley Alison, then a strikingly unconventional young diplomat. Born in Cannes, the daughter of an English mother and Scottish father who had inherited an Australian fortune, educated in France, Australia, Malaya and Kent, Barley had been a debutante in London just before the war, but was then recruited into SOE (the Special Operations Executive) and sent to Algiers, where she worked under Duff Cooper briefing and debriefing the agents who were being landed in occupied France to 'set Europe ablaze'. When Cooper was appointed ambassador to liberated Paris in 1944 he took Barley with him. Despite her lack of formal qualifications she quickly became a Third, then Second Secretary – a rare distinction for a woman in the diplomatic service. In post-war Paris she knew Sartre, Cocteau and Camus, then moved in 1949 to the Foreign Office in London where she continued to mix in literary and artistic circles. It is not clear when she met Jenkins, but a letter she wrote him years later indicates that she knew him before he was thirty, so probably during 1950. Her name starts to appear in his engagement diary from the beginning of 1951. She was petite, dark, quick, exotic and evidently fascinating. By the summer of 1952 Jenkins was writing her passionate letters, some of which survive.

From a holiday cottage on the north coast of Brittany where he was staying with Jennifer and the two children – plus Tony Crosland – he wrote that he thought about her 'almost incessantly', but was careful not to mention her name in conversation.[72] A few days later (by which time he was on his way to give a lecture in Berlin) he told her very frankly what was lacking in his marriage and wondered whether Jennifer knew about Barley or was deliberately closing her mind to the knowledge. He was missing Barley very much and longed to see her again.[73] These letters were addressed to 'my love', but signed off with the same curious calibration of affection as his wartime letters to Jennifer: 'Too much love', 'Quite a lot of love' or 'At best an average amount of love'.[74] By 1953 the affair had cooled, but Roy still saw Barley as a confidante. Touring America that autumn, he wrote her long letters describing his impressions of the various cities he visited. 'Every time I think of a good remark about America I long to have you to make it to. I know this will confirm your view that I merely treat you as an audience, but you are without question the best in the world!'[75] By now Barley seems to have realised that a relationship with a married man who was not going to leave his wife offered her no future; she ended the affair, though Roy tried to keep it going a bit longer. In 1953 she left the Foreign Office and, after a short spell of travel and freelance journalism, went into publishing. She joined George Weidenfeld as his fiction editor and over the following years built up a remarkable list of authors including Saul Bellow, Vladimir Nabokov, Piers Paul Read and Margaret Drabble, until in 1967 she left (taking her authors with her) to set up her own imprint, the Alison Press, as part of Secker & Warburg. Their affair gradually petered out, but she and Jenkins remained good friends. In 1954–5 they still met almost weekly for lunch or a drink or dinner; but Barley would also come to lunch or dinner at Ladbroke Square, where her brother Michael (later a Tory MP) was for some years the Jenkins' basement lodger. She was now a family friend, to the extent that she was godmother to the Jenkins' third child, Edward (born in 1954), and gave them all presents at Christmas.* Barley had several more relationships and some heartbreaks over the years but never married. She remained an extraordinarily original and vibrant figure on the London literary scene, famous both for her parties – she was never without a drink in one hand and a cigarette in the other – and for her devotion to her authors. When she

* A list, in Roy's writing, of Christmas presents received, which has survived among his papers, includes presents from Barley for Roy, Jennifer and the two elder children. 'Soap etc for Jennifer. Cig. holder for me. Snakes + ladders (Ch). Cy. Fish'.[76] It would seem to date from *c*.1955.

died in 1989, aged only sixty-nine, but now a white-haired *grande dame* looking much older than her years – her *Times* obituary celebrated 'one of the most outstanding and enterprising personalities in contemporary publishing'.[77] Jenkins remained on good terms with her to the end and attended her funeral.

Barley Alison was unusual among Jenkins' lovers in that she was not married. All the others were. Another probable early mistress was Helena Tiné, the wife of a young French diplomat based in London in the mid-1950s. She and her husband too became lifelong friends. Many years later, when Jenkins was President of the European Commission, Jacques Tiné was also in Brussels as French Ambassador to NATO, and he and Helena were frequent dinner guests. Jenkins' two most important and enduring extramarital relationships, however, dated from the late 1950s and early 1960s. The first was Caroline Gilmour, the wife of the owner/editor of the *Spectator* and (from 1962) Tory MP, Ian Gilmour. Born Lady Caroline Montagu Douglas Scott, she was the daughter of the eighth Duke of Buccleuch (owner of some 280,000 acres spread over four estates in the Scottish Borders) and an aristocrat to her fingertips – slim, elegant, cool and slightly aloof. The second – a much softer and gentler personality – was Leslie Bonham Carter, the American-born daughter of Condé Nast (founder of the magazine empire), who was briefly married to the second Baron St Just, before marrying in 1955 Jenkins' Balliol contemporary, now his publisher, Asquith's grandson Mark Bonham Carter. Both women in their different ways exemplified the sort of upper-class society that Jenkins now inhabited in his private life when he was not being a Labour MP.

There has been much discussion about whether Gaitskell's secret relationship with Ann Fleming was an appropriate liaison for the leader of the Labour party, and whether it influenced his politics. His most recent biographer, Brian Brivati, insists that Ann 'meant nothing' to him politically. 'The picture of Gaitskell being sucked into a Tory world and turning his back on the class to which he was committed underestimates the man . . . She appealed to another part of himself entirely, and his ability to keep separate people who appealed to different parts of him had been illustrated over and over again in his life.'[78] The same questions have been asked about Jenkins, and in his case it is difficult to be as confident as Brivati is about Gaitskell. For one thing, Gaitskell was a Wykehamist to start with, so he was less likely to be dazzled by upper-class society. For the same reason Gaitskell was always acutely conscious of his need, as a middle-class

Labour leader, to cultivate his working-class support and was assiduous in attending trade union events and conferences – something Jenkins rarely felt the need to do. Jenkins compartmentalised his life only to the extent that he kept Birmingham separate from London. He performed his constituency duties conscientiously; but the rest of his political, literary and social life merged into one quasi-Edwardian round as his political style became self-consciously Asquithian. The widening of his social circle in the 1950s undoubtedly coincided with the dropping of his more left-wing ideas, most obviously towards the public schools. In an article in *The Current* on the defection of the spies Burgess and Maclean in 1955 he went out of his way not to criticise the number of Etonians in the Foreign Office, insisting that Eton was an excellent school and you would find a lot of Old Etonians among successful men in any sphere.[79] In sending his own children to private schools he was by no means unusual in the Labour Party of the day, whose upper ranks from Attlee and Gaitskell down were dominated by public-school boys. Even the grammar-school products like Harold Wilson often sent their own sons to private schools without drawing serious criticism. In that respect Jenkins was no different from many others. 'I do not think it is any worse for a Socialist to do this,' he argued, 'than it was for my father to pay my fees at Balliol before the war.'[80] Nevertheless the impression that the company he kept accelerated his evolution away from socialism is difficult to deny.

Tony Crosland was not best placed to criticise Gaitskell or Jenkins in this respect. But when Susan Barnes reminded him of his own 'Dukes' Daughters period' he explained to her – as she reconstructed his conversation many years later – that there was actually 'a basic difference':

Going to bed with some little actress . . . is hardly likely to affect one's political standpoint. If you choose to associate, as Hugh does, with intelligent people whose political values are the opposite to your own, an insidious erosion of your political values can occur. I mightn't think that if I hadn't seen what's happened to Roy.[81]

Jenkins did have one other interest which helped keep his feet on the ground. From 1953 until he entered government in 1964 he worked about one and a half days a week as a financial consultant for the John Lewis Partnership. This came about at the invitation of John Spedan Lewis, the son of the founder of the firm, who had read *Pursuit of Progress* and been impressed by it – though, according to Susan

Crosland, the job was first offered to Tony, who turned it down.[82] The profit-sharing philosophy of John Lewis made it a suitable sideline for a Labour MP, as well as a useful supplement to his income, as Spedan Lewis made clear in offering Jenkins the job:

> You may, I hope, feel that an inside view of an enterprise of this kind might give some useful light upon pressing and weighty problems of the peaceful evolution of capitalism towards a healthier and more decent society. The supreme purpose of the Partnership's creation was to throw light upon those problems.[83]

In a later letter Lewis hoped that the John Lewis Partnership could 'resemble in a tiny way but to an appreciable extent the Athenian democracy in its best days'.[84] When Jenkins – after consulting his leading supporters in Stechford – accepted, Lewis hoped it would prove 'a useful general experience at your stage in a career of statesmanship'.[85] Jenkins' job, according to the chairman, Sir Bernard Miller, was to attend monthly board meetings and 'give us an intelligent feel of what was happening in the economy, a broad economic picture, if you like'.[86] For this he was paid £1,212 a year, plus a bonus paid in shares, which at the time was more than his parliamentary salary, though the latter rose to £1,250 in 1954 and his literary earnings soon outstripped both. His freelance income in 1955 was already £1,666, rising to £1,838 in 1957–8 and £2,977 in 1959–60. In addition he and Jennifer made £194 in 1955 from letting the basement of Ladbroke Square; and Jennifer contributed small sums (£62 in 1956) in lecture fees. His total income from all sources in the mid-1950s was thus around £3,000 a year (about £60,000 today).[87] For comparison, Cabinet ministers at this time earned £5,000 and the Prime Minister £10,000.

For a few years he employed a literary agent – 'a splendid literary gent of the period, with fine handlebar moustaches and a permanent occupancy of one of the two window tables in the Etoile restaurant' – but soon dispensed with his services and did not acquire another until the 1980s.[88] He paid an accountant, originally based in Piccadilly until she moved to Edinburgh, to handle his finances, but here too he was quite hands-on himself: his personal accounts are detailed and scrupulous, but he did not like paying any more tax than necessary and was constantly challenging the Revenue's demands. He was also in frequent correspondence with his bank manager in Pontypool to renegotiate his overdraft. In July 1957 he assured Mr Dibble, confidently but as it turned out wrongly, that MPs' salaries were likely to be raised again shortly to £1,750 (in fact they were not raised again until 1964). Meanwhile he was owed £100 in repaid Indian income tax (presumably on his earnings from *The Current*); his new book (*Dilke*) was nearly finished; and he would deposit some shares (Hoover and John Lewis). By these means he hoped to keep within his £1,200 limit. Three years later, in 1960, as a result of Selwyn Lloyd's credit restrictions, his limit was cut to £700. Jenkins appealed and requested an increase to £850, which was agreed.[89]

Altogether he lived well, but worked hard for it. The experience of sustaining a comfortable lifestyle by supplementing his parliamentary salary mainly by writing gave him a special insight, years later, when he came to write his biography of Churchill: he devoted a whole chapter, which other writers might not have done, to Churchill's unending struggle to maintain Chartwell and support his family in the 1930s by a 'frenzy of authorship and journalism'.[90] Neither Jenkins' earnings nor his outgoings were on Churchill's scale; nevertheless his literary output and the range of his political and other activity in the 1950s should have been sufficient to refute the idea that he was lazy.

Meanwhile party politics were in a curious state of suspension. Churchill continued as Prime Minister, his failing health largely concealed from the public by a still-deferential press, repeatedly postponing his retirement in the belief that he alone could do a deal with Stalin to secure a lasting peace, and stretching the patience of his long-suffering heir apparent, Anthony Eden, almost to breaking point. On the Labour side, too, Attlee hung on as Leader of the Opposition mainly in order to block Herbert Morrison, while offering little sustained criticism of the government or sense of a dynamic alternative. Though the philosophical gulf between the parties was still wide, the practical difference between the economic policies of the Tory Chancellor, 'Rab' Butler, and his Labour shadow, Hugh Gaitskell, was so narrow – to the frustration of their more militant supporters on both right and left – that *The Economist* lumped them together as the composite centrist figure of 'Mr Butskell'. Almost the only excitement in politics derived from the continuing fratricidal war between Gaitskellites and Bevanites within the Labour party.

In this battle Jenkins was not just a devoted Gaitskellite, but now viscerally anti-Bevan. In December 1953 he explained the right's position candidly to Dick Crossman (himself a somewhat maverick Bevanite):

'They – I mean we – feel that every speech, every action must now be considered as part of the power fight within the Party. That's why we hate Bevanism. Before it began one could have free speech. Now one can't afford to.' He repeated several times, 'We on the right feel that every force of demagogy and every emotion is against us. In the constituency parties, which are now Opposition-minded, the Bevanites have it all their own way. I suppose one must wait for the tide to turn, as it slowly did in the 1930s, away from the opposition-mindedness of 1931 to constructive policies.'

I asked him why he thought it was so terribly important to defeat the Bevanites and he said, 'The electorate is extremely Conservative-minded and we can never win except with that kind of attitude represented by the right-wing leadership.' He also added that, for people like himself and Tony Crosland, the very existence of the Bevanites and their popularity was the major factor in making him loyal to Gaitskell. In the sort of hopeless fight that Gaitskell was waging, one had to stand by him.

What was interesting about the whole talk, which lasted for an hour and a half, was Roy's feeling that they were battling against the tide in the constituencies, that they must hang on for dear life. He also repeatedly emphasised that, just because the Bevanites were so strong, Gaitskell was more and more forced to rely on forces such as Arthur Deakin, which made him even further to the right than he would naturally be.[91]

It was the left's opposition-mindedness that exasperated Jenkins. He was already, by temperament and conviction, a man of government, interested in winning and using power, not in the emotional satisfaction of empty protest. He saw the division in the Labour party after 1951 as a fundamental difference between, on the one side, serious politicians whose concern was to get back into office in order to give a better life to the mass of the population, according to certain principles but recognising the constraints of the real world and ready if necessary to make hard choices between shades of grey; and, on the other, a gang of irresponsible play-actors, some of them warm-hearted romantics, others narrow-minded ideologues, temperamentally suspicious of power and only concerned to preserve their sense of righteous indignation. His fear was that the self-indulgent posturing of the left would prevent the right from regaining power to resume the pursuit of progress. This fear was perfectly crystallised by Bevan's second impulsive resignation from the Labour front bench in April 1954 over a relatively trivial disagreement with Attlee about Britain's role in SEATO (the South East Asia Treaty Organisation, intended as a sort of Asian equivalent of NATO), which had taken the heat off the Tories just when things seemed to be going Labour's way. Bevan, Jenkins wrote in *The Current*, 'will not become Prime Minister, but there seems a real danger that he may prevent any other Labour man in his lifetime from doing so either'.[92]

Yet he could be critical of Gaitskell too. When the following year Bevan staged another intemperate outburst on the floor of the House of Commons, subjecting Attlee to a humiliating interrogation about Labour's carefully fudged position on the use of nuclear weapons, he gave the disciplinarians in the Shadow Cabinet who wanted him out of the party what they thought the perfect excuse to withdraw the whip as a prelude to expelling him. After some hesitation, Gaitskell backed the hardliners led by Herbert Morrison. To Crossman, he revealed the depth of his paranoia by comparing Bevan to Hitler: 'There are extraordinary parallels . . . They are demagogues of exactly the same sort.' 'If Nye were out of the Party,' he argued, 'the main Tory propaganda for the next Election would be killed, whereas if the Executive failed to carry his expulsion the Tories would assert that Bevan is indispensable and the main master of the Party.'[93] But this sort of talk was too much for Gaitskell's younger acolytes, who recognised that Bevan, difficult though he was, had a large following and a legitimate place in the party, as Tony Crosland told Dalton: 'Tony . . . is very vexed with Hugh for taking, as he thinks, the wrong line over Bevan . . . He, with Roy Jenkins, Woodrow Wyatt, [Fred] Mulley and [Austen] Albu have been unconditional, unquestioning Gaitskellites, but now they are going to tell him what they think of this last incident.'[94] Three days later Crosland, Jenkins and Wyatt wrote their leader a warning letter. 'You must excuse this slightly formal letter,' they began, 'but we want you to consider seriously the views that it expresses.' They believed not only that the Shadow Cabinet was wrong to press for the withdrawal of the whip on this occasion, but that it had mishandled several previous episodes too:

> On all these occasions . . . we supported the platform with our votes . . . with various degrees of misgivings. There must, however, be a limit to the number of times on which one can vote the straight 'ticket' merely out of loyalty and regardless of our personal views. We therefore feel that we must in future have some freedom

of action; and we think you ought to know that this is our present
mood . . .

You know us well enough to realise that this in no way affects
our feelings of both personal and political loyalty to you. We are
pleased to be called 'Gaitskellites'; we want you to be leader of
the Party in the future and we shall do everything we can to see
that you are.

We have, of course, occasional differences, in particular over
Morrison. This is part of a wider view of ours that it is essential
that any 'Right wing' leader must have the fairly solid support
of the centre, which Attlee has, which Morrison does not, and
which we want you to have. Our difference of opinion only
arises because we believe that you and the 'Right wing' must in
the future carry many people whose support you did not have
last Wednesday morning.

Do not please think you have to write a reply to this – if one
comes we shall all be too frightened to open the envelope! Can
we not meet soon?

Yours ever

Roy, Woodrow, Tony[95]

Though happy to be Gaitskellites, Dalton's 'three wise young men'
were also anxious not to be identified too closely with the right. When
they met over a boozy lunch in Hampstead two weeks later they told
Gaitskell directly that he was 'getting labelled Right Wing. And must
devote more time and effort to attacking Tories.' In reply Gaitskell
retorted slightly peevishly that 'he had to do so much of the anti-Bevan
fighting because others did so little . . . some of his Trade Union
supporters sometimes asked him why his young intellectual supporters
didn't take a larger share.'[96] In the meantime, however, Attlee – the
object of Bevan's original outburst – had belatedly asserted himself in
the cause of unity and by a single vote (14:13) the NEC drew back
from the folly of expelling the party's most charismatic leader at the
beginning of what was likely to be an election year. Nevertheless
the whole prolonged rumpus was a wonderful gift to the Tories. Just
seven days after it was resolved Eden finally succeeded Churchill and
immediately sought his own mandate.

Jenkins recalled the 1955 General Election as the dullest he ever
fought. With a new, handsome and relatively young Prime Minister
pitched against an elderly and bitterly divided Opposition, the Korean
War over, a new Queen on the throne and the last vestiges of rationing

finally lifted, the Conservatives could hardly fail to increase their majority. In fact, as Jenkins – writing in a Birmingham local paper – correctly warned, the economic outlook was less rosy than it appeared.[97] Butler's spring budget, taking sixpence off income tax, was a blatant bribe that fed the summer feel-good factor, but had to be embarrassingly reversed in the autumn once it had achieved its electoral purpose. In the meantime Jenkins, like most other candidates, had to go through the motions of a contest whose result, despite substantial boundary changes, was never in doubt. In *The Current* – where he could be fairly sure that no one at home would read it – he confessed the unspeakable truth that 'most candidates would do equally well if they retired to the south of France for a fortnight's holiday and issued an election address from there!' But with characteristic precision he went on to give his Bombay readers a useful account of what electioneering in the 1950s involved – utterly different from half a century later.

He had already, he said, spent three days in Birmingham on 'preliminary work': drawing up his election address and getting it to the printers, writing several articles for local papers to appear during the campaign, and holding 'a workers' meeting . . . attended by about fifty of the keenest Labour party supporters, who were told the election plans by my agent and given a talk on general policy issues by myself'. Since then he had spent two days back in London clearing up other work, before going to Grantham to speak at three village meetings 'on behalf of my friend Woodrow Wyatt, who has had to leave his previous constituency and is to fight there'. The next day he would return to Birmingham to hand in his nomination papers to the Lord Mayor. 'Afterwards he will give us a drink and I will chat politely to my Conservative opponent, whom I have not yet met, and do the same rather less formally with some of the other Members for the City whom I knew in the last Parliament. Then we will have our photographs taken for the press, and the ceremony will be over.'

Since his seat was considered safe he would then do an evening meeting in a neighbouring marginal, before setting off on a three-day tour of the South-West arranged for him by Labour headquarters, doing two or three meetings every evening and one or two open-air meetings with a loudspeaker van during the day:

On Sunday, eleven days before the poll, I go back to Birmingham to start my own campaign in earnest. Apart from one quick visit to Southampton to speak for another close friend of mine who is fighting a very difficult seat,* I shall from then on be continuously in Birmingham. I shall hold twelve indoor meetings in my own constituency. These will take place in school halls with an average capacity of about 150 people. If the experience of 1951 is any guide they will all be very well filled. But some people take the view that the great spread of television in the last three-and-a-half years will make attendance at meetings far worse than was previously the case.

In addition, there will be a great rally in a large covered market in the centre of the City. One of the other candidates in Birmingham will be in the chair, I will address the meeting for twenty minutes to half an hour, and Mr Attlee will follow and speak for about the same time. On this occasion we hope to have an attendance of ten thousand. Three days later the Conservatives will be holding a similar gathering in the same place, when their principal speaker will be the new Prime Minister.

Whether all this will affect the result I cannot say. I know that at the end of it I shall be very tired. I know too that if one did not exhaust oneself there would be little possibility of getting one's supporters to work really hard. And their morale is of great importance. So perhaps it is all worth while.[98]

He was right about the effect of television on meetings. This was not because voters got their politics from the television – there was no election coverage apart from the official party broadcasts: the first election in which television played a significant part was 1959 – but simply because there was now better entertainment to be had by staying in. Compared with the three previous post-war elections, Jenkins wrote in a second article just before polling day, 'meetings are sparsely attended – in some . . . the platform outnumbers the audience – workers are fewer and less eager to help, and the busy cheerful hum of the committee room is absent'. As a result turnout fell from 82 to 76 per cent – and the Labour vote by 1.5 million. 'It is a far greater strain and a depressing business,' he concluded gloomily, 'to fight an election in an atmosphere of apathy, and it will be an enormous relief to candidates when it is all over.'[99]

The Tories gained twenty-two seats and increased their majority to

---

* This was Crosland, whose South Gloucestershire seat had been made unsafe by redistribution. Unfortunately Southampton, Test, turned out to be even less winnable, so he was out of the House for the next four years, until he secured Grimsby in 1959.

176

fifty-eight. Redistribution had shrunk the Stechford electorate by more than 20 per cent, but did not seriously affect its political balance, and Jenkins still had a comfortable margin over his new Tory opponent:

Roy Jenkins (Labour)	23,358
J.M. Bailey (Conservative)	16,618
Labour majority	6,740[100]

Today a defeated Opposition leader – certainly a seventy-two-year-old leader who had now lost two elections – would resign immediately. But in 1955 Attlee still hung on. His heir apparent was the sixty-seven-year-old Morrison. In a party that still respected the principle of Buggins' turn, Gaitskell felt himself – at forty-nine – too young and inexperienced to push himself forward and believed that Morrison must have his chance: he saw himself as the next leader but one. His friends, however, marshalled by Dalton, were desperate to jump a generation and bypass Morrison; and with Crosland and Wyatt both out of the House, Jenkins was now the most prominent of these younger supporters. 'Nobody has pushed the claims of Mr Gaitskell with greater zest and fervour,' the *Daily Express* noted. 'He is an able young man with a bright future.'[101] Gaitskell still insisted that there was no vacancy. But at the party conference at Margate he made a passionate avowal of his socialist faith which went a long way to humanise his appeal to those who had hitherto thought him merely – in Bevan's cutting phrase – 'a desiccated calculating machine'; then back at Westminster in November he led the attack on Butler's emergency budget with a force of moral outrage that comprehensively buried 'Butskellism': as in 1952, Jenkins was again part of his Shadow Treasury team, described by Crossman as 'the first effective fighting Opposition we've known for a long time'.[102] These performances helped convince Attlee that he could now safely retire, and at the beginning of December he suddenly resigned. Gaitskell still needed persuading to come forward, but Jenkins took a leading part in convincing him that Morrison's support was so weak that standing aside could let Bevan in. Helped by a brazenly cynical last-minute attempt by Morrison and Bevan to combine against him, which only discredited them both, Gaitskell won overwhelmingly on the first ballot with 157 votes against Bevan's seventy and a humiliating forty for Morrison.

For Jenkins, Gaitskell's victory was a 'Wordsworthian' moment which seemed to offer the prospect of a new dawn and boundless opportunity, both for Labour and for himself personally. 'Apart from my joy at his triumph,' he wrote in his memoirs, 'I felt that for the first time I had influenced major events.'[103] (Morrison evidently agreed, and did not speak to him again for seven years.) In *The Current* he wrote confidently that Gaitskell had now emerged 'beyond reasonable doubt' as the next Prime Minister of Great Britain. There was no reason why his tenure of office should not be 'at least as long as that of Lord Attlee'; and 'during that period it can hardly be doubted that there will be many years when he will enjoy the tenancy of no. 10 Downing Street'.[104] This was a perfectly reasonable expectation in December 1955. In reality Gaitskell was destined to toil for seven long years as Leader of the Opposition and die without ever reaching Downing Street; even had he lived to lead Labour back to power in 1964, he would have been the third Prime Minister after Eden. Nevertheless Gaitskell's replacement of Attlee marked a generational shift in the Labour Party of huge importance for Jenkins.

At the same time, he did not fail to pay due tribute to the retiring leader, who replied characteristically:

> My dear Roy,
>   Thank you and Jennifer for your kind good wishes.
>   It has been a great joy to me to watch Arthur's son growing in authority in the House.
>   I should like to live long enough to see you in office.
>   All good wishes.
>   Yours ever,
>   Clem[105]

9 The Liberal Agenda

G AITSKELL'S election as Labour leader in December 1955 did not, as might have been expected, propel Jenkins onto the front bench, but rather the reverse. The new leader's priority was not to reward his supporters, but to unite the party by reconciling former opponents to his leadership. Accordingly he ignored Bevan's truculent grumbling and offered him the job of Shadow Colonial Secretary, which he gratefully accepted; at the same time he sought to detach Harold Wilson from Bevan by appointing him to fill his own place as Shadow Chancellor. 'A minor side-effect of this,' Jenkins wrote in his memoirs, 'was that it made me much less eager to devote time to the minutiae of Finance Bills' than when it had meant working closely with Gaitskell.[1] He still spoke frequently in economic debates over the next few years, but from the back benches, expressing his own views often on quite technical questions of taxation or monetary policy, not as part of Wilson's front-bench team. But he also began to pursue wider – some might say more peripheral – causes, creating for himself a new identity as a leading advocate of liberalisation in a number of controversial areas of national life and, in the process, forging important alliances – and friendships – across party lines. It was also at this time that he discovered the second great theme of his political life: Britain's place in Europe.

He still remained close to Gaitskell, but their friendship was as much social as it was political. While Gaitskell, always very conscious of being a Wykehamist leader of a still predominantly working-class party, was assiduous in cultivating his trade union and constituency supporters, he also liked to relax when off duty; and now that he was leader he was determined to make more, rather than less, time for private friendship, parties and dancing. For Jenkins this energetic conviviality was a large part of Gaitskell's appeal (though he was not so keen on dancing). He too enjoyed the cross-party fellowship of politics and felt no guilt about accepting the hospitality of Tory hostesses like Ann Fleming and Lady Pamela Berry (wife of the chairman of the *Daily Telegraph*). While Gaitskell's strictly political performance at the dispatch box and in party management was generally hard to fault, criticism of his leadership soon focused on his social life, which seemed to more puritanical elements in the movement – not just on the left, but also among his backers on the trade union right – inappropriate for a Labour leader. Even a supporter like Anthony Wedgwood Benn (not then on the left, but quite close to Gaitskell) wrote after attending a party he gave for the failed American presidential candidate Adlai Stevenson in 1957: 'It was a little depressing to see the leader of the party half-way to being sozzled.'[2] At the same time there grew up a damaging impression that Gaitskell surrounded himself with a narrow clique of middle-class intellectuals – not just Jenkins and Crosland, but Douglas Jay and Patrick Gordon Walker, Frank Soskice, Frank Pakenham, Denis Healey and a few others who (as Jenkins freely told Crossman) met socially 'most Sunday evenings', usually in Hampstead where Gaitskell, Jay and Gordon Walker all lived.* Their easy access to the leader aroused the jealousy of less-favoured colleagues in the Shadow Cabinet or on the National Executive who felt excluded from these 'secret confabs'.[3] In terms of actual policy development the influence of this 'Hampstead set' was probably less than his critics thought; but undoubtedly Gaitskell's Hampstead friends shared the same broad understanding of how the party should be changing in the second half of the century. This under-standing was encapsulated by the publication in October 1956 of Tony Crosland's *The Future of Socialism*, which was immediately hailed as the seminal text of Labour revisionism – and correspondingly condemned by unreconstructed Bevanites as a betrayal of their core beliefs. 'Socialism?' queried the headline of *Tribune*'s review. 'How Dare he Use the Word?'[4]

Crosland's book was not in truth strikingly original. What it did was to pull together with some style and wit, but also a lot of dense socio-logical analysis, the sort of ideas that had been floated over the past five years in *New Fabian Essays* and books by Jay, John Strachey and others, including Jenkins' *Pursuit of Progress*, to redefine Labour's *raison*

---

* Jay, Gordon Walker, Pakenham, Soskice and Crosland were all public-school boys, educated respectively at Winchester, Wellington, Eton, St Paul's and Highgate; and all had been to Oxford – as, of course, had Jenkins and Healey.

d'être after 1951. It was less an economic blueprint than a manifesto for a new definition of socialism, based not on the old dogmas of public ownership and planning – now relegated to possible means, rather than defining ends – but rather on increased equality, the breaking down of class barriers and wider opportunities for personal fulfilment, all predicated on the most optimistic assumption of ever-increasing economic growth and future material abundance. In his final chapter Crosland conjured an alluring vision of what might be called 'socialist hedonism', involving 'personal freedom, happiness and cultural endeavour, the cultivation of leisure, beauty, grace, gaiety, excitement, and of all the proper pursuits . . . which contribute to the varied fabric of a full private and family life'. He hoped to see Britain become 'a more colourful and civilised country to live in', with 'more open-air cafés, brighter and gayer streets at night, later closing hours for public houses, more local repertory theatres, better and more hospitable hoteliers and restaurateurs, brighter and cleaner eating houses, more riverside cafés, more pleasure gardens . . . and so on *ad infinitum*'. Explicitly substituting the generous cultural vision of William Morris for the dour mechanistic socialism of the Webbs, Crosland famously concluded that 'Total abstinence and a good filing system are not now the right sign-posts to the socialist Utopia; or, at least, if they are, some of us will fall by the wayside.'[5]

This was Jenkins' philosophy too, and this part of Crosland's book doubtless reflected many long conversations over the past five years – though Jenkins was not one of those whom Crosland thanked for reading his manuscript. They had both come a long way from their undergraduate arguments about class war in 1939–40. Writing in *Forward* (the Gaitskellites' answer to *Tribune*), Jenkins hailed *The Future of Socialism* as 'the most important book on socialist theory' since Evan Durbin's *The Politics of Democratic Socialism* in 1940, and briefly summarised its thesis: the present economic system could no longer be called capitalist, Labour's short-term goals had been largely achieved between 1945 and 1951, and the ownership of industry no longer mattered, so socialism was now about two things – 'the relief of the distress and poverty which still persists in fairly large pockets in this country'; and 'the removal of the class barriers which still disfigure British Society', especially by educational reform. He, like Crosland, no longer advocated the abolition of the public schools but their 'rapid infiltration', whatever that meant. Above all he endorsed his friend's confidence that 'high and rising consumption standards' would naturally lead to greater equality, as in the United States. 'The difference between a rich man and an ordinary man is much less when the former has a Cadillac and the latter a Chevrolet than when only the former has a motor car at all. Accordingly, Mr Crosland is highly impatient of those who appear to be attached to austerity for its own sake.'[6]

Austerity had never appealed to Jenkins, either politically or personally, so Crosland's agreeable redefinition of socialism usefully countered any charge of inconsistency between his public policy and his private lifestyle – that combination of 'good living and liberal ideas' which Bill Rodgers noted when visiting Ladbroke Square. But *The Future of Socialism* also reflected his growing interest in libertarian social issues. Crosland specifically picked out 'the divorce laws, licensing laws, prehistoric (and flagrantly unfair) abortion laws, obsolete penalties for sexual abnormality, the illiterate censorship of books and plays, and remaining restrictions on equal rights for women', most of which, he declared, were 'intolerable, and should be highly offensive to socialists, in whose blood there should always run a trace of the anarchist and the libertarian, and not too much of the prig and the prude'.[7] Jenkins had already been focusing on this agenda for some years, as evidenced by his articles in *The Current*. In April 1954, for instance, he used the highly publicised trial of Lord Montagu of Beaulieu to call for the decriminalisation of homosexuality. The law should be changed, he argued, so that 'private relations between adult men are not an affair which concerns the state'.[8] In February 1953 he deplored the way a determined sabbatarian minority was able to block the reform of Sunday trading laws.[9] And in the same month he wrote that the execution of the nineteen-year-old (and mentally defective) Derek Bentley for a murder actually committed by his sixteen-year-old accomplice (who was too young to be executed) had greatly strengthened the case for the abolition of capital punishment.[10] These were all campaigns with which he would be prominently associated over the next decade.

But the cause that Jenkins was to make particularly his own was the censorship of books, which had suddenly assumed a new urgency in 1954 when the most illiberal Home Secretary since the 1920s, Sir David Maxwell Fyfe, launched a ferocious crackdown on allegedly 'dirty' books under the Obscene Publications Act of 1876. Even the harmlessly naughty postcards of Donald McGill were seized by police at several seaside resorts, while Swindon magistrates ordered the destruction of a scholarly two-volume edition of Boccaccio's *Decameron*. Among 132 prosecutions brought that year at least five were directed at reputable publishers of books of literary quality which could be freely published anywhere else in western Europe. Two of these prosecutions were successful, two failed and the jury was unable to agree on the fifth, so that publishers, printers and booksellers, all of whom could find themselves liable, did not know where they were. The Society of Authors established a committee chaired by the writer and veteran campaigner Sir Alan Herbert to campaign for a clarification of the law. As the only sitting MP on the committee (though Michael Foot, temporarily without a seat, and Norman St John Stevas, a young Tory barrister not yet in the House, were also members), Jenkins thus became the parliamentary leader of a campaign which was to occupy much of his energy for the next five years.

The government responded not by moving to liberalise the law, but to tighten it, specifically to deal with an influx (mainly from America) of what were known as 'horror comics'. The 1876 Act was based on Lord Cockburn's famous catch-all judgement of 1868, which defined obscenity as 'the tendency of the matter charged . . . to deprave and corrupt those whose minds are open to such immoral influences and into whose hands a publication of this sort may fall'. As Jenkins wrote, the Children and Young Persons (Harmful Publications) Bill introduced in the spring of 1955 by the new Home Secretary, Gwilym Lloyd George (son of the Welsh Wizard, but now a Tory scarcely less reactionary than Maxwell Fyfe), 'took all the objectionable features of Cockburn's 1868 judgement and applied them in statute form to a new field'.[11] In the House he called it 'a thoroughly bad Bill', which would make a bad situation worse by exposing serious literature to the same petty vigilantism as cheap pornography.[12] The next month he introduced under the Ten-Minute Rule an alternative bill that incorporated the Society's proposals.* Meanwhile he and a handful of allies concentrated on moving amendments to the government Bill; the closest they came to success was in attracting sixty-five votes (including both Gaitskell and the Liberal leader Jo Grimond) for a clause to allow a defence on grounds of 'literary merit'. 'The fact that we had to argue it exclusively within the context of strip cartoons did not make the task any easier!'[13]

A Private Member's Bill introduced by the Tory MP Hugh Fraser was talked out by a Home Office minister in 1956. The prospects improved marginally in the next session when Lord Lambton (whose courtesy title did not prevent him sitting in the Commons) won a

---

* The Bill was drafted by St John Stevas, whose book *Obscenity and the Law,* published in 1956, became the reformers' guiding text.

higher place in the ballot and took up the Society's Bill; and brightened again when Harold Macmillan – a publisher by profession – succeeded Eden in January 1957, and Rab Butler (who at the time was President of the Royal Society of Literature) became Home Secretary. Rather than send Lambton's Bill to a Standing Committee, however, Butler offered a Select Committee to enquire more widely into the case for reform. This was duly established, with Jenkins again a leading member. After examining witnesses from all sides of the argument – from the Director of Public Prosecutions and the Public Morality Council to T.S. Eliot and E.M. Forster – the committee issued a compromise report balancing liberalisation in some areas with increased police powers in others. By this time, however, Lambton's bill had fallen, so in 1958 (having failed to find another lucky Member willing to sponsor a Private Members' Bill, and three and a half years after his first effort) Jenkins introduced another Ten-Minute Rule Bill, with the hope that this time the government might give it a fair wind or even take it up itself. Informed opinion and the serious press, from *The Times* and *Telegraph* to the *Manchester Guardian* and the *New Statesman*, were unanimously supportive. But again Butler, while professing sympathy with the object of the Bill, prevaricated, allowing a handful of back-benchers, encouraged by the government whips, to deny it a Second Reading – until Herbert mischievously announced his intention to stand as an Independent in a forthcoming by-election in Harrow East, which would probably have allowed Labour to win the seat. This timely threat magically galvanised the government into giving parliamentary time for an unopposed Second Reading – only for the Law Officers to table a slew of amendments in committee, which tilted the balance heavily back towards the police.

The central purpose of his Bill, as Jenkins summarised it, was to narrow the definition of obscenity to take account of the author's intention:

The common law misdemeanour of obscene libel disappears and is replaced by a new statutory offence of which the essence is the guilty knowledge of the offender, who shall be judged by the likely dominant effect of his work on those among whom it is *intended* to circulate – not the *possibility* of its corrupting anyone into whose hands it *might* fall.[14]

The essential points were that a work should be considered as a whole – not condemned on the basis of a few titillating passages taken out of context – and that literary merit should be admissible as a defence. By giving up some lesser points (notably a provision that criminal proceedings should only be brought with the consent of the DPP) the reformers were able, after some tough horse-trading with the Home Office and Law Officers – the Attorney-General was the famously reactionary Sir Reginald Manningham-Buller – to preserve these gains. Butler still showed very little urgency to drive it forward. Writing to Jenkins in December 1958 (incidentally mentioning that he was enjoying *Dilke*), he admitted that 'people will say I was manoeuvring', but pleaded somewhat wearily that 'I had great difficulty finding time or opportunity for Obscene Publications. As one gets older one takes the criticisms of politics v. calmly.'[15] Once in Committee, Jenkins and his band of allies – who included Kenneth Robinson and the former Home Secretary Chuter Ede on the Labour side, Mark Bonham Carter (Liberal, just elected at a famous by-election in Torrington) and the Tories Hugh Fraser, Maurice Macmillan and Nigel Nicolson (the last four all Jenkins' Balliol contemporaries) – managed to carry most of the key votes by clear majorities: 10:5, 10:6 or 8:3. The Bill finally passed the Commons in April 1959, after the reformers had defeated (by 40:28) another government attempt at Report Stage to wreck it by widening its scope; but then the House of Lords passed more amendments, which Butler, with a hint of menace, advised Jenkins to accept if he did not want to lose his Bill altogether:

Quite frankly, I think that the worries which you and your friends have expressed about their possible effect have been exaggerated . . . We think these changes are entirely reasonable and I feel sure that, while you will of course have an opportunity to express your opinion during the discussion on the motions, you will want to think again about your idea of dividing the House.[16]

In the end, with time running out before the end of the session, the reformers had to settle for a more circumscribed measure than they had initially envisaged, which gave some protection to reputable publishers only at the price of giving the police increased powers to seize offensive material, and still leaving a lot of uncertainty to be tested by some celebrated cases (including *Lolita* and *Lady Chatterley's Lover*) in the next few years. Nevertheless the 1959 Act was a considerable personal triumph for its principal sponsor, who earned the gratitude of the Society of Authors' magazine: 'The tactical skill exhibited throughout by Mr Roy Jenkins MP may well assure that this long overdue Statute . . . will go down in history as the Jenkins Act.'[17] A private tribute came from one of his allies in the fight, Hugh Fraser:

> My dear Roy,
>   You have made a most useful piece of history . . . with great distinction. The better Balliol attributes fit you ever more closely as you mature. And what about patience! And quiet persuasive movements off stage! Most impressive, and gratifying to your friends.
>   Hugh[18]

Jenkins, for his part, thought it prudent to thank Butler for his 'great help' in getting the bill through: the whole struggle 'would have been unavailing had you not been basically sympathetic'.[19] This was generous. Reviewing the five-year saga in *Encounter* that autumn, Jenkins concluded that Private Members' legislation could still succeed with the right combination of luck, patience, all-party support, a sympathetic minister, determined allies and articulate extra-parliamentary support. 'When all these circumstances coincide it is possible to make some progress in a liberalising direction.' The great majority of MPs, he believed, were not so much hostile as indifferent, though some were frightened of their constituents – 'in most cases needlessly . . . for not one of mine has ever complained to me about my activities in this field'. Nevertheless he ended with a gentle but unmistakable dig at Butler. 'Libertarian reform . . . is undoubtedly a long and wearisome road for a private member. A determinedly liberal Home Secretary could do it much more quickly and much more surely.'[20] Six years later he was given the chance to prove the truth of his words.

Meanwhile, the seismic political event of the mid-1950s was the botched Franco-British operation to seize control of the Suez Canal in October 1956, which divided the political class more bitterly than any controversy since Irish Home Rule in 1912–14. By secretly colluding with France to invade Egypt – and then unconvincingly denying it – Eden betrayed his own reputation as a peacemaker and shattered the consensus between the parties on foreign policy that had existed since 1945; while for denouncing Eden's duplicity and opposing the invasion, Gaitskell was vilified in the Tory press for lack of patriotism, if not treason. Jenkins was of course firmly behind Gaitskell. Apart from his column in *The Current* and other occasional journalism, he had hitherto taken strangely little interest in foreign affairs. The first time he spoke in the Commons on any foreign issue was in March 1956 on the subject of Malta. By his own admission, 'I lacked confidence in the subject and never dared open my mouth in the House of Commons throughout the Suez crisis.'[21]* But at the height of the crisis on 4 November – the same day that Bevan memorably castigated the Prime Minister in Trafalgar Square – Jenkins spoke at another Labour rally in Birmingham Town Hall, where he deplored Eden's 'squalid imperialist adventure' for damaging the United Nations, NATO, the Commonwealth and Britain's reputation in the world, as well as for making it impossible to condemn the Russians' simultaneous crushing of the Hungarian uprising against Soviet rule in Budapest.[23] Two years later he wrote that 'Suez was a totally unsuccessful attempt to achieve unreasonable and undesirable objectives by methods which were at once reckless and immoral; and the consequences, as was well deserved, were humiliating and disastrous.'[24]

The humiliation of Suez brought home to the British foreign-policy establishment what it had been strenuously attempting to deny since 1945: that Britain was no longer a great power with the ability to act independently on the world stage. Diplomats and forward-thinking politicians were forced to take seriously for the first time the idea that Britain would do better inside the nascent European Economic Community than continuing to try to go it alone. The EEC was then no more than an economic community comprising just six countries – France, West Germany, Italy, Belgium, the Netherlands and tiny Luxembourg – which came together in 1957 to sign the Treaty of Rome, though its architects' long-term political ambitions were already clear. Britain stayed away from the founding conference at Messina in 1955 in the lofty belief (shared equally by Churchill and Eden, Attlee and Bevin) that her special bond with the United States on the one hand and the Commonwealth on the other gave her global interests and responsibilities far beyond Europe. This confidence in Britain's distinctiveness was badly shaken by Suez; and the shock was perhaps greatest on Harold Macmillan who, as Chancellor at the time and initially a hawk for military action, was most sharply exposed to Britain's

---

* That did not stop him penning in *The Current* a withering condemnation of Selwyn Lloyd's appointment as Foreign Secretary. Rightly suspecting that Eden wanted a malleable stooge at the Foreign Office, Jenkins told his Bombay readership that Lloyd was 'to my mind one of the most overrated men in British politics. He has never done a memorable thing or made a memorable speech or associated himself in the public mind with any policy other than that accepted by the generality of the Conservative Party . . . I hope he will make a better Foreign Secretary than I think he will. I find it impossible to believe that he will make a distinguished one.'[22]

economic weakness in the face of American disapproval. On succeeding as Prime Minister following Eden's ignominious resignation he began to inch towards a reassessment of Britain's role in the world.

Jenkins, as he always admitted, was not in the vanguard of this reassessment; but he was a relatively early convert, some way ahead of Macmillan. As a very young MP in 1950 he had unquestioningly toed the Labour party line by voting against British participation in the Schuman Plan; in 1951 he attended a European Movement weekend in Brussels, but still argued what he later called 'the boring old case' against Britain's full involvement; in 1953, however, he accompanied Attlee to a conference in Wiesbaden, which pricked his interest; and in 1955 he was appointed one of the twelve-strong Labour delegation to the Council of Europe in Strasbourg. Over the next two years – covering, as he wrote in his memoirs, precisely the period from the Messina Conference to the Treaty of Rome – 'I spent a total of about seven weeks in Strasbourg or in committee meetings from Palermo to Berlin . . . and I have no doubt that those experiences sowed the seeds of my subsequently persistent conviction . . . I learned a lot from those two years of watching Britain throw away its opportunity to play a formative role in the shaping of the Common Market.'[25]

In October 1956, as rapporteur to one of these committees, he made a speech in Strasbourg which caught the attention of *The Times*:

> A concise and most effective statement of the British case, which was much remarked on in the lobbies afterwards, came from Mr Roy Jenkins . . . Illustrating his arguments with a quotation from Gladstone, he suggested that the Common Market was an affair of men just as much as of packages,* and thought that the greatest drawback of not being associated with it would not be economic – although there would certainly be grave economic disadvantages – but political, for thus a new political division would be created in Europe.[27]

This success was doubtless gratifying but, looking back from 1991, Jenkins took little pride in a speech that still contained 'all the fallacies

---

* In 1841 the thirty-two-year-old Gladstone was disappointed to be offered by Peel no more than a junior position at the Board of Trade and complained that where he had hoped to be concerned with the affairs of men, he had been 'set to governing packages'.[26] This is Jenkins' first recorded use of one his favourite quotations, which he used repeatedly when distinguishing between the economic and political aspects of European unity for the next forty years.

which were to bedevil our relations with [the EEC] for most of the next thirty-five years'. While wishing to be 'associated' with the Common Market, he still accepted the conventional wisdom that Commonwealth commitments made it impossible for Britain to consider joining a full customs union with a common tariff against the outside world, though it might join some sort of free-trade area. But he was still a step ahead of the government. By the time Macmillan in 1958 came up with the European Free Trade Association (EFTA) – a loose alliance with six smaller countries, intended as an alternative to the EEC – Jenkins was already clear that EFTA offered no real substitute, but was merely 'a foolish attempt to organise a weak periphery against a strong core'.[28] Britain's proper place was to be part of the core. By 1959 he was explicitly arguing the case for EEC membership as a way of exorcising the imperial illusions so disastrously exemplified by Suez:

> The chief danger for a country placed as we are is that of living sullenly in the past, of believing that the world has a duty to keep us in the station to which we are accustomed, and showing bitter resentment if it does not do so. This was the mood of Suez; and it is a mood absolutely guaranteed, not to recreate our past glories, but to reduce us to a level of influence and wealth far lower than that which we need occupy . . .
>   Our neighbours in Europe are roughly our economic and military equals. We would do better to live gracefully with them than to waste our substance by trying unsuccessfully to keep up with the power giants of the modern world.[29]

This was a central theme that he would continue to sound for the rest of his life. But the lesson had still not been learned at the time of his death.

Jenkins' enthusiasm for Europe was another eccentric preoccupation which both advertised his growing independence and distanced him from the bulk of the Labour party, which was still for the most part either insular and xenophobic or sentimentally attached to the Commonwealth. Even among the Gaitskellites, Douglas Jay was famous for his loathing of 'abroad' while Gaitskell himself – a child of the Raj – was far more emotionally attached to India than to Europe. Tony Crosland was at this time an equally ardent Europhile, seeing France in particular, with its street cafés and restaurants, all-day drinking and relative lack of censorship, as the antithesis of the grey 1950s England he had denounced in *The Future of Socialism*. But most of the left and centre of the party still viewed the Common Market as a capitalist club which would block Britain's progress to socialism. Jenkins' commitment to Europe reflected the increasingly important cross-party and non-party friendships – diplomatic, literary and academic – that he was forging across what became known around this time as the 'Establishment'.

A particularly important new friend whom he first met in February 1957 was Ian Gilmour. Gilmour was a wealthy young Eton-and-Balliol heir to a baronetcy who in 1954 had bought the ancient but staid *Spectator* magazine and turned it into the liveliest voice on the political scene. It was nominally Conservative but libertarian, anti-Suez, pro-European and persistently critical of the Macmillan government. Its chief political columnist was Henry Fairlie, who coined (or at least popularised) the term 'the Establishment'; while the irreverent young Bernard Levin made his name by pioneering a new genre of satirical political sketch under the Disraelian pseudonym 'Taper'. Alan Brien, Alan Watkins, Katharine Whitehorn and many others also cut their teeth on Gilmour's *Spectator* in its late 1950s/early 1960s heyday; and Jenkins was part of this golden age. He wrote his first article for the paper – on the literary censorship struggle – in March 1957 and continued to contribute with increasing regularity for the next five years (he had dropped *The Current* in 1956). In 1959 Gilmour, while remaining proprietor, gave up the editorship to Brian Inglis in order to concentrate on finding a seat in Parliament; but this in no way reduced the frequency of Jenkins' contributions. During 1960 he contributed eight articles and no fewer than thirteen book reviews. Henceforth reviewing, for a variety of papers, provided not only a steady source of income for the rest of his life, but a useful platform which enabled him to indulge his favourite hobby by passing judgement on practically every political biography, diary and contemporary memoir as it appeared.

Meanwhile Gilmour became one of his best friends, and his wife Caroline one of his most enduring girlfriends. The Gilmours and the Jenkinses holidayed together in France in 1958, and again in America (to observe the Nixon–Kennedy presidential election) in 1960. By this time Roy and Caroline had become lovers. It is not clear whether it was on this American holiday or earlier that their relationship began. But on 24 October Roy had to return from Chicago to Britain. The same day Caroline wrote him – in pencil on flimsy airmail paper – a long passionate letter:

My love,

No words can describe the utter *desolation* of returning to the Ambassador yesterday afternoon without you. I felt completely lost and shell like as though the major part of me had gone with you. I just lay and *ached* for you – unable to read or write or watch the television . . .

With the help of several pills I managed to sleep for nearly 12 hours and woke feeling just as miserable but slightly less tearful. I imagined you arriving feeling as desolate (I hope) with less sleep, Boeingitis & being immediately thrown into a maelstrom of Labour upheavals . . .

Promise to burn this immediately. I hope to heaven it arrives safely

My love – I miss you so desperately at the moment that the thought of our [illegible] two days together causes really acute pain – but when the gnawing ache has gone I am sure that they will permanently sit on a high pedestal suffused by rainbow like rays of happiness – and I tremendously hope they will for you too.

So much of my fondest love

Caroline[30]

Two days later she wrote again.

My love,

I still miss you so enormously and get terrible twinges and pangs and go into mammoth glooms . . . I will obviously have to make a vast effort otherwise Ian might notice I suppose . . .

I feel so unable to cope without having your eye to catch across the room.

I long and long to hear from you but do be careful as I shall have to show it to Ian.

I pine for you in every way.

My immense love

C[31]

Clearly at this stage Ian did not know what was going on. Later he certainly did. Initially he was not very happy about it, but he was already enjoying affairs of his own, so he had no choice but to accept it; and Roy and Caroline's relationship continued as a more or less open secret for the next forty years. Jennifer too accepted it, though she never warmed to Caroline, and somehow the quadrilateral relationship between the four of them remained intact for the rest of their lives – Roy and Jennifer were frequent summer visitors to the Gilmours' house in Tuscany – though it was all so discreet that their children were unaware of the truth until many years later.

Jenkins' increasingly high-profile journalism added a new string to his political bow. Having established his historical credentials with *Mr Balfour's Poodle* and *Dilke*, he brought a quasi-academic detachment to his observation of the Westminster scene. In November 1957, for instance, he questioned the constitutional propriety of the Chancellor of the Exchequer's use of outside economic advisers.[32] In March 1958 he reviewed a defence debate almost as if it were a theatrical performance.[33] And in May 1959 – by which time he had started work on *Asquith* – he contrasted the declining interest shown by the modern House of Commons in its own debates with the packed attendance for the far longer Finance Bill debates of 1909 – not that he was particularly good at attending himself – and called on the Speaker to do more to ensure a real clash of argument.[34] But sometimes he was more partisan. In August 1959 he contributed to a series of articles on the meaning of 'radicalism' and took the opportunity to debunk the fashionable notion of 'Tory radicalism' promoted in a previous article by Lord Altrincham – the historian and biographer John Grigg, a close friend (and Tuscan neighbour) of Ian Gilmour, who occupied a similar perch on the far left of the Tory Party. A streak of iconoclasm, Jenkins argued – citing Lord Randolph Churchill as an example – did not make a man a radical; while the most truly radical Prime Ministers of the past century (Gladstone, Asquith and Attlee) were all in their private lives men of distinctly conservative temperament. This was a favourite paradox to which he often returned. With some exceptions, he argued (thinking of his allies on the Obscene Publications Bill), Tory claims to radicalism on social and colonial questions were quite untenable. On a whole range of social issues – hanging, homosexuality, licensing, betting, Sunday observance, divorce, theatre censorship, policing and abortion – there was 'immensely more to be hoped for from a Labour Home Secretary than from the most liberal Conservative Minister'; while Tory colonial policy (this was soon after the brutal suppression of the Mau Mau rebellion in Kenya) threatened to make Africa 'the Ireland of the twentieth century':

> The Radical tradition still exists in British politics, but it has not become spattered over the political spectrum. As has always been the case, it remains concentrated well to the Left of the Conservative Party.[35]

By this time Jenkins rarely called himself a socialist, but he vigorously laid claim to the label 'radical'.

The next month, however – by which time Macmillan had fired the starting gun for the 1959 election – he launched (still in the tolerant columns of the *Spectator*) a more direct attack on the Tory government. Abandoning any pretence of objectivity, while still affecting a historical overview, he lambasted its colonial policy and its economic policy, but above all its duplicity (or what we now call 'spin'):

> Nothing can be shown for what it is. Everything has to be dressed up and presented as another great triumph of our infallible rulers. The besetting sin of Mr Macmillan and his colleagues is a degree of intellectual dishonesty which has not been seen in British politics for a long time past. If a Government can continue with this, and can make the criminal mistakes which have been made since 1955 in the foreign and colonial fields, and still be re-elected, the prospect, not only for policy in the next five years, but for the whole tone of politics in this country, will be an appalling one.[36]

This assumption of moral superiority was beginning to grate with some observers. Their irritation had been reflected in a sharp *New Statesman* commentary by the Bevanite MP J.P.W. Mallalieu in November 1957 which recognised Jenkins' quality while conveying a vivid picture of his distinctive mannerisms:

> Jenkins is not everyone's favourite, for his public manner suggests arrogance. But he is reputed to be so close a confidant of Mr Hugh Gaitskell that only the keenest observer can detect where Mr Jenkins' mouth ends and Gaitskell's ear begins. So when he speaks in the House, others grudgingly listen for the sound of things to come. On Tuesday, he spoke with his easy, controlled fluency, glancing occasionally at his notes more for pause and effect than from any need to refresh his memory. Only the movements of his hands seemed uncalculated. These hands twisted and writhed in front of him like snakes, and though from time to time he would thrust them deep into his pockets or plant them firmly on his hips beneath his wide open coat, back they would come in a few seconds to twist and writhe as before.[37]

With all his outside interests, Jenkins was beginning to be seen as a bit of a dilettante. But he was still a serious politician – on his own terms. Outside the House he devoted a good deal of time to the Fabian Society. He had been a member of its executive since 1949, attending weekend conferences and writing earnest papers on price control or fiscal policy; in 1954 he went on a Fabian jaunt to Austria, and by 1957–8 it was his turn to be chairman for a year. He took the job seriously and made a point of speaking at Fabian meetings all round the country – a commitment that not only repaid a debt to his past but also forged a key political relationship for his future, since he was frequently accompanied on his speaking trips by Bill Rodgers, the then twenty-nine-year-old general secretary of the Society who became MP for Stockton-on-Tees in 1962. A robust Gaitskellite who was initially more dazzled by Crosland than by Jenkins, Rodgers switched his allegiance on Gaitskell's death in 1963 to become over the next thirty years Jenkins' most loyal political supporter and right-hand man. In 1957 he found Jenkins an admirably decisive chairman who would get through executive meetings in an hour;[38] but he also remembers Jenkins fretting about his lack of public recognition and deciding to make more speeches to raise his profile.[39]

Since he never belonged to a trade union, apart from the Society of Authors, this involvement with the Fabian Society was Jenkins' sole connection with one of the affiliated organisations of the Labour movement beyond Westminster. But he made a point of speaking practically every year at the party's annual conference – 1956 at Blackpool, 1957 at Brighton, 1958 at Scarborough. (By contrast, Crosland never bothered with conference after 1953.) In 1956 his interest in equality was recognised by his co-option onto a party committee on the subject (chaired by Gaitskell and including Wilson, Barbara Castle and the leading Bevanite Ian Mikardo); and at conference that year he spoke in the debate on its report, entitled *Towards Equality*, arguing that society was still 'disfigured' by class divisions and urging the taxation not just of large incomes but of inherited wealth by making death duties 'a reality and not a fraud', and by tackling tax avoidance.* He still thought private education an important preserver of inequality, but he increasingly recognised the

---

* Back in July he had defended the case for higher taxation in a letter to *The Times*, responding sharply to familiar Tory criticism of 'the politics of envy':

> It is hard to understand why an attempt to get more of the national product for those who at present get least is to be dismissed as pandering to envy, while an attempt to tilt it the other way by securing more concessions for the discontented Conservative electors of Tonbridge is not denounced as rapacity, and why the one is manifestly more worthy than the other.

> Restraining consumption, he argued, was vital to achieving growth, and fairness vital to achieving restraint.[40]

political difficulty of doing anything about it since – unlike excessively high incomes – the best possible education was in itself a good thing. One could level down great wealth, but should not try to lower educational standards.[41]

In 1957 he made a combative speech in the debate on nationalisation. Trying to forge a compromise around which Gaitskellites and Bevanites could unite, the National Executive had come up with a report, *Industry and Society*, which largely accepted the revisionist view that large-scale nationalisation on the Morrisonian model of 1945–51 was outdated and proposed instead a range of more flexible, small-scale forms of public enterprise. Though Bevan himself wearily accepted it, *Industry and Society* was furiously attacked by unreconstructed old left-wingers like Manny Shinwell who wanted no retreat from full nationalisation. In a heated debate opened by Wilson and wound up by Gaitskell, Jenkins made the best speech from the floor defending the report. None of the powerful speeches opposing the report, he asserted, offered any constructive alternative except 'back to 1945'. But the position in 1957 was very different. A resolution moved by the Hornsey constituency party called on the next Labour government to nationalise the 512 biggest companies; but the President of the Board of Trade already had enough trouble trying to run three industries! Ownership without full control was the worst of all worlds, which would certainly lose Labour the election after next. Instead, the party must embrace the mixed economy and recognise the need for even publicly owned enterprises to make a profit. (Even the Co-op, Jenkins pointed out, made a profit, but called it a surplus.) 'The key issue is not whether you make a profit, but what happens to it when it has been made.' The essence of socialism was that the whole community should share it. Thus *Industry and Society* was not a retreat from socialism. 'You will get more socialism by accepting it than by rejecting it. You have to win the next election before you get any public ownership at all.' And *Industry and Society* gave Labour its best chance of doing that.[42]

The next year at Scarborough he urged another part of the revisionist case. 1958 was a 'stop' year in the 'stop–go' economic cycle of the 1950s. The previous July Macmillan had famously boasted that 'most of our people have never had it so good'.[43] But since then production had slowed and unemployment had risen, reaching 600,000 in January 1959. This, Jenkins urged, gave Labour the chance to present itself as the party of expansion: a difficult trick to pull off at a time when living standards were still rising rapidly, but politically vital, to counter the persistent association of Labour in the public mind with 'drabness, rationing and restriction'; as well as economically right, since wages were rising ahead of production. Jenkins did not underestimate inflation (as Macmillan arguably did). What he argued in 1958–9 was that only in an expanding economy could living standards rise without inflation. Growth was the key, but growth combined with wage restraint. This was the theme of several speeches that he made in the House that year, and also of his speech to conference. On the one hand, he warned at Scarborough, 'our bias must be for investment and against consumption'. On the other, 'we must be a party of a rapidly rising standard of living, and I am very suspicious of those people, sometimes on the left, often with a standard of living well above average, who claim to see the corrupting effects of more motor cars or more washing machines, or other material benefits'. What he was doing was trying to combine the hair shirt of Stafford Cripps – which still had an appeal on the left: even Bevan railed that the workers were being bought off with consumer goods – with the socialist hedonism of Tony Crosland. Without mentioning Europe, he concluded with his characteristic call for the country to look forward positively, not resentfully backwards as at Suez. 'The best antidote . . . is a buoyant economy, a rising standard of living and a faith in our economic future.'

An important sub-theme that he sounded repeatedly was the need for Britain, as part of the process of shaking off the burdens of empire, to rid itself of the obligations of the sterling area.* Labour should be 'very sceptical', he declared at Scarborough, 'about this mystique of sterling as a world currency, and we must think that that may be too high a price to pay if it has to be got at the price of stagnation and restriction at home'. It was 'lunatic' for the government to celebrate the first autumn for years without a sterling crisis by liberating dollar imports and moving towards restoring full convertability.[45] This probably went over the heads of most of the delegates in the hall. But the problem did not go away: it blighted the first three years of the next Labour government in 1964–7, and it was not until Jenkins himself became Chancellor of the Exchequer, still fending off recurrent threats to sterling in 1968–9, that he was able finally to begin winding up sterling's anachronistic obligations as a reserve currency.

In the run-up to the 1959 election Jenkins was given an opportunity

---

* In December 1957 Gaitskell had appointed Jenkins to chair a policy sub-committee on the future role of sterling, following criticism by the economist Andrew Shonfield. His fellow economists Alan Day and Robert Neild backed Shonfield's view that the sterling area was a burden on Britain, but they and Jenkins failed to prevail against the pro-Commonwealth convictions of Wilson and Douglas Jay, supported by Thomas Balogh.[44]

that many of his fellow backbenchers would have killed for, when he was invited by Penguin to write one of three instant paperbacks setting out the programmes of the three parties. *The Conservative Case* was written by the current chairman of the Tory Party, Lord Hailsham (though it was actually a windy rehash of a book he had first published in 1947); while the historian Roger Fulford contributed *The Liberal Case*. Jenkins wrote *The Labour Case* (60,000 words, for which he received an advance of £500) very quickly in the early months of 1959 and delivered it in April; it was published, with its two companions, in July, in good time for the expected election, which Macmillan duly called in October. In his preface Jenkins stressed that his was an entirely personal and unofficial statement of Labour policy:

> There is, fortunately, no rigid orthodoxy in the Labour Party. There is room for a wide variety of beliefs under its umbrella. It may therefore be worth while to set down why one person, holding rather moderate views, believes it to be of overwhelming importance that the General Election should result in a Labour Government.[46]

His presentation of Labour's aims accordingly bent over backwards to reassure those uncommitted voters whose support the party needed to regain power. There was little about nationalisation and still less of the confiscatory zeal that had still figured on his previous personal agenda five years earlier, or even two years earlier. He actually admitted that 'the post-war Labour Government tilted the balance too much towards the austerity of fair shares, and too little towards the incentives of free consumers' choice'.[47] The objective was still to abolish remaining pockets of poverty and promote a more equal society; but this, Jenkins now argued, could be achieved almost entirely by levelling-up, via the magic of growth, without the need of punitive levelling-down. In his opening chapter he conceded that eight years of Tory government had produced a modest increase in general prosperity, but claimed that the country was still 10 per cent worse off than it need be ('The principal fault of the British economy today is that it does not grow').[48] Living standards could rise much faster if the economy were run at full capacity, which would be greatly assisted if Britain would give up striving vainly to maintain the position of a world power, spent less on defence and adjusted to its position as a middle-sized European nation (though he respected party sensitivities to the extent that he did not explicitly advocate joining the Common Market). There were a couple of somewhat dutiful chapters on specific Labour policies – Crossman's proposed superannuated pensions scheme, and plans to raise standards in state education as an alternative to doing anything directly about public schools; and some detailed suggestions of how Labour would revitalise the economy by directing investment more productively than the Tories ('It requires the most skilful use of all the available weapons').[49] By the Thatcherite standards of thirty years later it was still a strongly interventionist programme. But the unquestioned assumption was that a broad range of progressive policies – better schools, higher benefits, improved social services and more provision for the arts – could be paid for out of the proceeds of 17½ per cent growth over five years ('the same rate of growth that our neighbours in Western Europe are confidently expecting'), which would still leave room for 'substantial tax reductions' (balanced by some increased taxation at the higher level, notably a capital gains tax and closing loopholes).[50] Three years after *The Future of Socialism*, *The Labour Case* represented the high-water mark of revisionist Labour confidence in an effortlessly expanding social democratic future.

Within this optimistic scenario, Jenkins gave special prominence to his own particular agenda with a final chapter entitled 'Is Britain Civilised?' in which he set out a shopping list of reforms whose prospects – although not party commitments – would be advanced by the election of a Labour government. The list was headed by the abolition of the death penalty ('this presumptuously fixed penalty'), followed by the legalisation of homosexuality; the abolition of the Lord Chamberlain's theatre censorship; reform of the licensing and betting laws; divorce law reform; reform of the 'harsh and archaic' abortion law; decriminalisation of suicide and attempted suicide; and the humanisation of immigration law. He concluded, echoing Crosland:

> Let us be on the side of those who want people to be free to live their own lives, to make their own mistakes, and to decide, in an adult way and provided they do not infringe the rights of others, the code by which they wish to live; and on the side of experiment and brightness, of better buildings and better food, of better music (jazz as well as Bach)* and better books, of fuller lives and greater freedom. In the long run these things will be more important than the most perfect of economic policies.[51]

---

* Jenkins had not yet caught up with the new phenomenon of rock-and-roll; in so far as he was aware of it, he probably saw it as a youthful variant of jazz.

These were the concluding words of Jenkins' personal manifesto, published by Penguin as if it represented the general view of the Labour party, which it emphatically did not. Many ordinary party members and trade unionists must have been enraged by his cavalier interpretation of socialism: his book surely played a part in stoking the left's campaign against the proposed rewriting of the party constitution by the 'Hampstead set' that surfaced after Labour's loss of the election. Perhaps that overstates its importance, among the many thousands of words poured out in the course of an election campaign. But the most revealing passage in *The Labour Case* perfectly embodies the mature political philosophy at which Jenkins had arrived by 1959, and from which he never subsequently departed: coolly pragmatic, undoctrinaire and increasingly centrist. 'Of course,' he conceded, 'the Labour Party does not stand only for economic expansion and a touch of realism about Britain's world position' (that 'only' must have raised some eyebrows). 'Since its earliest days it has been infused by a desire to promote a more just as well as a more prosperous society'. (Again, the word order is unusual):*

> At the same time it is a practical party. It is quite as much concerned
> with immediate reforms as with ultimate purposes. These reforms
> must be in the right direction. Any radical party must specify this,
> for without a sense of moving towards a goal, the idealism which
> is essential to the momentum of a left-wing party could not be
> generated. But the Labour Party does not ask its supporters to
> buy a ticket for the whole journey. It is always difficult to see
> how the course of politics will develop. The solution of one set
> of problems invariably uncovers new ones, the nature of which
> often cannot be seen in advance. And living as we do under a
> party system in which at least two of the parties have firm bases
> of support, alternating governments will no doubt continue to be
> the pattern of British politics.[53]

He added that Labour 'had never conceived its purposes as extending only to this country'; and *The Labour Case* included a remarkable chapter on the Commonwealth, in which he not only called for early majority rule for Southern as well as Northern Rhodesia (Zimbabwe as well as Zambia), but warned that by 2000 'the relationship between peoples of different coloured skins . . . will almost certainly have transcended the importance of the cold war issue of Communism against the West'. If it was not amicably defused, the white races could become a 'hated minority' in the world like the whites in South Africa, 'clinging to their privileges, afraid to mingle with the stream of world progress, and listening with anxious foreboding to the rumblings of the volcano beneath them'.[52] This was a strikingly prescient, progressive and surprisingly passionate excursion on a subject Jenkins very rarely wrote about.

It was his sense of history that led Jenkins to accept that alternating governments were not just inevitable, but positively healthy. He never believed that any government should stay in power for too long. At the same time he believed firmly in what Sir Keith Joseph later called the 'ratchet effect', by which Labour governments would advance the march of progress, but Tory governments, while temporarily halting it, never – until Mrs Thatcher – attempted to reverse it. In later year. he attached the same importance to maintaining momentum, without worrying too much about the ultimate destination, to the cause of European union. The journey, not the arrival, mattered. For a very clever man it was a curiously woolly, unenquiring and almost fatalistic cast of mind.

Most comment on *The Labour Case* thought the book revealed more about its author than about the likely policies of a Labour government. At least two reviewers already wondered how long Jenkins could remain in the Labour party. 'The merit of Mr Jenkins, book,' opined *The Economist*, 'is that it charts the direction in which the Labour party, if it is ever to be really acceptable to the British public, must go. Unfortunately a Labour government, if elected, would not be made up of people like him. 'The stratified remains of socialism,' the anonymous writer concluded, 'are an uneasy legacy for an undogmatically radical man.'[54] In the *Spectator* Bernard Levin led up to a similar conclusion with an admiring sketch of Jenkins' parliamentary style:

> First, there is Mr Roy Jenkins, he of the bland and carefree countenance, the erudite dome, the wagging forefinger, the courteous approach, the gentle humour, the collar one point of which insists on riding up over his waistcoat (and frequently over his lapel). Mr Jenkins, as many a Minister has reason to know, carries the fastest statistic in the West, and will shoot the pips out of an inaccuracy at thirty paces.

But what was such an intelligent, rational man doing wasting his time in politics when he should be writing elegant history books? (Jenkins' answer could have been that he managed to do both.) 'Mr Jenkins,' Levin suggested, 'is the last surviving member of the eighteenth-century Enlightenment.' He was a member of the Labour Party 'because his reason tells him to be, and while the Labour Party can continue to attract – and hold – such reasonable men, it will survive.'[55]

Jenkins' belief in alternating governments certainly led him to hope for a Labour victory in 1959. He thought the Tories were tired, cynical incompetent and reactionary and he desperately wanted to see Gaitskell as Prime Minister – in which event he could probably expect some sort of office. But privately he was not optimistic. Sometime that spring a group of young Labour candidates, including Bill Rodgers, Peter Shore, Dick Taverne and Gerald Kaufman, took him to dinner at a scruffy Greek restaurant. Labour was ahead in the polls, but Jenkins was positive that they would not win.[56] For a couple of years after Suez it had seemed all but certain that Labour would win comfortably. The government had led the country into a humiliating debacle, while Labour's family quarrel had been successfully patched up, with Bevan now working reasonably harmoniously under Gaitskell as Shadow Foreign Secretary. In January 1958 Dick Crossman wrote that power after the next election was 'now assumed to be inevitable'.[57] But by a remarkable personal display of style and nerve, helped by an increasingly widespread sense of rising 'affluence', Macmillan turned the tables. A giveaway budget (ninepence off income tax), a hot summer and a glossy advertising campaign ('Life's Better With the Conservatives. Don't Let Labour Ruin It') propelled the Tories into a commanding lead by the time Macmillan called the election for 9 October 1959. Actually Gaitskell fought an excellent campaign and seemed to be closing the gap again, until he made what Jenkins in his memoirs – forgetting what he had written at the time – called 'the most terrible mistake' by promising that a Labour government would not increase the standard rate of income tax. In view of Labour's ambitious spending plans this seemed either dishonest or irresponsible, and the Tories had a field day. 'It was unwise, out of character,' Jenkins wrote, 'and had the undesirable effect of putting Gaitskell on the defensive for the rest of the campaign.' With hindsight, however – and contrary to the contemporary view of David Butler and Richard Rose in their Nuffield study of the election – he did not believe it decisively affected the result. 'The underlying current of the election . . . was that the hidden mood of the country was against the Labour party . . . In the circumstances no radical leader could have won.'[58] Most historians would now agree.

The swing to the Tories on 9 October was particularly marked in the Midlands, where Labour lost ten seats, and Jenkins felt the effect of it in Stechford. 'I did not exert myself unduly,' he recalled. He ventured beyond his home territory only to speak for friends – Crosland, Woodrow Wyatt and David Ginsburg, all of whom were contesting new seats (Grimsby, Bosworth and Dewsbury respectively), which they all won. On arriving with Jennifer at his own count, however – having already heard gloomy pointers to the national result – Jenkins found

some of his supporters worried that he had lost.* 'I can assure you tha
you've won,' the Tory agent reassured him, 'but I don't know what'
happened to your majority.'[60] In fact he did not come seriously close
to losing, but he suffered a swing 'worse than the Birmingham average
and much worse than the national average'. His 1955 majority wa
more than halved to just under 3,000 – its lowest level in nine contests
over twenty-six years:

Roy Jenkins (Labour)	21,919
J.M. Bailey (Conservative)	18,996
Labour majority	2,923[61]

Nationally Labour lost twenty-three seats, enough to double the
Tories' overall majority from fifty to exactly one hundred. It wa
the fourth consecutive election since the great landslide of 1945 a
which Labour had lost seats. The post-mortem began almost
immediately.

* Roy and Jennifer had been dining with Solly Zuckerman and his wife Joan, as he di
frequently during the campaign. Though he still stayed with the Hitchmans in Stechford
the Zuckerman house in Edgbaston 'provided a lot of meals and high-quality wine' at th
end of the campaigning day. Zuckerman was then Professor of Anatomy at Birmingham
University, as well as the Macmillan government's chief adviser on nuclear weapons, 'bu
did not find the latter role incompatible with providing me with hospitality and encour
agement in Birmingham'.[59]

10 'Fight and Fight Again'?

J ENKINS may have anticipated Labour's defeat in 1959, but the reality of it was still hugely disappointing. On the Saturday after the election, Hugh Dalton wrote in his diary that Roy and Jennifer had come round for a drink, 'very crushed, especially she'.[1] The next morning the leader's friends gathered in Hampstead. Those present were Gaitskell, Dalton, Jay, Gordon Walker, Jenkins and Crosland, plus Herbert Bowden (Chief Whip), John Harris (then an adviser to Gaitskell) and Jennifer Jenkins. This meeting was subsequently portrayed by the left as the launch of a concerted effort to wrench the party to the right. It was actually much less organised than the conspiracy theorists imagined. It lasted only a couple of hours – after which Jenkins took Dalton off to lunch – and was mainly an opportunity to lick their wounds and compare experiences of the campaign. It was just one of dozens of such primarily social post-mortems: in the two weeks after the election Roy and Jennifer dined with the Daltons, the Jays, the Wyatts and the Benns, and themselves entertained Tony Crosland, the Healeys and the Gordon Walkers (plus Denis Howell, who was one of those who had lost his seat in Birmingham). But there was clearly some serious discussion that first Sunday morning at Frognal Gardens, since 'at one stage we all sat in a circle and each expressed our view as though at a seminar'.[2] On this occasion Jay took the lead in urging that Labour should drop any talk of further nationalisation, loosen its links with the unions and possibly even change the party's name, in order to broaden its appeal from the old cloth-cap image of the past. 'We are in danger,' he warned, 'of fighting under the label of a class which no longer exists.'[3] Jenkins largely agreed, though he never favoured changing the party's name. But their view was by no means universally accepted.

Dalton thought Jay's ideas 'rather wild, pouring out the baby with the bathwater and throwing the bath after them'; Crosland said 'practically nothing'; while Gaitskell let the discussion flow without at this stage revealing his own thinking.[4] Nevertheless he was happy to encourage a public debate. A few days later Jay published his proposals in an article in *Forward*, which attracted a lot of attention. Meanwhile Jenkins had been due to leave (with Jennifer) for a month's lecture tour in the United States, arranged for him by J.K. Galbraith. At Gaitskell's request he postponed his trip so that he could take a leading role in Labour's inquest.* Indeed, over the next four weeks he threw himself into it with unusual energy.

First he appeared on the BBC's flagship current affairs programme *Panorama*, where he took very much the same line as Jay. Tony Wedgwood Benn watched the broadcast and saw Jenkins 'advocating very modestly that you should drop nationalisation, watch out for the dangers of union links and not rule out an association with the Liberals'. But on his way home to Ladbroke Square he and Jennifer called in on Benn in Holland Park Avenue and they had a 'flaming row'. 'I was very calm and collected,' Benn wrote in his diary, but 'he got into a semi-hysterical state'. ('Usually it's the other way round', Benn noted.) '"We must use this shock to drop nationalisation entirely at this forthcoming Conference," he said . . . I concentrated on the dangers to our integrity if we were to be so reckless. In the end he half-apologised for his temper and went off with Jennifer.'[5]

When Parliament reassembled a few days later Dick Crossman too found Jenkins 'in a state of neurotic frenzy', or at least 'in a mood for heroic crusading', demanding 'shock tactics . . . to shake the Party into dropping nationalisation altogether'. ('After all', he said, 'you taught me . . . that in order to educate, one must shock.') Crossman was as surprised as Benn to find himself 'cool and reasonable, with Roy frantic'. Crossman told Jenkins that he was actually making it harder for Gaitskell to drop nationalisation. '"How can Mr Bevan drop nationalisation because you and Jay order him to?" . . . However Roy stormed out, saying he would make a great speech this morning' at the party meeting – as indeed he did. Following a similar appeal by Christopher Mayhew and a robust speech from a Durham miner who told Jay bluntly to go and join the

---

* He would presumably have had to cancel his tour entirely if Labour had won the election, since Gaitskell would surely have given him some sort of office – perhaps in the Treasury or the Home Office. So either the American trip was arranged some time before Macmillan called the election, or Jenkins' signing up to it is confirmation that he did not expect Labour to win.

Liberal party, 'Roy Jenkins weighed in with his great plea to cut away from nationalisation' – which, *The Times* reported, was not altogether well received:

> Mr Roy Jenkins, one of the Party's younger intellectuals, made some of his colleagues bristle by what seems to have been a complicated and almost theologically subtle exploration of the damage that the two firm election pledges to nationalise steel and long distance road haulage had done to the party image. When Mr Jenkins was challenged to put the argument in words of one syllable he seems to have decided to move warily. He is said to have given no positive answer.[6]

Crossman conceded that both Jenkins' and Mayhew's speeches 'were very well delivered and thoughtful and were received thoughtfully. It was the highest level of debate I have heard for a long time.' Nevertheless, he concluded, 'the Jenkins/Jay line has no chance whatsoever of being accepted . . . Most of the Party were deeply shocked by what they felt was a betrayal by Gaitskell's closest friends.'[7] The week ended 'with the Hampstead poodles in complete rout'.[8]

The trouble was not that the 'Hampstead poodles' had launched a coordinated coup, but on the contrary that (in the words of Gaitskell's biographer Philip Williams) they 'organised no conspiracy and agreed no objectives, but put up a cacophony of individual contributions' – of which Jay's *Forward* article and Jenkins' *Panorama* interview were only the most provocative – which 'greatly harmed their own cause'.[9] Driving Crossman home after a dinner at the French Embassy on 27 October, Jenkins admitted that there had been 'grave tactical errors in the activities of the Hampstead group'.* But he did not ease up. In early November he gave a Fabian Society lecture in which he again blamed Labour's defeat on the unpopularity of nationalisation ('We must kill the misplaced view that the Labour Party is a dogmatic nationalising party, existing primarily to pop more and more industries into the bag')[11] and wrote another similar analysis of the result for the *Spectator*. 'I also made political speeches in both Oxford and Cambridge, addressed

---

* Over dinner they had another 'snappy' argument when they discovered that they were both reviewing the memoirs of the former Tory party chairman Lord Woolton (Jenkins in the *Spectator*, Crossman in the *New Statesman*). Crossman said that Woolton was 'a Keynesian Liberal, like the American Democrats. At once Jenkins spotted what I was at when I added, "What really distinguishes a Socialist is the belief in public ownership and State trading."'[10]

a *Socialist Commentary* lunch, and proselytised the French and Italian embassies as well as the *Time* magazine London bureau, the *Observer* newspaper and all the editors of the Westminster Provincial Press group about the virtues of the new revisionism.'[12] At the same time he was careful to keep his Stechford activists onside with what he was doing. In his *Spectator* piece, published just before the party conference, he dismissed as 'a complete fallacy' the idea that the reformers would 'take the stuffing out of politics' and reduce Labour to 'a sort of junior Conservative party'; and he listed seven 'great issues of today and tomorrow' which would still divide Labour sharply from the Tories:

1. Britain accepting her new place in the world;
2. colonial freedom;
3. whether, as we grow richer, this new wealth is used exclusively for individual selfishness or for the growth of necessary community services and whether, in consequence, we follow or escape the American precedent of great private affluence surrounding rotting public services;*
4. whether we reverse the present anarchy sufficiently quickly to prevent the permanent destruction of the amenity of life in this overcrowded island;
5. the right of the individual to live his private life free from the intolerant prejudices of others or the arrogant interference of the State and the police;
6. whether we can expose and destroy the inefficiencies of contemporary private industry without offering only the sterile alternative of an indefinite extension of public monopoly;
7. whether, as existing class barriers break up, they are replaced by a new and nasty materialist snobbery or by a fresher and more co-operative approach.[14]

There were more questions in this list than answers. The key question of public versus private ownership came notably low down. But thirty years later Jenkins still thought his agenda constituted 'rather a good radical programme' – though not, he admitted, a socialist one.[15]

Having delivered this parting manifesto he left on his delayed American tour, thus missing the stormy party conference at which Gaitskell

---

* This was a direct lift from J.K. Galbraith's *The Affluent Society*, published the year before, which first drew attention to the phenomenon of 'public squalor in the midst of private affluence'.[13]

outraged the fundamentalists by proposing to amend Clause Four of the party's 1918 constitution: the key clause that committed the party to 'the common ownership of the means of production, distribution and exchange' – in other words the nationalisation of practically the whole economy. Ironically this was one reform that neither Jay nor Jenkins, Crosland or any of his other friends had urged on him; keen as they were to modernise the party's image and policies, they all thought it reckless to challenge its Holy Writ. At Blackpool Gaitskell's face was only saved by Bevan, who finally gained the advantage in their decade-long feud with a brilliant unifying speech – only to fall ill almost immediately and die nine months later. But the furore Gaitskell provoked at Blackpool was only the first round in a renewed battle with the left which almost tore the party apart again over the next three years. In that battle, despite his doubts about Gaitskell's choice of ground, Jenkins was once again firmly, but much less frenetically, behind his leader.

While he was away the *Sunday Times* printed a rumour that Gaitskell intended to appoint Jenkins Shadow Chancellor in place of Wilson. It was almost certainly nonsense, though Gaitskell may possibly have toyed with the idea. Some time before the election he had told Crossman disparagingly that Wilson was not an economist and urged him to 'talk to an economist like Jenkins or Crosland';[16] and during the campaign he told Benn, who was handling the party's communications, that he should ignore the second eleven and build up 'the up-and-coming generation – Crosland, Jenkins, Healey, and you can include yourself in that category'.[17] Doubtless all these would have got junior office if Gaitskell had formed a government in 1959. But none of them was yet in the Shadow Cabinet – Healey was elected for the first time that autumn, while Jenkins (having stood once unsuccessfully in 1957) did not even stand – so in a party as hierarchical as Labour it would have been suicidal to have elevated a favourite in this way. Gaitskell told the editor of the *Manchester Guardian*, Alastair Hetherington, that 'there wasn't a word of truth in it'.[18] But the fact that it could even be suggested reflected the way both Gaitskell and Jenkins were viewed by their critics. It is clear from Crossman's diary that Wilson believed it; Jenkins thought the story 'cast a shadow over his [Wilson's] relations with me for several years'.[19] As it was, he was one of five aspirants under forty (only just, in his case) to be given junior frontbench roles,* and he joined – briefly – Wilson's Shadow Treasury team. In this

---

* The other four were Tony Benn, Roy Mason, Reg Prentice and George Thomson – all future Cabinet ministers under Wilson.

capacity over the next eight months he asked one or two questions and moved Opposition amendments to the Finance Bill (opposing reducing import duty on sherry, trying to cut the tax relief on 'golden handshakes'), but made only one substantial speech. This was in the debate on Heathcoat Amory's 1960 budget, in which he rejected the usual Tory clamour for tax cuts with his favourite Galbraith line about private affluence and public squalor: 'If we are to devote absolute priority constantly to shrinking the total of public expenditure as a proportion of our national income, what sort of community are we to live in?'[20]

Such was the uproar caused by his questioning Clause Four that for a time Gaitskell thought he might have to resign. In an article in the American journal *Foreign Affairs* – not exactly bedside reading on the Labour left – Jenkins loyally explained that the Clause as it stood was 'both inadequate and misleading': inadequate because it omitted all Labour's other objectives ('international, colonial, social, educational, libertarian') and misleading because it falsely suggested that Labour wanted to nationalise everything. Gaitskell had merely proposed to bring 'the theoretical position into line with what has long been the practical position. And on grounds of intellectual honesty alone, this is always a good thing to do.' The left, he suggested, clung to nationalisation as 'a sort of emotional raft', arising from its 'essential defeatism'.[21] But Gaitskell had taken on a battle he could not win. The unions refused to countenance any change to the constitution, and long before the 1960 conference he was forced to settle for an expanded but woolly 'statement of aims' which left the 1918 aspiration intact until Tony Blair finally consigned it to history nearly half a century later. 'It is perhaps always a mistake to raise matters of dogma in a left-wing party,' Jenkins wrote philosophically in the *Spectator*. 'They are probably best left to be made irrelevant by the development of practical policies.'[22] Gaitskell's blunder threw the revisionists on the defensive just when they had hoped to seize the initiative.

Meanwhile another equally emotive but more substantive row blew up over nuclear weapons. It was the 1945 Labour government which had committed Britain to developing its independent nuclear deterrent: Ernest Bevin was determined to have a British bomb 'with the bloody Union Jack on top of it' to maintain Britain's position as a great power.[23] Up to 1957 the party in opposition, still dominated by the right-wing unions, had held to that commitment, with even Nye Bevan, in an emotional speech to the 1957 conference, horrifying his unilateralist supporters by refusing to send a future Labour Foreign Secretary – he meant himself – 'naked into the conference chamber'.[24] But by 1960 the balance in the party had shifted. Bevan was dead, a new generation of left-wing leaders led by Frank Cousins of the TGWU had taken over the unions, and the left, already gunning for Gaitskell over Clause Four, seized on unilateral nuclear disarmament as a new stick to beat him with. The Campaign for Nuclear Disarmament (CND) held its first march from London to Aldermaston (later the other way round) in 1958 and quickly attracted a mass membership. Over the summer of 1960 one union conference after another carried unilateralist motions and Gaitskell faced a second defeat at Scarborough in the autumn. Given his concern that Britain should scale back her military pretensions and adjust to a more modest role in the world, Jenkins might have been expected to feel some sympathy with CND. But on this issue he was still a firm Cold Warrior, devoted unquestioningly to the Atlantic alliance. Privately he actually thought Gaitskell could have afforded to fudge a bit on the detail: at a heated meeting at Ladbroke Square in May, for instance, Jenkins, Crosland and Gordon Walker all thought the leader's 'extreme and provocative clarity' likely to be counterproductive and were exasperated by his stubbornness.[25] But Jenkins' overriding worry was that the left's lurch into unilateralism was just another symptom of irresponsible opposition-mindedness that threatened to make Labour unelectable.

When the AEU (the engineering union) voted for unilateral disarmament (as well as sweeping new targets for nationalisation and against any change to Clause Four), he agreed with Dalton that 'the position had become impossible for Hugh'. They both thought Gaitskell should declare that if the party went unilateralist, he could no longer lead it. But Jenkins wanted him to go further and 'say something positive and forward-looking to attract support from non-members, e.g. an anti-Trade Union declaration. We couldn't go on being pushed about, on matters of policy, by snap decisions at Trade Union Conference by narrow margins, while delegates were waiting for tea.'[26] In other words, it was the method of making policy, as much as the policy itself, that he objected to. (He accepted that he had not objected to the union block vote when it was controlled by the right, but argued that it was different now that it was being used to oppose the leadership rather than to support it.) In June he held a press conference in Stechford and issued a stark warning of what was at stake if the unions tried to impose unilateralism on the parliamentary leadership:

For the conference to force such a policy upon these men could hardly fail to destroy the Labour Party as we know it today. Either they would have to stand up in the House of Commons and say things which everybody knew they did not believe, and inevitably sacrifice the respect of the country, or they would have to resign and leave the party virtually leaderless. Either alternative would be catastrophic for Labour's electoral prospects.

The vote at Scarborough would not rid the world of nuclear weapons; but it could easily 'destroy the hope of a Labour Government for a generation'. He begged other local parties to follow the lead of the Birmingham Labour Party and reverse their position.[27]

Over the summer many did so – Stechford followed his advice by a margin of 5:1 – so that by the time they came to Scarborough most of the delegates in the hall had swung back behind the official multi-lateralist line. The trouble was that most of the big union block votes, headed by Cousins' TGWU, were long ago tied up the other way. So when Gaitskell made his famously defiant speech ('There are some of us, Mr Chairman, who will fight and fight and fight again to save the Party we love') he had already won the argument but lost the vote. He still lost the vote, but by a much narrower margin – just under 300,000 in a total vote of six million – than had seemed likely a few weeks earlier.[28] Jenkins was moved 'to tears and total commitment' by Gaitskell's speech.[29] The next day he spoke in the debate on Clause Four and directly confronted the left's destructive hostility. 'I hope we can conduct the rest of this debate,' he began, 'without the personal bitterness and rancour which seems to have been previous speakers' main contribution to socialist aims.' The party was actually pretty united on practical measures. 'There may be a small minority who think we can achieve our aims only through cataclysm and misery. But the majority know we must change radically, but not destroy, society, and build on the foundations which exist.' He mocked the 'unyielding conservatism' of those who would admit no change to the party consti-tution, and also their chauvinist insularity:

> We exist to change society. We are not likely to be very successful if we are horrified at any suggestion of changing ourselves . . . One of the things from which we are suffering is a misplaced national complacency: a belief that we do things better than anyone else . . . Do not let us be too afraid, in the Labour Party, to learn from some of our friends abroad.

Roy aged three with his mother.

Aged six, posing with his parents
Arthur and Hattie (seated and
standing right) on the day Arthur
was released from prison in 1927.

Arthur Jenkins leaving
10 Downing Street
after his appointment
as junior Education
minister in August 1945.

Eduard Beneš, exiled president of Czechoslovakia, addresses the Oxford Union on 7 March 1940, with Madron Seligman in the chair, Jenkins at the secretary's table, Tony Crosland and Ted Heath behind Beneš.

The Union Committee with visiting speakers Lord Londonderry and Arthur Greenwo in February 1940, with Seligman as President (seated centre), Jenkins and Crosland toge (standing right), Heath (seated second left) and Nicko Henderson (seated second from ri

Roy and Jennifer on their wedding day, 20 January 1945.

in Jenkins and Major Denis Healey with other delegates at the Labour Party conference
May 1945, six weeks before the General Election at which they were both candidates.

(*Above and right*) The dapper Labour candidate meets old soldiers and building workers while canvassing in the Central Southwark by-election, April 1948.

Jenkins with Clement Attlee in 1959.

GENERAL ELECTION, 1950
POLLING DAY — THURSDAY, FEB. 23rd — 7-0 a.m. to 9-0 p.m.

ROY JENKINS
THE LABOUR CANDIDATE FOR STECHFORD

Jenkins' election address at Stechford in the 1950 General Election.

...s of the Stechford Parliament...

...OUR P... ...PLE FIRST

...ector,

...our Candidate for the new ...vision, I ask for your support ...this General Election. I ask ...back the Labour Government, ...ay continue with its policy of ...ment and fair shares for all. ...native would be a return to ...ne Conservative Party, with its ...ased up a little for electoral ...urt with its basic ideas the same ...ee than in pre-war days, for the ...destroyed many of the advantages ...re used to enjoy in our trading ...with other countries. Tory ideas ...u be intolerable; and Tory ...now be intolerable; and Tory ...of our productive basic industries, ...larly of the vital basic industries, ...was dangerous enough fifteen years ...would now mean national disaster.

...DUCTION UP

...ready, under the Labour Government, ...h of this pre-war neglect has been made ...Our basic industries are being put ...their feet again. A full part in this ...cess is being played by nationalisation, ...ich our opponents will tell you is a ...arile and doctrinaire creed. When you ...ar this accusation, I ask you to remember ...se coal industry. The thirty-three years ...om 1913 to 1946 had become an industry ...uninterrupted decline in the industry— ...che country's major economic difficulty, ...and threatened to stultify our whole re- ...covery effort. Three years of public owner- ...ship have effected a vast change. The ...trend of decades has been sharply reversed,

...product... ...has be... ...pre-wa... ...cultura... Output to... ...to the 1938 level. This re... ...to the British people and a rebu... Tory charge that the workers have not been pulling their weight.

NO DOLE QUEUES

For the first time in peace-time for many, many years, we are using our resources to the full. Industrial disputes are no longer draining away the life-blood of our pro- ductive effort. For every working day lost in this way in the three years after 1945, twenty-two were lost in the comparable period after 1918. And, most important of all, the waste and the misery of mass unemployment have been banished. Be- tween the wars there were never less than 800,000 unemployed, and the average figure was 1,750,000. To-day there are dole queues, and this has had an enormous effect, both on our productive effort and on the status of every worker.

TORIES WORRIED

Our opponents are very worried by our success in this direction. They seek to explain it away by saying that it is due entirely to world conditions, or to Marshall Aid, or to some other external cause. But the hard fact remains that in many other countries—Belgium, Italy, Western Germany and even the United States, affected by the same external conditions, the return of large-scale unemployment. So it would be here after February 23rd if the Labour Government's mechanism of planning and control were to be destroyed.

...aw has been increased. Old Age ...nywhere in the world. ...Pensions have been abolished, Old Age Allowances have been instituted, Family tion for industrial injuries has been placed upon a new basis, the National Insurance Act, with its comprehensive benefits, has been brought into full operation, and the Health Service has become a reality. Many of these advances have been made against Conservatism opposition. Labour does not merely talk about the benefits of social security at election time. It acts to create them.

HOMES FOR THE PEOPLE

A great housing drive is going on, and over a million new homes have been provided since 1945. The results still lag behind the need (particularly where Tory- dominated Councils have not co-operated fully in carrying out the Ministry of Health's policy), but Britain's progress in this field has outstripped that of every other country in the world, with the solitary exception of Sweden. Every priority is given to the building of houses to let—at reasonable rents, and this policy will be continued.

PRICES

At this Election much attention will be devoted to high prices. We have been living in a period of world inflation, and some rise in the cost of living has therefore been inevitable. Our opponents will make much play with the 3s. 8d. fall in the pur- chasing power of the £ which they say has taken place since 1945. They will not tell you that, in the United States, where their "free for all" methods have been tried,

...ly built up ...lso shared ...er before. ...the con- ...of social

the fall in the value of a corresponding unit of money has been 4s. 10d. and that in most other countries the decline has been still sharper. Nor will they tell you that their Conservative proposal for abolishing the food subsidies would add about 14s. to each housewife's weekly shopping bill. The Labour Party is not complacent about the price level. It believes that much can be done to cut distributors' margins, particularly in the case of fruit and vege- tables, and it intends to take resolute action in this direction.

YOU AND TO-MORROW

I do not seek to put before you a picture of an easy future with no difficulties. This would be dishonest and foolish. Our enormous economic problems are still vital to us, even though it has done no more than counterbalance the help which we ourselves have been giving to the rest of the world—will soon come to an end. We must replace it by our own efforts. The question you have to answer is whether this can best be done by Labour's policy of high and rising production or by the traditional Tory method of creating a pool of un- employment and making the people too poor to buy the imports and the other goods which they need. Since 1945 we have had, for the first time, a Parliament which has carried out its pledges to the nation, and which has worked for the whole community, and not just for a selected few. I ask you to elect another such Parlia- ment on February 23rd.

Yours sincerely,

Roy Jenkins.

The Labour Candidate

VOTE
LABOUR

ROY JENKINS, son of the late Arthur Jenkins, M.P., the miners' leader, was born in 1920 at Pontypool, in Monmouthshire.

From the local elementary school he made his way to Oxford, where he gained a first class honours degree in Philosophy, Politics and Economics.

At the 1945 General Election, he fought the Solihull Division and succeeded in polling 21,000 votes for Labour—an all-time record for the area. At a Bye-Election in 1948 he was elected to the House of Commons as Member for Central Southwark, a seat which disappears under redistribution. He is married, with one child.

JENKINS | X

Printed by The Birmingham Printers, Ltd., 42-44 Hill St., B'ham, & Published by S. G. Cooke, 116, Oxmoore Road, B'ham, 26.

Canvassing with Tony Crosland
in Grimsby in 1959.

Hugh Gaitskell

Jenkins speaking in the Common
Market debate at the Labour Party
conference in Brighton, October 1962.
Gaitskell listens sceptically.

Barley Alison

Caroline and Ian Gilmour

Ann Fleming,
Mark and Leslie
Bonham Carter

Roy and Jennifer at East Hendred in April 1969, with their two
younger children, Cynthia & Edward.

Jenkins in his study at Ladbroke Square in the mid-1960s.

Socialist parties all round the world, Jenkins pointed out, had been modernising themselves in recent years – most famously the West German SPD at its Bad Godesberg conference in 1959, but also the Scandinavian, Austrian, Israeli and New Zealand Labour Parties – and doing very well as a result; the last wholly unreconstructed socialist parties left were the Australian and the French. To haul itself back into a position to win again, Labour must show that its principles were relevant to the 1960s, not keep refighting 'old battles with old slogans'.[30] He was booed for his pains. But Jenkins, for all his fastidious manner, never shrank from telling conference what it did not want to hear.

Having survived Scarborough, the next challenge Gaitskell faced was from Harold Wilson, who felt obliged to stake his claim to Bevan's inheritance by standing against Gaitskell for the party leadership in November. He stood on a somewhat spurious unity ticket, claiming that Gaitskell's style of leadership was 'divisive'; but to the right, his candidacy only confirmed his reputation as an ambitious little twister. Writing in the *Daily Telegraph*, Jenkins was confident that Gaitskell would be able to reverse the unilateralist vote next year, and was contemptuous of Wilson's cynical suggestion that the nuclear argument could somehow be fudged:

It is peculiarly difficult to see how Mr Wilson, were he by chance to achieve success, would view his new position. He is clearly not a unilateralist . . . To pretend that compromise is always possible and that policy statements can mean both everything and nothing is a certain recipe for the continued erosion of the Labour vote.[31]

Gaitskell comfortably defeated Wilson by 166 votes to 81; but the two-to-one margin underlined the continuing tribal division in the party. Analysing the result in the *Spectator*, Jenkins jeered that if Wilson had been prosecuting in the recent *Lady Chatterley* trial he would doubtless have argued that 'with goodwill there should be no difficulty in reaching a compromise between publication and suppression'. He went on, more seriously, to assert that there was no point compromising with the left, which only wanted to remain the left. To win again, Labour must reconnect with its potential supporters in the country:

Unless the Labour Party is determined to abdicate its role as a mass party and become nothing more than a narrow sectarian society, its paramount task is to represent the whole of the leftward-thinking half of the country – and to offer the prospect of attracting enough marginal support to give that half some share of power.[32]

That was precisely the objective of a new organisation, the Campaign for Democratic Socialism, founded that autumn to lead a grass roots fightback against the domination of the left. Jenkins attended the first meeting, in a Chelsea pub in May 1960, which decided on the name. Tony Crosland helped write the manifesto (with two Oxford city councillors, Frank Pickstock and Philip Williams), and at least one of the early meetings was held in Jenkins' house. But CDS, though it soon attracted the declared support of forty-five Labour MPs, the covert sympathy of most of the Shadow Cabinet and the endorsement of Attlee, was primarily an extra-parliamentary movement of younger candidates, councillors and local activists, including many of the rising stars of the next generation. The chairman and part-time paid organiser was Bill Rodgers; Denis Howell and Dick Taverne were also on the executive; while others who cut their teeth in CDS included Shirley Williams, Brian Walden and David Marquand. All of these entered Parliament in the next few years: Rodgers, Howell and Taverne at by-elections in 1961–2; Williams and Walden at the 1964 election; Marquand in 1966. All would be more or less closely associated with Jenkins over the next three decades, and all but Walden and Howell were founder members of the SDP in 1981. CDS was in fact a clear precursor of the SDP, successfully fighting within the Labour party much the same battle against the influence of the left that later drove the Social Democrats to leave the party. CDS was the first major exercise of Bill Rodgers' unmatched organising talents, and was largely instrumental in enabling Gaitskell to beat back the unilateralist challenge at the 1961 conference in Blackpool. Compared with the other leading members of the 'Hampstead set', however, Jenkins himself did not play a very active part in CDS, even behind the scenes. 'I was aware of your relative absence,' Rodgers told him in 1990 when commenting on his draft memoirs. 'I began to wonder if you were serious about politics.'[33]

He was not the only one. Jenkins was at this time, by his own admission, a 'semi-detached MP'.[34] After his uncharacteristic burst of energy immediately after the 1959 election he seemed to prefer writing about politics to full participation. That autumn he started work on his most ambitious literary project yet, a full-scale biography of the last Liberal Prime Minister, H.H. Asquith. The following summer, after a mild tiff with Gaitskell, he slightly petulantly resigned his frontbench post in order to be free to speak about Europe. 'I have no general policy disagreement,' he explained. 'It is only on this one issue.'[35]* But he actually spoke very little over the next two years, preferring to use the *Spectator* as a platform from which to comment on the political scene in lofty and often somewhat disillusioned terms. For the *Sunday Times* in October 1961 he wrote a 'long and adulatory' – but anonymous – profile of Gaitskell in which he attributed his recovery of authority less to CDS than to his own exceptional qualities: his 'stubborn intellectual integrity' combined with (ironically, as it turned out) 'extraordinary resilience of mind and body'. With Wilson 'talented but isolated', he asserted, and Gaitskell now buttressed by a group of right-wing colleagues (George Brown, Patrick Gordon Walker, Jim Callaghan and Denis Healey) with whom he worked well, Labour looked like an alternative government again.[37]

For the *Spectator*, however, and in his own name, he wrote a considerably more critical assessment of the 1961 conference.† Despite the leadership's victories on the main issues, the tone of the debates was still worrying, with too much ignorant applause for 'farragos of half-baked Marxist nonsense' from an irreconcilable minority who were 'far more interested in the destruction of Mr Gaitskell than in the return of a Labour Government'. There was a disturbing lack of interest 'whenever a matter of internal party dispute was not being touched on'. The reason, he suggested, was 'the feeling of impotence produced by the years without power':

> The party is now suffering from ten years of passing too many programmes without any of them being carried into effect. What it now needs above all is not more policy proposals but the ability to carry through some of those it already has. It would then begin to be more interested in constructive solutions.

There were still 'a lot of faults in the party's structure', as well as 'a sizeable irreconcilable element' within it. 'But it may be,' he concluded cautiously, 'that, with a little more help from the Conservatives, these

---

* 'It's a slight exaggeration to say I resigned,' he told Robin Day a few years later. 'I was doing a very small job and I asked not to be reappointed . . . It wasn't a very dramatic gesture.'[36]
† Ever mindful of his creature comforts, he had not looked forward to going back to Blackpool. 'It takes a long time to get there, the sea front is hideous, the hotels are inadequate' and the weather was usually bad.[38] This time, however, he found the place 'slightly more agreeable than I had remembered it . . . The food was better, the weather was less wet and the illuminated tramcars were most impressive.'[39]

are containable until after the next general election and not incompatible with victory when it comes.'[40]

But his great cause in 1960–62 was the Common Market. By now Jenkins was clearly established as the leading Labour advocate of entry, which he presented primarily as a progressive cause to set against the 'ghastly complacency . . . bound up with insularity . . . which, under Mr Macmillan's example and inspiration, is settling upon the country', and he attempted to link it with the youthful optimism aroused by the election of President Kennedy in the United States. He took as his text a pamphlet published in October 1960 by the sociologist Michael Young (author of *The Rise of the Meritocracy* and founder of the Consumers' Association), entitled *The Chipped White Cups of Dover.**

> An effective Labour party must be against retiring behind this rather squalid and insubstantial fortification, against the dangerous isolationism which is implicit both in unilateralism and in much of Mr Macmillan's foreign policy, and in favour of the steady merging of British sovereignty . . . A major task of the Labour party is to see that we do not remain the last bastion of misplaced self-satisfaction.[41]

His problem was that it was the Tories, not Labour, who were becoming the pro-European party. In the summer of 1961, after much cautious testing of the ground, Macmillan finally brought his Cabinet to agree to open negotiations for British membership, to be conducted by Ted Heath. Jenkins became deputy chairman of an all-party Common Market Campaign. Chaired by the former ambassador to Paris, Lord Gladwyn, it comprised a careful mix of parliamentarians, industrialists, mandarins and one or two trade unionists (including the former Durham miners' leader, Sam Watson); its newsletter was initially edited by Bill Rodgers. But its cross-party character and City funding, plus the fact that it seemed to be supporting the Tory government, was a handicap in winning Labour support; so after a few months Jenkins set up a separate but overlapping Labour Common Market Committee, with himself as chairman and Jack Diamond, who was already treasurer of the parent body, as treasurer. (Diamond, Labour MP for Gloucester, was another long-term ally who would serve with Jenkins in the Treasury and later in the SDP.) At its launch Jenkins claimed the support

---

* With his twin enthusiasms for Europe and consumer protection, Young – later Lord Young of Dartington – was an almost perfect combination of Roy and Jennifer.

of eighty Labour MPs. The division in the party was broadly right/left, with a majority of Gaitskellites (including Crosland) in favour and the old Bevanites like Michael Foot and Barbara Castle the most vociferous opponents; but there were plenty of cross-currents. Some left-wingers like Eric Heffer and the veteran Fenner Brockway supported entry; while several leading CDS supporters, including Jay, Gordon Walker, Michael Stewart and Denis Healey, leaned against. Gaitskell at this stage tried to hold the balance; but only three members of the Shadow Cabinet – George Brown, Ray Gunter and Douglas Houghton – could be counted as definitely pro-Market. So Jenkins' committee faced an uphill task.

In the Commons on 28 June – a purely temperature-testing debate with no vote – Jenkins spoke with what Macmillan in his diary called 'luminosity and sincerity' in favour of early entry,[42] but was heckled from both sides of the House. The Common Market issue, he wrote in the *Spectator* a few days later, cut across party lines to an unprecedented degree, uniting the far left in incongruous alliance with the far right: Sydney Silverman with Lord Hinchinbrook, *Tribune* with the *Daily Express*. 'They all share a grossly exaggerated and completely outmoded view of Britain's importance in the world and her capacity for independent action.' The Suez mentality and unilateralism were reverse sides of the same coin. At the same time he dismissed equally scornfully Douglas Jay's illusion that Britain could find a viable alternative in the Commonwealth and Denis Healey's simple Atlanticism, pointing out that the Kennedy administration itself wanted to see Britain inside Europe. Healey, he wrote more tactfully, had now fallen back on 'the most subtle and intellectually credible presentation of the Commonwealth argument': that Britain must keep clear of 'colonialist' Europe in order to exercise leadership in the emerging Third World. But this too was nonsense, since the emerging nations did not want leadership from Britain: they wanted independence and aid. It was a 'pathetic illusion' to imagine that everyone wanted leadership from Britain. 'Whether or not we join the EEC is now subsumed by a bigger question: whether we live in an atmosphere of illusion or reality about our position in the world.'[43]

Jenkins next took his argument to the floor of the Blackpool conference, where he met the argument that he was supporting the Tory government by pointing out that he had supported joining the Common Market long before Macmillan and only wished that Labour had taken the initiative first. Again he insisted that Labour objections to the Common Market were mistaken. The Commonwealth would not suffer but benefit from British membership; while there was nothing necessarily anti-socialist about the EEC. Nothing in the Treaty of Rome would prevent Britain nationalising industries; within the Community France had more effective economic planning; both France and Germany had better social services; and every socialist party in the Six wanted Britain in. To use the European issue to attack the government, he urged, would be dangerously xenophobic for an internationalist party, dangerously backward-looking for a progressive party, and dangerous electorally:

Think of fighting a General Election with the *Daily Herald*, the *Daily Mirror*, the *Guardian* and the *Observer* against you! And who would be our allies – the *Daily Express* and the *Daily Worker* . . . Let us put such thoughts from our minds, and remember that as an international and an adventurous party, we should be moving towards and not away from Europe.[44]

The pro-Market resolution was overwhelmingly defeated. For the moment Labour resolved, without a vote, to await the outcome of Heath's negotiation. For most of 1962 Gaitskell reserved his position, trying to hold his party together by keeping the pressure on the government, while his pro- and anti-European friends competed to win him to their side. At the turn of the year Jenkins thought the whole political outlook deeply depressing. On 12 January, in what turned out to be his last column for the *Spectator*, he delivered a withering assessment of the government, charging Macmillan with sidelining his ablest colleagues (Butler and Hailsham) while surrounding himself with mediocrities. 'The result is that we have a weak Chancellor of the Exchequer [Selwyn Lloyd], a foolish Foreign Secretary [Lord Home] and a general Cabinet intellectual level which is such that it seems perfectly natural to have Dr Charles Hill in charge of all land use planning, of housing and of local government reform.' But he was scarcely less despairing of Labour:

The recovery from the sudden fever of unilateralism has been quick and fairly complete, but the disappearance of the disease did not take with it the underlying and independent debility which was there before Scarborough and is still present today. As a result, the decline in the Government's support reflects itself in almost everything other than an increase in those who say they will vote Labour.

The government, he concluded, seemed to be immune from the electoral consequences of failure. 'Few things could be worse for the whole tone of British politics.'[45]

The same month Woodrow Wyatt (now back in the House as MP for Bosworth) floated the idea of a pact with the Liberals, who were then enjoying, under the dashing leadership of Jo Grimond, the first of many deceptive 'revivals'. (In March they scored a famous by-election victory at Orpington after which their Gallup poll rating jumped temporarily into the mid-twenties, compared with just 6 per cent in 1959.) Gaitskell was furious and threatened to drum Wyatt out of the party. In public Jenkins backed his leader. Though he was currently writing about Asquith, counted Grimond and Mark Bonham Carter among his best friends and was actively cooperating with them on Europe, he had little faith in the Liberals as a serious political force. There was no agreement, he had written in 1960, 'between the civilised radicalism of Mr Grimond and his immediate colleagues on the one hand, and the outlook of large numbers (perhaps the majority) of Liberal voters on the other', who were more 'Poujadist' than radical and voted Liberal merely as a protest; their 6 per cent of the poll in 1959 actually overstated their genuinely Liberal support.[46] In January 1962 he still maintained that a Lab–Lib pact would offer no better prospect of defeating the government than Labour on its own. 'Every practical politician knows that all talk of a re-alignment of forces on the left is now quite out of the question, at least until after the next election.'[47]

Yet there are signs that privately he would have liked to see some form of cooperation. According to Wyatt – admittedly not the most reliable witness – Jenkins thought Gaitskell's rejection of the idea 'irrational' and told Jennifer: 'Woodrow has more political sense than Hugh sometimes.'[48] As a historian, Jenkins held that Attlee's Labour party had simply replaced the Asquithian Liberals as the single progressive party representing 'the whole of the Left-leaning half of the electorate' in a two-party system. But when the Liberals showed signs of taking a significant slice of the vote, thus splitting the anti-Conservative forces – as they were to do more and more regularly from 1974 onwards – his instinct was always to try to bring them together. At this time, however, when his lukewarm socialism and his passionate advocacy of the Common Market, combined with his prolific writing in Tory papers and his sybaritic social life, already made him an object of considerable suspicion to much of the party, he probably thought it unwise to add another heresy to his charge sheet.

Too many of his colleagues, while acknowledging his ability, already felt he barely belonged in the Labour Party at all. An *Observer* profile just after the 1959 election noted that 'Mr Jenkins . . . with his polished, adenoidal voice is one of the smoothest of the Labour members . . . Much though the Labour leaders enjoy good parties, there are some rank-and-filers who feel, after observing him hobnobbing with a duchess or in company with Princess Margaret, that he may be too socially successful.'[49] Even Gaitskell, who mixed happily in Tory circles himself, told Crossman (a fellow Wykehamist) that he was worried about his younger friend's social life, with a delicately class-conscious explanation of why what was all right for himself was bad for Roy:

He is very much in the social swim these days and I am sometimes anxious about him and young Tony. We, as middle class Socialists, have got to have a profound humility . . . Now that's all right for us in the upper middle class, but Tony and Roy are not upper and I sometimes feel they don't have a proper humility to ordinary working people.[50]

A vivid snapshot of this 'social swim' is glimpsed in a letter from Ann Fleming to Evelyn Waugh in August 1962, describing what she called 'a noisy evening' with the Avons and the Devonshires (that is Anthony Eden, now the Earl of Avon, and his much younger wife Clarissa, and the forty-two-year-old Duke of Devonshire who was married to the youngest of the Mitford sisters), plus the Tory MP Nigel Birch (another Old Etonian married to the daughter of a peer):

It was very civilised till Lord Avon's bedtime, then there was great uproar between Andrew and Nigel and lots of four-letter words: Debo [Devonshire] said to Roy Jenkins 'Can't you stop them by saying something Labour?' but this is something Roy has never been able to do.[51]

Jenkins was perfectly at ease in high Tory company – as often as not without Jennifer – but this suggests that he was treated by some of his hosts as a sort of Labour mascot.

Jenkins' busy social life, however, was just his way of relaxing; he also worked deceptively hard. Colleagues who sat gossiping in the bars of the House of Commons all day – something he almost never did – imagined Jenkins to be lazy and self-indulgent, but his output of writing, in a range of different outlets, was prodigious. As well as *Asquith*, which he wrote mainly on holiday, and his regular articles and book reviews for the *Spectator* (up to 1962), he also contributed heavyweight articles (mainly on the progress of the Common Market negotiations) to *Encounter* and other highbrow journals,* as well as a steady stream of articles and book reviews for daily and weekly papers, including the *Sunday Times*, both *Telegraphs*, the *Listener* and anyone else who asked him, so that his journalistic earnings considerably exceeded his parliamentary salary. Then in 1962 he began a long association with the *Observer*, then at its liberal zenith under the enlightened proprietorship of David Astor, who (like Ian Gilmour at the *Spectator*, but for much longer) edited his own paper. Though its political allegiance was loosely Conservative, Astor made the *Observer*, from 1948 when he inherited it to 1976 when he sold it, for Jenkins, 'and I believe for many others, the paper with which, across the whole spectrum of British journalism . . . they most identified and were most proud to be associated'. In an article celebrating its bicentenary in 1991 he handsomely acknowledged his debt: 'I know how much David Astor's *Observer* contributed both to developing me as a writer and to sustaining the causes for which I cared in politics.'[52]

Between 1962 and 1964 he undertook four major pieces of investigative journalism for the *Observer*. The series began when Astor – presumably remembering his interest in the 1954 Savoy takeover battle – invited Jenkins to write a detailed account of a recent takeover struggle between the textile giants ICI and Courtaulds, to be spread over three successive review fronts and running to some 8,000 words.[53] This was a quite new departure in Sunday journalism, combining close analysis with vivid narrative and anticipating the *Sunday Times* Insight page, which began the following year. Jenkins gave Astor all the credit – 'The concept was entirely his, although the treatment was entirely mine'[54] – but it won him that year's *What the Papers Say* award for innovative journalism. The following year he wrote another equally extensive analysis of the papal conclave by which Pope Pius VI was elected following the death of John XXIII in June 1963 – an improbable subject, which he treated slightly cynically as an exercise in pure

---

* *Encounter* was a political and literary journal, founded in 1953 and initially edited by the poet Stephen Spender. Its reputation was later tarnished when it was revealed to have been funded by the CIA as an anti-Communist weapon in the Cold War; but in the 1950s and 1960s it was an influential magazine.

politics ('My account paid more attention to the temporalities than to the spiritualities of the Church') on the basis of just a week in Rome interviewing cardinals and others.[55] For an unbeliever of Welsh Nonconformist background he had a curiously persistent interest in the papacy. His opening sentence gives a good flavour both of the narrative style and of his characteristic choice of incidental detail: 'On a Tuesday evening in June, 24 hours before the start of the 1963 Papal Conclave, the Cardinal Archbishop of New York left his apartment in the Grand Hotel, one of the six Roman establishments to which the Italian edition of the *Guide Michelin* gives five roofs, and drove up the hill towards the Pincio.'[56] He always took a close interest in Michelin stars.

The same year he also wrote a blow-by-blow account of the Cuban missile crisis, based on interviews conducted in January with all the leading members of the Kennedy administration from the President down, and published as a single long article on the anniversary of the crisis in October – just a month before Kennedy's assassination. As well as showing off his Washington connections, the self-consciously states-manlike conclusion of this piece could have been seen as a job applica-tion for a position in the Foreign Office when Labour finally returned to government.[57] In the event it was his fourth *Observer* commission that probably secured him the job he did get in October 1964. This was another two-part investigation into the problems of BOAC – the British Overseas Aircraft Corporation, which was merged ten years later with BEA (British European Airways) to form British Airways (BA). The question was specifically whether BOAC could afford to support the domestic aircraft industry by buying the British-built VC-10 or should make a hard-nosed commercial decision to buy American Boeings. But Jenkins placed the blame for the Corporation's difficulties and the wider crisis of the British industry squarely on the government's failure to set a clear policy and priorities. When the two articles were reprinted in hard covers three years later it was under the uncompromising title 'How Not to Run a Public Corporation'.[58] By that time Harold Wilson had given Jenkins the chance to apply his own prescription by appointing him Minister of Aviation to sort out the mess.

In the meantime Europe remained his central preoccupation. As the Macmillan government moved closer to a definite application to join the Community, Jenkins was engaged in a desperate effort to stop Gaitskell committing Labour against it. First he tried to convince him of the economic case for British entry. Then he sought to inspire him with the vision of a united Europe. To this end he arranged a meeting between Gaitskell and the founding prophet of European unity, Jean Monnet, by inviting Monnet to address a dinner of the XYZ club which Gaitskell would attend. The occasion was a resounding failure. 'I have never seen less of a meeting of minds,' Jenkins wrote. 'I think I fondly imagined that Monnet would lucidly meet all Gaitskell's points and dissolve his doubts.' Instead he brushed them aside as trivial and urged Gaitskell to 'have faith'. Gaitskell replied coldly, 'I don't believe in faith. I believe in reason and you have not shown me any.' Douglas Jay, who was present, was delighted and dated Gaitskell's firm conviction that he could not support entry from that night. Jenkins, by contrast, 'drove Monnet back to the Hyde Park Hotel in deep depression'.[59]*

Finally he tried to change Gaitskell's mind by appealing to tactical considerations. Normally, as a professional writer, Jenkins disliked writing other than for money: he much preferred talking over a good lunch. But at the beginning of May 1962 he sat down and wrote his leader a six-page handwritten letter. 'My dear Hugh,' he began, 'Perhaps because I am so unused to disagreeing with you (and greatly dislike it) I find arguing rather wearing, and as a substitute for doing so I thought I would send you a letter.' His first argument was that Macmillan and Iain Macleod (the current Tory party chairman) would like nothing better than for Europe to become an election issue, with Labour having come out against the Market. All the evidence of the polls ('and you have never been inclined to discount them when dealing with unilateralism') indicated that the Tories would gain votes and Labour lose them on the issue. But even on present voting intentions, 'I still think that the issue is an immensely dangerous one for us.'

---

* The next month Jenkins wrote a long letter to the *New Statesman* refuting in great detail an article by Jay 'more rooted than usual in false premises and exaggerated conclusions', condemning 'the backward-looking insularity which is the foundation of his whole case':

> He assumes throughout that the Britain of 1949 with its high direct taxes, its subsidised food, its detailed physical controls and its import restrictions had provided the ultimate answer to all social and economic problems. And he sees all outside problems by putting the wrong end of a specially opaque British telescope to his blind eye.[60]

Generally speaking, Jenkins did not quarrel with his political opponents. But this letter infuriated Jay, who accused him of using a deliberate misquotation to discredit his argument. In his memoirs Jay described the bitter ending of their friendship around this time. 'It is hard in my experience to feel personal affection towards those who are actively working to destroy . . . something for which one cares deeply.'[61]

He was still confident that Labour would win the next election, but he also assumed that the Liberal revival would be maintained; in which case 'it seems as near certain as can be that we shall have to do it on 35–40% of the votes'. In a hung Parliament the Liberals would much rather put Labour in (with Grimond perhaps taking a seat in the Cabinet) than back the Tories. But if the Common Market issue was not settled and Labour was against it, they would have 'no alternative but to keep the Tories in to carry it through'. Alternatively Labour might win a small majority and be able to form an independent government, but in that case it would still be in a very weak position. 'A left-wing govt needs more moral strength than a right-wing one, and it is a great disadvantage to start with, say, 38% of the votes.'

Moreover, he went on, 'if you have fought on an anti-C.M. ticket you add two other special, important and unnecessary weaknesses to the govt'. First, Gaitskell would 'immediately run head on into a major clash with Kennedy about the whole organisation of the West . . . I have no doubt at all that you would find the issue dominating every Anglo-American discussion and that your good relations with him would founder on it.' Second, Gaitskell would find that 'the whole of what may be called non-Tory establishment opinion' was very hostile to him on the issue. By this he meant Whitehall mandarins like Lord Plowden and Sir Robert Hall as well as most of the serious press, who would not support an anti-Common Market line:

> The position you face is therefore this: you have to try to govern on ⅔ths of the votes, with Kennedy hostile and with neutral intelligent opinion here unnecessarily disaffected. I do not believe that you or anyone else could be a successful Labour P.M. in these circumstances.

Gaitskell might claim that he was trying to keep open the possibility of supporting entry. 'But . . . there is not a single person I know, whether one of your own friends or a detached journalist, who does not believe you are moving in the other direction.' By going against his natural supporters, Jenkins warned, he was making political difficulties for himself in the future. It was no good waiting to see the terms negotiated by the government before deciding the issue, since 'people's attitudes to the terms are overwhelmingly likely to turn on their prior position'. The Labour party could still be swung in favour of entry; 'but not without a lead, and not by always stressing the conditions . . . and never the advantages'. If Gaitskell allowed the party to swing into opposition, he concluded, 'then we will face the dangers I have tried to outline at the beginning of this letter'.[62]

This was a classic expression of Jenkins' identification with the liberal establishment and his belief in the importance of being in the right company. In reply Gaitskell agreed that it would be better that the Common Market should not become an election issue; but he was more concerned with holding Labour together than with giving a lead:

> You will, I am sure, appreciate that it is not really a matter of what I think; it is a question of carrying the party in this matter . . . I suspect that if I were to do what you want, we should be more likely to lose control altogether.[63]

In a television broadcast that evening Gaitskell was still careful to hold the scales fairly even: 'To go in on good terms would, I believe, be the best solution . . . Not to go in would be a pity, but it would not be a catastrophe.' But it was increasingly clear that his emotional priority was the Commonwealth. 'To go in on bad terms which really meant the end of the Commonwealth would be a step which I think we would regret all our lives and for which history would not forgive us.'[64]

Over the summer of 1962 Gaitskell gave different people differing impressions of the way his mind was moving. He accepted the argument that he should not separate himself from his natural supporters, and would have preferred the familiar position of taking on the left. But at the same time he was irritated by those of his friends who saw Europe as a matter of semi-religious principle; he was disappointed that they could not reassure him that British membership of the Community would not damage under-developed countries. 'Roy Jenkins, Tony Crosland and one or two other friends had no specific replies to these points,' he told Alastair Hetherington. 'He had rather hoped that they would have, but they didn't.'[65] In these circumstances it was always likely that Gaitskell would find unacceptable terms which Macmillan, in his eagerness for a successful negotiation, would be prepared to recommend. Defending his position to President Kennedy, Gaitskell persuaded himself that 'Roy Jenkins, the leader of the pro-Market minority . . . did not demur.'[66] But Jenkins did demur. By mid-September he was so resigned to a breach with his leader on an issue he thought more important than party that he was actually prepared to consider dumping him; failing that, he preferred Macmillan's continuance as Prime Minister till British entry was achieved. 'Roy privately not optimistic – nor I,' Austen Albu recorded after a gloomy meeting of pro-Europeans at Ladbroke Square. 'Some discussion of H.G. as leader – agreed no-one else in sight . . . Roy and Strachey said at present Macmillan better P.M. than H.G.'[67]

Two days later, in his capacity as chairman of the Labour Common Market Committee, Jenkins held a press conference at which he tried to rally the pro-Market forces before the party conference, claiming that Labour MPs were about equally split, with eighty or ninety in favour, another eighty or ninety against and the same number undecided. He was careful to criticise the government's poor handling of the negotiations, but insisted that Britain could still, by negotiating hard but positively, win better terms:

> Mr Gaitskell's statement seems to stress too harshly the hostile point of view. We should negotiate for better terms, but we want to negotiate in the context of going in and not staying out.
>
> We do not intend to embarrass anybody, but we do intend to show that there is a substantial body in the Labour movement that still believes that one can get into the Common Market on reasonable terms, and this should be the aim.[68]

Though Jenkins was at pains to deny it, the *Observer*'s Mark Arnold-Foster presciently saw in this press conference the seeds of a Labour split more serious than its predecessors since, unlike the nuclear weapons or Clause Four battles, this one could actually determine events. 'Mr Jenkins and his men could help to decide history by making it possible for the Government to get Britain into Europe, despite Mr Gaitskell and its own murmuring Tory rebels.'[69] This was acute, but premature. It would be another nine years before Jenkins and his supporters made it possible for the Heath government to take Britain into Europe against the opposition of the Labour party and a rump of Tory rebels.

For the Labour conference in Brighton two weeks later the NEC produced a fudged document which still committed the party to keep negotiating for better terms. But when Gaitskell spoke on the Wednesday morning he blew this compromise out of the water with an emotional speech that was as traumatic for his supporters on the right as Bevan's speech rejecting unilateralism in the same hall five years earlier had been for the left. He began by repeating that he was not against entry on principle, only the terms on offer; but then he invoked the sacrifices of Commonwealth soldiers at Gallipoli and Vimy Ridge and declared that for Britain to consent to become 'a Texas or California in the United States of Europe' would mean 'the end of Britain as an independent nation state . . . the end of a thousand years of history'.* He sat down to a standing ovation led by his old enemies on the left, which most of his friends refused to join. Jenkins did reluctantly stand ('Afterwards I worked out a sophistical theory that standing was a tribute to the man, whereas clapping would have been a tribute to the speech');[71] but Jack Diamond, Bill Rodgers and others stayed firmly seated with their arms folded. Dora Gaitskell whispered to her neighbour, Charles Pannell: 'Charlie, all the wrong people are cheering.'[72]

This was a painful breach, personally as much as politically. For some weeks afterwards Jenkins and Gaitskell had no contact. It was Gaitskell who took the initiative to repair relations by inviting Roy and Jennifer to Frognal Gardens on a Sunday evening in late November where they were quickly back on friendly terms. They met again the following weekend in Paris. Jenkins was making a tour of European capitals for *Encounter* to assess the mood as the British negotiations reached the point of decision; Gaitskell was there to see de Gaulle's Foreign Minister, to make sure the French government understood Labour's position. They nevertheless enjoyed 'a very jolly party' with Jacques and Marie-Alice de Beaumarchais 'in a restaurant . . . near the Odeon, where we ate a lot of shellfish and drank a lot of wine'.[73] But the next morning Gaitskell felt unwell. Just before Christmas he went into hospital with a mystery virus. Jenkins visited him once, with no idea that he was seriously ill, before leaving for Washington on 12 January 1963 to research his article on the Cuba crisis. He was still in America when he heard first that Gaitskell was dying and then, on 18 January, that he was dead.

He was given the news by the New York office of the *Daily Express*, which somehow tracked him to Connecticut and asked him for a tribute. When he could not instantly oblige, the reporter said that Harold Wilson had given them a very moving one. 'Yes,' Jenkins replied bitterly, 'but you have to remember that he was very fond of Gaitskell.'[74]

He decided not to return immediately. 'I find Hugh's death almost

---

* After this speech Jenkins was heard to declare bitterly that if Gaitskell lost the next election he could always become chairman of the Commonwealth War Graves Commission.[70]

totally shattering,' he wrote to Bill Rodgers. 'Politics apart, I really adored him, and find the thought of coming back to an England without him almost unassimilable. It is rather as though an H-bomb had fallen in one's absence.'[75] Despite their disagreement over Europe, all his political hopes had been bound up in Gaitskell's success. As it happened, that disagreement no longer mattered since on 14 January General de Gaulle had abruptly vetoed Britain's application to join the Common Market. This ruthless démarche not only removed Europe as a source of contention from British politics for the immediate future, but also torpedoed the Macmillan government's flagship policy, thus greatly boosting Labour's chances of winning the next election. Had he lived, Gaitskell would surely have become Prime Minister within two years. As it was, the prize was cruelly snatched away and now seemed likely to fall to his successor – who was most likely to be Harold Wilson.

The bereaved Gaitskellites tried desperately to prevent this outcome, but they were torn between two candidates. Their front runner was George Brown, who had been deputy leader since 1960 and only two months earlier had beaten off a challenge from Wilson by 133 votes to 103. Brown was one of the last working-class, non-university-educated figures in the Labour leadership. He was colourful, forceful, often brilliant, robustly anti-unilateralist and strongly pro-Market; but he was also volatile and unpredictable, especially when he had been drinking. Jenkins always had a high regard for him. He had 'an untutored mind of the highest speed and quality', he wrote in an obituary tribute in 1985. On the big issues, 'he nearly always showed wisdom, verve and foresight . . . In a Cabinet with an unusual and excessive Oxford predominance, he had at least as good a brain as anyone around the table . . . He cared about causes more than himself. He had vision. He was a good friend. He enhanced life.'[76] He deserved better than to be remembered as a drunk. But the fact was that in 1963 it was difficult to see him as Prime Minister. The right's alternative was Jim Callaghan – a far more canny figure of similarly unprivileged background, a safer pair of hands, but in those days lacking personality. Callaghan was the choice of those who could not stand the thought of Wilson but thought Brown too much of a liability.

Jenkins believed that they must stick with Brown, *faute de mieux*. When he could bear to think about the succession he wrote to Rodgers from Washington on 23 January, expressing both his antipathy for Wilson and his dim view of Callaghan:

I am clear that Brown is the best available, and I hope Callaghan can be dissuaded from standing, as that is surely more likely to help Wilson than anything else. The decisive argument against Wilson, I think, is not the policy he would pursue, at any rate in the short run, or even his effect on wavering public opinion, but his undesirability as head of the Govt. A complete lack of trust at the top would infect relations all the way down, and make it a nightmare in wh. to serve. Callaghan's faults are not these, but he has no real standing of his own in the country, so cannot be urged on that ground . . . He would be easily swayed by different gusts of pressure within the Party.

He added that he would certainly be back in time for the first ballot on 7 February, but could not manage Gaitskell's memorial service at Westminster Abbey on 31 January without cutting short his Washington interviews. 'I would really rather have gone to the small funeral service, wh. Jennifer went to today. I think the memorial service will be vast & impersonal.'[77]

Rodgers replied five days later, reporting that the Gaitskellites were 'very evenly divided . . . I lean to Brown but am still open to persuasion . . . Tony leans to Callaghan but is open to persuasion too.' In fact Crosland had already decided to back Callaghan and lobbied Brown to stand down, thus placing himself for the first time in the opposite camp from Jenkins and putting down a marker which earned its reward thirteen years later.* There was some talk of Frank Soskice or Patrick Gordon Walker; but neither of these commanded serious support. Rodgers did not think the division of the anti-Wilson forces had done any harm. 'On the contrary, the whole series of meetings we have held and the canvassing we have done . . . has resulted in a clearer anti-Wilson feeling than might have otherwise emerged.' His prediction was that Wilson would lead Brown by 105:95 on the first ballot, with forty-five for Callaghan; but that Brown would sneak it 'with a majority of fewer than ten votes' on the second. But this was 'the sheerest speculation'.[79]

In the event he underestimated Wilson's vote and overestimated both Brown's and Callaghan's (the figures were Wilson 115, Brown 88, Callaghan 41). Had either Brown or Callaghan stood aside, the other might possibly have won on a straight right–left vote. But with Callaghan

---

* Crosland also calculated that if Wilson won on the second ballot, 'he will know who put him there'.[78] But this part of his calculation did him less good than he hoped.

eliminated, most of his (and probably some of Brown's) votes switched behind the front-runner, giving Wilson a comfortable victory by 144:103. While old Bevanites like Crossman and Barbara Castle – and even Tony Benn, who had fallen out with Gaitskell – rejoiced at the sudden improvement in their prospects, Jenkins, Crosland and the other Gaitskellites faced a bleak future. Crossman had lunch with Roy and Jennifer at the Athenaeum on the day of the second ballot (when the result was already all but certain):

> Both of them were completely knocked out by Gaitskell's death. It makes a huge gap in their personal lives, bigger even than the gap in Crosland's. I felt them to be generally in mourning for Gaitskell and not particularly enthusiastic for Brown . . . Nevertheless Roy was as implacable as ever and I spent most of lunch trying to make him say what makes him support a thug like Brown against a man of Wilson's quality. Jenkins found it surprisingly difficult. First he tried to call Harold intellectually dishonest but he really couldn't pretend that Douglas Jay or Patrick Gordon Walker show greater intellectual integrity. All Roy could say was that it was worse in Harold's case because he was more gifted . . . Finally Roy said, 'The fact is that Harold is a person no-one can like, a person without friends.' 'So much the better for him as Leader,' I replied. 'You admired Attlee. That loneliness was Attlee's quality.' Roy was indignant at the comparison and both of us finished lunch genuinely baffled as to what it was that caused the revulsion in each of us that the other didn't share.[80]*

Such was Jenkins' revulsion from Wilson's leadership that he thought about leaving politics altogether. He was under strong pressure the other way from Rodgers, who lost no time after Gaitskell's death in telling him, 'You are our leader now,' and urging him to spend more time in the House of Commons. 'I take what you say about the H. of C.,' Jenkins replied, 'and will try to act upon it.'[82] In fact he spoke even less in 1963 than he had done in 1961–2: with Europe now off the agenda, he spoke just three times – on the government's defence White Paper in March, when he came out

---

* Reviewing Anthony Howard's biography of Crossman many years later, Jenkins recalled that Crossman spent this lunch denouncing Gaitskell 'as though a poisonous plague had been removed from the Labour party. I was more struck . . . by Crossman's self-destructiveness than by his malevolence.'[81]

against Britain attempting to maintain an independent nuclear deterrent; on the budget in April; and in June in support of the Bill which allowed hereditary peers to disclaim their titles (while complaining that it did not address the broader question of reform or abolition of the House of Lords).[83] In appointing his new front bench Wilson had extended one olive branch to the Gaitskellites by making Gordon Walker Shadow Foreign Secretary. (He was stuck with a predominantly right-wing Shadow Cabinet whether he liked it or not, telling his Bevanite friends that their time would come.) But with Jenkins he had no contact at all for nine months. In May, after a long talk with Crosland at a party, Tony Benn wrote that 'with Hugh's death his old courtiers feel out in the cold – exactly as I felt with Hugh. Roy Jenkins is bitter about it and jealous of what he conceives to be my relationship with Harold, which frankly is similar to his relationship with Hugh.'[84] 'In a slightly flat way,' Jenkins wrote, 'I just got on with *Asquith*, my other (mainly *Observer*) writing commitments, picking up the pieces from de Gaulle's veto . . . advising John Lewis's and pursuing my over-active social life.'[85]

He also wrote a chapter for a tribute volume about Gaitskell, edited by Bill Rodgers, which appeared the following year with a dozen other contributors, including John Betjeman, Maurice Bowra, Arthur Schlesinger and Willy Brandt. To the question 'What was Gaitskell's legacy?' he gave a three-part answer:

First, the promise of being a great Prime Minister, not because he would necessarily have avoided mistakes, but because he would have infused the whole Government with a sense of loyalty and purpose . . . Second, a Labour Party with both the will and capacity for victory . . . And third, a memory which is a standing contradiction to those who wish to believe that only men with cold hearts and twisted tongues can succeed in politics.[86]

Jenkins and Crosland were joint literary executors; and Crosland agreed that Jenkins should write the official biography. This was almost certainly a bad idea. He was not exactly in a client relationship, as he had been to Attlee; but he was much too devoted to Gaitskell's memory to be objective. Fortunately the pressures of office soon forced him to abandon the commission. He and Crosland then appointed Philip Williams – an Oxford academic and one of the founders of CDS – whose immensely long, highly detailed, but excessively discreet volume (he drew a veil over Gaitskell's relationship with Ann Fleming) finally appeared in 1979.* By that time Jenkins had written another substantial biographical essay for *The Times* in 1973, later published in *Nine Men of Power*. Gaitskell remained his political hero, and a photograph of the lost leader stood on the mantelpiece in the dining room at East Hendred for the rest of his life.

Leaderless and depressed, Jenkins was, in his own words, 'an obvious sitting target for a job outside politics'. And in July there came an offer which seriously tempted him: the editorship of *The Economist*. Though not then boasting the international circulation and prestige it enjoys today, it was a venerable and respected title. The chairman and former editor, Sir Geoffrey Crowther, pressed him to accept. Jenkins was 'surprised, flattered and excited'.[88] The money was more than twice a Cabinet minister's salary, while he had no confidence that he would get any sort of office from Wilson. On the other hand, as a writer used to his own byline, he would have chafed at *The Economist's* anonymity; and editors cannot write too much themselves. Above all, he would have had to leave the House of Commons, and when it came to it he really did not want to make that break. Still he was tempted. He asked to be allowed to consider it over the summer, when he, Jennifer and the family went to stay near the Beaumarchaises in south-western France. It was Marie-Alice who told him that instead of trying to guess Wilson's intentions, Roy should go and ask him. So he did. He saw Wilson in the Leader of the Opposition's room at the Commons on 12 September, and immediately afterwards wrote a note of their conversation which was a good deal more detailed than the account he gave in his memoirs.

Wilson was impressed by the *Economist* offer, which probably raised Jenkins' standing in his eyes, so he was sympathetic to his dilemma. But at first he tried to play Jenkins along, suggesting that he postpone a decision in case there was an autumn election, or hinting that he could take the job and still join the government in a couple of years – maybe as some sort of ambassador to the EEC. When Jenkins objected that he would have no seat, Wilson said that seats could always be found. But Jenkins closed that avenue by saying that if he accepted *The Economist*, he would feel morally bound to stay at least five years.

---

* Tactfully Jenkins chose not to review Williams' book. Years later, however – after Williams' death – he revealed what he thought of it when reviewing another, less reverential biography by Brian Brivati. 'Alas, as Williams was a person utterly unlike Gaitskell, lacking his gaiety, his half-suppressed hedonism and his occasional frivolous warmth, it was inevitably not much good on the private Gaitskell.' By contrast he commended Brivati for dealing 'honestly, yet not pruriently or obsessively, with Gaitskell's late-life intoxication with Mrs Ian Fleming . . . a passion which says more for Gaitskell's astringent taste than for his political caution.'[87]

When Wilson asked what sort of job he would like in government, Jenkins said that he had started as an economist but had developed other interests, in defence and some home departments – almost everything, in fact, except social services. Transport he would find 'fascinating'. When Wilson suggested a job in an overseas department he did not demur. Wilson assured him that his name was ringed for a 'substantial' job. But when Jenkins asked what that meant, they embarked on a delicate haggle between hypothetical options. Clearly, Wilson suggested, if he could be Chancellor, he would refuse *The Economist*. Jenkins agreed, but said that he would not decline *The Economist* just to be Financial Secretary. Wilson did not respond to this, but asked if he would take the Board of Trade. Jenkins said that yes, he would rather be President of the Board of Trade than editor of *The Economist*. Not surprisingly, he came away thinking that Wilson had half promised more than he possibly intended.[89]

In his memoirs Jenkins wrote that by this time Crowther too was cooling on the offer, under pressure from Lord Robbins, chairman of the *Financial Times* (the principal shareholder in *The Economist*), whose 'half-free-market soul was rather shocked by the idea of having a Labour MP as editor of Bagehot's journal'. Though discussions continued for another few months, 'they were never serious after 17 September 1963'.[90] In fact correspondence in his papers shows not only that Crowther remained keen to get Jenkins right up to Christmas, but that Jenkins too remained keen to keep the offer open until after the election, in case Labour lost or Wilson did not give him a job. When Alan Watkins (then writing the Crossbencher column in the *Sunday Express*) accurately reported his dilemma on 15 December, he wrote anxiously to Crowther hoping that the publicity would 'not do too much damage'.[91] But maybe he was just keeping his fallback option open. Eight years later – by which time it was abundantly clear that he had made the right choice – Jenkins admitted to the *Birmingham Post* that he had thought seriously about the *Economist* offer. 'But I couldn't really see myself doing it. Politics is my life. I've never wanted to do anything else. I knew that, when it came to the point, I couldn't and wouldn't quit. And I didn't.'[92] The following year Alastair Burnet was appointed.

Meanwhile Jenkins had demonstrated his commitment to politics by standing for election to the Shadow Cabinet, for the first time since 1957. In fact he and Tony Crosland both stood – possibly influenced by another Crossbencher column which described the two of them, in its inimitable style, as 'Tweedledum and Tweedledee':

Both Mr Jenkins and Mr Crosland went to Oxford and excelled at the Union. Both are economists. Both move in smoothly elegant circles and know their Latour from their Mouton Rothschild. Both were utterly loyal friends of Mr Gaitskell. And in a Gaitskell government both would have been set for a swift rise to the Cabinet.

But I fear they have something else in common. A profound distrust of their new party leader which they scarcely bother to hide. Is their personal dispute with Mr Wilson too deep to be bridged? Unless they chuck it these two able, arrogant men will face a miserable choice: either to leave public life – or else put up with a seat on the back benches for ever.[93]

Whether jolted by this or not, they both put their names in for the annual beauty contest in November. According to Susan Crosland (who married Tony the next year), Bill Rodgers urged Tony against standing, since he would only take votes from Roy. The idea that he was now seen as the junior partner 'came as a surprise'.[94] Tony stood anyway, and actually got more votes than Roy – 72 to 64. Neither came near to getting elected: they were eighteenth and nineteenth respectively, fifty or sixty votes adrift.* But at least by standing they had shown a willingness to play in Wilson's team.

The day after the Shadow Cabinet elections President Kennedy was assassinated in Dallas. This was the second shatteringly unexpected death in a year. It is no exaggeration to say that Jenkins adored the Kennedys. Almost all his American friends, like Ken Galbraith and Arthur Schlesinger, were New England Democrats and he was naturally swept up in their enthusiasm for 'Camelot' (as the Kennedy groupies romantically christened the administration). He and Jennifer, with Ian and Caroline Gilmour, had stayed with the Galbraiths in Vermont for the Nixon–Kennedy election in 1960 and spent a day trailing Kennedy on the stump around New York, hearing him make five speeches ('All of them were invigorating, one or two of them were moving. His command of widely contrasting audiences was complete').[96] Over the following three years he visited Washington several times – usually staying at the

* Michael Stewart topped the list with 184, followed by Jim Callaghan. Twelfth and last of the successful candidates was the seventy-three-year-old Dick Mitchison, with 123. Denis Healey (143) was the only successful candidate under fifty (and the only one younger than Wilson). Tony Benn was fifteenth with eighty-two votes.[95]

British Embassy with the ambassador, David Ormsby-Gore, who was exceptionally close to the Kennedy White House – and loved the sense of being at the centre of the democratic world. The dinner-table talk in Georgetown, he gushingly declared in 1990, might be excessively political, 'but it is at least conducted by the most famous journalists vying with the most favoured ambassadors to produce the most sophisticated witticisms about the most powerful cabinet officers to be found in any capital'.[97] He loved the 'confidence and vigour' of the people around Kennedy – his brother Bobby, Robert McNamara, McGeorge Bundy and the rest – as he wrote in the *Birmingham Mail* in February 1963:

> They all work incredibly hard, but also lead very active social lives. Most of them get to their offices soon after eight . . . and stay there till seven in the evening. They then rush home and change to go out to dinner or to some small informal dance, which goes on until midnight or later. And at eight next morning they are back at their desks again. They work on Saturdays too, but not quite so hard.[98]

He did not have much contact with JFK himself. In 1962 he wrote in the *Observer* a slightly cool review of Kennedy's student thesis (about appeasement, recently published under the title *Why England Slept*), treating it as a fairly callow effort while insisting that the still-youthful President had matured since 1940.[99] But in January 1963 he was granted a forty-minute interview, which made a deep impression on him:

> He asked a series of rapid-fire questions about all sorts of subjects – economic growth, Europe and de Gaulle, the Labour Party. He interrupted the answers, he gave his own views, he followed up a weak or unconvincing reply by forcing one hard against the ropes.

The whole experience was 'peculiarly intellectually testing'. Moreover, Jenkins concluded, Kennedy 'contributed two pieces of original, rather unconventional, analysis. That, again, was unexpected from any Head of State.'[100]

That January he also interviewed Bobby Kennedy, McNamara, Dean Rusk and all the other key players in Washington's handling of the Cuban missile crisis. Naturally he concluded that in calling Khrushchev's bluff and facing down the Soviet Union's attempt to site nuclear missiles barely a hundred miles from the US mainland, Kennedy had 'led the world with almost faultless skill and precision through the most dangerous crisis in its history':

> The essence of his strength was his ability to watch the cases for and against the different courses of action being built up or destroyed, without rushing into prior commitment to one or another; and then, when all the relevant information and arguments were available, to make a clear decision in favour of the one that seemed best.[101]

This was exactly the sort of cool decision-making that Jenkins also admired in Asquith; and which, when he came very soon to exercise executive office himself, he tried to emulate.

On Friday 22 November 1963 he had gone to Wales for the weekend when the news came in that Kennedy had been shot. David Astor rang to ask him to write a tribute for the *Observer*. Jenkins barely slept that night. He wrote his piece the next morning, then went to Gloucester for a Fabian Society engagement which he tried to get out of, amazed that such routine events should still be carrying on. His article, including the judgements quoted above, appeared the following day:

> Compared with the greatest Presidents of American history . . . he inevitably leaves more promise and less achievement behind him. Yet, aided perhaps by the manner of his death, it is difficult to believe that his name will not live with theirs. He will be the great 'might-have-been', the symbol of fate in its most vicious and retaliatory mood.[102]

Though written in shock within hours of Kennedy's death, this was a judgement that he would never modify. Twenty-eight years later, by which time the romance of 'Camelot' was badly tarnished, Jenkins still rated JFK 'the best president of the past four decades' – that is, since Franklin Roosevelt and Harry Truman.[103]

Though he met Jack only once, Jenkins got to know other members of the Kennedy clan well – particularly Bobby (about whom he wrote a long, admiring essay in 1972) and Jackie, and also Jackie's sister Lee Bouvier, who had married (as her second husband) a Polish count, Stanislaw Radziwill (which somehow made her a princess). Lee now lived in England, where she featured regularly in the gossip columns, and was rumoured to be another of Jenkins' lovers.* Bobby he met in London two months after Dallas, when he was still 'completely disoriented',† and thereafter two or three times a year in London, Washington or New York until he too was assassinated in 1968.[106] With Jackie – now the beautiful, tragic widow – he developed an affectionate friendship. He took her to a New York performance of his *Right Honourable Gentleman* (the play made from his Dilke biography) in 1965; and the next year he escorted Jackie and Lee to *Juno and the Paycock* at the National Theatre in London. He saw less of Jackie after she married Aristotle Onassis in 1968; but after Onassis' death in 1975 they again used to lunch together whenever she was in London or he in New York, and they exchanged letters for the rest of her life.

A typical – and very funny – letter was one Jackie wrote from Gstaad in January 1966, where she was skiing with her children and the Galbraiths, trying to escape the press and social life by 'violent physical exertion'. ('You don't have time to think about anything. You do your stint on the mountain & stumble to your bed. I have a luxurious but tiny chalet where we just squeeze in. When Caroline has a friend for the night, John sleeps in my bed & the nurse I don't like to imagine where.') It ends:

> This whole letter makes me laugh – as I have just read it over to see if it makes sense – & it sounds just like something Diana Cooper's gardener wrote to Margot Asquith's chambermaid. Travelling with Ken & writing to you could do wonders for one's style . . . Dear Roy – so much is ahead of you – I shall always hope to see you somewhere, & hope for so much for you. Love [signature illegible].[107]

Meanwhile, at the end of 1963, Jenkins had begun his relationship with Leslie Bonham Carter. They had known each other ever since Leslie married Mark Bonham Carter in 1955, but the moment when

---

* This affair occasioned a rare flash of mild jealousy from Caroline Gilmour who wrote to 'Darling Roy' sometime in the mid-1960s: 'I was deeply shocked to see that, so great is your passion for the princess that you had to copy her bedroom at East Hendred! Which visit, incidentally, I greatly enjoyed, and feel it was almost like the old days (before the affairs of state and the little lot monopolised you).'[104]

† This may have been the same dinner party at the American Embassy described by Ann Fleming in a letter to Clarissa Avon in February 1964. She was seated between Roy and Bobby, whom she did not like. 'He seemed humourless and aggressive with the nasty American desire for facts, not my strong point . . . It was a pleasure to turn to Roy Jenkins.'[105]

the spark ignited was at a New Year's Eve party at Mark's brother Raymond's house in Golders Green. They had lunch together two days later. Leslie's understanding was that his relationship with Caroline Gilmour had ended; this was not so, though there may have been a temporary interruption. He continued to see both of them almost equally frequently for the rest of his life. Leslie was a gentler personality than Caroline, and Jennifer liked her more: indeed they remain good friends to this day. Mark too quietly accepted the relationship. In getting to know Leslie, Roy also became close to her children: in particular the eldest, Laura Grenfell, her daughter by Lord St Just, who would come to play an important part in his life in the late 1970s; but also her three younger daughters, one of whom (Jane) in time became a Liberal Democrat peer. From the time he started work on *Asquith* in 1959 the whole extended Bonham Carter clan became an increasingly important part of Jenkins' world.

As the 1964 election loomed his priority was finishing *Asquith*. He was lucky that the election was delayed till the last possible moment. Already damaged by the Profumo and other scandals, Macmillan was forced by ill health to resign in October 1963, but contrived – to general ridicule – to have himself succeeded by Lord Home, who took advantage of the new law to disclaim his ancient hereditary earldom in order to descend to the Commons as Sir Alec Douglas-Home, and then carried on as Prime Minister until October 1964. This just gave Jenkins time to finish his book. He had been writing in concentrated bursts since 1959. After the success of *Dilke* he had wanted another biographical subject, preferably another Liberal, but this time a first-rank figure. Asquith practically chose himself. He was, with Attlee, the embodiment of that cool liberal intelligence which Jenkins most admired in politics; yet there had been no major life since the official biography in 1932. Moreover his publisher, Mark Bonham Carter, was Asquith's grandson and held the copyright on a major unpublished source, the enormous sequence of intimate letters written by Asquith, at the height of his premiership, to Venetia Stanley. This was gold for any biographer. In addition he was allowed to take away – six boxes at a time – Asquith's political papers, owned by Balliol but housed in the Bodleian Library. These two collections apart, Jenkins used no other primary sources; but he scarcely needed to.

He worked on the papers during 1960 and did most of the writing over the next three summers – 1961 in the south of France near Saint-Tropez; 1962 at Jakie Astor's house near Cambridge; 1963 near the Beaumarchaises in the Basque country near Saint-Jean-de-Luz – ending with a final burst at Nicko and Mary Henderson's house in Berkshire at the beginning of 1964: a pattern characteristic of his lifelong habit of working holidays, usually staying in other people's houses while the rest of the household revolved around him. In this way he completed the 220,000-word manuscript – in longhand – in time for publication by Collins in October 1964. But there was a last-minute problem. It turned out that Asquith's surviving daughter and fierce guardian of his reputation, the formidable Lady Violet Bonham Carter (Mark's mother), was unaware of her father's letters to Venetia – her contemporary and close friend – and was horrified by them. She had thought the early chapters 'rather dull & flat', and was already 'shattered' by the unflattering description of her own mother, Asquith's first wife, who died young.[108] She then read some more '& got a *terrible* shock when I reached Chapter 22. I cannot believe that Mark *did* have contemplated publishing it. It is a betrayal of intimacies of private life second to none.' When Mark told her that it was necessary to let Roy publish the letters in a responsible way in order to forestall Lord Beaverbrook doing worse with them, she wrote that this was 'like burning down your own house for fear an enemy might burn it down tomorrow! The remedy is worse than the disease.'[109] In reality Beaverbrook had copies of the letters, given to him by Venetia's daughter, but did not own the copyright, so he could not have done anything with them. Mark Bonham Carter wanted to publish them on purely commercial grounds and did not share his mother's filial scruples. She reluctantly read the whole correspondence 'with pain – and astonishment. It is so strange to *know* that I was quite unaware of what was passing between 2 human beings'[110] – the closest people in her life at that time – and was horrified at the idea of exposing her father's '"infatuation" . . . which must *inevitably* cheapen him and reduce his stature to posterity'.[111] She was particularly upset by the revelation that Asquith wrote to Venetia during Cabinet meetings. 'This wld shock others terribly, as indeed it has shocked me.'[112] Right up to the verge of publication she begged for cuts. 'She did not exactly exercise censorship,' Jenkins wrote after her death, but 'we argued a good deal. In the majority of cases she generously gave way to me. In a few I gave way to her.'[113] He finally agreed to cut some passages of Asquith's most desperate pleading ('Shall I try to tell you what you have been and are to me? First, outwardly and physically, unapproachable and unique . . .').[114] He always insisted that these cuts did not significantly bowdlerise the truth; but he did take the opportunity to restore them when the book was republished, after Lady Violet's death, in 1978.

Asquith was an almost perfect match of subject and author. Jenkins not only admired Asquith, but already in 1964 seemed to be modelling himself on him. The effortless Balliol gloss superimposed on a relatively humble background, the smooth intellect hiding a strong competitive streak, the self-consciously Edwardian style and what Asquith recognised in himself as 'a certain capacity for the enjoyment of comfort and luxury, with a moderate fondness for social pleasures and (perhaps) a slight weakness for the companionship of clever and attractive women' – all these were already clearly present in Jenkins. Further career parallels were yet to unfold: both the Home Office and the Treasury within the next five years, though of course Jenkins, unlike his model, never made it to Number Ten; a country house near Oxford; and, most uncanny, a late return to the House of Commons at a famous by-election for a Scottish constituency. But there was enough similarity already for the parallel to be levelled at Jenkins by political opponents, particularly in the Labour Party, who always suspected him of complacent elitism and closet Liberalism. Once when he was Home Secretary an unusually literate graffiti artist scrawled 'ASQUITH' on the pillars of Ladbroke Square.[115]

Asquith is, with some mild criticisms, an almost wholly admiring portrait which describes the supporting personalities and expounds the sometimes tortuous crises of 1911–16 with an economy and concise clarity lacking in Jenkins' later biographies of Gladstone and Churchill. It remains probably his best book. His facility with elegant historical parallels is already developed; while his penchant for elaborately sustained metaphors has not yet got out of hand. But much of it reads like a self-portrait. Jenkins notes Asquith's 'lack of interest in speculative thought', and writes that 'There was always in his character a surprising but strong streak of recklessness'. Asquith wrote for the *Spectator* as a young man, was of course a member of Brooks's, and shared Jenkins' dinner-table passion for rating historical figures in order. 'He had an intellectual self-confidence which left him in little doubt about the rightness of his own decisions', but also a 'steadily developing belief in an economy of intellectual effort'. He saw no harm in appointing his friends to important offices, but was 'a little too concerned with "Athenaeum opinion"'. He enjoyed 'a constitution which required no austerity of life to keep it unimpaired'; and 'an extraordinary taste for relaxing with pen and paper'. His 'capacity for the swift and almost effortless transaction of business was always such that he never worked excessively long hours'; but 'in spite of his "guise of lethargy" he rather despised those who liked living at half-pressure'. Every one of these passing comments on Asquith could equally be applied to Jenkins himself.[116]

The reviews were good without being unanimously ecstatic. 'There are few political historians writing today,' wrote Kenneth Rose in the *Sunday Telegraph*, 'who so agreeably blend scholarship with imagination, authority with liveliness'; while Michael Foot in the *Evening Standard* called Jenkins 'a skilled, generous and graceful biographer'. Some of the kindest comments came from friends like Asa Briggs ('lucid, fascinating and highly readable') and John Grigg ('intelligent and suggestive and above all readable').[117] *The Times* rather surprisingly invited Lady Violet to write a stirring defence of her father, accepting the praise, refuting the few criticisms and ignoring the Venetia letters entirely (she wrote in her diary that she wished she 'had not lived to see this week').[118] But some reviewers thought the book a bit too bland, notably Robert Rhodes James in the *Spectator*, who thought that 'Asquith was surely a tougher, stronger, more acute man . . . than Mr Jenkins would have us believe . . . We required a Sutherland; but we have got an Annigoni';[119] and A.J.P. Taylor in the *Observer*, who typically charged Jenkins with covering up Asquith's drinking and wondered what else he had omitted in deference to Lady Violet: 'A biographer has an overriding duty: he is the servant of the reading public, not of the family.'[120] ('Poisonous' was Lady Violet's verdict on Taylor.)[121]* Nevertheless the book did well. It sold about 20,000 copies in hardback, more in paperback, and has been reprinted several times. It is a bit dated now, as a wider range of sources has become available, but for half a century it has remained unchallenged as the best biography and is rightly regarded as a classic.

Labour went into the October 1964 election confident of victory. By his energetic performance as Leader of the Opposition against a tired and scandal-damaged Tory government, Wilson had papered over – at least temporarily – the old Bevanite–Gaitskellite split, and the party enjoyed commanding leads in the opinion polls for the last two years of the Parliament. Even Jenkins conceded that Wilson, building on his inheritance, had done well. 'I was one of the large minority which did not support him for the leadership,' he wrote in the *Observer* in September 1963. 'But I find that many of my doubts have gone.' Wilson's great theme – that after the 'thirteen wasted years' of backward-looking

* Taylor was a great champion of Lloyd George, whose much more vigorous love life he revealed a few years later by publishing his toe-curling letters to his secretary/mistress Frances Stevenson, as well as her diary.

old-school Toryism, Labour would somehow harness 'the white heat of the technological revolution' to stimulate a much higher rate of planned economic growth – was exactly what Jenkins had been saying for years. 'Industrially, educationally, socially,' he believed, 'we must move 25 years in the next five'; and he looked forward optimistically to a Labour government that would be 'as adventurous as it is undogmatic'.[122] Concentrating on the Common Market question for the past few years, he had rather neglected economics; but each year in the budget debate he had berated successive Chancellors for their failure to promote investment and exports. 'We have never accepted the view,' he lectured Selwyn Lloyd in 1962, 'that the most likely way of dealing with balance of payments difficulties is by restriction rather than expansion.'[123] The following year he condemned Reginald Maudling's 'half-hearted approach to expansion'.[124] Even in 1964, when it was plain that Maudling was actually fuelling an unsustainable pre-election boom, he still criticised a 'budget of missed opportunities'.[125] Like Wilson, Jenkins believed unquestioningly that Labour would be able to conjure growth where the Tories had failed.

In his Stechford election address – printed in red, with the slogan FOR A NEW BRITAIN LET'S GO WITH LABOUR and a very smooth photo of the candidate – he promised an end to 'Stop–Go', with 'a fair incomes policy . . . an attack on monopolies and market rigging . . . effective planning and a better taxation system' to build up exports and save imports:

> By these means [a Labour Government] would cut the knot which at present throttles our ability to expand production without running into economic crisis. We could then go ahead like many other countries at a steady 4 or 5 per cent a year.

'This steady expansion,' he confidently predicted, 'is the key to paying for the great schemes of social advance which Labour puts forward.' He mentioned housing, education and pensions, with a nod to helping the poorer countries of the world – but no specific mention of Europe.* There was also a message from Jennifer on 'women's issues', specifically (wearing her Consumers' Association hat) the need for compulsory

---

* Jenkins accepted that de Gaulle's veto had knocked Europe off the agenda for the moment. But his commitment remained undimmed. 'The problem,' he wrote in the *Daily Telegraph*, 'will present itself in a new form in a few years' time. As a convinced "European", I am not unhopeful about what a Labour Government, learning from the facts of international life, might do then.'[126]

labelling and dating of food in the shops; and the usual family group with the three children – now aged fifteen, twelve and ten – in the back garden of Ladbroke Square.[127]

This was the last election Jenkins would fight as a purely local figure. He held his usual round of meetings in Stechford schools, chaired the big rally when Wilson came to the Birmingham Bull Ring, and spoke for Woodrow Wyatt in Bosworth, George Brown in Belper and a few more friends and pro-European candidates elsewhere. He wrote several newspaper articles – on Labour's economic policy in the *Daily Mail*, a magisterial survey of foreign policy in the *Daily Telegraph*[128] – but did no television and was barely reported in the national press. In one characteristic sally he described Quintin Hogg as 'the nearest thing we have to Senator Goldwater of British politics'* and – with the authority of his official biographer – refuted the idea that Gaitskell would not have supported all of Wilson's policies.[129] In another, when it was clear that whichever government was elected would face a balance-of-payments deficit in the region of £600 million, he followed the party line in asserting that the Tories were already planning to impose import restrictions in November:

Only Mr Maudling has to protest that everything is all right. He sits heavily but apprehensively on top of the Treasury like a chairman of an anti-volcanic society meeting on the top of Vesuvius and hoping he can get the vote of thanks over before the gurgles underneath him turn into another eruption.[130]

Despite recognition of a looming crisis, however, the polls narrowed. Wilson paraded his slide rule to emphasise his economic expertise, while Douglas-Home confessed that he used matchsticks to work out economic problems; yet the public still turned back to the Tories. All Labour's talk of growth began to look a bit too facile. In the end Labour's vote actually fell slightly compared with 1959; but the Tories' fell more, while the Liberals doubled their share to three million, helping Labour to a bare overall majority of just four (Labour 317, Conservative 304, Liberals nine). After thirteen years in the wilderness Labour was back, but scarcely with the ringing mandate Wilson had hoped for, and facing a dire economic inheritance.

---

* Barry Goldwater was the Republican candidate opposing Lyndon Johnson in that year's US presidential election. He was regarded as an extreme right-winger and lost by a landslide.

In Stechford, Jenkins nearly doubled his personal majority from its low point in 1959:

Roy Jenkins (Labour)	22,421
D.L. Knox (Conservative)	17,033
Labour majority	5,388[131]

After sixteen years in Parliament, he finally had the possibility of office. The next six years would transform him from a semi-detached literary dilettante to a central figure in British politics and a potential Prime Minister.

11 Office at Last

A s soon as it was clear that Wilson would be able to form a government Jenkins, like every other Labour MP hopeful of office, was
plunged into an agony of anticipation mixed with apprehension, exactly
as satirised in the opening episode of *Yes, Minister*. Would he get a job
at all and, if so, what? After his reassuring talk with Wilson the year
before he had reasonable grounds for confidence that he would be
offered something. But it might not be in one of the departments he
wanted: there was considerable speculation that he might get Education.
Almost as important was how any offer compared with what was
offered to others.

He did not hurry back to London while the last votes were being
counted on Friday morning, but stayed in Birmingham to give lunch
to his party workers; then he drove back to take part in a television
discussion at Lime Grove during which the first Cabinet appointments were announced: notably Jim Callaghan to be Chancellor,
with George Brown in charge of a rival economic ministry, the
Department of Economic Affairs (DEA). This division – designed
primarily to provide a suitable niche for Brown, but supposed to
encourage 'creative tension' in economic policy – had been planned
several months earlier. Brown had then pressed Jenkins to be his
number two, but Jenkins resisted. 'High though was my regard for
many aspects of Brown's brilliant but uncontrolled personality, I
thought this would be more a recipe for emotional exhaustion than
for calm ratiocination and effective decision-taking.'[1] But what might
he get instead?

Next morning he had a drink with Tony Crosland at his flat in
Chelsea; he was relieved that Tony had not heard anything either, but

jumped whenever Tony's phone rang. After a nervous walk with Jennifer in Richmond Park in the afternoon he came home to a message – the phone having been answered by ten-year-old Edward – to ring 10 Downing Street immediately. When Jenkins did so he was summoned for 10.30 the next day. He then took Charles and Edward to see the new James Bond film *Goldfinger* at the Kensington Odeon. Bill and Sylvia Rodgers came to Ladbroke Square for dinner; they had just reached the cheese when Brown telephoned to tip Jenkins off that he was to be offered the Ministry of Aviation – outside the Cabinet, but heading his own department – while Rodgers was to be an Under-Secretary in the DEA. Brown summoned them all to his flat in Marble Arch, where they found the Croslands and learned that Tony was to be Brown's Minister of State. One might imagine that for Labour's ambitious young economists the DEA, which was supposed to be the powerhouse of the new economic planning, was the place to be, even in a subordinate position. But this was not how Crosland saw it: he was already in a furious altercation with Brown over devaluation. 'Tony was in a black mood,' Rodgers remembered, 'because he did not want to become . . . George's Number 2, least of all when Roy was to have a department of his own.'[2] In the Whitehall pecking order, having your own ministry – any ministry – is better than being number two in any other department. This was a critical moment: the first of a series of steps by which Jenkins decisively overtook his old friend over the next few years, from which their relationship never fully recovered.

Wilson's choice, setting aside past differences, showed that he already saw Jenkins as a clear-sighted problem-solver who could be placed straight away at the head of a complex department. In their conversation in October 1963 he had already hinted that he was thinking of giving him a job on the foreign affairs/defence side of the government, so Jenkins' wider international interests, going beyond economics, probably gave him an edge over Crosland. But when he saw the Prime Minister in Downing Street the next morning Wilson took an age to come to the point, so he was grateful for Brown's tip-off. Being fore-warned, he had time to bargain. Before the election Wilson had planned to break up the Ministry of Aviation, putting civil aviation under Transport or the Board of Trade and leaving only the military side.[3] But Jenkins, having taken an interest in the problems of BOAC for his *Observer* articles, was keen to keep the civilian side as well; and Wilson needed little persuasion. He was less cooperative over personnel. Jenkins asked for Tom Bradley as his junior minister, but Wilson insisted ('unusually brusquely for him') that he must have John Stonehouse.[4] Jenkins appointed Bradley his PPS instead.*

Aviation might not sound like a key job in an incoming Labour government, but in 1964 it was a high-profile assignment with several big decisions to be made concerning both military and civilian aircraft. Jenkins' appointment was generally well received. 'Youngest Minister Gets Tough Air Job' was the *Daily Mirror's* front-page headline (Jenkins was forty-three at the time);[5] while the *Spectator* predicted that 'Mr Roy Jenkins will shine brightly at the scarcely impossible task of doing better than Mr Julian Amery'.[6] Jenkins himself, both in his *Observer* articles and during the election (when he had no reason to expect to get the job himself), had criticised his Tory predecessor's handling of BOAC in highly personal terms:

> For a public corporation to work well there must be relations of trust between the top management and the Minister. Mr Amery is a thousand miles from creating such trust, and completely unsuited to his job.[7]

But BOAC was only one of the problems facing him. He had also to review – with Denis Healey at the Ministry of Defence – the prospects and the proper size and structure of the struggling British aircraft industry; and most immediately he had to take a view on whether to go ahead with the Anglo-French supersonic airliner, Concord (as it was still spelled in Britain).

Jenkins had barely found his office – on the second floor of the huge new Ministry of Defence building off Whitehall, with a fine view over the river – and was just beginning to read himself into his new responsibilities when he was plunged into a rough baptism. On joining the government he was obliged to sever his connection with John Lewis; but he was determined that ministerial office should not affect his lifelong insistence on lunching with someone practically every day, so on his third day he was about to give a farewell lunch to the chairman, Bernard Miller, at Brooks's when his Permanent Secretary, Sir Richard Way, hauled him out – in person – to warn him of Whitehall rumours that the

---

* Tom Bradley had been an official of the Transport Salaried Staffs' Association before becoming MP for Leicester North-East in 1962; he was a faithful supporter who followed Jenkins to the Home Office and the Treasury, and much later into the SDP. Stonehouse, also from a trade union background, was a high flyer who rose quickly through several departments in 1964–70 before coming spectacularly unstuck in the 1970s when he ran into money troubles and was sent to prison for faking his own death.

Cabinet had decided the previous day, as part of the spending cuts required by the £800 million deficit, unilaterally to cancel Concord. Here was the disadvantage of being outside the Cabinet. 'The issue was plumb within the responsibilities of the Minister of Aviation, and I had not been consulted.'[8] He was not in fact particularly committed to the project. His *Observer* article the previous summer had concluded sceptically that 'The Concord . . . needs much harder economic analysis than it ever received.'[9] The estimated cost had more than doubled in just four years since Amery had signed the agreement with the French. As the costs spiralled, the likelihood of being able to sell the plane diminished, so that even BOAC and Air France might need to be subsidised to fly it; while the so-called 'sonic boom' was proving worse than anticipated, threatening operating restrictions which would further affect its commercial viability. There was no great demand for supersonic travel; and scarce technological resources might be better employed in a multiplicity of less glamorous projects than one or two 'prestige' ones. The problem was that Amery had signed not just a commercial contract to co-produce the aircraft, but a full-blown treaty. It would be not only expensive but internationally humiliating to withdraw. Whatever his private doubts, both as a departmental minister defending his patch and as a proponent of European cooperation, Jenkins had to fight the decision.

The next day he attended the second meeting of the new Cabinet – for Item 5 on the agenda only – where he argued, first, that there would be no immediate savings from cancellation and, second, that relations with France would be damaged and future cooperation on other projects put in jeopardy. He urged the Cabinet at least to hold back from an immediate announcement.[10] But Callaghan was insistent, while Patrick Gordon Walker, who as Foreign Secretary might have been expected to be concerned for Anglo-French relations, was strangely unsupportive. Jenkins was deputed the tricky job of explaining the government's decision, first to the manufacturers (the British Aircraft Corporation and Bristol Siddeley) and then to the French. Before flying to Paris on 29 October he was warned by the Foreign Office that he would be met by an 'atmosphere of cold enmity'.[11] On arrival he suffered an awkward lunch with the British ambassador, Sir Pierson Dixon, at which – horror! – 'the wine was lightly corked . . . So we proceeded to the key meeting . . . without much prior fortification'.[12] This actually went better than expected. His opposite number 'gave absolutely nothing away from the French point of view, but he was perfectly courteous and even friendly throughout'.[13] Jenkins' next hurdle was the House of Commons.

The occasion was the debate on the Address, when the Tories decided at short notice to focus on Concord, forcing Jenkins to make his first speech as a minister, with little time for preparation, in reply to an attack by his new shadow, Angus Maude. In those days the winding-up speeches in a packed (and well-lubricated) House before the ten o'clock vote were highly charged gladiatorial events. It was another testing baptism, but Jenkins achieved a parliamentary triumph, defending the government's decision to seek an 'urgent review' of the project, and blaming both Amery for concluding an agreement with no break clause and the outgoing government for leaving Labour such a crippling deficit.[14] It was, wrote the *Daily Telegraph*, 'a tremendous rapping fighting speech':

> In little more than half an hour he established himself as one of the most formidable and powerful debaters on the Government Front Bench . . . Rarely has a new Minister made so decisive an impact on the House.[15]

Just three weeks after the General Election, Jenkins had already announced himself as a star of the new government. But he remembered it as a nerve-racking initiation. 'My whole recollection of those first weeks of government,' he wrote in a book review thirty-three years later, 'is of feeling like a rather bad and inexperienced skier being swept down a steep slalom course, trying desperately to stay on my feet.'[16] Even at the time he confessed to Walter Terry of the *Daily Mail*: 'It was like having to dodge bulls without knowing the size of the arena. I had certain patches of knowledge about the aircraft industry . . . but it was five weeks or so before I was able to see the full picture.'[17] At a Cabinet committee on 16 November he set out a range of alternatives to outright cancellation; but he was still having to argue a case in which he did not really believe, between the 'brutal economisers' (as Crossman called them) – the economic ministers, Callaghan and Brown – on one side and the 'internationalists' – Crossman, Crosland and (ironically) Douglas Jay – on the other. (As President of the Board of Trade, Jay already had the embarrassment of explaining to Britain's EFTA partners the government's unilateral imposition of import charges.) The economisers inevitably won, and Jenkins 'went away with instructions to negotiate from an impossible position'.[18] But the French still refused to give an inch. On 20 January he had to announce that Concord would go ahead after all. Although the British government still retained 'some doubts about the economic and financial aspects of the project', they had been impressed by French confidence and were resolved to stand by the treaty.[19] The truth was that the Cabinet could find no way to renege on it. Legal opinion presented by the Attorney-General, Elwyn Jones, suggested that France could be awarded as much as £200 million in compensation at The Hague if Britain unilaterally cancelled. This made it more expensive to cancel than to carry on; so Callaghan and Brown bowed to the inevitable and Concorde (the British eventually accepted the French spelling) survived.

With hindsight, Jenkins believed that if the government had either consulted Paris in the first place or else persisted and called the French bluff, they too would have been happy to abandon the project: it was the hasty unilateralism of Britain's initial announcement that caused the French to dig in. He came to wish they had cancelled it, as it turned into 'a tremendous financial albatross'.[20]* Concorde never operated at a profit, was never sold to any other country and singularly failed to herald an age of supersonic travel. Only twenty planes were ever built and these were finally taken out of service in 2003 after a fatal crash in Paris. The failure to cancel was a somewhat inglorious start to Jenkins' ministerial career; yet the decision was not his, but the Cabinet's, and by pinning the blame squarely on the Tories he contrived to come out of it with his reputation enhanced.

He had made such an instant impression that he was first in line for promotion when the government faced its first enforced reshuffle. Patrick Gordon Walker had been appointed Foreign Secretary in October even though he had lost his Smethwick seat to a nasty racist campaign. Another constituency was quickly found for him, but the voters of Leyton objected to having a defeated minister foisted on them and in January 1965 he lost that too, after which he could not carry on. Needing a new Foreign Secretary, Wilson thought seriously of appointing Jenkins.[22] Somehow the veteran chairman of the parliamentary party, Manny Shinwell, got to hear of this and tipped Jenkins off, so that when called to see the Prime Minister he walked up Downing Street in a delirium of anticipation. In fact Wilson had decided to play safe and appoint the colourless figure of Michael Stewart, previously Secretary of State for Education; it was this vacancy that he offered to Jenkins, whom he and Burke Trend, the Cabinet Secretary, had already identified as 'by far the outstanding success among ministers outside the Cabinet'[23] – even though Wilson knew it was not a job he coveted.

* On the day Jenkins announced its continuation, the cartoonist Vicky drew him dolefully surveying a large white elephant with the face of General de Gaulle.[21]

Disappointed, Jenkins prevaricated. He first objected that all his children were at private schools, but Wilson brushed that aside. (So, he pointed out, had his own been: it was not a problem for Labour politicians in the 1960s.) Then he asked for a couple of hours to think about it and summoned Jennifer for a sandwich lunch in his office. The sandwich was unusual, but at every key moment in his career he always discussed his big decisions with her. She inclined towards acceptance; but Roy decided that he was enjoying Aviation too much to want to give it up after three months, even for a seat in the Cabinet. Education was frankly not a subject that excited him. It did not at that stage, he later confessed, occur to him that someone else would necessarily leapfrog over him. He went back to the Commons and told Wilson, who once again was impressed. He probably realised that Jenkins was gambling that the next vacancy would be the Home Office. Even so, he wrote in his memoir of the Labour government, it was 'a brave decision: few politicians would refuse their first chance of joining the Cabinet'.[24] A few hours later Jenkins heard that Tony Crosland had been appointed, and 'experienced an inevitable stab of jealousy that I had surrendered my brief lead over this great friend but formidable rival'.[25] He quickly restored his advantage, however, by letting it be known that he had been offered the job first. Crosland was not amused.

Two days later Jenkins wrote Wilson a slightly grovelling letter of thanks. 'I am very struck by how well you have treated me ever since I came to see you to discuss the Economist offer. Each time you have been a little better than your word. May I also be permitted to say what a great pleasure it is to work closely with you on a problem.'[26] From disliking and even despising Wilson, Jenkins had come to appreciate both his political skill and how much he stood to gain from getting on with him.

Despite having no previous executive experience of any sort, Jenkins took to government like a duck to water. He had been reading and writing about the exercise of power for the past fifteen years; and in Asquith he had a model of how to be an effective minister. From the beginning his civil servants thought him first-class: 'He is highly intelligent, extremely agreeable, very quick on the uptake, and he works very fast.'[27] Though he generally preferred reading to verbal briefing, he believed in listening to all available advice before making a decision; he would then adjourn the meeting, take time to think out his line and then announce his decision at the start of the next meeting. Coming into a scientific department where he had to deal with technical specifications and – on the military side – complex weapons systems, he made it a rule not to pretend to understand something if he did not: the memory of Bletchley, where he had at times been frankly out of his depth, still scarred him. Above all he was determined not to spread himself too thinly. 'One has to decide what are the main areas of policy and confine oneself to, say, three or four issues at a time', he told the *Daily Mail*.[28] He was also determined – like Asquith – to keep up his social life and make time for general reading. After just four months he gave an interview to the *Observer* in which he described his working day with remarkable confidence and candour:

> I wouldn't say that in the last few months in office I've been excessively overworked. I arrive at about 10 in the morning and work through till about 1.15 fairly solidly: meetings, work on papers and so on. I then go out and lunch with somebody; I don't always talk business then by any means. I have an hour and a half for lunch. If there's not something arranged I go to the House of Commons or Brooks's Club.
>
> In the afternoon my hours are a quarter-to-three to a quarter-to-eight. Apart from this I do perhaps an average of an hour working on papers outside the office. I do half-an-hour every day in the car; that's one of the advantages of having a chauffeur-driven car, which I've never had before in my life. I can get through a lot of papers between Ladbroke Square and my office.

Note the refusal to take work home in the evening – the bane of most ministers' lives.

He actually thought being a minister less demanding than writing, which cannot have endeared him to his hard-pressed colleagues:

> In a sense I work very hard as a Minister; but in another sense I don't think I work as hard as I used to: I only regard writing as real work. The most difficult thing is sitting down at a desk with a blank sheet of paper; and unless you write the thing there will be nothing there. As a Minister you hardly write anything. You have something in draft form: you can rewrite it if you want to; or approve it; or say, 'do you mind redrafting it?' But I think the most difficult thing of all is to sit faced with a blank piece of paper . . .
>
> As a Minister . . . I suppose you sometimes take fairly responsible decisions; but you don't have this extreme form of mental effort, which is starting from blank. There's a momentum in a Minister's

work . . . Even if you're not on best form, you have a certain number of people to see and drafts to approve, and so you get through the morning's work because the morning's work doesn't have to be created by oneself . . .

Despite his testing initiation he found that he worried less than he had done before:

I don't mean that I don't think terribly carefully about what I should do. But I'm much less a prey to destructive worry – thinking about things one cannot alter – than I used to be . . . There have been moments of high tension, certainly; but regrets and destructive worry less than before. Certainly I have thought, 'God, it matters terribly how I do that in the next half-hour.' And occasionally there's an absolutely sickening feeling that one's going to do it badly. But I draw a great distinction between worry about the future and worry about the past. Worry about the future is sometimes good; worry about the past is almost always debilitating.[29]

A second expensive aeroplane that the incoming government was determined to review was the nuclear-strike bomber, the TSR-2, designed as a replacement for the old Canberra, commissioned in 1959 and now being built by Hawker Siddeley in Coventry. There were actually three British-built military aircraft under threat in the November 1964 defence review. The HS681 was a short take-off transport plane, a replacement for the Argosy, and the P1154 was a supersonic vertical take-off fighter intended to replace the Sea Vixen and the Hunter. But it was on the TSR-2 that controversy centred. The decision raised in acute form the question of whether the RAF should fly British planes, at greater expense if necessary, to support the survival of the independent British aircraft industry, or go for American planes which, being built for a bigger market, could be bought more cheaply. The Ministry of Defence, under Denis Healey, was moving towards scrapping all three British planes and buying instead the swing-wing F-111A (in the case of the TSR-2), Hercules Transport planes (in place of the HS681) and Phantoms plus more British Buccaneers (in place of the P1154).

In the House of Commons on 9 February Jenkins defended the scrapping of the HS681 and the P1154, but still held out some hope for the TSR-2. At Cabinet the day before, however – which he again attended for this item only – he had recommended scrapping that too, even though Hawker Siddeley had made an 'almost embarrassingly good' new offer on costs and delivery time.[30]* In the House he reviewed the whole future of the aircraft industry, which consumed 25 per cent of the government's research and development spending to produce models that were then unsaleable and now made up only 2½ per cent of British exports. (The death knell had sounded for the TSR-2 in 1963 when the Australian government decided to buy the F-111A instead.) The lesson from the TSR-2 – whether it went ahead or not – was that the aircraft industry must never again tie up all its resources in one or two commercially uncertain projects. The future must lie (and here Jenkins could restore his European credentials) in international cooperation:

> Whatever decisions we have taken in the past weeks, and whatever decisions we may take in the next few months, we are at the end of the road as far as exclusive British manufacture of complicated weapons systems for an exclusive British market is concerned. We can afford to make the products only if others will buy them. The corollary is that we must be prepared to buy some of the products of others. An all-British industry equipping an RAF flying all-British planes is out, whether we like it or not.[32]

'A masterly speech,' *The Times* enthused. 'In less than 45 minutes Mr Jenkins took the aircraft industry and shook it inside out.'[33] Among the private congratulations were notes from Shirley Williams ('The best speech I've heard so far here' – though admittedly she had only been elected the previous October) and Michael Foot ('Mr Asquith at his peak could not have done it better'); while the *Sun* quoted a Labour MP, not previously an admirer, saying, 'I'll be damned . . . but I think he could be Prime Minister.'[34]† Still the Cabinet had to take the decision on the TSR-2. Healey's proposal to make a straight substitution of the F-111A ran into strong opposition from the defenders of British industry, led by Cousins, Jay and Crossman (a Coventry MP) and backed by marching aircraft workers. But the Chancellor was adamant,

* Denis Healey's unpublished diary suggests that Jenkins initially wanted to go on with TSR-2, out of concern for the jobs at stake. If so, by February 1965 he had changed his mind.[31]
† The *Sun* was still the new incarnation of the stodgy old TUC-owned *Daily Herald*, launched in 1964. Not until 1969 was it bought by Rupert Murdoch and transformed into a raunchy tabloid.

particularly after the failure to cancel Concorde, that TSR-2 could not be kept going at the cost of £4 million a month and he was determined to announce the cancellation in his budget. Over two long Cabinet meetings on 1 April Jenkins argued for cancelling TSR-2 without replacing it at all. 'My scepticism about a continuing British East of Suez role predisposed me in favour of doing without either.'[35] The Cabinet was split evenly three ways: between cancellation; cancellation with an option to buy the F-111A; and carrying on with the TSR-2. At the end of the second meeting, however – for which Jenkins had postponed a visit to New York – Healey, backed by Wilson, got his middle way. By a majority of 12:10, well after midnight, it was agreed to cancel, but with an option on the F-111A; and a year later the American plane was duly bought, as the MoD had clearly intended all along.[36] Once again, however, Jenkins was seen to have done well, as Crossman noted: 'The only man who has come out on the defence side with a will and a mind of his own is Roy Jenkins at Aviation . . . Roy Jenkins is an example of a non-Cabinet Minister who has steadily raised his status.'[37]

In the Commons the Tories moved a censure motion, which gave him another parliamentary triumph. If his speech in February had been impressively reasoned, this was back in his most combative vein. After only six months the government was already in trouble: the loss of the Leyton by-election had halved its already tiny majority, the economic outlook was gloomy and the party was rapidly becoming demoralised. But Jenkins rallied the troops, as *The Times* described:

As if to prove that they can still win in the place where it matters, the Government pulled off a huge victory in the House of Commons last night, defeating the Opposition censure motion on the cancellation of the TSR-2 by a clear 26 votes.

The end came after a thunderous tub-thumping display by Mr Roy Jenkins, Minister of Aviation, which set the Commons alight after what had been – by censure debate standards – a rather dull day.

What Mr Jenkins had to say hardly mattered, even if the House had been able to hear more than a fraction of it. In fact it was largely a repetition of what Mr Healey had said earlier, but Mr Jenkins' style was so belligerent that he could have spoken Swahili and still provoked a riot.[38]

The third major decision to occupy Jenkins during his fourteen months at Aviation was the one he had addressed in his *Observer* articles in 1964: what to do about BOAC? The problem was the same one in civil guise: whether the national airline should fly the flag or buy the cheapest in an effort to make a profit. In 1963 Amery had appointed a new chairman, Sir Giles Guthrie, with instructions to make a profit. Guthrie's response had been to cancel BOAC's order for thirty British Super VC-10s in favour of American Boeing 707s. Jenkins had argued that this was unacceptable: though BOAC should in principle fly the cheapest plane available, the corporation was too far committed to Vickers to scrap its order now. The government should make good the financial disadvantage to BOAC in this instance and write off its £80 million past loss, but with the instruction that it should operate as economically as possible in future.[39] In office a few months later he followed his own advice, except that the amount of debt written off was actually £110 million, to be accompanied by a restructuring of the corporation's relationship with the government. Announcing this in the Commons on 1 March, he again made short work of the Opposition: 'The Minister chopped Mr Maude down to size with a few cutting phrases before going on to speak at length of his own decision.'[40]

Meanwhile he had set up a small but high-powered inquiry intended – as he wrote much later – to 'shine a searchlight of sceptical judgement upon a somewhat cushioned industry',[41] and persuaded Lord Plowden to chair it. Edwin Plowden, formerly chief planner at the Treasury, more recently chairman of the Atomic Energy Authority, was one of the most revered figures in Whitehall, so he was quite a catch and an example of Jenkins' networking skill (Plowden was a member of Brooks's). He reported towards the end of the year, recommending – as Jenkins hoped – that the industry should concentrate on a small number of cost-effective projects with a guaranteed export market, and more collaboration with Europe. He also proposed that the government should take a stake in the largest air-frame manufacturers, BAC and Hawker Siddeley. This too was something Jenkins had privately supported even before he became the responsible minister. 'Although I am very far from being a fanatical nationaliser,' he wrote in August 1964 to the Labour-supporting industrialist Michael Montague, 'I think that public ownership would now probably be a good thing for the aircraft industry and, I daresay, for the efficiency of the economy as a whole.' His only doubt was that nationalisation had caused the Labour Party such trouble in recent years that it might be politically unwise. 'I think one has to have a certain amount of regard for these rather "cowardly" considerations. But I would certainly keep the matter open for the next Labour Government to consider.'[42] In the event Jenkins was moved on before he could act on Plowden's recommendation; his successor Fred Mulley tried to implement it by merging the two companies under public control; but that plan fell through and it was not until 1977 that they were nationalised by the Callaghan government as British Aerospace – only to be privatised again by Mrs Thatcher in the 1980s.

One lasting piece of reorganisation that Jenkins did achieve was to set up the British Airports Authority to run Heathrow, Gatwick and Stansted (Scottish airports were added later), while devolving smaller government-owned airfields to the relevant local authorities. Typically he took the opportunity to visit every one, including those in the Scottish highlands and islands, in a small plane. 'I am not sure it greatly helped the passage of the Bill,' he wrote, 'which in any case John Stonehouse was mostly conducting, but it gave me a grid of geographical knowledge which became useful when I entered Scottish politics seventeen years later.'[43] The BAA too was privatised in the 1980s.

By now, however, he was ready to move on. Indeed he claimed somewhat arrogantly in his memoirs that he began to lose interest in Aviation after just six months. As soon as the TSR-2 question was settled in April 'I began to feel that I was no longer in the front line. At first this was a relief, then it became rather boring.'[44] Frank Soskice had not been a success as Home Secretary and was expected to retire soon on health grounds. This was the next job Jenkins had his eye on, and the press was lining him up for it. But Wilson really wanted to put him into an economic department. 'He was one of the few people who was familiar with financial and economic subjects,' he told Alastair Hetherington, 'and could deal with them both by knowledge and by instinct. In a way, he was the kind of person one wanted as Chancellor.'[45] He probably thought the Home Office a waste of a good economist. In September Lord Longford warned Jenkins that this was how the Prime Minister was thinking; so once again Jenkins went see him, on some Aviation-related pretext. Wilson assured him that he wanted to bring him into the Cabinet very soon, as one of 'a series of moves' following Soskice's resignation. Jenkins deliberately let his disappointment show. 'You surely wouldn't like to be Home Secretary, would you?' Wilson asked; and when Jenkins said that he would like it very much indeed, he said, 'Well, that makes it all much easier.'[46] Wilson should not have been surprised. Did he not recall the last chapter of *The Labour Case*, in which Jenkins had set out his detailed list of reforms which he thought a Labour Home Secretary should undertake? Maybe they were all metropolitan issues like homosexuality, censorship and abortion, which Wilson, ever-conscious of his Nonconformist northern roots, thought traditional Labour voters would not stomach: his every move at this time was geared towards an early General Election to secure a working majority. But on reflection he may have welcomed the chance to restore the government's credit with its *Guardian*-reading supporters while shuffling off these difficult causes to someone who believed in them. At any rate Jenkins came away with the impression that he would be appointed almost immediately.

On the strength of this he counted his chickens before they were hatched. In early October he set off on an eighteen-day trip to Australia and New Zealand, confidently expecting to be called back to London halfway through. But in his absence Cecil King – the megalomaniac chairman of the *Daily Mirror*, who at this time saw himself as a confidant of the Prime Minister – wrote in his diary that Soskice was not keen to go and Wilson was too soft-hearted to sack him, even though he had already offered the job to Jenkins, 'who had told his friends and had even done a little celebrating'.[47] Wilson also disliked having his appointments leaked in advance and had decided – as Crosland took 'some pleasure' in telling him – to show Jenkins who was boss by letting him stew for a bit.[48] In the end he had to wait until just before Christmas before the reshuffle was finally announced.

No one questioned that Jenkins had earned his promotion, though it was slightly overshadowed by the simultaneous promotion of Barbara Castle to Minister of Transport, which shocked the newspapers because she did not drive. Jenkins was actually in Bonn, discussing German participation in the European airbus, when the call from Number Ten came through; and this underlined the only criticism of his appointment: that he should be leaving Aviation just when big decisions were needed to implement the Plowden report. 'It is incredible,' Ted Heath – now Leader of the Opposition – charged, 'that having brought the aircraft industry into its present difficulties Mr Jenkins should now abandon it at such a crucial stage.'[49] But *The Times* reflected the general view in welcoming his switch to the Home Office:

> It is not simply Mr Jenkins' liberal outlook which recommends him, for liberalism and judgement are not invariably yoked. His administrative competence and power of decision make it a most promising appointment.[50]

The *Daily Telegraph* entered a note of caution:

It remains to be seen whether MR ROY JENKINS . . . will be able to retain, in so daunting a department, that peculiar combination of toughness and charm which have so far marked his political career.[51]

But the *Birmingham Post* had no doubt. By his cool handling of the problems of aviation Jenkins had shown himself a fighter, not a dilettante. 'If it came to the fight of his life,' it predicted, Labour MPs 'would find him tough as steel . . . Here was not only a leader, but a leader among leaders.'[52] This was putting it a bit high; but across the Atlantic the potential significance of his advance was noted by *Time* magazine:

Jenkins is not yet a serious rival for Wilson's succession. But with his youth, he may become the very model of a leader for the 1970s: pro-Europe, moderate in social philosophy, possessed of a feel for the past as well as an openness towards the future in an era of rapid change for both the Labor Party and Britain.[53]

The announcement released a flood of congratulations from an immense range of friends, running from Attlee ('How pleased your father would have been') through political colleagues from both sides of the House, Balliol contemporaries (Nicko Henderson, Madron Seligman), journalists (Walter Terry, Jeremy Isaacs, Ludovic Kennedy, John Grigg) and academics (Noel Annan, John Sparrow, Christopher Hill, Hugh Thomas), to girlfriends (Barley Alison, Caroline Gilmour) and other lady friends (Ann Fleming, Pamela Berry, Marietta Tree and Jackie Kennedy). The fat file of letters in his papers – all immensely flattering, often comparing him to Asquith and many of them explicitly hoping that he would in due course follow his model all the way to Number Ten – give a flavour of the admiration that Jenkins aroused among the liberal establishment and the hopes now vested in him. Caroline Gilmour wrote from Scotland: 'Darling Roy, Many, many congratulations. What a gigantic relief to have the uncertainty over. I am *so* pleased for you . . .'; Ann Fleming more teasingly from Sevenhampton: 'Dearest Roy, *Please* time your next visit when your box is crammed with the Pennine murders evidence – better reading than Plowden. I thought you *looked* like a Home Secretary the other night . . .' Generously swallowing any jealousy he may have felt, Tony Crosland was typically sardonic:

Had thought to see you at Cab. Thurs. Then called at Lad. Sq. this morning, but only stillness & silence.

All goes to show (a) pessimism never justified, (b) people have their just deserts, & (c) you've lost nothing by a few months delay.

So many congratulations: & please make abortion compulsory at earliest date, thus winning plaudits of *Observer* & easing my problems in the schools. (Tho' in fact still think you've gone to the wrong Dept.)[54]

One wonders which department he thought Roy should have gone to.

Jenkins spent the Christmas holiday with the family in the dower house at Hatley, replying to all these letters while reading himself into his new responsibilities. It was a happy Christmas.

12 'A More Civilised Society'

THE Home Office was in many ways a surprising department for an ambitious politician to set his sights on. Though supposedly one of the three 'great offices of state', it has more often than not been occupied by second- or even third-rank figures who advanced no further, or occasionally by a first-rank player on the way down. The Home Secretary has no concern with economic policy, which is where the real power in modern government lies; his (or her) responsibilities cover a ragbag of somewhat miscellaneous administrative functions, ordinarily routine but with an unusual potential for controversy. There is no subject on which the press more stridently seeks a scapegoat when things go wrong – a policeman murdered, or a prison riot – than the web of interconnected social problems known collectively as 'law and order'. For this reason the Home Office is usually regarded as a graveyard of reputations rather than a launch pad: in the previous sixty years the only former Home Secretary to reach the premiership was Winston Churchill – and it took him thirty years and a world war.

It was just because it had so long been a backwater of timid illiberalism, however, that Jenkins saw in the Home Office the opportunity for a determined reformer to make his mark. During the long years of Tory rule he had derided the wilful obscurantism of David Maxwell Fyfe (1951–4), Gwilym Lloyd George (1954–7) and Henry Brooke (1962–4), but had been especially disappointed by the one – Rab Butler (1957–62) – who might have brought to the office both a more liberal outlook and the authority of a senior minister. As a backbencher trying to steer his Obscene Publications Bill onto the Statute Book in 1958, Jenkins had experienced at first hand the power of the department to obstruct reform; now he was eager to have the resources of the Home

Office under his command in order to advance it. Rarely does a new minister come into office with his personal agenda so clearly mapped out as he did in December 1965: Prime Ministers are usually careful to keep potential rivals away from their areas of expertise. It is to Harold Wilson's lasting credit that he gave Jenkins the opportunity he craved.

Jenkins' two years at the Home Office – actually less than two years – are a classic example of the right man in the right job at the right time. Half a century later his brief tenure still excites admiration and controversy in equal measure. Coinciding with the height of Beatlemania, the miniskirt, the contraceptive pill and 'Swinging London', but also with the Rolling Stones, the drug scene and the first Vietnam war demonstrations, the period 1965–7 now appears, for good or ill, a turning point in the social history of the country – a halcyon time of personal liberation or the onset of national decadence. While Jenkins himself always spoke unapologetically of the 'more civilised society' he helped to inaugurate, Mary Whitehouse in the 1970s and Margaret Thatcher in the 1980s denounced him as the chief corrupter of morals who loosed the demon of 'permissiveness' in the land. Of course Jenkins did not create, but only reflected, the new moral climate which twenty years of peace and growing affluence suddenly produced in the mid-1960s. It was not he, nor even the Labour party, that had abolished National Service in 1960; curtailed the use of the death penalty in 1957; given the green light to high street betting shops and bingo; opened the door to new Commonwealth immigration; and titillated the country with the Profumo scandal in 1963. But he was far more in tune with the changing times than most Home Secretaries. He was openly on the side of the youth revolution, not against it, and if a forty-five-year-old balding politician could hardly be its patron saint, he was certainly its benevolent sponsor. To an extent, of course, he was lucky: there was a steadily building consensus (at Westminster and in most of Fleet Street, if not necessarily in the country) in favour of libertarian reforms – from the permanent abolition of hanging and the legalisation of homosexuality to the relaxation of licensing laws and the ending of theatre censorship – for which the moment (and after March 1966 a parliamentary majority) was now ripe. But no one had done more over the last ten years to promote this liberal agenda. So Jenkins deserved his luck; and it still required a committed Home Secretary to push it through. He was not in place long enough to deliver the whole list. The death penalty had already been suspended a few months before he took office – one thing Frank Soskice did achieve for which Jenkins was deeply grateful. But he ended flogging in prisons; secured government time to ensure the passage of Private Members' Bills on both homosexuality and abortion; initiated the ending of theatre censorship; and introduced a groundbreaking Race Relations Bill. It was a remarkable record in just twenty-three months.

And this was not even the main focus of his activity. Taken as a whole, Jenkins' period at the Home Office was by no means a time of liberalism run mad. Like every other Home Secretary, his first priority had to be the maintenance of law and order, the more so since he took office in the middle of what was then seen as an unprecedented crime wave, and suffered his full share of the political embarrassments Home Secretaries are heir to. His liberal reputation made it imperative to demonstrate that he was not 'soft' on crime. Here too he succeeded, winning the confidence of the police by overhauling their administrative structure and improving their equipment, while putting through a major Criminal Justice Bill incorporating important reforms of court procedure. 'I see the central purpose of the Home Office as being that of striking a very difficult balance between the need to preserve the Queen's peace and the need to preserve the liberty of the individual,' he told Robin Day in a thoughtful interview a few days after taking office. 'I certainly don't regard the fact that I consider myself broadly a libertarian means that I don't consider myself as having a great responsibility for trying to do something effective about organised crime.'[1] On the whole he held this delicate balance between liberty and order extraordinarily well.

His first priority was to transform the ethos of the Home Office itself, starting with his own room. It was 'a rather formidable office physically', he told Day, 'with a very high ceiling and a slight atmosphere of Victorian punishment about it . . . I hope to make certain changes . . . which will make it look a little more in accordance with how I see my role.'[2] He replaced the Secretary of State's forbidding desk with a long dining table (an idea he had inherited from Julian Amery at Aviation and thought a good one); replaced the small ancient electric radiator with a coal fire burning in the grate; changed most of the pictures; and symbolically banished the grim board – 'somewhat in the form of a billiard marker'[3] – which had recorded the names of murderers awaiting execution and replaced it with a refrigerator, presumably well stocked. More importantly, he wanted to change the way the department worked, and much of the senior personnel. If he needed any prompting, Kenneth Younger, a Home Office minister under Attlee who was now chairman of the Howard League for Penal Reform, wrote to tell him that all his contacts in the prison service were 'desperately hoping that you will be able to shake things up'. Generally, Younger wrote, the officials were 'decent, liberal men with a reasonably intelligent approach to their work. But compared with the top officials one knows in, for instance, the Treasury or the Foreign Office, they are seriously lacking in drive and self-assertion and seem to be brought up to believe that their first duty is to keep their political chief out of trouble at Question Time.'[4]

To change anything, however, Jenkins had to overcome the Permanent Secretary, Sir Charles Cunningham, a formidable Scot who had been in post since 1957 and expected things to be done his way. He was almost sixty, but had been assured by Soskice that he could stay on beyond the normal Whitehall retirement age. Jenkins had other ideas. Again the opening episode of *Yes, Minister* was very near the mark, with the difference that Jenkins – unlike Jim Hacker with Sir Humphrey Appleby – was determined to have his way, and did so. Cunningham, who had come to the Home Office from the much smaller Home and Health Department of the Scottish Office, operated an 'intensely hierarchical' system by which all advice to ministers was submitted exclusively by himself. Instead of a full exposition of the alternative courses of action with the supporting arguments for each, allowing the Secretary of State to question a range of subordinate officials and form his own judgement, 'everything came on one or two sheets of thick blue paper, boiled down to a few hundred words of lucid explanation, and boldly initialled "C.C.C."'.[5] The Home Secretary had either to agree or face a major confrontation. Jenkins was certain from the moment he entered the department that this must change. He also insisted that Cunningham himself must go; proposed to replace several of the older deputies and under-secretaries with new blood from other departments, 'to correct a tendency to inbreeding and inward-looking'; and requested three specific individuals of his own choosing. He wanted David Dowler, his private secretary from Aviation, to head his private office; John Harris from the Foreign Office to handle his press relations; and Jeremy Hutchinson, QC, as a part-time legal adviser. He presented these demands at a difficult meeting on Monday, 11 January 1966. The next morning, in a stiff note of protest, Cunningham resisted them all.

First, while ostensibly acceding to the minister's wishes, Sir Charles made clear his preference for his own method of submitting advice:

> You asked that the practice of submitting matters of importance requiring a decision by Ministers in the form of a self-contained minute . . . ending with a recommendation should be discontinued

and that we should revert to the former Home Office practice (which I personally regard as inefficient) of submitting all business in relevant files. Instructions have been given accordingly.

'An inevitable consequence of this change of practice', Cunningham claimed, was that the junior ministers would be less fully informed.[6] But this was the opposite of the truth. When Cunningham tried to enlist them to support his rearguard action – 'a nicely calculated attempt', in Jenkins' words, to stir up the 'distinguished but slightly prickly trio' whom he had inherited from his predecessor – they realised that a more open procedure offered them more input, not less. So Cunningham got no joy there.[7]

Then he strongly defended all the officials whom Jenkins wanted to replace; asserted that moving Dowler from Aviation was contrary to Civil Service rules; and objected to the secondment of Harris: 'I regard as most undesirable an arrangement under which an individual officer who ought to work as a member of a team has a special relationship of this kind.' He particularly deplored the proposal to bring in Hutchinson, 'which will be regarded, if it is given effect, as a reflection upon a most distinguished and competent Home Office legal adviser'.[8] No doubt, by established Whitehall convention, there was justice in all these objections. Nevertheless Jenkins got most of what he wanted. He managed to shift three of the five under-secretaries that he targeted. He was allowed to bring in Dowler and, after a short delay, Harris. He failed to get Hutchinson, but secured the appointment of another liberal-minded QC, Anthony Lester, instead. Above all, Sir Charles himself reluctantly moved on to become head of the Atomic Energy Authority. Jenkins told Barbara Castle on 14 January that he had had 'an emotionally exhausting time' battling with Cunningham. 'He was furious, but I've got my way.'[9] His new Permanent Secretary, Sir Philip Allen, had spent much of his career in the Home Office, but had most recently served in the Treasury, so 'he did not count as a troglodyte' and Jenkins quickly formed an excellent relationship with him.[10]

Jenkins' determination to bring in his own people was characteristic of his way of working, which led to some criticism – in the Home Office and later at the Treasury and in Brussels – that he relied too much on his private office rather than using the full resources of the machine at his disposal. Certainly Dowler, until his early death, and Harris, in various roles for the rest of his life, were his closest advisers. Dowler, born in 1930, had joined the Ministry of Transport and Civil

Aviation straight from Cambridge and was quickly identified as a high-flyer; as Principal Private Secretary from January 1965 he proved so congenial that Jenkins insisted on taking him with him, against all normal practice, first to the Home Office and then to the Treasury. He was by all accounts brilliant – in Jenkins' words, 'one of the best and most consistently alert critical minds that I have ever encountered' – with good political antennae and effective at driving progress.* But Dowler was also a bit of a bully, sharp-tongued and could be insufferably rude: decades later one former colleague remembered him as 'pure poison'.[12] When he died suddenly of a congenital heart defect in January 1970, Jenkins wrote a warm appreciation in *The Times*: 'I shall greatly miss his advice. But, even more, I shall miss the sheer pleasure of his company.'[13] To another former secretary who had served under his 'iron rod', however, he acknowledged that Dowler was 'a wonderful private secretary to me, but I suppose not altogether easy to work under'.[14] Like many shy men who shrink from confrontation, Jenkins often needed someone else to do his dirty work for him.

John Harris, the same age as Dowler, had been around Gaitskellite circles for some years. He had started life as a journalist before becoming personal assistant to Gaitskell in 1959 – he was present at the Frognal post-mortem after the election that year – then served as Labour's director of publicity up to 1964, when he went to the Foreign Office as special assistant to Patrick Gordon Walker and stayed on under Michael Stewart until poached by Jenkins. This was the beginning of a long, exceptionally close, but sometimes controversial association. Though paid as a civil servant, Harris acted as Jenkins' personal spin doctor, infuriating his rivals by keeping his name constantly in the headlines; even before he officially started he was already advising Jenkins how to secure maximum coverage for his first big speech and which lobby correspondents he should invite for a drink.[15] When Jenkins returned to the Home Office in 1974 he persuaded Wilson to make Harris a peer so that he could become – as Lord Harris of Greenwich – a junior minister in the department. In later life he became a slightly comic clone of his master, affecting many of the same mannerisms and intonations; but Jenkins valued him highly as 'a counsellor of buoyancy, humour, flair and instinctive political wisdom'.[16] Sometimes his activities probably did Jenkins more harm than good; but at every

★ Sir John Chilcot, who served as an assistant secretary under Dowler, remembered that one way Jenkins helped shake up the Home Office was by introducing ringing telephones. Previously the phones had only flashing lights and the office was as silent as a public library.[11]

important moment of his career, from the Home Office to the SDP, Harris played a key role.

Jenkins had little time for his first three junior ministers, all considerably older than himself, who were already in place when he arrived and understandably resented his promotion over their heads. Alice Bacon, the Minister of State, a no-nonsense Yorkshirewoman and long-standing right-wing member of the National Executive, positively disliked him; she was eventually moved to Education, but not until August 1967. The two Under-Secretaries were George Thomas, the slightly sanctimonious Welsh Methodist who later achieved national recognition as the first broadcast Speaker of the House of Commons; and Lord Stonham, a former Labour MP and prison reform campaigner who had been given one of the first life peerages in 1958. Jenkins was relieved when Thomas was moved to the Welsh Office after the 1966 election and Wilson gave him instead Dick Taverne, a Gaitskellite barrister who was to become one of his closest associates. At the same time he managed to have Maurice Foley transferred from the DEA to deal more positively with race relations. Thus he gradually got a ministerial team that was more to his liking.

One aspect of the job that he found aggravating was the convention by which the Home Secretary, as head of the Metropolitan Police, had a constable permanently stationed outside his front door. One Ladbroke Square neighbour, having heard him talking on television about the shortage of police, wrote to ask, 'Is it *really* using a police officer to good advantage having one standing outside your front door?!'[17] A few weeks later Jenkins himself wrote to the Commissioner questioning the practice; it was not only doubtfully necessary, in pre-terrorist days, but it provided 'maximum boredom and discomfort for the police and minimum convenience' to himself and his family; Jennifer thought the constable's presence when they were at home and his absence when they were away an invitation to burglary.[18] Eventually Jenkins got the protection withdrawn. But he still had a Special Branch detective shadowing him wherever he went. He once asked this bodyguard if he could stop him being assassinated. 'I doubt it,' the officer replied, 'but being so close to you I could write a much better report.'[19] And sometimes they could be useful. Over Easter 1966 – the fiftieth anniversary of the Easter Rising in Dublin – Roy and Jennifer joined a weekend party at Ann Fleming's country house at Sevenhampton. Ann wrote characteristically to Nicko Henderson:

Roy had two detectives because of the Easter rebellion, marvellous at moving furniture for the Roys and a boon and blessing for children because of revolvers in holsters under armpits and more than ready to give demonstrations.[20]*

By the time he left the Home Office, Jenkins had grown used to them and confessed that when he moved to the Treasury he rather missed them.

Having lost no time in stamping his will on the department, Jenkins set out his intentions to Parliament in a judicious, carefully non-partisan speech of 'incisive vigour' in the Commons on 2 February, followed by a press conference five days later, both emphasising the priority he would give to fighting crime.[22] But he had not been in office more than two months before Wilson judged the moment right to try to convert his precarious toehold on power into a secure majority, and called a General Election for 31 March 1966. This was the first election Jenkins had fought as a senior minister. He not only spoke much more widely beyond the West Midlands, but he fronted one of Labour's morning press conferences and was chosen to deliver the party's last radio broadcast, two days before polling day, in which he spoke authoritatively about the government's record so far – constrained by the deficit left by the Tories – and its ambitions for the next five years: first to stimulate the economy by 'a mixture of competition and planning', regional policy and prices and incomes policy, and then to distribute the results fairly so as to eliminate 'the remaining islands of poverty and hardship' while giving 'proper rewards' to the wealth creators. This was the standard Labour line, in retrospect naively optimistic. But Jenkins also sounded two characteristic themes of his own. First, without mentioning Europe, he urged that a key issue for the future was Britain finding her 'proper role in the modern world':

A strong economy and a secure balance of payments position would do ten times as much for Britain's influence as the one

---

* This house party, fairly typical of Jenkins' social circle at this time, also included Lady Diana Cooper and the literary historian Peter Quennell and involved 'much tennis and coming and going with the Astors'. When Jenkins was first appointed, Ann wrote him an outrageously (by modern standards) politically incorrect postcard:

Dear Home Sec: *Do* be the first Home sec to employ a negro detective, he'd 'mash' (Jamaican for murder) P. Worsthorne and rape P. Berry for you. Love, A. P.S. and think what fun for your friends.[21]

Presumably Peregrine Worsthorne, then deputy editor of the *Sunday Telegraph*, had written something critical about Jenkins; but what had Pam Berry – Lady Hartwell – done to offend him?

new aircraft carrier which the Conservatives want to build, or the base at Aden which they say they would not give up.

Second, he wanted to 'put behind us Britain's reputation for meanness in matters affecting the arts, sport and general amenities of life'. The government's aim was 'to use prosperity as a means to a more civilised and tolerant community'. On this rosy prospectus he asked the country to give Labour the 'clear and decisive majority' that he believed it had earned.[23]

The voters did as he asked, and Labour was returned with a landslide majority of ninety-eight and a share of the poll – 47.9 per cent – marginally higher even than in 1945. On this high tide, Jenkins in Stechford won 64 per cent of the poll and more than doubled his majority, despite the intervention of a third candidate:

Roy Jenkins (Labour)	24,598
David Knox (Conservative)	12,727
W. Dunn (Communist)	998
Labour majority	11,871[24]

Labour now seemed to have secured the platform it needed to become a great reforming government on the model of 1906 and 1945.

From his study of Asquith, Jenkins told Robin Day, he had learned that to succeed as a minister 'you should concentrate on relatively few issues on which you think you can really do something decisive . . . not dissipate your energies over too wide a field'.[25] If other colleagues wanted to make territorial raids on bits of his sprawling empire, he suggested a few days later – Fred Peart (Agriculture) to take over responsibility for wild birds, Kenneth Robinson (Health) drugs or Arthur Bottomley (Commonwealth Relations) the Isle of Man – that would be 'OK by me'.[26] His 'core function' was holding the balance between order and liberty; and here his first concern was to improve the organisation and equipment of the police. His most radical step was to cut the number of small local forces from 117 down to forty-nine (and later forty-three), which meant treading on a lot of local pride and more than seventy Chief Constables losing their jobs. This was, as *The Times* put it, 'the greatest upheaval in policing since the time of Peel', going a good deal further than the recommendations of a Royal Commission which had reported in 1962, and further than the Home Office thought he could get away with. Soskice had been waiting for the report of another Royal Commission on local government; but Jenkins just got on with it. The strongest resistance was in Lancashire, where thirteen local forces were merged into one. But reform was overdue, and Jenkins' boldness was generally applauded.[27] One of those who lost out, the Chief Constable of Leicester, Robert Mark, wrote in his memoirs that 'the enforced amalgamation of police forces against the strong opposition of chief constables, local authorities and some civil servants . . . took real courage and determination . . . but proved so obviously right that Jenkins was quickly accorded the reward to which he was entitled, the enhanced respect of police and public alike'.[28] This 'sweeping and courageous' reform, in Mark's view, produced 'immeasurable improvements in organisation, equipment, procedures, accountability and in common or shared services' and began the transformation of the police 'from a fragmented, essentially artisan service, often dominated by local politics or the central government, to a well-organised professional body much better equipped to resist outside pressures and to speak for itself'.[29]

Jenkins had already identified Mark as an exceptionally able and intelligent policeman, so he quickly found other roles for him and then appointed him Assistant Commissioner of the Metropolitan Police, with the deliberate intention of putting him in line to become Commissioner. This was another brave move, since the Met had a jealous tradition of promoting only from within its own ranks: only one provincial policeman had ever been appointed to such a high rank in the London force, and he lasted just three years. When Jenkins offered him the job at the end of 1966 Mark asked him: 'Have you consulted the Commissioner, and does he agree?'

There was a lengthy silence while Jenkins surveyed the ceiling. At last, choosing his words with typical Jenkinsian skill, he replied, 'He has loyally promised to abide by my decision.' It could hardly have been plainer, but for me, of course, it was Hobson's choice. I therefore accepted with as good grace as I could muster.[30]

He was not made welcome. But Jenkins' decision was abundantly justified when Mark eventually succeeded as Commissioner in 1972 and set about vigorously rooting out the corruption that was endemic in the London force.

Next Jenkins gave the police better equipment. In September 1966 he visited Chicago to study policing methods there.* He had originally planned to go in June, but had to postpone his trip to deal with a prolonged seamen's strike which was blocking the ports: as Home Secretary he chaired the Cabinet Emergencies Committee charged with keeping essential supplies moving. What he saw in America led him to accelerate two major reforms, which the police had long been pressing for. First, he greatly increased the provision of two-way radios so that policemen on the beat were no longer isolated units but could be sent quickly wherever they were needed. In 1965 the Met had had just twenty-five radios for the whole force: Jenkins upped that to 2,500, with similar increases over the whole country.[32] Second, he equipped the police with more radio cars, which had a double-edged effect: it made them more mobile, but also took them off the street, making them less visible and more anonymous. The public, preferring *Dixon of Dock Green* to *Z-Cars*, has been calling for more 'coppers on the beat' ever since.

All this could be done without legislation. Jenkins' biggest challenge was to put together and carry a major Criminal Justice Bill. He outlined his proposals to Cabinet in August 1966, and by the end of the year he was ready to introduce what he described in a notably lucid and thoughtful party political broadcast as 'the most far-reaching piece of Home Office legislation we have had for a very long time'. It brought together a somewhat miscellaneous ragbag of measures with a single purpose, 'to strengthen the hand of those engaged directly in the war against crime'.[33] They ranged from tighter controls on the purchase of shotguns (closing a loophole in the most recent legislation) through the streamlining of committal proceedings, the banning of 'sprung' (that is, last-minute) alibis and the introduction of majority verdicts in jury trials, to various measures to reduce the soaring prison population: release under licence, easier bail, suspended sentences and earlier parole, attachment of earnings instead of imprisonment for debt.† These, he insisted, were not designed to make prison 'softer'. 'I am searching urgently for means of limiting the prison population, not because I dismiss the value of prison in the fight against crime, but because I

---

* While in Chicago, Jenkins called on the city's notorious Mayor Daley, who was 'distinctly vague about the role of a British Home Secretary' and later described him on television as 'that London police official who called on me this morning'. 'I, rather proud of having been recently promoted to the office of Peel and Palmerston, Asquith and Churchill, was not too pleased to be regarded as a sort of precinct captain.'[31]
† The daily average prison population in England and Wales had risen from 29,000 in 1964 to nearly 35,000 in 1966 (compared with just 11,000 before the war). But Jenkins' Bill checked the growth only briefly: by the time he became Home Secretary for the second time in 1974 the figure was more than 40,000, and today it is 85,000.

want to use it as a much more effective weapon that it is today.'[34] 'I want to sharpen and not blunt the deterrent effect of prison, and I believe we can best do this by not acclimatising men to prison unless we have to.'[35]

By far the most controversial innovation was majority verdicts, designed to prevent the 'nobbling' of juries, which was allowing a lot of hardened criminals to escape conviction. Senior policemen – Robert Mark prominent among them – had been pressing for this for some time. But tampering with the ancient requirement of unanimous verdicts was an affront to legal conservatives and civil liberties watchdogs alike. *The Times* published several outraged letters and thundered editorially against 'the abandonment of a principle of unanimity in a society that has known no other for six hundred years'.[36] To guard his flanks Jenkins was careful to get both Michael Foot, the leading tribune of the Labour left, and his new Tory shadow, Quintin Hogg (later, as Lord Chancellor, a crusty defender of legal precedent), onside. Both agreed to support the clause. Hogg in particular had to withstand considerable pressure from colleagues both legal and political who saw an opportunity to defeat the government; but as he wrote in his memoirs, 'I kept my word to Jenkins and backed his proposals for all I was worth as a welcome, if minor, rationalisation, of the creaking old eighteenth-century ox-wagon of our criminal law.'[37] When it came to the vote in April 1967 Jenkins generously adjourned the debate to allow more passionate objections to be voiced from both sides of the House: seventy-four Tories – including the Shadow Energy spokesman, Margaret Thatcher – a dozen Labour members and most of the Liberals voted against. But the contentious clause was carried by 180 votes to 102 and has never subsequently been seen as anything but common sense.

The rest of the Bill, which Jenkins introduced in December with 'an hour-long speech of didactic clarity',[38] aroused no comparable furore and passed into law the following summer. More controversial was his determination to deliver a new Race Relations Bill. Soskice had already passed one Race Relations Act in 1965; but though it broke new legislative ground it was a timid measure which established a Race Relations Board to investigate allegations of discrimination but excluded housing and employment from its remit, which made it virtually useless. From the moment Jenkins came into office Anthony Lester was pressing him to beef it up. Lester drafted a major speech for Jenkins to give to the National Committee for Commonwealth Immigrants, and was very critical of the 'disastrous' draft that the department had written for him. (It was perhaps significant that the relevant assistant secretary,

J.T.A. Howard-Drake, had come from the Colonial Office.) 'I respect Roy more than anyone else in British politics,' Lester wrote to Maurice Foley, whom Jenkins had brought into the Home Office from the DEA specifically to deal with immigration issues:

> If he makes the speech in its present form he will lose the right to be regarded as liberal and creative on race relations . . .What he says on 23rd May will set the tone for future Government policy . . . If the speech is delivered in its present form it will create universal dismay and hostility in the immigrant communities.[39]

Similar advice came from Mark Bonham Carter, whom Jenkins had appointed as the first chairman of the Race Relations Board. The department had been seeking a chairman for months, trawling through dozens of worthy names, who either declined or were for one reason or another judged unsuitable. (The great West Indian cricketer Learie Constantine was vetoed by the Prime Minister of Trinidad; Dora Gaitskell was thought to lack relevant experience; they also tried Gaitskell's younger brother Arthur, an expert on African development.) Jenkins immediately added Bonham Carter to the list and quickly offered him the job.[40] 'I have never seen any objection to appointing friends,' he explained years later, 'provided they are good enough; and if they are not, maybe there is something wrong with one's choice of friends.'[41] Bonham Carter was an excellent appointment. Asquith's grandson, who had stuck loyally to the Liberal party through its leanest years, winning a famous by-election at Torrington in 1958 but then losing the seat again in 1959, had been disappointed in his hopes of a political career: this was a good way of giving him some role in public life. He was initially doubtful that he could combine the chairmanship with his directorship at Collins and his commitments to the Liberals: but when persuaded that he could, he threw himself into it with energy and success. Jenkins tacitly encouraged him to press for greater powers and he did. American experience, he urged, showed that strong legislation was needed to combat racial discrimination: in the build-up to Jenkins' big speech, he echoed Lester in urging him to stress the positive benefits of immigration, not just the problems, and suggested that he should make reference to his own Welsh heritage.[42]

Jenkins did that, and also spoke warmly of the contribution made by successive waves of immigrants from 1066 to the 1930s; he called for faster integration, which he defined 'not as a flattening process of assimilation but as equal opportunity accompanied by cultural diversity, in an atmosphere of mutual tolerance'. Such a process was essential, he insisted, 'if we are to maintain any sort of world reputation for civilised living and social cohesion'. A lot could be done under the 1965 Act – he could hardly rubbish his predecessor's legislation completely – but he dropped a clear hint that 'my mind is far from being closed about future changes to the Act'. British policy-makers at this time were acutely conscious of the racial violence that was beginning to erupt in inner cities in the United States: the following year Enoch Powell grimly foresaw 'the river Tiber flowing with much blood' unless large numbers of immigrants were 'repatriated'. Their aim was to pre-empt such trouble in Britain by wise legislation now. Compared with America's bitter legacy of slavery, Jenkins suggested, Britain started with a relatively clean slate:

> The problem we are discussing today makes less demands [*sic*] upon our capacity for tolerance and change than many which we have successfully surmounted in the past. But the way in which we face it, particularly in the next few years, can have a great effect upon our future. If we overcome [it] we shall have a new message to offer the world. If we fail we shall be building up, both inside and outside the country, vast difficulties for future generations of English people.[43]

This speech was known to his advisers as his 'We Shall Overcome' speech. Lester, Dowler, Harris, Foley and Bonham Carter all had a hand in it, while Howard-Drake did his best to emasculate it; but, as he always did with major speeches, Jenkins wrote and polished it carefully himself. For the present he did not press for a government Bill. The next month Maurice Orbach, the Labour MP for Stockport who had won a high place in the ballot for Private Members' Bills, published a Bill, drafted by Lester and Foley and supported by a range of Labour and Liberal Members, to extend the scope of the 1965 Act; while the veteran Fenner Brockway introduced a similar Bill in the Lords. In the Cabinet Legislation Committee Jenkins cited the inevitable flaws of Orbach's Bill to argue that the subject could be properly dealt with only by a government Bill, fully negotiated between the interested departments.[44] But he faced a stiff battle, since both the TUC and the CBI were lobbying against any further legislation, while the Treasury, the DEA and the Ministry of Labour – already embattled with them over prices and incomes policy – were reluctant to open another front of conflict. Beyond Westminster there was still a lot of casual racism in the workplace (hence the unions' opposition), while organisations like the Society for the Preservation of All Races (formerly the Racial Preservation Society) called openly for the separation, not integration, of races and the abolition of the 'provocative and un-British' 1965 Act. Bonham Carter's first report, however, made it clear that the existing Act was not working – only a quarter of the complaints the Board received fell within its powers – and threatened to resign if it was not given more teeth, which would have embarrassed the government. So in April 1967 the Cabinet agreed to let Jenkins have his Bill in the next session; he brought his proposals to Cabinet in July and announced them to the Commons the following week. He insisted that the new legislation must outlaw discrimination in employment, though he drew back from the minefield of religious discrimination.[45] He had moved to the Treasury by the time the Bill was ready to be introduced, leaving it to his successor, Jim Callaghan, to pilot it through; but in an interview the following year Jenkins judged announcing the legislation 'probably the most important thing I did' at the Home Office.[46] Praising his 'patience and tactical skill', the *New Statesman* recognised what he had been up against. 'In confronting his own party, the Commons and Labour in the country, he exhibited a masterly, even noble, capacity to nullify prejudice, to achieve what he believed right in the face of serious odds.'[47] The strengthened Race Relations Act became law in 1968.

In another area of racial policy, however, Jenkins was lucky. The question of what to do about a possible influx of 200,000 Kenyan Asians – holders of British passports who were being driven out by the 'Africanisation' policy of the Kenyan government – was a tricky one for a self-consciously liberal Home Secretary. In October 1967 he brought the problem to the Cabinet's Home Affairs Committee, warning that the government could not let them all in, yet had no power to keep them out. Despite 'formidable' legal objections, he feared a white backlash if he did nothing, so he asked for a slot in the legislative programme for an emergency Bill in case the trickle (currently 500 a week) turned into a flood.[48] By the time this appeared to be happening, however, just four months later, Jenkins had left the Home Office and it fell to Callaghan to incur the odium of introducing 'racist' legislation to deny British passport holders their right of entry. The Commonwealth Immigrants Bill, based on Jenkins' draft, honoured the promise, but tried to stagger the numbers by imposing a quota of around 7,000 a year, enforced by a voucher system. No longer departmentally responsible, however, Jenkins now felt free to oppose Callaghan's Bill in Cabinet, as Crossman recorded, 'partly because he hates him and partly because [he] was convinced that if we plunged into this in the kind of spirit Callaghan showed we would have offended every decent instinct. Roy pleaded for delay whereas Harold was ready to impose the quota that very day.'[49] The Bill was rushed through all its stages in a single week in February 1968, honourably opposed by thirty-five Labour Members, fifteen Tories (including Ian Gilmour) and ten Liberals. Jenkins voted for it on Second Reading, but not on Third.

In subsequent interviews Jenkins claimed that he would not have introduced the Bill:

> I can't say that it is inconceivable that I would have done it, because I did say that a draft Bill could be prepared. But I certainly gave no approval in principle to a Bill being brought in, and I do not think I would have taken the view that the influx or the threat of influx was such as to justify this highly divisive measure.[50]

Rather he blamed himself for not having fought it more strongly. 'I am afraid I behaved a good deal less than heroically when the Bill was discussed by the Cabinet,' he told Anthony Howard in 1970, excusing his failure by claiming that he was too busy with the economy.[51] In reality there can be little doubt that he would have had to introduce very similar legislation had he still been Home Secretary. What he wrote in 1973 about Gaitskell's opposition to all controls on Commonwealth immigration in 1962 applied equally to himself in 1968: 'It was a position to which it is now difficult to believe that he could possibly have held. As a practical democrat he would have had to move. But he would have suffered great anguish in the process.'[52] Jenkins was fortunate to be spared that anguish. Callaghan, on the other hand, felt understandably aggrieved that he got the blame for introducing Jenkins' Bill while Jenkins escaped with his liberal reputation largely intact.[53]

Meanwhile he had been coming under fire from the other direction for being too liberal. After a relatively easy first few months, a sequence of the sort of unexpected crises to which the Home Office is so vulnerable suddenly blew up in the autumn of 1966. First, in August, three policemen were shot dead at Shepherd's Bush, West London, in the course of a robbery that went wrong. To the right-wing press this was a natural consequence of the suspension of the death penalty, and a 'soft' Home Secretary who had been a prominent supporter of abolition was an easy target. Jenkins insisted that there was no connection – murder was one of the few crimes that was not increasing; but strident demands to 'bring back the rope', at least for the murder of police officers, continued until a Commons vote in November re-affirmed its suspension by a solid 292:172. Then, in September, Maidstone magistrates ordered the birching of a young prisoner serving a life sentence for murder, following a riot in the local prison. But the sentence required the confirmation of the Home Secretary; and since he was already committed to abolishing corporal punishment in prisons as part of the Criminal Justice Bill, Jenkins reversed it, to the fury of the *Sunday Express* and other papers.[54]* Next, on 18 October he announced a posthumous free pardon for Timothy Evans, who had been hanged in 1950 for a murder which it was now clear he did not commit. This was a notorious miscarriage of justice, which had greatly assisted the cause of the abolitionists; but two days later he had to address the London Police Federation, which did not see it that way. The whole force was said to be 'seething with discontent over pay and capital punishment'; he was booed when he mentioned Timothy Evans and the Maidstone birching case, and there was a 'howl of derision' at his suggestion that the police should recruit some black officers. The press reported that 300 officers walked out (though Jenkins claimed it was only about twenty).[56] Even so, this was 'one of the roughest and most disagreeable meetings I have ever had', Jenkins wrote. 'When it was over I went to Brooks's with David Dowler and John Harris and sat exhausted over a large drink.'[57]

Two days later the Soviet spy George Blake escaped from Wormwood Scrubs. Less famous than Philby, Burgess and Maclean, but arguably more damaging than any of them, Blake was an MI6 agent who had passed secrets to the KGB and allegedly caused the deaths of forty British agents before he was exposed in 1961 and sentenced to a record forty-two years. He escaped by scaling the perimeter wall with a nylon ladder reinforced with knitting needles.† Embarrassing at any time, this came when high-profile escapes were already a scandal and becoming a cartoonists' joke. In the past two years two of the so-called 'Great Train Robbers', Charlie Wilson and Ronnie Biggs, had escaped from

---

* When the *Sunday Express* renewed its attack in October, alleging that Jenkins was 'tender to prisoners and out of sympathy with the police' on account of his father's imprisonment during the General Strike, Dick Taverne urged him to sue, force a retraction and give the enormous damages to the Police Benevolent Fund. Wisely Jenkins did no such thing.[55]
† Blake later turned up in Moscow, where he was hailed as a national hero. In 2007, aged eighty-five, he was honoured by Vladimir Putin.[58]

Cummings, *Daily Express,* 22.10.66 (Cartoon Archive, University of Kent)

Winson Green and Wandsworth respectively. Nine long-term prisoners had escaped from Parkhurst in May; and four more had walked out of Wormwood Scrubs in June. Jenkins heard the news on Friday evening when he had just arrived at Hatley to spend the weekend with Jakie and Chiquita Astor. He immediately rang Wilson 'in a great stew', according to Crossman, who was with Wilson at Chequers when he took the call. 'When Harold put down the receiver he turned to me and said, "That will do our Home Secretary a great deal of good. He was getting too complacent and he needed taking down a peg."'[59] 'Whatever snide comment he may have made to Crossman', however, Jenkins noted at the time that Wilson 'took the whole thing reasonably calmly. He is always good in a situation of that sort, no note of recrimination, although obviously slightly agitated himself by what had happened.'[60]

Over the weekend Jenkins decided to set up an inquiry, not just into Blake's escape but into prison security in general, and asked Lord Mountbatten to chair it. The Queen's cousin, the last Viceroy of India and just-retired Chief of the Defence Staff, Mountbatten was a clever choice, which somewhat wrong-footed the Tories. Nevertheless Heath and Hogg gave Jenkins a rough ride in the Commons on Monday. 'Anger, recrimination and insult rocked the chamber as they pressed their view on an uncomfortable Mr Jenkins.'[61] By insisting on a wider inquiry while refusing to be drawn on the possibility of Russian involvement in the 'springing' of Blake, Crossman wrote, 'poor Roy Jenkins . . . seemed obstinate and a little stupid'.[62] But he stuck to his guns; and when Heath decided to table a full-dress censure motion the following week Jenkins was ready for him.

He knew his career was on the line. He spent most of the preceding weekend working on his defence. He even bought a new suit for the occasion. When the three-hour debate started, in a packed Chamber, he was visibly keyed-up.* Hogg opened, charging that Jenkins had practically invited Blake's escape by relaxing special precautions put in place by his Tory predecessor, Henry Brooke. Duncan Sandys intemperately reinforced the indictment from a back bench, charging first that Mountbatten was an inappropriate choice as chairman who was clearly intended to deliver a cover-up, and more widely that Jenkins had demoralised the police and strained the loyalty of the prison service. The former Solicitor-General, Sir Peter Rawlinson, suggested that Jenkins would 'adorn every single office in the Cabinet, save for one': he was 'unfitted to be Home Secretary'. A Labour Member loyally interjected that he was 'the best Home Secretary we have ever had in the history of the country', while Patrick Gordon Walker and Jeremy Thorpe also defended him, before Enoch Powell wound up. Heath did not speak, but was present throughout. The Tories complained that Jenkins waited till the end of the debate before replying; but when he did respond his reply was a parliamentary tour de force, as Crossman recorded:

Before he got up he sat there next to me rubbing his hands and looking as nervous as hell but the moment he started one realised he'd prepared that speech with tremendous care. He demolished Quintin's case and demonstrated that no special precautions had been taken by Henry Brooke. The demolition job was so total that when the vote came many of the Tories just weren't there.

* Leslie Bonham Carter wrote him a supportive letter earlier that day: 'Darling Roy, I am thinking about you all the time and am in agony about today – *not* because I have any doubts about the way you will scatter your foolish and ill-advised adversaries. I have none about this, and nor should you. But all the same the nervous strain must be appalling at this moment . . . If it is at all possible will you ring up when it is all over? I know that you will be marvellous. With love, Leslie.'[63]

It was a tremendous reversal achieved by sheer debating skill – the first really good evening the party has had since we came back from the recess.[64]

Jenkins began combatively by rejecting as 'typically disgraceful and totally unfounded' the charge that he had demoralised the police and prison service, and repeatedly slapped down Sandys when he tried to repeat it. When Tory backbenchers bayed, 'What about Blake?', he told them: 'If the hon. Members opposite will give up their tribal bleating I will immediately come to Blake.' (One Tory told him to 'calm yourself down a little'.) As well as refuting the allegation that he had relaxed Brooke's precautions on Blake, he also demonstrated that prison escapes generally had not suddenly increased but had been running at a roughly similar level since the early 1960s. 'The striking change is not in the figures but that we are now doing something about them.' Moreover, if Blake should not have been in Wormwood Scrubs in the first place, it was Rab Butler who had put him there! He comprehensively demolished the Tories' 'trumped up motion', since enquiring into Blake's escape was specifically part of Mountbatten's remit, and directed his scorn very personally at Heath. The problem of prison security would be solved by constructive measures, he concluded. 'It will not be met by that combination of procedural incompetence and petty partisanship which is the constant characteristic of the right honourable gentleman's parliamentary style.'[65]

'To deafening applause,' the *Daily Mirror* enthused, 'Jenkins triumphantly turned the tables on the Tory leaders . . . It was a Commons victory unequalled by a minister since Labour returned to power.'[66] *The Times* was equally admiring:

> With imperious contempt and a flow of invective rarely heard in the House of Commons these days, Mr Roy Jenkins . . . tonight swept aside an Opposition censure motion on his refusal to set up a specific enquiry into the escape of George Blake.
>
> The voting figures were 331 to 230, a Government majority of 101. But the figures scarcely mattered. The cruel slashes of Mr Jenkins' verbal sabre, lacerating the Opposition Front Bench while his cohorts roared him on to greater bloodshed, told the whole story.
>
> Mr Heath, castigated as a procedural incompetent, so obsessed by personal pique that he failed to read the terms of reference of the Mountbatten enquiry before framing the motion, never stood

a chance. His shoulders seemed to shake with laughter at the end, but he might well have been sobbing.[67]

'That half-hour,' Jenkins wrote in a magazine article thirty years later, 'was the nearest I have ever got to experiencing the thrill which I imagine big game hunters felt when they shot a tiger, or matadors when they inserted the blade in the right spot of the bull* . . . It was all slightly farcical, for it neither helped to recapture Blake nor to make me a better (or worse) Home Secretary.'[69] Nevertheless it was 'by far the greatest parliamentary triumph that I ever achieved';[70] and it had serious political consequences, as Bill Rodgers recalled:

Your Blake speech moved you immediately into the next-leader stakes in the eyes of many who had not previously seen it that way. I remember Bob Brown [MP for Newcastle West] walking through Westminster Hall with glazed eyes and stopping me to say, 'He'll be our next leader.'[71]

The next day the Tories tried to hit back. Brooke issued a statement contesting Jenkins' account, on the basis of which Hogg alleged that the Home Secretary had misled the House: a serious charge, if he could have made it stick. But Jenkins, after consulting Dowler, Harris, Sir Philip Allen and his chief information officer Tom McCaffrey,† flattened Hogg again by securing Brooke's permission to publish a minute of August 1964, which effectively supported his slightly flip paraphrase of it. 'I do not know where Blake is now,' Brooke had written – a fairly extraordinary admission – 'but if he were to escape or be rescued it would be as disastrous as if another of the train robbers were to get out.' Despite this professed concern, Jenkins insisted that 'there was no tightening in 1964 and no slackening afterwards . . . The departmental records show that Lord Brooke took no action following this minute, and no new precautions were taken.' Second collapse of Tory opposition. Nevertheless Dowler took Hogg's charge seriously enough to make a special 'note for the record' of how they refuted it.[72]

Meanwhile the serious business of prison security was devolved to

---

* When an outraged reader objected to this comparison, Jenkins dismissed the objection as 'ridiculous'. 'I have never shot an animal in my life, and like you rather disapprove of blood sports . . . But this does not affect the fact that many people certainly get such a thrill; and I am not willing to see vivid similes banned.'[68]
† McCaffrey was later Jim Callaghan's chief press officer in 10 Downing Street in the 1970s, and then worked for Michael Foot when he was Leader of the Opposition until 1983.

Lord Mountbatten, assisted by (among others) Jenkins' favourite policeman, Robert Mark. (He tried to get another good friend, Solly Zuckerman, to serve as well; but the government's Chief Scientific Adviser was, unsurprisingly, too busy.) Mountbatten reported quickly, within two months. His recommendations included electronic alarms, closed-circuit television and the use of dogs; classifying prisoners by security risk; and various suggestions for improving prison officers' morale and reducing overcrowding, which the Criminal Justice Bill was already addressing. But his most controversial proposal was that the most dangerous prisoners should all be held together in a single maximum-security prison to be sited on the Isle of Wight. Most other advice was against this and Jenkins referred it to another inquiry; his successor, Jim Callaghan, eventually decided on a policy of dispersal instead. Nevertheless Jenkins was condemned by prison reformers for giving way to demands for a tougher prison regime; he himself subsequently felt that he had tipped the balance too far towards security at the expense of rehabilitation. But it was a difficult time. Just before Christmas he faced another press and parliamentary storm when a gangster named Frank Mitchell, known as 'the mad axeman', was sprung from Dartmoor by his friends the Krays while on a loosely supervised outdoor working party; and there were several more well-publicised escapes over the holiday. 'My nerve was a bit shaken,' Jenkins admitted. 'I ought to have been steadier under fire, but it is easier to say this in retrospect than it was to sustain it during the barrage of daily bombardment.'[73] In fact he did quite a lot in 1966–7 to try to humanise the prison system – though, like every other Home Secretary for the next thirty years, he failed to end the primitive practice of 'slopping out'. It is during his second tenure in 1974–6 that he can be criticised for not doing more.

As a member of the Cabinet, Jenkins was now more involved with economic policy than he had been at Aviation, though still outside the inner circle. The critical decision was whether to devalue the pound. Despite the £800 million deficit and heavy pressure in the money markets, Wilson had agreed with Callaghan and Brown, on the very first day after the 1964 election, before the rest of the Cabinet had even been appointed, that for a mixture of political and patriotic reasons the value of sterling must be preserved. On the one hand, Wilson remembered Stafford Cripps' 1949 devaluation and did not want Labour to be cast again as the party of devaluation; on the other, the parity of sterling was held to be the symbol of Britain's credit in the world. The decision was taken, and defended with stubborn resolution for three years, in defiance of most of the government's economic advisers who saw it as a futile distraction of resources from the government's real purposes and doomed to failure in the long run anyway. There was undoubtedly a political case for not devaluing straight away in 1964, when the government's very survival was precarious. By 1966, however, when Labour had secured its landslide majority, there was none. Moreover the balance of the Cabinet had changed, with Tony Crosland, Barbara Castle and Tony Wedgwood Benn, as well as Jenkins, replacing some of the older loyalists whom Wilson had felt obliged to appoint in 1964. These four plus Crossman – the 'intellectuals' of right and left – all believed that what Wilson had declared 'the unmentionable' must not merely be discussed but should be accepted and got over with as quickly as possible if the government was ever to break free of recurrent financial crises which required repeated doses of painful deflation to appease the bankers. They were joined by George Brown, an increasingly loose cannon, who was disillusioned with Wilson, drinking too much and constantly on the verge of resignation. But Brown was a doubtful asset to the devaluationist camp, since left-wingers like Barbara Castle would not defeat Wilson to make him leader.

In mid-July 1966 sterling suddenly came under renewed pressure, due largely to the seamen's strike. Even Callaghan began to think devaluation was inevitable, before he recovered his nerve to demand another package of spending cuts and tough deflationary measures, including a six-month wage freeze. In Cabinet the devaluers called for a complete change of strategy if the deflation was to be made to work. In turn Crossman, Jenkins ('quietly but convincingly'), Benn and Castle argued that it was impossible to maintain full employment and a healthy balance of payments at the present parity. The Cabinet minutes do not name individual speakers, but the assertion that Britain must be prepared to 'abandon a very substantial part of our oversea [sic] commitments' expressed Jenkins' long-held view. The counter-argument, led by Callaghan and supported by the Foreign Secretary Michael Stewart, was that devaluation would still have to be accompanied by deflation, would not necessarily help and would have incalculable international consequences. 'One after another,' Barbara Castle wrote, 'the "do-nothing yet" brigade mowed us down.'[74] Wilson was able to sum up that the majority was still against devaluation, though Brown insisted that his disagreement be specially recorded.[75] When Crossman, Jenkins and Healey tried to argue that the Cabinet must discuss contingency plans in case it became unavoidable, Wilson re-imposed his ban on even uttering the dreaded word.[76]

So Wilson got his way for the moment; but the July crisis marked the postponement of all the government's socialist aspirations – so resoundingly endorsed by the electorate less than four months earlier – and permanently damaged both his reputation and his self-confidence. From now on he began to see enemies everywhere. The failed Cabinet revolt fuelled his growing suspicion that the devaluationists had been plotting to replace him, though he contradicted himself about whether Brown, Callaghan or Jenkins was the intended beneficiary. In August his devoted political secretary Marcia Williams told Peter Shore (then a junior minister at the Ministry of Technology), who in turn told Tony Benn, that 'the events of the last weeks have absolutely shaken Harold to the core. He is convinced that a plot was conceived to get rid of him . . . Roy Jenkins and his gang decided to get rid of George Brown and to make Callaghan no. 2, with a view to getting Roy in as No. 1.' This was palpable nonsense, if only because Jenkins would never have plotted with Callaghan against Brown; but it reflected Wilson's suspicion that Jenkins had a 'gang' ceaselessly pushing his cause. Benn, though he recognised that Jenkins 'may well have his eye on Number 10 in the long run', sensibly did not believe a word of it, realising that Wilson lived 'in an atmosphere of intrigue, encouraged by George Wigg, who is a completely crazy adviser, Marcia who gets a bit hysterical, and Gerald Kaufman'.[77]

It seems to have been Wigg – a deeply unpleasant former army officer, Labour MP for Dudley since 1945 and now Paymaster-General and Wilson's unofficial security adviser – who planted in his mind the idea that the 'July plot' had been hatched over the weekend of 16–17 July (when Wilson was away in Moscow) at Ann Fleming's country house at Sevenhampton where Jenkins had again been staying. 'If any of you knew your job,' Wilson charged Barbara Castle in October, 'you would find out who attended that weekend meeting at her place last July when I was in Moscow.'[78] 'Amazing scandal,' Mrs Fleming wrote excitedly to Nicko Henderson when the story leaked. 'It seems that Mr H. Wilson imagined or was wrongfully informed that the July weekend you spent here with old pals, I was entertaining Callaghan, Crossman (some say Crosland) and Jenkins, hatching a plot to uncrown Wilson and crown Callaghan.'[79] The truth was much more mundane. No other Cabinet minister stayed at or visited Sevenhampton that weekend, though there is some dispute about who exactly was there. Jenkins' memoirs, based on his engagement diary, record that only Mark and Leslie Bonham Carter stayed, though John Sparrow, the Warden of All Souls, and the philosopher Stuart Hampshire came to lunch on the Saturday, presumably with their wives. (He seems to have forgotten about Henderson.)[80] To add to the confusion, Lord Goodman later claimed that he was there too (and told Wilson that 'the principal occupations had been scrabble and croquet').[81] Whoever was present, Hampshire remembered it as 'an entirely social occasion . . . There was no intrigue. It was light gossip which prevailed on that sort of occasion with that particular set.'[82] In imagining anything else Wilson entirely misunderstood the nature of Ann Fleming's weekends, which were strictly for relaxation, not high politics.*

This is not to say that there was not some serious politicking going on in Wilson's absence. Over the weekend Jenkins spoke (by phone) to both Brown (who was at the Durham Miners' Gala) and Callaghan (on his farm in Sussex); and on his return to London he had a drink with Crosland. But these conversations were all about trying to win support for devaluation before Tuesday's Cabinet, not about replacing the Prime Minister. Admittedly if he had succeeded in persuading Callaghan to stick to his wobble, a joint front of the two senior economic ministers would have made Wilson's position impossible; but changing the Prime Minister's mind, not forcing him out, was the purpose of the exercise. Jenkins had no wish by now to see the increasingly erratic Brown as Prime Minister, and he was never a fan of Callaghan; while he himself, though beginning to be touted as a future leader, was not yet a credible challenger. After barely seven months he was enjoying the Home Office too much to wish to move on so soon. Fantastic though it was, Wilson's unshakable belief in a 'July plot' illustrated the feverish paranoia now at the heart of the government.

One way Wilson tried to divide the devaluers was by telling Crossman and Barbara Castle that they had been 'taken for a ride by the Europeans, who only want to devalue to get us in' (to the Common Market).[84] When Crossman tackled Jenkins directly about this, Jenkins admitted that the two issues were linked, though not inseparably:

> I mean we will have to do something about sterling in order to enter Europe. This might mean devaluation; but in my view a floating pound gives a certain freedom of action, either to enter

---

* Ann liked entertaining the more amusing Labour politicians, but her own politics were thoroughly Tory. If Labour got back with an increased majority, she wrote in March 1966, 'it won't be tiptoe through the tulips with Tony and Roy, but Harold may put Foot on the pedal', which would be bad news for 'an old reactionary like me'.[83]

Europe or to do anything else, and what we are trying to do . . .
is to regain freedom of action. If we go on as we are we remain
prisoners of the situation and prisoners of our own weakness.[85]

Paradoxically, Wilson himself was just coming round to making a
fresh attempt to join. The first hint of his shift, immediately after the
1966 election, was his appointment of George Thomson, a convinced
pro-Marketeer, to be Minister for Europe (as Chancellor of the Duchy
of Lancaster, the office Ted Heath had held while negotiating for
Macmillan in 1961–3). Then in August he switched Brown from the
DEA – whose *raison d'être* had been destroyed by the July cuts – to
the Foreign Office; and in November he devoted most of three Cabinets
to discussing a new approach to Europe, at the end of which it was
agreed – despite the profound suspicion of the anti-Marketeers – that
there were 'no insuperable obstacles' to joining.[86] In the New Year the
Prime Minister and Foreign Secretary, in uncomfortable double harness,
toured the capitals of the Six to demonstrate Britain's renewed commitment and persuaded themselves that this time General de Gaulle would
lift his veto. Five more Cabinets in March and April 1967 were devoted
wholly or largely to the issue, as Wilson deviously manoeuvred his
divided Cabinet towards agreeing to make an application. Again the
minutes do not record individual contributions, but the various diarists
– Crossman, Castle and Benn – suggest that Brown made most of the
running. 'Roy Jenkins never says much in Cabinet,' Crossman wrote
after one of the autumn meetings, 'but he knew that we all regarded
him as deeply committed and he didn't see why he should say anything.'[87]
He was doubtless pleased that Wilson appeared to be converted to the
cause, but did not believe another application had much chance of
success so long as de Gaulle was President of France, so did not expend
too much energy on supporting it. For the same reason the antis did
not fight very hard against, since they confidently expected de Gaulle
to do their work for them, as indeed he did. The whole application,
in fact, was a bit of a charade. But when the Commons voted, after a
three-day debate, by 488 votes to 62 to submit a formal application to
join – actually a more definite approach than Macmillan's, which was
merely an exploration of possible terms – thirty-five Labour Members
voted against and another fifty-one abstained: a clear warning that a
substantial section of the party remained deeply opposed. (Likewise the
party conference voted by only 2:1 to support the application.) When
the General duly applied his second veto in November 1967, Wilson
defiantly declared that Britain 'would not take no for an answer', and

Brown successfully insisted that the government should leave its application 'on the table'.[88] This meant that when de Gaulle resigned in
1969 it had only to be picked up and dusted off and Labour went into
the 1970 election still committed to negotiate, but this time with a real
prospect of success.

Jenkins was now generally acknowledged as the Cabinet's rising star:
almost the only member of a floundering government who was steadily
enhancing his reputation. But the tide of admiring profiles – the
Guardian thought him the best Home Secretary of the century 'and
quite possibly the best since Peel';[89] Ian Trethowan in *The Times* called
him 'a superb debater, skilful in his deployment of argument, sensitive
to the mood of the House, sometimes commanding in his use of
language';[90] while the *Sunday Times* tipped 'this clever, sophisticated,
liberal-minded ambitious Welshman' as Wilson's likeliest successor –
inevitably aroused the jealousy of his colleagues. 'Jenkins' rapidly
emerging strength as a candidate for eventual party leadership has . . .
sparked off some curious psychological warfare by his rivals,' the *Sunday
Times* reported. There was no evidence at all that he had plotted against
Wilson in July, 'but plenty of evidence that a hostile Cabinet colleague
had been spreading the story'.[91] All three diarists clearly resented what
they saw as Jenkins' tireless self-promotion. Benn – even though he
dismissed the Ann Fleming story – wrote in August 1966 that a *New
Statesman* piece puffing 'Labour's Crown Prince' 'confirms my view
that Roy is working hard with Bill Rodgers, Bernard Donoughue and
the old Campaign for Democratic Socialism – Europe Group to take
over the leadership of the party at some stage'.* In the meantime 'he
obviously hopes to be made Chancellor of the Exchequer . . . in the
autumn reshuffle'.[92] A few days later Tony Crosland told Benn that he
was 'getting awfully sick of Cabinet Ministers telling the press what
jobs they would like' – the 'main culprits' being Callaghan (who was
angling for the Foreign Office) and Jenkins, 'who uses John Harris and
Roy Hattersley . . . as his agents in dealing with the press'.[93] Irritated
by all the inspired speculation, Crosland demanded of his PPS,
Christopher Price: 'Why the fuck don't I ever read about Crosland for
PM; what the hell are you doing about it?'[94] And when Crossman
suggested to Crosland, the following summer, that he should warn
Jenkins, as his oldest friend, that Harris' activities were damaging him,

* Bernard Donoughue was then a young LSE lecturer who had been active in CDS; he
later headed the Number Ten Policy Unit under Wilson and Callaghan in 1974–9. He
became a Labour peer in 1985 and served briefly in the first Blair government.

Crosland replied that he entirely agreed but unfortunately could not help, because 'he and I have ceased to know each other at all intimately . . . I think he is behaving in a very funny and remote and ambitious way.' Crossman concluded that 'Tony is completely on his own and Roy is running his drive for power completely on his own.'[95]

Crossman observed his colleagues carefully in Cabinet, and pointedly contrasted the performance of 'our two leading Europeans':

> Roy keeps himself to himself with extreme care. He's the most conspiratorial member of the Cabinet. I watch him as he sits opposite me. He speaks very little but when he does it's always terse and to the point, as though he had kept a lot in reserve. Tony Crosland is proving himself a jolly good departmental Minister, but in Cabinet he's curiously lightweight.[96]

Barbara Castle too recorded her shrewd assessment of Jenkins after the *Sunday Times* profile. Like Crossman, she recognised his ability and enjoyed good working relations with him; but they belonged to different tribes within the Labour party, and she – the feisty left-wing battler who saw permanent exhaustion as a badge of seriousness – always thought he was essentially a dilettante:

> I was interested to read that Roy works at the Department only till 7.30 p.m. My day's work is just beginning then. I think the explanation is that Roy carefully contracts out of anything ancillary, e.g. I never see him at Party meetings. Ambitious he may be, but he isn't going to sacrifice himself. Personally I believe he is temperamentally incapable of leading the Party. Despite all his care, his instinctive high-handedness will slip out.[97]

The idea that Jenkins was lazy was a canard sedulously propagated by the old Bevanites, which reflected a mixture of jealousy and disapproval that he managed to maintain such a busy social life while still being – they could not deny – an extremely effective minister. He achieved it partly by a remarkable ability to concentrate intensely for short periods, absorb information and then take decisions quickly; and partly by his deliberate policy of focusing on certain key areas and letting the rest go. He quite consciously made reserving time for his social life a priority, first to keep himself refreshed, believing (unlike Mrs Castle) that an exhausted minister was unlikely to make good decisions; and, second, to keep himself widely informed. To this end he had lunch with someone outside the department practically every day. This might be anyone from Tony Crosland, Mark Bonham Carter or Caroline Gilmour (with whom he lunched about once a fortnight) to the Governor of the Bank of England or the editor of *The Times*. Unless there was an official lunch or other unavoidable appointment, his officials had to leave his diary clear for an hour and a half to two hours in the middle of the day: he never ate a sandwich at his desk. Barbara Castle might sneer, but he believed this break actually made him a better minister. He drank wine with his lunch, but it did not affect his capacity to work in the afternoon. This was not in the least unusual. 'A politician of the day,' Alan Watkins recalled, '– Anthony Crosland, Richard Crossman, Denis Healey and Iain Macleod come to mind – would think nothing of enjoying a large aperitif beforehand, sharing a bottle of wine with the meal and having some brandy afterwards with his coffee . . . Tomato juice and mineral water . . . came in during the 1980s, to the detriment of politics and journalism alike. Roy belonged to an earlier and better age.'[98]

It was the same in the evening. Quite often he would have an official dinner or a speech to make; but he also dined out privately – sometimes with Jennifer, often without – a couple of times a week. John Chilcot, then serving under Dowler in his private office, vividly remembers seeing Jenkins coming down the main staircase of the Home Office one evening flanked by Jackie Kennedy, her sister Lee Radziwill and Barbara Castle, all dressed to the nines.[99] He belonged to an astonishing number of dining clubs – both The Club and the Other Club, the Literary Society and Grillion's – and was a regular attender at all of them.* He would generally do his boxes before going to bed; but he did not like going to bed late, and also made a point of keeping up his non-departmental reading: on being appointed to the Home Office he claimed to have re-read the whole of Proust (unfortunately he did not record how long it took him). At weekends he frequently had to make a speech or address a conference somewhere; but he very often managed to structure this around a country house visit, whether

---

* Jenkins was invited to join The Club by the Lord Chamberlain, Lord Cobbold, in April 1966. 'It is the oldest dining club in London (straight from Dr Johnson) & I have found it the most agreeable . . . I think you might find it entertaining.' But Cobbold admitted there was some prejudice against Labour members: when Gaitskell had been proposed for membership he was blackballed.[100] Jenkins was already a member of the marginally less Establishment Other Club, founded by Churchill and F.E. Smith in 1911, whose rulebook famously stipulated that 'nothing in the rules or intercourse of the Club shall interfere with the rancour or asperity of party politics'.[101]

to Ann Fleming at Sevenhampton, the Astors at Hatley or some other welcoming host. He now also had a country house of his own.

He and Jennifer had bought St Amand's House in the (then) Berkshire village of East Hendred, ten miles south of Oxford, in the autumn of 1965 and moved in after minor building work the following spring. Jennifer had spotted it in a newspaper advertisement and bought it at auction in Abingdon a few days later. It is an attractively rambling old house with fourteenth-century foundations and cellar, mainly eighteenth-century, but enlarged in the nineteenth: not a vicarage, but with church connections. (St Amand was a local saint, and it is still a strongly Roman Catholic area.) Its glory is the garden, big enough for both a tennis court and a croquet lawn as well as several well-shaded sitting areas. It was said to have been bought with the proceeds of *Asquith,* which says something about the sales of political biography half a century ago; more relevant perhaps is the fact that ministerial salaries were raised in 1965 from £5,000 to £8,500. Roy and Jennifer bought most of the furniture together at a sale in Cirencester. It became a comfortably cluttered family home, not in the least grand, which rather surprised both Crossman and Barbara Castle when they visited.* For the rest of Jenkins' life it provided an escape from London where he could relax, but also entertain friends and (more rarely) colleagues at weekends. Its location was to some extent fortuitous – they had also looked at East Anglia – but neatly reflected Roy's identification with Asquith, whose country house at Sutton Courtenay was only a couple of miles away. It was not too far from Birmingham, and once the M4 motorway was completed in 1971 only forty-five minutes from Heathrow, which turned out to be convenient both for flying to Brussels in the late 1970s and to Glasgow in the 1980s. It was even more perfectly situated when Jenkins became Chancellor of Oxford University in 1987. So altogether it was a most happy purchase.

Jennifer's career too was taking off, with the children all now in their teens. In 1965 she became chairman of the Consumers' Association, then a rapidly growing organisation reaching 600,000 members in 1969 and very much part of the 1960s consumer revolution. As well as testing

---

* 'I was most curious to get this new glimpse into Roy's environment,' Mrs Castle wrote in April 1969. 'Their cottage is authentically old and beautiful with uneven floors, low doors and a number of rooms full of character. It is furnished with taste but by no means lavishly . . . It is a lovely village but I personally could not stand being in a garden overlooked by houses on all sides . . . I couldn't help wondering occasionally whether some enterprising journalist might be eavesdropping on the other side of the garden wall.'[102] She herself had recently bought a rather more secluded old farmhouse in Buckinghamshire.

washing machines and toasters, *Which?* that year reported on wine for the first time, as well as on corkscrews. One American journalist called Jennifer 'the closest thing to a British Ralph Nader'.[103] * She and Roy continued to lead very close yet independent lives; but the work of holding the house and family together fell entirely on her. Barbara Castle, on her one visit to East Hendred, found 'the contrast between Roy's poise and polish and her general air of rather untidy harassment . . . fascinating'. 'The garden was rather neglected and Jennifer complained that she had to do all of it, whereupon Roy drawled that gardening really wasn't his strong point. "It would be nice if you could do the lawns,"' Jennifer retorted. 'Supper was a very domesticated affair. Jennifer's eked-out chicken pilaff was fully adequate in quantity but I wasn't surprised that Roy has a taste for expensive meals out in restaurants.'[104] But Jennifer had never pretended to be a fancy cook; she thought it good for Roy to eat plainly when at home. For lunch parties she usually got a local woman in to do the cooking, but the food was still unpretentious – unlike the wine, which was Roy's one responsibility.

The children were all growing up. Charles, the eldest, having had a difficult time at Winchester, was much happier at Holland Park comprehensive, where he met the extrovert daughter of a Yugoslav diplomat who, nearly fifty years on, is still his wife. Roy hoped that Charles might go to Balliol, and in December 1965 wrote slightly tentatively to the Master, Christopher Hill, explaining his switch of schools – 'I do not know how the combination of educational experience will work out' – but hoping he might be good enough.[105] In fact Charles won a place at New College. Cynthia was still at St Paul's Girls' School and Edward at the City of London School, both London private day schools. Jennifer told the *Sunday Times* in 1966 that none of them had inherited Roy's combination of qualities. 'I mean one of them might be very intelligent,' she explained, clearly thinking of Charles, 'but not very buoyant.'[106] The first time Crossman visited East Hendred in 1968 all three children were there, plus Jennifer's parents. 'I hadn't at all expected this family atmosphere. It shows how little one knows about one's colleagues. So Roy has got a real family to cope with at home, I thought.' He noted the difference between the two boys. Charles, 'a tall willowy young man at New College . . . with his girlfriend . . . is certainly a difficult son'; whereas Edward, 'the rumbustious boy', was 'an object lesson of what Patrick [Crossman] may be if we let him talk

---

* Ralph Nader was the leading American campaigner for consumer rights and environmental protection who stood for the presidency five times between 1992 and 2008.

all the time, busting and crashing into the conversation'. 'Roy gave us some excellent claret,' he concluded, 'and . . . in the noise of the family talk he told me about his conversation with the Prime Minister.'[107]

Perhaps Jenkins was able to combine politics and private life so successfully because he made little distinction between them: his friends were almost all in the broadest sense political, so while he did not talk shop over his lunches and dinners, all his conversations served to inform his approach to his work. He moved within an extensive, yet at the same time quite narrow, political elite in which he knew and made a point of cultivating everyone who mattered. His meticulously kept engagement diaries allow us (apart from the difficulty of deciphering his tiny handwriting) to trace his movements every day. One week in June 1966 is fairly typical. The weekend began with lunch with Michael and Pandora Astor at their house in Oxfordshire; he or they (one can never be sure whether Jennifer was with him) then moved on to Jakie and Chiquita Astor in Hertfordshire, where Noel and Gabrielle Annan and Rab Butler were also staying, and David and Sylvia Harlech came to dine. On Sunday there was tennis and Selwyn Lloyd came to lunch; and in the evening Roy dined (possibly back in London) with Victor and Tess Rothschild. On Monday 6th he took John Harris to lunch at Brooks's, and in the evening attended a dinner for the Prime Minister of Northern Ireland, Terence O'Neill, at the Savoy.* On Tuesday morning he had a Northern Irish meeting at the Home Office at 10.15, saw Wilson at Number Ten at 11.00, lunched at the Beefsteak Club (unusually he did not record with whom) and visited Wormwood Scrubs prison in the afternoon, before dining for once at home and going to see the film of the moment, *Tom Jones* (starring Albert Finney and Susannah York). On Wednesday he had the Home Affairs Committee of the Cabinet in the morning; lunch with Hugh Cudlipp, chairman of the *Daily Mirror*; an appointment with his doctor at 6.00; and Ronald and Doreen McIntosh to dine at Ladbroke Square at 8.00. Thursday was full Cabinet at 10.00, followed by lunch with Michael Stewart at Brooks's, then dinner at the Other Club in the evening. On Friday he flew to Newcastle, where he met the police, gave a press conference, had lunch with the Lord Mayor and met the notorious

---

* The 'troubles' in Northern Ireland hit the headlines only in 1968, just after Jenkins had left the Home Office, so one would not think that the province featured highly in his concerns. Nevertheless he may have had some influence in encouraging the first tentative steps by a Northern Irish Prime Minister to try to bridge sectarian differences. 'Home Secretaries come and go,' O'Neill wrote in December 1967, 'but I have never worked so closely with anyone else before.'[108]

former leader of the council, T. Dan Smith (now head of the North Eastern Planning Council), flew back to London and dined at Ladbroke Square before driving to East Hendred. Ann Fleming came to lunch on Saturday, after which he drove to Cardiff for what was probably a constituency dinner for George Thomas, preceded by a drink with his old schoolfriend Derek Powell. He got back to East Hendred at 2 a.m. and lunched there on Sunday before returning to London for tennis in Ladbroke Square followed by a quiet dinner. In the morning he started again with an equally packed schedule for the next week.[109]

And yet he was unquestionably an ambitious minister who took his work as seriously as his social life. Far from neglecting his office, Jenkins was thought by Crossman – as Leader of the House – to be always pushing for more than his share of the legislative timetable. On top of the Criminal Justice Bill already going through Parliament, he irritated his colleagues by wanting 'a second major Bill this Session . . . to deal with the extraordinary consequences of Rab Butler's measures for legalising gambling. This has turned London into the gambling head-quarters of the world and Roy insists that we must act to control the activities of this vast and dangerous new industry.'[110] At first he seemed to get his way, but when it got squeezed out he wanted a bipartisan Dangerous Drugs Bill instead. When that too fell through because the Tories would not cooperate, Jenkins went back to gambling. 'Well now, look,' he pressed Crossman, 'if I lose the Gaming Bill can I have a little Commons time for the Bill about the Registration of Clubs which is just going through the Lords?' 'It's a minor Bill and I think we can just fit it in,' Crossman conceded, 'but he is certainly an intrepid pusher and shover and we have to push and shove back to get the programme right.'[111]

By the end of 1966 Jenkins was becoming disillusioned with Wilson's failure to give the government a clear sense of direction. When Crossman, coming out of Cabinet on 8 December, grumbled that 'I wish we could have been given a clearer vision of his long-term vision for Rhodesia', Jenkins replied tartly: 'I'd give anything for evidence that we have a long-term plan for any part of this Government's policy, thank you very much, Dick' and walked off – doubtless to share his depression with Dowler and Harris over lunch at Brooks's.[112] When Labour suffered a pasting in the local elections at the beginning of May 1967 – winning only eighteen out of a hundred seats on the Greater London Council in what had always been a Labour strong-hold – he decided to make his concern public in a major speech to the London Labour Conference which set out his vision of where the government should be heading and was inevitably taken as a coded challenge to the Prime Minister.

He began, typically, by introducing a bit of historical perspective by reminding his audience that all parties suffered 'periods of short-term electoral gloom': the Tories had suffered 'equally crushing and wide-spread reverses' in 1952, but had gone on to enjoy the longest uninter-rupted period of power that any party had achieved in modern times. But his message was 'not one of comfort, still less of complacency'. In taking the painful short-term measures that were necessary to achieve long-term prosperity, the government had seemed to lose sight of its social objectives – the elimination of poverty, slum schools, and so on – on which action must be taken soon. But such measures were not the core of the problem:

> The core of the problem is to give the party and the nation a clear sense of direction: a lifting of the sights, a view at once sharp and far-reaching, of where we want to get to by the end of this Parliament, an exposition of the purposes, a good deal more elevated than merely keeping the Tories out, for which this Government exists.

This was a pretty clear swipe at Wilson's 'A week is a long time in politics' style of leadership. The rest of his wide-ranging speech focused particularly on his two pet themes: Europe and the 'civilised society'. First, he argued more explicitly than ever that Britain should stop trying to 'cling on to our precarious position as the third of the great powers'. The military overstrain caused by trying to police large parts of the world had undermined the economy over the past twenty years, which in turn neutralised Britain's military capacity. 'To maintain a role which has to be paid for by others bailing us out is neither dignified nor effective.' The answer lay in Europe, which was now back on the agenda. 'Europe . . . offers the prospect of living amongst equals, and exercising great influence through our co-operation with them, instead of straining ourselves into weakness by trying vainly to keep up with the power giants of the world.' He made the economic case for joining the Common Market too: access to a large unified market, stimulus to investment, bigger companies to secure economies of scale, both mergers and competition – a balance which would be easier to achieve in a bigger market. He admitted that food prices would rise, but this would be offset by lower prices of manufactured goods and faster growth, so that 'after five years it would all be net gain'.

He still banged the drum for faster growth, which had been 'the core of our electoral appeal' in 1964 and remained 'fundamental to our other objectives', despite the admitted failure to achieve it so far due to the vast inherited deficit. Despite that, he claimed that the government's record – he mentioned higher pensions, redundancy payments, school building and housing subsidies – was a proud one in the circumstances. And he called for a 'fair' taxation policy 'directed firmly in favour of those to whom unrestricted economic forces would be most harsh and unjust':

> That is an essential duty of a Labour government, and anyone who believes the reverse would be willing a society so grossly unfair that the consequences would be unacceptable to anyone with a social conscience.

At the same time, however, he warned against 'the disincentive effect which very high taxation of earned incomes might have', insisting, perhaps contradictorily, that 'We desperately need a competitive and thrusting business climate.'

Finally, turning to his own responsibilities as Home Secretary, he restated his vision of 'a more civilised, more free and less hidebound society', insisting that there was no conflict between this and measures to control the crime wave, which he claimed were already having some success:

> I have never seen the slightest contradiction between being tough where we need to be tough, and striving at the same time to enlarge the area of human freedom. We gain nothing, and lose a great deal, by keeping subject to the penalties of criminal law, personal actions and conduct which should be matters of personal choice and do no harm to society.

Here he foreshadowed, without specifying them, 'several measures, sponsored by Private Members, but aided by the Government', which he hoped soon to see on the Statute Book, and reminded his audience that 'to enlarge the area of individual choice, socially, politically and economically, not just for a few but for the whole community, is very much what democratic socialism is about'. After a powerful statement of the moral case for a stronger Race Relations Act ('For a Labour Government to fall down on this would be a betrayal without excuse of everything for which the Labour Party has ever stood') he repeated that the government's objective must be 'not merely to govern well, important thought this is, but also to change and improve society'. On that basis the party could 'repair the damage of this spring and lay the foundations of another period of Labour power'.[113]

This was a remarkable personal manifesto, serious, thoughtful and statesmanlike, which if it was not an immediate challenge to Wilson, unmistakably announced Jenkins' emergence as a potential future leader. In the meantime, however, the two measures for which his tenure at the Home Office is primarily remembered were almost simultaneously approaching completion. One, the legalisation of homosexuality, stands as an historic milestone in the enlargement of human rights, now almost universally accepted; the other, allowing easier access to legal abortion, remains a contentious and emotive issue – though not, thankfully, as divisive in Britain as in America. Both were on Jenkins' 1959 shopping list of reforms which a determined Home Secretary should be able to deliver. But both were too controversial and too marginal to most voters' concerns to be appropriate for government legislation.

There is an established convention that issues of personal morality are decided by MPs voting according to their consciences on a free vote, usually on a Private Members' Bill. But this is a tortuous and uncertain process, as Jenkins had discovered with reference to Obscene Publications in the 1950s. Even with a clear majority in both Houses in favour, reform requires, first, a Member who is willing to take up a controversial subject winning one of the top three or four places in the ballot for Private Members' Bills; and, second, a sympathetic government ready to give enough parliamentary time to get the Bill through. Thus Jenkins' reforming ambition was wholly dependent on finding Members ready to sponsor the necessary Bills; and then on his ability to persuade a sceptical Cabinet to give them time. The first problem was partly solved when David Steel won third place in the Private Members' ballot. Steel was a young Liberal who had won a Scottish Borders seat at a by-election in 1965 and managed to hold it at the General Election in 1966. His first idea was to promote a Scottish Borders development Bill; but the Scottish Secretary, Willie Ross, was against it, so that was a non-starter. Jenkins initially hoped that Steel would take up the homosexuality bill which Lord Arran had already carried through the House of Lords. But Steel chose – partly because Arran's Bill did not apply to Scotland – to take on abortion instead, picking up another measure successfully carried through the Lords by Lord Silkin. The Labour MP Leo Abse then undertook to introduce a homosexuality Bill under the Ten-Minute Rule.

Steel's Medical Termination of Pregnancy Bill aimed to tackle the scandal by which dozens of poor, desperate women were dying every year at the hands of unscrupulous and inexpert back-street abortionists, who were estimated to be performing anything between 40,000 and 200,000 illegal operations a year: the numbers are necessarily inexact. The Bill allowed foetuses up to twenty-eight weeks to be legally aborted, with the approval of two doctors, to preserve the physical or mental health of the mother, or at any stage to save the life of the mother or if the child was likely to be severely handicapped. It did not, as its critics insisted, sanction 'abortion on demand'; nevertheless it was a highly sensitive issue, which the twenty-eight-year-old Steel handled with remarkable maturity and skill. Jenkins gave his strong personal support, arguing that the existing law was 'uncertain . . . harsh and archaic, and . . . consistently flouted by those who have the means to do so. It is, therefore, very much a question of one law for the rich and one for the poor'.[114]* The Bill passed its Second Reading in the Commons by a deceptively comfortable majority – 223:29 – in July 1966. But its opponents – led by Norman St John Stevas (Jenkins' old ally in the obscenity battle, but a leading Roman Catholic) – fought it line by line in committee in early 1967 and it was clearly going to fail to get through its Report Stage unless the government granted it more time. In Cabinet Lord Longford (Lord Privy Seal and another prominent Catholic), the Scottish Secretary Willie Ross and the Minister of Housing, Anthony Greenwood (worried about the Catholic vote in Lancashire), argued that it would be politically dangerous for the government to take sides on the issue;† but Jenkins maintained that it did not breach the government's neutrality to allow the Commons to decide on a free vote, while the question would come back year after year unless it was dealt with.[117] It was agreed to grant an all-night session on 29 June; but when that was not enough he had to ask for another, eventually set for 13 July. Crossman thought he was 'throwing his weight around a bit . . . trying to decide the allocation of parliamentary time', but nevertheless promised Steel that the House would

---

* Jenkins tended to steer clear of the religious and ethical arguments about abortion. But thirty years later he revealed his essentially practical motivation in reply to a correspondent who accused him of murdering five million unborn babies since 1967. 'You presumably think that the addition of hundreds of millions (I cannot much distinguish conceptually between contraception and early abortion) of unwanted children would make the world a better place. I do not.'[115]
† While Greenwood was speaking, Barbara Castle, also a Lancashire MP but a strong supporter of the Bill, threw Jenkins a note across the table: 'What a contemptible man he is.'[116]

sit until the bill had completed all its stages.[118] Still the opponents did not give up, so the supporters of the Bill had to be sure to have 100 Members on hand all night to keep the debate alive and vote whenever necessary. Jenkins himself voted in every division. But finally, just before noon on 14 July, the Bill was given its Third Reading by 167 votes to 83. Jenkins paid tribute to Steel's coolness under often emotional attack. 'I think that the hon. Member, as a young Member of the House with a marginal constituency and without a great party machine behind him, has shown exceptional courage in carrying on with the Bill in these circumstances.'[119] Though Jenkins and Steel actually had few direct dealings during the passage of the Bill, this was the foundation of an important relationship of mutual respect, which would bear fruit fourteen years later. After a brief scare in the Lords, the Bill received the Royal Assent on 26 October.

Abse's Sexual Offences Bill – to decriminalise homosexual acts 'between consenting adults in private' – had a closely parallel passage, though it commanded even less enthusiasm within the government. Back in 1961 Wilson had warned that supporting the recommendation of the Wolfenden Report would cost Labour six million votes.[120] Both the senior working-class ministers, Brown and Callaghan, were deeply opposed to changing the law; and even Crossman feared that it was 'twenty years ahead of public opinion'.[121*] But from the moment he succeeded Soskice, Jenkins pressed for government time and assistance to be given to a Private Members' Bill introduced by the Tory MP Humphrey Berkeley which in February 1966 was given a Second Reading by 164 votes to 107, despite crusty old Tories like Sir Cyril Osborne and Sir Cyril Black inveighing furiously against pansies and national decadence. Again Jenkins himself spoke powerfully, on a personal basis, in favour of tolerance, while insisting that 'full penalties' would be retained 'for any offence touching the corruption of youth'.[122] Unfortunately Berkeley lost his seat at the General Election with an above-average swing against him, which seemed to bear out the fears of those who thought the issue best left alone; on the other hand Labour's big majority, with a large influx of younger, university-educated new Members, made it easier to press ahead without regard to the electoral consequences. (In fact an NOP poll in 1965 had shown 63 per cent support for legalisation, and the opponents were not so

---

* Willie Ross, Secretary of State for Scotland, was so vehemently opposed that he refused to countenance a parallel reform on his patch, with the result that homosexuality remained illegal in Scotland until 1980 (and in Northern Ireland until 1982).

geographically concentrated as the Catholic opponents of abortion.)[123] No MP successful in the Private Members' ballot was willing to take up Berkeley's Bill. But in July Leo Abse – the eccentric amateur Freudian MP for Jenkins' native Pontypool – had been given leave by a substantial majority (244:100) to introduce a Ten-Minute Rule Bill; and in October Jenkins argued in Cabinet that 'we shall be under considerable criticism, mainly from our own supporters, if we fail to provide a little time for Mr Abse's Bill to make progress'. If nothing was done it would become increasingly difficult to enforce a law that both Houses of Parliament had twice pronounced against. Partly on the basis that it was better to get an unpopular measure out of the way well before the next election, Wilson reluctantly summed up in support of granting half a day for a Second Reading, with no promise of support through further stages.[124] Just before Christmas, however, the bill passed that stage unopposed on a technicality when its opponents were caught napping by an early closure.

Abse's flamboyant (though heterosexual) showmanship was the exact opposite of Steel's soft-spoken seriousness. 'He wasn't exactly the person I would have chosen to be the sponsor of the Bill,' Jenkins told a historian of the legislation many years later, 'but given that he didn't do it badly at all.'[125] Abse antagonised many supporters of his Bill by his equally passionate opposition to the abortion Bill. (On the other hand, St John Stevas, the leading opponent of the abortion Bill, was a strong supporter of legalising homosexuality: the two measures drew on overlapping but not identical support.) But he cleverly wrong-footed his opponents by unexpectedly conceding that homosexuality should remain an offence in the merchant navy, after which they had no other amendments ready, so the committee stage went through in an hour. The diehard opponents were not many – no more than a couple of dozen – but they were persistent, delaying the Bill by tabling innumerable new amendments; while with many working-class Labour members unwilling to be seen to be supporting a 'Buggers' Charter', Abse had some difficulty keeping up the quorum needed to defeat them through an all-night filibuster on the Report Stage and Third Reading on 3–4 July 1967.[126] The Bill was eventually carried by ninety-nine votes (plus two tellers) against fourteen.

On both these measures Jenkins was criticised for lending the government's authority and government time to get the legislation through. Sir Charles Taylor, the Tory Member for Eastbourne, for instance, typified the opponents' apoplectic outrage at the homosexuality Bill:

One would have thought that the Home Secretary had enough on his plate to deal with crime . . . without taking the time of the House to deal with a Bill which nobody ever really wanted. I am glad to say that nobody in my constituency wanted it . . . The Government are completely out of step with the people, who do not believe in buggery.[127]

Jenkins had no difficulty mocking Sir Charles' narrow-mindedness ('untypical even of his constituents') and repeatedly insisted that the government was doing no more than making it possible for the clear majority opinion of the House to be expressed without being blocked by small minorities. While recognising that same-sex attraction was not a matter of choice, but a fact of life for a significant number of the population, however, he was still careful to emphasise that the Bill was not intended to promote homosexuality:

It would be a mistake to think that we are giving a vote of confidence or congratulation to homosexuality. Those who suffer from this disability carry a great weight of loneliness, guilt and shame. The crucial question, which we are nearly at the end of answering decisively, is, should we add to those disadvantages the full rigour of the criminal law?

Unlike Hogg, who somewhat churlishly called it 'a small measure which will have very little effect on our social life', Jenkins celebrated the Bill as 'an important and civilising measure'.[128]

Of course Jenkins was not solely responsible for these Bills; Steel and Abse who sponsored them; Crossman and the Government Chief Whip, John Silkin, who controlled the parliamentary timetable; Wilson, who appointed Jenkins to the Home Office knowing his agenda and then allowed him to pursue it; the 200-odd mainly but not exclusively Labour and Liberal Members who voted for them, and the greater number in all parties who abstained – all were equally essential. But these reforms would not have happened when they did – well ahead of most other European countries – without Jenkins' drive and determination; and down the years he received the largest share of odium from those who continued to abhor them, as well as the credit from those who approved or were quietly grateful. He accepted that the detailed provisions of the Abortion Act would require periodic modification the time-limit was reduced from twenty-eight weeks to twenty-four in 1990. He probably did not envisage the positive flaunting of gay and lesbian culture that would explode a generation on, let alone the legalisation of same-sex marriage. But he never resiled from the belief that both these Bills were socially beneficent measures and he never apologised for having assisted their passage. Just two years later, now Chancellor of the Exchequer, in a quite minor speech opening a Labour party bazaar at Abingdon (five miles from East Hendred), he demurred from the phrase 'the permissive society', widely used to describe these and other liberalising developments of the decade. 'What I prefer to ask is whether the changes recently made . . . have made us a more civilised society. And to that I unhesitatingly answer yes.'[129] The newspapers immediately paraphrased his words into a soundbite – 'The permissive society is the civilised society' – which was not quite what he said. But 'I never made a very strenuous attempt at correction,' he wrote years later, 'because it was not all that far from my meaning.'[130]

In the 1980s Margaret Thatcher and Norman Tebbit, among others, regularly blamed Jenkins for the breakdown of families, disrespect for authority and decline of social responsibility which they believed flowed from the liberalisation of the 1960s – ignoring the contribution of their

THE CIVILISED SOCIETY

Cummings, *Daily Express,* 8.8.69 (British Cartoon Archive, University of Kent)

own economic policies. 'Thus was sown the wind,' Tebbit charged in 1985, 'and we are now reaping the whirlwind.'[131] But Jenkins always pointed out that Mrs Thatcher voted for both the abortion Bill and the homosexuality Bill, though she did oppose Lord Gardiner's relaxation of the divorce law (Tebbit was not yet in the House) and that her governments with their huge Tory majorities never made any attempt to repeal any of them. The Thatcher government did pass the infamous Clause 28 of the 1988 Local Government Act, which outlawed the 'promotion' of homosexuality; but no prosecution was ever brought and it was repealed in 2003. Since 1967 no one has ever seriously suggested recriminalising homosexuality between consenting adults.

Another overdue reform that Jenkins was not quite able to see onto the Statute Book before he left the Home Office was the repeal of the Lord Chamberlain's power of censorship of live theatre. This was an absurd anachronism under which playwrights had chafed for years: it was brought to a head in 1965 by the banning of a production of Edward Bond's *Saved* at the Royal Court. Frank Soskice had maintained that the system 'continued to work by and large remarkably well' and claimed that a more logical system might be harder to operate.[132] Jenkins immediately set up an inquiry, which reported predictably in favour of abolishing the Lord Chamberlain's role; and in July 1967 – just a few days after the abortion and homosexuality Bills had gone through – he pressed the Home Affairs Committee of the Cabinet for a bill to implement its recommendation. ('Roy Jenkins is getting more imperious every day,' Crossman grumbled.)[133] He resisted those – headed by the Lord Chamberlain himself, Lord Cobbold – who recognised the anachronism but wanted to see his role taken over by a board of theatre censors analogous to the Film Censorship Board, arguing instead that plays should be treated in the same way as books under the Obscene Publications Act and the ordinary law of libel. The Cabinet initially agreed, until the Prime Minister began to worry about the representation of living people on stage. He claimed to be thinking of the Queen or foreign leaders; but it was not coincidental that a play was just about to open at Joan Littlewood's theatre in Stratford East based on the *Private Eye* spoof, *Mrs Wilson's Diary*. The Lord Chamberlain declared the script 'so cheap and gratuitously nasty, and so completely worthless that it is not recommended for licence'.[134] Wilson, Brown and Callaghan all read it, and eight scenes were cut before the play was allowed to open in September 1967; it quickly transferred to the West End, where it ran for another eight months.

When Crossman warned him against defying the Prime Minister and the Palace, Jenkins allegedly replied (this is Crossman's paraphrase, probably not his actual words): 'I'm not prepared, as a liberal and radical Home Secretary, to have my reputation ruined by being ordered to impose worse conditions on the live theatre than they are getting now under the Lord Chamberlain.' He 'made it quite clear that he was thinking of the threat of resignation in order to get his way'.[135] Fortuitously the veteran Labour MP and former minister George Strauss won a place in the Private Members' ballot and planned to introduce a Bill concentrated the government's mind. Jenkins proposed to assist Strauss with the drafting of his Bill; the Cabinet could then decide at Second Reading whether to take it over as a government Bill. With reference to the representation of living people he argued that political satire was simply too popular to ban: no one had enjoyed the ridicule of Harold Macmillan by *That Was The Week That Was* more than the Labour party, and you could not logically enforce tighter restrictions on the stage than were applied to television.[136] When Callaghan took over at the Home Office he agreed; Strauss's Bill thereafter proceeded unopposed and received the Royal Assent in July 1968. Thus the Lord Chamberlain was finally consigned to history, and the hippy musical *Hair* – with its few seconds of dimly lit nudity – opened in London a few weeks later.*

There were other extensions of personal freedom foreshadowed in *The Future of Socialism* and *The Labour Case* that Jenkins did not manage to deal with in 1965–7. One was the licensing laws; another was Sunday Observance – a Bill sponsored by Lord Willis passed the House of Lords in 1966, but never made progress in the Commons; a third was drugs. Jenkins was studying the case for making a distinction between 'hard' and 'soft' drugs and legalising the recreational use of cannabis, but had not yet made up his mind when he was moved on; Callaghan took a much less liberal view and immediately shelved the issue. Jenkins later wished he had dealt with it while he had the chance. He still took an interest in the continuing propensity of the police to seize serious books like William Burroughs' *The Naked Lunch*, published by 'obviously reputable publishers', and as minister responsible for the Met was embarrassed when they made themselves ridiculous by raiding an exhibition of pictures by Aubrey Beardsley.[137] He was not responsible

---

* During its run *Mrs Wilson's Diary* was continually updated to keep up with events. When Jenkins became Chancellor in November he was added to the script and played by Nigel Hawthorne.

for the closure of the hugely popular 'pirate' radio stations which broadcast illegally from ships moored just off the coast, since broadcasting came under the remit of the Postmaster-General, Ted Short. But he was responsible for the unpopular experiment with 'double summer time', which ran for three years from 1968 to 1971; his old ally A.P. Herbert led a spirited campaign against what he called 'Jenkins Time', which he predicted would prove lethal for the government.[138] Here again, as with the Kenyan Asians legislation, Jenkins was lucky to have moved on before its unpopularity came home to roost.

One last episode gave him another parliamentary triumph at the very end of his time at the Home Office. In the summer of 1967 a whistle-blower made serious allegations of excessively severe use of corporal punishment at Court Lees 'approved school' – that is, a school for young offenders – in Surrey. A quick inquiry by a leading QC revealed a thoroughly corrupt regime run by 'an inbred oligarchy', most of whom were related to one another; Jenkins was 'particularly incensed' that ten more beatings took place after he had ordered the inquiry. He promptly sacked the headmaster, dispersed 116 inmates and closed the school. (It later reopened, with a new name, under the aegis of Surrey County Council.) 'I acted quickly and I believe I was right,' Jenkins told Alastair Hetherington. His only misgiving was that it was bad luck on this headmaster to be singled out, when there were 'probably at least ten other approved schools that were as bad as Court Lees'.[139] But his action raised another furious storm from the defenders of corporal punishment. When Parliament returned in November the local Tory MP, Sir John Vaughan-Morgan, accused him of 'butchering' Court Lees so that he could go off on his Italian holiday. 'He was more concerned with a theatrical gesture and with the preservation of his own image as a liberal-minded Home Secretary' than with justice.[140] Quintin Hogg piously condemned him for sacking the headmaster without a hearing, saying that he himself could never have done such a thing. But Denis Howell – now an education minister – briefed Jenkins that this was nonsense: Hogg when Education Secretary must have sacked dozens of teachers without a hearing – it was normal procedure. Jenkins intervened to put this to Hogg. 'It was a knock-out blow. Hogg never recovered and the Home Secretary wound up the debate with a devastating speech.'[141] 'Mr Jenkins', *The Times* reported, 'had an easy time with some revelations about the close family ties of the Court Lees Board of Management', who failed to realise the seriousness and the allegations and were only concerned to discredit and sack the whistle-blower. 'The Tory case . . . was razed to pretty near ground level by Mr Roy Jenkins.'[142]

But this was Jenkins' last stand as Home Secretary. That same morning – Thursday 16 November – the Cabinet was told that Wilson and Callaghan's vain battle to maintain the parity of sterling had finally failed. The Six-Day War in the Middle East, the Arab oil embargo and the closing of the Suez Canal had increased the pressure; a dock strike in September was the last straw, and devaluation had become inevitable. On the previous Monday Jenkins took Barbara Castle to lunch at the Connaught Grill. ('Nothing very significant about it,' he told her, 'just the feeling that we all ought to keep in touch more.)' Neither of them was on the Economic Strategy Committee, so they were both completely in the dark; but they agreed that they should both be ready to resign rather than accept another deflationary package without devaluation; and she urged him to 'probe at Cabinet tomorrow about what was being cooked up behind our backs', even though Wilson would suspect a conspiracy. "'He really does believe I'm plotting, doesn't he?" Roy mused. "It really is very absurd."' They found that they agreed about a lot of things, except Europe. 'An affable and delicious lunch. Roy can be very charming when he likes,' she concluded. 'But I left him in no doubt that I didn't think anyone could lead the party but Harold.'[143]

The next day at Cabinet, Jenkins did probe. 'The Home Secretary suggested that it would be useful for the Cabinet to have a general discussion in the near future about the economic situation.'[144] 'After a whispered conversation', Wilson promised a full discussion in two or three weeks' time.[145] This, Mrs Castle wrote, 'was hardly reassuring and Roy said so . . . Jim and Harold looked like a couple of schoolboys caught with their hand in the till.'[146] Their embarrassment was not surprising, since the decision to devalue by around 17 per cent had already been taken. Two days later they told the Cabinet, though the public announcement was not for another two days after that – leading to a further disastrous outflow of reserves as Callaghan tried unconvincingly to deny that it was imminent. 'This is the unhappiest day of my life,' the Chancellor told his colleagues. 'I will not pretend that it is anything but a failure of our policies.' (Wilson, by contrast, drew only ridicule by trying to play down the humiliation on television.) Barbara Castle doubted that the devaluation was big enough, and suggested floating the pound; but she found no support, 'not even from Crosland or Roy'.[147] Crossman objected to Callaghan's proposed list of spending cuts – 'announced verbally and so fast there was only just time to write it down' – and Jenkins backed him up. "'Why do we have to pre-announce a winter budget?" he asked. "This will give us the worst of both worlds . . . We can't have these decisions taken in a split second.'"[148] The next day he and Crossman agreed that the way devaluation had been announced had been 'utterly chaotic . . . We had to have a package with a social philosophy.'[149] It would very soon be his job to provide one.

It was taken for granted that Callaghan would resign as soon as he had completed the immediate practicalities. The question was who would succeed him. For at least a year there had been widespread speculation that it should be Jenkins. But Wilson had been increasingly irritated by the press puffing of Jenkins. Earlier that year he had been furiously jealous that the Home Secretary scooped most of the headlines over the successful operation to contain a huge oil spill from a tanker, the *Torrey Canyon*, which ran aground off the Scilly Isles – Wilson's own holiday retreat – over Easter. As chairman of the Cabinet Emergencies Committee it was Jenkins' decision, on scientific advice and with the Prime Minister's assent, to bomb the stricken vessel in order to burn off the oil that threatened the Cornish beaches. But Wilson complained bitterly to Crossman that 'the moment he took over on that Sunday afternoon he tried to create the impression that he found everything in a shemozzle and that no decisions were taken until he, the decisive Roy Jenkins, took command. That's an impression I resent . . . He's rigged the whole Sunday press as well.'[150] Three months later Crossman was still writing of Jenkins as 'the man [Wilson] detests and whose influence he really hates in Cabinet'.[151] And in September Wilson was childishly delighted with his latest reshuffle in which he had moved Tony Crosland to the Board of Trade (in place of Douglas Jay). 'I managed to increase my crown princes from two to six . . . Now I've got seven potential Chancellors and I've knocked out the situation where Jenkins was the only alternative to Callaghan. You know . . . this is one of the most successful political operations that's ever been conducted.'[152] Quite how Wilson worked this out, or whom he considered his six crown princes or seven potential Chancellors, is not obvious; what is clear is that he both saw Jenkins as the front runner and was determined not to be cornered into appointing him.

Crosland was very doubtful about moving to the Board of Trade. He desperately wanted to be the next Chancellor, and was afraid that the move to a lesser economic department might rule him out. But Callaghan congratulated him on his 'step nearer the centre': Crosland would still 'have to put up with me – but you would prefer that than having to put up with Roy'. His chances of going to the Treasury were 'not prejudiced – on the contrary, I would say'.[153] Crossman too told him that his new job put him 'at least on a level with Roy in his chances of becoming the next Chancellor', and wrote in early November that Crosland 'looks to me like the man booked for the Treasury'.[154] There is no doubt that Crosland thought himself far better qualified for the job than Jenkins: he had found his old friend's speech in May trumpeting the need for growth 'almost more than flesh and blood could stand'.[155] Academically he was – as Jenkins always admitted – unquestionably the better economist. Yet in Cabinet he came across as 'curiously lightweight' and he was equally unimpressive in the House of Commons. Callaghan wanted Crosland to succeed him, and assured him the day after devaluation that the job was practically his;[156] he also told Jenkins on 23 November that Crosland was going be the new Chancellor.[157] But the succession was not Callaghan's to bestow; and several factors changed Wilson's mind.

First, Jenkins had proved himself, initially at Aviation and then at the Home Office, the more effective minister, both in his capacity to take tough decisions and in his ability to defend them robustly in the House. Once devaluation had been decided on, it was not economic expertise but political personality that would be needed to force the painful consequences through the Cabinet and convince the party, the country and the markets that Britain was now on the right track. On his record since 1964 there could be no question that Jenkins was the better option. As Alan Watkins wrote in the *New Statesman*: 'As a parliamentary performer . . . Mr Jenkins is a class apart from the rest of either front bench . . . He not only looks superior: he is superior.'[158] Crossman urged Wilson that moving Jenkins to the Treasury would 'give us the kind of lift we need'.[159] So, crucially, did the Prime Minister's closest confidante, his personal secretary Marcia Williams, who recognised Jenkins' appeal to non-Labour opinion. But more Macchiavellian calculations also came into it. Though Wilson was wary of Jenkins, he thought he could best secure his loyalty and bind him to himself by giving him the Treasury; at this moment the challenger he feared most – paradoxically, after the humiliation of devaluation – was a resentful Callaghan. He knew that Jenkins would never combine with Callaghan against him; whereas Crosland, Callaghan's protégé, might make a very dangerous combination with him. Despite his suspicion of Jenkins' ambition and mockery of his glossy lifestyle, Wilson thought he could work well with him, as indeed proved to be the case. They shared a similar fascination with obscure statistics – 'railway timetables or Wisden-like political records'[160] – whereas real intellectuals like Crosland (and Denis Healey, another possible candidate) made him uncomfortable.

Finally, the most practical and possibly decisive consideration was what to do with Callaghan. The Home Office was a suitably senior position for a former Chancellor to which, as a former adviser to the Police Federation, he was eminently suited; the simplest option then, once Callaghan had decided that he wanted to stay in the government, was a straight job-swap between Callaghan and Jenkins, which avoided the need for a wider reshuffle.

Jenkins was called out of a meeting about House of Lords reform on 28 November to go and see the Prime Minister: Wilson immediately offered him the Treasury and he accepted without hesitation – though not without a good deal of apprehension. It was a tough moment to be taking on the second job in the government: as he admitted in a speech a few days later, the Treasury was 'the only post which could make the Home Office look almost like a bed of roses'.[161] He had some regrets about leaving the Home Office with a certain amount of unfinished business, but he must have reflected with satisfaction that this promotion continued his close emulation of Asquith's career path – with the difference that Asquith was fifty-three before he reached the Treasury, while he was only forty-seven. The press reception of his appointment, ranging from 'Roy's the Boy' in *The Economist* to 'Jenkins the Cash has the Makings of a First-class Chancellor' in the *Daily Mirror*, with major profiles in all the papers over the weekend, was, in his own words, 'exceptionally favourable, really rather frighteningly so'.[162] *The Times* set the tone:

> There is something almost alarming about the relief and hope which have greeted MR ROY JENKINS' appointment as Chancellor. It is natural that he should arouse new hope. His combination of economic understanding, parliamentary skill and political judgement makes him the most promising appointment to the Exchequer since Hugh Gaitskell in 1950, though that was a mixed blessing.[163]

There was general agreement on the great opportunity his appointment represented. 'Thanks to the new situation created by devaluation,' the *Financial Times* declared, 'the Treasury becomes for the first time a job worth having by an ambitious politician. With luck, firmness and patience he might even find himself presiding over the long-delayed British economic miracle.'[164] But there was equal appreciation that the stakes were high. The *Sunday Telegraph* called him 'the Last-Chance Chancellor';[165] while the *Sunday Times* went so far as to suggest that the whole future of the economy, of the Labour Party and even the survival of parliamentary democracy in Britain depended on his success.[166]

· But Crosland was devastated to have the prize for which he felt pre-eminently qualified not merely snatched from him but given to his younger friend whom he had always regarded as his junior partner. No one but the two of them knew quite how close they had been at Oxford twenty-seven years before; but they cannot have forgotten. Through their early careers they were written of as a pair of rising stars; but Tony had always been seen – first by Dalton, then by Gaitskell – as the more brilliant of the two. But this was the third time in three years that Wilson had preferred Roy: first for a department of his own in October 1964, then for Education and membership of the Cabinet in January 1965, and now for the Treasury. Tony was bitterly jealous, and their friendship, already under strain, never fully recovered. It was rather like the moment in 1994 when Tony Blair snatched the Labour leadership from his older friend and early mentor Gordon Brown, who never forgave him. To rub salt into Crosland's wound, the first thing he had to do – before Jenkins' appointment was officially announced – was fly to Paris to represent Callaghan at an OECD meeting. As a result he and Roy did not meet until he got back on the following Monday. In the circumstances, Jenkins wrote, 'he behaved remarkably well'. Crosland did not hide his disappointment, but regretted having moved from Education to the Board of Trade in August. He now felt that any achievements in the economic field would redound to Roy's credit, and possibly to Wilson's, but certainly not to his; he would therefore welcome another move to a different area entirely. In fact Wilson kept him at the Board of Trade until October 1969 before switching him to Local Government, so he and Jenkins were obliged to work quite closely together – with Jenkins now the senior – for the next twenty-three months, which was difficult for both of them; and the hurt festered longer than that, with enduring consequences, as Jenkins reflected in his memoirs:

It would be idle to pretend that these events of November 1967 did not leave a scar on Crosland which had the effect of crucially damaging the cohesion of the Labour right over the next eight or nine years. Had he and I been able to work together as smoothly as did Gaitskell and Jay or Gaitskell and Gordon Walker a decade before it might have made a decisive difference to the balance of power within the Labour Party and hence to the politics of the early 1980s.[167]

Denis Healey had less hope than Crosland of becoming Chancellor himself; but he too was disenchanted at seeing his younger Balliol contemporary promoted over him. As Giles Radice described in his triple biography *Friends and Rivals*, published in 2002, by promoting Jenkins Wilson effectively divided Gaitskell's heirs for years to come.[168]

Meanwhile Jenkins was facing the biggest challenge of his life.

13 'Two Years' Hard Slog'

WHEN Jenkins and John Harris crossed the bridge that connected the old Home Office with the Treasury on 29 November 1967, Harris recalled, it was 'like entering the French General Staff's Headquarters at Sedan in 1870, so pervasive was the gloom and defeatism'.[1] In the aftermath of the devaluation it had fought so long to avoid, the Treasury was a thoroughly demoralised department. No other Chancellor in modern times – except perhaps Sir Kingsley Wood in the rather different circumstances of May 1940 – has entered on his inheritance in such grim conditions. Having been deliberately kept away from any detailed knowledge of the economy for the past three years, Jenkins had to start from scratch, picking up the pieces of a failed policy. Yet this gave him three advantages. First, he was generally thought to be a good appointment, both economically literate and tough. Second, he was known to have been one of those who had argued for devaluation at least as far back as July 1966, so he came in with no responsibility for the failure but personally vindicated by the debacle. Third, he took office when the critical decision had been taken, with a clean slate to write on and the responsibility, but also the opportunity, to make a success of a new, post-devaluation strategy. In this respect, therefore, Jenkins could be said once again to have been lucky in his timing.

In addition to the overwhelmingly positive press coverage of his appointment, he received a mountain of congratulatory letters which bore witness to his wide circle of admirers. They came from both sides of the political spectrum – from Rab Butler, Quintin Hogg and Selwyn Lloyd as well as from Michael Foot; from leading journalists; from old school friends (and his old headmaster) in Abersychan and members of his constituency party in Stechford; from senior policemen and prison officers who had appreciated his work at the Home Office; as well as from several of his female fan club (Barley Alison, Ann Fleming, Pam Berry, Marietta Tree and Lee Radziwill) – almost all of them assuring Roy that he was the man to save the country and hoping that he would soon go on to become Prime Minister. Ian Gilmour reminded him of how fortunately the cards had fallen for him:

> It is funny to think that if dear old Hugh had been PM he would probably not have been able to promote you so fast for fear of ill-founded charges of nepotism . . . It is even more peculiar to remember that you might have disappeared into the recesses of the *Economist*. In the circumstances what an escape![2]

While from the Ministry of Defence, Denis Healey wrote generously:

> My dear Roy, Just to say how delighted – and relieved! – I am at your move. I'm afraid in some respects I may find you a more formidable adversary than Jim, but I am certain you are just what the country, the Government and the Party need as Chancellor.[3]

Tony Crosland did not find it in himself to be quite so generous. But Michael Shanks – the author of an influential Penguin Special, *The Stagnant Society*, which embodied all the hopes, so far unrealised, that the leftish intelligentsia had placed in the Labour government – was not alone in seeing the combination of the two leading Gaitskellites now taking over the top two economic jobs (Jenkins as Chancellor with his old friend Crosland as President of the Board of Trade) as offering the government a second chance. 'A tremendous responsibility,' he wrote in *The Times*, 'rests on the shoulders of this suave, rational, Kennedy-like man of cool nerves and radical instincts.'[4] Jenkins was of course delighted to be Chancellor. But all the hopes invested in him and the dire predictions of the consequences if he should fail imposed a frightening degree of pressure. Normally a sound sleeper, he confessed that in these first few weeks at the Treasury he slept badly, waking early with a dread of what the day ahead might bring. He also started smoking again, having given up a few months earlier: during the long Cabinet battle over spending cuts in early 1968 he got through a dozen cigars a day, before managing to give them up again in February. Yet he contrived to keep up a front of unruffled confidence. Dining at the

Annans' on 7 December – his diary shows that his promotion barely affected his social habits – one of the other guests, Cecil King, noted that 'Roy was his usual suave self, showing no sign of pressure or any idea that this is the crisis of his life.'[5]

Much was made of the fact that Jenkins was 'an expansionist, first and foremost, recognising that faster economic growth is the only respectable objective of economic policy'.[6] But his expansionist instincts were, in the short and medium term, irrelevant. Growth was still the ultimate goal; but sustained growth depended on restoring a stable currency no longer at the mercy of the international money markets, as it had been since 1964; and that could be achieved only by getting the balance of payments – the balance of exports over imports – back into surplus after five consecutive years of deficits. In the immediate aftermath of devaluation the absolute imperative was to use the temporary competitive advantage that devaluation gave to restore the balance of payments: only this could make sterling secure at its new value. The new Chancellor therefore had no choice but to impose a further massive dose of deflation – by a mixture of spending cuts, taxation and other controls – to switch resources from domestic consumption into exports. Ironically this was where Jenkins had come in as a young MP, just in time to see Stafford Cripps, Labour's famously austere 'Iron Chancellor', facing almost exactly the same challenge in 1948: no two men could have been more different, but Jenkins was obliged to follow closely Cripps' example. The very lack of options, however, was another source of political strength. No one seriously advocated any other strategy; and Wilson could not afford to lose a second Chancellor. The whole Cabinet, and even the Labour left, recognised that any premature relaxation would immediately suck in more imports and put fresh pressure on the pound, bringing the dismal cycle quickly back to square one. The only question was whether he was being tough enough. After three wasted years vainly trying to postpone the inevitable, deflation was thus inescapably still the order of the day: 'two years' hard slog', as Jenkins promised in his first budget speech, 'with no weakening and no short cuts'.[7] But at least it was now deflation with some prospect of ultimate success. Ministers were no longer trying to defy the facts of life. 'For the first time since it came to office,' Samuel Brittan of the *Financial Times* wrote in 1969, 'the Government had a rational strategy which at least had a chance of working.'[8]

Nevertheless Jenkins got off to a slightly hesitant start. He immediately published Callaghan's Letter of Intent to the International Monetary Fund – an initiative hailed by Wilson as 'a new exercise in open government'[9] – setting a target (which proved over-ambitious) of a surplus of at least £200 million p.a. by the second half of 1968 and a borrowing requirement below £1,000 million; and lost no time in seeking deep spending cuts from every department. But he decided – on Treasury advice – to delay a further squeeze on consumption until the budget. This Jenkins soon recognised as a mistake. Everyone knew that tax increases were on the way, and that prices would rise as a result of devaluation; the result was a pre- (and post-) Christmas buying spree as the public sensibly rushed to spend their money while the going was good: imports rose 10 per cent (by volume) in the first three months of the New Year. It was clear to most commentators, as Nicholas Davenport put it, that 'the extra taxation should have been imposed at once to prevent the fever rising'.[10]

One reason for this misjudgement was that senior officials from the Permanent Secretary, Sir William Armstrong, downwards were simply exhausted by the failed effort to avert devaluation. Another was that it took the new Chancellor several weeks to get his private office sorted out. As at the Home Office, Jenkins wanted to have his own trusted confidants around him. The Principal Private Secretary he inherited from Callaghan, Peter Baldwin (later Permanent Secretary at the Department of Transport), was anxious to move on. The Civil Service candidate to replace him was Robert Armstrong (later Mrs Thatcher's Cabinet Secretary – no relation of Sir William); but Jenkins was determined to have David Dowler, and he was in a strong enough position to insist, until Wilson resolved the situation characteristically by suggesting that he should have both! This, Armstrong recalled, was 'a profoundly unsatisfactory arrangement': Dowler enjoyed Jenkins' confidence but was new to the Treasury, while Armstrong knew the Treasury but not the new Chancellor.[11] Somehow they made it work for nine months until Armstrong was promoted, but the awkward interregnum – with Baldwin still in post until January 1968 – helps to explain Jenkins' failure to spot what he later recognised as bad advice. For nearly six weeks, he wrote in his memoirs, he was dependent on John Harris, 'who would not at that stage have claimed much economic expertise'.[12] But he should not really have needed to be told that action was required urgently. 'We lost a few months in early 1968,' he admitted soon after leaving the Treasury, 'but the effect was not decisive. The turnaround in the Balance of Payments may have been delayed by a few months, but not by more.'[13] At the time, however, it felt a good deal more serious.

Meanwhile he set out, in consultation with Wilson, a programme of spending cuts designed to fall equally heavily on domestic and overseas commitments. At home, Jenkins' most controversial proposals were the restoration of prescription charges and postponing the raising of the school leaving age. Both were highly emotive issues within the Labour party. Prescription charges were the sacred cow over which Nye Bevan had resigned in 1951. The incoming government had abolished them in a symbolic act of socialist piety in 1964: for a leading Gaitskellite to restore them again, only three years later, was a slap in the face for Wilson's old Bevanite supporters. Raising the school leaving age to sixteen (known as ROSLA) was another long-cherished Labour ambition, which had been announced to take place in 1970–71. Jenkins' proposal to defer it for another four years was opposed particularly bitterly by the elementary-educated members of the Cabinet like Brown, Callaghan and Ray Gunter, who felt that it denied opportunity to people from poorer backgrounds like themselves.* There were also severe cutbacks on planned expenditure on housing and road building.

These were regrettable postponements of desirable objectives, which caused much anguish on the Labour benches. But Jenkins was also determined to use the economic squeeze to achieve his long-held ambition to cut Britain's anachronistic and unsustainable military commitments, which helped to placate the left. Once again, he was the right minister in the right place at the right time. Wilson had come into office as determined as any Tory to honour Britain's post-imperial obligations; he even made an exceptionally foolish statement that Britain's frontier was still – in 1965! – on the Himalayas.[14] Realism had actually forced him to announce some withdrawal from bases in the Far and Middle East by the mid-1970s as part of the July 1966 package of economies. But when Jenkins proposed to accelerate the withdrawal to 1971 he still encountered fierce opposition from a powerful section of the Cabinet who shared the Prime Minister's hankering to preserve Britain's status as a global power: George Brown, Denis Healey and George Thomson (Foreign, Defence and Commonwealth Secretaries respectively) were backed by the former Chancellor, Jim Callaghan, and the former (and future) Foreign Secretary, Michael Stewart. Washington too applied heavy pressure to the government to maintain a military presence East of Suez: Brown reported a 'disturbing and distasteful discussion' with the American Secretary of State, Dean Rusk,

---

* ROSLA was eventually carried through by the next Conservative Education Secretary, Margaret Thatcher.

who had told him, 'For God's sake act like Britain.'[15] The Prime Minister of Singapore, Lee Kuan Yew – an old friend of several Labour ministers – also flew to London 'in a very excitable state' to beg the government to think again.[16]

Before taking his proposals to Cabinet, Jenkins went a long way to disarming his potentially difficult colleagues by meeting them individually, not formally in the Treasury, but socially, as was his preferred way, over a meal. Denis Healey, with whom he was particularly anxious to maintain good relations, he took to lunch in a private room at Brown's Hotel on 14 December, with a return engagement the following week in Healey's flat in Admiralty House. Patrick Gordon Walker (Education) he lunched at Brooks's on 28 December; and Barbara Castle (Transport) he invited to East Hendred. Then, since she was ill, he visited her at her farm in Buckinghamshire on New Year's Eve, on his way to the Radziwills' nearby. 'I am interested in the way he is handling all these interviews himself,' Mrs Castle noted, 'without officials present . . . I am interested in the way, too, that he never seems over-pressed with work. Come what may, he would always take life in a relaxed way.'[17] She characteristically fought the cuts to her road programme; but Gordon Walker accepted the postponement of ROSLA, preferring to protect university funding instead, which made it hard for others to oppose it; while Kenneth Robinson (Health) and Anthony Greenwood (Housing) put up no great resistance. As always it was a matter of international confidence. The Cabinet reluctantly accepted Jenkins' insistence that 'the re-introduction of prescription charges had, rightly or wrongly, come to be regarded as a symbol – at home and abroad – of the Government's determination to take all the measures required to restore the economy'.[18] The major battle was thus over withdrawal from East of Suez. Departing from his strategy of one-to-one interviews, Jenkins agreed to meet Healey, Brown and Thomson all together, with their officials, in Brown's room at the House of Commons (and hence under his chairmanship):

> They all proceeded to defend Britain's worldwide role with an attachment to imperial commitments worthy of a conclave of Joseph Chamberlain, Kitchener of Khartoum and George Nathaniel Curzon . . . I quickly learned that a Chancellor should never see together a group of spending ministers with a common interest, and is unwise to see them even singly except on his own territory and with the initiative firmly in his own hands. I never made these simple mistakes again.[19]

The battle to get his package through the Cabinet occupied an unprecedented eight meetings in twelve days between 4 and 15 January 1968, some thirty-two hours in total. These were still the days of real Cabinet government. Jenkins faced different combinations of ministers opposing him on each front – he made careful lists of who voted which way on which item; but he refused to do deals, taking the view that his proposals had a balance and philosophical unity which would unravel if once he started to give ground, and he ultimately got everything he wanted by very narrow majorities on each issue, with just one unimportant resignation – Lord Longford (Lord Privy Seal), who was high-mindedly unable to accept the postponement of ROSLA. Tony Crosland tried to argue that the cuts were too severe and wanted to do more by increased taxation, which would be 'politically acceptable in the present climate'; he gained some support, but Jenkins successfully insisted that 'it would be disastrous if the Government's measures were thought to be too timid'. He himself would have preferred still deeper cuts and was still looking at other possibilities: delaying the switch to decimal currency (due in 1971) or the development of Stansted airport.[20] Both the principal Cabinet diarists, Dick Crossman and Barbara Castle, admired (almost despite themselves) the lucid and persuasive way in which he argued each part of his package. 'On the whole I feel much happier than I ever thought I would be,' Mrs Castle wrote when it was all over. 'Roy has shown many of the right instincts and we are certainly a long way from the crude sell-out of 1931. The package is a sophisticated combination of principle and expediency, and that is what politics is about.'[21]* Crossman particularly admired the way Jenkins defeated Brown and Healey over the defence cuts. 'He did far better than the Prime Minister in fencing with Denis, undermining him first on the economic side and above all on the political side . . . Denis was no match for Roy.'[22]

Reluctantly converted by economic necessity, Wilson gave steady but generally passive support, while leaving most of the running to Jenkins. To Lee Kuan Yew he conceded a nine-month delay from March to December 1971; but when President Johnson threatened to break off defence cooperation if Britain withdrew precipitately, he stood firm, insisting that Britain too had to consult its national interest. 'Believe me, Lyndon,' he wrote to the President on 15 January, 'the decisions

* Labour in the 1960s was still haunted by the 'great betrayal' of 1931 when Ramsay MacDonald and Philip Snowden insisted on cuts, particularly to unemployment benefit, which fell most heavily on the poorest, and then, when the Cabinet split, abandoned Labour to form a 'National Government' with the Tories to force them through.

we are having to take now have been the most difficult and the heaviest of any that I, and I think all of my colleagues, can remember in our public life'; but they were unavoidable, to allow Britain to find her 'new place on the world stage'.[23] Jenkins himself could not have put it better. Cruelly caricatured at the time as Johnson's poodle, Wilson actually stood up to American pressure pretty well, notably by refusing to send British troops to Vietnam, but also in relation to East of Suez generally.

The narrowest margin was over the F-111, the American fighter-bomber that was supposed to fill the gap left by the cancellation of the TSR-2 in 1964. It only made strategic sense in the context of a continued presence in the Far East; and as part of that withdrawal Jenkins was determined that it should go. But to the old imperialists it was a symbol of the intention to retain some world role. Healey dug in to defend it, supported by Brown, Callaghan and the whole rightward-leaning half the Cabinet, leaving Jenkins to find support largely from the left. 'It was part of the skill of Harold Wilson in making me Chancellor,' he wrote, 'that I was now going to have to fall back on the support of him and his Cabinet "tail" in order to defeat a substantial part of the old Labour right.'[24] 'Once again,' Barbara Castle wrote, 'I had to admire Roy's courteous but steely inflexibility. Arguing quietly but firmly, he pitted intellectual reasoning against emotion.'[25] Despite his frequent claims to the contrary, Wilson always counted heads in Cabinet. On this issue, after several hours of often heated debate on 12 January, the Cabinet divided 12:11 in favour of cancellation. But in view of the closeness of the result, Healey asked for it to be reconsidered; and in the interval he succeeded in persuading Longford to change his vote, which he thought would be enough to swing the decision his way. But when the Cabinet reassembled later the same day he found that Jenkins too had been busy and had 'turned' two ministers – Gordon Walker and Cledwyn Hughes (Wales) – now making a 13:10 majority for cancellation. Game, set and match to Jenkins. Wilson had expected Healey to resign if he lost;[26] but he was persuaded to stay on. 'Denis behaved with enormous dignity and courage in the face of a shattering blow, quite as great for him as devaluation was for Jim Callaghan,' Tony Benn recorded. 'I must say my opinion of Roy rose,' he conceded grudgingly. 'I don't regard him as having any principles, but today in argument, getting all that he wanted from his colleagues, he was very impressive.'[27]

Despite their history of mutual suspicion, the Prime Minister and his new Chancellor stood shoulder-to-shoulder throughout this key battle, forging the basis of a surprisingly good working relationship over the next two and a half years. Both in their memoirs paid tribute to the other's staunchness. 'My greatest asset,' Wilson wrote, 'was the firmness and determination of the Chancellor in the presentation of his balanced package.'[28] But when it came to presenting it to the House, Wilson was determined to do it himself. 'With this build-up of Roy,' he told Crossman, 'I can't possibly afford not to make the Statement myself.'[29] But he did it very badly, rattling through it without conviction; whereas Jenkins did the television broadcast that evening and did it well, admitting (as Wilson could never do) that devaluation had been a defeat, but showing how it could be 'a springboard to real economic success in the future', while subtly underlining his own victory for realism. 'We are recognising that we are no longer a superpower . . . There is no greater recipe for disaster than a persistent refusal to face unwelcome facts.'[30] The division of responsibility demonstrated the shift of power between them: 'Six months ago,' wrote Ian Trethowan in The Times, 'who could imagine the Prime Minister not going on the box himself, however bad the news?'[31] 'It is now openly hinted that he may be on the way out,' Barbara Castle recorded;[32] and Benn wrote that 'All the papers are now effectively calling for Roy Jenkins to take over.'[33]

Jenkins' preoccupation, however, was the budget. He did consider bringing it forward but was persuaded, wrongly as he later admitted, to leave it for another two months (though 19 March was still several weeks earlier than normal). From the moment he started thinking about the budget he knew it would have to be an extremely severe one. The Treasury's initial view was that he would need to raise £400–600 million by extra taxation. But Jenkins saw 'some psychological advantage' in going even higher, and he was keen to do as much as possible in his first budget so that he did not have to keep coming back for more.[34] In the end he raised taxes in this budget by more than £900 million. But he rejected the initial advice of the Governor of the Bank of England, Sir Leslie O'Brien, who wanted sixpence on income tax.[35] He preferred to raise as much as possible by indirect taxation, while mitigating the regressive effect of this by differentiating between earned and unearned income – a distinction first made by Asquith in 1908. Faithful to his own past, he also wanted to explore the possibility of some form of wealth tax. He wanted to tax betting more heavily; and he was keen to introduce a national lottery. Treasury papers and the diary of the chief economic adviser, Sir Alec Cairncross, show Jenkins gradually narrowing the options; after discussion with his officials he would often take papers away to East Hendred for the weekend and come back on Monday morning having made his decision.* During February he was gradually persuaded – mainly by Harold Lever, the Financial Secretary and, unusually for a Labour minister, a wealthy man himself – that a wealth tax was impractical and would be counterproductive, and settled instead for a one-off 'special charge' on unearned incomes over £3,000 a year, following the precedent of Stafford Cripps in 1948. He was also reluctantly persuaded against increasing betting duty as steeply as he would have liked. He did get Cabinet approval for a national lottery: a Private Members' Bill to establish one had already passed its Second Reading and Jenkins proposed to incorporate it in the Finance Bill. But this was unexpectedly defeated on a free vote by 'a combination of Labour puritanism and Conservative opportunism' and was not revived for another twenty-five years.[36]

The key choice turned on what to do about Selective Employment Tax – a controversial and not very effective tax on service industries, designed to favour manufacturing, introduced by Callaghan in 1965 on the advice of Nicky Kaldor, one of the two Hungarian economists (Thomas Balogh was the other) who famously advised the Wilson government. Jenkins initially resisted Kaldor's wish to raise it, since 'the only people I have met who have a word to say in favour of SET are in this room'.[37] Eventually, however, it came to seem the least bad option. Two weeks before the budget, given that he had determined not to raise income tax, he had a choice between raising SET, raising petrol duty or extending purchase tax to biscuits, crisps and pet food. Over the weekend of 9–10 March he chose the first two, reckoning that the third would be too unpopular (and risked the budget as a whole being dubbed 'the Pedigree Chum or even the potato crisp Budget').[38] The final package, however, was still extremely tough. He warned the Cabinet on 7 March that 'a second devaluation would occur within three months if the budget didn't restore confidence in sterling'. This, Crossman wrote, was 'the big stick with which he decided to beat the Cabinet into accepting a tremendous budget'.[39] In all he raised £923 million in new taxation, an unprecedented figure, largely

---

* In addition to David Dowler, John Harris and Robert Armstrong, the principal officials involved in composing the 1968 budget were the Permanent Secretary, William Armstrong; Alec Cairncross; Professor Kaldor; and two special economic advisers, Michael Posner and Kenneth Berrill (later head of the government 'think tank'). The two second-tier ministers were Jack Diamond (Chief Secretary) and Harold Lever (Financial Secretary), whose instincts were entirely opposed: Diamond cautious and miserly, Lever naturally expansionist. Dick Taverne was initially Minister of State until he replaced Lever in 1969.

from every Chancellor's traditional sources: drink and cigarettes (though he excluded beer); purchase tax; petrol duty (up 4d a gallon); road tax (up from £17.10s to £25); and a 50 per cent rise in SET. In addition his one-off 'Special Charge' on personal incomes (on top of income tax and surtax), beginning at two shillings in the pound between £3,000 and £4,000 p.a. and rising to nine shillings in the pound over £8,000 p.a. raised another £100 million. One mitigation was that he increased family allowances, finding the money by cutting child tax allowances. He also decided not to tighten hire-purchase restrictions, as had been widely expected, in order to keep something in reserve in case it was needed later in the year.

Once again the old Bevanites were impressed by Jenkins' unexpected radicalism when he unveiled his proposals to the Cabinet on Monday 18 March. 'It was genuinely based on socialist principle,' Crossman wrote, 'fair in the fullest sense by really helping people at the bottom of the scale and by really taxing the wealthy.'[40] Even Barbara Castle could not withhold her 'sneaking admiration' for the 'Special Charge': 'No punch-pulling here . . . I must say he has a greater grasp of principle than Jim ever had.' Callaghan in fact – 'who can't be relishing Roy's success' – was the one minister to strike a sour note, complaining that Jenkins was only aiming to hit the same economic targets that he had been aiming at before devaluation, so devaluation had been unnecessary. Jenkins told him firmly that without devaluation they would have been unrealisable.[41]

Before this, however, he had nearly been thrown off course by a sudden sterling crisis over the weekend. One result of Britain's devaluation was that the speculators turned their attention to the dollar, which was vulnerable because of the escalating cost of the Vietnam war, triggering a rush to buy gold which in turn led to further heavy selling of the pound. 'As was invariably the case in the 1960s,' Jenkins recalled, 'whatever currency the gale was directed against, the side-winds were devastating for sterling.'[42] By Thursday 14 March Britain was haemorrhaging hundreds of millions of pounds a day from the reserves and a second devaluation was looking horribly likely when the Americans, late that evening, threw out a lifeline by requesting the closure of the London gold market, which provided cover for closing the foreign exchange market as well by declaring Friday a bank holiday. But this required an Order in Council to be proclaimed by a quorum of four Privy Councillors in the presence of the Queen. Unable to locate George Brown – though he may not have tried very hard – Wilson roped in Peter Shore to make up the numbers (the Queen's private secretary made the fourth) and they all trooped off to the Palace at half past midnight. By the time they got back to Downing Street, Brown had heard what was afoot and was complaining furiously that he had not been consulted. Unluckily the House was sitting all night on Barbara Castle's Transport Bill, which enabled Brown to round up half the Cabinet to go across to Number Ten and support his complaint: Jenkins had to explain to them what he and Wilson had done and why there was no time to consult. Most accepted that there was no alternative, but Tony Crosland and Michael Stewart were still unhappy and Brown refused to accept Wilson's version of events and walked out, slamming the door.[43] The next day he resigned, not for the first time. This time, however, Wilson accepted his resignation, bringing a sad end to a remarkable career. Then Crossman came on the phone saying that the House was in ferment and would not be satisfied until the Chancellor came and explained what was happening. So at 3.20 a.m. Jenkins was obliged to go over and make an exceptionally tricky statement: one false word might have pushed sterling over the brink. 'I had never,' he wrote later, 'previously understood the full force of the expression "walking on eggshells".'[44] But he rose to the occasion, calmly making it clear that the crisis on this occasion originated in America, not in Britain, that the banks would reopen for normal business on Saturday – in fact they had to keep them closed on Saturday as well – and that he would be presenting his budget on Tuesday as planned. Mrs Castle, sitting beside him on the front bench, vividly described the release of tension:

> Roy handled every supplementary very skilfully, with Harold patting him on the back with an exuberance of bonhomie every time he sat down. I noticed for the first time that Roy has a funny little habit of fingering his buttock every time he stands up and I was relieved to know that I am not the only one who feels the strain on these kind of occasions. But he certainly came out on top.

'Once more,' she concluded gratefully, 'we were a credible Government.'[45]

But that was not the end of it. As the price of acceding to the American request to close the gold market, Britain still needed to secure yet another American credit to surmount the immediate crisis. Jenkins sent William Armstrong, Leslie O'Brien and Harold Lever to Washington to negotiate it. On Saturday he went through the traditional pre-budget ritual of posing for photographs with the family at East Hendred; but on the Sunday he had to break his weekend by going

Illingworth, *Daily Mail*, 26.2.68 (supplied by Llyfrgell Genedlaethol Cymru/ National Library of Wales)

back to London for more crisis meetings to decide what to do if a sufficient loan was not forthcoming: should they float the pound, block the international sterling balances, or both? Not until late on Sunday night did Armstrong telephone that he had secured just over $4 billion – only two-thirds of what they had wanted, but it was enough. It was not the ideal preparation for Jenkins' first budget; fortunately it had been pretty well finalised the previous week.

On the Monday he disclosed its contents to the Cabinet, made another statement to the House about the financial crisis, saw the Queen for an hour and spent the rest of the day polishing his speech and writing (with David Dowler) his budget broadcast.* Then on the Tuesday he woke 'with a small dagger-like headache going down into one eyeball' and spent two and a half hours alone rehearsing his speech, feeling like 'a boxer told to relax before a prize fight on the result of which all the trainers and seconds had invested more money than they could afford'. He walked in the garden of Number Eleven for half an

---

* Of his royal audience he wrote in his memoirs that he found the Queen 'informed and interested'. But in the notes he recorded at the time he was rather more specific. 'She . . . asked a number of questions, not about the Special Charge, in which she showed no interest at all, partly perhaps because she doesn't pay direct taxation, but a good deal more about SET, which she does pay. In other words she showed individual rather than class self-interest! . . . I found her more intelligent and interesting than on any previous occasion' – to which he added in 1970 'or any later one'.[46]

hour, then lunched with Harris, Dowler, Robert Armstrong, Tom Bradley (still his PPS) and Jennifer, and 'drank a fair amount . . . The wine seemed to do my headache more good than the fresh air had done.' Finally he went over to the House, opened Gladstone's famous dispatch box and ploughed through his speech from 3.45 to 6.15 p.m., now feeling like a Channel swimmer losing sight of Dover long before he could see Calais. 'When I eventually sank back into my seat there was to my amazement and great relief a demonstration of unusual support from the Government benches. Nearly everyone stood up and waved their order papers.'[47]

Jenkins had managed to pull off the rare feat of pleasing both the Labour back benches and the press. 'He had just enough for the Left Wing,' Cairncross noted, 'but it was astonishing to hear them cheer a speech imposing over £900m in taxation, mostly indirect.'[48] Barbara Castle likewise thought the budget's 'brilliance . . . proved by the fact that the most swingeing Budget in history left our people positively exultant'.[49] Leslie Bonham Carter was in the gallery – as was Jennifer – and wrote gushingly but also shrewdly to tell 'Darling Roy' that he was 'absolutely magnificent':

> It seemed to me a near miracle that in spite of what you *had* to do the effect you achieved was yet one of exhilaration. The whole gallery behind me was a-buzz with praise – even from those who had been punched in their sensitive unearned incomes. I admired you today more than I can possibly say.[50]

Cairncross was not the only observer who wondered if, in cheering the Chancellor, the Labour benches were not perhaps 'cheering an alternative leader to H.W.'[51]

But Jenkins – after staying to listen to Ted Heath grudgingly denouncing 'a hard cold budget, without one glimmer of warmth'[52] – had only about half an hour to enjoy his success before he had to go back to Number Eleven to record his budget broadcast, which went out at nine o'clock that evening. He spoke gravely, straight to camera, explaining the country's critical economic situation in terms remarkably like those of the Conservative–Liberal coalition in rather different but equally dire circumstances in 2010. 'This has been an extremely harsh budget,' he began bluntly. 'It had to be. I had no alternative. If we let the opportunity of devaluation slip through our fingers, we would just find ourselves quickly slithering back to the sort of economic crisis which has beset us on at least eight occasions since the war.' Unlike his successor forty-two years later, he carefully avoided party point-scoring, pointing out that the record of economic failure had persisted under governments of both parties. Britain had been 'living in a "fool's paradise"' for years, 'importing too much, exporting too little and paying ourselves too much', yet still enjoyed a lower standard of living than Germany and France. His budget – 'the harshest budget for a long time' – was designed to produce a 1 per cent cut in living standards in the coming year. But now, with a competitive exchange rate and by cutting the defence burden to what the country could afford, he asserted, Britain could in five years become again one of the most prosperous countries in Europe. 'If we face the challenge we can end a long period of retreat . . . It's up to all of us.'[53]

'You spoke as an adult to adults,' one admiring friend, John Grigg, told him, 'but also with a distinction and authority all your own.'[54] 'He presented the facts in straightforward fashion and without trying to wriggle,' wrote the London *Evening Standard* the next day, contrasting Jenkins' directness with Wilson's slippery broadcast after devaluation. 'By continuing in this way he could do much to reduce the present cynicism about politicians.'[55] On the substance of the budget, too, the verdict of Fleet Street was overwhelmingly positive. The *Guardian* grumbled about a 'bankers' budget',[56] but most commentators echoed the economics editor of *The Times*, Peter Jay:

Roy Jenkins has risen fully and magnificently to the occasion. Yesterday's Budget was really everything that was economically needed. It should give devaluation a virtually certain guarantee of success . . . Britain has now beyond any shadow of doubt done everything required to correct the fundamental weakness of the economy and the balance of payments . . . This offers the prospect of a distinctly liberal Budget in two years' time when most of the debt should be paid off.[57]

From the most unpropitious circumstances Jenkins had achieved an astonishing personal triumph. Labour continued to trail twenty or more points behind the Tories in the opinion polls, and lost a string of by-elections over the next year by enormous margins, while the balance of payments still took an agonisingly long time to respond to his harsh medicine. During 1968 the Bank still had to shell out £1,400 million to support sterling in the exchange markets – nearly as much as in the three years before devaluation taken together – and the turnaround did not come until mid-1969. Yet in an unpopular government, under a severely discredited Prime Minister, Jenkins had established a position of personal authority that raised huge expectations. He was now widely seen as Wilson's natural and inevitable successor, with constant suggestions that he should seize the reins sooner rather than later. But these siren voices only added extra pressure to his situation, pulling him in different ways. After three and a half years in office, the 1968 budget marked the end of his period of apparently effortless ascent. From now on his choices would become much more difficult.

After he left office in 1970 Jenkins wrote for the *Sunday Times* and *Observer* two thoughtful articles comparing the Home Office and Treasury, based on his recent experience of running both. He contrasted the intellectual self-confidence and informality of the Treasury, where officials habitually addressed each other by their Christian names, with the much greater defensiveness and formality of the Home Office, where surnames still prevailed. More seriously, he contrasted the way decisions had to be taken in each department. The climate of the Home Office, he wrote – remembering the Blake escape, the Shepherd's Bush shootings, the Maidstone birching case and the Court Lees affair – was 'one of tropical storms that blow up with speed and violence out of a blue sky, dominate the political landscape for a short time, and then disappear as suddenly as they arrived'. Meanwhile there was a heavy permanent workload of administration and legislation:

> The climate of the Treasury, on the other hand, during most of my time there, was that of a long dark arctic winter, only slowly melting into a tentative spring. Changes, whether pleasant or unpleasant, could usually be foreseen at least a few weeks ahead, and were part of a general ebb and flow of events rather than some unexpected occurrence.

The Chancellor introduces no legislation apart from the Finance Bill and has relatively little routine administration in his own department. But he has to take a close interest in what is going on in every other department. 'He has to attend all major ministerial meetings, and nearly always be either protagonist or antagonist.'[58] Above all, given the centrality of the economy in modern government, he is seen to carry the whole fate of the government on his shoulders while peculiarly vulnerable to international forces outside his control. So it is a uniquely burdensome and stressful job.

Jenkins had a difficult baptism at the Treasury, and he was not initially impressed by what he found there. He blamed Sir William Armstrong for giving him bad advice about the timing of the budget; and when Sir Douglas Allen succeeded Armstrong as Permanent Secretary in May 1968, he wrote Allen a stiff letter saying that 'a good deal of reorganisation and shaking up' were needed to remedy some serious failures. A recent meeting about the bank rate was 'I think the worst prepared on a major question in my experience as a minister'; while the contingency planning division that he had asked to be set up in February still did not exist. If they were forced into a second devaluation with as little planning as in November 1967 it would be 'a major public scandal' – for which he naturally did not want to be responsible. 'There are obviously a lot of highly-talented and hard-working people in the Treasury,' he concluded. 'But as a coordinated and reliable machine it is not what I would have expected to find. It is living too complacently on its reputation, and if it does that for much longer the reputation will have disappeared.'[59] Allen accepted the criticism, but pleaded in mitigation that contingency planning for devaluation had been hampered by the Prime Minister refusing to allow the possibility to be discussed.

Generally, however, Jenkins got on much better with Allen than he had with Armstrong and soon had the department working the way he wanted. Unlike Callaghan, who had frankly struggled with economic concepts, he found the work of the Treasury 'intellectually satisfying' and had the self-confidence to take his own decisions.[60] Several senior mandarins testified how much they enjoyed working with him. One wrote in retirement that these two and a half years were 'the happiest of my professional career. For the first time for many years a Chancellor was rising fully to his responsibilities.'[61] Alec Cairncross too thought Jenkins 'the ablest of the four Chancellors I served' (the others were Selwyn Lloyd, Reggie Maudling and Jim Callaghan):

He listened to advice, but made up his own mind, explaining to his advisers the grounds for his decision. He was at times able to foresee contingencies of which his staff had not warned him, such as the possible devaluation of the French franc . . . He was not afraid to take extreme measures to overcome major dangers, adding more to taxation and cutting more from public expenditure than his advisers suggested and showing a sound judgement of what was at stake. This resoluteness . . . enabled him to carry the Cabinet with him after three years in which they had shrunk from much milder action.[62]

As at the Home Office, however, he aroused some resentment by relying too exclusively on his small circle of trusted advisers, in particular David Dowler and John Harris whom he had brought with him from the Home Office. Even Cairncross worried about 'the Chancellor's tendency to discuss policy with his little "court" . . . and then call together officials briefly to hear judgement before he invites them to give evidence';[63] and Jenkins' engagement diaries confirm that before practically every big speech or major decision he would lunch with Dowler and Harris at Brooks's. Even Douglas Allen once found that the only way he could get a real talk with the Chancellor was by booking the seat next to him on a flight to Washington. Many years later Jenkins recalled that at the farewell party the Treasury gave for him after Labour's defeat his old Oxford friend Leo Pliatzky (then an Under-Secretary) slightly spoiled the eulogistic atmosphere by telling him that he could have been a better Chancellor if he had made more use of the middle ranks. 'I muttered defensively that I had been trying desperately to avoid a second devaluation rather than to organise a running seminar for assistant and under secretaries.'[64] He certainly preferred small purposeful meetings to large wool-gathering ones, largely because he disliked wasting time; he also stopped minor questions being referred to him so that he could concentrate on the big picture, and delegated as much routine as possible to his junior ministers.* The result was that while some of those who worked closely with him admired him greatly, others found him remote.

Above all he was determined to break the departmental culture of working long hours for their own sake. 'He had the greatest difficulty in dissuading officials from working far into every evening as a matter of course,' Samuel Brittan wrote in 1969.[65] Harold Wilson used to complain that Jenkins left work every day at seven o'clock to go out to dinner; and the same charge recurs throughout the diaries of Crossman, Castle and Benn. 'The way that man refuses to sacrifice his social life to his political duties never fails to astonish Harold and me,' Barbara Castle expostulated in July 1968, 'but he obviously feels strong enough to get away with it.'[66] In so far as it was true, however, it was not due to laziness, but was a deliberate policy designed to avoid exhaustion. Jenkins believed strongly that tired and harassed ministers do not make good decisions, and that those who let their job take over

---

* For example, Jenkins had very little to do with the change to decimalisation. The big decision had already been taken in 1966. The new coins started to circulate in 1968–9 before the changeover in 1971, but the practicalities of the transition were handled by his junior ministers.

their whole life lose their sense of perspective. He did not exactly work short hours as Chancellor, as he described in the *Observer*:

> The hours were testing but not killing. It was only after I had been there for five months that I first had a day completely free from Treasury work. Subsequently I avoided such continuous over-application. Even so, I habitually worked on boxes of official papers or wrote speeches for at least six hours of each of the two weekend days, and from Monday to Friday I did something like a 12-hour day. But I very rarely worked after midnight, and still more rarely did I start, even in bed, before 7.30 a.m.[67]

Of Stafford Cripps' habit of doing four hours' solid paperwork before breakfast every day he wondered, 'What on earth did he do? It is not necessary, particularly for a man of quick mind and weak body, to steal this additional four hours from sleep or leisure for the administration of the Treasury.'[68] Jenkins' mind was very quick and his health – unlike Cripps' – was excellent. Like Asquith he had the power of dispatching work exceptionally rapidly, economically and decisively: not only did this leave time for relaxation, but after such concentrated exertion he positively needed it. Unlike Wilson, who used to sit up late in Downing Street gossiping obsessively with his 'kitchen cabinet' – Marcia Williams, Joe Haines and Gerald Kaufman – Jenkins liked to get away from politics in the evenings and at weekends.* He did not hang around Westminster any more than necessary and was rebuked by the Chief Whip for his poor voting record. (Only Crosland's was worse.)[70] He believed that this determination to recharge his batteries actually made him a better minister. Reviewing the published diaries of his former colleagues in the 1970s and 1980s, Jenkins disputed Crossman's suggestion that he lacked 'industriousness' ('a quality which I think Crossman confuses with freneticism') and mocked Barbara Castle's account of her own working habits. 'She was always "dragging" herself to early meetings, "crawling" with exhaustion out of Cabinet, and finally "creeping" home" to a tired bed. She made exhaustion into a political virility symbol, and was foolishly critical of those who did not believe that decisions were best taken in a state of prostration.'[71] The third Cabinet diarist, Tony Benn, had some sympathy with Jenkins' determination to protect his sanity. When Peter Shore complained that the Chancellor

---

* In fact even Wilson had his relaxation. He found time to play golf seventy-three times in the first ten months of 1968, usually with Marcia's brother.[69]

'couldn't work as hard as he and I did, and had to have weekends off, didn't work in the evenings and, generally speaking, operated like a pre-1914 Minister', Benn commented that this routine might upset the Treasury, 'but it is the way to survive; frankly the pressure of life at the moment is too much for me'.[72]

Any idea that Jenkins was not thoroughly on top of his job is belied by his record as one of the most successful Chancellors of the past half-century. If Crossman, as Social Services Secretary, sometimes complained that he was poorly briefed on the intricacies of pensions, for instance, that was because pensions were, to the Treasury, a relatively marginal issue. Far more often both Crossman and Castle were forced to recognise his authority and effectiveness on the major issues on which he concentrated his effort. ('When Roy wants to he takes trouble,' Crossman noted in September 1968. 'This morning he was really briefed from top to bottom and got exactly what he wanted.')[73] The central function of the Treasury on which he certainly did not skimp was the preparation of his annual budget. Jenkins presented three of them – the same number as Asquith – and he took immense care that they were all elegantly structured and intellectually coherent. He had studied the budgets of previous Chancellors: not only Asquith's three, but Lloyd George's (rather less exemplary) six, as well as those of Dalton, Cripps and Gaitskell. Above all, he considered that Callaghan's three budgets between 1965 and 1967 had 'lacked cohesion or purpose' and was determined that his should be in a different class.[74] He started thinking about the shape of the budget as soon as Christmas was out of the way: in 1969 he wrote down his first budget thoughts on the evening of Christmas Day.[75] He deliberately broke the convention of strict 'purdah' surrounding the Chancellor in the run-up to the budget by discussing his options confidentially with the two colleagues whose views he most valued, Tony Crosland and Denis Healey, as well as with Wilson. Then, after he had decided on the detailed measures, he would spend many hours, alone or with David Dowler, writing, polishing and rehearsing his speech. In the tribute that he wrote on Dowler's early death he recalled a passage in the economic analysis of the 1969 budget 'which, through successive drafts, we could not get right', until Dowler came in early one morning 'to get the points in their correct logical sequence . . . Thereafter we had no trouble with the structure of the argument.'[76] It was this perfectionist attention to detail that gave Jenkins' three budgets their literary quality and contributed to their political success. Another important innovation was that he started publishing the economic forecasts on which the budget was based. This, wrote

Samuel Brittan, 'was rightly hailed as a major step forward'.[77] William Davis in the *Guardian* thought it typical of Jenkins' 'adult approach and it merits the full cooperation of the press'.[78]

Every Chancellor's crucial relationship is with his Prime Minister. Nigel Lawson's experience under Margaret Thatcher and Gordon Brown's tense rivalry with Tony Blair are only the most recent examples of how a dysfunctional relationship can undermine a government. Jenkins and Wilson, despite their different tastes and lifestyles – 'good claret and good HP sauce', as one journalist put it[79] – actually worked pretty well together most of the time. Whereas Wilson and Callaghan 'met only at times of crisis' and the interconnecting door between Numbers Ten and Eleven was usually closed, Marcia Williams wrote that in 1967–70 'the door was always unlocked and very often open', and the Prime Minister and Chancellor talked almost every day.[80]* This was partly because Jenkins clearly held the upper hand. Wilson had been damaged by devaluation and could not afford to lose another Chancellor, so Jenkins was effectively unsackable. An early example of Jenkins exerting his strength occurred in April 1968, soon after his first budget, when Wilson wanted to move Barbara Castle to the DEA. Jenkins had seen the results of divided responsibility for the economy when George Brown had been at the DEA, and he did not want another strong personality disputing his territory, so he vetoed the appointment, successfully flattering Mrs Castle that it was a compliment to her quality that he did not want her there. ('Relations between us would be bound to be strained and I should regret that.')[83] Wilson backed down and created a new job for Mrs Castle as Secretary of State for Employment and Productivity instead, leaving the more light-weight Peter Shore effectively to wind up the DEA. There were limits to Jenkins' influence – Wilson ignored his suggestion that he should make Denis Healey Foreign Secretary when Brown resigned, and

---

* Unlike most new Chancellors, Jenkins already knew Number Eleven from when his father had been Attlee's PPS during the war. But Jennifer and the children hated living there. 'As a family we loathed it,' Jennifer told the *Birmingham Evening Mail*. 'It is gloomy and inconvenient . . . You cannot go out without crowds of sightseers watching . . . The kitchen is miles from the dining room and the washing machine is 50 steps up and round a passage.' Moreover the Ministry of Works was only responsible for the ground floor. She tried to improve it by collecting pictures and cartoons of former Chancellors and got Roy Strong, director of the National Portrait Gallery, to hang them up the stairs like the pictures of former Prime Ministers in Number Ten.[81] But Cynthia and Edward, now teenagers, hated it so much that in 1969 they moved back for a time to Ladbroke Square, so that (as Barbara Castle wrote) 'poor Jennifer has to commute between two homes'.[82] At this time she was still chairman of the Consumers' Association, and was also able to resume sitting as a magistrate when Roy left the Home Office.

reappointed Michael Stewart instead; and he played little part in foreign policy. But over the whole field of economic policy he was determined that he should be seen to be in charge: he later criticised some of his successors, even Lawson, for having tolerated 'a degree of Prime Ministerial control over exchange rate policy, the core of Treasury responsibility, which I would never have accepted'.[84] Wilson, though often jealous of Jenkins' laudatory press, expertly spun by John Harris, accepted this, partly because he respected Jenkins' competence and recognised that the reputation of the government depended on his success, and partly because most of the time he did not seriously believe that Jenkins was after his job. Jenkins, for his part, though still often critical of Wilson's crablike methods and impatient with his chronic time-wasting, was genuinely grateful to the Prime Minister both for having given him the job and for his loyal support, and even grew quite fond of him.* They were in fact bound together: they needed each other, and they both knew it.

Looking back over his career, Jenkins recognised that 1968–9 was the time when he could have become Prime Minister himself. Wilson was at the nadir of his popularity and Labour trailed by huge margins in the polls. Jenkins seemed to be the one minister with a chance of turning the situation round in time to win the next election, and there was constant press speculation that he could and should push Wilson aside and move next door. Moreover he had a devoted band of supporters working to promote this result. The 'Jenkinsites' were now a recognised group within the Parliamentary Labour Party, largely drawn from the 1964 and 1966 intakes. There were some older members and one or two trade unionists, but most were youngish, ambitious, middle-class and university-educated, bereaved Gaitskellites like Bill Rodgers who had cut their teeth in CDS in the early 1960s and had seen the light go out of their political life with Gaitskell's death in 1963; or David Owen, an abrasive young hospital doctor who had won a Plymouth seat in 1966. They had never quite been able to see George Brown as a credible successor, but having come into politics under the influence of *The Future of Socialism* looked initially to Tony Crosland as their leader. Some, like Owen and Roy Hattersley, still saw Crosland as their philosopher, but had been persuaded by Jenkins' much more

---

* Jenkins used to recall, however, that when he went to see the Prime Minister, Wilson would pour him half a tumbler of whisky and then talk endlessly without coming to a decision. 'You had to be prepared to come out drunk two hours later in order to get five things agreed.'[85] As a strong believer in lunch and dinner, he also found it tiresome that Wilson did not observe proper mealtimes.[86]

decisive performance in office – and greater care to advance their careers – to switch their allegiance to him as their potential leader. The strong tribal identity within the group, Rodgers explained to David Butler in an off-the-record interview before the 1970 election, was based on an almost visceral antipathy to Wilson, who – however much his policies might disappoint the left – was not, in their view, a Social Democrat. 'His style, attitudes values are not ours,' Rodgers told Butler. 'I see Harold as a usurper of my mother, Gaitskell' – in the same way that the grieving Kennedys resented Lyndon Johnson. Rodgers' picture of the Gaitskellite 'family' was rose-tinted:

> From Roy and Tony downwards there is a striking sense of kinship, affection and loyalty . . . Roy embodies this to a great extent: integrity, intellectual distinction, political *nous* and an un-meanness. These were the qualities we looked for in Gaitskell. The Home Office was a complete and logical part of the Gaitskellite achievement. I'm very fond of Roy. All of us will do anything for each of us.[87]

This turned out to be not quite true of all of them. But it vividly captures the emotional quality of Rodgers' devotion to his leader.

But the Jenkinsites faced three problems in 1968. First, even on the most generous estimate they only constituted a minority of the PLP and not the most popular with their colleagues; they included some of the brightest talents, certainly, but people like Owen and Hattersley, Dick Taverne, John Mackintosh and David Marquand were widely seen as arrogant intellectuals, out of touch with the working-class movement they were supposed to represent – much like Jenkins himself. The solid centre of the party, still in those days containing a high proportion of down-to-earth trade unionists, frankly distrusted them, as naturally did the Tribunite left. Second, there was no support among senior members of the Cabinet for a change of leader. However much their loyalties were sometimes strained, old Bevanites like Crossman and Castle would always ultimately stick with Wilson. Brown was gone; Callaghan was still bitterly resentful of Jenkins and, from the low point of his resignation, was steadily rebuilding his own position as an alternative contender; while Crosland and Healey were both too jealous and too ambitious themselves to wish to see their younger contemporary leapfrog them into the leadership. 'We discussed the mechanics of how [Wilson] might be replaced endlessly,' Rodgers recalled. 'But Roy would never have supported Jim and Jim would never have supported Roy.' Nor would Tony or Denis. 'They all belonged to the same generation and they all wanted to be Prime Minister.'[88] Wilson was safe so long as his senior colleagues could not agree on a replacement.

Third, they lacked clear encouragement from Jenkins himself. He never denied that he 'very much' wanted to be Prime Minister. He thought he had the 'intellectual capacity' to do the job, and never seemed worried by his lack of rapport with the industrial side of the labour movement.[89] 'The old cloth cap idea is dead,' he over-confidently told the journalist Anne Scott-James.[90] But he did not think that his time was yet. In mid-1968 he had only been a minister for three and a half years and Chancellor for a few months. He thought he must prove himself a success in that role before he could credibly aspire to the leadership, and for the moment he was too busy worrying about sterling to have any energy left for plotting. Having studied history, written three political biographies and reviewed dozens more, he was almost too well aware that – as he had written about Rab Butler's failure to seize his moment back in 1952 – '"There is a tide . . ." but it does not often continue at the flood for very long, nor does it often recur.'[91] But he calculated that his best chance of succeeding Wilson was by natural succession, not by a *coup d'état*; and he knew that if he tried to grab the prize he would inherit a divided party that would face certain defeat at the next election. 'Unlike Callaghan,' Gerald Kaufman shrewdly told David Butler, Jenkins 'wanted to be PM, not just leader of a broken party.'[92] So when his followers urged him to go for it, he hesitated. To some, like David Owen, his hesitation raised doubts for the first time about whether he had the necessary ruthlessness for leadership. For others his honourable caution was exactly why they had supported him in the first place.

The aborted coup is documented in the diaries of two of the senior plotters, Patrick Gordon Walker and Christopher Mayhew, both of whom had their own grievances against the Prime Minister. Gordon Walker's ill-starred ministerial career had ended in April 1968 when he was replaced as Education Secretary by Ted Short. Mayhew, a dashing young Foreign Office minister under Bevin in 1946–50, had been brought back by Wilson to the MoD, but resigned over cuts to the Royal Navy in 1966. Neither could expect any further advancement under Wilson. During the war Mayhew had taken part in the ill-fated Dieppe raid in 1943; and in his memoirs Jenkins fancifully likened the plotters of 1968 to 'a dedicated group of commandos, waiting as it were with their faces blackened for the opportunity to launch a Dieppe raid against the forces of opportunism'.[93] By May 1968 they had put together an inner group of nine or ten, including several ministers, who met in one another's houses to go through lists of names. On 7 May Mayhew reported to Jenkins that they had sixty who would be ready to sign a letter to the Chief Whip calling for Wilson to go. But Jenkins, while happy to say that he was 'utterly fed up with Harold' – their relations were just then going through a bad patch – thought sixty was not enough, as Mayhew recorded:

> '80?' I asked. '100,' he replied, and then as an afterthought: 'I suppose really one ought to go for a majority of backbenchers.' I said this would be about 120, statistically speaking.

A few days later, at another meeting at Dick Taverne's house, the rebels reckoned they could count on thirty-five 'certainties', thirty-nine 'probables' and sixty-three 'possibles', with another seventeen potential supporters whose views were still unknown. 'It no longer seemed impossible that a majority of backbenchers against Harold was out of the question.'

But three weeks later Jenkins again raised the bar. '"I don't intend to do a Ramsay MacDonald," he said. "I must have a substantial part of the Party with me." "Fifty–fifty," I queried. "Seventy–thirty," he replied.' If Mayhew's account can be believed, Jenkins was already playing with the idea of breaking the party system itself:

> I put it to Roy that simply to take over the leadership and to struggle on trying to maintain a semblance of unity and morale would at best allow him two years as prime minister before a shattering election defeat which would in effect end his political career altogether. The only hope would be to combine the takeover of the leadership with an entirely fresh revolutionary political approach. We should embrace the biggest political issue of all – far-reaching constitutional reform aimed at ending the farce of the present party struggle and the kind of ludicrous performance we were now getting in Parliament . . . He most warmly agreed. 'I would not agree to lead without getting out of this appalling nonsense' – he nodded in the direction of the Chamber – 'We must break loose from the present political straitjacket.'[94]

There was no possibility of this in 1968. But this is the first record of Jenkins' disillusion with the existing political system, even when he was at the peak of his conventional success within it.

'The Conspiracy is now in full swing,' Gordon Walker wrote excitedly on 17 June. But while Taverne was keen to 'come out into the open and hot things up', others, including Mayhew, wanted to wait until the autumn, while Jenkins himself still had no intention of putting his head above the parapet unless he could be certain of success:

> Roy Jenkins thought better not move now. He did not want to say, at any time, that we should move. He wanted to be consulted and might advise against action – but, otherwise, he would leave it to us. He clearly did not want to be implicated in actually launching an action.[95]

On 19 July the majority agreed that they had 'missed the bus' for the moment, and should try again in the autumn.[96]

But the autumn, with another sterling crisis in November, turned out to be too fraught a time. They did gear up for another attempt in the spring of 1969, when a group now including Robert Maclennan and David Marquand, meeting in Ivor Richard's chambers on 7 May, decided that it was now or never: 'no better chance would ever recur'. The local election results were certain to be terrible, and any later would be too close to the next election. Fifty MPs were said to be ready to sign a letter to the chairman of the PLP, Douglas Houghton, which they thought would be enough to call a meeting at which they would have sufficient votes to force Wilson to stand down. But now Jenkins sent word via John Harris that they should not move while Barbara Castle's Industrial Relations Bill was dividing the party: 'The centre of the party would not move against HW while this issue was still open.' More importantly, Callaghan had by now, by his opposition to the Bill, re-emerged as a serious challenger. So once again at Donald Dewar's flat on 12 May the plotters agreed to wait, but to hold themselves ready.[97] In fact the moment never did recur and the Jenkinsite revolt petered out. In retrospect, Jenkins thought that the previous year was the closest he ever came to becoming Prime Minister:

> Looking back . . . I think that those troubled summer days of 1968 were for me . . . the equivalent of . . . 1953 for Rab Butler. Having faltered for want of single-minded ruthlessness when there was no alternative to himself, he then settled down to a career punctuated by increasingly wide misses at the premiership. People who effectively seize the prime ministership – Lloyd George, Macmillan, Mrs Thatcher – do not let such moments slip.[98]

Jenkins would have had to be a different character to have seized his moment in 1968; and he did not, at the end of his life, seriously regret not having acted out of character.

This capacity to see his own career as a biography in the making probably inhibited his capacity for decisive action at critical moments. Ambitious though he was, he could seem curiously detached. Barbara Castle put her finger on this quality at the height of the Mayhew plot in May 1968. After lunch with him alone at Number Eleven – by the end of which she confessed, 'I liked him more . . . than I have ever done before' – she concluded:

> Despite his concern that things are really serious, he seemed remarkably relaxed, but then I think he is in some strange way an observer of politics rather than a practitioner. I have the feeling that it would not really break his heart if the Government fell, provided he could write its history.[99]

Crossman too doubted whether Jenkins really had the necessary desire to be Prime Minister:

> When I sit beside him I feel that he has a patrician air – a little like Balfour,* disdainful, detached – plus a delicious boyish humour. He also likes his tennis and his croquet and is much more of a family man than I realised. But throughout his political career he has always succeeded in remaining to some extent uncommitted. If he became Prime Minister I'm sure he could live up to the big hours – the big broadcasts, the big speeches. But could he show the energy to do the endless fixing and arranging which is Harold's daily life? I don't know two more sharply contrasted men.[100]

Jenkins would not have quarrelled with these judgements. When push came to shove he had too many other interests, and too healthy a sense of perspective, to give his whole being obsessively to politics.

'Things' continued to be serious throughout 1968 – too serious for playing politics. Jenkins' draconian budget achieved its purpose

---

* Arthur Balfour succeeded his uncle, Lord Salisbury, as Prime Minister in 1902 and held the job for three years before leading the Conservatives to a heavy defeat in 1906.

335

eventually, by switching resources into exports; but in the short run the impact of devaluation was that imports were now more expensive and continued to rise faster than exports – the 'J-curve effect' – so that the balance of payments got worse before it could get better and sterling remained vulnerable to rumours of a second devaluation. The drain on Britain's reserves was still running at around £500 million every quarter, while a succession of traumatic international events – the French *événements* in May, the still-escalating Vietnam War, the Soviet invasion of Czechoslovakia in August – further buffeted the money markets, with every puff of wind threatening to blow sterling off its precarious new parity. Alec Cairncross's Treasury diary is a record of almost unmitigated gloom as the economy staggered from one crisis to the next. In April Jenkins had to fly to Washington to negotiate another standby loan of $1,400 million from the IMF, while the Treasury prepared all sorts of contingency plans for floating the pound if necessary, including import deposits and a secret plan for blocking the sterling balances held around the world by other (mainly Commonwealth) countries, codenamed with typical Treasury classicism 'Operation Brutus.'* (Various alternative plans were named 'Hecuba', 'Priam' and 'Orestes'.) Jenkins had long argued that these sterling balances – worth more than five times the value of Britain's foreign exchange reserves – were a source of weakness, not strength, to Britain. Many years later he likened sterling's over-extended world role to 'too large a sail on an unsteady small boat', which constantly threatened to capsize it.[102] But that July Harold Lever and the Governor of the Bank persuaded a meeting of central bankers in Basle to share the burden by providing a $2 billion credit, under cover of which Britain could begin the gradual dissolution of the sterling area. This was a long-term achievement comparable to the withdrawal from East of Suez.

The August trade figure was unexpectedly better, and there was also a slight fall in unemployment (currently around half a million), so Jenkins had a slightly more positive backdrop against which to make his first speech as Chancellor to the Labour Party conference at the end of September. Since he was not a member of the National Executive, it was not certain that he would be allowed to speak from the platform

---

* While Jenkins was in Washington, Martin Luther King was assassinated in Memphis. Jenkins decided to attend the funeral in Atlanta three days later. He flew down with the Governor of New York, Nelson Rockefeller, and joined the four-hour march behind the coffin under a blazing sun, partly in company with Rockefeller and other liberal Republican governors, senators and congressmen, and partly with Bobby and Ethel Kennedy – an emotional occasion of which he wrote a memorable description in 1973.[101] Just eight weeks later Bobby himself was assassinated in Los Angeles.

– by the strict rules he could have been limited to just five minutes from the floor – but eventually the brothers relented and he grasped the opportunity to spell out the hard truth of the country's economic situation. 'I took a great deal of trouble with my speech,' he recorded, 'and worried about it more than about almost any other speech ever.' Britain, he explained, was not paying its way, but was being subsidised by other countries:

> I do say to you, therefore, that it is not some malevolent quirk of international bankers which makes a balance of payments surplus necessary for this country, it is the hard facts of life.

The 'shackles' of the IMF, he said, were often exaggerated:

> But if you want to have less to do with bankers, if you want fewer IMF visits here, the answer is straightforward: help us to get out of debt. [Applause] It is no good urging independence and denying us the policies to that end.[103]

In other words, he was begging the party, and the trade unions in particular, to accept the government's incomes policy, which had imposed a 3½ per cent ceiling on wage rises. That did not stop conference voting overwhelmingly against the policy later that day; but his speech was surprisingly well received: 'a near triumph but not quite one', as he characteristically scored it. (Dowler and Harris, monitoring its reception in the hall, thought that 'if Wilson had got to his feet, two-thirds of the audience would have too, and very good applause would have turned into a standing ovation'.)[104] At least he was not booed, as Denis Healey was when making a somewhat similar speech to a much more hostile conference in 1976.

But then the autumn was bad again. First, domestic consumption was still rising too fast, so he proposed to tighten hire-purchase restrictions – the extra shot he had deliberately left in his locker at the time of the budget. But this was strictly a matter for the Board of Trade, which gave Tony Crosland the chance to make difficulties of a sort that Jenkins found increasingly characteristic: his old friend was 'half in favour, half against, but always opposed to an immediate decision on any particular course. His view (very typically) was that we ought to do something different from the proposition currently under discussion, maybe more drastic, maybe less but certainly much later.'[105] Jenkins wanted to take moderate action quickly: he got his way eventually, but the announcement (made by Crosland on 1 November) was delayed ten days longer than it should have been.* This was 'a classic example of split control and fully justified my refusal to allow a revival of the DEA'.[107]

Then, after three better months, the October trade figures were disappointing, which triggered yet another sterling crisis – 'perhaps the most palpitating of all', in Cairncross's view.[108] Once again sterling was caught up in wider international instability caused by an expected devaluation of the franc and upward revaluation of the D-mark: in a single day (15 November) the Bank had to spend £250 million, about one-eighth of its reserves, to stop the pound going through its floor. Watching helplessly as the reserves flowed out, the Treasury was seriously considering another 5 per cent devaluation, before Jenkins decided – 'in a kind of last fling' – to use the 10 per cent regulator (further increasing purchase tax and excise duty) and impose import deposits (requiring 50 per cent upfront deposits from importers). His officials disliked the latter; but Jenkins overruled them, insisting that he could

---

* The deteriorating relations between Jenkins and Crosland were illustrated by a sour little spat in September 1969 when Jenkins objected to Crosland making a statement about the August trade figures without consulting him about it. Crosland's reply recalled the prickliness of their letters of thirty years before:

> I was at first astonished, then saddened, to receive so hectoring and pompous a communication from an old friend and Cabinet colleague. It was tempting to reply in kind. I refrain for the sake of our future relationship which, apart from anything else, is not unimportant to the Government and the Party.
> Your tone was curiously ungracious. There will always be some tension between the Treasury and the Board of Trade, the Chancellor and the President, and no doubt us two personally. But as virtually everyone in the Treasury knows perfectly well, you are very lucky to have had me at the Board of Trade in the last 2 years; and the degree of constructive tension between our Departments is just about right.

Crosland insisted that Presidents of the Board of Trade always made statements about the trade figures, and he would continue to do so: Roy would just have to trust his judgement, not bicker about 'trivia'. But Jenkins declined to back down:

> I would not have written to you in the terms I did if I had not felt strongly about the matter and if this feeling had not accumulated over some time. If, as you say, you attach importance to our relationship (which I most certainly do), I wonder why you do not give more consideration to the reason for my attitude.

His objection was that Crosland's statement could have had a serious effect on the foreign-exchange market:

> This is of great importance, and I bear the responsibility. This is not worrying about 'trivia'. It is a point on which the principle of consultation is essential. You know perfectly well that I do not seek to interfere with your judgement on any other aspect of Board of Trade work.
> Having said that I am content to let the matter rest, and like you I look forward to a long friendly talk as soon as possible.[106]

not hit the public again without also being seen to act directly against importers.[109] This mini-budget added another £250 million of extra taxation on top of the £923 million raised in March.

The next day he flew to Bonn for an emergency meeting of the Group of Ten finance ministers. This, he wrote years later, was 'one of the most chaotic and ill-organised monetary conferences ever to have plagued the Western world', thanks largely to the 'pedagogic verbal diarrhoea' of the German chairman, who must have talked 'for a good twelve of the fifty hours we were in Bonn'.[110] He was further frustrated by his European opposite numbers holding long meetings among themselves from which he and the Americans were excluded, which powerfully confirmed his conviction that Britain needed to be inside the EEC. Moreover the conference proved abortive, since the Germans stubbornly refused to revalue and the French – following a characteristic démarche by General de Gaulle – ultimately decided not to devalue after all, leaving sterling no less (but for the moment no more) exposed than it was before. After getting to bed at 4 a.m. Jenkins had to fly back to London after only two hours' sleep to make a statement to the House of Commons announcing the latest measures. Writing his speech all the way – 'the last page came out of the typewriter as we taxied in at London Airport'[111] – he was whisked to Westminster with a mortorcycle escort in seventeen minutes flat, just in time to get to his feet at 4 p.m. and managed once again to turn a tricky assignment into a remarkable parliamentary success. Three days later, after a weekend at East Hendred to recover, he further affirmed his authority by demolishing Ted Heath in the Chamber ('Roy did brilliantly,' Barbara Castle enthused) and then, at the party meeting upstairs, even managed to get Labour MPs of left and right eating out of his hand.[112]

Sterling then stabilised for ten days; but at the beginning of December there was another extraordinary scare when the City was swept by rumours that both Jenkins and Wilson had resigned, which caused another crazy run on the pound. At one point Jenkins was handed a message in Cabinet that the Bank had lost $100 million in forty minutes, before the markets rallied. But this turned out to be the darkest hour before the dawn. A couple of days later the November trade figures showed exports hitting a record £561 million and the deficit down to just £17 million – the lowest since July 1967. Sterling was not out of the woods yet – more encouraging figures in January 1969 were followed by a setback in February – but at least the balance of payments was now moving in the right direction. Alec Cairncross left the Treasury at the end of this traumatic year confident that devaluation was working.[113]

This was the background to Jenkins' second budget in April 1969. Many years later he wrote in his book *The Chancellors* – apropos Philip Snowden – that 'the difficulties inherent in a second budget after a considerable triumph with the first . . . are at least as great as those of writing a successful second novel'.[114] His problem was that he wanted to convey the message that the economy was on the right track, but could not yet risk easing the pressure on consumption. Once again the Treasury papers chart the process of narrowing the options. At the early meetings of the budget committee in the New Year the discussion leaned towards a neutral budget; but as the improvement in the trade figures still seemed fragile the consensus moved towards another round of belt-tightening. The budget judgement was 'more delicate than last year', when there was no question that very big measures were needed.[115] At the end of January Jenkins confessed that 'his difficulty in considering individual measures was that he was not yet clear about what was to be the main theme and purpose of the Budget'. He had some sympathy with Harold Lever's argument that more deflation would only damage confidence, with no economic effect.[116] He was still against increasing income tax or surtax, but still wanted to find new ways of taxing the better-off. He could not repeat his 'Special Charge'; a wealth tax was impractical; and he could not increase the differential against unearned income in what was to be billed as a 'savings budget'. He was still keen to tax convenience foods and pet food, also perhaps hairdressing and antiques, and (leading by example?) to increase the tax on wine. But there were awkward arguments against all of these. John Harris warned that 'we would pay an exceedingly high political price' for taxing convenience foods.[117] By early March Jenkins was looking to take another £200–250 million, but his officials were pressing for decisions: 'We have now reached the stage where the Chancellor must be told the deadlines for decisions on all candidates for his budget.'[118] In the end he took another £340 million, partly from some of the things discussed (potato crisps, wine, petrol, bingo and betting shops), but also from a 2½ per cent rise in Corporation Tax and another hike in SET, while simultaneously finding the money to raise the basic state pension by ten shillings (to £5) and raise personal allowances again to take 1.1 million more people out of tax altogether.*

---

* Jenkins' desire to tax the rich was largely unaffected by mixing with them at weekends, as Ann Fleming found when he and Jennifer lunched at Sevenhampton in October 1969. 'I *very very* mildly and for the first time criticised the CHANCELLOR,' she wrote to Nicko Henderson:

    I *only* said that if they brought in a wealth tax then everything I loved and to

It was a shrewdly balanced package, 'so ingeniously disposed', to Crossman's relief, 'that it won't hurt too much and will only increase the cost of living by ½ per cent'. Tony Crosland congratulated Jenkins on 'a good, fair and civilised Budget' which 'could well mean a real change in our political fortunes' – though he added: 'Needless to say there were bits I could have done without.'[120] Once again Crossman thought Jenkins' presentation of it to the Cabinet 'masterly . . . each item beautifully prepared by Roy and beautifully rehearsed . . . It only marks the contrast with the flaccid, indecisive bungling of Harold's central direction.'[121]

Jenkins' speech in the House was almost as long as the previous year and equally admired. 'In style at least,' the *Daily Telegraph* acknowledged, 'Mr Jenkins' 2½ hour effort yesterday was just about everything a good Budget speech should be: elegant as well as eloquent, good-humoured as well as having humourous touches, and well-planned.' Both sides of the House particularly enjoyed his twitting of the moustachioed Tory showman Gerald Nabarro, who had run a loud campaign against an increase in road tax: Jenkins timed perfectly his announcement that any such increase had been ruled out the previous December. But the budget itself was much less well received than the previous year. *The Times* thought it 'pusillanimous in its economic intentions and somewhat class-conscious in its detailed provisions' and condemned 'the niggling discrimination that mars so many of his choices of tax changes'. The *Financial Times* judged it, slightly more generously, 'a holding operation against the national and international uncertainties of the autumn'. But the mass circulation papers characteristically rubbished 'a dog's dinner of a Budget, with dearer potato crisps thrown in' (*Daily Mail*) and 'a Budget that is going to creep up on you like a pickpocket for the next 12 months' (*Daily Express*). Only the *Sun* (not yet owned by Rupert Murdoch and still Labour-supporting) was relieved that it was not more severe, giving the Chancellor credit for putting most of the burden in the right places.[122] In his memoirs Jenkins pointed out that it was his much harsher but highly praised 1968 budget that actually proved inadequate, while that of 1969 was if anything more severe than necessary, since it led to the first surplus of revenue over total expenditure since

which he was not averse would end – e.g. country houses and large tracts of unspoiled countryside; that Squire Eyston probably protected much of the beauty of East Hendred. I had hoped Jennifer was out of earshot, but no, she intervened with alarming vehemence; naturally I retreated, since I have always recognised the seagreen incorruptibility of the female of the species! She is far more formidable than Roy, not handicapped by the wish to please.[119]

1936/7 and, within a few months, the longed-for turnaround in the balance of payments – thus illustrating the dictum, attributed to Iain Macleod, that the instant judgement on budgets is almost invariably wrong.[123]* But at the time – accustomed to praise for practically everything he did – Jenkins was depressed by the negative verdict.

His depression deepened the next month when new fears of a French devaluation – sparked by General de Gaulle's sudden resignation – set off a fresh wave of selling of the pound, which in turn necessitated a 'sticky negotiation' with the IMF for a further standby loan. In his memoirs Jenkins remembered Friday 16 May as 'the nadir day of my whole Treasury experience', when he felt for the first time that 'I had used all the shots in my locker'. He vividly described how, returning from a visit to his constituency – alone, unusually – he settled down in the front first-class section of the 7.55 from Birmingham to Didcot for what he called 'a hundred minutes of intensive ratiocination'. He concluded that unless there was a clear and unmistakable improvement in the trade figures for May and June, the strategy he had pursued since devaluation would be seen to have failed. Far from replacing Wilson as Prime Minister, he would be 'a used-up Chancellor' – like Callaghan in 1967 – and would have to resign. If the pound was forced to float he could even see himself – like Snowden in 1931 – facing 'the dilemma which . . . every non-doctrinaire Labour politician . . . most dreaded': a conflict between the national and the party interest, which might destroy the Labour Party for a generation. At that time, he insisted, he saw no attractions in a coalition, which many on the

---

* Macleod, then Shadow Chancellor, was one of the few senior figures in politics with whom Jenkins could never get on friendly terms, finding him consistently petty, petulant and partisan. Maybe it stemmed from his having written a critical review of Macleod's 1961 biography of Neville Chamberlain. But according to Kenneth Baker, who as a young MP was part of the Tory team opposing the 1968 Finance Bill, 'Iain could not stand Roy Jenkins, who he thought represented the worst element of the soft left.'[124] In June that year Jenkins wrote to Macleod to try to improve their relations:

> I must confess that I feel more aggressed against than aggressing. No doubt you feel otherwise . . . But as you are one of the leading politicians on either side whom I most respect, it does seem a great pity. I would welcome a talk . . . I do not in any way wish to still controversy between us. But even when we disagree most strongly, we ought to be able to speak to each other![125]

But his olive branch was not accepted. 'When I eventually got him to lunch alone at 11 Downing Street (probably a mistaken venue) he sulked throughout the meal, declining both conversational gambits . . . and alcoholic refreshment.' In fact Jenkins did not rate Macleod very highly. Some years after his death he wrote that he was constantly struck by 'the contrast between the splendour of his phrases and the vacuity of his economic prescriptions'.[126]

left suspected him of wanting: he was still totally committed to Labour. 'It was merely that I could begin to see, as an added complication in a web of gloom, the emergence of a case for it.'[127]

Before getting off the train he wrote down the criteria that he judged would constitute success, and 'so felt rather easier in my mind, as perhaps do those who have just completed writing a suicide note'.[128] And within a few weeks the figures started to improve. First, Crosland's statisticians at the Board of Trade discovered a substantial underestimate in the export figures going back several years, which was a bonus in itself and incidentally gave Jenkins another parliamentary triumph later in the year when Heath and Macleod, 'with the almost incredible unwisdom which sometimes afflicts frustrated oppositions', accused him of falsifying the correction.[129] Then the May and June figures turned out better than he had dared hope – the monthly deficit down to £20 million – giving grounds for confidence that they really had turned the corner. There was still one last scare in August when the French did finally devalue without warning. Jenkins was on holiday, ironically in the south of France, where in the days before direct international dialling he was dependent on very poor telephone connections as the pound plunged again. He had to break his holiday and return to London (under cover of an emergency Cabinet called by Wilson to deal with the Northern Ireland situation, which had suddenly exploded); but this time the reserves took the strain, and within a couple of weeks the

"WHILE WE MUSTN'T PLACE TOO MUCH RELIANCE ON THESE WILDLY FLUCTUATING MONTHLY REPORTS - YIPPEE!"

Garland, *Daily Telegraph*, 16.9.69 (British Cartoon Archive, University of Kent)

reality of recovery was confirmed. Jenkins, appropriately, had just opened the Export Services Exhibition at Earls Court on 8 September, where he had given a cautiously optimistic speech, when John Harris gave him the August figures. "'£40m minus?" he asked. "No, £40m, plus," came the answer.'"[130] This, *The Times* reported when they were published a week later, 'far exceeded the most optimistic guesses abroad and in the City . . . The figures were greeted in Whitehall yesterday as proof that an export-led expansion of the economy was finally under way.'[131] Sterling immediately rose twenty-nine points. Jenkins' 'long dark arctic winter' was finally seeing the spring. His 'two years' hard slog' had almost achieved their purpose.

At that year's Labour party conference – having once again flown overnight from Washington, but this time after a much easier meeting with the IMF – Jenkins could bask in the delegates' relieved applause; but at the same time he warned that there could be no easing up on the need to build a strong competitive economy. He looked forward to a surplus of at least £450 million, maybe £500 million, over the coming year. But 'the fact that a big surplus now appears to be building up is no reason for premature relaxation'. In other words, he hinted, there would be no pre-election distribution of goodies. 'In the exuberance released by the Chancellor's good news,' *The Times* noted, 'many delegates clearly did not immediately take in the significance of his statement that the surplus is not going to be spent (by him at any rate) on all those worthy causes that the Labour rank and file have so closely at heart.'[132] Instead they actually cheered a social vision which some commentators thought had more in common with liberal Toryism than with Labour's traditional understanding of socialism. 'One of the central purposes of democratic socialism,' he declared, 'is to extend throughout the community the freedom of choice which was previously the prerogative of the few.'[133] This was a vision of personal liberation consistent with the sort of social reforms he had advanced at the Home Office, and which he had recently defended in his 'civilised society' speech at Abingdon in July. But 'choice' was not a word much associated with socialism in the past; still less would it be heard on the lips of Labour activists over the next fifteen or twenty years. Uttered by a successful Chancellor widely seen as the next Prime Minister, however, it was a striking marker of the direction in which Jenkins might have tried to take the Labour party if the electoral cards had fallen differently over the next few years: 'New Labour' twenty-five years before Tony Blair. This was perhaps the high point of Jenkins' career. Many years later he told a journalist that he still looked back on 'sipping a dry martini in the bar of the Grand Hotel, Brighton . . . sleepless but with the journey [from Washington] and the speech behind me, as the most pleasurable moment of my often bumpy Chancellorship'.[134]

If righting the balance of payments was the great success of Jenkins' Chancellorship, there were significant failures to set against it which between them dashed the government's prospects of re-election, on which his succession to the premiership depended. First was the perennial, ever-contentious problem in the 1960s and 1970s of incomes policy. In 1966 Callaghan had imposed a complete statutory wage freeze. In his first budget Jenkins relaxed this to the extent of setting a 3½ per cent ceiling on pay rises for the next eighteen months. Both were of course bitterly resisted by the trade unions and did lasting damage to relations between the unions and 'their' government. Jenkins disliked statutory control as much as anyone, but saw it as essential to appease the bankers. 'If we are not seen to deal strongly with wages,' he told Barbara Castle just before the budget, 'we can't avoid a second devaluation, world monetary confusion and the destruction of this Government.'[135]*

As Secretary of State for Employment and Productivity, Mrs Castle had the prime responsibility for selling the policy to the unions: she bit the bullet and defended wage restraint on socialist grounds as a necessary component of a planned economy. From their different standpoints, she and Jenkins worked surprisingly well together, with considerable mutual respect – though she often felt that he let her carry the can for unpopular policies. (On the other hand, she had much better relations with the union leaders, so it made sense for her to take the lead.) But then the question of income control became complicated by the government's even more unpopular attempt to reform trade union law on the lines of Barbara Castle's famous White Paper entitled, in a cheeky echo of Nye Bevan, *In Place of Strife*. As a sweetener to try to push this through, Jenkins announced in his 1969 budget that the powers to control wages would not be renewed, but would be replaced by a voluntary 'norm' of 2½–4½ per cent rises. This might well have been unenforceable anyway; but by the time the government had

---

* Ahead of his time, Jenkins also attempted to control inflation by squeezing the money supply: he was the first Chancellor to get daily reports on the Bank's money operations, and he actually fined the banks for lending too much. Enoch Powell – practically the only declared monetarist in Parliament at that time – applauded him for quietly doing the one thing that would reduce inflation, while pretending to do it by incomes policy, which merely transferred the blame for it from the government to the public.[136]

thoroughly antagonised the unions by *In Place of Strife* and then backed down in the face of union opposition, it did not stand a chance. The resulting pay explosion – average earnings rose by 13 per cent between the last quarter of 1969 and the last quarter of 1970 – fuelled the rampant inflation of the early 1970s which undid most of Jenkins' achievement in restoring the balance of payments. In economics, victory in one part of the battlefield is so often balanced by defeat in another.

The government's ignominious surrender to the unions over *In Place of Strife* probably contributed more than anything else to Labour's defeat the following year. Jenkins' performance in respect of this doomed policy – first backing it, then abandoning it – was, on his own admission, inglorious; in his defence, his attention was primarily focused on the repeated crises of sterling. The policy, championed by Barbara Castle with the full support of the Prime Minister, was designed to deal with the wave of unofficial strikes which was damaging industrial output (and hence exports). She saw it as a balanced package, which guaranteed union rights in return for outlawing unofficial strikes; but the unions – backed somewhat cynically by Jim Callaghan in a successful bid to rebuild his support with the party – saw the attempt to bring legal sanctions into industrial relations as an attack on union privileges and fought it tooth and nail. Jenkins persuaded himself that legislation to curb strikes would make up for dropping the incomes policy, which was threatening to become counterproductive. 'I thought . . . this was a good bargain,' he wrote in his memoirs.[137] But it was not, since the unions did not accept it. He would have done better to have heeded the advice of Andrew Graham (then a young adviser to Wilson, much later Master of Balliol) who warned that 'while a policy to improve industrial relations may be complementary to an incomes policy, it *cannot* be a *substitute* for it . . . and to push ahead with it *at the expense* of incomes policy would, in my view, spell disaster'.[138] It did: the government ended up with neither an incomes policy nor legislation on industrial relations. But having decided to back legislation, Jenkins committed himself to it as strongly as Castle and Wilson and even insisted on announcing it himself in his budget speech, with Mrs Castle giving the details the next day. This was his second mistake, since it made trade union reform look like an economic sop to please the IMF, which only heightened opposition on the left. It was 'an odd political decision', wrote the *Guardian*'s labour correspondent Peter Jenkins, 'by a Minister who was beginning to get the reputation for "keeping his head below the parapet"':

Nobody was asking him to go to the lengths of mingling his blood publicly with Barbara Castle's. He was exceeding by far the terms of their demarcation agreement . . . Chivalry to a lady colleague was verging on the quixotic. It was a political error for an ambitious man.[139]

Thus at the very moment when Mayhew's plotters were waiting for a signal from him to launch their coup to make him Prime Minister, Jenkins had bound himself not only to Barbara Castle, but to Wilson. By early summer 1969, as opposition to the bill mounted, his supporters were begging him to back off. Tom Bradley, his PPS, told him several times that 'the bill was the only thing standing between me and the premiership'.[140] Roy Hattersley recalled visiting East Hendred in an unsuccessful attempt to move him. His 'lofty refusal even to contemplate deserting Barbara Castle both dashed any hope I had of his becoming Prime Minister and made my suggestion of a premature strike for Downing Street seem profoundly squalid'. Instead they sat in the garden academically discussing other potential Prime Ministers who had missed the bus.[141] If Jenkins' refusal was honourable, it was also realistic, since unlike the previous year he was no longer the only alternative to Wilson. By leading the opposition to the bill from within the Cabinet, Callaghan had reinvented himself as a powerful contender who probably commanded wider support across the party: any attempt to replace Wilson now, Jenkins told Hattersley, would lead to a 'bloodbath' and the new government would not last a year.[142] Moreover – this he did not tell Hattersley – his own position was weaker than it seemed, since this was exactly the moment when he was contemplating having to resign in a couple of months if the balance of payments did not come right. So this was not really such a missed opportunity as it seemed.*

But then he did renege after all. At the critical meeting of the Cabinet on 17 June – actually two meetings – at which the Chief Whip, Bob Mellish, warned that they would not be able to get the Bill through the parliamentary party, Crossman, Crosland, Shore and others backed Callaghan in urging compromise. Wilson, defiant for once, refused to capitulate and threatened to resign if the Cabinet did not support him. Jenkins was conspicuously silent, 'looking pretty worried', according to Barbara Castle, and intervening just once to warn, rather

---

* Hattersley's visit to East Hendred is not recorded in Jenkins' normally very detailed engagement diary. But he has described it so vividly more than once that one hesitates to doubt his memory.

feebly, that they were leaving her in a very difficult position.[143] On the one hand, he had told Crossman that morning, he felt duty bound to support Barbara, 'though I really believe in the policy less and less'. On the other, Crossman too was dangling the premiership under his nose, urging him to think of the party: if he resigned with Wilson and Castle he would leave Callaghan to take over unchallenged. They actually discussed the mechanism for replacing the Prime Minister: 'how the Party meeting should be called and whether Roy could go to the Palace direct'. Jenkins promised to stand if Callaghan made a bid for the leadership.[144] Before the second meeting he asked Mrs Castle to come to his room at 4 p.m.:

> There he told me, with that evasive look he has been developing lately, that I would have gathered that he no longer thought the fight was worth the cost. I replied that, yes, I had noticed it. But he would realise that Harold and I could not back down. If we could not get an acceptable compromise we would both resign. He looked unhappier than ever, saying that this would have a very bad effect on the Party morale, 'More because of your resignation than Harold's, if I may say so' . . . I replied that . . . it was impossible for Harold and me to capitulate . . . Now he was looking even more unhappy as a crash seemed inevitable.[145]

At the second meeting he said even less. In the end the Cabinet, to save Wilson's face, agreed to give him a free hand to negotiate with the TUC; and the next day he and Mrs Castle secured a 'solemn and binding' assurance that the union leaders would use their best efforts to prevent unofficial strikes. Wilson did his utmost to present this as a satisfactory outcome; but no one was fooled. This was his second humiliating defeat on a major policy, which left him further damaged. But no one came out of this episode with much credit. In his memoirs Jenkins regretted the 'sad failure of Mrs Castle's trade union policy'.[146] With hindsight, having once supported it, he would have done better to have had the courage of her convictions and stuck with it. The combination of Prime Minister, Chancellor and First Secretary might have been able to force it through. Alternatively he could have strengthened his position in the party by distancing himself from the start. As it was, his late defection left him with the worst of all worlds. He not only lost the policy for which he had given up his incomes policy, but he confirmed the suspicion of his critics (and some of his supporters) that he was not a fighter. David Owen was one who judged it a fatal mistake to 'ally himself to a sinking ship and then abandon it'. The defeat of *In Place of Strife*, on this view, marked the beginning of Labour's takeover by the unions and the militant left in the 1970s. Had the government stood up to the TUC in 1969, Owen believed, Labour would have won the 1970 election and Jenkins would have become Prime Minister in a year or two.[147] This is probably exaggerated, typical macho posturing after the event. But the important thing for the future was that Owen came to believe it.

In time the unions had cause to regret opposing *In Place of Strife* so bitterly. Two years later they defeated very similar (though more legalistic) legislation brought in by Ted Heath's Tory government (with Wilson and Mrs Castle now opportunistically egging them on); then – ironically – they used their untamed muscle to destroy Jim Callaghan's government in the 'Winter of Discontent' in 1978–9. Only when Mrs Thatcher and Norman Tebbit in the 1980s passed a series of Acts that really did emasculate them did they realise, too late, that *In Place of Strife* was a very moderate and constructive attempt to regularise the conduct of industrial relations which they would have done better to have accepted. In the long run, as Jenkins acknowledged, Wilson and Barbara Castle actually 'emerged with more credit than the rest of us'.[148]

Three months later, the humiliation of *In Place of Strife* seemed to have been magically exorcised by the improvement in the economy. September's stunning trade surplus was not a flash in the pan, but was followed by similar figures in the following months, so that the final balance for 1969 showed a surplus of £387 million (compared with deficits of £461 million in 1967 and £398 million in 1968) and sterling ended the year comfortably above its $2.40 parity for the first time since devaluation. From trailing the Tories by twenty-four points (55:31) in the Gallup poll in July, the government cut the margin to single figures (46:37) in September and to almost nothing (46:44) in October. Suddenly, from the certain prospect of defeat, it seemed possible that Labour could win the next election after all. In a series of cautiously boastful speeches around the country in November Jenkins claimed, with characteristic precision, that the economy had been turned around in 731 days – that is, exactly two years from devaluation (1968 was a leap year) – and looked forward to a balance of £500 million in 1970.[149] The question he now faced was what to do with his hard-won surplus. The squeeze of the past two years having achieved its purpose, how much relief could he afford to give to taxpayers and consumers? His last critical challenge as Chancellor would be the 1970 budget.

At the beginning of February he asked the Treasury for comparative projections for three options: a neutral budget, a £100 million expansion, or a further £100 million restriction.[150] All the official advice pointed to a broadly neutral budget. Jenkins was determined to do nothing to jeopardise the balance of payments. Nevertheless he thought that the Treasury was taking prudence too far. He interpreted 'neutral' as allowing tax reductions up to £100 million, and asked for a fourth diagram showing the effect of a £200 million expansion.[151]* While his junior ministers – Jack Diamond (Chief Secretary), Dick Taverne (now Financial Secretary) and Bill Rodgers (Minister of State) – all wanted to cut the standard rate of income tax, by threepence or even sixpence, Douglas Allen warned that too generous a budget would damage foreign confidence. Jenkins' preference was to take more lower-paid workers ('at least 2 million') out of tax and extend tax relief further up the scale.[153] He also wanted to help the elderly.[154] In the meantime, however, he was becoming worried about soaring public-sector pay. At Cabinet on 12 February, when every spending minister in turn pitched for his own department's deserving claimants – teachers, nurses, postal workers, the armed forces – he delivered what Barbara Castle called 'a typical Chancellor's sermon' warning that an 'avalanche' of claims (now running up to 20 per cent) would lead back to another round of deflation by the summer if it was not halted. With unblinking cynicism, Wilson proposed phasing in the increases so that the impact was not felt until after the election:

> If the Labour Party were then returned to power, it would no doubt be distasteful to have to introduce a policy of restriction immediately thereafter; but this situation would have to be faced. If, on the other hand, they lost the Election . . . the Conservative Party . . . would have to shoulder the responsibility for dealing with the potentially inflationary problem which they would have inherited.[155]

In other words, Barbara Castle paraphrased, 'He would rather win the election and have a November Budget than have July measures and lose the election. It was all pretty crude and Roy reacted loftily: "I would rather lose the election than jeopardise our economic

---

* These elliptical diagrams were known in the Treasury as 'MacDougall's Flying Saucers', after the new chief economic adviser, Sir Donald MacDougall. Jenkins was a good enough statistician to be fascinated by them. He would take them back to East Hendred for the weekend, and often asked for more elaboration on Monday morning.[152]

success.'"[156] What Jenkins actually said, according to the official minutes, was marginally more nuanced:

> It could be argued to be better for the Labour Party that they should lose the next Election but should leave behind them a record of sound management of the economy than that they should put that record at risk in order to achieve an electoral victory which might be no more than marginal. He could not endorse this course; and . . . he would judge it wiser to continue to resist excessive wage claims.[157]

Tony Benn was equally disgusted by Wilson's cynicism, and his account confirmed the other two.[158] All three Cabinet diarists, however, were worried that Jenkins' high-minded attitude would lose Labour the election. That weekend, after he and his family had all been to lunch with Roy and Jennifer (and Edward) at East Hendred, Crossman described what he took to be the Chancellor's dilemma:

> Roy is now making up his mind about his budget. He can be cautious and conventional, and keep his reputation as Chancellor, making an election defeat absolutely certain and keeping himself in position to seize the leadership afterwards, or he can conceivably take the other risk and have a more expansionist budget, which could give us a chance of election victory but could also ruin his reputation if it went wrong. I wonder.[159]

Three days later Mrs Castle, Benn, Peter Shore and Tommy Balogh all dined at Crossman's and tried to guess which way Jenkins would jump. They all took it for granted that he would do whatever he thought would serve his own interest, and were afraid he reckoned his best chance of becoming leader was following an election defeat. 'If Roy thought we were going to win the election he would produce a Budget that would help us,' Benn summed up, 'and if he thought we were going to lose he would produce a Budget that would allow him to leave as the Iron Chancellor, with his reputation unaffected . . . Barbara said that Roy would then go into the City and get a well-paid job and this was his real interest.'[160] Crossman thought rather that he feared that if Labour won 'the whole thing will continue in the same way with Harold and Jim at the top and Roy as number three. Then he might join me in writing books.'[161] (Crossman was leaving Parliament at the election to become editor of the *New Statesman*.) Benn believed

" CAN I GIVE YOU A HAND ?"

Garland, *Daily Telegraph,* 17.3.70 (British Cartoon Archive, University of Kent)

that Jenkins probably did want Labour to win 'because he wanted to be Foreign Secretary, and subsequently Prime Minister when Harold was got rid of'.[162] They agreed that they must somehow persuade him to have a popular budget. 'It was settled that Dick and I should try to dine with him next week,' Mrs Castle recorded, 'and convince him that, if he made a Budget that contributed to our defeat, he would be finished politically.'[163] One way or another, as Crossman put it, they all felt that the government's fate lay in the hands of 'this strange, in-scrutable young man, this extraordinary mixture of ingenuousness, feminine petulance and iron determination'.[164]*

At a special meeting of the 'Inner Cabinet' (about half the full Cabinet) at Chequers on Sunday 8 March Crossman and Mrs Castle were joined by Tony Crosland in pressing for a 'class redistributive budget' with big tax concessions targeted at the lower paid. Mellish begged emotionally, 'Don't do a Stafford Cripps on us, Roy.' But Jenkins stood firm:

He insisted that we had invested so much political capital in solving the balance of payments that confidence in the Government depended on our maintaining a good surplus . . . It was far better

---

* Youth is of course relative. Jenkins was forty-nine – but Crossman was sixty-two, and Barbara Castle fifty-eight.

not to do too much in the Budget and reflate selectively in the summer by other means if the outlook was propitious.[165]

Crossman despaired of Jenkins' 'conventional, rigid, narrow, low-risk' strategy, aimed solely at protecting the balance of payments. 'But it was quite clear he had swung Harold to his side and that Callaghan and Healey were also with him.'[166] Crosland apart, it was a broadly left–right split. Jenkins did agree to dine with Crossman and Castle three days later; but after the Chequers meeting he was not prepared to talk any further about the budget, so Crossman expanded the event into a social evening with spouses. 'It was good fun,' Barbara recorded. 'But we didn't succeed in getting much out of Roy, except that he needs a lot of sleep and never works in the evenings. When I asked him casually what job he would like other than Chancellor, he headed me off.'[167]

Maybe Jenkins was more influenced than he let on, since back in the Treasury the next day he told his officials that the projected £100 million giveaway was too pessimistic: he now thought he could afford to boost demand by £150 million.[168] At least one academic adviser, Michael Posner, was alarmed that '£100 million between friends has increased by about 50%.'[169]* But MacDougall's latest forecast supported the case for a mildly reflationary budget. Whatever his final judgement, Jenkins was anxious to present it as positively as possible, leading to some discussion between his officials about how to massage the figures. 'On this basis,' Douglas Wass (who had succeeded David Dowler as Jenkins' Principal Private Secretary in 1969) minuted William Ryrie on 3 April, attaching the most favourable formulation he could contrive, 'the Chancellor would reasonably be able to show that his proposals come very close indeed to forming a £200m Budget.'[171] In the end Jenkins announced a giveaway of £220 million, composed mainly of increased personal allowances for the lower-paid and raising the earnings limit for pensioners. But this was widely regarded as disappointing, and it was in truth a remarkably dull budget, delivered with something less than his usual style. The only welcome novelty was the abolition of stamp duty on cheques (which was Bill Rodgers' idea). Labour backbenchers were visibly unenthusiastic ('Muted welcome for a Scrooge-like Budget' was the *Times* headline);[172] while the Treasury's press digest summarised the consensus of the rest of Fleet Street:

---

* In his memoirs Jenkins remembered this slightly differently. He recalled Posner resolving the dispute between the Chancellor and his more cautious officials by saying that '£100 million or so between friends is nothing much to worry about.' Either Posner changed his mind or Jenkins' memory was wrong.[170]

The *Telegraph* finds it dull. The *Guardian* says it's almost too cautious. The *Mail*, *Sketch*, *Express* and *Star* are more disappointed. The *Star* talks of a few crumbs after a 2-year hard slog. The *Express* also talks of crumbs, and the *Sketch* of a miserable share out of the petty cash.[173]

Significantly, however, both the *Daily Mirror* and the *Sun* dubbed it 'an honest budget'.[174] And curiously, in view of their earlier anxiety, the diarists were surprisingly positive. Crossman thought the limited giveaway 'the correct, prim and proper thing to do, and it is also positively socialist, because the remission only apples to people with incomes between £16 and £19 a week';[175] and Barbara Castle conceded that 'psychologically he [Jenkins] is striking the right note of sustained growth, much as I would have liked him to do more. We have now invested so much political capital in his strategy we had better stick with it.'[176]

On television that evening Jenkins adopted the tone of the responsible bank manager. He celebrated the fact that Britain's trading position was now 'one of the strongest in the world' and the pound once again 'a strong currency', and explained that his purpose in the budget was to 'consolidate success' by pursuing 'a sensible middle course, neither rash nor mean'. He warned against excessive pay rises ('If wages were not going up so fast I would have been able to make more concessions in the budget. That is simple common sense. You cannot have things twice over'), but stressed that while it was not a soft budget, 'virtually everything in it is a benefit'. There was 'no effective increase in tax for anybody. And nothing to cause or justify an increase in prices.' In short, he concluded, 'I believe it is a fair budget', which had been made possible by the hard work and national success of the past two years: 'a budget not just for today but for the year as a whole, and for the future as well'.[177]

Gradually over the next few days it appeared that the public – reflecting the *Mirror* rather than the *Express* – appreciated his responsibility. Within a week the polls were showing Labour, for the first time since 1967, moving into a lead over the Tories. David Butler interviewed Labour party workers and found them attributing the swing explicitly to the budget. 'Jenkins' Budget had made a good impression because it was without tricks or gimmicks and . . . Jenkins himself made a very good impression on television,' said one regional organiser. The Transport House Press Officer admitted that 'Roy Jenkins' budget was now seen to have been a very good thing. It really would not have done Labour any good to offer goodies in an election year.'[178] Even Crossman now conceded that 'not having an election budget might have been electorally the cleverest thing to do. It is clear that Roy's posture has paid off. He is honest Roy, Aristides the Just.'[179]

After Labour lost the 1970 election Jenkins' over-fastidious refusal to bribe the voters with a giveaway budget was widely blamed, particularly by the left, for the result. Barbara Castle, for one, quickly reverted to her earlier view and spent the next thirty years bitterly propagating it. 'I remain convinced,' she wrote in her memoirs, 'that Roy Jenkins' Budget was the primary cause.'[180] Once Jenkins had become a hate-figure – first over Europe in 1971–2 and later for defecting to form the SDP – it became a settled part of Labour mythology to make him the scapegoat for the government's defeat. But this mythology flies in the face of the facts. If anything, it was Jenkins' budget that very nearly won Labour an election it had never looked like winning before. All the evidence is that voters were sick of transparently cynical pre-election giveaways and responded positively to Jenkins' more adult approach. The economic wisdom of the budget is still contested. With hindsight Jenkins himself came to believe that the Treasury advice had been too cautious, overstating the level of demand already in the economy, so that he could have afforded to give away a little more than he did (though even that was more than they approved). The counter-argument, made at the time only by *The Economist*, is that unchecked wage inflation was already doing quite enough to stimulate the economy.[181] Given that the Conservative government inherited both rising inflation and rising unemployment, either position is tenable. 'Purely economically', Jenkins later reflected, the budget might have been a bit too restrictive. 'But politically it was the best budget we could have had.'[182] Arguably it was too popular. The only way the 1970 budget can be said to have contributed to Labour losing the election two months later was that its success tempted Wilson to go to the country too soon, before the turnaround in the balance of payments was incontrovertibly established – thus inviting the very charge of opportunism to which he was most vulnerable.

Actually Wilson claimed to have pencilled in a June election ever since 1966: among other things, he hoped to gain a boost from England successfully defending the football World Cup in Mexico. But up until the budget most calculations had assumed an autumn election, and most press comment immediately afterwards assumed that its caution confirmed this expectation. It was the sudden leap in the polls, confirmed by good local election results on 7 May, that led Wilson to gamble on

June. Jenkins was initially doubtful. 'Roy was clearly in favour of waiting until October,' Crossman wrote on 4 May.[183] But the local elections, plus the enthusiasm that he encountered on a visit to Birmingham, brought him round. By 10 May he was 'beginning to think that we ought to work on the June assumption', if only because the government could not put the genie back in the bottle once it had been released.[184] The rest of the Cabinet acquiesced without much difficulty, and on 18 May Wilson announced the election for 18 June. John Harris did point out that the May trade figures were due to be published on 15 June. But in the prevailing mood of over-confidence neither Jenkins nor Wilson listened.

'After the event,' David Butler and Michael Pinto-Duchinsky wrote in their Nuffield study of the 1970 election, 'it is difficult to record how completely the astonishing Labour upsurge in the polls had swept most commentators and politicians off their feet.'[185] With far more polls than ever before, Labour began the campaign with a lead averaging around 7 per cent, which barely moved over the next three weeks. This had been enough to secure a landslide majority in 1966, so there was virtual unanimity in Fleet Street that Wilson, after all the vicissitudes of the past four years, was coasting back to Downing Street with another comfortable majority. As the principal architect of the government's recovery, Jenkins naturally played a leading part in trumpeting Labour's record and ridiculing Heath's increasingly desperate warnings that the economy was not as sound as he pretended. He spoke more widely around the country, accompanied Wilson at four of Labour's morning press conferences and gave several television interviews.* Britain's balance of payments was now the strongest in the world, he told Robin Day on *Panorama*, and sterling was strong. To talk about another devaluation in these circumstances, he insisted, was 'absolute nonsense'; while Tory scares about a looming crisis were 'pure moonshine'.[187] Delivering what was generally reckoned to be the best of Labour's five television broadcasts – the others were given by Wilson, Callaghan, Short and Wilson

---

* Ann Fleming mischievously attended a meeting he addressed at Swindon on 5 June, standing conspicuously at the back in a fur coat (in June!), having promised not to heckle. Nicko Henderson (then Ambassador to Poland, but home on leave) went too. 'I was struck by how fit he looked, as if, despite the election campaign, he had spent the last weeks on holiday in the Mediterranean. By contrast, the others on the platform looked distinctly pale.' They all met up the next day for lunch at a *Good Food Guide*-listed pub, the White Hart in Hamstead Marshall, which was full of wealthy Tories. '"Roy's much more likely to get eggs thrown at him here than in Swindon Town Hall," I suggested to Ann as we arrived. "Yes," she replied, "but they will be *oeufs en cocotte*, much more suitable for our Roy than raw eggs."'[186]

again – Jenkins claimed the economic turnaround as 'a great national success story in which the nation as a whole is entitled to take pride', and promised that Labour would now use Britain's new economic strength to promote growth by means of regional policy and positive action to eliminate poverty, protect the environment (a newly fashionable concern) and improve the quality of life. 'This is one of the biggest gulfs between the two parties,' he asserted. 'We believe the community must do a lot of the job. They believe it can mostly be left just to happen, but it won't . . . Only you can help us maintain this advance.'[188] He might not use the word very often, but Jenkins in 1970 was still in a real sense a socialist.

He did not expect to carry on as Chancellor, however. It was an open secret that Wilson had virtually promised him a move to the Foreign Office, where he would have responsibility for overseeing Britain's renewed application to join the Common Market. Before accepting, Jenkins told George Thomson that he had secured Wilson's assurance that he was absolutely committed to achieving entry this time.[189] Talking freely to David and Debbie Owen when he visited Plymouth during the campaign, he said that he wanted to 'move fast towards Europe' while recognising that it would be necessary to 'nurse the Left and Right wings of the Labour Party through the European transition'. At the same time he promised to 'break the Government's "absurd, almost craven silence" over Vietnam' and openly criticise 'the whole of the US's Vietnam policy'. (In this view Owen thought he was influenced by his Democrat friends in the US.)[190] Jenkins was greatly looking forward to becoming Foreign Secretary, which would have given him a full hand of the great offices of state as preparation for becoming Prime Minister.

Though privately critical of much of Labour's record, particularly the waste of the first three years, and of Wilson's often devious performance as Prime Minister, he still felt that the government deserved to be re-elected. At just 2.2 per cent, growth between 1964 and 1970 had actually been slower than in 1959–64. But with a projected current account surplus of £735 million for 1970 and £1,058 million in 1971, he believed that he had laid the foundations that would allow Labour to advance in the next Parliament the social reforms that it had promised but generally failed to deliver since 1964; and which he himself had a reasonable expectation of succeeding Wilson in a couple of years. (Wilson told him that he intended to step down once he had overtaken Asquith's tenure, which would be in June 1973.) In fact Jenkins was not only over-confident, but over-sanguine about the inheritance he left to his – as it turned out Tory – successor. The balance of payments was stronger, certainly, and sterling temporarily secure; but both higher inflation and higher unemployment were in the pipeline: the dreaded combination later dubbed 'stagflation'. In his only Commons speech as Chancellor before his early death, Iain Macleod – getting his own back for Jenkins repeatedly wiping the floor with him over the past three years – asserted: 'I do not see how anybody . . . could conceivably claim that it is a happy heritage that we have taken over'.[191] And during the election it seemed that Macleod's and Heath's warnings did finally get through to the electorate, raising doubts about Wilson's and Jenkins' sunny optimism.

The Tories' most successful television broadcast showed a pound note being snipped away by a pair of scissors to produce what they called 'Labour's ten-bob pound' – a graphic illustration of the effect of inflation, which was not countered by Jenkins' warning that Tory policies would make it worse. But the most serious blow to Labour's success story was delivered by the publication of the May trade figures on 15 June: exports were somewhat down on recent months, while the import figure was swollen by the exceptional delivery of two jumbo jets costing £18 million, giving a deficit of £31 million. Jenkins and Wilson had actually known about this ticking bombshell since 1 June, but the figure was so clearly an aberration, and would be announced so late in the campaign, that they decided against either trying to fiddle the figures or changing their narrative. In the event Heath had a field day, claiming that the one great achievement on which Labour based its case for re-election had been rumbled. Jenkins toured the television studios trying to limit the damage, but 'it is difficult to look self-confident when running round trying to plug holes in a dyke'.[192] The Tories' private polls – which they immediately released to the press – showed an increasing number of voters inclined to believe their warning of another crisis and saying they trusted a Tory more than a Labour government to handle it: this was clearly the crucial switch in voting intention.[193] Even so, it only showed up in one little-noticed opinion poll (ORC) published on polling day, which gave the Conservatives a 1 per cent lead; the others (Gallup, Marplan, Harris and NOP) all still pointed to a comfortable Labour victory. On the way to his count in Stechford, Jenkins was still confident enough to discuss with the family whether they should continue to spend weekends at East Hendred or at the Foreign Secretary's country house at Dorneywood.

The result – the loss of seventy-six Labour seats, turning Labour's 1966 majority of ninety-eight into a Conservative majority of thirty

– was a shock, but not, Jenkins claimed in his memoirs, a devastating one. 'I was surprised but in no way incredulous . . . My belief in a Labour victory had been firm, but skin-deep, for I had not believed in it for long . . . While disappointed, I was not shattered by what had occurred.'[194]* For one thing, he had long maintained that the regular alternation of administrations every few years was generally healthier than one party holding office for too long; and he personally, after the intense strain of the past six years, was ready for a period of recuperation. He had enjoyed a rapid rise, in those few years, from semi-detached backbencher to the second place in the government; but he was still only forty-nine and felt that he had plenty of time ahead of him to take the next step. He had no inkling that this was actually the peak of his career, or of how quickly his position in the Labour party would deteriorate in opposition.

---

* Jenkins' personal result in Stechford showed a higher-than-average swing against him – 7.1 per cent against a national swing of 4.7 per cent and a West Midlands swing (boosted by the local influence of Enoch Powell's lurid warnings about immigration) of 5.6 per cent. His majority, though still quite safe, was almost halved, taking it roughly back to its 1964 level, though on a lower turnout he still won 56 per cent of a substantially enlarged electorate:

Roy Jenkins (Labour)	22,559
J.B. Stevens (Conservative)	15,848
D. Hardy (National Democrat)	1,438
S. Pegg (Communist)	298
Labour majority	6,711[195]

14 Europe before Party

LOSING office is a shock – especially when defeat is as unexpected as it was for Labour in June 1970. Writing in 1971, Jenkins compared the experience to that of a prisoner released after several years inside. 'There is a sense of release, but also a certain apprehension that the props of a familiar routine and the well-known jailers have been removed. A combination of greater freedom but greater responsibility for one's own life stares one sternly in the face.' He found himself initially not only without an official car or office, but with no staff: even his long-time secretary, Bess Church, was on holiday, and he was hopeless at coping by himself. He soon regained one of his familiar props by persuading Collins, his publisher, to employ John Harris as his part-time research assistant at £1,000 a year; and in 1972 he acquired another younger aide, Matthew Oakeshott, paid for by the Rowntree Foundation.* Meanwhile since Jennifer's ancient Morris 1300 was mostly kept in East Hendred, he used taxis to get around London until, as he noted in his diary with due self-mockery, he ventured onto the

---

* As an Oxford undergraduate in 1966 Oakeshott had been involved in a breakaway from the left-dominated Labour Club uncannily like that which Jenkins and Crosland had led twenty-six years earlier. In 1972 he and David Lipsey successfully answered advertisements to become aides to Shadow ministers. Jenkins had them both to lunch (separately) at East Hendred and chose Oakeshott – partly, Lipsey believed, because he (Lipsey) had the temerity to beat Jenkins at croquet, but probably more importantly because Jennifer approved of Oakeshott.[1] Lipsey was then assigned to Crosland. Both became closely identified with their respective patrons over the next few years. Oakeshott went with Jenkins to the Home Office as a special adviser in 1974, filling the role hitherto taken by John Harris; he was closely involved in the creation of the SDP in 1981, fought Cambridge for the Alliance in 1983 and became a Liberal Democrat peer in 2000. Following Crosland's death, Lipsey stayed with Labour and became a Labour peer in 1999, but served on Jenkins' inquiry into the voting system in 1998.

Underground for the first time in six years on 16 July. For a few weeks he felt disoriented. 'In July I felt lost. In August I had a holiday [five weeks in Tuscany]. In September I got back to normal.'[2]

'Normal', however, was a life very different from that he had lived up to 1964. Then he had been a semi-detached backbencher, as much a writer as a politician. Now he was an ex-Chancellor of the Exchequer, still Labour's principal economic spokesman and widely seen as the next leader, with a major decision to make immediately. Despite having led the government to defeat, Wilson had no intention of stepping down as leader; but George Brown's loss of his seat in Belper had created a vacancy for deputy leader. The deputy leadership was in truth not much of a job: since it was created to save Herbert Morrison's face in 1951, no deputy had ever succeeded to the leadership and it was by no means always held by the second man in the party. Nevertheless, when vacant it provided an opportunity for an important test of strength, as much between the different wings of the party as between individuals. Most of those who now considered themselves Jenkinsites – Bill Rodgers, George Thomson, David Owen, Dick Taverne, David Marquand and Bob Maclennan – thought it essential that Jenkins should stand for the Gaitskellite right against Michael Foot, the standard-bearer of the left, and he had little hesitation in agreeing. With hindsight he might have done better to have followed the example of Jim Callaghan and let it go. But Callaghan already had a seat on the National Executive as party treasurer, whereas the deputy leadership would give Jenkins a formal position in the party which he had hitherto lacked. Wilson encouraged him to go for it, possibly in order to bind his most dangerous rival to his leadership. Barbara Castle, however – whose unpublished diary for these years provides a vivid commentary on the deep split which quickly reopened in the party – was furious that the job was being 'carved up for Roy', and objected to Jenkins being handed a power base on the NEC 'to which he could never get elected'. She threatened to stand herself until Wilson firmly discouraged her.[3] In the event Fred Peart (the former Minister of Agriculture and Leader of the House) stood as a third candidate on an anti-Common Market ticket. The result was by no means a foregone conclusion; but on 8 July Jenkins was comfortably elected on the first ballot with the votes of 133 Labour MPs against sixty-seven for Foot and forty-eight for Peart (though no fewer than thirty-nine abstained). 'It really is ironic,' Mrs Castle fumed, 'that the party had endorsed so wholeheart-edly the man who denied them growth.'[4] But the vote, which seemed to confirm Jenkins as front-runner for the eventual succession, was

'Heir today, gone tomorrow—eh Roy?'

Gibbard, *Guardian*, 9.7.70 (British Cartoon Archive, University of Kent)

widely hailed as evidence that Labour was now a responsible governing party interested in regaining power as quickly as possible and was not, as so often in the past, going to swing left in opposition.

That soon turned out to be a mistake. But the deputy leadership contest did furnish one ominous pointer to the future. Jenkins had naturally hoped that Tony Crosland would support him; but Crosland declined to give him any such assurance, indicating that he would probably back Callaghan. When Callaghan did not stand, Crosland was possibly one of those who abstained rather than support his old friend. This, Jenkins noted, was 'a phase, an important one . . . in the deterioration of our political relationship'.[5] It was also an important symptom of the fragmentation of the Labour right.

Jenkins soon found the chores of frontbench opposition more demanding than ministerial work. For one thing he was expected to spend far more time in the House of Commons. 'As Chancellor,' he wrote in the *Observer*, 'I answered questions once a month and made perhaps six speeches and six Ministerial statements a year. In opposition I find it necessary to be present for Question Time and part of the debate for at least three and possibly four days a week.'[6] For a man who liked to spend every minute of his day purposefully, either at work or in relaxation, hanging about listening to other people's speeches was intensely aggravating. As a star performer, he loved the big debates in the Chamber with the back benches cheering him on; he never stayed on to gossip in the bars and tea-rooms afterwards, preferring to escape to his own haunts with his own coterie. When forced to mix with his fellow MPs his awkwardness and evident reluctance only increased his reputation for aloofness and elitism. He could still shine in set-piece debates: reappointed as Shadow Chancellor – not, as he might have hoped, Shadow Foreign Secretary – he replied effectively to Iain Macleod's one speech as Chancellor before his death, refuting the charge that he had left behind an economic crisis.[7] His speeches on these occasions were invariably carefully prepared and powerfully delivered. But he soon found it harder to be authoritative in opposition than in government with the resources of the Treasury behind him; and the first time he substituted for Wilson at Prime Minister's Questions on 17 November he was 'badly carved up' by Ted Heath, which dented his confidence for a time.[8]*

As well as weekly meetings of the Shadow Cabinet, where as Shadow Chancellor he still spoke with authority, Jenkins had a new obligation as deputy leader to attend the National Executive – an uncongenial body dominated by the trade union leaders and the resurgent left, on which he found himself increasingly out of place. Over the twenty-one months that he sat on the NEC he attended seventeen out of twenty-three full meetings; he was also an *ex officio* member of all sub-committees, and attended about half the meetings of the Home Policy committee and the International committee, as well as various other party bodies like the National Council of Labour. But the Finance and Economic Affairs committee, which he chaired, met only four times; he was determined to keep economic policy to himself in consultation with his former Treasury colleagues like Dick Taverne and Harold Lever and other chosen advisers, excluding left-wing members

---

* In reality Heath merely patronised him – 'The right honourable Gentleman will have to do rather better than that if he is permanently to occupy the place of his right honourable Friend the Leader of the Opposition' – but in the House of Commons bearpit that is enough.[9]

of the NEC like Ian Mikardo: this proved an expensive dereliction, which allowed Mikardo and others to develop a far more left-wing programme in the Industrial committee.[10] Jenkins also had to make a lot more speeches to Labour audiences around the country, and was expected to attend the whole of the party conference in October. He had always disliked the conference – especially when it was held at Blackpool – and privately described the 1970 gathering as 'a thoroughly disagreeable week', adding typically that 'The gloom and strain were added to the filthy, oppressive, damp, muggy weather.'[11] Now entitled to speak from the platform, he made what the *Guardian* called a 'powerful and statesmanlike' speech in the economic debate, attacking the new Chancellor, Tony Barber, for frittering his inheritance, which Tony Benn thought had 'entrenched him strongly with the delegates'.[12] But in a sign of the rapidly changing mood of the party he was heckled by Eric Heffer and other prominent left-wingers. 'That week in the Fylde,' he wrote in his memoirs, 'took some of the edge off my zest for the politics of opposition.'[13]

He got back with much more enthusiasm to writing. Even as deputy leader and Shadow Chancellor he had no more intention of treating politics as a full-time job than when he was a backbencher. He noted in his memoirs that he received no offers from the City of the sort he was pretty sure would have been made to an outgoing Tory Chancellor. He was not greatly worried by this, however, partly because he never had any interest in finance or money-making for its own sake, but mainly because he could earn more from writing. Privately he confessed to being 'a little surprised and disappointed' that John Lewis did not want him back.[14]* But within weeks of losing office he was negotiating with publishers and newspapers a package of contracts worth several times more than his parliamentary salary. His diary shows him lunching with Ian Chapman of Collins on 30 June and 16 July, with Harold Evans of the *Sunday Times* on 15 July, and with William Rees-Mogg of *The Times* on 21 July. First he undertook to write for *The Times* over the next three years a series of ten biographical essays (10–15,000 words each) on a number of recent historical figures, for £1,500 each,

---

* In fact he did get one offer: he was invited by Leslie O'Brien to become a non-executive director of the Charterhouse Group at a salary of £2,000 a year for one meeting a month; he declined for the moment, and again two years later when he was sure he did not need the money. His tax return for 1972–3 also shows that he received £3,000 from Rothschild's for services unspecified. That year he declared a total income of £35,135, mainly from writing, of which his parliamentary salary plus expenses comprised just £5,546. (His salary as Chancellor had been £8,500.) He paid his secretary Bess Church £1,300.[15]

plus an unspecified number of articles on issues of the moment. Then he resumed book reviewing for the *Observer* at £120 per review. In this first year he also wrote for both the *Observer* and the *Sunday Times* the long, thoughtful pieces already quoted reflecting on his contrasting experience of the Home Office and the Treasury. Most substantially – having abandoned the idea of writing Gaitskell's biography – he contracted with Collins (for £30,000 over three years) and the American publisher Doubleday for a book comparing several pairs of American and British leaders, to be entitled *The Presidency and the Prime Ministership*, which was also to be serialised in the *Sunday Times*. He assured Harold Evans that it would be 'based on a good deal of research' and told him in January 1971 that he was already working on Franklin Roosevelt and Lloyd George.[16] All that appeared, however, were two very bland articles in the *Sunday Times Colour Magazine* in August and September 1973. The contract was renegotiated later that year, but the book never materialised, though he did write some 50,000 words which eventually formed the basis of his 1984 biography of Stanley Baldwin.

What did appear steadily over this Parliament were his biographical essays for *The Times*, eventually published in book form in 1974 (one having fallen by the wayside) as *Nine Men of Power*. Jenkins' first list of possible subjects included several – Lord Beaverbrook, Jawarhalal Nehru, Iain Macleod and Nye Bevan – whom he later dropped, probably because he could not have trusted himself to be fair to them. The final selection perfectly reflected his political sympathies and perspective. Three were Labour figures: Gaitskell (written for the tenth anniversary of his death in 1973 – 'For many of us there is a sense of long term deprivation which, as the years go by, persists and even increases'); Ernest Bevin (of whom he wrote memorably that when he became Foreign Secretary 'there was no other position in the Foreign Office, unless it was that of a rather truculent liftman on the verge of retirement, which it would have been possible to imagine him filling'); and Stafford Cripps ('almost the only post-war Chancellor' – until Jenkins himself is the unspoken implication – 'to depart with his colours flying high'), who additionally fascinated Jenkins, as a student of career patterns, as one who 'for a short time exercised an authority as great as it is possible to achieve without occupying the premiership itself, and who came to it by a route which is one of the least obviously charted in the history of British politics'.[17]

Three were American, reflecting Jenkins' close identification with the post-Roosevelt Democratic Party: classless, progressive, liberal and outward-looking, his model of what the Labour Party could be, if it would only shed its antiquated commitment to old-time socialism. FDR himself – the architect of the New Deal – he left to his planned book on Presidents and Prime Ministers; but two of the three Americans in *Nine Men of Power* represented different aspects of his legacy. Adlai Stevenson, the Democratic candidate for the presidency twice defeated by Eisenhower in 1952 and 1956, was to Jenkins an American Gaitskell: a civilised liberal who would not stoop to conquer, but nevertheless 'inspired a generation'. Jenkins had got to know him well in the early 1960s and had spoken to him on the phone, arranging for him to come to lunch at Ladbroke Square the next day, an hour before he collapsed and died in a London street in 1965. He admired both Stevenson's modesty as a candidate ('I don't *have* to be President') and his grace in defeat ('He was too old to cry, but it hurt too much to laugh').[18] Even his inability to decide whether to run again in 1960 Jenkins portrayed as part of his attraction. He felt a lot of sympathy with Stevenson in his own dilemmas in 1970–73.

Robert Kennedy was a very different sort of Democrat. Under the influence of J.K. Galbraith and Arthur Schlesinger and his continuing friendship with Jackie, Jenkins still romanticised the Kennedys. Jack he had hardly known, but Bobby he came to know quite well, and in *Nine Men of Power* he wrote of him very movingly – first with the world at his feet before Jack's assassination, then 'completely disoriented' after it; finally, the last time they met, walking together at Martin Luther King's funeral in Atlanta eight weeks before Bobby too was shot. Like others, Jenkins by then saw in Bobby much more than the ruthless Irish machine politician he had once been, and wrote poignantly of his rapidly maturing statesmanship, his compassion, vision and surprising rapport with 'the dangerously alienated elements of American society', and of his great potential had he lived.[19] Jenkins may have been a bit star-struck, but there is love in this essay.

Jenkins felt no love at all for his third American, the Communist-hunting Republican Senator Joe McCarthy, the 'black joker' in his pack, of whom he could never have written a full biography, but whom he thought a phenomenon worth the three to four weeks he spent on each of these studies. His remaining three subjects were Lord Halifax (another odd choice, but an instructive career); the interwar French socialist leader Leon Blum (a nod to his father here); and J.M. Keynes, the only non-politician of the nine and the only one Jenkins never met or even saw ('It is a great deficiency which I wish I could retrospectively repair. There is no figure of the past generation (with the possible exception of Roosevelt) with whom I would more like to have talked').[20] The interest of their subjects apart, these nine essays represent the consummation of Jenkins' mature style: polished, urbane and epigrammatic, breathing a perfect confidence in his own political assumptions and historical judgement. The book is studded with passages of excellent writing; but one sentence from the essay on Blum illustrates both its quality and its limitations:

> He was the one man who, from a dismal continent, with Hitler creating a new barbarism in Germany, with Mussolini grooming Italy for the role of predatory auxiliary, with Spain on the verge of eruption into the cruellest and most international of civil wars, with power in England about to pass from the fading benignity of Baldwin to the harsher defeatism of Chamberlain, might have sent back an answering light to the uncertain signals of encouragement which came across the Atlantic from Roosevelt.[21]

The long sentence is superbly constructed and reads impressively. Yet it contains no thought that is in the least original; rather a catalogue of solidly conventional judgements complacently accepted as received truths. The effect is achieved by the arresting choice of words, particularly adjectives, and the final graphic image. Jenkins' writing always relied heavily on pictorial metaphors, often extended to ingenious length. These made for vivid reading, but at the risk of running away with the meaning, so that content could come to be determined by style. A facility with images seems to be a peculiarly Welsh characteristic, exemplified by those other great Welsh orators Lloyd George and Aneurin Bevan; it was an important part of Jenkins' force as a politician. But in his writing it carried the danger that once he had hit on an image he was pleased with, he would pursue and elaborate it to wearisome and sometimes comic effect: he wrote quickly and disliked revising what he had written, because he thought in images rather than ideas. This is one reason why he was an effective populariser, but never an original historian.

Jenkins wrote these nine essays mainly in the recesses of the parliamentary year, starting with Bevin in October 1970 between the Blackpool conference and the return of Parliament (though it is still hard to see when he found the time, since his engagement diary was as packed as ever with lunches and other meetings filling every day); then Kennedy over the Christmas holidays at East Hendred, with the rest following over the next three years until the February 1974 election spared him the necessity of deciding on a tenth.

In addition to this lucrative hobby he also managed a good deal of travelling on his usual mixture of business and pleasure. In December 1970 he visited New York and Washington, where he delivered one economic speech, but also managed to meet all the leading Democratic contenders for the presidency (Teddy Kennedy, John Lindsay,* Ed Muskie and George McGovern) and fitted in a visit with Arthur Schlesinger to Roosevelt's house at Hyde Park. (While in New York he stayed with Lindsay in the Mayor's mansion; in Washington he stayed at the British Embassy, as he usually contrived to do on his travels to foreign capitals.) A year later he returned to America to deliver three foreign policy lectures at Yale, combined as always with a whirl of Washington and New York dinner parties. The lectures, published as a slim volume entitled *Afternoon on the Potomac?*, Jenkins himself described in retrospect as 'a slightly tiresome sermon to the Americans telling them that they had to adjust from total pre-eminence to being merely *primus inter pares* . . . expressed in florid prose'.[22†] Later in this Parliament he made further trips, usually with Jennifer, to Persia (as Iran was still known), Singapore, India and newly independent Bangladesh, in February 1972; to Africa (January 1973); and to China and Australia (October 1973). On all these visits he combined sightseeing with meetings with the national leaders (the Shah, Mrs Gandhi, Deng Xiaoping, Gough Whitlam), and then wrote up his impressions in lengthy articles for *The Times*, very much in the style of his political travelogues for *The Current* in the 1950s, but now with the added gravitas of a senior statesman and potential Prime Minister.

Politically it soon became clear that he faced a difficult time. The first sign that Labour in opposition was going to repudiate much of what it had advocated in office came with the party's decision to fight the Tory government's Industrial Relations Bill, even though it was substantially similar to Barbara Castle's aborted White Paper of barely eighteen months before. Mrs Castle herself, in an undignified effort to repair her credit with the unions, vowed to fight her successor's Bill 'tooth and nail, line

---

* Lindsay was then a Republican, but switched to the Democrats in 1971 to contest the Democratic nomination.
† *Afternoon on the Potomac?* met with mixed reviews in Britain, ranging from the *Times Literary Supplement* ('frank and statesmanlike') to Patrick Cosgrave in the *Spectator*, who loathed 'the narcissism of Mr Jenkins' style', his 'mean and pampered mind', his 'tepidity of spirit' and his 'assumed hauteur . . . that so many of his colleagues in the Labour Party find repulsive'.[23] Under new ownership, the *Spectator* was now virulently Conservative.

by line . . . We shall destroy this Bill.'[24] Jenkins thought this not only hysterical but hypocritical. At the Shadow Cabinet on 8 October 1970 he warned that the public wanted something done to curb the abuse of union power: Labour should therefore offer 'moderate but not screaming opposition' until the committee stage, and then 'hammer them' on some of the detail.[25] But screaming opposition was what the unions demanded; Wilson – at the time more interested in writing his self-vindicating account of the Labour government – tamely agreed, and as deputy leader Jenkins had to toe the line. As the complex Bill ground its way through Parliament in early 1971, accompanied by mass demonstrations and 'days of action' (that is, strikes), he earned Mrs Castle's contempt by complaining that all-night sittings left him more tired than he had been as Chancellor. (To be fair, Crosland and Lever complained too.) Jenkins was told he could go home early the next time, so long as he was back by 8 a.m.[26] The Bill finally carried, but was rendered unworkable by the unions' refusal to implement it. Meanwhile this battle set the tone for Labour's determination to paint the Heath government as the most reactionary since the 1930s, to be opposed by every possible means, as the left increasingly made members of the previous government eat dirt to make up for their failures in office.

At an all-day meeting of the Shadow Cabinet in January 1971, recorded by Barbara Castle, Jenkins tried to argue for a more responsible approach to opposition. Labour's aim should not simply be to regain power, but to prepare itself to make a greater success of the next government than it had of the last. Incomes policy he now believed was crucial, more so than reforming industrial relations, so that he came close to apologising for *In Place of Strife*. ('I attached too much importance to what could be done legislatively with IR. The trade off in my budget was false.') The Tory government, he argued, was 'doctrinaire and uninspiring', but not necessarily incompetent. 'They will be changing things; we mustn't just be in favour of keeping things as they are.'[27] Sadly neither the official minutes nor Mrs Castle recorded the upshot of this discussion. A few weeks later, however, Jenkins was 'clearly disturbed' by Jim Callaghan's support for Reginald Maudling's Immigration Bill, frankly designed in response to Enoch Powell's stirring of the racial pot, which many believed had helped Heath win the election. It tried to restrict the number of 'New Commonwealth' (that is, black and Asian) immigrants entering the country by creating a new provision for 'patrials' – those with parents or grandparents born in Britain, who were by definition largely white citizens of the 'Old' Commonwealth. 'It was surely an entirely new principle of English law,' Jenkins objected, 'that you go round asking people who their grandfather was.'[28] Despite their differences, Barbara Castle at this stage still could not help liking Roy. 'He may not be a Socialist,' she reflected, 'but at least he is a radical. Jim is neither.'[29]

Far more serious was the party's reversal on Europe. In June 1970 all three parties had gone into the election supporting a renewed application to join the Common Market. For most of the past decade the heat had been taken out of the European controversy by General de Gaulle's veto of the Macmillan government's application in 1963. Labour's anti-Marketeers had not been too worried by Wilson's conversion to making a second attempt, since it clearly had no chance of success so long as the General ruled France: in 1967 he duly repeated his veto. But Labour's application still lay on the table; and following de Gaulle's retirement in 1969 his successor, Georges Pompidou, was known to look more favourably on British membership. In this situation a Labour government re-elected in 1970, with Jenkins as Foreign Secretary and George Thomson as chief negotiator, would have re-presented its application and Wilson as Prime Minister would have remained committed to its success. ('Not just committed,' he assured Jenkins, but 'dedicated'.)[30]* In government, Wilson could have overridden the confirmed antis and kept the majority of the party substantially united on a pro-Europe line. Instead it was Ted Heath who picked up the historic opportunity to renew the negotiations for which he had been personally responsible in 1962. Within days of the election Tony Barber, as Minister for Europe, submitted the application which had been prepared for Thomson. But almost as quickly Labour began to backtrack. All the party's old suspicion

---

* Indeed the recently published official history of Britain's relations with the European Community has revealed that Wilson and Jenkins were committed not just to joining the existing Community, but to early movement towards a single currency. Visiting Paris as Chancellor in February 1970, Jenkins assured his French opposite number, Valéry Giscard d'Estaing, that Britain would have no difficulty in moving 'as far and as fast as any member of the Six'. When Giscard suggested that 'in due course there might be only two currencies of any importance – the European currency and the US dollar – Jenkins did not demur and confirmed that the British Government "did not want to reserve the monetary field from the Community and were prepared to move far in this field". When Wilson saw the record of this conversation, he minuted his approval: "Yes. Interesting. Chancellor seems to me to have given all the right answers."'

Five weeks later Wilson and Jenkins together met the Swedish Prime Minister, Olof Palme, in London and told him that there was 'a new momentum within the Six towards some form of monetary union, to be achieved by the end of 1978 or 1979. Jenkins . . . thought the date a little optimistic and that it might slip into the 1980s . . . Wilson did not gloss what Jenkins had said in any way.'[31] No commentator seems to have picked up this revelation of how deeply Britain was committed to the single currency more than forty years ago.

of Europe was fanned back to life by the loss of the election and its loathing of Heath; and in the interest of party unity and the doctrine that the Opposition's job is to oppose, Wilson began to equivocate about what terms of entry Labour would find acceptable.

The very day after the election he told Barbara Castle that it was 'not inconceivable that the terms they get . . . will not be acceptable to us'. 'So that's what the wily old devil is plotting!' she noted with delighted admiration.[32] The next day Tony Benn – hitherto pro-Market – hinted that he too was 'having second thoughts about the market and ready to challenge the Tories on it'.[33] Dick Crossman, now editing the *New Statesman*, used its columns to lead the shift to outright opposition; while the defection of Eric Heffer, a leading left-winger who had previously supported entry, was an important indicator that Europe was being shaped into a left–right divide, with the centre increasingly siding with the left. By the turn of the year the antis had gathered 100 signatures for an Early Day Motion opposing entry, and the supporters of entry – which had been the policy of the Labour government just six months before – were being made to feel like a beleaguered minority.

Thus opened the critical battle of Jenkins' career: a battle which, in the course of 1971, quickly destroyed his position in the Labour Party and eventually drove him out of it. The pros and cons of membership of the Community soon became subsumed in the wider question of political morality and ultimately the very purpose and direction of the Labour Party. On the first question he remained resolute. He refused to get bogged down in niggling about the terms of entry. 'I am in favour of strong bargaining,' he wrote in *The Times* in May 1971 when the Tory negotiations were nearly complete. 'But we must not lose sight in the process of the purpose of the exercise', which was to get Britain in. 'The terms themselves are not in any circumstances going to sound overwhelmingly attractive. An admission fee never does . . . But anything will appear extortionate unless we have a lively idea of why we want to join.' Taking almost for granted that access to the European market would stimulate Britain's sluggish economy, he emphasised more than ever the political and psychological benefits of membership: Britain's political opportunity inside Europe as a counterweight to France and Germany, and a united Europe's power for good in the wider world as a counterweight to America and Russia and a source of aid to the developing world:

Good transitional terms are necessary. So are honourable arrangements for those overseas who are economically dependent upon us. But necessary too is a full appreciation of the wider issues involved and a clear appraisal of the opportunities before us. What this country needs is a little more realistic self-confidence. Without it we face a future of narrowing horizons. With it we can find a new role as rewarding as any in our history.[34]

Even more impassioned now than such repeated statements of his old faith, however, was Jenkins' stand on the principle that Labour must not deny in opposition what it had proclaimed in office. When Jim Callaghan, his finger as always on the pulse of party feeling, signalled his intention to oppose entry not merely on the likely terms, but on any terms – claiming, quite irrelevantly, to be defending 'the language of Chaucer, Shakespeare and Milton' – Jenkins retorted sharply. Speaking in Birmingham on 18 June, the first anniversary of the election, he was careful to begin by blaming the Tories for 'a rapid devaluation of the standards of British politics'. Elected on 'an utterly bogus prospectus' to reduce prices and unemployment, they were now watching helplessly as both soared. But his point was that Labour must not mirror this duplicity, but rather make a stand for 'honesty and consistency' in public life:

I can see no basis on which it was right to seek entry in 1967, and to persist in this enterprise in 1968, 1969 and the early part

" .. AND HE MARCHED THEM DOWN AGAIN .... "

Garland, *Daily Telegraph*, 29.7.71 (British Cartoon Archive, University of Kent)

of 1970, but to oppose it in principle in 1971 . . . unless we believe that a party should take a different attitude to the nation's interests and say different things in Government than in opposition. I do not believe that.

Public opinion, he conceded, might have swung against entry; but it had swung before and could swing again. 'In any case, I do not believe that it is always the duty of those who seek to lead to follow public opinion.'[35]

This was widely interpreted as a challenge to Wilson. The cartoonists had a field day – Garland in the *Daily Telegraph* depicted Jenkins as a noble Brutus honourably stabbing Caesar in the front[36] – and the pro-European commentators once again contrasted his shining integrity with Wilson's slippery opportunism as he prepared to follow Callaghan's lead. 'The great build-up of Roy Jenkins and the denigration of Harold is in full flow,' Barbara Castle complained. 'Really the lengths to which the press is prepared to go these days to discredit anti-Marketeers are limitless.'[37] Wilson bitterly resented the denigration, but insisted that he knew what he was doing. His job, he told her, was to hold the party together and avert a split. 'That means I have to come out against the terms in my own time and in my own way. I am about to go through the worst three months . . . in my political life. The press will crucify me. But I will bring the party out of this united and then I am seriously giving up the leadership.'[38] By the time he finally gave it up in 1976, following a cosmetic renegotiation of Heath's terms and the constitutional innovation of the 1975 referendum, he could claim to have succeeded, after a fashion, while ensuring that Britain did in the end remain in Europe with solid public endorsement. Indeed it could be said that it was the anti-Europeans whom Wilson ultimately double-crossed.

By the end of his life Jenkins was half prepared to recognise this backhanded achievement. But at the time he believed that Wilson could have achieved both his objectives by playing it very differently, without dragging his own reputation though the mud. Labour was badly split on Europe, with deeply held views on both sides; its own recent record made nonsense of its opportunistic desire to oppose; and the likelihood was that Heath's application would succeed whatever Labour did. In these circumstances, Jenkins maintained, 'the only sensible course was to let the Heath Government get on with it, show complete tolerance to its large pro-European minority and generally play the issue in a minor key. Instead it did exactly the reverse, with predictably disastrous consequences.' By the time he came to write his memoirs in 1991 Jenkins had developed a theory – based on the Tories' split over tariff reform after 1903 and David Owen's behaviour in relation to nuclear weapons in the 1980s – that political parties cannot resist returning obsessively to the issues that most divide them, instead of leaving well alone and focusing on those that unite them.[39] Wilson's manoeuvring over Europe did not, after all, hold Labour together in the long run. Though the party did not formally split until 1981, five years after his retirement, the seeds of that rupture were sown by his allowing the left to hound and harass the pro-Europeans in 1971–2.

Jenkins had no wish to challenge Wilson in 1971; he would rather have supported him in holding the European line against Callaghan, who posed a far more dangerous threat to his leadership, and in a friendly conversation on 9 June he told him so. But Wilson would not be placed in a position of dependence on the Jenkinsites; he was determined to play it his own way.* On 23 June, however, he could not prevent the NEC voting by a narrow majority (13:11) to hold a special one-day conference in London on 17 July, which widened the rift. (Ironically the vote was swung by Shirley Williams, an ardent pro-Marketeer, switching sides because she thought it the proper democratic thing to do.) In the meantime Wilson's attempt to limit the argument to the detail was demolished when the government published the terms it had obtained from the Community, and George Thomson – the minister who would have led Labour's negotiation – promptly declared that he would have accepted them, supported by all three of the others who had held responsibility for Europe between 1966 and 1970 (George Brown, Michael Stewart and Lord Chalfont). But the terms were now irrelevant. The mood of the special conference was expressed by a newly elected Welsh firebrand, the twenty-nine-year-old Neil Kinnock, who declared uncompromisingly that 'Because I want to see the Tories beaten, and because I am willing to use any weapon to beat them, I am against EEC entry on these terms at this time.'[41] On the other side John Mackintosh (MP for Berwick, but also Professor of Politics at Edinburgh University) made the most passionate pro-European speech. No vote was taken; but in his closing speech Wilson edged closer to outright opposition to entry on any terms.'It was like watching someone being sold down the river into slavery,' Jenkins wrote, 'drifting away,

---

* He may well have been right not to trust the Jenkinsites. 'If Wilson loses his support on the left,' Bill Rodgers was reported to have said, 'he won't have any at all. And we'll cut his bloody throat.'[40]

depressed but unprotesting.'[42] Just as they had done with Gaitskell's 'thousand years of history' speech nine years earlier the Jenkinsites sat grimly, refusing to applaud.

As part of the minority on the NEC, Jenkins was not allowed to speak at the special conference. But two days later his frustration burst out in one of the most powerful speeches of his life at a meeting of the parliamentary party. He agreed that a Labour Cabinet would have accepted the so-called 'Tory terms', which were as good as anyone could have realistically hoped for: to suggest that Labour would not have accepted them was to say that the whole 1967 application had been a sham from the beginning. Exempting those like Barbara Castle and Fred Peart who had opposed the application all along, he bluntly condemned Wilson's and Callaghan's cynicism and derided their alternatives. Wilson's 'kith and kin' argument that Britain had a duty to protect the Commonwealth was mere sentimentality: Australia was 'the toughest, roughest, most self-interested Government with which I ever had to deal'. Callaghan's prescription he dismissed with contempt:

> Jim Callaghan offered running the economy flat out for five years. That is not a policy: it is an aspiration. We were not lacking in aspirations during the early days of the last Government. What we were lacking was results.

The third alternative was the left's: 'Socialism in one country'. 'That is always good for a cheer. Pull up the drawbridge and revolutionise the fortress. That is not a policy, either; it's just a slogan' – unconvincing in itself and hypocritical when dressed up as Labour's contribution to international socialism. If Britain rejected Europe, Jenkins warned, she would not have 'rugged independence', but merely greater dependence on the USA:

> I beg the party not to follow this recipe for disappointment and decline but to face problems realistically and to lift its eyes beyond the narrow, short-term political considerations of the moment.[43]

'It was a powerful speech,' Tony Benn conceded, 'and the arguments carried a great deal of weight.' But it was also 'an arrogant and an elitist speech', which was immediately seen as 'a direct attack on Harold Wilson and also on Healey and Crosland, who had climbed off the fence against the Market'.[44] Among the Jenkinsites it aroused enormous enthusiasm, with great banging of desks 'in which quite clearly many of the floating voters of the party joined'.[45] But its defiant tone and personal gibes also gave huge offence. If Jenkins had intended only to defend his own position, he soon realised that he had gone too far, allowing the anti-Europeans to portray him as the splitter. 'It could have developed into a standing ovation at the drop of a hat,' wrote Barbara Castle, who had spoken earlier and was furious that she had been persuaded to keep her speech low-key. 'I realised then why he had insisted on speaking last and why the room was so packed'; it was 'as clearly organised a demo as I have ever seen, and an anti-Wilson demo at that'. In the dining room afterwards, when Jenkins stopped at her table, she told him 'savagely' that she had always liked and trusted him, but never again. 'Roy was obviously shaken, bridled nervously and moved away.' (Jenkins himself recalled this encounter in very similar terms.) Wilson too, she recorded, 'was obviously shaken by the night's events . . . As we walked together to the division lobby, he agreed that this was war. "Perhaps you will now listen to some of us," I pleaded with him. "They've always been out to get you and they think this is their chance." He said grimly that he had some hard thinking to do.'[46]

The next day Tony Benn found Wilson still 'extremely agitated about Roy Jenkins' great speech' and determined to slap him down: 'I don't know why I go on. But I'll smash CDS before I go.'[47] The old Bevanite–Gaitskellite divide – almost healed between 1964 and 1970 – was reopened with a vengeance. The next day Wilson charged the Jenkinsites with operating 'a party within a party' (exactly the charge that Attlee had levelled at the Bevanites in 1952) – 'no less so because it meets outside the House in more socially agreeable surroundings'[48] – and wondered sarcastically how people like Bill Rodgers and Roy Hattersley could sully their purity by accepting Shadow spokesman-ships. Rodgers immediately sought a meeting with Wilson to ask whether pro-Europeans were now ineligible to sit on the front bench. Wilson assured him this was not so, and a fragile front of tolerance was restored. At the Shadow Cabinet on 21 July Michael Foot told Jenkins that he should make it clear in his speech in the European debate the next day that he was not challenging the leader. 'Roy looked affronted at this and said haughtily that he would make his own speech in his own way and so we left it.' Barbara Castle thought this 'a healthy bloodletting', but reckoned characteristically that 'we came off best'.[49] In the House the next day, while repeating his commitment to Europe, Jenkins did pay qualified tribute to Wilson's leadership; and when he sat down he received 'a pat on the back which looked almost complimentary'.[50]

The summer recess brought a month's respite. After a week together in Lebanon, Roy and Jennifer holidayed separately – she in Greece, he in Italy, where he stayed in turn with a succession of British friends in agreeable villas: two days with Bill and Sylvia Rodgers (plus the Hattersleys) on Lake Bracciano; a week with Mark and Leslie Bonham Carter at Policastro in the far south; four days with Ronald and Marietta Tree in Florence and two with Isaiah and Aline Berlin near Portofino; with a busy round of other house guests, lunches and dinners in each place, leavened by sightseeing, tennis and bathing. For once he does not seem to have done much writing. The looming vote on the government's application to join the EEC, to be taken at the end of October, can never have been far from his mind.

At the beginning of October the party conference – that year in Brighton – carried overwhelmingly the NEC's motion to reject the Tory terms.* But at a pro-European fringe meeting Jenkins made clear that he and others would refuse to toe the line. Less provocatively than in July, he claimed 'no monopoly of rightness or sincerity':

I do claim that we are entitled to stick to the beliefs which we have long held. I do not apologise for doing so. I reject utterly the view that . . . we are supporting the Tories. My aim is to increase the future opportunities and influence of the Labour Party.

To underline his anti-Tory credentials he used his speech in the economic debate to accuse Heath and Barber of 'the most abject and deliberate betrayal of election promises in modern British history', but also repeated his plea for Labour by contrast to restore integrity to politics.[52] 'He is the figure dominating this Conference; there is no question about it,' Benn wrote.[53] But the more the press lauded him as the only man of principle, the more pressure he came under from the party loyalists.

Back at Westminster, there were two big questions: whether Labour would impose a three-line whip and, if it did, whether the deputy leader could defy it without resigning. For three weeks the Jenkinsites agonised. 'Roy Jenkins presided over endless discussions about the possibility of a "free vote",' Roy Hattersley remembered, 'and how we

---

* The margin was officially 5:1. But this was almost entirely due to the block votes of the unions, only one of which balloted its members. Analysis of the constituency parties showed a much narrower margin of just 3:2 against Europe.[51]

should react if the Shadow Cabinet decided on rigid discipline. Most of the meetings were no more than the search for safety in numbers.'[54] Beyond the inner core of his supporters there were still sixty or seventy, perhaps as many as ninety, long-standing pro-Marketeers, including several robustly independent characters like Tam Dalyell, Willie Hamilton and Betty Boothroyd, whom they hoped to keep on board. There was huge pressure from the whips, their colleagues and constituency parties that they could salve their consciences while preserving party unity by abstaining; but Jenkins' unwavering determination, helped by Bill Rodgers' skilful whipping, helped to keep them solid. From the outset Jenkins was clear that the vote on 28 October would be an historic occasion comparable to the Great Reform Bill, the repeal of the Corn Laws or the vote that brought down Neville Chamberlain in May 1940, and he conveyed this sense of destiny to his followers. 'People didn't want to say when asked in the future what did you do in one of the great divisions of history, "I abstained".'[55]

Up until the last week he still hoped to persuade the Shadow Cabinet to allow a free vote (as both Wilson and the Chief Whip, Bob Mellish, had earlier promised) or at least a reasoned amendment which the pro-Marketeers could support. On 18 October he proposed a form of words: 'That this House, recognising the deeply held differences of view about the terms negotiated for entry into the EEC, has no confidence in the ability of the Government to deal with the consequences that will come after our entry.'[56] But positions had hardened since the summer, and Wilson was now determined on outright rejection. But then the government – calculating that the Labour pro-Europeans substantially outnumbered the Tory antis – announced a free vote on its side. For a moment Wilson believed that Labour would have to allow a free vote too: Heath's reluctant granting of a free vote torpedoed the idea that, by voting for Europe, Labour MPs would be keeping alive the hated Tory government, since it could no longer be regarded as a confidence motion. But Benn – occupying a key position as that year's party chairman – insisted that Labour MPs could not have a free vote when conference had determined its view; and a second meeting of the Shadow Cabinet summoned at short notice at 7.15 that evening decided that the government's statement 'in no way altered the decision taken by the Committee earlier in the afternoon'.[57] Unfortunately Jenkins was absent, having already gone out to dinner (with David Watt of the *Financial Times*). Next morning he protested furiously, claiming that he had only left the House at 7.07. He was not the only absentee: just twelve members of the Shadow Cabinet were present. But Wilson was unyielding, suggesting only that Heath's 'apparent liberality' should be countered by demanding a General Election. Shirley Williams picked this up and proposed a motion recognising the deep divisions in the party, condemning the government's divisive economic policies and calling for 'a free vote of the people' through a General Election.[58] Michael Foot offered to consider this if Jenkins undertook to try to limit the number voting with the government. But Jenkins, according to Barbara Castle's account, would have none of it. '"Tony and Michael must accept that some of us are determined to vote with the Gov[ernment]. I cannot accept Michael's bargain." So that was that.'[59] The majority voted to confirm the earlier decision for a straight 'No' vote with a three-line whip. Both were endorsed by a party meeting later that evening. But Michael Stewart's motion to support the government was defeated only by 151:87 – showing the number of potential rebels holding up well – and Willie Hamilton's plea for a free vote failed only by 140:111.*

The vote came at the end of a six-day debate in which, once again, Jenkins and the other pro-European members of the Shadow Cabinet (George Thomson, Harold Lever, Shirley Williams and Douglas Houghton), bound by collective responsibility, were debarred from speaking. In the final days the pressure on them mounted from all sides: 101 Labour MPs signed a round robin begging Jenkins to think again, for the sake of the party which was bigger than any of them. Thirty-seven Birmingham councillors and aldermen signed a petition calling on all the city's Labour MPs to vote against. (But Jenkins was covered on this front, having already obtained the backing of the Stechford party to vote according to his conscience.) Others, including 'quite a lot of fairly good people', begged him to abstain in order to maintain Labour as a viable alternative government, without endangering Britain's joining the Community.[61] On 27 October the NEC carried by 15:8 a strongly worded motion with a touch of menace: 'The NEC believes that the overwhelming will of the Party is to end the present economic and social evils of this Government and expresses the hope that this will be regarded as the absolute priority on 28 October.'[62] To one correspondent who urged him to abstain ('kick for touch'), however, Jenkins gave the same high-minded answer that he gave to many others:

---

* On the first vote Tony Crosland, having earlier defected to the anti camp, voted with the pro-Marketeers, to Barbara Castle's disgust: 'So he has re-ratted! Really that man is the flabbiest figure in national politics.'[60]

In addition to the considerations you mention, however, it is also very important in my view that I should not join the queue of those who, as you rightly point out, have sacrificed their credibility and consistency in the past few months.[63]

Years later he insisted that he had never considered abstaining. 'This was not a difficult time,' he recalled, 'because my mind was absolutely settled . . . One just thought one was walking with destiny . . . It was never conceivable to me that one was going to abstain in this key division.'[64]

On the day of the vote he lunched at Brooks's with John Harris and Roy Hattersley, who warned him of possible violence in the lobbies; in the afternoon he listened to some of the debate; then dined at Lockets with Jennifer and the Thomsons (later joined by Taverne) before going back to the House to hear Callaghan and Heath wind up. He then walked firmly through the government lobby with Douglas Houghton, followed by another sixty-seven Labour MPs. A further twenty – including Tony Crosland – abstained, while thirty-three anti-European Tories, including Enoch Powell, voted with Labour, giving an emphatic pro-European majority of 112 (356:244). This was the proudest moment of Jenkins' career. For fifteen years, second only to Heath, he had been the most prominent advocate of Britain belatedly joining the Community; and now, by leading the principled revolt against Labour's U-turn, he had played the decisive role, second only to Heath, in making it happen. Through all the traumas of the next few months and years, 28 October 1971 remained a moment of high exhilaration for all the Jenkinsites. But it was all downhill from here. There was no actual violence against them, but furious anger in the loyalist ranks. Walter Harrison, the deputy Chief Whip, was 'almost beside himself with rage', Barbara Castle recorded: '"We now know who the buggers are, don't we?" he said to me. "We won't forget." There is deep bitterness in the loyalist ranks at what we all felt were the "traitors" . . . Everyone felt that a deep rift had been opened up in the party which will take a long time to heal.'[65] Neil Kinnock again voiced the simple partisan view. Conscientious support for Europe was accepted, he wrote in *Tribune*. 'But what kind of conscience permits Labour MPs to save the creators of a million unemployed?'[66] Three days after the vote the political editor of the *Sunday Times,* James Margach, wrote that 'The unconcealed objective of the Left now is either to humiliate Roy Jenkins and his allies into submission – or drive them from the party.'[67]

The means of humiliating them immediately presented itself. For, as Wilson declared that evening, the vote on 28 October was 'not the end but the beginning' of a long process.[68] The Commons had only voted in favour of the principle of joining the EEC: to make accession a reality now required detailed legislation, involving dozens more divisions over several months. Douglas Houghton – who as chairman of the PLP was in almost as exposed a position as Jenkins – came up with a compromise formula by announcing that having cast his one dissenting vote on the principle, he would henceforth vote the party line against the enabling legislation, on the argument that it was up to the government to find its own majority for legislation. Several others, including Hattersley and Joel Barnett, told Jenkins that for the sake of party unity they intended to do the same. The danger from a pro-European perspective was that, without the sixty-nine Labour rebels, the government might be unable to get the legislation through. Jenkins abhorred, as they all did, the prospect of voting against legislation which he ardently wanted to see passed, and the real possibility that their historic vote of 28 October could yet be undone. But he also respected the deep desire of most of his allies – many of them under intense pressure from their constituencies – to demonstrate their loyalty by getting back onside. His own position was complicated by the deputy leadership, which was up for re-election in three weeks' time. He had chosen not to resign, despite voting against a three-line whip, arguing that to resign and immediately stand again would have been 'a somewhat mock-heroic gesture . . . I do not like mock-heroic gestures – so I did not resign'.[69] If he could be re-elected despite his vote, his position would be greatly strengthened and his offence might in time be forgiven. But in order to be re-elected he had to be seen to place party unity above his commitment to Europe.*

In a speech in Barnett's Lancashire constituency on 29 October, therefore, Jenkins endorsed the Houghton formula and promised not to vote with the government again. 'The Government must be prepared to get legislation through on its own votes . . . If it cannot get its own

---

* Only one of his supporters urged him to go further and challenge Wilson for the leadership. He would not win, Bob Maclennan argued, but he would attract a good vote – 'probably well over a hundred' – and do more to strengthen his position than by hanging on for another year as deputy. 'In retrospect,' Jenkins wrote in his memoirs, 'I think he was right.'[70] 'The greatest tactical mistake of his career,' he told Robert Harris in 1996, 'was not standing for the leadership . . . against Wilson in 1971.'[71] But this is very doubtful. By setting himself openly against the leader Jenkins would have been seen as even more divisive than he already was, and he would surely have won fewer votes than he did in the election for deputy.

legislation through, the Government is not in command of the House of Commons and must take the consequences.'[72] But he only promised not to vote with the government, not to vote against it. ('So he only pledges to "abstain",' Barbara Castle wrote in disgust. 'And he gets a standing ovation for it!')[73] Pressed to clarify his position before the PLP meeting on 4 November, he composed a carefully worded statement, designed (in Roy Hattersley's words) to be 'conciliatory without sounding penitent',[74] in which he made 'absolutely no apology' for his vote the previous week – 'the only time I have gone against a 3-line whip in 23 years in this House' – but drew a distinction between that vote and the coming series of votes:

> That is not, let me say it myself, a strictly logical position. But I have to try to balance two commitments, both to keep alive the European cause in the Labour Party and to build up the strength of the Labour Party I believe the country needs.

Accordingly he promised not to vote with the government, and to vote against it whenever he could:

> But in the absence of knowledge of what is being proposed I cannot undertake to cast a vote which would be directly contrary to the clearly thought out vote on the major central principle which I gave last Thursday night.

That was clear enough. But after urging the party not to concentrate its whole effort on fighting the European legislation, which merely exacerbated divisions and discredited Labour with 'a significant part of the country', and warning against any sort of 'witch-hunt' against pro-Europeans in their constituencies, he ended with an unwise admission which undermined his previous stance: 'I shall recognise that, when an immediate election is not pending, any deputy leader cannot continue if he is unable to accept majority decisions.'[75]

At the time this failed to satisfy the left. Barbara Castle (who was not at the meeting because her husband Ted was having a heart operation) heard that Jenkins had been 'pretty uncompromising';[76] while Benn's interpretation was that he had 'made it absolutely clear that he did not commit himself . . . to vote with the Party throughout the year'.[77] But in fact Jenkins had given more of a hostage than they realised, or he intended. He should have simply said, 'You know my beliefs, you know my record, vote for me if you want.' But his team was desperate to maximise his vote, so he gave an undertaking that he soon regretted. 'It was a weak and equivocating and yet tying statement as it absolutely bound me . . . I had to vote for everything or resign. This was a major tactical error.'[78]

In the short run it seemed to work. Opposed by both Foot and Benn, Jenkins actually gained seven more votes than in 1970 (Jenkins 140, Foot 96, Benn 46) and came within two votes of winning on the first ballot. He must have retained the votes of at least fifty MPs who had voted against the EEC on 28 October, showing that he still commanded wider support than just the pro-Europeans. But then on the second ballot, with Benn eliminated, he picked up no more votes; or, if he did, he lost the same number, since he still had only 140 to Foot's 126. Some who had backed him on the first ballot in order to defeat the left – Callaghan supporters, he guessed, possibly including Crosland – abstained when they thought his victory was assured.[79] So his re-election was not after all a ringing endorsement. Mrs Castle was jubilant. 'The best news for a long time is that Mike has run Roy so close for the deputy leadership.'[80]*

And then he only retained the job for another four months. Before and after Christmas Jenkins twice escaped the toils of domestic politics, in December to visit America and deliver his three lectures at Yale, in January on his whistlestop Asian tour taking in Iran, Singapore, India and Bangladesh, hobnobbing with Indira Gandhi and the Shah. (The Head of Chancery at the British Embassy in Delhi attended the interview with Mrs Gandhi and wrote that he handled her with great skill, 'penetrating the ice-barrier which begins to form after about 10 minutes and ending up with the lady eating out of his hand'.)[82] But on his return he was instantly plunged back into the next phase of the European battle. On 22 January 1972 Ted Heath had signed Britain's formal accession to the EEC, to take effect from 1 January 1973; and on 26 January the government published the European Communities Bill. Instead of the expected mammoth 'Bill of a thousand clauses', the parliamentary

---

* Houghton was re-elected even more narrowly, by 139:130. But if the left had hoped to punish Thomson, Lever and Williams in the Shadow Cabinet elections, they were disappointed. All three leading pro-Europeans actually improved their ranking, while Mrs Castle was surprisingly knocked off. 'Roy came up to me with one of those serious faces which he normally reserves for exchange crises,' she wrote. '"I want you to know how sorry I am."' He admitted that he had not voted for her this year 'for obvious reasons', but wanted her to know how sorry he was.[81]

draughtsmen had managed to reduce it to just twelve clauses and four schedules, making up just thirty-seven pages. Not that this eased the agony of the sixty-nine Labour Europeans as they faced the first critical vote on Second Reading on 17 February. Most of them, under threat of expulsion or deselection, had already promised to fall into line; and by his statement on 4 November Jenkins felt himself bound to do the same or else resign, which he did not then want to do. But there was a real danger that if they all obeyed the whip, while enough of Powell's Tory rebels held firm, this might indeed 'undo' their vote of 28 October.* This time, unlike October, Heath declared it a vote of confidence, so Labour really could defeat the government and force a General Election if the whole party voted together. In this situation Jenkins had no choice. But there were, among the sixty-nine, enough stubborn old lags – mainly those who had already declared their intention not to stand again – to ensure the passage of the bill by quietly staying away. While Jenkins and most of his younger supporters swallowed their self-respect and voted miserably against their deepest conviction alongside fifteen unrepentant Eurosceptic Tories in the Opposition lobby, six of these Labour veterans were absent unpaired, just enough to ensure that the government squeaked through with a majority of eight (309:301). 'There were fantastic scenes in the House,' Benn recorded, 'and great rage that some Labour people who had abstained would have carried Heath absolutely to the brink of defeat if they had voted.'[84] Anger was also directed at the Liberals, five out of six of whom (including Jeremy Thorpe, Jo Grimond and David Steel) voted for the Bill and could therefore be said to have given the government its majority. On this occasion Thorpe was physically assaulted by one of the Labour whips.

Over the next five months there were another ninety-six divisions on the detail of the legislation, culminating in the Third Reading on 13 July. Not all were three-line whips, and Jenkins contrived not to vote in all of them. (He actually voted against the legislation fifty-five times, was paired thirty-four times and absent unpaired seven times.)[85] But most of the Labour Europeans were obliged to go on voting unhappily night after night, while just enough were always absent to ensure that the government was never defeated, though the majorities often fell to single figures. Labour loyalists, repeatedly thwarted by this

---

* Over lunch at Brooks's on 11 January Jenkins tried to persuade Foot that the Labour pro-Europeans were just as principled as the Tory antis. But Foot, who had an inexplicably soft spot for Enoch Powell, persisted in regarding the Tory rebels as honourable patriots who put their country before their party, while the Labour Europeans were unpardonable traitors. 'We parted in total mutual intellectual incomprehension.'[83]

handful of blacklegs, suspected collusion and they were right: John Roper (MP for Farnworth) acted as unofficial whip liaising discreetly with the Tory whips to keep the numbers up (or down) as required. Bill Rodgers, David Owen, Roy Hattersley and others have all written of the shame and misery of this period; Jenkins described the embarrassment of sheltering behind others whom he characteristically distinguished as 'old men who had decided their political fate no longer mattered and young men with the gallantry of 1916 subalterns . . . It is never comfortable to be dependent on men braver than oneself.'[86]*

Jenkins' embarrassment was magnified by the fact that he had just been awarded the Charlemagne Prize for his part in promoting European unity; this was a great honour whose previous recipients had included Churchill, Adenauer, Jean Monnet and Ted Heath. 'It was not something which any European in his right mind would lightly decline.'[87] But before accepting he was obliged to warn the prize committee that he was committed to vote against the European legislation; while at home the announcement only confirmed the suspicions of those who thought him more interested in collecting foreign gongs than in serving the Labour party. 'I suppose it was impossible for him to refuse it,' Barbara Castle commented, 'but he is intelligent enough to know that it hasn't done him any good with the party as a whole.'[88] He collected the prize at a splendid ceremony at Aachen in May.

He came very close to resigning the deputy leadership after voting twice more against his conscience on 21 and 22 February. At least two of his inner circle, Dick Taverne and Bill Rodgers, were reported to be urging this course, though Rodgers later claimed he was only playing devil's advocate to get the option discussed.[89] He was pulled back by the weight of others – Denis Howell, Joel Barnett, Tam Dalyell, John Smith and Neville Sandelson among them – urging that his resignation now would be 'disastrous' or 'madness'. Several were highly critical of Rodgers and Taverne. Roy Hattersley told Barbara Castle that he had 'just spent four of the most hectic days of his Parl[iamentary] life fighting the madmen who were trying to get Roy to resign';[90] Phillip Whitehead warned against 'a handful of romantics with a Thermopylae

---

* The most prominent of the former were Christopher Mayhew (who was actually only fifty-six, but on his way to joining the Liberals), Austen Albu and George Strauss, an old left-winger who had been a minister in the Attlee government. The most suicidal of the latter was the thirty-nine-year-old Michael ('Mickey') Barnes, whose Brentford and Chiswick constituency was due to disappear under redistribution. Barnes and his wife Anne were at this time good friends and Notting Hill neighbours of Roy and Jennifer, and Anne was one of Jenkins' regular lunch dates.

complex';[91] while Gwynoro Jones begged Jenkins to resist those with 'a martyrdom complex':'It should be your aim over the coming months to be seen to be moving away from this happless [*sic*] magic circle, and assert your undoubted connection with other spectrums of the Parliamentary Party.'[92] These divided counsels were summarised by Austen Albu after a 1963 Club dinner at which John Smith and Alex Lyon argued that Jenkins' role as leader of the 'militant moderates' was so essential that 'he should not put himself in a position in which he might be forced to resign'. The majority of those present, however (Taverne, Mayhew, David Marquand, David Owen, John Roper, Patrick Gordon Walker and Albu himself), 'in varying degrees thought this not possible – partly because R's strength in the party depended on his strength outside and partly because for him, as for many of us, Europe was the supreme issue' and he would lose credibility if he toed the party line. He would become – perhaps had already become – Wilson's prisoner, and he would corrode his own soul. 'Although there were therefore differences of view and emphasis there was overwhelming agreement against immediate resignation but in favour of escalation of opposition to H.W. and the antis – even if, in the end, this led to resignation.'[93]

This position was elaborated at length by David Marquand, who had initially wanted Jenkins to resign immediately but now thought that he should wait a bit longer and choose his moment. He should make 'a very belligerent speech' sometime in the next few weeks, 'staking out your territory and laying down your terms . . . in such a way that Harold couldn't accept it'. Then he should resign. What was at stake, Marquand argued, was 'the whole future . . . of the democratic left in this country'. Jenkins was the only person who could stop Wilson selling the pass, and this was the only way to do it.[94] David Owen argued similarly that he should widen his attack in a way that might lead to resignation, but that they should not keep on defying the whip. 'Persistent abstaining by a major group,' he warned, 'will lead to a new party' – evidence that a breakaway was already seen as a possibility. 'I hope you have no doubt of one thing,' he ended. 'Whatever your decision if you resign – I resign and I will support your decision to the hilt.'[95]

It is significant that all those listed as taking this more aggressive view later joined the SDP; whereas most of those counselling against resignation, notably Smith and Hattersley, ultimately stuck with Labour. The fault line within the Jenkinsites was already visible. For the moment Jenkins was persuaded to hang on – a decision made easier by the

Shadow Cabinet's decision not to press a three-line whip on every vote. To Neville Sandelson (MP for Hayes and Harlington), who had written urging that the European battle had been won and there were now wider issues involving the whole shape of the party on which his leadership was essential, Jenkins replied on 28 February: 'I hope we can get through without upheaval, but this will require a touch of steel on our part as well as sense and caution. But I am more optimistic after last week.'[96] His strategy, following Marquand's advice, and Sandelson's, was to try to move beyond Europe and reassert his credentials as an alternative leader by setting out his own vision and programme in a series of wide-ranging speeches over the spring and summer.

The first was delivered in John Roper's Farnworth constituency (in Greater Manchester) on 11 March. It was largely written by Marquand, but harked back to Jenkins' long standing concern with poverty and inequality. 'In the 1950s,' he admitted, 'many of us thought the inequalities would diminish as society became more prosperous. It is now clear that this view was at best over-simplified, and at worst just wrong.' Confessing that the 1964–70 government, despite its achievements in certain areas, had been a disappointment in this respect, he asserted ambitiously that 'the next Labour Government can be content with nothing less than the elimination of poverty as a social problem'. The problem was that the poor were now a minority, while the bulk of Labour's traditional supporters were relatively well off. Formed to fight for the poor majority against the wealthy minority, the party's new challenge was to 'enlist the majority in a struggle on behalf of a poor minority':

> We have to persuade men and women who are themselves reasonably well off that they have a duty to forgo some of the advantages they would otherwise enjoy for the sake of others who are much poorer than they are. We have to persuade motor car workers in my constituency that they have an obligation to low-paid workers in the public sector.

'Our only hope,' he concluded, 'is to appeal to the latent idealism of all men and women of goodwill – irrespective of their income brackets, irrespective of their class origins, irrespective in many cases of their past political affiliations.'

Here was a clear anticipation of the SDP. (Marquand even included a quotation from Andrew Marvell about Cromwell 'casting the Kingdoms old into another mould', and coined a phrase later adopted by the SDP: 'We have to break the mould of custom, selfishness and apathy which condemns so many of our fellow countrymen to avoidable indignity and deprivation.') But this was not the part of the speech that attracted attention in 1972. What made the headlines were a couple of sentences at the beginning, which were read as a barely veiled attack on Wilson:

> When the next election comes, we shall not be judged by the vehemence of our perorations, still less by the dexterity with which we follow the transient twists and turns of public opinion. We shall be judged by the quality of the programme we put before our fellow citizens, and by the consistency and courage with which we advocate it.

And if this was not clear enough, right at the end he called again for Labour to put 'in place of the politics of opportunism, the politics of principle. Only so can we hope to succeed. Only so will success be worth having.'[97]

Trailed in advance as a major political event, the speech was carefully timed to catch the Sunday papers, which duly made it their front-page lead. But then Jenkins took fright, decided he had gone too far and drove into Oxford on Sunday morning to re-record a radio interview he had already given to *The World This Weekend* to deny that he intended to stand for the leadership. He was merely trying to open a debate on some fundamental issues. 'And I rather resent it when the whole press reacts to this as though it is a personal issue, which it is not, and tries to create a great leadership crisis which does not exist.'[98] Those like Marquand and Owen who thought they had finally screwed him up to the point of issuing a clear challenge were in despair at this bathetic climbdown, which seemed to confirm the view that he was not, when push came to shove, a fighter. At the same time he conspicuously declined to say 'yes' or 'no' when asked if Wilson still had his support, so he got the worst of both worlds, appearing 'willing to wound but yet afraid to strike'.* Barbara Castle was initially furious at Jenkins 'getting all these press hallelujahs for plagiarising ideas on which some of us have been working quietly and constructively in the NEC groups for months'. But she still felt he was more a victim of 'press

---

* The phrase, from Pope, comes from a passage describing a politician remarkably like Jenkins: 'Blest with each talent, and each art to please, / And born to write, converse and live with ease.'[99]

sensationalism' than actively bidding for the leadership; and she was delighted when his botched coup – 'carefully planned in his little group' – seemed to have rebounded on him. 'I think Roy must be regretting it now: the whole business has done him enormous harm.'[100]

Resignation was still very much on his mind. He told the editor of the *Guardian*, Alastair Hetherington, on 9 March that he had been reading about historic resignations, particularly that of Anthony Eden, who almost resigned as Neville Chamberlain's Foreign Secretary four or five times before he finally did. Jenkins knew quite well that resignations are usually mistimed and the last straw is often quite trivial. He recognised that if he resigned, others would feel obliged to go with him, leaving vacancies in the Shadow Cabinet which would be filled by 'one extremely right-wing anti-marketeer [Reg Prentice] and three or four left-wing anti-marketeers' (Barbara Castle, Eric Heffer and John Silkin), pushing the party still further to the left. But he was afraid that Wilson was already being driven towards a commitment not merely to oppose entry, but to withdraw from the Community, and in that case he would have to resign.[101] Up to the end of March, however, he still intended to 'stagger on uncomfortably as deputy leader through the summer and perhaps to re-election in the autumn'.[102] But then within a few days came three fresh setbacks. First, on 28 March George Thomson told him that he had decided to accept an offer to become one of Britain's two Commissioners in Brussels when the country joined the Community in January 1973. Jenkins did not try to dissuade him; but Thomson, a heavyweight of robust Scottish good sense and humour, was 'by far the best and steadiest and most important' of his allies, and his loss would be 'a major blow'.[103] Then the next day the NEC, after a long procedural wrangle and on the casting vote of Tony Benn as chairman, appointed the left-wing and anti-European Ron Hayward to be the party's next General Secretary, rather than the right-wing, pro-European and (in Jenkins' view) much more able front-runner for the job, Gwyn Morgan. This was 'a serious defeat because it both symbolised and reinforced a significant leftward shift in the control of the party machine'.[104] Third, later the same day, the Shadow Cabinet reversed its previous position and voted to support Benn's call for a referendum before Britain joined the Community.

Jenkins had always opposed referenda on principle, subscribing to Attlee's view that they were 'a splendid weapon for demagogues and dictators', which would be a serious brake on progressive legislation.[105] Way back in 1954 he had argued in a letter to *The Times* that 'Representative democracy demands a clear division of function between the electors and the elected.' The former could dismiss the latter, but meanwhile they must be free to exercise their own judgement. 'Any form of referendum is an infringement of this freedom, and the more complex and detailed the issue upon which it is held the more absurd an infringement it becomes.'[106] Moreover he believed that a referendum on Europe, with members of the Shadow Cabinet taking opposite sides, could only widen the division within Labour. As a matter of fact, as he came to acknowledge after 1975, the referendum turned out to be the means by which the party reconciled the opposing views without splitting, at least in the short term. But in 1972 it was not just the referendum *per se*, but the way the Shadow Cabinet once again reversed itself within the space of a fortnight that he could not stomach. For more than a year Benn had been a lone voice pressing the idea: the 1971 party conference had rejected the proposal – so much for the sanctity of conference decisions – and on 15 March he found just four supporters in the Shadow Cabinet. But then on 22 March he persuaded the NEC, with Wilson, Callaghan and Jenkins all absent (Jenkins was attending a PLP meeting on the budget), to vote 13:11 to refer it back to the Shadow Cabinet, where (on 29 March) Wilson seized on the pretext that President Pompidou had just announced a referendum in France to execute another tactical U-turn.

Foot, Shore and Benn led the case for supporting a dissident Tory motion demanding a referendum, backed by Fred Peart and Bob Mellish. Jenkins spoke strongly against, dismissing Pompidou's announcement as an irrelevance dictated purely by domestic politics and warning that 'the intrusion of referenda was harmful to left-wing policies'; he was supported by Shirley Williams, Harold Lever, Houghton, Thomson and (for once) Tony Crosland. But Wilson, in self-pitying mood, complained that while he had never doubted the pro-Marketeers' integrity, 'none of the pro-market leaders . . . had ever publicly given him credit for similar integrity. None of them had gone to his help despite the fact that he was bitterly attacked by enemies of the Party.' He admitted that the French precedent was irrelevant, but nevertheless 'thought we might have to come to a position where we supported a referendum'; at which Jim Callaghan pitched in to say that losing the amendment would be a serious defeat for the government, 'and as he thought getting rid of the Government was more important than the question of the Common Market he agreed with Mr Wilson'. Ted Short, though a pro-Marketeer, then changed sides; and since Denis Healey and Willie Ross, both opponents of referenda, were absent, the decision came out 8:6 in favour of supporting the referendum.[107] Benn hailed 'a tremendous victory',[108] while the Jenkinsites were 'stunned'. Having been 'sandbagged in the morning' at the NEC, Jenkins wrote, they had been 'garotted in the afternoon'.[109] He drew the conclusion that the anti-Europeans would stop at nothing till they drove him out, while Wilson no longer had any intention of trying to hold the balance.

But that was no reason to give his enemies what they wanted. For ten days over Easter he stayed at East Hendred, taking advice from his most trusted associates. On Easter Monday he drafted a resignation letter which he read over the phone to Thomson and Houghton and to others (Owen, Marquand, Maclennan and Barnes) who came to lunch over the next week. Bill Rodgers, a hawk in February, now wrote him a long letter arguing on balance against resigning. The European argument was won; the referendum, if carried, might be a nuisance but was not disastrous. Jenkins could still be the next leader if he just sat tight for two or three years and waited for the storm to pass. If he resigned now, 'You would lose a valuable platform as the price of winning your freedom.' It might not matter if Foot became deputy leader, but if Short, Crosland or – 'most dangerously' – Healey succeeded, 'he might be hard to dislodge and Wilson could choose his moment to go with the deliberate purpose of dishing you'. Having set out the case for hanging on, however, Rodgers accepted that Jenkins might feel that lying low for two years would be intolerable and assured him that 'I am with you whatever course you choose.'[110] David Owen also argued against resigning but undertook to follow his judgement.[111]

Jenkins made his decision at the end of the week, when his most important sounding board, John Harris, flew back from Chicago (where he had been covering the Democratic primaries for *The Economist*) and came straight to East Hendred. He had been traced by Roy Hattersley, who had expected him to be an ally against resignation; but he turned out to be strongly in favour. That Sunday the Thomsons and Bradleys came to lunch. Jenkins' account of their arguments, dictated five weeks after the event, is rather different from the more polished version he wrote two decades later in his memoirs and crucially includes Jennifer's reluctant conversion. Tom Bradley's advice, he wrote, was broadly the same as Rodgers': 'Never resign, hold on, accept humiliations, wait for the leadership to drop into your lap.'

But Thomson argued very strongly that this was not a possible position, that it would erode me externally and internally and indeed, which was strongly my view, that at the end of the day I would hardly be in a state to be leader even assuming I could be, because I would have destroyed my own self-confidence and self-respect. This I think was the view which Jennifer also accepted, although she during the week had taken a good deal of convincing and really I think came to be in favour of resignation not because she thought it was tactically wise but because she thought it was personally necessary to me.[112]

It was 'a hideous error', he acknowledged in a television interview some years later, had his sole ambition been to become leader; but he still maintained it was the right decision, since he would not have been a good leader if he was not happy in himself.[113] That may well be true; but as a political leader Jenkins can still be blamed for putting his personal feelings before his responsibility to his supporters and the wing of the party that he led. As he had anticipated, Thomson and Lever resigned from the Shadow Cabinet with him (though Shirley Williams, who was rather in favour of referenda, noticeably did not); and David Owen, Dick Taverne, Dickson Mabon and Lord Chalfont resigned their lesser positions outside the Shadow Cabinet. (Rodgers had already been sacked by Wilson in January.) This represented a serious weakening of the front bench, which surrendered the field almost entirely to the anti-Europeans and the left. Meanwhile Hattersley, Denis Howell, Joel Barnett and Ivor Richard chose to stay in their posts, and Hattersley accepted promotion to defence spokesman (taking Thomson's place), which as *The Economist* wrote 'shattered the concept of the Jenkinsites as a coherent, well-trained political force'.[114] Meanwhile Wilson appointed Denis Healey to be the new Shadow Chancellor, telling Barbara Castle that he felt 'liberated' by Jenkins' self-removal ('I'm impregnable now') and claiming that Healey would 'really get stuck into the Finance Bill' in a way that Jenkins never did ('Do you know Roy never attended a single meeting of the committee last year?'). With Taverne gone as well ('good riddance'), he would now be able to build 'a really effective Treasury team'.[115]

Jenkins' resignation of the deputy leadership was a watershed for the Labour party comparable in its consequences with Nye Bevan's resignation from the Attlee Cabinet in 1951. In Roy Hattersley's view it was 'the moment when the old Labour coalition began to collapse' and the eventual formation of a new centre party became inevitable.[116] But whereas Bevan's resignation had split Labour into two warring tribes, Jenkins' split it into three. It both signalled and accelerated the mounting disillusion of the core Jenkinsites – those who later left to form the SDP – with the takeover of the party by the left; but it also divided the right, leaving the two mutually suspicious camps less able to combine to fight the left. Hattersley was the symbolic figure here: pilloried in the press as 'Rattersley' – the Jenkinsite who betrayed his master – he spent the next decade protesting his unshakable loyalty to Labour, right or wrong, and ended up (ironically) as deputy leader under Neil Kinnock.* Still more important in the short term, it widened the rift between the Jenkinsites on the one hand and Crosland, Healey and their smaller bands of supporters on the other. Relations between the three Oxford contemporaries had been strained since 1967; but it was the perception on the part of the other two that Jenkins was leading his own clique, intent on making him leader and willing to sacrifice the party to preserve their own moral superiority, that wrecked any possibility that the former Gaitskellites would be able to contain the rise of the new hard left.

The breach between Jenkins and Crosland was particularly bitter because they had once been so close. The Jenkinsites considered Crosland's defection on Europe especially unforgiveable because he had once been as strongly pro-European as Jenkins. In fact he did not quite defect: he actually abstained in the vote on 28 October. But he adopted a pose of lofty boredom towards the issue, claiming that it was not really very important and certainly not worth splitting the party for, which the Jenkinsites thought dishonest as well as infuriating. For his part Crosland was jealous that Europe had become so much Jenkins' issue. Candidly assessing his prospects at the beginning of 1972, he recognised that 1971 had been a bad year for him in which he had done poorly in Shadow Cabinet and NEC elections.

> For 1st time reputation as trimmer, ditherer, lack of consistency & courage . . . Not for 1st time, but more acutely uncomfortable & ambivalent relationship c. CDS Eur. Right, wh. now totally Jenkinsite.

He now planned to distance himself from the 1963 Club, which he thought had become narrow, elitist, Euro-obsessed and 'now wholly Royite', which was 'v. embarrassing & being No. 2 intolerable'. He particularly objected to Rodgers' whipping ('Bill bullying quite

---

* Hattersley noted slightly bitterly that Shirley Williams attracted no such opprobrium for not resigning. 'For the first time I realised that Shirley is surrounded by a beatific light that shields her from harm and criticism, which would be heaped on ordinary people.' She has 'an enviable . . . capacity to be loved and admired whether she deserves it or not'.[117]

unacceptable'). He still saw himself as a possible future leader, however – even though he admitted he might not be a very good one! – and was anxious to widen his support among the anti-European right and centre.[118] When Jenkins resigned, therefore, he stood for the deputy leadership. But in a show of pettiness of which Jenkins subsequently felt ashamed, the Jenkinsites decided to back Ted Short – even though Short had also abstained on 28 October and voted the 'wrong' way on the referendum proposal, while Crosland had voted the right way: Rodgers justified this partly as a means of 'punishing' Crosland for his apostasy, but also as a blocking move to keep the seat warm for Jenkins' possible return.[119] The result was that Crosland got only sixty-one votes to Short's 111 and Foot's eighty-nine; Short then beat Foot 145:116 on the second ballot to become the least distinguished of all Labour's deputy leaders. With the Jenkinsites' forty-odd votes, Crosland would have won easily. By missing the chance to heal, or at least contain, the division on the right the Jenkinsites played into the left's hands.*

'What a mess he has made of things!' Barbara Castle wrote:

He ought to have abstained in the first place and not run for the office. Lying low for a bit would have saved both his own position and the party's unity. Now he – and the fanatics who have been egging him on – have the nerve to argue that it is those who are supporting the party line on the C.M. [Common Market] who are 'splitting the party'. Middle-of-the-roaders seem to disapprove of Roy's step.[121]

She was at least half right. Jenkins was probably right that he could not honourably abstain in the historic European vote in October 1971. But voting against the whip as deputy leader put him in an inherently false position. He would have done better – had he known how swiftly the party was going to reverse its position – not to have stood for the job in 1970; and he would certainly have saved himself a lot of agony

* David Owen wrote Crosland a convoluted letter explaining why he was not voting for him. He was desperate to get rid of Wilson, so did not want to tie Crosland to him; what he really wanted was a Callaghan/Crosland leadership. He had never believed that Jenkins was the only possible successor and thought that his resignation gave the party the chance of uniting in the short term around a compromise figure – Callaghan 'or just possibly Ted Short' – with 'Roy coming back into the collective leadership before the next election and you Denis Jim Roy and hopefully Michael agreeing to work together'. Failing that, he feared that Benn would become a real possibility, in which case he shuddered for the future.[120] His analysis was prescient, but his hope that all the big beasts would pull together was sadly optimistic.

had he not stood again – that is, effectively resigned – in November 1971, instead of staggering on to resign five months later. As it was, he looked both indecisive and self-indulgent. The possibility of a referendum – which the Commons comfortably rejected anyway, with sixty Labour abstentions and only fourteen Tory rebels – was a poor issue to resign on, which made him appear anti-democratic.

He did win plaudits from his cheerleaders in the liberal press, notably *The Times*, where the extravagantly hyperbolic Bernard Levin was supported in magisterial editorials by the editor, William Rees-Mogg, who hailed 'an act of political courage and principle . . . [which] contrasts with the stricken lack of policy or understanding of too many other members of the Shadow Cabinet'. Describing Jenkins as 'a remarkable and serious statesman . . . who can be seen to set himself the standards of an earlier and stronger age of British statesmanship', he predicted (wrongly) that by driving the Europeans out of the Labour leadership, 'anti-Europe has probably secured Conservative government for most of the rest of the 1970s'.[122] *The Economist* too, after suggesting initially that he had made 'a disastrous mistake', concluded that 'Mr Jenkins has shown that he has the guts to put his political future totally at risk, not only for the sake of a credible, principled Labour party but for parliamentary politics.' It was now up to moderate Labour MPs and supporters to follow his lead.[123]

He received a huge postbag of letters – 80 per cent of them supportive. There were dozens from friends on both sides of the House of Commons and from senior ornaments of the liberal establishment (Lords Longford, Gladwyn and Shawcross); from bishops (Mervyn Stockwood), journalists (Samuel Brittan, Harold Evans) and playwrights both old and young (Terence Rattigan, Michael Frayn); from America (Pierre Salinger and Arthur Schlesinger) and further afield (Lee Kuan Yew), all expressing congratulation, admiration, sympathy and support. But there were as many from ordinary members of the public praising his integrity and courage as 'a breath of fresh air' and 'restoring their faith in politics', several of them urging him to form a new centre party and almost all hoping that he would soon be Prime Minister.[124] If Jenkins began to show increasing signs of vanity and self-righteousness, such flattering fanmail might have turned anyone's head.

On the other hand, there were letters from Labour loyalists saying 'good riddance', calling him Judas, a fascist and a traitor to the working class, and telling him to get out of the Labour party, where he had never belonged. Many were racist ('dirty Welsh bastard') or xenophobic:

You are no bloody good, to yourself or anybody else. You have ponced on the people long enough. Now piss off. And take that yid and scotchman [that is, Lever and Thomson] with you. You git, you soft git, go on now, piss off.[125]

Jenkins replied carefully to all the positive and rational ones, and ignored the abusive ones.

The printable view from the left was expressed in a letter to *Labour Weekly* from London NW5:

April 10, 1972 will go down in history as a great day of purification for the Party and the Labour movement. Without Roy Jenkins and his pals on our backs we can go forward in unity to a landslide for Socialism in the next General Election. I have never before felt as proud to be a member of the Labour Party as I am today.[126]

15 *What Matters Now*

JENKINS' problem was what to do next. Should he widen his area of disagreement from Europe to the whole future direction of the party, with a view to challenging Wilson in November? Or do his best to restore unity by lying low and mending his fences until the European storm had passed, then hope to resume his position in the leadership?

On the one hand, Wilson was still very vulnerable to a determined challenge. Even Barbara Castle admitted that 'everyone – including Harold's friends – now think Harold is so discredited that he cannot continue as leader';[1] and the *New Statesman* (now edited by Anthony Howard) wrote that 'his very presence in Labour's leadership pollutes the atmosphere of politics'.[2] Moreover in this vacuum of leadership the left was continuing to gain ground, not just over Europe and opposing the Industrial Relations Bill, but by committing the party to a more sweeping programme of nationalisation than it had contemplated since the 1940s (including plans to take over banks, insurance companies, building societies and development land), while making life increasingly unpleasant for several of the Jenkinsites – though not Jenkins himself – in their constituencies. (It was partly because of trouble with his local party in Dundee that Thomson had decided to give up and go to Brussels.) By his stand on Europe Jenkins had – despite his wobble between October and April – built a strong identity as an alternative leader with a clear and different vision and a considerable following both within the party and beyond. His wide appeal was demonstrated by an ORC poll published in *The Times* in September, which found strong support for an alliance between 'moderate Labour' and the Liberals. In this hypothetical scenario, the Lab/Lib combination scored

35 per cent against the Conservatives' 27 per cent and 'Socialist Labour's' 23 per cent.

The accompanying editorial, entitled 'Twelve Million Jenkinsites', assumed that the Liberals would provide the necessary organisation and believed that money would be no problem. 'The Liberal–Labour coalition, if it was to work at all, would create a public enthusiasm which would make it more than self-financing from popular subscription. It could produce an explosion of support from frustrated voters.' If the next election were a presidential contest between Heath, Wilson and Jenkins, 'Mr Jenkins would be the Brigadier Gerard of the race' – in other words, he would win hands down. (Brigadier Gerard was the leading racehorse of the moment.) It would not happen, the paper concluded, because the pro-Europeans would not leave Labour. 'Nevertheless the most disquieting fact in this poll is that two to one agreed that the present party system no longer works properly.'[3] Jenkins was just beginning to reach the same conclusion; but he was not yet ready to act on it. In retrospect – since the moderates did lose control of the party over the next decade and it did eventually split – he came to believe that he should have come out boldly and fought in 1972 before it was too late, as some of his more hawkish supporters like Bill Rodgers and Bob Maclennan were urging.

'I fear the thinning of the ranks,' Maclennan warned:

If you don't go now what do you do before the next election is lost? The slide will continue . . . And when we finally are rejected by the electorate as unfit to govern you will be blamed for not speaking up. No, for not standing up and putting HW to the test. For not giving the Party the opportunity to choose its way . . .

If you stand you will not win, but you will bring the succession nearer. If you do not stand I think you will seem more isolated than you are [and] the appearance will gravely damage your prospects.[4]

Rodgers recalled that Wilson had not done himself any harm by challenging Gaitskell in 1960 and questioned Jenkins' stomach for a fight:

The question is what do you want: a relatively quiet and untroubled life with the prospect of the crown, although diminishing; or a bid for the leadership continuing over three to five years, unpleasant sometimes, unrewarding often, but with a distinctly better than fifty–fifty prospect of success. I can see the attractions of the first. But with no regrets?

So why not this year? What is there to lose? And will you not lose something if Mayhew stands and you don't?[5]

But Jenkins was not temperamentally a rebel and he did not want to risk splitting the party. Those like Tony Benn and Barbara Castle who suspected that he was itching to break away and form a new party underestimated the pull of his Labour roots. He still believed that with clear leadership Labour could be brought back to sensible policies, as it had been after previous lurches to the left in 1931 and 1951. But was he the man to give such leadership? In a shrewd review of *Afternoon on the Potomac?* in June, the deputy editor of the *Guardian*, John Cole, suggested that Jenkins was 'more of an architect than a builder':

He can see the vision. But can he shift the bricks? . . . The question . . . is whether Mr Jenkins can harness his considerable powers of persuasion and his limited powers of patience to the task of convincing people of his view at a time when it matters. That is what political leadership is about.[6]

So he took the course of least resistance. After his resignation he carried on with the series of speeches that he had launched in March. They were good, thoughtful speeches, delivered to constituency and trade union audiences in Blackpool, Edinburgh, Leicester, London and Carmarthen between May and September 1972, addressing poverty and inequality, regional and industrial policy, the environment and the needs of the Third World, and still advocating strongly interventionist solutions including substantial (though selective) public ownership. But they were largely written for him by Judith Marquand and Matthew Oakeshott, with input from David Marquand and David Owen; for the most, Jenkins took little interest in their preparation (with the exception of the one on cities, always a particular interest), delivered them without conviction and singularly failed to follow them up. They were published in a Fontana paperback (priced 30p) in September, just in time for the party conference, under the seemingly urgent title *What Matters Now*, and sold well – evidently bought by a good many of *The Times'* twelve million Jenkinsites. For publication he included his speech accepting the Charlemagne Prize – anticipating Britain's role in an increasingly united Europe – and added a short postscript reaffirming his long standing conviction that Labour, in order first to win elections

399

and then to implement lasting reform that would change society for the better, could not afford to be a narrow socialist party imposing unpopular left-wing nostrums on the basis of a minority vote, but must aim to 'represent the hopes and aspirations of the whole leftward thinking half of the country . . . A broad-based, international, radical, generous-minded party,' he concluded, 'could quickly seize the imagination of a disillusioned and uninspired British public' and win the sort of positive victory needed to sustain a successful Labour government.[7] But he made no attempt to test this belief by using his speeches as a platform from which to challenge Wilson: he was only putting down his marker for a future contest – probably after Labour had lost another election. At Blackpool in October he spoke only at fringe meetings and said nothing controversial, beyond repeating his commitment to British membership of Europe. His decision not to speak in the Common Market debate – which might have been counterproductive – was vindicated when Wilson succeeded in keeping Labour's options open by persuading conference to reject an outright commitment to withdraw in favour of a promise to 'renegotiate' the terms. From the point of view of keeping Britain in the Community, Jenkins commented, this was 'not ideal, but it could have been a great deal worse'.[8]

Above all, he declined openly to support Dick Taverne, who after a particularly acrimonious struggle with his constituency party in Lincoln was deselected for voting against the whip the previous October. The NEC – on which Jenkins of course no longer sat – upheld the decision; and on the last day of conference Taverne announced his intention to resign and fight a by-election on the principle of an MP's right to follow his own judgement, not the dictation of a party clique. Most of the other Jenkinsites (several under similar threat themselves) tried to dissuade him. Only Jenkins thought he might win. Taverne pressed Jenkins to come and speak for him, arguing that his victory would then be Jenkins' victory, which could be the launching pad for a centre party. But Jenkins did not believe the time was ripe for a significant defection from Labour; apart from anything else they would need to attract a lot of councillors, who could not be expected to defect before the local elections in May.[9] Given that none of his other supporters was yet ready to contemplate the unthinkable, he was unquestionably right. By speaking at Lincoln he would merely have invited instant expulsion, which a majority of the NEC would have been delighted to enforce. But his heart was with Taverne; and it was noted that John Harris did help in an advisory capacity. Jenkins came under considerable pressure to speak against Taverne – as both Healey and Crosland did. But though he spoke loyally at two other by-elections in February 1973 (at Chester-le-Street and Dundee) he told the national agent, Reg Underhill, that it would not be 'appropriate' – in view of 'our past connection and his very loyal service to me in two departments' – for him to speak at Lincoln.[10] He was delighted when Taverne, standing as Democratic Labour, won a momentous victory, beating the official Labour candidate out of sight with a majority of more than 13,000.* The result confirmed that there was huge public support for moderate Labour and that the militants could be beaten if they were faced head-on. As events developed over the next few years Jenkins felt that he had taken the coward's path by not supporting Taverne, who remained a scar on his conscience ever after.

For the present, however, he was concerned to reaffirm his loyalty to Labour and stamp on any suggestion that he was considering forming a centre party. In a speech to the Oxford University Labour Club a week after Lincoln he insisted that he found the idea 'profoundly unattractive' for four reasons – all of which would be gleefully quoted against him eight years later when he did lead a breakaway. First, he did not believe that such a grouping would have 'any coherent philosophical base':

A party based on such a ragbag could stand for nothing positive. It would exploit grievances and fall apart when it sought to remedy them. I believe in exactly the reverse sort of politics. It is the duty of leaders to seek to synthesize and give reality to people's aspirations, not to separate and exploit their conflicting grudges.

Second, he believed that a centre party would only benefit the Conservatives by destroying the prospect of an effective alternative government – which was why some Tory newspapers were so keen on it. 'The most likely result would be chaos on the Left and several decades of Conservative hegemony almost as dismal and damaging as in the twenties and thirties.' Third, he claimed to have no wish to drive the left out of the mainstream of British politics, which would only 'increase and not diminish the divisions in our society'. Fourth, and

---

* Taverne had wanted to call himself a Social Democrat, but was persuaded that Democratic Labour would be better understood. The official Labour candidate was Margaret Jackson, then a hard-left local activist who later reinvented herself as the model Blairite Margaret Beckett.

more personally, 'the Labour party is and always has been an instinctive part of my life':

> The most moving speech I ever heard was Hugh Gaitskell saying he would 'fight, fight and fight again to save the party we love'. That was the right message in 1960, and I believe it is still the right message today . . . But I believe there is a lot of fighting to be done.

Labour was self-evidently in a bad way, performing very poorly in by-elections against an unpopular government.* 'There is something very wrong indeed with an opposition party which in mid-term and in the winter of the Government's discontent cannot do better than this.' But it was 'standing sense on its head' for those who had enjoyed 'almost undisputed control' for the past two years to blame those who had argued for 'a more responsible, more consistent approach'. Labour would only regain public support by adopting sensible and honest policies, and he offered three tests for every new policy proposal: Was it necessary to creating a better society? Was it able to be carried out? And would it win, rather than alienate support? Every policy should pass at least two of these tests. But 'all too often none of the three are given serious consideration'. Harking back to the distinction he had drawn in *Pursuit of Progress* twenty years before, he warned that Labour must decide what it was about. 'Are we offering people the prospect of steady progress towards better living, a fairer distribution and a more idealistic society? Or are we seeking salvation through catastrophe?' Those prepared to put the country through 'the needless misery of complete national failure' were a tiny minority, but they exerted an influence disproportionate to their numbers. The great majority of Labour members and – just as important – supporters wanted a radical party, but also responsibility and consistency. 'It is time we started talking sense to the British people.'[11]

This was all very fine, but it was hopelessly vague. 'It is a fault of Mr Jenkins,' wrote David Wood in *The Times*, 'that when he comes to

---

* At Chester-le-Street Labour's majority slumped from 20,000 to 7,000, with the Liberal winning 38 per cent of the vote, while in Dundee East Labour only narrowly held off the Scottish Nationalists and the Tories in a three-way cliffhanger. Meanwhile the Liberals were enjoying a spectacular revival. Having won Rochdale from Labour in October and Sutton and Cheam from the Tories in December 1972, they went on to take Ely, Ripon and Berwick from the Conservatives during 1973, while consistently scoring around 20 per cent in the polls, making the likelihood of Labour winning a clear majority at the next election increasingly remote.

the point he tends to hit hard with a feather duster.'[12] The speech was an elegant analysis, but it neither offered a clear lead to his supporters nor made clear which left-wing policies he objected to, while offering the left an easy target. In two speeches in the West Country the next day Barbara Castle laid into him unmercifully. 'Let there be no mistake about who is causing the splits . . . Roy Jenkins and Roy Jenkins alone is responsible for starting up all these old rows all over again':

> Does anyone really believe that the Labour Party lost the last election because it was too left? Some of us who loyally supported our colleagues in government even when we disagreed with them . . . are getting sick and tired of the attempt of some of them now to pre-empt for themselves all the claims of probity, courage and consistency.[13]

'Wonderful, Barbara,' Wilson congratulated her. 'When I said I would not comment on Roy's speech I also said there was one person I hoped would; you. He has boobed this time.'[14]

The weakness of Jenkins' position was that by emphasising responsibility and sense he had ceased to sound remotely radical. There was some justice in the complaint of three Bradford councillors who wrote to *Labour Weekly*: 'The truth is that Mr Jenkins is indistinguishable from the liberal wing of the Conservative party.'[15] The previous year he had actually set out a lot of quite detailed policies on poverty, industrial policy and urban regeneration; and he still advocated increased public ownership. Condemning the Heath government's efforts to 'hive off' parts of the nationalised industries and return them to the private sector, he declared that 'We should move firmly in the other direction. We should seek to hive on parts of the private sector to the nationalised sector, and encourage the nationalised sector to diversify wherever it sees a good opportunity.' To this end he proposed a State Holding Company, backed by a Regional Development Bank, on the model of the Italian IRI. This was not very different from the left's proposed National Enterprise Board, which became official policy in 1973 and formed the centrepiece of Labour's 1974 manifesto. The difference was that Jenkins envisaged – as Crosland had advocated in the 1950s – a patchwork pattern of public ownership for the purpose of stimulating regional investment, *not* the wholesale nationalisation of entire industries and major companies:

> I have always believed that public ownership should be judged more by the results it will produce than by abstractions and

preconceived views. I have not been convinced that it contains the key to the elimination of injustice between individuals . . . But I am increasingly convinced that injustice between the regions cannot be dealt with except by a significant expansion of the public sector.[16]

But he failed to sound as if he really meant it. In a Radio 4 debate with Enoch Powell, Michael Foot and Reggie Maudling, chaired by Robin Day, he was asked if he still spoke of socialism. 'Yes, I use that word,' he replied cautiously. 'I certainly use it.' But he was 'happy to be called a social democrat'. He dismissed as 'foolish' the NEC's latest plan to nationalise twenty-five unnamed major companies ('I think it's a number drawn out of a hat, and I've no idea what is intended to be achieved') and declared himself still 'an unrepentant believer in a mixed economy'. He professed to think that 'on the whole the balance of that mixture tilts, and tilts rightly, and should be helped to tilt as time goes on, in favour of the elected government of the country playing a greater part in determining what happens'.[17] But he scarcely sounded in a hurry to speed up the process. This was never going to inspire anyone. He also continued to insist that the next Labour government, like the last, would have to maintain some form of incomes policy to control inflation – just as the Heath government had been driven, against its original intention, to introduce one. But this was another part of the record of 1964–70 which the Shadow Cabinet, under pressure from the unions, had repudiated. The result was that on the three most contentious issues of the moment – Europe, nationalisation and incomes policy – Jenkins appeared irredeemably right-wing: not only was he opposed to the official policy of the party, but on two of them he was in agreement with the Tory government.

Released from frontbench duties, Jenkins had more time for writing: he got on with his biographical essays which appeared at regular intervals in *The Times*. He also travelled a good deal, making several longer journeys as well as his regular jaunts to America and Europe. He spent the whole of August 1972, unusually and not very happily, at Aspen, Colorado, enjoying the company of a large gathering of the Democratic great and good, including such pillars of the Kennedy White House as Robert McNamara, McGeorge Bundy and Arthur Schlesinger, but oppressed by both the rainy weather and the high altitude: the effect of the latter was that he could not consume his usual quantity of alcohol without getting a hangover. In January 1973 he and Jennifer, accompanied by Matthew Oakeshott, visited Africa (not his favourite continent), moving rapidly through Nigeria, Ethiopia, Kenya, Zambia and Tanzania in two and a half weeks. That summer they spent August in Italy as usual. Then in September Jenkins was invited to give a lecture in Australia and managed to tack onto it two weeks in China on the way. This was only a year after President Nixon's historic visit; Roy and Jennifer were given the full tour of approved sites – the Great Wall and the Forbidden City – but also schools, factories, exhibitions and performances of revolutionary opera. Roy met the recently rehabilitated Deng Xiaoping (by whom he was not particularly impressed) for a formal exchange of geopolitical perspectives: the Chinese were keen on a united Europe as a counterweight to both the Americans and the Russians. China was then sufficiently unknown that he kept (and later circulated privately) a journal of the trip, recording in somewhat dutiful detail not only their impressions of the country and its inhabitants, but what they had to eat and the difficulty of getting decent wine. (On the train to Nanking, they 'secured a Moselle-like bottle of Chinese wine. Tasted like a mixture of sherry and Orvieto.') Characteristically Jenkins tried to classify every town and landscape they saw by comparison with places they reminded him of in Europe or America. Thus Peking resembled working-class Paris in the 1930s; apartment blocks in Shanghai were like Glasgow tenements; the Yangtze was 'not unlike the Thames between Tower Bridge and Tilbury'; while the Pearl River at Canton was 'about the size of the Rhone at Lyon'. Best of all, they stayed in a wonderful old pre-Communist hotel in Shanghai, which made their hotel in Peking 'seem like a dour Mongolian barracks':

> The lifts have clock-face floor indicators outside exactly like the ones I remember in Selfridges in my childhood, the corridor carpets are the height of 1934 fashion, the windows are Crittall leaded casements, the doors dark-stained, the bedroom reminiscent of a very good Cunard state room . . . and the 11th floor dining room exactly like the restaurant in the departed *Queen Mary*.

He did like his comforts. On arriving in Hong Kong he noted: 'I had been looking forward to pre-luncheon Martini (there is no ice or gin in China, and we had even run out of whisky for previous 36 hours) but alas it was over-vermouthed.'[18]

In his memoirs Jenkins claimed that 'China made a deep impact on me'; but what that impact was is far from clear, since he rarely referred to the experience again and signally failed to foresee the rise of the 'sleeping dragon' in the next century. From Hong Kong ('brash') he went on to Australia ('provincial') to deliver his lecture in Melbourne, plus a number of other speeches, and flew home via Singapore (Lee Kuan Yew again), arriving back on 24 September, a week before the Labour party conference (once again in Blackpool).[19]

There he made a five-minute speech from the floor, which as an ordinary backbencher was all he was allowed, and another vain appeal for realism. There was a case for a significant extension of public owner-ship, he conceded. But it was 'no good taking over a vast number of industries without a clear plan as to how and by whom they are going to be run'. More to the point, you could not do it without clear public support:

> It is not much good talking about fundamental and irreversible changes in our society and being content with a 38 per cent Labour voting intention . . . Democracy means that you need a substantially stronger moral position than this to govern effectively at all, let alone effect a peaceful social revolution.[20]

For this heretical suggestion he was rebuked by the next speaker, an USDAW-sponsored MP named Charles Loughlin, who had been a junior minister in various departments in 1967–70:

> I regret that Roy Jenkins came to this rostrum to resuscitate the outmoded idea that this party can cater for the middle-class, that we ought to fashion our policies to cater for the mythical floating voter . . . If I may say so . . . one of the difficulties of those of us who were members of the Government was with the Treasury, and he was in charge of the Treasury.[21]

This was the tribal mindset he was now up against.

Sooner or later he had to decide what to do. Should he stand boldly for the leadership, at the risk of splitting or even breaking up the party? Or continue to bide his time, swallow his dissent from most of its current policies and stand again for the Shadow Cabinet? 'One couldn't stay out indefinitely on the back benches.'[22] Though he still floated the possibility with friendly journalists like Tony Howard and John Cole, and his lieutenants were still keeping lists of definite and possible supporters who might back him if he stood, it was fairly clear that he was not going to challenge Wilson this side of an election. Wilson was belatedly showing signs of standing up to the left, first by vetoing the NEC's call to nationalise twenty-five top companies and then by persuading conference not to commit the party to withdrawal from the EEC, but merely to 'renegotiate' the Tory terms and submit the result to either a referendum or a General Election. Jenkins thought renegotiation was nonsense, but realised that it could provide a fig leaf for staying in. The idea of rejoining the Shadow Cabinet was not appealing – particularly if it committed him to joining another Wilson government if Labour won. Friends outside the party, including significantly David Steel, with whom he lunched in July, and Nicko Henderson, now ambassador in Bonn, urged him to keep his distance. But his allies inside the party all urged that only by coming back could he regain his position in the hierarchy and be a candidate for the leadership after the election, if Labour lost. The Jenkinsites needed their man back at the Cabinet table. And Jennifer agreed. So a week after conference he announced his intention to stand; and he did remarkably well.

He came fifth, with 143 votes, behind Callaghan, Foot, Reg Prentice (then still a party favourite, as a robust right-winger who was anti-Common Market) and Tony Crosland. But they were all closely bunched and he was only seven votes behind Callaghan; with just a few more he could have topped the poll, which would have been a triumph. As it was, his vote indicated a clear willingness among Labour MPs to close ranks and present the strongest possible team to the electorate. On this ground at least Wilson appeared pleased to have him back. But what was he to do with him? With Healey and Callaghan established as Shadow Chancellor and Shadow Foreign Secretary respectively, the only appropriately senior job left was Shadow Home Secretary, which meant displacing Shirley Williams. Jenkins felt bad about this, but she took it well, stepping down without complaint to Shadow Consumer Protection.

Jenkins' return in a diminished role was not easy. The minutes show that he attended all sixteen Shadow Cabinet meetings between November 1973 and March 1974, but he could not hope to overturn the party's settled policies and did not seriously try. In late November, however, he got embroiled in support of Prentice, who was the one prominent right-winger to call publicly on Labour moderates to 'stand up and be counted' against the domination of the 'Marxist' left. He was answered in kind by Tony Benn, at which point Wilson called a special meeting of the Shadow Cabinet to demand that colleagues should clear their speeches in future with Transport House. When Jenkins declared that this was 'unacceptable to him', Wilson complained about leaks and briefings – an old obsession of his – implying that they had only started up again since Jenkins' return. Jenkins in turn objected to inaccurate briefings about what he had said. He got some support from Shirley Williams; but Crosland characteristically thought his intervention 'pompous and bumbling'.[23]*

His better stage, however, was the House of Commons, and here he soon scored another debating triumph. At the end of 1973 the Heath government ran into the combination of crises which sank it. First, the Arab–Israeli war led to the quadrupling of the price of oil, on top of already soaring prices for imported food and other commodities (copper, rubber, zinc and so on), giving a powerful external boost to inflation, which Heath and Barber had already racked up by their reckless dash for growth (the so-called 'Barber boom'). Then the National Union of Mineworkers, having already humiliated the government once by extorting a 30 per cent pay rise by strike action in 1972, realised that the oil price hike gave them increased bargaining power to demand a further massive increase in 1973, threatening to smash the elaborately detailed statutory incomes policy which was the heart of the government's economic strategy. On 12 November they announced an overtime ban, which immediately cut the output of coal by 40 per cent. On 3 December, after intensive talks had failed to reach a settlement, Heath put the country on a three-day working week to save energy; and on 13 December Barber introduced a drastic package of spending cuts, which brought the boom to a grinding halt. The following week there was a two-day debate on the crisis. Wilson opened for Labour on the first day and Healey on the second. Jenkins – despite no longer holding an economic portfolio – was allowed to wind up, and comprehensively upstaged them both.

'I did not attempt to dine,' he wrote in his memoirs, 'but I can remember sitting and fortifying myself in the smoking room with Bob

---

* Wilson later claimed that they had another spat over the Arab–Israeli war, when Wilson, always strongly Zionist, wanted to impose a three-line whip on a motion condemning the government's refusal to supply arms to Israel. When Jenkins objected, Wilson retorted: 'Look, Roy, I've accommodated your ******* conscience for years. Now you're going to have to take account of mine. I feel as strongly about the Middle East as you do about the Common Market.' Wilson's official biographer, Philip Ziegler, repeats this story (from Wilson's book *The Chariot of Israel*) as though it happened in Shadow Cabinet. But the Commons vote (on which Labour MPs were actually allowed a free vote) was on 18 October; and Jenkins did not rejoin the Shadow Cabinet until 7 November. Was this then just Wilson's imagination? There must have been some ground for his remembering the incident.[24]

Maclennan and one or two others until about 8.15, when I returned to the chamber in as great a state of neurosis intermingled with terror as I have ever managed to produce before a speech.'[25] Shirley Williams wrote him an encouraging note: 'Dear Roy, You will have to "speak for England" – no-one else has yet! Or will –.'[26] But nervous tension always fired his best performances. Once on his feet, he lambasted Barber first for his entire economic record – for 'having taken over an economy with a £1000m surplus and running it into a £2000m deficit'; for having conducted the national finances 'with such profligacy that the accounts are out of balance as never before'; for having 'presided over the greatest depreciation of the currency at home and abroad in history'; and for leaving the country 'at the moment of test far weaker than most of its neighbours' – and then for his 'trivial and irrelevant' measures to deal with the current crisis, which he described as 'a mixture of economic lunacy and fiscal inequity'. Jenkins did not deny that it was a real crisis, but warned – with an eye to some in his own party – that it was not just an economic but a social crisis, which posed 'a greater threat to the effective workings of our democratic institutions than most of us have seen in our adult lifetimes'. Heath, he suggested, lacked the imagination and persuasiveness that the situation demanded. What was required to resolve the miners' dispute was 'neither an imposed solution nor an open hand at the till'. As a Labour spokesman seeking to restore his credit with the party, he could not be seen to criticise the NUM. So 'the task of statesmanship', he concluded, 'was to reach a settlement as quickly as possible, but to do it in a way that opens no floodgates', somehow securing 'the differentials which the miners need and deserve and the nation needs them to have'.[27]

How this miracle was to be achieved he did not reveal: in fact the whole speech was a fairly standard piece of Opposition posturing, condemning the government without saying what he would do instead. But it delighted the Labour benches, as *The Times* reported:

Mr Roy Jenkins came back with a thunderclap into the front rank of the leadership tonight . . . Where Mr Healey . . . had uttered mainly party political bombast and Mr Wilson . . . had been full of recrimination and bickering, here was the voice of authority and leadership that the Labour Party has so sadly lacked in the long months since Mr Jenkins retired to the back benches over the European issue.[28]

Shirley Williams was one of many Labour MPs to congratulate him. 'Thanks – that was a truly magnificent speech.'[29] 'Your winding up speech,' Betty Boothroyd wrote, 'sent me through the Division Lobby with head held high – what a splendid tonic it was'; and Andrew Faulds – the bearded ex-actor who was one of the most colourful characters on the Labour benches: 'That was one of the best speeches I have heard in the House – and the closing minutes certainly the greatest. How rarely politicians rise to the occasion. Thankyou. There is a sort of wholesomeness about the place tonight.'[30]

While this was exactly the sort of response he needed to confirm his comeback – even Dennis Skinner was said to have declared that Jenkins would now 'certainly' be the next leader[31] – his situation at the turn of the year remained uncomfortable. As the government's emergency measures took effect, with industry on a three-day week, reduced street lighting, a 50 m.p.h. speed limit and television shutting down at 10.30 p.m., Heath hesitated about whether to call an election to try to resolve the deadlock. Jenkins was not sure whether he wanted an early election or, if one came, that he wanted Labour to win it. In his memoirs he was quite frank that his personal interest required Labour to lose, triggering an immediate leadership election and an opportunity to challenge those whose policies had led it to defeat.[32] Failing that, it was better for him that Labour should win well, allowing Wilson to form a government strong enough to deal with the crisis and keep Britain in the EEC, then hand over in a couple of years, by which time he might have re-established his position as the heir apparent. What he most feared was the sort of result he had been warning of in recent speeches: a hung Parliament or a narrow Labour victory on a minority vote which would give it no authority to deal with the crisis, while perpetuating divisions within the party.

In the Shadow Cabinet he counselled moderation, warning that the Tories might try to hold a scare election, as in 1931, and pleading that Labour's response should be responsible, not opportunist. People were 'bewildered and apprehensive and the Party must be realistic in assuaging their fears. We had to be careful in seeing that what was promised was capable of being fulfilled.'[33] Labour should seek to cool the situation, not inflame it. 'The Party had to battle for the marginal voter who would be lost if things were "stirred up" at Westminster.'[34] By 19 January 1974 he thought that Heath had missed his best moment and the danger of an early election had passed.[35] But then on 4 February – following the breakdown of all attempts to find a formula that would buy off the miners without allowing every other union to demand the same treatment – the NUM escalated its dispute by voting for a full-scale strike; and Heath felt he had no remaining option but to call an election to be held on 28 February.

Though it was not clear what an election would achieve, all the polls suggested that he would win. In this expectation, Jenkins rallied to the Labour cause like a professional, submerging his doubts about the wider implications of the contest in the argument that it was Heath's mismanagement that had landed the country in an unnecessary crisis. His appeal to middle opinion was recognised with a role in Labour's campaign almost as prominent as in 1970. He featured alongside Wilson in several of the party's morning press conferences and – at Wilson's insistence – in one of its television broadcasts, and toured a number of marginal seats in Yorkshire and Lancashire as well as speaking for several of his personal supporters, like David Owen in Plymouth and Bob Maclennan in Caithness and Sutherland. 'As in previous campaigns,' David Butler and Dennis Kavanagh wrote, 'Roy Jenkins was brought in to sound a note of civilised idealism and to recognise, unlike anyone else on television, a responsibility to the outside world.'[36] Generally he tried to strike a moderate note, following Wilson's line that Heath's 'confrontational' policies had divided the country and it was Labour's job to heal it; on the central issue of the miners' strike he repeated his loftily vague formula that 'Statesmanship demands a solution which recognises that the country has a special need for the miners and that others must not seek to exploit it so that we are all damaged in the process.'[37] Asked at a press conference what he thought of Heath, he replied diplomatically:

> According to which way you look at it, Mr Heath has stubbornness or determination. Nobody becomes Prime Minister of this country without qualities. The tragedy is that he doesn't accompany those qualities with judgement, persuasiveness or the imagination to see across a chasm of disagreement and into the minds of others whose experience of life is different.[38]

But the adrenalin of the hustings brought out more partisanship than he really felt. He nursed a particular animus against Barber for dissipating the hard-won balance-of-payments surplus he had bequeathed him. At Plymouth on 18 February he described his successor in uncharacteristically personal terms as 'a dated disaster shot through with political viciousness'.[39] Barber may have been a bad Chancellor, but he was scarcely a vicious one. Remembering the fuss the Tories had made in 1970 about his one unlucky monthly deficit of £31 million, however, Jenkins felt entitled to attack the record deficit of £383 million that Barber had to announce for January. When the Tories claimed that they were better able than Labour to deal with the problem he commented sarcastically that 'the Government appeared to regard each fresh disaster as a reason for voting for it'.[40]

Some Labour people still suspected that his heart was not in it. The former MP for Hampstead, Ben Whitaker, who had lost his seat in 1970 and was now working in Wilson's office, wondered of Jenkins and his friends: 'Do they really care who wins this election?'[41] But Jenkins did appeal to intelligent middle opinion which despaired equally of Heath and Wilson. The Oxford historian Raymond Carr wrote that he was 'deeply impressed' by his television broadcast. 'It was the only morally & intellectually respectable speech of the whole lot & left you head & shoulders above every other politician in the country.'[42] Terence Rattigan wrote similarly, wishing Jenkins could somehow be Prime Minister.[43] And the Labour MP Raymond Fletcher (pro-European, but not a Jenkinsite) wrote a week before polling day thanking him for his television appearances, saying that his constituents in Ilkeston liked his style even when they disagreed with his views. He feared that Labour had lost, but thought that this would be Jenkins' opportunity:

> This, of course, will enlarge the role which you will have to play in the coming period of national disintegration and decline. You can rise to this challenge. Please do it in the style you brought to this otherwise degrading election campaign.[44]

Campaigning more for others than for himself, Jenkins spent as little time as possible in Stechford, which he found increasingly dispiriting. Such canvassing as he did – using for the first time a counting machine in his pocket to record exactly how many people he had spoken to – impressed him with the persistence of tribal voting. A lot of Labour supporters told him that they disagreed with his views on Europe or capital punishment, but would nevertheless vote for him; while Tory and Liberal voters assured him that they would have voted Labour if he had been leader. When he asked how they could want him to be Prime Minister and yet not vote for him as their MP ('Cannot you see that massive local support would help to make me leader?'), they replied doggedly that he was not the leader: 'Mr Wilson is.' 'This experience left me feeling that . . . the British party system was so rigid as to make it almost impossible to build up a cross-party constituency base, such as any well-known American senator easily achieves.' He felt particularly aggrieved that the Liberals – fielding a candidate against him for the first time since 1950 – attracted so much support. 'I already regarded myself as such a closet Liberal that I naively thought they ought nearly all to have come to me.'[45]

At his eve-of-poll meeting he claimed to see a late swing to Labour, which offered the only way out of Heath's 'blind alley of gloom, despondency, division, selfishness and frustration'.[46] But going to his count he still anticipated a comfortable Tory majority of about fifty. Instead the early results pointed to a narrow Labour victory. 'You know,' he told Matthew Oakeshott gloomily, 'I think we're going to win this bloody election.'[47] The final result was thoroughly inconclusive. Labour gained fourteen seats, several of them by the tiniest majorities, which was enough to give them four more than the Tories – 301:297 – but with 230,000 fewer votes (37.1 per cent against 37.9 per cent); while the Liberals, who had campaigned openly for a hung Parliament and a government of national unity (supported by Dick Taverne, who narrowly retained Lincoln), won more than six million votes (19.3 per cent), but were rewarded with just fourteen seats. The Scottish and Welsh nationalists took another nine between them, while the imposition of Direct Rule in Northern Ireland meant that the twelve Ulster Unionists could no longer be counted as Conservatives.* This outcome called the fairness of the electoral system seriously into question for the first time since the 1920s. Moreover it was exactly the result Jenkins had dreaded, since after a weekend of uncertainty while Heath tried to cobble together a deal with Jeremy Thorpe – which did not stand up, since the Tories and Liberals together still fell short of an overall majority – he was forced to contemplate what job he should seek, and what job he was willing to accept, in a minority Labour government still led by Harold Wilson, committed to a lot of left-wing policies and more than ever in the pocket of the unions.

Back in July 1973, when Jenkins decided to rejoin the Shadow

---

* Jenkins' personal result showed a modest recovery from its 1970 dip, despite a strong performance by the Liberal:

Roy Jenkins (Labour)	23,704
D.J. Wedgwood (Con)	13,472
G.A. Gopsill (Lib)	7,221
R. Bull (WRP)	280
Labour majority	10,232[48]

Cabinet, his supporters had pressed him to insist on going back to the Treasury when Labour regained power. He had refused then, and he was no more enthusiastic now. On the Friday evening after the election, following an afternoon meeting which endorsed Wilson's determination to form a minority government if he got the chance, Bill Rodgers called at Ladbroke Square to re-emphasise their view. 'Roy was very tired and depressed and had drunk a fair amount.' He reiterated his reluctance, but agreed that he might go back for a short time.[49] He also rang his old friend Ronnie McIntosh, 'very depressed' and saying that 'he felt like a prisoner'. McIntosh too tried to persuade him that his bargaining position was very strong, since the electorate had clearly voted for the things he stood for. But Jenkins felt that Wilson was bound to give the job to Denis Healey, who had been Shadow Chancellor for the past two years.[50] More to the point, he really did not want to return to the Treasury at such a difficult time: the only job he coveted was the one great department he had not already experienced, the Foreign Office. But that was earmarked for Jim Callaghan and was out of the question anyway while the party was committed to renegotiating the Common Market terms. Jenkins justified his position by arguing that no one could be a successful Chancellor without the Prime Minister's full confidence. 'To force myself into the Treasury over the reluctance of my colleagues, and to believe that I could then command their loyal acceptance of what I laid down was a non-starter.'[51] This was probably realistic. But over the weekend his mood changed, partly under continued pressure from Rodgers and David Owen (with whom he and Jennifer lunched on the Sunday), but more as a result of hints from a number of sources that Wilson – himself pressured by Marcia Williams – did want him back at the Treasury after all. If that were really so, he did not think he could refuse. He actually got as far as drafting a memorandum setting out the terms on which he would accept. On Sunday evening Rodgers found him 'a good deal more cheerful' about the prospect; and Jenkins told McIntosh that he had 'become quite nostalgic for his old job as Chancellor of the Exchequer'.[52]

But then Wilson found that he could not break 'the Healey/Callaghan matrix'. He had hoped – or so he told Jenkins – to send Callaghan to sort out industrial relations and give Healey the Foreign Office, allowing Jenkins to return to the Treasury. That would actually have been the best deployment of his available talent. But Callaghan was determined to have the Foreign Office, and was strong enough to get his way. Unwilling to tell Jenkins himself, Wilson initially sent Bernard

Donoughue* to convey the news, provoking an uncharacteristic outburst in a House of Commons corridor, which spoke volumes about his edgy state:

> Roy explodes in an extraordinary fashion, shouting, 'You tell Harold Wilson he must bloody well come and see me and if he doesn't watch out, I won't join his bloody government.' He repeated this several times, on a public staircase. He was very angry . . . Roy shouted again, 'This is typical of the bloody awful way HW does things.'[53]

Wilson was sufficiently anxious to have Jenkins on board that – reversing normal practice – he did go to see him in his small room at the top of the Palace of Westminster, 'puffing his pipe and panting for breath after the unwonted exercise of the stairs'.[54] But he could still only offer a return to the Home Office, with a clumsy attempt to enhance it by throwing in Northern Ireland. Jenkins had no difficulty refusing the latter, but weakly accepted the former without using his window of bargaining strength to try to influence the shape of the government – the only appointment he objected to was the possibility of Peter Shore as Trade Secretary having charge of negotiations with the EEC – or to insist on suitable jobs for his own supporters.

He went on almost immediately to meet a large group of them at Harry Walston's rooms in the Albany, where he ran into 'a wall of disappointment and dismay' when he told them what he had done.[55] The usually loyal Rodgers led the attack, bitterly blaming him for letting them all down by not insisting on the Treasury. As Chancellor, Jenkins would have been the central figure of the government and still a challenger for the leadership; but as Home Secretary he would be marginalised. 'We can't mount a political campaign on the basis of penal reform.'

> I said it was a defeat and we must recognise it as such . . . Roy reacted to my view by saying that he had no choice and we always had greatly exaggerated his position. I said, 'Did you want the job? Did you make clear you wanted the Treasury?' Roy was very angry. He said that he had no choice. 'If you're not the Prime

---

* An academic at the London School of Economics, Bernard Donoughue had been seconded to Downing Street as an adviser to the Prime Minister. He became a Labour peer in 1985.

Minister you can't make these decisions' – and at one point that if we went on like this he was going to leave.[56]

They were both shocked by this open row. On reflection, Rodgers wrote the next day, 'I suppose I'm disappointed in Roy':

Not that he's disloyal – he's a terribly loyal person, a terribly affectionate person – but in an odd way he hasn't got the muscle or the will for the ugliness or the in-fighting. On this occasion his distaste for the idea of a Wilson government, his hesitation about coming back at all, the extent to which he's been very flat since Jennifer's mother died – all these have made him even less of a fighting man.[57]*

As well as failing to secure the Treasury for himself, the Jenkinsites felt particularly sore that he had failed to insist on jobs for his friends. Apart from Shirley Williams (Prices and Consumer Protection) and Harold Lever (Chancellor of the Duchy of Lancaster) – both in the Cabinet – they were all ignored in the first tranche of appointments to the new government. Jenkins himself quickly recognised that he had let them down. Only a few months earlier he had written that Adlai Stevenson, in accepting the post of ambassador to the United Nations from President Kennedy, had made sure that his associates all got good jobs too. 'He was as loyal to them as they had been to him.'[58] And yet he failed to do the same for his associates. Rodgers, Owen, David Marquand, Dickson Mabon and Bob Maclennan ('almost choking') were among those disappointed; while Cledwyn Hughes, who had held two Cabinet posts in 1966–70, first as Secretary of State for Wales and then as Minister of Agriculture, was in Rodgers' words: 'the saddest looking man last night as the most senior, most deserving, most unkindly treated two years ago and most let down now by Roy'.[59] Jenkins took Rodgers for a depressing lunch at Brooks's on the Wednesday, at which Rodgers told him he had never imagined that Jenkins would go back into government without him; Jenkins said miserably that he had not realised he felt like that and 'had he known this on Friday he would certainly have said to Wilson that it was a condition of his returning' that Rodgers should get a good job.[60] This was a strange

---

* Jennifer's mother, Lady Morris, had died on New Year's Day, while staying at East Hendred over Christmas, as a result of falling from an upstairs window. She was in her early eighties. But the incident evidently affected both Jennifer and Roy very badly, if Roy was still depressed by it two months later.

failure of imagination towards his chief lieutenant. In fact it was not too late. Jenkins saw Wilson that afternoon and again the next morning to plead his supporters' cause, as a result of which Rodgers was offered Minister of State at the Ministry of Defence, while Owen and Maclennan became Under-Secretaries at Health and Prices respectively. Rodgers was so fed up that he nearly refused until Jenkins urged him to accept; while Maclennan wrote slightly tartly to thank Jenkins for his advocacy:

> I am the more conscious of my good fortune in the light of the position of others among your friends who have not been so favoured. Paul Rose is feeling particularly bruised and you may want to have a word with him. Dick Mabon seems the most philosophical – admirably so.[61]

Paul Rose, MP for Manchester, Blackley, since 1964, was a pro-European barrister, more left-wing than most of the Jenkinsites, who had been an employment spokesman in 1970–71, but lost his job after voting the wrong way in October 1971. He now wrote bitterly to Jenkins that people like himself faced blighted careers, 'feeling that one has been a pawn sacrificed in a gambit that failed', while 'those who played it both ways have been suitably rewarded'. 'I have taken it upon myself,' he wrote, 'to say what others undoubtedly feel. You were in a strong position to prevent this massacre of the innocents and did not use that strength.' While it must be galling for Jenkins not to return to 'your rightful place as Chancellor', several of them – 'Bob, David, Dick, Cledwyn and those who might have followed us' – now faced a future as 'permanent lobby fodder . . . as the casualties of a battle in which . . . we were made the scapegoats'. He was now wondering 'whether to soldier on . . . or to break out before it is too late':

> If there is no future, and you must know Harold's mood better than we do, then please be frank about it so that I for one can fight my political battles elsewhere and build up a different future from the one I had some fragile hope of no more than three years ago.[62]

This was really rubbing Jenkins' nose in the responsibilities of political leadership. He wrote on Rose's letter that he would reply verbally (as, frustratingly for his biographer, he often did). His diary gives no indication of when they met, but his advice cannot have been encouraging, since a year later Rose wrote again that, acting on it, he had built up his Bar practice successfully and intended to leave Parliament at the next election – as indeed he did.[63]* Of the others he mentioned as feeling similarly aggrieved, Marquand also left Parliament in 1976 and Cledwyn Hughes lost his seat in 1979; Maclennan did belatedly get a job from Wilson in 1974, and Mabon from Callaghan in 1976. But it would be fair to say that they all felt disillusioned with Jenkins at this time. He had failed once too often to stand up for himself and them when the chance was there, and they all felt – as did Rodgers, David Owen and Shirley Williams – that he had shot his bolt as a potential leader and their generation should begin to look elsewhere for leadership. This was the end of the Jenkinsites as a cohesive force.

One other recently elected supporter was not yet disillusioned, though he sounded as if he thought he might soon be. Giles Radice – the victor of the Chester-le-Street by-election held the same day as Lincoln in March 1973 – wrote to Jenkins that even though not Chancellor, he was still strategically 'the most powerful man in the Cabinet', since everyone knew that 'in present circumstances there can be no Labour administration without you'. The knowledge that he would be willing to resign, as in 1972, if pushed too far gave him 'a formidable strength inside the Cabinet – a strength which nobody else has'. Radice urged Jenkins to 'forget what happened last week – and use your power fearlessly and ruthlessly in the Cabinet. Your admirers still believe in you. Please don't let them down.'[64]

Others of a more coalitionist tendency still hoped that the combination of a hung Parliament and a continuing national emergency might yet be Jenkins' opportunity. Madron Seligman – who from Balliol onwards had managed to remain a good friend of both Jenkins and Ted Heath – wrote to congratulate him on his return to the Cabinet: 'I feel you are ideally placed to bring maximum influence to bear, when the present equivocal stage comes to an end.'[65] An even older friend, Derek Powell from his Pontypool schooldays, was afraid that by sending him back to the Home Office, Wilson had given him 'the bum's rush', but still hoped that he might yet be called upon to lead a National Government that would command a huge majority.[66]

But how much of this did Jenkins himself believe? He knew he had suffered a serious defeat. For an ex-Chancellor, going back to the Home Office was a clear demotion, and the upward momentum of his career

---

* Rose continued to be politically active in the areas of civil liberties and human rights, and was a leading campaigner against the National Front. In 1981 he joined the SDP, but did not stand again for Parliament.

had clearly stalled. In 1967 he had been a rising star; now, like so many Home Secretaries, he was probably on the way down. In appointing him – confident that he was no longer a dangerous rival – Wilson was friendly and even renewed his previous hints that, with Labour back in office, Jenkins would be his favoured successor when he stood down, probably in a couple of years. He accompanied this with the suggestion that 'if, as was perhaps inevitable for a time, I wanted to be a semi-detached member of the Government', the Home Office was 'the most suitable department from which to play such a stand-off role'. Jenkins called this 'one of the oddest remarks that a Prime Minister has ever made to a colleague in a new Cabinet'.[67] In fact he had made the same point himself in his 1971 article comparing the Home Office with the Treasury, writing that 'A man could, I believe, be a tolerable and even a good Home Secretary while not on speaking terms with most of his principal colleagues.'[68] The hard fact was, however, that for all his seniority he was not going to be a central figure in the new government: with Healey at the Treasury, Callaghan at the Foreign Office and Michael Foot at Employment (charged with ending the miners' strike and keeping the unions happy), Jenkins was barely on speaking terms with his senior colleagues. Tony Crosland at Environment was still outside the big four, but now more clearly on the up than his old rival. So was Tony Benn, boosted by his triumph in committing Labour to hold a referendum on Europe and now Secretary of State for Industry, charged with setting up the National Enterprise Board and enforcing planning agreements on private industry. Nor could Jenkins console himself with going back to unfinished business at the Home Office: the liberalising chapter of the 1960s had been written – if anything the backlash had begun – and he felt no enthusiasm for a second bout of wrestling with prisons and the police. For all these reasons he went back to the Home Office in March 1974 with a heavy heart, quite unlike his first arrival there full of hope and energy, nine years before.

16 Back to the Home Office

JENKINS' second period at the Home Office was very different from his previous tenure nine years earlier. Then he had been a rising star, the youngest Home Secretary since Churchill, widely tipped as a future Prime Minister, with a clear agenda of reforms he wanted to pursue and a liberal social climate which supported his programme. Now, though still only fifty-two, he was a senior but marginalised member of a minority government, returning without enthusiasm to a job he had done before, against a much more anxious and illiberal national mood dominated by economic crisis, industrial militancy and Irish terrorism. The optimism and confidence of the 1960s had given way to the fractious and disillusioned 1970s. Jenkins was thoroughly out of sympathy with the colleagues he had reluctantly rejoined – Wilson a tired and tarnished Prime Minister; Healey initially out of his depth at the Treasury; Callaghan cynically Eurosceptic at the Foreign Office; Michael Foot in the Department of Employment bent on giving the unions everything they wanted. At the Home Office his in-tray was dominated by an escalating campaign of IRA bombings, spreading in 1974–5 from Northern Ireland to the British mainland; while on the wider political front he increasingly feared that the combination of roaring inflation and left-wing militancy could lead to social breakdown and a threat to democracy itself. The one positive priority he set himself was to ensure a 'Yes' vote in the Common Market referendum which he now accepted as inevitable.

Unlike most incoming ministers in a new department, Jenkins made little secret of the fact that he did not want to be there. Once again he did not begin to feel happy until he was able to surround himself with some of his own people. The Permanent Secretary since 1972, Sir

Arthur Peterson, was not as hidebound as Sir Charles Cunningham in 1965, but nor was he as congenial as Philip Allen, or Douglas Allen at the Treasury, and Jenkins never formed the same sort of bond that he had enjoyed with those two. But he soon managed to bring in some familiar faces, starting with the faithful John Harris, no longer as a mere special adviser but now as Minister of State (in charge of prisons and the police), for which purpose he was given a peerage as Lord Harris of Greenwich. It was said that Harris was the first peer created by a Home Secretary; but in fact the promotion suited Wilson admirably and may even have been his idea, diverting Harris from the day-to-day polishing of his master's image – which had created such irritation and jealousy in 1964–70 – by giving him defined responsibilities of his own. His elevation also provided a useful precedent for the equally unusual translation of Marcia Williams into Lady Falkender two months later. It raised some eyebrows at first, but Harris quickly proved himself an effective departmental minister, so much so that he not only stayed on under Merlyn Rees when Jenkins went to Brussels in 1976, but was then appointed chairman of the Parole Board by Willie Whitelaw in 1979. He remained Jenkins' most trusted adviser, still on hand whenever he was needed and a frequent lunch companion. But he was no longer ever-present in his private office.

The Principal Private Secretary he inherited from Robert Carr was a Home Office lifer named Syd Norris – 'an able assistant secretary,' Jenkins wrote in his memoirs, 'but not in my view a natural private secretary'.[1] After six months Jenkins got Peterson's agreement to replace Norris with his deputy, the thirty-one-year-old Hayden Phillips, who thus stepped into the role filled in 1965–9 by David Dowler: the indispensable official with the intellectual self-confidence and the zest for good living to become an inseparable companion – one of his first duties was to accompany Jenkins to the Colchester Oyster Festival – and a lifelong friend.*

A still younger long-term confidant was Mathew Oakeshott, his Rowntree-funded special adviser since 1972, whom Jenkins now brought into the Home Office, partly to keep an eye on the Common

---

* Norris was hurt by Jenkins' description in his memoirs and wrote to protest, leading Jenkins to apologise. All he had meant, he explained tactfully, was that 'at that stage my interest was much more on general Cabinet politics than on the Home Office, and that yours was the reverse . . . I must have been very difficult to work for in the spring and summer of 1974, owing to my generally downbeat mood and the fact that, for the first few months at least, I did not do my job at all well.' Norris thanked him for the clarification, insisting that he had enjoyed working for him and did not share Jenkins' recollection of his own performance.[2] He retired in 1997 as Director of Finance in the Prison Service.

Market 'renegotiation' by forging close links with George Thomson's *cabinet* in Brussels, but also to keep him in touch with Labour party feeling and help write speeches and newspaper articles. Anthony Lester, who had edited Jenkins' speeches in 1967, thought Oakeshott tended to over-egg them, writing to Jenkins that his 'remarkable ability to emulate your magisterial political style can be a disadvantage. At its worst it can become a parody, too verbose and a tiny bit pompous and complacent.' He should write more briskly, 'leaving you to add the flourishes, the metaphors and the irony'.[3] But Jenkins disagreed: he thought Oakeshott's speeches extraordinarily good – 'enough in my style to enable me to deliver them with conviction [but] in a slightly harder and more extreme form than I would have used myself'.[4] Oakeshott was delighted when *The Times* praised the Home Secretary's use of English. Finally Jenkins brought Lester into the department as his special adviser on legal and racial policy. Lester provided the initiative for the two principal legislative achievements of his second term at the Home Office, the Sex Discrimination Act of 1975 and the Race Relations Act of 1976.

After a few months these three – Phillips, Oakeshott and Lester, in their different (slightly competitive) roles – formed a sort of inner *cabinet* which gave Jenkins the support he needed to enjoy the job again and to prove once more, in difficult circumstances, a pretty good Home Secretary. Those officials outside the close circle of his confidence still found him chilly and remote: he was shy, and could be 'brusque and dismissive'.[5] But others actually thought him better than the first time round: less driven, more experienced and more reflective. He still enjoyed long lunches and his mind was often on wider matters, but when he attended to Home Office business he listened carefully to all views and then made decisions quickly and judiciously. And it can be argued that the legislation he introduced in these years, promoting gender and racial equality, actually affected the lives of more people than the homosexuality and abortion Acts of 1967.

The Northern Ireland conflict had exploded since he was last in the Home Office. It was Jim Callaghan who had sent troops onto the streets in 1969, initially to protect the Catholics, since when they had become a target for the Provisional IRA who saw them as an occupying force. In 1972 the Heath government suspended the devolved parliament at Stormont and imposed direct rule from London while successfully negotiating a power-sharing agreement. But when this broke down in 1974 in the face of Protestant strikes, the IRA took its campaign of indiscriminate murder from Ulster to the British mainland. London and other cities became sickeningly resigned to regular attack. The bloodiest atrocities came later in the year; but Jenkins had an early taste of the policy dilemmas thrown up by terrorism as early as May, when two young sisters, Marian and Dolours Price (aged twenty-three and twenty respectively), sentenced to twenty years for helping to plant bombs outside the Old Bailey and New Scotland Yard which killed one person and injured 213, went on hunger strike in Brixton prison. They had been forcibly fed since December, but now withdrew the necessary minimum degree of cooperation. Their aim was to be allowed to serve their sentences in Northern Ireland. It was a relatively modest request, and because they were young girls it attracted noisy demonstrations and some sympathy. (Four male hunger strikers, one of whom died, drew far less attention.) As their condition worsened Jenkins as Home Secretary came under enormous pressure to grant their wish: humanitarian appeals from the Catholic hierarchy were backed by warnings of terrible retribution if the girls should die, and the pragmatic argument that only the IRA would benefit from creating a new pair of youthful martyrs. 'The difficulty,' Jenkins reflected some years later, 'was that there was no particular reason why they should not be moved . . . One had to try to . . . enable them to be moved to Northern Ireland at some stage in the future without doing it under pressure of their threats.'[6]

Over the May bank holiday weekend he decided that the prudent course was to announce a date when the girls would be transferred. But when he tried to frame the case for doing so, 'the words simply failed to come . . . To be respectable I had to pretend I was not acting under duress. But as that was in fact what I was doing I could find no convincing words to act as a cloak.' In his memoirs he gives credit to Anthony Lester for showing him that he could not do it, because he knew it was wrong. Over lunch at East Hendred – 'fortified by one of Roy's dangerously potent dry Martinis'[7] – Lester 'argued with force and cogency that the correct thing was to make it absolutely clear that I was not moving under threat and that if the sisters were determined to kill themselves we must allow events to take their course' – while holding out the possibility of a move at some time in the future.[8] After clearing it with Wilson, Jenkins announced his decision in a statement, repeated in a television broadcast, in which he weighed the alternatives with gravity and compassion before concluding that 'After deep thought, I am clear that I must not be forced into a decision about their future location or an unwarranted promise as a result of any intimidation, however harrowing may be the consequences.'[9] His broadcast was widely admired. 'In his judgment and explanation,' George Hutchinson wrote in *The Times*, 'he has delivered . . . one of the finest statements of principle heard from any minister in recent years . . . in words of such simple, compelling dignity as to elevate the public debate. This is Prime Ministerial language.'[10] It is still remembered forty years later. Moreover it worked. After informal assurances from a string of mainly Roman Catholic intermediaries, the girls were persuaded to start taking liquid food again and the crisis passed. Six months later they were moved to Durham prison; and the following March, with little publicity, to Northern Ireland. Essentially Jenkins had given them what they wanted; but with Lester's help he had finessed his concession very skilfully. The most important thing from the British perspective was that the sisters were not allowed to die: their death, he believed, would have triggered 'a wave of retributive violence which would have dwarfed even the other incidents of that bloody year'.[11] That at least was prevented. Meanwhile the praise heaped on him from all sides helped greatly to restore his self-confidence.*

Over the summer of 1974 IRA activity increased in intensity, with further bombings in London, Manchester and Birmingham. Jenkins had repeatedly to come to the House to report on the latest outrage, promising that the perpetrators would be brought to justice while urging vigilance on the public. The horrors climaxed in the autumn with attacks in Guildford on 5 October, where five people were killed and sixty-five injured by bombs planted in two pubs frequented by soldiers; and in Birmingham on 21 November, when twenty-one were killed and nearly 200 injured in city centre pubs packed with young people. Jenkins was dining with an American lady friend at Lockets restaurant in Westminster when he was told of the Birmingham attack, by far the worst yet. He returned immediately to the Home Office where he was joined by John Harris; they quickly decided to bring forward emergency legislation already prepared. Jenkins got Wilson's agreement on the phone that evening and announced it in the Commons the next morning, before hurrying to Birmingham to inspect the damage and visit the mutilated survivors. The fact that it was his own city that had been targeted made a deep impression on him: touring the familiar streets, he was oppressed by the 'stench of death and carnage' in the air, but also by the 'pervading atmosphere of stricken, hostile

---

* The sisters were released under the Royal Prerogative in 1980. Dolours then married the actor Stephen Rea, who later voiced the words of Gerry Adams when he was banned from the airwaves by Mrs Thatcher. Both sisters remained unrepentant Republicans who opposed the Good Friday Agreement and were linked to bombings carried out in 2009–11 by the 'Real IRA'. Marian was sent to prison again in 2011–13. Dolours died in 2013.

resentment such as I had never previously encountered anywhere in the world'.[12] As well as predictable demands to bring back hanging there were ugly calls to deport the entire Irish population. Accompanied by Denis Howell – who had himself been the target of a car bomb just the week before – he called on the Lord Mayor and the police; but he also made a point of visiting the Roman Catholic bishop to try to stem the growth of anti-Irish feeling.

The legislative response – the ironically named Prevention of Terrorism (Temporary Provisions) Act – was finalised over the weekend. Home Office draftsmen came to East Hendred on Sunday morning and Jenkins presented it to the Cabinet on Monday morning. Hitherto the police had insisted that they already had all the powers they needed to pursue terrorists. But public reaction to the slaughter in Birmingham demanded that more must be seen to be done. So the IRA – which as recently as June had openly staged the paramilitary funeral in Kilburn of the one hunger striker who had died – was declared an illegal organisation. A proposal to introduce identity cards was rejected as 'disproportionate'; but the police were given the power to hold suspected terrorists for forty-eight hours without charge, plus a further five days with the consent of the Home Secretary; and the Home Secretary was given the power to deport suspects to Ireland and – most controversially – bar Northern Irish suspects from mainland Britain. The Cabinet raised concerns about civil liberties, and Merlyn Rees, as Northern Ireland Secretary, objected to the discrimination between UK citizens; but by promising that the 'unprecedented' and 'draconian' provisions would run for only six months, renewable for another six months by Affirmative Order, Jenkins got his package agreed.[13] He explained it to the Commons that afternoon, and to the country on television that evening. The Bill was published on the Wednesday and rushed through all its stages in the Commons over Thursday night (28–9 November) and in the Lords on Friday morning, to become law the same day. During the all-night committee stage Jenkins – supported by the Law Officers, but doing most of it himself – spoke more than a dozen times, defending his proposals from critics who thought them either excessive or insufficient (Enoch Powell characteristically mocked the 'almost humorous optimism' of imagining that you could prevent terrorism by legislation at all)[14] while fortifying his team, and disarming critics, with champagne in his room. He finished up at Brooks's for 'a large late breakfast' with Harris and Phillips.[15]

By introducing the Prevention of Terrorism Act, Jenkins wrote years later, 'I provided a *locus classicus* for the permanence of the provisional.'[16]

As the Irish troubles persisted, the supposedly temporary Act was renewed annually for the next twenty-five years – he himself renewed it twice – until, to counter the still greater threat of Islamist terrorism from 2001, it was replaced by ever more restrictive measures by the Blair government. The seven-day limit on detention without charge was extended to fourteen and then to twenty-eight days, with the government in 2008 actually seeking to extend it to ninety days before Parliament finally rebelled. Jenkins naturally felt some qualms in later years that he had introduced this Frankenstein's monster: a paradoxical legacy for an avowed liberal. But in his memoirs he justified it as necessary at the time, 'both to steady opinion and to provide some additional protection', though he would have been horrified to be told it would still be in force three decades later.[17] In truth it was probably the minimum any Home Secretary could have done. Once again his relatively measured response – and particularly his television broadcast – drew admiration from his friends in the liberal establishment. 'I simply cannot tell you how thankful I am that, faced with our present difficulties . . . we have you as Home Secretary,' wrote Sir Robert Birley, the former head of Eton;[18] and the former royal secretary Sir Alan Lascelles wrote that he had never heard a better ministerial announcement at a time of national stress – and that included Asquith, Lloyd George and Churchill.[19] Even Denis Healey wrote generously: 'My dear Roy, Just to say I thought you were superb . . . on TV last night. It could not have been done better.'[20]

Public anger against the IRA also led to new calls for the restoration of the death penalty, at least for terrorists. As a prominent abolitionist and a Birmingham MP as well as Home Secretary, Jenkins bore the full force of this demand: he received 'a bigger volume of nasty disagreeable mail than I had ever had from Stechford on any issue previously . . . much of it couched in very bitter and hysterical terms'.[21] For a time it seemed that enough MPs of both parties might join the public clamour to reverse Parliament's previous decision. Jenkins was as determined as ever to stand against it. Quite apart from his long-standing personal abhorrence of capital punishment, he had just confronted the likely consequences if the Price sisters had starved themselves to death: their potency as martyrs would have been many times greater if they had been executed, like the rebels of 1916. He considered 'nearly insane' the argument of his Tory shadow, Keith Joseph, who still claimed to be an abolitionist while making an exception for terrorists.[22] Fortunately Willie Whitelaw (a former Northern Ireland Secretary) and Ted Heath (still just clinging on as Tory leader) held firm, so that following a highly charged debate the motion to restore hanging was heavily defeated, to Jenkins' immense relief, by 369 votes to 217. He had always maintained that he could not have served as Home Secretary had the job still involved the power of life and death. He was not of course responsible for the fact that the police subsequently arrested, and the courts convicted, the wrong men for both the Guildford and the Birmingham bombings. In the 1980s he worked hard behind the scenes with Cardinal Hume and others to secure the eventual pardon and release of the 'Guildford Four' and the 'Birmingham Six' in 1989 and 1991 respectively. That experience made him more than ever thankful that they had not been executed in 1975.

On the wider issue of Northern Ireland, however, Jenkins nursed private doubts about whether Britain should be there at all. He had in fact once ventured this view in print. In his 1972 Yale lectures, published as *Afternoon on the Potomac?*, he told his American audience that he had 'long regarded it as a clear lesson of history that the British political genius, great though it may be in certain fields, does not extend to a peculiar talent for settling the affairs of Ireland'.[23] (His point had been to suggest delicately that the same applied to the Americans in South-East Asia.) Now, after Guildford and Birmingham, he told the Cabinet committee on Northern Ireland on 4 December that 'everything he heard made him more convinced that Northern Ireland had nothing to do with the rest of the UK. He said that although the whole discussion was about how to impose the civilised standards of Britain on Northern Ireland, the real prospect and danger was of the barbaric standards of Northern Ireland spreading to the rest of us.'[24] This view hardened during 1975 as the IRA campaign continued. According to Bernard Donoughue (who as a member of the Prime Minister's Policy Unit sat in on Cabinet committees), quite a few ministers supported the withdrawal of troops; but Jenkins and (perhaps surprisingly) Wilson were the only two looking for complete separation of Northern Ireland from Britain in the long term.[25] Publicly, however, Jenkins never did more than hint at this heresy.* For the moment he was stuck with dealing with the violent consequences of the union.

These included several more bombings in London – at Selfridges, Harrods and Ted Heath's house in Belgravia – in December 1974 and a further twenty-nine incidents, which killed another ten people, in

---

* Reviewing Garret FitzGerald's memoirs in 1991 he confessed that his prejudices were 'much more green than orange. I am a poor Unionist, believing intuitively that even Paisley and Haughey are better at dealing with each other than the English are with either.'[26]

1975. One failed attack on a Mayfair restaurant in December led to a dramatic siege, when four fleeing IRA men holed themselves up in a flat in Marylebone with two elderly hostages. By chance the police had recently faced a very similar siege (nothing to do with the IRA) resulting from a bungled robbery at an Italian restaurant in Knightsbridge. On that occasion, Jenkins wrote in his draft memoirs, the Metropolitan Commissioner, Sir Robert Mark, was 'jumpy in the first 24 hours and might easily have done some foolish shooting without a firm political lead. Once given it, he accepted it and carried the thing out very skilfully.'[27] Through patience, the latest surveillance techniques and good psychology, the hostage-takers were persuaded to give themselves up without bloodshed after six days. The lessons learned at the Spaghetti House were successfully applied in Balcombe Street three months later with the same result, and the four men – the right ones this time – were taken out of circulation until released as part of the Good Friday Agreement in 1999.*

There were other threats to order, unrelated to Ireland, which added to the sense that the country was becoming ungovernable: anti-American riots in Grosvenor Square; an anti-National Front rally, which resulted in the death of a student in Red Lion Square; the attempted kidnapping of Princess Anne in the Mall. Against this unpromising background, Jenkins nevertheless tried to press on with some constructive legislation, prompted by Anthony Lester. By contrast with his liberal agenda in the 1960s, Jenkins was frankly much less interested in either the 1975 Sex Discrimination Act, which legislated for the first time for gender equality and set up the Equal Opportunities Commission to enforce it, or the 1976 Race Relations Act, which closed some major gaps in the two previous Acts, notably by extending their application to private clubs. But he strongly supported them in principle; he lent his authority to Lester to get on with them, so long as he worked through the Home Office officials; and he pushed them through the Cabinet and the Commons with his usual lucidity. There was in truth not much opposition to the Sex Discrimination Act – except within the department from one 'dedicated Under-Secretary' (ironically a woman) who 'did try to sabotage it. I had to come down with firm Secretary of State authority on her.' (This, Jenkins claimed, was the

---

* Two of the Balcombe Street gang had earlier carried out the murder of the journalist Ross McWhirter, co-author of the *Guinness Book of Records*, who had offered a reward for information leading to the arrest of IRA terrorists. McWhirter was shot on his own doorstep in North London. Such incidents meant that Jenkins and other ministers dealing with Northern Ireland now had to be heavily guarded wherever they went.

only issue in either of his two spells at the Home Office on which he encountered any official obstruction.)[28] The Bill was approved by the Cabinet in July 1974 and given its Second Reading in March 1975 with Opposition support – Ian Gilmour was now Jenkins' Tory shadow – and just a handful of unreconstructed mavericks like Enoch Powell voting against.

The Race Relations Bill was more contentious. In order to minimise opposition, Jenkins and Lester made a deliberate decision to introduce the gender Bill first in 1974–5, and then model the new race Bill on it the following year. Within the race relations industry the most controversial decision was to merge the quasi-judicial function of the Race Relations Board with the campaigning role of the Community Relations Commission, to create a new Commission for Racial Equality (to be chaired by the Conservative MP David Lane) on the model of the Equal Opportunities Commission. On this Jenkins chose to follow the advice of Mark Bonham Carter rather than of Lester, who argued that this would weaken the Board's powers of enforcement.[29] Lester was probably right. The CRE was never a wholly successful organisation before it was merged into the new all-encompassing Equality and Human Rights Commission in 2006. In Parliament the Bill was supported by the official Opposition, but faced determined obstruction from a small group of Tories led by Enoch Powell (again) and Norman Tebbit. Powell, still pursuing his furious campaign against non-white immigration, insisted that the real threat to good race relations arose from the birth rate of the immigrant population; while Tebbit earned his reputation as a political skinhead with a lot of crude *ad hominem* sniping at Jenkins as the claret-swilling godfather of the permissive society. 'There is nothing permissive in our society now,' he complained ironically. 'We are not permitted to decide whom we want to work with and whom we want in our own clubs.'[30] It took an all-night sitting on 8–9 July 1976 to force the Bill through its committee stage. Stoutly supported once again by his latest shadow, Willie Whitelaw, Jenkins had to see off a whole series of filibustering divisions, though the opponents never mustered more than thirteen votes. The Third Reading was finally carried at lunchtime the following day by eighty-two votes to three. These turned out to be Jenkins' last speeches in the Commons as a minister.

Ever since Powell's 'rivers of blood' speech in 1968 the question of immigrant numbers had been an explosive issue. Jenkins had been lucky to leave the Home Office just before the influx of Kenyan Asians which Callaghan had to deal with. In 1971 the Heath government had tried to buy off Powell by introducing tighter restrictions on those without a 'patrial' connection with Britain – though it did honour Britain's obligation to the expelled Ugandan Asians with British passports. Coming back to the Home Office in 1974, Jenkins knew there could be no question of restoring an 'open door' policy; but he was determined to apply the existing legislation as humanely as possible. First he implemented a pledge given by Shirley Williams in opposition to grant an amnesty to illegal entrants who had arrived before 1973. Second, he allowed women already settled the same right to bring in their husbands as men had to bring in wives. On the former, he brushed aside objections from the Foreign Office (represented in Cabinet committee by David Ennals), saying that 'he really couldn't have his policy dictated by the fact that the FO had failed to man its posts adequately'. ('Roy's drawl always lengthens when he is angry,' Barbara Castle noted, 'which heightens the effect of contempt.')[31] The latter concession raised a storm in the Commons, with the Tories claiming that it would be abused by thousands of young men from the Indian sub-continent taking advantage of arranged marriages. Meanwhile Powell kept up a stream of allegations that the government was fiddling the statistics to disguise the projected growth of the ethnic population: he was triumphant when the Home Office was obliged to correct some of its figures. Jenkins managed to explain this as a clerical error rather than a conspiracy; but in this climate he had constantly to hold a balance between his own liberal instincts and public opinion, of which as a Birmingham MP he was only too well aware.

This led to mounting friction with his Minister of State with responsibility for immigration and race, Alex Lyon, whom he characterised privately as 'Cromwellian, dogmatic, Quakerish and well-meaning'. Egged on by his private secretary Clare Short, whom he later married – she went on to become a notably feisty Labour MP and Cabinet minister herself – Lyon saw himself as the immigrants' champion whose job, in every disputed case, was to take the individual's side against the bureaucracy. After eighteen months Jenkins had to tell Lyon bluntly that he was 'the worst of all the 14 junior ministers I had ever had'.[32] He had already asked Wilson to move him, before Callaghan finally did so in March 1976. Lyon then gave a number of bitter interviews claiming that he had started out as a Jenkinsite, but had become disillusioned when he realised that Jenkins 'wasn't remotely interested in socialism but only in himself'.[33] He subsequently found his niche as chairman of the UK Immigrants Advisory Service.

The police and the prison service still bulked large among the Home

Secretary's responsibilities. Prisons were one subject on which Jenkins frankly failed. Visiting them visibly distressed him. Like other Home Secretaries since, he would have liked to cut the prison population, then around 40,000 (in England and Wales) – up from 35,000 when he was last responsible for it. He warned in July 1975 that if it reached 42,000, 'conditions in the system would approach the intolerable and drastic action to relieve the position will be inescapable'.[34] The following year he told the Police Federation conference bluntly that, for many prisoners, prison did not 'work': he urged them to 'look at the evidence and to recognise how little the widespread use of prison reduces crime or deals effectively with the individuals concerned'. Faced with concerted booing, he gave his hostile audience a lecture on democracy. The rule of law in a democratic society did not mean 'our pet prejudices', but the rule of Parliament as applied by the courts:

> You cannot have a rule of law while dismissing with disparagement Parliament, the courts and those who practise in them. That is not the rule of law. It is exactly what the pressure groups you complain about seek to achieve by demonstration. Your job, and mine, is to apply the law as it is, not to decry it.

He respected their right to put their views to him. 'You will no doubt respect my right to tell you that I do not think all the points in sum amount to a basis for a rational penal policy.'[35]

He did what he could to encourage community service and other alternatives to prison and encouraged judges to pass shorter sentences. But nothing had much effect; the population passed 42,000 in October 1976 and went on rising. Thirty-eight years later it has more than doubled, to 87,000. Despite Lester's urging, Jenkins also failed to do anything about squalid conditions in many prisons. But in his second spell at the Home Office he did make another long-overdue reform of the criminal justice system by introducing for the first time an independent element into the system for investigating complaints against the police, against the determined opposition of the Commissioner of the Met, Sir Robert Mark. Mark was Jenkins' favourite policeman whom he had appointed Assistant Commissioner in 1966: since becoming Commissioner he had made a big impact by rooting out corruption – with the memorable remark that 'a good police force is one that catches more crooks than it employs' – and generally he and Jenkins had a high regard for one another.[36] But Mark took a strictly 'military' view of policing and believed that independent investigation of complaints would undermine the authority of chief constables. Jenkins was not deterred and introduced his Police (Complaints) Bill to the House in December 1975. Typically he managed to persuade the eminent former Treasury mandarin Sir Edwin Plowden – whom he had previously used to chair his inquiry into the aviation industry in 1964 – to chair his new investigative board. The Bill was condemned by the Tories (echoing the Police Federation) for damaging police morale, and by the left for not being independent enough.[37] Jenkins stuck to his guns – while leaving most of the piloting of the Bill to his third junior minister, Shirley Summerskill – and it eventually passed in June 1976. Mark carried his opposition to the point of resigning when the new system came into effect in January 1977. Since then, of course, the complaints procedure has been repeatedly strengthened as public trust in the police has steadily declined.

The Home Secretary, as Jenkins told the Police Federation, was the guardian of the rule of law. But in a Labour government concerned as never before to please its trade union masters, he found himself exposed to pressure from the party and even his colleagues to bend the law in their favour. First Michael Foot, as Employment Secretary, wanted to give pickets in industrial disputes the right to stop the movement of lorries: this was vehemently opposed by the police and Jenkins, with the support of the Lord Chancellor, Lord Elwyn-Jones, eventually succeeded in blocking it. Second – though this was not a Home Office matter – he was sickened by Tony Crosland's readiness (as Environment Secretary) to grant an amnesty to eleven Labour councillors in Clay Cross, Nottinghamshire, who had been surcharged in 1973 for refusing to raise council house rents in accordance with the Tory government's Housing Finance Act and had in consequence become heroes of the Labour movement to rank with the Tolpuddle Martyrs. Susan Crosland's biography of her husband makes it clear that Crosland knew perfectly well that retrospectively validating law-breaking was wrong: the difference between him and Jenkins was that Crosland was prepared to prostitute his integrity to appease the left, whereas Jenkins would not have done – as was demonstrated by a third related issue that was firmly on the Home Secretary's plate.[38]

The case concerned two men, Des Warren and Eric Tomlinson, convicted in December 1973 for intimidation and affray in connection with an industrial dispute in Shrewsbury and sentenced to three and two years respectively. They were released in June 1974 pending an appeal; but when their appeal was dismissed (in October) they were sent back to prison. Once again the left hailed the 'Shrewsbury Two' as 'political prisoners' unjustly jailed for defying an oppressive Tory government, and confidently expected a Labour Home Secretary to quash their convictions. Several delegations of MPs and the entire Finance and General Purposes Committee of the TUC called on Jenkins in person to press their cause. He listened politely, but having reviewed the case decided that there were no grounds for early release: Warren and Tomlinson, he later wrote, were 'rough thugs who in my view deserved their sentences' and he declined to intervene. 'I had the impression that the bulk of the deputation was not so much angry as amazed that I would not accede.'[39] An unnamed minister commented admiringly that this was 'the first time that this Government had told the Labour Conference and the TUC where to go'.[40] For months afterwards Jenkins was hounded wherever he went by demonstrators chanting 'Free the Two'. There were suggestions that he should have been sympathetic because of his father's wrongful imprisonment in 1926; but he saw no comparison and refused to budge. The episode underlined not only the growing gulf between Jenkins and a large part of the labour movement, but how much the movement had changed since his father's day.*

Wilson had suggested, in appointing him, that the Home Office was a department in which it was possible to remain semi-detached from the rest of the government; and this was very much Jenkins' position in 1974–6, particularly in the first few months. Bernard Donoughue, from his ringside seat in Number Ten, regretted his passivity. 'What a pity Roy Jenkins has completely disappeared from the Labour political scene,' he wrote in July 1974:

He has completely dropped out of the government, never speaking, never appearing anywhere to defend the government. He is just a sleeping partner. Yet he could have *worked* at it, distinct from HW and disagreeing with the left, but working as a member of the team to earn his passage. Instead he stands aloof, disdainful, unhappy, trying to avoid contamination from his own party. Maybe he is proving himself a worthy coalition leader, as Joe [Haines] suggests. What is certain is that his Labour support is dwindling.[41]

One former admirer whom he alienated at this time was the future leader, John Smith. 'As a junior minister in that administration,' Smith

---

* 'Ricky' Tomlinson, as he was now known, later achieved fame as an actor in the TV series *The Royle Family*.

wrote much later, 'I recall him chairing Cabinet sub-committees with a lack of interest [amounting] almost to disdain which was disagreeably unattractive to his junior colleagues.'[42]

Joe Haines' suspicion was not entirely unfounded. Jenkins always denied hankering for a coalition and he was certainly not actively working for one; but he was becoming increasingly disillusioned not only with the Labour party, but with the party system itself. In June he told his old Balliol friend Ronnie McIntosh – still director of the NEDC (the National Economic Development Council, known as 'Neddy') – that if Labour won a second General Election in the autumn he would not join the new government. This would get him free of 'people he didn't agree with' and give him room for manoeuvre. He was, he confessed in confidence, 'thinking increasingly in terms of a government of national unity'. When McIntosh objected that such a government would only drive the unions further to the left, Jenkins said this was 'a risk he was very conscious of'. But McIntosh concluded that 'I don't think that in his heart of hearts he cares – or knows – much about the trade union movement.'[43]

Very early in the life of the new government, believing that the patently inequitable result of the February election had made the subject unavoidable, he raised in Cabinet the idea of electoral reform, suggesting that it would be better to refer it to a Speaker's Conference 'in a low pressure way' before the Liberals did so. He immediately ran into furious opposition led by Foot, Bob Mellish and Willie Ross, who warned that 'If we were not careful we could see the end of any possibility of a Labour Government.' Wilson thought it 'obviously best to let this sleeping dog lie as long as possible'. So, Barbara Castle wrote happily, 'We sent Roy away with a flea in his coalition ear.'[44] But he did not give up. Eighteen months later in November 1975 – now with some encouragement from Wilson, who had decided that a Speaker's Conference might after all be the best way to kill the issue – he tried again, proposing not just a Speaker's Conference but, 'as a sweetener', an independent inquiry to consider the various systems of proportional representation. Again he was 'slapped down'. Most of the Cabinet thought PR 'totally unacceptable' and believed that, if ignored, the demand would blow itself out.[45] He was supported only by those Mrs Castle called 'the hard-core coalitionists': Shirley Williams, Harold Lever and Reg Prentice. 'But these rightists will go on beavering away . . . until they have finally destroyed the Labour Party's independence and power to govern single-handedly.'[46] This, Donoughue wrote, was 'a bad defeat for Jenkins'.[47]

Jenkins with
George Brown –
Labour Party
conference,
Blackpool, 1968.

Bill Rodgers, newly appointed to
the Department of Economic Affairs,
October 1964.

John Harris, Jenkins' closest
adviser over thirty years.

Jenkins, as Home Secretary, inspecting the London Fire Brigade, July 1966.

Visiting the scene where three policemen were shot in Shepherd's Bush in August 19

The Chancellor of the
Exchequer arriving
at the Treasury, 1968.

...g 11 Downing Street
...ent his first budget,
...rch 1968.

A confident Chancel
and Prime Minister,
few days before the
General Election.

The Opposition
Front Bench after
the election: from l–r:
Barbara Castle,
Denis Healey, Harold
Wilson, Roy Jenkins
and James Callaghan.

Tennis at East Hendred, 1969 and 1976.

Speaking at the
Labour Party s[...]
conference on [...]
Common Mar[...]
26 April 1975.

Jenkins with Jeremy Thorpe and Edward Heath during the
European Referendum campaign, May 1975.

A television debate
between Jenkins and
Tony Benn, chaired
by David Dimbleby,
June 1975.

Struck by a flour
bomb while speaking
for Reg Prentice at
Newham Town Hall,
September 1975.

Jenkins in his study at East Hendred, mid-1970s.

Receiving an award to mark twenty-five years as MP for Stechford, 1975: with onlook
including Denis Howell, Roy Hattersley, George Canning, Brian Walden and Jennife

He met similarly entrenched opposition when he tried to reform the notoriously catch-all nature of the 1911 Official Secrets Act, under which any information down to the colour of the toilet paper in the Welsh Office could be classified as secret. 'Unlike most in Whitehall,' Anthony Lester wrote, Jenkins 'really did believe in the need for more open government'.[48] In January 1975 he visited the United States to study the effect of freedom of information legislation (taking the chance while there to fit in a busy diary of lunches and dinners with Henry Kissinger, Nelson Rockefeller and other old friends); and later that year he took to Cabinet committee a package of proposals based on the recommendations of Lord Franks. But again he was shot down by his senior colleagues, led this time by Callaghan and Elwyn Jones, tacitly supported by the Prime Minister, on grounds of protecting national security. Afterwards, Donoughue recorded, Wilson 'was chuckling away at the opposition to Jenkins and seemed delighted there would be no progress on Official Secrets'. Jenkins found this reactionary attitude 'shocking'.[49] But it soon emerged that the Cabinet Office and the Lord Chancellor's department – backed again by Wilson – actually wanted a more restrictive Act:

> It was quite clear that the majority of the committee – led by HW, Callaghan, Elwyn Jones, [Roy] Mason and [Peter] Shore – were for tightening everything up. Roy Jenkins would not have that and lost his temper several times. He said if we were not going to keep our promise of liberalisation then he would rather do nothing.[50]

He got some support from Denis Healey and Ted Short, but could not prevail against the overwhelming culture of secrecy. Not until 1989 was the discredited Section Two of the 1911 Act finally scrapped and then – following the Clive Ponting case – it was replaced by even tighter restrictions on information relating to defence, international relations, the security services and the police. Only in 2000 did the Blair government bring in the Freedom of Information Act, which implemented some of what Jenkins had wanted a quarter of a century earlier.

For the first five months of the new government's life, as Bernard Donoughue noted, Jenkins kept his doubts about the central thrust of the administration's policy largely to himself. Wilson was in any case primarily concerned with treading water until he could go to the country again in the hope of winning a working majority. But in July he broke cover with an uncompromising speech at Haverfordwest, in deepest Pembrokeshire. He was actually encouraged to range beyond his departmental brief by the Prime Minister, who doubtless calculated that Labour-voting moderates needed some reassurance. But Wilson got rather more than he bargained for. Jenkins took the chance to lay down four fundamental principles which he believed were under insidious attack and on which Labour's commitment needed to be made 'crystal clear'. Europe, for once, was not among them.

The first, in the light of Clay Cross and the campaign for the Shrewsbury pickets, was the rule of law. 'No-one,' Jenkins insisted, 'is entitled to be above the law. If we weaken on that principle, we can say goodbye to democratic socialism, because what is sauce for the goose will be sauce for the gander.' Second, Britain's commitment to NATO. 'If anyone wants a Britain poised uneasily between the Western alliance and the Communist block they can, in the immortal words of Mr Sam Goldwyn, "include me out".' With this he coupled belief in an open trading economy, not a siege economy – the left's pet solution to economic difficulties. His third fundamental principle was the mixed economy, though he conceded that the mix might change. He still claimed to support 'sensible and well-argued extensions of public owner-ship . . . But I am also in favour of a healthy, vigorous and profitable private sector.'

Finally he stressed the absolute priority of fighting inflation, currently running at 16.5 per cent. He had been privately appalled by Healey's electioneering mini-budget, just four days earlier, which had cut VAT and introduced various subsidies to try to cut the cost of living. 'This,' Jenkins wrote in his memoirs, 'seemed to me a frivolous way of proceeding . . . like throwing stones at a potential avalanche.'[51] Without explicitly criticising the Chancellor, he warned that 'the greatest threat to the cohesion of our society today is the still increasing rate of infla-tion'. He was still enough of a party politician to lay the blame on Tony Barber, though partly also on world conditions, which made the problems he had had to deal with in 1967–9 look small by comparison. It was not of course his own or Labour's fault: 'We left a relatively healthy situation, and we came back to desolation and decay.' But the country was now facing 'an economic crisis without precedent since the growth of post-war prosperity':

> The country will not for long put up with it. If we cannot solve it by tolerable and civilised methods, then someone within a few

years will solve it by intolerable and uncivilised ones. And we shall all – Government and Opposition and other parties alike – look irrelevant and ineffective.

He was not, he insisted, calling for a coalition. He still wanted Labour to form a majority government. But in order to win a majority, he reminded the party once again that it needed to attract 'the great body of moderate, rather uncommitted opinion . . . It cannot be done upon the basis of ignoring middle opinion and telling everyone who does not agree with you to go to hell.'[52] This might be thought obvious – he received another huge postbag from ordinary members of the public, 90 per cent of it supportive – but it was heresy to the left, who accused him once again of 'anti-socialist claptrap' (Sidney Bidwell) and splitting the party (Neil Kinnock). 'Everyone was talking about Roy Jenkins' disastrous speech on Friday,' Barbara Castle wrote. 'When Ted and I saw him on TV I said, "That has cost us the election."'[53] Nevertheless she criticised Bidwell, Mikardo and others for attacking him in public. She preferred to speak to him privately and did so the next day.

'Roy,' she began, 'I wanted to have a word with you in the greatest friendliness because I am very fond of you. I think that once again you have listened to very bad advice . . . Of course the press is waiting to egg you on: you are their mouthpiece for Europe and they are using you. But your friends ought to know better. They are driving you into a course that can only ruin your political career.'

At this point, red in the face with sudden emotion, Roy said violently, 'What makes you think I care about my political career? All that matters to me is what is happening in the world, which I think is heading for disaster. I can't stand by and see us pretend everything is all right when I know we are heading for catastrophe.' More calmly he added, 'It isn't only Europe. It is a question of whether this country is going to cut itself off from the Western Alliance and go isolationist.'

Mrs Castle was uncomprehending. '"I simply don't see where you get that fear from. Are you suggesting we are going Communist?" No, he said, it was not as crude as that.' But at this point they were interrupted by a division bell. 'We stood up and Roy said, smiling affectionately, "But I repeat what I told you in the corridor the other day. I think you are a very good Minister and 70 per cent of the time I agree with you in Cabinet. I appreciate that you have spoken in friendliness."'

He squeezed my hand. As we made our way downstairs I persisted: 'But what exactly do you want the Government to do that it isn't doing? What is *your* remedy for our troubles?' . . . He had no answer. Awkwardly he said, 'Let us have a talk some time,' and disappeared thankfully.[54]

Barbara Castle was not alone in thinking that Jenkins' speech lacked positive content. 'His remarks were variously interpreted as an attack on Mr Wilson, a call for coalition, a rallying-cry to pro–Europeans and a warning on the dangers to parliamentary democracy,' *The Times* commented; but apart from a professed openness to nationalisation there was nothing specifically Labour about it at all – no mention of equality, for instance, 'which to the mind of Hugh Gaitskell was what the whole thing was about': in fact nothing with which a Liberal or moderate Tory would disagree.[55] Jenkins would not have disputed this. To escape the furore that his speech had caused he and Jennifer went to the cinema with Ronnie and Doreen McIntosh. (The film was *The Sting*.) Over supper beforehand Jenkins said that he was becoming 'an extreme moderate' and was 'thoroughly fed up with the party system, which he regarded as a conspiracy against the people'.[56] It was in Italy that summer, he wrote later, that he first began seriously to question the two-party mould. Tuscany, however, worked its balm. On his return he told McIntosh that he was now feeling 'much more cheerful about the government and the election'. He believed Wilson had finally stirred himself to curb Benn's influence and that the manifesto would be all right, so he would after all be willing to carry on if the government was re-elected. There would still probably be 'a great bust-up after six months or so, but he might as well wait till then before doing anything drastic'.[57]

Once again it could be said that Jenkins had issued a challenge but then shrunk from following it up. Contrary to what Barbara Castle imagined, however, most of his friends were urging him to work for a Labour victory. Unlike in February, Lester told him, he could fight the coming election genuinely wanting Labour to win, since his only remaining chance of winning the leadership when Wilson stepped down was as a loyal member of a government with a mandate to tackle the economic crisis: in that situation his record as the Chancellor who had righted the ship after devaluation would give him a strong platform.[58] On 12 September Donoughue – a closet Jenkinsite even while working for Wilson – went with Lester to press this course on him:

> We went into Roy's enormous room . . . and had several large gin and tonics . . . I said what I thought – that Roy should take a more active part leading the Right, and also in the campaign showing his loyalty to the party, including knocking any idea of joining a coalition; that I thought HW thought more of Roy than vice-versa; that HW was a much improved figure. (Here Roy agreed strongly, saying that in 1964–70 most of their time was spent discussing plots and press smears) . . . After two hours . . . Roy summed up . . . by saying in future he would 'try to love HW more'.

Donoughue went home 'feeling drunk but cheered'.[59]

Jenkins made a reasonable stab at fighting the October election with conviction. His election address in Stechford featured a picture of him looking exceptionally grim. 'Whereas in the past twenty-five years we have been arguing about how fast the standard of living could increase, we now face a real struggle to prevent it being cut.' Inflation, he warned, could destroy 'not merely our money but our society'. But at the same time he asked for renewed trust in the Labour government, which had been 'remarkably faithful to the limited number of promises it made in February', and insisted that Labour's 'Social Contract' – the government's supposed bargain with the unions, about which he was in fact deeply sceptical – offered the best hope of beating inflation.[60] He spoke widely around the country in a number of key marginals (Stockport, Bosworth, Carmarthen, Peterborough and North-West Norfolk) as well as for friends and supporters (John Mackintosh in Berwick, Bob Maclennan in Caithness, Tom Bradley in Leicester) and his two junior ministers, Shirley Summerskill in Halifax and Alex Lyon – despite their differences – in York (another marginal), as well as for Matthew Oakeshott who was standing in Horsham and Crawley. In his dictated notes he glumly remembered only 'an endless series of breakfasts – quite good breakfasts – in British Rail restaurant cars, looking out at a sodden countryside in the early morning just after dawn'.[61] But Lester – who accompanied Jenkins on some of these trips – told Donoughue that he was 'enjoying his canvassing tour and was very good at it'.[62] He also appeared at two of Labour's press conferences – the first alongside Wilson and Healey, the second with Wilson and Barbara Castle – and in one television broadcast, in which he highlighted Labour's commitment to equality for women by plugging his Sex Discrimination Bill. He rejected with scorn Ted Heath's half-hearted overtures for a government of national unity; at his second press conference, two days before polling day, Donoughue thought him 'superb, hammering the coalition idea out of sight'.[63] Generally, *The Times* commented, 'Mr Jenkins has pitched his campaign at a high level, speaking with almost religious zeal about political morality and the broad-based conscience and reform approach for which the Labour Party "does and must stand".'[64] After Wilson, he was the second most-quoted figure on the Labour side in the television news bulletins, just one mention behind Michael Foot and ahead of Healey.[65]

He did his best to say nothing contentious about Europe. He swallowed a certain amount of humble pie by admitting that there was after all 'substantial scope' for renegotiation of the terms of entry and claiming to be 'optimistic . . . that a position will come out which will be more favourable to this country and more helpful to the Community generally'. And in return for Wilson agreeing to keep open the option of another General Election, rather than a referendum, he declared that he accepted, by one means or another, 'the desirability of reconciling British public opinion to membership of the EEC'.[66] But his hand was forced by Shirley Williams, who unguardedly blurted out at a press conference that if the public voted against staying in Europe, she would resign from the government, resign her seat and leave politics. Jenkins was immediately pressed to say whether he agreed. He initially tried not to comment, but eventually issued a rather more qualified statement to the effect that he would 'naturally' not be able to serve in a Cabinet that was obliged to withdraw, but not that he would leave politics altogether; he hoped the renegotiation would succeed so that the question would not arise.[67] This successfully defused the issue. In any case Europe by now came well down the list of the voters' concerns.

On the last weekend his campaign was disrupted by a different sort of explosion: the IRA bombing of Guildford. Hayden Phillips arranged with Number Ten for a private plane to fly him from Norfolk – where he had been staying with Solly and Joan Zuckerman – to Guildford on Sunday morning to inspect the damage and visit the victims, then on to Birmingham in the afternoon to join Wilson – dramatically late – at his regular final weekend rally with all the local candidates in the town hall. Despite this, Jenkins judged it 'the dullest election since 1955'.[68] Both Wilson and Heath were tired and shop-soiled leaders; but Wilson managed to keep a lid on the left while projecting an air of hard-won experience and making a virtue of Labour's close relations with the unions, while the Tories were still fatally damaged by the memory of the three-day week, and the Liberals were unable to build on their advance in February. The electorate, unimpressed by a second election in eight months, showed no enthusiasm for any party and turnout fell to 72 per cent. Labour gained eighteen seats, giving a lead of forty-two over the Tories, but with the Liberals, Scottish and Welsh nationalists and Ulster Unionists between them picking up a total of thirty-nine seats, it had an overall majority of just three. It was very far from the repeat of 1966 that Wilson had been looking for, but another inconclusive result, which confirmed Jenkins' belief that the winner-take-all electoral system no longer reflected the national will. The government was returned with just 39 per cent public support.

In Stechford – where the turnout fell to 64 per cent – Jenkins' personal vote held up well, while both the Tory and the Liberal votes fell back, giving him a slightly increased majority:

Roy Jenkins (Lab)	23,075
D.J. Wedgwood (Con)	11,152
G.A. Gopsill (Lib)	5,860
Labour majority	11,923[69]

The following September the local party held a dinner dance to mark Jenkins' twenty-five years as their MP. But this election turned out to be his last in Stechford.

17 Victory and Defeat

W ITH the October election out of the way, Jenkins' attention – so far as the IRA permitted – turned back to his top political priority: making sure that Britain, having finally joined, stayed in the Common Market. Over the summer he had continued to fight a rearguard action against a referendum, maintaining that it would be divisive, detract from the sovereignty of Parliament and could not be binding anyway.[1] But by December it was clear that he had lost that battle: a referendum, with Cabinet ministers exceptionally allowed to campaign on opposite sides of the argument, was actually the only way the government and the Labour party could be kept united, and the only way – as he later acknowledged – to settle the European question for the foreseeable future. He eventually voted for it on the assurance from Wilson and Callaghan that, once the renegotiation was complete, the government would recommend a 'Yes' vote. A MORI poll in January 1975 showed for the first time a majority for staying in, if the government recommended it – the first clear encouragement to the pro-Europeans that they could win a popular vote. In March Jenkins (along with Heath, Shirley Williams, Jo Grimond and others) attended the twenty-fifth anniversary meeting of the Anglo-German Konigswinter conference, which he had first attended in the 1950s, where he announced that he was 'beginning to savour the scent of battle in my nostrils'.[2] At the end of the proceedings Nicko Henderson and his wife gave a ball at the British Embassy in Bonn at which Jenkins took to the floor and danced for the first time in nine years; but 'he soon got the hang of it,' Henderson recorded, 'and was still galumphing around at 2.30 a.m.'[3]

Two days later the Cabinet began its two-day deliberation which formally endorsed the outcome of the largely cosmetic 'renegotiation'. Explaining his pragmatic reconversion, Callaghan claimed that the EEC had changed since the early 1970s: it had abandoned the ambition of economic and monetary union (EMU) – originally planned for 1980 – and other 'federalist concepts'; the Commission was less powerful and the Council of Ministers more powerful; and the Community was supposedly more open to the world and more responsive to its members' national interests.[4] On the second day Wilson too weighed in, stressing the dangers of withdrawing. The antis made their last stand. Tony Benn warned of a 'tragic decision' which would lead to the break-up of the UK and possibly the Labour party. Barbara Castle linked her opposition to the Common Market to Labour's objection to electoral reform: the Council of Ministers, she argued, was in effect a permanent coalition, 'and the Labour party had always been united in its opposition to the notion of coalition government. Our virility as a nation would be weakened if we remained a member of the Community.' These two were still supported by Foot, Shore, John Silkin, Willie Ross and Eric Varley, but by no others. Jenkins felt no need to speak until the very end. The Cabinet then voted 16:7 to accept the renegotiated terms.[5] After all the wriggling of the past five years this was an historic moment.

The wider party was still divided. When the Commons voted after Easter, Labour MPs split almost equally – 145:137 against, with thirty-three abstaining: even ministers were only 45:38 in favour. With the Tories still overwhelmingly pro-Europe, however (despite Margaret Thatcher having replaced Heath as leader in February), the terms were approved by 396:170: an even bigger margin than in October 1971. This time it was the antis' turn to suffer for defying the latest reversal: Eric Heffer lost his ministerial job for speaking against the government line. Then yet another special conference on 26 April voted heavily for a 'No' vote. Thus the referendum, set for 5 June, pitched the Labour government directly against the Labour party.

There was a plethora of competing campaign organisations. On the 'Yes' side Jenkins accepted the presidency of the all-party umbrella grouping, Britain in Europe (BiE). (Ted Heath, who might most appropriately have headed it, was now considered too divisive.) Heath and Whitelaw for the Tories, Shirley Williams for Labour and Jo Grimond for the Liberals were named as vice-presidents, while Shirley Williams also chaired the separate Labour Campaign for Europe (LCE), which held its own meetings, untainted by the suspicion of coalitionism. There were suggestions that she was deliberately shunted into this less prominent role by the Jenkinsites; but she told David Butler that she found BiE 'too professional and too upper-class for her taste' and preferred to campaign within the Labour fold.[6] Jenkins himself admitted that the leaders of BiE looked like 'well-fed men who had done well out of the Common Agricultural Policy'.[7] On the 'No' side an incongruous ragbag of opponents ranging from the extreme left to the far right were pulled together as the National Referendum Campaign, chaired by the Tory MP Neil Marten. Each side received £125,000 from the government, plus a leaflet putting its case delivered to every household in the country. But Britain in Europe, overwhelmingly backed by business and the City, was able to raise and spend another £2 million on glossy propaganda, while the NRC raised just £166,000. So the spending ratio was around twelve to one.[8] Moreover the print media – both the broadsheets and the tabloids – were almost unanimously for a 'Yes' vote. The only papers in the 'No' camp were *Tribune*, the Communist *Morning Star* and the High Tory *Spectator*. The anti-Marketeers, who had campaigned so long for a referendum and confidently expected to win it, were entitled to feel unfairly outgunned. With the government adding a statement of its own official recommendation, even the leaflets through the door were two-to-one in the 'Yes' campaign's favour.

Not that this imbalance worried the pro-Europeans. The sense that the leadership of all three main parties, all the newspapers and virtually the whole establishment were on one side, opposed only by the mavericks, romantics and extremists of all parties – Michael Foot and Enoch Powell, Tony Benn and Ian Paisley, the Communists and the National Front – only confirmed that they were right and that their hour had come. For Jenkins in particular the referendum, bringing together all the sensible people in public life in a common cause, came at exactly the moment when he had been losing faith in the rigidly tribal party system which forced him to work with old colleagues with whom he disagreed while dividing him from others with whom he increasingly felt more comfortable. He had always believed in cross-party alliances to secure goals like the abolition of hanging or reforming censorship. But now the experience of sharing platforms up and down the country with leading Tories (not only Heath and Whitelaw, but Reggie Maudling, Lord Carrington and others) and Liberals (Jo Grimond, Jeremy Thorpe and David Steel) as well as longstanding Labour Europeans like Cledwyn Hughes and the former General Secretary of the TUC, Vic Feather, was both very civilised and immensely liberating. It did not make him any keener to get into bed with the Tory party – particularly now that it was led by Mrs Thatcher (who kept a conspicuously low profile in the campaign). But it did convince him that the public rather liked the spectacle of politicians of different parties working together instead of endlessly blaming each other; and, most important, it confirmed that he now had more in common with the Liberals than with much of the Labour Party. Admittedly he did not have much time for Thorpe, whom he thought lightweight and untrustworthy. But the experience renewed the high regard he already felt for David Steel. 'Of all the people I worked with during the campaign,' he wrote soon afterwards, 'he was one of the best. A man of great sensitivity, reliability, imagination, somebody certainly well worth a major Cabinet place if he belonged to a major party.'[9] The referendum planted a seed which would bear fruit in six years' time.

Jenkins was reinvigorated by the campaign in which, as president of the 'Yes' campaign, he played an almost Prime Ministerial part. Only Heath was as prominent. (Wilson, like Mrs Thatcher, took a relatively back seat.) Between 14 May and 4 June he was flown around the country in a small plane, often with Willie Whitelaw, speaking at nine big BiE rallies from Aberdeen to Plymouth, all enthusiastically attended by audiences numbering between 1,000 and 2,000, and at five LCE meetings which were much less well attended and where he faced some heckling from Labour and far-right anti-Marketeers. (The contrast again made an impression on him.) He also chaired steering-group meetings most mornings in London, usually followed by a press conference, gave interviews, wrote articles and appeared on innumerable TV programmes. At the same time he still had to deal with essential Home Office business (though he had arranged with Arthur Peterson to keep this to a minimum). Hayden Phillips or Matthew Oakeshott usually accompanied him on his speaking trips to help him handle it, but fortunately no major crises cropped up.

The European debate had been going on so long that there was really nothing new to say. Jenkins stuck mainly to his well-worn argument that Britain must take its rightful place among other medium-sized powers in Europe, where her real influence would be enhanced as part of a larger entity, rather than seeking to go it alone in an increasingly hostile world, with the added point that the country was now in the Community:

> I believe that both the security and the prosperity of the country
> depend upon a Yes vote. Not to have gone into Europe would
> have been a misfortune. But to come out would be on an even

greater scale of self-inflicted injury. It would be a catastrophe. It would leave us weak and unregarded, both economically and politically.[10]

He made relatively little of the economic case for staying in and steered firmly clear of the heated arguments about how much food prices would rise inside the Community, pitching his tent firmly on the high ground of Britain's role in the world and the vaguely defined goal of European unity. Subsequently he and Heath were blamed for failing to spell out what exactly this might mean in the longer term, and thus for having taken Britain into Europe on a dishonest prospectus. In his memoirs he sought to refute this charge:

> Heath and I . . . agreed that it was always the high arguments, the broad discussion of the country's future orientation in both foreign policy and economic terms, which most captured the attention and fired the imagination of audiences. Neither did either of us attempt to play down the importance of the issues or to suggest that all that was at stake was a narrow trade policy decision. It was political Europe in which we were interested. A common market, which existed and of which we were a part, was a vital step on the road but it was not the ultimate goal or the primary purpose.[11]

This may have been true. But it is also true that they never disclosed what the next steps were, let alone the ultimate goal. If they said anything at all about the single market, tax harmonisation, majority voting, enlargement or a single currency – all ideas that would become contentious reality over the next thirty years – it was not reported. They never seriously addressed the issue of national sovereignty, doggedly pursued by Enoch Powell and others, beyond repeating that sovereignty was an outdated illusion in the interdependent modern world, to be shared, not hoarded. Jenkins' line was still, as it had always been, that one could not know exactly how the Community would evolve and it was foolish to try: the important thing was to be a part of it and to maintain the momentum.

One of the pleasures of the Cabinet's 'agreement to differ' was the licence it provided to criticise colleagues. Tony Benn had been making headlines with the claim that membership of the EEC had already cost the country half a million jobs. Since the unemployment figure was currently about 800,000, this amounted to claiming that outside the

EEC Britain would have been enjoying – in the middle of a world recession – the lowest unemployment since the war. At his press conference on 27 May Jenkins demolished this absurdity, suggesting that Benn's method seemed to be simply to think of a number and then double it, before adding, quite deliberately: 'I find it increasingly difficult to take Mr Benn seriously as an economic minister.'[12] This 'public brawl' brought a sharp rebuke from Wilson, who objected not so much to the refutation of Benn's figures – which he echoed – as to the implication that Benn should be moved from the Department of Industry: either Jenkins was putting 'irresistible pressure on me and limiting the options in a reshuffle', he charged, or he was implying that he was 'already privy to my intentions, which of course is not the case'.[13] In fact Wilson already intended to move Benn if the referendum returned a 'Yes' vote, but he did not want to seem to be dictated to by Jenkins.

The following Monday, by chance, Jenkins and Benn were booked to go head-to-head on *Panorama* in an unprecedented debate between two Cabinet ministers, chaired by David Dimbleby. This was a highlight of the campaign, watched by some eight million people. But anyone expecting an acrimonious dust-up was disappointed: Dimbleby barely had to intervene at all. 'With firm ministerial politeness,' David Butler and Uwe Kitzinger wrote in their Nuffield study of the campaign, 'they achieved a decidedly more lucid and intricate level of discussion than is commonly seen on political television.'[14]* It was an open question who came off best, as John Whale scored it in the *Sunday Times*:

The contrast between the two men's styles was complete: Jenkins rapid in speech, Benn measured; Jenkins qualificatory, parenthetical ('Curiously, on a point of reminiscence . . .'), Benn simple ('Be commonsensical, Roy!'); Jenkins anxious to deal with everything that came crowding into his head ('Well, there are a lot of points there, and I'd like very quickly to run through one or two, if not three of them'), Benn banging one point repeatedly ('This erodes the importance of the vote'); Jenkins eager to peg out common ground ('I don't think Tony would disagree with this . . .'), Benn quite prepared to come through with the moralising rebuke ('A

---

* A letter to *The Times* contrasted the high quality of this extended debate with the usual brief studio discussion chaired by an intrusive interviewer, noting that 'the exasperated incredulity of Mr Jenkins in the face of Mr Benn's statistical agility . . . revealed far more subtly than a shorter confrontation could have done the personal rivalry that lay behind their careful cordiality.'[15] The writer was the present author.

joke about weather is not really right when we're talking about people's jobs'); Jenkins worrying about truth, Benn intent on making a case.

On the page, Whale felt that Benn's evasion of Jenkins' persistent questioning about jobs and alternatives might have looked shifty; on television, however, 'it seems likely that his single point will have stuck more in viewers' minds than any of Jenkins' did'. But television was never Jenkins' medium. As a throwback to the age of Asquith and Lloyd George, he was far more at home on the platform:

> At the Newcastle meeting he tried physically to keep his chairman from intervening so that he could deal with his hecklers himself; at the Philharmonic Hall in Liverpool he totally outshone his fellow speakers, Jeremy Thorpe and Reggie Maudling, laying an incantation on his audience with his most characteristic gesture, right arm outstretched, hand tilted up, fingers spread; in an ill-filled Birmingham Town Hall [this was an LCE meeting], on the very last weary night before polling, he could still speak with such verve as to prompt a woman in the gallery to call out as he sat down: 'I'm glad he's my MP, anyway.'[16]

At the last London meeting at the Central Hall, Westminster on 2 June – having already taken part in a three-hour television debate in the morning and recorded the Benn encounter in the afternoon – Jenkins found a new image for his favourite theme. For Britain to withdraw from Europe, he warned, would be to retire into 'an old people's home for fading nations', adding tartly: 'I do not think it would be a very comfortable old people's home. I do not like the look of some of the prospective wardens.'[17] Since the start of the campaign the polls had consistently forecast a clear victory for the 'Yes' camp. The pro-Marketeers' only worry was a low turnout, which, Jenkins warned at his final press conference, might yet allow the antis to question the verdict, prolong the uncertainty and still try to prevent Britain from pulling its full weight in the Community. Therefore, he concluded, 'Let us vote decisively to settle the issue overwhelmingly and free us from the continual debilitation of being hesitant and reluctant partners.'[18]

The result matched his highest hopes. On a 64 per cent turnout the public voted by a margin of slightly more than two to one – 17.3 million to 8.4 million, evenly spread across the country – to stay in the Community. Labour voters were reckoned to have voted 'Yes' by a margin of 5:4. With no individual count to attend, Roy and Jennifer were able to watch the exit polls at Ladbroke Square with Bill and Sylvia Rodgers, the Harrises and Anthony Lester. The next day Jenkins welcomed the 'massive and heartening majority' and hailed 'a day of satisfaction and jubilation', noting characteristically that 6 June was the thirty-first anniversary of D-Day, when Britain had ended a previous period of exclusion from Europe.[19] It was indeed a famous victory, which only a few months earlier had looked unlikely. The long saga of dithering and wrangling, failed applications and renewed applications, which had lasted since 1961, was finally – so it appeared – over. Britain was at last, for better or worse, in Europe. But Jenkins did not get much credit from his colleagues. When the Cabinet met a few days later there were no congratulations:'Callaghan,Wilson, Healey, Crosland were all what one might best describe as fairly po-faced.'[20] It was clear that they were going to do as little as before to make Britain's membership a reality. So on 19 June Jenkins celebrated with those who had borne the heat of the battle by hosting a dinner at Brooks's attended by Heath, Whitelaw, Steel, Grimond and the rest, the only result of which was to reignite Wilson's suspicion that he was hatching a coalition plot.* The possibility was now certainly in his mind. The next day he told George Canning, his long-standing constituency chairman in Stechford, that the Labour government might not be able to survive on its present basis and 'one could not exclude the possibility of some political realignment'. Canning was shocked, but loyal.[22] But still he did nothing serious to advance it.

In retrospect, when he came to write his memoirs, Jenkins rather regretted that he had not done more. 'Looking back, I think that I should have been more and not less "disloyal" in 1975.'With the government facing enormous difficulties, the Labour Party becoming ever more fractious and many moderate Tories alarmed by Mrs Thatcher, the referendum had temporarily brought together a combination of people who might possibly have been kept together for wider cooperation even after the European campaign had been won:

---

* Still worse, Wilson told Barbara Castle, he had learned from a reliable source that Heath had been 'secretly' to lunch at East Hendred.[21] Typically, his spies had misled him. Heath had indeed been to East Hendred, but for dinner (not lunch) on 1 April, when the other guests were Sir William Hayter (former ambassador to the USSR, now Master of New College, Oxford) and his wife, and Evangeline Bruce (wife of the former American ambassador to Britain, David Bruce) – a typical mixed party, not obviously coalition-hatching material.

All in all I look back on 1975 as a great missed opportunity for Heath and Whitelaw and a whole regiment of discarded Conservative 'wets' as much as for Shirley Williams and Steel and me. They and we could have had much more the sort of government we broadly wanted than anything which was in office in the 1980s, and the country would in my view have greatly benefited.[23]

But if anyone is to blame for not having done more to make it happen, it is Jenkins himself. There were plenty of people outside politics urging him to take his courage in his hands. The historian Hugh Thomas, for instance – one of a number of prominent intellectuals whose despair with Labour eventually led them to embrace Mrs Thatcher – wrote urging him, as soon as the referendum was over, to 'break out on your own with a new movement in politics. You would soon see that you would be very far from being "on your own". . . .You have, as you must be aware, a very large national constituency.'[24] Jenkins, however, was still too much a prisoner of the tribal politics he was hankering to transcend. Not until he put a physical distance between himself and Westminster did he see his way clearly enough to act. In the immediate aftermath of the referendum he was quickly sucked back into Labour's internecine battle by the need to fight his corner – specifically to defend his most outspoken ally in the Cabinet, Reg Prentice, who was under serious threat from the hard left in his Newham constituency. Playing off left against right as usual, Wilson determined to balance the removal of Benn from Industry to Energy by the simultaneous demotion of Prentice from the Department of Education, even though he had explicitly promised Jenkins that Prentice's position was safe. When he heard of this, Jenkins abandoned his dinner (and his dining companion) at the White Tower to demand an immediate meeting with Wilson at which he threatened to resign himself if Prentice was sacked. In his memoirs he gave a pretty frank account of their interview; but the contemporary note on which his published account was based was even stronger:

> I cannot recall my exact words but they were several times in a form which left no doubt that I regarded him as a squalid little man who was using squalid little arguments in order to explain why he was performing so much below the level of events, as well as going back on a firm undertaking which he had given me, and that this was not the way in which I was prepared to do

business . . . I only made my offensive remarks . . . in reply to extremely offensive dribbles from him.

With some reason he feared that this – 'almost the most disagreeable row of my political life' – might have 'a long-term effect on my relations with Wilson'.[25] A stronger Prime Minister would have accepted Jenkins' resignation; in fact it was a measure of Wilson's weakness that he swiftly backed down, calling Jenkins back within the hour to concede that 'provided we were dealing with a statement of consequences and not a threat, he was prepared to relent and keep Prentice in the Cabinet'.[26] He then offered Prentice a move back to Overseas Development (a job he had held in 1967–9, but now upgraded to the Cabinet) at the cost of displacing Judith Hart, for whom Foot, Benn and Castle had fought as furiously as Jenkins did for Prentice. Altogether this was an utterly pointless shuffle, which fully bore out Jenkins' criticism of the Prime Minister's trivial and devious modus operandi: it had nothing whatever to do with good government, but at least Jenkins could take some comfort from the fact that the upshot was to shift the balance of the Cabinet marginally to the right.*

Prentice turned out to be an unfortunate ally on whom to stake his own position, since when he finally lost his reselection battle in Newham the next year he abandoned Labour and crossed the floor to join the Tories: he was quickly rewarded with a safe seat and office in Mrs Thatcher's government, thus seeming to confirm the left's charge that those who opposed them were closet Tories all along. But in 1975 Prentice was the most robust right-winger in the Cabinet whom Jenkins – remembering his failure to support Dick Taverne – felt bound to fight for: just three years earlier he had topped the Shadow Cabinet elections. So in September Jenkins and Shirley Williams (accompanied by Jennifer, Bill and Sylvia Rodgers, Matthew

---

* Three years later Jenkins elaborated his regret over this incident to John Grigg, who reported the conversation to his wife:

> R. himself feels that his only chance to split the Labour Party and bring about a coalition was two days after the EEC referendum. He then had a blinding and 'particularly squalid' row with Wilson, demanding that Prentice should not, as W. wished, be dropped from the Cabinet. W. gave way but R. clearly thinks that some other and much better excuse for resignation could have been found at that time, and that if he had been ruthless enough to do it the result would have been a Coalition. He is convinced that a number of leading Tories, including Ian [Gilmour], would have joined him. The whole idea seems to me highly debatable, but it's fascinating that he regards that as the great opportunity missed.[27]

Oakeshott and the Annans, plus his Special Branch detective and his driver) went to East London to show solidarity with him. The occasion turned into a roughhouse when both the far left and the far right turned up to barrack him and fight each other. Jenkins had difficulty making himself heard above the Socialist Workers and the Workers' Revolutionary Party (WRP) chanting 'Free Des Warren', but he had the good sense to stop the stewards from calling in the police, reckoning that the demonstrators made his point for him; he also managed to retain his dignity when hit full in the chest by a flour bomb thrown by a member of the National Front (protesting against the Race Relations Bill) which made a dramatic picture all over the next day's newspapers. Jenkins was 'magnificent', Prentice told the press: 'He was angry, but he showed his scorn and contempt for these people and delivered his prepared speech.'[28] He attacked both tribes of extremists, but particularly the left, recalling that Vanessa Redgrave, standing for the WRP against Prentice the previous October, had won just 570 votes, while their candidate in Stechford in February had managed only 280: now these tiny hard-left groups had realised that by infiltrating local Labour parties they could win 20,000 or 25,000. Reaching once again for Gaitskell's old promise to 'fight and fight and fight again as long as we have political breath in our bodies', he warned that if Prentice was deselected 'an axe was being laid' to the Labour party itself:

> If tolerance is shattered, formidable consequences will follow. Labour MPs will either have to become creatures of cowardice, concealing their views, trimming their sails, accepting orders, stilling their consciences, or they will all have to be men far to the left of those whose votes they seek. Either would make a mockery of parliamentary democracy. The first would reduce still further, and rightly reduce, respect for the House of Commons. It would become an assembly of craven spirits and crooked tongues. The second would, quite simply, divorce the Labour Party from the people.[29]

In the short run the publicity given to the scenes at Newham won Jenkins, and Prentice, a good deal of support and sympathy. But it did nothing to halt the takeover of the party. 'If there was any sort of extreme behaviour,' a member of the Newham executive maintained with a straight face, 'it came from the platform, because they should not have been there.'[30] No one else in the leadership – not Callaghan nor Healey nor Crosland – showed any willingness to refute this sort of nonsense. A number of younger MPs (most of whom would later join the SDP) formed the Manifesto Group to try to counter the influence of the left in the Commons. But where it mattered – that is, on the NEC – Shirley Williams and Tom Bradley were isolated and helpless as the majority voted tamely to uphold Prentice's deselection and steadfastly refused to act on the clear evidence of far-left 'entryism' which ultimately destroyed Labour as a party of government for a generation, precisely as Jenkins had warned it would.

With just a handful of middle-ranking supporters – Prentice, Shirley Williams and Harold Lever – Jenkins was equally isolated in the Cabinet. Throughout 1975 both Barbara Castle and Bernard Donoughue recorded him sounding increasingly apocalyptic warnings about the coming 'catastrophe'. In February Andrew Graham (now in the Number Ten Policy Unit) told Donoughue that on the Economic Strategy Committee 'nobody except Jenkins raised any concern about the progress of the economy. "They are just going to sit and wait for it to hit them."'[31] As inflation climbed inexorably past 20 per cent (it eventually peaked at 26.9 per cent in August) he warned that it was not only 'bankrupting all sorts of institutions . . . but it was also bankrupting civilised government . . . "We have got to stop it in its tracks . . . The survival of society is threatened"',[32] and privately worried that 'we were living through an equivalent of the summer of 1939'.[33] Against this grim background he did what he could to protest against what he saw as damaging or irrelevant policies: he successfully resisted Foot's attempt to extend union closed shop legislation to journalism, opposed the nationalisation of aircraft and ship-building – 'Roy murmured gloomily that he hoped nationalisation would not provide the most expensive programme yet for subsidising uneconomic aircraft'[34] – and opposed the hasty devolution of power to Scotland and Wales (though he later changed his mind on this). In December 1975 he and Shirley Williams alone opposed the government rescue of the Chrysler motor company.[35] He was briefly cheered when Healey, under severe pressure from the markets, belatedly forced through a package of 'voluntary' price and income controls (with statutory powers in reserve). Critical as he was of Healey's tardiness to grasp this nettle, Jenkins was thankful that he was not Chancellor again himself: 'The last thing I wanted was to have to try and show people for a second time running that the golden coach was a pumpkin.'[36] When Healey finally imposed deep cuts in public spending, however, he supported him not just as a matter of economic necessity, as it had been in 1968, but out of ideological principle.* This was a moment of truth in his journey from socialism.

Hitherto, while rejecting the fundamentalism of the left, he had remained faithful to the revisionist doctrine formulated by Gaitskell and Crosland in the 1950s, which took it for granted that ever-higher public spending – including new forms of public ownership – was still an essential means of creating a more equal society. Now, after some rumblings in Cabinet over the previous year, he publicly repudiated this central article of Labour faith. In January 1976 he used a speaking engagement in Anglesey (Cledwyn Hughes' constituency) to deliver what he called 'my most provocative speech . . . since Haverfordwest', eighteen months earlier. (He had a habit of making major speeches in remote corners of Wales.) Knowing it would provoke a storm, he deliberately delayed clearing it with Healey until it was too late: by the time the Chancellor's office caught up with him to try to stop it Hayden Phillips was able to say that Jenkins was already on his feet. Since 1964, he asserted in the critical passage, the proportion of GNP taken up by government expenditure had risen from 44 to 60 per cent, while producing no commensurate improvement in public services or social welfare. This could not go on. There was a limit to how far one could go on taxing the rich: further taxation would have to bite deep into average and below-average incomes. He concluded by drawing a line in the sand:

> I do not think that you can push public expenditure significantly above 60 per cent and maintain the values of a plural society with adequate freedom of choice. We are here close to one of the frontiers of social democracy.[39]

'How these people come out in their true colours!' Barbara Castle had exclaimed when he tried out this line in Cabinet the previous summer.[40] To her, it was all of a piece with Jenkins' closet coalitionism. Even former supporters like Roy Hattersley felt that he had sold the pass and used this speech as an excuse to distance himself. In fact

---

* Oddly, however, he wanted to exclude defence, claiming that 'our national credibility depended on no more cuts in Defence'.[37] 'If we adjusted our Defence so rapidly,' he argued in May, 'we would become a third-class power in the eyes of the world.' This would not help the economic problem, but would actually make it worse, 'because of its depressing psychological effect on the British people'. Wilson and Callaghan agreed, and defence was spared.[38] But it was a strange argument from one who had always urged Britain to reduce its military ambitions in accordance with its economic strength.

Jenkins had only dared to voice an insight that was coming to be widely shared even within the Cabinet. Crosland had already warned local authorities that 'The party is over.'[41] Nine months later Callaghan, now Prime Minister, would tell the party conference that Keynesianism had run its course: 'We used to think that you could just spend your way out of a recession . . . I tell you in all candour that that option no longer exists.'[42] Yet when Jenkins said much the same he was seen to be detaching himself from Labour.

'It was a thesis of truth and relevance,' he wrote in his memoirs, 'and it did not appear to cause offence to the Anglesey audience.' Nevertheless it was 'a crazy sermon to deliver to the Labour party' at that particular moment – and curiously enough he knew it. He had been tipped off a few weeks before, at Ann Fleming's house on Boxing Day, by Wilson's confidential 'fixer' Lord Goodman that Wilson intended to resign around his sixtieth birthday in March. This inside knowledge, which he immediately shared with Jennifer, John Harris, Hayden Phillips, Bill Rodgers and David Owen, 'ought to have galvanised me into the most intense politicising of my life', if he was to give himself a last outside chance of winning the leadership.[43] Instead it had almost the reverse effect: partly because he had flu that winter; partly because (like many others) he could not quite believe that Wilson would ever really step down voluntarily; but partly also because he did not want to believe it. He knew that if there was a leadership election he would have to stand. But he also knew that he was now unlikely to win; and deep down he no longer truly wanted to lead the ugly, fractious party that Labour had become, even if he could have been elected. He was already – subconsciously, perhaps – looking for a way out; and the day before he went to Anglesey, Wilson, ironically, offered one.

He saw Wilson on the Friday evening for what he called 'an hour's routine ramble around the ramparts of the Home Office and other government business of mutual interest',[44] in the course of which he told the Prime Minister that he was nearing the end of what he could usefully do at the Home Office. 'Unless he saw some role for me to play, a major role either in economic or foreign or constitutional affairs – I had devolution a little in mind at that stage . . . I probably wouldn't wish to stay on indefinitely.' Without referring to his own intentions, Wilson said that both the Treasury and the Foreign Office were filled but suggested that replacing Short as Leader of the House, in charge of devolution, might be a possibility. But then he mentioned that the presidency of the European Commission would fall vacant in January 1977 and there was a 'predisposition' in favour of a British candidate, if a sufficiently senior figure was available: French President Giscard d'Estaing and German Chancellor Helmut Schmidt would be willing to accept either Jenkins or Heath. 'I was caught completely off balance by this,' Jenkins wrote soon afterwards, 'because I had never considered it before.' He immediately declined, telling Wilson almost reflexively that he was 'a British political animal' and wanted to stay in the House of Commons.[45] But Donoughue thought he looked 'unhappy and distracted as he left'.[46] And over his Welsh weekend – where he was opening a police station at Wrexham as well as speaking in Anglesey – he began to have second thoughts. On the Monday he wrote to Wilson withdrawing his refusal:

> If, as seems likely, there seems little prospect of my being able to play a major foreign policy, economic or constitutional role in this country, I think I ought seriously to consider, in spite of my dislike of the place, whether I could not best spend the next four years in Brussels.[47]

Neither accepting nor refusing, he asked for more time to consider his options.

The problem was the unspoken and unmentionable possibility of Wilson's resignation triggering a leadership contest which he would feel bound to enter. So long as there was a chance of winning he did not want to rule himself out. Even if he did not win, he might at least get the Foreign Office, which would be better than going to Brussels. On 29 January he tried to get Donoughue to confirm Goodman's tip-off; but Donoughue felt obliged to keep mum.[48] In February he went to Paris, nominally on Home Office business, but actually to see Giscard, who pressed him – speaking for Schmidt as well as himself – to take the European job. This was not only flattering, but encouraged Jenkins to believe that with their support the job would be worth doing; it also made him less dependent on Wilson's favour. Before leaving he went to see the eighty-seven-year-old Jean Monnet, who also urged him to accept. 'Insofar as I was increasingly tempted,' he wrote in the introduction to his *European Diary*, 'I was exhilarated by being blessed by the spiritual as well as the temporal authorities of Europe.'[49] But others whom he consulted counselled him the other way. Nicko Henderson – newly translated from Bonn to Paris – urged him to 'stop the band-waggon' at once. He was surprised that Giscard seemed to want Jenkins. 'I am also increasingly doubtful in my own mind whether it is the job for you. In the next few years, European policy is not going to be made by the Commission. Both Giscard and Schmidt will see to that.'[50] And his old friend Jacques de Beaumarchais (now French ambassador in London) likewise told him that he would have far more influence as Foreign Secretary.[51]

His mind was still not made up when Wilson resigned. In spite of all the hints and tip-offs, Wilson's announcement still came as a bombshell to most of the political world. As his sixtieth birthday passed (on 11 March), even Jenkins had begun to discount it.* But on Tuesday 16 March Wilson read out a twenty-five-minute statement to his astonished Cabinet. After thanking them for their services over the past dozen years he pointedly reminded the claimants to his job – who comprised about a quarter of the Cabinet – that being Prime Minister was nowadays 'a full-time calling . . . These are not the easy, spacious, socially-oriented days of some of my predecessors.' This barb could only have been aimed at Jenkins. He added that being over sixty should not be a disqualification: a barely coded endorsement of Jim Callaghan, who was sixty-four.[52] By chance, Jenkins was lunching that day with the 'Walston group' of his supporters at the Albany. They all took it for granted that he would stand. This was the moment they had been anticipating for the past eight years. There was a general recognition that he had lost a lot of ground since resigning the deputy leadership in 1972, but there was still a hope that when it came to electing a new Prime Minister in the middle of an economic crisis enough Labour MPs would put aside their personal reservations and choose the best-qualified man for the job. After all, Jenkins had clearly been a better Chancellor than either Callaghan or Healey. That evening he dined at Brooks's with Bill Rodgers, John Harris and his PPS, Ian Wrigglesworth, and appointed Wrigglesworth to run his campaign.

Callaghan was the clear favourite, despite his age and undistinguished record in all three of the great offices of state. Since defying Wilson over *In Place of Strife* he had rebuilt a formidable reputation as a re-assuring heavyweight with a sure feel for party and public opinion.

* As Westminster and Fleet Street struggled to take it in and rumours abounded that Wilson had resigned to pre-empt some looming scandal, Jenkins started a mischievous explanation of his own: that Wilson had forged his birth certificate and was actually ten years older than he pretended, which would account both for his youthful precocity and his seemingly premature retirement![53]

Three days after Wilson's announcement, *Labour Weekly* quoted odds of 2:1 on Callaghan, with Jenkins second on 5:1 followed by Crosland on 12:1 and Foot and Benn on 14:1 (Healey had not yet declared). All Labour leadership elections in those days came down to the leading candidate of the right against the candidate of the left, with the former always likely to win unless he carried too much personal baggage – like George Brown in 1963, which had let Wilson sneak through. This time Foot would be the champion of the left and would probably top the first ballot. To have a chance of winning Jenkins therefore had to get more votes than Callaghan on the first ballot, after which he should easily beat Foot on the second. Five years earlier he had commanded 140 votes for deputy leader. But the parliamentary party had changed since then, with two new intakes in 1974 replacing a lot of older Members who had known him since 1950: the memory of how he had dominated the House in 1966–70 was a dwindling asset. There were too many younger Labour Members whom he had never taken the trouble to get to know. One MP of moderate views was reported to have said that he would vote for Jenkins if he once said 'Good evening' to him in the division lobby; but he didn't, so he didn't.[54] More seriously there was real doubt as to whether he could unite the party in the country. Not only on Europe, but on the trade unions, industrial policy and the economy he had set his face firmly against the majority of party activists, while his libertarian views on hanging, homosexuality and immigration were out of step with the bulk of Labour voters.

In *The Times* his faithful cheerleader Bernard Levin argued that Jenkins would bring back to Labour many former supporters who had abandoned it since 1970 and mop up the Liberal vote: the left called him divisive, but he would unite the country as no other potential Prime Minister could, while actually standing well to the left of Callaghan on most issues.[55] But Establishment endorsement of this sort was counterproductive: in the same paper the cartoonist Mark Boxer drew one willowy toff saying to another: 'If you really want Roy to win, what about *not* announcing your support?'[56] 'No amount of encomiums from Bernard Levin,' Phillip Whitehead wrote in the *New Statesman*, 'are worth the vote of a single ward party.' One MP who failed to vote for Jenkins told Whitehead sadly: 'I could have done it if there had been a glimmer of support for him in the constituency.'[57] And a famous story went the rounds alleging that when one of Jenkins' supporters tried canvassing a group of miners' MPs in the tea-room he was met with a kindly brush-off: 'Nay, lad, we're all Labour here.'[58]

The fact was that Jenkins simply did not look or sound like a Labour leader.*

He did not canvass, realising that it would have looked false if he had suddenly appeared in the bars and tea-room pressing the flesh; but he made himself available in his room for interviews with wavering supporters. Several whose votes he could have counted on a few years earlier told him frankly that they no longer believed that he could lead the party: notable defectors included Leo Abse, Roy Hattersley and Edmund Dell. At least two who later joined the SDP, Edward Lyons and Colin Phipps, also failed to vote for Jenkins in 1976. He still had some committed supporters outside the ranks of the core Jenkinsites – Shirley Williams, Shirley Summerskill, Betty Boothroyd, Willie Hamilton and his old Balliol friend David Ginsburg. But his Birmingham colleague Denis Howell voted for him only after much heart-searching; and even a close ally like Harold Lever told Donoughue that he supported him because 'in the end he is a Jenkins man', despite having frequently felt snubbed by him.[60] Despite this lack of enthusiasm he fought, in his own way, a good campaign. A lot of people thought he wiped the floor with Healey and Foot on *Panorama* – Callaghan preserved his position as front-runner by declining to appear, while Crosland, to his fury, was not invited† – insisting that he could work with the unions and unite the party. Afterwards he told Ronnie McIntosh that he still expected Callaghan to win, but he 'clearly has some hope that he may pull it off, and admitted that he felt exhilarated by the whole thing'.[62] There is nothing like an election for stimulating unreal hopes.

He had a lot of letters from old friends wishing him luck. His one-time girlfriend Barley Alison desperately hoped that he would win but, failing that, hoped that he would become Foreign Secretary and succeed to the leadership in a couple of years, 'so you can trounce Mrs T'.[63]

---

* After the election Bill Rodgers compared Jenkins with Gaitskell, who had led the party successfully despite an equally middle-class lifestyle. Rodgers did not believe that Jenkins' lifestyle counted against him, but thought his manner did:

> There is no doubt that Roy can be brusque and off-putting. He can be difficult to approach and to talk to. Telephone calls can be cold and abrupt. His accent, his use of words, his pronunciation, the way he holds his head, the way he shows interest (or impatience) – all these are obstacles to easy contact. The fact that there is shyness does not come through: it can seem like arrogance and indifference.[59]

† Crosland had been determined to stand in the deluded hope that he could 'beat Roy on the first ballot' by picking up the votes of the 1974 intake. 'I cannot believe that it will happen,' Donoughue commented. From the moment Wilson resigned he thought the contest was 'all sewn up for Callaghan'.[61]

459

His boyhood playmate from Abersychan, Derek Powell, feared that Callaghan would win, which he thought would be a disaster, and told Roy that he should never have resigned as deputy leader.[64] This was plainly true, but unhelpful.

As the first ballot approached, some of his team were still optimistic that he could poll well enough to have a chance of winning on the second or third. John Roper actually put him in second place with 84 votes to Foot's 90 and Callaghan's 79, with Healey, Benn and Crosland sharing 57 between them. 'I stick my neck out,' Matthew Oakeshott wrote, 'and say you will get 80 votes tomorrow. That already would represent a substantial chance of victory.' Bill Rodgers was a little more realistic, but still substantially overstated: 'My best guess is that you will get 68 votes. But there is a good prospect that this will rise to about 75.' These estimates were based on a printed list of all 318 Labour MPs marked up in four classes, A, B, C or D: certain, possible, unlikely and definitely hostile. This gave just 44 As and 82 Bs. Roper, Oakeshott and Rodgers all misjudged the number of Bs Jenkins would actually get. Jenkins' own prediction, written down the evening before the ballot, was the most accurate: Foot 90, Callaghan 85, Jenkins 62, Healey 38, Benn 25, Crosland 12.[65] He was spot-on with Foot, one off with Callaghan, but still overestimated his own vote by six, Healey's by eight, and underestimated Benn by twelve and Crosland by five. The actual result, declared the following afternoon, was Foot 90, Callaghan 84, Jenkins 56, Benn 37, Healey 30, Crosland 17.

This outcome – 'about ten votes less than I had realistically hoped for' – he characteristically described as 'a considerable, but not a shattering disappointment to me'.[66] Analysis in the *New Statesman* suggested that he won the votes of only just over half the 100-odd committed pro-Marketeers, and just seven votes from the other 227 who were lukewarm or hostile to Europe. Both Foot and Healey won more of the 'middle' than he did; Foot attracted wider support beyond his left-wing core than Jenkins did beyond the right; while eleven of Crosland's seventeen votes came from the left.[67] In retrospect he was inclined to regret that another dozen votes taken from Callaghan, plus a handful more from Healey and Crosland, would have given him the chance to beat Foot on the second ballot and win the premiership. Perhaps he should have worked a little harder to win back the doubters? But in reality these figures show that his support was just too narrow and he could never have commanded the party.

That afternoon Rodgers had written him 'a long, powerfully argued letter' considering what he should do if he did not win. If he was more than about ten votes behind Callaghan, Rodgers reckoned, he probably would not be able to close the gap. If Healey and Crosland won forty-five between them – nearly right – they would have to switch two-to-one for Jenkins on the second ballot, and 'I just don't believe it, given the instinct to back the winner'. More likely, his vote might actually fall, and the gap between him and Callaghan widen, thus losing the benefit of having run him close on the first ballot. Therefore, Rodgers advised, it would be better to bank his winnings and withdraw at once. 'My strong sense is that, if on the most hard-headed analysis you can't win, you should make a virtue of necessity with a quick decision to withdraw.'[68]

Jenkins agreed. He thought the country needed a new Prime Minister quickly, not a protracted struggle stretching over three or four rounds. Of his supporters who gathered in his room after the result, only three disagreed. One – who arrived late as usual – was Shirley Williams. She wanted Jenkins to negotiate a deal with Callaghan: a promise of the Foreign Office in return for his withdrawal. But Jenkins rejected both this and any sort of deal with Healey. He lost no time in issuing a statement to the press that he was stepping aside, and Dickson Mabon was dispatched to break the news to the Callaghan camp, who were mightily relieved. Jenkins then went off to the monthly dinner of the Other Club with Nicko Henderson, 'where not unnaturally in all the circumstances we consumed a good deal of alcohol'.[69]

Barbara Castle was 'staggered' by his decision to withdraw. 'This further display of political daintiness proves conclusively what I have always known: that Jenkins will never lead the Labour Party. I bet Denis stays in the ring, despite his derisory thirty votes. But then, he's a pugilist, not a patrician.'[70] In her memoirs she added that David Owen – her junior minister at the Department of Health – 'did not attempt to hide his disgust from me'.[71] Healey did stay in, but picked up only eight more votes on the second ballot, on which Callaghan narrowly took the lead (Callaghan 141, Foot 133, Healey 38) before winning convincingly on the third (Callaghan 176, Foot 137). At the party meeting to announce the result on 5 April, Jenkins made what Tony Benn called 'a most ponderous, rather Victorian speech' marking the change of leadership:

> He looked shattered – this contest has been as much of a death for him as Herbert Morrison's execution at the hands of Hugh Gaitskell in 1955. I think Roy does now realise he can't ever be Leader of the Labour Party.[72]

Much of his speech was a surprisingly warm tribute to the departing Prime Minister. Wilson was touched by it, and asked for a copy. Jenkins obliged, with a covering letter generously burying the hatchet after their often fraught relationship since 1964:

> I am sorry we had a number of differences – some of them a bit rough – over the past five years. They do not in any way blot out for me the recollection of close earlier co-operation . . . In retrospect I think I never allowed enough for your ability and determination to achieve medium and long-term aims at the expense of short-term sacrifices of esteem.

In his original draft Jenkins had added an apology 'for my occasional (or perhaps more frequent) shortsightedness'. But this was perhaps going a bit too far and he deleted it.[73]

Callaghan's succession marked the end of Jenkins' dwindling hope of the premiership. He now had to decide whether to stay in British politics or take up the offer to go to Brussels. His answer depended on what inducement Callaghan offered him. He rather assumed – as did most of the press – that he was the obvious candidate to fill Callaghan's place at the Foreign Office. This was the one senior department of state he had not occupied, for which he felt well qualified and where he could see an important role for himself, making the most of Britain's now-confirmed membership of Europe. Callaghan, however, had other ideas. He initially wanted Healey as his Foreign Secretary – the job for which Healey too had been preparing all his life, for which he was far better equipped than for the Treasury. But Healey could not leave the Treasury for the present (he was about to introduce his third budget) and generously told Callaghan he 'must offer the FCO to Roy'.[74] Meanwhile Foot warned that the party would not stand Jenkins as Foreign Secretary: the anti-Marketeers might have lost the referendum, but they would not accept an ardent pro-Marketeer conducting a love-in with Europe. Foot wanted Peter Shore to have the job. When Jenkins saw Callaghan on the morning of 6 April, therefore, he was disappointed to be offered not the job he coveted, but only the possibility of the Treasury in six months' time when Healey would be free to move to the Foreign Office. In the meantime he would presumably stay at the Home Office:

> I was dismayed by this. The thought of going back to the Treasury, particularly in a much weaker Cabinet position than

had been the case in 1966/70 and trying to fight through sensible policies with Foot and Jones to deal with struck me as appalling.* I therefore immediately said that I thought I would have to pursue policies so rigorous that they would break the Government.[75]

Callaghan disagreed and said he believed Jenkins could do it; but they parted inconclusively. Jenkins lunched with his inner circle of advisers – Jennifer, John Harris, Hayden Phillips, Anthony Lester and Matthew Oakeshott – all of whom more or less endorsed his reluctance to go back to the Treasury (Lester and Oakeshott less certainly than the others), especially as it was only a promise for the future. By the time he saw Callaghan again the next day he had resolved to take the Foreign Office or nothing. He was at least as well qualified as Healey. Was the Prime Minister really saying that a pro-European could not be Foreign Secretary? If so, he would rather go to Brussels. Callaghan was regretful but unbudging. The next day he rubbed vinegar in the wound by appointing Tony Crosland Foreign Secretary.

This was the latest (and, as it turned out, the last) twist in the game of leapfrog that Jenkins and Crosland had been playing ever since Oxford: Tony's revenge for Roy beating him to the Treasury in 1967. It had never occurred to Jenkins that Crosland – who had never shown the least interest in foreign affairs – might be a rival for the Foreign Office, and he confessed to feeling, as in 1965 when Crosland had accepted Education after he refused it, 'a twinge of rather discreditable jealousy'. 'My relations with Crosland have of course been odd over a number of decades,' he wrote in his memoir notes – before substituting 'equivocal' for 'odd'. As in 1965, he took some malicious pleasure in the fact that Crosland was widely considered a poor appointment, 'on the ground that he knew remarkably little about foreign affairs'.[76] On the other hand Crosland had been the better-qualified economist when he missed out in 1967, so there was rough justice there. Lack of knowledge did not stop Crosland being 'exultant' at getting his own back.[77] For his part, Jenkins did not believe that Foot had vetoed him, but rather that Callaghan was jealous of his greater success at both the Home Office and the Treasury in 1965–70. 'I think he was determined that this pattern should not repeat itself a third time,' he wrote, 'and

* Jack Jones was the left-wing leader of the Transport & General Workers' Union, widely held to wield undue influence over the government.

THIS LITTLE PIG STAYED AT HOME ...

Garland, *Daily Telegraph,* 9.4.76 (British Cartoon Archive, University of Kent)

had no desire to go around Europe or the world or to deal with foreign affairs with me as a Foreign Secretary with a fairly widespread world reputation and perhaps having my attitude contrasted with his rather ungracious insularity.'[78] The complacency of this consolation does not mean that it was an inaccurate analysis. Callaghan was much more comfortable with a Foreign Secretary who shared his own weary scepticism towards Europe. The appointment was also Crosland's reward for having backed Callaghan for the leadership as far back as 1963. There is sometimes gratitude in politics.

Jenkins really did not want to go to Brussels if he could have stayed. His first instinctive recoil from Wilson's suggestion was genuine. But the only two British jobs he really wanted had been denied him and he did not wish to stay in the Cabinet as a lame duck. He was afraid that his poor showing in the leadership election would have damaged his authority. He now felt that he might have held a stronger bargaining hand if he had not withdrawn from the leadership contest so quickly. In other circumstances, he told Lester, he might have been interested in taking on devolution and other constitutional reforms, 'but not if his authority is gone'.[79] All sorts of people – friends, journalists and others – urged him not to go. 'For heaven's sake stay in politics and don't desert us for Europe,' Ann Fleming begged him. 'You will be needed here more than you ever were.'[80]* More seriously David Watt of the *Financial Times*, with whom he lunched (at the Ritz) on 30 March, understood his wish to get out, but told him that Brussels was not the job for him at this time: there was still a lot for him to do at home and he might yet succeed Callaghan.[81] Janet Morgan, then a young Oxford academic who was editing the Crossman diaries, wrote flatteringly:

> The more I plod through the Crossman diaries . . . the more clear it becomes that while Wilson & Callaghan & Castle & Foot and all the rest of them are a past generation of politicians, you are not. You are forward-looking and looked to, in a way that is not true of much of the 1964–70 and 1974–76 front bench, and you are, though it may not seem like it now, still on the upward rise of the curve. Please don't go.[82]

Some of his most trusted supporters, by contrast, were telling him more or less delicately that he was finished. Even before the final result of the leadership election, when he was still hoping to get the Foreign Office, David and Debbie Owen had come to East Hendred for tennis and dinner and over the course of the evening Owen rather encouraged him to go to Brussels. It was of course his decision to stay or go, but either way he must realise that his campaign for the leadership was over: 'I mustn't expect to run a group as I had done in the past.' Owen talked almost exclusively of his own prospects and ambitions. 'His attitude struck both Jennifer and me as being a little cold and self-interested.'[83] In the *New Statesman* Phillip Whitehead likened Jenkins' anticipated departure to the death of Peel in 1846 which allowed the Peelites – above all Gladstone – to move on to make their own careers.[84] Historical parallels always resonated with Jenkins and he duly noted this one. The next day Bill and Sylvia Rodgers came to lunch: Rodgers was friendlier than Owen, but his advice was much the same. Just as he had done over the deputy leadership, he thought Jenkins must follow his own instinct. There was no point staying in the government if his heart was not in it. 'There is no point acting against nature':

> I prefer to think of you in the House of Commons, not across the Channel. But equally, to be your own man in Brussels influencing

---

* She also wondered what she should say to her other Labour favourite. 'I don't know what to write to Tony?' she wrote. 'Perhaps advise a more elegant way of smoking and look generally less scruffy.'

the future of Europe, must be more attractive than being a prisoner in an uncongenial Cabinet . . . My conclusion is that while I – and many others – want you to stay, the logic (the logic of who you are and what you feel) may point the other way.[85]

That was Jenkins' view too. Accordingly on 8 April he wrote formally to Giscard d'Estaing accepting the Presidency of the European Commission.[86] 'He realised it might be the end of his career in British politics', Ronnie McIntosh wrote in his diary, 'but he couldn't see any future for himself in the Labour Party, as at present constituted, anyway.'[87]

His appointment was widely welcomed, both in Europe where it was hoped that a heavyweight politician might raise the profile of the Commission after a succession of rather dim bureaucrats like the outgoing French President, François-Xavier Ortoli, and in Britain where it was hoped that a British President would increase Britain's clout in the Community – though there was some regret that Jenkins had taken the job only after he had missed out on the premiership, confirming 'the popular view of the Commission as a well-paid grazing ground for played-out politicians'.[88] It was almost universally assumed that there was no way back. 'No previous incumbent has been wholly successful in managing a re-entry into national politics,' *The Times* commented. 'Certainly none has returned to a career of great eminence or distinction.'[89] In his own mind, however, Jenkins always kept open the possibility that he might come back. To the Prime Minister of Luxembourg, Gaston Thorn – who four years later was to be his successor – he wrote on 5 May that he regarded going to Brussels 'not as the termination of my political life, but as its development in the most useful way that I could envisage for the next two years'. (The appointment was initially for two years, though he made it clear to Giscard that he expected to have four.) 'The future beyond that I would leave entirely open, both in my own mind and in public statements.'[90] And he received some support for this secret hope from John Grigg, who assured him that he could still become Prime Minister. 'For one thing,' Grigg wrote, 'age is very much on your side.' Callaghan and Foot were the two oldest candidates in the recent election, 'so the Labour Party seems to be healthily biased towards the gerontocratic principle'. Moreover, by going to Brussels he would be absolved of responsibility for whatever Labour did in the next four years:

You will be making a success of yet another job (having never made a balls of any that you have done), and absence may very well make the hearts of your colleagues grow fonder. It seems to me that Providence may not have played you quite such a dirty trick after all in denying you the leadership now.[91]

Meanwhile he agreed to stay on for another few months as Home Secretary, while preparing for his new responsibilities. Having failed to get the job he wanted for himself, he did this time try – over a series of 'bad-tempered' telephone calls with Callaghan – to look after his supporters.[92] In his own department he wanted Shirley Summerskill or Tom Bradley promoted in place of Alex Lyon, with Ian Wrigglesworth becoming an Under-Secretary. Callaghan made no difficulty about sacking Lyon, but proposed moving Bill Rodgers to the Home Office. Jenkins rejected this, saying that this would be no promotion and bad for Rodgers' career. Callaghan then appointed Brynmor John – 'something of a crony of his' – without further consultation, and found no place for Wrigglesworth. He also ignored Jenkins' urging of a job for David Marquand, who decided instead to give up his seat and follow Jenkins to Brussels.[93] The reality was that Callaghan felt no need to do any favours for a defeated rival who was on the way out. But in the reshuffle that followed Jenkins' final departure in September he did bring Rodgers into the Cabinet as Transport Secretary.

There were no more major terrorist incidents in these last few months, but there were a number of racial flare-ups – riots in Southall in June after an Asian man was stabbed, and trouble at the Notting Hill Carnival in August – leading to questions about the policing of black communities. Jenkins still had to see his Race Relations Bill onto the Statute Book in July. He also had to secure Cabinet approval for two new bills for the 1976–7 session: a Conspiracy and Criminal Law Reform Bill, and another Criminal Justice Bill, both of a fairly technical nature.[94] He set up a Royal Commission to look into the law on gambling, chaired by Lord Rothschild (the former head of Ted Heath's think tank). Beyond these departmental responsibilities he tried again to advance some of his own pet reforms before he left. He had another go at trying to get electoral reform considered by a Speaker's Conference, but did not press the matter;[95] and he had another try at liberalising the Official Secrets Act, but was thwarted on this occasion by Tony Crosland who – to Donoughue's disgust – simply read out his Foreign Office brief against any relaxation.[96] Jenkins joined forces with Tony Benn in refusing to sign a restrictive undertaking about publishing ministerial memoirs.[97] He published a Green Paper, written by Anthony Lester, backing the incorporation of the European Convention on

467

Human Rights into British law; but this too ran into opposition and was quietly buried for another twenty-two years.[98] In an interesting echo of an old controversy that came to Cabinet in May he also argued strongly against a proposal by the Education Secretary, Fred Mulley, that in ratifying the UN Covenant on Human Rights the government should reserve the right to outlaw independent schools. The freedom to choose private education, Jenkins now insisted, was itself a human right: the government could still squeeze the public schools, but threatening to abolish them would simply stir up a lot of trouble to no benefit. No other country was thinking of such a thing. Strong views were expressed on both sides, but Callaghan summed up against making such a reservation.[99]

One major issue on which Jenkins changed his view between 1974 and 1976 – one that was to be unexpectedly important for his future – was devolution. The Scottish Nationalists had won their first seat at a by-election in 1967, but had only become a serious force when they won seven seats in February 1974 and eleven in October, taking 30 per cent of the vote in Scotland. (Plaid Cymru meanwhile won three seats with 10 per cent of the Welsh vote.) Fuelled by the discovery of North Sea oil and the heady slogan 'It's Scotland's Oil', the SNP's advance posed a potentially mortal threat to Labour's dominance in Scotland, without which it could never hope to form a government in the United Kingdom. In a desperate effort to defuse this challenge the government had hastily committed itself to introducing some form of devolution to allay nationalist sentiment some way short of independence, and put Ted Short in charge of framing it. When Short first brought his ideas to Cabinet in July 1974 Jenkins, as Barbara Castle recorded, 'clearly disapproved of the whole business: "I am horrified at the idea of rushing into a decision in the last fevered weeks of July which could affect the shape of Great Britain for a hundred years."'[100] A week later he supported Healey and Crosland in arguing that they should put the brakes on: 'We should announce the minimum commitment and announce that we will deal with this properly after the election.'[101] Even then, when the SNP had gained another four seats, he still thought devolution 'a most frightening prospect' and passed a note to Crosland in Cabinet committee blaming Willie Ross – a longtime opponent of devolution who had now decided that it was irresistible – and particularly Short ('the revered headmaster') for 'approaching it with a lack of imagination or ability + knowledge . . . which would be a severe disadvantage to drawing up a school curriculum, let alone a new constitution for the U.K.' ('I agree,' Crosland wrote back.)[102] At

Chequers in January 1975 Jenkins again 'spoke long and impressively. He said frankly he was a "go-slower" because he "didn't like the look of the destination". He was "afraid of the slippery slope of separatism". He saw no reason to rush things and exposed some inconsistencies in Short's arguments.' According to Donoughue, Jenkins took the lead, supported by Crosland, Prentice and Benn, in stopping Wilson from railroading it through.[103] In June Jenkins, Crosland and Healey were still leading 'a big move to retreat' on the issue.[104]

Yet by September 1975 he was beginning to be converted. He was still not happy with the proposals on the table, warning that retaining a power for Westminster to 'override' the devolved assemblies would be 'meaningless' and would 'frighten Westminster more than the Scots'.[105] But characteristically, if there was going to be major constitutional reform, he wanted to do it by all-party agreement – arousing equally knee-jerk opposition from Michael Foot and Barbara Castle:

> Mike and I both said 'no' in a loud voice. I said our interests and the Tories' in this matter were diametrically opposed, while Mike pointed out that it would hardly do our cause any good in Scotland to be advocating a consensus policy.

While admitting to her diary that 'the implications of devolution *are* worrying', Mrs Castle considered that Labour had no alternative and thought it 'a bit much for Roy Jenkins and co. to express their alarm at the break-up of the unity of the UK when they have done so much to destroy its sense of sovereignty by impaling us on the horns of the EEC.'[106]

By the beginning of 1976, however, Jenkins was fully persuaded. After due consideration he now believed that the demand for devolution reflected 'a firm change in Scottish opinion' – less so in Wales – and that to resist it would be to ignore the lessons of history (specifically Irish history) and carry a greater risk of breaking up the United Kingdom than would be run by acceding to it. The important thing was to establish clear lines between devolved and UK functions. He was afraid that the government's White Paper, published in March, was too centralist and would create a recipe for endless friction between Edinburgh and London, which could only lead to separation; he wanted a process of judicial review, on the US model, to resolve disputes. On 26 March – ten days after his withdrawal from the Labour leadership contest – he made a long-gestated speech in Greenock (Dickson Mabon's constituency) announcing his view. He did not go into detail about precisely what powers should be transferred, but declared his support for 'a coherent and enduring constitutional framework which recognises the legitimate demands for Scottish control over Scottish affairs with the equally legitimate requirements of democratic and effective United Kingdom government'.[107] Four days later he astonished Barbara Castle by the vehemence of his position: 'I am absolutely convinced now that we must go ahead with our devolution policy. There can be no going back whatsoever.' For a day or two he played with the suggestion that if he could not be Foreign Secretary, he might take over responsibility for devolution. Mrs Castle was horrified. 'We should end up with PR, a written constitution and a Bill of Rights.'[108] The idea foundered when Jenkins decided that he would take the Foreign Office or nothing. But he had reason to be grateful that he had put his support for devolution firmly on record six years before he ever imagined that his comeback to British politics would depend on fighting a Scottish seat.

He made his last Commons speeches as Home Secretary before the House rose for the summer recess. First, on 5 July, he had to defend the government's policy on admitting the dependants of immigrants in an adjournment debate opened by Willie Whitelaw: he promised to close loopholes and root out abuses, but refused to do anything to endanger good race relations: 'We cannot afford not to make a success of the multiracial society.' The Tories officially abstained, but a number of diehards – including Norman Tebbit, Nicholas Ridley and Alan Clark (but also, oddly, Douglas Hurd) – forced a vote and were defeated by 68:18.[109] Three days later he had to speak and vote several times during an all-night sitting on the Race Relations Bill, before it was finally carried with just three dissenting votes at lunchtime on 9 July. These were to be his last speeches from the government front bench. He attended what turned out to be his final Cabinet on 3 August before his usual month-long summer holiday, divided between Italy (staying with the Gilmours) and France (staying with Jacques and Marie-Alice de Beaumarchais). He missed Cabinet on 9 September because he had gone to Paris for the day (lunching with Nicko Henderson at the British Embassy), came back the next day for what he thought was going to be a meeting about the seamen's strike, but was upset by Callaghan rushing the reshuffle and left without the graceful exchange of compliments he would doubtless have liked. 'I watched him go out for the last time,' Donoughue wrote, 'after his interview with the P.M., head down, arms swinging, somehow not happy.'[110] Merlyn Rees took over as Home Secretary and Jenkins' ministerial career was over.

There remained only his farewells to Stechford, where he stayed on as MP until the end of the year. At the time, and later, he always maintained that leaving Stechford was a greater wrench than leaving the House of Commons. Though he never felt much love for Birmingham as a city, nor for Stechford as a particularly characterless slice of it, he had over nearly twenty-seven years forged warm relationships with a good many individuals in the local party – Joe Balmer, George Canning, Dink Hitchman (Austin had died in 1965) and Dennis and Alannah Brennan – real friendships, which he kept up for years after he left the constituency. Nevertheless Stechford, like other constituency Labour parties, had changed in recent years as younger militants moved in and pushed out the old loyalists. Jenkins had not hitherto faced the sort of open hostility that Dick Taverne had provoked in Lincoln or Reg Prentice in Newham; but by 1976 his support was rapidly eroding. In his contemporary notes he described an unpleasant meeting of the general management committee in April – just after the leadership election – at which Alannah Brennan was elected secretary (temporarily replacing her husband who was ill) only by Canning's casting vote as chairman:

> The room was divided into two parts in a way I had never known it before. The youngish middle-aged in the party seemed to have disappeared. There was a young group of IS [International Socialists], aggressive, completely without warmth or sentiment towards me, and the older group, sad, disillusioned, bitter, hating this invasion and talking a great deal about moving out of the party. Perhaps from the point of view of the end of a long marriage it was depressing but salutary.

If this was the modern Labour party, he reflected, maybe he was lucky not to have been elected leader.[111]

Announcing his resignation in July when his appointment to Brussels was formally confirmed, he urged the local party to select as his successor a candidate 'with broad appeal to the electorate', not a narrow left-winger.[112] They actually took his advice by choosing a local businessman, Terry Davis, who had briefly been MP for Bromsgrove between 1971 and 1974. In the grim political climate of the time, however, after Denis Healey was forced to seek an emergency bail-out from the IMF in October, Davis was unable to defend Jenkins' nearly 12,000 majority and lost the by-election the following March.* Jenkins kept up his

---

* Davis regained the seat at the General Election in 1979 and held it (redrawn and renamed Hodge Hill) until 2004. After holding various frontbench spokesmanships under Michael Foot and Neil Kinnock in the 1980s, he became leader of the Labour group on the Council of Europe, before becoming its Secretary-General from 2004 to 2009.

"Farewell old things, and the best of British luck !"

Franklin, *Sun,* 20.12.76 (British Cartoon Archive, University of Kent)

constituency surgeries on the third Friday of every month over the autumn until he bowed out with a farewell party on 10 December. He had not spoken in the House, and rarely attended, since July; but he cast his last vote four days before Christmas at the end of an adjournment debate on the economy on which the Labour left rebelled, but the Tories abstained, giving a government majority of 219:51. He did not stay for another vote on tobacco duties, but slipped away for what he must have thought would probably be the last time.

There was a round of valedictory lunches and dinners, both private and public. Bill Rodgers organised a dinner for his supporters at the House on 29 November. The Parliamentary Press Gallery gave him a lunch on 8 December at which he looked forward to the new challenge facing him in Brussels, but also back over his twenty-eight years at Westminster. Deploring the increasingly 'gladiatorial' conduct of politics and 'the utopianism of opposition' – the belief that all problems could be solved by a change of government – which was strangling rational debate, he warned that without greater independence of speech and probably greater freedom of voting 'the strains will build up to an extent that will burst the banks of our present parliamentary system'.[113]

This was now almost explicitly his hope. Interviewed on *Panorama* in October, he had hinted as never before at the desirability of coalition; and privately he wondered 'a little wistfully . . . whether he had been right to leave British politics at this time'.[114] When the *Daily Telegraph* misreported his Press Gallery speech as a definitive farewell, he wrote quickly to correct it: he 'could not guarantee that Parliament had seen the last of me'.[115] Distinguished friends who begged him not to burn his boats included Jeremy Hutchinson, QC – 'Nobody knows more about the extraordinary twists of politics than you, and it may well be that the 1980s will hold all manner of surprises . . . I sincerely hope you won't become a Lord!'[116] – and Hugh Thomas, who looked forward to him returning from Brussels in four years' time, still much younger than General de Gaulle in 1958, and suggested setting up some sort of shadow party to prepare for the moment.[117]

But the Establishment world in which he now largely moved was best typified by the dinner given by a group of his closest male friends on 13 December. It was hosted by Jakie Astor and Victor Rothschild, and the other guests were Ian Gilmour and Mark Bonham Carter, John Grigg and Woodrow Wyatt, Noel Annan, David Harlech, Claus Moser (head of the Government Statistical Service since 1967 and chairman of the Royal Opera House) and Robert Armstrong (just about to take over, on Jenkins' recommendation, as Permanent Secretary at the Home Office and, within three years, as Cabinet Secretary). There was only one ex-Labour man among them! They drank Château Lafite Rothschild 1945 and Quinta do Noval port, also 1945. It was an aptly symbolic way to say goodbye to Labour politics.

18 'Le Roi Jean Quinze'

J ENKINS felt almost childishly excited in the summer and autumn of 1976 as he prepared to go to Brussels. Once he had made up his mind, he felt liberated by the prospect of escaping the drudgery and dishonesty of domestic Labour politics; and he anticipated the new challenge of Europe with unrealistic optimism. While still Home Secretary until September, he started reading intensively about the history and institutions of the Community, with briefing papers prepared for him by Michael Jenkins (no relation, *chef de cabinet* to George Thomson, who was just finishing his term as one of the two existing British Commissioners) and Christopher Audland (deputy Secretary-General of the Commission) – plus a useful list of Dos and Don'ts from the other outgoing British Commissioner, Christopher Soames. He also visited all the Community capitals at least once – except Brussels, which he deliberately avoided till he took up his post in January 1977 – meeting the Prime Ministers and foreign ministers, and lunched in London with Emile Noël, who had been Secretary-General since 1958. Noël was a classic French diplomat of immense wisdom and subtlety who – Jenkins later wrote – 'knew every strand in the history and practice of the institutions of Europe as a spider knows every filament in its web' and composed 'inimitable minutes, where *mots justes* jostled with subjunctives in every sentence'.[1]

This highlighted his first challenge, which was to improve his schoolboy French so as to be able to appreciate these subtleties. He worked hard at it, compiling – as he had with his German at Bletchley – long lists of vocabulary to learn, reading simple French authors like Voltaire and Simenon and practising conversation with Leslie Bonham Carter. He achieved a functional level of communication, but was never comfortable in French.

He always distrusted those who claimed to be able to understand a language but not to speak it, insisting on the contrary that 'it is much easier to speak a language simply than to take in the nuances of what someone is saying to you'.[2]* Despite his love of Italy he had never learned any Italian – his many holidays there were spent entirely among British friends – and his German remained rudimentary. Fortunately the business of the Community was done almost entirely in French and English, and most of the non-French-speaking leaders and officials spoke good English. Nevertheless his lack of fluency in French remained a handicap.

He also had to appoint his *cabinet* – his team of personal advisers – and staff. His first intention, characteristically, was to take Hayden Phillips from the Home Office as his *chef de cabinet*. But Phillips had no experience of Brussels and spoke no better French than Jenkins did. So he was persuaded to interview several Foreign Office high-flyers from whom he eventually chose Crispin Tickell, who had served as private secretary to successive Europe ministers during Britain's successful entry negotiations in 1970–72. Tickell went on to a distinguished career, culminating as Mrs Thatcher's ambassador to the United Nations; more unusually he was one of the first to highlight the threat of climate change – an interest that appealed to Jenkins' obsession with the weather.† Jenkins admired his intellect, and Tickell served him well; but he was an abrasive character whose perceived arrogance made enemies in Brussels – rather as David Dowler had done in Whitehall. He tended to assume that the Commission should function like the British Civil Service, with a clear command structure, which it did not. The more emollient Phillips, who became his deputy, had to spend a lot of his time mending fences and smoothing ruffled feathers, while there was some competition between them for their master's ear.

For the rest Tickell recruited for him two more Britons – 'both of them Balliol economists as it happened'[5] – a German and a Luxembourgeois, and a British press spokesman. In addition Michael Jenkins stayed on for some months to ease the transition; and David Marquand gave up his safe seat at Westminster to take on a somewhat undefined role supposedly liaising with the European Parliament. There was some criticism that the personnel of his *cabinet* was too British.

---

* In later years he used to claim to have read the whole of Proust in French; but Jennifer was 'sharply sceptical' of this claim.[3]
† Jenkins was influenced by Tickell to take climate change seriously, and by 1988 was voicing his 'increasing conviction that the planet will be in greater danger by the year 2000 from man's peaceful activities than from the threat of nuclear war'[4] – not, it must be said, that he made it one of his major concerns.

This was not surprising – Jenkins always needed to be surrounded by people with whom he felt comfortable – and previous Presidents had shown no less preference for their own nationality. The more valid criticism in the early days was their inexperience of the ways of the Community, which stirred some resentment among old Brussels hands that the British had joined Europe late but now expected to throw their weight around. Some of this naturally reflected on Jenkins himself, and some wit soon christened him 'Le Roi Jean Quinze'.

On a practical level, Jenkins also had to find a house in Brussels. The President of the European Commission, he later complained, 'was the only head of an international organisation in the world who did not have a residence provided'. From the moment of his appointment the British press focused relentlessly on what it saw as his enormous salary – around £50,000 plus expenses: this was in line with European pay levels, but more than twice the British Prime Minister's salary, with three years' severance pay and a generous pension on top. But Jenkins claimed that more than half his salary 'went straight into providing what had to be in effect a small embassy'.[6] He did not accept that he was overpaid. 'The position was obviously more than tolerable, but hardly the Croesus-like existence constantly presented . . . to the British public . . . I do not think that I saved anything during my four Brussels years.'[7] He declined to take over the grand mansion occupied by Christopher Soames, but settled for what he called 'a small art nouveau town house' – found by Jennifer – in the rue de Praetère to the south of the city near the Bois de la Cambre.[8] John Grigg, visiting in 1978, described it to his wife as 'a solid bourgeois house more or less out of *Villette*, with a porte-cochere, high ceilings and an atmosphere of rather drab prosperity . . . The drawing room, for instance, has rather a dentist's waiting-room air.' Roy and Jennifer, he added, 'are not particularly good at making their houses attractive . . . But on the whole the house is comfortable and certainly the drink flowed.'[9] They undoubtedly did a lot of entertaining there. The dining room could not seat more than ten, but Jenkins wrote that 'it was a rare week in which we did not entertain thirty or forty people, visiting ministers, ambassadors, other Commissioners, staff and friends'.[10] To cater for all this they took over from Soames (another noted gourmand) his 'skilled but sometimes forbidding cook . . . a Belgian lady of uncertain age, confirmed spinster-hood and untitillating appearance' named Marie-Jeanne, who was kept very busy over the next four years.[11]*

---

* Jenkins also took over secretaries from his two British predecessors: Sue Besford from Soames and Celia Beale from Thomson. Sue Besford stayed with him for two years before

Jennifer was not there much of the time. She had given up the Consumers' Association in 1976, but was now chairman of the Historic Buildings Council, among numerous other appointments. 'There is no real work for me out there,' she told *The Times*. 'It is not like being an ambassador's wife.'[12] She usually came out to Brussels one or two weekends a month, while Roy normally went home one weekend a month, so he was on his own a good deal of the time; except that he hated being alone and invited a constant stream of staff, colleagues or friends from England to keep him company, so that he very rarely lunched or dined alone. In particular he brought over Laura Grenfell – Leslie Bonham Carter's twenty-six-year-old daughter from her first marriage – to act primarily as his hostess, though she also acted as his diary secretary and was effectively part of his *cabinet*, with her own office in the Berlaymont building. Many in Brussels assumed that Laura must be his mistress; she was not, but Jenkins loved her 'zest and intelligence and buoyancy which make my spirits rise whenever I see her'.[13] He was delighted when she married Hayden Phillips, and bereft when Phillips felt he should go back to the Home Office after two years and he and Laura both moved back to London.

His most important task before taking up his post was to appoint his fellow Commissioners: two from each of the four larger countries (France, West Germany, the UK and Italy) and one each from the five smaller (Belgium, the Netherlands, Luxembourg, Ireland and Denmark). But here he came up sharply against the realities of the job. Having never taken a close interest in how the Community actually worked – he liked to joke that he had supported the church of European unity for the past twenty years 'as a buttress rather than a pillar'[14] – he had imagined that he would be something like a Prime Minister of Europe with the power to choose his own colleagues. A report by the former Belgian Prime Minister, Leo Tindemans, had indeed proposed that the President should have more say in appointing his colleagues; but in practice the member governments jealously guarded their own right to appoint whom they wanted – invariably chosen for domestic political reasons and not necessarily the best person for the job. On his summer visits to the various capitals Jenkins had to haggle to try to secure the

being replaced first by Patricia Smallbone and then by Sarah Keays. Celia Beale stayed with him until 1983. Bess Church continued as his London secretary until 1980, when she was replaced by Patricia Smallbone. Another vital member of his personal support team was his driver, Peter Halsey, whom Jenkins took with him from the Home Office and who helped out in all sorts of practical ways, as well as getting him unfailingly to meetings and airports on time.

477

names he wanted. Some of the outgoing incumbents he was happy to keep on, notably the Frenchman Claude Cheysson and the Dane, Finn Olav Gundelach, and he eventually agreed that his French predecessor, François-Xavier Ortoli, should stay on as part of the price of getting Giscard to reappoint Cheysson. After delicate bargaining he was also happy with the two whom the Italians were determined to appoint. But the Dutch and Irish and, more importantly, the Germans all insisted on nominations who would not have been his choice and did not turn out to be conspicuously successful.

He naturally took a close interest in the choice of the second British Commissioner, who for reasons of political balance had to be a Conservative (thus ruling out the possibility of Thomson staying on). Jenkins first tried to interest Lord Carrington in the job. Carrington professed himself 'flattered' and replied that 'there is nobody with whom I would rather work'. He admitted – 'rather indiscreetly' – that he was not happy with the direction in which Mrs Thatcher was leading the Tory Party, but did not feel he could jump ship. 'Your problem is wholly different but perhaps you will understand.'[15] Jenkins then successfully resisted Mrs Thatcher's attempt to nominate John Davies – her first Shadow Foreign Secretary, whom she was now trying to be rid of – and considered a number of other candidates, including Ian Gilmour, before persuading Callaghan to appoint the thirty-nine-year-old MP for the Cities of London and Westminster, Christopher Tugendhat. His thinking was that he wanted a younger man with his career to make, not another ageing retread.[16] Callaghan was delighted to annoy Mrs Thatcher in this way, and Tugendhat fully repaid his appointment by becoming an effective if unflashy Commissioner, as well as a good friend of both Roy and Jennifer.

Having finally assembled his team, Jenkins next faced the nightmarish jigsaw puzzle of trying to allocate portfolios among his twelve colleagues. Each must have his own area of responsibility, but there were not enough real jobs to satisfy individual and national pride. Again it was a shock to discover that he had very limited authority and everything in Brussels had to be horse-traded. He quickly decided that nothing less than Economic and Monetary Affairs would do for Ortoli (given that he wanted Cheysson to retain Overseas Development, on which Giscard also insisted). That meant that one of the two Germans, Wilhelm Haferkamp or Guido Brunner, neither of whom he really rated, must have External Affairs. The coalition government in Bonn wanted Brunner – a prickly career diplomat whom Jenkins thought lightweight; he preferred Haferkamp, a somewhat sybaritic trade unionist, whom he wanted to prise out of the economic brief to make room for Ortoli.

478

In an effort to bang heads together he brought the whole team together, with their wives, for a dismal weekend at Ditchley Park in Oxfordshire just before Christmas which still left a good deal of the jigsaw unresolved. By this time his initial exhilaration had evaporated and he approached the moment of departure for Brussels at the turn of the year with gloomy trepidation.

Back in October he had spoken confidently of the fresh impetus he intended to bring to the Community. He had been appointed as a politician, not a civil servant, he told David Dimbleby on *Panorama*. 'I want to introduce some political content, to have direct contact with the Governments, with the peoples of Europe in a way that perhaps non-politicians have not been able to do to the same extent.' He frankly admitted that he would rather have become Prime Minister, but was now fully persuaded that Brussels was 'the most difficult job open to me at the present time . . . in fact the most difficult I have ever done, but I regard it as a crucial next stage in my life.' He was not turning his back on Britain. 'I think I can help this country just as much by what I am going to do in Brussels as by anything which it would be open for me to do here.'[17]

In a farewell speech to the Parliamentary Press Gallery in December he repeated his intention to be a more active President than his recent predecessors: his aim would be to try to get the Community moving forward again after the stagnation of the past few years when the momentum had been lost following the 1973 oil shock.[18] How he was going to do this, however, he had little idea. In an interview with *The Times* he set out his goals with his usual combination of seeming certainty and studied vagueness about the ultimate destination:

My wish is to build an effective united Europe. Now I've never sought to define exactly what I mean by this, but I've got an absolutely clear sense of direction. I've never been frightened about the pace being too fast, I have been frightened about the pace being too slow. I do not think it's terribly useful to lay down blueprints as to whether one will be federal or confederal in the year 2000 and beyond. I want to move towards a more effectively organised Europe, politically and economically, and as far as I am concerned I want to go faster, not slower.[19]

The problem was that he inherited no clear agenda. The most successful Presidents of the Commission both before and after him – Walter Hallstein in 1958–67 and Jacques Delors in 1985–94 – came in with broadly agreed mandates to drive forward the Common Agricultural Policy and the single market respectively. The only things on the agenda in 1977 were enlargement, with negotiations already under way to admit Greece, and direct elections to the European Parliament, neither of which was very exciting. Jenkins was going to have to find his own way forward and at first he was barren of positive ideas. Meanwhile his inability even to appoint his own colleagues had brought home to him how limited his powers of initiation were. He had accepted the job in the belief that Giscard and Schmidt wanted a political heavy-weight – one who might have been Prime Minister in his own country – to raise the profile of the Community, but it was already becoming clear to him that they were resiling from this view and that Giscard in particular had no wish to see a more activist Commission. Friends like Bill Rodgers and Mark Bonham Carter did their best to reassure him that it would be better once he got there,[20] but he was horribly afraid that he was going to be no more than a glorified civil servant after all.

He travelled to Brussels on 4 January 1977 and was formally inaug-urated as President two days later on what he called 'the cliff-face day'.[21] For the only time in his life he started keeping a diary to record his moods and impressions as he worked his way into the job. Actually he did not write it every day but dictated it every few weeks, using his detailed engagement diaries to fix the framework of his days. He published an edited – indeed lightly polished – version of it in 1989, when it aroused a good deal of mockery for its relentless cataloguing of lunches and dinners in restaurants and embassies as he flew, drove and trained from capital to capital around the Community, recording his conversations with leaders, foreign ministers, parliamentarians and Popes. In fact there was even more about food and drink in the original than in the published text. But Jenkins was always fascinated by matters of protocol and etiquette and by the different practices of different countries. He was a sharp observer, amused as well as frustrated by the absurdities of diplomatic life; and if there is too little for the serious historian about the high politics of European integration, his portraits of the leaders with whom he had to deal are shrewd and vivid. Above all it is an unrivalled record of his stamina, his resilience and his fluc-tuating moods – which were always heavily influenced by the weather.

He arrived in Brussels in miserable weather – foggy, cold and raw, just the sort of conditions he most hated – and it stayed miserable for most of his first six months. 'Creature comforts,' he noted after chairing his first Commission, 'were clearly going to be well looked after':

Large open boxes of Havana cigars round the table, boxes of mineral water, coffee placed beside one almost as soon as one had sat down, and huissiers waiting to answer the touch of a bell and bring anything else one wanted. But this was hardly a recompense for the intimidating prospect which confronted me.[22]

Immediately he was plunged into a bruising all-night session to resolve the allocation of portfolios. The essential difficulty was still over the two Germans – stiffening Haferkamp's uncertain desire for the External Affairs job, while denying it to Brunner – but there were plenty of minor headaches in trying to divide up the available responsibilities so as to give everyone something that satisfied their home governments that they were not being snubbed. In the end Tugendhat successfully held out for the Budget portfolio, and the main loser was the Irish Commissioner, Richard Burke, who did not finally accept a ragbag of ill-assorted scraps until five-thirty in the morning. After a press conference and five television interviews Jenkins then adjourned with Tickell, Michael Jenkins and Celia Beale for 'a large bacon and eggs breakfast' at a nearby hotel, which he described as 'by far the best hour I had had in Brussels so far'.[23]

The next day, Saturday, he slept late to recover from this exertion, then went for a rainy drive with Jennifer and Laura round the 'sodden suburban battlegrounds' of Waterloo, twenty miles from Brussels, followed by an 'excessively heavy, excessively expensive lunch', more sleep in the afternoon and 'an extremely good dinner with very good wine' given by Peter Halsey, his British-born driver, and his wife, who also worked for the Commission.[24] On the Sunday Roy and Jennifer lunched with some old friends, Jacques Tiné (now in Brussels as French ambassador to NATO) and his wife Helena, whom they had known since 1955. This was typical of his weekends over the next four years.

Then it was down to the tedious work of trying to master the Brussels bureaucracy. His office was on the thirteenth floor of the Berlaymont building, an 'architectural monstrosity'[25] situated in a particularly nondescript area of the city, well described by *The Economist*:

An X-shaped glass and steel tower . . . rising from the drab Brussels streets . . . the Berlaymont . . . is as cosy as a space station and about as baffling. Floor after floor of corridors lined with identical offices are filled with toiling but well-paid Eurocrats. The 13th – top – floor covered with enough green carpet for a football pitch and altogether lusher than the rest, contains the 13 commissioners.[26]

The bureaucracy was not in reality all that large, numbering around 7,800, some 1,400 of them translators and interpreters – roughly one-third of the size of the British Home Office that Jenkins had just left and smaller than a single London borough. But it was peculiarly complex, divided into twenty directorates-general with detailed responsibilities for trade and agriculture, of which Jenkins was entirely ignorant. 'I was an enthusiast for the *grandes lignes* of Europe,' he later confessed, 'but an amateur within the complexities of its signalling system.'[27] In practice he concentrated on the *grandes lignes* and left the signalling to others. But even that left him a very wide range of duties, as Crispin Tickell testified:

> The job . . . is exacting. He has to keep the member governments sweet, he has executive responsibilities in quite large areas, he's got meetings with the Council of Ministers, meetings with others . . . It's a curious system, with the European Parliament, the European Court, the Council and the Commission. Playing these relationships with each other is quite complex.

'Roy Jenkins did it,' Tickell concluded, 'and did it very well.'[28]

The job, at least as Jenkins interpreted it, involved an immense amount of travelling between Brussels, Strasbourg – where he spent two to four days every month – and the other capitals of the Nine, as well as beyond Europe to America, Japan and elsewhere. He was rarely in his office, or even in Brussels, for a whole day, but often flew to Rome or Dublin or London and back the same day. While he attached most importance to forging direct relationships with the heads of government, much of his diplomacy was necessarily at a lower level. Within the Community 'the key body from the point of view of the day-to-day working of relations between the member states and the Commission' was the Committee of Permanent Representatives (known as COREPER);[29] while there were in Brussels another 100 accredited ambassadors to the Community from the rest of the world, all of whose credentials he received in person.[30] Many of these contacts, of course, were lubricated by good lunches and dinners. But at the same time Jenkins was easily bored by people he did not think worth his time – and sometimes showed it. Diplomacy was not really his forte. He had made his reputation in Whitehall as a decisive executive and at Westminster as a forceful debater. In Brussels he found that he had few executive powers and no opportunity, beyond formal speeches, to put his case.

'The job is more difficult to get hold of and less rewarding than I thought,' he reflected ruefully at the end of his first year. 'Also I in many ways am not particularly well suited to doing it, lacking patience, perhaps at times resilience, certainly linguistic ability . . . (this notwithstanding the fact that my French . . . has improved very significantly during the year but is still far from magnificent), and possibly application to administrative detail as well.' Neither the parliament nor television afforded the sort of platform he had been used to in domestic politics. 'On the other hand,' he told himself, 'I think I am able to run the Commission itself, as opposed to the Berlaymont, reasonably well.'[31] Others agreed. While he did not attempt to micro-manage, Tugendhat acknowledged, 'he was exceptionally skilful in getting his team of fellow commissioners to work together'; and Tickell praised his 'remarkable powers of sympathetic persuasion'.[32] Generally emollient and genial, he was usually able to defuse tensions around the table, though his love of elaborate metaphors sometimes baffled the interpreters. In practice he relied heavily on three of his more experienced colleagues: Ortoli ('probably the nicest of all my colleagues'); Gundelach, who 'held the vital Agricultural portfolio'; and the flamboyant Belgian, Etienne ('Stevy') Davignon ('taken in the round . . . the best member of my Commission'), who handled Industry and the Internal Market.[33] These three formed his inner circle, at the expense of the others who sometimes resented their exclusion. But this was always Jenkins' way. In fact he was rather disappointed that they, with homes and wives to go back to, did not mix Commission business with social life quite as freely as he liked to do. They rarely invited him (with or without Jennifer) back to their homes; and he frequently complained that when he took them to dinner at expensive restaurants they never offered to pay or host a return meal.[34] So he surrounded himself perhaps too much with the British members of his *cabinet* and a stream of friends from England. Just as it had been in Whitehall, Tugendhat wrote, 'Roy's habitual weakness of surrounding himself and working through a praetorian guard of devoted officials was resented.'[35]

His French was not quite good enough to do anything else. According to *The Times*, soon after he took up the job it was 'painful but grammatically accurate'.[36] Nicko Henderson, with an old friend's cheerful candour, thought his accent 'perfectly appalling'.[37] Jenkins' diary frequently records the strain of speaking French for any length of time, so he could not properly socialise or joke in French; nor was he comfortable speaking it formally. His press spokesman, Roger Beetham (seconded from the Foreign Office), found his job difficult, particularly in the early days, 'not least because of his [Jenkins'] reluctance to speak French'. It was partly that he was simply shy:

His vocabulary was incredible, he read Simenon in the original. But he was very reluctant to use his French, except socially. There were a few occasions when this was almost provocative, trying to represent, as I was, a European President who declined to speak the Brussels language. It wasn't that he couldn't; and it did make things difficult.[38]

In August 1977 he was still trying to read Simenon on his summer holiday, but not getting on very well; at the same time he confessed that he was reading Jean Monnet's *Memoirs* in English.[39]

Frustrated by the 'oppressive strangeness' of the job, suddenly cut off both from the Westminster and clubland society in which he had lived and breathed for the past twenty-five years and from Jennifer's emotional and practical support; already under criticism in Brussels for being too British, painfully conscious of the disappointment of those who had invested such high hopes in him, but unsure of how to set about realising them, Jenkins admitted to feeling lost and lonely in his first six months in Brussels. 'I missed the actual detail of both Stechford and the House of Commons much more than I had expected . . . and found that I was constantly dreaming, literally dreaming in my sleep, about both.' Had he known what it was going to be like, he would not have come. 'Even as late as mid-July I was in depths of, not continuous but occasional, suicidal depression with resignation thoughts hovering round my mind.'[40]

His gloom was deepened barely a month after his arrival by the sudden death of Tony Crosland, who suffered a massive stroke on 14 February and died five days later. This triggered all sorts of complicated emotions: memories of their youthful intimacy overlaid by more recent rivalry (though Jenkins claimed that they had restored much of their old friendship in the last few months), but also inevitably speculation that he might now have had the Foreign Office after all, if he had stayed in the Cabinet. Ironically, since Britain held the rotating chairmanship of the Community for the first half of 1977, Crosland had chaired the Council of Ministers during January: Jenkins had thought him 'a pretty effective chairman'.[41] He had actually been receiving a visit from Denis Healey when they heard the news of Crosland's collapse. Two days later the Foreign Office Minister of State David Owen – in Brussels to open fisheries negotiations with the Russians – assured

Jenkins that Crosland was already 'morally and mentally dead', with no possibility of recovery.[42] So it was no more than mildly spooky that he woke early on Saturday morning in Rome 'having had a vivid dream about Tony being present and saying in an absolutely unmistakable, clear, rather calm voice, "No, I'm perfectly all right, I am going to die but I'm perfectly all right."' An hour and a half later he heard that Crosland had died at exactly that moment.* He quickly recorded a tribute, which the BBC was able to use on the eight o'clock news; and then wrote a 650-word piece for the *Sunday Times* in the car en route to an official lunch with Italian officials, which brought 'the immense closeness of our earlier relationship flooding back into my mind . . . I found I was much more affected than I had been during the previous week, even though I had already realised that he was dying.'[45] For all their recent differences, he wrote, Tony Crosland had remained 'the most exciting friend of my life';[46] and his death left a big emotional gap. He found the memorial service in Westminster Abbey on 7 March an 'impressive and harrowing' occasion.[47] Susan Crosland told him that Tony would have felt exactly the same had it happened the other way round.[48]

To general surprise, Callaghan filled the vacancy at the Foreign Office with the minimum disruption by promoting David Owen, making him – at thirty-eight – the youngest Foreign Secretary since Anthony Eden in 1935. Jenkins professed himself 'greatly pleased' by the appointment;[49] but it can only have rubbed salt into his sense of what might have been. Nicko Henderson was impressed that Roy showed 'not the slightest resentment at Owen's great good fortune'.[50] But Jenkins confessed to his diary that there was 'undoubtedly a slight problem of adjustment' on meeting Owen in his new role. 'When somebody has been a loyal, young, junior supporter for a long time, it is a little difficult to get used to his suddenly being Foreign Secretary.' Not unnaturally, he added with a characteristic mixture of perspective and egotism, Owen was 'very pleased with himself . . . because he had after all just had a most remarkable political breakthrough – certainly one of the greatest ones since I became Chancellor in '67, and probably a still greater one than that.'[51] Henderson 'was not quite sure that Owen reciprocated such loyalty in equal measure', noting 'his determination to do nothing that might displease Callaghan to whom, after all, he

---

* Oddly, Jenkins had told in his *Dilke* a somewhat similar story of Joe Chamberlain having a premonition of Dilke's death.[43] Even stranger, he had the same dream about Tony Crosland again on the anniversary of his death the next year.[44]

owes his promotion'.[52] Very quickly Jenkins found that talking to Owen, even socially at East Hendred, 'does now remind me slightly of talking to Tony in the last four or five years. There is a certain reticence on both sides . . . I hate being slightly in the position of a *demandeur* with David.'[53] Owen realised that it was awkward for Jenkins, but inevitably their relationship had changed. 'Slowly,' he wrote in his memoirs, 'our friendship ebbed away.'[54] For some time already there had been signs of the ambitious Owen growing impatient with Jenkins' leadership; but his sudden elevation from subordinate to equal, or even superior, was going to make working together in the future very difficult.[*]

Meanwhile Jenkins' first major test was to establish his right, as President of the Commission, to attend G7 summits. These originally informal get-togethers of the heads of government of the seven leading Western economies had been inaugurated by Giscard d'Estaing in 1975 and continued by President Ford in 1976.[†] The next was to be held in London in May 1977. Since they were specifically economic, not political or military in purpose, the five smaller members of the EEC ('the little five') thought the Community should be represented by the President of the Commission. But Giscard firmly resisted this, partly from a wish to keep the meetings small but also, it increasingly appeared, from a determination to stop the Commission getting above itself. The summits, he argued with perfect French logic, were meetings of sovereign states; the EEC was not a sovereign state, therefore it could not be represented. Under pressure from the 'little five' to fight his corner, Jenkins thus found very early in his presidency that 'my credibility as an effective new President was therefore somewhat at stake'.[56] Seeking support from Helmut Schmidt on 18 March, he told the German Chancellor that 'French arguments for excluding the Commission were palpably poor.' Crispin Tickell's minute recorded the exchange that followed:

> Herr Schmidt said somewhat defensively but with emotion that he did not want a row with his friend Valéry Giscard d'Estaing whatever the Dutch, the Belgians and others might want . . . Mr Jenkins said that if he were excluded from the Summit he would

---

[*] Henderson also noted that Jenkins already considered Owen 'well and truly right wing'.[55]
[†] The seven at that time were the United States, Britain, France, West Germany, Italy, Japan and Canada.

legitimately ask himself why he was doing the job he was. He had been chosen as a politician and not as a bureaucrat.[57]

Here was the problem that Jenkins faced throughout his time in Brussels – *mutatis mutandis* the same problem that successive British governments have faced down the years, whether with Kohl and Mitterrand or Merkel and Sarkozy – the unshakable axis of the French and Germans to fix things in the Community between themselves without giving their other partners much of a look-in. Jenkins had enormous regard for Helmut Schmidt, whom he considered the most constructive Western statesman of his generation. Compared with Giscard, he thought Schmidt by far 'the more considerable figure of the two . . . Schmidt had wider vision, better balance, and greater depth of personality and character . . . He talked far more engagingly and eclectically than did any other European leader of the late Seventies' – even if his talk did not always lead to action.[58] Giscard he found (like most others who had to deal with him, not least Mrs Thatcher) impeccably polite but cold, supercilious and arrogant, with an extraordinary sense of the precedence due to him as a head of state. Yet to his frustration, Schmidt – still convinced thirty years after the war that West Germany must not attempt to punch its true weight – would rarely take up any position in opposition to Giscard, whom he always called 'his only real friend'.[59]

The Italians strongly backed the 'little five' in pressing for Jenkins to be invited, and the Americans had no objection; but the British government, which might have been expected to welcome another British voice at the table, played a typically ambivalent role. Callaghan was bluffly unhelpful to his old rival; and Owen, now chairing the Foreign Affairs Council, followed his lead, though he claimed in his memoirs that he was more supportive behind the scenes than Jenkins knew.[60] After tortuous negotiations between the heads of government in Rome in March, Giscard, finding himself isolated, made a partial climbdown, agreeing that Jenkins could attend some sessions of the summit but not others and some of the accompanying meals – where most of the real business was done – but not others. The result was that at London he was subjected to a series of farcical snubs. Callaghan, in the words of one experienced official, 'made him as welcome as a polecat'.[61] At dinner on the first evening, which Giscard boycotted in protest at Jenkins' presence, he was placed not at the top table with the leaders, nor even with the foreign ministers, but at the third level with the finance ministers ('This was a gratuitous piece of nonsense by Callaghan').[62] He was then excluded from the Saturday session (on the world economy), but admitted to the Sunday morning session (on the so-called 'North–South' dialogue) where, according to Tickell, he 'did very well with measured interventions that were well received'.[63] He was allowed to dine at Buckingham Palace on the Saturday evening, where he had 'no contact with Callaghan at all, which was probably as well', but some slightly edgy joshing with Giscard ('Ah, mon ami Jenkins, bonsoir') and a bizarre conversation with the Queen in French ('Her French is somewhat better than mine, but not much I guess').[64] On the Sunday he was relegated again to lunch with the foreign ministers to draft the communiqué, which he did mainly with the US Secretary of State, Cyrus Vance. (Owen, 'acting too much as Callaghan's office boy . . . was less good . . . than I had expected.')[65] At the final press conference he was allowed to sit with the heads of government – but without a microphone.

This was all intensely embarrassing for Jenkins, since in fighting for his right to be present it looked as if he was concerned solely for his personal dignity rather than for the place of the European Community on the world stage. His old colleague Barbara Castle – whom Callaghan had sacked on becoming Prime Minister – was bitchily delighted to read of Jenkins being forced to wait in antechambers and 'eat below the salt'. 'It almost makes me a Callaghan fan,' she wrote in her unpublished diary.[66] In fact, as Christopher Tugendhat wrote, 'there was a major issue of principle at stake':

> If he had lost the battle, the Commission would have been relegated to being a Secretariat like that of the OECD. By winning, Roy secured for himself and his successors the right to speak as practically an equal of prime ministers and presidents both at the G7 and within the community itself. This made the Commission a political force in its own right, which in turn gave it the self-confidence and clout to relaunch the idea of European Monetary Union and later, under Delors, the Single Market programme.[67]

London was only a partial victory, but it was a foot in the door. At subsequent meetings – Bonn in 1978, Tokyo in 1979 and Venice in 1980 – Jenkins' presence was accepted and he made increasingly confident contributions. At Bonn he had a microphone at the final press conference, but chose not to use it; at Tokyo and Venice he had a microphone and used it. 'By then,' Tickell wrote, 'the precedents had been set and were carefully followed. The absurdity of the London experience in 1977 had been largely forgotten, except of course by Giscard.'[68] In fact Giscard never quite gave up trying to clip his wings. He threw a petty tantrum in 1979 when Jenkins dared to take a marginally different line at a joint press conference in Paris, and insisted that in future the President of the Commission should hold his own press conference or speak only after the President of France had left. He later consented to stay for Jenkins' statement, but left before his questions.[69] By this time, however, Jenkins had established his position. Once he had found his feet in the job he became both effective and respected. The other leaders, in the Community and beyond, treated him as an equal because they knew that – unlike Ortoli before him or Gaston Thorn after – he could easily have been Prime Minister of a major country, and probably should have been. As a result he permanently raised the standing of the Commission within Europe, and of Europe in the world. This was supposedly what Schmidt and Giscard had intended in appointing him in the first place.

But this breakthrough was yet to come in the summer of 1977. He was still depressed and wishing he had never taken the job when he was shaken by 'a particularly disobliging article' in *The Economist*, which he read on the way to a picnic with Jennifer in the Forêt de Soignes on 16 July. Reviewing his first six months, the writer (anonymous, as always in *The Economist*)* declared that Jenkins was 'visibly bored by Brussels' and lacked his predecessor's grasp of issues like fish and steel; the Commission worked poorly as a team and staff morale was low, partly because all but one of his personal staff were British and his *chef de cabinet*, though undoubtedly a first-class brain, was 'a little short on tact':

> His own press conferences have fallen flat, mainly because he does not seem to appreciate that the commission is more of a think-tank than a government. He tells the press where he has been travelling, but not what he has been saying, and he is ultra-cautious about criticising governments.

As a result the Brussels press had all but given up on him. Jenkins was being made a scapegoat for recession and the member governments' refusal to pool sovereignty. But there was little he could do about it,

---

* The *Economist*'s Brussels correspondents at the time were Stephen Milligan, later a Tory MP who died in bizarre circumstances in 1994, and Chris Huhne, who became a Liberal Democrat MP in 2002, twice contested the party leadership and was Energy Secretary in the Cameron coalition until his enforced resignation in 2012 and subsequent imprisonment for obstructing the course of justice.

the writer concluded: the expectations vested in him had been too high.[70]

This was depressing because he knew that much of it was true (though there were actually two non-Britons in his *cabinet*) and because *The Economist* was widely read in Brussels. He was in danger of being written off as a failure halfway through his first year. But it also gave him a salutary shock, as he described in his memoirs: 'After moaning under the beech trees I was given a great talking to by Jennifer, and began to feel that if I wanted to escape from these doldrums rather than wallowing in self-pity I had better strike out with some major new initiative.'[71] Jenkins rather gives the impression that he had to cast about to find such an initiative. In fact he already knew that he needed an eye-catching departure to give his presidency a purpose and had a good idea what it should be. As long ago as January, in his very first speech to the European Assembly, he had spoken of the Ortoli Commission having had to 'live in winter quarters':

I do not yet feel any benign stirrings of the breezes of spring. But what I do feel is that there comes a time when you have to break out of the citadel or wither within it. That time is now very close upon us.[72]

Among other possible ideas – direct elections, reform of the CAP (Common Agricultural Policy), ways to engage the young – he touched on economic convergence in the broadest terms. He did not specifically mention monetary union. But, scarred by his experience as Chancellor trying to defend sterling, he had long criticised both the vulnerability of competing fixed exchange rates and the instability (since 1972) of floating exchange rates; and in an interview for American television in January and again in an interview with *The Times* in April he had floated the idea of European monetary union as a desirable objective. It was not a new idea: before losing office in 1970 he and Wilson had been ready to accept a single currency as the next step forward for the Community they then hoped to join, and in 1973 Pompidou, Brandt and Heath had set a target to achieve it by 1980. But that was before the 1974 oil shock put a stop to such optimism. Jenkins' bold initiative was to put it back on the agenda.

He began, slightly oddly, by trying it out at home. Just five days after his 'great talking to' by Jennifer in the Forêt de Soignes, he paid an official visit to London. This was a slightly strange experience, being entertained in familiar places as the representative of an outside organisation and holding formal conversations with everyone from the Queen and the Prime Minister down – including his first meeting with Mrs Thatcher as Leader of the Opposition. Callaghan he found far friendlier than in May. 'He even sounded rather pro-Europe . . . He was sufficiently forthcoming that I began to think he must have had some news . . . that all North Sea oil was turning out to be salt water, and that they needed the Community more than I thought!'[73] According to Tickell's minute, Jenkins told the Prime Minister firmly that 'his own considered view was that members of the Community should work out a phased programme over 10 years towards monetary union'. Callaghan was sceptical, thinking there was too much divergence between the various economies; he was not impressed by any scheme he had heard so far, 'but he knew that Mr Jenkins would give one practical sense and meaning. He looked forward to hearing more from Mr Jenkins.'[74] The next day Jenkins called on Tony Benn at the Department of Energy and told him of his plan for EMU within ten years. 'Mr Benn expressed interest.'[75]

Next, he broached it with his *cabinet*. He summoned them all to East Hendred for a strategy meeting on 2 August and seven of them – plus Jennifer and John Harris, with Laura Grenfell taking the minutes – sat in the garden in hot sunshine discussing the mistakes of the past six months and the way forward. Jenkins' introductory remarks, distinguishing subjective factors from objective difficulties, were frankly critical of his own performance:

[I] underestimated . . . taking over a highly complicated, to me wholly new organisation, with its own methods of work both internally & in relation to the Council, Parlt., Press etc + have not yet clearly & confidently worked out what one's style shd be. That is nobody's fault but mine, and the Cabinet in my view has worked almost superlatively well in the circs.

The first objective difficulty had been dealing with the British presidency. But a deeper basic difficulty was that 'none of the three major powers are prepared to support the Commission in any major initiative. Only Italy + the small ones. Not enough.'

So what should they do? There were two possible courses. Either they could settle for making 'such limited advances as we can', but the options were limited: they could not just be an intermediary between governments – 'Schmidt/Giscard axis precludes that.' Alternatively, 'we have to proclaim a new way forward'. In that case they could either go for monetary union, which would enthuse the Commission (with two important exceptions) but not the governments; or reform of the CAP, which would split both the Commission and the governments, 'but has to be done'. 'How far,' he asked, 'should we strike this controversial role & let the Governments go to hell? How far will this damage our ability to deal with ongoing business?'[76]

It was clear that Jenkins wanted to go for monetary union, on lines set out by one of his Balliol economists, Michael Emerson. But the Italian Renato Ruggiero – present as head of his press department – took the lead in urging him not to stake his reputation on such a risky venture;[77] and others too stressed the difficulties and the need to get other Commissioners and the Parliament on board if he were to have any chance of success. Jenkins agreed, but believed – on what basis is not clear – that the German government would support it. He thought a speech in Bonn in December would be 'a good platform to put forward some of the problems, and proposals for solution'.[78]

In fact he accelerated this timetable. In mid–September, having discussed it intensively with various friends (the Gilmours, Bonham Carters, Beaumarchais and others) over his summer holiday in Italy, he held another strategy weekend with his fellow Commissioners at a hotel in the Ardennes at which he overcame the doubts of his predecessor, Ortoli, and won the support of all but two of them (not the two he had predicted) for 'an early leap forward'.[79] Then he expounded his plan to the foreign ministers of the Nine at another weekend get-together in Belgium on 8–9 October. 'David Owen was sceptical, but not particularly hostile or indeed particularly informed'; but the other eight were encouragingly positive.[80] By now he had decided to launch his big idea in a lecture that he was due to give in honour of Jean Monnet in Florence on 27 October. But he had already trailed it quite fully in advance. On 24 September *The Economist*, which had sparked his moment of epiphany barely two months earlier, applauded his ambition while doubting that he would succeed. Restating the goal of monetary union, it conceded, was 'an astonishingly bold idea for Mr Jenkins, himself nursing a thousand political cuts in his new Brussels role, to espouse':

> Mr Jenkins is right to be radical. It is, or should be, his job . . . At the very least he is giving a little spark of that leadership in the midst of economic crisis that national governments are manifestly failing to give. Whether that will make him friends in the chancelleries and treasuries of Europe must be doubted.

Brave though he is to attempt it, monetary union in the absolute form Mr Jenkins is suggesting is all too likely to prove a bridge too far.

The Economist doubted whether divergent exchange rates were the real constraint on growth and presciently questioned whether Germany would wish to subsidise the weaker economies of Europe. Rather than replace the existing currencies, it proposed making more use of the European Currency Unit (ECU) for internal transactions alongside them.[81]

In his speech at Florence Jenkins gave seven reasons why he believed this approach did not go far enough. First, he argued that monetary union would promote 'a more efficient and developed rationalisation of industry and commerce than is possible under a Customs Union alone', allowing business to take full advantage of the single market. Second, he urged that 'a major new international currency' backed by the economic strength of the EEC would form 'a joint and alternative pillar of the world monetary system', leading to greater international stability. 'Economic welfare in Europe would be improved substantially if macro-economic policy was not subject to present exchange rate and external financial risks.' Third, he maintained that monetary union would help reduce inflation by controlling the money supply. At this point he conceded that this would involve some loss of national sovereignty, but argued that 'governments which do not discipline themselves already find themselves accepting very sharp surveillance from the International Monetary Fund' – as Britain had just discovered. Fourth, he believed that monetary union would stimulate employment. And, fifth, he suggested that it would do far more than existing policy instruments to even out regional differences, protecting the weaker regions while assuring stable markets for the stronger. Without wanting to push the analogy too far he argued that the United States fifty years before had far greater regional inequality than Europe in 1977.

His sixth and seventh arguments were more political. He believed that monetary union could be reconciled with the demand in almost all member states for more decentralised government, and with the reluctance to cede sovereignty. There was no need for social and welfare spending – around 25 per cent of GNP in most states – to be centralised. But some functions were better done at the European level. Monetary union, he reckoned, need take 'only' 5–7 per cent of GNP. He envisaged 'a highly decentralised type of monetary union in which the public procurement of goods and services is primarily in national, regional or other hands. The public finance function of such a Community could be stripped down to a few high-powered types of financial transfer', run by 'a quite small central bureaucracy'.*

He admitted that such a step had major political implications; but this, for him, was the whole point:

> The relocation of monetary policy to the European level would be as big a political step for the present generation of European leaders as for the last generation in setting up the present Community. But we must face the fundamental question. Do we intend to create a European union or do we not?

Real national sovereignty over monetary issues, he insisted, was already a chimera for medium-sized European countries. 'The prospect of monetary union should be seen as part of the process of recovering the substance of sovereign power. At present we tend to cling to its shadow.'

This was the clearest statement Jenkins had ever made that his ultimate goal was a full-blown European union. He had now decided that early monetary union was the best way to forge it. He concluded his case, characteristically, with a metaphor: 'Let us think of a long-jumper. He starts with a rapid succession of steps, lengthens his stride, increases his momentum, and then makes his leap.' Europe had taken a lot of small steps since 1945, was now lengthening its stride in several areas – 'external policies, establishing more democratic and thus accountable institutions, elaborating more coherent industrial and regional policies, and giving our financial instruments the means to keep the whole movement on a balanced course'. It was now ready to take a qualitative leap: 'We have to look before we leap, and know when we are to land. But leap we eventually must.' He finished by invoking the founding father in whose honour he was speaking. Politics, Jean Monnet had said, was 'not only the art of the possible, but . . . the art of making possible tomorrow what may seem impossible today.'[82]

This Jenkins later described as 'the most fructuous speech of my life'.[83] But the immediate reaction was predominantly sceptical. In Britain *The Times* was surprised that he should have 'attached himself so firmly and personally to the idea' of monetary union, and raised

---

* The fact that Jenkins envisaged monetary union taking 'only' 5–7 per cent of GNP is noteworthy, since the single currency when eventually established in 1999 was backed by just 1 per cent of the EU's collective resources – which possibly explains its fragility after the crash of 2008.

two major objections: first that it ran 'clean counter' to the process of enlargement, which would be difficult enough anyway; and, second, that it *would* require a massive central budget to support the weaker countries.[84] Before leaving Italy Jenkins extracted an assurance from the Prime Minister, Giulio Andreotti, that he could count on his support; but there was 'no echoing applause from the Elysée or the Bundeskanzlei, let alone Downing Street'.[85] Over the next few weeks he toured the major capitals trying to sell his vision to the various leaders. On 10 November he had a typically gloomy conversation with Schmidt, who said that he would welcome EMU in theory, but was afraid that it would push German inflation up to 8 per cent: 'Mr Jenkins said that perhaps it would be the other way round, and the Germans would impose their inflation rate on the others.'[86] On the 19th in Paris he found Giscard's Prime Minister, Raymond Barre, quite supportive, happy to agree in principle to make EMU 'a firm objective' rather than a mere aspiration, promising Giscard's goodwill, but non-committal in practice.[87] In London on the 25th Callaghan cheerfully admitted that he had not actually read the Florence speech.[88] By contrast when Mrs Thatcher visited Brussels a week later she had read it: she acknowledged the force of Jenkins' argument that the world monetary system needed a European pillar to balance the decline of the dollar, but homed in unerringly on the problem of the weaker economies. 'Mr Jenkins explained that he thought these problems could be solved.' Douglas Hurd, who accompanied her, assured Tickell later that her attitude was 'one of scepticism rather than hostility. He felt that she was open to persuasion.'[89]

Afterwards Mrs Thatcher lunched with members of the Commission. 'She wasn't tiresome,' Jenkins wrote rather superciliously, 'but left one with not the faintest sense of having been in the presence of anyone approaching the high quality of a great statesman or stateswoman, or even of someone who was likely to grow into this; she just seemed slightly below the level of events.'[90] The next day he noted that Christopher Tugendhat seemed 'a bit too oppressed by Mrs Thatcher. He doesn't make enough jokes about her.'[91]

At the European Council (in Brussels, under Belgian chairmanship) on 5–6 December Jenkins presented his proposals formally to all the leaders together. Andreotti and the 'little five' were all enthusiastic, but of those whose support he really needed Giscard was cool, Schmidt reserved and Callaghan the friendliest of the three. 'However,' he recorded, 'we got enough of what we wanted for the moment . . . I think that my tactic of not having a great row with Ortoli [who still

##

wanted to go cautiously] and not presenting the European Council with too hard a choice at this stage has been correct.'[92] Back in London just before Christmas, Jenkins dined at the Savoy with Edwin Plowden's 'now slightly ageing but still very powerful businessmen', who had continued to entertain him regularly ever since he was Chancellor, and had 'a good discussion on EMU' with them. 'They were all in favour of it but totally sceptical as to whether it would be possible for the politicians ever to do anything so imaginative.'[93]

So his mood at the end of the year was much more positive than in July, but still uncertain. He no longer felt suicidal – if he ever really did – but he still felt 'a certain continuing regret at the loss of my position in British politics', particularly since the British economy (under the tutelage of the IMF) seemed to have turned a corner during 1977. 'Was I wise?' he asked himself. 'Who can possibly tell?'

Clearly had I taken Callaghan up on his offer to stay as Home Secretary and then become Chancellor again in six or so months' time this would, in retrospect, have been a more enticing prospect than it looked at that stage. Would he have stuck to the bargain? I don't know. But had I been there in the Government and available it might have been very difficult for him, under pressure, not to have moved Healey and put me in in the late autumn of last year, and clearly that would have been very much buying at the bottom of the market with fortuitously and no doubt undeservedly, an enormous reputation developing over the next six or nine months for having put things right a second time. However this would have been a fortuitous reputation and so I suppose one should not regret not getting things which one would not have totally deserved. In any case, my mind had become sufficiently detached from the general current of opinion in the Government that it was reasonable I should leave.[94]

Nevertheless he could not help reflecting that 'if I had become Chancellor fourteen months ago I would obviously have been in an extremely strong position politically now':

But that is all water over the dam, and I find that British politics, viewed from outside, while not as disastrous as I had thought previously, looks a pretty flat and unattractive landscape with no great figures on either side, although Callaghan and Healey are obviously the most dominating. There are no significant debates in the House of Commons such as we used to have in the late sixties, and therefore no great tug from that point of view.

On the other hand, if he had expected to leave a gap in British politics he found it chastening to realise how little difference the almost simultaneous departure from the scene of both himself and Crosland seemed to have made. 'The country seems perfectly happy with a government of not very significant figures,' he noted, faced by an even less impressive Opposition. He now regretted the opportunities he had missed earlier in the decade 'through not being quite sure what tactical political line I wanted consistently to pursue'. He consoled himself with 'a tolerable life in Brussels, something clearly well worthwhile though not at all easy and not immensely rich in achievement'. But one year in, his mind was already turning to life after Brussels. 'But of the future . . . who can possibly tell, and the future is of course becoming nearer all the time.'[95]

For four months after Jenkins' Florence speech it seemed that nothing very much was going to come of it. In Paris on 21 February 1978 he found Giscard, distracted by imminent assembly elections, still 'favour-able in theory [but] non-committal in practice'.[96] But five days later the picture suddenly changed when, in the course of what he had expected to be a routine meeting in Bonn, Chancellor Schmidt 'elec-trified me by announcing his conversion to a major scheme of European monetary integration':[97]

> You may be shocked, you may be surprised at what I intend to do, but as soon as the French elections are over, probably at Copenhagen . . . I shall propose, in response to the dollar problem, a major step towards monetary union.[98]

'I shall never forget how my heart leaped during that exposition,' Jenkins wrote in his memoirs. 'It was one if the few occasions in my life when that cliché could justifiably be used.'[99] Tickell's minute precisely corroborated his account, and his delighted reaction:

> Herr Schmidt said that after careful consideration he believed that a dramatic move forward was necessary after the French elections towards monetary integration. It was more than ever necessary to make a common front against the dollar . . . There were of course

terrible risks. The Community might break up if such an initiative were to fail. Mr Jenkins said that he thought the risk should be taken. Herr Schmidt said that the risks of doing nothing seemed to him greater than now doing what he proposed.[100]

What had converted Schmidt was primarily the weakness of the dollar, which had fallen from DM2.30 the previous October to DM2.02 in February (and would fall further to DM1.76 by September), a collapse which made it, in Jenkins' words, 'increasingly difficult to regard it as a satisfactory pivot or arbitrator of a world monetary system'.[101] 'The flow of dollars into the Federal Republic had reached crisis proportions,' Schmidt had concluded, threatening dangerous levels of inflation.[102] His response was influenced by his low opinion of President Carter. 'He had long believed in the American captaincy of the West,' Jenkins wrote many years later. 'But when the American ship of state began to founder, he thought that it was time to take to the European lifeboats.'[103] At this February meeting he swore Jenkins to 'utmost secrecy' – he was especially not to tell his colleagues Ortoli and Haferkamp – but said he would break his decision to his friend Giscard 'very soon'.[104]

As soon as he had secured his parliamentary majority (which saved him from having to share power with a socialist Prime Minister), Giscard signed up to Schmidt's initiative and between them they gave the drive to monetary union a momentum – and the necessary political muscle – which resulted in the launch of the European Monetary System (EMS) within eighteen months of Jenkins proposing it, an almost unprecedented speed of movement in the normally sclerotic EEC. They revealed their hand at the Danish-chaired Copenhagen summit in April, when Schmidt expounded the whole scheme after dinner, proposing 'a kind of European IMF', and Giscard spoke of 'a new Bretton Woods system within the Community'.* The only doubts were raised, predictably, by Callaghan, who said it 'went a great deal further than anything he had expected' (only because, in Jenkins' view, he had not taken in what Schmidt had told him when he visited Bonn in March) and worried that it might seem anti-American.[105] As they broke up, though it was after midnight, he asked Jenkins back to his hotel to talk him through it with his officials, one of whom – the man from the Treasury

---

* Bretton Woods was the name given to the system of international currency management established in 1944 based on convertibility to gold. It ran successfully until 1971, when the United States unilaterally came off gold.

– kept repeating in classic Sir Humphrey mode: 'But it is very bold, Prime Minister . . . I don't know what the Americans will say about it. It's very bold.'[106] Next morning Schmidt pressed Jenkins to help bring Callaghan on board. But at this stage the whole plan was still secret. The press reporting of the summit was all about plans for co-ordinated growth and the possibility of expanding the existing 'snake' which linked several currencies – but not the franc – loosely to the Deutschmark. But there was no hint of what was actually under discussion. At his final press conference – to some 600 journalists – Jenkins declared himself 'encouraged, even excited' by the reception given to his ideas, without giving away too much.[107]

Before the next summit at Bremen in July Jenkins did his best to bring the British along. But Callaghan, while friendly, remained unconvinced. 'Frankly he was a little miffed about the way Herr Schmidt and M. Giscard had fixed things up between them after the promises of co-operation which both had made at Copenhagen.' He had stopped fretting about the American reaction – Carter was actually strongly in favour – but he was worried about transferring more resources to Europe when the UK was already paying more than its share: 'If the British were to accept additional burdens, then something must be done to alleviate present ones.' Jenkins conceded the point, but reminded Callaghan that, as Foreign Secretary, he had accepted the budget settlement in 1974 and urged that if Britain wanted reform in some directions, like the CAP, she should not block advance in others. Callaghan replied that he wanted to be constructive, but needed a quid pro quo: 'He would not sign any old piece of paper. He wanted to see the colour of the horse.'[108]

Callaghan wanted more time, but Giscard and Schmidt were determined to press ahead, with or without Britain. At Bremen – where the Commission, to Jenkins' satisfaction, occupied 'a far more nodal position than at previous European Councils'[109] – eight of the nine member countries agreed to pool 20 per cent of their gold reserves to create a $50 million central fund and a European currency unit, the ECU (or *ecu*) – a weighted average of members' currencies – to come into operation in January 1979. The participating currencies would be brought into a narrow band of fluctuation against each other (1 per cent for the hard core, wider for the weaker currencies). Callaghan still reserved his position, but Jenkins' patient diplomacy at least prevented him from committing himself definitely against or attempting a veto. At the final press conference (which he took alongside Schmidt), Jenkins explained that the EMS would be stronger than the existing 'snake' because the European Monetary Fund would have more reserves than the IMF. He said that he had never dreamed that so much could be achieved so quickly.[110]

There was still a hiccup at Brussels in December, when Giscard suddenly introduced a new, highly technical difficulty about agricultural subsidies (otherwise known as Monetary Compensation Amounts), which almost resulted in Italy and Ireland deciding to stay outside; in the end the French dropped their objection as inexplicably as they had raised it, both Italy and Ireland overcame their doubts and the first stage of the EMS came into operation three months late in March 1979. Only Britain, to Jenkins' disappointment, stayed out. Over the autumn Schmidt had lost patience with Callaghan's foot-dragging. He thought the British just wanted to use the EMS as an opportunity for another renegotiation. This, he told Jenkins on 30 November, was 'out of the question. They used the Community as a scapegoat for their own economic failures. Mr Jenkins agreed.'[111] In an earlier conversation in London Jenkins had tried to persuade Callaghan that it was not a question this time of Britain joining an existing mechanism, 'but of whether Britain should participate in the creation of something new' and help to shape it. It was a question of national self-confidence. 'The French instinctively looked to see how they could benefit from EMS, while the British instinctively looked to how it might damage them.' Callaghan 'rather sadly said that perhaps that was right'.[112] But the upshot was still, when it came to the point, that Britain stayed out. Callaghan explained that he was afraid of being locked in at too high a rate, which would prevent him dealing with unemployment. Mrs Thatcher – in opposition still maintaining the Tories' staunch pro-Europe line – called his decision 'a sad day for Europe'. It was 'a sad reflection on the performance of this Government that . . . the Prime Minister is content to have Britain openly classified among the poorest and least influential members of the Community'.[113] Jenkins could reasonably have hoped that if the Tories won the forthcoming election she would reverse the decision. In fact, when he visited her for the first time in Downing Street soon after the election she prevaricated, on the opposite ground that she was afraid of being locked in at too low a rate, which would stop her dealing with inflation; and the longer she stayed in office the more viscerally opposed to joining she became. For the whole of the 1980s Jenkins was left to lament Britain once again missing the opportunity to get in on the ground floor of a European development and then complaining that the arrangements did not suit them, while continuing to suffer from both higher inflation and higher unemployment than any of the participating countries.

'Without sterling the system is frankly incomplete,' he wrote in 1980. 'Without participation, Britain is not playing its full part in Europe.'[114] He was also frustrated that the other leaders did not press on as fast as he would have liked to stage two, with the EMF taking on the full powers of a central bank controlling the issue of ECUs. Nevertheless Jenkins was able to celebrate a considerable success which marked the high point of his presidency. By the time he left Brussels he could boast that 'In a turbulent sea, the Europe of the Community has been an island of exchange rate stability.'[115] And for the next decade the system continued to work well, facilitating the creation of the single market in 1986 and the evolution of the European Economic Community into the fully fledged European Union. Only in 1992 did problems arise, when both Britain – just sixteen months after Mrs Thatcher was finally persuaded to join, at the wrong rate and at the worst possible moment – and Italy were forced to leave the EMS. The problem was the anticipated one: that a single exchange rate did not suit all countries equally. Jenkins had consistently minimised this difficulty, believing that maintaining the momentum towards unity was what mattered and that economic differences would be ironed out in time. 'I believed then, and I believe now,' he still insisted in 1992, 'that if you only advance when all the conditions are ripe you never advance at all. Monetary union is more likely to be the cause of economic convergence than the result of it.'[116] This was more an article of faith than a reasoned proposition. In his Florence speech and in all his subsequent wooing of European leaders he argued that enlargement of the Community to include Greece, Portugal and Spain made monetary union more urgent – to provide 'a stronger bone structure', as he told Raymond Barre – rather than making it more difficult.[117]* He clearly foresaw the Europe of the future working as a single economy, in which transfers of resources between richer and poorer countries would be as normal as they already were within countries. 'Some regions,' he

---

* It was not as though Jenkins was unaware of the tendency of some applicant countries to bend the rules to gain admission. Very early in his presidency, in February 1977, he told Giscard that the Greeks, whose application to join the Community was already well advanced, 'seemed curiously unwilling to negotiate seriously. They tended to agree with every proposition put to them by the Commission and were clearly proceeding from the position that it was better to join quickly and allow problems to be dealt with once they were inside the Community.' When Giscard asked if they were ready to accept regulations on state aid and competition, 'Mr Jenkins replied that . . . it was difficult to get the Greeks to come to grips with these questions. The Commission sometimes felt like a man boxing with a pillow.'[118] Despite these doubts, Greece was nevertheless allowed to join the Community in 1981 – and later the euro.

told Irish ministers in Dublin in February 1978, 'had large balance of payments deficits', but this was not a decisive objection. 'There was already a massive but largely invisible transfer of resources within Member States to cope with this problem.'[119] He evidently envisaged the same sort of evening-up on a European scale to enable the weaker economies to live with the same exchange rate as the stronger. But this was utopian, as became clear when the next generation of European visionaries, undeterred by the experience of 1992, pressed on with the creation of a single currency – the euro – without a European Central Bank or a single economic authority to manage it.

By helping to launch the EMS, Jenkins could claim to be the god-father of the euro. It was not his fault that economically weaker countries like Greece and Portugal were encouraged to join the eurozone without meeting the criteria for membership, and then allowed to run up massive debts which they could not repay when the financial crisis struck in 2008. But the EMS and then the euro were intended to promote ever-closer European unity: in practice the euro – by tying the weaker economies into a common exchange rate, preventing them devaluing their way out of trouble and forcing the richer countries to bail them out to stop them defaulting – has sown only recrimination and disunity. With hindsight, Jenkins must bear some of the blame for foisting a flawed vision on the continent before it was ready for it.

19 'Home Thoughts from Abroad'

O NCE the EMS was successfully launched, Jenkins' focus shifted back increasingly towards Britain. Not that he had ever really taken his eye off domestic developments. He actually read the British papers more avidly than ever – noting after just two weeks in Brussels that 'it is curious that away from London or East Hendred one finds much more to read in the combination of the *Sunday Times* and *Observer* and *Sunday Telegraph* than would be the case at home'.[1] On his regular hops back to London he was assiduous in keeping up with all his British friends, political and otherwise: his engagement diaries show that he filled every minute of every visit with lunch, a quick drink here or a social call there, squeezed in between formal calls on the Prime Minister or the Foreign Secretary, usually followed by an official dinner or a meal at one of his many dining clubs.* Weekends at East Hendred – roughly one in four – were equally packed with mixed lunch parties, often on both Saturday and Sunday, usually followed by tennis or croquet, though guests rarely stayed the night.

His schedule for the ten days of his first Easter break in 1977 was entirely typical. He flew back to London on Wednesday 6 April. The next day he and Jennifer looked at a house they were thinking of buying and visited the British Council to choose some pictures for his office in Brussels; he then fitted in a visit to his doctor and a haircut before seeing Callaghan for an hour at 12.20. This was followed by lunch with Leslie Bonham Carter and a call on his publishers (still

---

* At the Other Club in February 1978 Jenkins was the recipient of Willie Whitelaw telling him 'how absolutely ghastly life was with that awful woman' and asking his advice on whether he should resign from the Shadow Cabinet. Jenkins advised him not to resign, but to 'distance yourself'.[2]

Collins) at 3.45, after which he and Jennifer drove to East Hendred. On Good Friday they lunched with the Michael Astors, preceded by tennis and followed by croquet. On Saturday Nicko and Mary Henderson and Woodrow and Verushka Wyatt came to lunch. Easter Sunday was a family lunch, followed by an afternoon visit from the Owens; Monday was Bill and Sylvia Rodgers with Matthew Oakeshott and his wife. On Tuesday 12th they went to the Davenports for lunch and tennis. On Wednesday Roy lunched with Caroline Gilmour and her mother, the Duchess of Buccleuch, near Kettering before going on to Jakie Astor at Hatley for the night, and then on Thursday to Victor Rothschild for a 'spectacularly good dinner' at Cambridge.[3] Friday was lunch with Noel and Gabrielle Annan and Jennifer at one of their favourite pubs, the Blue Boar at Chieveley; and on Saturday the American writer and academic Douglas Cater and his wife came to lunch at East Hendred with Ian and Caroline Gilmour, Ann Fleming and Peter Quennell. The next morning, his holiday over, Jenkins flew to Washington for five days of meetings with President Carter and other American leaders, fitting in another busy schedule of lunches and dinners with Democratic friends in both Washington and New York before returning to Brussels. The whole of his life was like this.[4]

During 1977 Roy and Jennifer sold their house in Ladbroke Square after twenty-three years, and bought instead a large, somewhat cavernous flat in Kensington Park Gardens on the other side of the square, which would serve as their London base for the next twenty-five.* Leaving the house where they had raised their family, entertained the Gaitskells and played tennis until they bought East Hendred was a wrench; but Jenkins consoled himself that the new flat, 'with its vast drawing room, is in many ways better than Ladbroke Square'.[5] They still overlooked the same communal garden, but he liked the fact that the sun now rose and set in the opposite direction.[6]

He also encouraged a stream of visitors to the rue de Praetère, who often did stay the weekend – sometimes when Jennifer was there, frequently when she was not: again a mixture of political friends, social, literary and diplomatic friends and girlfriends – Gilmours, Griggs, Bonham Carters, Annans, Beaumarchaises and others. One who invited himself (for four days!) in 1978, but was not made welcome, was Harold Wilson, in retirement suddenly a somewhat pathetic figure. Jenkins (as he told John Grigg, who came to stay a few days later while filming

---

* They bought this flat in 1977 for £55,000 and sold it shortly before Roy's death for £1.25 million – an almost twenty-three-fold increase over twenty-five years.

a television programme on Great War battlefields) 'didn't see why he should have him to stay and offered only to give him lunch at the Commission'.[7] There Wilson talked exclusively about 'the most recondite details of English politics, which hardly anyone except him and me . . . could be expected to understand', and claimed to have 'specially timed his resignation in order to be as helpful to me as possible'. Now he begged his former Chancellor not to cut himself off from British politics:

> I might well be needed in the future, he said. Callaghan was too old, Owen was too young. The whole thing was very bad . . . He did not think there was much future for the Government, or indeed the Labour Party. A coalition government would almost certainly be necessary; he would bless it from outside, but would not serve.

'Altogether, an extraordinary visit,' Jenkins concluded. 'He was thoroughly agreeable, except for being an absolute caricature of himself.'[8]

Jenkins took Wilson's gloomy prognostications with 'several pinches of salt'. He told Grigg that he now wished he had resigned after his row with Wilson immediately following the 1975 referendum: that was the moment, he now believed, when he might have forced a coalition. Since then he thought Callaghan had done well enough as Prime Minister that Labour might yet be re-elected. Jennifer shared this view, but had already decided to vote Liberal.[9] That autumn, when Callaghan postponed the expected election, they were irritated by a story started by *Tribune* (but gleefully taken up by all the papers) that they had not paid their Labour Party subscription for several years. The story – 'obviously . . . motivated by a malicious Trot in the North Kensington Labour Party' – was plausible because it reflected their obvious disillusion with Labour. In fact they had switched (as long ago as 1968) to paying by banker's order and their payments were up to date. On the plane to London Roy drafted 'rather a good letter' for Jennifer to send to *The Times*, humorously but firmly detailing her efforts to squash the story, which she compared to 'trying to catch a very vigorous eel by its tail'.[10] It cost them £300 in legal fees, which they never recovered. But the story only ran so strongly because, though wrong in detail, it was substantially true in spirit.

In January 1979 – by which time Labour's chances of re-election had been all but destroyed by the wave of public-sector strikes dubbed by the press the 'winter of discontent' – Jenkins had a gloomy conversation with Shirley Williams (now Education Secretary) at a Labour Committee for Europe dinner. They agreed that their mistake was not to have supported Dick Taverne in 1973. 'Everything had got worse since then . . . She thought the election lost whenever it came and that the party would be in a very bad state after it, and she was thinking very clearly in terms of splits and anxious for me to come back.'[11] Jenkins was already pretty certain that he could not return to Labour; but talk of splits kept him interested in the idea that there might be some other way back for him. At the European Council in Paris a few weeks later, Callaghan – in the gents' lavatory – casually offered him the governorship of Hong Kong. 'Certainly not, Jim,' he replied. 'I have never heard a more preposterous suggestion.' Callaghan then assumed that he would go to the Lords when he came back from Brussels. 'Probably not,' Jenkins replied, 'as I told you when you last suggested that to me. Not for the moment, certainly. I want to come back and look around and keep options open.' 'You might find it quite difficult to get back into the House of Commons,' Callaghan warned him. 'And you might not like it when you got there . . . It has deteriorated a lot.' 'Yes, yes,' Jenkins fended him off. 'All I intend to do is come back and look around at the political landscape, Jim, and certainly not become Governor of Hong Kong.'[12]

He was actively considering other options. In 1979 he was offered the headship of at least two Oxbridge colleges: St Catherine's, Oxford ('Not . . . I fear, a particularly tempting offer') and Corpus Christi, Cambridge.[13] Declining St Catherine's, he wrote that 'I am totally committed in Bx [Brussels] until 1981, and after that I cannot as yet see clearly.'[14] Towards the end of that year he was flattered to be pressed to stay on in Brussels and did not rule it out.[15] Of course he was also thinking about getting back to writing. Ian Chapman at Collins was keen to publish his half-written biography of Baldwin, possibly paired with an American subject: Jenkins was initially keen on Franklin Roosevelt, but thought there might be nothing new to say about him and began to consider Eisenhower or Truman instead. During 1980 he had several offers from the City – making up for its marked lack of interest in him ten years earlier. In June he was surprised to be invited to become a consultant for Deloitte's. ('Rather a strange idea,' he noted. 'I had never thought of accountants as having people who were not professionally qualified.' But it had 'certain possible attractions'.)[16] In August Claus Moser pressed him to join Rothschild's.[17] And in September Morgan Grenfell made him a more substantial offer, which he accepted. Over dinner with three of the bank's directors in November

– only a month before he was due to leave Brussels – it was 'more or less fixed up that I would start with them on a sort of three day a week basis sometime in the spring'. In subsequent negotiations he asked for £30,000 for a three-day week; they countered that his 'infrastructure' (office, secretary, car plus chauffeur and pension) would cost £25,000 and offered only £20,000. They were happy for him to be politically active, but if his political profile became too high they would renegotiate; he could join a clearing bank and an accountancy firm as well, if he wished, but not an American investment bank.[18]

But still what he really wanted was to get back into politics. When Callaghan lost a confidence vote in the Commons at the end of March 1979 and could delay the election no longer, Jenkins was genuinely unsure what result he hoped for. Residual allegiance to Labour warred with a feeling that the country needed a change of government and the hope that Mrs Thatcher might be more positively disposed towards Europe – plus the calculation that a Labour split following the party's defeat might give him his best opening. The day before polling day (3 May) both Shirley Williams and Bill Rodgers rang in alarm at a rumour that he was about to issue a statement supporting the Tories. He assured them that he was making no statement at all. Neither did he vote – though Jennifer did indeed vote Liberal.* They watched the results together in Brussels with Laura, Celia Beale and Thea Elliott (the widow of Jenkins' old Balliol friend Anthony Elliott, who had drowned while serving as ambassador to Israel in 1976). Jenkins thought Mrs Thatcher's victory probably the best outcome, 'but one can't pretend that one has any real pleasure in it. Thea I think was the most solid Labour supporter amongst us, though we were all somewhat torn.'[20] But next day he was shaken by the 'totally unexpected and dreadful news' of Shirley Williams' defeat in Hertford and Stevenage.[21]

Historically – in 1931, 1951 and 1970 – Labour in defeat had invariably swung left. Now in 1979 the Bennites and all the various factions of the hard left were better placed and more determined than ever to take control of the party, while Mrs Thatcher was driving the Tories determinedly to the right. Between them these developments left a wide political space in the centre and opened a real prospect for some form of new party. Jenkins spent much of the weekend after the election on

---

* Less diplomatically Wilson had let slip in an interview that his wife intended to vote for Mrs Thatcher. A few days after the election Jenkins met them both at an Open University degree ceremony in London where 'Mary, amazingly, more or less confirmed the story . . . She said that she had to deny it, "which meant that I couldn't vote for her" [Mrs Thatcher] – the clear implication being that she would otherwise have done so.'[19]

the telephone, speaking to Bill Rodgers, Shirley Williams and David Owen on one side and to Tory friends including Ian Gilmour and Peter Carrington (the new Foreign Secretary) on the other. At a dinner in Edinburgh the following week he sat next to Joe Gormley – Ted Heath's nemesis in 1974 and still President of the NUM – and noted that even such an old trade union stalwart was 'making a great number of centre party noises'.[22] For the next few days he was on Commission business in Brussels, Copenhagen and Munich; but on 16 May he was back in London to address a big CBI dinner where his large audience included half the Cabinet and almost half the Shadow Cabinet, as well as all the leaders of British industry – 'one of the most formidable gatherings I had ever addressed'. While speaking mainly about Europe he took the chance to deliver 'a good plug for centrist politics', begging the new Tory government to 'spare us too many queasy rides on the ideological big dipper'.[23] This was an old theme, but one whose time suddenly seemed that it might have come.*

By lucky chance Jenkins had already accepted an invitation from the Director-General of the BBC, Ian Trethowan, to give the televised Dimbleby Lecture later in the year – an unrivalled opportunity to address an even bigger audience on a subject of his choice. The seven previous lecturers since 1972 had been Noel Annan, Robert Mark, Arnold Goodman, Huw Wheldon, Quintin Hailsham, Jack Jones and Victor Rothschild, so he was only the second active politician to be invited. The BBC probably expected Jenkins to speak about Europe, but he quickly determined to use the occasion to propose 'a new anti-party approach to British politics' and devoted much of what he called his 'working leisure' that summer to thinking about what he wanted to say.[25] In focusing his ideas he was considerably influenced by an article by David Marquand in the July issue of *Encounter*. After an unhappy eighteen months in Brussels when he had failed to find a satisfactory role, Marquand had left to take up a chair in politics and contemporary history at the University of Salford, to which he was far better suited. His *Encounter* article reflected his experience as a Labour intellectual – born, like Jenkins, into the party purple: his father was a middle-ranking minister under Attlee – who had seen people like himself increasingly driven out of the party. It was, he wrote, the influx of middle-class radicals between the wars that had transformed Labour

---

* He had made at least one previous foray onto this territory since coming to Brussels: a lecture at the Royal Institution in November 1977, which was reprinted in *Encounter* in February 1978 under the broad title 'What's Wrong and What Could be Set Right: Reflections after 29 Years in Parliament'.[24] But this attracted little attention.

from a narrow trade union pressure group into a broad-based governing party, replacing the Liberals as the main vehicle of the centre left. All its leaders since 1935 (Attlee, Gaitskell, Wilson) as well as many of its leading figures from Cripps and Dalton to Crossman and Crosland had come from that class, contributing crucially to its thinking and its appeal. The changed ethos represented by the deselection of moderates like Taverne and Prentice was symbolised for Marquand by the 1976 leader-ship election and the choice of the least intellectual candidate – Callaghan – over his five university-educated rivals. Labour, he argued, had become increasingly conservative and backward-looking since 1970, intolerantly proletarian and wedded to an outdated socialism. As an instrument of progressive social reform it had 'outlived its usefulness', and the middle-class radicals who had found it a comfortable home in the past needed to find a new vehicle for their ideas – implicitly a new party.[26]

Marquand sent Jenkins an advance copy of his article at the end of June, saying that he was coming to Strasbourg the next month and wanted to talk to him about it – 'particularly about the possible implications for your own position of the conclusion I come to that it's a waste of time for Social Democrats to go on working within the Labour Party & that some new structure is needed instead'.[27] This was music to Jenkins' ears, providing academic backing for the conclusion he had already reached. Marquand came to Strasbourg on 19 July for the first meeting of the directly elected European Parliament – about which he was writing a book – and he and Jenkins had dinner together. Another significant conversation around this time was with David Steel (Liberal leader since 1976), who came to dinner (alone) at rue de Praetère on 14 June. Jenkins recorded in his diary 'a rather gossipy talk with him, more about the election than the current and future political situation'. Steel was at pains to emphasise that though the Liberals had not done particularly well, he personally had had a good election and was now 'a major public figure, possibly the best-known after Callaghan, Heath and Mrs Thatcher. In other words, he was, I think, underlining in the nicest possible way that in any future political arrangement he wasn't to be treated as an office boy.'[28] Though they did not yet discuss it in any detail, the idea of future cooperation was already in both their minds.

Jenkins started trying to write his Dimbleby Lecture at East Hendred in August (he and Jennifer did not holiday in Tuscany that year, but had ten days staying with the Griggs in Spain). But it did not come easily. In October he showed an incomplete first draft to the BBC producer Eddie Mirzoeff, who was unimpressed ('Quite right too prob-ably, though it depressed me mildly at the time').[29] Then on 1 November, with three weeks to go, he settled down at East Hendred again to break the back of it. He wrote solidly for eight and three-quarter hours, broken only by a pub lunch with Jennifer. 'I was very pleased to discover that I could still concentrate as hard as this on writing something for myself and produce nearly three thousand words in a single day.' That evening Bill and Sylvia Rodgers came to dinner and Jenkins read bits of it to Rodgers, who did not fully take it in – 'perhaps because I was full of claret and sleep'[30] – but 'showed no sign of reacting with deep shock or hostility'. Jenkins judged that Rodgers had 'moved quite a bit' since the summer, when he had tried to persuade Roy that he could still come back for a Labour seat.[31]*

The next day the Gilmours came to lunch and Jenkins got Ian to read it. Gilmour (now number two at the Foreign Office) was the wettest of the Tory 'wets'. He thought Jenkins' text 'too right-wing' – he objected particularly to the phrase 'the social market economy', which was just coming into use as code for privatisation and increased competition – and thought the Yeats quotation with which he proposed to end ('The best lack all conviction . . . the centre cannot hold') too hackneyed.[33] Jenkins accepted the first of these suggestions but not the second, and kept on tinkering. When he reread his draft the next weekend he was 'really rather pleased with it. It seems to me, now, taut and good and sensible, nearly all of it right.'[34] But a few days later Marquand made a critical contribution, harking back to his *Encounter* article by suggesting that Jenkins should talk not just about the centre, but about 'the *radical* centre'.[35] After more rewriting over the weekend of 17–18 November, Jenkins finally sent off his text on the 20th, borrowing from Browning the title 'Home Thoughts from Abroad' (Browning's poem, starting with the famous lines 'Oh, to be in England / Now that April's there', was an apt reference for an exile beginning to sense the first shoots of a political spring at home). In his diary he complained that an unusually heavy load of Commission meetings that week – leading up to a critical European Council in Dublin starting on the 29th – was not the best way to 'prepare and be fresh for . . . the long-awaited, and with much foreboding, Dimbleby day' on the 22nd, which was clearly his priority.[36] The Dimbleby Lecture was only a *ballon d'essai*, but it was potentially an even more momentous one than his Florence speech two years earlier.

---

* Birmingham, Northfield, a previously safe Labour seat which had fallen to the Tories in May, was said to have put out feelers, 'although I don't think that would attract me, even if a Labour seat did at all'.[32]

He finally delivered it at the Royal Society of Arts, live on television, with most of his friends in the audience and the whole BBC top brass sitting in the front row. He began with a historical analysis of the decline of the two-party system since 1951, developing the case he had started making five or six years earlier when he was still a contender for the Labour leadership. Even now he did not explicitly disavow the Labour party, only the leftward path on which it seemed irrevocably set. What was new was what he called an 'unashamed plea for the strengthening of the political centre', building on his 1973 theme that the tendency of both main parties towards the extremes was disenfranchising a large part of the electorate:

> In 1951 83% of the electorate voted, and no less than 97% of those who went to the polls voted for one or other of the two big parties. In the second 1974 election only 73% of the electorate voted, and only three-quarters of those . . . voted Labour or Conservative. To put it another way: the Labour Party in 1951 polled 40% of the total electorate . . . and it just lost. In October 1974 it polled 28% of the electorate and it just won. Even in 1979, with some recovery in the total vote and a substantial victory, the Conservatives polled only 33% of the electorate.

The missing voters, Jenkins argued, were alienated by the false hopes and unredeemed promises held out by both parties over the past twenty years and the alternation of governments each claiming a monopoly of wisdom and rushing onto the Statute Book a mass of ill-digested legislation founded on little popular support and promptly reversed by its successor. Good government demanded not an avoidance of controversy – he cited the great Reform Bills, the repeal of the Corn Laws, the curbing of the power of the House of Lords and the Beveridge revolution as measures bitterly contested at the time which quickly became inviolable parts of the social fabric – but the assurance, before embarking on any major reform, that it would last, because no succeeding government would dare repeal it. 'All this implies a certain respect by politicians for the opinions of their opponents.' Exaggerated partisanship, the pretence that everything was the fault of the other side and each successive government either 'the most reactionary since . . . Lord Liverpool or some other hobgoblin figure shrouded in the past' or 'the most rapacious, doctrinaire and unpatriotic conspiracy to be seen this side of the Iron Curtain', was no longer convincing to most of the electorate, whose aspirations, he believed, 'pull far more towards the centre than towards the extremes'. The job of politicians was 'to represent, to channel [and] to lead the aspirations of the electorate'.

That being so, he believed that the case for proportional representation had become 'overwhelming'. Already in 1974–6 he had tried to have the possibility examined by a Speaker's Conference. But now, fortified by his experience in Europe, he believed that the demands of equity could no longer be denied by the argument that first-past-the-post produced strong government compared with the weakness and instability of coalitions:

> Do we really believe that we have been more effectively and coherently governed over the past two decades than have the Germans? . . . Do we really believe that the last Labour Government was not a coalition, in fact if not in name, and a pretty incompatible one at that? I served in it for half its life, and you could not convince me of anything else.

All democratic government, he now asserted, depended on some form of coalition:

> The old Labour Party of Attlee and Gaitskell was a coalition of liberal social democrats and industrially responsible trade unionists. Willy Brandt and Helmut Schmidt have governed the Federal Republic of Germany with a coalition of Social Democrats and Liberals for the past decade. Sometimes the coalitions are overt, sometimes they are covert. I do not think the distinction greatly matters. The test is whether those within the coalition are closer to each other, and to the mood of the nation they seek to govern, than they are to those outside their ranks.

Proportional representation might indeed produce coalition:

> I would much rather that it meant overt and compatible coalition than that it locked incompatible people, and still more important, incompatible philosophies, into a loveless, constantly bickering and debilitating political marriage, even if consecrated in a common tabernacle.

The last word was straight out of the political vocabulary of the 1890s. It was typical of Jenkins that he did not talk down even to a mass audience on television, but used his own – sometimes slightly recondite – language. For this he was mocked as an elitist. Unabashed, he concluded this part of his argument with a line from *Hamlet*:

> The great disadvantage of our present electoral system is that it freezes the pattern of politics, and holds together the incompatible because everyone assumes that if a party splits it will be electorally slaughtered. They may be right. They may be wrong. I am not so sure. I believe that the electorate can 'tell a hawk from a handsaw' and that if it saw a new grouping with cohesion and relevant policies it might be more attracted by this new reality than by old labels which had become increasingly irrelevant.

Turning specifically to the Labour party, he conceded that there was nothing inherently objectionable about the left's current demands: the mandatory reselection of MPs, NEC control of the manifesto and the leader to be elected by an electoral college. They were contentious because they were the battleground between two incompatible views of the party. This brought him to his call to arms, couched in a favourite military metaphor:

> The response to such a situation should not be to slog through an unending war of attrition, stubbornly and conventionally defending as much of the old citadel as you can hold, but to break out and mount a battle of movement on new and higher ground.

By changing the political structure, strengthening the centre and ending the see-saw alternation of irrelevant dogmas, he contended, Britain might go a long way towards restoring national prosperity. 'Our great failure, now for decades past, has been a lack of adaptability': the economic system mirrored the political. 'The paradox is that we need more change accompanied by more stability of direction.' Specifically he called for acceptance of 'the broad line of division between the public and private sectors' so that those in the private sector were not constantly threatened with nationalisation or expropriation, setting out an even-handed middle way between the excesses of Thatcherism and Bennism:

> You encourage them without too much interference to create as much wealth as possible, but use the wealth so created both to give a return for enterprise and to spread the benefits throughout society in a way that avoids the disfigurements of poverty, gives

a full priority to public education and health services, and encourages co-operation and not conflict in industry and throughout society. You use taxation for this purpose, but not just to lop off rewards . . .

You recognise that there are certain major economic objectives . . . which can only be achieved by public action, often on an international scale . . . You use market forces to help achieve these objectives, but do not for a moment pretend that they, unguided and unaided, can do the whole job.

Finally he repeated the libertarian themes that had been his particular hobby-horse since the 1950s:

You also make sure that the state knows its place . . . in relation to the citizen. You are in favour of the right of dissent and the liberty of private conduct . . . You want the nation to be self-confident and outward-looking, rather than insular, xenophobic and suspicious. You want the class system to fade without being replaced either by an aggressive intolerant proletarianism or by the dominance of the brash and selfish values of a get-rich-quick society.

All these objectives, he believed – adopting Marquand's paradoxical formulation – could be assisted by 'a strengthening of the radical centre'. Without explicitly advocating the formation of a new party, he anticipated that such an initiative would tap a huge unfilled demand:

I believe that such a development could bring into political commitment the energies of many people of talent and goodwill who, although perhaps active in many other voluntary ways, are at present alienated from the business of government, whether national or local, by the sterility and formalism of much of the political game. I am sure that this would improve our politics. I think the results might also help to improve our national performance. But of that I cannot be certain. I am against too much dogmatism here. We have had more than enough of it. But at least we could escape from the pessimism of Yeats's 'Second Coming' where

The best lack all conviction, while the worst
Are full of passionate intensity

and

Things fall apart; the centre cannot hold.[37]

To most of the political commentators and professional cynics, Jenkins' thesis was as hackneyed as his concluding quotation. Talk of realignment had been going on for as long as anyone could remember, and nothing had ever come of it. The idea of a 'radical centre' was either a contradiction in terms or woolly naivety. Moreover it seemed singularly self-serving for Jenkins to advance it now, after he had done very well out of the old two-party system for the past twenty years, but now needed a new system (and a new party) to facilitate his re-entry from lucrative exile in Brussels. Fred Emery in *The Times* was amazed that the BBC should have granted him 'fifty minutes of prime time, free of charge' for a blatant job application: 'a personal political broadcast by someone preparing to come back from the EEC Commission Presidency to oust Conservative and Labour alike. Marvellous.'[38] The BBC's house magazine, *The Listener*, reprinted the full text and then invited a number of politicians, academics and journalists to comment on it. From Enoch Powell and Paul Johnson on the right to Jack Jones and Professors John Griffith and Bernard Crick on the left they were unanimously contemptuous: the most respectful, remarkably, was Neil Kinnock, who alone conceded that Jenkins' views had 'the appeal of reason and the authority of demonstrated commitment', but thought him misguided on the ground that Britain had already suffered centre government for the past thirty years. Even Jo Grimond was grudging. instead of welcoming Jenkins' revelation, he complained that it was twenty years too late and invited him, if he was serious, to 'come down into the battle' and join the Liberals:

> Let him shove with the rest of us. All too many social democrats have gone off into banking, consultancy, TV, academic life etc. It is Mr Steel who has been in the scrum. Will they join him? The opportunity is indeed great . . . but time is very short.[39]

Paul Johnson – the former editor of the *New Statesman*, now turned Thatcherite – likewise accused Jenkins of wanting 'the palm without the dust':

> A call to battle by Jenkins might have been useful, even well-received. Instead he drops a hint that if the system is changed and

provided the breakaway works and once the dust has settled – and always assuming he hasn't been offered a better job in the meantime – then he might consider accepting the leadership.[40]

Some of the editorials, including *The Times*, *Sunday Times* and *Observer*, were more positive; but even among those sympathetic to his analysis there was widespread scepticism that any change of the sort Jenkins advocated was practical politics. Since neither Labour nor the Conservatives would ever agree to proportional representation, there was general agreement that no hypothetical new party could have any realistic hope of breaking through. Where he struck a chord, however, was with the public – or at least that section of it to which he had attempted to appeal: those 'many people of talent and goodwill' who felt themselves disfranchised by the 'sterility and formalism' of current politics and longed for a new movement to which they could relate. Within days letters were pouring in from all sorts of people, which were overwhelmingly supportive. The numbers were not enormous (around 300), but the quality was unusually high. He had never before, Jenkins declared in a second speech six months later, received such a weight of mail 'which was, first, 99% friendly; second, 99% sane; and third, revealed, often argued over 400 or 500 words, such a degree of desire for release from present political constraints and for involvement in the future'.[41] These were the people who would flock to join the SDP as soon as it was launched. The 1 per cent of letters that were not supportive, he noted in his diary, were 'dotty rather than against'.[42]*

Most of his friends and long-standing supporters in the Labour Party – those whom he would need to carry with him out of the party, if his new venture were to take off – were more or less enthusiastic, or 'certainly not hostile'.[44] The exception at this stage (perhaps because he was not invited to the lecture) was David Owen, who immediately made a defiant speech scorning Jenkins' appeal as a diversion and vowing to carry on the fight for Labour from within:

> The trouble in the past was that too often the centre right of the party has disdained from fighting from within, has not been prepared to muddy its feet on doorsteps, not fought for a place

---

* An example of those he would have classified as 'dotty' came from a Mrs Brown, telling him not to come back to Britain: 'We had enough of you when you were here before, with your policy of turning this country into a BLACK STATE, after which you marched your arse off to Brussels . . . You are a useless money and glory-grabbing dolt . . . In fact you are hated by many people in this country.'[43]

on the National Executive, not taken the battle enough into the constituency parties.

He urged the centre of the party to 'stand firm. We will not be tempted by siren voices from outside, from those who have given up the fight from within.'[45] Bill Rodgers, on the other hand – far more deeply rooted in the party than Owen – told Jenkins that 'suddenly in the course of the lecture he had a vision of himself sitting in the headquarters of the new party with his sleeves rolled up, actually organising things'. This, Jenkins confided to his diary, 'I took to mean – I hope rightly – that Bill had passed over some intellectual watershed.'[46] In the published version of his *European Diary* he changed 'intellectual' to 'emotional'.[47] Either way, it actually took Rodgers longer than Owen to reach the point of breaking with Labour. Between the Dimbleby Lecture and the launch of the SDP there was still to be a long and rocky road. Jenkins himself still had another year to serve in Brussels before he was in a position to show the doubters that he was ready to come down into the arena and muddy his feet on doorsteps. But in the immediate aftermath of Dimbleby he had reason to be encouraged by the strong public response to his trial balloon. Looking ahead at end of 1979 to the coming year and the coming decade, he felt 'slightly intimidated by the thought of having let a genie out of its bottle'.[48]

Meanwhile, now that he had recovered his self-confidence and knew that he could discharge the job successfully in his own way, Jenkins was reasonably happy to serve out his time in Brussels and make the most of what the European gravy train had to offer. Brussels itself he never much cared for. Rather like Birmingham, he confessed in his last completed book, *Twelve Cities*, 'it does not clutch at my heart strings'.[49] But it had its good points: notably the Forêt de Soignes ('a Brussels asset which surpasses Hyde Park, the Bois de Boulogne or Central Park in New York'); twenty-seven theatres and some fine art galleries (though it was 1980 before he visited the Musées Royaux for the first time); and above all – the most important criterion by which he judged any city – its restaurants, which he rated 'formidably good, at least comparable . . . with the range and quality of those in Paris'. His favourites were the Villa Lorraine ('which by its sylvan but not rustic location . . . between the Bois and the Forêt recalls both Pré Catalan in the Bois de Boulogne and Ledoyen in the Jardin des Champs

Elysées'); L'Ecailler du Palais Royal ('to my mind the best of all fish restaurants'); and Comme Chez Soi ('the highest peak of the lot, now secure in its three stars, but set in the far from glossy Place Rouppe . . . in London terms a sort of Clerkenwell location').* But the suburbs too were 'littered with Michelin two-stars', while the attractive old Flemish towns within easy distance – Ghent, Leuven, Bruges, Antwerp – were also 'rich in restaurants'. 'Flemish menus,' he was happy to confirm after thorough research, 'are far from being just an affair of *moules* and *frites*.' The wine lists too were 'of great depth and quality . . . overwhelmingly French and overwhelmingly red', but not as he had been led to expect biased towards burgundy. 'The claret lists,' he noted, 'are at least as strong' – adding with a real oenophile's precision, 'with perhaps a more subtle trade-route discrimination, compared with a rare English list of equal quality, in favour of the right-bank and overland-moving St Emilions and Pomerols as opposed to the left-bank Medocs and Graves which were more easily shipped to Britain, Scandinavia or America'.[51]

Jenkins made no apology for enjoying good food, the best wine and large cigars; but he was a demanding customer and his diary is full of critical comments on meals that failed to meet his standards. Quite early on, in May 1977, he had a very good, expensive lunch with Helena Tiné, followed by dinner the same day with Laura Grenfell and Michael and Maxine Jenkins, which was only 'tolerable' and almost as costly. 'Moral,' he concluded: 'Unless you go somewhere really cheap it is always better in Brussels to go to restaurants of the *grande classe*.'[52] His comments on the quality of the airline meals and many of the official dinners he was obliged to eat were often withering, though he was sometimes surprised by the quality of the wine: Château Lafite on the fourteenth floor of a modern hotel in Halifax, Nova Scotia, for instance (even if it was not the best year), or 'ludicrously good wine, Haut-Brion '62' in Ghana.[53] He could be intimidating to entertain, as Nicko Henderson noted after having Roy and Jennifer to dinner at the Paris Embassy in June 1978:

> Roy was satisfied, I think, with the Lynch–Bages 1960. He brought his own cigars with him, so we did not have the usual trouble arising from inadequate hospitality in this respect on my part.[54]

---

* Comme Chez Soi was 'spectacularly good and spectacularly expensive'. Dinner for four in December 1977 cost £160.[50] But that did not stop Jenkins going there remarkably frequently.

He always enjoyed guessing the wine and was delighted when he got it right. On his first foray into Brussels society, a private dinner where the wine was 'outstanding', he got it 'nearly but not sufficiently right'. He guessed a Medoc Premier Grand Cru of middle age (1953, possibly 1961) but *not* a Lafite, when it was in fact Château Lafite '53. 'It was a pity to have got so near, but to have failed so completely at the last fence.'[55] His expertise was largely confined to claret, however – though he was once very pleased with himself for correctly guessing 'an extremely good Californian'.[56] At a heads of government dinner in Paris in March 1979 'both the wines . . . were Burgundies so it was a little difficult for me to judge how good they were'.[57] Crispin Tickell used deliberately to serve him Spanish wine, which he confessedly knew nothing about.[58] But so long as it was red he was reasonably happy. He had no time for white at all – except champagne. 'One must remember not to go to Rome for official dinners on Fridays,' he reminded himself in January 1980, 'as it always means not particularly good fish and no red wine.'[59]

Despite his expensive tastes, he was scrupulous about his expenses. He certainly claimed every allowance to which he was entitled, and these were undeniably generous. But he was careful not to exceed them and was annoyed when the German Commissioner Willi Haferkamp was exposed by *The Economist* for running up excessive bills – partly for being accompanied on foreign visits by an interpreter who was also his mistress – which resulted in a searchlight being thrown on the alleged extravagance of the whole Commission. 'No doubt my own predilections assisted the caricature,' Jenkins wrote. 'But in fact it was largely unjustified.'[60] Compared with the representatives of the national governments or other organisations like NATO, he insisted, he and his staff and colleagues lived relatively modestly and largely at their own expense. Whenever he and Tickell stayed in Paris, for instance, they stayed in a grand suite at the Hôtel de Crillon if paid for by the French government, but at the less expensive (though scarcely spartan) Ritz if the Commission was paying.

At weekends he liked to get out of the city on excursions of one sort or another, usually including a good restaurant, and made a practice of taking visitors to sites of historical interest, like the battlefields of Waterloo and Passchendaele or the war memorial at the Menin Gate. Two relatively new friends – made through Jennifer's Historic Buildings work – who came out to Brussels several times were Henry and Shirley Anglesey. He was the seventh Marquess and a noted military historian, author of a multi-volume history of the British cavalry; she was the daughter of the now largely forgotten novelist Charles Morgan and an active stalwart of all sorts of arts and conservation quangos. In February 1980 Jenkins took them, in filthy weather, to Waterloo, where they managed to find the place where the first Marquess's leg was buried after he lost it in the battle; the next day he took them to Malines, where they witnessed the installation of the new Archbishop in the presence of an impressive turnout of cardinals. The Angleseys, he noted approvingly, were 'very good guests, full of enthusiasm and interest'.[61] They became good (if eccentric) friends over the next twenty years, and their stately home, Plas Newydd, with its Rex Whistler murals and stunning views over the Menai Strait, was one of his favourite places to stay. They in turn thanked him for a weekend of 'superb wines and delicious meals . . . gourmandising and good company and talk.'[62]*

Jenkins had inexhaustible curiosity about places, buildings, countries and people: he loved to compare and contrast, categorise and rank them. So he enjoyed the non-stop travel around the Community and beyond. In addition to the constant meetings in his role as President, he delivered an enormous number of speeches, addresses and semi-academic lectures at universities and ceremonies of all sorts all over the world. His diary is thus an exhaustive record of flights and train journeys, meetings and meals, commenting favourably or unfavourably on the airlines, hotels, hospitality and habits of different countries. He loved to compare the varying diplomatic protocol between the smaller countries of Europe and the large – the grand palaces, blank modern conference centres or nineteenth-century suburban châteaux where European Councils were staged with more or less pomp; the French *motards* who swept important dignitaries though the Paris traffic at hair-raising speed; the fact that the Prime Minister of Luxembourg could eat quite modestly in an ordinary restaurant without anyone batting an eyelid; the informality of the Dutch or Spanish royals compared with the stuffiness of the British court; or the etiquette of inspecting guards of honour at the Vatican or the Elysée. All this was material for his amused observation. He pretended to mock, but really loved it when he was awarded honours such as the Grand Cross of Charles III, which he was given by the King of Spain for opening the negotiations for Spanish entry into the Community – 'a splendid decoration with an enormous blue and white sash, though of course one can think of no possible occasion

---

* Henry Anglesey's eccentricity manifested itself in meticulously hand-decorated postcards, which he used to send, sometimes six or seven at a time, to Roy and Jennifer, full of the most florid and archaic compliments.[63]

when one could wear it'.[64]* He was 'slightly irritated' when he subsequently had to decline a grand Italian decoration, 'owing to the ridiculous British Government rules ... about not accepting foreign decorations'.[66]

Above all, as a biographer and keen observer of global politics Jenkins relished the opportunity to meet, talk with and critically assess all the great men and women of his day, from Giscard, Schmidt and Mrs Thatcher to Jimmy Carter, Deng Xiaoping, Pope John Paul II and Indira Gandhi, as well as a lot of lesser lights. He did this with the self-confidence of one who clearly saw himself as their equal, if not superior, judging them for intelligence and penetration – often admiring, sometimes a touch patronising and curtly dismissive of those he considered second-rate. A typical snap judgement was that on Al Haig, supreme NATO commander in Europe 1974–9 and later Ronald Reagan's Secretary of State:

> Haig appeared as usual as a nice man, plenty to say, right-wing views but not offensively so. He has been a good SHAPE commander and believes, though I have my doubts, that he may have a great political future, but he is not to my mind a great man.[67]

Pope John Paul he found disappointing:

> He has a wonderful smile and, even without the smile, looks agreeable (forceful as well) and made of very good material ... While it was a much more agreeable, intimate talk than I had ever had with either of the two previous Popes whom I have met, the sheer human and intellectual impact on me was less than I expected.[68]

Deng Xiaoping, however, with whom he had 'one and half hours of extremely fast, taut, intensive conversation' in Peking in 1979 – through an interpreter, obviously – impressed him:

> Compared with when I had last seen him five and a half years ago ... Deng looked younger ... and he has gained enormously in authority. He is now an extremely tough, impressive personality

---

* In *Twelve Cities* he wrote that he did sometimes wear it to Buckingham Palace banquets, 'partly as a tease and partly as a bit of peacockery'.[65]

by the highest world standards, with a great grasp of the details of international affairs, accompanied of course by an extremely hard line.[69]

One leader with whom he got on particularly well – with no language barrier – was Garret FitzGerald, Irish Foreign Minister during Jenkins' first year in Brussels and later Taoiseach. 'He listens well, is serious, and takes in what is said.'[70] This was always an important attribute, in Jenkins' book. Of his old friend Lee Kuan Yew of Singapore he wrote in 1979: 'Harry Lee may have political faults, but he is almost unique amongst world leaders in being an extremely good talker and a very good listener as well.'[71] Reviewing FitzGerald's memoirs more than a decade later, Jenkins recalled almost enviously his effortless cosmopolitanism when he spoke in excellent, elegant French at the opening of the new European Parliament building in Strasbourg. 'There, I thought, spoke the Ireland of Joyce and Synge and the Countess Markiewicz . . . It was he who made me feel provincial.'[72] It was not often that Jenkins, the great European and world statesman, admitted to feeling provincial!

He travelled a good deal beyond Europe in these years: to America frequently, as always, but also on official visits to Japan in 1977; to Sudan and Egypt (a semi-holiday, accompanied by Jennifer and Laura Grenfell, as well as Hayden Phillips), and Canada in 1978 (plus Greenland, which as a province of Denmark was then part of the EEC); to three West African countries – Senegal, Mali and Ghana – in January 1979 (which confirmed that Africa was not his favourite continent); to China in February; to Japan again (for the Tokyo G7 summit in June); to Egypt again in October; and to India in 1980. All these trips he described in his diary in the political travelogue style he had developed in the 1950s, recounting not only his meetings with the local leaders, but his impressions of the country, various sightseeing adventures (riding an elephant in India, for instance) and innumerable more or less ghastly meals. One of the most spectacular was in Timbuctoo:

We had a rather nasty lunch in a rather nasty hotel. After having consumed bits of three or four courses I assumed that the lunch was over, but there was a sudden stirring at the windows which were thrown open . . . and in came the most enormous roast camel, trussed like a sort of monstrous turkey, though about seventeen times as big, borne in upon a stretcher and laid down with great cheering. Then they performed the old desert trick of taking a whole roast sheep out of the inside of the camel, a whole roast chicken out of the inside of the sheep, a little pigeonneau out of the inside of the chicken, and an egg out of that, and one had to eat a little of everything. The camel seemed to me to have rather a bland taste, not nearly as objectionable as its milk. Then back to Bamoko for a Government dinner with speeches and the presentation to me of another Grand Croix du Legion d'Honneur.[73]

Most reviewers of his *European Diary* commented on Jenkins' stamina. But in fact the constant flying, with high-level meetings to be prepared for and speeches to be made as well as the heavy eating and drinking, was a considerable strain on his health. Behind the urbane manner he was actually very highly strung. He expended a lot of nervous energy before any sort of encounter, after which he would be physically and emotionally drained and would need time to recover. 'An hour and twenty minutes of detailed conversation with a Head of State,' he wrote after his first official meeting with Giscard, 'is quite exhausting' – even though on this occasion Giscard deigned to speak English ('and spoke it very well');[74] while even a televised interview with half a dozen European journalists would require 'about 36 hours of mental and psychological preparation'.[75] His morale was always surprisingly fragile and sometimes it cracked. In December 1977, for instance, he recorded that he woke at five in the morning feeling under-prepared for a European Council. 'I haven't had such a gloomy panicky morning for a long time.' Jennifer had to postpone her return to London in order to help him pull himself together.[76] In fact it went perfectly well. But as late as July 1979 he still confessed to suffering weekly attacks of gloom lasting twenty-four hours. 'However it is sustainable if it isn't more than that out of a week.'[77]

Between engagements he frequently went back to the rue de Praetère or his hotel for a sleep in the afternoon (this was a detail he omitted from the published diary). And he worried constantly about his health. Practically every time he visited London he fitted in a visit to his Harley Street doctor – an elderly Austrian named Gottfried – to have his blood pressure checked. He knew he ate and drank and smoked too much, but was incapable of giving up. In 1977 he tried to give up cigars for Lent ('even with the temptation of free Commission cigars'); but he lasted only eight days.[78] So that summer at East Hendred he took up running as a way of trying to look after himself. Like everything else, he took it very seriously:

Instead of going for a walk I decided to attempt a jogging session which had been recommended to me as producing five times more exercise per minute than walking. Accordingly jogged round the croquet lawn, with a few pauses, for two miles between 8.40 and 9.00: considerable exhaustion but good liver effect afterwards.[79]

Back in Brussels in September he forced himself to carry on his exercise regime, meticulously recorded. He would leave home at 8.15, walk for twenty-one minutes through the Bois de la Cambre to the lake, where he would jog for seven and a half minutes, walk for two to two and a half and jog for another six and a half, 'before collapsing in the car and being driven back to the Rue de Praetère with the newspapers for bath, breakfast [and] newspaper reading'. After this, he was 'rather late in the office, but these times suit my pattern and I think it is well worth it in terms of effectiveness when one gets there'.[80] After a while he started being driven to the Bois as well as back: but he kept up his routine, with some variations, most of the time he was in Brussels, except when it snowed or he had hurt his ankle or felt otherwise unwell, or when an assassination scare led the police to urge him to vary it. His friends were satirical about his 'new addiction' (as Nicko Henderson called it). 'Every morning he seeks redemption from overeating and overdrinking by jogging for two miles in the Bois,' John Grigg reported to his wife. 'I only hope the exertion won't be too much for him.'[81]

By the end of 1978 his blood pressure was down; but then he started suffering from debilitating colon pain, and by early 1980 his blood pressure was high again and he was getting headaches. Gottfried had retired, forcing him to find a new doctor named Bott (recommended by Solly Zuckerman) whom he did not like: he was 'too bouncing, too English' and wore an Old Harrovian tie ('always a bad sign').[82] So he went back to Gottfried, now semi-retired in Wimbledon – 'creeping back to him in a period of worry, rather like somebody going back to their wife'.[83] Gottfried confirmed that his blood pressure was up, 'not dangerously so but higher than it ought to be, I think 170 over 110', and put him on a heavy dose of pills.[84] The next month Jennifer persuaded him to go on a diet. For a few weeks he ate light lunches, with white wine or Vittel, and sometimes no dinner, which seemed to do the trick. But by July the colon pain was back, he was sleeping badly and getting depressed again as the end of his time in Brussels loomed. In August, with much trepidation, he saw a specialist who found nothing seriously wrong. 'Really rather an anticlimax,' Jenkins reflected characteristically. 'One of those visits which are very satisfactory at the time, but a little less so subsequently. At first you are suffused with the relief of a negative diagnosis, but after a bit realise that you have not been cured.'[85] The truth is that Jenkins was bit of a hypochondriac, and his pains were probably largely psychosomatic. In October Dr Bott – to whom he had to return when Gottfried finally retired to Switzerland – found his blood pressure improved again; but he never seriously reformed his eating and drinking habits.

Jenkins used up so much nervous energy in his ceaseless round of travel, work and equally strenuous relaxation that he needed his summer holidays to recover; though by most people's standards he worked pretty hard on holiday too. With his compulsion to account for every minute of his days he drew up charts meticulously recording how many hours he had spent on different activities – work, exercise and reading – and what books he had read. He usually worked in one form or another for four or five hours a day, divided between a certain amount of unavoidable Commission work, English reading, French reading, writing (articles, reviews and letters) and dictating and correcting his diary, which he took very seriously. He also ran, walked or (depending on whom he was staying with) swam a certain number of miles or lengths every day, and played tennis and/or croquet. The rest of the day would be taken up with lunching and sightseeing. Most years his holiday reading comprised around a dozen books, both fiction and non-fiction. In 1978, for instance – staying with the Beaumarchaises at their country house in the Pyrenees – he got through six contemporary novels (Barbara Pym, Kingsley Amis, Edna O'Brien, J.I.M. Stewart, Angela Huth and – in French – Simenon); two newly published memoirs (Lord Drogheda and Robert Mark), which he was reviewing; three biographies (Arthur Schlesinger's *Robert Kennedy*, Robert Gittings' *Young Thomas Hardy* and Charles Douglas-Home's *Evelyn Baring*); and (in typescript) a book on Birmingham by Joan Zuckerman for which he had undertaken to write a preface.[86] He recorded a similar list every year for the rest of his life. In 1980 (in Italy with the Bonham Carters) he read several books about Franklin Roosevelt, but also the latest novels by Iris Murdoch, Barbara Pym and Angus Wilson, Graham Greene's autobiography, three Lytton Strachey essays and one or two other things.[87] Year on year it amounts to a formidable catalogue. What other recent politician, with the possible exception of Harold Macmillan in more leisured times, could claim to have read half as much?

★

Jenkins' last year in Brussels was dominated by a protracted crisis over Britain's contribution to the Community budget. The problem was that, five years after Wilson and Callaghan's 'renegotiation' of Heath's entry terms, Britain was about to become the largest net contributor to the Community, despite being now (measured by GDP) one of the poorer members. The reason was that the Common Agricultural Policy remained far and away the biggest item in the budget while Britain, as a primarily industrial country, drew from it the least benefit. Some of the other initiatives, like regional policy, from which Britain was supposed to gain compensation, had never fully taken off. Callaghan had been gearing up to demand a rectification of this imbalance before he lost office; now Mrs Thatcher had taken up the cudgels and was determined to get what she called 'her' money back. As President of the Commission, Jenkins was keen to promote a settlement, partly on the merits of the case, because he believed that Britain was indeed paying more than her fair share; and partly because it became increasingly clear during 1980 that Mrs Thatcher's single-minded focus on getting her way ensured that no progress would be possible on any other front until she was satisfied. He became exasperated with her counter-productive method of fighting her case, which merely antagonised her partners and alienated potential allies. But it was a peculiarly awkward issue for him, just because it involved his own country. Hitherto he had been careful to give his colleagues and critics in Brussels no ground for thinking he was a British stooge. That had not been a problem over the EMS; but over the BBQ (the British Budgetary Question, or the 'Bloody British Question', as it came to be known in Brussels) it was difficult for him not to seem to be taking Britain's side. It did not help that the other Commissioner whose portfolio included the budget was Christopher Tugendhat.

He had his first meeting with the new Prime Minister just two weeks after she took office on 21 May 1979. She was 'very anxious to be pleasant' and began by offering him a drink, which he 'primly refused', thinking twelve o'clock a little early. 'Let us have one at 12.30,' he suggested. 'It will give us something to look forward to if the conversation goes badly.'[88] In fact it went quite well. Mrs Thatcher was 'very determined to get something on the budget', but at this stage she also wanted to be positive. She intended to fight for British interests, but wanted to be a better partner than the previous government, and even held out hope of joining the EMS, though not immediately. As they talked, however, she became more worked up. There had to be 'give and take in the Community', she conceded, 'but so far as Britain was concerned it was all give' and this was 'fundamentally unjust. She could not understand why the others did not understand this.' Jenkins disputed some of her figures and warned her not to be too demanding. 'Without goodwill on the British side and readiness to co-operate', the others would be 'very tough'. They did not accept the argument that Britain was relatively poor. On the contrary, the Europeans – he was doubtless thinking particularly of Helmut Schmidt – felt that 'the British had great human resources, they had immense oil and coal reserves, and their industrial problems were in many ways their own fault'. Mrs Thatcher had to agree with this, but claimed that Britain's unfair budget contribution was inhibiting her efforts to put them right.[89] Jenkins came away reasonably encouraged – except by her tendency to equate the EEC with NATO and 'one or two frankly foolish remarks about starving the Arabs to death by cutting off North American wheat supplies' – and went straight on to lunch with Leslie Bonham Carter at the White Tower, before recording a television interview in the afternoon and attending a dinner in the evening.[90]

It was at her first European summit in Strasbourg a month later that the other leaders realised what they were up against. When Giscard and Schmidt tried to patronise her, Mrs Thatcher 'immediately became rather too shrill' and then picked an unnecessary quarrel with Schmidt, 'which was silly because he was absolutely crucial to her getting the result she wanted'. Jenkins – whose role at summits was now accepted – had to intervene to keep the peace.[91] Three weeks later he was invited to dine at Chequers, which gave him another chance to advise her on how to press her case: he told her that she should 'endeavour to break up the endless exhibition waltz between Schmidt and Giscard which has been going on for too long, and which left the Little Five, and indeed Italy as well, as rather bored wallflowers sitting at the edge of the room' – in other words, that she should seek allies and not expect to get what she wanted simply by demanding it.[92] Unfortunately this was advice she failed to heed.

This dinner – the first time he had been to Chequers for several years – was a curious occasion. The only others present were Denis Thatcher and Jenkins' old friend Woodrow Wyatt, now an ardent Thatcherite and an intimate confidant of the Prime Minister. 'Woodrow', he noted with some surprise, 'is on very close terms with her, talks freely, easily, without self-consciousness, says anything he wants to.' Denis, too, 'while a caricature of himself in some ways, is not in the least afraid of her and talks a good deal, perhaps because he had had a few drinks by that time. But he doesn't talk altogether foolishly . . .

Whether he is exactly out of his depth I don't know. He is rather his own man, I think.' The third thing that struck him was that Mrs Thatcher was 'remarkably indiscreet in front of me', though she was tactful enough to criticise his particular friends in the Cabinet (Gilmour, Carrington and Whitelaw) only by implication, by pointedly leaving them off a list of 'the sound men – Howe, Biffen, Joseph, Nott . . . (a slightly frightening list) – who were fighting tooth and nail on her side for public expenditure cuts'. He was disappointed that there was only white wine with dinner ('two moderately good German wines'), but he must have drunk quite a bit of it because he drove himself back to East Hendred 'rather gingerly – it is a long time since I have driven myself any distance home after dinner'.[93] He did not normally worry about drink-driving.*

The first real effort to resolve the BBQ came at the Dublin summit in November. Before that, in late October, Jenkins had another 'rather wild and whirling interview with Mrs Thatcher, lasting no less than an hour and fifty minutes':

> She wasn't, to be honest, making a great deal of sense, jumping all over the place, so that I came to the conclusion that her reputation for a well-ordered mind is completely ill-founded.

'On the other hand', he acknowledged, 'she remains quite a nice person, without pomposity'.[95] Crispin Tickell's minute as usual gives the full flavour of her anti-European prejudice and Jenkins' mild attempts to counter it. She began by threatening to withhold payments above a certain level. Jenkins warned her that this would break Community law:

> Mrs Thatcher said that she would fight by the Queensberry rules so long as others did so; but if they did not abide by the rules she would hit below the belt. Mr Jenkins said that he understood Mrs Thatcher's feelings, but the essential was for her to get the result she wanted . . . Something manifestly illegal would not help the British cause.

---

* He had already noted Mrs Thatcher's lack of interest in wine at the Tokyo G7 in June, when he was seated opposite her at dinner. 'I decided during dinner that my new friend Mrs Thatcher . . . doesn't know very much about wine because she refused the Lafite and also asked Giscard whether the Dom Perignon was French champagne. Furthermore when Giscard responded to this . . . by asking whether they had a good wine cellar at Downing Street, she said "Alas, no", whereas the wine cellar in effect is Government hospitality, which is extremely good and far better than anything you ever get from the French Government.'[94]

Then – 'if he could venture a word of warning' – he urged Mrs Thatcher not to expect to get everything she wanted at Dublin. After an argument about precise figures, during which Mrs Thatcher said that 'she would not continue to fill the begging bowls of other members of the Community', Jenkins told her it was a mistake for any member to think it would always be in balance. She disagreed vehemently, saying the CAP and fisheries agreement had been 'catastrophic' for Britain and demanding what benefit Britain had so far got from membership of the EEC (Jenkins, rather weakly, was unable to give a snap answer). Warming to her theme, Mrs Thatcher then alleged that 'the French were trying to take her money and her fish and she would not let them have a penny piece . . . France was the kept woman of Europe.' When Jenkins urged her at least to get Chancellor Schmidt on her side, she agreed that Schmidt was 'the kind of man to do business with', but repeated several times that the others were 'a pack of squealing children' and generally 'a rotten lot'. She thought she had joined a reasonable club, 'but as far as she could see the British were the only decent members of it'. Jenkins 'enquired what the British had done in recent months to show their particular decency'. When Mrs Thatcher replied that they had made their contribution to the Lomé Convention (a trade-and-aid agreement with fifty-odd Third World countries) he answered that so had everyone else.

Repeatedly Mrs Thatcher insisted that she wanted a rebate of £1,000 million and would accept nothing less. 'She knew what she wanted at Dublin and she would get it.' At one point she came close to threatening to leave the Community: 'She could not help thinking that Britain would do better with its own food policy, its own fish, its own industrial policy, its own customs tariff, with of course its particular clout on defence.' 'Mr Jenkins said that Mrs Thatcher should occasionally see the problem through other people's eyes'. He told her that she would do well to get two-thirds of what she was demanding and begged her not to lose the possibility of a substantial victory by saying that it was not enough. He repeated that she would need allies and would be wise to have some constructive points up her sleeve. 'He was not against Mrs Thatcher giving M. Giscard a piece of her mind but she should always seek to avoid finding herself alone.' When he explained that the Commission could only lay possibilities on the table and could not impose a settlement, Mrs Thatcher told him crossly that in that case 'the Commission must be a rotten organisation too'.[96]

Jenkins came out 'slightly reeling after this extremely long tirade', hoping that he had 'put a little sense into her head' on one or two points. 'I was left with no sense that she had any clear strategy for Dublin, except for determination, which is a certain quality I suppose.'[97] A few days later he spoke by telephone to Helmut Schmidt, who said that he had told Mrs Thatcher it was 'impossible' to give her everything she wanted and that 'if she insisted on the full satisfaction of her demands she might find herself obliged to take Britain out of the Community next year'. Jenkins now foresaw 'a real danger that Britain might in the end leave the Community'. This would not only be 'a disaster for Britain', but might also – it is not clear why – 'lead to the break-up of the Community'.[98] Both Schmidt and Giscard claimed to want to help Britain at Dublin, but both insisted that Mrs Thatcher's demands were 'unrealistic'.[99] Jenkins thus found himself rather helplessly caught in the middle. Just before Dublin – and four days after the Dimbleby Lecture, which 'at least had the advantage that I could not worry too much about Dublin': another revelation of where his priorities now lay[100] – he had another session with Mrs Thatcher. This time he found her 'more restrained', adamant that she had no intention of leaving the Community, but still determined that she could accept nothing less than her full demand, confident that the Community would crack before she did. He shared with her some of his own difficulties with Giscard – 'rarely had he seen M. Giscard so casuistical and unimpressive' as at their last meeting – and tried to persuade her that a gesture towards joining the EMS would have 'a big impact'. 'It would greatly help if the British Government could give some meaning to its repeated statements of commitment to Europe.' Mrs Thatcher simply repeated that she was not being unreasonable, but 'she could not take half a loaf'.[101] In his diary, oddly, Jenkins wrote that he 'could not quite make out whether she intended to compromise or not'.[102] But Tickell's minute makes it pretty plain that she would not.

At Dublin on 29–30 November she was offered only £350 million – one-third of her 'loaf' – and duly dug her heels in. She started fairly reasonably ('a bit shrill as usual, but not excessively so') and won 'quite a good initial response'. But then as the evening went on she became 'far too demanding'. In his diary Jenkins analysed her performance:

> Her mistake, which fed on itself subsequently at dinner and indeed the next morning, arose out of her having only one of the three major qualities of an advocate. She has the nerve and determination to win, but she certainly does not have a good understanding of the case against her . . . which means that her

constantly reiterated cry of 'It's my money I want back', strikes an insistently jarring note. 'Voila parle la vraie fille d'épicier', someone . . . said. She also lacks the third quality, which is that of not boring the judge or the jury, and she bored everybody endlessly by only understanding about four out of the fourteen or so points on the British side and repeating each of them twenty-seven times.[103]

What infuriated her was that after a bit no one bothered to argue with her. Giscard ostentatiously read a newspaper while Schmidt pretended to go to sleep. She foolishly – and irrelevantly – antagonised the smaller nations by upbraiding them for their 'pusillanimous' attitude to nuclear weapons. In the end – after she had 'kept us all round the dinner table for four interminable hours' – Jenkins decided that the only possible course was to postpone the issue. Schmidt and Giscard were unwilling to accept this unless Mrs Thatcher promised to approach the next Council (in Luxembourg in April) in a spirit of compromise. Finding her the next morning installed – 'perhaps incarcerated is the better word' – for security reasons in Dublin Castle (in the very room where James Connolly had passed his last night before his execution by the British in 1916), Jenkins managed to persuade her to accept a postponement; then Lord Carrington persuaded her – 'the words coming out of her with almost physical difficulty' – to give the required promise.[104] The leaders left Dublin with relief, to try again another day.*

The 'Bloody British Question' dominated the first five months of 1980. 'Not only I but the whole Community was rarely allowed to think about anything else during this period,' Jenkins wrote later.[106] He gave his 'total priority' to attempting to broker a solution: trying to get the others to contribute and Mrs Thatcher to accept a rebate of around £700 million (in euro-speak, 1,000 million ECUs) or two-thirds of her 'loaf'. In trying to achieve an acceptable compromise he found himself for the first time seeming to play a British hand, which strained his relations with his fellow Commissioners as never before: once he found himself (with Tugendhat) in a minority of two.[107] In a long, gloomy conversation with Schmidt in January – 'well over three hours with no dinner, one or two drinks I thought rather reluctantly brought

---

* Three months later Granada Television staged a dramatised enactment of the Dublin summit, with journalists playing the leaders, which Jenkins thought 'remarkably good'. Sarah Hogg took the part of Mrs Thatcher 'in a way worthy of Sarah Bernhardt', and Schmidt and Giscard were equally convincing. 'Stephen Milligan played me, accurately in substance, but I thought without style.'[105]

in, a few *kleine essen*, and nothing else' – he found that the Chancellor's position had hardened since Dublin.[108] But they decided that the best way of trying to shift Mrs Thatcher might be through Carrington: Jenkins agreed to set up an opportunity for the German Chancellor and the British Foreign Secretary to meet informally over dinner at East Hendred: this took place on 23 February, though Jenkins was not sure it achieved very much.[109] Jenkins himself had several meetings with Carrington during February: over breakfast (never his favourite meal) at the rue de Praetère on the 5th he got Carrington to agree – 'not exactly reluctantly but extremely nervously' – to try to sell Mrs Thatcher a settlement around 1,000 million ECUs.[110] He evidently got nowhere with this since at dinner at the British Embassy in Rome on the 18th they agreed that a solution looked more distant than ever and there was a real possibility of Britain leaving the Community.[111] Meeting Mrs Thatcher again in Downing Street on 17 March, however, Jenkins found her 'a good deal calmer' than previously and formed the impression that she might be willing to contemplate a deal, 'provided the actual phrase was avoided'.[112] In a speech to the political committee of the European Parliament two weeks later he pointed out that the gap between the two sides amounted to no more than about two weeks' cost of the CAP. 'My sum was based on the unspoken premise that there was hardly anybody who was not willing to go to 700 million and I believe the British would settle at 1100 million if not a little less.'[113] For this he was portrayed in the French press as a British agent, which 'though ridiculous and unwarranted was mildly depressing and threw me slightly off balance . . . for a day or two'.[114]

But again Tickell's minute of his 17 March meeting with Mrs Thatcher gives little basis for Jenkins' optimism. She still threatened to break the law if necessary ('If the French could get away with defiance of the Court, why should not the British?'), still declined his plea that she could change the whole atmosphere by announcing her willingness to consider joining the EMS and still insisted that she must have 1,500 million ECUs.[115] Robert Armstrong – her Cabinet Secretary – assured Tickell that Mrs Thatcher 'had great respect for Mr Jenkins. He was one of the few people to whom she listened'; and, on another occasion, that Carrington (unlike most of his colleagues in the Cabinet) was 'pretty robust . . . and Mrs Thatcher was rarely tempted to take him on'.[116] But there was little sign in the run-up to Luxembourg that she was prepared to act on their advice. And so it proved. Mrs Thatcher was initially 'much quieter, less strident, less abrasive than at Dublin'.

In a weary effort to settle the issue, Schmidt and Giscard made her what was widely taken to be a pretty good offer of 2,400 million ECUs over the next two years. But, to general astonishment, when she came back to the table after a long adjournment she again rejected it. When Jenkins tried to persuade her that she was making a great mistake she told him firmly, 'Don't try persuading me, you know I find persuasion very counterproductive.'[117] Schmidt and Giscard – and all the other leaders who had backed the deal – were furious; Jenkins was embarrassed; but Mrs Thatcher, at a time when her domestic policies were becoming deeply unpopular, was delighted with the headlines that her handbag-wielding intransigence won her in the British press. The next day Jenkins left for his week-long visit to India: he thought of cancelling it in view of the crisis in the Community, but was actually glad to get away.

Initially he blamed Mrs Thatcher's senior advisers – Carrington, Armstrong and the head of the Foreign Office, Sir Michael Palliser – for not putting enough pressure on her to accept a good deal. But in the end a settlement was achieved only by outflanking her. The Commission spent the next four weeks working up 'approximately the same deal in somewhat different form', lasting for three years instead of two, which was then put to the Council of Foreign Ministers in Brussels at the end of May.[118] (It was typical of Jenkins' mixing business with pleasure that he spent the previous weekend staying with the Gilmours in Tuscany, and then had Gilmour, Michael Jenkins and another senior Foreign Office man, David Hannay, to dinner at rue de Praetère the evening before: there was some ground for French suspicion that he was hand-in-glove with the British.) But it was still not easy. The Council sat from 3.30 to 8.30 p.m., adjourned for dinner till 11.15, followed by an all-night session during which Jenkins and the Italian Foreign Minister, Emilio Colombo, saw all the other foreign ministers individually or (in the case of the Benelux countries) together, with several intervals 'during which', Jenkins wrote, 'I had to sustain myself with Irish whiskey, which I do not much like, for the bar for some curious reason had run out of all other supplies'. There was one highly technical sticking point, concerning agricultural payments, which Carrington could not accept, but which the others (including Jenkins' three most powerful colleagues in the Commission) all insisted on, which brought them very close to another failure. They resumed after a short break at 7.15 a.m. and finally achieved a breakthrough around 10 a.m. when Emile Noël, 'with a sudden shaft of subtle brilliance', came up with a formula that both sides accepted. 'It was a prodigious achievement,' Jenkins noted with relief, but one 'made necessary only by a stubborn woman's foolish whim a month before. The new settlement was only cosmetically different from that which Mrs Thatcher had turned down at Luxembourg.'[119] He gave credit to Colombo for what he called 'the finest piece of sustained chairmanship I have seen in decades of public life';[120] and to Carrington, who had proved 'a more skilful and sensible negotiator than his head of government. He knew when to settle. She did not.'[121]

He went back to the Berlaymont, had 'a few glasses of champagne to celebrate', followed by a large breakfast at the rue de Praetère at noon, and got back to East Hendred by two o'clock, where he 'slept fairly contentedly all the afternoon'.[122] Meanwhile Carrington and Gilmour went straight to Chequers, where they received a frosty reception. 'Had we been bailiffs arriving to take possession of the furniture,' Gilmour wrote, 'we would probably have been more cordially received.'[123] Furiously Mrs Thatcher accused them of selling Britain down the river and vowed to resign rather than accept their deal. But when they got back to London Gilmour ignored her reaction and briefed the press that they had secured a diplomatic triumph, which the press the next day duly hailed as a victory for her hard bargaining. Grudgingly she had to swallow her objections and accept it. It was still only an interim settlement; but it shelved the issue for three years, by which time two new leaders of the Paris–Bonn axis, François Mitterrand and Helmut Kohl, realised that they would get no peace until Mrs Thatcher got what she wanted and concluded a final deal at Fontainebleau in 1984. By that time Jenkins had long gone from European affairs. But he deserved a lot of credit for the interim achievement. He generously acknowledged the role of Colombo and Carrington; but Carrington gave much of it to him. 'You were splendid on Thursday–Friday,' he wrote on 2 June. 'It would not have been possible without you & your advice and experience . . . I feel as if a black cloud has been lifted off the top of my head. And for you it means a tremendous success as you near the end of your term as President.'[124]

But Jenkins still felt it was an unnecessary row, which not only soured his last year in Brussels but blighted Britain's relations with Europe for years to come. He had hoped that the return of a Conservative government would bring a more positive British attitude to the Community after the ambivalence of Wilson and Callaghan; instead the row over the budget stoked Mrs Thatcher's latent suspicion and contempt for Europe and set her on the Euro-bashing path which led her by the end of the decade – and eventually most of the Tory

Party – into full-blown Europhobia. More widely, Jenkins thought it 'a dreadful diversion of energies', which damaged the whole Community. If only it could have been settled earlier, he reflected in an encomium to Emile Noël on his retirement in 1987, instead of hijacking successive European Councils in fruitless efforts to devise new formulae to bridge a relatively trivial difference, 'I am convinced that Europe could have escaped slipping so far behind both the U.S. and Japan, from technological, growth and employment points of view, as it did in the early 1980s.'[125]

The long-term solution Jenkins was pushing in his last months in office was to reduce the proportion of the budget spent on agriculture – not primarily by cutting back on agriculture, which was politically almost impossible, but by extending Community activity into new areas (industrial, energy, social and regional policy) from which Britain could expect a more equitable return, in pursuit of his goal of a more fully integrated Community. This, he argued in a Winston Churchill memorial lecture in Luxembourg in November 1980, was the next step forward, the only step 'commensurate with the vision of our founding fathers'. There was no future either in 'Europe *à la carte*', of which British non-participation in the EMS was a lamentable example, or in drift. 'Some governments,' he warned, mentioning no names, 'will wish simply to patch things up, shrink from tackling the agricultural problem, and leave the imbalance of the budget to be settled by a continuing series of *ad hoc* arrangements.' 'The most difficult and most desirable course', on the contrary, would involve 'a substantial reshaping of both our revenue system and our expenditure system'. The size of the budget, he proposed, should be tripled – from 0.8 per cent to 2–2.5 per cent of the Community's total GNP – by transferring to the Community industrial and social functions at present funded nationally. The Community's resources should be increased primarily by raising from 1 per cent to perhaps 3 per cent the proportion of each member's VAT payable to it; there might also be a tax on imported oil (which would benefit Britain as an oil exporter). This, as he had stressed in his Florence lecture in 1979, would still be very little compared with a true political union like the United States, where federal expenditure accounted for 25 per cent of GNP; but it would still be enough to transform the EEC from 'an agricultural community with political trimmings' into something much more all-embracing. 'Here is the means,' Jenkins proposed, 'by which we can on the one hand deal with the problems of economic divergence and the future industrial base, and on the other establish that better balance within the budget which is indispensable.'

It could not, he acknowledged, be done overnight. 'But I strongly believe that we should set ourselves on the budgetary path which would permit the development of a Community of this scale and function.'[126]

Mrs Thatcher, unsurprisingly, did not buy this vision at his last meeting with her on 3 November.[127] But neither did anyone else – then or later. With all the developments that have taken place since Jenkins' time – extension of the single market, the Social Chapter and numerous other harmonising directives leading to the evolution of the European Economic Community into the European Union in 1992 and the adoption of the single currency in 2000 – the EU budget still comprises no more than 1 per cent of the now twenty-seven members' total GNP (though the share consumed by agriculture has been gradually reduced). So Jenkins left Brussels at the end of 1980 with a considerable sense of frustration. Even the EMS was not developing as fast as he had hoped after its initially rapid launch. In a valedictory statement to the Luxembourg European Council on 2 December he listed what he saw as his achievements. The EMS was certainly one: 'a modest but substantial' success, which had already made the EEC 'an island of monetary stability' in an unstable world. The directly elected Parliament was another, though after a good start in 1979 when it had attracted a number of major European figures, including several past and future prime ministers, who briefly turned it into something like a real parliament, it quickly relapsed into bickering anonymity.* A third was the Lomé II agreement with Third World countries in which Jenkins himself

---

* He had been 'secretly dreading direct elections,' Jenkins told David Butler, 'and had feared that they would be a terrible fiasco and that the new Parliament would be a dreadful anti-climax'. But initially he felt he had been wrong. 'There was far more life, and one's speeches got a better response. To make a speech to an audience including Brandt, Berlinguer, Craxi, Chirac, Debré, Tindemans and Madame Veil . . . was a quite different experience from speaking to the rather lack-lustre figures in the old Parliament.'[128] But Barbara Castle – who as a lifelong anti-Marketeer had rather surprisingly got herself elected to the new parliament – gave a rather different impression in her memoirs, recalling Jenkins replying to a prim and tedious debate in which members read their speeches onto the record before going off to dinner. 'When Roy rose to reply about 10 pm, there were about five MEPs left in the chamber, including me. Roy was furious and stumbled angrily through his detailed reply.' Years later she teased him: '"You know, Roy, you hated the European Parliament." He replied, with one of those slow smiles of his, "Barbara, you cannot expect me to abandon the beliefs of a lifetime."'[129]

Shortly before he left Brussels he asked her out to dinner, when they reminisced together over three bottles of wine. She felt he regretted leaving his old colleagues.[130] He had been reading her just-published diary of the 1974–6 government and enjoyed his evening with her. 'She was very talkative, slightly tipsy I think is the right word . . . as self-obsessed as ever . . . half sensible and half incorrigible.'[131]

played little part, but which, he congratulated himself, had 'successfully resisted protectionism'.[132]

Enlargement was a fourth achievement about which he was more ambivalent than he could let on. He was always dubious about the imminent admission of Greece ('in my view the least qualified for membership'), despite his high opinion of its Prime Minister, Konstantin Karamanlis, and not much more positive about Spain and Portugal, with whom negotiations were opened under his presidency, which led to their joining in 1986.[133] He had no doubt that they must all be admitted for political reasons, to cement democracy as they emerged from recent dictatorships. 'To keep them out would involve the Community betraying its purposes . . . But I had no illusions,' he confessed in 1987, 'about the additional strain which increases in numbers would put upon the already creaking decision-making process.' He hoped that the accession of new members would make it more necessary to 'strengthen the sinews' of the Community; but he recognised that they could simply make it more unworkable, and he was 'very cautious' about further enlargement, which might end up with nothing but an enlarged customs union.[134] Above all he agreed with Giscard in 1978 that Turkey was not eligible for membership, quite simply because it was 'not a European country'.[135]

'About the future,' he confessed, 'I am apprehensive, although certainly not despairing. I do not think we can stand still . . . Yet as yet there is no consensus emerging between Governments as to how we should move forward.'[136] This underlined, after four years' experience, the limitations of the job he had taken on in 1977. He had hoped to be able to make more of a difference. But the President of the Commission was only the servant of his political masters: he had no independent powers of his own to drive things forward. On first coming into office he had spoken ambitiously of 'grafting the idea of Europe into the lives of the people', so that the individual citizens of the nine nations should become aware of the EEC 'not as an abstraction . . . but as a continuum extending from world influence to job opportunity'.[137] Four years later he confessed in his final press conference that he had not succeeded in changing the image of the Commission as a remote and irrelevant bureaucracy. In a valedictory report the Brussels correspondent of *The Times* voiced the disappointment of those who had expected him to make a bigger impact:

Those who had hailed his arrival in Brussels . . . looked to him for more than the role of a clubbable honest broker. They were hoping for a President who would be prepared to court the wrath of member governments in defence of policies that amounted to more than the lowest common denominator of what was acceptable in national capitals. To the disappointment of many, Mr Jenkins seldom put his head above the parapet.[138]

Jenkins rejected this criticism. He had learned the hard way, he said, that 'you have to proceed by persuading governments. It would be nice to think that you could operate by generating a tide of public opinion that would sweep governments aside. But that is an illusion.'[139] What success he had was indeed achieved by working directly with, and on, the heads of government. From that point of view his victory over Giscard in establishing his right to be present and play an active role not only at EEC but also at international summits was perhaps his most important legacy to his successors. His tireless travelling and high-level networking undoubtedly raised the profile of Europe on the world stage. Jenkins never pretended to take much interest in running or reforming the Brussels machine – though here again it was the heads of government who in his last year blocked the implementation of the Spierenburg Report, which recommended a number of sensible improvements. But the EEC had had faceless technocrats before – such as his predecessor François Ortoli – good at oiling the bureaucratic wheels, but lacking the ambition or the political weight to do much more. Jenkins was appointed as a politician, and as a politician he probably had as much success as could be expected with no independent base of his own, wholly dependent on whatever personal influence he could bring to bear on Schmidt and Giscard, Callaghan and Mrs Thatcher. He ducked the problem of agricultural spending, which did not excite him. But he did launch, in defiance of the cautious wisdom of the time, one big idea and saw it carried at least partly into effect. That is not a lot to show for four years: but that is the nature of international organisations. It is arguably a waste of a major politician to condemn him to the frustrations of Brussels; and yet it takes a major politician to achieve even as little as Jenkins did. Of his five successors, only Jacques Delors has made more impact.

'I have lost a little of my superficial European idealism,' he confessed. 'But I have lost none of my underlying conviction that a united Europe is essential for itself, for every one of the member states, and for the world.'[140] 'I am glad I came,' he told his farewell press conference on 5 January 1981, 'and glad that I did the job. I would not have wished to spend the past four years otherwise.'[141] At the end of his life he still looked back on them as 'on balance a well worthwhile segment of my life'.[142] But he had never seen Brussels as more than an interlude. And the next day – just two months after his sixtieth birthday – he returned to Britain to embark on the boldest gamble of his political life.

20 The Gang of Four

A FTER the Dimbleby Lecture, Jenkins still had thirteen months more to serve in Brussels. It was an anxious year. While the public response to Dimbleby had been encouraging, confirming his sense that there was a large untapped reservoir of support for some sort of middle way between the extremes of Thatcherism and Bennery, it was not at all clear how or whether he could channel it into an effective political movement. On the one hand he had aroused a considerable sense of anticipation which his potential followers now expected him to follow up. 'Until now,' one correspondent wrote to *The Times*, 'I believed that Roy Jenkins was the best Prime Minister we never had. Now, I believe that he is the best Prime Minister we will have.'[1] Opinion polls still suggested – as they had done since the early Seventies – that a hypothetical alliance of Labour moderates and Liberals would attract substantial support. On the other hand there was widespread scepticism at Westminster and in Fleet Street first about whether such an opportunity really existed outside the fantasies of naive herbivores; and, second, about whether Jenkins, a notoriously pleasure-loving Brussels fat cat who had retired hurt from the domestic dogfight four years earlier, had the stomach or the stamina to re-enter it when a more comfortable life in academia or the City beckoned. He sometimes doubted it himself. While still heavily preoccupied in Brussels with the wretched British budget problem, therefore, he devoted much attention on his regular visits back to Britain during 1980 to sounding out potential allies, testing the water and weighing up his options.

There were four or five separate groups of possible supporters whose different agendas he somehow needed to hold in balance. First, he kept in close touch with David Steel, who he hoped would be able to deliver some sort of arrangement with the Liberals. Jenkins always recognised that the Liberals already occupied a substantial bridgehead in the centre ground – up to 19 per cent in 1974, still nearly 14 per cent in 1979 – and, unlike most Labour people, he was personally well-disposed to them: some of his best friends were Liberals and he had always been happy to call himself a liberal. Second, there was a core of long-standing Jenkinsites from the Wilson years – Dick Taverne, David Marquand, Michael Barnes and others, now out of Parliament but still loyal to him as their unquestioned leader: to these could be added Anthony Lester, John Harris (now President of the Parole Board, but still Jenkins' most trusted adviser) and Matthew Oakeshott. The third group was a somewhat maverick collection of virulently anti-left Labour councillors and failed parliamentary candidates who had already broken with Labour and were impatient for him to raise the standard of a new democratic party of the centre-left. Fourth, he knew that no new party would have a serious chance of success without a significant defection of sitting Labour MPs, including one or two frontbenchers – specifically Shirley Williams and Bill Rodgers. Finally Jenkins also hoped to attract some 'one nation' Tories unhappy with the direction in which Mrs Thatcher was leading their party.

He had already established a basis of understanding with Steel four months before the Dimbleby Lecture, when Steel came to dinner in Brussels in July. Now they had another long meeting at East Hendred at the beginning of January 1980. 'He is very agreeable, sensible and curiously mature,' Jenkins recorded in his diary. (He was also struck by the fact that Steel looked remarkably like Hayden Phillips.) It was at this meeting, according to Jenkins, that they agreed that there was 'no question of me or anybody else joining the Liberal Party'. There would be more chance of securing a significant number of Labour defectors, and Labour voters, by forming a new social democratic party, working in alliance with but separate from the Liberals – but with the option, if things went well, of 'an amalgamation after a general election'. This diary entry makes it clear that more than a year before the formation of the SDP Jenkins already anticipated a merger at quite an early date. For his part, Steel claimed to have 'overwhelming' Liberal support for this strategy.[2] Thanking Jenkins for a 'splendid lunch', he wrote that he was planning an article for the *Sunday Times* outlining 'the broad agenda for a Government of National Reform', which should help to 'keep nervous Liberals happy, since most of it will flow from established Liberal policies'. He conceded that there were 'a number of anti-social democrat noises coming from Liberals, but I hope to deal with the appropriate bodies in the spring'.[3] Discounting Jo Grimond's sour comments about Dimbleby, he said that Grimond was just jealous because Jenkins looked as if he might succeed in doing what he had been urging unsuccessfully for the past twenty years.[4] Jenkins and Steel kept in touch during 1980, but they did not need to meet very often because they both knew exactly the outcome they were hoping to achieve.

Jenkins met his 'Jenkinsite' supporters for what he called 'a plotting meeting' followed by dinner at Brooks's a few days before Christmas 1979: Taverne, Marquand, Barnes and Lester were joined by two still-sitting MPs, Bob Maclennan and, 'unexpectedly but extremely agreeably', John Horam (MP for Gateshead West). They were all more or less enthusiastic, Jenkins recorded, and all thought a split 'inevitable and desirable'; but there was already some difference of emphasis about whether they should be appealing simply to disaffected Labour supporters or trying to cast their net more widely.[5] The least enthusiastic at this stage was Lester, who wrote to Jenkins a few days later pressing the case for 'a new centre-left party led by you and Shirley and Bill, not a new centre-right party led by you alone': the latter, he warned, would lead nowhere 'beyond a successful by-election and the Liberal Party'.[6]

The immediate shock troops for a breakaway from Labour seemed to be offered by a prickly pair of Greater London councillors, Douglas Eden and Stephen Haseler, both polytechnic lecturers, who in 1975 had founded an outfit called the Social Democratic Alliance to fight the influence of the hard left. (Haseler had earlier written a book about Gaitskell's battle with the left in the early Sixties.) After the Dimbleby Lecture they were joined by Jim Daly, a former chairman of the GLC transport committee; Clive Lindley, a wealthy businessman who had made his money in motorway catering; and Colin Phipps, an oil geologist who had been MP for Dudley for five years before losing his seat in 1979. Jenkins met these 'conspirators' in different combinations over some months for exploratory talks. 'They were all quite sensible and I hope they are all right,' he noted slightly nervously after one such meeting in January 1980. 'It is going to be very difficult to manoeuvre everyone into position.'[7] During the year the two groups came together to form a Centre Party Preparation Committee (CPPC) to prepare the ground before Jenkins' return from Brussels at the beginning of 1981.[8] But a clear division soon emerged between those who wanted to move quickly and those who wanted to wait for the optimum moment to attract a significant number of heavyweight defectors; in the first camp were Haseler, Eden, Phipps and Barnes, in the second Marquand, Daly, Lindley and John Harris, with Taverne somewhere between the two. Marquand warned in August that a preparing committee would only scare away potential defectors, forcing Rodgers and Williams to distance themselves, while Eden and Haseler were distrusted by the Liberals. Apart from his own natural caution, Jenkins was always more likely to be influenced by those he liked. Phipps he found 'opinionated' and 'tiresome';[9] while Haseler and Eden looked like 'hard-faced men who have done badly out of the Labour Party. The difficulty is that they are interested in spoiling tactics, which I am not.' At a difficult meeting that he and Jennifer attended at Phipps' flat in July, it was agreed to make no overt move till after the Labour conference. 'In the meantime,' he wrote, 'the SDA could do what they liked as long as they did not implicate me, and those who are longing for action, like Mickey Barnes and Colin Phipps and maybe Dick, could associate themselves with them to the extent that they liked.'[10]* He agreed with Marquand and Harris that he should wait for Rodgers and Shirley Williams to reach their personal breaking points.

Jenkins knew from the outset that he needed Bill and Shirley, though his relationship with the two of them was very different. Bill Rodgers had been his most faithful lieutenant since Gaitskellite days – secretary of the Fabian Society when Jenkins was its chairman, organiser of CDS in the early 1960s, one of his junior ministers at the Treasury in 1969–70, unofficial whip of the pro-European rebels in 1971, organiser of his leadership campaign in 1976. It was as difficult to imagine Jenkins launching any major initiative without Rodgers' support as it was to imagine Rodgers ultimately failing to follow Jenkins wherever he led. Rodgers looked up to Jenkins as his 'elder brother' in politics;[12] while Jenkins characterised Rodgers somewhat unfairly in his diary as 'above all a fighting colonel . . . He is a very good short-term operator, but very much needs somebody to give him the orders and tell him what is the overall objective.'[13] (It should be said that he soon revised this view and came to consult Rodgers almost daily, paying close attention to his advice.) While Jenkins had been in Brussels, however, Rodgers

---

* In an addition to Colin Phipps' *Times* obituary in 2009, Douglas Eden gave the SDA version of these tensions. At what turned out to be the last meeting of the group, Eden wrote, Phipps attacked Jenkins' reluctance to found a new party. 'It turned out that Roy preferred a Parliamentary realignment under his leadership that could take power quickly, rather than lead a movement in the country that could replace Labour. Colin pressed him so much that he lost his temper (the only occasion I ever saw this happen), informed the group that he would not meet them again and stormed out of the house. Thanks to Colin at least we all knew where we stood.'[11] But Jenkins' diary makes no mention of this episode.

had become a Cabinet minister in his own right (as Transport Secretary) and increasingly sceptical as to whether Jenkins was 'a big enough risk-taker' or had the stomach for 'the massive job which would be entailed in trying to mobilise a centre consensus'.[14] With a five-figure majority in Stockton-on-Tees he was deeply rooted in the Labour Party and had no intention of being driven out of it. In an important speech in South Wales a week after Jenkins' Dimbleby Lecture, however, he warned that Labour had 'a year, not much longer, in which to save itself'.[15] On his way back to London he stopped off at East Hendred, where Shirley Williams also came, and the three of them established 'a fairly good identity of view'.[16] But neither Rodgers nor Williams was yet ready to break with Labour, and Jenkins was careful not to push them. On 3 January 1980 Rodgers wrote one of his long letters to Jenkins stressing that his hope was still to save the Labour party, not to found a fourth party.

'This may prove impossible,' he conceded, 'and my own optimism continues to diminish. But unless some of us can say – and show – that we have tried and failed, we shall not carry with us the troops that we shall need if the break should come.' He was afraid that people like Dick Taverne risked discrediting the idea by jumping the gun. He was also wary of the Liberals: he recognised that an electoral pact would be essential, but wanted only 'an arms-length relationship' with them, and ultimately to absorb them. To succeed, a fourth party must be unambiguously a party of the left and aim to take 'over 90% of the existing Labour vote'. 'I'm not sure whether we agree about this,' he concluded. 'But I have no confidence in (and no great warmth towards) a party of the Centre. It would not work . . . A Fourth Party will only succeed if it sets out to usurp the traditional Labour vote.' Otherwise it would only split the left, to the benefit the Tories.[17] A few days later he assured Giles Radice that he had no interest in a centre party: 'A breakaway party would not get anywhere unless it could take people like me [that is, Radice] and Phillip Whitehead with it.'[18]

Shirley Williams had never been so close to Jenkins. She felt great respect for him, had fought for many of the same causes in Cabinet and on the NEC, but was never a fully paid-up Jenkinsite: an archetypal bluestocking, she moved in quite different circles and rather disapproved of his chummy male dining clubs and country house weekends. He in turn admired her courage, her passion and her common touch, but found her disorganisation and chronic lack of punctuality maddening. In March she came to Brussels to make a speech and stayed the night at the rue de Praetère, where she and Jenkins sat up talking – 'unbelievably' – till four in the morning (Jenkins normally disliked going to bed much after midnight). He felt she was 'in a sense lonely, not that she does not have plenty of people around, but perhaps people she can't talk to very easily'. She had been half-persuaded by Denis Healey that if he won the Labour leadership when Callaghan retired he was ready to be 'an absolutely ruthless social democratic leader' and take on the left; but having lost her seat in May she was not sure she wanted to stay in politics – she might be more tempted by something like the chairmanship of the BBC or a visiting professorship at Harvard.[19]* Of this meeting Jenkins wrote in his memoirs: 'I never came away from an encounter with her without being encouraged, bewitched and inspirited, yet also totally mystified about what she was going to do next.'[21] Later in the year, however, when she was still undecided about what to do, he wrote less kindly that 'She was as engaging and muddled as ever . . . but as is always the case with Shirley one never knows quite where she is, not because of any dishonesty on her part but because she does not think things out schematically and is almost incapable of making up her mind.'[22] Nevertheless she had such a following in the Labour Party that she was the recruit Jenkins was keenest to secure.

Finally, in pursuit of his broader view of what the new party should aim to be, Jenkins was anxious to try to recruit some of the Tory 'wets' who were most unhappy with Mrs Thatcher's policies – above all Ian Gilmour, with whom he lunched at Brooks's on 3 January. Gilmour was in principle sceptical about a centre party, yet thought it 'well within the bounds of possibility that we might achieve success more quickly than is within the bounds of my imagination'. If Conservative support collapsed, they might even win the next election:

> He would obviously be very torn in these circumstances, though I didn't raise this with him in any way and wouldn't have dreamed of doing so. He thought we would get no Tory members of the

---

* She came bearing 'some sort of message' from Denis Healey offering Jenkins the Foreign Office in a future Labour government. He told her that 'apart from my having burnt too many Labour Party boats, I really could not stand being Foreign Secretary under Denis. He would lecture one every day on every subject under the sun.' This did not mean, he added in his diary, that he would not serve under anyone. 'I could serve under David Steel or under Shirley herself, I think, but not with somebody quite as pedagogic and know-all and lecturing as Denis.'[20]

H of C in the short run while the Government was in, but would get an awful lot of Tory votes and probably a lot of Tory members after a successful breakthrough and after the Government had collapsed.[23]

Gilmour was letting his loathing of his leader run away with his judgement. When he and Caroline came to lunch at East Hendred three months later he still confidently expected Mrs Thatcher's government to collapse. In that event he hoped to see Jenkins join forces with Ted Heath: 'You and Ted would be a formidable combination.' 'He also indicated that while he probably could not do anything until after the election he would be very pulled towards it.'[24] In June Heath too came to lunch at East Hendred on his way to his boat in the Solent; but he was full of the report of the Brandt Commission (on Third World development) on which he had sat, and showed very little interest in Jenkins' plans. The truth was that Tories like Heath and Gilmour were so sure that Mrs Thatcher was a temporary aberration who could not last long that they never thought seriously of jumping ship. The SDP did eventually draw a lot of its members from disillusioned Tories; but it was one of the weaknesses of Jenkins' social approach to politics that he only really thought of recruiting his friends at the top of the Tory party who – unlike their Labour equivalents – were not going to leave a party which they were confident would in time come back to them. Though several others had serious talks about the possibility of joining, both before and after the party was launched in 1981, only one Tory MP – the member for North-West Norfolk, Christopher Brocklebank-Fowler – actually did so, and he was a lone maverick who brought no followers with him.

In much the same way Jenkins failed to see the importance of attracting some serious trade union support. John Grigg – one 'wet' Tory who did join the SDP – wrote to him the day after Dimbleby warning shrewdly that 'Unless a Labour split involves the industrial as well as the political wing of the movement it will be doomed, as in 1931 . . . So long as the trade unions remain politically monolithic, there is no hope of making any change in the system effective.'[25] This was absolutely right. In practice, however, Jenkins' chances of winning trade union support were pretty minimal, as was exemplified by the one possible recruit he did attempt to woo: the robustly right-wing electricians' leader, Frank Chapple, with whom he lunched at Brooks's in September. 'He had recently been excluded from key committees of the TUC,' Jenkins recorded, 'but was nevertheless in a cocky, aggressive, agreeable mood':

> He agrees with me on absolutely every aspect of policy, but still does not want to contemplate a break . . . He believes that everything can be won by a tough battle from within, including committing the Labour Party to a nuclear missile in everybody's back garden almost. Curious that he should have this element of political unrealism. It was nonetheless well worth seeing him, probably a pity I did not do so earlier.[26]

After six months of these private soundings Jenkins put up another trial balloon in a speech to the Parliamentary Press Gallery on 9 June. This was a less friendly audience than the BBC's invited guest list in November, mainly composed of 'hard-boiled journalists seasoned by a few parliamentary guests like Neil Kinnock'.[27] He gave them a more sharply political but somewhat muddled speech, which went a good deal closer to announcing his intention to form a new party, but was, as a result, less well received than his more elegant Dimbleby *tour d'horizon* seven months earlier. Broadly it repeated his previous analysis that the existing two-party structure, rooted in outdated class allegiance and entrenched by the first-past-the-post voting system, not only militated against sensible and consistent policies but no longer represented the aspirations of a more sophisticated and less tribal electorate. He began by describing the weight and quality of the mail he had received from members of the public after his Dimbleby Lecture, which had convinced him of the need to see the political battlefield in much more fluid terms than hitherto, expressed in a characteristic metaphor:

> It is inadequate to see British politics as two and a half bottles, one labelled Conservative, the next Labour, the third Liberal, and then to think in the fixed quantities of exactly how much you could pour out of each of the first two bottles and put alongside the third. We must think much more in terms of untapped and unlabelled quantities – and when you look at the low level of participation today . . . there is no reason to doubt that they exist.

But then the bulk of the speech was aimed squarely at Labour's further 'lurch to the left' since leaving office. The NEC's latest policy document, entitled *Peace, Jobs, Freedom*, adopted at a special conference at Wembley at the end of May, had saddled Labour with what Jenkins called 'a near neutralist and unilateralist' defence posture which would 'make meaningless our continued membership of NATO', and 'a commitment to practical non-cooperation with the European Community leading in all likelihood to a firm proposal for complete withdrawal in the near future', which together amounted to 'the total reversal . . . of the carefully-built and democratically endorsed long-term direction of our economic and foreign policy'. With plans for 'a massive further extension of the public sector' and a squeeze on private enterprise unmatched in any other democratic country, this was not 'by any stretch of the imagination a social democratic programme', nor did it 'represent the views of the great majority of moderate left voters'.

This analysis was clearly directed at Rodgers, Williams and the others still hesitating about breaking with Labour. But if this emphasis could be taken to imply that Jenkins' aim was merely to woo disenchanted Labour voters by re-creating a more Atlanticist, pro-European and enterprise-friendly Labour party, his concluding paragraphs reverted to his more ambitious vision, couched in another graphic metaphor, which over the coming months was a gift to the cartoonists. Likening his proposed new party to an experimental aeroplane, he admitted that the forces of political inertia might be too strong:

> The likelihood before the start of most adventures is that of failure. The experimental plane may finish up a few fields from the end of the runway . . . But the reverse could occur and the experimental plane could soar in the sky. If that is so, it could go further and more quickly than few now imagine [*sic*], for it would carry with it great and now untapped reserves of political energy and commitment.

He ended with a historical flourish by recalling George Dangerfield's once-famous book about the political crises of 1910–14, *The Strange Death of Liberal England*. 'That death,' he suggested, 'caught people rather unawares':

> Do not discount the possibility that in a few years' time someone may be able to write at least equally convincingly of the strange and rapid revival of liberal social democratic Britain.[28]

Jenkins had originally written 'Liberal and Social Democratic Britain', with capital letters and a connecting conjunction, which would have emphasised cooperation between the existing third party and his hypothetical fourth party, which in his diary he invariably called a 'centre' party. But this was too explicit for Shirley Williams, on whom he had tried out the speech over the phone the day before. That very day, protesting too vehemently her determination not to leave the Labour party, Williams had declared in a radio interview that a centre party would have 'no roots, no principles, no philosophy and no values' – a foolish statement, which it was instantly predictable she would live to regret.[29] But Jenkins – 'thinking that if Paris was worth a mass, Shirley was certainly worth an "and" (and a lower case)' – accepted her amendment, 'after which we rang off on terms of great amity. She said she was sure we would all be together in six months or so.'[30]

As it turned out, they were. But in the short term Jenkins' latest feeler was a damp squib. On television that evening Denis Healey – still seen by most wavering social democrats as the last best hope of saving Labour – dismissed it robustly as 'absolute bunk', quoting Shirley Williams' rash words effectively in support. Most commentators still believed that the stand against the left had to be made within the Labour party; few believed that Labour would actually split or, if it did, that the right would rally to Jenkins' centrist standard. Over the weekend Shirley Williams, Bill Rodgers and David Owen had responded jointly to a move to commit Labour definitely to leaving the EEC by insisting that 'there are some of us who will not accept a choice between socialism and Europe. We will choose both.' Without these three, *The Times* mocked, the new venture would appear simply as 'Mr Jenkins' dining club going public'.[31] There was still a general refusal to take his musings seriously. 'Almost everything Mr Jenkins says is true,' *The Economist* conceded. 'It is all magnificent, but it is not war.'[32] The rudest comment came from the *Spectator:*

The residual image Mr Jenkins conveys is that of a fat, flabby and nearly-extinct bird endeavouring to fly but lacking the muscle and momentum to take flight. Mr Jenkins might soar: he is altogether more likely to crash.

A fourth party, the writer concluded, could only fragment the centre. If Jenkins really wanted to strengthen it, he should join the Liberals 'and give them the helping hand they need. It can only be ambition and self-conceit which prevent him from volunteering to serve under Mr Steel.'[33] Amid the general ridicule just one voice came to his defence – David Steel himself, who wrote calmly: 'Roy Jenkins is simply ahead of his' time.'[34]*

Thrown by this response, Jenkins fell into 'a thorough gloom', feeling that the speech had been 'a grave mistake'. Unlike the Dimbleby Lecture, he wrote later, he felt he had misjudged the moment and left himself 'stranded halfway up a cliff, committed to some dramatic political action, but lacking the strength and resources single-handedly to launch a new political movement'.[36] If no major allies would join him he began to wonder if he should not just quietly join the Liberals after all. This mood lasted the rest of the summer, exacerbated by ill health – the colon pain which affected him from June to September – and miserable weather. Jennifer remembered this as the one time in his life when he was seriously depressed.

But then from the late summer things began to move again in his direction. First David Owen, who had hitherto been some way behind the other two, joined again with Bill Rodgers and Shirley Williams to write a letter published in the *Guardian* on 1 August warning that, while they did not support a centre party, they might, if Labour continued on its present course, be forced to consider setting up 'a new democratic socialist party'.[37] From now on they were dubbed in the press the 'Gang of Three'. The tipping point for Owen had been the experience of being shouted down when he tried to make an anti-unilateralist speech at the special conference in May. He had shallower roots in Labour than the other two, and was now the most impatient to make a break. When he and Debbie came to lunch at East Hendred on 31 August, Jenkins noted 'a remarkable change in him since the last time I had talked to him' the year before: Owen had not only 'stiffened and toughened a lot' vis-à-vis Labour, but was personally 'a great deal more agreeable' than he had been since before he became Foreign Secretary.[38] The first was undoubtedly true, but the second was a misjudgement.

---

* The extent to which Jenkins had been written off even by some who had once admired him is illustrated by the scornful comments of Bernard Donoughue, who told the *Sunday Times* journalist Hugo Young that he was 'a pretty well dead duck. Just unwilling to do the necessary. Always has been. A fatal flaw of social aspiration, elitism etc. Thought the brilliant Roy Jenkins could get anywhere on his own while still preferring Covent Garden to the National Union of Railwaymen . . . He is a 60-year-old failure who no-one wants to get committed to. Whereas he could have been the best Prime Minister we ever had, if he had any real idea of political seriousness.' He might possibly win a by-election as a Liberal. 'But there is no serious chance for a man so cut off from all roots and organisation.'[35]

Labour's annual conference at Blackpool at the end of September pushed the 'Gang of Three' closer to the exit by definitely adopting the unilateralist, anti-European and nationalisation policies proposed in *Peace, Jobs, Freedom* plus the full Bennite agenda of constitutional changes to require mandatory reselection of MPs and an electoral college to elect the leader – measures designed to ensure the left's control of the party in perpetuity, while their senior Shadow Cabinet colleagues who should have led the fightback (Denis Healey, Roy Hattersley, Eric Varley, Gerald Kaufman, Merlyn Rees) all kept their heads down. Jenkins watched the first day on television in Kensington Park Gardens with satisfaction:

> Benn madder than ever, the conference in an ugly mood, Shirley in a great fighting mood [at a fringe rally] . . . No great tugs upon the heart strings, but great interest and things look as though they are going worse even than I thought they would.[39]

The day after the conference ended Bill and Sylvia Rodgers invited themselves to lunch at East Hendred. Jenkins had spent the intervening days in Brussels with a flying visit to Madrid, but as the pace increased he was now spending more weekends in Britain. He was still not confident that Rodgers was ready to give up on Labour, but thought him 'certainly a lot nearer to it than nine months ago', which reassured him that his strategy of waiting for the 'Gang of Three' had been the right one. 'I certainly feel much easier about the political situation and whatever it may hold. I do not feel myself boxed in, in the way that I did in June and July and early August.'[40] His health was better too. Back in Brussels he revealed his returning confidence over lunch at the Berlaymont with a group of British lobby correspondents, one of whom – Fred Emery of *The Times* – wrote it up as a front-page story ('Mr Jenkins Paves Way for a Political Comeback'), reporting that he believed that events had vindicated his Dimbleby Lecture and now planned a further series of speeches:

> Mr Jenkins . . . intends to set out his view of a true and sensible alternative to both Mrs Margaret Thatcher's monetarism and the mass nationalisation policies embraced by the Labour Party Conference before deciding whether to form a new political grouping in alliance with the Liberal Party.[41]

This, Jenkins wrote in his diary, was 'quite satisfactorily put from my point of view'.[42]

The next day – seventeen months after losing office – Callaghan finally announced his resignation, launching a critical leadership election. For most of that time the wavering social democrats had seen Healey's succession as the moment when the fight to regain control of the party would begin. Healey was seen as a tough right-winger, a former Defence Secretary and former Chancellor of undoubted prime-ministerial calibre, who would bring the party back to its traditional values. In his letter to Jenkins after Dimbleby, Rodgers had confessed to a sneaking hope that Healey might make him Shadow Chancellor.[43] Shirley Williams had come to Brussels in March with an olive branch from Healey offering Jenkins the Foreign Office in a future government. Owen had been a junior minister under Healey at the MoD and was personally closer to him than either of the others. By October, however, they had all lost any belief that Healey would take on the left: behind his bluff image he had already compromised too much and still seemed more concerned with appeasing the left in order to secure the leadership. When a delegation of MPs from the Manifesto Group of moderate MPs went to see him, he told them bluntly that they had nowhere else to go. He was wrong. By his failure at this moment to give the leadership they were looking for, Healey was, as Peter Jenkins later wrote, 'effectively one of the founders of the SDP'.[44] Briefly Rodgers thought of standing against him.[45] Owen talked of abstaining.[46] So long as Healey was the probable next leader, however, they felt obliged to stick with Labour and give him the chance to prove them wrong. Opposed only by Peter Shore and John Silkin, he would probably have won. But then Michael Foot was persuaded to throw his hat into the ring. A romantic veteran of the Bevanite left, loved even by the right, Foot was seen as the one man who could unite the divided party – even though scarcely anyone saw him as a credible Prime Minister. On the first ballot on 4 November he took eighty-three votes to Healey's 112. Silkin with thirty-eight votes and Shore with thirty-two both dropped out, switching their support to Foot, which raised – Jenkins noted from Brussels – 'a perfectly good possibility' of Foot beating Healey in the second ballot: 'A rather exciting prospect.'[47] A week later he rushed back to the rue de Praetère after entertaining the Norwegian Prime Minister to hear the result – Foot 139, Healey 129 – with undisguised delight:

> Sensational result: Foot elected by ten votes. I cannot pretend that I was other than elated, as it clearly opened up a much greater prospect of political realignment. Dined with Jennifer at home, discussing this urgently and excitedly.[48]

This was a turning point. It was suspected (and later admitted) that at least six MPs who had already decided to abandon Labour voted for Foot to give themselves a pretext for what they were going to do anyway, deliberately saddling Labour with a weak and unelectable leader as a cynical parting gift. It is just possible that Healey, had he been narrowly elected, would have changed his tune sufficiently to prevent the SDP defection. But it is equally arguable that he had already sold the pass. What is certain is that Foot's election made it much easier for the Gang of Three to conclude that Labour was beyond salvation and start firming up their plans accordingly. Foot's election was not quite, as David Owen called it, 'the final straw': that did not come till January 1981.[49] But in the meantime they all signalled their disaffection in different ways. Owen declined to stand again for the Shadow Cabinet and started actively gathering a group of potential defectors. Rodgers did stand and was re-elected, but then declined the uncongenial portfolios (Northern Ireland and Health) that Foot offered him. Shirley Williams stayed on the NEC for the moment, but announced that she would not stand again for her former seat in Stevenage. Meanwhile Jenkins watched and waited, like a fat spider, for them to fall into his web.

He was prepared to wait for them; but they were much less sure that they wanted to join him. The problem which blighted the SDP from the outset was that the two streams which eventually came together to form it – Jenkins and his friends on the one hand, none of them any longer in Parliament; the Gang of Three and their handful of embattled MPs on the other – had different ideas about the sort of party they were trying to set up. Jenkins, effectively out of the Labour party for the past four years and impressed by the vague public yearning revealed by his Dimbleby Lecture – frankly wanted a centre party that, in alliance with the Liberals, would tap new reservoirs of support from those who felt unrepresented by either of the old class-based parties. Rodgers, Owen and Williams, however – still constrained by emotional loyalty to Labour and obligations to their constituency parties – needed to believe that they were not betraying their Labour allegiance, merely seeking to preserve it in a new form: they wanted nothing to do with a centre party, but insisted that they were in the business of creating a new Labour party, purged of the dogmatism, utopianism and intolerance of the Bennites. Jenkins knew that he needed a substantial breakaway from Labour to make his venture credible; but he did not want them to define it. They equally did not want to be seen to be merely joining him: they welcomed Jenkins' somewhat lofty blessing, but they had all regarded him since 1976 as a bit of a spent force. They did not share his belief in untapped reservoirs of uncommitted support or his enthusiasm for the Liberals. They were still fighting inside the Labour Party and – if they were eventually driven to leave it – for the soul of the Labour party.

David Owen in particular thought Jenkins a liability to any new venture they might found. 'The essential,' he told a friend in America, 'is that a new party is not cast in Roy Jenkins' image.'[50] But image rather than policy was what his objection to Jenkins was all about. Owen liked to see himself as more 'radical' than Jenkins; but on any normal left–right scale he was actually more right-wing – as the evolution of his thinking after 1983 rapidly confirmed. With the shallowest Labour roots of any of the Gang of Four and even less connection with the unions than Jenkins, it was nonsense for Owen to pretend to be any sort of socialist: ideologically rootless but temperamentally impatient, seeking a reforming, egalitarian, democratic party that would be strong on defence and not in hock to the unions, he should really have been a prime candidate for a centre party.* But what mattered more to him than any policy was that the new party should appear young, fresh, dynamic, modern and decisive, with none of the 'fudging and mudging' he had despised in the Labour party; in other words, a party formed in his own brash image. He frankly thought Jenkins by 1980 an old, lazy, sybaritic has-been, while under the influence of his American wife he saw himself – in Bill Rodgers' later view – as 'J.F. Kennedy reincarnated'.[53] 'David's unease at Roy's re-emergence onto the political stage,' Rodgers wrote shrewdly, 'was rather like the resentment of an adolescent boy on discovering that his rejected father is dangerously attractive to his girlfriend and still a fast mover on the football field.'[54] In December, Owen circulated to Williams and Rodgers a ten-page memorandum on how they must try to prevent Jenkins becoming leader by default. 'The whole key to success for any initiative,' he insisted, 'is that it is new, different, young and fresh-looking.'[55] 'From the beginning,' he claimed in 1984, 'I knew it would have been better without involving Roy . . . In the

---

* During 1980, when he was still hoping to save the Labour party, Owen wrote a big rambling book entitled *Face the Future* in which he tried to formulate his ideas. Published in January 1981, three days after the Limehouse Declaration, it was still studded with references to 'socialism'. For the second edition later that year these were all changed to 'social democracy'. In his memoirs he claimed that *Face the Future* foreshadowed his later ideas on competition and internal markets.[51] But Bill Rodgers thought it 'confused and almost unreadable'.[52]

beginning it was truly a Gang of Three and we should have kept it that way.'[56]

On 29 November he went to East Hendred to tell Jenkins this to his face:

> He told me firmly for the first time that he was prepared to form a new party, and that he thought Shirley would come too, though he was curiously less sure about Bill. He was also . . . very firmly geared up to tell me that he thought that Shirley should be leader . . . because of her great popularity etc. And it was made clear that it was in his view to be not a centre party but a 'Socialist International' party, in other words to some extent my joining them rather than vice-versa.

Jenkins played him skilfully, careful not to seem to assume the leadership; but in his diary he was still quietly confident that things were going his way:

> We will see how that works out, but at any rate it is a great advance which no-one would have thought possible some time ago. There will now be a real break in the parliamentary party, and I may well get, at the end of the day, much more the sort of party I want than the sort of party that for the moment he wants. But we will see.[57]

In trying to marginalise the older man, Owen underestimated Jenkins' undimmed competitiveness. When he and Jennifer had lunched at the Owens' country house in Wiltshire in October, Jenkins noted characteristically that he had 'played three games of ping-pong after lunch, again satisfactorily beating them both'.[58] It was the same in politics: once fully committed to launching his project, Jenkins played to win.

When he finally came back from Brussels, the Gang of Three formally became the Gang of Four. After spending Christmas and the New Year at East Hendred, Jenkins returned to Brussels on 5–6 January 1981 to clear his office and hand over to his successor, the former Luxembourg Prime Minister Gaston Thorn, with a round of farewell meetings, lunches and dinners – lunch with his retiring Commissioners, dinner with his *cabinet* and a final lunch at Comme Chez Soi with Maxine

Jenkins. But then he was back in Britain to launch the greatest gamble of his life. Though Owen still tried to speak of Jenkins attending 'our' meetings, his seniority as a former Chancellor and deputy leader, plus the drama of his return and his well-trailed intention to launch some new initiative, ensured that all the press anticipation and speculation centred on Jenkins. The 'Gang' met four times in each other's houses during January to formalise their coming together. The first time was at East Hendred on Sunday 11th: not for lunch, unusually, but a business meeting lasting from 3 p.m. till 8 p.m. (though on this occasion Rodgers was absent with a bad back). The second was at Shirley Williams' Westminster flat the following Wednesday evening (14 January) from 8 p.m. to 11.10, with no mention of dinner. The third meeting on Sunday 18th was due to be at East Hendred again – possibly because it was Jennifer's sixtieth birthday and there was a family party for her on the Saturday night; or maybe because Shirley Williams was already nearby attending a conference at Ditchley Park. Whatever the reason, this one almost never happened. His new colleagues had their first experience of Jenkins' (or John Harris') talent for briefing the press, which had so infuriated Wilson in the 1960s. The previous Tuesday he had lunched with John Cole and Adam Raphael of the *Observer*; a photographer came to East Hendred on the Saturday, and Sunday's paper ran a story about the intended meeting, illustrated with a picture of Jenkins standing at his gate looking like the lord of the manor waiting to greet them. Shirley Williams was furious at the implication that he had summoned them as his junior partners and refused to come. Only when the meeting was switched to Rodgers' house in Highgate was she persuaded to attend; and only when she was finally pacified – 'with Roy contrite and at his most conciliatory and, of course, disowning all knowledge of the story,' as Owen wrote[59] – were they able to get down to drafting a joint declaration of intent.*

The next day Jenkins flew to Washington for five days to witness (though only on television) Ronald Reagan's inauguration and give a lecture at Georgetown University. In his absence the Three met again in Highgate to continue drafting, while Michael Foot made a last half-hearted appeal to them to stay with Labour. Jenkins returned on Saturday 24 January just in time to watch television coverage of Labour's latest

---

* Each of them was accompanied on this occasion by a trusted political adviser: Matthew Oakeshott (for Jenkins), John Lyttle (Shirley Williams), Alec McGivan (Owen) and Roger Liddle (Rodgers). All four continued to play active roles in the early days of the SDP, with McGivan as the party's national agent and Oakeshott and Liddle on the steering committee.

special conference (at Wembley), which after a series of chaotic votes adopted an electoral college to elect the leader which gave the unions 40 per cent of the votes and the constituency parties and the MPs 30 per cent each. If they had any last-minute doubts, this was the final push the defectors needed to leave the party. On Sunday morning (25 January), the Gang of Four – with their four 'sherpas' – met again at David Owen's house in Docklands to finalise and issue what immediately became known as the Limehouse Declaration: not yet declaring the formation of a new party, but announcing in nine short paragraphs their intention to establish a Council for Social Democracy as a clear staging post towards that end.

Their accounts all differ about who contributed what. According to Owen, 'The best and most elegant words came as usual from Roy Jenkins, the substance of policy came largely from me, the quotable pieces for the press from Shirley and practical sense from Bill.'[60] But Rodgers' recollection was that Owen contributed the least.[61] It is generally accepted that the ringing opening sentence – 'The calamitous outcome of the Labour Party Wembley conference demands a new start in British politics' – was Williams' and Rodgers'; and the crucial final sentence – 'We believe that the need for a realignment of British politics must now be faced' – was included at Jenkins' insistence. Over the past two weeks the word 'realignment', implying a definite break with Labour, had caused Williams and Rodgers more heart-searching than anything else. Its inclusion, in Jenkins' view, 'gave clear notice that we were moving outside a Labour party laager . . . There must be somebody with whom to realign. And the most obvious although not necessarily the only people whom this embraced were the Liberals.'[62]

In his memoirs David Owen claimed that the Declaration was still clearly Labour-oriented and *not* a rallying cry for a centre party; somewhat contradictorily, however, he now (1991) believed that he should 'in honour' not have signed it, since he had come to realise that Jenkins' goal was always merger with the Liberals.[63] There was admittedly no mention of cooperation with the Liberals, of proportional representation or indeed of any political strategy at all; the Declaration was purely a statement of principles. So to that extent it was less than wholly candid. Nevertheless the whole thrust of the Declaration is pure Jenkins, explicitly appealing not only to unhappy Labour (and lapsed Labour) activists but to others not previously involved in politics. 'We do not believe that the fight for the ideals we share and for the recovery of our country should be limited only to politicians. It will need the support of men and women in all parts of our society.' And again:

The Council will represent a coming together of several streams: politicians who recognise that the drift to extremism in the Labour Party is not compatible with the democratic traditions of the Party they joined and those from outside politics who believe that the country cannot be saved without changing the sterile and rigid framework into which the British political system has increasingly fallen in the last two decades.

We do not believe in the politics of an inert centre merely representing the lowest common denominator between two extremes. We want more, not less, radical change in our society but with a greater stability of direction.

In other words, what Jenkins had called in his Dimbleby Lecture 'a strengthening of the radical centre'.

For the rest, the Declaration looked to create 'an open classless and more equal society [which] rejects ugly prejudices based upon sex, race or religion'. It wanted a healthy mixed economy without frequent 'frontier changes' – that is, neither more nationalisation nor privatisation; it aspired to 'eliminate poverty and promote greater equality' without either stifling enterprise or excessive bureaucracy; insisted that it was possible to combine high employment with low inflation; and aimed to re-create a self-confident, outward-looking Britain playing its full role in Europe, NATO, the United Nations and the Commonwealth, promoting multilateral disarmament and help for the Third World. Not only the objectives but the very phrasing echoes everything Jenkins had been advocating since the 1950s. The Declaration concluded with a recognition that for many who had given much of their lives to the Labour party the decision to leave it would be 'deeply painful', but urged that the need for 'realignment' must now be faced.[64]

Having finalised the text, they broke for lunch while Debbie Owen typed it up. (The Owens did not have a photocopier, so Oakeshott and McGivan had to find somewhere to get it copied for the press. There were no copy-shops in those days and Parliament was in recess; they eventually copied it in the Savoy Hotel.) Meanwhile the four leaders were joined by four of the nine Labour MPs who were committed to joining them: Bob Maclennan, Ian Wrigglesworth, John Roper and Mike Thomas.* Then at four o'clock the Gang of Four went out to pose for photographs, standing somewhat awkwardly on

---

* The other five were Tom Bradley, Tom Ellis, John Horam, Neville Sandelson and Richard Crawshaw.

a small bridge in Narrow Street in the fading light. So little thought had been given to this photo-call that Shirley Williams had to borrow a blouse from Debbie Owen, while Oakeshott was dispatched across town again to fetch a skirt from her Westminster flat. Jenkins was in his usual dark suit while Owen changed into a smart light one; but Rodgers still wore a casual jumper. Despite the amateurishness of this beginning, however the public response was immediate and overwhelming. They received 8,000 letters of support in the first week, 25,000 in the first month, many of them including small donations, and an instant opinion poll gave the still notional new party 27 per cent support (on top of 11 per cent for the Liberals). The sudden momentum was well caught by a *Guardian* cartoon showing the four leaders in a small boat hurtling away from Foot and Healey left behind on the pier, borne up by a seal (the seal of public approval!), with Jenkins in the bow holding on to his hat and Rodgers at the stern saying: 'What do you mean, can't we slow down a bit? We haven't even started the motor yet.'[65] 'After Limehouse,' Jenkins wrote, 'the Gang of Four or any individual member of it could no more have stopped launching a new party than logs could prevent themselves being swept down a mountain torrent.'[66] 'We found that we had placed ourselves in the leadership of an army already formed and waiting,' Rodgers recalled. 'The momentum was irresistible and we decided to bring forward the launch to 26 March.'[67]

The public response vindicated Jenkins' belief that there was huge untapped support just waiting for an outlet, though even he had not anticipated quite this rush; but the scale of it took the others by surprise. There was still a good deal of scepticism in the press. Jenkins' seniority ensured that he was seen as the leading figure; but his wine-bibbing image invited relentless mockery. Geoffrey Wheatcroft in the *Spectator* dubbed the embryonic party 'Lafite – The League of Agreeable Fellows Incommoded by Tiresome Extweemism' – and repeated Ferdinand Mount's cutting paraphrase of Jenkins' Press Gallery speech the previous June: 'Keep the yobs away from the best claret.'[68] Meanwhile it was pointed out that the Gang of Three were just three middle-ranking ex-ministers of limited achievement – one over-promoted and arrogant, one well-meaning but muddled, the third a quintessential political back-room boy. The fact that they had only announced the formation of a Council for Social Democracy (whatever that was) rather than going straight for a new party suggested that they were still hesitating on the brink.

On 5 February a full-page advertisement was published in the *Guardian* naming 100 members of the great and good who were pledging their support to the new movement. Nearly half had been active in Labour politics, including four former Cabinet ministers, headed by the once-deputy leader George Brown (now Lord George-Brown), another nine former MPs like Dick Taverne and David Marquand, and several figures prominent in local government, including Frank Pickstock (a veteran of the Gaitskellite CDS in the early 1960s), Clive Wilkinson (current leader of Birmingham city council), George Canning (Jenkins' longtime agent and then chairman in Stechford, recently Lord Mayor of Birmingham) and Jim Cattermole (his agent even longer ago in Solihull, subsequently a Labour party regional organiser and active pro-European). The rest of the list was heavily weighted towards academics, journalists, retired civil servants and leading figures from medicine, the law and other professions: it included Alan Bullock and Philip Williams, biographers respectively of Ernest Bevin and Hugh Gaitskell; Lord Flowers, rector of Imperial College, London, and Walter Perry, vice-chancellor of the Open University; Sir Alec Cairncross, Jenkins' chief economic adviser at the Treasury in 1967–9, and Anthony Lester, his adviser at the Home Office in 1974–6; Michael Young, founder of the Consumers' Association, and Eirlys Roberts, the former editor of *Which?*; Anthony Sampson of the *Observer* and Polly Toynbee of the *Guardian*; Rabbi Julia Neuberger, the actress Janet Suzman and the opera singer Sir Geraint Evans. Notable by their absence, however, were trade unionists: the only current union leader was Frank Chapple – and he, like Clive Wilkinson and one or two others who lent their signatures, ultimately declined to leave the Labour Party.[69]

Over the next few weeks two more Labour MPs (John Cartwright and Edward Lyons) and one Conservative (Christopher Brocklebank-Fowler) announced their support; more significant was the number who did not. The SDP was launched with just fourteen MPs; over the next year, as its fortunes soared, a further trickle came aboard, amounting in the end to twenty-nine. It was a substantial breakout, but not a decisive one. The Gang of Four had a list of around eighty Labour MPs whom they would have liked to persuade to join them, ranging from leading members of the Shadow Cabinet like Roy Hattersley and Eric Varley to rising younger moderates like John Smith, Phillip Whitehead, Giles Radice and George Robertson; but all of these elected to stick with Labour and work to turn around the party from within. Without them the SDP had no chance of replacing the Labour Party, as Owen, Rodgers and Williams initially hoped to do. Jenkins congratulated himself on the near-unanimity with which his former ministerial colleagues and PPSs in the Treasury and the Home Office followed him into his new party; he also liked to claim that it was mainly the libertarians who came over and the more socially conservative who stayed put.[70] But this only reinforced the impression that it was essentially a party of his friends. If there was a larger group that might have been expected to follow him it was the sixty-nine who had voted for the Common Market in 1971; but of the thirty who were still in Parliament ten years later, only eleven joined the SDP: nineteen – including respected figures like Tam Dalyell and Betty Boothroyd – did not. Nor were all of those who did join particularly pro-European; twenty-two of them had been in the House, but only half of these had defied the whip in 1971. By any analysis, therefore, those who defected were not an easy group to classify. They were in truth a somewhat disparate collection of individuals, some with deep roots in the party, others less so; some with their careers ahead of them, others near retirement; all with their own personal or constituency reasons for choosing to break with Labour. They certainly did not constitute anything near a majority of the Labour right, or of the most able or promising among them.[71]

Right at the outset, before the party was even formed, they lost the moral high ground, and arguably missed an opportunity to cash in on the early enthusiasm, by declining to resign their seats to fight by-elections under their new colours. David Owen and one or two others who were confident of their local support were keen to do so. Jenkins with hindsight thought that perhaps some at least should have done, but claimed that since he was not in the House it was not for him to press them.[72] Bill Rodgers, however, argued persuasively that Labour would have controlled the timing of any by-elections and would have delayed and staggered them to its own advantage, so that the defectors would simply have been 'picked off one by one'.[73] In fact the example of Dick Taverne at Lincoln in 1973 suggests that most would have been triumphantly returned, which would have given the new party democratic legitimacy and an enormous boost – as well as improving their chances of holding their seats in 1983. As it was, they were vulnerable to the charge of betraying the voters who had elected them as Labour MPs. 'Renouncing a political allegiance is a defensible political act,' Neil Kinnock declared five days after the Limehouse Declaration. 'Making a meal of the hand that fed them is indefensible political morality.'[74] In characteristic vein a fortnight later Kinnock denounced the defectors as 'political lounge lizards' whose brand of 'pink Toryism' would delight every 'multinational boss, judge and general' by offering them 'the malleable Common Market-loving, NATO-worshipping, trade union bashing, PSBR-saving, permanent PR coalition that they have longed for'.[75] The day before the SDP finally launched, it was again Kinnock who moved at Labour's NEC that the defectors had 'no moral or democratic right to continue to sit as MPs without presenting themselves again to their electorates'.[76] Their failure to do so was not only morally questionable, but bad politics.

In the meantime the four leaders set about creating a major new party from scratch in just eight weeks. They quickly established a collective leadership with a steering committee, initially numbering fourteen, which they took it in turns to chair, a month at a time. The four of them lunched together every Monday, initially at each other's London flats or houses, later at an Italian restaurant in Westminster called L'Amico, before the steering committee at three o'clock. But from the beginning there were tensions arising from Jenkins' natural tendency to assume that he was the senior partner and Owen's equal determination to resist this assumption. A few days before the first meeting of the steering committee they met at Shirley Williams' flat to divide up the leadership responsibilities. Owen proposed that he should chair the parliamentary group, Rodgers take charge of organisation and Shirley Williams look after publicity, while Jenkins should be confined to fund-raising. Jenkins was 'taken aback', Rodgers recalled, and 'obviously hurt', until the other two rejected the suggestion as 'preposterous'. It was then agreed that Jenkins should take charge of policy, though not entirely: another four-way division gave him responsibility for economic policy while Owen, Williams and Rodgers would take the lead on foreign, home and industrial policy respectively. This was duly accepted at the first meeting of the steering committee on 9 February.[77]

Neither the name nor the logo of the party gave much difficulty. They considered calling themselves 'The Radicals' or – thirteen years before Tony Blair – 'New Labour'; but the press had long been calling them the 'social democrats' and it was easiest to go along with that. To Edwin Plowden, who thought it would have been better to have retained the word 'Labour' in the party name, Jenkins confessed to some misgivings:

I was myself very doubtful about the title Social Democrats in the early stages, but it seems to have caught on quite well, and in any event the momentum is now such that I do not think we could change it. 'Labour' obviously has historic advantages, but it may also have disadvantages for an appeal to the 'soft' Conservative vote, of which there is a good deal at the moment.[78]*

A desire to appeal to Tory voters might also be thought to have influenced the choice of party colours; but in fact the logo was the brainchild of Mike Thomas – a marketing man before he entered Parliament – who was more interested in targeting the patriotic Labour vote. As early as 2 February Thomas proposed that they should follow the example of the West German SPD and simply use the three letters (in their English order) in red, white and blue (instead of black, red and yellow) and underlined in red. This, he suggested, would tap into an established and successful social democratic pedigree with positive associations with Willy Brandt and Helmut Schmidt:

> The use of the red, white and blue would not have any 'Empire Loyalist/Union Jack' implications . . . but would touch on a national desire to pull Britain up by the bootstraps that people really do feel in the present economic mess.
>
> It would also be cheap, quick and easy to do and avoid all the tedious arguments that might otherwise ensue about a symbol.[80]

This brilliantly simple solution was accepted with no recorded discussion, and the logo was designed in good time for the launch.

Meanwhile Ian Wrigglesworth found temporary offices in Queen Anne's Gate, where the twenty-eight-year-old Alec McGivan was installed as national agent. One of his first tasks was to prepare a breakdown of the thousands of letters pouring in, ensure that they all received a reply from the Gang of Four inviting them to join the new party and enter their names on a central register: to much mockery from the old parties the SDP set out to be the first computerised party, with subscriptions paid by credit card. There was a lot of discussion at the early meetings of the steering committee over the level at which to fix the subscription, balancing the need for money with the wish to maximise membership and appear open to all: the decision was eventually made to 'suggest' a £9 subscription but allow members to pay as much or as little as they could afford. Thomas was given charge

---

* There had actually been an earlier Social Democratic party in British politics: the Social Democratic Federation founded by the Victorian Marxist H.M. Hyndman in 1881, which Jenkins described in his biography of Attlee as preaching 'a rigid doctrine of class war and economic determinism'.[79] But if he remembered this he prudently never mentioned it.

of arranging the launch and brought in advertising agencies and professional event organisers to give it as much impact as possible.

Jenkins played relatively little part in these details, though he chaired the steering committee in the four weeks up to the launch. He concentrated on his policy brief. First he drew up a seven-point statement of aims, based on his well-trailed ideas, to which Shirley Williams added some more down-to-earth matters like training, social services and education in which he never took much interest, as well as a commitment to gender and race equality: this eventually became 'Twelve Tasks for Social Democrats' in time for the launch.[81] More importantly, he made several major speeches designed both to flesh out the party's alternative to Thatcherism and Bennery and assert his claim as leader presumptive.* First, at the Institute of Fiscal Studies on 23 February he delivered – with the authority of a former Chancellor widely regarded as the most successful since the war – a comprehensive demolition of Mrs Thatcher's monetarist experiment, which was threatening to destroy Britain's industrial base, comparing his own record on jobs, inflation and growth between 1967 and 1970 with Geoffrey Howe's since 1979. Control of the money supply was important, he conceded; but it was only one 'crude and flickering' indicator among many, and trying to fly a modern economy on one instrument was 'like trying to fly a Jumbo Jet on a small car's speedometer'. The result of the government's blinkered policy was that on present trends Britain would fall behind South Korea in five years and 'soon cease to qualify as a major industrial country':

I simply do not understand the attitude of those who believe that behind the façade of falling production and mounting unemployment something triumphant is occurring. There are certain fields in which, according to one's beliefs, a purification of the spirit may be achieved through mortification of the flesh. The management of economic policy is not one of them. It is essentially a material process, using material means to attain material ends. Its success is to be judged by wealth creating results and not by moral purpose or virility tests.

* If he felt any hesitation about this he was encouraged by letters from friends and admirers like Jack Diamond, who wrote to him a week before the launch: 'I want you to have no shred of a doubt about your being the man of the hour, the one – and the only one – who will be able to lead and to stimulate our people into their near-maximum achievement.' He should have no doubt that he was 'peculiarly fitted and indeed called to this great task'.[82] With unusual bluntness Jenkins himself told an American academic who wrote an early book about the SDP: 'I was the founder . . . The others could never have done it without me.'[83]

What was his answer? Salvation lay in the windfall of North Sea oil. 'The central issue is how we deal with the years of oil abundance in order to leave ourselves in the best possible position to live without the oil in the future.' It was clear what a wise government should do:

It is essential that we use a large part of the oil revenue for productive public sector investment: railway electrification, public transport generally, the expansion of British Telecom, energy saving and insulation work, the development of renewable resources, the renewal of outdated water and sewerage systems.

'In spite of the traditional objections to the hypothecation of revenue,' he suggested, 'a special North Sea Oil revenue Investment Fund may be the right way to proceed here.'

To contain inflation he tentatively proposed Professor James Meade's idea for 'an employment-oriented Pay Commission', some way short of a full-blown statutory pay policy. (Meade was one of the 100 supporters listed in the *Guardian*.) 'I do not pretend to a complete answer,' Jenkins concluded modestly, 'but I think this offers the right direction.' No economic policy was ever perfect:

But the present mix is something very near to disaster. It will not destroy inflation, although at a great price it may modify it. It will permanently damage a large part of our economy and it will make the worst rather than the best use of the limited period when the oil is in flood.[84]

Then, at a public meeting at the Oxford Union on 9 March, he set out his historian's vision of the opportunity to fundamentally reshape the landscape of politics:

Something approaching a geological movement is occurring. It is certainly the greatest period of flux in British politics for sixty years – since the break-up of the old Liberal Party of power and its replacement by the Labour Party of the Twenties.

More specifically he spelled out the new party's modus operandi and its ambition, explicitly assuming alliance with the Liberals:

We look for a mass membership. We shall welcome the formation of local groups. We shall mount a major campaign of meetings.

We shall be prepared to fight by-elections. But our sights will be essentially concentrated upon the next General Election – probably about 2½ years away . . . At the election, clearly working in close and friendly arrangement with the Liberals . . . our aim will be no less than complete victory: a majority in the House of Commons, a Social Democratic/Liberal Government of Britain. In the present state of public opinion . . . that is a perfectly feasible possibility.

The fallback position would be to hold the balance of power and force the introduction of proportional representation.* But he saw no reason to be so modest. The response to the Limehouse Declaration encouraged him in his wider ambition to radically realign the centre left and draw a lot of talented new people into politics. 'This we can do,' he told his predominantly young audience. 'It can happen in the next three years . . . I ask you to join us in this great venture.'[86]

The Gang of Four also did a lot of wooing of the press in these weeks. Jenkins' engagement diary shows that he and David Owen lunched with the editor of the *Daily Mail*, David English, on 17 March and with Lord Hartwell, proprietor and editor-in-chief of the *Telegraph*, on 24 March; the same day he and Shirley Williams had three *Guardian* journalists for a drink at Kensington Park Gardens; he lunched with Fred Emery of *The Times* on 11 March and with Peter Jenkins of the *Guardian* at Brooks's on the 25th; he also met Charles Douglas-Home and David Watt of *The Times* at Ann Fleming's house on Sunday 22nd.†

Most crucially, perhaps, the whole Gang of Four were invited to lunch at Gray's Inn Road on the 20th by Rupert Murdoch, who had just been allowed by a grateful Margaret Thatcher – grateful for the *Sun*'s support in 1979 – to buy *The Times* and *Sunday Times* in addition to the *Sun* and the *News of the World*. The occasion, unsurprisingly, was not a success. Hugo Young, who was there, recorded that Jenkins arrived last, rather grandly, looking 'fat and sleek, and just like they say in the nasty newspapers'. He led off by summarising their critique of

---

* Such was the optimism generated by the huge public support at this time that in another speech a few days later he confidently predicted: 'We can and shall achieve proportional representation in the 'eighties and very likely before the middle of the decade. It is not a panacea, but it is an essential step to the regeneration of Britain.'[85]
† Typically, perhaps, they concentrated their attention almost entirely on the 'quality' press. But Jenkins did write – or at least put his name to – an article in the *Sun* on 24 March proclaiming that Britain was 'on the brink of . . . a peaceful revolution'.[87]

Thatcherism, which doubtless went down like a lead balloon. When Murdoch asked how they differed from Callaghan, Jenkins and Owen said they would be tougher on the unions and on public spending. But they differed among themselves when Owen and Shirley Williams insisted that they were not a centre party but still democratic socialists who wanted to introduce a wealth tax; Jenkins dissented, saying it would be too expensive to collect. After they had gone Murdoch characteristically declared them to be 'all crap', saying they had failed to answer his questions on policy, that only Owen had 'delivered on toughness' and they all clearly hated one another's guts. Young thought this 'quite wrong'. 'Obviously they disagree,' he noted, 'but the main thing is their excitement at having got the show on the road so fast and so well.'[88] Under William Rees-Mogg for the past fourteen years *The Times* had been strongly supportive of Jenkins' positions on Europe and in the Labour party; and for a few months under Murdoch's first editor, Harold Evans, it remained broadly sympathetic without actually endorsing the SDP. Within a year, however, Evans had gone and all Murdoch's papers were thereafter staunchly supportive of Mrs Thatcher.[89] Since the *Guardian*, despite the support of individual columnists, remained editorially faithful to Labour, no national newspaper ever positively endorsed the SDP – which rather belies the repeated allegation from both Labour and Conservative opponents that it was a party 'of the media, by the media and for the media'.[90]

Nevertheless the launch on Thursday 26 March was an undoubted media event, brilliantly staged by Mike Thomas. The world's press was summoned to the Connaught Rooms near Covent Garden at the early hour of 9 a.m. Five hundred journalists and television crews packed the hall and their reports and pictures dominated the news bulletins for the rest of the day (though Mrs Thatcher did her best to steal their thunder by making an announcement clearing the former head of MI5, Sir Roger Hollis, of suspicion of having been a Soviet spy). The four leaders sat on the platform with the red, white and blue letters SDP forming a frieze behind them: Jenkins at one end, Owen beside him, then Rodgers with Shirley Williams at the other end; and they spoke in the same order, each highlighting their own particular angle. Jenkins spoke with historical perspective about breaking the mould and bringing in those previously uncommitted or alienated from politics, and the signs that 'we may succeed beyond our hopes':

We offer not only a new party . . . but a new approach to politics; we want to get away from the politics of outdated dogmatism and class confrontation . . . to release the energies of the people who are fed up with the old slanging match.

He hoped for a realignment of the left-centre 'without even a temporary weakening of the force of the anti-Conservative challenge'. Owen stressed the youthful, democratic character of the new party and its commitment to one-member-one-vote; Rodgers stressed his Liverpool working-class background and fidelity to traditional Labour values; while Shirley Williams recalled her education in the United States and her admiration for American classlessness. They answered questions, in the course of which Rodgers, off the cuff, stated that in an electoral pact with the Liberals the SDP would expect to fight 'about half' the seats.[91] The four then left separately to spread the word around the country. Jenkins took a train to Cardiff for a 1.15 press conference followed by TV interviews, then flew to Manchester for another press conference at 5 p.m., an interview on Granada TV and a speech in the evening (and went on to Liverpool the next morning). Owen followed a similar schedule in Southampton and Plymouth, Rodgers in Leeds and Newcastle, and Shirley Williams in Birmingham and Edinburgh. Meanwhile Alec McGivan had set up banks of phones manned by volunteers to take the calls that poured in from members of the public keen to join the party.

Within days they had 43,000 members and some £500,000 raised in contributions, while the first Gallup poll after the launch gave the SDP 36 per cent on its own or 48 per cent in putative alliance with the Liberals, eclipsing both the other parties.[92] Labour and Tory opponents tried to mock both the media hype and the pioneering use of new technology, as if it was merely trendy and elitist. 'It's very convenient,' a cartoon in the *Guardian* jeered. 'You can join with a credit card and at the same time write everything they stand for on the back of it.'[93] Roy Hattersley scorned the vision of 'a Britain free for credit card holders'.[94] The Tory party chairman, Lord Thorneycroft, tried a different tack to dismiss the SDP with a cheap dig at Jenkins: 'I rather thought of joining myself. After all, it isn't a party, it hasn't a programme, and I'm told the claret is very good.'[95]* But privately both parties were

---

* Thorneycroft was a throwback to an earlier generation: Macmillan's Chancellor for twelve months in 1957–8 until he resigned in protest at the level of public spending, he was surprisingly brought back into front-line politics by Mrs Thatcher in 1975.

more worried than they admitted, each fearing that the impact of the new party would benefit the other: Labour thought splitting the left could only help Mrs Thatcher, while Tories worried by the SDP's appeal to 'wet' Tory voters feared it could open a way to Downing Street for Michael Foot. As a result, while they tried to dismiss the alarming phenomenon as an evanescent media bubble, there was a lot of intensive analysis of where exactly the SDP's support was coming from and which of the old parties it might damage most.

The answer that eventually emerged vindicated Jenkins' belief in a new constituency of uncommitted voters waiting to be tapped, rather than his three colleagues' hope for a Mark II Labour party. Analysis of the membership in November, at the height of the party's electoral success eight months after the launch, found that 72 per cent had never previously belonged to another party; only 15 per cent had been members of the Labour party and many of those had long been lapsed, 36 per cent had voted Labour in 1979, 35 per cent Liberal and 27 per cent Tory.[96] The SDP was thus an awkward mix: a core of old pros who bore the scars and cynicism acquired in internecine battles in council chambers and smoked-filled committee rooms over decades, and a membership of so-called 'political virgins' who brought idealism, valuable skills and expertise from outside politics but little or no political experience. The former tended to retain the habits and assumptions of their old allegiance – not least a dim view of the Liberals – while the latter aspired to a more inclusive, ecumenical, but sometimes naive approach. In every new area party, as they were quickly formed up and down the country – the SDP deliberately created area units comprising several constituencies to try to prevent the domination by small unrepresentative cliques which had corrupted the Labour party – the same coming together of odd bedfellows was repeated. In the enthusiasm and excitement of the early months these differences could largely be ignored; but over the next few years, as the going got harder, tensions arising from this fundamental difference of outlook came to poison some of the early idealism.

In one respect the SDP mirrored other political parties: the most active tended to be more committed to their particular hobby-horses than the broader membership, which had a vaguer faith in the power of goodwill and moderation. But even among the activists the party's instant historians detected three distinct but overlapping strands associated with the four leaders. First there was an old Labour strand represented by Bill Rodgers, which wanted essentially to re-create the party of Attlee and Gaitskell, purged of the new hard left. Then there was a new self-consciously young, modern, classless party – avowedly 'radical' but light on ideology – which David Owen aspired to create in his own image. Shirley Williams sat somewhere between these two, splicing feminist, internationalist and green concerns onto her old Labour roots. And then there was Jenkins' unashamedly centrist vision, seeking to draw in public-spirited supporters from all parties and none, to transcend the sterile tribalism of the old politics and build a new consensus around his long-held fusion of liberal, moderately progressive, Atlanticist and pro-European views based firmly on alliance with the Liberals.

These different visions raised acutely the question of which of them was going to be the leader. For the moment they had no choice but to talk up the benefits of the collective leadership. These were real, both in sharing the load of creating a new party and in maximising the party's appeal to different strands of potential support. There were also practical reasons for postponing a decision until the party had approved its constitution and drawn up rules for the election of a leader; and a strong case in fairness for postponing it while the two most popular of the four founders still lacked seats in Parliament. But it was clear that the four-headed leadership could not continue for ever. It made life difficult for those struggling to set up the party organisation, leading to duplication and unclear lines of command; and there were continuing tensions between them, with Rodgers (clearly, as he wryly entitled his memoirs, the 'fourth among equals') frequently having to act as mediator between the other three. Above all, the media wanted to focus on a single leader. At first Shirley Williams was widely assumed to be the favourite. She had much the biggest personal following among Labour voters – much less among Tories who blamed her for abolishing grammar schools when Education Secretary in 1976–9 (though she actually closed fewer than Mrs Thatcher had in 1970–74). She also seemed more likely than Jenkins to be able to fight an early by-election to return to the House of Commons. She was certainly not unambitious: Bill Rodgers, who had known her since Oxford, thought her 'the most ambitious person he knows in politics'.[97] Nevertheless those who worked with her found her indecisive and maddeningly disorganised – not good qualities in a leader. She also lacked self-confidence to push herself forward, due largely to problems in her private life. Around this time an anagram of her name began to circulate around Queen Anne's Gate ('I whirl aimlessly'), which years later she admitted was 'both wounding and clever'.[98] She attributed it to 'Roy's acolytes' – specifically Matthew Oakeshott, who she felt set out deliberately to undermine her, which sowed new seeds of resentment towards Jenkins and drove her temporarily towards David Owen.

Meanwhile the most pressing question facing the new party was relations with the Liberals. Again, the four leaders fell initially into three camps. From the time of his first conversation with David Steel in 1979, Jenkins had always envisaged the closest possible cooperation: in his case, electoral realism – recognising that a fourth party would have no chance at all in competition with the third – was bolstered by his historical attachment to the Asquithian tradition and his close friendship with members of the Asquith family. There was some truth in the gibe that the only Liberals he actually knew were Bonham Carters and Grimonds. He would have had no difficulty joining the Liberals had he not judged that a new party would attract wider support; and even after the SDP was formed he would have been happy to allow joint membership of both parties. In a speech to the Gladstone Club just five days after the launch he acknowledged differences between the Liberal and social democratic traditions, but claimed to see no differences of substance and called for a 'partnership of principle' to seize the present opportunity.[99] Rodgers and Williams started out with a much more typical Labour view of the Liberals as cranky and irrelevant: they shared none of Jenkins' fondness for them – they both admitted that they had previously had very little to do with them – but quickly realised that there was no future in fighting them and came to see their positive qualities as campaigners on the ground. Owen was different again: he had made his career in the West Country where the Liberals were historically strong. He had fought his first election against Mark Bonham Carter at Torrington in 1964 and took an instant dislike to his superior Balliol manner.[100] Since 1966 his marginal seat in Plymouth had been threatened by successive Liberal candidates who always won a vote bigger than his majority: he accordingly regarded them as unprincipled spoilers, and his view was shared by other recruits to the SDP – from both Labour and Conservative – who had spent years fighting the Liberals in their own areas and had no wish to get into bed with them now.

These sharply contrasting views were impossible to reconcile. Just a week after Owen had warned his co-leaders that 'David Steel is pushing us all the time, for obvious reasons, on his timetable . . . Nothing could be more damaging for us than to be forced into an Alliance before we are ready',[101] Jenkins was at the Gladstone Club openly calling for a 'partnership of principle'. The first meeting of the SDP steering committee after the launch accepted the necessity of a pact, but betrayed the new party's assumption of seniority by agreeing that they should 'continue to show magnanimity' towards the Liberals.[102] This attitude was resented by many Liberals who felt that they had been building up their strength on the ground locally for years and did not take kindly to a few failed Labour grandees swanning in late in the day expecting to harvest the fruits of their hard work. The outspoken Cyril Smith (ex-Labour himself) spoke for many grass-roots Liberals when he called for the SDP to be 'strangled at birth'.[103] Bill Rodgers' off-the-cuff suggestion that the two parties should fight 'about half' the seats each thus outraged the partisans on both sides equally. The Liberals thought he had a cheek expecting so much – even Steel initially only imagined the SDP fighting around 100 seats – while Owen thought he had fatally compromised the SDP's identity by conceding the Liberals so many. In his memoirs Owen still maintained that the SDP could, and should, have established itself clearly as the third party, ahead of the Liberals, by taking them on and beating them in some early by-elections, before contemplating making an alliance with them.[104] In practice Rodgers' fifty:fifty division was quickly accepted as the obvious middle way; but it took a lot of hard negotiation over the next two years to nail down the detail, which went a long way to sour the willing union of hearts and minds that Jenkins had hoped for.

That union was brought a great deal closer by a fruitful meeting between Rodgers and Shirley Williams, on the one hand, and Steel and Richard Holme (that year's President of the Liberal party), on the other, when they all met at the annual Königswinter Anglo-German Conference in Bonn in early April. 'Well away from the basilisk eye of the British media', as Shirley Williams put it, they took the chance to discuss their future relationship and semi-formalised it in the form of a 'Königswinter Compact', written down by Richard Holme and initialled by the four of them.[105] This was the first time Rodgers and Williams had properly talked with Steel and they got on like a house on fire. It could be said that he played them very skilfully. But in the enthusiasm of the moment they exceeded their authority, and at the next meeting of the steering committee, in Owen's words, 'all hell broke loose among the SDP MPs' who demanded a special meeting the next day to discuss the matter.[106] Practically every member of the now nineteen-strong committee spoke, and they divided almost equally. Rodgers and Williams defended what they had agreed, winning support from David Marquand, Tom Bradley and three or four others (Dick Taverne was absent); but Ian Wrigglesworth 'felt very strongly that the

Social Democrats were being constantly "bounced" by David Steel on all aspects of the Lib/SD relationship': it was 'nonsense', he argued, to deal with the Liberals on a basis of equality when the polls showed far higher support for the SDP. Edward Lyons felt that 'we were in bed with the Liberals far too early and this could damage recruitment'. Mike Thomas thought the public saw the Liberals as failures, the SDP as 'new and positive', and wanted no discussion of electoral arrangements at all for twelve to eighteen months. Even such a loyal Jenkinsite as Bob Maclennan, who had considered joining the Liberals himself if the SDP had not come about, backed the objectors. Owen and Jenkins spoke last. Owen accepted that they did not want an open dispute with the Liberals, but warned that they were in 'a political bargaining situation' with them. Jenkins, in the chair, was forced to agree that the two parties should retain their separate identities: 'There was no idea of merger.' He admitted the difficulty of negotiating with the Liberals, but was anxious that Steel's determined support of the SDP should be reciprocated; in return he thought that Steel should be asked privately – presumably by himself – to halt the selection of Liberal candidates in winnable seats.[107]

Owen thought Königswinter was where 'relations with the Liberals went critically wrong' and accused Rodgers and Williams of 'selling the SDP down the river'.[108] But he acquitted them of acting dishonourably: he believed they honestly changed their minds about the necessity of working with the Liberals. His lasting bitterness was reserved for Jenkins, who he believed had plotted with David Steel to amalgamate their two parties all along. 'I find it impossible to escape the conclusion that Roy Jenkins misled me and some of the other MPs who left the Labour Party . . . about his real intentions,' he wrote in his memoirs. 'Roy used the SDP. It would have been more honourable to have joined the Liberals in 1981.'[109] Jenkins' denial in his own memoirs is unconvincing. It is clear from his Brussels diary that he did envisage a merger with the Liberals sooner rather than later. Of course he always wanted an organic union that would evolve naturally through cooperation on the ground – as to a great extent it did; but he was keen for that to happen as rapidly as possible. He was also probably right that under the first-past-the-post electoral system there was no room for two competing parties in the centre: the idea that the SDP could have simply brushed the Liberals aside underestimated their deep roots and resilience. Had the SDP really been able to take 90 per cent of Labour's vote, as Bill Rodgers had once hoped, then indeed the Liberals might have been irrelevant; but it was already clear by the time of the launch that this was not the sort of party the SDP was, and it was not going to push Labour to the margin. It could be argued that without Jenkins the SDP might have made more appeal to Labour supporters and attracted more defectors. But in practice they had no option, as Rodgers and Williams quickly recognised, but to cooperate as harmoniously as possible with the Liberals. Jenkins achieved the sort of party he had wanted, and he soon got his alliance with the Liberals, which for a time was extraordinarily successful. His political judgement was better than Owen's, whose independent SDP successfully fighting all three other parties at once was always a fantasy. In truth Jenkins' view of the party's ultimate future was never in much doubt. But to the extent that he claimed throughout the formation of the SDP and beyond that there was 'no idea of merger', it must be admitted that he did mislead Owen, Thomas, Wrigglesworth and the others who wanted no such thing.

Despite their grumblings, the 'Königswinter Compact' led to the establishment of two joint working parties and a 'Joint Statement of Principles', which Steel and Shirley Williams unveiled in June, sitting together on the grass opposite Westminster Abbey like a pair of 'super-annuated student lovers'.[110] But it was the momentum of events which really forced the two parties together. Politics is all about elections. The SDP decided early on that it was not ready to contest the local elections in May. But the leaders always knew that they must be ready to fight by-elections wherever they might occur. As it happened, the first came up in a constituency that they would not have chosen – the safe Labour seat of Warrington in Cheshire, where the sitting Member who had held the seat since 1961 resigned in late May to become a circuit judge. With a Labour majority of 10,000 and a Liberal vote of less than 3,000 to build on, Warrington was 550th on Matthew Oakeshott's calculation of winnable seats.[111] Nevertheless they knew they had to fight it and the immediate assumption was that Shirley Williams should be the candidate. The SDP needed to field one of its national figures to establish its credibility, and a traditional Labour seat was more obviously suited to her 'demotic appeal' – as Jenkins called it – than to his, especially as Warrington had a substantial Roman Catholic population.[112] A *Sun* poll on 4 June suggested that she would win it easily.[113] Had she done so it would have made her front-runner for the leadership; and she would very probably have been able to hold it at the General Election. But, for a combination of personal reasons, she declined.

'If ever a constituency was made for me,' she wrote in her memoirs, 'this was it.' Turning it down was 'probably the single biggest mistake of my political life'.[114] David Owen was appalled, believing that if she had taken it on and won, the whole history of the SDP would have been transformed. In an interview some years later she admitted, 'I could kick myself . . . for not having fought Warrington.' But she explained that she had commitments at Harvard to complete and a book to finish and was still not sure she wanted to go back into the Commons at all.[115] In her memoirs she added that after her divorce in 1974 she was a single mother with a teenage daughter and no money; if she failed to win she would find herself without a job and damaged by a second defeat. 'I did not dither,' she insisted. 'I quailed.'[116] But she appeared to dither, and her standing in the party never recovered. The opportunity fell instead to Jenkins, whose standing conversely was hugely boosted by the way he accepted the challenge.

Bill Rodgers thought that Jenkins only 'stepped reluctantly into the breach'.[117] ('"I suppose I'll have to fight it," you said wearily when Shirley made clear she wouldn't,' he recalled in 1990.)[118] David Owen, on the contrary, thought he was keen to stand. 'He was like an old stallion, sniffing the smell of the racecourse, hoping that if the favourite withdrew he might take her place at the starting line.'[119] The truth is that he was keen to show his paces, but knew that a bad result would set back both the fledgling party and his own chance of leading it. He also knew he had to gamble. Shirley Williams announced her decision to the steering committee on 1 June. The following weekend, to avoid publicity, Jenkins asked Jennifer to reconnoitre Warrington while he was speaking at a conference in Lausanne. It was actually a less grim prospect than it first appeared: unlike many declining manufacturing towns in the North-West, Warrington was not dependent on a single industry but still boasted a relatively mixed economy based on brewing, distilling (the famous 'Vladivar vodka from Varrington'), detergents and light engineering. Unemployment was lower than on most of Merseyside: there was no inner-city blight, just sprawling council estates – rather like Stechford, in fact. Unlike Stechford, however, it had some history and a compact old centre with a covered market.[120] Jennifer thought it would be 'a hard nut to crack', but it was not entirely unpromising territory.[121]

Jenkins received plenty of advice. Jack Diamond urged that he must be prepared to 'fight his way to No. 10', not expect the others simply to concede the leadership to him;[122] while the *Guardian* columnist Peter Jenkins – the extent of whose private commitment to the SDP might have surprised his readers – was equally sure that he was right to go for it, especially after Shirley Williams' damaging refusal:

> There is everything to gain and nothing to lose. In your case, to be seen to be taking on the tough one is exactly right for the king returned from across the water . . . On the basis of the *Observer* poll I would say it is just winnable. The campaign is bound to generate intense media excitement and the Labour party is likely to do everything in its power to assist the SDP cause. We should throw everything we've got into the fight, cash in on the underdog status (how can one be a claret-drinking underdog?) and turn it into the most exciting and important by-election of the post-war period.[123]

That was pretty much what Jenkins did. He announced his willingness to stand after the Monday meeting of the steering committee on 8 June and travelled up to Warrington on the 11th, where he was enthusiastically adopted by the small local SDP group and then met the local Liberals to ask for their support. They sought four assurances: that the Liberals should have first option at the next by-election; that they should have one of the two new seats when Warrington was split at the next election; that he should 'affirm publicly the value of Liberal support' during the campaign; and that he should describe himself as 'Social Democrat with Liberal support' on the ballot paper. 'To each of these,' the chairman reported to David Steel, 'Mr Jenkins replied unequivocally and enthusiastically "Yes".'

The Media were then allowed in and Mr Jenkins spoke for 10 minutes. His enthusiasm for a full Liberal partnership was so vigorous and persuasive that he cut a swathe through any Liberal doubts and he was adopted as candidate with total Liberal support.[124]

There was much mockery of 'Woy' Jenkins, with his famous speech defect, fighting a seat he could not even pronounce – JAK in the London *Evening Standard* showed him arriving with his suitcases on a rainswept railway platform to be told by a porter: 'No lad, this is Warrington, Wowington must be up near Rochdale'[125] – and still more scepticism at the pampered Brussels fat cat descending to a gritty northern town that most metropolitan commentators had never visited. But in his adoption speech he rejected the suggestion that he would be out of his element:

The idea that I have served my political life among rolling pastures or leafy suburban avenues . . . is ludicrous. I have represented one of the most industrial seats in Birmingham for 27 years. I believe I had happy relations with them. I certainly won nine elections there.[126]

During the next fortnight he paid only two more short visits to the constituency, which led the Liberals to complain that the SDP lacked 'a sense of urgency about this by-election'.[127] But from 25 June he established himself with Jennifer at the Fir Tree Motel on the southern edge of the town, giving himself three weeks of solid campaigning before polling day on 16 July – which he described in his memoirs as 'much the longest continuous series of nights in one place that I had spent for at least five, maybe ten, years past'.[128] For the whole three weeks he denied himself both country weekends and London restaurants – though he did find an acceptable French restaurant in nearby Knutsford to which he escaped two or three times.*

After a slightly nervous start he surprised himself by enjoying canvassing more than he had ever done in Stechford, and everyone else by the energy with which he threw himself into it, as his belief in what he was doing overcame his natural shyness. He had a lot of outside support. The other members of the Gang of Four, all the SDP MPs and David Steel came several times, as did other Liberals like Jo Grimond and Cyril Smith who had been critical of the SDP, plus busloads of enthusiastic new SDP members from as far afield as Lincoln and Birmingham and experienced Liberal workers from Liverpool. George Brown came and did a breezy walkabout (making much more impact than Harold Wilson, who made a rather shamefaced appearance for Labour on the eve of polling day); while old friends like Ronnie McIntosh and Mark and Leslie Bonham Carter also came to help. Jenkins held relatively few public meetings, but mainly canvassed in the street and house-to-house and visited factories, talking personally to as many people as possible.† *The Times'* sketch-writer Frank Johnson wrote of an 'Avalanche of Charm as Jenkins Sweeps In'. Johnson started

* In several interviews and newspaper profiles at this time – for instance, with John Mortimer in the *Sunday Times* – Jenkins was careful to claim that he liked 'very simple food' like shepherd's pie and fishcakes and mostly drank 'rather cheap wine'.[129] This clearly depended on how one defined 'rather cheap'.
† His visit to the Vladivar factory, where he sampled the product, was seized on gleefully by the cartoonists with jokes about vodka and claret, and fully exploited by the company, which published its own by-election newsletter reprinting several of the best cartoons and promoting its own fictional candidate, a leggy stripper named Fiona Vladivar.[130]

out by mocking Jenkins' incongruously patrician accent as he strolled around a shopping centre – 'What did the people make of him, one wondered, as he bade them "good morning" and asked if they shopped here "orphan"[131] – but by the second week he had changed his tune. He still wondered what the voters of Warrington thought of 'the grand, stupendously distinguished but largely incomprehensible magnifico from another world who has been introducing himself with a courtly bow of his smooth shiny head to incredulous passers-by', wooing them with 'that incomparable voice, beside which Sir John Gielgud sounds like rough trade'; but concluded, to his surprise, that people really rather liked him.[132] Others were impressed by the way Jenkins listened to their concerns and did not talk down to them. 'Mr Jenkins is a famous and civilised man,' *The Economist* commented after it was over. 'He worked hard and argued seriously. Snobbish London journalists were wrong to suppose that working-class Warringtonians would not appreciate this . . . He got credit for putting Warrington on the map.'[133]

The main pitch of his campaign was to blame Mrs Thatcher's 'stubborn theories' for increased unemployment – 'the worst fall in industrial output suffered by any major industrial country since the war' – while condemning the irrelevant extremism of Labour's siege-economy alternative and promoting his own record as a prudent and successful Chancellor. (Adult unemployment in Warrington had been only 995 when he left office in 1970, he boasted, but 3,124 when Denis Healey left in 1979.) Mrs Thatcher claimed credit for sticking to her guns, he charged in one of his relatively few set-piece speeches on 18 June, but the guns were 'often trained on our own people' and were reducing 'whole regions' of the country, including Merseyside, to 'industrial wastelands'.[134] Jenkins' unashamedly Keynesian alternative was a six-point programme of infrastructure investment backed by incentives to employers and wage control, which was designed to take one million people off the dole within two years: the £2–3 billion annual cost was said to be substantially self-financing, but in any case, he claimed, was less than Geoffrey Howe's margin of error. 'These are positive proposals,' one of his leaflets boasted, 'which offer a workable alternative both to the heartless job destruction of Mrs Thatcher and to the wildly spendthrift policies of Mr Foot.' His formal election address featured a spread of pictures of Jenkins talking earnestly with local people – and one with Willy Brandt, to emphasise his international statesmanship – and a message from Jennifer regretting how Labour had changed. 'We are fighting to change the old party system,' it concluded. 'Warrington can change the political map of Britain.'[135]

His message was helpfully reinforced first by the bitter battle between Healey and Benn for the Labour deputy leadership, which was unfolding that summer, and then by the wave of riots and looting which began in nearby Liverpool on 3 July and quickly spread to Manchester, Birmingham and a dozen other cities, which seemed to vindicate the warnings her opponents had sounded about the damage Mrs Thatcher's policies were doing to the social fabric. On the one hand, Jenkins naturally condemned 'the dark forces of violence and irrationalism' sweeping the country and, as a former Home Secretary, called on the police to uphold the law. But at the same time, in a speech on 10 July, he seized on the need to ameliorate the conditions that led to rioting and tried to promote Warrington, which was so far 'an oasis of relative peace with violence on both sides of it', as a model:

> It has civic pride and industrial versatility. It can send to the nation a message of reconciliation and hope, a message at once of fairness and understanding. Britain needs a new deal, and it can start here in Warrington, next Thursday.[136]

Labour tried to repel the SDP challenge in one of its heartlands by personal ridicule and abuse. Their candidate Doug Hoyle, a Bennite member of the NEC with a record of admiration for the Soviet Union, dismissed Jenkins as 'a retired pensioner from the EEC', a merchant banker and a class traitor;[137] while Peter Shore, now Shadow Chancellor, targeted him as 'the most articulate exponent of all that they [the SDP] stand for – from the sick, overriding passion for the Common Market, through the obsession with proportional representation and the so-called restructuring of British politics, to the specious and dangerous dependence, not on the support of individual men and women, but upon the good opinion of the media' – and called on the voters of Warrington to 'strangle the monster at birth'.[138] Meanwhile the Conservative candidate, an amiable London bus driver whom the Tories had put up almost as a sacrificial victim, called him a socialist. Between them his two principal opponents did Jenkins one big favour by supporting the 1967 Abortion Act, which might otherwise have been a difficult issue for him with the large number of Catholic voters.* On one other issue Jenkins made a slightly surprising but little-noticed shift of position.

---

* There were eight other candidates, ranging from the Ecology party to Commander Bill Boaks' ever-hopeful Democratic Monarchist/Public Safety/White Resident Party. Two spoilers who changed their names to Roy Jenkins also attempted to stand, but were debarred by the Returning Officer.

While still firmly opposed to unilateral nuclear disarmament, he questioned Mrs Thatcher's decision to buy from the Americans the new Trident missile system. Britain should retain her independent deterrent, he suggested, so long as Polaris lasted, 'but not necessarily renew it at limitless cost in the future'.[139] This would become a clear point of difference between him and David Owen.

In one respect the SDP/Liberal campaign was disappointing. The polls persistently failed to reflect the enthusiasm they felt they were arousing on the ground, barely moving from 29 per cent at the beginning to 31 per cent at the end. In an internal SDP memo entitled 'What Counts as a Good Result in Warrington?' Mike Thomas was at pains to manage expectations so that the media did not write off a good result as a disappointment. It was important to get across that '25% of the vote in Warrington is a *very creditable* performance. 30% or over . . . is an *excellent* performance. This would not only be good public relations, but the plain electoral truth.'[140] By the last weekend of the campaign they had created something of a carnival atmosphere, with Jenkins 'cavalcading' around the streets on the back of an open truck, waving at what he called 'nodal points', and Bill Rodgers providing a running commentary over a loudhailer, interspersed with the theme music from *Chariots of Fire* and Aaron Copland's 'Fanfare for the Common Man'; and they were confident of at least a respectable result. Jenkins, always cautious, hoped for 35 per cent. In fact he won 42 per cent and, by squeezing three-quarters of the Tory vote (from 9,000 in 1979 down to just over 2,000), cut Hoyle's 10,000 majority to just 1,759. The eight fringe candidates took just over 200 votes between them.

E.D.J. Hoyle (Labour)	14,280
R.H. Jenkins (SDP with Liberal support)	12,521
S.J. Sorrell (Conservative)	2,102
+ eight others	219
Labour majority	1,759[141]

After the declaration Hoyle made a 'sour and truculent' speech in which he claimed a 'magnificent victory' against an unprecedented media campaign, which had sold the SDP 'like soapflakes'. In response – discarding his prepared speech – Jenkins congratulated Hoyle on achieving 'the lowest Labour vote in this constituency for fifty years' and described the result as at once the first parliamentary election he had lost since 1945 and 'by far the greatest victory in which I have ever participated'.[142] 'What a marvellous result and what a speech!' John Grigg wrote the next day. 'If you had *paid* the horrific Hoyle to set the thing up for you he could hardly have done the job better. But you turned the situation to electrifying account, and with a vast unseen audience.'[143] (The polls closed at nine o'clock in those days and the declaration was broadcast live on television soon after eleven.) Another who admired Jenkins' 'perfectly-judged' reply to Hoyle's 'deplorably ungracious and offensive speech' was the rector of Warrington, who thanked him for putting Warrington on the map. 'I have never known anything remotely like the excitement and intensity of feeling generated by the campaign . . . The whole community of Warrington seemed to come alive.'[144]

The next day's headlines were all the mould-breakers could have wished for, from *The Times* ('A Triumph that May Change the Course of British Politics') to the *Sun* ('A New Age of Politics is Dawning in Britain'), reflecting a sudden realisation that the SDP must be taken seriously.[145] 'There have been false dawns before,' the *Guardian* cautioned, 'but there has been no time when a fundamental change in the pattern of British politics looked more likely to come than it does this morning.'[146] Jenkins himself – discounting the most extravagant projections, which would have given an SDP/Liberal combination practically all the seats in the House of Commons – declared that the 'experimental plane' that he had dared to imagine just thirteen months earlier was now 'cruising high. We have to accomplish the passage and landing, but the take-off has been securely achieved.' Warrington, he predicted, might mark the beginning of 'a change in British politics such as we have not seen since the First World War'.[147] One Labour moderate who had declined to join the breakaway, Giles Radice, acknowledged in his diary that Jenkins' 'astonishing 42% of the vote' was 'a splendid result for the Social Democrats and a sombre warning to the Labour Party that it cannot go on like it has without substantial working class defections'.[148]

Another result of Warrington was that Jenkins – though still lacking a seat in Parliament – was now firmly installed as the favourite for the leadership. Both the way he had risen to the challenge and the unexpectedly close result put an end to the caricature of a lazy fat cat who would never fight for anything except a restaurant table. With the sudden possibility that the SDP might really form at least a part of the next government, a poll of members found that 49 per cent now wanted him as leader compared with 29 per cent for Shirley Williams and 19 per cent for David Owen.[149] Even Owen was impressed by his 'campaigning spirit' and temporarily reconciled to Jenkins becoming leader.[150]

A third consequence of Warrington was the consolidation of the SDP–Liberal Alliance on the ground. The Liverpool Liberals' energetic contribution to Jenkins' campaign swept aside the reservations of many of those in the SDP who had wanted to preserve a distinct identity. 'There was no inter-party friction,' Jenkins wrote in his memoirs, 'and everybody got along together very well.'[151] The burgeoning love affair was consummated two months later when he and Shirley Williams, with David Steel and Jo Grimond, addressed a packed fringe meeting at the Liberal Assembly in Llandudno in September. (Bill Rodgers was also there but did not speak.) There had been apprehension that some Liberal purists might reject Steel's strategy of working together; in fact they gave Jenkins and Shirley Williams a rapturous welcome and endorsed the Alliance the next day by the overwhelming margin of 1,600:112. This was the famous and subsequently much-mocked occasion when Steel told his troops to 'go back to your constituencies and prepare for government'.[152] In his brief speech at the fringe meeting Jenkins went beyond the 'partnership of principle' that he had proclaimed in March and – reviving 'an old Gladstonian phrase' – called for 'a union of hearts' to make a reality of the prospect of a Liberal/Social Democrat government after the next election: 'a reality which breaks the stultifying monopoly of power which the two big parties have for too long enjoyed; a reality which means full scale electoral reform at the earliest possible moment so that the unfair and damaging monopoly cannot remain; a reality which frees the electorate from the false choice between the equally unwelcome extremes of Mrs Thatcher and Mr Benn; a reality which offers a new and widely sought-after hope to the British people'.

We can of course let all this slip. You can fall back on your ancient purity and we can console ourselves with our exciting novelty. But what fools we would be if we did! Mrs Thatcher and Mr Foot would heave sighs of relief. Still more important, a great part of public opinion would experience a sense of disappointment and let-down. The monopoly would survive, unloved, uncreative and almost unscarred. This will not happen. We have jointly made an unprecedented opportunity. Let us seize it together in an alliance of mutual respect and mutual trust.[153]

In his memoirs Jenkins regretted that David Owen was absent from this love feast, and wondered if his subsequent attitude to the Alliance might have been warmer had he been there. 'It is, I suppose, more likely that his absence was due to his coolness rather than the other way round.' But he believed that Llandudno shaped the future attitudes of all of them to the Alliance:

> The three of us who were there henceforth regarded it, even in moments of occasional exasperation, *con amore*, as a union of hearts as well as a partnership of principle. The one who was not there regarded it as a marriage of convenience, necessary and requiring the respectful observance of forms in public, but not to be confused with affection.[154]

There was a minor tiff between the two parties over who should fight the next by-election that came up: Croydon North-West. It was a Tory seat where the same Liberal candidate had already stood three times with conspicuous lack of success – indeed, his vote had fallen at each of the last three General Elections, in 1979 to just 10 per cent. After Jenkins' near-miss at Warrington there was strong pressure from the SDP for Shirley Williams to fight Croydon. Steel and other leading Liberals would have been happy with this, and this time she was willing. But the agreement made before Warrington gave the Liberals first stab at the next by-election; and the local Liberals stubbornly refused to jettison Bill Pitt.* Owen and others in the SDP who thought like him argued that Shirley should stand anyway. 'I did not leave the Labour Party after 43 years . . . so I could support . . . the Liberal Party,' one ex-MP wrote furiously to Bill Rodgers. 'The Liberal Party is dying – let it die in peace.' Rodgers replied that this would be electoral suicide. 'We are playing for very high stakes and to elbow the Liberals out of the way is not, in my view, consistent with our long term interests.'[157] In the end Pitt stood for a fourth time with SDP support – all four of the Gang of Four went to speak for him – and such was the tide now flowing behind the Alliance that he romped home in October with 40 per cent of the vote in a three-way contest, with

---

* 'We tried to kill him with flattery, food and drink,' Steel wrote, but Pitt refused to budge.[155] Sharing the widespread frustration that his candidacy would deny the Alliance a victory that Shirley Williams could win, Laura Grimond suggested that 'Mr William Pitt is really a case for Andrew Gino Newton or rather some more capable hit-man!'[156] Andrew Newton was the man allegedly hired by the former Liberal leader Jeremy Thorpe to kill his blackmailer Norman Scott, but who only shot his dog.

13,800 votes to the Tories' 10,546 and Labour's 8,967. This was in many ways a more striking result than Warrington because it was achieved without a star candidate.

Meanwhile the SDP had held its first conference – or rather (to break away from the stale seaside venues of the old parties) a 'rolling' conference, which started in Perth, moved on to Bradford and finished up at the Central Hall, Westminster, with two days in each. At Perth, Jenkins – now very much the leader presumptive – gave the opening speech reminding the party how far it had come in just six months and fixing its eyes on the General Election perhaps less than two years ahead. In London he gave a more substantial speech on the economy, once again lambasting the government for its 'uncomprehending and misdirected' monetarism, which was creating unemployment worse than the 1930s, and Labour for its utopian mix of nationalisation, protectionism and withdrawal from Europe, which would debase the currency and snuff out the last vestiges of confidence in the private sector. As a positive programme he repeated his Warrington plan to cut unemployment in the short term, whose arithmetic, he claimed, had never been challenged – 'not even by our complacent Chancellor, who came to Warrington just a few days later, exactly when he would, if they could have worked one out, have tried to present a counter-attacking Treasury brief'. Second, he proposed an 'inflation tax' on excessive pay rises, which would be 'relatively straightforward to collect' and would damp down 'the vicious process of wages following prices and prices following wages', allowing an SDP/Liberal government to 'revive expansionary forces in the economy and set unemployment on a permanently downward path'. Third, for the long term, he repeated his advocacy of a North Sea Oil fund to invest the temporary windfall constructively for the future. All this, he concluded – never shying away from words beginning with 'r' – was in line with 'the great tradition of radical responsible reform, which has been dead for too long and to which we are the true heirs'.[158]

'That was, quite simply, the finest speech that you have ever made,' Anthony Lester congratulated him. 'No-one who heard or reads it could doubt your future. I wish you health and strength for what lies ahead.'[159] Six weeks later the apparently unstoppable momentum of the Alliance bandwagon was demonstrated by another smashing by-election victory in the formerly rock-solid Tory seat of Crosby on the Lancashire coast. This time Shirley Williams announced her candidacy unilaterally, without consulting anyone, during the Bradford leg of the rolling conference. It was, on the face of it, a most unsuitable seat for her (and winning it tied her to a constituency she would be unable to hold in 1983). But the now road-tested Alliance machine moved into the sleepy Victorian suburb, taking 49 per cent of the vote and turning a Tory majority of nearly 20,000 into an SDP/Liberal one of more than 5,000. This was a staggering swing, which appeared to leave no constituency in the country beyond the reach of the Alliance's ambition. The next Gallup poll in December gave the Alliance 51 per cent, with 24 per cent for Labour and 23 per cent for the Conservatives.[160] At that moment nothing seemed impossible. But Crosby turned out, for various reasons, to be the zenith.

21 'Prime Minister Designate'

WHEREAS 1981 had been a year of almost unimaginable success for the SDP, 1982 turned out to be one of increasing difficulty, frustration and disillusion. First, there were already signs by the turn of the year that the government's harsh economic medicine was beginning to show some results: unemployment was still rising, but inflation was falling and the economy was showing signs of recovery. The summer riots had petered out in the 'fairytale' royal wedding of Prince Charles and Lady Diana Spencer, and Mrs Thatcher had reasserted her authority by sacking or demoting several of the 'wets' from her Cabinet, while at the same time quietly abandoning the strict interpretation of monetarism. For her the worst was over and her poll rating was beginning to recover, even before the Falklands war transformed her standing. Then Labour too, once Healey had narrowly defeated Benn for the deputy leadership, was presenting a slightly more moderate face to the electorate. Over the summer and autumn another dozen Labour MPs defected to the SDP, but none of them was very high-profile and there were to be only two more. Had Benn beaten Healey and maintained the momentum of the left's advance, many more substantial figures and even some right-wing unions like the engineers (AEU) might have switched allegiance, which would have transformed the political dynamic. Third, visible strains were beginning to appear between the Gang of Four as the euphoria of the launch was replaced by the serious prospect of power and Owen felt himself consistently outvoted by the other three. 'I don't look forward to lunches where David behaves like an arched cat,' Jenkins told Rodgers;[1] and after Warrington the weekly lunches at L'Amico dwindled to monthly. A serious policy difference also began to emerge within the parliamentary party over

Norman Tebbit's abolition of the trade union 'closed shop': some of the MPs still closest to their Labour roots were determined to oppose what they saw as typical Tory union-bashing, while others – notably Owen – wanted to support the government. Jenkins thought Tebbit's Bill negative and bigoted, but nevertheless thought the SDP right to vote for it in the hope of amending it in committee, believing that ordinary trade unionists deserved better than 'a choice between unelected extremists who pervert these values and uncaring Conservatives who despise them'.[2] In the key division in February 1982 seventeen of the twenty-seven SDP MPs voted for the bill, five against and five abstained.[3] This was the first real test of the party's coherence in the division lobby and a three-way split was not impressive.

Finally, all the camaraderie of Warrington, Croydon and Crosby could not prevent, but rather exacerbated, conflict between the two Alliance parties over which one was to fight which seats at the General Election. Jenkins and Steel might agree over their fortnightly lunches that they should fight roughly equal numbers of winnable seats; but the fact that they were expecting to win far more seats than the Liberals had ever won on their own made the argument in constituencies up and down the country anything but academic.* The Liberals were a famously decentralised party (or, in some SDP eyes, an undisciplined rabble). After Bill Pitt's fourth-attempt victory in Croydon, seasoned Liberal candidates were not lightly going to hand over their chance of emulating him to one of the SDP's political virgins or ex-Labour retreads on the say-so of their leader. Bill Rodgers led the negotiations for the SDP, region by region and seat by seat; but he found it hard to make any broad agreement stick in the face of Liberal localism. Eventually at the end of December he decided to go public, leaking his exasperation to the *Observer*, which made the breakdown of the negotiations its front-page story on 3 January. The revelation that the two supposedly 'nice' parties could not agree was extraordinarily damaging to the image of the Alliance. And it came just as Jenkins faced a second – but almost certainly his last – opportunity to claim the leadership by winning a by-election.

Once again the vacancy occurred in a seat that he would not have

---

* Jenkins usually took Steel to lunch at Brooks's, but Steel felt unable to reciprocate by inviting Jenkins to the National Liberal Club because the food there was so bad, so he had to find alternatives. He once took Jenkins to a Chinese restaurant that he knew had taken over a well-stocked cellar. Jenkins was initially doubtful but then delighted, declaring that the wine was 'spectacular'. Steel was always amazed by the amount he drank at lunch while remaining apparently unaffected by it.[4]

chosen: Glasgow, Hillhead – the one Tory-held division in that over-whelmingly Labour city. The Alliance had long had its eye on it, since the sitting Member, Tam Galbraith, was heir to a hereditary peerage and his father was ninety; but in fact it was the son who died on 2 January. Jenkins' story was that Tom Bradley rang him at East Hendred early on the Sunday morning to tell him cryptically that 'Galbraith is dead' before ringing off, leaving Roy and Jennifer under the sad misap-prehension that their good friend, the economist J.K. Galbraith, had died in America until they learned the truth much later in the day.[5] This is contradicted, however, by Bill Rodgers' recollection that Jenkins rang him early that morning when the row over seat allocation was splashed in the *Observer* to tell him, 'You have just lost me Hillhead.' It was the only time in their long association that he saw Jenkins so angry.[6] Whatever the timing, the row over seats made an awkward backdrop against which Jenkins had to decide whether to go for a constituency where once again the Liberals already had a candidate in place.

The biggest difficulty was that it was in Scotland. Once upon a time thoroughly English figures like Asquith and Churchill had thought nothing of sitting for Scottish seats in East Fife and Dundee respectively; but that was in less nationalistic days. Now it could be tricky for an anglicised Welshman with no Scottish connections who would inevitably be painted as a carpetbagger. Hillhead was also a marginal constituency, where Galbraith had a majority of just 2,000 over Labour: instead of being able to squeeze the Tory vote (as in Warrington) or the Labour vote (as in Croydon and Crosby) there was a danger that the Alliance, building on quite a small Liberal base, might itself be squeezed. There would also be an SNP candidate, making it a four-way fight. Against this, the character of the constituency was very unusual and, on closer inspection, tailor-made for the SDP and Jenkins in particular. Comprising most of the West End of central Glasgow, it contained not only Glasgow University, but the Glasgow School of Art, Glasgow High School, Jordanhill College of Education, the Western Infirmary (and two other teaching hospitals), two major art galleries (Kelvingrove and the Hunterian) and several other artistic and educational institutions, a high proportion of whose staff – including no fewer than 1,300 doctors – lived in the constituency. It was in fact the most highly educated constituency in Scotland and arguably in Britain, filled with just the sort of intelligent professionals who had flocked to the SDP banner. It did also have its share of solidly working-class Labour voters concen-trated along the Clyde. As he got to know the constituency Jenkins liked to describe it as divided between 'the river and the hill': his potential voters comprised 'the hill' and there seemed to be enough of them to warrant him taking the gamble.

But unlike Warrington it really was a gamble, since this time he absolutely had to win. 'Another good second place,' he wrote in his memoirs, 'would be no use to me at all.' If he lost he would have to give up trying to get back into Parliament, and with it any claim on the leadership. 'To fight two bye-elections had elements of valour. To fight three would have been ridiculous.'[7] Also he confessed to feeling nervous of Glasgow itself, which he had visited less frequently than most British cities – that is, only about ten times since 1959 – and still saw as strange and 'slightly sinister';[8]* and on top of this there was the complication of relations with the Liberals.

One of the most intractable constituency disputes was over Greenock, where the Scottish Liberals were refusing to stand aside for the sitting MP, Dickson Mabon, who had joined the SDP only in October. A Scottish Office minister in 1964–70, then responsible for North Sea oil under Callaghan, Mabon was the most senior figure to defect from Labour after the Gang of Four. He had been one of the sixty-nine EEC rebels in 1971 and resigned with Jenkins from his frontbench spokesmanship in 1972: Jenkins was reluctant to queer his pitch by insisting on fighting Hillhead, and very nearly pulled out, especially since Steel was doubtful about his chances in a Scottish seat. Bob Maclennan, however, who had grown up in the constituency, knew better than anyone that Hillhead was perfect for him and worked hard to persuade the Scottish Liberals to withdraw their candidate, a young computer engineer called 'Chick' Brodie (Maclennan wrote later of 'the horrendous row I had with the Liberals to prise the seat from the sainted Chick Brodie').[10] Eventually Brodie and his constituency chairman travelled down to Kensington Park Gardens on Sunday 10 January and after three hours agreed to stand down in Jenkins' favour. In his memoirs Jenkins gratefully acknowledged him as 'a major artificer of the Alliance'.[11]†

---

* He had in fact recently had a foretaste of what he would come to love about Glasgow when he gave a lecture at Strathclyde University in 1979. 'After the lecture I dined agreeably . . . with the academic weight of Strathclyde, and then returned to the Central Hotel. It really is a rather magnificent hotel, old railway style at its best, expressing all the weight, solidity and splendour of 1890 Glasgow: tremendously good woodwork . . . not at all rundown.'[9]
† After the by-election Jenkins took Brodie to lunch at Brooks's and offered to help him in any way he could. Twenty years later Brodie did approach him for help in finding a business opening in Europe. Jenkins promised to try, but nothing came of it.[12] Brodie stood three times as a Lib Dem candidate in 1992, 1997 and 2001, but then joined the SNP and is now a member of the Scottish Parliament.

Jenkins was formally adopted by both parties the following Thursday. He was still unsure that he was wise to stand. To Edward Lyons he explained that he 'rather reluctantly decided to do Hillhead in order to prevent the Alliance falling apart in Scotland';[13] and to another former MP who urged him not to stand for a Scottish seat, he replied, 'You may be right about standing for a Scottish constituency, but events have rather taken over and I am now committed. Let us hope it will be for the best.'[14] In his adoption speech, however, he promised to fight 'a memorable Hillhead campaign and I believe secure a famous victory'. He invoked the example of one of his political heroes, Franklin Roosevelt, promising to 'substitute hope for fear' and show the country that 'there is an alternative':

> A hundred years ago this month Franklin Roosevelt was born. Fifty-one years later he started to give a depressed America a new deal, a new confidence, a new freedom from fear. He did it without doctrinaire ideological baggage, without out-of-date class dogma, but with a determination to make things work better and give his great nation an opportunity to escape from its head down attitude and restore its verve and its greatness. We need a touch of that in the heart of Scotland and in Britain as a whole today. Let us try to infuse this campaign with such a message of unifying hope.[15]

Then he set about getting to know the constituency and the city. The next day he held a press conference and gave a lot of interviews, then spent the rest of the weekend quietly exploring on foot and by car, before flying back to London on Monday morning. After Crosby the Tories were in no hurry to call another by-election sooner than they had to, so it was going to be a long campaign: not until late February was polling day fixed for 25 March. So for the first month he went back to Glasgow only one or two days a week. But he used his visits well, concentrating initially on meeting 'opinion formers' – the editors of local papers, the principals of the colleges and heads of professional organisations, medical professors and religious leaders. Then from 1 February he started holding unofficial advice bureaux as if he was already the MP; and from 19 February he began meeting small groups of voters at informal coffee mornings in the houses of local supporters. This, he wrote, was an effective way of 'penetrating the gentility of Kelvinside, Dowanhill, Broomhill and Jordanhill [which] could have worked only in the relatively large sitting rooms of the

What does Roy Jenkins wear under his kilt ?

Garland, *Daily Telegraph*, 12.1.82 (British Cartoon Archive, University of Kent)

hill'.[16] The ladies of Hillhead were charmed and flattered to have the great man in their homes and duly spread the word to their neighbours. Once the election was called he established himself permanently in the Pond Hotel on the Great Western Road and started serious canvassing in shopping centres and door-to-door, slogging up and down the solid sandstone tenements; only after several weeks of this did he start holding public meetings. Even more than in Warrington a lot of his grand friends as well as the whole of the SDP and Liberal top brass poured in to help, to the extent that David Steel worried that his campaign was far too English – and posh southern English at that.[17] One quint-essentially Kensington lady drew satirical attention for running up and down some of the poorest tower blocks in shocking lilac tights. Steel cringed when Jenkins initially ducked the question of whether he would undertake to live in the constituency by saying that he owned two houses already, but would acquire 'a wesidence' – that difficult consonant again – in Hillhead.

He focused on three main issues: unemployment again – a national issue, renewing and expanding the plan he had unveiled at Warrington;

education, particularly the government's cuts in higher education – an issue specifically tailored to Hillhead's particular electorate; and devolution – an unavoidable issue in Scotland. On this, somewhat fortunately, Jenkins was able to point to the speech he had made in March 1976 declaring his conversion to the case for a Scottish assembly with revenue-raising powers to prove that he had not embraced the subject just because he found himself standing for a Scottish seat. But undeniably devolution henceforth took a rather higher place in his programme for the renewal of British democracy, and he set out his view both of the principle and of the necessary safeguards in a major speech on 10 March.[18] In addition he made targeted appeals to all sorts of specific interest groups: at an Indian Association of Strathclyde dinner he recalled his record of race relations legislation at the Home Office and talked about Third World aid;[19] to a Hillhead businessmen's lunch he talked about Keynesian economic management;[20] his diary was packed with daytime meetings in schools and hospitals, with the Scottish Development Agency, the Glasgow Housing Association and similar organisations.

While addressing local issues, however, he fought unashamedly on his record as a national and international statesman. As well as harping on Labour's links with the far left – particularly the fellow-travelling utterances of that year's Scottish Labour chairman, George Galloway – his leaflets made much of the anonymity of most of Glasgow's thirteen other MPs (all Labour, none of them, with the exception of Donald Dewar, at all distinguished). 'Do you really want another member of this losing team as your MP?' . . . 'Hillhead Needs a Voice that will be Heard . . . Scotland needs a real alternative to Mrs Thatcher's Conservatism.'[21] His opponents were of nowhere near the same stature. Labour's candidate was a nineteen-stone community worker, bearded and sporting an earring, lacking the personality or eloquence to convince any but the most committed loyalist. The Tories selected a young Catholic lawyer, Gerald Malone (later MP for Aberdeen South and later still for Winchester). He was articulate and personable, and had been born and bred in the constituency; but sectarian feeling still ran strongly in Glasgow and the militant Protestant pastor Jack Glass ran a virulent anti-Catholic campaign against him which probably siphoned off more of the Protestant vote than the 388 he actually received. Another Tory without that handicap might well have held the seat.[22] In addition to the SNP and Pastor Glass, the by-election circus again attracted several fringe candidates, including another spoiler who changed his name to 'Roy Jenkins': this time he was allowed to stand, so that volunteers had to be posted outside every polling station to remind voters that 'The Real Roy Jenkins is No. 5.' The counterfeit polled nearly 300 votes, which might easily have been crucial.

Jenkins' time in Brussels was not as much of a liability as might have been expected. The story was told of one man, strongly anti-European, who said he was going to vote for him: when reminded that Jenkins had been President of the EEC, he replied, 'Aye, but he jacked it in, didn't he?'[23] The Tories tried to make something of his reputation as the godfather of the permissive society by reproducing a letter from Mary Whitehouse alleging that 'Pornography . . . was legalised by the Obscene Publications Act of 1959, sponsored by none other than Mr Roy Jenkins': Alec McGivan had to put out a note reminding canvassers that the Bill had been carried with the support of a Tory Home Secretary and that Jenkins did not support pornography or sex shops on every high street.[24] Meanwhile Labour banged away at his claret-swilling image: at an eve-of-poll meeting no less a figure than Denis Healey thought to shock the Glaswegians by asserting that Jenkins had brought with him a supply of 'an Italian wine called Valpolicella', which he presumably thought would sound wickedly foreign and expensive.[25] But all this was froth. The real worry for the Jenkins camp was that, as in Warrington, his message did not seem to be getting through. The Alliance's national standing had already fallen from the mid-forties to the mid-thirties as a result of the seat allocation row; and the local polls, which had initially shown Jenkins winning, now indicated that he was falling back. Jenkins himself had a filthy cold; the weather, which always affected his mood, was cold and wet; and he was becoming increasingly tense and agitated as he faced a second defeat. The nadir was an NOP poll in the *Observer* on 14 March, which put him in third place with just 23 per cent, with Labour leading.

But it was just around this time that the tide began to turn, as the long campaign peaked with a series of ten public meetings, all packed, at which Jenkins was supported by a varying cast of back-up speakers, both SDP and Liberal; the most memorable was on 18 March, a week before polling day, when the four members of the Gang of Four all spoke together on the same platform at Hyndland school and then went out in turn to address another thousand people waiting outside in the moonlight in the frosty playground. The enthusiasm and the seriousness of the audiences were alike astonishing. Jenkins wrote later that the SDP, in the heady twelve months since its launch, had revived the almost defunct tradition of the political meeting: at Hillhead he calculated that around a quarter of the entire electorate came to at least one of his meetings – though it was a measure of the interest aroused that both

Benn for Labour and Ted Heath, ambiguously for the Tories, drew similar crowds.[26] In the last week the weather and the whole mood changed: the sun came out, the constituency was suddenly gay with purple crocuses and the polls turned up at last. One on 19 March put Jenkins ahead for the first time (by a single point); then in the last days the *Glasgow Herald* put him 4 per cent ahead, and NOP in the *Daily Mail* and MORI in the *Express* put him six points clear (though differing on who was second). In the collective sigh of relief at the Pond Hotel, Jenkins told Celia Goodhart that she could wear her lilac tights again, and was confident enough to brush off as an aberration a final poll showing him third. The last day saw him visibly relaxed, beaming broadly as he 'cavalcaded' around the streets in a decorated Land Rover driven by David Astor and plunged into shopping centres to shake hands – Bob Maclennan at his shoulder, Bill Rodgers ahead playing John the Baptist with a megaphone, and Jennifer (her right arm in a sling because of a poisoned finger) gamely shaking hands with her left; and polling day confirmed his perfectly timed spurt to the wire:*

Roy Jenkins (SDP/Liberal)	10,106
Gerald Malone (Conservative)	8,068
David Wiseman (Labour)	7,846
George Leslie (SNP)	3,416
+ 4 others	853
SDP/Liberal majority	2,038[27]

On a poll of 76 per cent (higher than the General Election) Jenkins took 33.4 per cent of the vote, with a swing of 19 per cent – less than at Warrington, but a greater achievement in that it was won against an ebbing tide. For an advocate of proportional representation it was ironic to win with twice as many votes against him as for; but that was the first-past-the-post system. Nevertheless his victory was widely recognised as a personal triumph. 'Reckless Roy Comes Out On Top: The Gambler Who Hit The Jackpot', ran the *Daily Mail*'s headline; while *The Times* hailed 'The Second Coming of Saint Roy' and reflected a general assumption that the result – proving that he was not just an elder statesman, but still an effective vote-winner – gave him 'an irresistible claim' to the SDP leadership.[29]

---

* The result was in such doubt up to the last minute, however, that the *Times* pocket cartoonist Mel Calman drew two alternative frames, according to whether Jenkins won or lost. In the first, passing a placard announcing 'Roy loses', his little man thinks: 'Perhaps he's too civilised for politics.' In the second ('Roy wins') he thinks: 'Hooway!'[28]

The President of the European Commission off-duty on an official visit
to Timbuctoo, January 1979.

...sident Jenkins in session with his fellow Commissioners in the Berlaymont building,
Brussels, 1977.

Jenkins with (*top left*) French President Giscard d'Estaing; (*top right*) West German Chancellor Helmut Schmidt; (*above*) British Foreign Secretary David Owen, 1977; (*right*) US President Jimmy Carter and Margaret Thatcher in Venice, June 1980.

Delivering the Dimbleby Lecture, November 1979.

The Gang of Four after the Limehouse Declaration, 26 January 1981:
Bill Rodgers, Shirley Williams, Jenkins, and David Owen.

Jenkins announcing his intention to fight the Warrington by-election for the SDP, June 1981.

(*Above and right*) Canvassing in Warrington.

... ng in the rain,
... gton, July 1981.

... Returning to the
... se of Commons
... Shirley Williams
... fter winning the
... ead by-election,
... March 1982.

... LLHEAD
... BERALS
for
... ROY

The leaders of the Alliance: Jenkins and David Steel campaigning in the 1983 General Election.

Jennifer and Roy on Great Yarmouth beach during the SDP conference, 1982.

Jenkins in procession as Chancellor of Oxford University, June 1988.

Writing in Tuscany, 1993.

Winning the Whitbread Biography Award for *Gladstone* in 1995.

Roy and Jennifer in 1999.

Calman, *The Times*, 26.3.82 (British Cartoon Archive, University of Kent)

On a personal level Jenkins' victory at Hillhead was perhaps the high point of his political life. Achieved on the very anniversary of the SDP's birth, it seemed to crown the journey he had plotted since the Dimbleby Lecture and to give him at least a very good chance of leading the Alliance into government within the next two years. He drew particular pleasure from the uncanny parallel that by staging a triumphant come-back in a west of Scotland seat he was precisely emulating Asquith, who had gained a similar victory – after losing his seat in 1918 – at a famous by-election at Paisley in 1921. The next day, by chance, Jenkins was due to address the Scottish Liberal conference in St Andrew's (in Asquith's former constituency of East Fife), from where he returned via a dinner in Edinburgh to another SDP celebration in Paisley: a day, as he admitted, of 'almost excessive Asquith pietism'. Unfortunately the precedent was not a good one. Asquith's victory 'heralded one of the greatest false dawns in twentieth century politics';[30] and his own victory at Hillhead sadly turned out to be another. Nevertheless Hillhead, and the city of Glasgow as a whole, unexpectedly became one of the two great loves of the last period of his life.

He and Jennifer did buy a 'residence': a small flat in an elegant Georgian terrace on the Great Western Road – 'the most architectur-ally distinguished façade behind which we have ever lived' – and spent about one weekend a month there, plus other visits, so long as he remained the MP.[31] Jenkins actively enjoyed Hillhead as he had never enjoyed Stechford. He delighted in showing off the under-appreciated glories of Glasgow to visiting friends (particularly American friends) and celebrated the city in several lectures and articles, culminating in a full chapter in his last book, *Twelve Cities*, in which he firmly rated Glasgow 'upon grounds of site, metropolitan atmosphere, industrial history, visual impact, educational and cultural resources and the splendid mixture of early- and late-Victorian exuberance in its architecture . . . as one of the outstanding non-capital cities of the world, almost compar-able with Chicago or Barcelona'.[32] Despite the appalling redevelopment of the 1960s (for which as Chancellor at the time he took a share of the blame) he judged Glasgow to be 'architecturally the finest Victorian city in the world', by comparison with which Birmingham, the largest provincial city in England, was just a manufacturing town – 'a Detroit to Glasgow's Chicago' – while classical Edinburgh was like 'a splendid salmon laid out on a slab', handsome but dead.[33] Even London he considered 'a much less European city than Glasgow . . . an essentially suburban city'. He attributed much of Glasgow's character to its 'God-given' site, ranking the Clyde estuary as 'the most dramatic piece of seascape at the gates of a major city anywhere in the world, with the possible exception' – he always had to add a qualification – 'of Vancouver Sound and the Bosphorus'.[34] But he also loved (at least at a distance) 'the cranes of Govan, still to be seen on the drive in from the airport [which] proclaim that this is Glasgow as emphatically as the Eiffel Tower identifies Paris, or the Statue of Liberty does New York, or the bridge and the opera house do Sydney'.[35] Above all he admired the 'quiet self-confidence' of the people of Glasgow, which he defined as 'a curiosity about outside things accompanied by a contentment within one's own skin'.[36] He and Jennifer made a number of lasting friends in Hillhead, most notably Donald Macfarlane, a local GP, and his wife Elsa, with whom they continued to stay on their visits to the city after he had lost his seat and they had given up their flat.* On another of the criteria by which he judged cities, Glasgow offered at least two restaurants that met his standards: the Ubiquitous Chip off Byres Road (Michelin-starred, despite its unpromising name) and Rogano (with wonderful 1930s decor in the style of a Cunard liner)

---

* He also kept in touch with several of his Hillhead party workers, even after he lost the seat: for instance, he used to telephone one, Les Goodall, every Christmas right up till his death. 'How many politicians of Roy's stature,' Goodall's daughter wondered, 'would have bothered over all those years to telephone an aged and confused retired party worker of no importance whatsoever?'[37] It should be said that he did the same with some of his old Stechford supporters.

in the city centre. All in all he derived immense pleasure and took great pride in having been a Glasgow MP: as a collector of political arcana, he also relished the curious distinction that he believed himself to be the only person to have represented in Parliament all three of the United Kingdom's biggest cities: London, Birmingham and Glasgow.

Jenkins' victory at Hillhead might seem to have put his claim to the SDP leadership beyond doubt, with the premiership now firmly in his sights. He received a whole file of congratulations not only from his usual army of friends but from a wide range of political opponents on both sides of the House of Commons, including Julian Amery and Douglas Hurd, Fred Mulley and Tam Dalyell, many of them confidently assuming that he would soon be Prime Minister.[38] His old girlfriend Barley Alison looked forward to being able boast that she had known he was going to be Prime Minister when he was still in his twenties;[39] while the Oxford political scientist Vernon Bogdanor wrote to reassure him that he was 'not Asquith at East Fife, but Gladstone at Midlothian in 1880 . . . following which he led three administrations!'[40] Yet there were still mutterings within the SDP that he should not be leader. David Owen, Mike Thomas and others still wanted Shirley Williams to stand; and she herself suggested publicly in a speech in East London that Jenkins might perhaps be leader of the Alliance but not of the SDP, urging that the party should not rush into a leadership contest, but stick with the collective leadership: 'The SDP must not slip towards a hierarchy dominated by a single person, however wise or brilliant.'[41] Opinion polls, on the other hand, showed that while Jenkins had decisively replaced Shirley Williams as the best leader of the SDP, the public preferred Steel as leader of the Alliance. These differences were raised explicitly at the steering committee ten days after Hillhead, when Jenkins made it very clear that he did not intend to be marginalised:

RJ explained that he could see no reason for placing himself in limbo within the SDP by becoming Alliance Leader but not SDP leader. He proposed to be a candidate in any leadership election within the SDP and if defeated in that election he would not be Alliance Leader. He pointed out that the question of a Leader for the Alliance did not arise at this stage. Instead, the Alliance should prepare for a General Election with a candidate for Prime Minister. To discuss an Alliance Leader further now could cause confusion and damage to the party.[42]

Unfortunately his return to the House of Commons was an immediate disappointment. He took his seat on the Tuesday after his election, introduced by Bob Maclennan and Dickson Mabon, and made his first intervention, suitably enough, following a statement by Mrs Thatcher about the latest European Council in Brussels in which she reiterated her refusal to make progress on other matters until she got what she wanted on the Community budget.[43] Jenkins' intervention was acidly described by the Tory diarist Alan Clark:

> Thereafter Jenkins, with excessive and almost unbearable gravitas, asked three very heavy, statesmanlike non-party-political questions of the PM. I suppose he is very formidable, but he was so portentous and long-winded that he started to lose the sympathy of the House about half way through and the barracking resumed. The Lady replied quite brightly and freshly, as if she did not particularly know who he was, or care.[44]

He never really got any better. In the five years he had been away the House of Commons had deteriorated enormously – as Jim Callaghan had warned him. Instead of the set-piece debates at which he had excelled, climaxing in substantial half-hour speeches from the dispatch box by a minister replying to his Opposition shadow, cheered on by the packed ranks of their usually post-prandial supporters before the ten o'clock vote, the focus had moved decisively to the cheap point-scoring of Prime Minister's Questions which, he later lamented, 'bear about as much resemblance to traditional eloquence as a game of snap does to the skills of bridge or chess'.[45] At the same time the serious reporting of the business of the House was increasingly replaced by satirical sketch-writing exemplified by Frank Johnson in *The Times* and Edward Pearce in the *Daily Telegraph*. Jenkins was not good at cheap point-scoring and he was an easy target for satire. Lacking either a dispatch box to rest his notes on or supportive benches behind him, he had to speak unsupported from the front or second row below the gangway. All third-party leaders – David Steel, David Owen, Paddy Ashdown – have struggled to be heard from this position, but Jenkins was mercilessly heckled by Dennis Skinner, Bob Cryer and others of the Labour awkward squad who usually bagged the front row and sat looking up at him, putting him off his stride with gibes about claret, his Brussels pension or 'Roy, your flies are undone'. He never found a way of coping with this new style of parliamentary sniping; and the Speaker – his old Welsh rival George Thomas – did too little to protect him. The only good speech he made after his return to the House was against the restoration of the death penalty, a non-party issue which gave him the chance to rehearse familiar arguments from twenty years before.[46]

His discomfort was exacerbated by the crisis which erupted out of a clear sky just a week after his election when Argentina invaded and occupied the Falkland Islands in pursuit of its longstanding claim to sovereignty. After the immediate sense of shock at the seizure of British territory, Mrs Thatcher's decisive reaction in sending a naval task force to recapture the islands saved her reputation and transformed the entire landscape of politics up to the General Election. Jenkins was lucky that the invasion took place seven days after his by-election: had the Argentines moved ten days earlier he would almost certainly have been swept away by the tide of patriotic outrage. As it was, the expectation that his return to Westminster would re-invigorate the flagging momentum of the Alliance was instantly dashed by an unexpected war which not only suspended all normal political controversy about unemployment and monetarism, making it practically certain that the next election would be a landslide for the Tories, but cruelly exposed his particular limitations. Despite his three years in uniform during the war and his liking for military metaphors in his writing, Jenkins was temperamentally utterly unsuited to talking about war, which offended his whole concept of rational international relations.

He was attending an SDP dinner in Cambridge when news of the invasion broke: his immediate reaction was that it was a serious humiliation for Mrs Thatcher, but it never occurred to him that she would try to reverse it by military force.[47] For some weeks he managed to avoid making any reported comment about the crisis at all, leaving it to David Owen, in the Commons and on radio and television, to promise the SDP's firm support for whatever action was needed to retake the islands. Owen was not only an MP for Plymouth (with its strong naval tradition) with a close interest in defence matters, but temperamentally far more in sympathy with Mrs Thatcher's belligerent response: he could also, as Foreign Secretary in 1978, claim to have deterred a previous Argentine attempt to threaten the Falklands by sending an aircraft carrier, thus effectively balancing his support for the government with criticism of its negligence in allowing the crisis to occur in the first place.* Jenkins' first intervention, in a question to the

---

* According to Bill Rodgers, however, Owen's first instinct was to oppose sending the task force, until persuaded by Rodgers that they must support it. Shirley Williams, on the other hand, shared Jenkins' uneasiness about the war.[48]

Prime Minister on 20 April, was at once trivial and almost laughably portentous, and was duly guyed by Frank Johnson ('Jenkins rolls a jowl at the Falklands') and brushed aside by Mrs Thatcher ('I must confess I had expected a more fundamental point from the right hon. Gentleman').[49] When finally forced to declare his position, Jenkins naturally condemned the Argentine action and reluctantly supported the sending of the task force. But he continued to urge that some form of negotiated settlement, possibly resulting in UN Trusteeship of the islands, was preferable to military engagement. He kept harking back to Suez, insisting that the most important lessons to be learned from 1956 were to avoid dividing the nation and to preserve international support.[50] But this just made him sound like a dinosaur: Suez might seem like yesterday to him, but to most of the voting public it was ancient history, scarcely relevant to the present situation. In 1982 the nation was not seriously divided – despite some disquiet over the sinking of the Argentine battleship, the *General Belgrano* – and thanks to some skilful diplomacy in New York and Washington (not least by Jenkins' friend Nicko Henderson, now ambassador in Washington) Britain had UN backing for its position. It might have been different if General Galtieri had shown any willingness to compromise; but so long as he did not, Mrs Thatcher's determination to expel the invader by force seemed the only option. Nevertheless Jenkins stuck to his pacific line. 'At the end of the day,' he warned on 14 May, 'whether there is more fighting or not, we have to get a negotiated settlement. That is because we cannot indefinitely defend islands 8,000 miles away in a hostile environment.'[51] He refused to be carried away by the emotion of the moment in defence of 1,800 islanders, but foresaw the absurd distortion of defence policy which the recapture of the islands would entail for decades ahead.

He loathed Mrs Thatcher's flag-waving jingoism during the war and her triumphalism when it was over. Speaking at a by-election in Beaconsfield a few days before the British forces went ashore on 21 May – an election which a few weeks earlier the Alliance would have hoped to win, but where it could now only hope to come a distant second – Jenkins took the Prime Minister to task for speaking as if a small war in the South Atlantic could 'regenerate the nation and bring forth the glories of a new Elizabethan age'. This, he said, was 'dangerous nonsense', and he accused her of exploiting the war for party advantage: 'Mrs Thatcher must understand that the Conservative Party is not the nation.'[52] Less than three weeks later – actually some days before the Union Jack flew again over Port Stanley – he called for magnanimity in victory and a sense of perspective. Writing in *The Times* under the headline 'Our honour upheld: now comes the time for statesmanship', he ridiculed Churchillian comparisons with the spirit of 1940: 'We have carried through a limited operation extremely well. That ought to help us not to reach beyond our grasp. We have assuaged our honour. Let us now show foresight in victory.'[53]

David Owen by contrast had a good war, lending Mrs Thatcher critical support at every stage and greatly raising his own profile at the same time. Where Jenkins appeared flabby and long-winded, Owen was tough and pithy: quite suddenly he was seen as a serious challenger for the leadership of the SDP. At a meeting of the communications committee on 25 May Shirley Williams worried that only one member of the Gang of Four was getting any media coverage.[54] Yet Jenkins' doubts about the war were more representative than Owen's. At the steering committee on 14 June – the day Mrs Thatcher announced that the islands were wholly back in British hands – Polly Toynbee, normally a strong Owenite, argued that the party had been too supportive of the government, while John Roper, the party's Chief Whip, reported that a majority of the MPs backed Jenkins' line on sovereignty and UN Trusteeship. The committee agreed that it had been a peculiarly difficult time for the party, putting its belief in 'cool rationalism' in conflict with its 'opposition to internal factionalism'; but now that the war was over, it agreed to 'push for a long-term international solution, and oppose any move towards a "Fortress Falklands".'[55] Owen was in the chair, but Jenkins' view clearly prevailed.

As soon as Shirley Williams and Jenkins were both back in the Commons the steering committee had decided to bring forward the contest for the leadership, with the result that the starting gun was fired while the war was still going on. While Jenkins, supported by Bill Rodgers, had hoped that he might be elected unopposed, both Owen and Shirley Williams were determined that the new party's democratic credentials required a contest, not a coronation which would be seen as a stitch-up. This difference of view was magnified by a row over how the leader should be elected. Having made the case for internal democracy one of his key reasons for breaking with Labour, Owen believed that one-member-one-vote elections should be a matter of principle for the SDP; moreover he believed that Jenkins had agreed to this at their meeting at East Hendred in November 1980. Many of Jenkins' strongest allies, however, including Rodgers, adhered to the traditional view that a party's MPs, who observed the candidates at first hand every day, were better placed than the wider membership to judge their qualities. Jenkins himself claimed not to feel so strongly about this; but he also claimed to have no recollection of any undertaking to Owen and allowed himself to be persuaded by his friends, 'well after I could see that it was both difficult to argue and unnecessary in my own interest'.[56] Owen was incensed by what he still called in his memoirs a decade later 'the shabbiest act that I have ever witnessed . . . His change of mind meant only one thing: he was in so much of a hurry that he could not give a damn for the Party that he had helped found. The SDP was just a disposable vehicle for his ambition to be Prime Minister.'[57] In the event the party's constitutional conference in mid-February – more than a month before Hillhead, when it was still not certain that Jenkins would be eligible to stand – voted to let the membership decide the question by ballot; and they in turn voted decisively for one-man-one-vote.

Owen's fury was based partly on the expectation that the MPs were more likely to vote for Jenkins, and the membership for a supposedly more radical candidate, Shirley Williams or himself. In fact the opposite turned out to be the case. When Williams once again declined the heat of the kitchen and Owen determined to stand instead, he won the support of nearly half of the party's twenty-nine MPs, while Jenkins' support was stronger among the ordinary members. An exchange of letters between Bill Rodgers and Shirley Williams reveals some of the tensions within the Gang of Four that led her – and a dozen others – to back Owen. Rodgers recalled that the previous August she had agreed that Jenkins would make the best leader and she would not challenge him; but subsequently she had changed her mind 'in view of a campaign on the part of some of Roy's friends that was personally damaging to you'. He argued that since she had 'personally exonerated Roy, and absolutely rightly', this was not reason to change her mind about his suitability as leader:

> We need someone to pull the party together, achieve a working relationship with the Liberals and lead us in Government if we win. Why should anything that may have been said by Roy's friends – however mistaken and hurtful to you – invalidate the qualities that . . . led you to support him?

He went on to say that he had always thought a combination of Roy as leader with Shirley as president was the most powerful for the party, while his own 'relative advantage' lay in organisation. 'It seemed to me that David – for all his high qualities – had lots of time ahead. I hoped that all of us would put the overall interest of the party ahead of self-indulgence.' He regretted that this was now to be set aside in 'a contest of personalities with the best interests of the party in second place':

> Given David's style and mood and his personal antipathy to Roy, his behaviour is at least predictable. I had hoped that you would see matters in a different light.
>
> I appreciate that you may decide not to stand against Roy, although you would be a stronger candidate than David. But, if you nominate David or otherwise support him, it will still be a clear breach of our understanding of last summer.

'The Gang of Four,' he concluded, 'has been a remarkable achievement and much good has come of it.' But it would now be much more difficult to maintain a collective leadership. 'For the first time since the party was launched I am profoundly depressed.'[58]

Williams did not reply for more than week, by which time she had announced her nomination of David Owen – not, she explained in her memoirs, because she expected him to win, but because (wrongly as it turned out) 'I thought he would hold the new Party to the left of centre. I did not want to see the Jenkinsites uncontested.'[59]

> My dear Bill,
>
> Thank you for your letter. I've kept my word and won't oppose Roy. I have both respect and affection for him. But one cannot wholly divorce anyone from their friends and supporters . . . I'm not wholly certain that he would not be more influenced by them than by the rest of the four – and that's why I've consistently argued for a collective style of leadership.
>
> Frankly, I believe there is a perfectly legitimate right for any of us to stand as leader . . . I believe many Party members would believe they had been led up the garden path at the time of the vote on the method of election otherwise . . .
>
> I hope you won't be too depressed. I think the Party had to have a contest, and that once the contest is over . . . we will move forward decisively again.
>
> Yours ever,
Shirley[60]

Owen's high profile during that Falklands summer made the outcome much less certain than had previously been assumed. Both candidates promised to keep the contest gentlemanly, with no public campaigning and no overt criticism of one another: they were each limited to a 750-word statement which was sent with their ballot papers to all 65,000 paid-up members of the party. Outwardly the Queensberry rules were pretty much observed. The two principals spoke mainly to meetings of local area parties. But their supporters waged a proxy campaign in the media which was a good deal less squeamish, while Jenkins' diary shows that he lunched with a good many influential journalists and wrote several newspaper articles implicitly pressing his claim: he also (as Owen saw it) 'broke his own ban and went on TV, no doubt feeling disadvantaged by my Falklands-related TV appearances'.[61] Behind the comradely façade it was a tensely fought contest between sharply opposed personal styles and strategies. The visible contrast was entirely one of image: Owen the young, handsome, brash, impatient challenger, claiming to be the more 'radical'; Jenkins nearly twenty years older, Home Secretary before Owen was even in Parliament, only sixty-one, but presenting the image of a wise old owl. Jenkins was assumed to be more conservative just because of his age and manner, though real policy differences between them were hard to find, and Owen's instincts – on the Falklands, for instance, and on nuclear weapons – were in reality more right-wing. Owen's streak of puritanism, strongly anti-tobacco and personally sparing with alcohol, contrasted with Jenkins' famous enjoyment of his pleasures. 'Abrasive David or Rounded Roy?' was Hugo Young's summary in the *Sunday Times*; 'Bossyboots *versus* the Drinker's Friend' was Alan Watkins' more memorable encapsulation in the *Observer*.[62]

The one difference of substance between them was over relations with the Liberals: Owen's desire to protect the distinct identity of the SDP against Jenkins' vision of ever-closer cooperation leading to eventual merger. There appeared to be a genuine difference of strategy here, with implications for the party's appeal to the voters: Jenkins wanting to draw support from both sides of the political spectrum, Owen still keener to replace Labour. Edward Lyons, one of the original defectors who decided to back Owen, explained his decision apologetically to Jenkins by arguing that the SDP needed 'a personality distinct from the Liberal Party . . . and to have a left of centre image attractive to the Labour voter. I am also uneasy that the SDP is becoming the junior partner in the Alliance . . . I am so very deeply sorry.'[63] But even here the distinction was more of tone and image than of substance. In an article in the *Observer* on 13 June Jenkins made it clear that he too saw 'the historic role of the SDP – and indeed of the Alliance' as being 'to push the Labour Party out of the arena of government, and to make ourselves the effective alternative to the Conservatives'. But he saw more clearly than his critics that this required winning Tory votes as well as Labour ones: otherwise, he warned – since the Labour Party could not be expected to disappear altogether – the SDP would simply re-create 'the scenario of the 1920s', offering the prospect of political realignment 'at the price of a period, maybe a generation, of Conservative hegemony':

> This has been one aspect of breaking the mould which has from the beginning given me pause. I do not wish to repeat this part of the political history of the inter-war years . . . I cannot under-stand why it is regarded as the 'left-wing' strategy, for it is a gift to the Right.
>
> My view . . . is that it should in the future be perfectly possible over the country as a whole to take approximately two votes from a terminally sick Labour Party for one vote from an inflated Conservative support, to add this to a significant Liberal base, and by doing so create a new radical majority without the penalties of fifty or sixty years ago. This is the correct centre-left strategy. This is the true breaking of the mould.[64]

The problem for this strategy was that it had been upset by the Falklands. So long as the Tories under Mrs Thatcher could be presented as being as ideologically extreme and economically disastrous as Labour, it was possible to see the Alliance coming through the middle by taking votes from both. Once Mrs Thatcher's reputation had been transformed by victory in the South Atlantic, making her re-election a foregone conclusion, the country was indeed set for a period of Conservative hegemony. Since Labour did not implode, but gradually moved back towards the centre, all the SDP and the Alliance could achieve over the next decade was, precisely as Jenkins feared, to split the anti-Conservative vote and entrench that hegemony.

Owen's strategy was in practice no different from Jenkins'. Of course he too wanted Tory votes as well as Labour ones: he was in reality just as much of a centrist and he accepted that an alliance with the Liberals was at least temporarily unavoidable. The difference between them was Owen's barely concealed contempt for the Liberals and his illusion – delusion – that the SDP could become a viable distinct fourth party while keeping the third party at arm's length. So in fact it came down to a difference of image and personality after all. In their respective statements each underlined his own particular qualities while subtly undermining the other's. Jenkins led with a reminder of Warrington, Hillhead and the Dimbleby Lecture, to make the point that it was he, not Owen, who had originated the SDP (while 'those still active in party politics were still wrestling with their loyalties') and borne the heat of its first campaigns. Similarly Owen began with a reminder that the election was by one-member-one-vote (which he had supported and Jenkins opposed), called for a spirit of adventure, 'guts' and 'drive' (which by implication Jenkins lacked) and beat a drum for 'rational patriotism' (a reminder of Jenkins' ambivalence on the Falklands). On the necessity of the Alliance both sought to blur their difference by stealing the other's clothes. Jenkins praised the 'partnership of principle' with the Liberals while taking care to stress 'our distinct SDP philosophy and membership'; Owen emphasised the SDP's distinctiveness, but was equally careful to mention 'our principled partnership' with the Liberals. Insisting, like Owen, that the SDP was 'a radical party, and must remain one', Jenkins gave more substance than Owen ever did to what he understood the word to mean:*

> But our radicalism does not spring from the need to seek a particular segment of votes. We are radical because the country is in desperate need of change: constitutionally, industrially, socially. We need change that will stick, not the largely irrelevant and too easily reversible changes of recent Governments which have paradoxically left us an almost uniquely hidebound and unadaptive society.

He listed as priorities tackling unemployment; 'democracy in the voting system and in industry'; 'a constructive commitment to Europe' and 'our determination to attack poverty and prejudice at home and abroad'. Owen by comparison was wordy, but surprisingly vague: the SDP, he proclaimed, should be 'determined, practical and imaginative' yet also 'open, democratic and classless'. While Owen merely promised to work hard for victory, Jenkins ended with a leader's authoritative words of encouragement to the troops:

---

* In a sentence cut from his draft, Jenkins questioned whether a 'radical' party in his sense of the word would in fact attract Labour votes: 'Apart from anything else, I am no convinced of the radicalism of the right-wing Labour working-class vote.'[65]

We have come an immense distance in a very short time. If we keep our nerve and our sense of direction we can make the breakthrough at the next crucial General Election.[66]

Jenkins was still *claiming* the leadership as the Alliance's obvious Prime Minister in waiting, while Owen was merely challenging for it on the back of his sudden rise to prominence over the Falklands. One Jenkinsite MP, Tom Ellis, warned the party against a 'khaki' election 'in which, as a result of a collective emotional spasm, we elect the wrong leader'.[67] Another loyal supporter, Anthony Lester, privately sympathised with Jenkins being faced with 'Dr Death in his ugly prime. I strongly disagree with the line which he has taken over the Falklands, and deplore his efforts to diminish your standing.' It was probably too late to curb him now, 'but I suspect we will all live to regret his lovely war'. The party was currently drifting 'without captain or rudder or charts or compass', he lamented, before concluding confidently: 'Once you are leader that will all change . . . Yours devotedly, Anthony.'[68] The trouble was that the case for Jenkins depended heavily on the assumption that the winner had a serious prospect of becoming Prime Minister within the next two years. From the moment this no longer seemed very likely, his claim was severely weakened. If what the SDP was electing was not after all the next Prime Minister but merely an effective leader of a minority party for the long haul of opposition over at least another six or seven years, then Jenkins' age became a liability and his experience of high office irrelevant. On this argument both *The Times* and *The Economist* came out for Owen. 'It has been Dr Owen who . . . has shown the vigour and the ruthlessness needed for the task of storming fortress Labour,' *The Economist* concluded. 'The SDP should take its courage in both hands and send for the doctor.'[69]

For a moment Jenkins was afraid that he was going to lose. An NOP poll in the *Observer* showed that potential Alliance voters – as opposed to the SDP members who were going to make the decision – thought Owen would make a better leader by a margin of 57 per cent to 33 per cent. Significantly, however, they preferred David Steel to either; and this slightly dampening verdict probably contained the clue to Jenkins' victory. For Steel made little secret that his good working partnership with Jenkins was critical to the functioning of the Alliance, which would be imperilled if Owen were to become SDP leader. Should they be in a position to form an Alliance government after the next election, he would be happy to take second place under Jenkins – but not necessarily under Owen. Other leading Liberals made it still clearer that they fully reciprocated Owen's unflattering view of them. When Owen, towards the end of the non-campaign, suggested that once proportional representation was achieved the two Alliance parties could go back to fighting each other before possibly forming a coalition as separate parties, Jenkins insisted that such a scenario would fatally undermine the Alliance. The public, he believed, had responded to 'a partnership of principle', but would not vote for a cynical 'marriage of convenience'.[70] In voting for Jenkins a clear majority of ordinary SDP members asserted their belief in the positive vision of the Alliance which he had proposed in the Dimbleby Lecture and embodied at Warrington and Hillhead, and which they did not want to see jeopardised. But the margin of his victory, by just 26,256 votes to 20,864 (56:44 per cent, on a 75 per cent poll), was far from overwhelming and carried the seeds of serious strains ahead.

Jenkins admitted to being relieved by the result and told reporters – with some exaggeration – that he was getting used to 'winning from behind'.[71] It was a sufficient margin to be decisive, without humiliating Owen. On the contrary, Owen was arguably the moral victor: he had certainly established himself as the undisputed leader-in-waiting breathing down Jenkins' neck. But he had come to believe that he might win; and he was disproportionately depressed by his defeat. A week after the result his fellow Plymouth MP Alan Clark found him 'still in an agitated state' and talking of refusing to serve in Jenkins' shadow team.[72] He eventually agreed to carry on as foreign affairs spokesman. But two months later he was still frustrated at losing when he thought he had it in the bag, telling Clark that he now thought he was 'blown'. His only hope was an early election that would smash both Labour and the Alliance – in other words, a Thatcher landslide – after which he might be able to rebuild the SDP, independent of the Liberals, but drawing on the old Labour Party. By the next year he was afraid that Labour would have recovered and the Liberals have become dominant in the Alliance, leaving him with nothing.[73] In this black mood he was an even more difficult colleague than before. Bill Rodgers wrote that Owen went into 'a prolonged sulk', obstructing Jenkins' every attempt to assert his leadership.[74] Those smiling pictures of the Gang of Four on the bridge at Limehouse less than two years earlier were a distant memory. With reason Jenkins believed that the leadership contest, far from raising the party's profile as Owen and Shirley Williams had hoped, did it immense damage that never healed.

★

Jenkins was sole leader of the SDP for eleven months; but it was an unhappy period, which ended in bitter disappointment, for which he took a large share of the blame. Quite simply, having secured the prize, he turned out not to be a very good leader. Of course there were other reasons, already mentioned, for the Alliance's failure to recapture its heady momentum of the previous year. With hindsight it can be seen that the SDP was launched at a moment when both the old parties seemed to have rushed to ideological extremes and the established party system really did feel on the brink of collapse, creating an unprecedented opportunity for the sort of radical realignment that Jenkins had proclaimed. But by the spring of 1982 that moment had passed and normality was beginning to be restored. The Alliance was still polling better than the Liberals on their own had ever done, but instead of the 50 per cent they had touched the previous autumn they were back in the thirties, with all three parties roughly level-pegging. At that point a hung Parliament looked the most likely result of the next election, which would probably have meant the Alliance forming at least part of the next government, with the chance to extract proportional representation as the price of its participation, so that realignment was still a real possibility. That prospect evaporated with Mrs Thatcher's victory in the Falklands. Now the Tories' rating soared into the forties and stayed there until the General Election, leaving Labour and the Alliance stuck in the mid-twenties scrapping for second place, which instantly destroyed Jenkins' unique selling point as a wise and statesmanlike alternative Prime Minister to lead the country through a crisis. As an opposition leader he did not cut the mustard: his moderate, sensible policies suddenly seemed platitudinous and his prime ministerial pretensions merely pompous.

In addition Jenkins was exhausted, suffering from what he himself called 'battle fatigue' after fighting three strenuous elections in the past year. Four weeks after finally winning the leadership he and Jennifer disappeared for his usual August holiday in France and Italy: one week with Michael and Maxine Jenkins in the Vaucluse, a second with the Gilmours near Lucca and a third with Marietta Tree near Siena, all with the usual flow of English visitors. On holiday he swam and walked and played tennis, but he also slept a lot. Back in England he resumed his running – in Ladbroke Square when in London, or round the tennis court in East Hendred – in an effort to get himself fit for the trials ahead. But he was still overweight, and he was also beginning to suffer from a thyroid condition, not diagnosed until the following year, which left him frequently tired and lacking energy: he still slept in the afternoons whenever he could. The result was that he looked and sounded old, flabby and long-winded on television, which was now – far more than in his 1960s prime – the critical medium of political communication. In the Commons he was ponderous at Prime Minister's Questions and had few opportunities to make the sort of speeches with which he used to command the House.* Paradoxically he was now a much better performer at public meetings and out on the stump than he was in Parliament. As SDP leader he worked hard in his own way, making scores of speeches around the country, many of them essentially the same speech tailored to his particular audience and the issue of the moment, but others major policy statements to which he gave a lot of thought; he also wrote a great deal of newspaper articles. These were the old-fashioned formats – familiar to Asquith or Gaitskell – at which he still excelled. But he was not good at the quickfire exchange of pithy soundbites that had become the staple of modern politics, at which David Owen – and David Steel – excelled. Nor did Jenkins have the patience or stamina for the more tedious chores of party leadership: as Barbara Castle and others had said when predicting that he would never be Labour leader, he was not interested in organisation and was too shy for back-slapping and morale-boosting. The importance he attached to maintaining his private life (his lunches with women friends, literary dining clubs and country house week-ends) had not stopped him being a good minister in the Sixties and Seventies, when he could alternate periods of intense activity with such periods of relaxation that he needed to recover. But the demands of leadership, particularly of a small party challenging to smash the existing mould of politics, were continuous and never-ending, and Jenkins did not have the right sort of energy for it. For all these reasons of personality, temperament and aptitude he was ill-equipped for the position he had striven for, in the circumstances in which he finally achieved it.

One of the chores of leadership was the continuing battle between the two Alliance parties over the allocation of seats, made more fractious by their falling polls. As the early euphoria began to fade, Rodgers warned Jenkins in July that the Liberals in some areas wanted to reopen agreements that he regarded as settled. As it stood, if the Alliance were to win 100 seats, the Liberals would probably win at least sixty of them,

* To David Butler he admitted that he 'had come to regard Tuesdays and Thursdays as a source of misery'. In a typically shrewd piece of self-analysis he reckoned that he had been successful in the House of Commons as a batsman, but was no good as a bowler.[75]

yet some Liberal members were 'militant for more'. Rodgers believed the SDP had made enough concessions and he now had his 'back to the wall'; Jenkins might need to intervene directly with David Steel to knock some heads together.[76] This was deeply distasteful to Jenkins, whose experience at Warrington and Hillhead had given him a somewhat rosy picture of the extent of goodwill between local activists on the ground; but his reluctance to fight the SDP's corner only confirmed the Owenites' suspicion that he did not really care about its distinct identity. In September Mike Thomas wrote him a stiff letter warning that any further concessions would threaten the party's very existence:

What I want to communicate to you is that you are not here dealing with a little political awkwardness that has to be circumvented or overcome, you are approaching a fundamental sticking point, not just for me but, I believe, for many in our Party. I don't want an Alliance party. I don't want to be a part of parachuting a few people into the upper echelons of what is essentially the Liberal Party. I want a true partnership between two distinct forces – each of which brings to the Alliance its own strengths and convictions. That is why, for me, the outcome of the negotiations with the Liberals is actually about preserving the capacity of our own party to survive and develop, and thus contribute to a genuine alliance.

'In common with a substantial proportion of our members,' he concluded, 'that is something I feel very strongly about . . . With every step down this slippery slope I feel my energy and enthusiasm sapping away . . . I impute nothing but the best of motives in the approach you are pursuing, but I think you should be clear how it looks from where I am sitting.'[77]

No reply survives: Jenkins always preferred to reply to letters with a phone call or an appeasing private word, rather than on paper. Two weeks later Thomas wrote again, repeating his complaint that the SDP was being left 'invisible and defenceless in the face of a tide of propaganda for the Alliance'. This time it was Rodgers who replied. He acknowledged that giving up some good seats to the Liberals had been painful, but insisted that the Alliance was overwhelmingly more attractive to the electorate than competing parties and denied that it was a slippery slope to merger:

Perhaps I may add that I think that Roy's experience over the last few days has taught him a great deal about the difficulties of negotiating with the Liberals. He has become impatient of attempts to re-open agreements (something of which both of us have much experience).[78]

In the end Jenkins did have to become involved. At the end of September, just before the Liberal assembly, he and Steel exerted their authority to enforce a settlement of outstanding disputes which was accepted in all but a handful of constituencies. Owen thought Jenkins had once again sold the pass. 'This week,' he wrote in his diary, 'Roy Jenkins has finally tipped the seat negotiations across a threshold which could be fatal for the independence of the party.'[79] 'Once again,' he wrote in his memoirs, 'we gave ground in order to avoid a row.'[80] Years later Mike Thomas called this moment 'the death knell of the SDP'.[81] It was true that Jenkins was anxious above all to avoid a row which he thought damaging to the Alliance. But an idea of what the SDP negotiators were up against is furnished by the example of Liverpool, Broadgreen, one of three seats where the local Liberals declined to accept the leaders' ruling and refused to stand down for Dick Crawshaw, one of the first wave of SDP defectors, thereby splitting the Alliance vote and ensuring the loss of a seat he might otherwise have held. The SDP – Jenkins included – were often frustrated by what they regarded as the anarchic character of the Liberals, who prided themselves on their local autonomy; but there was little Steel could do about it and he actually did well to get as many adopted Liberals to stand down for SDP candidates as he did. In the end the two parties fought roughly equal numbers of seats: 311 against 322. Outside the thirty seats the SDP was defending, the Liberals did fight more of those that were judged most winnable. But Bill Rodgers still believed in December 1982 that if the Alliance were to return 100 MPs, the SDP would have between forty-five and fifty-five of them.[82] Of course they did not win anything like that number, so the bitter arguments based on over-optimistic expectations turned out to be academic. Nevertheless the arguments were another factor that took much of the shine off the Alliance's dwindling appeal in 1982–3.

There was another public row at the autumn conference. This was another 'rolling' event, which travelled from Cardiff to Derby to Great Yarmouth, but not so successful as the previous year because – typifying the party's loss of momentum – the train broke down. The row, at Great Yarmouth, was over the old chestnut of incomes policy. Jenkins still favoured a statutory policy, and had got it agreed by the party's national committee; but Owen did not. In his memoirs he denied that he encouraged his research assistant, Ruth Levitt, to move an amendment opposing a statutory policy; but he applauded her speech vigorously from the platform, so when her amendment was overwhelmingly carried, it was inevitably seen by the press as a calculated challenge to Jenkins' leadership. Jenkins, by Owen's account, was 'incandescent with fury':

> I was summoned to his hotel as if he were a headmaster hauling in an errant schoolboy and I had to listen to a tirade about a 'petty ploy over an insubstantive issue' and how ruthlessly, calculatingly, personally ambitious I was. He was so incoherent with rage that there was little point in arguing . . . Despite my repeated apologies he was incapable of listening.

The effect of this episode, according to Owen, was to 'sever all personal relations between us'.[83] In fact relations were already pretty bad, and Owen's attempts to paint himself as the innocent party do not square with others' recollection of his behaviour following his defeat in the leadership election. Bill Rodgers wrote that Jenkins tried hard to accommodate Owen, but found his 'black moods' difficult to handle. He normally hated confrontation, so the incident at Great Yarmouth was unusual and shows the strain he was under. Rather than risk further unpleasantness he abandoned his intention to put Rodgers in charge of election planning, in deference to Owen's objection, but failed to appoint anyone else: this was not the action of a strong leader.[84] There were other signs of tension within the party organisation (now housed in an elegant Queen Anne House in Cowley Street, five minutes from the House of Commons). In November Bernard Doyle, the previously unpolitical businessman who had been the Gang of Four's surprising choice as Chief Executive in 1981, tried to resign, saying that his relations with Alec McGivan (the national organiser) and others – he specified Mike Thomas and Christopher Brocklebank-Fowler – were making his position 'untenable'. He was persuaded to carry on, but complained to Jenkins that the MPs were now (by contrast with the party's first year) 'obsessed with infighting'. To restore its momentum the party needed 'strong political leadership of a visible kind', which Jenkins evidently was not providing.[85]

Two weeks later Jenkins tried to give a pep talk to the national committee – an unwieldy body now numbering thirty-six members.

With the Alliance's poll rating now down to just 21 per cent, he told them that 'the first essential [was] to show buoyancy, optimism and determination' and still insisted that they must 'go for the major break-through at the next election'. He recognised that one way of dealing with the party's declining 'visibility' in the media would be to 'go for instant comments'; but typically thought that much of the party's success had been due to 'its ability to stand back'. He insisted that there was 'no question of a merger' with the Liberals, or of 'either of them ceasing to exist'. Finally he urged that the SDP should aim to 'raise the level of political argument . . . and not get involved in day-to-day insults'. He wanted the national committee to be 'a symbol and vehicle of unity within the party'; and the party to take 'a very firm line on key issues'.[86] Even allowing for the blandness of official minutes, this was an extraordinarily vague and platitudinous call to arms.

A telling comment on Jenkins' failure as SDP leader – specifically his failure at Westminster, where he should have been at his best – was made by the *Daily Telegraph*'s parliamentary sketchwriter Edward Pearce, pointing out that he had had behind him a party of thirty MPs, or forty with the Liberals.

> If that party had played Parliament hard, if it had attended in full numbers, used questions intelligently, organised its set-piece speeches and generally gone for impact, the outcome would have been very different . . . Three minutes' harsh irony should have carved up Skinner so that he never walked again . . . With a team forty strong and not short of talent, he could and should have made the Alliance a parliamentary force and a national one.[87]

Unfortunately the combination of Jenkins' shattered self-confidence in the Chamber and personal tensions within the Gang of Four, which were reflected right through the parliamentary party, meant that he fluffed the opportunity.

In January 1983, at the beginning of what seemed certain to be an election year, the Alliance held its first joint rally at the Central Hall, Westminster, billed optimistically as a 'relaunch'. In its own terms it was a considerable success. Jenkins made an excellent speech in which he looked back over the ups and downs of the past three years and insisted that there was all still to play for:

> I reject utterly the defeatist view that our correct strategy is to go for a balancing bridgehead in the next Parliament . . . Total

victory is perfectly possible. And this, and nothing less, is our objective.

He drew encouragement from an uncanny 'rhythm of history' going back 150 years, which suggested that major reforming governments came to power at almost precisely thirty-eight-year intervals.* The Whig government of Lord Grey, which passed the 1832 Reform Bill, took office in 1830; Gladstone formed his first great Liberal administration in 1868; the landslide election of 1906 led to Asquith's Liberal government, Lloyd George's 'People's Budget' and the beginnings of social insurance; and thirty-eight years on again, the great Labour victory of 1945 brought in the Attlee government and the full flowering of the welfare state. Another thirty-eight-year gap naturally pointed to . . . an SDP/Liberal Alliance government in 1983, led – though of course he did not say it – by himself, thereby emulating two of his three great political heroes, Asquith and Attlee! It was an alluring vision with which to inspire himself and rouse the troops, but one has to wonder whether he really believed it.

For the rest he damned the Labour Party on the one hand for its unilateralism, its protectionism, its anti-Europeanism and the leadership's appeasement of the hard left; and Mrs Thatcher on the other for her 'immoral' tolerance of unemployment and her deluded belief that she had made British industry more competitive, 'while in fact she has destroyed much of it'. He rehearsed once again his 'detailed, practical, carefully costed programme' for tackling unemployment, but placed it in a wider context with an additional three-point plan for concerted international expansion, 'greater flows of finance to the poor world' and British membership of the EMS, which would help form 'a tripod of stability' between the ECU, the dollar and the yen. He ended with a stirring call for 'radicalism in the cause of reconciliation' – almost deliberately seeking out those 'r's again – and 'the regeneration of our country'.[89] 'It was the nearest approach to a triumph that I had during that difficult winter,' Jenkins recalled in his memoirs, 'and good for morale':

But it was also a striking example of the self-indulgence of oratory. Both I and the audience of party faithful thought that we had

---

* Jenkins had first noted this pattern nearly thirty years earlier in an article on 'The Labour Party Today' in an unidentified paper in November 1953.[88] Did he even then have his long-distance sights set on 1983?

accomplished something because I had made a good speech and they had cheered vociferously. But we had only given each other a good evening out. There was no evidence that we had lifted the Alliance off its temporary floor.[90]

The event which did temporarily lift the Alliance off the floor was Simon Hughes' by-election victory in the London Docklands constituency of Bermondsey, caused by the resignation of the former Labour Chief Whip, Bob Mellish. After a sequence of disappointing by-elections since Hillhead – even Dick Taverne had been unable to make much impression in Peckham in October, though he came a decent second behind Harriet Harman, pushing the Tory, John Redwood, into a poor third – Bermondsey was a huge boost for Alliance morale. But it was a slightly fortunate result, since Labour shot itself in the foot by selecting a young, left-wing community worker, Peter Tatchell, whom Michael Foot had initially declared he would never accept before having to turn round and endorse him after all. Tatchell was also fairly obviously (though not in those days openly) gay, which recommended him still less to traditional Labour voters. The Alliance campaign did not scruple to exploit this homophobic prejudice, despite the fact that Hughes himself turned out years later to be gay himself: so it was a morally flawed victory. Nevertheless it seemed to show that Labour was still intent on alienating its old working-class base – though from a narrowly SDP point of view it was annoying that it was a Liberal who had reaped the benefit, while the SDP had so far only managed to capture Tory seats.

The SDP had its chance at the next by-election a month later in Darlington, a Labour marginal where the adopted Alliance candidate was one of their own. Unfortunately Tony Cook, a popular local television presenter, illustrated the downside of the party's appeal to 'political virgins'. He might have been an adequate candidate at a General Election, but under the spotlight of a by-election he was cruelly exposed as 'a lightweight, with neither ideas nor passion' (Bill Rodgers' rueful description),[91] whereas Labour this time had the sense to field an experienced local councillor who successfully kept the left out of sight. Having started with a lead in the polls and a wonderful opportunity to project the Alliance as the real opposition to the Tory government, Cook finished the campaign a poor third with just a quarter of the vote, while Labour's Ossie O'Brien held off the Conservative with a majority of 2,400.[*] Darlington was a salutary reminder that, in a by-election at least, the quality of the candidates still mattered. But Tony Cook's unravelling prompted angry recriminations within the Alliance. David Owen thought him 'a flabby centrist' (code for Jenkinsite) and 'a typical left-wing Liberal community politician' (and a unilateralist to boot) who should never have been selected;[92] while senior Liberals blamed the SDP, saying Cook was no worse than Bill Pitt at Croydon, but had not been properly coached.[93] In his memoirs Jenkins blamed himself for not imposing an experienced national figure like Dick Taverne, but claimed that had he tried, 'the still resentful Owen faction' would have objected on grounds of party democracy. ('I ought to have been tougher'.)[94] Publicly he put a bold face on the setback, calling it 'a disappointment but not a disaster', from which the Alliance would bounce back at the next by-election, due in Cardiff North-West (but actually pre-empted by the General Election).[95] But it was too late. As the last by-election before the General Election, Darlington remained seared on all their hearts as the single moment when the SDP blew its chance to break the mould. 'It remains tragically the case,' Rodgers wrote to Jenkins in 1990, 'that, with a good candidate, we would probably have won and then pushed Labour into third place in the General Election'. And he might have held his own seat in nearby Stockton.[96]

When Mrs Thatcher called the election for 9 June – a year earlier than it need have been, taking advantage of her Falklands 'bounce' – the Alliance was back at 20 per cent or less in the polls, way behind Labour which in turn was way behind the Tories. Yet Jenkins was still committed to his proclaimed strategy of aiming for a major breakthrough, not a bridgehead. 'We are going in with victory as our aim,' he insisted at his opening press conference.[97] This meant directing most of their fire at the Tories, presenting the Alliance as the only serious alternative government while trying to dismiss Labour as irrelevant because no longer fit to govern. It would have been more realistic – and therefore more credible – to have accepted that they were in a life-or-death battle with Labour for second place and concentrate on trying to knock Labour out of the ring. This would have been Owen's preferred strategy. Alternatively they should have aimed to hold the balance in a hung Parliament, stated their terms for supporting either a Labour or a Tory government, possibly without Michael Foot or Mrs Thatcher, and tried to secure proportional representation that way. But

---

[*] O'Brien failed to retain the seat at the general election less than three months later, however, making him one of the shortest-serving MPs on record.

Jenkins as leader was still absolutely committed to his all-or-nothing strategy – frankly, in Owen's view, because at the age of sixty-two it represented his one remaining shot at becoming Prime Minister.[98]

The agreement between Jenkins and Steel the year before, that Jenkins should be put forward as the Alliance's 'Prime Minister Designate' – a title Jenkins later dismissed defensively as 'a bit of portentous nonsense'[99] – was actually a perfectly sensible way of meeting the media's demand for a single leader at a time when an Alliance government seemed a real possibility and Steel naturally deferred to Jenkins' superior credentials to lead it.* By 1983, however, when 87 per cent of respondents, according to Gallup, expected a Tory victory, the decision to promote Jenkins as the alternative to a now-rampant Mrs Thatcher invited only derision, most of it heaped on Jenkins personally, while concentrating the media spotlight on him at the expense of Steel, who was a far better performer, especially on television, and far more popular: one poll found that voters would have preferred Steel by a margin of 61:25 per cent, and even SDP supporters preferred Steel by 49:47 per cent. 'Rightly or wrongly,' Ivor Crewe and Anthony King concluded, 'voters appeared to give less weight to ministerial experience than to television images when judging potential prime ministers.'[102] It was a cruel reality that politics was now a television game and Jenkins appeared to belong to a pre-television age.

The Alliance campaign was fought very much on Jenkins' agenda. Despite all the earnest policy work that had been done by innumerable party committees over the past two years, the manifesto was hastily drawn up by the SDP's director of policy, Christopher Smallwood, and approved by the two leaders plus Alan Beith (for the Liberals) and John Roper (for the SDP). It comprised all Jenkins' now-familiar themes – an unashamedly Keynesian attack on unemployment; some form of

---

* There survives among his papers a list of names with the jobs they might fill in a putative Alliance Cabinet, written out in Jenkins' handwriting. It was probably no more than a mischievous party game, since it assigns David Owen to Northern Ireland! But the other notional appointments probably give an accurate idea of how he regarded his colleagues and how he might have deployed them if he had ever had the chance. David Steel is listed as Home Secretary and Leader of the House, Shirley Williams as Foreign Secretary and Bill Rodgers as Chancellor. Other horses for courses are Dick Taverne (MoD), David Marquand (Education), Tom Bradley (Employment), Ian Wrigglesworth (DHSS), Bob Maclennan (Scotland), Lord Scarman (Lord Chancellor) and Anthony Lester (Attorney-General). The list gives the Liberals only six out of twenty-three places: Steel and Scarman plus John Pardoe, Russell Johnstone, Richard Wainwright and Jo Grimond (as Lord Privy Seal).[100] Steel says it can only have been a joke since he and Jenkins never discussed appointments and, as a Scottish Member, he could not have been Home Secretary. In fact John Reid served as Home Secretary in 2006–7 despite sitting for a Scottish seat.[101]

prices and incomes policy (with a vague commitment to industrial democracy); neither more nationalisation nor privatisation; proportional representation (presented as the key to simultaneously rejuvenating and stabilising politics); and a renewed commitment to the EEC and NATO.[103] It was all thoroughly sensible, but it lacked anything to fire the electorate's enthusiasm: it was well described – in a phrase that stuck because it was so accurate – as offering 'a better yesterday'.[104] While rightly condemning the harsh consequences of Mrs Thatcher's economic and social policies, it failed to recognise the extent to which she had a global wind of free market liberalisation and deregulation behind her and had already torn up many of the statist assumptions with which Jenkins had grown up. Back in 1972, in his essay on Keynes in *Nine Men of Power*, he had written that so-called 'crude Keynesianism' had its limitations, 'but it is a great advance on crude pre-Keynesianism'.[105] That unswerving view still underpinned his almost visceral contempt for Thatcherism in the 1980s. From the perspective of 2014, following the financial crash of 2008, his scepticism about the benefits of the unregulated market begins to look prescient again; but in 1983 it was spitting in the wind. Keynesianism as an economic panacea had been badly discredited by its perceived failure over the past twenty years.

In the four weeks of the campaign Jenkins made fifteen major speeches at public meetings up and down the country, mainly written for him by Christopher Smallwood, many of them in support of sitting SDP Members defending their seats: Bill Rodgers in Stockton, Tom Bradley in Leicester, Christopher Brocklebank-Fowler in Norwich, John Roper in Worsley (Manchester) and Shirley Williams in Crosby. (It was noticeable that he did not speak in Plymouth.) He also appeared with David Steel at 'Ask the Alliance' meetings in Birmingham and London, a television-style format chaired by friendly celebrity interviewers, Magnus Magnusson and Ludovic Kennedy. He visited more than sixty constituencies – characteristically he made a handwritten list of them – doing the sort of street canvassing he had perfected in Warrington and Hillhead. Defending a marginal seat, however, he also had to spend more time than as party leader he would have liked in Hillhead: five visits involving part of seven days, more street canvassing and several meetings, one of them with Shirley Williams. The rest of the time, while he toured the country, Jennifer bore the brunt of holding the seat for him, which she did heroically.

All this was good old-fashioned politics, trying to re-create the extraordinary excitement which the SDP and the Alliance had aroused by direct contact with the voters in individual constituencies in 1981. But in a General Election what mattered was national television. Unfortunately the focus on Jenkins as 'Prime Minister Designate' resulted in him doing the first two big television interviews for the Alliance: *Weekend World* with Brian Walden on Sunday 22 May and *Panorama* with Robin Day the next day. On both programmes he came over as 'ponderous and ill at ease', hesitant and defensive where he needed to be clear and positive. 'His two performances . . . were generally thought to have been unhelpful at best, ghastly at worst.'[106] He also featured prominently in two of the Alliance's four election broadcasts, to the despair of the advertising agencies engaged to handle the campaign, which thought his personality hopelessly at odds with the modern classless image they were trying to project. 'Jenkins,' one professional complained, 'was like a rhinoceros in the corner, a huge ugly problem that everyone tried to ignore.'[107] There was also friction between different agencies reflecting the rivalries at the top of the Alliance. Shirley Williams (as SDP President) had hired Gold Greenlees Trott to handle the campaign; but Jenkins additionally involved Charles Guggenheim, an American who had directed the 'Yes' campaign in the 1975 referendum, while Steel had his own PR consultant, Justin Cartwright (later a successful novelist), and they all got in each other's way. Trying to project Jenkins and Steel as joint leaders, Cartwright found Roy 'extremely uncooperative', insisting on using his man, Guggenheim.[108] Steel and Jenkins also had separate press officers (John Lyttle for Jenkins and Paul Medlicott for Steel), which made for a lack of coordination compounded at every level by an overall lack of direction. Under the pressure of a joint campaign that was clearly not going well tensions spilled over: when it seemed that the SDP big guns were adding nothing to the sort of results the Liberals had achieved at previous elections on their own, even such a key architect of the Alliance as Richard Holme complained to David Butler that he found Shirley Williams 'silly and random', Bill Rodgers 'lazy and arrogant' and David Owen 'independent and difficult': Jenkins, he judged, 'had the best mind in the Alliance, but he was not always tactful at putting his point' and Steel chaired meetings much better.[109]

Hence there was mounting pressure, particularly – but not only – from the Liberal side of the Alliance to replace Jenkins with Steel as Alliance leader. This was brought to a head on 24 May by an opinion poll which suggested that while the Alliance still trailed badly with Jenkins as leader (Conservatives 45 per cent, Labour 32 per cent, Alliance 20 per cent), it would do dramatically better – almost neck-and-neck with Labour – if Steel were to replace him: Conservatives 42 per cent, Labour 29 per cent, Alliance 28 per cent.[110] The next day, with some embarrassment, Steel put the idea to Jenkins over breakfast following a joint press conference in London. Jenkins then set off for a day's campaigning on his battle-bus through Kent ('one of the prettier days of the campaign') promising to think about it. In his memoirs he wrote that 'the last thing I wanted was to be an incubus to the Alliance for the sake of clinging to a position which had abruptly ceased to give me any satisfaction'. Nevertheless, considering Steel's proposal 'in the interstices between Sittingbourne High Street, the Ashford railway workshops and the Tonbridge shopping enclave', he concluded that changing horses in mid-stream would do neither the Alliance nor Steel himself any good. This was not an entirely selfless calculation: he also feared that 'abdication . . . would destroy my position with press and public, not least in Hillhead'.[111] But he was stiffened in his view by a supportive letter from Jack Diamond, who was supposed to be coord-inating the Alliance campaign from Cowley Street, who warned firmly that any such change in mid-campaign would be disastrous. This, he wrote, was not just the advice of friendship and loyalty – 'albeit a little of those qualities would not come amiss in this sea of gutless foolish-ness in which I am swimming'. Steel, he believed, must hold to 'his present firm honourable line' and Jenkins to his 'good-humoured and dismissive line', and the Liberals should get on with talking up Jenkins' irreplaceable experience.[112] Thus encouraged, Jenkins sent a negative reply to Steel and hoped that was the end of the matter.

The following Sunday, however, the Alliance leaders were due to hold a photogenic 'summit' – planned partly to draw publicity from Mrs Thatcher attending a G7 summit in the United States – at Steel's house at Ettrick Bridge in the Scottish Borders. They were supposed to converge by helicopter, but bad weather prevented that, so they all arrived late from various directions by car: Jenkins, with Jennifer, came from Glasgow. The main participants have all given slightly conflicting accounts of what happened at Ettrick Bridge, but piecing them together the basic facts are clear. As soon as they had all arrived John Pardoe, the pugnacious Liberal MP for North Cornwall (whom Steel had beaten to the party leadership in 1976), surprised three of the Gang of Four (but not Owen, whom he had warned in advance) by reopening the question of the leadership. 'His denunciation of Roy's role in the campaign was brutal,' Shirley Williams wrote. 'He told him in short order to relinquish the leadership position.'[113] Rodgers and Williams furiously rejected any change, though Shirley conceded that Roy was not good on television and suggested that more of that could be done by 'David, David and me'.[114] They then moved on to other matters until Pardoe raised the leadership again, this time backed by Steel, who actually produced a draft statement for Jenkins to agree. Rodgers and Williams again opposed, strongly supported by Jack Diamond; and Williams went so far as to say that she would withdraw from the campaign if Jenkins was dumped. According to Jenkins' account, this 'killed it dead'.[115] But others are not so clear-cut. According to Williams, Jenkins himself sat silent, 'shaking' and 'absolutely shattered' to be so betrayed by Steel. Afraid he might yield to 'this extraordinary battering', she mouthed 'no, no, no' to him across the table, until he nodded.[116] Whereas Richard Holme's memory was that 'On the whole, Roy just kept quiet and let others defend him',[117] others suggest that he offered to stand aside if it would help, but repeated his view that it would be 'counterproductive'; while Steel's version, slightly different again, is that 'After frank discussion it became clear that he would not be budged.'[118] Pardoe still wanted to pursue it, but Steel said they had better drop it. It was agreed that they should try to give Steel a higher profile for the remainder of the campaign – which in fact was due to happen anyway – without explicitly demoting Jenkins.

After lunch – a strained occasion at which Jennifer was even angrier than Roy and had to be restrained by John Lyttle – Jenkins and Steel gave a blandly upbeat joint conference to the press assembled outside.* Amazingly, no word of what had really gone on inside leaked out. The BBC news that evening reported that 'Mr Jenkins is not being written out of the Alliance election show, but Mr Steel is to take the starring role, especially on television'; while the next day's papers likewise got the message of an enhanced role for Steel – 'Alliance to Move Jenkins out of the Limelight' (*The Times*); 'Steel takes over from Jenkins as Front Runner for the Alliance' (*Guardian*) – without presenting it as a humiliation of Jenkins.[120] In fact the summit made a positive news story for the Alliance. Paddy Ashdown thought it a brilliant success, which essentially achieved what the Liberals wanted without the bad publicity that would have attended an open coup.[121] And in fact the Alliance did begin to rise in the polls from around this point.

But a good deal of bitterness remained, not least surrounding the

---

* John Pardoe believed that Jennifer's presence was critical in stiffening Jenkins' refusal to stand down. 'Roy was firmly uncooperative, firstly because it would damage his chances at Hillhead, secondly because it would annoy the party regulars, and thirdly, probably much the most important, because of Jennifer Jenkins who was an iron lady.'[119]

role of David Owen, who was noticeably silent at the meeting. It was clear that he tacitly agreed with the Liberal criticism of Jenkins' leadership, but did not want to be seen to wield the knife. He claimed soon after the election that if Jenkins could have been persuaded to stand down it would have added 4 or 5 per cent to the Alliance vote (in his memoirs he put it at 'ten to fifteen extra seats'); but he 'would not be the Brutus'.[122] 'At Ettrick Bridge,' he told an American academic, 'Steel tried to dump the whole thing in my lap. I would have none of it.'[123] His line, then and in his memoirs, was that Steel had got himself into a mess, first by backing Jenkins for the leadership of the SDP and then by yielding him the leadership of the Alliance, so he must get himself out of it. 'If there was to be a change it had to be done absolutely voluntarily with a good grace by Roy Jenkins. Even then it was a high risk game and must be presented in an utterly convincing way.'[124] In 1987 he claimed that 'In all my years in the Labour Party I had never seen such a ruthless and savage deed' as Steel's attempted coup;[125] but at the time he was rather less squeamish. As Bill Rodgers drove Owen and Shirley Williams back to Edinburgh airport Owen let slip, of Steel, 'I never knew he had it in him!'[126] 'I glanced at David in the passenger seat beside me and caught a half-smile of genuine admiration, perhaps his first and last for David Steel in the six years of Alliance.'[127] It is clear that Owen felt that Jenkins' poor performance as leader vindicated his decision to stand against him the year before; and that he was poised to stage his own coup the moment the election was over.

David Steel, on the other hand, was rather ashamed of the part he had played at Ettrick Bridge. To be fair, he was under such pressure from Liberal candidates and colleagues that he had to say something, but after Jenkins' initial rejection he felt he should not have raised it a second time. 'This time,' he acknowledged in his memoirs, 'Roy did resent my pressure', and the episode 'nearly led to a break between me and Roy which would have been my fault had it happened'.[128] But Jenkins bore no lasting grudge; he retained a high regard for Steel, and treated his action as 'an error of judgement rather than of motive' in the stress of an election campaign. Ten days after polling day they dined together at Brooks's, where Steel apologised and was forgiven.[129] But Steel still felt a need to put his apology on paper and wrote to Jenkins the next day, thanking him for dinner:

Having considered what you said, I think I owe you a rather more formal apology for my piece of paper at Ettrick Bridge. You can attach this to it. No-one else saw it, but it was a lapse of judgement on my part not to show it to you privately, and I am deeply grateful that you are not allowing it to spoil our excellent personal relations.

'This' was his handwritten draft of a statement to be read out by Jenkins saying that he was dropping the title of Prime Minister Designate, which he had never wanted, so that Steel would be seen unambiguously as leader of the Alliance campaign. In the event of the Alliance winning the election it would be up to the MPs of both parties to choose the Prime Minister, but Steel undertook that he would not be a candidate.[130] Of course this was now academic. At the time Jenkins was undoubtedly hurt by Steel's support for Pardoe's attempted coup, but he found Steel's uncharacteristic behaviour easier to forgive than Owen's persistent hostility.

Despite or because of Ettrick Bridge, the Alliance did start to close the gap on Labour in the last ten days of the campaign. They had more enthusiastic meetings and better press coverage, and Jenkins was widely felt to have become more forceful; while both Denis Healey and Neil Kinnock scored own goals by clumsily accusing Mrs Thatcher of exploiting the Falklands for her own glory. While still far from looking like an alternative government, the Alliance did begin to look like an alternative Opposition. By election night they had come within touching distance of matching Labour's share of the vote – 25.4 per cent against 27.6 per cent.* On the criterion that the Alliance was the only party to increase its vote over the course of the campaign, it could be said to have achieved a considerable success. But in reality it was a crushing failure. The SDP held on to only five seats (Jenkins in Hillhead, Owen in Plymouth, Bob Maclennan in Caithness, John Cartwright in Woolwich and Ian Wrigglesworth, by a whisker, in Stockton South) and unexpectedly gained one (the twenty-four-year-old Charles Kennedy in Ross, Cromarty and Skye), while the Liberals gained just six, giving them seventeen MPs and the Alliance twenty-three in all: a scandalously poor return for 7.7 million votes. By comparison Labour – while dropping sixty seats and more than three million votes – still

---

* The overall result gave Mrs Thatcher 397 seats and a landslide majority of 144, with just 42 per cent of the vote. The Conservatives actually won nearly 700,000 fewer votes in 1983 than in 1979. But clearly the huge majority of the Alliance's additional three million votes – 7.7 million compared with the 4.3 million the Liberals had won in 1979 – were taken from Labour, thus fulfilling the predictions (and Jenkins' fear) that the only effect of the SDP would be to split the anti-Conservative opposition.

won 209 seats with 8.4 million votes.[131] If the Alliance had won just fractionally more of the national vote than Labour it would have gained a moral victory, which would have made its tally of seats indefensible and the demand for proportional representation irresistible. As it was, the rough justice of first-past-the-post left them a distant third, with an insignificant representation in the new House. In reality it was the best performance by a third party since the days of Asquith and Lloyd George in 1923, right at the beginning of the Liberal party's post–First World War decline, a comfortable improvement on the modern Liberal party's high-water mark – 19.3 per cent in February 1974 – and nearly double the 13.8 per cent they had achieved on their own in 1979. In comments after the result Jenkins called it 'a tantalising triumph', claiming that the Alliance had lost a battle but 'begun to win a war' because of the obvious unfairness of the result. The Alliance, he predicted, would now become the real opposition to the government, leading to 'still greater success at the next election'.[132] In reality it was a cruel disappointment after the soaring hopes of 1981 – salved for Jenkins only by his successfully hanging on to Hillhead.

The constituency had been significantly redrawn since the by-election fifteen months earlier, tipping the social balance towards 'the river' at the expense of 'the hill' by adding about 18,000 mainly working-class electors down by the Clyde. (Jenkins could have contested this, but only at the cost of renaming the seat Kelvin. Already sentimentally attached to the name Hillhead, he admitted, 'I attached too much importance to the label rather than the contents of the bottle.')[133] As a result it was a much tougher proposition to retain the seat and in the circumstances, largely thanks to Jennifer making up for his necessarily limited appearances, a considerable triumph that he did so. Contrary to his lordly English image he had actually worked hard at being a good constituency Member: his leaflets stressed that he had bought a flat in the constituency, held regular surgeries and had – with the help of an enthusiastic local organisation – dealt with more than 1,000 individual cases in fifteen months and helped to get important projects moving. 'I believe,' he claimed, 'that the constituency has seen more of its MP than it had for a long time past.'[134] This time he faced a challenge from a strong Labour candidate, Neil Carmichael, a former minister who had lost his neighbouring seat in the redistribution. But the combination of national exposure and local effort was just enough. In a substantially enlarged electorate his majority was roughly halved:

Roy Jenkins (SDP/Alliance)	14,856
Neil Carmichael (Labour)	13,692
Murray Tosh (Conservative)	9,678
George Leslie (SNP)	2,203
+ three others	627
SDP/Alliance majority	1,164[135]

Retaining Hillhead was a relief. But the prospect of continuing as leader of a tiny, divided parliamentary party, exposed to the taunts of Dennis Skinner in the Commons and with David Owen breathing down his neck in the national committee, was not attractive. Bill Rodgers, Shirley Williams and most of the other colleagues who had made parliamentary life tolerable had lost their seats. By the time of the next election he would be sixty-six or sixty-seven. He had already decided before the election that if the Alliance did not make a substantial breakthrough he would not carry on. So the only question was when to go. He could have stayed on over the summer and bowed out at the party conference in September. But Owen wasted no time in telephoning him on the Saturday morning to tell him that unless he stepped down immediately he (Owen) would force a leadership ballot in July. Jenkins thought his demand 'somewhat incontinent', but had no will to fight him.[136] So he summoned the Gang of Four plus John Roper and Jack Diamond to East Hendred on the Monday and announced his intention to resign at once. Shirley Williams, Roper and Diamond tried to persuade him to change his mind; but he had already discussed the timing with Bill Rodgers, who had advised him to 'go at once, given D. Owen's attitude: life would be intolerable if you did not'. Owen, as Rodgers recalled, 'grudgingly conceded that you could go on until July if you wished. That was as good as settling the matter the other way. Yes, we were bullied,' he concluded, 'but I don't think that you could have hung on, especially if your illness was already casting its shadow before.'[137] He did not believe Jenkins could have beaten Owen in a second leadership ballot.

Steel was shocked when told – not by Jenkins, but by Rodgers – and thought he should have been consulted; but when he remonstrated with Jenkins (this was before their reconciliatory dinner) he got 'a pretty sharp answer'.[138] He had no idea that Jenkins was suffering from thyroid problems and doubtless did not look forward to having to work with Owen. Others too were disappointed by Jenkins' decision. Jo Grimond declared himself 'bewildered' by the news. He had – from a slightly detached perspective – thought the election campaign a great success, until he heard 'horrifying stories' about Ettrick Bridge. He was not surprised that Jenkins had had enough, but his resigning was 'a severe blow to many of us'.[139] This was just one letter among a huge postbag, mainly from ordinary SDP and Liberal members, expressing regret, commiseration and thanks for Jenkins' role over the past three years. At the next meeting of the national committee – not preceded by the usual lunch – on Monday 20 June, Shirley Williams paid tribute and added the party's thanks:

> The Party owed a great deal to him: he was the first to see the need to break the mould of British politics. Few British Prime Ministers in this century would have contributed as much to Britain, Europe and the world as he had.

In reply Jenkins said that he had always intended to relinquish the leadership if the Tories won a clear majority, but put as positive a gloss as he could manage on the election:

> The campaign had been well fought with no own goals by the Alliance. The morale in the Party had been good . . . and he was convinced that the Alliance would form at least part of the next Government.[140]

The next day Owen was elected to the leadership unopposed. Jenkins professed himself delighted that he had succeeded smoothly, 'without fraying speculation or hint of disunity'.[141] But he knew that Owen's election spelled trouble ahead. In a Sunday newspaper article he voiced his fear that Owen's leadership could jeopardise the Alliance and gave unmistakable notice of his intention to defend it:

> Anyone who seeks to destroy it . . . will be betraying the wishes of many who voted . . . They will also be destroying everything I have endeavoured to build over the past 30 months. But this will not happen. The Alliance is secure because our joint campaigns have established deep loyalties in the hearts of our supporters.[142]

In his new role as the party's elder statesman he set himself to fight for his vision of the SDP against David Owen's.

22 Elder Statesman

AFTER his bruising experience of the past eleven months, and nineteen years as a fully committed front-rank politician, Jenkins was happy to give up the responsibility of leadership and return to being what he had been in the 1950s and early 1960s, a part-time politician, semi-detached commentator and writer. Despite the disappointment of the election result he thought the Alliance had actually done quite well, building a solid platform for the next election. Suppressing some doubts, he was happy to endorse David Owen as the dynamic young leader to take the SDP forward. 'I could feel,' he wrote in his memoirs, 'that I had not left the Alliance in a quagmire but put it on a springboard.'[1] In the first by-election of the new Parliament (caused by Willie Whitelaw's immediate elevation to the Lords) the Alliance showed that it was still a force to be reckoned with by cutting Whitelaw's large personal majority in Penrith and the Border from 15,000 to a bare 500. Jenkins departed for what he regarded as a well-earned summer holiday in France and Italy in good heart.

He came back to a depressing SDP conference – depressing not least because it was held in Salford – at which Owen lost no time in imposing his authority by ruling out not only any prospect of an early merger between the Alliance parties, but even any moves towards closer cooperation, such as joint selection of candidates or a single team of frontbench spokesmen. Liberated not just by Jenkins' semi-withdrawal but by Shirley Williams and Bill Rodgers both having lost their seats, the new leader set about redefining his little party of just six MPs in his own image. Jenkins was alarmed both by Owen's increasingly autocratic style and by his defiantly separatist strategy, which went against the whole purpose of the SDP as he had envisaged it, as a catalyst for a more inclusive style of politics. In his memoirs he described the unpleasantly factional atmosphere which now prevailed in the national committee, which reminded him of the Labour National Executive in the early 1970s. In his speech to the Salford conference he begged the party – and implicitly Owen – to let the Alliance continue to evolve organically as it had done since 1981. Echoing Parnell in reference to Ireland ('No man has a right to fix the boundary of the march of a nation') he urged the conference: 'Do not set a limit to the march of the Alliance.'[2] Most of his political energy for the next four years was devoted to trying to keep the idea of cooperation alive without challenging Owen directly, while broadening and deepening his attack on Thatcherism. He also took on the presidency of an all-party campaign for proportional representation, with Ian Gilmour for the Tories and Austin Mitchell from Labour as vice-presidents representing the minorities in their respective parties. Even as a part-time politician in uncertain health he continued to make two or three speeches a week to various audiences all round the country. In the last four months of 1984, for instance, he listed thirty-three engagements, eighteen of which he asterisked as 'difficult'.[3]

But his health was a worry. In April 1984 he was diagnosed with a thyroid problem, which retrospectively helped to explain his relative lack of energy over the past year. Curiously, this was the same condition that had afflicted Ted Heath in 1973–4 and is generally thought to have explained his tired and uncharacteristically indecisive behaviour in the crisis of his premiership in early 1974. In Jenkins' case it required six weeks' rest at East Hendred – a good excuse to stay away from SDP committees, which nevertheless did not preclude fairly frequent visits to London for lunch and other more agreeable purposes. Then at the end of 1984 he developed a serious prostate condition, which required emergency surgery and forced him to spend Christmas in hospital. This operation was not immediately successful, so he had to undergo several more over the next eighteen months before the problem was sorted out in July 1986. These troubles dispelled any lingering regrets he might have had about giving up the leadership in 1983.

Meanwhile enforced 'rest' gave him more time to get back to serious writing. He began by going back to his 1970s idea of back-to-back studies of British Prime Ministers and US Presidents. He had then thought of pairing Stanley Baldwin with Franklin Roosevelt, but now decided there was nothing new to say about Roosevelt, so switched to Harry Truman instead. He had already written a good deal of *Baldwin* and had somehow made a start on *Truman* during 1982, but now took the latter up again and finished it in 1984–5 for publication by Collins in January 1986. He then revised and lengthened his 1970s draft of *Baldwin*, which appeared in a matching format a year later in February 1987. Both were modest little books, only around 200 pages and making no pretence to original research, longer than his biographical essays for *The Times*, but well short of full-scale biographies. Deftly written, urbane, slightly bland assessments, his long absorption in politics on both sides of the Atlantic reinforcing his own experience of high office, they received respectful rather than enthusiastic reviews. One of the kindest notices of *Baldwin* was by Enoch Powell in the *Daily Telegraph*, who had himself written a similar-length biography of Joseph Chamberlain in 1977. 'I thought it by far the most perceptive review,' Jenkins wrote to thank him. 'As Gladstone, I think, said after he had addressed an audience of actors, they (you) understood what I was trying to do.'[4] These were not major books, but they got him back into historical writing and whetted his appetite for bigger subjects to come.

Then he started editing his Brussels diary, which he described as 'very satisfactory hospital work'.[5] In fact he not only cut but polished and quite significantly improved the dictated text, though without seriously misrepresenting its original thrust. He showed it to his agent, Michael Sissons of A.D. Peters (soon to become Peters Fraser & Dunlop), who was enthusiastic and sold it to Collins for an advance of £25,000, to deliver by the end of 1987.[6] Jenkins missed that deadline, but the fat volume eventually appeared in March 1989 preceded by three weeks of serialisation in the *Observer* (which largely focused on his dealings with Mrs Thatcher and the genesis of the SDP, rather than on Europe) and launched with a lavish party at Brooks's to which Jenkins invited practically everyone mentioned in the text, including a lot of leading Europeans (Schmidt, Andreotti, Ortoli, but not Giscard) and Americans (Henry Kissinger, Robert McNamara), as well as all his usual friends and former colleagues. Crispin Tickell read a draft typescript and objected that it contained too little about what Jenkins actually did as President of the Commission. 'A casual reader could all too easily conclude that what you were doing was seeing a succession of distinguished people, whizzing about Europe and the world, and wining and dining to agreeable purpose . . . You must be careful to avoid self-parody.'[7] This accurately anticipated the response of many of the reviewers. Tom Bower, for instance, in the London *Evening Standard* claimed that the words 'lunch' and 'dinner' occurred 2,000 times in 700 pages.[8] It is indeed a shamelessly self-indulgent book, much concerned with the author's stomach, and at times a little self-important, assuming that minor details of his life are of interest to the reader; but it is also tirelessly curious about the leaders, customs and etiquette of the European diplomatic circus and vividly conveys the frenetic experience of rushing by plane, train or *avion-taxi* from one capital to another. What it fails to convey, as Tickell rightly complained, is any sense of what it was all for. Some of Jenkins' friends were embarrassed by the book, thinking that it did not show him in his best light. Nevertheless it sold far better than a more earnest account of European politics would have done, notching up 5,000 copies in the first fortnight, and served as a useful (if substantial) hors d'oeuvre before his memoirs, to which he turned in 1988.

All the time he kept up an enormous output of book reviews – principally for the *Observer*, for whom he contributed about six a year (at £400 a time), rising to nine in 1989, but also for the *Spectator, Sunday Telegraph* and several other papers, including local Glasgow papers or SDP publications if they asked him and he was interested in the book. He mainly covered twentieth-century political history and biography, with occasional excursions into the nineteenth, enabling him not only to keep his encyclopaedic knowledge of the genre up to date, but also to pass lapidary judgement on the memoirs and diaries of practically all his contemporaries. He was a fair-minded reviewer but also a conscientious one, who frequently complained that the excessive length of books made them difficult to hold up in bed and took too many hours to read, and he usually commented on the structure, literary quality and index as well as the content. His own style was becoming increasingly florid, often involving elaborate metaphors so extended as to become distracting and faintly ridiculous. At his best, however, he could summon an excellent pithy image. Martin Gilbert's 700,000-word final volume of the official Churchill biography, for instance, was 'a formidable slab with which to seal up the tomb';[9] and he brilliantly saw the disgraced President of Austria (and former Secretary-General of the United Nations) Kurt Waldheim as 'a tawdry individual who is a sort of national portrait of Dorian Gray, exhibiting all their own [that is, the Austrians'] hidden faults and sins'.[10] Such bravura touches illuminate most of his reviews.

As a connoisseur of political careers he loved drawing carefully shaded comparisons across decades, which would not have occurred to anyone else. Of Selwyn Lloyd, to take one example, he commented that he was 'among Liverpool barristers not merely well behind advocates like F.E. Smith and Shawcross, but not quite up to Maxwell Fyfe', before going on to compare him with Edward Grey (one of his few historical bêtes noires):

> They both landed the country in disastrous wars. Grey's was won after four and a half years of slaughter. Lloyd's was lost after twenty-four hours of humiliating miscalculation and chicanery. But there the comparison stops, for Grey's foreign policy under an easy-going and domestically oriented Prime Minister was very much his own, whereas Lloyd's, under a fretful and externally obsessed one, was very much his master's.

He was characteristically generous to Lloyd's biographer, D.R.Thorpe, who, Jenkins wrote, had entered a plea of 'guilty but with heavily diminished responsibility because of a mind enfeebled by excessive loyalty and inadequate self-confidence. It can hardly be a ringing exculpation, but I think he achieves it. In any event his Suez chapter is a very good one, fair, convincing and compelling.'[11]* Few serious writers got a really bad review from Jenkins.

Reviewing the first instalment (covering 1963–7) of the voluminous diaries of his former colleague, rival and Notting Hill neighbour Tony Benn, however, he calculated that 'within the field of Labour history alone, I must have spent at least 250 solid hours of reading time on the combined output of Dalton, Gaitskell, Crossman and Mrs Castle. It has been an agreeable enough way of passing the time, although the precipitate of new information or insight gained per hour of reading time has been fairly low.'[13] In fact he enjoyed Benn's diary and wrote to tell him so. Benn replied equally warmly that he was 'touched' by Jenkins' letter and 'given your own literary achievements honoured that you enjoyed the diaries', adding with typical disingenuousness:

> They were momentous times in British politics – and for those of us who worked together in government. For my part I am really sorry that the disintegration which followed should have so damaged the radical tradition in both the Labour and the Liberal parties – and I still wonder if it was inevitable.[14]

---

* 'This is a model biography of a middle-rank politician,' he concluded. 'I would count myself very lucky if I were eventually done by someone as balanced, sympathetic and well-informed as Mr Thorpe.'[12]

Benn may have been less pleased by Jenkins' review, however, which was a good deal sharper than these courtesies suggested. Benn's facts he judged to be for the most part 'wholly accurate', but he thought he had 'practically no sense of proportion . . . His description of his early period as Postmaster-General is a manual on how not to be a minister.' While the class warrior of the Seventies and Eighties was yet to come, he concluded witheringly, 'Mr Benn in the Sixties emerges as nice, honest, not very clever, but full of gimmicky talent.'[15] Like Churchill ensuring that history would be kind to him by writing it himself, Jenkins used his unrivalled platform in the *Observer* and elsewhere to pass Olympian judgement on his contemporaries.

As well as book reviews – which were a hobby – Jenkins also kept up a steady stream of topical articles on issues of the day, usually with a historical perspective, often on constitutional questions, for the *Observer* (which paid £2,000 a time), *The Times* and other papers. A.D. Peters additionally got him a lot of lucrative bookings on the conference and after-dinner speaking circuit, for which he was always willing, if the money was good enough. In October 1988, for instance, he was invited to address Honeywell Computers on the single European market for a fee of £1,000. ('They certainly ought to pay more,' he wrote to Sissons. 'But, as you say, I cd. do it.')[16] Sometimes he was too greedy. When invited to speak to a City audience on 'Europe and the City' in 1989 he asked for £2,000–2,500, which was more than they were prepared to pay. He may have been boasting when he told Woodrow Wyatt in 1987 that he could get £10,000 a time for lectures around the world. ('He says he has a very good agent,' Wyatt commented enviously. 'He must have.')[17] An international conference in Finland in 1990 (where he would have appeared with Boris Yeltsin) dropped him when he asked for £7,000; but he did get £5,000 the previous year for a speech in Frankfurt. With no City directorships or international consultancies of the sort other former leaders and Chancellors enjoyed, Jenkins nevertheless racked up a substantial income from speaking as well as writing to keep himself in claret in these years.

But he also found time to read a lot purely for pleasure, and listed what he read meticulously. On his 1983 summer holiday, immediately after giving up the SDP leadership, for instance, he got through ten books, some admittedly for review (Gaitskell's diary, Richard Shannon's biography of Gladstone), some memoirs not for review (A.L. Rowse, John Mortimer), but also novels by Brian Moore, William Boyd, Simenon (in French), Clive James and Dick Francis; and he continued to keep up with contemporary novels, particularly by women writers.[18] When the John Menzies bookshop asked him, as part of a promotion, to list twenty favourite books, fifteen of those he offered were fiction. His choice comprised some familiar favourites (Anthony Powell, Proust, Evelyn Waugh and Trollope) and some classics (George Eliot, Hardy, Austen);* several modern British women (Virginia Woolf, Elizabeth Bowen, Rosamond Lehmann, Iris Murdoch), two more British men (E.M. Forster and Aldous Huxley) and two Americans (Scott Fitzgerald and Willa Cather). Of the other five, three were biographical collections (Churchill's *Great Contemporaries*, Lytton Strachey's *Eminent Victorians*, Harold Nicolson's *Some People*), only one straight history (D.W. Brogan's *The Development of Modern France*) and one architectural (Pevsner on Oxfordshire).[20] It was in some ways a safe list; but it is a good guide to the furniture of his mind.

Of course, in recording the amount of time Jenkins had for reading and writing one must remember that he lived, by most people's standards in the late twentieth century, an extraordinarily pampered life. All his domestic needs were taken care of: at home Jennifer (with some help) organised his meals, his clothes and the shopping, cooking and laundry – chores with which other husbands were increasingly expected to help. When they had lunch guests at East Hendred the only thing Roy was responsible for was the wine (and in winter the wood for the fire). Away from home he stayed in hotels or with friends – frequently in the British Embassy – and ate in restaurants or one of his clubs. If he had a lot of time to read and write, it was because there was literally nothing else he was required to do except eat, drink and talk. In October 1987 he spent a recuperative long weekend at a health spa in Hampshire, where he presumably ate and drank rather less than usual. Over the five days, as well as a lot of swimming, saunas and massages, he recorded that he read or wrote (including newspapers and letter-writing) for an average of nine hours a day: forty-six hours in total.[21] But the pattern of his life was not very different at other times. Wherever he was, at home or staying with friends, the household revolved around him: he would emerge for meals, tennis or croquet, a walk or a drive, but the rest of the time he spent alone reading or writing, like an old-fashioned bachelor academic whose college took care of all his practical arrangements. He unquestionably worked hard,

---

★ Here again he loved classifying. He read *Middlemarch* 'properly' for the first time in 1988, and judged it (in the *TLS*) 'a great novel, more penetrating than Thackeray, less circumscribed than Austen'. Its only fault was that the two stories did not really fit together: 'It is like one of those old big railway stations where one half has been built by one company and one half by another.'[19]

and fast; but if one is inclined to be astonished at his literary and journalistic output, one needs to remember the extraordinarily tolerant support team — primarily Jennifer — who made it possible.*

Jennifer remained remarkably tolerant of his girlfriends, too, who continued to be an accepted and central part of his life — though by this time, following his prostate operation in 1984, the physical element had almost certainly waned. Whatever else he was doing, he still usually contrived to have lunch with Caroline Gilmour at least once a fortnight and often weekly, at a variety of London restaurants (the White Tower in Fitzrovia was one favourite, a French restaurant in Holland Park Avenue called La Pomme d'Amour another) and with Leslie Bonham Carter almost as frequently. He would also often call in for an hour or two at the Ferry House, the Gilmour house on the Thames at Isleworth — particularly handy for Heathrow — or the Bonham Carters' house in Victoria Road, Kensington. Both Caroline and Leslie would also come to Kensington Park Gardens or to East Hendred when Jennifer was not there, and sometimes when she was. There was nothing secretive about these visits. Jennifer knew all about them — she would often drop Roy off at the Ferry House and meet up again later to drive back to East Hendred — and so did Ian Gilmour and Mark Bonham Carter, who had long ago accepted the position, and both had extramarital relations of their own. Once a year Roy and Caroline would spend a weekend together in Scotland, staying with trustworthy friends on the way up or down. It was a remarkably Edwardian arrangement — aristocratic or Bloomsbury — which was possible because all those concerned had several houses and of course there were no mobile phones enabling — nowadays virtually requiring — spouses to keep constant track of one another. It was, in a favourite Jenkins word, very 'civilised', so long as no marriage was threatened and there was no scandal, which there never was.†

Jenkins was not exactly open about these relationships, but he was not apologetic or dissembling about them either. In a feature in *The*

---

* In 1994 he fell off a table when attempting to change a light bulb. Luckily he did not hurt himself, but he was deterred from attempting anything similar again. One friend wrote mock-sympathetically that there was 'something endearingly risible in . . . the thought of you attempting to change an electric light'.[22]
† The press, or certainly a large number of journalists, must have known about his relationships, but nothing ever appeared even in the gossip columns. In June 1983, for instance, just a week after the General Election, the *Times* Diary carried a trivial item reporting that Jenkins had been seen drinking white wine with his cheese at the three-Michelin-starred Chelsea restaurant La Tante Claire. But it omitted to mention that his lunch companion was Caroline Gilmour.[23]

Times in 1993 in which various public figures were asked to describe 'My Perfect Weekend' he declined to say who his perfect companion would be, since everyone else 'cloyingly' named their husband or wife, 'whether or not that would be true'.[24] In his own books he was uncensorious of his subjects' sexual irregularities, and in reviews he often criticised biographers who brushed them out of sight. He usually declined to answer questions from students who asked him about politicians' mistresses; but in the last year of his life he gave a revealing answer to one correspondent who asked him about Churchill's unusual marital fidelity and wondered about other post-war Prime Ministers, compared with at least two notably randy American Presidents. Reflecting on 'the absence of British Kennedys and Clintons and the propriety of post-war Prime Ministers', Jenkins thought Eden was 'the only exception I could put up. Maybe they would have been more interesting had they been less narrowly focussed on politics, although Eden is not an encouraging example.'[25] The clear suggestion is that an affair or two would have made certain recent Prime Ministers less one-dimensional.*

In an interview he gave a few years earlier to Sarah Bradford in connection with her biography of Jackie Kennedy, Jenkins speculated on why Jackie did not marry his friend David Harlech – British ambassador in Washington during the Kennedy years – after JFK's assassination:

> My view is, having known both of them quite well, that if Jackie had asked him to marry her he probably wouldn't have been able to resist it but . . . he had a very good sense of self-preservation and he had a very good hedonistic calculus . . . My view is that he would have had the sense to see that life married to Jackie would have had a lot of disadvantages and wouldn't really have suited him.[26]

Whether or not this is true, the phrase that Jenkins here applied to Harlech – 'hedonistic calculus' – perfectly described his own approach to life, which governed not only his relationships with women, but his enjoyment of all his other pleasures, which could have threatened his marriage and arguably did damage his career. With Jennifer's long-suffering acquiescence he calculated that he could enjoy his food and

---

* Jenkins never had much time for John Major as Prime Minister. But he might have thought him less one-dimensional if he had known about Edwina Currie.

drink and women and clubs and high society and still stand a good chance of becoming Prime Minister, if the political cards had fallen right. If he was required to give up all his other pleasures in order to get to Number Ten, that was a price he would not pay. He thought that he could 'have it all' – and very nearly succeeded. If in the end he failed, he reckoned that he enjoyed his life a good deal more than most of those who did make it. 'Hedonistic calculus' was a principle which did not let him down.

Inevitably very few letters from his women friends survive. Caroline Gilmour's diary is still in the family. There are in the Jenkins papers just two letters from Leslie Bonham Carter to 'Darling Roy' dating from 1990. They are both quite trivial, but they give a flavour of their relationship – not least Leslie's easy acceptance of both Caroline and Jennifer. The first teases Roy about the fact that the picture of Lord Young on the cover of his just-published memoirs looked unnervingly like Roy, while Caroline looked like Mrs Thatcher:

> Which do you think has the greater cause for worry Caroline or you with your look-a-likes? It's a nice point. By a narrow margin I think Mrs T. is slightly less frightful.
>
> You are a real gadabout. Let's try to talk Thursday morning when I gather you are spending an hour in the UK. With my love, Leslie.[27]

The second, six months later, suggests rather more the loving mistress:

> I thought I might have solved the vexed question of your silk handkerchiefs with a selection like the one I enclose. I think it's beautiful – do you? The only thing that stopped me buying a quantity was a discreet little label which caught my eye at the last moment saying HAND WASH ONLY. I am sure that Jennifer would welcome the chance to round out her day in this way? Let me know. I hope you are feeling svelte and well. Love Leslie.[28]

Jenkins was in the fortunate position of having no fewer than three discreet and devoted women all dedicated to looking after him.

Over his last four years as a Member of Parliament after giving up the SDP leadership Jenkins made an average of four substantial speeches in the House each session, plus about a dozen questions or shorter interventions. The latter were mainly either questions to Mrs Thatcher after European summits (which she usually batted away with no difficulty or turned tartly back on him) or Scottish questions with an eye on his electorate in Hillhead. Even though the SDP had only six MPs he declined to take an official spokesmanship under Owen, but exercised his right to speak as a senior Privy Councillor as and when he wanted. Thus he always spoke in the budget debate in March and again after the Chancellor's autumn statement, and once or twice more on other issues of particular interest to him like Europe, the security services or – again for the benefit of the Scottish press – regional policy or the survival of ship-building on the Clyde. His speeches were short, weighty and could be a little pompous, invoking his authority as a former Home Secretary and Chancellor, but they were generally heard with respect. The heckling that had thrown him as SDP leader gradually died away as the Labour awkward squad realised that he was a more powerful critic of Thatcherism than most of their own front bench. In 1986 he was actually awarded the *Spectator*'s 'Parliamentarian of the Year' award – a remarkable accolade on the basis of so few speeches. Over the whole Parliament he steadily refused to be impressed by Nigel Lawson's hubristic and self-congratulatory management of the economy, partly because of what he called Lawson's 'clamant, know-all discourtesy'[29] – 'I wish that I was as certain of anything as the Chancellor is of anything,' he complained in 1986[30] – but more seriously on three main grounds of criticism.

First, Jenkins continued to insist that the 'unending plateau of the highest unemployment in a major country in the industrialised world was 'simply not acceptable'.[31] He complimented the ingenuity of some of Lawson's tax changes, but branded him 'fundamentally complacent for tolerating such a level of unemployment.[32] The 1986 budget, he complained, was 'the Budget of a minister of taxation who accepts the economic weather', not of a Chancellor who tried to make it.[33]* By now he conceded that Lawson was presiding over a partial recovery

---

* As an unapologetic Keynesian, Jenkins spoke, with J.K. Galbraith, at an event in Cambridge to mark Keynes' centenary in December 1983. Much of his contribution was a rehash of his biographical essay in *Nine Men of Power*, but he also stressed Keynes' Liberalism and claimed his posthumous support for the Alliance. ('The Alliance was made for him. I wish he were here to help make it.') So-called 'crude Keynesianism', he conceded, might have had 'some limitations, but it was a great advance on crude pre-Keynesianism'. What was needed now in Downing Street and the White House, he concluded, was 'some of the rational panache which Keynes showed nearly fifty years ago. We may not see his like again, but let us at least hope that the world economy is not ruined by his denigrators.'[34]

but believed that the destruction of manufacturing in 1979–82 had been both disastrous and self-inflicted. 'Judged by results,' he declared in November 1984, 'the Chancellor's attempt to portray the last four years as a golden economic age looks not merely wrong but ludicrous.'[35] He insisted that services alone could not sustain a prosperous economy and repeatedly called for more active government intervention of the type that less ideologically dogmatic competitors like the Americans – even under Reagan – and the Japanese took for granted to support their industries.[36] In 1985 he joined with Healey and Hattersley from Labour and sacked Tory wets like Jim Prior and Francis Pym, plus a host of other concerned members of the great and good under the chairmanship of Professor Richard Layard, in a cross-party Employment Institute to call for some reflation – 'or merely less vicious deflation';[37] and he frequently drew attention to the unprecedented consensus stretching from Ted Heath and the ninety-two-year-old Harold Macmillan (now Lord Stockton), the CBI and an experienced Select Committee of the House of Lords to both main opposition parties and the TUC, all pressing the same case on the government's deaf ears.* Though unemployment finally peaked – at nearly 3.5 million – in 1986 he predicted correctly that Lawson's policies would not bring it below three million before the next election.[39]

Next, he warned the government constantly not to waste the temporary windfall of North Sea oil. 'The second problem which dominates my mind,' he declared in his televised response to Lawson's first budget in 1984 (summarising his speech in the House), 'is . . . how are we going to earn a living when North Sea oil begins to run out?' This, he believed, was the most menacing economic challenge the country had faced since 1945. In fact oil extraction did not peak quite as soon as he anticipated; but his essential point was surely right. 'I believe the primary duty of our Government is to use the remaining period of oil spate to put Britain in the best possible shape for a difficult future' by rebuilding the national infrastructure – roads, railways, communications and industrial capacity – and educating a skilled workforce. The danger was not, as Lawson maintained, bequeathing a burden of debt to the next generation: by comparison with the post-war years the real level of debt was not particularly high. 'The real danger is bequeathing

---

* Jenkins frequently found himself in these years speaking in the House immediately after Heath, and taking much the same line as the ex-Prime Minister, as he ironically acknowledged in March 1985. 'I do not know what effect losing the leadership of the Conservative party is said to have had on his temper, but it has had a remarkably good effect on the sense and sweep of his judgement and view of the world.'[38]

a run-down Britain without the skills or the tools to earn its living.' 'The Alliance,' he concluded, 'wants the Government to launch a major programme of re-equipping Britain.'[40] Right up to the 1987 election he kept on berating the Thatcher government, which claimed to believe in thrift and good housekeeping, for frittering away a one-off capital asset in short-term tax cuts and a personal consumption boom. (In November 1985 he even charged the government with 'improvident financing on a scale which makes . . . General Galtieri almost Gladstonian'.)[41] From the perspective of the twenty-first century it is clear that he was right.

Third, he was contemptuous of the government's incompetence in allowing sterling to yo-yo up and down – from $1.60 to $2.40, down to $1.07, then back to $1.60, all within eighteen months – 'like lift-dwellers in a department store',[42] instead of pegging it to greater stability by joining the Exchange Rate Mechanism of the EMS. Following a fiasco in January 1985 when Mrs Thatcher appeared to say that she did not mind if the pound fell to parity with the dollar, obliging Lawson hurriedly to raise interest rates to 14 per cent to shore it up, Jenkins wrote a scornful letter to *The Times* mocking 'the extraordinary pantomime-horse act of 10 Downing Street and the Treasury over last weekend':

A large part of the trouble stems from the combination of the present Chancellor's insensitivity and the Prime Minister's unamiable tendency always to blame something or someone other than herself. As a result she handles the exchange rate with peculiar ineptitude. It cannot, of course, be commanded by any Government. But it can be considerably influenced by a firm and consistent policy to behave less erratically and more in our national interests.

It could not be achieved by 'treating market forces as though they were junior ministers, first patted on the head as her own special progeny, then sternly ordered to stop behaving independently and improperly, and finally assailed with a flailing mass of misleading statistics'.[43]

In January 1986 Jenkins used an SDP Opposition day to open a debate urging immediate entry to the ERM. Since its creation, he claimed, the EMS had been a 'limited but substantial success', affording European currencies some stability against the violently fluctuating dollar. He repeated his story of Callaghan and Mrs Thatcher each keeping Britain out for opposite reasons, and urged that so long as Britain remained outside her influence in Europe would inevitably be reduced.[44] The Treasury put up a junior minister to answer him; another who spoke against entry in the short debate that followed was the young Tony Blair (first elected in 1983). With both big parties whipped against it, Jenkins' motion was rejected by 397 votes to twenty-two. But as it became obvious that most of the Prime Minister's senior colleagues, including both Lawson and his predecessor Geoffrey Howe (now Foreign Secretary), wanted to join, while her excuses for resisting became increasingly threadbare, Jenkins kept up the pressure to wear down her stubborn opposition.

At the same time after every European summit he pressed her to be more positive towards Europe generally. He hoped that the result of the General Election would finally lay to rest any possibility of Labour taking Britain out of the Community and encourage Mrs Thatcher to settle the British Budget Question, which she eventually did at Fontainebleau in 1984. He continued to insist that she could have got much the same deal with far less hassle years earlier and deplored the way other countries had followed her penny-pinching example, 'turning every successive meeting into an accountants' wrangle'. A favourite theme was that after several decades of catching up, Europe was again falling behind America and Japan. 'The combined national income of the Community countries,' he wrote in *The Times*, 'has fallen back to ninety-three per cent of that of the United States.'[45] 'In these circumstances,' he believed, 'to spend all our time in Europe quibbling about a few hundreds of millions of pounds is something which in the context of wider issues looks totally disproportionate.'[46] As always he was anxious to see Europe moving forward again, without ever spelling out exactly where it should be going. He was keen to see Spain and Portugal admitted as soon as possible (they finally joined in 1986). He wanted to see the proportion of the Community's resources devoted to agriculture 'sealed off' so that more could be spent on other sectors; and as such a rebalancing of the budget would be very much in Britain's interest, he constantly pressed Mrs Thatcher to agree to more majority voting – what he called 'rolling back the use of the veto'[47] – to make this and other developments possible. Otherwise the Community would stagnate. 'We must get our head out of the groceries,' he urged in 1985, 'and regain the vision, nerve and perspective of those who more than thirty years ago were responsible for the European Community's creation.'[48]*

---

* In fact Mrs Thatcher did support a considerable extension of majority voting as part of the Single European Act – something she later regretted.

As much as specific policies, Jenkins abhorred the whole style and ethos of Mrs Thatcher's government: her narrow-minded certainty and moralistic self-righteousness offended him – though of course she and her supporters thought him equally dogmatic in his own way. Distaste for her values dripped from his lofty intervention at Prime Minister's Questions during the Westland crisis in January 1985, when she got herself into a tangle – and lost two Cabinet ministers – over the sale of a small West Country helicopter company to her preferred (American) buyer rather than a European consortium:

> Is the Right Hon. Lady aware that as she and her Government sink deeper into the bog of deceit and chicanery, almost her only remaining memorable words will be that there were commercial decisions involved, and that Governments before hers have been activated by considerations higher than that?[49]

On this occasion Mrs Thatcher replied defensively that commercial decisions did carry legal obligations. Jenkins also deplored the government's penny-pinching cuts to the Foreign Office budget, its 'foolish and short-sighted' withdrawal from UNESCO and its stingy level of relief for a famine in Ethiopia – all at a time when it was happy to spend billions on buying Trident and defending 'Fortress Falklands'. Thatcher and Lawson, he charged in November 1984, had 'little sense of history, proportion or compassion, and the absence of all three qualities in confluence is a devastating weakness'.[50] He was severely critical of Mrs Thatcher's neglect of Parliament ('The Government treat this House with a discourtesy that I have never seen parallelled in 39 years in the House');[51] her emasculation of the Cabinet by purging anyone who disagreed with her, so that by the middle of the decade there was more rejected talent on the Tory back benches than on the front; and her systematic politicisation of public bodies like the BBC, the Bank of England and the National Coal Board by appointing only Tories who could be relied upon to do her bidding.[52] Above all he was withering about the government's farcically doomed attempt to suppress the memoirs of a rogue MI5 officer, Peter Wright, by sending the Cabinet Secretary – Jenkins' former private secretary Robert Armstrong – to be humiliated in an Australian courtroom. Once again Jenkins did not scruple to condemn the Prime Minister's 'combination of exceptional ill-judgement and exceptional stubbornness' in the most personal terms. Drawing attention to 'the peculiarly unacceptable hypocrisy of a Prime Minister whose stock-in-trade is leaks from the top accompanied by prosecutions lower down', he concluded by questioning her truthfulness:

> The Prime Minister, with the possible exception of Anthony Eden for a few unfortunate weeks exactly thirty years ago, is undoubtedly the most self-righteous Prime Minister since Neville Chamberlain, in the wholly relevant sense of despising her opponents . . . and being convinced of her own moral superiority. In these circumstances it is peculiarly unfortunate that whenever attention is focussed on some activity in which she has been involved, as in Westland, as here, there should be a trail of dissimulation left behind.[53]

This speech was also notable for Jenkins' refusal to believe the wild suggestions in Peter Wright's book that Harold Wilson had been a Soviet spy:

> Many criticisms can be made of Lord Wilson's stewardship – I have made some in the past and I have no doubt that I may make some more in future – but the view that he, with his too persistent record of maintaining Britain's imperial commitments across the world, with his over-loyal lieutenancy to Lyndon Johnson, with his fervent royalism and with his light ideological luggage, was a likely candidate to be a Russian or Communist agent, is one that can be entertained only by someone with a mind diseased by partisanship or unhinged by living for too long in an Alice-Through-The-Looking-Glass world in which falsehood becomes truth, fact becomes fiction and fantasy becomes reality.[54]

As Home Secretary, Jenkins had always been sceptical of the activities of the spooks, and Wright's revelations of their dirty tricks confirmed his conviction that it was time to rein them in. In a letter to *The Times* in 1985 he had already proposed that the security services should be subjected to parliamentary scrutiny by a committee of senior Privy Councillors. He did not believe that phone-tapping was as widespread as some conspiracy addicts alleged – 'I hope and believe that nothing improper was done in my periods of office . . . Most of those who think themselves to be tapped are suffering from illusions of grandeur' – but nevertheless considered that MI5 had become 'more trouble than it is worth' and concluded that 'on grounds of utility I would now close down the political side of its activities'.⁵⁵*.In the debate following the *Spycatcher* affair – opened by David Owen, but very much on the lines of Jenkins' letter – he gained the support of one or two maverick Tories like Jonathan Aitken; but the Alliance motion was crushed as usual by 232 votes to twenty-four.

Jenkins' critique of Thatcherism rested on a wider base than just distaste for her personality. In late 1984, following the collapse of the Johnson Matthey bank and a series of City scandals involving Lloyd's and other prestigious financial institutions, he wrote for the *Sunday Times* magazine a remarkably prescient article criticising the increasing dominance of the City of London, the massive salaries now being earned there ('the greed factor') and the lack of effective regulation (this was *before* the deregulation introduced by the so-called 'Big Bang' in 1986). He also noted the increasing carelessness of MPs in declaring their outside interests. He acknowledged the difficulty of legislating against greed, but warned that the 'exuberance' of the City made a mockery of the government's appeals for pay restraint and was drawing too much talent away from industry and public service. Quoting Baldwin's semi-serious remark that a man who made a quick million 'ought not to be in the House of Lords but in jail', he concluded that the City needed more authoritative and more austere leadership if it was to escape 'a severe financial jolt'.⁵⁷ The fact that it took another thirty years to come about does not detract from the prescience of the warning. In the Commons that autumn Jenkins also warned of a looming 'financial catastrophe' in the form of an international debt crisis, which might force governments to buy up bad debts in order to avert bank failures.⁵⁸

In one of his last speeches in the House, criticising Lawson's tax-cutting pre-election budget in March 1987, Jenkins protested against the whole trend of the government's policies since 1979 – showing that he had moved some way, but not so far as his critics alleged, from the concerns he had first expressed in *Fair Shares for the Rich* more than thirty years before:

* In a sentence that he cut from the letter as published, Jenkins was more specific about his criteria for authorising surveillance: 'To avoid euphemism . . . I would probably have signed a warrant against Mr Scargill, not because of the strike, but because of his stated general desire to overthrow our system of government, and refused them against Mrs Ruddock, Monsignor Kent, Ms Hewitt or Ms Harman.'⁵⁶ Joan Ruddock and Bruce Kent were leading anti-nuclear campaigners; Patricia Hewitt and Harriet Harman – later model Blairites – were then seen as Labour left-wingers.

Not only . . . is this no Budget for jobs, but it is no Budget for the growing number of the deprived in our society. I do not believe in the almost mechanical egalitarianism of the right hon. Member for Sparkbrook [Roy Hattersley, now Labour's Shadow Chancellor], but I believe . . . it is the duty of the state to lean firmly but unvindictively in favour of greater equality – for the natural forces all lean the other way, and, if left untrammelled, produce results that might shock even the Chancellor's conscience. But, for eight years, the Government has leaned the other way. Two-thirds of the tax concessions have been given to the top 20 per cent. The effect has been accentuated by the splurge of City and some other incomes.

The government's apologists argued that 'if the rich are made rich enough, some wealth will spill over to make the poor less poor'. Unfortunately, he asserted, there was no sign of this so-called 'trickle-down effect' happening:

> On the contrary, the gap has widened. The number of those below the poverty line and with little hope of rising above it has grown inexorably . . . If I were Chancellor I would be deeply apprehensive for the future cohesion of our society under his policies, even if . . . his luck holds.[59]

By this time, as the 1987 election approached, Jenkins had accepted Owen's invitation to return to the front bench as the Alliance's Shadow Chancellor – Owen having finally conceded the principle of joint spokesmen in January 1987. Jenkins was probably no keener to take on the role than Owen was to offer it, but neither could deny the enhanced credibility it brought to the Alliance team. Over the previous four years the Alliance had continued to perform remarkably well under the uneasy dual leadership of Owen and David Steel. Contrary to the retrospective myth that this was the high noon of rampant Thatcherism, the government actually suffered a succession of political challenges and embarrassments in these years, ranging from the year-long miners' strike, the Greenham Common women's peace camp and the unpopular abolition of Ken Livingstone's Greater London Council (GLC) to the self-inflicted Westland imbroglio and the Americans' bombing of Libya from British bases, as a result of which it trailed in the polls about half the time between June 1983 and June 1987. Labour under Neil Kinnock had regained a good deal of credibility, but still never polled above

40 per cent, so that the Alliance was never squeezed out of sight, but fluctuated between a low point of 19 per cent (early in the Parliament) and a high of 39 per cent (briefly in September 1985). It was normally third, but over forty-eight months was six times second behind the Tories, seven times second behind Labour and three times actually led.[60] In addition it notched up four more exciting by-election victories, taking Portsmouth South, Brecon and Radnor (in South Wales) and Ryedale (in Yorkshire) from the Tories and – just before the General Election – Greenwich from Labour; the Alliance now controlled or held the balance on more than 100 local councils. Despite the disappointment of 1983, six years after the formation of the SDP three-party politics appeared to be firmly established, with a serious prospect of the Alliance forming at least a part of the next government.

Nevertheless Jenkins was increasingly alarmed by Owen's leadership of the SDP, on several counts: first, by his continued determination to maintain the SDP's separate identity and resist the evolution of the Alliance into a single party; second, by his paradoxically unambitious strategy, aimed only at holding the balance in the next Parliament, not at the complete breakthrough which Jenkins was convinced was still possible; and above all by the increasingly right-wing flavour of some of Owen's policies and his undisguised admiration for the Prime Minister's abrasive style. He put down a clear marker against all these tendencies in a lecture in July 1984 in honour of the economist R.H. Tawney (whom the SDP was endeavouring to co-opt as an intellectual forebear). Denying the existence of any major ideological differences to prevent the two parties coming together – 'I honestly believe the Alliance is ideologically about as cohesive as any decent democratic grouping ought ever to be, substantially more so than either the Labour or Conservative parties' – he quoted Churchill in the summer of 1940 likening the Anglo-American alliance to the mighty Mississippi: 'Let it roll on in full flood, inexorable, irresistible, benignant, to broader lands and better days.' Insisting that if the Alliance held true to its founding principles it could still 'at the second run, make a reality of the great prospect which opened up before us in 1981', he explicitly rejected the idea that the SDP was 'on the way to becoming a sort of junior Thatcherite party' ('"Not while I'm alive it ain't," as Ernest Bevin said about Aneurin Bevan being his own worst enemy'). 'The whole spirit and outlook of the SDP,' he insisted, 'is and must be profoundly opposed to Thatcherism.'[61] The following year – just in time for the party conference in Torquay – he contributed to an SDP magazine the *New Democrat*, a warning that the country would not want ' sub-Thatcherite alternative' at the next election, so the Alliance must campaign boldly 'for power, not balance'. Noting the irony that he had once been considered the most right-wing of the Gang of Four, while the self-declared 'radical' of 1982 had then aspired to replace Labour, he concluded pointedly: 'We must be clear about the political orientation of our party . . . We should keep our radical cutting edge well honed and endeavour to cut as deep in Durham as in Devon.'[62] The challenge to Owen could hardly have been more explicit. Though Jenkins did not actually say any of this at the conference, when he spoke only about unemployment, the delegates had read what he had written and gave him a rapturous reception.*

The tensions within the Alliance – and between Owen and the other three members of the Gang of Four – boiled over in 1986 when Owen deliberately provoked a split over what he saw as the Liberals' 'softness' on defence. Admittedly there was a unilateralist minority in the Liberal Party which had succeeded in carrying a vote at the party's 1984 conference to remove American cruise missiles from British soil. But it was a minority, which was firmly opposed by Steel and the rest of the leadership. Since the SDP was solidly multilateralist there was no danger of the Alliance being committed to unilateralism. Precisely to scotch this possibility, however, a joint commission composed of senior figures from both parties – including Bill Rodgers – was set up to consider an agreed Alliance policy, including the open question of whether Britain should replace its ageing Polaris system with American Trident missiles. Jenkins was, of course, no unilateralist. He accepted that nuclear weapons existed, could not be disinvented and could be a deterrent. 'To proclaim a local nuclear-free zone and to believe that this gives safety is to erect a bamboo fence against a hurricane,' he declared in a rare speech on defence in 1984. The only route to nuclear disarmament was multilateral, by NATO negotiating weapons limitation with the Soviets, with the British and French forces included in the mix.[63] Nevertheless he was sceptical about replacing Polaris and did not believe that a decision to buy Trident had to be made immediately, while arms-limitation talks were still going on and the accession of Mikhail Gorbachev to power in Moscow raised hopes that they might succeed. This was also the conclusion of the Alliance commission which reported in the summer of 1986. But Owen chose to see this as a

---

* Just before the 1985 conference Clive Lindley edited a selection of Jenkins' writings and speeches about the making of the Alliance, entitled *Partnership of Principle*. Starting with the Dimbleby Lecture and his speeches at Warrington, Llandudno and Hillhead, it also included his Tawney lecture and an introduction based on his *New Democrat* article.

cop-out, which, he told an SDP conference at Southport in May, 'would get and deserve a belly laugh from the British electorate'.[64] He was overreacting to a misleading interview David Steel had given to the *Scotsman*, saying – correctly – that the commission would not commit the Alliance to replacing Polaris. This the paper mischievously headlined as a defeat for Owen ('Owen's Nuclear Hopes Dashed'), prompting Owen to decide unilaterally to pre-empt the report before it was even published. This high-handed behaviour was the last straw for the other three members of the Gang of Four, especially since it was quite unnecessary. When told what had provoked Owen to make his intemperate démarche, Jenkins reportedly exploded: 'In that case the man's totally unfit to hold public office';[65] and a few weeks later he took the opportunity of running into Owen in the Commons to take him into the smoking room to tell him exactly what he thought of him. 'I gave him a piece of my mind,' he wrote in his memoirs, 'of which the burden was that he ought to ask himself why he sooner or later quarrelled with everyone with whom he was politically closely associated.'[66]

Owen, Jenkins reflected, 'was something of a nuclear fetishist. He could talk about missiles with a discriminating enthusiasm which some men reserved for horses or women or wine.' His obsession with nuclear weapons bore out one of Jenkins' favourite observations – usually illustrated by reference to Joseph Chamberlain's tariff reform campaign, which split the Tories in 1903, and Labour's contortions over Europe in the 1970s – that political leaders can never keep away from the subject that will do them the most damage. 'Once he [Owen] had decided with some justification that nuclear weaponry was the most dangerous subject for the coherence and success of the Alliance, he came increasingly to talk about little else.'[67] His gratuitous exaggeration of a minor difference of emphasis to justify his contempt for the Liberals punctured the Alliance's momentum just when it was on a roll – two weeks after the Ryedale by-election – knocking its Gallup poll rating from 32 per cent in the spring to 22 per cent by the autumn; and the damage to the parties' mutual trust was permanent. His action actually played into the hands of the Liberal unilateralists, who managed (by the narrowest of margins) to carry an anti-nuclear resolution at the party's autumn conference, which was less a vindication of his intransigence than a consequence of it. Steel was just as dismayed by the Eastbourne vote as Owen was. In fact the two leaderships managed to patch up a formula in time for the election, by which they agreed to keep Britain's independent deterrent until it could be negotiated

"PERHAPS IF YOU TRIED GETTING INSIDE ..."

Garland, *Independent,* 16.6.87 (British Cartoon Archive, University of Kent)

away as part of a wider deal, as a result of which the Alliance's poll rating climbed back into the low thirties. The whole row was an unnecessary storm in a hypothetical teacup. But, with sad hindsight, Jenkins believed that 'the Alliance began to die on that wet Southport Saturday afternoon'.[68]*

At the very end of 1986 Harold Macmillan died, a few weeks short of his ninety-third birthday. Among his other honours the former Prime Minister had been since 1960 Chancellor of Oxford University. This was a largely ceremonial but prestigious position, which Jenkins confessed to having had his eye on since the mid-1970s, though the

---

* Reflecting in his memoirs on his own and Owen's different view of the Liberals, Jenkins concluded sagely: 'He essentially regarded the Liberals as a disorderly group of vegetarian bearded pacifists . . . I treated them as the statesmanlike heirs of Gladstone and Asquith. The truth was no doubt somewhere between the two, but I am sure that my method pushed them in the right direction from an SDP point of view, and that his pushed them in the wrong direction.' He regretted having failed to engage successfully with Owen in this period, but it had become 'an extraordinarily difficult thing to do. If one spoke softly . . . he interpreted it as weakness. If one spoke harshly he took deep umbrage. I have never tried to work closely with anyone with whom it was so difficult to talk things out.'[69] In 1987 – after the election – Jenkins told Woodrow Wyatt that the trouble was that 'David must either be an acolyte or have acolytes. He can be nothing in between. He cannot deal with equals.'[70]

odds would always have been against him since the titular head of Oxford (unlike Cambridge) was a highly politicised elective post, elected by the resident Fellows and those graduates willing to go to Oxford to vote in person, in which almost any Conservative candidate, however dim, could be expected to defeat any non-Conservative, however distinguished. The classic case was Asquith, in 1925 clearly the most eminent living Oxonian, who was humiliatingly rejected by the Tory dons and country clergy who then still dominated the university in favour of the then Lord Chancellor, Lord Cave – described by Jenkins in his biography of Asquith as 'the least distinguished occupant of the Woolsack of the first thirty years of this century'.[71] In 1960 Macmillan, Tory Prime Minister at the time, defeated the former ambassador Sir Oliver Franks and lived to stamp the office with his style, theatricality and wit for twenty-six years. For most of that time Jenkins assumed that he would have little chance of succeeding: 'I think I probably saw myself more as a left-of-centre candidate willing to lose' – probably to Quintin Hailsham – 'than as a likely winner.'[72]* But Macmillan's longevity worked to Jenkins' advantage, since the current Tory Prime Minister bitterly divided the university. In 1985 a majority of voting dons, infuriated by her government's attack on universities in general and science funding in particular, had run a successful campaign to deny Mrs Thatcher the normally uncontested award of an honorary degree, to the equal fury of others who thought such pettiness only dishonoured the university. In the wake of this row the Tory camp was split. Ted Heath was determined to stand and immediately drew a lot of anti-Thatcher support, while the pro-Thatcher loyalists put up Robert Blake, Provost of Queen's College and the leading historian of the Tory Party, as an internal, academic candidate. Between the two of them and their squabbling supporters Jenkins appeared almost as the non-political candidate, as well as arguably the most distinguished and certainly the most entertaining company at High Table.

Jenkins' supporters ran a brilliant campaign, drawing on his wide cross-party fan base among the great and the good, so many of whom had flocked to the SDP. It was publicly fronted by Sir Alec Cairncross (his former economic adviser at the Treasury); the former chief

---

* It was probably with a view to his eligibility for the Chancellorship that Jenkins decided in 1972, when given an honorary doctorate, that he should take his MA, which he had never done. He wrote to Christopher Hill, the Master of Balliol, hoping it could be awarded *in absentia* with little fuss, 'as I do not relish the faint ridiculousness of a middle-aged baptism'.[73]

government statistician Sir Claus Moser; the Provost of Worcester College, the historian (and old friend from Bletchley days) Asa Briggs; the economic historian Patrick O'Brien; and the philosopher Isaiah Berlin. Anthony Kenny, the current Master of Balliol, and Michael Brock, Warden of Nuffield, were discreetly active in the background; while Celia Goodhart ran the London end of the campaign like a by-election, chasing up supporters to canvass their friends and persuade them to go to Oxford to vote. They collected and published week by week in the *Oxford Gazette* an impressive list of nominations drawn from all the colleges and including women – unlike Heath, whose nominators incredibly were all from Balliol and all male. Jenkins' final tally of 410 included twenty-six present or former heads of college, two Nobel Prize-winners, three holders of the Order of Merit and twenty-seven members of the Royal Society or the British Academy. By contrast, Heath secured only 160 nominations and Blake just sixty-seven.

Alec Cairncross's pitch in the *Oxford Magazine* stressed, in addition to his other achievements, six reasons why Jenkins would make the best Chancellor: he would be immensely proud of the distinction, and would discharge the duties assiduously; he lived nearby and would therefore be readily available for university occasions; he would provide 'the elegance and wit' which, after Macmillan, the Chancellor's speeches were expected to display; he would bring international prestige to the university and speak for the university to the government; and he would 'oppose the philistinism and short-sightedness which now colour prevailing attitudes towards the universities' [74] It can fairly be said that Jenkins delivered on all these promises.

The contest was intensely political and excited tremendous interest in the national – and international – press. The two Tory candidates each believed that the other should not have stood, and neatly cancelled one another out. In the absence of a Labour candidate – Healey was sounded out, but declined to stand – most of the 'left' voters who still saw Jenkins as a class traitor backed Heath as the strongest anti-Thatcherite; but Heath was equally seen as a traitor by many Tories. 'The petulance and bitterness he has shown in his sterile campaign against the Prime Minister,' the *Daily Telegraph* advised its readers, 'should disqualify him from the Oxford Chancellorship.' Jenkins, the paper admitted, was 'a figure of much grace and dignity' who would be 'an ornament to the university'. But Blake had charm and distinction and an undoubted commitment to academic values. 'If Oxford wishes to give a clear signal of its commitment to restoring its threatened greatness, its members will elect Robert Blake.'[75] The Tory whips, however, sent out mixed messages: after seeming initially to back Blake, they switched to Heath at a late stage. Blake subsequently blamed his defeat on 'the *treachery* . . . of the Tory Establishment who threw their weight behind Ted Heath . . . solely because they erroneously reckoned that he had a better chance of beating Roy than I had . . . The row in the Tory party,' he wrote to a friend, 'is bitter and furious, I am glad to say.'[76]* By contrast he had no quarrel with Jenkins and sent him a friendly postcard a few days before the poll, quoting Macmillan's description of the 1960 contest as a cross between 'Eatanswill, a gaudy and a two-day cricket match' and hoping to see him at Grillions or The Club before too long.[78] Nor did Jenkins' now quite warm relations with Heath suffer.

Polling was on Thursday 12 and Saturday 14 March. Such was the interest aroused that about 6,000 graduates came back to their old colleges to vote on the Saturday, causing traffic jams and long queues in the spring sunshine; most of the colleges laid on lunch for their alumni, creating a jolly reunion atmosphere. These 'outvoters' were crucial: whereas in 1960 only 3,673 votes were cast in total, this time there were more than twice as many: 8,307, of whom only about 2,500 were resident in Oxford. These gave Jenkins a clear majority with 3,249 votes to Blake's 2,674 and Heath's 2,348 (there was also a fourth candidate who got thirty-eight votes). Some thought it ironic that the great champion of proportional representation should owe his victory to first-past-the-post; but Jenkins dismissed any doubts this cast on the result, reckoning that he would have won enough of Heath's second-preference votes to win anyway. At any event he was absolutely delighted to win. At his installation in June he declared that 'Nothing in my life has given me greater pleasure than my election as Chancellor.'[79] And he meant it.

It was indeed the best thing that could have happened to him and came at just the right moment, given that he was to lose Hillhead at the General Election just three months later. He lived to enjoy the office for another fifteen years. It was the perfect retirement job for him and he was nearly perfect for it. He loved the ceremonial side

---

* The novelist Anthony Powell − an ardent Thatcherite − was initially inclined to vote for Jenkins, 'not only as a friend, as also most suitable for the job'. But he was so disgusted by the university refusing Mrs Thatcher a degree that he was 'unwilling to lend public support to anyone even moderately tainted with Leftism like Roy'. He also objected to Mrs Goodhart telling him how to vote between two Balliol men.[77] His journal does not reveal how he did vote.

– the academic dress, the processions, the speeches in Latin and the formal dinners, representing Oxford all around the world – but he also loved the opportunity to dine informally in the colleges and savour the academic life that he had been too young and too intensely political to take advantage of as an undergraduate. At the same time there was just enough serious content, acting as a sort of constitutional monarch to the Vice-Chancellor, with no power but the right to be consulted, to advise and exercise influence behind the scenes, to keep him intellectually stimulated. Speaking up for Oxford and universities in general gave him in his last decade a new political cause in which he had not hitherto taken much interest. (He had declined Education when offered it in 1965.) And it turned out to be extraordinarily convenient that twenty years earlier he and Jennifer had made their country home just twenty miles south of Oxford: he could be a highly visible Chancellor, attending all sorts of university and college events, and still sleep in his own bed every night. Above all, perhaps, nothing would have given more pleasure to his father, who had been so determined that Roy should go to Oxford, than that he should finish up as Chancellor of the university. In Arthur's book that probably beat being Prime Minister; while Jenkins himself took great satisfaction from having attained the one coveted prize that Asquith's glittering career had missed.

He took the honour very seriously and threw himself into it with characteristic thoroughness. He immediately started a programme of dining at all the colleges – Merton in October 1988 was his twenty-fourth in eighteen months – usually making a well-researched little speech with some neatly turned compliments to famous alumni, past and living. At a St Hilda's gaudy in July 1989 he risked some rather daring comparisons between the changing characteristics of the women's colleges as they had been in his day and as they were now.[80] As early as April 1988 he was telling a dinner in Washington that 'I sometimes think I do little but respond to toasts at college dinners.'[81] But in his first two years he also spoke to every other sort of university audience, some of them beyond his normal range, from the University Church to the University Air Squadron and the pre-match dinner before the Oxford v. Cambridge rugby match. (The last he called his second most difficult Oxonian task' since becoming Chancellor – the most difficult being A.J. Ayer's memorial service.)[82] In March 1989 he watched the University Boat Race for the first time since 1959, following the crews in the Oxford launch alongside the Duke of Edinburgh, in his capacity as Chancellor of Cambridge, in the

Cambridge launch.* Altogether in these first years he reckoned to fulfil forty to fifty engagements a year in Oxford itself and a good many more around the world – for instance, attending the anniversary celebrations of other universities, ranging in age from Bologna (900 years) to Chicago (100) – calculating with typical precision that the job took 'a good quarter of my time and energy', but provided 'something more like half of my interest'.[84]

In his first year a new Chancellor is allowed to nominate his own choice of distinguished people to receive honorary degrees at his inaugural Encaenia. Jenkins took the opportunity to honour a dozen selected friends and admired contemporaries from different parts of his life – with the notable exception of British politics. His list comprised five resident members of the university, all of whom had certainly voted for him: Isaiah Berlin, Anthony Kenny, the chemist Dorothy Hodgkin, the philosopher/novelist Iris Murdoch and the current Vice-Chancellor, Patrick Neill, plus (a nod to Hillhead) the principal of Glasgow University, Alwyn Williams; two Americans, Robert McNamara and Arthur Schlesinger; from his Brussels years the King of the Belgians; President Cossiga of Italy and the former Irish Taoiseach Garret FitzGerald; and his old friend Nicko Henderson, ambassador successively to Bonn, Paris and Washington. Henderson wrote an amusing account of the accompanying festivities, starting with dinner for the Americans – McNamara and Schlesinger, plus Joseph Alsop, Kay Graham and Marietta Tree – the night before the ceremony at the Berlins', where Aline Berlin served 'a sumptuous dinner and a 1945 Château Lafite'. The next day there was lunch in All Souls, then a dinner at Balliol, which was awkward because most of the dons had backed Heath as 'the more vociferously anti-Maggie' candidate. Henderson thought Jenkins made a good speech, but got a frosty reception ('Balliol was not prepared to respond'); while McNamara made a serious speech about the Cuba crisis.[85]

There were private occasions too. In 1988 Jenkins gave a dinner at Balliol to mark the fiftieth anniversary of his arrival at the college as a not-quite-eighteen-year-old undergraduate. The guests on this occasion were all Balliol contemporaries: Ted Heath, Mark Bonham Carter

* In 1991 Jenkins had to deal with a cross letter from Prince Philip complaining about being misquoted in the new *Oxford Dictionary of Modern Quotations*. Jenkins could only reply that: (a) Oxford University Press was independent of the university and (b) he was used to being misquoted himself; but he could not resist pointing out to his opposite number that the recent *Cambridge Guide to English Literature* had received terrible reviews.[83]

Madron Seligman, Ronnie McIntosh, David Ginsburg, Philip Kaiser, Julian Amery, Ian Bancroft, Neil Bruce, Nigel Foulkes, Admiral of the Fleet Sir Roger Keyes and the Bishop of London, Graham Leonard – demonstrating both the ubiquity of Balliol men in public life and the care Jenkins took all his life to keep up with his contemporaries, including those who were not close friends. Thanking him, McIntosh wrote that 'the food and wine surpassed one's expectations of Balliol cuisine. You struck just the right note of informality in your speech and it was nice to hear Ted respond so gracefully';[86] while Bancroft (head of the Civil Service until sacked by Mrs Thatcher) called it 'a memorable evening of such disarming elegance . . . astringent rather than nostalgic: so much energy (still) there too'.[87] The last decade of Jenkins' life was to be punctuated by frequent such dinners to mark significant birthdays and anniversaries.*

As Chancellor, he loved showing off Oxford to visiting friends – particularly Americans and particularly American women – much as he had loved showing off Glasgow. Afterwards they wrote him gushing letters of thanks. Marietta Tree, for instance, the wealthy, witty Washington socialite and former mistress of Adlai Stevenson, wrote in 1989 to thank him for a memorable visit and a lunch at East Hendred (with the Donaldsons, Macfarlanes and the President of Magdalen, Anthony Smith), which synthesised 'all that is best and most delightful about your country. The dramatis personae combined with the delicious lunch and lavish bottle [*sic*] of wine, could never happen anywhere else save with the unique inspiration and organising genius of R & J Jenkins.'[89] Two years later he invited Jackie Kennedy to that year's Encaenia, along with Marietta Tree again, Jakie Astor, Andrew Devonshire

---

* He marked his own seventieth birthday in November 1990, for instance, with a dinner for ninety at Brooks's – all real friends, no-one *ex officio*, so no David Owen, and no Shirley Williams either, though she sent two bottles of claret; David Steel was invited, but could not come. The seating plan was interesting. At an E-shaped table, Charles, Cynthia and Edward each sat at the head of one arm, with Roy in the middle of Edward's side, Jennifer on Cynthia's. Roy's immediate companions were Marie-Alice de Beaumarchais on his right, Frankie Donaldson on his left and Caroline Gilmour opposite him, with Nicko Henderson, John Grigg, Jeremy Hutchinson and Claus Moser the other men within talking distance, and Leslie Bonham Carter one place beyond John Grigg. Noel Annan spoke and Roy replied. Jakie Astor commented on the 'spontaneous and prolonged applause' for Jennifer.[88] A week later there was a second celebration in New York with a company including Arthur Schlesinger, J.K. Galbraith and Marietta Tree; and in December Ian Aitken of the *Guardian* hosted yet another dinner at the Garrick Club, at which the company was mainly journalists – Robin Day (who gave the main speech), Peter Jenkins, Alan Watkins, Tony Howard, Charles Wilson, Bill Keegan, Hugh Cudlipp, Frank Johnson – but also included Bill Rodgers, Anthony Lester, Graham C. Greene and Peter Parker. It was a cosy world.

and Solly Zuckerman. Afterwards she wrote to him from the Ritz, clearly star-struck:

> Dear Dear Roy,
> All the emotions of the last few days, what I've seen and what I've felt − I feel a bit weakened by it, yet perfectly happy and grateful. It is your great heart that made it all happen . . .
> And you at Oxford, the glory of your robes and your Latin and the architecture; the theatre and the great hall and the honored seat from which you let me see it all. And the House of Lords. It will be hard to top for company standing there with you and Solly and the Archbishop of Canterbury . . .
> Please tell [Jennifer] how happy it made me to see her again. Going home is sad because I will miss you both and would so love to have more hours together. I hope you will both come to New York.
> You deserve every good thing that will ever come your way because you are such a kind and generous man. So many good things have, and that makes me very happy for you.
> Dear Roy − I thank you with all my heart. Jackie[90]

Jenkins loved talking and writing about Oxford, and over the next decade gave countless lectures and wrote innumerable articles celebrating its glories. He particularly enjoyed comparing it with Cambridge − sometimes seriously, more often tongue-in-cheek, but invariably to Oxford's advantage. For example, in a speech at Brasenose in 1990 he gave Oxford the architectural palm:

> The combination of the Clarendon Building, the Sheldonian Theatre, the Bodleian, the Radcliffe Camera and St Mary's Church is unparalleled anywhere in the world. The grandeur of individual colleges, particularly Trinity and King's, may be greater in Cambridge, but there is no comparable ensemble of university buildings.[91]

And in an article for the *American Oxonian* he claimed that Oxford not only had the better buildings, but also overwhelming political predominance, having educated eleven of the last twenty-one British Prime Ministers plus several overseas ones, though not yet − this was pre-Clinton − a US President. 'Most unusually,' he noted, 'there are more Cambridge than Oxford men in the present Cabinet, although this is perhaps more than outweighed by the predominance of one Oxford woman.' Oxford could also boast more major novelists (Graham Greene, Anthony Powell, Iris Murdoch, Kingsley Amis and Penelope Lively) and now, he questionably asserted, equalled Cambridge in science. Moreover – the clinching point – Oxford was always listed first: 'In spite of the alphabet, Cambridge and Oxford simply does not come off the tongue.'[92]

But he also saw his role as standing up for Oxford in the corridors of power. 'The University today,' he declared in his installation speech, 'needs a voice who will speak out, if necessary, against ruling opinions.' Oxford was 'an immensely valuable national asset at a time when this country needs to cling with an iron determination to those few roles which it can pre-eminently perform' and resist 'the depredations of the wave of anti-intellectual philistinism which sometimes seems to be sweeping this country and its government'.[93] He was particularly exercised by some of the provisions of Kenneth Baker's 1988 Education Reform Bill which threatened both academic freedom and university funding, and immediately went into battle to try to limit the damage. 'By great good fortune,' he wrote, 'my switch from one legislative chamber to another in 1987 proved a great bonus . . . The House of Lords was a much more favourable forum than the House of Commons would have been for putting forward and carrying an amendment which at least limited the evil.'[94] In May 1988 he introduced an amendment to the proposed abolition of tenure – that is, job security – for university lecturers:

> to ensure that academic staff have freedom within the law to question and test received wisdom, and to put forward new ideas and controversial or unpopular opinions, without placing themselves in jeopardy of losing their jobs or privileges they may have at their institutions.[95]

It was carried by 152 votes to 126 and subsequently accepted by the government. He also joined with other academic peers – Michael Swann (the former chairman of the BBC, now Provost of Oriel College, Oxford and Chancellor of York University, Max Beloff and Conrad Russell, among others, to oppose both specific provisions and the government's whole mercenary approach to the universities.

After initially hoping that fund-raising was not part of his job, he quickly recognised that it very definitely was. 'I note with mild dismay,' he confessed in a lecture as early as May 1988, 'that three-quarters of

my conversations with theVice-Chancellor . . . is devoted to this subject
. . . Yet I accept that it is inevitable.'[96] Or again, two years later:
'Fundraising is frankly not one of the most enjoyable aspects of being
Chancellor. It is not the core of my "idea of a university" . . . But it
is absolutely necessary . . . to keep Oxford secure amongst the handful
of world-class universities.'[97] Jenkins was of the generation that had
grown up expecting the state to provide. But he recognised that since
the great expansion of universities in the 1960s this was no longer
realistic. Without private funding, he warned on another occasion,
Oxford would by the end of the century slip 'quietly but ineluctably
out of the small group of six or eight universities, or at most ten, which
are indisputably in the world league . . . This would be a major national
and indeed international misfortune . . . So I am a resolute fundraiser'
– even though he feared that reliance on private benefaction could
only widen the gap between Oxbridge and less-favoured universities.[98]
As a result much of his time and effort over the next decade was spent
in travelling the world seeking to squeeze money from businesses and
philanthropists for new buildings, new chairs and new bursaries. He
did not mind the travelling, particularly to America, but his ill-concealed
distaste for the process and for many of the people to whom he was
obliged to go cap-in-hand meant that this was one aspect of the job
to which he was not well suited.* His successor, Chris Patten, has been
more effective in this role.

As the 1987 election approached, Jenkins still hoped to be able to hold
Hillhead – maybe even to return to office as part of a post-election
coalition if the Alliance held the balance of power. After its autumn
plunge in the polls the Alliance had recovered surprisingly strongly and
he could feel the scent of battle once again in his nostrils. Des Wilson
– the former director of Shelter, now the Liberals' campaign director –
noted that 'Jenkins had over the past few months rediscovered his f
orm'. After 'a brilliant speech, witty, incisive and loudly cheered' at the
SDP's autumn conference, and another ('heavyweight but spiced with
wit') at the Alliance's latest 're-launch' at the Barbican in January,[100] he
took on the role of economic spokesman and unveiled his own

---

* 'As the Chancellor of Oxford University, married to the Chairman of the National
Trust', he joked in 1989, he feared that he and Jennifer 'must jointly be one of the most
predatory couples in Britain, and I am increasingly amazed that anyone any longer dares
to ask us anywhere.'[99] Jennifer had joined the board of the National Trust in 1985 and was
its chairman from 1986 to 1990.

'alternative budget' in March, placing the emphasis (not altogether to Owen's liking) on jobs and 'fairness' instead of Lawson's tax cuts. The victory of the fresh-faced young SDP candidate Rosie Barnes against a hard-left Labour candidate at Greenwich in February, followed by good local election results in May, lifted the Alliance's poll ratings back to 30 per cent – ahead of Labour for three months running. This was a far better platform than at the equivalent stage in 1983, and Jenkins still believed that if the Alliance pulled together and raised its sights it could yet achieve the sort of breakthrough it had just failed to make four years earlier.

On policy the two parties did actually pull together pretty well: even on defence a formula was found that both could live with – though Owen was too easily provoked by Mrs Thatcher claiming that Alliance policy was effectively unilateralist. The fatal mistake, in Jenkins' view, was Owen's insistence on a 'realistic' strategy of aiming only for the balance of power, which inevitably drew attention to the different instincts of the two leaders as to what they would do in the event of their achieving it. Steel saw the primary goal of the election as defeating Mrs Thatcher, and found it hard to foresee any circumstances in which the Liberals would be willing to support a minority Tory government or join a coalition while Mrs Thatcher was still Tory leader. His instinct would have been to join with Labour to throw her out. Owen, on the other hand, had no time for Kinnock or Labour and plainly would have had no difficulty taking the SDP into coalition with Mrs Thatcher. When asked on television, as they were endlessly, which party the Alliance would support if put in a position to choose, they struggled to conceal the difference in their approach – which allowed both the other parties to frighten wavering supporters by warning that a vote for the Alliance would let the other in, while making no positive case for the Alliance itself.

The second problem compared with 1983 was that Labour fought a much slicker and more professional campaign. Even though the party still advocated getting rid of Britain's nuclear weapons and coming out of Europe, while Kinnock was scarcely more plausible as a potential Prime Minister than Michael Foot, he had clearly brought Labour halfway back towards electability, so that it was once again the primary vehicle for anti-Thatcher votes, making nonsense of the Alliance's claim to be the only real opposition; moreover the novelty of the Alliance's middle-of-the-road appeal had inevitably worn off when neither Labour nor Conservative seemed as extreme as they had in 1983.

All these factors made it more difficult for Jenkins to retain the seat he had won so spectacularly in 1982, even though he spent most of the four-week campaign in Glasgow. Despite his role as economic spokesman he played only a minor role in the national campaign. He took part in one Alliance broadcast – speaking about unemployment and the government's waste of North Sea oil – and one press conference, at which Des Wilson thought his performance 'magisterial but dull',[101] and appeared on a number of TV programmes, where he deplored the parochialism of the election: 'the most insular campaign I have ever fought';[102] but he was restricted mainly to the role of senior grandee so as not to detract from the youthful appeal of the two Davids, and was very little reported. His only forays outside his own constituency were to support old SDP allies (Ian Wrigglesworth fighting to hold his seat on Teesside; Bill Rodgers and Shirley Williams trying to get back for Milton Keynes and Cambridge respectively), and two of his favourite Liberals (Richard Holme, still trying vainly to win Cheltenham, and Menzies Campbell, who was at last successful in North-East Fife). But his effort in Hillhead came too late. In his memoirs he half-blamed Owen's neo-Thatcherism for making it harder for him to win in Scotland; but he also admitted that he had done too little over the last four years to counter the changed make-up of the constituency since 1982. He had been lucky to hold on in 1983, when he had been helped by his national exposure as SDP leader. Since then, though he had been assiduous in holding his monthly advice bureaux and chasing constituency problems, he had allowed himself to be identified too much with the affluent residents of 'the hill' and neglected the rougher neighbourhoods on 'the river'. Moreover this time he was up against a formidable Labour opponent in the person of the thirty-two-year-old George Galloway, against whose charismatic militancy his statesmanlike gravitas was peculiarly ill-matched.* His campaign literature stressed his national distinction – 'The MP whose Voice is Always Heard' – but this only made him appear more remote from the gritty realities of the Clyde.[103]

He went into the count still hoping he might pull it off, but soon found that he had lost by more than 3,000 votes. He actually held his own share of the vote, but the Tory vote fell by more than 3,000 while Galloway gained more than 4,000; almost certainly Jenkins picked up a lot of previously Conservative votes, but lost more to Labour:

---

* Jenkins was urged to make capital of the already widespread allegations of corruption surrounding Galloway, specifically concerning his stewardship of the charity War on Want, of which he had been general secretary since 1983. But he refused to stoop to such tactics.

George Galloway (Labour)	17,958
Roy Jenkins (SDP/Alliance)	14,707
B.D. Cooklin (Conservative)	6,048
W. Kidd (SNP)	2,713
A. Whitelaw (Green)	443
Labour majority	3,251[104]

So he was out. He was not unduly disappointed. He was sad to lose his connection with Glasgow, which had given him such pleasure, but not at all sorry to leave the House of Commons, which now held very few attractions since the Alliance had come a poor third with just 23 per cent of the vote, down from 25 per cent in 1983, and only twenty-two MPs – seventeen Liberal and five SDP – facing another three-figure Tory majority.* The only immediate prospect was of mutual recrimination between the two parties of the Alliance and arguments over whether and when to merge. He was well out of it. Above all, Jenkins had his triumph at Oxford three months before as a wonderful compensation. 'By winning in Oxford,' he consoled himself, 'I at least avoided an exact emulation of the fate of my favourite biographical subject: Asquith lost both the University election and a Clydeside constituency within the same twelve months.'[105] He was free to concentrate on Oxford.

In the hour of her third victory, Mrs Thatcher claimed to be horrified by Jenkins' defeat. 'A man of such great distinction and stature. It was dreadful,' she told Woodrow Wyatt, adding characteristically: 'It tells you something about the Scots.'[106] She immediately offered him, through Wyatt, the second consolation of a peerage. He had some doubts about accepting it, partly because he did not want to be on a party list ('He's very vain, you know,' Mrs Thatcher remarked) and partly because, from *Mr Balfour's Poodle* onwards, he had been pretty scathing about the Lords and he retained some admiration for those historical figures who had remained plain 'Mr Gladstone' or 'Mr Chamberlain' to the end of their days. He had said nothing, however, that made it actually hypocritical to accept and, like most ageing politicians, he wanted to retain a foothold in Parliament. He was also pleased to able to pay tribute to his old constituency (not Stechford, which he had represented for twenty-six years, but Hillhead, which he had represented for just five) and his birthplace by taking the title Baron Jenkins of Hillhead, of

---

The five surviving SDP Members were David Owen, Bob Maclennan, John Cartwright, Charles Kennedy and Rosie Barnes.

Pontypool in the County of Gwent. (He had to be known as Lord Jenkins of Hillhead to distinguish himself from an existing Labour peer, Lord Jenkins of Putney.) His elevation was announced in July, but did not take effect until December, when he was introduced into the Upper House by Jo Grimond and Jack Diamond, following – of course – a good lunch with Jennifer and all three children and their spouses plus Mark and Leslie Bonham Carter, the Grimonds, the Diamonds, John Harris and his wife, and Sir Alexander Cole, Garter King of Arms, who had facilitated his choice of title. Characteristically Jennifer declined as far as possible to be known as Lady Jenkins, preferring to stick with her own title, awarded in 1985, as Dame Jennifer.

No sooner was the election over than David Steel – determined not to be pre-empted by an Owen veto, as in 1983 – proposed an early merger of the two Alliance parties; and Jenkins immediately backed him, using a Sunday lunchtime radio interview to put his view (which was also Bill Rodgers' and Shirley Williams') 'firmly but non-provocatively' on the record before Monday's meeting of the SDP national committee.[107] Unfortunately Steel's somewhat clumsy initiative irritated a number of the SDP hierarchy who felt that he was making a crude takeover bid. Most of Jenkins' closest friends and supporters agreed with him in seeing merger as the natural way forward; but all four (initially) of Owen's surviving parliamentary colleagues, most of the SDP peers and both the party's trustees (David Sainsbury and Leslie Murphy), as well as his devoted band of (mainly female) admirers on the national committee, still clung to their separate identity – though Charles Kennedy fairly quickly switched sides to join the pro-merger camp. Jenkins was deeply depressed that the venture which had been launched with such optimism should have descended to such bitter squabbling. 'Rarely, even in the voluminous history of family feuds,' he wrote in his memoirs, 'can there have been such unrelenting argument over the details of a will while the whole inheritance was manifestly being allowed to slip down the drain.'[108] But after three 'horrible' meetings over the following weeks Owen was able to carry an 18:13 majority against merger and for a referendum of the membership in early August.

'I have a nagging feeling that I ought to have done more to transcend the mood of destructive bitterness which seized the party,' Jenkins reproached himself with hindsight. 'I ought to have done something though exactly what it was I still do not know.'[109] In truth he underestimated the strength of opposition to something that seemed to him so obviously right. What he did was to write several newspaper articles putting the case for merger, while privately trying to win round those of his old friends – notably Bob Maclennan and Jack Diamond – who were opposed. In the *Sunday Times* on 12 July he wrote of his distress at the division in the party, but insisted that he was not dismayed because he was so sure that the creation of a single party with a single leader was the only way to protect and build on what had been achieved. 'I always saw the SDP as a catalyst which would change the face of British politics and not just as a like-minded sect.' Steel might have been a bit precipitate in forcing the issue, he conceded, but he was only voicing the feeling of every Alliance committee room. Two General Elections had shown how hard it was for a third force to crack the two-party monopoly. 'The idea of that challenging force achieving anything if it is itself split into a third and fourth force is simply preposterous.' Of course there were minor differences between the two halves of the Alliance; but 'the only certain way of having no policy differences', he sharply reminded the Owenites, 'is to have a party so exclusive that it is little more than a private army. But private armies do not win great political campaigns.' To do that a party needed to make a wide appeal, as the Alliance had done in 1981–2. 'I am as proud of the SDP as anyone,' he concluded, 'but it is its capacity for political creativity, not for narrow exclusivity, which excites my enthusiasm. Neither Britain nor the SDP should be isolationist.'[110]

Bob Maclennan – not at all a natural Owenite, but in his quiet way one of the most loyal Jenkinsites going right back to 1966 – wrote three days later that he hated finding himself on the opposite side of the argument. 'As you probably know from your experience with Hugh Gaitskell over Europe it is bitter indeed to disagree profoundly with those whom you love and admire.' But he believed the Alliance could be saved only by 'managed convergence', not by 'enforced merger'.[111] He saw no more hope for the survival of a separatist SDP than Jenkins did. But merger would not work either if it was forced too soon. 'I think it still lies within your power to save the Alliance by proposing something short of full merger . . . Surely there is an alternative? Must the fate of the Alliance be decided by the Ultras?'[112] The problem for Maclennan and others who wanted to carry on as two parties primarily in order to avert the break-up of the SDP was that Owen was happy to split the SDP – as early as 17 June he was proposing an 'amicable divorce'[113] – so long as he could still lead his own pure SDP uncompromised by the despised Liberals and Jenkinsites, who in his view had plotted from the beginning to betray it. No compromise was possible because Owen did not want one.

A revealing insight into Owen's essentially solipsistic thinking emerges from his response to John Grigg, who wrote begging him not to withdraw into 'bitter isolation' and copied his reply to Jenkins. 'Why does it have to be bitter?' Owen wrote. 'And I'm not even sure I will be all that isolated.' Ironically he deplored Grigg's 'lack of historical perspective'. Who could predict what would happen three or ten years ahead? He was still only forty-nine and could afford to wait. 'I'd like to be proved wrong, but if it turns out that the new merged party is the Liberal Party writ large, maybe my being on the outside could help restore the credibility of the centre?' (What did he mean by that?) Even if he agreed to join the merged party, he argued, he would not carry with him a lot of dedicated SDP activists. 'These people are essential – they are not dining room social democrats, they are the backbone of the SDP. What is on offer is for me to lead a party that has no backbone. No thanks, it is simply not for me, and all my family agree.'[114]

The eventually agreed wording of the ballot paper offered a choice between (Option 1) supposedly seeking to negotiate 'a closer constitutional framework for the Alliance, short of merger' or (Option 2) 'a merger of the SDP and the Liberal Party into one party'. But this was disingenuous, since Owen's whole purpose since 1983 had been to resist closer relations with the Liberals and it was dishonest to pretend that a closer partnership was what he intended now. Nevertheless the apparent reasonableness of Option 1 persuaded a substantial minority of SDP members – afraid of the consequences if the party's biggest hitter chose to walk away – to vote for it. Following a bitter public campaign in which each side accused the other of wishing to destroy the party they both professed to love, the result, declared on 6 August, was a clear but far from overwhelming majority for merger: 25,897 to 19,228 (57:42 per cent) on a very respectable 77 per cent turnout. Owen promptly resigned the leadership, but quickly made clear his intention of leading a rump party that would claim to be the continuing SDP. This was a claim that Jenkins thought preposterous. The minority was 'uncomfortably large', he told the party's autumn conference at the end of August; nevertheless the result was decisive. If the vote was to be ignored, how could the party retain the principle of one-member-one-vote – the very principle of which Owen had been the great champion – at the heart of its constitution?

> It must be accepted that a majority vote is a majority vote. Those who contributed to . . . that result cannot within any practice or theory of one member one vote be treated as the dissidents, the

deserters, the disrupters – and the minority as the sole repository of the true faith. Once that simple democratic principle is fully and freely accepted, then I believe the difficulties can be unravelled.[115]

One at least of Owen's supporters recognised this truth. Bob Maclennan – the co-author of the SDP's constitution in 1981 – accepted the result and reluctantly took on the leadership in order to negotiate the merger that the majority had voted for. This was a messy process with which Jenkins was thankful not to be involved, but it eventually resulted in the emergence of a new party, initially called the Social and Liberal Democrats, but soon simply the Liberal Democrats.* After all the ructions within the SDP there was some speculation, when the negotiation was complete, that the Liberals might at the last minute baulk at giving up their historic identity. Jenkins was in America promoting his Truman biography, but he was pressed to fly back to speak at the special Liberal assembly convened to approve the marriage. 'Houston,' he noted in his memoirs, 'is the one city in the US from which you can fly to Europe after a dinner speech.' Catching a midnight flight to Paris and changing again at Heathrow to fly on to Manchester, he was on his feet in Blackpool seventeen hours after he had sat down in Texas.[118] In fact his dash was unnecessary, as the Liberals backed merger by an overwhelming margin of nearly six to one. But at least he was able to celebrate the moment over dinner with Ming and Elspeth Campbell, Ludovic Kennedy and the Goodharts.

In *The Times* he looked forward with satisfaction to an 'honest marriage' of the two parties, noting that 'nearly all the best features of the SDP constitution have been accepted', while the potential difficulty over nuclear weapons had been resolved with a statement 'in no way tinged with British or Western unilateralism' that Hugh Gaitskell would have had no quarrel with. Altogether, he believed, the merger negotiations had produced 'a satisfactory prospectus for an electable

---

* Jenkins would have preferred to retain the word Alliance in the party's name. 'We ought to have called ourselves "The Alliance of Liberal and Social Democratic Parties", or "The Alliance" for short', he wrote in his memoirs. 'This would have linked us in to the substantial reservoirs of goodwill which survived from past campaigns, as well as making it much more difficult for the rump Owenite party to confuse legitimacy by appropriating the SDP name to themselves. Instead we called ourselves the Social and Liberal Democrats (SLD) and spent eighteen months of identity crisis compounded by trying to escape from the herbivorous and unrespectful sobriquet of "Salads".'[116] On the other hand he told Paddy Ashdown in September 1989 that 'he had always been rather in favour of Liberal Democrat' and was happy to use that name.[117]

left-of-centre alternative to Thatcherism', such as the SDP had always aimed at providing, free of the dogmas of both left and right, but with the emphasis firmly towards the left:

A controlled economy is not much use at producing consumer goods. But 'the market', in terms of protecting the environment or safeguarding health, schools, universities or Britain's scientific future, cannot run a whelk stall. And if asked which is under greater threat in Britain today, the supply of consumer goods or the nexus of civilised public services, I unhesitatingly answer the latter.

It was not a question of choosing socialism over capitalism, or regulation over freedom, he insisted. 'It was precisely to free the British people from that false two-dimensional choice that we were created . . . I hope that this weekend we can lay the foundations for returning to a period of effective challenge. Unless we do, I fear that the middle ground of British politics will be barren and chaotic for many years to come.'[119]

The middle ground remained chaotic for another two years while the Liberal Democrats struggled to establish themselves under the fresh leadership of Paddy Ashdown, and the rump SDP predictably failed to make any independent headway and finally wound itself up after coming a humiliating seventh behind the Monster Raving Loony Party at the Bootle by-election in 1990.* Jenkins welcomed its demise, insisting once again that Owen's party was *not* the SDP, which had voted democratically to merge in 1987 into the new party in 1988, but 'a loose cannon crashing around the deck of a warship'. With the field to themselves he now hoped that the Liberal Democrats could move on. Having demonstrated his continuing commitment by taking on the leadership of the Lib Dem peers in 1988, he now saw two possible roles for the party in the 1990s, depending on whether Labour's move back towards the middle ground enabled it to win the next election. 'If it does win,' he wrote in the *Observer*, 'which I would prefer to a fourth dose of Thatcherism, there will be need for a liberalising force on its flank. If it loses, there will be need of an alternative challenger for the future.' The ambition was more modest than in 1981, but he believed

---

* 'It was perhaps appropriate,' Ivor Crewe and Anthony King concluded in their history of the SDP, 'that what one journalist had dubbed "the Monster Raving Ego Party" should in the end have been destroyed by the Monster Raving Loony Party.'[120]

the Lib Dems now had 'a better chance to perform one of these roles'.[121]

Meanwhile he used the House of Lords – plus a steady output of newspaper articles and letters to the press – to maintain his wholesale excoriation of Thatcherism. The Upper House suited him very well as a platform where he could deliver magisterial, somewhat lofty speeches to a respectful audience of his similarly ennobled contemporaries, free of the heckling of the Commons. He made his maiden speech during a debate on taxation in February 1988, pointing out characteristically that it was actually his second maiden speech in that chamber, since when he was first elected to the Commons the Lower House was still sitting in the Lords while its own chamber was restored after its bombing in the war. Recalling that earlier maiden speech, on Stafford Cripps' 1948 budget, he explicitly recanted his youthful enthusiasm for penal taxation – 'my certainties have perhaps become a little less angular over the passage of four decades' – but still disputed the currently prevailing view that 'the supreme duty of statesmanship is to reduce taxation'. There was certainly no virtue in taxation for its own sake, he conceded. 'But a decent fiscal rectitude is a great deal preferable to a Gadarene rush to tax reduction at all costs' – as should be clear from the experience of the United States, which had managed in seven years to reduce itself from 'the world's greatest and richest economy . . . to the world's greatest debtor'. ('Keynes, the alleged father of permissive finance,' he added in an article in *The Times* on the same theme a few weeks later, 'would have turned in his grave at the improvidence of Reaganomics.')[122]

There is no doubt . . . about the ability of a low-taxation, market-oriented economy to produce consumer goods, even if an awful lot of them are imported, far better than any planned economy that ever was or probably ever can be invented. However, I am not convinced that such a society and economy, particularly if it is not infused with the civic optimism which was in many ways the true epitome of Victorian values, is equally good at protecting the environment or safeguarding health, schools, universities or Britain's scientific future.[123]

Jenkins deliberately got that relatively uncontroversial maiden speech out of the way in order to be able to move a serious resolution the following week condemning the Prime Minister's relentless centralisation of power to Whitehall generally and herself personally. This speech – consciously echoing John Dunning's famous motion of 1780 (directed at George III) that 'the influence of the Crown has increased, is increasing and ought to be diminished' – was described by the historian of Whitehall, Peter Hennessy, as 'a *tour de force* on the condition of institutional Britain'.[124] In addition to his previous criticism of Mrs Thatcher's abuse of Cabinet government and her intolerance of such independent centres of influence as the Church of England, the universities and the BBC, he focused in particular on the emasculation of local government, recalling that when he became a young MP the town clerks of cities like Birmingham were powerful, austere figures, 'the guardians of legality and the near equals of the permanent secretaries in Whitehall'. Their autonomy had been severely reduced by the reorganisation of local government by the Heath government in 1973; but the Thatcher government, by its rate-capping of 'loony left' councils in London, Liverpool and elsewhere, had driven the process much further:

> They have used every weakness of local government as an excuse for making it still weaker and every political extravagance, by a few authorities, as a reason for also penalising the responsible ones and transferring still more power to the centre. The result has been a degree of civic degradation . . . which it would be difficult to imagine being imposed in any other democratic country.

It was inconceivable, he suggested, that President Reagan or President Mitterrand could simply abolish the mayors of Washington or Paris, as Mrs Thatcher had abolished Livingstone's GLC.[125] London was now unique among the capitals of the Western world in having no single elected voice.*

In other speeches in 1988–90 Jenkins defended the Foreign Office against Mrs Thatcher's style of 'megaphone diplomacy and government by indignation' ('Each morning we read, by courtesy of Mr Bernard Ingham and the lobby system, a daily report on a kind of Richter scale about the force of the previous day's volcanic eruptions');[127] moved an amendment to the government's reformed Official Secrets Act attempting (unsuccessfully) to allow a 'public interest' defence for whistle-blowers;[128] and another – also rejected – to postpone for a year the introduction of student loans to allow anomalies in the legislation to be ironed out.

---

* In a later speech on the folly of the poll tax – after it had been abandoned by the Major government at a cost of at least £10 billion – Jenkins commented tartly that 'if anyone in local government had been able to pursue their dogmas with a tenth of the reckless determination of the former Prime Minister and her accomplices . . . they would have been surcharged to and over the edge of personal bankruptcy.'[126]

In the course of this speech, commenting on the flood of ill-thought-out legislation in the government's third term, he reflected on 'the fatal frenzy which seizes governments when the basis of their support becomes ever narrower' – likening the present situation to the Callaghan government's nationalisation of ship-building in 1976 (which to his shame he had voted for in his last days as a Labour MP).[129] But his most contemptuous dismissal of the government's record over the previous eleven years came when he moved a resolution in March 1990 condemning Nicholas Ridley's handling of the Fayed brothers' contested takeover of Harrods (an 'emporium', he was careful to point out, that he did not himself patronise):

> We live in a society which is increasingly awash with money. I grow ever more sceptical of the alleged economic achievements of this Government. Curing inflation was supposed to be the centre-piece, but our exceptionally high rate is now pointed to almost with pride . . . by the Prime Minister as a still compelling reason for not entering the ERM . . . Thrift was made the theme of the recent Budget. But if this is the desideratum, the Government have presided over a decade of disaster. Savings have collapsed and have been far more than outweighed by erecting the maximum use of personal indebtedness into a socially compelling way of life. The core of the achievement, such as it is, is that this Government has made some people rich and, as some of them are articulate and grateful, they have elevated this into a national triumph.[130]

Above all Jenkins kept up continuous pressure on Mrs Thatcher over Europe, charging that her increasingly undisguised hostility to all things European worked consistently against the national interest and risked leaving Britain more isolated than at any time since Suez. In January 1988 he was scathing about her failure to reappoint Lord Cockfield, the British Commissioner who had been largely responsible for driving the single market, on the ground that he had supposedly 'gone native' in Brussels:

> She wishes British industry to have the benefit of a large single market, and would like to exercise a political leadership role within it. But her self-righteousness and instinctive nationalism makes it difficult for her to see that these objectives can only be achieved on a basis of give and take and respect for both the legitimate self-interest and the European idealism of others.[131]

By refusing to join the ERM, keeping Britain out of moves towards a common currency and a European Central Bank – both 'serious probabilities for the Nineties' – he asserted repeatedly that she would damage British industry and endanger the pre-eminence of the City, repeating the historic errors of 1951, 1955–7 and 1978. 'We could soon find ourselves relegated to the *de facto* status of a second-rank member,' he lamented in December 1989, 'almost as though we had stayed in Efta. It was not for this that we went through the long struggles of the 1960s and 1970s, picked ourselves up after two de Gaulle rebuffs and fought through the referendum campaign of 1975 to the outcome of a massive pro-European majority.'[132] 'Europe is now moving so fast,' he wrote a month earlier, following Nigel Lawson's resignation and the removal of Geoffrey Howe from the Foreign Office, 'that exclusion is more damaging and its subsequent rectification more difficult. Mistakes could be made in the next couple of years (against the better judgement of most senior members of the Cabinet) for which this country will pay long after Mrs Thatcher has ceased to be responsible for their consequence.'[133] He consoled himself, however, that the Prime Minister's 'increasingly shrill determination to turn her back on nearly 30 years of Conservative commitment to Europe' was so clearly out of step with her own senior colleagues that it must eventually provoke a split in the Tory Party comparable with the repeal of the Corn Laws in 1846 or Joseph Chamberlain's tariff crusade in 1903. 'I find it difficult to believe that our politics have become so supine that she will be allowed to do so without a degree of political turbulence comparable with those two dates 153 and 86 years ago.'[134]

Here Jenkins almost seemed to anticipate Mrs Thatcher's overthrow yet he could not quite believe it would come through a revolt of her own party. The government, he wrote in the spring of 1990, was exhausted but still dangerous, passing legislation that no one wanted – the poll tax, electricity and water privatisation, student loans – all whipped through Parliament 'to save the face of a First Minister whose self-righteous stubbornness has not been equalled, save briefly for Neville Chamberlain, since Lord North'. Tory MPs voted tamely for policies they did not agree with, making the government 'an inverted pyramid of foolish dogmatism'. But retribution would only come through 'a great electoral revolt', which he feared 'may well go too far' – presumably back to Labour.[135] In the *Independent* in April he likened the seething discontent in the Tory Party to the febrile plotting against Wilson in 1968, when 'I was the Michael Heseltine of the situation', which signally failed to unseat Wilson and led only to the election of Ted Heath.[136]

He could only welcome Mrs Thatcher's belated agreement to join the ERM – forced on her by John Major and Douglas Hurd during the Tory Party conference in October 1990 only because she could not afford to lose another Foreign Secretary and another Chancellor – but insisted that she had finally done it at the worst possible time for the wrong reasons at the wrong exchange rate. ('During the 138 months when Britain was outside the ERM,' he later calculated, 'the system had worked satisfactorily and quietly . . . Of these months at least 130 in my view would have been better points of entry than the one which, largely for reasons of internal party politics, was eventually chosen.'[137] A month later in the Lords he equally welcomed Geoffrey Howe's lethal resignation speech, which 'almost precisely endorsed' everything he had been saying for several years past about Mrs Thatcher's counterproductive xenophobia.[138] Eight dramatic days later she was gone, deserted by nearly half her MPs and abandoned by her Cabinet. As a result, Jenkins wrote in the *Observer*, 'November 1990 will undoubtedly rank as one of the classical crisis months in British political history', comparable to December 1916 or May 1940. Mrs Thatcher would live in history, if only for her longevity and her sex. But, he asked, what ultimately did she achieve? 'Judged by all the hard criteria, inflation . . . balance of payments, investment, prospects for growth, Britain remains as it was in 1979 a second-rate economy in danger of falling into the third rank.' Despite her pious talk of thrift and self-help, the government's most consistent success had been high consumption 'achieved by a steady policy of living above our means'. She had downgraded the public service in every sphere, yet increased centralisation; and, despite her boasts, she had not increased Britain's influence in the world.[139] Altogether his final verdict on her premiership was almost wholly negative.

But he was not impressed by Major, either. For a time he gave the new, almost unknown Prime Minister the benefit of the doubt, hoping that his professed ambition to put Britain 'at the heart of Europe' signalled a real change of direction. But he was soon pressing Major too to be more positive towards Europe, insisting that the federal European 'superstate' Mrs Thatcher was now warning about from the back benches was a fantasy. Europe, he believed, would 'never become an analogue of the United States because its people have not turned their backs on their countries of origin, have not been through a melting pot, and do not have a common language'. At the same time it was still not clear where he would draw the line between federalism and pooled sovereignty, since he went on:

On the other hand Britain being effectively part of the dynamic Europe which has evolved since 1985 will undoubtedly involve some substantial pooling of an increasingly elusive sovereignty and also significant elements of federalism, some of which are indeed there already . . . National identity is not an issue. Some considerable merging of sovereignty is.[140]

He still believed in maintaining the momentum of 'ever closer union' and still refused to say where he thought that evolution should end.

More than anything he simply wanted Britain to be part of the process, wherever it led – not, as so often in the past, grumbling from the sidelines. In the run-up to the signing of the Maastricht Treaty in December 1991 he was afraid that Major would try to finesse the issue, like Wilson in 1970–75, by opting out of the Social Chapter and moves towards a single currency in order to appease his party critics, when the experience of the 1975 referendum showed that the public would respond to a clear cross-party lead, using Labour and Liberal Democrat support (Labour having performed another U-turn on Europe) to overcome Tory opposition. 'Put country before party, Mr Major,' he urged in the *Observer*, begging the Prime Minister to commit Britain now to joining the single currency from the start. A 'poultice for the Tory party' was not the same as the national interest.[141]

As the 1992 General Election approached, Jenkins was in no doubt that he wanted to see the Tories thrown out, if only on the ground that thirteen years of one party was enough. A decade earlier, he reflected in another Tawney lecture, the SDP had been formed to bring some stability to the see-saw swings of two-party politics; now the country was suffering from the opposite problem, 'desperately needing a change of government yet half frightened to achieve it'. The Tory government was like 'a sad old dog needing to be put out of its misery'.[142] Single-party rule, he wrote in the *Observer*, was bad for democracy, bad for civil servants and bad for the government itself:

It is bad for governments to be able to behave as incompetently as this one has done since 1987, both in its handling of the economy and in the shambles of its legislation (poll tax on and off, Broadcasting Act, Football Spectators Act and various educational nonsenses) and still get away with it.[143]

The electorate, he believed, wanted change but did not fully trust Neil Kinnock. This gave the Lib Dems – now firmly established under Ashdown's 'Action Man' leadership, winning by-elections again and back to 20 per cent in the polls, with the Conservatives and Labour neck-and-neck at around 37 per cent – 'considerable relevance and opportunity'. It was vital that they should do well in order to 'oil the rusty springs of change' and act as a midwife to constitutional reform.[144]* Shrewdly he suspected that a Labour government elected in 1992 was likely to be too cautious rather than too radical, drawing a characteristic parallel with the 1930s:

> I think its loss of ideological conviction and its desperate search for respectability has made it more likely, in the field of economic policy at least, to model itself more on Philip Snowden than on Franklin Roosevelt.

History taught that in the hung Parliament of 1929–31 MacDonald and Snowden should have heeded the ideas of the Liberal 'Yellow Book' promoted by Lloyd George and Keynes at the 1929 election and not the conventional prescriptions of the City. The Lib Dems could not deliberately campaign for a hung Parliament, which in any case he warned was 'not an easy hand to play for the third party . . . Nevertheless, while it is by no means necessarily a bonanza for the third party it may well be in the interests of the country and may well be the hand that we have to play.'[146] In that eventuality, he told Paddy Ashdown, the Lib Dems should insist on at least four ministers in the Cabinet: Ashdown himself, Steel, Ming Campbell and Alan Beith.[147] As so often before, however – and again in the future – the Liberal dream of exerting influence by holding the balance was not to be.

For most of the campaign – in which Jenkins played almost no active part – the likeliest outcome did seem to be either a small Labour majority or a hung Parliament. Either way Jenkins was by no means alone in anticipating the end of Tory rule. At The Club – the most Establishment of all the dining clubs to which he belonged, founded in the eighteenth century by Dr Johnson and friends – those present on 31 March, ten days before polling day, placed bets on the outcome:

---

* In the same article he voiced his fear that another five years of Tory refusal to concede devolution to Scotland would lead to the growth of separatism, as in Ireland in the late nineteenth century. 'It would be a supreme irony, but even more of a supreme tragedy, if in the fourth quarter of this century it were to produce the same severance along the Scottish border. Yet five more intransigent years would carry a real danger of that.'[145]

only three out of twelve predicted a Tory victory. Jenkins predicted a Labour majority of thirty.* In fact Major was returned with a much-reduced but still clear overall majority of twenty-one, while the Liberal Democrats won only twenty seats (on 18 per cent of the poll). Tory hegemony was thus confirmed for another Parliament; Labour still had some way to go before it would be trusted with government again, and the Lib Dems were no nearer breaking the mould than the Liberals had been in 1974.

Roy and Jennifer watched the results in Kensington Park Gardens with Hayden and Laura Phillips, the Bonham Carters and Bill and Sylvia Rodgers. Rodgers told Hugo Young that he and Jenkins were 'both depressed by the results as they came in. We didn't want another Tory government. But we thought Kinnock no good as a potential PM.'[149] In fact – unless he was being completely hypocritical – Jenkins had higher hopes of Kinnock than this suggests. A week after the election, when Kinnock had resigned the Labour leadership, he wrote him a remarkably sympathetic and generous letter (remarkable considering how mercilessly Kinnock had mocked him a decade earlier):

Dear Neil,

May I send you a note of greeting and sympathy? I thought you fought a very good campaign. I would have been happy to see you Prime Minister, and I think you might have made a very considerable one. I also thought you handled things well on the dreadful night.

I hope you find satisfactory things to do. In my experience people who do not become Prime Minister are often happier than those who do. The misfortune is sometimes for the country, not for the individual!

Yours ever,
Roy[150]

The result of the 1992 election meant that those who had warned back in 1981 that the only effect of the SDP would be to perpetuate Tory rule had been vindicated for a third time. Jenkins had recognised the risk, but hoped the Alliance could make a sufficient breakthrough to negate it. He was almost more disappointed by this failure than he

---

* The winner, ironically, was a non-politician, the banker and former chairman of the Stock exchange, Sir Nicholas Goodison, who scooped the £60 pot by guessing a Tory majority of seventeen.[148]

had been in 1983 or 1987. In the next Parliament he would begin to think seriously about some form of reunification of the centre left to harness what he still believed was an anti-Conservative majority in the country just waiting to be mobilised.

Meanwhile, in September 1991, he had published his long-planned memoirs. In the Introduction he confessed that he had been reluctant to put pen to paper from fear that there was 'inevitably a touch of "ending up" about it'.[151] In fact he had another full decade of active life ahead of him. But as a compulsive writer and avid consumer of others' memoirs he never doubted that he would one day write his own. 'Of course,' he told Robin Day in a television interview in 1966, 'one always thinks about one's autobiography. One has to live on something when one's retired.'[152] As a reader, he was sceptical of the value of most political memoirs. Reviewing Hugh Dalton's third volume in 1962, he wrote that 'the fallibility of elderly memory and most men's desire for self-justification combine to erect a fairly thick screen between the reader and events as they actually happened', and he had not changed that view in the intervening thirty years; but he thought Dalton an exception, because he was 'at least half a diarist'.[153] Jenkins himself had never kept a regular diary, except for his four years in Brussels. But from 1964 onwards he had dictated a note of every major episode in his career soon after the event; and he had also kept meticulously detailed engagement diaries since 1945, in which he recorded not only all his engagements but exactly how long they lasted, as well as everything else he had done that day – how far he had walked, run or swum; journey times; whom he had lunch with and where; even the weather – so that he could (as can his biographer) reconstruct with extraordinary precision what he was doing every day of his adult life. That at least gave him a framework for accurate recollection, though he was well aware, as he told the Royal Society of Literature in 1972, 'how quickly and almost inevitably a film of retrospective wishful thinking clouds the memory'.[154]

The possession of all this primary material, however, and his forty years' experience as a biographer in knowing how to use it, lent his book, when he finally came to write it, a quality of reflective detachment almost unique among politicians' memoirs. *A Life at the Centre*, as he chose rather banally to call it, is a genuine *auto*-biography – a biographer turning his skills upon his own life almost as if it were someone else's, able to balance the record of what he thought at the time with the longer perspective of hindsight. As a result he can often be attractively self-deprecating: the older man shaking his head at the follies of the younger, while not seeking to deny them. At the same time there is an undoubted vein of vanity in the book: as in the *European Diary* an assumption – perhaps inevitable in any autobiography – that quite small details of his life are of interest to the reader, and an unshakable self-satisfaction (notwithstanding the self-criticism relating to specific episodes) that his views have been broadly consistent and right all along.

Coming to autobiography for the first time, he was uncertain of the right tone of voice, so rather than start at the beginning with his childhood, he began with the easier part and plunged in (in Italy in the summer of 1988) with his first appointment to ministerial office in 1964, followed by the next dozen years of high-level politics under Wilson: the Home Office, the Treasury, the civil war in the Labour Party over Europe and his failure to become Prime Minister. Only then did he go back to Pontypool, Oxford, Hugh Gaitskell and his years as a semi-detached backbencher in the 1950s, before revisiting Brussels – the least compelling part of the book, perhaps because he had covered it so recently in his published *Diary* – and going on to the excitement and disappointment of the SDP, writing (as was his habit) in various locations and holiday homes around Europe and finishing in the autumn of 1990. For the first time, apart from a couple of minor exceptions, he abandoned his longtime publishers Collins, mainly because the personnel had changed – neither Mark Bonham Carter nor Ian Chapman was still there – and took this book to Macmillan, from whom Michael Sissons managed to extract the huge advance of £130,000.[155] *A Life at the Centre* was launched with a party at Brooks's on 11 September to which, as usual, practically the whole liberal establishment was invited.

The general tone of the book was urbane and generous, even to political opponents and rivals. Jenkins did not gloss over his sharply critical view of Wilson over the European issue, but on reflection was much more understanding of the difficulties he had faced. He allowed himself a few digs at Denis Healey, Jim Callaghan and Tony Benn; but the one person he could not forgive, since their dispute was so recent and the damage inflicted on his most cherished project so painful, was David Owen. He pulled no punches in his account of the way Owen's vanity, impatience and self-deluding intransigence had destroyed the idealism and unity of the SDP and then of the Alliance. By chance Owen's own enormous memoir, *Time to Declare* (at 800 pages one-third longer than Jenkins', covering a far shorter career) was published almost simultaneously, so the press coverage of both books focused heavily on what each said about the other. Owen maintained that he had not intended to rehearse his quarrel with Jenkins in such detail, but that having seen Jenkins' criticism of himself in proof he felt obliged to sharpen his own account, defending his own actions and setting out his charge that Jenkins had used the SDP dishonestly as a vehicle for his own ambition and should have joined the Liberals in the first place.[156] By the time his book came out his rump SDP had folded, so it was inevitably seen as an overlong and unconvincing justification of his essential failure, by comparison with Jenkins' elegant retrospect of a life well lived.*

In his final chapter, entitled 'Establishment Whig or Persistent Radical?', Jenkins attempted to sum up his own career, acknowledging that his hedonistic tastes and social life might have sometimes given a false impression but insisting that his views had all along remained consistently radical. He placed himself, for instance, clearly to the left of both Jim Callaghan and Denis Healey, let alone David Owen, and summarised his abiding convictions in a single paragraph:

> My broad position remains firmly libertarian, sceptical of official cover-ups and uncompromisingly internationalist, believing sovereignty to be an almost total illusion in the modern world, although both expecting and welcoming the continuance of strong differences in national traditions and behaviour. I distrust the deification of the enterprise culture. I think there are more limitations to the wisdom of the market than were dreamt of in Mrs Thatcher's philosophy. I believe that levels of taxation on the prosperous, having been too high for many years (including my own period at the Treasury), are now too low for the provision of decent public services. And I think that the privatisation of near-monopolies is about as irrelevant (and sometimes worse than) were the Labour Party's proposals for further nationalisation in the 1970s and early 1980s.[158]

Did he, looking back, regret having devoted so much of his life to politics? He certainly believed that he had been too narrowly focused

---

On the second day of the Liberal Democrat conference in Bournemouth the booksellers reported, perhaps unsurprisingly, that they had sold 450 copies of *A Life at the Centre*, but only five of *Time to Declare*.[157]

on politics as a young man, first at Oxford and then as a young MP,
when he was 'too much of a party loyalist, thinking more about the
game than about the merits of issues'. But he believed that he found
a better balance from the mid-1950s, when his second career as a writer
gave him 'both the material and the intellectual detachment to treat
party machines with scepticism'. From this time onwards he believed
that politics, 'not always taken in excessive doses', had given him 'more
satisfaction than I could have obtained from any other way of life':

> It has inevitably produced its ration of boredom, pettiness, frustra-
> tion, exhaustion and dismay, but less I think than I would have
> found in any profession or other occupation. And to offset these
> low points there has been greater variety and stimulus, a more
> frequent sense of widening horizons, at least as many friends, and
> a wider acquaintanceship both with people and with places than
> I would have been likely to find elsewhere.

He believed that his Home Office reforms in the 1960s had been
significant and worthwhile. His stint at the Treasury, on the other hand,
while important and largely successful at the time, left no comparable
legacy. ('Economic management by its very nature leaves no footprints
in the sand. The tide of the next Chancellor washes them away.')
Paradoxically he thought his contribution in opposition to helping
secure Britain's entry to the EEC would have 'a longer-term effect'
and he believed the creation of the EMS during his time in Brussels
would prove 'not merely durable but seminal'. The SDP had sadly
proved less durable, 'although not necessarily less seminal'. Altogether
he felt he had had more influence on events than he could have realistically hoped for when he embarked on a political career, and hoped
he had done more good than harm. 'But I do not feel certainty about
this, for my beliefs have become much less dogmatic and my outlook
far more relativist than at the beginning.'[159]

Finally he asked himself whether he regretted not having been
Prime Minister, when the opportunity had several times seemed to
be within his grasp. There had been moments in 1968–9 and again in
1972–3 when a more determined effort on his part might have snatched
the prize; alternatively, had he kept his head down in 1971–2, finessed
the European issue and retained the deputy leadership, he might have
been well placed to succeed Wilson in 1976. There was also 'a brief
flickering moment' in 1981–2 when the early success of the SDP
seemed to give him another chance. The fact that he raised th

question showed clearly that he did at least half-regret his failure. Judging his career against earlier 'nearly men', he consoled himself that 'some non-prime ministerial politicians – Joseph Chamberlain, Ernest Bevin and R.A. Butler, for example – put more imprint on British politics than did, say, Campbell-Bannerman, Anthony Eden or Alec Home'. Nevertheless he quoted Melbourne's remark that it was 'a damned fine thing' to have been Prime Minister, even if only for two months. 'It puts one in a sort of apostolic succession of forty-nine men and one woman descending from Walpole, for which no amount of explaining how narrowly or even honourably it was missed is a compensation.' (Gaitskell, he characteristically added, was 'a considerably greater man than either of his two immediate Labour successors, yet there is no contesting the fact that because he was out of that list and they are in he has become more quickly forgotten by those who did not know him.')[160]

Yet he insisted that he did not really regret that he was not on the list, since he suspected that he would not actually have enjoyed it very much. He valued too many other things more, and lacked the single-minded ambition of those – he mentioned Napoleon, Lloyd George and Churchill – who craved power for its own sake and were at ease with it. 'Although I think that I was a decisive and even an adventurous politician at various stages in my life, and had more sensible views about how to lead a government than many of those who have actually done it, I nonetheless lacked at least one of the essential ingredients of a capacity to seize power.'* He was sorry to have let down those who had looked to him as their leader. But looking around him at the afterlives of those who had been Prime Minister – this was a theme he was to develop more strongly as the 1990s went on – he was not inclined to envy them. He had had a good life, with 'a lot of friends and a lot of interests'. He had been 'married for forty-six years to the same wife' and was on 'good and even close terms' with his three children. These, he coolly reflected, 'are not negligible fixed points. There are also seven grandchildren who have so far brought much more pleasure than pain.' 'It seems to me,' he ended, 'that I would be inexcusably churlish if I concluded with any note of complaint against fate, or events, or almost anyone with whom I have been closely

---

* In a book review written at just the time he was writing this conclusion, Jenkins contrasted Austen Chamberlain's gentlemanly failure to become Prime Minister with the success of his half-brother Neville, 'a good narrow Conservative who looked on most of his opponents as "dirt" and hence qualified to get to the top in a way that Austen never did'.[161]

associated.'[162] The characteristically precise qualification of that final
'almost' can surely only have been aimed at David Owen.

A Life at the Centre received mainly generous reviews – a good many
of them, it must be said, written by his friends – and is now regularly
named, with Denis Healey's *The Time of My Life*, as one of the two
best political memoirs of recent years. Most reviewers praised Jenkins'
historian's perspective and his ability to laugh at himself and admit his
own mistakes. John Grigg in the *Times Literary Supplement*, for instance,
called it 'a marvellous account of high politics by a participant writing
with honesty, irony and sustained narrative verve';[163] while Anthony
Quinton in the *Spectator* thought Jenkins 'a confident commentator on
his own performance . . . He is not afraid to praise himself and earns
the right to do so by unfudged self-criticism.'[164] But several regretted the
absence of any serious discussion of political ideas or much personal
revelation;* and some – mainly Labour writers who could not forgive
the SDP – thought him insufferably self-satisfied. The historian Ben
Pimlott admired the writing, but criticised Jenkins' 'arrogance to believe
that the world could be his oyster on his own terms';[166] and John Smith
– then Shadow Chancellor, soon to succeed Kinnock as Labour leader,
a Gaitskellite right-winger who had declined to join the SDP – was
caustic about Jenkins' disloyalty to the party that had made his career:
he did not fight to save the party he loved, Smith charged, because he
did not love it, but was all along an ambitious careerist solely interested
in furthering his own career.[167†] Between these poles, Peter Hennessy,
writing in the *Times Educational Supplement*, was perhaps the most
objectively laudatory:

> These are beautifully written recollections. The vocabulary, the
> quality of the language, the mixture of weighty judgements light-
> ened by phrases glowing with characterful insight into other

---

* John Grigg commented knowingly that Jenkins' reticence about private matters left
plenty for his biographers. Quintin Hailsham, conversely, actually managed to refer to
Jenkins' 'impeccable private life, married to the same wife for 46 years'.[165] Was this discreet
Establishment solidarity, or did he really not know about Caroline and Leslie?

† The book was published in America in 1993 under the title *Memoirs of a Radical Reformer*,
with a few thousand words substituted or rewritten for the American audience. *Truman*
had sold disappointingly in the States, Jenkins wrote, so this book needed to do well 'if
my literary New York life was not to lag well behind its political and social counterparts'.[168]
An interesting review in the *New Yorker* (by Adam Gopnik) called him 'by the brutal
standards of American politics a failure'. What Gopnik thought striking was that Jenkins,
'though a much worse failure in domestic politics than he is inclined to admit, was a
much greater, and more prophetic, success as an international administrator than he is
inclined to recognise'.[169]

figures, paragraphs infused with the spirit of place and (unexpectedly this) sections of truly brilliant comic writing, make *A Life at the Centre* a deeply pleasurable read.[170]

A Life at the Centre marked the end of Jenkins' active political career. But it marked a new beginning of his career as a writer. The next decade would see him move on to three more big biographical books (two of them highly praised bestsellers) as well as two or three slighter ones, exercising continuing political influence behind the scenes. He was by no means finished yet.

23 History Man

'ONE of the most difficult feats for a successful politician,' Jenkins wrote in one of his biographical essays in 1998, 'is to manage a semi-retirement so that it gives at least as much satisfaction as, and maybe more happiness than, the battles to which it is a postscript.'[1] This was a theme to which he recurred frequently in his later writings: among twentieth-century Prime Ministers he reckoned only Attlee and Macmillan had achieved it (and he was probably wrong about Macmillan). Jenkins never achieved the topmost rung of the ladder, but he considered that he had managed for himself a pretty satisfactory final decade.* While still maintaining an astonishing output of journalism, he took his serious historical writing to a new level with two full-scale, prize-winning and bestselling biographies of the two biggest beasts in nineteenth- and twentieth-century British politics. The Chancellorship of Oxford still gave him a dignified, fulfilling but not-over-demanding public position; while he was still able to exercise considerable political influence behind the scenes in trying to achieve vicariously some of the long-term objectives he had been unable to complete in his own

---

* In 1978, in a letter condoling with Quintin Hailsham on the death of his wife in a riding accident, Jenkins wrote: 'You, more than almost anyone else I know, deserved different chapters in the latter part of the book' – a perfect statement of his belief that life was a lived biography.[2] Hailsham was a political opponent with whom Jenkins maintained an ambivalent relationship over the years. They had a particularly sharp exchange of feline courtesies in 1988 when Hailsham asserted that it would be unconstitutional for the House of Lords to amend the poll tax. 'Throughout a long career,' Jenkins wrote to *The Times*, 'Lord Hailsham has whirred with the noise of impartial statesmanship while almost invariably alighting on the bough most convenient for the Conservative leadership of the day.' 'Despite his undoubted brilliance, courtesy and charm,' Hailsham retorted, 'Lord Jenkins of Hillhead is rather out of his depth on constitutional matters.'[3]

career. And right to the end he was able to keep up the same inexhaustible social whirl on the interface between the political, literary, diplomatic and academic worlds: lunching, dining and corresponding continuously with everyone who mattered in the liberal establishment, including not only his contemporaries and old friends as they gradually thinned out, but a remarkable range of new younger friends as well. Despite increasing health problems, it was an object lesson in how not to be diminished by advancing age.

In a satirical profile in 1998 Boris Johnson poked fun at 'the Duke of Omnium and Lord High Everything Else, Lord Jenkins of Hillhead, Baron Pontypool in the County of Gwent, Chancellor of Oxford University and holder of just about every gong going from the Robert Schuman Prize to the Legion of Honour (Senegal) and the order of the Infante Henrique (Portugal)'.[4] But the award that set the seal on Jenkins' status as the grand panjandrum of the British Establishment was the Order of Merit in 1993. This is the most coveted honour because it is awarded personally by the Queen to leading figures from the arts and sciences, the military and the public service. There are just twenty-four members at a time and vacancies are normally filled within a year or two of a member dying. Very few politicians receive it, fewer still who have not been Prime Minister: Lloyd George, Churchill, Attlee and Macmillan all got it, and Mrs Thatcher was awarded it within weeks of stepping down in 1990. The next four recipients were the opera singer Joan Sutherland, the scientist Francis Crick, the director of the Royal Ballet, Dame Ninette de Valois, and the mathematician Sir Michael Atiyah. Jenkins was awarded it in December 1993 along with the painter Lucian Freud, filling the shoes of Oliver Franks and Solly Zuckerman. This was exalted company, which could hardly fail to feed his sense of self-importance. He recorded 167 letters of congratulations, plus another 102 verbal expressions of pleasure. Bill Rodgers and Mark Bonham Carter organised a celebratory dinner – for eighty-four invited guests – at Brooks's. Only the *Sunday Times* pooped his party by running an anonymous profile blaming Jenkins for the permissive society and generally judging him a pompous overrated failure.[5]

In January 1995 Roy and Jennifer celebrated their golden wedding with a relatively small lunch – just twenty-five – at the Savoy (where they had held the original reception fifty years before). It was mainly a family occasion (the wine bill included thirty-two Coca-Colas), but the guests also included the Rodgerses, the McIntoshes, the Donaldsons and Roy's oldest boyhood friend from Pontypool, Hugh Brace, who had spent his life working for the Patent Office and wrote gratefully a few days later:

> It would have been so easy, after the war, when our paths were manifestly destined to be so divergent, for our friendship to fade and lapse. That it did not was entirely due to initiatives on your part.

He also paid tribute to Jennifer's selfless support of Roy while raising the family and pursuing her own career:

> You have between you a mighty synergy, the attributes of each enhancing the effectiveness of the other; above all you have forged a strong bond of love and affection fortified by tolerance and good humour.[6]

Nine months later Jenkins spoke at Denis and Edna Healey's golden wedding. After ironically recalling their rivalry (and Healey's maddening one-upmanship) from Balliol onwards, he somewhat daringly described Denis and himself as 'two remarkably uxorious politicians', exceeded only by Gladstone, Lloyd George ('a bit shaky on other marital aspects'), Baldwin, Alec Home and Harold Wilson 'and by practically no-one else'.[7] Devoted to Jennifer though he undoubtedly was, everyone in the room must have known that he was at least as 'shaky' on some aspects of marriage as Lloyd George, so it was a cheeky claim, which came close to being publicly exposed six months later in a television programme made by the master of televised political biographies, Michael Cockerell. Cleverly subtitled *Roy Jenkins: A Very Social Democrat*, this was for the most part an affectionate and admiring portrait – most memorable for a sequence showing Jenkins getting his daily exercise by walking purposefully around the tennis court at East Hendred for exactly forty-five minutes ('Shorter would be too short and longer would be a waste of time'). Cockerell and his producer Alison Cahn spent a good deal of time filming at East Hendred. Roy and Jennifer were therefore upset – Jennifer particularly – when they saw an early cut of the programme in which Cockerell made explicit reference to Roy's girlfriends.

At their request some changes were made before it was broadcast on 26 May 1996. Photographs of Caroline and Leslie were dropped and a new section added emphasising Jennifer's career. 'Everyone who has seen the programme has said she comes across as a very appealing and strong, personality,' Alison Cahn wrote to Jenkins three days before transmission. 'We did try our best to make a fair and honest portrait of you.'[8] Not cut, however, was a section of interview in which Cockerell asked Jenkins directly about his lovers. Momentarily thrown, he nevertheless recovered and parried the question skilfully by saying that it was generally better not to admit or deny these things: it was 'ungallant' either way. Pressed on whether he was not worried that he might be found out, he replied calmly: 'No, I don't think I've done things I'm ashamed of.' Jennifer too was impressively unfazed. 'Everybody's marriage goes up and down. It's not true we've never had a disagreement, but we've certainly never had a serious rift.'[9] Their combined sangfroid successfully killed the story. But the advance publicity for the programme had sparked a flurry of wide-eyed speculation, mainly focusing on 'Princess' Lee Radziwill – almost the only time Jenkins' girlfriends were openly mentioned in the press. Roy and Jennifer felt that Cockerell had betrayed their hospitality. To their surprise, however, most of the feedback from friends was strongly positive. Shirley Anglesey thought the programme 'very good . . . much better than the gossip columnists had led us to expect'.[10] 'You were so amusing, witty and good-tempered throughout,' Elizabeth Longford assured Roy. 'You handled it perfectly.'[11] And Christopher Audland (former deputy Secretary-General of the European Commission) wrote warmly: 'The picture which came through was very much the genuine Roy we both know: straightforward, witty, understated, reflective and wise. How little you have changed over the years.'[12]

In the light of these reactions Jenkins wrote again to Cockerell generously revising his earlier complaint. 'Truth and fairness constrain me to say that the great majority of our friends and friendly acquaintances who have seen the programme . . . think it was a favourable and interesting portrait,' he acknowledged. This was 'well short of a unanimous view', but the minority who dissented did so mainly on what he called 'Hattersley grounds': that it trivialised politics by focusing too much on personality:

Jennifer and I, as you will be aware, were not at all happy, particularly with the advance publicity, which mostly appeared between our seeing the first version and the public showing. We both also thought that to go back to that old mountebank Abse . . . [verb illegible] the same story out of which he has made a metier for the past 30 years, was boring. It would have been better to have had some serious opponent, Tebbitt [*sic*] or Benn say, analysing my weaknesses. All this led us to feel that we had perhaps been too forthcoming and reposed too much confidence in you and Alison.

However there is no doubt that at the time we enjoyed working with you, that you showed yourself a very skilful interviewer, giving full and favourable opportunities to both Jennifer and me, that the photography was excellent, and that on balance a strong and on the whole helpful impression was left on many people's minds. And, of course, subjects are far from necessarily the most detached or best critics of portraits.

Yours ever,
Roy[13]*

Not until after his death did anything more appear in the press about his lovers.

By now Jenkins had settled confidently into his role as Chancellor of Oxford. He understood perfectly the limitations of his function and never tried to exceed them, seeing himself as a constitutional monarch – the dignified face of the university's government – with no power but the right to be consulted, to encourage and to warn. ('Why does Oxford need a Chancellor?' Macmillan once asked, and answered: 'Because without one there could not be a Vice-Chancellor, and without a Vice-Chancellor there would be no-one to run the university.')[15] In his fifteen years Jenkins worked with four Vice-Chancellors: Patrick Neill, a lawyer (1985–9), who was in post when he was elected; Richard Southwood (1989–93), a zoologist; Peter North (1993–7), another lawyer and finally Colin Lucas (1997–2003), a historian whom he was influential in appointing and the one with whom he got on best. He had little say in the two earlier appointments, which were relatively uncontested; but in 1997 he thought neither of the front-runners up to the

* A few months later, when the former Archbishop of Canterbury Robert Runcie complained that his biographer Humphrey Carpenter had betrayed his trust by publishing material that he had thought off-the-record, Jenkins wrote to him sympathetically in the light of his own experience with *A Very Social Democrat*:

> Both Jennifer and I devoted a great deal of time to it, and Cockerell very successfully worked his way into our confidence. Then we felt rather let down by some at least of what appeared, and had a miserable week when we first saw the video before its public showing. But then, a further twist, we discovered that about 70% of people, friends and others, thought that both of us . . . came out of it well, and that it had enhanced our reputations.[14]

job and took the initiative in widening the search to approach Lucas, then just forty-seven, who had been Master of Balliol since 1994 (a plus point, naturally) but was not an Oxford insider as he had made his name in Chicago. Jenkins saw him as a moderniser, and Lucas was widely recognised as a good appointment. Jenkins was also instrumental in extending the Vice-Chancellor's term from four years to five; but he failed to persuade Lucas to continue for a second term. At the time of his death he was chairing the committee to choose Lucas' successor. He would have liked to go for Alison Richard before she was pinched by Cambridge, and would probably not have supported the ill-starred choice of John Hood, which was made after his death.

Jenkins got on perfectly adequately with Neill, Southwood and North, but he formed a particularly close partnership with Lucas: they shared the same historical interests and Lucas consulted him more than his predecessors had done. They would talk informally on the phone, lunch together in local pubs or at East Hendred and became good friends. Lucas found Jenkins easy to talk to and full of shrewd advice, a 'consummate politician' with 'great powers of accommodation and persuasion', always looking to steer sensible change by agreement without losing sight of the objective, and came to rely on him more and more.[16] Within the wider Oxford community Jenkins in turn relied for advice primarily on the former Master of Balliol, Anthony Kenny; the philosopher Bernard Williams; and the historian Keith Thomas. In the book of essays edited by Thomas and Andrew Adonis after his death, Kenny wrote that Jenkins, compared with his two most activist predecessors, 'worked much harder for the University than Chancellor Macmillan ever did, and inspired much more affection than Chancellor Curzon ever did. He has a good claim to have given more to Oxford than any other twentieth-century Chancellor.'[17]

A good example of his style was the question of whether Somerville should follow other former women's colleges and admit male undergraduates and fellows. In 1992 the governing body voted to do so; but opponents of the change, both present students and alumnae, objected that they had not been consulted and appealed formally to Jenkins in his *ex officio* capacity as Visitor of the college. Jenkins considered the case carefully before delivering an even-handed judgement, ruling that the college had acted perfectly legally, but should have consulted more widely first: he proposed a year's delay, by which time a lot of the heat had gone out of the controversy. The first men were then admitted without fuss in 1994. He also played a discreet role, with others, in persuading the Oxford and Cambridge Club (in Pall Mall) to admit lady members. He was less successful, however, in attempting to persuade the University Press to reverse its decision to cease publishing poetry.[18]

In 1996 Jenkins got involved in a public spat with the historian Alistair Horne, who wrote to *The Times* accusing Oxford of cravenly refusing a bequest from a German industrialist, Dr Flick, on the grounds that the money was tainted by his grandfather's association with the Nazis, attributing the decision to a 'gang of politically correct trendies'.[19] Jenkins responded with a withering demolition of Horne's 'misleading ignorance', pointing out that the university's Ethics Committee had actually accepted the bequest: Flick had withdrawn it, regrettably, in the face of outside criticism, 'whipped up mostly by those of tenuous connection with Oxford'. 'This has been an isolated unhappy incident,' he concluded, 'in the university's extremely successful record of fund-raising over the past seven-and-a-half years.'[20] Horne apologised, after which Jenkins characteristically invited him to lunch at an Oxfordshire pub much nearer Horne's house than his own. 'I have to say I came with some trepidation,' Horne wrote, 'but left having enjoyed *every second* of it! . . . We seemed to cover an immense amount of ground, and I don't think I found myself disagreeing on any point.'[21] This is a good example of Jenkins' way of smoothing over disagreements over lunch.

He continued to enjoy the ceremonial side of the Chancellorship, though he struggled with the correct modern pronunciation of the Latin in his formal speeches, which he rehearsed laboriously with the Public Orator beforehand. 'His conscientious efforts were not always rewarded with success,' Kenny noted, 'and the audience could perceive a sense of relief and a quickening of pace as he arrived at the final unvarying part of the formula: *auctoritate mea et totius Universitatis . . .*'[22] He particularly enjoyed the awarding of honorary degrees to visiting statesmen. When Bill Clinton, early in his presidency, came back to Oxford, where he had been a Rhodes scholar in the Sixties, to receive an honorary degree, Jenkins made the most of the occasion. Evangeline Bruce – wife of the former US ambassador in London and one of his coterie of American lady friends – wrote to him: 'You set the tone from the start – all was so sumptuous and orderly and yet not pompous. Beautiful, too. The Clintons, it was clear, felt loved and consequently at their most charming and receptive.' Even a noisy demonstration outside the Sheldonian merely gave the President the opportunity for 'a graceful reference to the home of free speech'.[23] *The Times* reported acidly that if Clinton's often cool view of Oxford was revived by 'the plummy condescension of Lord Jenkins', it did not show.[24] Jenkins was keen to milk every opportunity to raise Oxford's fund-raising profile in the States. In subsequent years he likewise entertained and honoured Mikhail Gorbachev, Václav Havel and the President of Ireland, Mary Robinson, as well as cultural luminaries like Seamus Heaney and David Hockney.*

But he also widened his role beyond Oxford to become a powerful spokesman for the British university sector as a whole (he claimed to have visited every one, including all the converted polytechnics). Having, as he confessed, taken little interest in higher education since 1941, he reckoned that the 1980s had given him an unusual opportunity to appreciate the universities' difficulties from three very different vantage points: respectively, as he called them in one of his less happy metaphors, 'the proud peacock of Oxford . . . the 441-year old eagle of Glasgow . . . [and] the enthusiastic young pouter pigeon of Strathclyde'. By 1990 all three were suffering from 'a decade of debilitating financial restriction' – driven, he alleged, less by real financial stringency than by a climate of anti-intellectualism, free-market ideology and a desire to curtail critical thought:

> The Government policies of the 1980s towards the universities were, I believe, the most short-sighted that Britain has ever had the misfortune to encounter. Nearly every previous administration of whatever party had been responsible for some major advance . . . in our academic framework. That one alone was distinguished for creating nothing and for inflicting great damage on teaching, research, morale and students.[26]

The political scientist Vernon Bogdanor – subsequently famous for having been David Cameron's tutor – wrote to thank Jenkins for being 'almost the only politician in Britain to speak out against money-making as the be-all and end-all of life'.[27] As the Major government floundered to its end in the mid-1990s, Jenkins hoped for better from the incoming Blair government.

Jenkins never pretended to be an academic, but he enjoyed talking with scholars and was usually good company at High Table – though he could be rude, if bored by the person he was seated next to. Some

---

* In conferring an honorary degree on Gorbachev in 1996, however, Jenkins – having perhaps lunched too well with Robert Harris – embarrassingly referred to him throughout as 'Mr Brezhnev'![25]

dons were snooty about the lack of original research in his books; but most were grateful to have a Chancellor who wrote books at all, who read a lot of books and could talk about books. In 1990 he agreed to give a lecture as part of a series marking the centenary of the death of Cardinal Newman, alongside five distinguished Newman scholars. 'As the date for the lecture came into the middle distance,' he confessed, 'I first thought that I must have taken leave of my senses in accepting and then decided that I had no alternative but to spend a month reading little except books by and about Newman.'[28] Thus prepared, he delivered a thoroughly respectable generalist's appreciation of Newman, whom he found 'a wholly absorbing even if sometimes provoking subject';[29] and Newman's 1852 lectures on 'The Idea of a University' became a fruitful starting point for his own thoughts about universities over the following years, as well as making a useful preparation for tackling the theological contortions of Gladstone.

While limbering up for that assault he published another collection of his shorter writings under the title *Portraits and Miniatures*. The core of this book was another set of six biographical essays which he had written for *The Times* in 1993 on the same lines as his *Nine Men of Power* in the early 1970s, but somewhat shorter. His chosen subjects this time were three front-rank British politicians (Rab Butler, Nye Bevan and Iain Macleod) whom he had known, one American (Dean Acheson) and two Europeans (Konrad Adenauer and General de Gaulle). He considered including Henry Kissinger and Helmut Schmidt, but stuck to his rule of not writing about living subjects. These by themselves were not enough to make a book, so he added his Newman lecture and another on 'Changing Patterns of Leadership' from Asquith to Mrs Thatcher that he had first given in 1987; a dozen more articles and lectures on a variety of subjects ranging from 'An Oxford View of Cambridge', celebrations of Glasgow and the bicentenary of *The Times* and a round-up of recent political biographies, to slighter pieces on wine and croquet; plus twenty-two of his book reviews, some historical and others – the memoirs of Nigel Lawson and Cecil Parkinson – very recent. This eclectic but entertaining potpourri was published by Macmillan in 1993 (for an advance of £10,000), to generally appreciative reviews and a private tribute from Mollie Butler, who wrote to thank Jenkins not only for his perceptive piece on Rab, but for all the others too, comparing him to 'a great lepidopterist, pinning your model to the page with the perfect *mot juste*'.[30]

After the success of his memoirs, however, he was ready for another big book. He had not written a full-scale biography since *Asquith* in

1964. But in 1992 Michael Sissons and Roland Philipps (then at Macmillan) persuaded him (for an advance of £75,000) to take on Gladstone. (Stuart Proffitt tried to get him to do Charles James Fox for HarperCollins, but Jenkins declined that one.) At first, he recalled later, he quailed at the prospect of the Grand Old Man's immense career, spanning practically the whole of the nineteenth century and encompassing four premierships. 'I thought Gladstone was too big a subject for me, and in particular I doubted my ability to get to adequate grips with his important but subsidiary pursuits, such as the theological and liturgical disputes of early Victorian England or his attempt to see Homer as part of the headwaters of Christianity.' But he was fascinated too, and excited by the challenge. 'He was the highest peak in the mountain chain, and as such the most enticing as well as the most intimidating.'[31] There had been no single-volume life since Philip Magnus in 1954 (though Richard Shannon had published the first part of a two-volume project in 1982), so there was a gap in the market. Nevertheless it was, as he wrote in his Preface, 'by far my rashest literary enterprise . . . like suddenly deciding, at a late state in life and after a sedate middle age, to climb the rougher face of the Matterhorn'.[32]

He had frequently, in reviewing other writers, condemned big books that were too heavy to hold up in bed. *Gladstone* was always going to break his own rule. Yet the research and writing took him only three years, from early 1992 when he started reading intensively, to the end of 1994. Of course his book was based entirely on secondary sources, apart from bits of the Dilke and Asquith papers which he had read thirty-five years earlier. His method now was frankly to synthesise the work of other historians and weld it into a fresh narrative, spiced with his own highly personal commentary. By far his greatest debt – which he fully acknowledged – was to the Oxford historian Colin Matthew, editor of the monumental Gladstone diaries, which had appeared in fourteen volumes between 1968 and 1994. These are not descriptive or reflective diaries in the Pepys or Crossman sense of the word, but an epic engagement diary – what Gladstone himself called 'an account-book of the all-precious gift of Time' – accounting to God in abbreviated shorthand for almost every minute of every day for more than seventy years: whom he had seen, whom he had written to, what he had read, how long he spoke for and where he stayed every night. (They are in fact extraordinarily like Jenkins' own meticulous engagement diaries, though even more detailed.) This amazing resource, mirroring his own obsession, enabled Jenkins to chart Gladstone's day-to-day activities, and particularly his social life, with a precision that lent his book a somewhat pedantic and antiquarian flavour. Jenkins was in one sense the perfect biographer of Gladstone, because he was almost the last person in England who knew or cared about the minute Trollopian gradations of Victorian society, the correct precedence between a duke and an archbishop and who was related to whom, the great houses, mealtimes, railway timetables, precise journey times and even fashions. ('There was by 1847 hardly anyone other than the first Marquess of Anglesey who habitually wore a blue coat in London.')[33] But arguably this sort of detail is overdone: it tells the reader more about Jenkins' own enthusiasms than about Gladstone, and does sometimes obscure the big historical picture.

At the same time *Gladstone* was the first of Jenkins' books in which his prose style – perhaps influenced by Gladstone's own – became at times almost unreadably convoluted and parenthetical. He could no longer resist including in the narrative extraneous curiosities of information that would have been better relegated to a footnote, while continually showing off his familiarity with the entire cast of nineteenth-century public life and assuming the reader's equal familiarity and interest.[*] Of one of Gladstone's early speeches he wrote that 'the subordinate clauses hung like candelabra throughout his oration with few of his sentences containing less than seventy words, and some twice as many'.[35] In this respect biographer and subject were almost too well matched. Nor was this the only similarity. Without forcing the parallels, Jenkins brought out in Gladstone innumerable characteristics that were extraordinarily like himself: not only his obsessive diarykeeping and precise accounting for time and distances, but his love of planning journeys, his special love of Italy, his devotion to 'the God-fearing and God-sustaining University of Oxford'[36] and his considerable consumption of wine. Almost the longest quotation from Gladstone in the entire book is a wonderful disquisition in praise of good wine.[37] He wrote of Gladstone's 'liking for country-house gatherings, the pleasures of which, however, hardly diminished the flow of his writing and reading';[38] and of his fondness, as he grew older, for staying at 'well-appointed Home Counties residences . . . in which the life of the house and the services of the household revolved around himself'.[39] 'It never occurred to him that they [his hosts] could expect anything in return except for the pleasure of knowing and serving

---

[*] But much of the incidental detail is unquestionably fascinating, such as Gladstone's comment on Queen Victoria's habit of drinking claret 'strengthened, I should have thought spoiled, with whisky'.[34]

him.'[40] He commented ironically on Gladstone's 'frequent and dutiful habit of riding in London . . . For the most part it was a solitary and somewhat contrived pursuit . . . Whether riding did his health any good, which was its ostensible purpose, seems more doubtful.'[41] Exactly the same could be said of Jenkins' jogging in Brussels and his walking round his tennis court. He also referred (not disapprovingly) to 'fragmentary but converging evidence . . . that Gladstone had a sexual drive to match the flash of his eye, the force of his oratory and the vigour of his intellectual and physical energy'.[42] He devoted considerable space to the question of Gladstone's famous 'rescue work' with prostitutes, concluding that it was probably not wholly innocent, hence the need to scourge himself to purge his feelings of remorse. Gladstone's statement at the end of his life that he had never 'been guilty of the act which is known as that of infidelity to the marriage bed' was 'obviously both precise and limited'.[43] And when Jenkins wrote of Gladstone's youthful friendship with Arthur Hallam that there was 'no evidence of any homosexual behaviour, but it is impossible to believe that there was not the electricity of infatuation and jealousy between them',[44] he cannot have failed to have in mind memories of his own intense undergraduate relationship with Tony Crosland.

As he wrote, Jenkins became increasingly absorbed and amazed by Gladstone, not so much for his politics, which – though broadly admirable – were in detail often extraordinarily wrong-headed, as for his personal qualities, the inexhaustible variety of his activities and his astonishing physical energy: reading enormously (some 20,000 books in his lifetime), writing, speaking, walking and chopping down innumerable trees. He did not try seriously to engage with Gladstone's tortuous theology. But by the time he finished he had 'no doubt that Gladstone was the most remarkable specimen of humanity who ever occupied 10 Downing Street'.[45] *Gladstone* is a tremendous achievement because it fully conveyed to the reader this prodigious energy and variety. As usual, Jenkins sent pre-publication copies to a wide circle of his friends. One, Isaiah Berlin, wrote back admiringly: 'How you manage to write first-rate books, of immense length and learning, with a degree of rapidity which equals almost that of Trollope and the other great Victorians, I simply cannot imagine. But you do.'[46] Another, Jim Callaghan, saw a resemblance not so much to Jenkins himself as to another of their former colleagues:

Did it strike you that Gladstone & Tony Benn share several characteristics? e.g. both are demagogues, both have inexhaustible energy, both are obsessive diarists, both are convinced that whatever opinion they happen to hold at any one time is the only possible course to follow, both are non-team players & both are a little mad! And who knows – perhaps Tony scourges himself![47]

The reviews – once again written mainly by his friends, not by specialists – were overwhelmingly favourable. In *The Times* Robert Blake (himself the unsurpassed biographer of Disraeli) praised the way in which Jenkins brought the insight of his own experience to bear on the not-so-dissimilar politics of Gladstone's day. 'He appreciates from personal knowledge how Budgets are made and changed, how Cabinets and parties are kept together or sundered. He knows how ministers have to be cajoled or persuaded . . . and the importance of oratory.'[48] John Grigg in the *Sunday Telegraph* noted the similarities between author and subject, but also the difference that Jenkins' sense of irony enabled him to see the comic side of Gladstone;[49] and Anthony Howard in the *Sunday Times* was one of several reviewers to think the book, at Jenkins' age of nearly seventy-five, a Gladstonian achievement in itself.[50] That autumn it won the Whitbread Biography Prize; it failed to win Book of the Year, losing out to Salman Rushdie's *The Moor's Last Sigh*, but it sold well and was translated into a large number of languages.* In 2001, amazingly, Jenkins was able to send Václav Havel a copy of the Czech translation.

All the time he was writing *Gladstone* Jenkins was still reviewing two or three books a month, now mainly for the *Observer* and *Daily Telegraph*, as well as contributing articles on political topics of the day to a whole range of papers, for which he could normally command a four-figure fee. He wrote regularly in *The Times*, *Telegraph*, *Independent* and *Observer*, occasionally in the *Financial Times*, *Sunday Times* and *Daily Mail*. In fact the only major title for which he practically never wrote was the *Guardian*, possibly because too many of its readers still regarded him as a traitor for having left the Labour Party, but also because he did not think it paid enough. When Philip Stephens asked him to write

* In 1999 the second volume of Richard Shannon's biography presented a very different view of Gladstone. Reviewing it in the *TLS*, Jenkins wrote that while he himself might have underestimated Gladstone's near-lunacy, he thought Shannon exaggerated it. He also thought Shannon's writing so dense that it was hard to read. ('Indeed it could be said that one of Shannon's major qualifications for getting inside Gladstone's mind is that he almost rivals the Grand Old Man in opacity.') Jenkins was sorry that, after devoting his life to Gladstone, Shannon did not seem really to admire him, 'and this leads him to write about him, often brilliantly, but also constantly on the verge of bad temper'. This was not, in Jenkins' view, the way to write good biography.[51]

occasional comment pieces for the *Financial Times* he agreed so long as the money was right, insisting, 'No *Guardian* fees! The F.T. is not only a respected but a very prosperous paper.'[52] While Max Hastings was editor of the *Daily Telegraph* he deliberately used Jenkins to try to move the paper towards the centre. They became good friends – another example of Jenkins' ability to keep making new, much younger friends – and when Hastings moved to edit the London *Evening Standard* in 1996 he continued to commission Jenkins to add weight to that paper for the rest of his life.

Wearing his literary hat, Jenkins was regularly asked, often by more than one paper, to nominate his book (or books) of the year – usually, but not always, books he had reviewed – or sometimes his holiday reading. His choices for the latter illuminate his compulsion to keep on filling gaps in his knowledge: in 1992, for instance, he named a biography of Goethe and in 1993 Linda Colley's *Britons* ('because my eighteenth century history needs improving'), plus Alan Clark's *Diaries* ('because I do not think I can hold out indefinitely against reading what everyone else finds entertaining even if unadmirable').[53] But his lists also included the latest fiction: Anita Brookner, Sebastian Faulks and in 1992 Hilary Mantel's *A Place of Greater Safety* – even though he generally disliked historical novels – because 'her *Fludd* of two years ago was so unforgettable that I am willing to try anything she writes'.[54] When the *Financial Times* asked him in 1999 for his three books of the century, however, he went back to old favourites: his first was Proust, his second Evelyn Waugh's *Sword of Honour* trilogy, but his third, more surprisingly, was not Anthony Powell – on the grounds that he was too similar to Waugh. He would have picked a Thomas Hardy, but he was the wrong century, so he plumped for Virginia Woolf's *Mrs Dalloway*. These, he said, were the books that had given him 'the most persistent and recurring pleasure' over his adult lifetime. Paradoxically, he noted, for a writer of non-fiction, they were all fiction, for even the best non-fiction was 'relatively evanescent' by comparison.[55]*

---

* His choices were admirably consistent. In a previous, slightly longer list in 1991 he had named Proust, Waugh, Powell and *Mrs Dalloway*, plus George Eliot (*Middlemarch*), Trollope (*The Duke's Children*), Scott Fitzgerald (*Tender is the Night*) and Hardy (*The Trumpet Major*). Of Proust he said that he had 'read the whole four times, twice in Scott Moncrieff, once in French and once in Kilmartin . . . I still hope to read it once or twice more.'[56] Some years later he called Proust 'by a long head the greatest novelist of the twentieth century . . . a richly comic writer, with an unique gift for the evocation of landscape and for the meticulous cartography of social nuance as well as for the minute analysis of human emotions, particularly those of love and jealousy'. 'The meticulous cartography of social nuance' is a quintessential Jenkins phrase, which perfectly encapsulates what he loved in Proust.[57]

How did he manage to read so much? His habit was to wake early and read in bed for one and a half or two hours before getting up. 'It is one of the few benefits of old age,' he reflected in 1998, 'that I need less sleep.'[58] Jennifer was not disturbed because for some years now they had slept in separate rooms.[59] 'Perhaps inspired by Gladstone,' he confessed in a lecture at Hawarden, 'I have taken to keeping a list of what I read, and it comes out remarkably steadily at between 75 and 80 a year.'[60] His tally actually varied between sixty-seven in 1992 (seventeen of them for review) and 108 in the last year of his life, 2002, though that included a good deal of rereading: nowhere near Gladstone's 250-odd a year, but still a remarkable weight of reading.

And as well as reading and writing he still, in his last decade, maintained an exhausting schedule of speaking to all kinds of audiences, from serious semi-academic lectures at universities at home and abroad to literary lunches and after-dinner speeches to bodies such as the College of Estate Management or the Thames Valley Police – often about Europe, but sometimes on Baldwin or Gladstone or some other aspect of British politics. In 1996, for instance, he listed seventy speaking engagements of all sorts, and in 1999 a hundred. He kept trying to refuse invitations, pleading that he was 'fighting a constant battle against . . . over-commitment',[61] but then kept finding reasons for accepting. In April 1998, for example, he agreed to speak about Gladstone at Liverpool John Moores University in October, saying he would have refused almost any other request but that Liverpool – Gladstone's birthplace – must have something in his centenary year (the centenary of his death, that is).[62] He would almost always speak for friends. In November 1998 he was in Edinburgh to speak (for Elspeth Campbell) at the annual Patrons' dinner at the National Gallery of Scotland; and the next day he was back in London to give a London Library lecture on Gladstone's reading habits (for John Grigg). 'Your stamina amazes me,' Grigg wrote to him the next day, 'but I must impertinently insist that you should perhaps consider taxing it rather less severely. None of my business, of course, but I think Jennifer agrees.'[63] Maybe he listened, for the next month he declined to speak to the Society of Bookmen. 'The plain fact is that I have been accepting far too many speaking engagements. I had four last week and three this week. And I do not do them easily (i.e. without preparation). The result is not only exhaustion but a serious bar to getting on with my own writing work.'[64]

Finally, he continued to appear regularly as a panellist on *Any Questions?* on Radio 4 and *Question Time* (now chaired by David Dimbleby) on BBC1, where he invariably gave good value. 'It is a relief to a chairman,' Dimbleby wrote to him after one appearance in 1994, 'to know that he can turn to a guest confident that something funny or of substance or both will ensue.'[65] In 2001 he was invited to appear on the satirical panel game *Have I Got News for You?*, where he would have been subject to merciless ribbing at the hands of Angus Deayton and Ian Hislop; he was tempted, but sensibly declined.[66] Back in 1989, however, he was a guest on *Desert Island Discs*, then hosted by Sue Lawley. His choice of records was thoroughly middlebrow, but autobiographically honest. His taste in music was not sophisticated, though he was happy to go to Covent Garden when invited and often had opera playing while he was writing. Along with pieces of Elgar (*Enigma Variations*), Haydn (the 'Oxford' symphony), Verdi (*Un Ballo in Maschera*), Saint-Saëns (*Samson and Delilah*) and Hamish MacCunn (*The Land of the Mountain and the Flood*) he picked the 'Soviet Airman's Song' (which reminded him of Oxford and the war), the Glasgow Orpheus Choir singing 'We'll Keep a Welcome in the Hillside' and the theme from *Chariots of Fire* (which reminded him of campaigning in Hillhead). His book was *Who Was Who* and his luxury, inevitably, a case of claret.[67] He never pretended to be what he was not.

In September 1992 the Major government, unexpectedly re-elected just four months earlier, suffered a catastrophic humiliation when it was forced to leave the ERM, which Britain had finally joined only two years before. Its reputation for economic competence never recovered, though it staggered on for a full parliament until finally put out of its misery in 1997. In newspaper articles in the *Independent* and the *Daily Telegraph* Jenkins naturally blamed this 'crushing defeat' for Major's proclaimed ambition to put Britain 'at the heart of Europe' not on the wisdom of having joined in the first place, but on Mrs Thatcher's stubbornness in refusing to join when the going was good, and then joining at the worst possible moment and at the wrong rate just before her fall. 'The defeat lies in the fact we have added another and peculiarly dismal chapter to the almost incredible story of the mismanagement of our relations with the continent of Europe over the past 40 years.'[68] In the *Telegraph* he compared the fiasco unfavourably to the 1967 devaluation, which by comparison with 'the sad farce of last Wednesday could almost be described as elegant'. Writing as a former Chancellor, he concluded that Norman Lamont should resign, as Callaghan had done in 1967 and as he himself would have done in 1968 if the balance of payments had not come right, since his moral authority would have been exhausted. Lamont had 'never been strong on moral authority' and would be 'completely bereft of it' in the future, 'wholly dependent on Mr Major's attempt to protect him'. 'To be the creature of the Prime Minister,' he warned, 'is never good for a Chancellor.' Though the failed policy was actually more Major's than Lamont's, he did not think Major should resign since Prime Ministers – with the exception of Eden after Suez – did not resign for failure. The hard rule was that 'Departmental ministers . . . should pay the price of abject departmental failure.'[69]*

Nevertheless Jenkins soon decided that Major was not fit for his high office, either; and for the next four and half years he pursued him relentlessly and very personally. 'Looking back on nearly half a century in Parliament,' he declared that autumn, 'I have never seen this country worse governed than it is today . . . Neither in breadth of personality, nor in depth of knowledge and expertise, is the Prime Minister up to the job.' There had been bad periods before. 'But the present utter inadequacy of both men and measures is unique.'[72] He condemned not only Major's feeblenesss towards Europe, but also 'the weak and whining jumping from improvisation to improvisation which has recently passed for economic policy',[73] and the 'ultimate dogmatism' of rail privatisation, driven by 'the very small minority of partisan activists . . . completely insulated from the wider body of supporters whom they are supposed to represent', which he again likened to the Callaghan government pushing through the nationalisation of the docks in 1976.[74] In January 1994 he widened his critique to lambast the whole frenetic, inbred culture of modern politics:

> The unwanted upheaval of rail privatisation, the threat of yet another local government reorganisation . . . and the actuality of the seventh education bill and the fifth criminal justice bill within

---

* Two months after 'Black Wednesday' Jenkins appeared with Lamont on *Question Time* and dismissed him to his face as 'not up to the job'. When Lamont retorted that he did not think anyone was, apart from himself, Jenkins drawled that 'Stafford Cripps wasn't bad'.[70] After the programme, according to Lamont, Jenkins went 'white with anger' and refused to speak to him, 'as though *I* had made a personal attack on *him*'. Lamont got his own back three years later with a sarcastic article in the *Daily Mail* on the occasion of Jenkins' seventy-fifth birthday, attacking his pomposity, self-importance, responsibility for current social problems and outdated economic thinking: 'What does Lord Jenkins, on his chaise longue, know of the Tiger Economies of the Far East? . . . Maybe he will take them seriously only when they threaten to buy up all the world's claret.'[71] There were very few people in politics with whom Jenkins did not try to maintain friendly relations, but Lamont was one of them.

a decade, demonstrate not calm continuity but flailing and ineffective restlessness . . . If governments concentrated on using well
the period of power they have already won rather than accepting
any humiliation for themselves and any misfortune for the country
provided it comes right on the night of the quinquennial decision,
politics and politicians might not be held in as low esteem as is
currently the case.[75]

Was this just an ageing politician moaning about his successors, or did
he have a point? The experience of the last twenty years has tended
only to vindicate his view.

He was particularly scathing about Major's rash proclamation of 'Back
to Basics', which predictably collapsed in a flurry of sexual and financial
scandal. 'No-one with any sense of history or realism,' he wrote in the
Telegraph, 'can pretend that sexual purity has been the outstanding
characteristic of great political leaders, or that its absence is consequently
a sensible disqualification for high office.' Churchill and de Gaulle were
outstanding exceptions; but Gladstone once said that of the thirteen
Prime Ministers he had known, eleven were adulterers:[*]

> So there is no room for mounting high moral horses about sexual
> peccadilloes. Indeed, it would be more plausible to argue that the
> energy and charisma which are necessary for successful leadership
> (and sadly lacking today) are mostly accompanied by an unusual
> sexual drive which has rarely contained itself within monogamous
> bounds.

Major, he allowed, could not be held responsible for his third-rate
colleagues. But he was responsible 'for having opportunistically and
thoughtlessly adopted a slogan which was disastrously ill-suited to the
rather louche band he had to lead . . . This casts further doubt on
whether the Prime Minister, so signally lacking in either touch or luck,
is not also fatally hobbled by a lack of judgement and shallowness of
personality for the effective leadership of a government.'[76]
'The sense of a decadent political scene, a decadent Government
and a decadent party hammers away at the mind,' he wrote in June
1993, recalling for comparison the last days of other governments –
Balfour in 1903–5, the Hoover administration in the United States in

---

[*] The other two, Jenkins guessed, were probably Aberdeen and Rosebery, 'whose tastes
lay in another direction'.

1930–32, the Callaghan government in 1976–9 – which had run out of steam long before the electorate put them out of their misery. The problem was that while the Tories were exhausted and discredited, incapable of tackling the serious issues facing the country, there was no credible alternative ready to take over. Labour, now led by John Smith, enjoyed massive leads in the polls, but still did not look like an alternative government; it was the Liberal Democrats under Paddy Ashdown who were once again winning by-elections (Newbury and Christchurch in 1993, Eastleigh in 1994). Hence Jenkins believed that 'a convincing alternative Government will not emerge without a substantial measure of Labour and Liberal Democrat co-operation', which would have to be imposed on the parties from the bottom up. Otherwise there was 'an uncomfortable likelihood that many of us will live the rest of our lives under Conservative governments'.[77] He now looked to unofficial tactical voting by the electorate to determine the balance between the opposition parties. 'But whatever that balance may be, and however firmly the official parties, as is their wont, reject formal collaboration, the voters will in my view try very hard to construct an unofficial anti-Tory front.'[78]

Jenkins had already identified Tony Blair as his best hope for bringing this about before John Smith suddenly died on 12 May 1994. Anthony Seldon in his biography of Blair states that the two men had no significant contact before Blair wrote to Jenkins 'out of the blue' asking his advice on economic policy, and that they had no serious meeting before mid-1994.[79] In fact they had already been in touch at least eighteen months earlier, when Blair was still Shadow Home Secretary and looking back to Jenkins' famous tenure of the Home Office in the 1960s as the model of what a reforming Labour Home Secretary – tough both on crime and on its social causes – could achieve. He was also frustrated by Smith's resistance to what he saw as urgently necessary modernisation of the party. On the second day of 1993 Jenkins invited the Blairs to lunch at East Hendred (with Dick Taverne and his wife, which suggests the way he was already thinking). Thanking him both for lunch and for his 'very kind' letter, Blair wrote: 'There are times, at present, when a very cold breeze seems to be blowing around my ankles! However I live in hope that a sensible debate will break through.' He added that he had not read *A Life at the Centre* but would love to do so. 'I suspect it would be more than a little illuminating.'[80] Jenkins duly sent him a copy.

When Smith died and Blair outsmarted Gordon Brown to snatch the Labour leadership the following July, Jenkins immediately hailed him, in *The Times*, as 'the most exciting Labour choice since the election of Hugh Gaitskell in December 1955' – the highest praise in his book – quite explicitly seeing him as the man to forge a united moderate/progressive front and realise the thwarted ambition of the SDP. Blair's emergence, he wrote, gave new hope to 'the great number of the non-socialist public who are now longing for a change of ministers'. It was 'the alienation of this Gaitskellite constituency' which had led directly to 'the long period of Labour's unelectability'. In order to reverse that exclusion he urged Blair to seek friendly relations with the Liberal Democrats, 'within whose ranks are many whose thoughts and instincts are very close to his own'. It would require at least two Parliaments to repair the damage done by the Tories, and Labour was unlikely to be able to win two consecutive terms on its own. In the meantime he warned Blair not to lead Labour any further down the road of embracing the free market. Good work had been done by Smith and Kinnock in jettisoning nationalisation and other left-wing policies. 'But the market cannot solve everything and it would be a pity to embrace the stale dogmas of Thatcherism just when their limitations are becoming obvious.'[81] Within hours of Blair's confirmation as leader Jenkins was already worried that Blair might take Labour too far to the right.

Jenkins was not alone in thinking that Blair's emergence changed the whole picture. Bill Rodgers and Shirley Williams were almost as quick to echo his enthusiasm, and over the next couple of years as 'New Labour' systematically ditched most of the last remnants of 'Old Labour' policies – towards Europe, defence, trade unions, the public sector, free markets and internal party structure – a steady stream of lesser figures who had defected to the SDP returned to Labour. Roger Liddle was just one who wrote to Jenkins explaining that he was rejoining Labour because Blair had re-created the excitement of the early SDP and he wanted to help. 'Hope this doesn't upset you too much. For most of the past quarter century I've regarded you as my political leader and mentor. It's because Tony is so clearly the man to carry forward the torch you've held high that I've determined on this course.'[82] Jenkins, Williams and Rodgers knew they could not do the same without letting down all those who had followed them into the Liberal Democrats. But they were all equally keen not to let narrow party allegiances obstruct the election of a left-of-centre government. 'We . . . are interested in Big Politics', Rodgers told Hugo Young only weeks after Blair's election (but after Roy and Jennifer had spent some days with Bill and Sylvia in Tuscany). 'Many Lib Dems are interested in Little Politics.'[83] It was awkward for the Lib Dems, having struggled for five years to establish their own identity, now to have their senior leaders openly praising the leader of a rival party, which called into question their very *raison d'être*. But from the moment he became leader in 1988 Jenkins had forged a close relationship with Paddy Ashdown. 'I hardly knew him at the time,' he wrote later. 'But I had the instinctive feeling that he had the stuff of leadership in him.'[84] Over the next five years, Jenkins as leader of the Liberal Democrat peers strongly supported Ashdown's leadership; so that in 1994 Ashdown needed little convincing to abandon the party's previous stance of 'equidistance' between Labour and the Tories and quickly threw his effort into positioning the Lib Dems as the junior partner in an informal anti-Tory alliance, as Jenkins had long advocated.* Jenkins now devoted himself to acting as a 'bridge' to bring Blair and Ashdown together. 'I think Tony treats me as a sort of father figure in politics,' he told Ashdown in October 1995. 'He comes to me a lot for advice, particularly about how to construct a Government.'[86] Nothing could have flattered Jenkins more than the opportunity to act – like Lord Melbourne with the young Victoria – as mentor to a young leader with no experience of government who was very likely to be the next Prime Minister.

That September – just before Blair's second party conference as Labour leader – Tony and Cherie lunched again at East Hendred, this time with two of their children (Euan and Nicky, then aged eleven and nine), with Edward and Sally Jenkins and their children making it a family occasion. Jenkins sent Tony away with an advance copy of *Gladstone*, which Cherie wrote the next day he had 'already started'.[87] This was the start of a deliberate strategy to get Blair to read some history, which as a law student he had barely done and now regretted.† Jenkins was keen to impress on Blair the idea that now gripped his mind: that whereas the division of the centre left between the Liberals and Labour after 1918 had allowed the Conservatives to be the dominant party for most of the twentieth century, a reunion of those forces – by means of an electoral pact, potentially leading to a coalition government and possibly even a merger of the two parties, reinforced

---

* Their only serious difference was over Jenkins' wish to have several of his old supporters like Dick Taverne, John Roper and William Goodhart raised to the Lords, whereas Ashdown was determined to nominate only those he believed would really contribute to the new party. All three eventually got their peerages, but the issue temporarily caused some tension between them.[85]

† Jenkins also got Ashdown reading *Gladstone*, so that he too became excited by the parallels between the fluidity of mid-nineteenth-century politics and the present.[88]

by proportional representation – would enable them in turn to dominate the twenty-first century, making the Tories the minority party. Blair was excited by this vision, and his enthusiasm was shared by some (but crucially not all) of his close allies, notably Peter Mandelson and the pollster Philip Gould. Both Mandelson and Roger Liddle in their 1996 book *The Blair Revolution* and Gould in *The Unfinished Revolution* (1998) made it one of the central planks of New Labour, explicitly acknowledging Jenkins' influence. Converting this ambitious vision into reality became known to Blair, Ashdown and their respective advisers as 'the project': their secret conversations were recorded in exhaustive detail in Paddy Ashdown's diaries, and a joint commission headed by Robin Cook (a rare supporter of PR on the Labour side) and Bob Maclennan for the Lib Dems was set up to look at possible areas of agreement on constitutional reform – not just PR, but devolution, human rights, freedom of information and House of Lords reform. The fatal trouble was that neither leader took his own party into his confidence. Most Lib Dems would probably have swallowed some arrangement in return for a definite commitment to proportional representation. But most of Blair's senior colleagues – most critically Gordon Brown, John Prescott and Jack Straw – wanted nothing to do with either the Lib Dems or PR. Over the next two years both Jenkins and Ashdown allowed themselves to be blinded by Blair's plausible assurances to the fact that he was never going to be able to sell the idea to his party.

In particular they persuaded themselves that Blair was serious about PR, when in truth he was never fully convinced. Jenkins simply could not believe that someone so sensible on most other subjects could fail to see the case for PR. In October 1995 he thought Blair's position 'rather "unthought-through" and "ill-considered"', but still believed he was 'moveable'.[89] 'I will do what I can to put pressure on him,' he promised Ashdown. 'It is a ridiculous position. He must realise how much is at stake here.'[90] Ashdown in turn convinced himself that 'the overwhelming majority of New Labour favoured PR' and that Blair recognised it as the key to securing a two-term government.[91] The next month, after lunching with Mandelson who assured him that Blair was indeed 'moving' on PR, Jenkins again told Ashdown that he 'would really press this matter home with Blair'.[92]

The fundamental problem, which Jenkins strangely failed to see, was that Blair, while wholly sharing his ambition to heal the Labour/Liberal divide to create a 'progressive' majority that would keep Labour in power for two or three parliaments, had no strategic interest in conceding proportional representation, which would only preserve the Liberal

Democrats' existence as a separate party. Blair frankly wanted to draw the Lib Dems into his 'big tent' in order to swallow them up – Labour supporters of 'the project' actually called it 'the hoover strategy' – whereas the Lib Dems had no wish to be swallowed, so they were bound to make PR their absolute condition for cooperation. The two parties' interests were in this respect incompatible.[93] That Jenkins failed to grasp this was not just the wishful thinking of an old man in a hurry. It was also consistent with the fact that he had always seen the SDP (and by extension the Lib Dems) as essentially a catalyst to the restructuring of the centre left, not as a long-term end in itself. Almost subconsciously, perhaps, while campaigning to break the mould, he had really always hankered to get back to the two-party system which had prevailed in his prime from 1945 to 1975 and previously in the High Victorian/ Edwardian period that he loved as a historian. Once, when Robert Harris asked if he thought Labour and the Lib Dems would one day merge, he replied unhesitatingly: 'Oh yes. Absolutely.'[94]

In January 1996, as part of his mentoring effort to prepare his pupil for the realities of government, Jenkins gave a dinner at Kensington Park Gardens to enable Blair and his chief of staff, Jonathan Powell, to meet the Cabinet Secretary, Sir Robin Butler, and four more top mandarins. Beforehand Butler sent Powell some background on those invited, who included two future Cabinet Secretaries, Andrew Turnbull and Richard Wilson, and Hayden Phillips, now Permanent Secretary at the Department of National Heritage. 'While I am entirely content to defend this occasion if necessary,' he cautioned, 'I hope it will remain private.'[95] 'I found it hugely interesting and even enjoyable!' Blair thanked Jenkins afterwards. 'I will get your ratings of the various people when we next meet – though I am not sure I was quite able to judge.'[96] 'It was an excellent opportunity for Tony to meet the key Permanent Secretaries prior to the opening of official contacts later this month,' Powell wrote. 'He was, as you could tell, impressed. Tony has also firmly registered your points about electoral reform.'[97] For his part, Jenkins thought Blair 'more impressive than some of the permanent secretaries' – though Jennifer more shrewdly sensed he was not really very inter- ested[98] – and hoped that he was indeed 'becoming convinced intel- lectually' on PR, though still afraid that it would split the Labour party.[99] Richard Wilson (then Permanent Secretary at the Home Office) wrote to thank Roy and Jennifer for a memorable evening, which could easily have been awkward. 'It was very good of you to take so much trouble to oil the wheels of the constitution and very helpful.'[100]

Of course the press did get to hear of it. Under the headline 'Traitor

Roy's Lessons in Leadership: Labour's most hated deserter is now teaching Blair how to run No. 10', the *Sunday Express* splashed a big story by Peter Oborne alleging that 'Twaiterous Woy, the pompous claret-sipping defector' had been seen mingling easily with New Labour at the launch of Peter Mandelson's book at the Reform Club. 'So enamoured has Mr Blair become with Lord Jenkins that he is now privately taking lessons from him in how to run the country . . . regular classes in the art of government.' An accompanying cartoon portrayed Jenkins as a schoolmaster (with mortar board and cane) and Blair as a schoolboy (in shorts and cap) in front of a blackboard saying: '1. Sign up to Single Currency. 2. Stamp on Unions. 3. Ditch the Left. 4. Drink Claret.' Labour MPs were said to be 'incredulous'. 'It is absolutely wrong for the Labour leader to be having the sort of relationship with a politician from another party – and it stinks that he is talking to scum like Roy Jenkins.' The number of double-defectors from the SDP like Liddle and Andrew Adonis now running Blair's office was taken as further evidence that 'Mr Blair plans to turn his party into an SDP Mark II'.[101]

The Permanent Secretaries' dinner was not repeated, but the social contacts continued throughout 1996 and into 1997. Tony and Cherie dined again at Kensington Park Gardens on 24 April and brought the children to another family lunch at East Hendred on 1 September; Roy and Jennifer dined with the Blairs in Islington in January. At first Jenkins was 'ebullient', telling Ashdown after their April dinner that Blair had told him 'three or four times' that he intended to include two or three Liberal Democrats in the Cabinet even if Labour won an outright majority; and (again) that he was 'moving towards PR'. While he acknowledged that selling it to the Labour Party might be difficult, 'I think he means it.'[102] In June he came up with a characteristic visual metaphor for Blair's historic task:

> He said he had formed an image of Blair, which he had described to him, that he was like a man with a very large, utterly priceless crystal bowl, condemned to walk miles and miles down slippery passageways, with events like the Harman affair [a controversy about Harriet Harman's decision to send her children to private schools] bowling around blind corners to knock him over. His role in history was to get to the other end without dropping the bowl. Blair had apparently laughed at this and said it was very accurate.

'I am not sure that he will make a great Prime Minister,' Jenkins told Ashdown. 'But I think of all the people I know in British politics I enjoy meeting and talking to him most . . . I can think of no other Prime Minister or possible Prime Minister who would be so self-deprecating – I find it rather attractive.'[103]

In August 1996 he sent Blair off to Tuscany with a pile of history books to read; and after their post-holiday lunch at East Hendred wrote to Ashdown that he had 'no doubt at all about his [Blair's] philosophical commitment to a radical centre strategy. It is the nuts and bolts which pose the problems, e.g. PR. But I think he will ultimately subordinate them to the wider strategy.'[104] In an interview with the Glasgow *Herald* in September he tried to play down exaggerated expectations, but set out the four minimal objectives he hoped to see from a Blair government: a better deal for the poor; improved public services; improved relations with Europe; and an end to single-party government.[105] By the New Year, however, the likelihood of the last was fading as Ashdown warned him that Blair was growing cool on the idea. Jenkins promised to talk to him – 'I know Roy's influence on Blair will be strong.'[106] But the morning after his dinner in Islington Jenkins reported gloomily: 'My brain did not seem to be working last night. Tony and I had a good dinner. But I am bound to agree with you that the project is not looking good. He feels he cannot now deliver what he promised you.'[107]

Others were coming to the same conclusion. Anthony Lester told Hugo Young that the Lib Dems were being 'hoodwinked' by the Cook–Maclennan commission, since Labour would give nothing on PR and was stubborn on House of Lords reform. 'A general disillusionment. Shirley almost wants to break off all talks. Jenkins, Rodgers, Cornford etc. etc. are all disillusioned.'[108]* When Jenkins tried to break the deadlock by raising publicly the goal of eventual merger, Shirley Williams quickly disassociated herself on the ground that such talk destroyed both the case for PR and the Lib Dems' bargaining power vis-à-vis Labour. He was entitled to his view, but she and Bill Rodgers should have been consulted. 'I appreciate that you feel much more at ease with New Labour than I do, and you know Tony Blair and I don't. I very much hope you are right. On the other hand, Labour's recent stances on Home Office bills aren't encouraging.'[109]

---

* James Cornford was a former politics professor, director of the Institute for Public Policy Research and a tireless campaigner for freedom of information and constitutional reform He was a special adviser in the first year of the Blair government, but soon became disillusioned and resigned.

Blair, on the other hand, thanked Jenkins for his 'excellent' speech, keen to assure him that 'the project' was still on course:

I hope all is well on the Lab/LibDem front. But the next few weeks are bound to be difficult as the parties fight each other on the ground. But the launch of the document [the Cook–Maclennan report] went well, I thought. Let us stay in touch and if anything is happening which concerns you, don't hesitate to call . . . Fingers crossed. I remain as committed as ever to what we both want to achieve.

Yours ever, Tony.[110]

Peter Mandelson wrote similarly a few days later: 'We've started well but there's a long way to carry our priceless vase across that slippery floor.'[111]

The same day Major finally called the General Election for 1 May. Jenkins again played little active part in the campaign. Richard Holme told Hugo Young that he would be used 'sparingly, on grounds of image' (whereas Shirley Williams would be used a lot); though Jenkins was going to do a rally in Harrogate – where Norman Lamont had sought refuge after his safe seat in Surrey was abolished – 'with much relish'.[112] He did one press conference with Ashdown and Steel two days before polling, where Ashdown thought him 'on wonderful form . . . dismissive of Blair in a light-hearted way. He said he had been disappointed "by Blair's timidity".'[113] Apart from that his main visibility (as in 1992) was appearing on BBC television three mornings a week during the campaign to comment as an 'Elder Statesman' with Norman Tebbit and Roy Hattersley (replacing Denis Healey) under the chairmanship of Robin Day. But his diary was as packed as ever with mainly non-political lunches, dinners, talks and meetings. In the penultimate week, for instance, he lunched with Nicko Henderson on Monday, Caroline Gilmour on Tuesday (followed by dinner at the Italian Embassy in the evening), Laura Phillips on Wednesday, Sir Robert Fellowes (the Queen's private secretary) on Thursday (with a speech to the Institute of Directors in the evening) and Robert Harris (in Oxfordshire) on Friday, topped off with a recording of *Any Questions?* (from Northamptonshire) in the evening. That weekend he worked on his next book in the intervals between lunching with Max Hastings on the Saturday and entertaining the Goodharts and Tickells at East Hendred on the Sunday. On the Monday morning he was back in the Elder Statesmen' studio in London at 8 a.m., followed by lunch with Ronnie McIntosh and a talk at the Bath Literary Festival in the evening, before driving back to London. Tuesday morning was his press conference with Ashdown and Steel, followed by Nancy Seear's funeral, lunch with Shirley Anglesey and a meeting of the Pilgrims' Trust in the early evening. On Wednesday morning he did his last 'Elder Statesmen' programme, then took the train to Glasgow, where he did a number of meetings in Hillhead, then on to St Andrews for an eve-of-poll rally for Ming Campbell. Finally back to London on Thursday for lunch with Leslie Bonham Carter, before Bill and Sylvia Rodgers came to Kensington Park Gardens to dine and watch the election results (until 3.15 a.m.).[114] And this was a man of seventy-six.

Like many others, he must have gone to bed immediately after the defeat of Michael Portillo in Enfield, which was announced at 3.10 – the moment that crowned the overwhelming rejection of the Conservatives after eighteen years. Labour won 418 seats (with 43 per cent of the poll), reducing the Tories to just 165 (from 31 per cent), while Ashdown's Liberal Democrats more than doubled their number to forty-six (from 17 per cent – though this was actually their lowest vote since 1979). The result clearly revealed an informal pact whereby Labour and Lib Dem supporters voted tactically for whichever was better placed to beat the Tory – just as Jenkins had hoped, but with no promises as to what should happen next. He was up again at 6.15 to write a quick piece for the *Evening Standard* and then meet Paddy Ashdown and Richard Holme to discuss what the Lib Dems should do in the new situation created by Blair's huge majority, as he no longer had any need of their support. Jenkins suggested that if Blair still offered a full coalition agreement, with at least two Cabinet ministers plus some policy changes like independence for the Bank of England, they should accept it, 'but if they didn't we had better not. Broadly, he was in favour.' But he later confessed that he would be relieved if Blair made no such offer – as of course he did not. He claimed to think that Labour's big majority might actually make it easier to work with them.[115] In his *Evening Standard* article he welcomed the scale of Blair's victory, despite his vague manifesto, arguing from history that great reforming governments – the Liberals in 1906, or Franklin Roosevelt in 1932 – were often elected on vague mandates. Unlike Wilson in 1964, Blair was lucky to face no immediate crisis. But Jenkins urged him to seize his opportunity. 'I would expect a cautious beginning with old Labour's dogma left well behind, and the hope that some green shoots of boldness may fairly soon begin to show.'[116]

For a year the mutual flattery continued. Jenkins used his newspaper columns to praise the government's first steps, while Blair kept on assuring Jenkins that he still wanted to bring their two parties closer together. They spoke on the telephone twice in the new government's first three days; and three weeks after the election Blair wrote to thank Jenkins for his good wishes:

> Of all the letters I have received, none has meant more to me. You have been an inspiration to me throughout. Yes, the vase arrived intact, but now I feel I am carrying a new one – altogether more valuable! Government beats Opposition. But I fear for when, as will inevitably happen, things get very rough. Incidentally we are proceeding on the Lib Dem front.[117]

What that meant was that a joint consultative committee was established to give the Lib Dems some unofficial input into the government's proposed constitutional reforms. (It soon turned out to be little more than a sop, however: it met only quarterly, achieved little and was wound up in 2000.) Three weeks later Jenkins and Ashdown dined with the new Prime Minister and Peter Mandelson (now a minister in the Cabinet Office) in the flat at Number Eleven Downing Street to discuss the way forward.* In another of his graphic images Jenkins compared the two parties to two teams of mountaineers on either side of the Alps, very close but separated by a formidable barrier. But on this occasion his talk of Labour and the Lib Dems forging a 'permanent and ever closer' relationship was too much for Ashdown, who was not interested in merging his party out of existence: he preferred the word 'durable'. Blair still professed to want to bring the Lib Dems into coalition eventually, and Mandelson and Holme were charged with drawing up a timetable. But Ashdown's immediate objective was still proportional representation. Before the election Blair had promised an inquiry into the possible options for electoral reform, and Ashdown now pressed him that Jenkins was the obvious person to chair it.[118]

In accepting this suggestion, Blair can have been in no doubt that Jenkins would recommend moving to some form of proportional system; while Jenkins made it clear that he would not accept the commission unless Blair practically promised him that he would act on his recommendation. Blair had some difficulty getting the commission's remit agreed by Jack Straw, the Home Secretary, who was 'opposed root and

---

The Blairs were living in Number Eleven, rather than Number Ten, because it had more space for their young family, leaving Number Ten to the then-unmarried Gordon Brown. Jenkins was thus going back to the flat where he and Jennifer had lived nearly thirty years before.

branch' to PR and tried to get 'proportionality' removed from its brief.[119] But eventually – in late October – he acceded to Jenkins' blandishments and overruled his Home Secretary. Relaying this to Ashdown, Jenkins became 'quite emotional', telling him that 'This is a very big event indeed' and complimenting Ashdown on the way they had worked together to achieve it. 'I think I can say that I have never enjoyed a closer or more constructive relationship in politics.'[120] A week later in Number Ten, in the presence of three officials, they thought they had definitely pinned Blair down to an irreversible commitment. Jenkins denied having said he would only take the job if Blair promised to accept his recommendation:

> I couldn't conceivably ask that of a prime minister. However, I don't want to take this on unless you have, at least, a strong dispos- ition to accept what I recommend. Ultimately, if you feel you must reject it you must do so. But I will want to know at the start that you are at least minded to accept.

Blair assured him that he was. As they walked back down Whitehall, Ashdown and Jenkins agreed that they had 'crossed a historic watershed'. 'We have got what we want,' Ashdown wrote in his diary. 'Just a little work to be done tying up the loose ends.'[121] When his chairmanship of an 'Independent Commission on the Voting System' was announced on 24 November, Jenkins believed that Blair would find it 'almost impossible now to turn down the recommendations of the commission'.[122]

He really thought he had been handed the opportunity to redesign the electoral system according to his own prescription. He had a good idea of what he proposed to recommend before he started, but he was determined that it should be a thorough and authoritative piece of work, so he took it extremely seriously and made sure he carefully considered all the possible options. It was not a one-man job: Blair and Straw gave him four colleagues to share the load, representing all parties but all broadly sympathetic to their 'proportional' remit. They were David Lipsey, once Tony Crosland's political adviser, now an *Economist* journalist; Baroness (Joyce) Gould, until recently Labour's director of organisation; Robert ('Bob') Alexander, a QC, former chairman of the Bar Council, now a Tory peer and chairman of the NatWest bank; and Sir John Chilcot, once Jenkins' private secretary in the Home Office, recently retired Permanent Secretary in the Northern Ireland Office. Jenkins himself gave up the leadership of the Lib Dem peers (after ten years) to focus on his task. He used all his diplomatic skill to bring his four colleagues along with him; but there was never any doubt that it was going to be his report. They were provided with an office where they met and with secretarial and research support by the Home Office; they invited written submissions from the political parties and other interested bodies, held public consultations around the country and made a number of journeys to study different electoral systems in other countries, including Ireland, Australia and New Zealand, though Jenkins did not himself go on all of these. In fact the only overseas trip he went on was to Bonn to study the West German system, which, he later wrote, 'had far more influence upon us than any other system'.[123] The report occupied him for the first nine months of 1998. During that time David Lipsey thought his 'stamina, humour, patience and drive would have been extraordinary in anyone; in a man of seventy-eight they were beyond belief'.[124]

Though they all contributed, Jenkins wrote most of the report himself: his first draft, completed in July 1998, comprised sixty-six closely handwritten pages. The result was exceptionally well written for a public document, enlivened by characteristic stylistic flourishes. ('Vintage stuff,' Andrew Rawnsley called it in the *Observer*, 'Grand Cru Jenkins 1998.')[125] It opened with a lucid exposition of the four 'not entirely compatible' objectives the commission was required to take into account:

(i) broad proportionality;
(ii) the need for stable government;
(iii) an extension of voter choice;
(iv) the maintenance of a link between MPs and geographical constituencies.

Fortunately none of these 'requirements' was absolute, so they had done their best to reconcile all four criteria. They were not, Jenkins insisted, 'being asked to impose a new electoral system on the British public':

What we are being asked to do is to recommend the best alternative system which will then be put to the British electorate in a referendum . . . The one proposition which is guaranteed a place upon the referendum ballot paper is the maintenance of the *status quo*. Our role is merely to recommend what the alternative should be.

While no system was perfect, 'some systems are nonetheless much better than others, and we have endeavoured to seek relative virtue in an imperfect world'.[126]

There followed a concise and readable account of the theory and purpose of representation and the virtues and increasingly glaring defects of first-past-the-post (FPTP), illuminated both from history and from Jenkins' own experience of the past forty years, followed by a brief examination of other, more proportional, systems used in other countries, rejecting most of them. Turning to possible alternatives for Britain, the report considered first the Alternative Vote (AV) and other systems that allowed the retention of single-member constituencies; then the Single Transferable Vote (STV) in multi-member constituencies; before making the case for a mixed system by which the majority of MPs would be elected in single constituencies by AV, topped up by a proportion – not more than one-fifth – who should be elected on a regional basis to ensure a broad parity between votes and members. This, the Additional Member System (AMS), came to be known as AV Plus.* The report was published with appendices providing dummy ballot papers and a map dividing the country into eighty large 'top-up' constituencies. It was not entirely unanimous: Bob Alexander insisted on including a reservation accepting the principle of AMS, but preferring that the constituency members should be elected by FPTP, not AV. But this was a detail.

Jenkins delivered, as he had intended, a powerful and authoritative case for major change. He disappointed the Electoral Reform Society and diehard Liberals who had long campaigned for nothing less than STV – the only fully proportional system – partly because the fourth criterion of his remit effectively required him to retain a majority of single-member constituencies. He recognised that AV was not proportional and could produce anomalies, but thought its defects could be compensated for by AV Plus, and did not believe that there would be a serious difference in esteem between the two types of MP. Nor did he accept that AMS was too complicated for the British voter to understand. He accepted that his recommendation was a compromise; but he was concerned more with political realism than with theoretical perfection, and judged that AV Plus was a system that Blair should be able to get the Labour party to accept, while retaining enough of the existing system to satisfy both Labour and Conservative traditionalists.

---

* This conclusion was very similar to that of the last inquiry into electoral systems, set up by the Hansard Society under the chairmanship of Robert Blake, which reported in 1976 and also opted for AMS.

At first Blair still gave out encouraging signals. In March 1998 he told Ashdown that the government would accept the Jenkins Report, 'provided it contains what we think it will'. At the same time, however, he said it would be 'a Cabinet decision which we will take together' – a pretty clear warning, in view of the known opposition of his most powerful colleagues.[127] In July – by which time rumours of Jenkins' conclusions were beginning to leak out – Mandelson acknowledged that the report would split the Cabinet 50:50, but reported that Blair was still confident he could 'bring them round';[128] and Andrew Adonis (now working in the Number Ten Policy Unit) told Jenkins that 'the electoral reform waters are starting to move fast'.[129] In the *Daily Telegraph* Boris Johnson – possibly to spook his mainly Tory readers – pretended to foresee 'The Final Twiumph' of Woy. After a lot of gentle mockery of his 'air of drawling, whiggish, Lafite-swilling, toff totty-chasing, *de haut en bas* benevolence', he suggested that everything Jenkins wanted to see was coming about. 'Wherever one looks, the political landscape is suffused by his froglike beam.' The Prime Minister was his faithful pupil:

And if proportional representation is endorsed, what a stunning triumph for Woy . . . If and when Britain joins EMU, the final piece of the Jenkins jigsaw will be in place; a liberal, devolved Britain, densely integrated into a federal Europe and with the constitution gerrymandered so as to keep the Tories out.[130]

It was not to be. Jenkins put the finishing touches to his report in Tuscany in August and presented it to Blair in September, still believing that he had come up with a politically acceptable middle way. But Blair was already warning Ashdown that he could not get it past the Cabinet: the best he could do was welcome the report, but postpone the promised referendum until after the next election. Ashdown correctly took this to mean that 'the project is dead in the water'.[131] Jenkins agreed that it was 'a very bad moment', but tried not to give up hope. Lunching with Giles Radice – who thought him 'a phenomenon' for his age: 'He still looks like a sleek and worldly porpoise, though his complexion is more claret-coloured than ever' – he was pleased with his report, but admitted to being worried about its reception: he wanted Radice to lobby for it, but Radice thought it too complicated.[132] He was not alone. As well as the dyed-in-the-wool defenders of FPTP, other commentators like the psephologist Peter Kellner in the *Evening Standard* dismissed it as an unholy mess:

Such a semi-proportional system will be difficult to sell to the electorate, for it looks like a fudge. There is a case for proportionality, and a case for a system that elects MPs for individual seats as now; but it is hard to detect a principled argument for a system that is not quite proportional and not quite constituency-based.

Giving people two votes, Kellner believed, would lead to 'utterly perverse outcomes', which would be bad for democracy. 'Lord Jenkins should think again.'[133]

When the report was finally published in late October, Blair duly thanked its author, but made it very clear that nothing was likely to come of it in the foreseeable future:

This is just the beginning. But at least now the advocates of change have a coherent proposition to argue for.

I've spoken to Paddy. I've said to him we have to build greater support within Government for the notion of cooperation and its value, first; & then construct the support for change. I'm sure that is right.

Meanwhile, again, thank you. It will be a great contribution to the reshaping of British politics in the way we want.

Yours ever, Tony[134]

There was some press support. In the *Observer* Andrew Rawnsley hailed the content of Jenkins' report as well as its inimitable style:

Roy, his prose as plummy as his complexion, begs to be teased. But his report is a work of high seriousness with the capacity to transform our democracy. Where most Government-commissioned tracts are dry and unpalatable, this is elegant and witty, full-bodied with metaphor and succulent with allusion, suffused with history, scholarship and common sense, and richly deserving of all the praise that has been lavished on its author.[135]

But for the most part it ran into the same sort of entrenched hostility to change that sank the AV referendum in 2012. In the Commons, Straw made no pretence of welcoming the report, but openly mocked it, 'playing to the Tory gallery' as Ashdown complained. Jenkins watched the beginning of the debate on television, but soon 'turned it off in disgust'. Ashdown protested to Blair, who apologised for Straw's

Willson, *The Times,* 26.10.98 (British Cartoon Archive, University of Kent)

'outrageous' negativity and promised to get Alastair Campbell to put out 'a strong counterspin'. But with 'an overwhelming majority of the Cabinet' now against any form of PR, Blair's warm words were worthless.[136] A few days later Blair and Ashdown issued a joint statement announcing continuing cooperation on constitutional reform; and over the following months Jenkins carried on promoting his scheme in articles and interviews, in public speeches and at private dinners – a fund-raising dinner for the Make Votes Count campaign at the Reform Club, dinner with leading businessmen at Brooks's – but he was bitterly aware that his baby was effectively stillborn.

In January 1999 Ashdown announced his resignation of the Lib Dem leadership after ten years in which he had brought the party from its fractious birth to the largest third-party representation for seventy years and a sniff, at least, of power. In the *Evening Standard* Jenkins paid generous tribute to him and denied that 'the project' had been a failure. New Labour, he claimed, had been most radical in precisely the area – devolution – where the Lib Dems had had most influence: proportional representation had been accepted as the method of electing the Scottish and Welsh Assemblies, the European Parliament and the Mayor of London, so that the retention of FPTP for Westminster alone had become increasingly anomalous. 'I am still hopeful that the October Report of my Commission will not be allowed to slumber for too long.' Meanwhile, if the government would only grasp the challenge of joining the euro – his next great cause – 'the fruits of the Ashdown policy will be plain for all to see'.[137]

His preferred choice for the succession was Ming Campbell, of whom he had always thought highly, probably thinking Charles Kennedy was still too young.* Ashdown was 'absolutely livid' with Jenkins for tipping Campbell off about his intention to resign so that he could declare his candidacy quickly.[139] But Campbell was not sure he wanted to stand – he had his eye on the Speakership, asking Jenkins to sound out Blair to see if it was a realistic possibility[140] – and in the end did not, so Kennedy it was. In a millennium article for the *Sunday Express* Jenkins wrote that Blair had lost 'an exceptional ally' in Ashdown and would now have to work out a new relationship with his 'different but highly talented' successor.[141] Kennedy was bound to pull back a bit from the close – if ultimately unconsummated – relations Ashdown had formed with Blair, but he hoped the Lib Dems would nurse no bitterness against the government. 'Charles takes things with calmness and humour,' he wrote in the *Independent*. 'There's quite a lot to be said for both qualities – and they're rather appealing to the electorate.'[142] It was still, he told a correspondent who asked him why he did not go back to Labour, 'the main remaining object of my life to promote a close Lib–Lab relationship'.[143]

To that end he made a point of cultivating several of the 1997 Labour intake whom he regarded as promising and congenial. There are in his papers a remarkable number of letters thanking him for lunch or other kindnesses. He wrote to congratulate the German-born (and then pro-European) Member for Edgbaston, Gisela Stuart, for instance, on her appointment to the government.[144] He declined to give an interview to Stephen Twigg's research assistant, pleading too many such requests. 'On the other hand I have a great interest in and admiration for you, and would like to know you better. Would you come and have lunch with me one day?'[145] (Twigg was chair of the Labour Campaign for Electoral Reform.) Other Labour figures with whom he maintained regular lunching relations were Giles Radice, Peter Mandelson (whom

---

* In 2002, when Campbell was close to leaving politics and applied to join the Scottish bench, Jenkins wrote him a fulsome reference. 'I . . . have the highest possible regard for his qualities, not only as a politician but in a much wider sense, including particularly his judgements on many aspects of human life. He is one of barely two handfuls of people throughout the world whose opinion I would value most highly.'[138]

he practically adopted as his political son and staunchly supported in all his political and personal difficulties) and Derry Irvine – whose expensive refurbishment of the Lord Chancellor's apartments in the House of Lords he publicly defended, even though he privately thought him 'arrogant (although with a fair amount to be arrogant about) and very politically unstreetwise'.[146] He was even reconciled to Roy Hattersley. But he remained on 'thoroughly bad terms' with Jack Straw.[147]

The postponement of any early prospect of PR, however, was just one of several areas in which New Labour disappointed him. Wearing his Oxford hat, he had hoped that the Blair government would bring a more positive attitude towards the universities; but it quickly appeared that its main concern was with attacking the 'elitism' of Oxford and Cambridge, maintaining the Tories' squeeze on funding while simultaneously announcing an unrealistic goal of enabling half the country's school-leavers to go to university. Jenkins was all in favour of widening access – never forgetting that he himself had got to Balliol from a very ordinary school in Pontypool – but he was an unrepentant believer in the national importance of maintaining the standing of the two ancient universities (and one or two others, such as Imperial College, London) among the top dozen in the world. One of the first acts of the new universities minister, Tessa Blackstone, however, was to announce that the government would no longer pay student support to the Oxbridge colleges, but henceforth only to the university. Jenkins immediately used his access to Blair to send him a 'stiff note' complaining about the lack of consultation, pointing out that the colleges were not all wealthy and that starving them would damage the whole ethos and quality of Oxford and Cambridge. Blair promised to look into the issue – 'My loins are now girded up. I shall see what I can do'[148] – and did impose some modification of the policy; but the colleges still lost about one-fifth of their income over the next ten years.[149] Jenkins protested to Blair again in May 2000 when Gordon Brown made a singularly ill-informed speech highlighting the case of a state-school pupil from Tyneside, Laura Spence, who had failed to win a place at Oxford despite having ten A★ GCSEs and four predicted As at A-Level, attributing it to 'old school tie' prejudice against the state sector. 'Nearly every fact he adduced,' Jenkins fumed in the House of Lords, 'was false.'[150] In an article in the *Mail on Sunday* he pointed out that Laura Spence was one of twenty-three candidates with equally good grades competing for five places. Which did Brown think Magdalen should have rejected to accommodate her? Oxford was already working hard to widen its social base and in the past five years had exactly reversed the private/

state-school proportions from 53:47 per cent to 47:53 per cent. Of course there was still some way to go. 'We just have to hope that the grandstanding over the last few days . . . will not set back the progress we are making to encourage the brightest and best candidates – whatever their background – to apply to this country's top universities.'[151]* Blair was embarrassed, and there was tacit acceptance that Brown had blundered; but six weeks later Jenkins still thought it 'intolerable that . . . no withdrawal or apology has been forthcoming from him or any other member of the Government'.[153]

While pleased by the swift introduction of Scottish and Welsh devolution and the creation of an elected mayor for London, he was unimpressed by the government's proposed reform of the House of Lords, which he thought half-baked and illogical. In December 1998 he emphatically denied a newspaper report that he now wanted to chair a commission on Lords reform. 'I completed the last task with relief,' he wrote to the editor, 'and one commission is more than enough in two years.'[154] Though he approved of the removal of most of the hereditary peers, he did not favour an elected second chamber that would rival the Commons, still less a partially elected one, as the government eventually proposed, which he thought 'a total nonsense'. Since joining the Upper House he had realised that it actually functioned a good deal better as a check on the executive than did the Commons, which had sunk so low in popular esteem that it was 'little more than an electoral college for the choice of the government of the day'. He would really have preferred a wholly nominated House, appointed not by the Prime Minister but by an independent body, with more cross-benchers and no guaranteed government majority.[155] (In 2000 he criticised Blair's 'shoal of not very distinguished nominations' – widely derided as 'Tony's cronies': 'Even if you leave out some of the more rococo edges of Harold Wilson's lavender list,' he wrote in the *Spectator*, 'I think they were better nominations than this lot.')[156] By 2002, however, he had come to the view that it was too late for a wholly appointed House. So in one of his last speeches in the Lords he argued for a small regionally elected House of no more than sixty to sit not in the present chamber 'with its gilt, its red and its flummery' but in 'a nice cosy utilitarian council chamber'. He confessed that he would personally rather the House could have stayed roughly as it was

---

* In July Jenkins lunched at Brooks's with Peter Lampl of the Sutton Trust, then as now the leading campaigner for wider access, who acknowledged that 'you have made real progress over the last three years', but thought there was still 'an opportunity to go further and faster'.[152]

with more restrictions on patronage. 'But I am sure that we should face the logic of one course or the other and not fish around in the ill-thought-out and muddled middle.'[157]

More generally Jenkins was disappointed by New Labour's illiberalism, as Blair and his successive Home Secretaries, Jack Straw and David Blunkett, tried to ensure that they could not be outflanked by the Tories on the right. Straw he judged to be no improvement on his predecessor, Michael Howard. ('He gives the impression that there is hardly a liberal bone in his body.')[158] More than thirty years after his own liberal heyday at the Home Office Jenkins reaffirmed his libertarian approach to social policy in the *Evening Standard* in March 2001:

> Libertarianism, which I define as allowing people to order their lives and choose their own patterns of behaviour – social, sexual, recreational – unless there is a clear case that by so doing they impinge upon the rights, not just the prejudices, of others, should be a central purpose of a radical government.

He was critical, among other things, of the government's restriction of the right to trial by jury, the 'emasculated' Freedom of Information Bill, Straw's failure to do anything about 'the appalling conditions in the prisons' and 'the kneejerk irrationalism of both major parties' avoidance of any sensible discussion of the law about cannabis'.[159] Personally he voted in the Lords for equalising the age of consent for gays and for repealing the notorious Clause 28 prohibiting the 'propagation' of homosexuality – unsuccessfully on both occasions.[160] But above all he condemned the government for wasting so much time and energy on trying to ban fox hunting to please some of its backbenchers. 'I am not a great fox-hunter,' he told Boris Johnson – perhaps unnecessarily – in the *Spectator*. 'I'm not a fox-hunter at all, but I believe even more strongly that if people want to do it, why the hell shouldn't they do it?'[161] 'If the unspeakable want to pursue the uneatable,' he wrote in the *Independent*, 'they should be free to do so . . . It shows an extraordinary order of priorities to push large numbers of people onto the wrong side of the criminal law on the basis of such a flimsy and socially divisive case.'[162] Banning hunting was 'a final act of illiberalism'. Even at a late stage in its passage through Parliament, he urged just before the 2001 election, it would be an act of statesmanship on Blair's part to abandon it.[163]

Despite these disappointments he remained determined not to lose faith in Blair's potential to be a great Prime Minister. Increasingly he believed – and asserted in innumerable articles and lectures – that the supreme test of Blair's historic calibre was whether he had the guts to defy the Europhobe Tory press and take Britain into the euro. This became the last great – and, as it now seems, doomed – mission of his final years. In *Gladstone* Jenkins had written that 'The frequent menace of old age is that it imprisons its victim in a departure lounge of life' – he credited the 'starkly memorable phrase' to Robin Day – 'awaiting with a mixture of apprehension and impatience the announcement that the aircraft is ready'; but that the aged Gladstone's belief that he had one last cause to fight 'was a tremendous prophylactic against senile futility'.[164] Seeing Britain into the euro was just such a cause for Jenkins as he neared his eightieth birthday as Irish Home Rule had been for Gladstone. Just as with electoral reform, he allowed himself to be too easily taken in by Blair's assurances that he really wanted to join. But as early as October 1997 he was already afraid that Blair was letting Gordon Brown control the timing, and he believed Brown's five economic tests were spurious. 'You are in great danger of having this issue of Europe undermine your government,' he warned Blair, 'just as it did for so many prime ministers before you, including Mrs Thatcher. But if you "seize this moment, then you can shape events and not have events shape you".' When Blair argued that public opinion was strongly hostile and he needed time to turn it round, Jenkins riposted that negative opinion polls could be turned around by clear leadership, as the pro-Marketeers had shown in 1975. 'Look, I will be very blunt with you on this. You have to choose between leading Europe or having Murdoch on your side. You can have one but not both.'[165]

'Tony Blair in my view undoubtedly has more instinctive European feeling than any of his predecessors since Edward Heath,' he wrote in 1998. 'But I hope that Mr Blair is not deceiving himself about the possibility of achieving a leadership role in Europe without full participation in its central activities . . . There is no getting away from the issue of the Single Currency.' It was going to happen, and there was no way that Britain could continue to enjoy the benefits of being in Europe while staying outside its defining project.[166] By early 1999 he was hopeful that Blair 'might at last be prepared to take on the tabloids' and go for it. He cited a poll showing that 'the overwhelming majority of the public have become convinced of Britain's inevitable participation in the single currency, and believe that this is already the Government's firm but unproclaimed intention'. But the government needed to make a positive case in order to win a referendum, which should have been held the previous summer when its public standing was at its highest.[167] That spring he travelled to Aachen to see Blair become the third British statesman (after himself and Heath) to be awarded the Charlemagne Prize for services to European unity – though it is far from clear what Blair had done to earn it; and two weeks later he told an audience in Dublin that he now expected the referendum to be held in 2001 or early 2002: with strong cross-party support from senior pro-European Tories like Kenneth Clarke and Michael Heseltine, he was confident it could be won.* Jenkins was still on flatteringly close terms with Blair and still believed he had his ear. In August he and Jennifer stayed with Tony and Cherie in Tuscany – where they were staying courtesy of Silvio Berlusconi – after which he wrote for *The Times* a characteristically unabashed defence of Blair's much-criticised acceptance of free holidays, which only followed the excellent precedent of Gladstone and Churchill:

> One of Tony Blair's wiser attributes is that he likes reasonably long holidays . . . He also has the attribute of liking going to rather sophisticated places. Tuscany and Gascony make a rather good pair of upmarket destinations . . . How much better than Disneyland or the Costa del Sol . . . Do we really want to be governed by pygmies in boarding houses in Bognor?[169]

In November he congratulated Blair on becoming a father for the fourth time (at the same age as Churchill).† 'After your generous hospitality in Italy we clearly owe you a meal' – maybe over Christmas – 'either *à quatre* or with a few other congenial people.'[171] But by the turn of the year – the turn of the century – he was becoming worried that Blair was going to let him down again. 'I have three great interests left in politics,' he told friends, 'the single currency, electoral reform and the union of the Liberals with Labour. And all three are languishing.'[172] In January 2000, lunching with Giles Radice, he was 'very depressed about Tony Blair's excessive caution about the euro'.[173] He was also critical of the *Guardian* for failing to make the case, writing to the editor, Alan Rusbridger, that it should be countering the 'fanaticism' of *The Times* and *Telegraph*, not wobbling around in the middle.

---

* After lunching with Jenkins in January 1998, six months after losing the Tory leadership to William Hague, Clarke had sent him a thank-you note, adding: 'I suppose events are now pushing you and me closer and closer together.' According to Ashdown, 'Roy thought this "very significant".'[168]
† Blair in return confided that he was 'much more fed up with the new baby than he lets on in public'.[170]

He called himself a 'fairly dedicated' *Guardian* reader, but was now wondering if he should not switch to the *Independent* as his third paper.[174] Writing in the *Independent* three weeks later he called the decision definitely to postpone joining the euro until Brown's 'famous but imprecise five conditions' were met 'the worst week for British European enthusiasts since Harold Wilson switched the Labour Party in 1971 against the policy of British entry that he had espoused in government, or even, maybe, since General de Gaulle vetoed Harold Macmillan's attempt at entry in 1963'. He publicly begged Blair to show some leadership or he would lose a lot of his cross-party liberal support, which was already disillusioned on civil liberties, the environment and electoral reform, but was still clinging to its hopes on Europe; and he gave the Prime Minister four pieces of advice:

> First, stop worrying about the result of the next general election . . . Second, regard popularity and high poll ratings, which you enjoy in rare abundance, as a springboard for resolute action and not as a store of value to be hoarded at all costs . . . Third, remember that the great Prime Ministers . . . are those who make the political weather and not those who skilfully avoid its storms and shelter from its downpours . . . Fourth, great administrations need to be based on a coalition . . . of support.[175]*

Doubtless he made all these points forcefully when Blair came to dinner at East Hendred again a few days later.

In April 2000, in an article comparing Blair's first three years with previous Labour governments, Jenkins judged it – Straw apart – not a bad record, but was only cautiously optimistic. 'It is unwise to tip the waiter until the meal is over . . . He has clearly shown himself a competent Prime Minister. Whether he will be a great one remains to be seen. But I am not unhopeful.'[177] A few weeks after this, however, there was a minor hiccup in their relations when Jenkins gave a wide-ranging interview to Boris Johnson, then editor of the *Spectator*, in which Johnson quoted Jenkins saying that Blair had a 'second-class mind': an apparent put-down gleefully taken up by the rest of the press. Jenkins immediately wrote to *The Times* to explain that he had been quoting Walter Lippmann's 'once famous remark about Franklin

* In the *Guardian* Roy Hattersley was delighted by Jenkins' loss of faith in Blair. 'I can think of nothing that will do more to restore grassroots support for Tony Blair than the knowledge that Roy Jenkins no longer regards him as his political heir . . . Roy Jenkins' dissatisfaction makes Labour look less like a cautious mutation of the SDP.'[176]

Roosevelt' – that he had a second-class mind but a first-class temperament, and the latter was more important – but should have known it
would be abbreviated and distorted.[178] He sent a copy to Blair with a
grovelling apology:

> I am sorry for the apparent discourtesy and indeed unfriendliness
> which, needless to say I hope, I do not feel. The fault was entirely
> in agreeing to do the interview with the clever and charming,
> but also bitchy and irresponsible Boris Johnson. Vanity, I fear, was
> my undoing. I thought that I could handle him (as I could have
> in a TV interview) but not be controlled the print [*sic*]. Even at
> my advanced age, there is much to learn.
>   Yours ever, Roy[179]

Blair rang to assure him that he had taken no offence. Jenkins' gaffe
was actually intended as high praise. He did not think first-class intel-
lects necessarily made good politicians – Tony Crosland being a prime
example – whereas Roosevelt was one of the towering figures of the
twentieth century. But he was mortified to be told by a *New York Times*
journalist that it was actually Oliver Wendell Holmes, not Walter
Lippmann, who had made the remark about Roosevelt[180] – especially
as he had once (in a 1973 lecture published in his *Gallery of Twentieth
Century Portraits*) got it right himself: an uncharacteristic lapse of
memory.[181]
    As the 2001 election approached he still hoped for a drawing together
of Labour and the Liberal Democrats. That summer two centre-left
'think-tankers,' Neal Lawson and Neil Sherlock, edited a book entitled
The Progressive Century: The Future of the Centre Left in Britain, which
explicitly sought to revive his pre-1997 vision. 'Roy Jenkins' famous
call for the strengthening of the "radical centre",' they wrote in their
Introduction, 'is at the heart of the progressive cause and his historical
analysis is the inspiration for this book':

> The challenge for the centre-left remains the same – how to unite
> the strands of social democracy and liberalism and give voice to
> a new social democratic liberalism that can dominate the twenty-
> first century.[182]

The two dozen contributors comprised a mixture of Labour and
Lib Dem politicians, including Robin Cook, Peter Mandelson, Ruth
Kelly and Stephen Twigg from one side and Paddy Ashdown, Chris

Huhne, Ming Campbell and Don Foster from the other, plus a clutc
of journalists and commentators including Polly Toynbee, Will Hutto
Steve Richards, Matthew Taylor and David Marquand. Jenkins contrib
uted a Foreword expressing his disappointment that the hopes of 1994–
had not been fully realised, but still hoping that Blair's second terr
might be 'much more adventurous and historically productive than h
first'. Prior to 1997 he had understood that Blair shared his vision t
make the twenty-first a 'progressive century': 'I do not believe that M
Blair has resiled from that intention.'[183]

But he played no part in the election. Two years earlier when Charle
Kennedy had asked him to undertake a Highland tour, he replied tha
his campaigning days were over:

> I think you most flatteringly forget how old I am . . . I do
> what I can to look after Oxford, get on with my writing, give
> political advice, but only when asked for, and to keep a benign
> eye on Bill [Rodgers'] success as my successor in the House of
> Lords. I also occasionally give a particular talk or lecture. But
> ground campaigning days – no. I think that in the 1980s and
> 90s I earned my retirement from that! Let us have lunch one
> day soon.[184]

The result was essentially a repeat of 1997. Labour was returne
with its massive majority over the Tories barely dented, while the Li
Dems under Kennedy gained a handful more seats, but not enoug
to change the balance between the parties. Blair no more neede
the Lib Dems than he had in 1997. In the *Evening Standard*, under th
headline 'Now Blair must take risks and be ready to offend', Jenkin
made one more plea to his erstwhile pupil – now that he had achieve
what had often seemed to be his central purpose, to be the firs
Labour leader ever to be elected for two full terms – to claim hi
place in history by *using* his newly confirmed power. Blair was, Jenkin
believed, 'intellectually convinced' that the euro was the crucia
question:

> If he can grasp the nettle, face and win a referendum, take Britain
> in and by so doing give us for the first time a voice as powerful
> for the future of Europe as that of Germany or France, then he
> will on this count alone have earned his place as a commanding
> statesman. But if he dodges the issue, lets Gordon Brown persist
> with his largely meaningless conditions (which are really just a

front for saying 'I and the Treasury will decide') then Mr Blair will be seen as joining the already too long column of fudgers and sludgers.

The other major issue facing the government was the quality of public services, and here Jenkins was true to his old Labour roots, insisting that they could only be improved not by privatisation and internal markets, but by spending more money, like the French (with their investment in high-speed rail transport) and the Germans (who spent 10.5 per cent of national income on health, compared with Britain's 7 per cent). He allowed himself a mild complaint that Blair had kicked his 'much worked upon and substantially unanimous report . . . firmly into the long grass'. But he came back to his central belief that the euro was the critical test of New Labour's second term.[185]

Privately, however, Jenkins had virtually given up on Blair. In July he had lunch with Peter Mandelson – now out of the government again, following his second enforced resignation, but still loyal to the Prime Minister.* Their exchange of letters over the next fortnight reveals that Jenkins' disillusion went far deeper than he let on in public. Over lunch Mandelson had defended Blair by reference to his problem with Brown, who was too powerful and successful (for the moment) at the Treasury to be overridden. 'When the economics move,' Mandelson wrote, 'so will Tony, and it will not be hard to manage the £ down when the time comes.' ('And do not underestimate', he added, 'the thoroughly malevolent influence of Ed Balls in *all* these matters.') Blair

---

* Jenkins had been a staunch supporter of Mandelson through his various troubles. After his first resignation from the Cabinet in 1998 (for accepting a loan from a colleague, Geoffrey Robinson, whose business dealings his department was investigating), Jenkins invited him to lunch and wrote a remarkable defence of his financial irregularities in the *Evening Standard*:

> We are . . . rapidly turning politics into a zero-sum game by which the prurience of the press and the apparent appetite for scandal of the public ensure that only the greyest of the grey and those whose interests are tightly bounded by politics will think it worth the constant threat of the searchlights of investigative journalism – almost like the knock of the secret police in the night – being suddenly turned upon them . . . Without question the present climate would have made it impossible for Disraeli, Gladstone and Churchill and many others of note and talent to have functioned in politics. Do we want an age of party apparatchiks, pygmies and eunuchs?[186]

After his second resignation in January 2001 (for allegedly using his position to influence a passport application) Mandelson thanked Jenkins for inviting him to his eightieth birthday party: 'Amid the gloom of my life at present, your birthday dinner greatly raised my spirits.'[187] And later that year he thanked Jenkins again for his advice, writing plaintively that 'I have almost no Counsellors of my own.'[188]

was fighting a mighty battle over public-service reform. 'It would not be wise (and not necessary) to fight a simultaneous war on both fronts with Gordon.'[189]

'I am tremendously impressed by your loyalty, in spite of everything,' Jenkins replied. 'But . . . I would be even more of a saint than you (which I am not) if I did not feel a deep sense of let-down.' He listed frankly the four remaining things he cared about in politics:

(i) Lib-Labery: the project as it was called. Now dead.
(ii) Electoral reform: even deader . . .
(iii) A liberal policy at the Home Office, where Straw is now widely regarded as having been no better than Howard. (To be fair Blunkett does show some signs of being keen to stand up to the police.)
(iv) Europe (which is really top of my list), I would be prepared to bet you a large sum that there will be no referendum this Parliament.

So you must excuse my language last week, although you were quite right to say that you would report it to Tony.

I have so far refrained from mentioning the Tube, which shows every sign of being a stubborn cock-up which will rival the Poll Tax.[190]

By the time of his death Jenkins had concluded that Blair had wasted his second landslide, as he had his first, and would not go down as a great Prime Minister. (He now ranked him merely 'between Wilson and Baldwin'.)[191] He did exercise some influence in one area of policy once more wearing his Oxford Chancellor's hat. In 1998 the government had introduced means-tested tuition fees for university students capped at £1,000 a year, replacing maintenance grants with loans. But Jenkins had become convinced – as he told the House of Lords in December 1999 – that the only way Oxford and other leading universities could maintain their standards was by charging higher fees.[192] This went against his lifelong belief in state provision; but in a climate of ever-falling government support for higher education he concluded that there was no alternative – there was a limit to how much could be raised from private benefactions – and set about convincing Blair. Here was one area in which Jenkins was reluctantly converted to market forces, and one on which Blair needed little persuading. Labour had gone into the 2001 election still promising no top-up fees; but within eighteen months this pledge was forgotten and a new ceiling of £3,000 was announced in January 2003 – though Jenkins would have liked to see the ceiling allowed to go higher still. But this was small beer compared with the heady vision of the mid to late 1990s when he had seen Blair as the man to carry through all the unfulfilled ambitions of his own career. He thought Blair allowed himself to be dangerously distracted by the 9/11 attacks on New York and Washington in 2001, and he would have hated, had he lived to see it, the disastrous decision to join in America's ill-conceived and irrelevant war in Iraq on the coat-tails of George W. Bush in 2003. Yet he still could not help liking the man, and he remained determinedly unbitter. He and Jennifer were due to dine with the Blairs over Christmas 2002. But by then Jenkins was too ill to go and they never met again.

All the while Jenkins never stopped writing. After *Gladstone* he did not immediately tackle another huge peak, but chose instead to write a collective biography of all the Chancellors of the Exchequer – nineteen of them – from Lord Randolph Churchill in the 1880s to Hugh Dalton in the 1940s. *The Chancellors* was a quintessential Jenkins project, never likely to excite his publisher, but just the sort of thing he loved doing, tracing what he called 'the river of British politics as it flowed from Gladstone to Attlee'.[193] The book gives full rein to his mania for classification, drawing biographical parallels and contrasts across the whole period from the late nineteenth to the mid-twentieth century, as if he knew each of his subjects personally and saw them as his peers: one can imagine him sitting round a dining table with them all, like the members of an exclusive club. The accumulation of a lifetime's study and experience of British politics, it is packed with shrewd observations and aphorisms, with a lot of sly digs at contemporary politicians and flashes of autobiography along the way – for instance, from the essay on Churchill's Chancellorship:

> A substantial minority of ministers are essentially supine. They take advice too slavishly . . . Then there is the middle group who sceptically query official advice but who end up [accepting it] . . . Those capable of both overcoming official opinion and of pushing ahead against the caution of colleagues are very rare.[194]

Jenkins would undoubtedly have included himself in this third category.

As in *Gladstone*, he manages to give the impression of close familiarity with both the gradations of the aristocracy and the topography of different parts of the country, sometimes in the same sentence: Michael Hicks Beach, for example, was 'the ninth holder of a baronetcy which dated from the first years of James I's creation of such a rank, and was well established in the triangle of good east Gloucestershire land between Cirencester, Lechlade and Bibury';[195] while Philip Snowden's Yorkshire birthplace 'epitomised the ability of Pennine villages, less than a thousand feet up, to give an almost Tibetan impression of being on the roof of the world. Snowden, like them, developed a habit of looking down on softer locations and weaker mortals.'[196] If there is an element of showing off in such comparisons, they do help to create vivid portraits of nineteen very different individuals. The book's limitation is that it was based almost entirely on the existing biographies, concisely summarised with Jenkins' commentary: where there was no biography, as in the case of Robert Horne – Lloyd George's Chancellor for eighteen months in 1921–2 – he had nothing to go on, so that essay is the shortest of the set at just nine pages.*

By the time *The Chancellors* was published in 1998 Jenkins was already planning his last and greatest mountaineering challenge. After Gladstone he wanted another big subject. 'I got rather hooked on absolutely major figures and I regarded most of the other possibilities . . . as being an anticlimax.'[199] The idea of tackling Churchill had probably already planted itself in 1994 when he reviewed Martin Gilbert's single-volume abridgement of his multi-volume official biography, which he read while attending a three-day Churchill conference in Texas. He complained that – at nearly 1,000 pages – it was too big. 'To hold it, particularly in bed but also in an armchair, is like trying to read through *Who's Who* on a beach picnic. Only a solidly constructed desk can comfortably bear its weight.' But he also felt that Gilbert's book had 'a certain lack of novelty and perspective', which must have sparked the thought that he could do better.[200] Later that year he attended another Churchill conference in Edinburgh, where he criticised 'this new school of revisionists who are so anxious to denigrate him' – specifically Clive Ponting ('dreary obsessional nonsense'), John Charmley

* 'Sir Robert Horne,' Jenkins characteristically began this essay, 'was a Chancellor whom it is easy to forget.' During the Hillhead by-election he was asked by an elderly voter who was the last Chancellor to have represented the seat. 'He was bowling me the equivalent of a long-hop, and I, whose mind is excessively cluttered with the minutiae of political careers, totally fluffed it.' The answer was of course Horne.[197] Jenkins committed another howler by describing Sir Kingsley Wood (1940–43) as the only Chancellor to die in office – forgetting, as a reader pointed out to him, Iain Macleod. 'Forgetting Macleod, who was my "shadow" and immediate successor, is as amazing as it is inexcusable.'[198]

(who 'argues a false case in a way that is nevertheless worth reading') and Andrew Roberts (whom he thought 'too keen on getting headlines' by quoting Churchill out of context). 'But while I reject, and as time goes on rather contemptuously reject, all these denigrations, I do not believe . . . that Churchill should be treated too reverentially.'[201] Here was the starting point for his own book.

He was slightly worried that Mary Soames, Churchill's surviving daughter, might not approve; on the contrary, she jumped at the idea of 'another Liberal study of my father', following too many that portrayed him as a reactionary Conservative.[202] He was also encouraged by Andrew Adonis – the young ex-SDP academic-turned-journalist now working in the Downing Street Policy Unit, who had become his latest confidant/adviser (in the mould of David Dowler, John Harris, Matthew Oakeshott and Hayden Phillips – he always needed one) while providing a useful link to Blair. He had no doubt of the magnitude of the challenge he was taking on. 'Yes,' he wrote to Raymond Bonham Carter, 'I am rashly attempting Mount Churchill. I envisage it very much as a companion volume to Gladstone – full life, same length. I have few no [*sic*] new sources – mainly an attempt at a new interpretation.'[203]* But he reckoned there was 'at least ten times' more existing literature about Churchill than about Gladstone. Another difference was that he had known Churchill, if only slightly, having been introduced to him by his father in 1941 and having overlapped with him in the House of Commons for sixteen years; as a young man he heard two of Churchill's wartime speeches from the public gallery. More important there were, in a modest way, several parallels between his own career and Churchill's. Not only had he held two of the same great offices, as Home Secretary and Chancellor, but he too was a writer/politician who had supported his family all his life by his books and journalism as Churchill did. Jenkins too had switched parties – though in his case only once. *The Times* even pointed out that they both suffered from mild speech impediments.[204] And there was another similarity. 'I was . . increasingly struck by Churchill's extraordinary combination of an almost puritan work ethic with a great capacity for pleasure, even for self-indulgence. I found that combination rather attractive'[205] – for the obvious reason that it mirrored his own 'hedonistic calculus'. 'I understand Churchill better than I did Gladstone,' he confessed in one of

---

* Raymond, a banker with S.G. Warburg until disabled by a botched operation in 1979, was the brother of Mark Bonham Carter and Laura Grimond, and father of the actress Helena Bonham Carter.

the dozens of lectures and interviews he gave after the book came out;[206] so that having previously pronounced Gladstone to be 'the most remarkable specimen of humanity' ever to have been Prime Minister, he ended up revising his opinion:

> I now put Churchill, with all his idiosyncrasies, his indulgences, his occasional childishness, but also his genius, his tenacity and his persistent ability, right or wrong, successful or unsuccessful, to be larger than life, as the greatest human being ever to occupy 10 Downing Street.[207]

After five months' preliminary reading, starting in the autumn of 1998, Jenkins wrote the whole book – in his tiny longhand – in a little over two years. By contrast with Churchill's small army of researchers, he had no assistance apart from one student who checked references for him. Once started, his method was to read up his sources a chapter or two ahead of where he was in the writing ('I am in front of the troops but not too far in front'), meticulously recording his progress as he went along.[208] Over Easter 1999 he wrote 15,800 words in 69¼ hours over twelve days, a rate of 229 words an hour; over Christmas/ New Year 1999 into 2000 another 34,000 words in twenty-three days. That summer he broke the habit of a lifetime by staying at East Hendred through August, 'writing hard', and going to Italy – where he still wrote every day – only in early September (missing the Lib Dem conference). 'After nearly 7 decades,' he apologised to Tom McNally, he and Jennifer felt that they had 'discharged our conference obligations, and this year we shall be in Italy'.[209] By now he was up to 1944, but he had just got to the Normandy landings when he fell ill; he had to spend three weeks in hospital (10 October to 1 November) having a heart bypass operation, complicated by a lung infection, which was nearly fatal, followed by another three weeks of 'rather difficult convalescence'.[210]* He appointed Adonis to finish the book for him if he were unable to complete it. In fact he recovered to write another 80,000 words – the last eight chapters – in two months between December and February

---

* His surgeon was supposedly the best in London, but he was 'not particularly strong on bedside manners', Jenkins wrote later. 'He came to see me a week after the operation looking worried. I asked if he thought I was very ill. "It could go one way or the other," he said. It was difficult to go to sleep after that.'[211]

During his three weeks in the Wellington Hospital he read nineteen books, including Alan Clark's diaries, Michael Heseltine's and Mary Warnock's memoirs and Max Hastings' *Overlord*, and reread several Anthony Powells. He received dozens of letters, including one from the Queen, and after the first week a stream of visitors.

2001, working five to seven hours a day, including 1,076 words on Christmas Day. By any standards this was a remarkable work rate. For a man just turning eighty it was phenomenal.

The book turned out to be little shorter than Gilbert's (the same number of pages, though the print is bigger), but much more readable – even though some of the writing is as baroque, the penchant for French phrases as pretentious and the metaphors, if anything, still more extended than in *Gladstone*: by this stage in his life Jenkins really needed a firmer editor than Macmillan provided. It was not, as he acknowledged, in any way original, except in one respect: the space he gave to Churchill's always precarious finances and the incessant journalism he needed to take on to maintain Chartwell and his extravagant lifestyle. But it was a magisterial work of synthesis in which, having absorbed all the existing literature, Jenkins used his own experience – both of high politics and of living by his pen – to weigh judiciously all the controversies of Churchill's career. After his criticism of the Charmley/Roberts school of revisionism it was no surprise that he broadly defended Churchill's conduct in most of them. This was his first venture into military history (if one discounts the 1914–16 chapters of *Asquith*). He sought advice in this area from Max Hastings, who told him, for instance, that he was too generous to Churchill over the ill-fated Dardanelles campaign of 1915: it was the almost unanimous view of military historians that the objective could never have been achieved with the forces made available, and Churchill should have realised this.[212] Jenkins half-accepted this, and added a grudging sentence to that effect; but generally he was reluctant to change what he had written. He once told Hastings that if he wanted a different sort of book he should write it himself.[213]*

Churchill was published in October 2001, with a lavish launch party at the National Portrait Gallery, and was the publishing hit of the year, selling 100,000 copies in hardback before Christmas.[215] Jenkins carefully noted the reviews – more historians and fewer friends this time, though the latter still included John Grigg in *The Times* – and graded them for favourability: in the eleven major papers he classified six as three-star and four as two-star, giving a score of twenty-six out of a possible thirty-three. The young revisionists were as laudatory as his old friends. 'Macaulay himself could not have done a better job,' John Charmley wrote in the *Guardian*;[216] and Andrew Roberts in the *Sunday Telegraph* hailed 'a first-class, well-sustained work of history and a masterpiece of

---

* Some years later Hastings did just that, and dedicated his *Finest Years: Churchill as Warlord, 1940–45* (2009) 'to the memory of Roy Jenkins and our Indian summer friendship'.[214]

biography – by far the best of Jenkins' 19 books . . . as much a work of literature as of history . . . To have written this splendid book at the age of 80 in only a little over two years is a simply astonishing achievement.'[217] 'Do we really need another life of Winston Churchill?' Robert McCrum asked in the *Observer*, and answered: 'Yes, if it's as magnificent as this study by Roy Jenkins.'[218] There was only one bad review, by the always acerbic Frank McLynn in the *Independent on Sunday*, who found it 'a grave disappointment' for lacking a point of view, ducking all the controversies and simply assuming Churchill's greatness. 'Aiming for balance,' he concluded, 'Jenkins achieves blandness.'[219] But his was a lone voice.

Before publication Jenkins wrote to the publicity director of Pan Macmillan: 'You will, I am sure, bear in mind that although not seriously diminished I like to think, I may not be up to quite such a strenuous schedule as we did for Gladstone six years ago.'[220]* But he still promoted his book at most of the major literary festivals – Cheltenham that October, Richmond in November, Charleston in May (preceded by lunch with Jim Callaghan) and Buxton in July (staying with Roy Hattersley) – and gave numerous other talks up and down the country. Since his operation, however, he was not allowed to travel alone, so Jennifer (or sometimes Leslie Bonham Carter) now always accompanied him. He also did a promotional tour in the United States, which included an event at the United Nations in New York and a dinner at the British Embassy in Washington hosted by the ambassador, Sir Christopher Meyer, and attended by Hillary Clinton, Robert McNamara and Karl Rove, among others. By the time of his death, not much more than a year later, sales in Britain and America had reached half a million; the American edition alone earned him $300,000. *Churchill* failed to win any prizes – it was shortlisted for the Samuel Johnson Prize, but lost out to Margaret Macmillan's account of the Treaty of Versailles – but nevertheless it made an amazing climax to Jenkins' literary career (and there were still two short books to come).

In these final years the pace of Jenkins' social life barely slackened. He kept up assiduously with old friends and contemporaries, going out of his way to mend relationships where they had been broken, and still making new friends in a constant round of lunches, dinners and weekends. 'How much more agreeable it is,' Jim Callaghan wrote

---

* But he refused to fill in a publisher's questionnaire for promotional purposes. 'It is exactly the sort of nonsense I have declined to answer for 80 years . . . and I am now much too old to change my habits.'[221]

to him in 1998, 'now that we can write to each other to express our genuine feelings now that the passions and frustrations of ambition have not only died down but have been broadly satisfied – in both our lives.'[222] 'After twenty years,' Roy Hattersley wrote, 'it seems that we are friends again, and that gives me real pleasure.'[223] He had become estranged from Woodrow Wyatt in the years when Wyatt had been an ardent confidant of Mrs Thatcher; but now Wyatt wrote recalling their 'jolly days' in the 1950s playing tennis with Tony Crosland and issuing 'our dramatic ultimatums to dear Hugh . . . You have always had a very special place in the furniture of my mind. Though sometimes we seem to disagree on politics I think we don't really do so very much *au fond*.'[224] When he knew he was dying, Wyatt asked for Jenkins to deliver the address at his memorial service, which he was delighted to do. Jenkins was also one of the few people to visit Harold Wilson in his sadly confused last days and wrote generously, even affectionately, about him in reviews of both the Ben Pimlott and Philip Ziegler biographies and in newspaper tributes on his death in 1995, greatly softening his often harsh criticism in the past.*

In his role as wise old cross-party elder he wrote equally generous letters of sympathy to former opponents when they were down: to Michael Heseltine after his heart attack in 1993; to Kenneth Clarke on losing the Tory leadership to William Hague in 1997; and to David Mellor on the loss of his seat in the same year. 'I received many charming letters following my demise,' Mellor wrote back, 'none as pithy and perfectly delivered as yours. You said it all in thirty words. I am really touched that you should write to me and in these terms.'[227] He even had John and Norma Major to lunch at East Hendred. When Neil Kinnock – that once-militant anti-Marketeer and scourge of the SDP – was appointed a European Commissioner in 1995, Jenkins invited him with Glenys to lunch at East Hendred to advise them about life in Brussels;[228] and when William Hague, after resigning the Tory leadership, was planning his biography of Pitt the Younger, Jenkins gave him 'valuable advice . . . in the highly appropriate surroundings of Brooks's Club'.[229] He took a similar interest in other young authors writing their first books – for instance, Adam Sisman, then writing a biography of A.J.P. Taylor, and Ruth Longford, who was writing the

---

* Marcia Falkender (the former Marcia Williams, with whom he had always got on well) wrote to thank Jenkins for his kind words about herself in his review of Ziegler's 'rather feline' biography of Wilson. 'If only we had won in 1970,' she lamented, '– or even lost in 1974!!'[225] At the same time Ziegler also thanked him for his 'generous' review of his book. I'm glad that you didn't find my treatment of her unreasonable.'[226]

life of her grandmother, Lloyd George's secretary/mistress Frances Stevenson. To these and many others who wrote to him for advice he showed extraordinary kindness. He turned down most requests for interviews, often PhD students asking about the 1960s, Europe or Bletchley, but he made a lot of exceptions for one reason or another, and always replied courteously and often interestingly even when he refused, scribbling his reply on the letter for his secretary to type up. He took extraordinary trouble to reply to every query, unless they were abusive; but always refused to fill in questionnaires, often sending correspondents a copy of one of his books instead.

His diary was increasingly punctuated by birthday celebrations and memorial services as his friends passed successive milestones or passed away: Isaiah Berlin's eightieth, Mark Bonham Carter's seventieth, Madron Seligman's seventy-fifth, Frank Longford's ninetieth, Nicko Henderson's seventy-fifth, Ludovic Kennedy's eightieth, Ted Heath's eightieth, J.K. Galbraith's ninetieth. This last was at Harvard, but most of the rest Jenkins hosted at either Brooks's or Balliol. Among those at whose memorial services he delivered an invariably felicitous address were Mark Bonham Carter ('my closest all-round friend'),[230] Solly Zuckerman, Laura Grimond, Gladwyn Jebb, Christopher Mayhew, Leo Pliatzky, Edwin Plowden, John Harris and Madron Seligman. Before Harris' service at St Margaret's, Westminster, he told the vicar that he would not need a rehearsal because he knew the pulpit all too well.[231] His encomium of Zuckerman was typical to the point of self-parody:

Everything to do with Solly was of the highest quality . . . Only he could produce Château Cheval Blanc 1961 and the Queen for a small country dinner party at his Norfolk flintstone house with his collection of early Sheffield plate upon the table and his conversational style which combined omniscient reminiscence with an optimistic interest in the future.[232*]

But he had made many younger friends too, among them the journalist-turned-bestselling-novelist Robert Harris. They met in 199? when Jenkins reviewed Harris's thriller *Enigma*, set in wartime at Bletchley Park – positively, despite some quibbles – and the publisher invited him to the launch party. Jenkins was then seventy-five, Harris thirty-eight, but they formed an immediate bond: Harris lived near

* In a Foreword to John Peyton's biography he wrote that 'No-one but Solly ever invited me to a country dinner *à cinq* with the Queen and Prince Philip.'[233]

Hungerford, just the other side of the M4 from East Hendred, and over the last seven and a half years of Jenkins' life they lunched together around 100 times at various favourite pubs between their two homes – lovingly listed in Harris' memoir of their friendship: 'the Blue Boar at Chieveley, the Harrow at West Ilsley, the Royal Oak at Yattendon, the Red House at Marsh Benham, the Fish at Sutton Courtenay, the White Hart at Hamstead Marshall and a large number of other congenial establishments spread around Oxfordshire and West Berkshire'.[234] Harris loved Jenkins' conversation and his positive attitude to life:

> He practised conversation . . . as an art form from a golden age, in the way that Evelyn Waugh once defined it: the apt joke, the shared confidence, the mutual building of a privately shared fantasy. His memory was prodigious, and he was generous in sharing it . . . But, for all his stories, and despite his age, he never passed into anecdotage . . . He would talk about the past, but he refused to live in it: he was always eager for the latest gossip, or to discuss the latest book or film . . . We would exchange news about publishing, publicity, sales figures, translations. Comparisons of daily output was a more contentious matter, since his was always so much greater than mine. He would return from a week's holiday and announce that he had added another 10,000 words: he produced three books to my one. And yet I do not think I had a friend who took a livelier interest in what I was writing.[235]

'I admire almost more than anything else about him this capacity . . . to get on with people thirty or forty years his junior,' Harris wrote in 1998. 'He is 78 next week, appears in good health, has phenomenal energy and mental stamina, but so many of his contemporaries are dead and dying: he must sense the gathering shadows . . . I guess this is why he likes to see me.'[236] At one of their last lunches, four years later, Harris found him in unusually low spirits. 'I've suffered rather a blow today,' Jenkins confided. He had heard that morning that Caroline Gilmour had cancer. 'Caroline is clearly the great love of his life, after Jennifer,' Harris realised. 'She was the one,' Jenkins told him. 'I didn't pursue it. There wasn't much I could say.'[237] Caroline actually outlived Roy, but only by a year.

Another new friend, slightly older but also conveniently within driving distance, was Max Hastings. As a young Tory journalist in the 1980s Hastings had covered the Hillhead by-election and taken a fairly satirical view of Jenkins; but when he got to know him a decade later he changed his mind and became devoted to him. Whereas Harris and Jenkins would usually lunch together in a pub, Hastings and his wife became friendly with Roy and Jennifer as a couple and they would lunch more often in each other's houses. In 2001 it was Hastings who hosted a dinner at Somerset House for Jennifer's eightieth birthday, attended by all the leading figures of the heritage industry, who lauded her work with the Historic Buildings Council and the National Trust;* and since Roy's death Max and Penny Hastings have continued to look after Jennifer, taking her to the theatre and twice on safari to Kenya. During Roy's lifetime there was some rivalry between Hastings and Harris about which was his favourite. But in 2000 they planned together to take Roy and Jennifer to Paris by Eurostar for his eightieth birthday, offering him a choice of two restaurants, which he found 'excruciating':

The Palais Royal plush elegance of the Grand Véfour I know but have not been to for nearly twenty years. A return visit would be very attractive. On the other hand L'Ambroisie is unknown and tempting and its three stars and Place des Vosges location very enticing. So I end up by weakly leaving it to you.[239]

In the event his illness intervened, but they went in April instead, staying at the British Embassy and dining at L'Ambroisie, where Harris reckoned that the food and six bottles of wine cost not far short of £2,000.[240]

A third, even younger friend was Andrew Adonis, whom Jenkins appointed in 1998 his official biographer – a remarkable act of faith considering the importance he attached to biography and the fact that Adonis had never written anything of the sort.† But having done so, he took Adonis closely into his confidence. 'When you put posterity in my hands, as it were,' Adonis wrote, congratulating Jenkins on his birthday, 'I had no idea that we would see so much of each other; still

---

* 'She was among the first to see conservation in the round, as a matter of whole areas and villages and towns and cities, rather than solely as a matter of grand old houses,' Hastings declared. 'She said briskly from the beginning that she was not in the business of handing out money to impoverished aristocrats.' Similar speeches were made by Sir Neil Cossons (English Heritage), Sir Angus Stirling (ex-National Trust), Marcus Binney (Save Britain's Heritage), Sir Jocelyn Stevens (ex-English Heritage) and Simon Jenkins, all emphasising Jennifer's immense contribution in their field.[238]
† Jenkins had previously considered Anthony Howard and David Marquand, and once hinted to Robert Harris that he would have liked him to do it. Harris declined to take the bait.[241]

less that we would become such friends. It has been one of the great pleasures of the last 2 years to me. It might even lead to a better book.'[242] So it might have done; but Adonis got drawn so deeply into government under Tony Blair and Gordon Brown that he eventually passed the project on.

Roy and Jennifer continued to entertain prodigiously at East Hendred, mixing old and new friends eclectically together. 'It was like turning up to a tutorial at a professor's house,' one guest, Tina Brown, recalled after Jenkins' death, 'and finding in the small garden a convivial little band of living legends, mixed with the younger critics, historians and novelists he collected and the invariable visiting American enjoying a pre-lunch Martini.'[243] It is invidious to take any particular company as typical; but to take just two examples, on 14 March 1994 it comprised the architectural historian and diarist James Lees-Milne and his wife, with Clarissa Avon (Anthony Eden's widow) and Jenkins' then publisher Roland Philipps and his wife; and on 23 July 1997 the historians David Cannadine and Linda Colley (both then in their forties) with the former chief government statistician Sir Claus Moser with his wife, and Donald and Elsa Macfarlane from Hillhead. In 1997 Jenkins noted that they held no fewer than fifty-five of these lunch parties at East Hendred – but only five dinners, which were usually for old friends who were staying, like Ronald and Doreen McIntosh, the Angleseys or the Macfarlanes. Altogether they entertained 257 people that year, with Roy at the head of the table pouring an abundance of superb claret, while Jennifer – with help from a local woman – supervised distinctly plain and exiguous food. You lunched at East Hendred for the wine and the conversation, not for the food.

Jenkins' own eightieth was spoiled by his illness. The major event was to have been a dinner at the Reform Club organised by Bill Rodgers, Celia Goodhart and John Grigg on 13 November 2000, two days after his actual birthday. Jenkins only reluctantly accepted, a few days before going into hospital in October, that it would have to be postponed. He was out of hospital and sufficiently recovered to have a family lunch party at East Hendred on the day (and watch *The Jewel in the Crown* on television in the evening). The dinner was then rearranged for 7 March 2001, when it was attended by 118 guests comprising practically the whole of the liberal establishment (Paddy Ashdown called it 'the project at dinner').[244] There were very few Tories – Ted Heath, Madron Seligman and Peter Carrington – and few Labour: just Peter Mandelson, Derry Irvine and Giles Radice. (Tony Blair was invited but could not make it: he promised a dinner at Chequers instead, but this never took place. 'It's rather like his approach to electoral reform or joining the euro,' Jenkins complained. 'No follow through.')[245] But there was a wide range of others from every period of Jenkins' life, from his boyhood friend, Hugh Brace, to his current secretary Gimma Macpherson with her husband, and his Harley Street heart specialist and his wife. There were twelve tables and Jenkins himself carefully composed the seating plan, placing Marie-Alice de Beaumarchais again on his left and Jean Kennedy Smith (sister of Jack, Bobby and Ted Kennedy) on his right, with Henry Anglesey, Thomas Bingham, Derry Irvine, Iona Carrington and Penny Hastings at the same table. On Table 2 Jennifer was flanked by Ted Heath and Arthur Schlesinger; Charles, Cynthia and Edward each hosted a table, while the other seven were headed by John Grigg, Paddy Ashdown, Celia Goodhart, Bill Rodgers, Ming Campbell, Crispin Tickell and Jeremy Hutchinson. Caroline Gilmour and Leslie Bonham Carter were both on Table 12 (the closest to Table 1), with Laura Phillips, Liz Stevens, Peter Carrington, Nicko Henderson, Dick Taverne and Peter Mandelson. Bill Rodgers acted as master of ceremonies and John Grigg, Shirley Williams and Arthur Schlesinger (with a message from J.K. Galbraith) spoke, before Jenkins made a 'refulgent' reply, elegantly accepting the praise of his devoted friends.[246] It must have been difficult not to think of Toad's speech at the end of *The Wind in the Willows*.

A more ambiguous view of his life's achievement was voiced in an ironic birthday tribute by Hastings' successor as editor of the *Daily Telegraph*, Charles Moore – Margaret Thatcher's official biographer – who saw Jenkins as (after Mrs Thatcher) 'the second most successful British politician of modern times', since he had seen most of what he had believed in come to pass. Britain was now irreversibly a 'liberal' society in his meaning of the word, in Europe and governed by a Labour government not dominated by the trade unions. This, Moore suggested from his High Tory perspective, was all due to Jenkins more than any other single person: 'True, the whole thing is pretty ghastly, and far from the "civilised" polity he wanted. But that is not because of any personal failing: it is simply because he is, by and large, in the wrong.' On this argument Moore should perhaps have made Jenkins the *most* successful politician of modern times; alternatively he should have blamed Mrs Thatcher for the state of the country. Even he, however, could not help acknowledging Jenkins' Trollopian integrity:

In persona, though clearly self-regarding and *de haut en bas*, he is also amused, self-critical, unbitter and detached. He is one of the few retired senior politicians who do not seem warped or broken by the career they have chosen.[247]

By now Jenkins had almost given up regular reviewing. But he still made an exception for books he wanted to read or authors he wished to help – for instance, he asked to review the posthumously published fourth volume of John Grigg's biography of Lloyd George in February 2002; and late that year he agreed to review a book on the Asquiths for the *Sunday Telegraph*. But he was still writing compulsively himself and still planning new books. In September 2000 – while still writing *Churchill* – he agreed to write the entry on Harold Wilson for the new *Dictionary of National Biography*, a major undertaking of around 12,000 words for which he reread both Pimlott and Ziegler. (He also contributed several shorter DNB entries, on Dilke, Tony Crosland, Mark Bonham Carter and David Harlech, though he declined several other subjects, including Woodrow Wyatt.) In 2001–2 he wrote the Introduction to a new edition of Churchill's *History of the English-Speaking Peoples*; another for a Folio Society volume on the 1980s; and a short essay on Churchill and France for a book on the centenary of the Entente Cordiale; as well as a still considerable output of occasional journalism.

His first book idea to follow *Churchill* was a semi-autobiographical study of European–American relations illustrated from his own experience of the Kennedy administration and his time in Brussels, to be called – fancifully – *The Bermuda Triangle*. In a draft prospectus he admitted that his lifelong love affair with the United States had not retained its 'pristine enchantment' in recent years, nor was he impervious to the 'frustrations and pettiness' of Europe; but he still believed it important to try to bridge both the Atlantic and the Channel and had had great pleasure over the years in trying to do so.[248] This project he abandoned, however, in favour of what he called 'a very lightweight book . . . on 12 cities which have either been intertwined with my life or have peculiarly aroused my interest and enthusiasm'.[249] This gave him the excuse to revisit several of his favourite places, with Jennifer or various friends, in order to write about them. The *Twelve Cities* of its title comprised three British (Cardiff, Birmingham and Glasgow), two American (New York and Chicago) and seven European (Paris, Naples, Bonn, Brussels, Dublin, Barcelona and Berlin). It is an exceptionally self-indulgent book: a rambling, digressive mixture of autobiography, name-dropping, architectural description and potted history, held together only by Jenkins' amateurish enthusiasm. Like *The*

Chancellors it is characterised to the point of self-parody by his compulsion to classify and compare everywhere by reference to somewhere else, assuming that the reader is a well-travelled man of the world like himself, familiar with all the places he cites as points of comparison. It is quite engaging in its way, but a book for connoisseurs of Jenkins' late style only. It was published in the autumn of 2002 to reviews that were generally more polite than enthusiastic.*

Before he finished that, he had agreed to revisit an old ambition by writing 'a 50,000 word booklet' on Franklin Roosevelt for a series on US presidents being edited by Arthur Schlesinger.[252] His last book, *Franklin Delano Roosevelt*, was actually rather tauter and less self-indulgent than some of its predecessors. But twenty years earlier he had backed off Roosevelt because he thought there was nothing new to say about him; and what interest this late essay contains lies less in what it says about Roosevelt than what it says obliquely about Jenkins himself. His fascination with FDR's family background and American class distinctions is characteristically overdone; but most intriguing are his reflections on Roosevelt's infidelities within what was nevertheless a strong marriage. First, he doubts whether Eleanor 'ever experienced any intense heterosexual desire, even at the height of her commitment to Franklin'.[253] As a result, some of their friends thought it 'amazing' that Franklin did not 'stray' earlier. 'However, stray he did, not casually but romantically and in an underlying sense not temporarily but to the very end of his life.'[254] Eleanor's discovery that he had a mistress – 'which sophisticates like Alice Longworth thought she should certainly have been expecting in view of the contrasting attitudes to relaxation and pleasure between

---

* Craig Brown wrote a wonderful parody in *Private Eye* entitled *Twelve Tube Stations*, which mocked Jenkins' orotund style to perfection. 'I first saw Totteridge and Whetstone when I was, I fancy, but fifteen years of age . . . I make no claim for it as a rival to, say, the sheer magnificence of the Place Vendôme in Paris, or, for that matter, the extravagant neo-Gothic of the Plaza de Colón in Madrid. It is set, a trifle clumsily, in surroundings that are not one must confess, greatly conducive to the pleasures of the table or, indeed, the amenitie of social intercourse. Neither High Barnet, its more northerly neighbour, on the far from undistinguished Northern Line, nor Woodside Park, its somewhat less trumpeted southern companion, offers overwhelming reasons for stopping. But Totteridge and Whetstone ha always possessed for me a certain creaky charm.' Or again, of Warren Street: 'It is not perhaps, a first-rate station, still less a second-rate station, but as the lower third-rate station go, I have always considered it ranks really rather high; if not at the very top, then quite near the upper-middle.'[250]
Jenkins enjoyed this so much that he wrote to thank Brown for it and even took credit for suggesting it. Jennifer found the postcard on his desk after his death. 'Dear Craig, I am glad you acted on my assurance to you . . . that Twelve Cities was infinitely parodiable. much enjoyed your Private Eye, thought it very funny, unwounding and even affectionate Yours ever, Roy Jenkins.'[251] This must have been one of the last things he ever wrote.

herself and her husband ... did not destroy the marriage ... but it changed its nature':

The relationship had never been physically passionate, although on Eleanor's side it had been deeply romantic ... Thereafter it became a powerful political partnership, but almost a limited liability one.[255]

Here Jenkins could have been writing about his own marriage. And again, weighing the possibility that Franklin had a second girlfriend at the very end of his life: 'It might ... be a mistake to assume that Roosevelt, who could keep so many political balls in the air at one time, would have found two ladies (plus a wife) an impossible challenge.'[256]

Then, in the last pages he wrote before he died, Jenkins included some unusually specific detail about FDR's heart disease and the remedies prescribed to control it:

Eventually it was agreed that he should take digitalis, cut back his smoking to six cigarettes a day, eat less, and take a short, sharp bout of exercise after lunch. He did as he was told, but never asked a question. Perhaps he did not want to know; perhaps he trusted fate, or God; perhaps he did not care.[257]

When he wrote this, Jenkins did not know how close to death he was himself; but he certainly knew that he had many of the same symptoms and might not have very long. For years Jennifer had been trying to get him to eat and drink less. He occasionally went on the wagon or limited himself to white wine (which he never thought really counted); he sometimes went without dinner; and he was diligent about taking carefully recorded quantities of exercise. But he refused significantly to compromise his lifestyle; he chose to enjoy his life rather than seek to prolong it by eschewing his pleasures. He had no expectation of an afterlife and his attitude to death was much the same as Roosevelt's.*

'Roy glows with the happy certainty of a life well-lived,' John Mortimer wrote in a late profile in the *Sunday Times*.[259] Donald Macintyre, interviewing him for the *Independent* in the autumn of 2002,

---

When in hospital near the end Jenkins had a supply of half-bottles of claret smuggled into his bedside. His son Edward suggested that rather than a statue or a scholarship, if anyone wanted to create an appropriate memorial they should endow a scheme to provide half-bottles to all patients in NHS hospitals.[258]

equally found him to be 'an inspiritingly undisappointed man'.[260] When John Major asked him over lunch if he ever regretted not having been Prime Minister, he was tempted to ask if Major regretted that he had been.[261] Likewise he refused to regret the SDP. 'One, we came near to spectacular success. That was worth the effort even though we did not quite achieve it. Two, I do not think that the Labour Party would have been dragged back from the wilder shores of lunacy without the shock of the SDP. I had higher hopes than that but at the lowest, we achieved that.' One regret he did admit to was the inability of himself, Tony Crosland and Denis Healey to work together in the 1970s to keep the Labour Party from lurching left in the first place. This was the theme of a group biography of the three of them entitled *Friends and Rivals*, published by Giles Radice in 2002. Jenkins thought the book 'fair and generous' and did not dissent from its thesis: he accepted that it had been difficult for the other two, both slightly older than him and arguably better qualified, to accept him as leader, in the way that people like Douglas Jay and Frank Soskice in the previous generation had accepted Gaitskell. He thought his failure to gain their allegiance was 'as much a criticism of me as it is of them'. Having initially described Crosland as 'an immensely close friend', he paused and corrected himself. 'No. I was an immensely close friend of his. He was the senior partner, that was the trouble. That's the parallel with Brown and Blair.'[262]

He watched the falling-out of Blair and Brown with some sympathy for the latter, despite his decisive role in keeping Britain out of the euro. Jenkins thought Brown had done well, 'admittedly in favourable circumstances', in maintaining a strong economy, and he was entitled to be ambitious. 'Most senior politicians tend to be motivated by a good deal of personal ambition. They wouldn't be senior politicians if they weren't. So I don't bitterly criticise him for that.' But Brown would now do better to settle for having been a dominating Chancellor rather than a 'tail-end Charlie' Prime Minister. There was 'an incredibly strong pattern' of Prime Ministers coming at the end of a long period of government by their own party being an anticlimax: Rosebery after Gladstone, Chamberlain after Baldwin, Eden after Churchill, Home after Macmillan, Major after Thatcher – 'and I wouldn't exempt Jim Callaghan after Wilson'. 'I rather wanted to be PM,' he reflected, 'and I suppose I would have been a tail-end Charlie.'[263]

He was dismayed by Britain tagging along behind the Americans' disastrous slide towards war in Iraq, which was the subject of his last speech in the Lords on 24 September 2002. He still professed his 'high regard' for Blair and was 'repelled by attempts to portray him as a vacuous man with an artificial smile and no convictions', which reminded him of 'similar attempts by a frustrated Right to suggest that Gladstone was mad, Asquith was corrupt and Attlee was negligible':

> My view is that the Prime Minister, far from lacking conviction, has almost too much, particularly when dealing with the world beyond Britain. He is a little too Manichaean for my perhaps now jaded taste, seeing matters in stark terms of good and evil, black and white, contending with each other, and with a consequent belief that if evil is cast down good will inevitably follow. I am more inclined to see the world and the regimes within it in varying shades of grey. The experience of the past year, not least in Afghanistan, has given more support to that view than to the more Utopian one that a quick 'change of regime' can make us all live happily ever after.

He worried about the Americans' 'vast preponderance of power and feeling that this gives it a right and a duty to arbitrate the world' without reference to international opinion or the United Nations, and questioned the connection between Saddam's alleged 'weapons of mass destruction' and the atrocities of 9/11. 'When we have embarked on a policy of taking out undesirable regimes by external armed force,' he asked, 'where do we stop?'

> There are a number of regimes which either have or would like to have nuclear weapons. I, and I guess the majority of your Lordships, would much rather they did not have them. But it would be difficult to justify a policy of taking them out seriatim with either common sense or international law.

'I am in favour of courage,' he concluded, 'but not of treating it as a substitute for wisdom, as I fear we are currently in danger of doing.'[264] These were his last words in Parliament.

That autumn he made his last foreign trip, taking the Eurostar to Brussels on 8 October, where he stayed the night at the British Embassy before going on by train to give a Churchill Memorial lecture in Luxembourg the next day, followed by a reception and dinner; then on to Zurich to speak again about Churchill at another dinner, after which he and Jennifer spent a week together in Venice before flying home. He also spoke at an Enigma conference at Christ Church and to a Barclays private clients' dinner, where he was 'a huge draw' and delivered a 'magisterial treat'.[265] At the end of October there was a dinner at the Athenaeum marking the centenary of the Order of Merit, followed next day by a service at the Chapel Royal and lunch at Buckingham Palace attended by most of the surviving members.* A few days later Jenkins wrote to thank the Queen for a 'splendid celebration' and the 'great privilege' of sitting next to her for part of the time. 'Looking back I am, if I may say so, greatly impressed by your benign buoyancy on what cannot have been a very easy day.' At the very end of his life the boy from Abersychan could even patronise Her Majesty; and he did not waste the opportunity for a little self-promotion: 'As you were kind enough to allow me to meander on for several minutes about my little book on Twelve Cities, I thought that I might be permitted to send you a copy in the hope that one or two of them might catch your eye.'[267]

Ten days after this he had a recurrence of heart trouble and had to go back into hospital, regretfully cancelling several more engagements, among them dinner with the Churchill Society of Toronto, from where he had been planning to go on to Montreal and New York. He was booked to appear on *Any Questions?* on 6 December, but had to cancel. On the 16th he lunched for what turned out to be the last time with Robert Harris. 'Mentally he was as sharp as ever, but physically he was manifestly ailing, hoarse-voiced, and walking with the aid of a stick. He said he was going into hospital straight after Christmas for electric shock treatment on his heart, and then immediately changed the subject.' They arranged to meet again in the New Year.[268] His last public act, just before Christmas, was to join with Geoffrey Howe, Peter Carrington and Douglas Hurd to sign a letter protesting at *The Times*' refusal to publish a pro-euro letter from eleven retired ambassadors (organised by Nicko Henderson) in response to an anti-euro one they had published previously.[269] He was still working six or seven hours a day to finish *Roosevelt* and reading as voraciously as ever. Among the last books he read were Orlando Figes' *Natasha's Dance*, Garret FitzGerald's *Reflections on the Irish State*, Bernard Williams' *Truth and Truthfulness* and a complex French novel (*A Life's Music* by Andreï Makine), all newly published, plus Anthony Powell (again) and Elizabeth Jane Howard. On Christmas Eve he sent Tony Benn a postcard praising

---

* Two years earlier Jenkins had been asked to advise on whether Tom Stoppard or Harold Pinter should be awarded the honour. He opted narrowly for Stoppard, 'but only after warning the Palace that Pinter would go wild with rage'.[266]

his latest volume of diaries.[270] On 3 January 2003 he lunched with Michael Sissons at the Hare and Hounds in West Hanney to talk about his next book, which was to be nothing less than a full-scale biography of President Kennedy. Sissons had no sense that Jenkins felt he might not live to write it. But two days later, on Sunday 5 January, Jennifer rang to say that he had died at nine o'clock that morning.[271] It was an enviably painless passing. His last words to Jennifer were to ask for 'two eggs lightly poached'. When she came back with them he was gone.[272]

He died at a good time for maximum coverage. Monday morning's newspapers did him proud. *The Times* put an almost quarter-page Gerald Scarfe caricature on the front page and most of the other papers had large photographs and tributes, with more inside from a variety of writers (Anthony Howard, Ben Pimlott, Robert Harris, Roy Hattersley) in addition to the formal full-page obituaries tracing his long career. Both the *Telegraph* and the *Guardian* called him 'the grand-father of New Labour'; even the *Daily Mirror* mourned 'a great Liberal, a great European and a truly great man'; and all gave prominence to Tony Blair's tribute: 'He was a friend and a support to me and someone I was proud to know as a politician and a human being . . . I will miss him deeply.' In the *Evening Standard* Max Hastings confessed frankly: 'I adored him'; while David Owen wrote warmly of happy times before their differences over the SDP and latterly over Europe, with an ambiguous conclusion:

> Roy died a fervent believer in a depth of integration that I continue to question. If he does get his wish posthumously, he will have played, for good or ill, a bigger role in reshaping the fate of Britain than any other Prime Minister or Cabinet Minister in the 20th century.[273]

The most dissenting note in the general chorus of admiration came from Denis Healey on the front page of the *Independent*, who praised Jenkins' first period at the Home Office, but went on to blame him unequivocally for letting Mrs Thatcher dominate the 1980s ('The SDP did not create New Labour: it delayed it') and ended with a typical final put-down: 'The problem . . . was that his judgment was not as sharp as his intellect, and that for him so many issues were matters of principle.'[274] Over the following days others recalled the Roy they had known. Alan Watkins in the *Observer* lamented that 'We shall not see a luncher of his like again.'[275] Ferdinand Mount gave a sharp twist to the same theme:

> I too have been lunched by Roy Jenkins . . . There can scarcely be anybody within a hundred miles of Westminster who has not at one time or another passed the hours between one and three in Lord Jenkins' company, at Brooks's or the Caprice or the Blue Boar at Chieveley.

But Mount questioned his enduring legacy:

> It feels rather like one of those fairy stories in which the hero's three wishes all come true but none of them delivers the expected delights . . . But Roy Jenkins was never one for the backward glance. As far as second thoughts went, he was irretrievably out to lunch.[276]

A different verdict was voiced by Vernon Bogdanor in the *Observer*, noting that 'the tone of the obituaries . . . has been almost uniformly elegiac, as if the causes for which he stood were those of the past'. On the contrary, Bogdanor asserted, 'Nothing could be more wrong.' Behind his Whiggish manner Jenkins was throughout his career 'both radical and contemporary':

> Roy Jenkins was the first leading politician to appreciate that a liberalised social democracy must be based on two tenets: what Peter Mandelson called an aspirational society (individuals must be allowed to regulate their personal lives without interference from the state); and that a post-imperial country like Britain could only be influential in the world as part of a wider grouping (the EU) . . . Jenkins was the prime mover in a form of social democracy which, being internationalist, is peculiarly suited to the age of globalisation and, being liberal, will prove to have more staying power than the statism of Lionel Jospin or the corporatist socialism of Gerhard Schroeder.[277]

Nothing in the decade since his death has contradicted that judgement.

The funeral was a low-key, informal occasion on the Friday following his death – 'a quintessentially English winter day, bone cold and damp'

Austin, *Guardian,* 6.1.03 (British Cartoon Archive, University of Kent)

– at the parish church of East Hendred, barely a hundred yards from St Amand's House, followed by refreshments (hot soup and sausages, but also, the papers noted, claret) in the village hall.[278] The fifty-minute service was conducted by the vicar and the Dean of Christ Church; Charles Jenkins gave an affectionate address emphasising the family man, not the statesman; and Cynthia and Edward both read lessons. Tony and Cherie Blair slipped in unobtrusively, 'with no handlers, aides or cellphones in sight', and stayed chatting for an hour; the rest of the congregation of about 300 included most of Jenkins' closest friends and longtime political allies: Bill and Sylvia Rodgers, Bob Maclennan, Charles Kennedy (Shirley Williams was away). Both Caroline and Leslie were there, of course; Jennifer, bare-headed, seemed to Tina Brown 'almost preternaturally calm'. The message on her flowers read simply: 'To Roy, my only love. 62 years and 5 months'.[279]

Two days later the *Mail on Sunday* splashed a large double-page spread headlined 'Woy, the Gweat Lothawio', illustrated with colour pictures of Caroline, Leslie, Lee Radziwill and a youthful Roy. 'Apart from an inability to pronounce his Rs,' it suggested, Jenkins was best remembered as 'one of the architects of the Swinging Sixties . . . blamed by some for the increase in promiscuity. But the full story of his own promiscuity has never been told – until today.' Only Lee Radziwill was actually specified as a lover, with the claim that she preferred 'portly, bespectacled' Roy to 'the young, strutting Mick Jagger at the peak of his sexual allure'. Caroline was quoted insisting that 'we were just good friends, no more'. But Leslie, Ann Fleming, Marie-Alice de Beaumarchais, Marietta Tree and even Shirley Maclaine were all named – most of them wrongly – in the context of his 'string of affairs' over three decades. 'He liked them to be beautiful, well bred, wealthy and intelligent – and had a special fondness for Americans. Some met all five requirements.' The article quoted Jenkins' evasive responses to Michael Cockerell's questioning on television in 1996; and finally suggested that he was 'fascinated by the sex lives of politicians of past ages' and in his books 'went into great detail' about Dilke's 'three-in-a-bed romp', Asquith's love letters to Venetia Stanley and Gladstone's picking up of prostitutes.[280] A few days later the *Daily Mail's* gossip columnist, Nigel Dempster, tracked down Lee Radziwill and quoted her – under the headline 'Why Women Wanted Woy' – saying that it was his 'fascinating mind' that attracted her. ('He could talk about anything with authority and could quote nearly anyone. Men like that are rare and such a pleasure to spend time with.') But she too denied that there was anything more than that.[281] After this flurry, however, the story died away and has scarcely been revived. Scandals usually flourish only when an aggrieved party spills the beans or seeks revenge. Jenkins conducted his affairs within a close circle of mutual friends. He adhered to two principles: first, that one should conduct affairs only within strong marriages; and second, that he could never love anyone who was not also very fond of Jennifer.[282] As a result, he did not leave a trail of broken hearts or broken marriages behind him and neither his lovers nor their husbands had any interest in talking to the press. He was not ashamed of his *amitiés amoureuses*, and would not have wanted his biographer to omit them. They were a very important part of his life. But as there was no scandal in his lifetime, neither should there be in death.

There was a memorial service at Westminster Abbey in March. Tony Blair asked to give the address, but to the relief of some family members he was in Washington for a meeting with George Bush, seven days after launching the assault on Iraq. Had he done it, he might have had to speak positively about electoral reform and the euro from the pulpit. But at short notice Shirley Williams spoke instead. It was a solemn state occasion, as Tony Benn characteristically described in his diary:

It was the British establishment en masse. I cannot think of a better description. Ted Heath was there. Jim Callaghan was there. The Dean of Westminster conducted the service. There was a choir of course. Bill Rodgers read something. Nicholas Henderson . . . read something. Shirley Williams delivered the address, which was a perfect account of Roy's life . . .

It was the memorial service of a Roman emperor, a man who had great talent, a great capacity for friendship, great charm, wildly ambitious, and who believed in maintaining the Establishment and the power of the Establishment, first in Britain and then in Europe. He split the Labour Party, which had made him what he was, and deserted it for the SDP. But he was friendly to me, liked the *Diaries*, was fond of Caroline [Benn's wife] and I knew him a long time, so I'm glad I went.[283]

The last few pages of *Roosevelt* were finished by the American professor Richard Neustadt – Shirley Williams' second husband – and published first in New York that autumn and then in Britain by Macmillan in 2004. It was Jenkins' twenty-second published title over a writing life of fifty-five years. He did a lot else besides, and left an enduring mark on British life and politics; and yet the best of his books – *Asquith, Gladstone, Churchill*, possibly *Mr Balfour's Poodle* and *Nine Men of Power* – may still be read long after his political achievements are forgotten or taken for granted.

He was buried in the village graveyard in East Hendred. On his gravestone Jennifer chose the simple epitaph:

ROY JENKINS
1920–2003
WRITER AND STATESMAN

In the end he would probably have been happy with that order of words.

Notes

Chapter One: His Father's Son

1. Interview, Denis Healey, 24.7.08
2. Leo Abse, *Private Member*, pp.34–6
3. Alan Watkins, *Brief Lives*, p.73
4. Roy Jenkins, *Twelve Cities*, p.2
5. *Daily Herald*, 27.4.46
6. *South Wales Argus*, n.d. See also Chris Williams, 'Arthur Jenkins', in the *Oxford Dictionary of National Biography*
7. Kenneth Harris, *Attlee*, p.58
8. *Kelly's Directory of South Wales and Monmouthshire*, 1920
9. Arthur Jenkins' diary, 11–14.11.20 [Jenkins papers]
10. *Sunday Express*, 5.11.72 (Drusilla Morgan)
11. ibid.
12. ibid. (Pita Karaka). Connie Peppin married D.F. Karaka in 1946 and Indianised her name.
13. ibid. (Derek Powell)
14. ibid. (Peggy Moseley)
15. ibid. (Derek Powell)
16. Pita Karaka, 'Youth', in Andrew Adonis & Keith Thomas, *Roy Jenkins: A Retrospective*, p.5; interview, 1982.
17. Pita Karaka, 'Youth', op. cit., p.4
18. Jenkins, *Twelve Cities*, p.205
19. *Spectator*, 3.8.96
20. Jenkins, *Twelve Cities*, p.191
21. Hugh Brace, 'Youth', in Adonis & Thomas, p.9
22. *Sunday Express*, 5.11.72 (Kathleen Tuck, née Tuttle)

23. ibid.
24. Jenkins, *Twelve Cities*, p.25
25. ibid., p.3; *Sunday Times*, n.d. 1998
26. Jack Branch to Roy Jenkins, 16.2.93 [Jenkins papers]
27. *The Times*, 31.8.26
28. ibid., 23.9.26
29. Arthur Jenkins' diary, 23.11.26 [Jenkins papers]
30. *The Times*, 29.11.26
31. House of Commons, 8.12.26 [Vol.200, cols 2115–16]
32. Abse, p.34
33. Watkins, p.73
34. Pita Karaka in Adonis & Thomas, p.5
35. Douglas Bence & Clive Branson, *Roy Jenkins: A Question of Principle?*, p.47, quoting Terry Coleman interview
36. Jenkins papers
37. Interview, Ivor Bulmer-Thomas, 26.5.82
38. Roy to Arthur, 9.4.30 [Jenkins papers]
39. Roy to Arthur and Hattie, 6.10.30 [Jenkins papers]
40. Norman Edwards to Roy Jenkins, 27.5.96 [Jenkins papers]
41. *Greenlands News*, 4.7.31 [Jenkins papers]
42. ibid., 4.3.33 [Jenkins papers]
43. Roy Jenkins, *A Life at the Centre* [hereafter *ALATC*], p.14
44. Hugh Brace in Adonis & Thomas, p.8
45. *Spectator*, 24.6.00
46. Jenkins papers
47. Article for *Daily Telegraph*, 29.8.95 [Jenkins papers]

48. Article for *Sunday Telegraph*, 10.10.93 [Jenkins papers]
49. *Sunday Express*, 5.11.72 (Peggy Moseley)
50. Hugh Brace in Adonis & Thomas, pp.8–9
51. Jenkins, *ALATC*, p.23
52. Jenkins, *Twelve Cities*, p.54
53. Speech to the Newport Model Parliament, 1949 [Jenkins papers]
54. Journal, 1–2.2.35 [Jenkins papers]
55. ibid., 5–6.12.35 [Jenkins papers]
56. ibid., undated [Jenkins papers]
57. Hugh Brace in Adonis & Thomas, p.8
58. Arthur Jenkins to Roy, 11.11.37 [Jenkins papers]
59. Article written for Cardiff University centenary volume, 1982 [Jenkins papers]
60. David Newsome to Jenkins, 12.2.94 [Jenkins papers]
61. Jenkins to Balliol College admissions tutor, 3.11.37 [Jenkins papers]
62. Balliol admissions tutor to Jenkins, 19.11.37 [Jenkins papers]
63. *Sunday Times*, n.d. 1998

Chapter Two: David and Jonathan

1. *Observer*, 24.7.88
2. Ronald McIntosh, 'Balliol', in Andrew Adonis & Keith Thomas, *Roy Jenkins: A Retrospective*, p.12. See also Philip M. Kaiser, *Journeying Far and Wide: A Political and Diplomatic Memoir*, pp.45–103
3. Interview, Madron Seligman, 16.3.82; McIntosh, pp.13–14
4. Roy Jenkins, *A Life at the Centre* [*ALATC*], p.32
5. Interview, David Ginsburg, 18.2.82
6. *Sunday Express*, 5.11.72
7. Derek Powell in *Sunday Express*, 5.11.72
8. David Ginsburg interview, 18.2.82
9. *Cherwell*, 3.11.89
10. Andrew Roth, *Heath and the Heathmen*, p.39
11. *Evening Standard*, 5.10.98
12. Roy Jenkins, *Twelve Cities*, p.36
13. Speech at Denis and Edna Healey's golden wedding anniversary, 1995 [Jenkins papers]
14. Jenkins, *ALATC*, p.34n

15. *Isis*, 25.1.39
16. ibid., 8.2.39
17. ibid., 2.3.39
18. Ronald McIntosh in Adonis & Thomas, p.15
19. Birmingham profile, February 1950 [Jenkins papers]
20. Jenkins, *ALATC*, p.35
21. ibid., pp.31–2
22. ibid., p.30
23. *Sunday Times*, 20.2.77
24. Jenkins, *ALATC*, p.32
25. Private information
26. Tony Crosland to Jenkins, n.d. December 1939 [Jenkins papers]
27. *Oxford Magazine*, 23.11.39
28. OULC *Bulletin*, 22.11.39
29. *Oxford Magazine*, 23.11.39
30. OULC *Bulletin*, 6.12.39
31. Address at Leo Pliatzky's memorial service, 21.7.99 [Jenkins papers]
32. OULC *Bulletin*, 17.1.40
33. David Walter, *The Oxford Union: Playground of Power*, p.113
34. Crosland to Hattie Jenkins, 18.1.42 [Crosland papers]
35. Crosland to Philip Williams, 13.3.45 [Crosland papers, ACP 3/26]
36. *Sunday Times*, 20.2.77
37. Jenkins to Crosland, 22.3.40 [Crosland papers, 9/1]
38. Arthur Jenkins to Crosland, 19.4.40 [Crosland papers, 9/1]
39. Crosland to Philip Williams, 10.7.40 [Crosland papers ACP 3/26]
40. OULC *Bulletin*, 30.1.40
41. ibid., 20.2.40
42. ibid., 22.4.40
43. *Oxford Magazine*, 2.5.40
44. Crosland papers, 2/22
45. ibid.
46. Denis Healey, *The Time of My Life*, p.46
47. Jenkins, *ALATC*, p.37
48. *Oxford Magazine*, 2.5.40
49. ibid., 9.5.40
50. ibid., 16.5.40
51. ibid., 23.5.40
52. OULC *Bulletin*, 14.5.40
53. *Oxford Magazine*, 6.6.40
54. *Sunday Express*, 5.11.72
55. Crosland to Jenkins, July 1940 [Jenkins papers]

56. Crosland to Jenkins, July 1940 [Jenkins papers]
57. Crosland to Jenkins, July 1940 [Jenkins papers]
58. Crosland to Jenkins, July 1940 [Jenkins papers]
59. Crosland to Hattie Jenkins, summer 1940 [Jenkins papers]
60. Crosland to Arthur and Hattie Jenkins, summer 1940 [Jenkins papers]
61. Jenkins to Jennifer Morris, 12.4.43 [Jenkins papers]

Chapter Three: The Gate at Dartington

All letters are from the Jenkins papers, unless otherwise credited.

1. Roy Jenkins, *A Life at the Centre* [*ALATC*], p.39
2. Jennifer to Roy, 10.8.42
3. Roy to Jennifer, January 1942
4. Roy to Jennifer, 29.4.42
5. Arthur Jenkins to Tony Crosland, 27.8.40
6. Jennifer to Roy, 13.12.40
7. Roy to Jennifer, 13.12.40
8. Roy to Jennifer, 16.12.40
9. Jenkins, *ALATC*, p.40
10. Francis Bennion in *The Times*, 9.1.03
11. *Oxford Magazine,* 28.11.40
12. Arthur to Roy, 23.11.40
13. Jenkins, *ALATC*, p.36
14. Crosland to Jenkins, 8.10.40
15. Crosland to Jenkins, 21.10.40
16. Crosland to Jenkins, undated, autumn 1940
17. Crosland to Jenkins, undated, autumn 1940
18. Crosland to Jenkins, 23.12.40
19. Crosland to Jenkins, undated, January 1941
20. Crosland to Jenkins, 26.1.41
21. Arthur Jenkins to Crosland, 31.1.41
22. Jenkins to Crosland, undated, February 1941 [Crosland papers 9/1]
23. Crosland to Jenkins, 10.2.41
24. Roy to Jennifer, undated, March 1942
25. Jennifer to Roy, 21.3.41
26. Roy to Jennifer, undated, March 1941
27. Roy to Jennifer, undated, April 1941
28. Jennifer to Roy, 20.4.41
29. Jennifer to Roy, 22.4.41

30. Jennifer to Roy, 12.5.41
31. Crosland to Jenkins, 11.5.41
32. Crosland to Jenkins, 3.6.41
33. Crosland to Jenkins, 18.6.41
34. Jenkins, *ALATC*, p.42
35. Interview, David Ginsburg, 18.2.82
36. Jenkins, *ALATC*, p.42
37. Roy to Jennifer, undated, May 1941
38. Roy to Jennifer, undated, April 1941
39. Roy to Jennifer, undated, May 1941
40. Jennifer to Roy, undated, June 1941
41. Jennifer to Roy, undated, January 1941
42. Roy to Jennifer, 8.3.41
43. Jennifer to Roy, 22.3.41
44. Jennifer to Roy, 24.3.41
45. Roy to Jennifer, undated, March 1941
46. Jennifer to Roy, 3.4.41
47. *Oxford Magazine,* 8.5.41
48. Roy to Jennifer, 4.5.41
49. Jennifer to Roy, 7.5.41
50. Jennifer to Roy, 12.5.41
51. Jenkins, *ALATC*, p.43
52. Attlee to Jenkins, 24.7.41
53. Jennifer to Roy, 23.6.41
54. Jennifer to Roy, 9.10.41
55. Jennifer to Roy, 19.7.41
56. Jennifer to Roy, undated, September 1941
57. Jenkins, *ALATC*, p.45
58. Roy to Jennifer, undated, October 1942
59. Jennifer to Roy, 6.10.42
60. Roy to Jennifer, 25.11.41
61. Jennifer to Roy, 25.11.41
62. Jennifer to Roy, 30.11.41
63. Roy to Jennifer, 18.7.44
64. Jennifer to Roy, 20.12.41
65. Roy to Jennifer, 15.1.42
66. Jennifer to Roy, 30.5.41
67. Jennifer to Roy, 30.10.41
68. Roy to Jennifer, undated, November 1941
69. Roy to Jennifer, undated, January 1942
70. Crosland to Hattie Jenkins, 18.1.42

Chapter Four: Captain Jenkins

All letters are from the Jenkins papers, unless otherwise credited.

1. Roy Jenkins, *A Life at the Centre* [*ALATC*], p.46
2. ibid., p.51
3. Roy to Jennifer, 16.2.42

4. Jennifer to Roy, 18.2.42
5. Roy to Jennifer, 2.5.42
6. Roy to Jennifer, 16.2.42
7. Roy to Jennifer, undated, March 1942
8. Roy to Jennifer, undated, May 1942
9. Roy to Jennifer, 24.4.42
10. Roy to Jennifer, 22.5.42
11. *Sunday Express*, 5.11.72
12. Roy Jenkins, *The Chancellors,* p.393
13. Roy to Jennifer, 2.7.42
14. Interview, Sir John Chilcot, 16.6.09; see also John Mortimer, *In Character*, p.143
15. Jennifer to Roy, 17.5.42
16. Jennifer to Roy, 24.12.41
17. Roy to Jennifer, undated, July 1942
18. Jennifer to Roy, 15.5.42
19. Jennifer to Roy, 2.9.42
20. Roy to Jennifer, undated, August 1942
21. Jenkins, *ALATC*, p.48
22. Jennifer to Roy, 29.4.42
23. Roy to Jennifer, undated, June 1944
24. Jennifer to Roy, 27.10.44
25. Jennifer to Roy, 17.12.42
26. Roy to Jennifer, undated, January 1943
27. Jennifer to Roy, 20.10.41
28. *Sunday Telegraph* magazine, n.d. 1993
29. Roy to Jennifer, 22.12.42
30. Jennifer to Roy, undated, March 1943
31. Roy to Jennifer, undated, March 1943
32. Jennifer to Roy, 21.4.43
33. June Morris, *The Life and Times of Thomas Balogh*, p.40
34. Jennifer to Roy, 27.4.43
35. *Sunday Express*, 5.11.72
36. Jennifer to Roy, 2.6.43
37. Jennifer to Roy, 21.5.43
38. Jennifer to Roy, 27.4.43
39. Jennifer to Roy, 4.5.43
40. Jennifer to Roy, 24.6.44
41. Jenkins, *ALATC*, p.49
42. Roy to Jennifer, 22.6.43
43. Jennifer to Roy, 7.8.43
44. Roy to Jennifer, undated, August/ September 1943
45. Roy to Jennifer, 30.9.43
46. Jennifer to Roy, 3.10.43
47. Jennifer to Roy, 23.3.43
48. Jenkins, *ALATC*, p.50
49. Arthur Jenkins to Roy, undated, July 1943
50. Roy to Jennifer, undated, June 1943
51. Roy to Jennifer, 22.6.43

52. Jennifer to Roy, 17.9.43
53. Roy to Arthur and Hattie Jenkins, 19.9.43
54. Jennifer to Roy, 17.10.43
55. Jennifer to Roy, 7.8.43
56. Jennifer to Roy, 19.9.43
57. Jennifer to Roy, 21.5.43
58. Jennifer to Roy, 16.7.43
59. Jennifer to Roy, 7.8.43
60. Jennifer to Roy, 13.7.43
61. Jenkins, *ALATC*, p.50
62. Roy to Jennifer, 16.11.43
63. Tony Crosland to Philip Williams, 12.2.44 [Crosland papers, 3/26]
64. Jenkins, *ALATC*, p.51
65. Paul Gannon, *Colossus: Bletchley Park's Greatest Secret*, p.164
66. Michael Smith, *Station X; The Codebreakers of Bletchley Park*, p.161
67. Jenkins, *ALATC*, p.54
68. Asa Briggs, 'Bletchley', in Andrew Adonis & Keith Thomas, *Roy Jenkins: A Retrospective*, pp.22–3
69. Jennifer to Roy, 26.3.44
70. Roy to Jennifer, 29.5.44
71. ibid.
72. Roy to Jennifer, undated, May 1944
73. Jennifer to Roy, 11.7.44
74. Jennifer to Roy, 14.3.44
75. Jennifer to Roy, 21.6.44
76. Jennifer to Roy, 11.7.44
77. Jennifer to Roy, 2.8.44
78. Jennifer to Roy, 18.9.44
79. Roy to Jennifer, 18.9.44
80. Jennifer to Roy, 21.9.44
81. Roy to Jennifer, 18.9.44
82. Jennifer to Roy, 21.9.44
83. Jennifer to Roy, 3.10.44
84. Tony Crosland to Hattie Jenkins, 22.2.44
85. Crosland to Roy, 21.9.44
86. Jennifer to Roy, 18.5.44
87. Roy to Jennifer, 29.5.44
88. Roy to Jennifer, undated, June 1944
89. Arthur Jenkins to Roy, 5.10.44
90. Jennifer to Roy, 3.10.44
91. Roy to Jennifer, *c*.7.10.44
92. Woodrow Wyatt, *Confessions of an Optimist*, p.105
93. Jenkins, *ALATC*, p.54
94. Address at Wyatt's memorial service, 1.4.98
95. Roy to Crosland, 28.11.44

96. Crosland to Roy, 10.10.44
97. Jennifer to Roy, 30.10.44
98. Roy to Jennifer, 18.9.44
99. Hattie Jenkins to Roy, 16.10.44
100. Ronald McIntosh interview, 23.7.08
101. Jennifer to Roy, 6.2.45
102. Jennifer to Roy, 9.2.45

Chapter Five: False Starts

1. *Labour Party Annual Conference Report*, 21.5.45
2. Roy Jenkins, *A Life at the Centre* [*ALATC*], p.56
3. *Birmingham Gazette*, 5.7.45
4. Roy to Jennifer, 24.7.45 [Jenkins papers]
5. Jennifer to Roy, 24.7.45 [Jenkins papers]
6. Roy to Jennifer, 24.7.45 [Jenkins papers]
7. *The Times*, 27.7.45
8. Jenkins, *ALATC*, p.63
9. Arthur to Roy and Jennifer, 14.7.45 [Jenkins papers]
10. Arthur to Roy, 26.6.43 [Jenkins papers]
11. Arthur to Roy, undated [Jenkins papers]
12. Edward Pearce, *Denis Healey: A Life in Our Times*, p.66
13. J.H. Lawrie, general manager of ICFC, typescript of an undated 1964 *Sunday Times* profile [Jenkins papers]
14. John Kinross, *Fifty Years in the City: Financing Small Business*, p.130
15. Memorial address for John Kinross, 8.11.89 [Jenkins papers]
16. ibid.
17. Jenkins, *ALATC*, p.63
18. ibid.
19. ibid., pp.63–4
20. Ben Pimlott, ed., *The Wartime Diaries of Hugh Dalton*, p.846 (4.4.45)
21. Jenkins, *ALATC*, p.65
22. ibid., p.66
23. *Monmouthshire Free Press*, 3.5.46
24. Tony Crosland to Hattie Jenkins, 29.4.46 [Jenkins papers]
25. *Monmouthshire Free Press*, 5.46
26. ibid.
27. Jenkins, *ALATC*, p.68
28. *The Times*, 27.4.46

29. Councillor Les Jackson in *Sunday Express*, 12.11.72
30. Leo Abse, *Private Member*, pp.34–6
31. Jenkins, *ALATC*, p.64
32. Jenkins papers
33. Speech to the Royal Society of Literature, 2.3.96 [Jenkins papers]
34. Roy Jenkins, *Mr Attlee: An Interim Biography*, p.19
35. ibid., p.97
36. ibid., p.74
37. ibid., p.132
38. Jenkins, *ALATC*, p.64
39. *The Times*, 21.4.48
40. Jenkins papers
41. *Manchester Guardian*, undated April 1948
42. *Observer*, 25.4.48
43. ibid.
44. Jenkins papers
45. *The Times*, 30.4.48
46. ibid.

Chapter Six: Baby of the House

1. Ben Pimlott, ed., *The Political Diary of Hugh Dalton, 1918–40, 1945–60*, p.430 (15.4.48)
2. Jenkins to Hugh Dalton, 1.6.48 [Dalton papers, 10/21]
3. Speech to Newport Model Parliament, 1949 [Jenkins papers]
4. Roy Jenkins, *A Life at the Centre* [*ALATC*], pp.73–4
5. David Eccles in the House of Commons, 3.6.48 [Vol.451, col.1252]
6. House of Commons, 3.6.48 [Vol.451, cols 1252–5]
7. Roy Jenkins, *Nine Men of Power*, p.83
8. House of Commons, 3.6.48 [Vol.451, cols 1252–5]
9. ibid. [cols 1255–68]
10. ibid., 5.7.48 [Vol.453, cols 93–8]
11. Walter Fletcher in the House of Commons, 5.7.48 [Vol.453, col.98]
12. House of Commons, 20.9.48 [Vol.456, cols 590–95]
13. ibid., 15.11.48 [Vol.458, cols 132–7]
14. *Tribune*, 17.9.48
15. ibid., 5.11.48
16. *Financial Times*, 8.11.48
17. Jenkins, *ALATC*, p.75
18. Jenkins papers. Jenkins also described his meeting with Croce in *Twelve*

Cities, pp.66–7. Boyd-Carpenter described the trip in his memoirs, *Way of Life*, pp.79–81

19. *Sunday Express*, quoted in Douglas Bence & Clive Branson: *Roy Jenkins: A Question of Principle?*, p.68
20. Jenkins, *ALATC*, p.76
21. ibid., p.62
22. House of Commons, 7.4.49 [Vol.463, cols 2238–47]
23. Jenkins, *ALATC*, p.73
24. House of Commons, 3.11.49, 11.11.49 [Vol.469, cols 637–44, 1569–73]
25. *Observer*, October 1990, reprinted in Jenkins, *Portraits and Miniatures*, p.255
26. Roy to Dalton, 31.10.50 [Dalton papers 9/10]
27. *Tribune*, 11.3.49, 13.5.49; *Socialist Commentary*, July 1949; *The Times*, 20.7.48, 23.7.49
28. Tony Insall: 'Haakon Lie, Denis Healey and the making of an Anglo-Norwegian special relationship, 1945–51' (Oslo Academic Press 2010), pp.110–11
29. *Picture Post*, 26.7.49
30. *New Statesman*, 26.2.49
31. *Labour Party Annual Conference Report, 1949*, p.143 (7.6.49)
32. *The Times*, 8.6.49
33. Jenkins, *ALATC*, p.77
34. ibid., pp.77, 82
35. Jenkins papers
36. *The Sphere*, 23.8.52
37. Roy Jenkins, *Twelve Cities*, p.52
38. HM Inspector of Taxes to Roy, 21.7.50 [Jenkins papers]
39. Notes for Stechford selection conference speech [Jenkins papers]
40. Stechford election address, 1950 [Jenkins papers]
41. *Birmingham Gazette*, n.d. [Jenkins papers]
42. *Birmingham Post*, 18.2.50
43. *The Times*, 25.2.50
44. *Birmingham Gazette*, 25.2.50

Chapter Seven: *Fair Shares for the Rich*

1. Jenkins papers
2. House of Commons, 19.4.50 [Vol.474, cols 208–13]
3. *Town Crier*, 24.6.50
4. Roy Jenkins, *Portraits and Miniatures*,

p.18; *A Life at the Centre* [*ALATC*], pp.83–4
5. Jenkins to Hugh Dalton, 31.10.50 [Dalton papers, 9/10]
6. Jenkins, *ALATC*, p.85
7. *Time and Tide*, 14.4.51
8. Roy Jenkins, *Fair Shares for the Rich*, p.16
9. *Review of Economics and Science*, n.d., in Jenkins papers
10. Woodrow Wyatt, *Confessions of an Optimist*, p.172
11. Roy Jenkins, *The Chancellors*, p.430
12. Ben Pimlott, ed., *The Political Diary of Hugh Dalton, 1918–40, 1945–60*, p.489 (29.9.50–6.10.50)
13. Dalton to Gaitskell, 19.5.52 [Gaitskell papers A 47]
14. Roy Jenkins, *Nine Men of Power*, pp.170–71
15. House of Commons, 12.4.51 [Vol. 486, cols 1248–57]
16. Dalton diary, pp.521–2 (9.4.51); Tony Benn, *Years of Hope: Diaries, Papers and Letters, 1940–1962*, pp.146–7 (11.4.51)
17. *Birmingham Gazette*, 28.4.51
18. *Birmingham Gazette, Birmingham Post*, 30.4.51
19. *Yorkshire Post*, 21.4.51
20. Dalton diary, pp.541–2 (11.5.51)
21. Jenkins papers, notes for 1951 eve-of-poll speech
22. *The Current*, 10.10.51
23. Jenkins papers, unidentified cutting
24. *The Times*, 27.10.51
25. John Campbell, *Nye Bevan and the Mirage of British Socialism*, p.258
26. *The Diary of Hugh Gaitskell, 1945–56*, ed. Philip M. Williams, p.311 (21.3.52)
27. Roy Jenkins, *ALATC*, pp.98–9
28. House of Commons, 22.5.52 [Vol. 501, cols 804–5]
29. ibid., 28.5.52 [Vol.501, col.1615]
30. Dalton diary, p.588 (29.5.52)
31. Roy Jenkins in W.T. Rodgers, ed., *Hugh Gaitskell, 1906–1963*, p.120
32. ibid., p.115
33. Wyatt, p.225
34. Jenkins, *ALATC*, pp.110–11
35. Michael Foot, *Aneurin Bevan, 1945–1960*, p.376

36. *The Times*, 6.10.52
37. Roy Jenkins to Gaitskell, 3.10.52 [Gaitskell papers p.50, in Williams, p.304]
38. Roy to Dalton, 31.11.50 [Dalton papers, 9/10]
39. Jenkins, *Pursuit of Progress*, pp.96, 104–5, 176
40. ibid., p.38
41. ibid., pp.44–5
42. ibid., p.24
43. ibid., p.37
44. ibid., pp.153, 158–60
45. ibid., p.161
46. Aberdeen *Press and Journal*, 18.4.53; Glasgow *Evening News*, 28.4.53; *National and English Review*, June 1953; *Manchester Guardian*, 12.6.53; *Daily Worker*, 11.6.53; *New Statesman*, 30.5.53; *Tribune*, 22.5.53; *The Economist*, 25.4.53
47. *Daily Telegraph*, 15.4.53
48. *Times Literary Supplement*, 17.4.53

Chapter Eight: Expanding Horizons

1. *The Times*, 6.1.03
2. Talk on New York radio, 9/53 [Jenkins papers]
3. House of Commons, 30.5.52 [Vol.501, cols 18935–42]; 16.3.53 [Vol.512, cols 2024–7]
4. Nigel Birch in House of Commons, 26.7.51 [Vol.491, col.706]
5. Sir Waldron Smithers in House of Commons, 8.4.54 [Vol.526, col.614]
6. House of Commons, 11.2.54 [Vol.523, cols 1383–94, 1401–8]
7. *Leeds Weekly Citizen*, undated cutting
8. Roy Hattersley, *Who Goes Home?*, p.11
9. *The Current*, 10.52
10. ibid., 9.53
11. Interview for *The Thatcher Factor*, 003/10 [LSE]
12. *Birmingham Post*, 6.5.71; Roy Jenkins, *A Life at the Centre* [*ALATC*], pp.106–7
13. Woodrow Wyatt, *Confessions of an Optimist*, pp.174–5
14. *Birmingham Gazette*, 2.10.55
15. *Birmingham Mail*, 10.11.55
16. *Sunday Telegraph*, 24.2.84
17. Roy Jenkins, *Twelve Cities*, p.51
18. ibid., p.43

19. Ben Pimlott, ed., *The Political Diary of Hugh Dalton*, p.542 [11.5.51]
20. Violet Bonham Carter, *Daring to Hope*, p.136
21. Jenkins, *ALATC*, p.96
22. Jenkins papers
23. Roy Jenkins: *Sir Charles Dilke: A Victorian Tragedy*, p.303
24. ibid., p.239
25. *The Times*, 23.10.58
26. *Observer*, 26.10.58
27. Conor Cruise O'Brien to Jenkins, 14.1.59; Jenkins to O'Brien, 2.2.59 [Jenkins papers]
28. Roy Jenkins, 'Sir Charles Wentworth Dilke', in the *Oxford Dictionary of National Biography*
29. *The Current*, 3.3.54
30. ibid., 10.6.53
31. ibid., 5.9.51
32. ibid., 5.1.55
33. ibid., 26.9.51
34. *Birmingham Mail*, September 1958
35. *Spectator*, 7.11.58, 14.11.58
36. Roy Jenkins, *Nine Men of Power*, p.183
37. Jenkins, *ALATC*, pp.100–1
38. *The Current*, 1.10.53
39. Jenkins, *Twelve Cities*, p.119
40. *The Current*, undated cuttings, 9–11.53
41. *New York Times*, 30.11.67
42. Jenkins papers
43. *Observer*, 3.12.67, quoted in Douglas Bence & Clive Branson, *Roy Jenkins: A Question of Principle?*, p.94
44. Bence & Branson, p.93
45. Roy Jenkins, *Franklin Delano Roosevelt*, p.50
46. Jenkins, *ALATC*, p.136
47. *Spectator*, 19.1.02
48. Jenkins, *Twelve Cities*, p.236
49. Tony Benn, *Years of Hope: Diaries, Papers and Letters, 1940–62*, p.256 (18.12.57)
50. Bill Rodgers' unpublished diary, 4.12.56
51. *House and Garden*, February 1992
52. Jenkins, *ALATC*, p.103
53. ibid.
54. Nicholas Henderson, *Old Friends and Modern Instances*, p.95
55. Kevin Jeffreys, *Anthony Crosland*, p.53
56. Wyatt, p.179
57. Benn, p.237 (25.5.57)

58. Susan Crosland, *Tony Crosland*, pp.57–8
59. Henderson, pp.93–4
60. Wyatt, p.178
61. Robert Harris diary, 26.7.96
62. Dalton diary, p.529 (12.4.51)
63. Roy Jenkins, *The Chancellors*, p.411
64. ibid., p.433
65. Jenkins papers
66. Nicholas Davenport, *Memoirs of a City Radical*, p.106
67. Jenkins, *The Chancellors*, p.262
68. Frances Donaldson, *A Twentieth Century Life*, p.176
69. George Weidenfeld, *Remembering My Good Friends*, p.172
70. Jeffreys, p.69
71. Interviews, Dame Jennifer Jenkins, Leslie Bonham Carter
72. Roy Jenkins to Barley Alison, 7.6.52 [by permission of Rosie Alison]
73. ibid., 10.6.52
74. ibid., 7.6.52, 19.9.52, 15.6.52
75. ibid., 10.9.53
76. Jenkins papers
77. *The Times*, 2.6.89
78. Brian Brivati, *Hugh Gaitskell*, pp.244–5
79. *The Current*, 5.10.55
80. Quoted in Bence & Branson, p.94
81. Susan Crosland, p.108
82. ibid., p.58
83. John Spedan Lewis to Jenkins, 8.6.53 [Jenkins papers]
84. ibid., 30.7.53
85. ibid., 15.8.53
86. Bence & Branson, p.98
87. Jenkins papers
88. Article for the Royal Society of Literature journal, dated 11.3.96 [Jenkins papers]
89. Jenkins papers
90. Roy Jenkins, *Churchill*, p.432
91. *The Backbench Diaries of Richard Crossman*, pp.280–81 (3.12.53)
92. *The Current*, 28.4.54
93. Crossman diary, p.411 (3.55)
94. Dalton diary, p.653 (18.3.55)
95. Jenkins, Wyatt and Crosland to Gaitskell, 21.3.55, in Philip M. Williams, ed., *The Diary of Hugh Gaitskell*, pp.394–5
96. Dalton diary, pp.663–4 (7.4.55)
97. *Birmingham Evening Dispatch*
98. *The Current*, 18.5.55

99. ibid., 3.6.55
100. *The Times*, 28.5.55
101. *Daily Express*, 12.12.55
102. Crossman diary, p.453 (2.12.55)
103. Jenkins, *ALATC*, p.112
104. *The Current*, 28.12.55
105. Clement Attlee to Jenkins, 13.11.55 [Jenkins papers]

Chapter Nine: The Liberal Agenda

1. Roy Jenkins, *A Life at the Centre* [*ALATC*], p.114
2. Tony Benn, *Diaries, Papers and Letters, 1940–62*, p.237 (31.5.57)
3. *The Backbench Diaries of Richard Crossman*, p.634 (26.11.57)
4. *Tribune*, 5.10.56
5. C.A.R. Crosland, *The Future of Socialism*, pp.520–24
6. *Forward*, October 1956
7. Crosland, p.522
8. *The Current*, 21.4.54
9. ibid., 11.2.53
10. ibid., 4.2.53
11. *Encounter*, October 1959, reprinted in Roy Jenkins, *Essays and Speeches*, p.103
12. House of Commons, 22.2.55 [Vol.537 cols 1089–97]
13. *Encounter*, October 1959
14. *Spectator*, 22.3.57
15. R.A. Butler to Jenkins, 19.12.58 [Jenkins papers]
16. ibid., 15.7.59
17. *The Author*, Autumn 1959
18. Hugh Fraser to Jenkins, 25.4.59 [Jenkins papers]
19. Jenkins to Butler, 9.8.59, in Anthony Howard, *RAB: The Life of R.A. Butler*, p.267
20. *Encounter*, October 1959
21. Jenkins, *ALATC*, p.103
22. *The Current*, 4.1.56
23. Speech notes [Jenkins papers]
24. Roy Jenkins, *The Labour Case*, p.14
25. Jenkins, *ALATC*, p.104
26. Roy Jenkins, *Gladstone*, p.67
27. *The Times*, 23.10.56
28. Jenkins, *ALATC*, p.105
29. Jenkins, *The Labour Case*, p.11
30. Caroline Gilmour to Jenkins, 24.10.60 [Jenkins papers]
31. ibid., 26.10.60 [Jenkins papers]

Notes

32. *Spectator*, 22.11.57
33. ibid., 7.3.58
34. ibid., 22.5.59
35. ibid., 14.8.59
36. ibid., 22.9.59
37. *New Statesman*, 2.11.57
38. William Rodgers, *Fourth Among Equals*, p.48
39. Interview, Lord Rodgers of Quarry Bank
40. *The Times*, 23.7.56
41. *Labour Party Annual Conference Report, 1956*, pp.121–2 (3.10.56)
42. *Labour Party Annual Conference Report, 1957*, pp.152–3 (2.10.57)
43. Speech at Bedford, 21.7.57
44. Jim Tomlinson, *The Labour Governments of 1964–70: The Economy*, pp.32–3
45. *Labour Party Annual Conference Report, 1958*, pp.157–8 (1.10.58)
46. Jenkins, *The Labour Case*, p.7
47. ibid., p.74
48. ibid., p.51
49. ibid., p.75
50. ibid., p.127
51. ibid., p.146
52. ibid., p.46
53. ibid., pp.11–12
54. *The Economist*, 3.10.59
55. *Spectator*, 18.9.59
56. Interview, Lord Taverne, 1.12.08
57. Crossman, p.654 (21.1.58)
58. Jenkins, *ALATC*, pp.126–7
59. ibid., p.127
60. ibid., p.128
61. *The Times*, 10.10.59

Chapter Ten: 'Fight and Fight Again'?

1. *The Political Diary of Hugh Dalton*, p.694 (10.10.59)
2. Roy Jenkins, *A Life at the Centre* [*ALATC*], p.129
3. Douglas Jay, *Change and Fortune*, pp.273–5
4. Dalton diary, pp.694–5 (11.10.59)
5. Tony Benn, *Years of Hope: Diaries, Papers and Letters, 1940–62*, p.318 (12.10.59)
6. *The Times*, 22.10.59
7. *The Backbench Diaries of Richard Crossman*, pp.793–5 (21.10.59)
8. ibid., p.796 (23.10.59)

9. Philip Williams, *Hugh Gaitskell*, p.543
10. Crossman diary, p.797 (27.10.59)
11. Speech to the Fabian Society, 4.11.59 [Jenkins papers]
12. Jenkins, *ALATC*, pp.130–31
13. J.K. Galbraith, *The Affluent Society*
14. *Spectator*, 27.11.59
15. Jenkins, *ALATC*, pp.130–31
16. Crossman diary, p.748 (14.5.59)
17. Benn diary, p.312 (15.9.59)
18. Alastair Hetherington diary, 13.2.59 [Hetherington papers 1/1]
19. Jenkins, *ALATC*, p.131
20. House of Commons, 7.4.60 [Vol.621, cols 569–82]
21. Roy Jenkins, 'British Labor Divided', in *Foreign Affairs*, April 1960
22. *Spectator*, 11.11.60
23. Peter Hennessy, *Whitehall*, p.707
24. *Labour Party Annual Conference Report, 1957*, pp.179–83 (3.10.57)
25. Patrick Gordon Walker, *Political Diaries, 1932–1971*, pp.259–60 (12.5.60)
26. Dalton diary, p.698 (4.5.60)
27. *Birmingham Post, Birmingham Mail* and *Daily Telegraph*, 20.6.60
28. *Labour Party Annual Conference Report, 1960*, p.201 (5.10.60)
29. Jenkins, *ALATC*, p.144
30. *Labour Party Annual Conference Report, 1960*, pp.211–12 (6.10.60)
31. *Daily Telegraph*, 25.10.60
32. *Spectator*, 11.11.60
33. Bill Rodgers to Roy Jenkins, 12.11.90 [Rodgers papers]
34. Jenkins, *ALATC*, p.109
35. *The Times*, 28.7.60
36. BBC2 interview 2.1.66, reprinted in Robin Day, . . . *But With Respect*, pp.61–2
37. *Sunday Times*, 1.10.61
38. *Spectator*, 23.9.61
39. ibid., 13.10.61
40. ibid.
41. ibid., 11.11.60
42. Alistair Horne, *Macmillan, 1957–1986*, p.353
43. *Spectator*, 7.7.61
44. *Labour Party Annual Conference Report, 1961*, pp.215–16 (5.10.61)
45. *Spectator*, 12.1.62
46. *Foreign Affairs*, April 1960

47. *Spectator,* 12.1.62
48. Woodrow Wyatt, *Confessions of an Optimist,* p.278
49. *Observer,* 25.10.59
50. Crossman diary, p.770 (13.8.59)
51. *The Letters of Ann Fleming,* pp.314–15 (2.8.62)
52. Roy Jenkins, 'David Astor and the *Observer*', in *Portraits and Miniatures,* p.246
53. *Observer,* 18.3.62, 25.3.61 and 11.4.61, reprinted in Roy Jenkins, *Essays and Speeches,* pp.143–64
54. Jenkins, *ALATC,* p.138
55. ibid., p.140
56. *Observer,* 14.7.63 and 21.7.63, reprinted in *Essays and Speeches,* pp.165–81
57. ibid., 27.10.63, reprinted in *Essays and Speeches,* pp.84–97
58. ibid., 12.7.64 and 19.7.64, reprinted in *Essays and Speeches,* pp.182–96
59. Jenkins, *ALATC,* p.145; Williams, p.708; Jay, p.282
60. *New Statesman,* 1.6.62
61. Jay, pp.283–4
62. Jenkins to Gaitskell, 1.5.62 [Gaitskell papers, C/2565]
63. Gaitskell to Jenkins, 8.5.62 [loc.cit.]
64. Williams, p.719
65. Hetherington diary, 11.9.62 [Hetherington papers 3/15]
66. Gaitskell memo to President Kennedy, 11.12.62, in Philip Williams, ed., *The Diary of Hugh Gaitskell, 1945–56,* p.668
67. Austen Albu diary, 18.9.62, in Williams, *Hugh Gaitskell,* p.731
68. *The Times,* 21.9.62
69. *Manchester Guardian,* 23.9.62
70. Jenkins papers
71. Jenkins, *ALATC,* p.146
72. Williams, *Hugh Gaitskell,* p.736
73. Jenkins, *ALATC,* p.146
74. ibid., p.147
75. Jenkins to Bill Rodgers, 23.1.63 [thanks to Lord Rodgers of Quarry Bank]
76. Roy Jenkins, *Gallery of 20th Century Portraits,* pp.44–5
77. Jenkins to Bill Rodgers, 23.1.63 [Lord Rodgers]
78. Peter Kellner & Christopher Hitchens, *Callaghan: The Road to Number Ten,* p.41
79. Bill Rodgers to Jenkins, 28.1.63 [Lord Rodgers]
80. Crossman diary, pp.978–9 (15.2.63)
81. *Sunday Times,* 14.10.90
82. Jenkins to Bill Rodgers, 23.1.63 [Lord Rodgers]
83. House of Commons, 4.3.63 [Vol.673, cols 107–18]; 8.4.63 [Vol.675, cols 996–1005]; 19.6.63 [Vol.679, cols 503–8]
84. Tony Benn, *Out of the Wilderness: Diaries 1962–67,* p.16 (10.5.63)
85. Jenkins, *ALATC,* p.149
86. Roy Jenkins, 'Leader of the Opposition', in W.T. Rodgers, ed., *Hugh Gaitskell, 1906–1963,* p.131
87. *Evening Standard,* 2.9.96
88. Jenkins, *ALATC,* p.149
89. Memo of conversation with Harold Wilson, 12.9.63 [Jenkins papers]
90. Jenkins, *ALATC,* p.151
91. Jenkins to Sir Geoffrey Crowther, 19.12.63 [Jenkins papers]
92. *Birmingham Post,* 6.5.71
93. *Sunday Express,* 29.9.63
94. Susan Crosland, *Tony Crosland,* p.117
95. *The Times,* 22.11.63
96. *Observer,* 24.11.63
97. Lecture to the Royal Philosophical Society of Glasgow, April 1990, in *Portraits and Miniatures,* pp.157–8
98. *Birmingham Mail,* February 1963 (typescript dated 14.2.63 in Jenkins papers)
99. *Observer,* 22.4.62
100. ibid., 24.11.63, reprinted in Jenkins, *Essays and Speeches,* p.96
101. ibid., pp.94–5
102. ibid., p.94
103. Jenkins, *ALATC,* p.142
104. Caroline Gilmour to Jenkins, n.d. (possibly August 1965) [Jenkins papers]
105. Ann Fleming to Clarissa Avon, 16.2.64, in *The Letters of Ann Fleming,* p.336
106. Jacqueline Kennedy to Jenkins, 29.1.66 [Jenkins papers]
107. Roy Jenkins, *Nine Men of Power,* p.216
108. Lady Violet Bonham Carter diary, in *Daring to Hope: The Diaries and Letters*

of *Violet Bonham Carter, 1946–69,*
pp.284–5 (9.2.64)
109. ibid., p.285 (6.3.64)
110. ibid., p.286 (17.3.64)
111. Violet Bonham Carter to Mark
Bonham Carter, ibid., p.286 (26.3.64)
112. Violet Bonham Carter diary, p.290
(31.7.64)
113. Roy Jenkins, *Asquith,* Preface to the
1978 edition
114. ibid., p.364
115. Personal knowledge
116. Roy Jenkins, *Asquith* (1978 edition),
pp.23, 29, 51, 63, 69, 161, 334, 256–7, 337
117. *Sunday Telegraph, Evening Standard,
Manchester Guardian,* October/
November 1964
118. Violet Bonham Carter diary, p.295
(1.11.64)
119. *Spectator,* 6.11.64
120. *Observer,* 1.11.64
121. Violet Bonham Carter diary, p.295
(1.11.64)
122. *Observer,* 29.6.63
123. House of Commons, 11.4.62 [Vol.657,
cols 1404–14]
124. ibid., 8.4.63 [Vol.675, cols 996–1005]
125. ibid., 15.4.64 [Vol.693, cols 482–90]
126. *Daily Telegraph,* 25.9.64
127. Election address, October 1964
128. *Daily Mail,* 29.9.64; *Daily Telegraph,*
25.9.64
129. *The Times,* 18.9.64
130. ibid., 1.10.64
131. ibid., 17.10.64

Chapter Eleven: Office at Last

1. Roy Jenkins, *A Life at the Centre*
[*ALATC*], p.157
2. William Rodgers, *Fourth Among
Equals,* p.77
3. Alastair Hetherington diary, 18.2.64
[Hetherington papers 5/5]
4. Jenkins, *ALATC,* p.158
5. *Daily Mirror,* 19.10.64
6. *Spectator,* 23.10.64
7. Speech notes, October 1964 [Jenkins
papers]
8. Jenkins, *ALATC,* p.161
9. *Observer,* 19.7.64, reprinted in Roy
Jenkins, *Essays and Speeches,* p.196
10. CAB 128/39, CC2(64)
11. Jenkins, *ALATC,* p.162

12. Roy Jenkins, *Twelve Cities,* p.12
13. Jenkins, *ALATC,* p.163
14. House of Commons, 5.11.64 [Vol.701,
cols 503–15], reprinted in Jenkins,
Essays and Speeches, pp.213–20
15. *Daily Telegraph,* 6.11.64
16. *New Statesman,* 7.2.97, reviewing
Gerald Kaufman, *How to be a Minister*
17. *Daily Mail,* 19.22.65
18. Richard Crossman, *The Diaries of a
Cabinet Minister,* Volume One, p.58
(16.11.64)
19. House of Commons, 20.1.65 [Vol.705,
cols 197–202]
20. Interview for *The Seventies*
21. *Evening Standard,* 21.1.65
22. *The Cecil King Diary, 1965–70,* p.23
(16.7.65)
23. Harold Wilson, *The Labour
Government, 1964–70,* p.100
24. ibid.
25. Jenkins, *ALATC,* p.171
26. Jenkins to Wilson, 24.1.65, in Philip
Ziegler, *Wilson,* p.187
27. *Sunday Times,* 10.1.65
28. *Daily Mail,* 19.2.65
29. *Observer,* 14.2.65
30. Crossman diary, p.152 (8.2.65)
31. Edward Pearce, *Denis Healey: A Life
in our Times,* pp.269–70
32. House of Commons, 9.2.65 [Vol.706,
cols 227–41]
33. *The Times,* 10.2.65
34. Jenkins papers; *Sun,* 9.3.65
35. Jenkins, *ALATC,* p.172
36. CAB 128/39, CC20(65) and CC21(65)
37. Crossman diary, p.203 (18.4.65)
38. *The Times,* 14.4.65
39. *Observer,* 12.7.64 and 19.7.64,
reprinted in Jenkins, *Essays and
Speeches,* pp.182–96
40. *The Times,* 2.3.65
41. Foreword to Lord Plowden, *An
Industrialist in the Treasury,* 24.11.87
[Jenkins papers]
42. Jenkins to Michael Montague, 21.8.64
[Jenkins papers]
43. Jenkins, *ALATC,* p.173
44. ibid.
45. Alastair Hetherington diary, 10.9.65
[Hetherington papers]
46. Jenkins, *ALATC,* pp.176–7
47. King diary, p.38 (14.10.65)

48. Jenkins, *ALATC*, p.178
49. *The Times*, 23.12.65
50. ibid.
51. *Daily Telegraph*, 23.12.65
52. *Birmingham Post*, 23.12.65
53. *Time*, 31.12.65
54. Caroline Gilmour, Ann Fleming and Tony Crosland to Jenkins, 12.65 [Jenkins papers]

Chapter Twelve: 'A More Civilised Society'

1. BBC2, *People to Watch*, 2.1.66, reprinted in Robin Day, *. . . But With Respect: Memorable Television Interviews with Statesmen and Parliamentarians*, pp.51–63
2. ibid.
3. Roy Jenkins, *Churchill*, p.183
4. Kenneth Younger to Jenkins, 29.12.65 [Jenkins papers]
5. Roy Jenkins, *A Life at the Centre* [*ALATC*], p.182
6. Sir Charles Cunningham memo, 11.1.66 [Jenkins papers]
7. Jenkins, *ALATC*, p.184
8. Cunningham memo, 11.1.66 [Jenkins papers]
9. Barbara Castle, *The Castle Diaries, 1964–70*, p.94 (14.1.66)
10. Jenkins, *ALATC*, p.184
11. Interview, Sir John Chilcot, 16.6.09
12. Private information [Sir Geoffrey de Deney]
13. *The Times*, 13.1.70
14. Jenkins to Margaret Clayton, 4.2.98 [Jenkins papers]
15. John Harris to Jenkins, 31.12.65, 4.1.66 [Jenkins papers]
16. *The Times*, 13.4.01
17. Dr Michael Gibson to Jenkins, 6.1.66 [Jenkins papers]
18. Jenkins papers
19. Donald MacDougall, *Don and Mandarin*, p.180
20. Ann Fleming to Nicholas Henderson, 13.5.66, in *The Letters of Ann Fleming*, p.379
21. Ann Fleming to Jenkins, n.d. [Jenkins papers]
22. House of Commons, 2.2.66 [Vol.723, cols 1120–35], reprinted in Roy Jenkins, *Essays and Speeches*, pp.232–42

23. Election broadcast, 29.3.66, in *Essays and Speeches*, pp.274–7
24. *The Times*, 2.4.66
25. BBC2, 2.1.66, in Day, p.56
26. Speech notes, 15.2.66 [Jenkins papers]
27. *The Times*, 19.5.66
28. Sir Robert Mark, *In the Office of Constable*, p.70
29. ibid., p.243
30. ibid., p.78
31. Roy Jenkins, *Twelve Cities*, p.142
32. *The Times*, 9.8.66
33. Party political broadcast, BBC Home Service, 1.12.66, in *Essays and Speeches*, p.252
34. Speech to London Labour Party conference, Hounslow, 12.9.66, in ibid., p.249
35. Party political broadcast, 1.12.66, in ibid., p.254
36. *The Times*, 10.12.66
37. Lord Hailsham, *A Sparrow's Flight*, p.364
38. *The Times*, 13.12.66
39. Antony Lester to Maurice Foley, 9.5.66 [HO 376/158]
40. Mark Bonham Carter to Jenkins, 7.2.66 and 15.2.66 [HO 376/161]
41. Address at Woodrow Wyatt's memorial service, 11.4.98 [Jenkins papers]
42. Mark Bonham Carter to Foley, 15.5.66 [HO 376/158]
43. Speech to NCCI, 23.5.66, in *Essays and Speeches*, pp.267–74
44. LG (66)124, in HO 376/15
45. HAC(67)74, in HO 3376/72
46. Interview.
47. *New Statesman*, n.d. quoted in *Roy Jenkins: A Question of Principle*, p.146
48. Cabinet paper, 17.10.67 [CAB 134/2858]
49. Richard Crossman, *The Diaries of a Cabinet Minister*, Volume Two, p.684 (15.2.68)
50. Phillip Whitehead, *The Writing on the Wall*, p.13
51. *New Statesman*, 17.7.70; interview for *The Seventies*, 003/8 [LSE]
52. Roy Jenkins, *Nine Men of Power*, pp.179–80
53. Bernard Donoughue, *Downing Street Diary: With James Callaghan in No. 10*, p.141 (2.2.77)

54. *Sunday Express*, 18.9.66, 23.10.66
55. Dick Taverne to Jenkins, 28.10.66 [Jenkins papers]
56. *The Times*, 21.10.66
57. Jenkins, *ALATC*, p.201
58. *Independent*, 6.10.09
59. Crossman diary, p.87 (22.10.66)
60. Jenkins, *ALATC*, p.202, and notes dictated in January 1967 [Jenkins papers]
61. *The Times*, 25.10.66
62. Crossman diary, pp.89–90 (24.10.66)
63. Leslie Bonham Carter to Jenkins, 31.10.66 [Jenkins papers]
64. Crossman diary, p.100 (31.10.66)
65. House of Commons, 31.10.66 [Vol.735, cols 115–66]
66. *Daily Mirror*, 1.11.66
67. *The Times*, 1.11.66
68. Jenkins to D. Paul Smith, 9.9.98 [Jenkins papers]
69. *High Life*, typescript dated 9.2.98 [Jenkins papers]
70. Jenkins, *ALATC*, p.203
71. Bill Rodgers to Jenkins, 12.11.90 [Rodgers papers]
72. David Dowler, 'Note for the Record', 4.11.66 [HO278/35]
73. Jenkins, *ALATC*, p.202
74. Castle diary, p.149 (19.7.66)
75. CAB 128, CC(66)37, Confidential annex (19.7.66)
76. Castle diary, p.159 (4.8.66); CAB 128, CC(66)42, Confidential annex (4.8.66)
77. Tony Benn, *Out of the Wilderness: Diaries, 1963–67*, p.466 (6.8.66) and p.472 (12.9.66)
78. Castle diary, p.172 (29.9.66–7.10.66)
79. Ann Fleming to Nicholas Henderson, 24.10.66, in *The Letters of Ann Fleming*, p.381
80. Jenkins papers
81. Philip Ziegler, *Wilson*, p.257
82. *Sunday Times*, 19.5.96
83. Ann Fleming to unspecified recipient, in *The Letters of Ann Fleming*, p.378n
84. Castle diary, p.149 (19.7.66)
85. Crossman diary, p.574 (18.7.66)
86. CAB 128, CC(66)53–5 (1, 3 and 9.11.66)
87. Crossman diary, p.116 (9.11.66)
88. Roger Broad, *Labour's European Dilemmas: From Bevin to Blair*, p.67

89. *Guardian*, 10.66, in Bence & Branson, p.144
90. *The Times*, 30.11.67
91. *Sunday Times*, 20.11.66
92. Benn diary, pp.463 and 465 (4.8.66 and 2.8.66)
93. ibid., pp.467–8 (9.8.66)
94. Kevin Jeffreys, *Tony Crosland*, p.119
95. Crossman diary, p.373 (8.6.67)
96. ibid., p.111 (6.11.66)
97. Castle diary, p.187 (21.11.66)
98. Alan Watkins, 'Backbencher', in Andrew Adonis & Keith Thomas, ed., *Roy Jenkins: A Retrospective*, pp.32–3
99. Interview, Sir John Chilcot, 16.6.09
100. Lord Cobbold to Jenkins, 29.4.66 [Jenkins papers]
101. Colin R. Coote, *The Other Club*, p.20
102. Castle diary, p.632 (8.4.69)
103. *Birmingham Mail*, 5.12.69
104. Castle diary, p.632 (8.4.69)
105. Jenkins to Christopher Hill, 16.1.66 [Jenkins papers]
106. *Sunday Times*, 20.11.66
107. Crossman diary, pp.778–9 (12.4.68)
108. Terence O'Neill to Jenkins, 1.12.67 [Jenkins papers]
109. 1966 engagement diary [Jenkins papers]
110. Crossman diary, p.169 (19.12.66)
111. ibid., p.251 (22.2.67)
112. ibid., p.159 (8.12.66)
113. Speech to the London Labour Party conference, 13.5.67, reprinted in *Essays and Speeches*, pp.278–89
114. House of Commons, 22.7.66 [Vol.732, cols 1140–46], reprinted in *Essays and Speeches*, pp.261–6
115. Jenkins to Ann Finnerty, 29.4.99 [Jenkins papers]
116. John Harris interviewed by Andrew Adonis [thanks to Lord Adonis]
117. Cabinet 1.66.67 [CAB 128, CC(67)35]
118. Crossman diary, pp.393–4, 412 (22.6.67, 6.7.67)
119. House of Commons, 13–14.7.67 [Vol.750, col.1366]
120. Andrew Holden, *Makers and Manners*, p.118
121. Crossman diary, p.407 (2.7.67)
122. House of Commons, 11.2.66 [Vol.724, cols 848–54], reprinted in *Essays and Speeches*, pp.256–60
123. Holden, p.123

124. Cabinet 27.10.66 [CAB 128, CC(66)53]
125. Holden, p.127
126. Leo Abse, *Private Member*, pp.157–8
127. House of Commons, 3–4.7.67 [Vol.749, cols 1509–10]
128. ibid. [cols 1510–11]
129. Speech at Abingdon, 19.7.69
130. Jenkins to Sir Frederick Bennett, 13.5.98
131. Norman Tebbit, Disraeli lecture 13.11.85, cited in Peter Thompson, 'Labour's "Gannex conscience"': Politics and Popular Attitudes in the Permissive Society', in R. Coopey, S. Fielding and N. Tiratsoo, *The Wilson Governments, 1964–70*, p.136
132. Holden, p.147
133. Crossman diary, p.433 (19.7.67)
134. Holden, p.153
135. Crossman diary, p.468 (7.9.67)
136. Cabinet 27.11.67 [CAB 128, CC(67) 186]
137. Jenkins to Tom Driberg, 7.9.67 [HO 302/41]
138. See *New Scientist*, 10.67
139. Alastair Hetherington diary, 6.9.67 [LSE]
140. House of Commons, 16.11.67 [Vol.754, cols 653–72]
141. Denis Howell, *Made in Birmingham*, p.190
142. *The Times,* 17.11.67
143. Castle diary, pp.321–2 (13.11.67)
144. Cabinet, 14.11.67 [CAB 128, CC(67)65]
145. *The Cecil King Diary, 1964–1970*, p.173 (8.2.68)
146. Castle diary, p.323 (14.11.67)
147. ibid., p.325 (16.11.67)
148. Crossman diary, pp.575–6 (16.11.67)
149. ibid., p.577 (17.11.67)
150. ibid., p.297 (3.4.67)
151. ibid., p.445 (27.7.67)
152. ibid., p.462 (5.9.67)
153. Callaghan to Crosland, 28.9.67 [Crosland papers 5/3]
154. Crossman diary, p.464 (5.9.67), and p.552 (3.11.67)
155. Alan Watkins, 'Mr Crosland's Clarion Call', in *Spectator*, 21.7.67.
156. Jeffreys, p.124
157. Jenkins, *ALATC*, p.214
158. *New Statesman*, 1.12.67
159. Crossman diary, p.593 (27.11.67)
160. Jenkins, *ALATC*, p.218
161. Speech at Meriden, 2.12.67 [Jenkins papers]
162. *The Economist*, 2.12.67; *Daily Mirror*, 30.11.67; Jenkins papers
163. *The Times*, 30.11.67
164. *Financial Times*, 30.11.67
165. *Sunday Telegraph*, 3.12.67
166. *Sunday Times*, 3.12.67
167. Jenkins, *ALATC*, p.217
168. Giles Radice, *Friends & Rivals: Crosland, Jenkins and Healey*, p.153

Chapter Thirteen: 'Two Years' Hard Slog'

1. Interview, Lord Harris of Greenwich, 19.5.82
2. Ian Gilmour to Jenkins, n.d. [Jenkins papers]
3. Denis Healey to Jenkins, 29.11.67 [Jenkins papers]
4. *The Times*, 1.12.67
5. *The Cecil King Diary, 1965–70*, p.163, (25.12.67)
6. *Spectator*, 1.12.67
7. House of Commons, 19.3.68 [Vol.761, cols 253]. He actually used the phrase for the first time two months earlier on 17 January [Vol.756, col.1805].
8. Samuel Brittan, *Steering the Economy* (1969), p.299
9. Harold Wilson, *The Labour Government, 1964–70*, p.595
10. Nicholas Davenport, *Memoirs of a City Radical*, p.220
11. Interview, Lord Armstrong of Ilminster, 3.3.09
12. Jenkins, *A Life at the Centre* [*ALATC*], p.221
13. *Money Management*, October 1971
14. Alan Sked & Chris Cook, *Post-War Britain, 1945–1992: A Political History*, p.199
15. CAB 128, CC(68)6 (12.1.68)
16. CAB 128, CC(68)7 (15.1.68)
17. Barbara Castle, *The Castle Diaries, 1964–70*, p.342 (31.12.67)
18. CAB 128, CC(68)2 (5.1.68)
19. Jenkins, *ALATC*, pp.224–5
20. CAB 128, CC(68)5 (12.1.68)
21. Castle diary, p.358 (15.1.68)
22. Richard Crossman, *The Diaries of a*

Cabinet Minister, Volume 2, p.647
(12.1.68)

23. Harold Wilson to Lyndon
Johnson, 15.1.68, in Philip Ziegler,
Wilson, p.285

24. Jenkins, *ALATC,* p.225

25. Castle diary, p.355 (12.1.68)

26. Alastair Hetherington diary, 13.12.67
[Hetherington papers 13/1]

27. Tony Benn, *Office Without Power:
Diaries, 1968–72,* pp.15–16 (12.1.68)

28. Wilson, p.608

29. Crossman diary, Vol.2, p.633 (3.1.68)

30. *The Times,* 17.1.68

31. ibid., 18.1.68

32. Castle diary, p.360 (19.1.68)

33. Benn diary, p.21 (19.1.68)

34. Robert Armstrong memo, 16.2.68
[T.171/829]

35. Sir Leslie O'Brien to James
Callaghan, 17.11.67, but shown to
Jenkins before his meeting with
O'Brien on 8.12.68 [T.171/829]

36. Jenkins to Raymond Snoddy, 3.11.99
[Jenkins papers]

37. Alec Cairncross, *The Wilson Years: A
Treasury Diary, 1964–69,* p.276 (21.2.68)

38. Jenkins, *ALATC,* p.233

39. Crossman diary, Vol.2, p.695 (7.3.68)

40. ibid., p.723 (19.3.68)

41. Castle diary, pp.405–6 (18.3.68)

42. Jenkins, *ALATC,* p.234

43. CAB 128/46 (note of a meeting at
1.15 a.m. on 15.3.68)

44. *The Times,* 31.10.87

45. Castle diary, p.399 (14.3.68)

46. Occasional journal, 'dictated Whitsun
1968' [Jenkins papers]

47. Jenkins, *ALATC,* pp.244–5

48. Cairncross, p.290 (19.3.68)

49. Castle diary, pp.406–7 (19.3.68)

50. Leslie Bonham Carter to Jenkins,
19.3.68 [Jenkins papers]

51. Cairncross, p.290 (19.3.68)

52. House of Commons, 19.3.68 [Vol.761,
cols 251–302]

53. Budget broadcast, 19.3.68

54. John Grigg to Jenkins, 20.3.68
[Jenkins papers]

55. *Evening Standard,* 20.3.68

56. *Guardian,* 20.3.68

57. *The Times,* 20.3.68

58. *Sunday Times,* 17.1.71

59. Jenkins to Sir Douglas Allen, 27.5.68
[Jenkins papers]

60. Interview, Lord Armstrong of
Ilminster, 3.3.09

61. Lord Bancroft to Jenkins, 20.4.90
[Jenkins papers]

62. Alec Cairncross, *Living with the
Century,* p.251

63. Cairncross, *The Wilson Years,* pp.336–7
(3.11.68)

64. Address at Sir Leo Pliatzky's
memorial service, 21.7.99 [Jenkins
papers]

65. Brittan, p.25

66. Castle diary, p.487 (15.7.68)

67. *Observer,* 20.6.71

68. Roy Jenkins, *Nine Men of Power,* p.103

69. Alastair Hetherington diary, 4.11.68
[Hetherington papers 15/5]

70. Robert Mellish to Jenkins, 8.5.69
[Jenkins papers]

71. *Observer,* 18.10.76 and 4.11.84

72. Benn diary, p.34 (11.2.68)

73. Richard Crossman, *The Diaries of a
Cabinet Minister,* Volume 3, p.194
(19.9.68)

74. Jenkins' obituary of Callaghan,
published posthumously in the
Sunday Times, 27.3.05

75. Interview with Anne Scott-James,
Evening Standard, 26.2.70

76. *The Times,* 13.1.70

77. Brittan, p.32

78. William Davis, *Three Years Hard
Labour,* p.181

79. Robert Carvel in *Evening Standard,*
30.11.67

80. Marcia Falkender, *Downing Street in
Perspective,* p.229

81. *Birmingham Evening Mail,* 9.70

82. Castle diary, p.726 (5.11.69)

83. ibid., p.419 (3.4.68)

84. *Daily Telegraph,* 17.9.93

85. Paddy Ashdown, *The Ashdown Diaries:
Volume One, 1988–97,* pp.252–3
(6.2.94)

86. John Cole, *As It Seemed To Me,* p.69

87. Bill Rodgers interviewed by David
Butler, 23.4.70 [David Butler papers]

88. Ben Pimlott, *Harold Wilson,* pp.504–5

89. Ashdown diary, p.130 (19.1.92)

90. *Evening Standard,* 3.5.68

91. *The Current,* 9.7.52

92. Gerald Kaufman interviewed by David Butler, 19.5.69 [David Butler papers]
93. Jenkins, *ALATC*, p.257
94. Mayhew's diary of events in 1968, sent to Jenkins 4.1.80 [Jenkins papers]; see also Christopher Mayhew, *Time to Explain*, pp.181–8
95. Patrick Gordon Walker, *Political Diaries, 1932–1971*, pp.322–3 (17.6.68)
96. ibid., p.324 (19.7.68)
97. ibid., pp.324–5 (7.5.69, 13.5.69)
98. Jenkins, *ALATC*, p.260
99. Castle diary, p.453 (31.5.68)
100. Crossman diary, Vol.2, p.784 (16.4.68)
101. Jenkins, *Nine Men of Power*, pp.207–8
102. *Observer*, 4.11.90
103. *Labour Party Annual Conference Report, 1969*, pp.135–8 (30.9.68)
104. Occasional journal, dictated August 1969 [Jenkins papers]
105. Jenkins, *ALATC*, p.261
106. Jenkins to Tony Crosland, 19.9.69; Crosland to Jenkins, 19.9.69; Jenkins to Crosland, 22.9.69 [Jenkins papers]
107. Jenkins, *ALATC*, p.261
108. Cairncross, *The Wilson Years*, pp.336–7
109. ibid.
110. Jenkins, *ALATC*, p.266
111. Occasional journal, dictated August 1969 [Jenkins papers]
112. Castle diary, p.557 (25.11.68)
113. Cairncross, *Living with the Century*, p.252
114. Roy Jenkins, *The Chancellors*, p.315
115. David Dowler to Jenkins, 3.1.69 [Treasury papers, T171/839]
116. Ann Fleming to Nicholas Henderson, 25.10.69, in *The Letters of Ann Fleming*, p.398
117. Treasury memo, 31.1.69 [T171/839]
118. John Harris to Jenkins, 3.3.69 [ibid.]
119. D.J.S. Hancock memo, 11.3.69 [ibid.]
120. Tony Crosland to Jenkins, 15.4.69 [Jenkins papers]
121. Crossman diary, Vol.3, p.437 (14.4.69)
122. *Daily Telegraph, The Times, Financial Times, Daily Mail, Daily Express* and *Sun*, 16.4.69
123. Jenkins, *ALATC*, p.274
124. Kenneth Baker, *The Turbulent Years*, p.29
125. Jenkins to Iain Macleod, 5.6.68 [Jenkins papers]
126. Roy Jenkins, *Portraits and Miniatures*, p.47
127. Jenkins, *ALATC*, pp.274–8
128. ibid., p.278
129. ibid., p.279
130. John Harris interviewed by David Butler, 29.9.70 [David Butler papers]
131. *The Times*, 16.9.69
132. ibid., 2.10.69
133. *Labour Party Annual Conference Report, 1969*, p.253 (1.10.69)
134. E-mail reply to *New Statesman* intern, Emily (illegible), n.d. [Jenkins papers]
135. Castle diary, p.393 (7.3.68)
136. House of Commons, 21.4.70 [Vol.800, col.111]
137. Jenkins, *ALATC*, p.287
138. PREM 13/2724, quoted in Jim Tomlinson, *The Labour Government, 1964–70: Economic Policy*, p.145
139. Peter Jenkins, *The Battle of Downing Street*, p.94
140. Jenkins, *ALATC*, p.288
141. Roy Hattersley, *Who Goes Home?*, p.68
142. Roy Hattersley's obituary of Jenkins, *Guardian*, 6.1.03
143. Castle diary, Vol.2, p.674 (17.6.69); Crossman diary, Vol.3, p.524 (17.6.69)
144. Crossman diary, Vol.3, pp.526–7 (18.6.69)
145. Castle diary, pp.674–5 (17.6.69)
146. Jenkins, *ALATC*, p.287
147. David Owen, *Time to Declare*, pp.156–8
148. Jenkins, *ALATC*, p.290
149. Speeches in Portsmouth, 7.11.69; Manchester, 28.11.69; Newcastle, 29.11.69
150. Treasury minute, 9.2.70 [T 171/855]
151. ibid., 17.2.70
152. Donald MacDougall, *Don and Mandarin*, p.17
153. Treasury minute, 20.1.70 [T 171/855]
154. ibid., 4.3.70 [T 171/865]
155. CAB 128, CC(70)7 (12.2.70)
156. Castle diary, pp.761–2 (12.2.70)
157. CAB 128, CC(70)7 (12.2.70)
158. Benn diary, pp.236–7 (12.2.70)
159. Crossman diary, Vol.3, p.819 (15.2.70)
160. Benn diary, p.240 (18.2.70)

161. Crossman diary, Vol.3. pp.824–5 (18.2.70)
162. Benn diary, p.240 (18.2.70)
163. Castle diary, pp.764–5 (18.2.70)
164. Crossman diary, Vol.3, p.835 (18.2.70)
165. Castle diary, pp.769–70 (8.3.70)
166. Crossman diary, Vol.3, p.851 (8.3.70)
167. Castle diary, p.772 (11.3.70)
168. Treasury minute, 12.3.70 [T 171/856]
169. ibid., 18.3.70
170. Jenkins, *ALATC*, p.294
171. Douglas Wass to William Ryrie, 3.4.70 [T 171/856]
172. *The Times*, 15.4.70
173. Treasury paper, 15.4.70 [T 171/868]
174. *Daily Mirror*, 15.4.70; *Sun*, 15.4.70
175. Crossman diary, Vol.3, pp.885–6 (13.4.70)
176. Castle diary, p.786 (15.4.70)
177. Chancellor's budget broadcast, 14.4.70 [T 171/868]
178. Paul Carmody and Percy Clark interviewed by David Butler, 5.5.70 [David Butler papers]
179. Crossman diary, Vol.3, p.898 (23.4.70)
180. Barbara Castle, *Fighting All The Way*, p.427
181. *The Economist*, 17.4.70, quoted in David Butler & Michael Pinto-Duchinsky, *The British General Election of 1970*, pp.132–3; see also Edmund Dell, *The Chancellors*, pp.366–7
182. Jenkins interviewed by Fiona Millar, 1992 [typescript in Jenkins papers]
183. Crossman diary, Vol.3, p.909 (4.5.70)
184. ibid., p.915 (10.5.70)
185. Butler & Pinto-Duchinsky, p.165
186. Nicholas Henderson, *Old Friends and Modern Instances*, pp.117–20
187. *The Times*, 2.6.70; *Financial Times*, 8.6.70
188. Party Election Broadcast, 12.6.70 [Jenkins papers]
189. Ziegler, p.337
190. David Owen, *Time to Declare*, pp.161–2
191. House of Commons, 7.7.70. [Vol.803, col.511]
192. Jenkins, *ALATC*, p.301
193. Butler & Pinto-Duchinsky, p.167
194. Jenkins, *ALATC*, pp.302–3
195. *The Times*, 20.6.70

Chapter Fourteen: Europe before Party

1. David Lipsey, *In the Corridors of Power*, pp.41–2
2. *Observer*, 20.6.71
3. Barbara Castle unpublished diary, 23.6.70 [Castle papers]; Bernard Donoughue, *Downing Street Diary: With Harold Wilson in No. 10*, p.34 (23.2.74)
4. ibid., 8.7.70
5. Dictated memoir material [Jenkins papers]
6. *Observer*, 20.6.71
7. House of Commons, 7.7.70 [Vol.803, cols 513–26]
8. Jenkins, *A Life at the Centre* [*ALATC*], p.313
9. House of Commons, 17.11.71 [Vol.806, cols 1032–7]
10. NEC minutes, 1970–72; Michael Hatfield, *The House the Left Built: Inside Labour Policy Making 1970–1975*, pp.46–7, 57
11. Dictated memoir material [Jenkins papers]
12. *Guardian*, 2.10.70; Tony Benn, *Office Without Power: Diaries, 1968–72*, p.307 (1.10.70)
13. Jenkins, *ALATC*, p.313
14. Dictated memoir material [Jenkins papers]
15. Jenkins papers
16. Jenkins to Harold Evans, 5.1.71 [Jenkins papers]
17. Roy Jenkins, *Nine Men of Power*, pp.180, 64, 83–4
18. ibid., pp.203, 197
19. ibid., p.223
20. ibid., p.x
21. ibid., p.29
22. *The Times*, 8.4.88
23. *Times Literary Supplement*, 23.6.72; *Spectator*, 17.6.72
24. House of Commons, 26.11.70 (Vol.807, cols 651–6)
25. Unpublished Castle diary, 8.10.70
26. ibid., 23.3.71
27. ibid., 18.1.71
28. ibid., 24.2.71
29. ibid., 7.6.71
30. David Owen, *Time to Declare*, p.162
31. Stephen Wall, *The Official History of*

Britain and the European Community:
Volume II, *From Rejection to*
Referendum, 1963–1975, pp.348, 358
32. Castle diary, 19.6.70
33. ibid., 20.6.70
34. *The Times*, 10.5.71
35. ibid., 19.6.71
36. *Daily Telegraph*, 21.7.71
37. Castle diary, 22.6.71
38. ibid., 24.6.71
39. Speech at Lancaster University,
    8.11.89
40. Ben Pimlott, *Harold Wilson*, p.583
41. Quoted in Roger Broad, *Labour's*
    European Dilemmas: From Bevin to
    Blair, p.80
42. Jenkins, *ALATC*, p.320
43. *The Times*, 20.7.71
44. Benn diary, p.358 (19.7.71)
45. Leo Abse, *Private Member*, p.264
46. Castle diary, 19.7.71
47. Benn diary, pp.358–9 (20.7.71)
48. Pimlott, p.587
49. Castle diary, 21.7.71
50. *The Times*, 23.7.71
51. Roger Broad, witness seminar
    12.6.90, in *Contemporary Record*, 1993,
    p.388
52. *The Times*, 4.10.71
53. Benn diary, p.377 (4.10.71)
54. Roy Hattersley, *Who Goes Home?*,
    p.105
55. Witness seminar, 12.6.90 (p.390)
56. Shadow Cabinet minutes, 18.10.71
57. Benn diary, p.379 (18.10.71)
58. Shadow Cabinet minutes, 19.10.71
59. Castle diary, 19.10.71
60. ibid.
61. Witness seminar, 12.6.90 (p.407);
    James Wellbeloved to Jenkins,
    10.10.71 [Jenkins papers]
62. NEC minutes, 27.10.71
63. Jenkins to David Rhydderch, 19.10.71
    [Jenkins papers]
64. Witness seminar 12.6.90 (p.407)
65. Castle diary, 28.10.71
66. *Tribune*, 5.11.71
67. *Sunday Times*, 31.10.71
68. *The Times*, 29.10.71
69. Speech at Heywood and Royton,
    29.10.71 [*Labour Weekly*, 5.11.71]
70. Jenkins, *ALATC*, p.333
71. Robert Harris diary, 22.4.96

72. Speech at Heywood and Royton,
    29.10.71 [*Labour Weekly*, 5.11.71]
73. Castle diary, 29.10.71
74. Hattersley, p.106
75. Speech notes in the possession of
    Roy Hattersley
76. Castle diary, 4.11.71
77. Benn diary, p.383 (4.11.71)
78. Witness seminar, 12.6.90 (pp.415–16)
79. Jenkins, *ALATC*, p.334
80. Castle diary, 18.11.71
81. ibid., 2.12.71
82. Head of Chancery, Delhi, to Jenkins,
    n.d. [Jenkins papers]
83. Witness seminar, 12.6.90
84. Benn diary, p.406 (17.2.72)
85. John Golding to Jenkins, 18.7.72
    [Jenkins papers]
86. Jenkins, *ALATC*, p.340; see also Uwe
    Kitzinger, *Diplomacy and Persuasion:*
    How Britain Joined the Common
    Market, pp.386–96
87. Reference mislaid
88. Castle diary, 9.3.72
89. Bill Rodgers to Jenkins, 7.4.72
    [Jenkins papers]
90. Castle diary, 22.2.72
91. Phillip Whitehead to Jenkins, 22.2.72
    [Jenkins papers]
92. Gwynoro Jones to Jenkins, 23.2.72
    [Jenkins papers]
93. Austen Albu to Jenkins, undated,
    February 1972 [Jenkins papers]
94. David Marquand to Jenkins, undated,
    February 1972 [Jenkins papers]
95. David Owen to Jenkins, undated,
    February 1972 [Jenkins papers]
96. Neville Sandelson to Jenkins, 23.2.72;
    Jenkins to Sandelson, 28.2.72
    [Sandelson papers 9/14, LSE]
97. Speech at Farnworth, 11.3.72,
    reprinted in Roy Jenkins, *What*
    Matters Now, pp.9–22
98. *The Times*, 13.3.72
99. Alexander Pope, *Epistle to Arbuthnot*,
    ll. 189–90
100. Castle diary, 12.3.72, 19.3.72
101. Hetherington diary, 9.3.72
     [Hetherington 19/22]
102. Jenkins, *ALATC*, p.340
103. Memoir material [Jenkins papers]
104. Jenkins, *ALATC*, p.341
105. There seems to be no agreed source

for this oft-quoted remark attributed
to Attlee.
106. *The Times*, 22.1.54
107. Shadow Cabinet, 29.3.72
108. Benn diary, p.421 (29.3.72)
109. Jenkins, *ALATC*, p.341
110. Bill Rodgers to Jenkins, 7.4.72
   [thanks to Lord Rodgers of Quarry
   Bank]
111. David Owen, 'Manoeuvres Towards
   the Referendum', in Mark
   Bainbridge, ed., *The 1975 Referendum
   on Europe*, p.126
112. Dictated memoir material [Jenkins
   papers]
113. Interview for *The Seventies* [LSE
   004/08]
114. *The Economist*, 15.4.76
115. Castle diary, 11.4.72, 12.4.72
116. Hattersley, p.109
117. ibid., p.114
118. Crosland papers, 6/2
119. Bill Rodgers to Jenkins, 12.11.90
   [thanks to Lord Rodgers]
120. David Owen to Tony Crosland,
   20.4.72 [Crosland papers, 6/2]
121. Castle diary, 10.4.72
122. *The Times*, 11.4.72
123. *The Economist*, 15.4.72
124. Jenkins papers
125. ibid.
126. Fred Silberman in *Labour Weekly*,
   14.4.72

Chapter Fifteen: *What Matters Now*

1. Barbara Castle unpublished diary,
   12.3.72 [Castle papers]
2. *New Statesman*, 26.5.72
3. *The Times*, 30.9.72
4. Robert Maclennan to Jenkins,
   undated, 10.72 [Jenkins papers]
5. Bill Rodgers to Jenkins, 21.7.72
   [Jenkins papers]
6. *Guardian*, 14.6.72
7. Roy Jenkins, *What Matters Now*, p.122
8. *The Times*, 5.10.72
9. Interviews, Dick Taverne, 4.8.82 and
   1.12.08
10. Jenkins to Reg Underhill, 20.1.73;
   Jenkins to Willie Hamling, 2.3.73
   [Jenkins papers]
11. *The Times*, 10.4.73
12. ibid.

13. ibid., 12.3.73
14. Castle diary, 12.3.73
15. *Labour Weekly*, 23.3.73
16. Jenkins, *What Matters Now*, pp.30–36
17. BBC Radio 4, 8.7.73 [transcript in
   Enoch Powell papers, POLL
   4/1/128]
18. Roy and Jennifer Jenkins, *China
   Diary*, 1973 [Jenkins papers]
19. Roy Jenkins, *A Life at the Centre*
   [*ALATC*], p.360
20. *Labour Party Annual Conference Report,
   1973*, pp.183–4 (2.10.73)
21. ibid., p.184
22. Interview for *The Seventies* [LSE
   004/08]
23. Shadow Cabinet, 28.22.73, 5.12.73;
   John Cole, note of lunch with
   Crosland, 28.11.73, in Alastair
   Hetherington papers, 21/39 [LSE]
24. Philip Ziegler, *Wilson*, pp.388–9,
   citing Harold Wilson, *The Chariot of
   Israel*, p.367
25. Jenkins, *ALATC*, p.362
26. Shirley Williams to Jenkins, 19.12.73
   [Jenkins papers]
27. House of Commons, 19.12.73
   [Vol.866, cols 1457–65]
28. *The Times*, 20.12.73
29. Shirley Williams to Jenkins, 19.12.73
   [Jenkins papers]
30. Betty Boothroyd to Jenkins, Andrew
   Faulds to Jenkins, 19.12.73 [Jenkins
   papers]
31. David Marquand, *The Progressive
   Dilemma*, p.188
32. Jenkins, *ALATC*, p.364
33. Shadow Cabinet minutes, 16.1.74
34. ibid., 30.1.74
35. Ronald McIntosh, *Challenge to
   Democracy: Politics, Trade Union Power
   and Economic Failure in the 1970s*, p.58
   (19.1.74)
36. David Butler & Dennis Kavanagh,
   *The British General Election of February
   1974*, p.162
37. *Birmingham Mail*, 14.1.74
38. *The Times*, 16.2.74
39. ibid., 21.2.74
40. Butler & Kavanagh, p.107
41. Ben Whitaker interviewed by Dennis
   Kavanagh, 14.2.74 [David Butler
   papers]

42. Raymond Carr to Jenkins, n.d. [Jenkins papers]
43. Terence Rattigan to Jenkins, 28.2.74 [Jenkins papers]
44. Raymond Fletcher to Jenkins, 22.2.74 [Jenkins papers]
45. Jenkins, *ALATC*, pp.366–7
46. *The Times*, 28.2.74
47. Interview, Matthew Oakeshott, 1.3.82
48. *The Times*, 2.3.74
49. Bill Rodgers diary, 3.3.74. (Unpublished. Thanks to Lord Rodgers of Quarry Bank.)
50. McIntosh, p.87 (1.3.74)
51. Jenkins, *ALATC*, p.369
52. McIntosh, p.89 (4.3.74)
53. Bernard Donoughue, *Downing Street Diary: With Harold Wilson in No. 10*, p.53 (4.3.74)
54. Jenkins, *ALATC*, pp.370–1
55. ibid., p.371
56. Rodgers diary, 4.3.74
57. ibid., 5.3.74
58. Jenkins, *Nine Men of Power*, p.203
59. Rodgers diary, 5.3.74
60. ibid., 6.3.74
61. Robert Maclennan to Jenkins, 11.3.74 [Jenkins papers]
62. Paul Rose to Jenkins, 11.3.74 [Jenkins papers]
63. ibid., 1.3.75 [Jenkins papers]
64. Giles Radice to Jenkins, 11.3.74 [Jenkins papers]
65. Madron Seligman to Jenkins, 12.3.74 [Jenkins papers]
66. Derek Powell to Jenkins, 12.3.74 [Jenkins papers]
67. Jenkins, *ALATC*, p.371.
68. *Sunday Times*, 17.1.71.

Chapter Sixteen: Back to the Home Office

1. Jenkins, *A Life at the Centre* [*ALATC*], p.375
2. Jenkins to Syd Norris, 31.3.93; Norris to Jenkins, 7.4.93 [Jenkins papers]
3. Lester to Jenkins, 20.5.74 [Jenkins papers]
4. Jenkins, dictated journal, 1975 [Jenkins papers]
5. Private information
6. Interview for *The Seventies* [LSE 004/08]
7. Anthony Lester, 'The Home Office Again', in Andrew Adonis & Keith Thomas, *Roy Jenkins: A Retrospective*, p.150
8. Jenkins, *ALATC*, pp.378–9
9. *The Times*, 3.6.74
10. ibid., 8.6.74
11. *Sunday Times*, 10.7.83
12. Jenkins, *ALATC*, p.395
13. House of Commons, 28.11.74 [Vol.882, col.669]
14. CAB 128/55, CC(74)49; House of Commons, 25.11.74 [Vol.882, cols 667–71]
15. Jenkins, *ALATC*, p.397
16. *Observer*, 3.11.91, reprinted in Roy Jenkins, *Portraits and Miniatures*, p.257
17. Jenkins, *ALATC*, p.397
18. Sir Robert Birley to Jenkins, 24.11.74 [Jenkins papers]
19. Sir Alan Lascelles to Jenkins, 25.11.74 [Jenkins papers]
20. Denis Healey to Jenkins, 28.11.74 [Jenkins papers]
21. Jenkins, dictated journal, 1974 [Jenkins papers]
22. Jenkins, *ALATC*, p.397
23. Roy Jenkins, *Afternoon on the Potomac?*, p.57
24. Bernard Donoughue, *Downing Street Diary: With Harold Wilson in No. 10*, p.254 (4.12.74)
25. ibid., p.562 (11.11.75)
26. Jenkins, *Portraits and Miniatures*, p.257
27. Jenkins, dictated journal, 1974 [Jenkins papers]
28. Jenkins interviewed 25.11.99, in Andrew Holden, *Makers and Manners*, p.14
29. Anthony Lester in Adonis & Thomas, p.159
30. House of Commons, 8.7.76 (Vol.914, col.1800)
31. Barbara Castle, *The Castle Diaries, 1974–76*, pp.71–2 (5.4.74)
32. Jenkins, dictated journal, 1976 [Jenkins papers]
33. Tony Benn, *The End of an Era: Diaries 1980–1990*, p.88 (12.2.81)
34. *The Times*, 22.7.75
35. ibid., 19.5.76

36. *Daily Telegraph* obituary, 1.10.10
37. House of Commons, 5.12.75 [Vol.901, cols 2076–2171]
38. Susan Crosland, *Tony Crosland*, pp.281–3
39. Jenkins, *ALATC*, pp.391–2
40. *Sunday Times*, 8.6.75
41. Donoughue, pp.158–9 (9.7.74)
42. *Scotsman*, 9.9.91
43. Ronald McIntosh, *Challenge to Democracy: Politics, Trade Union Power and Economic Failure in the 1970s*, p.120 (30.6.74)
44. Castle diary, pp.69–70 (4.4.74)
45. Cabinet, 18.11.75 [CAB 128/57 CC(75)49]
46. Castle diary, p.554 (18.11.75)
47. Donoughue, p.570 (18.11.75)
48. Anthony Lester in Adonis & Thomas, p.155
49. Donoughue, pp.527, 529–30 (13.10.75, 15.10.75)
50. ibid., pp.683–4 (3.3.76)
51. Jenkins, *ALATC*, p.386
52. *The Times*, 27.7.74
53. Castle diary, p.156 (29.7.74)
54. ibid., pp.159–60 (30.7.74)
55. ibid., 29.7.74
56. McIntosh, p.130 (29.7.74)
57. ibid., p.140 (5.9.74 – but Jenkins' engagement diary says he lunched with McIntosh on 6.9.74)
58. Lester to Jenkins, undated, July 1974 [Jenkins papers]
59. Donoughue, pp.184–5 (12.9.74)
60. Election address, October 1974 [Jenkins papers]
61. Jenkins, dictated journal, 1974 [Jenkins papers]
62. Donoughue, p.206 (2.10.74)
63. ibid., p.214 (8.10.74)
64. *The Times*, 4.10.74
65. David Butler & Dennis Kavanagh, *The British General Election of October 1974*, p.143
66. *The Times*, 5.10.74
67. ibid., 27.9.74
68. Jenkins, *ALATC*, p.389
69. *The Times*, 12.10.74

Chapter Seventeen: Victory and Defeat

1. Barbara Castle, *The Castle Diaries*, 1974–76, pp.155, 182–3 (25.7.74, 16.9.74); Tony Benn, *Against the Tide: Diaries 1973–76*, p.206 (25.7.74)
2. *The Times*, 15.3.75
3. Nicholas Henderson, *Mandarin*, p.84
4. Cabinet, 17.3.75 [CAB 128/56 CC(75)13]
5. Cabinet, 18.3.75 [CAB 128/56 CC(75)14]
6. Shirley Williams interviewed by David Butler [David Butler papers]
7. Jenkins, dictated journal, 1975 [Jenkins papers]
8. Roger Broad, *Labour's European Dilemmas: From Bevin to Blair*, p.116
9. Jenkins, dictated journal, 1975 [Jenkins papers]
10. Speech at Labour Party special conference, 26.4.75, quoted in the official 'Yes' leaflet [David Butler & Uwe Kitzinger, *The 1975 Referendum*, p.291]
11. Roy Jenkins, *A Life at the Centre* [*ALATC*], p.417
12. *The Times*, 28.5.75
13. Harold Wilson, *Final Term: The Labour Government 1974–1976*, p.105; Harold Wilson to Jenkins, 28.5.75 and 29.5.75, in Philip Ziegler, *Wilson*, p.430
14. Butler & Kitzinger, p.205
15. *The Times*, 6.6.75. The writer was the present author.
16. *Sunday Times*, 8.6.75
17. Butler & Kitzinger, p.183
18. ibid., p.188
19. *The Times*, 7.6.75
20. Jenkins, dictated journal, 1975 [Jenkins papers]
21. Castle diary, p.432 (23.6.75)
22. Jenkins, dictated journal, 1975 [Jenkins papers]
23. Jenkins, *ALATC*, p.425
24. Hugh Thomas to Jenkins, 13.11.74 [Jenkins papers]
25. Jenkins, dictated journal, 1975 [Jenkins papers]
26. Jenkins, *ALATC*, p.422
27. John Grigg to Patricia Grigg, 14.6.78 (thanks to Mrs Grigg)
28. *The Times*, 13.9.75
29. ibid.
30. ibid.
31. Bernard Donoughue, *Downing Street*

Diary: With James Callaghan in No. 10, p.316 (25.2.75)

32. Castle diary, p.400 (22.5.75)
33. Jenkins, dictated journal, 1975 [Jenkins papers]
34. Castle diary, p.199 (22.10.74)
35. Donoughue, p.608 (12.12.75)
36. Jenkins, dictated journal, 1975 [Jenkins papers]
37. Donoughue, p.379 (14.5.75)
38. ibid., p.594 (3.12.75)
39. *The Times*, 24.1.76
40. Castle diary, p.427 (20.6.75)
41. *The Times*, 9.5.75
42. ibid., 29.9.76
43. Jenkins, *ALATC*, pp.430–31
44. ibid., p.431
45. Jenkins, dictated journal, 1976 [Jenkins papers]
46. Donoughue, p.640 (22.1.76)
47. Jenkins to Harold Wilson, 26.1.76 [Jenkins papers]
48. Donoughue, p.650 (29.1.76)
49. Roy Jenkins, *European Diary*, p.5
50. Nicholas Henderson to Jenkins, 1.3.76 [Jenkins papers]
51. Jacques de Beaumarchais to Jenkins, n.d. [Jenkins papers]
52. Ziegler, p.483
53. CAB 128/58, CC(76)10
54. Gerald Kaufman, *How to be a Minister*, p.18
55. *The Times*, 24.3.76
56. ibid., 18.3.76
57. *New Statesman*, 16.4.76
58. Stephen Haseler, *The Tragedy of Labour*, p.119
59. Bill Rodgers diary, 27.4.76 (thanks to Lord Rodgers of Quarry Bank)
60. Donoughue, p.708 (22.3.76)
61. ibid., p.701 (17.3.76)
62. Ronald McIntosh, *Challenge to Democracy*, p.267 (21.3.76)
63. Barley Alison to Jenkins, 24.3.76 [Jenkins papers]
64. Derrick Powell to Jenkins, 24.3.76 [Jenkins papers]
65. Jenkins papers
66. Jenkins, dictated journal, 1976 [Jenkins papers]
67. Peter Kellner & Christopher Hitchens, *Callaghan: The Road to Number Ten*, p.171

68. Bill Rodgers to Jenkins, 25.3.76 [Jenkins papers]
69. Jenkins, dictated journal, 1976 [Jenkins papers]
70. Castle diary, p.705 (25.3.76)
71. Barbara Castle, *Fighting All The Way*, p.488
72. Benn diary, p.533 (5.4.76)
73. Jenkins to Wilson, 10.4.76, handwritten draft [Jenkins papers]
74. Callaghan papers
75. Jenkins, dictated journal, 1976 [Jenkins papers]
76. ibid.
77. Lord Goodman, *Tell Them I'm On My Way*, p.245
78. Jenkins, dictated journal, 1976 [Jenkins papers]
79. Donoughue, p.717 (2.4.76)
80. Ann Fleming to Jenkins, 9.4.76 [Jenkins papers]
81. David Watt to Jenkins, 30.3.76 [Jenkins papers]
82. Janet Morgan to Jenkins, 9.4.76 [Jenkins papers]
83. Jenkins, dictated journal, 1976 [Jenkins papers]
84. *New Statesman*, 16.4.76
85. Bill Rodgers to Jenkins, 5.4.76 [Jenkins papers]
86. Jenkins to Giscard d'Estaing, 8.4.76 [Jenkins papers]
87. McIntosh, pp.272–3 (14.4.76)
88. *The Times*, 27.4.76
89. ibid.
90. Jenkins to Gaston Thorn, 5.5.76 [Jenkins papers]
91. John Grigg to Jenkins, 5.5.76 [Jenkins papers]
92. Donoughue, p.19 (14.4.76)
93. Callaghan papers, Box 112/2733; Jenkins, *ALATC*, p.443
94. Cabinet 18.5.76, CAB 128/59 CC(76)
95. Cabinet 1.7.76, CAB 128/59 CC(76)12
96. Donoughue, p.61 (30.7.76)
97. Benn diary, p.569 (20.5.76)
98. See Anthony Lester, 'Back to the Home Office', in Andrew Adonis & Keith Thomas, *Roy Jenkins: A Retrospective*, pp.160–1
99. Cabinet 20.5.76, CAB 128/59 CC(76)6

100. Castle diary, p.153 (24.7.74)
101. Donoughue, p.170 (30.7.74)
102. Crosland papers 5/24
103. Donoughue, p.285 (17.1.75)
104. ibid., p.415 (13.6.75)
105. ibid., pp.493–4 (10.9.75)
106. Castle diary, p.497 (10.9.75)
107. *The Times*, 27.3.76
108. Castle diary, p.713 (1.4.76)
109. House of Commons, 5.7.76 [Vol.914, cols 972–87]
110. Bernard Donoughue, *Downing Street Diary: With James Callaghan in No. 10*, p.68 (10.9.76)
111. Jenkins, dictated journal, 1976 [Jenkins papers]
112. Speech in Stechford, 22.7.76 [Jenkins papers]
113. *The Times*, 9.12.76
114. McIntosh, pp.298–9 (11.10.76)
115. *Daily Telegraph*, 9.12.76
116. Jeremy Hutchinson to Jenkins, 17.9.76 [Jenkins papers]
117. Hugh Thomas to Jenkins, 10.11.76 [Jenkins papers]

Chapter Eighteen: 'Le Roi Jean Quinze'

1. Tribute to Emile Noël, 18.9.87, in Roy Jenkins, *A Gallery of Twentieth Century Portraits*, p.140
2. Lecture, Italian Institute, 17.11.92 [Jenkins papers]
3. Robert Harris diary, 8.4.01
4. Speech at St Mary's Church, Oxford, 24.10.88 [Jenkins papers]
5. Roy Jenkins, *A Life at the Centre* [*ALATC*], p.447
6. Mansion House dinner, 30.3.89 [Jenkins papers]
7. Jenkins, *ALATC*, p.449
8. ibid., p.447
9. John Grigg to Patricia Grigg, 14.6.78 [thanks to Mrs Grigg]
10. Jenkins, *ALATC*, p.448
11. Jenkins, *Twentieth Century Portraits*, p.166
12. *The Times*, 2.8.76
13. Birthday tribute, 16.7.00 [Jenkins papers]
14. Roy Jenkins, *European Diary*, p.2
15. Lord Carrington to Jenkins, 2.6.76. [Jenkins papers]
16. Interview, Lord Tugendhat, 18.2.11
17. *Panorama*, 11.10.76
18. *The Times*, 9.12.76
19. ibid., 5.1.77
20. Bill Rodgers to Jenkins, 22.1.76; Mark Bonham Carter to Jenkins, 22.1.76 [Jenkins papers]
21. Jenkins, *European Diary*, p.25 (6.1.77)
22. Unpublished diary, 6.1.77
23. Jenkins, *European Diary*, p.26 (7.1.77)
24. Unpublished diary, 8.1.77
25. Jenkins, *ALATC*, p.460
26. *The Economist*, 21.8.76
27. Jenkins, *European Diary*, p.2
28. Crispin Tickell interview, 28.1.99, British Diplomatic Oral History Programme
29. Lecture at Italian Institute, 17.11.92
30. Speech at De la Rue dinner, 2.6.88 [Jenkins papers]
31. Unpublished diary, 31.12.77
32. Crispin Tickell, 'President of the European Commission,' in Andrew Adonis & Keith Thomas, *Roy Jenkins: A Retrospective*, pp.208, 184
33. Jenkins, *European Diary*, pp.xiii–xvi
34. e.g. unpublished diary, 31.10.79, 5.11.79
35. Tickell in Adonis & Thomas, p.208
36. *The Times*, 22.1.77
37. Interview, Sir Nicholas Henderson, 10.7.08
38. Roger Beetham interview, 21.10.02, British Diplomatic Oral History Programme
39. Unpublished diary, August 1977
40. Unpublished diary, 31.12.77
41. Jenkins, *European Diary*, p.32 (18.1.77)
42. ibid., p.49 (16.2.77)
43. Roy Jenkins, *Sir Charles Dilke*, p.418
44. Jenkins, *European Diary*, p.223 (26.2.78)
45. ibid., p.50 (19.2.77)
46. *Sunday Times*, 20.2.77; Jenkins, *ALATC*, p.30
47. Jenkins, *European Diary*, p.60 (7.3.77)
48. Susan Crosland to Jenkins, 5.4.77 [Jenkins papers]
49. Jenkins, *European Diary*, p.52 (21.2.77)
50. Nicholas Henderson, *Mandarin*, p.140
51. Unpublished diary, 26.2.77
52. Henderson, p.140
53. Unpublished diary, 10.4.77

54. David Owen, *Time to Declare*, p.279
55. Henderson, p.140
56. Jenkins, *European Diary*, p.21
57. Minute of meeting with Chancellor Schmidt, Bonn, 18.3.77 [Jenkins papers]
58. Jenkins, *Twentieth Century Portraits*, pp.158–9
59. For example, at a meeting with Chancellor Schmidt, 18.3.77
60. Owen, pp.279–80
61. Roy Denman, *A Mandarin's Tale*, p.183
62. Jenkins, *European Diary*, p.96 (6.5.77)
63. Tickell in Adonis & Thomas, p.189
64. Unpublished diary, 7.5.77
65. Jenkins, *European Diary*, p.99 (8.5.77)
66. Barbara Castle, unpublished diary, 10.5.77 [Castle papers]
67. Christopher Tugendhat, 'The European Achievement', in Adonis & Thomas, p.206
68. Crispin Tickell in ibid., p.190
69. Jenkins, *European Diary*, pp.456–7, 467 (8.6.79, 22.6.79)
70. *The Economist*, 16.7.77
71. Jenkins, *ALATC*, p.462
72. *The Times*, 12.1.77
73. Jenkins, *European Diary*, pp.128–9 (21.7.77)
74. Tickell's minute of meeting with Callaghan, 21.7.77 [Jenkins papers]
75. Tickell's minute of meeting with Benn, 22.7.77 [Jenkins papers]
76. Speaking notes, East Hendred, 2.8.77 [Jenkins papers]
77. Michael Emerson to Jenkins, 16.7.98 [Jenkins papers]
78. Laura Grenfell's minute, East Hendred, 2.8.77 [Jenkins papers]
79. Jenkins, *European Diary*, p.143 (18.9.77)
80. ibid., p.152 (8.10.77)
81. *The Economist*, 24.9.77
82. Jean Monnet Lecture at the European University Institute, Florence, 27.10.77
83. Lecture at Italian Institute, 17.11.92
84. *The Times*, 28.10.77
85. Jenkins, *ALATC*, p.467
86. Tickell's minute of meeting with Schmidt, 10.11.77 [Jenkins papers]
87. Tickell's minute of meeting with Barre, 19.11.77 [Jenkins papers]
88. Tickell's minute of meeting with Callaghan, 25.11.77 [Jenkins papers]
89. Tickell's minute of meeting with Mrs Thatcher, 2.12.77 [Jenkins papers]
90. Unpublished diary, 2.12.77
91. ibid., 3.12.77
92. Jenkins, *European Diary*, pp.181–3 (5–6.12.77)
93. ibid., p.191 (21.12.77)
94. Unpublished diary, 3.11.77
95. ibid., 31.12.77
96. Jenkins, *European Diary*, p.221 (21.1.78)
97. ibid., p.197
98. ibid., p.224 (28.2.78)
99. Jenkins, *ALATC*, p.470
100. Tickell's minute of meeting with Schmidt, 28.2.78 [Jenkins papers]
101. Jenkins speech, 21.1.92. [Jenkins papers]
102. Tickell's minute, 28.2.78 [Jenkins papers]
103. *Independent*, 1.1.02
104. Tickell's minute, 28.2.78 [Jenkins papers]
105. Tickell's minute of European Council meeting, Copenhagen, 7.4.78 [Jenkins papers]
106. Jenkins, *European Diary*, p.248 (7.4.78)
107. *The Times*, 10.4.78
108. Tickell's minute of meeting with Callaghan, 3.7.78 [Jenkins papers]
109. Jenkins, *European Diary*, p.290 (6.7.78)
110. *The Times*, 8.7.78
111. Tickell's minute of meeting with Schmidt, 30.11.78 [Jenkins papers]
112. Tickell's minute of meeting with Callaghan, 3.11.78 [Jenkins papers]
113. House of Commons, 6.12.78 (Vol.959, cols 1424–5)
114. *The Times*, 13.2.80
115. Jenkins, *Twentieth Century Portraits*, p.168
116. Lecture at Green College, Oxford, 21.1.92 [Jenkins papers]
117. Tickell's minute of meeting with Barre, 19.11.77 [Jenkins papers]
118. Tickell's minute of meeting with Giscard d'Estaing, 28.2.77 [Jenkins papers]
119. Tickell's minute of meeting with Irish ministers, 23.2.78 [Jenkins papers]

Notes

Chapter Nineteen: 'Home Thoughts from Abroad'

1. Roy Jenkins, unpublished diary, 16.1.77 [Jenkins papers]
2. Roy Jenkins, *European Diary*, p.215 (2.2.78)
3. Unpublished diary, 14.4.77
4. Engagement diary, April 1977 [Jenkins papers]
5. ibid., 25.11.77
6. Roy Jenkins, 'Why I Live In Notting Hill', *Evening Standard*, 28.8.91
7. John Grigg to Patricia Grigg, 14.6.78 (thanks to Mrs Grigg)
8. Unpublished diary, 6.4.78
9. John Grigg to Patricia Grigg, 14.6.78
10. Unpublished diary, 19.10.78; *The Times*, 20.10.78
11. Jenkins, *European Diary*, p.387 (22.1.79)
12. Unpublished diary, 13.3.79
13. ibid., 8.3.79
14. Roy Jenkins to St Catherine's College, 8.3.79 [Jenkins papers]
15. Jenkins, *European Diary*, p.512 (23.10.79)
16. Unpublished diary, 19.6.80
17. ibid., 12.8.80
18. ibid., 25.11.80; Bill Mackworth-Young to Jenkins, 28.11.80 [Jenkins papers]
19. Unpublished diary, 10.5.79
20. ibid., 3.5.79
21. Jenkins, *European Diary*, p.443 (4.5.79)
22. ibid., p.445 (10.5.79)
23. Jenkins, *European Diary*, p.448 (16.5.79)
24. *Encounter*, February 1978
25. ibid., p.377
26. *Encounter*, July 1979
27. David Marquand to Jenkins, 28.6.79 [Jenkins papers]
28. Jenkins, *European Diary*, p.460 (14.6.79)
29. Unpublished diary, 15.10.79
30. Bill Rodgers, *Fourth Among Equals*, p.197
31. ibid., 1.11.79
32. ibid., 16.8.79
33. ibid., 2.11.79
34. ibid., 9.11.79
35. Jenkins, *European Diary*, p.520 (10.11.79)
36. Unpublished diary, 21–22.11.79

37. 'Home Thoughts From Abroad', reprinted in Roy Jenkins, *Partnership of Principle*, pp.9–22
38. *The Times*, 24.11.79
39. *The Listener*, 13.12.79
40. ibid.
41. *The Times*, 10.6.80
42. Jenkins, *European Diary*, p.528 (27.11.79)
43. Mrs S. Brown to Jenkins, n.d. [Jenkins papers]
44. Jenkins, *European Diary*, p.524 (22.11.79)
45. *The Times*, 24.11.79
46. Unpublished diary, 22.11.79
47. Jenkins, *European Diary*, p.524 (22.11.79)
48. ibid., 31.12.79
49. Roy Jenkins, *Twelve Cities*, p.149
50. Unpublished diary, 9.12.77
51. Jenkins, *Twelve Cities*, pp.157–9
52. Unpublished diary, 24.5.77
53. ibid., 9.3.78, 11.1.70
54. Nicholas Henderson, *Mandarin*, p.183
55. Unpublished diary, 26.1.77
56. ibid., 6.11.80
57. ibid., 12.3.79
58. Interview, Sir Crispin Tickell, 11.3.10
59. Unpublished diary, 11.1.80
60. Jenkins, *European Diary*, p.373
61. Unpublished diary, 2.2.80
62. Henry and Shirley Anglesey to Jenkins, 10.2.80 [Jenkins papers]
63. Jenkins papers
64. Unpublished diary, 3.10.80
65. Jenkins, *Twelve Cities*, p.74
66. Jenkins, *European Diary*, p.655 (15.12.80)
67. Unpublished diary, 9.4.79
68. Jenkins, *European Diary*, pp.499–500 (11.9.80)
69. ibid., p.407 (23.2.79)
70. ibid., p.105 (20.5.77)
71. ibid., p.459 (13.6.79)
72. *Observer*, 3.11.91
73. Jenkins, *European Diary*, p.384 (10.1.79)
74. Unpublished diary, 28.2.77
75. ibid., 11.1.77
76. ibid., 5.12.77
77. ibid., 30.7.79
78. ibid., 23.2.77
79. ibid., 5.8.77
80. ibid., 6.9.77

81. Henderson, p.183; John Grigg to Patricia Grigg, 14.6.78
82. Unpublished diary, 3.1.80
83. ibid., 15.2.80
84. ibid., 18.2.80
85. Jenkins, *European Diary*, p.624 (14.8.80)
86. Jenkins papers
87. ibid.
88. Jenkins, *European Diary*, p.450 (21.5.79)
89. Tickell's minute of meeting with Margaret Thatcher, 21.5.79 [Jenkins papers]
90. Jenkins,*European Diary*, p.450 (21.5.80)
91. Unpublished diary, 21.6.79
92. Jenkins, *European Diary*, p.479 (14.7.79)
93. Unpublished diary, 14.7.79
94. ibid., 28.6.79
95. ibid., 22.20.79
96. Tickell's minute of meeting with Margaret Thatcher, 22.10.79 [Jenkins papers]
97. Unpublished diary, 22.10.79
98. Tickell's minute of conversation with Schmidt, 7.11.79 [Jenkins papers]
99. Tickell's minute of conversation with Giscard d'Estaing, 23.11.79 [Jenkins papers]
100. Jenkins, *European Diary*, p.526 (25.11.79)
101. Tickell's note of meeting with Margaret Thatcher, 26.11.79 [Jenkins papers]
102. Unpublished diary, 26.11.79
103. ibid., 29.11.79
104. Jenkins, *European Diary*, pp.529–30 (29–30.11.79)
105. Unpublished diary, 28.3.80
106. Jenkins, *European Diary*, p.545
107. ibid., p.603 (29.5.80)
108. ibid., pp.564–5 (31.1.80)
109. ibid., pp.571–2 (23.2.80)
110. ibid., p.567 (5.2.80)
111. Tickell's minute of conversation with Lord Carrington, 18.2.80 [Jenkins papers]
112. Jenkins, *European Diary*, pp.579–80 (17.3.80)
113. ibid., p.585 (1.4.80)
114. Unpublished diary, 5.4.80
115. Tickell's minute of meeting with Margaret Thatcher, 17.3.80 [Jenkins papers]
116. Tickell's notes of conversations with Robert Armstrong, 22.2.80, 17.3.80 [Jenkins papers]
117. Jenkins, *European Diary*, p.593 (28.4.79)
118. ibid., p.547
119. ibid., pp.605–6 (29–30.5.80)
120. *The Times*, 30.5.80
121. Jenkins, *European Diary*, p.547
122. Unpublished diary, 30.5.80
123. Ian Gilmour, *Dancing with Dogma*, p.292
124. Lord Carrington to Jenkins, 2.6.80 [Jenkins papers]
125. Speech on the retirement of Emile Noël, Brussels, 18.9.87, in Roy Jenkins, *Gallery of Twentieth Century Portraits*, pp.139–43
126. Winston Churchill memorial lecture, Luxembourg, 20.11.80 (*The Times*, 21.11.80)
127. Tickell's minute of meeting with Margaret Thatcher, 3.11.80 [Jenkins papers]
128. Interviewed by David Butler, 19.7.79 [David Butler papers]
129. Barbara Castle, *Fighting All The Way*, p.522
130. ibid., p.524
131. Unpublished diary, 14.10.80
132. Statement at European Council, Luxembourg, 2.12.80 [Jenkins papers]
133. Jenkins, *European Diary*, pp.199–200
134. Speech on the retirement of Emile Noël, 18.9.87
135. Tickell's minute of meeting with Giscard d'Estaing, 12.7.78 [Jenkins papers]
136. Statement at European Council, Luxembourg, 2.12.80
137. *The Times*, 12.1.77
138. ibid., 31.12.80
139. Press conference, Brussels,.5.1.81 (*The Times*, 6.1.81)
140. Statement at European Council, Luxembourg, 2.12.80
141. Press conference, Brussels, 5.1.81
142. Jenkins, *Twelve Cities*, p.149

Chapter Twenty: The Gang of Four

1. Nikolas C. Hills, Walthamstow, to *The Times*, 23.11.79

2. Roy Jenkins, *European Diary*, p.553 (7.1.80)
3. David Steel to Jenkins, 23.1.80 [Jenkins papers]
4. Unpublished diary, 7.1.80
5. Jenkins, *European Diary*, p.540 (20.12.80)
6. Anthony Lester to Jenkins, 27.12.79 [Jenkins papers]
7. Jenkins, *European Diary*, p.552 (3.1.80)
8. Note of meeting, 4.7.80 [Jenkins papers]
9. Unpublished diary, 20.6.80
10. Jenkins, *European Diary*, pp.616–17 (11.7.80)
11. *The Times*, 12.2.09
12. Bill Rodgers to Jenkins, 27.11.90 [Jenkins papers]
13. Unpublished diary, 19.2.79
14. Bill Rodgers, 8.11.79, in *The Hugo Young Papers*, pp.134–5
15. Speech in Abertillery, 30.11.79 [*The Times*, 1.12.79]
16. Jenkins, *European Diary*, 1.12.79
17. Bill Rodgers to Jenkins, 3.1.80 [Jenkins papers]; also in Ivor Crewe & Anthony King, *SDP: The Birth, Life and Death of the Social Democratic Party*, pp.66–8
18. Giles Radice, *Diaries, 1980–2001*, p.6 (9.1.80)
19. Unpublished diary, 19.3.80
20. ibid.
21. Roy Jenkins, *A Life at the Centre* [*ALATC*], pp.523–4
22. Unpublished diary, 24.7.80
23. ibid., 3.1.80
24. ibid., 7.4.80
25. John Grigg to Jenkins, 23.11.79 [Jenkins papers]
26. Unpublished diary, 26.9.80
27. Jenkins, *European Diary*, p.609 (9.6.80)
28. Speech to the Parliamentary Press Gallery, 9.6.80 [*The Times*, 10.6.80]
29. *The Times*, 9.6.80
30. Jenkins, *European Diary*, pp.608–9 (8.6.80)
31. *The Times*, 10.6.80
32. *The Economist*, 14.6.80
33. *Spectator*, 14.6.80
34. ibid., 21.6.80
35. Bernard Donoughue, 3.9.80, in *The Hugo Young Papers*, pp.154–5

36. Jenkins, *European Diary*, p.549
37. *Guardian*, 1.8.80
38. Jenkins, *European Diary*, pp.625–6 (31.8.80)
39. Unpublished diary, 29.9.80
40. ibid., 5.10.80
41. *The Times*, 15.10.80
42. Jenkins, *European Diary*, p.637 (13.10.80)
43. Bill Rodgers to Jenkins, 3.1.80 [Jenkins papers]
44. Peter Jenkins, *Mrs Thatcher's Revolution*, p.144
45. Unpublished diary, 5.10.80
46. ibid., 19.10.80
47. Jenkins, *European Diary*, p.643 (4.11.80)
48. ibid., 10.11.80
49. David Owen, *Time to Declare*, p.458
50. ibid., p.466
51. ibid., pp.483–4
52. Bill Rodgers, *Fourth Among Equals*, p.208
53. Bill Rodgers, 14.7.87, quoted in Patricia Lee Sykes, *Losing from the Inside: The Cost of Conflict in the British Social Democratic Party*, p.111
54. Rodgers, p.201
55. Owen, pp.469–70
56. David Owen, 29.6.84, quoted in Sykes, p.111
57. Unpublished diary, 29.11.80
58. ibid., 19.10.80
59. Owen, p.476
60. ibid.
61. Bill Rodgers to Jenkins, 27.11.90 [thanks to Lord Rodgers of Quarry Bank]
62. Jenkins, *ALATC*, p.535
63. Owen, pp.481–3
64. *The Times*, 26.1.81; reprinted in Roy Jenkins, *Partnership of Principle*, p.28
65. *Guardian*, 2.2.81, reprinted in Ian Bradley, *Breaking the Mould: The Birth and Prospects of the Social Democratic Party*, p.96
66. Jenkins, *European Diary*, p.658
67. Rodgers, p.210
68. *Spectator*, 31.1.81
69. *Guardian*, 5.2.81
70. Jenkins, *ALATC*, p.544n.; *Sunday Times*, n.d. 1981, reprinted in John Mortimer, *In Character*, pp.142–8
71. Crewe & King, p.107

Roy Jenkins

72. Interviewed by David Butler, 11.6.83 [David Butler papers]
73. Bill Rodgers, 'SDP', in Andrew Adonis & Keith Thomas, *Roy Jenkins: A Retrospective*, p.217
74. *The Times*, 31.1.81, in Martin Westlake, *Kinnock: The Biography*, p.173
75. *Guardian*, 17.2.81, in ibid.
76. Westlake, p.173
77. SDP steering committee minutes, 9.2.81
78. Jenkins to Lord Plowden, 27.2.81 [Plowden papers PLDN 2/3/12]
79. Roy Jenkins, *Mr Attlee*, p.53
80. Mike Thomas to Bill Rodgers, 2.2.81 [Rodgers papers, Box 40]
81. SDP steering committee minutes, 9.3.81, 16.3.81
82. Lord Diamond to Jenkins, 19.3.81 [Jenkins papers]
83. Roy Jenkins, 19.6.84, in Sykes, p.112
84. *The Times*, 24.2.81, reprinted in Jenkins, *Partnership of Principle*, pp.71–7
85. *The Times*, 18.3.81
86. ibid., 10.3.81, and Jenkins papers
87. *Sun*, 24.3.81
88. *The Hugo Young Papers*, pp.161–2 (20.3.81)
89. Harold Evans, *Good Times, Bad Times*, pp.218–19
90. Peter Shore, speech to Labour Solidarity at Labour's Northern Regional Conference, Tynemouth, 23.3.81 [Shore papers, 13/69]
91. *The Times*, 27.3.81
92. Bradley, p.142
93. *Guardian*, 27.3.81
94. Bradley, p.108
95. Shore papers, 13/69
96. Crew & King, p.276
97. Bill Rodgers, 8.11.79, in *The Hugo Young Papers*, pp.134–5
98. Shirley Williams, *Climbing the Bookshelves*, pp.329–30
99. Speech at the National Liberal Club, 31.3.81, reprinted in Jenkins, *Partnership of Principle*, pp.31–2
100. Owen, pp.744–5
101. Owen to Jenkins, Williams and Rodgers, 23.3.81, in Owen, p.507
102. SDP steering committee minutes, 30.3.81
103. Bradley, p.90
104. Owen, pp.518–19
105. Williams, pp.286–7; Rodgers, pp.219–20
106. Owen, p.508
107. SDP steering committee minutes, 7.4.81
108. Sykes, p.113
109. Owen, p.519
110. Hugh Stephenson, *Claret and Chips: The Rise of the SDP*, p.77
111. Rodgers papers, Box 27
112. Jenkins, *ALATC*, p.539
113. Robert Maclennan papers, Box 9
114. Williams, p.288
115. Shirley Williams interviewed for *The Seventies* [LSE 004/9]
116. Williams, pp.288–9
117. Rodgers, p.216
118. Rodgers to Jenkins, 27.11.90 [Jenkins papers]
119. Owen, p.520
120. *The Economist*, 11.7.81
121. Jenkins, *ALATC*, p.540
122. Lord Diamond to Jenkins, 8.6.81 [Jenkins papers]
123. Peter Jenkins to Jenkins, 8.6.81 [Jenkins papers]
124. Moira Gallagher to David Steel, 14.6.81 [Rodgers papers, Box 27]
125. *Evening Standard*, n.d.
126. Warrington adoption speech, 17.6.81, reprinted in Jenkins, *Partnership of Principle*, p.51
127. John Holmes note, 17.6.81 [Maclennan papers, Box 9]
128. Jenkins, *ALATC*, p.540
129. Mortimer, p.148
130. Alec McGivan papers
131. *The Times*, 30.6.81
132. ibid., 6.7.81
133. *The Economist*, 25.7.81
134. Speech at Adelphi Hotel, Liverpool, 18.6.81
135. Warrington election literature [Jenkins papers]
136. Speech in Warrington, 10.7.81
137. *The Times*, 30.6.81
138. Peter Shore, speeches at Ely, 13.6.81, and Warrington, 7.7.81 [Shore papers, 13/69]
139. *The Times*, 15.7.81
140. Mike Thomas memo, n.d. [Rodgers papers, Box 33]

141. *The Times,* 17.7.81
142. Jenkins, *ALATC,* p.544
143. John Grigg to Jenkins, 17.7.81
[Jenkins papers]
144. Rev J.O. Colling to Jenkins, 22.7.81
[Jenkins papers]
145. *The Times,* 17.7.81; *Sun,* 17.7.81
146. *Guardian,* 18.7.81
147. Speech at the Oxford Union,
16.11.81 [*The Times,* 17.11.81]
148. Radice, p.49 (1.8.81)
149. *The Times,* 10.10.81
150. Owen, p.521
151. Jenkins, *ALATC,* p.543
152. David Steel, *Against Goliath,* p.226
153. Speech at Llandudno, 15.9.81,
reprinted in Jenkins, *Partnership of
Principle,* pp.33–4
154. Jenkins, *ALATC,* p.547
155. Steel, p.227
156. Laura Grimond to Jenkins, 2.8.81
[Jenkins papers]
157. Ken Lomas to Bill Rodgers, 22.6.81;
Rodgers to Lomas, 25.6.81 [Rodgers
papers, Box 40]
158. *The Times,* 10.10.81, reprinted in
Jenkins, *Partnership of Principle,*
pp.78–82
159. Anthony Lester to Jenkins, n.d. 10.81
[Jenkins papers]
160. Crewe & King, p.144

Chapter Twenty-One: 'Prime Minister Designate'

1. Bill Rodgers, *Fourth Among Equals,*
p.219
2. Draft of speech to SDP constitutional
convention, Kensington Town Hall,
14.2.82 [Jenkins papers]
3. House of Commons, 10.2.82
4. Interview, Lord Steel of Aikwood,
2.2.10
5. Roy Jenkins, *A Life at the Centre*
[*ALATC*], p.556
6. Rodgers, p.226
7. Jenkins, *ALATC,* p.559
8. Roy Jenkins, *Twelve Cities,* p.192
9. Unpublished diary, 5.4.79
10. Bob Maclennan to Jenkins, 11.4.82
[Jenkins papers]
11. Jenkins, *ALATC,* p.560
12. Brodie to Jenkins, 12.8.02, Jenkins to
Brodie, 20.8.02 [Jenkins papers]

13. Jenkins to Edward Lyons, 22.1.82
[Jenkins papers]
14. Jenkins to William Wells, 22.1.82
[Jenkins papers]
15. Hillhead adoption speech, 14.1.82,
reprinted in Roy Jenkins, *Partnership
of Principle,* pp.56–8
16. Jenkins, *ALATC,* p.561
17. David Steel, 25.3.82, in *The Hugo
Young Papers,* pp.178–80
18. Speech to Scottish Council for
Educational Technology, 10.3.82,
reprinted in Jenkins, *Partnership of
Principle,* pp.154–60
19. Speech to the Indian Association of
Strathclyde, 31.1.82 [Jenkins papers]
20. Speech to Hillhead businessmen,
22.2.82 [Jenkins papers]
21. Hillhead election leaflets [Jenkins
papers]
22. Interview, Dr Christopher Mason,
22.8.08
23. John Campbell, *Roy Jenkins: A
Biography* (1983), p.217n.
24. Alex McGivan papers
25. Personal recollection
26. Jenkins, *ALATC,* p.563
27. *The Times,* 26.3.82
28. *The Times,* 26.3.82. The unpublished
'Roy loses' is in the British cartoon
archive at the University of Kent.
29. *Daily Mail,* 26.3.82; *The Times,* 26.3.82
30. Jenkins, *ALATC,* p.564
31. ibid., p.571
32. Jenkins, *Twelve Cities,* pp.193, 199,
210–11
33. Speech at Glasgow Academy
Prizegiving, 29.6.89 [Jenkins papers]
34. Lecture to the Royal Philosophical
Society of Glasgow, April 1990,
reprinted in Roy Jenkins, *Portraits and
Miniatures,* pp.153–64
35. Jenkins, *Twelve Cities,* p.194
36. ibid., p.199
37. Ella and Ethel Goodall to the author,
31.7.08
38. Jenkins papers
39. Barley Alison to Jenkins, n.d. [Jenkins
papers]
40. Vernon Bogdanor to Jenkins, n.d.
[Jenkins papers]
41. Shirley Williams speech in Waltham
Forest, 30.1.82 [*The Times,* 31.3.82]

42. SDP steering committee minutes, 5.4.82
43. House of Commons, 31.3.82 [Vol.21, cols 310–11]
44. Alan Clark, *Into Politics*, p.310 (31.3.82)
45. Reference mislaid
46. House of Commons, 11.5.82 [Vol.23, cols 614–18]
47. Professor Peter Clarke
48. Rodgers, p.229
49. House of Commons, 20.4.82 [Vol.22, cols 121–2]; *The Times*, 21.4.82
50. Speech notes [Jenkins papers]
51. Speech in Hillhead, 14.5.82 [Jenkins papers]
52. Speech at Burnham Grammar School, 17.5.82 [Jenkins papers]
53. *The Times*, 4.6.82
54. SDP communications committee minutes, 25.5.82
55. SDP steering committee minutes, 14.6.82
56. Jenkins, *ALATC*, p.567
57. David Owen, *Time to Declare*, p.531
58. Bill Rodgers to Shirley Williams, 13.5.82 [Rodgers papers, Box 42]
59. Shirley Williams, *Climbing the Bookshelves*, p.299
60. Shirley Williams to Bill Rodgers, 22.5.82 [Rodgers papers, Box 42]
61. Owen, p.552
62. *Sunday Times*, 13.6.82; *Observer*, 13.6.82
63. Edward Lyons to Jenkins, 9.6.82 [Jenkins papers]
64. *Observer*, 13.6.82
65. Jenkins papers
66. *The Times*, 18.6.82, reprinted in Jenkins, *Partnership of Principle*, pp.61–3
67. *The Times*, 8.6.82
68. Anthony Lester to Jenkins, 20.5.82 [Jenkins papers]
69. *The Economist*, 26.6.82
70. *The Times*, 26.6.82
71. ibid., 3.7.82
72. Clark, p.341 (10.7.82)
73. ibid., pp.356–7 (10.9.82)
74. Rodgers, p.232
75. Jenkins interviewed by David Butler, 11.6.83 [David Butler papers]
76. Rodgers to Jenkins, 8.7.82 [Rodgers papers, Box 5]
77. Mike Thomas to Jenkins, 7.9.82 [Rodgers papers, Box 30]
78. Thomas to Jenkins, 20.9.82; Rodgers to Thomas, 21.9.82 [Rodgers papers, Box 30]
79. Owen, p.560
80. ibid., p.559
81. Transcript of witness seminar, 1991 [Rodgers papers, Box 45]
82. Rodgers to Alan Watkins, 6.12.82 [Rodgers, Box 30]
83. Owen, p.566
84. Rodgers, p.232
85. Bernard Doyle to Jenkins, 10.11.82 [Jenkins papers]
86. SDP national committee minutes, 22.11.82
87. Edward Pearce, *The Shooting Gallery*, pp.58–60
88. Jenkins papers
89. Speech at Westminster Central Hall, 20.1.83, reprinted in Jenkins, *Partnership of Principle*, pp.41–6
90. Jenkins, *ALATC*, p.572
91. Rodgers, p.236
92. David Owen interviewed by David Butler, 25.7.83 [David Butler papers]
93. Richard Holme interviewed by David Butler, 27.4.83 [David Butler papers]
94. Jenkins, *ALATC*, p.573
95. *The Times*, 25.3.83
96. Rodgers to Jenkins, 27.11.90 [Jenkins papers]
97. *The Times*, 10.5.83
98. Owen, p.563
99. Jenkins, *ALATC*, p.570
100. Jenkins papers
101. Interview, Lord Steel of Aikwood, 2.2.10
102. Ivor Crewe & Anthony King, *SDP: The Birth, Life and Death of the Social Democratic Party*, p.201
103. SDP/Liberal Alliance manifesto, 1983
104. This phrase is usually attributed to Ralph Dahrendorf, but no definitive citation has been found.
105. Roy Jenkins, *Nine Men of Power*, p.21
106. Crewe & King, p.201
107. Patricia Lee Sykes, *Losing from Inside*, pp.124–5
108. ibid., p.126
109. Richard Holme interviewed by

David Butler, 27.4.83 [David Butler papers]

110. David Butler & Dennis Kavanagh, *The British General Election of 1983*, p.125
111. Jenkins, *ALATC*, pp.575–6
112. Lord Diamond to Jenkins, 25.5.83 [Jenkins papers]
113. Williams, p.305
114. Crewe & King, pp.207–8
115. Jenkins, *ALATC*, p.576
116. Crewe & King, p.209; Williams, p.305
117. Richard Holme interviewed by David Butler, 27.4.83 [David Butler papers]
118. David Steel, *Against Goliath: David Steel's Story*, p.246
119. John Pardoe interviewed by David Butler, 20.7.83 [David Butler papers]
120. *The Times*, 30.5.83; *Guardian*, 30.5.83
121. Interview, Lord Ashdown of Norton-sub-Hamdon, 19.11.09
122. David Owen interviewed by David Butler, 25.7.83 [David Butler papers]; Owen, p.582
123. David Owen, 29.6.84, in Sykes, p.153
124. David Owen interviewed by David Butler, 25.7.83 [David Butler papers]
125. David Owen, *Personally Speaking*, pp.219–21
126. Rodgers to Jenkins, 27.22.90 [Jenkins papers]
127. Rodgers, p 237
128. Steel, p.244
129. Jenkins, *ALATC*, p.577
130. David Steel to Jenkins, 21.6.83
131. David Butler & Gareth Butler, *British Political Facts, 1900–1994*
132. Articles for *Daily Express* and *Social Democrat*, both written 17.6.83; *Sunday Standard*, 26.6.83
133. Jenkins, *ALATC*, p.572
134. Hillhead election leaflet, 1983
135. *The Times*, 11.6.83
136. Jenkins, *ALATC*, p.578
137. Rodgers to Jenkins, 27.11.90 [thanks to Lord Rodgers of Quarry Bank]
138. Jenkins, *ALATC*, p.577
139. Jo Grimond to Jenkins, 28.7.83 [Jenkins papers]
140. SDP national committee minutes, 20.6.83

141. Article for *Daily Express*, written 17.6.83
142. *Sunday Standard*, 26.6.83

Chapter Twenty-Two: Elder Statesman

1. Roy Jenkins, *A Life at the Centre* [*ALATC*], p.580
2. Speech at SDP conference, Salford, 14.9.83, quoted in Jenkins, *ALATC*, p.581
3. Jenkins papers
4. Jenkins to Enoch Powell, postcard, 6.3.87 [Powell papers, POLL 1/1/38]
5. Jenkins, *ALATC*, p.583
6. Michael Sissons to Jenkins, 1.7.86; Collins contract, March 1987 [Jenkins papers]
7. Crispin Tickell to Jenkins, 26.8.87 [Jenkins papers]
8. *Evening Standard*, 9.3.89
9. *Observer*, 29.5.88
10. *Sunday Telegraph*, 10.4.88; Roy Jenkins, *Gallery of Twentieth Century Portraits*, p.176
11. *Observer*, 19.2.89; Roy Jenkins, *Portraits and Miniatures*, p.277
12. ibid.
13. *Spectator*, 24.10.87
14. Tony Benn to Jenkins, 11.10.87 [Jenkins papers]
15. *Spectator*, 24.10.87; Jenkins, *Twentieth Century Portraits*, pp.39–40
16. Jenkins to Michael Sissons, 30.10.88 [Jenkins papers]
17. *The Journals of Woodrow Wyatt*, Vol.1, p.425 (22.10.87)
18. Jenkins papers
19. *Times Literary Supplement*, 11.88
20. Jenkins papers
21. Jenkins papers
22. Ba Eustace to Jenkins, 9.2.94 [Jenkins papers]
23. *The Times*, 18.6.83
24. ibid., 17.7.93
25. Jenkins to John Oliver, 16.1.02 [Jenkins papers]
26. Sarah Bradford, *America's Queen: The Life of Jacqueline Kennedy Onassis*, pp.437–8
27. Leslie Bonham Carter to Jenkins, 20.5.90 [Jenkins papers]
28. ibid., 5.12.90

29. House of Commons, 25.3.85 [Vol.76, cols 63–71]

30. ibid., 19.3.86 [Vol.94, cols 324–9]

31. ibid., 6.11.86 [Vol.103, cols 1123–7]; *The Times*, 16.3.84

32. House of Commons, 14.3.84 [Vol.56, cols 430–35]

33. ibid., 19.3.86 [Vol.94, cols 324–9]

34. Keynes centenary lecture, Cambridge, 1.12.83, in Roy Jenkins, *Partnership of Principle*, pp.90–98

35. House of Commons, 13.11.84 [Vol.67, cols 560–65]

36. ibid., 7.7.86 [Vol.102, cols 31–4]

37. ibid., 25.3.85 [Vol.76, cols 63–71]

38. ibid., 25.3.85 [Vol.76, col.63]

39. ibid., 22.11.84 [Vol.64, cols 442–5]

40. *The Times,* 16.3.84, in Jenkins, *Partnership of Principle*, pp.102–4.

41. House of Commons, 12.11.85 [Vol.86, cols 485–9]

42. ibid., 29.1.86 [Vol.90, cols 979–84]

43. *The Times,* 18.1.85

44. House of Commons, 29.1.86 [Vol.90, cols 979–84]

45. *The Times,* 13.3.84

46. Speech at *Financial Times* conference, 27.2.84, in Jenkins, *Partnership of Principle*, pp.138–44

47. House of Commons, 20.6.84 [Vol.62, col.295]

48. *New Democrat*, 1.85, in Jenkins, *Partnership of Principle*, pp.146–9

49. House of Commons, 23.1.86 [Vol.90, col.455]

50. ibid., 22.11.84 [Vol.68, cols 442–5]

51. ibid., 3.12.86 [Vol.106, cols 962–6]

52. Tawney lecture, 11.7.84, in *Partnership of Principle,* pp.161–9

53. House of Commons, 3.12.86 [Vol.106, cols 962–6]

54. ibid.

55. *The Times,* 10.3.85

56. Jenkins papers

57. MS article, late 1984 [Jenkins papers]

58. House of Commons, 13.11.84 [Vol.67, cols 560–65]

59. ibid., 18.3.87 [Vol.112, cols 965–70]

60. David Butler & Gareth Butler, *British Political Facts, 1900–1994*, pp.256–7

61. Tawney lecture, 11.7.84, in Jenkins, *Partnership of Principle*, pp.161–9

62. *The Times*, 4.9.85

63. Speech to the Council for Social Democracy, Birmingham, 15.1.84, in Jenkins, *Partnership of Principle*, pp.115–17

64. David Owen, *Time to Declare*, pp.649–50

65. David Steel, *Against Goliath: David Steel's Story*, pp.265–6

66. Jenkins, *ALATC*, p.591

67. ibid., p.589

68. ibid., p.590

69. ibid., pp.587, 591

70. *The Journals of Woodrow Wyatt*, Vol.1, p.425 (22.10.87)

71. Roy Jenkins, *Asquith* (Fontana paperback edn), p.579

72. Jenkins, *ALATC*, p.607

73. Jenkins to Christopher Hill, 21.12.72 [Jenkins papers]

74. *Oxford Gazette*, February 1987

75. *Daily Telegraph*, 3.3.87

76. Lord Blake to Christine Nicholls, reprinted in her obituary of Blake in the OUP magazine, 2003

77. Anthony Powell, *Journals, 1987–89*, pp.110–11 (12.1.87)

78. Lord Blake postcard to Jenkins, 7.3.87 [Jenkins papers]

79. Installation speech, 24.6.87, in Jenkins, *Twentieth Century Portraits*, pp.240–43

80. Speech at St Hilda's college, 22.7.89 [Jenkins papers]

81. Speech in Washington, 27.4.88 [Jenkins papers]

82. Speech to Oxford University rugby club, 12.12.89 [Jenkins papers]

83. Jenkins to the Duke of Edinburgh, 15.5.91 [Jenkins papers]

84. Jenkins, *ALATC*, p.611

85. Nicholas Henderson, *Old Friends and Modern Instances*, pp.169–77

86. Sir Ronald McIntosh to Jenkins, 14.10.88 [Jenkins papers]

87. Lord Bancroft to Jenkins, 10.88 [Jenkins papers]

88. Jakie Astor to Jenkins, 14.11.90 [Jenkins papers]

89. Marietta Tree to Jenkins, 4.7.89 [Jenkins papers]

90. Jacqueline Kennedy Onassis to Jenkins, 23.6.91 [Jenkins papers]

91. Speech at Brasenose college, 16.2.90 [Jenkins papers]

92. Article for the *American Oxonian*, 3.89 [Jenkins papers]
93. Installation speech, 24.6.87, in Jenkins, *Twentieth Century Portraits*, pp.240–43
94. *Independent*, 25.3.89
95. House of Lords, 19.5.88 [Vol.497, col.471]
96. Rede Lecture, Cambridge, 10.5.88, in Jenkins, *Portraits and Miniatures*, p.151
97. Speech at Brasenose college, 16.2.90 [Jenkins papers]
98. Goodman Lecture, 19.6.89 [Jenkins papers]
99. ibid.
100. Des Wilson, *Battle for Power: The Inside Story of the Alliance and the 1987 General Election*, pp.123, 138
101. ibid., p.251
102. David Butler & Dennis Kavanagh, *The British General Election of 1987*, p.97
103. Hillhead election leaflet, 1987 [Jenkins papers]
104. *The Times*, 13.6.87
105. Jenkins, *ALATC*, p.611
106. *The Journals of Woodrow Wyatt*, Vol.1, pp.369–70 (14.6.87)
107. Jenkins, *ALATC*, p.596
108. ibid., p.598
109. ibid., p.600
110. *Sunday Times*, 12.7.87
111. Robert Maclennan to Jenkins, 15.7.87 [Jenkins papers]
112. Robert Maclennan to Jenkins, 22.7.87 [Jenkins papers]
113. Owen, pp.713–14
114. David Owen to John Grigg, 16.7.87, copied by Grigg to Jenkins, 17.7.87 [Jenkins papers]
115. Speech at the SDP conference, Portsmouth, 31.8.87 [Jenkins papers]
116. Jenkins, *ALATC*, p.601
117. Paddy Ashdown, *The Ashdown Diaries*, Vol.1, p.64 (3.9.89)
118. Jenkins, *ALATC*, p.601
119. *The Times*, 30.1.88
120. Ivor Crewe & Anthony King, *SDP: The Birth, Life and Death of the Social Democratic Party*, p.440
121. *Observer*, 10.6.90
122. *The Times*, 8.4.88
123. House of Lords, 24.2.88 [Vol.493, cols 1214–16]

124. *Independent*, 4.4.88
125. House of Lords, 2.3.88 [Vol.494, cols 181–4]
126. ibid., 11.12.91 [Vol.533, cols 740–43]
127. ibid., 25.1.89 [Vol.503, cols 701–5]
128. ibid., 3.4.89 [Vol.505, cols 906–10]
129. ibid., 12.3.90 [Vol.516, cols 1327–30]
130. ibid., 28.3.90 [Vol.517, cols 916–19]
131. *Independent*, 1.8.88
132. *Observer*, 4.12.89
133. ibid., 5.11.89
134. ibid., 18.6.89
135. ibid., 11.3.90
136. *Independent*, 9.4.90
137. *Fordham International Law Journal*, 1998
138. House of Lords, 14.11.90 [Vol.523, cols 346–51]
139. *Observer*, 25.11.90
140. ibid., 23.6.91
141. ibid., 8.12.91
142. Tawney lecture, 7.3.92
143. *Observer*, 15.3.92
144. ibid.
145. ibid.
146. Tawney lecture, 7.3.92
147. Paddy Ashdown diary, pp.129–30 (19.1.92)
148. Jenkins papers
149. *The Hugo Young Papers*, p.433 (13.9.94)
150. Jenkins to Neil Kinnock, 16.4.92 [Jenkins papers; Kinnock papers KNNK 3/4/3/2]
151. Jenkins, *ALATC*, p.xi
152. Robin Day, . . . *But With Respect*, pp.62–3
153. *Spectator*, 9.2.62, in Roy Jenkins, *Essays and Speeches*, pp.47–8
154. Royal Society of Literature lecture 1972, in Jenkins, *Twentieth Century Portraits*, p.198
155. Jenkins papers
156. Lord Owen to the author, 5.5.09
157. *Guardian*, 10.9.91
158. Jenkins, *ALATC*, p.617
159. ibid., pp.616–18
160. ibid., pp.620–21
161. *Observer*, 21.4.91
162. Jenkins, *ALATC*, p.622
163. *Times Literary Supplement*, 6.9.91
164. *Spectator*, 14.9.91
165. *TLS*, 9.91; *The Tablet*, 14.9.91
166. *Evening Standard*, 12.9.91
167. *Scotsman*, 9.9.91

168. Roy Jenkins, *Twelve Cities*, p.100
169. *New Yorker*, 29.3.93
170. *TLS*, 27.9.91

Chapter Twenty-Three: History Man

1. Roy Jenkins, *The Chancellors*, p.101
2. Jenkins to Lord Hailsham, 15.5.78 [Hailsham papers, HLSM 8/6/4/7]
3. *The Times*, 26.4.88 and 28.4.88
4. *Daily Telegraph*, 22.7.98
5. *Sunday Times*, 12.12.93
6. Hugh Brace to Jenkins, 22.1.95 [Jenkins papers]
7. Speech at the Healeys' golden wedding, 6.11.95 [Jenkins papers]
8. Alison Cahn to Jenkins, 23.5.96 [Jenkins papers]
9. *A Very Social Democrat*, BBC2, 26.5.96
10. Shirley, Marchioness of Anglesey to Jenkins, 27.5.96 [Jenkins papers]
11. Elizabeth Longford to Jenkins, 28.5.96 [Jenkins papers]
12. Sir Christopher Audland to Jenkins, 27.5.96 [Jenkins papers]
13. Jenkins to Michael Cockerell, 7.6.96 [Jenkins papers]
14. Jenkins to Robert Runcie, 12.9.96 [Jenkins papers]
15. Roy Jenkins, *A Life at the Centre* [*ALATC*], p.606
16. Interview, Sir Colin Lucas, 27.7.10
17. Anthony Kenny, 'Oxford's Chancellor', in Andrew Adonis & Keith Thomas, *Roy Jenkins: A Retrospective*, p.269
18. Jenkins papers
19. *The Times*, 20.4.96
20. ibid., 23.4.96
21. Alistair Horne to Jenkins, 3.5.96 [Jenkins papers]
22. Kenny in Adonis & Thomas, p.260
23. Evangeline Bruce to Jenkins, 1.7.94 [Jenkins papers]
24. *The Times*, 9.6.94
25. Robert Harris diary, 31.10.96
26. Roy Jenkins, 'The British University Pattern', in *Portraits and Miniatures*, pp.222–3
27. Vernon Bogdanor to Jenkins, 30.5.91 [Jenkins papers]
28. *Independent* magazine, 17.3.90
29. Roy Jenkins, 'John Henry Newman and the Idea of a University', in *Portraits and Miniatures*, p.123
30. Mollie Butler to Jenkins, 8.10.94 [Jenkins papers]
31. *Journal of Liberal Democrat History*, January 1998
32. Roy Jenkins, *Gladstone*, p.xiii
33. ibid., p.88
34. ibid., p.243
35. ibid., p.91
36. ibid., p.630
37. ibid., p.223
38. ibid., p.368
39. ibid., p.561
40. ibid., p.432
41. ibid., p.173
42. ibid., p.43
43. ibid., p.115
44. ibid., p.16
45. *Daily Telegraph*, 21.10.95
46. Isaiah Berlin to Jenkins, 26.9.95 [Jenkins papers]
47. James Callaghan to Jenkins, 5.8.96 [Jenkins papers]
48. *The Times*, 12.10.95
49. *Sunday Telegraph*, 8.10.95
50. *Sunday Times*, 8.10.95
51. *Times Literary Supplement*, 16.4.99
52. Philip Stephens to Jenkins, 22.9.99 [Jenkins papers]
53. *Sunday Telegraph*, 5.7.93
54. ibid., 29.6.92
55. *Financial Times*, November 1999
56. *Mail on Sunday*, August 2000
57. Unidentified cutting [Jenkins papers]
58. Speech at Liverpool, n.d. 1998 [Jenkins papers]
59. *Evening Standard*, 17.3.89
60. Lecture at Hawarden, n.d. 1998 [Jenkins papers]
61. Jenkins to Michael Lee, 30.4.98 [Jenkins papers]
62. Jenkins to Lord Alton, 29.4.98 [Jenkins papers]
63. John Grigg to Jenkins, 18.11.98 [Jenkins papers]
64. Jenkins to Clive Bradley, 16.12.98 [Jenkins papers]
65. David Dimbleby to Jenkins, 4.2.94 [Jenkins papers]
66. Jenkins to Hat-Trick Productions, 27.3.01 [Jenkins papers]
67. *Sue Lawley's Desert Island Discussions*, p.196
68. *Independent*, 22.9.92

69. *Daily Telegraph*, 23.9.92
70. *Question Time*, BBC1, 12.11.92
71. *Daily Mail*, 9.11.95
72. *Observer*, 18.10.92
73. *Daily Telegraph*, 24.2.93
74. *Observer*, 10.10.93; *Daily Telegraph*, 24.2.93
75. *Daily Telegraph*, 7.1.94
76. ibid., 14.1.94
77. *Observer*, 13.6.93
78. ibid., 10.10.93
79. Anthony Seldon, *Blair*, p.267
80. Tony Blair to Jenkins, 11.1.93 [Jenkins papers]
81. *The Times*, 23.7.94
82. Roger Liddle to Jenkins, 23.4.95 [Jenkins papers]
83. *The Hugo Young Papers*, p.433 (13.9.94)
84. *Evening Standard*, 21.1.99
85. Jenkins papers; interview, Lord Ashdown of Norton-sub-Hamdon, 19.11.09
86. Paddy Ashdown, *The Ashdown Diaries*, Vol.1, p.346 (24.10.95)
87. Cherie Blair to Jenkins, 4.9.95 [Jenkins papers]
88. Ashdown, pp.419, 424 (9.4.96, 2.5.96)
89. ibid., p.346 (24.10.95)
90. ibid., p.360 (14.11.95)
91. *The Hugo Young Papers*, p.458 (27.11.95)
92. Ashdown, p.366 (12.12.95)
93. Interview, Peter Mandelson and Roger Liddle, 15.5.13
94. Robert Harris diary, 4.1.97
95. Sir Robin Butler to Jonathan Powell, n.d. [Jenkins papers]
96. Tony Blair to Jenkins, 18.1.96 [Jenkins papers]
97. Jonathan Powell to Jenkins, 17.1.96 [Jenkins papers]
98. Seldon, p.269
99. Ashdown, p.380 (17.1.96)
100. Sir Richard Wilson to Jenkins, 21.1.96 [Jenkins papers]
101. *Sunday Express*, 3.3.96
102. Ashdown, p.424 (2.5.96)
103. ibid., p.440 (20.6.96)
104. ibid., p.459 (17.9.96)
105. *Herald*, 6.9.96
106. Ashdown, p.508 (14.1.97)
107. ibid., p.509 (20.1.97)
108. *The Hugo Young Papers*, p.511 (29.1.97)
109. Shirley Williams to Jenkins, 2.3.97 [Jenkins papers]
110. Tony Blair to Jenkins, 8.3.97 [Jenkins papers]
111. Peter Mandelson to Jenkins, 17.3.97 [Jenkins papers]
112. *The Hugo Young Papers*, p.519 (17.2.97)
113. Ashdown, p.553 (29.4.97)
114. Engagement diary, 1997 [Jenkins papers]
115. Ashdown, pp.558–9 (2.5.97)
116. *Evening Standard*, 2.5.97
117. Tony Blair to Jenkins, 23.5.97 [Jenkins papers]
118. Paddy Ashdown, *The Ashdown Diaries*, Vol.2, pp.40–45 (12.6.97)
119. *The Hugo Young Papers*, p.552 (10.3.98)
120. Ashdown, Vol.2, pp.113–14 (30.10.97)
121. ibid., pp.123–4 (6.11.97)
122. ibid., p.131 (1.12.97)
123. Roy Jenkins, *Twelve Cities*, p.118
124. Seldon, p.274; see also David Lipsey, *In the Corridors of Power*, pp.190–203
125. *Observer*, 1.11.98
126. *The Report of the Independent Commission on the Voting System*, p.1
127. Ashdown, Vol.2, p.178 (4.3.98)
128. ibid., p.225 (7.7.98)
129. Andrew Adonis to Jenkins, 20.7.98 [Jenkins papers]
130. *Daily Telegraph*, 22.7.98
131. Ashdown, Vol.2, p.258 (11.9.98)
132. Giles Radice, *Diaries, 1980–2001*, pp.424–5 (28.10.98)
133. *Evening Standard*, 7.9.98
134. Tony Blair to Jenkins, 30.10.98 [Jenkins papers]
135. *Observer*, 1.11.98
136. Ashdown, Vol.2, pp.322–5 (3–7.11.98)
137. *Evening Standard*, 21.1.99
138. Jenkins to Sir Neil McIntosh, 29.7.02 [Jenkins papers]
139. Ashdown, Vol.2, p.373 (18.12.98)
140. Elspeth Campbell to Jenkins, 9.5.99 [Jenkins papers]
141. Undated text in Jenkins papers
142. *Independent*, 23.9.02
143. Jenkins to Ian Payne, 4.3.99 [Jenkins papers]
144. Gisela Stuart to Jenkins, 29.8.99 [Jenkins papers]
145. Jenkins to Stephen Twigg, 12.5.99 [Jenkins papers]

146. Jenkins to Raymond Bonham Carter, 7.5.98 [Jenkins papers]
147. Jenkins to Mary Robinson, 29.1.01 [Jenkins papers]
148. Tony Blair to Jenkins, 18.10.97 [Jenkins papers]
149. Noel Annan, *The Dons,* pp.298–302
150. House of Lords, 14.6.00 [Vol.613, col.1649]
151. *Mail on Sunday,* 28.5.00
152. Sir Peter Lampl to Jenkins, 12.7.00 [Jenkins papers]
153. *Independent,* 12.7.00
154. *Sunday Times,* 13.12.98
155. Jenkins to Sir Peter Baldwin, 1.12.98 [Jenkins papers]
156. *Spectator,* 24.6.00
157. House of Lords, 10.1.02 [Vol.630, cols 699–702]
158. *Evening Standard,* 27.4.00
159. ibid., 12.3.01
160. House of Lords, 20.4.99, 20.7.00
161. *Spectator,* 24.6.00
162. *Independent,* 12.7.00
163. *Evening Standard,* 12.3.01
164. Jenkins, *Gladstone,* p.565
165. Ashdown, Vol.2, p.104 (21.10.97)
166. *Fordham International Law Journal,* 1998
167. *Independent,* 2.1.99
168. Ashdown, Vol.2, p.156 (22.1.98)
169. *The Times*
170. Robert Harris diary, 24.3.00
171. Jenkins to Tony Blair, 23.11.99 [Jenkins papers]
172. Seldon, p.276; Robert Harris, 'A Late Friendship', in Adonis & Thomas, p.311
173. Radice, p.455 (19.1.00)
174. Jenkins to Alan Rusbridger, 18.1.00 [Jenkins papers]
175. *Independent,* 9.2.00
176. *Guardian,* 14.2.00
177. *Evening Standard,* 27.4.00
178. *The Times,* 26.6.00
179. Jenkins to Tony Blair, 26.6.00 [Jenkins papers]
180. Jenkins to Tony Lewis, 13.7.00 [Jenkins papers]
181. Roy Jenkins, *Gallery of Twentieth Century Portraits,* p.225
182. Neal Lawson & Neil Sherlock, *The Progressive Century: The Future of the Centre Left in Britain,* pp.vii–viii
183. ibid., p.ix
184. Jenkins to Charles Kennedy, 20.1.99 [Jenkins papers]
185. *Evening Standard,* 8.6.01
186. ibid., 4.1.99
187. Peter Mandelson to Jenkins, 12.3.01 [Jenkins papers]
188. Peter Mandelson to Jenkins, 14.7.01 [Jenkins papers]
189. ibid.
190. Jenkins to Peter Mandelson, 25.7.01 [typed copy of a handwritten letter, Jenkins papers]
191. Robert Harris diary, 13.7.01
192. House of Lords, 8.12.99 [Vol.607, cols 1284–90]
193. Jenkins, *The Chancellors,* p.10
194. ibid., p.325
195. ibid., p.90
196. ibid., pp.251–2
197. ibid., p.236
198. Jenkins to Nick Farnden, 1.12.98 [Jenkins papers]
199. *Yorkshire Post* interview, 11.10.01
200. *Independent on Sunday,* 7.4.91
201. Churchill Proceedings conference, Edinburgh, 21.5.94
202. Roy Jenkins, *Churchill,* p.xiv
203. Jenkins to Raymond Bonham Carter, 5.10.99 [Jenkins papers]
204. *The Times,* 25.9.01
205. Guildhall lecture, quoted in *Independent,* 16.11.01
206. *Yorkshire Post,* 11.10.01
207. Jenkins, *Churchill,* p.912
208. *Yorkshire Post,* 11.10.01
209. Jenkins to Lord McNally, 20.3.00 [Jenkins papers]
210. Jenkins to Lesley Abdela, 28.11.00 [Jenkins papers]
211. *Oxford Times,* 19.10.01
212. Max Hastings to Jenkins, 10.11.99 [Jenkins papers]
213. Interview, Max Hastings, 28.7.09
214. Max Hastings, *Finest Hours: Churchill as Warlord: 1940–45,* dedication
215. Jeremy Trevathan to Jenkins, 14.12.01 [Jenkins papers]
216. *Guardian,* 13.10.01
217. *Sunday Telegraph,* 7.10.01
218. *Observer,* 14.10.01

Notes

219. *Independent on Sunday*, 14.10.01
220. Jenkins to Philippa McEwan, 16.5.01
[Jenkins papers]
221. ibid., 20.9.01
222. Lord Callaghan to Jenkins, 2.6.98
[Jenkins papers]
223. Roy Hattersley to Jenkins, 10.8.94
[Jenkins papers]
224. Woodrow Wyatt to Jenkins, 5.2.90
[Jenkins papers]
225. Lady Falkender to Jenkins, 24.9.93
[Jenkins papers]
226. Philip Ziegler to Jenkins, 19.9.93
[Jenkins papers]
227. David Mellor to Jenkins, 5.97
[Jenkins papers]
228. Kinnock papers, KNNK 21/8
229. William Hague, *William Pitt the
Younger*, p.xvii
230. Address at Mark Bonham Carter's
memorial service, 27.10.94 [thanks to
Leslie Bonham Carter]
231. Jenkins to Canon Robert Wright,
18.9.01 [Jenkins papers]
232. Address at Lord Zuckerman's
memorial service, 1.4.93 [Jenkins
papers]
233. John Peyton, *Solly Zuckerman: A
Scientist out of the Ordinary*, p.xii
234. Robert Harris, 'A Late Friendship', in
Adonis & Thomas, p.308
235. ibid., pp.310, 313
236. Robert Harris diary, 1.8.98, 2.11.98
237. ibid., 20.6.02
238. *Evening Standard*, n.d. 2.01
239. Jenkins to Max Hastings, 5.4.00
[Jenkins papers]
240. Robert Harris diary, 8.4.13
241. ibid., 14.6.96
242. Andrew Adonis to Jenkins, 10.11.00
[Jenkins papers]
243. *The Times*,16.1.03
244. Radice, p.482 (7.3.01)
245. Robert Harris diary, 26.2.01
246. Interview, Sir Crispin Tickell,
11.3.01
247. *Daily Telegraph*, 28.1.01
248. Jenkins papers
249. *Spectator*, 19.1.02
250. Craig Brown, *The Lost Diaries*, pp.156,
246
251. Jenkins to Craig Brown, 30.12.02
[thanks to Craig Brown]
252. Jenkins to Scott Moyars, 12.12.01
[Jenkins papers]
253. Roy Jenkins, *Franklin Delano
Roosevelt*, p.28
254. ibid., p.36
255. ibid., p.37
256. ibid., p.144
257. ibid., p.151
258. Interview, Sir Anthony Kenny,
January 2009
259. John Mortimer, *The Summer of a
Dormouse*, p.205
260. *Independent*, 23.9.02
261. Robert Harris in Adonis & Thomas,
p.313
262. *Independent,* 23.9.02
263. ibid.
264. House of Lords, 24.9.02 [Vol.638, cols
892–4]
265. Michael Beloff, QC, to Jenkins,
9.10.02 [Jenkins papers]
266. Robert Harris diary, 11.2.00
267. Jenkins to the Queen, 3.11.02
[Jenkins papers]
268. Robert Harris in Adonis & Thomas,
p.314
269. *The Times,* 14.12.02
270. Tony Benn, *More Time for Politics:
Diaries 2001–2007*, pp.75–6 (4–5.1.03)
271. Interview, Michael Sissons, 3.10.12
272. Lord Rodgers of Quarry Bank in
House of Lords, 7.1.03 [Vol.642,
col.877]
273. *The Times, Guardian, Daily Telegraph,
Daily Mirror* and *Evening Standard*,
6.1.03
274. *Independent*, 6.1.03
275. *Observer,* 12.1.03
276. Ferdinand Mount, unidentified press
cutting
277. *Observer,* 12.1.03
278. *Daily Telegraph*, 11.1.03
279. *The Times,* 16.1.03
280. *Mail on Sunday*, 12.1.03
281. *Daily Mail*, 21.1.03
282. Interviews, Leslie Bonham Carter,
16.7.08; Marie-Alice de Beaumarchais,
1.10.08
283. Benn, p.108 (27.3.03)

Sources and Bibliography

David Butler papers (Nuffield College, Oxford)
James Callaghan papers (Bodleian Library, Oxford)
Barbara Castle papers (Bodleian Library, Oxford)
Anthony Crosland papers (London School of Economics)
Hugh Dalton papers (London School of Economics)
Hugh Gaitskell papers (University College London)
Lord Hailsham papers (Churchill College, Cambridge)
Robert Harris diary (thanks to Robert Harris)
Alastair Hetherington diary (London School of Economics)
Arthur Jenkins diary (East Hendred, now in the Bodleian Library, Oxford)
Roy Jenkins papers (East Hendred, now in the Bodleian Library, Oxford)
Neil Kinnock papers (Churchill College, Cambridge)
Alec McGivan papers (University of Essex, Colchester)
Robert Maclennan papers (University of Essex, Colchester)
Edwin Plowden papers (Churchill College, Cambridge)
Enoch Powell papers (Churchill College, Cambridge)
William Rodgers papers (University of Essex, Colchester)
Neville Sandelson papers (London School of Economics)
Peter Shore papers (London School of Economics)
Harold Wilson papers (Bodleian Library, Oxford)

Labour Party archive (The People's History Museum, Manchester)
Labour Party Annual Conference Reports, 1945–1976
The National Archives (Kew)
Parliamentary Debates, House of Commons, 1948–1987
Parliamentary Debates, House of Lords, 1987–2002
The Report of the Independent Commission on the Voting System, 1998 (Cm 4090–1)
Social Democratic Party archive (University of Essex, Colchester)
Interviews conducted for the British Diplomatic Oral History Programme (Churchill College, Cambridge)
Interviews conducted for Brook Productions' TV series *The Seventies* and *The Thatcher Factor* (London School of Economics)

Books by Roy Jenkins

Mr Attlee: An Interim Biography (Heinemann 1948)
Fair Shares for the Rich (Tribune 1951)
Pursuit of Progress: A critical analysis of the achievement and prospect of the Labour Party (Heinemann 1953)
Mr Balfour's Poodle: An Account of the Struggle between the House of Lords and the Government of Mr Asquith (Heinemann 1954)
Sir Charles Dilke: A Victorian Tragedy (Collins 1958)
The Labour Case (Penguin 1959)
Asquith (Collins 1964)
Essays and Speeches, ed. Anthony Lester (Collins 1967)
Afternoon on the Potomac? A British View of America's Changing Position in the World (Yale 1972)
What Matters Now (Collins/Fontana 1972)
Nine Men of Power (Hamish Hamilton 1974)
Partnership of Principle: Writing and Speeches on the Making of the Alliance, ed. Clive Lindley (Secker & Warburg 1985)
Truman (Collins 1986)
Baldwin (Collins 1987)
Gallery of Twentieth Century Portraits (David & Charles 1988)
European Diary, 1977–1981 (Collins 1989)
A Life at the Centre [ALATC] (Macmillan 1991)
Portraits and Miniatures (Macmillan 1993)
Gladstone (Macmillan 1995)
The Chancellors (Macmillan 1998)
Churchill (Macmillan 2001)
Twelve Cities (Macmillan 2002)
Franklin Delano Roosevelt (Times Books, New York 2003; Macmillan 2004)

Other books

Leo Abse: *Private Member* (Macdonald 1973)
Andrew Adonis & Keith Thomas: *Roy Jenkins: A Retrospective* (Oxford 2004)
Noel Annan: *Our Age: Portrait of a Generation* (Weidenfeld & Nicolson 1990)
——*The Dons: Mentors, Eccentrics and Geniuses* (HarperCollins 1999)
Paddy Ashdown: *The Ashdown Diaries, Volume 1: 1988–1997* (Penguin 2000)
——*The Ashdown Diaries, Volume 2: 1997–1999* (Penguin 2001)
Mark Bainbridge, ed., *The 1975 Referendum on Europe, Vol. 1: Reflections of the Participants* (Imprint Academic 2007)
Kenneth Baker: *The Turbulent Years: My Life in Politics* (Faber 1993)
Douglas Bence & Clive Branson: *Roy Jenkins: A Question of Principle* (Moat Hall 1982)
Tony Benn: *Years of Hope: Diaries, Papers and Letters, 1940–1962* (Hutchinson 1994)
——*Out of the Wilderness: Diaries, 1963–67* (Hutchinson 1987)
——*Office Without Power, Diaries, 1968–72* (Hutchinson 1988)
——*Against the Tide: Diaries, 1973–76* (Hutchinson 1989)
——*Conflicts of Interest: Diaries, 1977–80* (Hutchinson 1990)
——*The End of an Era: Diaries, 1980–90* (Hutchinson 1992)
——*Free at Last!: Diaries, 1991–2001* (Hutchinson 2002)
——*More Time for Politics: Diaries, 2001–2007* (Hutchinson 2007)
Tony Blair: *A Journey* (Hutchinson 2010)
Violet Bonham Carter: *Daring to Hope: The Diaries and Letters of Violet Bonham Carter, 1946–6* ed. Mark Pottle (Weidenfeld & Nicolson 2000)
Sarah Bradford, *America's Queen: The Life of Jacqueline Kennedy Onassis* (Viking 2000)

Sources and Bibliography

Ian Bradley, *Breaking the Mould: The Birth and Prospects of the Social Democratic Party* (Martin Robertson 1981)

Samuel Brittan: *Steering the Economy: The Role of the Treasury* (Penguin 1971)

Brian Brivati: *Hugh Gaitskell* (Richard Cohen 1996)

Roger Broad: *Labour's European Dilemmas: From Bevin to Blair* (Palgrave 2001)

Craig Brown: *The Lost Diaries* (Fourth Estate 2010)

David Butler & Gareth Butler: *British Political Facts, 1900–1994* (Macmillan 1994)

David Butler & Dennis Kavanagh: *The British General Election of February 1974* (Macmillan 1974)

——*The British General Election of October 1974* (Macmillan 1975)

——*The British General Election of 1983* (Macmillan 1984)

——*The British General Election of 1987* (Macmillan 1988)

David Butler & Anthony King: *The British General Election of 1964* (Macmillan 1965)

——*The British General Election of 1966* (Macmillan 1967)

David Butler & Uwe Kitzinger: *The 1975 Referendum* (Macmillan 1976)

David Butler & Michael Pinto-Duchinsky: *The British General Election of 1970* (Macmillan 1971)

Alec Cairncross: *Living with the Century* (Lynx 1998)

James Callaghan: *Time and Chance* (Collins 1987)

John Campbell: *Roy Jenkins: A Biography* (Weidenfeld & Nicolson 1983)

——*Nye Bevan and the Mirage of British Socialism* (Weidenfeld & Nicolson 1987)

——*Edward Heath* (Jonathan Cape 1993)

——*Margaret Thatcher: The Grocer's Daughter* (Jonathan Cape 2000)

——*Margaret Thatcher: The Iron Lady* (Jonathan Cape 2003)

Barbara Castle: *The Castle Diaries, 1964–70* (Weidenfeld & Nicolson 1984)

——*The Castle Diaries, 1974–76* (Weidenfeld & Nicolson 1980)

——*Fighting All The Way* (Macmillan 1993)

Alan Clark: *Diaries: Into Politics* (Weidenfeld & Nicolson 2000)

Richard Cockett: *David Astor and the Observer* (André Deutsch 1991)

John Cole: *As It Seemed To Me* (Weidenfeld & Nicolson 1995)

R. Coopey, S. Fielding & N. Tiratsoo, *The Wilson Governments, 1964–70* (Pinter 1993)

Colin R. Coote, *The Other Club* (Sidgwick & Jackson 1971)

Ivor Crewe & Anthony King: *The SDP. The Birth, Life and Death of the Social Democratic Party* (Oxford 1995)

C.A.R. Crosland: *The Future of Socialism* (Jonathan Cape 1956)

Susan Crosland: *Tony Crosland* (Jonathan Cape 1982)

Richard Crossman: *The Diaries of a Cabinet Minister*, Volume One, 1964–66 (Hamish Hamilton & Jonathan Cape 1975)

——*The Diaries of a Cabinet Minister*, Volume Two, 1966–68 (Hamish Hamilton & Jonathan Cape 1976)

——*The Diaries of a Cabinet Minister*, Volume Three, 1968–70 (Hamish Hamilton & Jonathan Cape 1977)

——*The Backbench Diaries of Richard Crossman*, ed. Janet Morgan (Hamish Hamilton & Jonathan Cape 1981)

Hugh Dalton: *The Political Diary of Hugh Dalton, 1918–40, 1945–60*, ed. Ben Pimlott (Jonathan Cape 1986)

——*The Second World War Diary of Hugh Dalton, 1940–45*, ed. Ben Pimlott (Jonathan Cape 1986)

Nicholas Davenport: *Memoirs of a City Radical* (Weidenfeld & Nicolson 1974)

William Davis: *Three Years Hard Labour: The Road to Devaluation* (André Deutsch 1968)

Robin Day: *... But With Respect: Memorable Television Interviews with Statesmen and Parliamentarians* (Weidenfeld & Nicolson 1993)

Edmund Dell: *The Chancellors: A History of the Chancellors of the Exchequer, 1945–1990* (HarperCollins 1996)

——*A Strange Eventful History: Democratic Socialism in Britain* (HarperCollins 2000)

Roy Denman: *The Mandarin's Tale* (Politico's 2002)

Frances Donaldson: *A Twentieth Century Life* (Weidenfeld & Nicolson 1992)

Bernard Donoughue: *Downing Street Diary: With Harold Wilson in No. 10* (Jonathan Cape 2005)

——*Downing Street Diary: with James Callaghan in No. 10* (Jonathan Cape 2008)

Harold Evans, *Good Times, Bad Times* (Weidenfeld & Nicolson 1983)

Marcia Falkender: *Downing Street in Perspective* (Weidenfeld & Nicolson 1983)

Ann Fleming: *The Letters of Ann Fleming*, ed. Mark Amory (Collins Harvill 1985)

Michael Foot, *Aneurin Bevan, 1945–1960* (Davis Poynter 1973)

Hugh Gaitskell: *The Diary of Hugh Gaitskell, 1945–56*, ed. Philip M. Williams (Jonathan Cape 1983)

J.K. Galbraith: *The Affluent Society* (Hamish Hamilton 1958)

Paul Gannon, *Colossus: Bletchley Park's Greatest Secret* (Atlantic Books, 2006)

Ian Gilmour, *Dancing with Dogma: Britain under Thatcherism* (Simon & Schuster 1992)

Lord Goodman, *Tell Them I'm On My Way* (Chapman 1993)

Patrick Gordon Walker: *Political Diaries, 1932–1971*, ed. Robert Pearce (Historians' Press 1991)

William Hague: *William Pitt the Younger* (HarperCollins 2004)

Lord Hailsham: *A Sparrow's Flight* (Collins 1978)

Kenneth Harris: *Attlee* (Weidenfeld & Nicolson 1982)

Stephen Haseler: *The Gaitskellites: Revisionism in the British Labour Party, 1951–1964* (Macmillan 1969)

——*The Tragedy of Labour* (Blackwell 1980)

Max Hastings: *Finest Years: Churchill as Warlord: 1940–45* (Harper Press 2009)

Michael Hatfield: *The House the Left Built: Inside Labour Policy Making, 1970–1975* (Gollancz 1978)

Roy Hattersley, *Who Goes Home? Scenes from Political Life* (Little, Brown 1995)

Denis Healey: *The Time of My Life* (Michael Joseph 1989)

Simon Heffer: *Like the Roman: The Life of Enoch Powell* (Weidenfeld & Nicolson 1998)

Nicholas Henderson: *Mandarin: The Diary of an Ambassador* (Weidenfeld & Nicolson 1994)

——*Old Friends and Modern Instances* (Profile 2000)

Peter Hennessy: *Whitehall* (Secker & Warburg 1989)

Andrew Holden: *Makers and Manners: Politics and Morality in Postwar Britain* (Politico's 2004)

Alistair Horne: *Macmillan, 1957–1986* (Macmillan 1989)

Anthony Howard: *RAB: The Life of R.A. Butler* (Jonathan Cape 1987)

David Howell: *British Social Democracy: A Study in Development and Decay* (Croom Helm 1976)

Denis Howell: *Made in Birmingham* (Queen Anne Press 1990)

Greg Hurst: *Charles Kennedy: A Tragic Flaw* (Politico's 2006)

Douglas Jay: *Change and Fortune* (Hutchinson 1980)

Kevin Jeffreys: *Anthony Crosland* (Richard Cohen 1999)

Peter Jenkins: *The Battle of Downing Street* (Knight 1970)

——*Mrs Thatcher's Revolution: The Ending of the Socialist Era* (Jonathan Cape 1987)

Philip M. Kaiser: *Journeying Far and Wide: A Political and Diplomatic Memoir* (Scribner's 1992)

Gerald Kaufman: *How to be a Minister* (Sidgwick & Jackson 1980)

Peter Kellner & Christopher Hitchens: *Callaghan: The Road to Number Ten* (Cassell 1976)

Cecil King: *The Cecil King Diary, 1965–70* (Jonathan Cape 1972)

——*The Cecil King Diary, 1970–74* (Jonathan Cape 1975)

John Kinross: *Fifty Years in the City: Financing Small Business* (John Murray 1982)

Uwe Kitzinger: *Diplomacy and Persuasion: How Britain Joined the Common Market* (Thames & Hudson 1973)

Sue Lawley's Desert Island Discussions (Hodder & Stoughton 1990)

Neal Lawson & Neil Sherlock: *The Progressive Century: The Future of the Centre Left in Britain* (Palgrave 2001)

Sources and Bibliography

David Lipsey: *In the Corridors of Power* (Biteback 2012)

Donald MacDougall: *Don and Mandarin: Memoirs of an Economist* (John Murray 1987)

Ronald McIntosh: *Challenge to Democracy: Politics, Trade Union Power and Economic Failure in the 1970s* (Politico's 2006)

Peter Mandelson: *The Third Man* (Harper Press 2010)

Sir Robert Mark: *In the Office of Constable* (Collins 1978)

David Marquand: *The Unprincipled Society: New Demands and Old Politics* (Jonathan Cape 1987)

—— *The Progressive Dilemma* (Orion 1999)

Christopher Mayhew: *Time to Explain* (Hutchinson 1987)

Ian Mikardo: *Back-Bencher* (Weidenfeld & Nicolson 1988)

Kenneth O. Morgan: *Callaghan: A Life* (Oxford 1997)

—— *Michael Foot: A Life* (HarperCollins 2007)

June Morris: *The Life and Times of Thomas Balogh: A Macaw among Mandarins* (Sussex Academic Press 2007)

John Mortimer: *In Character* (Allen Lane 1983)

—— *The Summer of a Dormouse* (Viking 2000)

Philip Norton, ed.: *Eminent Parliamentarians: The Speaker's Lectures* (Biteback 2012)

David Owen: *Face the Future* (Jonathan Cape 1981)

—— *Personally Speaking to Kenneth Harris* (Weidenfeld & Nicolson 1987)

—— *Time to Declare* (Michael Joseph 1991)

Edward Pearce: *The Shooting Gallery* (Hamish Hamilton 1989)

—— *Denis Healey: A Life in Our Times* (Little, Brown 2002)

John Peyton: *Solly Zuckerman: A Scientist out of the Ordinary* (John Murray 2001)

Ben Pimlott: *Hugh Dalton* (Jonathan Cape 1985)

—— *Harold Wilson* (HarperCollins 1996)

Edwin Plowden: *An Industrialist in the Treasury: The Post-War Years* (André Deutsch 1989)

Anthony Powell: *Journals, 1982–92*, 3 vols (Heinemann 1995, 1996, 1997)

Giles Radice: *Friends & Rivals: Crosland, Jenkins and Healey* (Little, Brown 2002)

—— *Diaries, 1980–2001: From Political Disaster to Election Triumph* (Weidenfeld & Nicolson 2004)

Robert Rhodes James: *Ambitions and Realities: British Politics, 1964–70* (Weidenfeld & Nicolson 1972)

William Rodgers: *The Politics of Change* (Secker & Warburg 1982)

—— *Fourth Among Equals* (Politico's 2000)

W.T. Rodgers, ed.: *Hugh Gaitskell, 1906–1963* (Thames & Hudson, 1964)

Greg Rosen: *Old Labour to New* (Politico's 2005)

Andrew Roth: *Heath and the Heathmen* (Routledge & Kegan Paul 1972)

Anthony Seldon: *Blair* (Free Press 2004)

Alan Sked & Chris Cook: *Post-War Britain: A Political History, 1945–1992* (Penguin 1993)

Michael Smith: *Station X: The Codebreakers of Bletchley Park* (Channel 4, 1998)

David Steel: *Against Goliath: David Steel's Story* (Weidenfeld & Nicolson 1989)

Hugh Stephenson: *Claret and Chips: The Rise of the SDP* (Michael Joseph 1982)

Patricia Lee Sykes: *Losing from the Inside: The Cost of Conflict in the British Social Democratic Party* (New Brunswick 1988)

Dick Taverne: *The Future of the Left: Lincoln and After* (Jonathan Cape 1974)

Jim Tomlinson: *The Labour Governments of 1964–70: Economic Policy* (Manchester University Press 2004)

Christopher Tugendhat: *Making Sense of Europe* (Viking 1986)

Stephen Wall: *The Official History of Britain and the European Community*, Volume II: *From Rejection to Referendum, 1963–1975* (Routledge 2012)

David Walter: *The Oxford Union: Playground of Power* (Macdonald 1984)

Alan Watkins: *Brief Lives* (Hamish Hamilton 1982)

George Weidenfeld: *Remembering My Good Friends* (HarperCollins 1995)

Martin Westlake, *Kinnock: The Biography* (Little, Brown 2001)

Phillip Whitehead: *The Writing on the Wall: Britain in the Seventies* (Michael Joseph/Channel 4, 1985)

Philip Williams: *Hugh Gaitskell* (Jonathan Cape 1979)

Shirley Williams: *Politics is for People* (Allen Lane/Penguin 1981)

——*Climbing the Bookshelves* (Virago 2009)

Des Wilson: *Battle for Power: The Inside Story of the Alliance and the 1987 General Election* (Sphere 1987)

Harold Wilson: *The Labour Government, 1964–70: A Personal Record* (Weidenfeld & Nicolson/Michael Joseph 1971)

——*Final Term: The Labour Government, 1974–1976* (Weidenfeld & Nicolson/Michael Joseph 1979)

Woodrow Wyatt: *Confessions of an Optimist* (Collins 1985)

——*The Journals of Woodrow Wyatt*, ed. Sarah Curtis, 3 vols (Macmillan 1998, 1999, 2000)

Hugo Young: *This Blessed Plot: Britain and Europe from Churchill to Blair* (Macmillan 1998)

——*The Hugo Young Papers: A Journalist's Notes from the Heart of Politics*, ed. Ion Trewin (Allen Lane 2008)

Philip Ziegler: *Wilson: The Authorised Life of Lord Wilson of Rievaulx* (Weidenfeld & Nicolson 1993)

Reference books

Annual Register

Kelly's Directory of South Wales and Monmouthshire

Oxford Dictionary of National Biography

Newspapers

Birmingham Evening Dispatch

Birmingham Gazette

Birmingham Post

Daily Express

Daily Herald

Daily Mail

Daily Mirror

Daily Telegraph

Evening Standard (London)

Financial Times

Glasgow Herald

Independent

Independent on Sunday

Manchester Guardian / The Guardian

Monmouthshire Free Press

Observer

South Wales Argus

Sunday Express

Sunday Telegraph

Sunday Times

The Times

Town Crier

Yorkshire Post

Journals and periodicals

Cherwell

The Current

The Economist

Encounter

Foreign Affairs

Forward

High Life

House and Garden

Isis

Labour Weekly

New Statesman

Oxford Magazine

Oxford University Labour Club Bulletin

Picture Post

Socialist Commentary

Spectator

The Sphere

Time

Times Literary Supplement

Tribune

Index

Index

Index